The State of the Union
Messages of the Presidents of
the United States

Volume I

The
State of the Union
Messages
of the
Presidents

1790-1966

★ ★ ★

with an introduction by

ARTHUR M. SCHLESINGER JR.

Editor: Fred L. Israel

VOLUME

I

1790–1860

NEW YORK

CHELSEA HOUSE PUBLISHERS

in association with the

R. R. BOWKER COMPANY

1967

Preface

The first clause of Article II, Section 3, of the Constitution provides the starting point for Presidential leadership in legislation—"He shall from time to time give to the Congress information of the state of the Union." Through custom, "from time to time" became annually and from George Washington to Lyndon Johnson, the "information of the state of the Union" also included recommendations, observations, and advice. These messages have become, as Charles Beard observed, "the one great public document of the United States which is widely read and discussed. Congressional debates receive scant notice, but the President's message is ordinarily printed in full in nearly every metropolitan daily, and is the subject of general editorial comment throughout the length and breadth of the land. It stirs the country: it often affects Congressional elections; and it may establish grand policy." While the style and content and even the manner of delivery have varied, the State of the Union messages tell dramatically the tribulations of a growing nation. Compiled and indexed for the first time, these documents present a sweeping view of American history as seen through the writings of the Presidents of the United States.

In 1839 the New York publishing firm of McLean and Taylor issued a 632 page volume containing the first compilation of the annual, special, and veto messages, proclamations and inaugural addresses of the Presidents through Van Buren's second State of the Union. Revisions, supplements and other editions followed sporadically. In 1894 Congress authorized the printing of 6000 copies of the Presidents' public papers. Under the editorship of Congressman James D. Richardson of Tennessee, the ten volume series *Messages and Papers of the Presidents 1789–1897* appeared between 1896 and 1899. Successive editions of Richardson brought the compilation through the Coolidge administration. Collections of the public papers of the Presidents from Hoover to Johnson have been published in separate Presidential series. In these three volumes we have compiled and indexed the full texts of the 178 State of the Union messages. These documents comprise a year-by-year chronicle of the nation's history. No other Presidential paper is as consistently comprehensive in coverage and analysis of major events and trends in the nation's history.

Volume One begins with Washington's State of the Union address, read before Congress on January 8, 1790, and concludes with Buchanan's fourth message of December 3, 1860. Washington presided over a new nation forged out of revolution. In seeking to fix the idea of Union, he datelined his address "United States" rather than New

York, the capital city. Buchanan, on the other hand, presided over a country tottering on the verge of disintegration. Seventy years of national successes and failures separate the two men. Running through these messages is the theme of the growth of Presidential power as well as the transformation of thirteen states into a mighty republic. Evident here, almost with the fatalism of a Greek tragedy, are issues pushing the nation toward the brink of self-destruction. Washington's faith in America sharply contrasts with Buchanan's pessimism. The messages and addresses of the Presidents presented in this volume form a cohesive pattern, which illustrates, among other things, why the conquest of a continent and the emergence of an Atlantic power resulted not in the fulfillment of Washington's hopes but in Civil War.

Fred L. Israel

The City College of New York
April 1966

Contents

JAMES BUCHANAN 1857–1861

Annual Messages of the Presidents: Major Themes of American History

by ARTHUR M. SCHLESINGER, JR.

★ ★ ★

*He shall from time to time give to the Congress Infor-
mation of the State of the Union, and recommend to
their Consideration such Measures as he shall judge
necessary and expedient . . .*

The Constitution of the United States
Article II, Section 3

The provision enjoining the President to inform the Congress regarding the state of the American Union and to submit programs and
policies to congressional consideration evidently struck the Constitutional Convention as entirely obvious and sensible. It provoked no recorded debate; as Hamilton wrote later in the 77th Federalist, "No
objection has been made to this class of authorities; nor could they possibly admit of any." Yet these innocuous phrases conferred on the
American President what has become, after vicissitudes, a basic tool in
his management of Congress and a potent instrument of national
leadership.

1

The Annual Message, as it was called through most of American
history, or the State of the Union Message, as it has been known since
1945, owed its origin to the first President of the republic. Washington,
indeed, had even directed his First Inaugural Address to his "Fellow-
Citizens of the Senate and the House of Representatives" (all subsequent inaugural addresses were directed to the nation as a whole); and
he followed this by the practice of appearing personally each year before
the Congress and offering his account of national problems and
prospects. The Houses of Congress made formal responses to the President, and each such response in due course received formal presidential
acknowledgment.

This ritual derived from the British practice of opening Parliament with "a speech from the throne"—a precedent which did not escape the notice of the zealously Republican party of Jefferson and Madison. When the Republicans won the Presidency after twelve years, Jefferson, coming to office in 1801, resolved to suppress what he considered a quasi-monarchical ceremony; he planned, as he liked to say, to "put the ship of state on its republican tack." The shift of the seat of government from Philadelphia to Washington seemed to provide a pretext, even if John Adams had been able to negotiate the muddy passage from the White House to the Capitol to deliver his Fourth Message in 1800. In any case, Jefferson a year later notified the President of the Senate, "The circumstances under which we find ourselves at this place rendering inconvenient the mode heretofore practiced of making, by personal address, the first communications between the legislative and executive branches, I have adopted that by message." In doing this, Jefferson explained, he had principal regard "to the convenience of the Legislature, to the economy of their time, to their relief from the embarrassment of immediate answers, on subjects not yet fully before them, and to the benefits thence resulting to the public affairs." He added other explanations privately. "By sending a message, instead of making a speech at the opening of the session," he told one friend, "I have prevented the bloody conflict which the making an answer would have committed them. They consequently were able to set into real business at once." Above all, he confided to another, his "great anxiety" was "to avail ourselves of our ascendancy to establish good principles and good practices; to fortify republicanism behind as many barriers as possible, that the outworks may give time to rally and save the citadel."

One inevitable effect of Jefferson's repudiation of Washington's precedent was to change the character of the Annual Message—and to set in motion its decay as a literary form. Under the first two Presidents the Message had been shaped and disciplined by the necessities of personal delivery. Though neither Washington nor Adams had pretensions as orators, their addresses nonetheless were composed with some care, were relatively coherent in structure and agreeably brief in text, and reflected and conveyed the presidential personalities. At the same time, they set the canon, passing on to future Presidents a set of standard genuflections: pious expressions of "profound gratitude to the Author of all Good for the numerous and extraordinary blessings we enjoy"; self-congratulatory statements about the national condition—"Is it too much to say that our country exhibits a spectacle of national happiness never surpassed, if ever equaled?"; and a methodical review of outstanding national issues. The next Presidents kept up the standards of the Messages for a while: Jefferson through literary grace and philosophical force; Madison through intellectual cogency; Monroe through the direct promulgation of policy (as in his celebrated Doctrine); John Quincy Adams through sweeping national vision; Jackson through bold executive initiative. But in time the Message became increasingly a perfunctory and bureaucratic document, made up of submissions from the executive departments lightly bound together by the passages of piety and self-congratulation.

Occasionally presidential preoccupations broke through and restored a personal tone and rhythm. So John Quincy Adams in 1826 concluded his Message with a reminder that a few months before, on the 50th anniversary of the Declaration of Independence, "two of the principal actors in that solemn scene—the hand that penned the ever-memorable Declaration and the voice that sustained it in debate—were by one summons, at the distance of 700 miles from each other, called before the Judge of All"; one, of course, was Jefferson, the other his own father. So Polk inserted into his Fourth Message in 1848 an extraordinary historical analysis and indictment of the American System of Adams and Clay. So Pierce in his Fourth Message in 1856 made a comprehensive and impassioned formulation of the case against the agitation of the slavery question. So Buchanan's messages from "an old public functionary" on the eve of the Civil War expressed the anguished helplessness of those who could bring themselves neither to approve nor arrest the drift toward disunion. So the war itself inspired Lincoln to the highest eloquence of all Annual Messages.

After the war Andrew Johnson delivered himself of bitter complaints about the policies of reconstruction; Grant in his final Message issued a pathetic defense of his stewardship ("Mistakes have been made, as all can see and I admit, but it seems to me oftener in the selections made of assistants appointed to aid in carrying out the various duties of administering the Government—in nearly every case selected without a personal acquaintance with the appointee, but upon recommendations of the representatives chosen directly by the people"); Cleveland poured out in moving language his sense of the moral decline of the nation; Theodore Roosevelt set forth with ardor and insight the need for national regulation of an industrial and urban economy. And from time to time Presidents stuck pet personal ideas of their own into their Messages: Jackson's proposal to abolish the electoral college and limit the President to a single term of four or six years; Andrew Johnson's desire for the direct election of senators as well as of Presidents and for the limitation of the terms of federal judges; Grant's support for the item veto (renewed by Arthur and again by Eisenhower); Arthur's wish (renewed by Cleveland) to clarify the question of presidential disability; Theodore Roosevelt's appeal for government subsidization of political campaigns, for a national divorce law and for capital punishment for rape; Taft's interest in giving cabinet members seats in each house of Congress and roles in congressional debates.

2

The day after Wilson's election in 1912 Oliver Newman, the chief editorial writer for the *Washington Times,* suggested to him that he restore the practice of the early republic and deliver his Annual Messages in person. Wilson at first rejected this idea; he feared it was too radical and would shock the Congress. Yet it was a logical development of his own philosophy of presidential leadership and, on reflection, he changed his mind. "Today I break another precedent by reading my message to Congress in person," he wrote a friend on April 8, 1913. "The town is agog about it. It seems I have been smashing precedents almost daily ever since I got here, chiefly no doubt because I did not know how it had been the custom to do and was not particularly careful to inquire, and proceeded to do it in the most simple and natural way—which is always and everywhere contrary to precedent. The President has not addressed Congress in person since John Adams's day—and yet what [could be] more natural and dignified? And a President is likely to read his own message rather better than a clerk would."

The announcement of this intention produced an excited senatorial reaction. "I am sorry to see revived the old Federalistic custom of speeches from the throne," said Senator John Sharp Williams of Mississippi. ". . . I regret this cheap and tawdry imitation of English royalty." Rather than risk debate over a resolution of unanimous consent for a joint session to hear the address, the Vice President quickly pronounced it a question of "high privilege on which unanimous consent was not required." When Wilson arrived in the Capitol, the atmosphere was tense. "Members of Congress," one cabinet member later wrote, "appeared to be a trifle nervous . . . Some . . . had a sullen look." Wilson began calmly:

> *I am very glad indeed to have this opportunity to address the two Houses directly and to verify for myself the impression that the President of the United States is a person, not a mere department of the Government hailing Congress from some isolated island of jealous power, sending messages, not speaking naturally and with his own voice—that he is a human being trying to cooperate with other human beings in a common service. After this pleasant experience I shall feel quite normal in all our dealings with one another.*

Driving home, Mrs. Wilson remarked to her husband that this was the kind of thing Theodore Roosevelt would have loved to do "if only he had thought of it." Wilson replied with a laugh, "Yes, I think I put one over on Teddy." Roosevelt's probable chagrin is unrecorded, but the general reaction was highly favorable. As for Oliver Newman, Wilson in June appointed him to the Board of Commissioners for the District of Columbia.

Though this first presidential return to the Hill was for a special message, Wilson delivered his Annual Messages in person every year except when illness prevented in 1919. His Republican successors followed this example only intermittently in the twenties (Harding twice, Coolidge once, Hoover not at all), but Washington's practice was nonetheless reestablished. Franklin Roosevelt seized on the idea with predictable relish, nor has any subsequent President foregone the opportunity to confront Congress face to face with his annual proposals. It is safe to suppose that the age of television has now made the State of the Union Message an occasion for national display which no future President will ever deny himself.

At the same time, Wilson brought about a revival of the Annual Message as a literary form. He charged his own addresses with an easy and lofty eloquence. "I have not so much laid before you a series of recommendations, gentlemen," as he put it in his final Message, "as sought to utter a confession of faith." Harding gave his messages the orotund phraseology of a midwestern newspaper publisher, Coolidge's had a dry and engaging terseness, and even Hoover's were embellished with sententious statements of social and economic philosophy. With Franklin Roosevelt, the Message became an oral address again and acquired in those skilled hands and with that golden voice new vitality and power.

The adoption of the 20th Amendment in the Thirties meant that, in those years when one President succeeded another by election, there would be two Annual Messages. Roosevelt therefore suggested in 1937 that "under this new constitutional practice" the retiring President should "review the existing state of our national affairs and outline broad future problems, leaving specific recommendations for future legislation to be made by the President about to be inaugurated." Since Roosevelt, this situation has arisen only twice. Truman observed Roosevelt's injunction by making his final message in 1953—one of the most remarkable of all Annual Messages—in effect a farewell address. Eisenhower in 1961, however, preferred to keep his final message relatively routine and, like Washington and Jackson, deliver a separate farewell address.

The 178 Annual Messages can by no means be relied on for a full and exact record of the state of the Union. Most of the time, as devices in the presidential management of Congress, they tended to employ the rhetoric of consensus, seeking to minimize differences, to mollify opposition and to court support. Abrasive issues were often swathed and submerged; thus one will look in vain in Monroe's Message of 1819 for mention of the question which would dominate that session of Congress and result in the Missouri Compromise, any more than one can find in Eisenhower's Messages any clear statement of his administration's policy of massive nuclear retaliation.

Yet, though sometimes in a muted and fitful way, major themes of American history nevertheless emerge in these texts: the security of the republic; the internal development of the continent; the place of ethnic minorities; the evolution of presidential power; and the significance of the experiment in democratic government.

3

National security. The preservation of national independence was the first necessity. The new republic wished to live at peace; but "if we desire to secure peace," as Washington put it, ". . . it must be known that we are at all times ready for war." The American people, he warned, could not "indulge a persuasion that, contrary to the order of human events, they will forever keep at a distance those painful appeals to arms with which the history of every other nation abounds." Peace thus required a strong navy and a strong militia: "The safety of the United States under divine protection ought to rest on the basis of systematic and solid arrangements, exposed as little as possible to the hazards of fortuitous circumstances." Nor could "such arrangements, with such objects, be exposed to the censure or jealousy of the warmest friends of republic government"; there was no incompatibility between defense and democracy. The pacific Jefferson soon agreed; writing in his First Message about Tripoli's requisitions on American commerce, he laconically said, "The style of the demand admitted but one answer. I sent a small squadron of frigates into the Mediterranean. . . ."

Peace also required a purposeful foreign policy. Safety lay in keeping out of power conflicts abroad. Like new states of Asia and Africa struggling for survival two centuries later, the young American republic committed itself to the course of neutralism. "The connection of the United States with Europe has become extremely interesting," said Washington in a moment of understatement in his Fifth Message; and his successors found themselves involved in harsh struggles to preserve American nonalignment at a time when the Western world was split into warring blocs. "We have seen with sincere concern," said Jefferson in his Third Message, "the flames of war lighted up again in Europe, and nations . . . engaged in mutual destruction." But America was "separated by a wide ocean from the nations of Europe and from the political interests which entangle them together," and Jefferson, emphasizing "the singular blessings of the position in which nature has placed us," instructed his countrymen to look on "the bloody arena" with total detachment. Even ideological sympathy could not be permitted to lead to political involvement. "That the people of the United States should feel an interest in the spread of political institutions as free as they regard their own to be is natural," said Van Buren in his Second Message; but their becoming "a party to any such struggle" was another matter.

This was true at least for Europe. The western hemisphere was a different question. The national struggles for independence in Latin America caused Madison in his Third Message to express a "deep interest" in "the great communities which occupy the southern portion of our own hemisphere." "We can have no concern in the wars of the European Governments nor in the causes which produce them," said Monroe. "The balance of power between them, into whichever scale it may turn in its various vibrations, cannot affect us. . . . But in regard to our neighbors our situation is different." The conviction that "with the movements in this hemisphere we are of necessity more immediately connected" led him to lay down his famous Doctrine in his Seventh Message.

Slowly the horizon of foreign policy enlarged. In becoming a continental nation, the United States became a Pacific power. In 1852 Fillmore complained that the office of commissioner to China remained unfilled; everyone had declined "on the ground of the inadequacy of the compensation. The annual allowance by law is $6,000, and there is no provision for any outfit." But, as he insisted the next year, "The general prosperity of our States on the Pacific requires that an attempt be made to open the opposite regions of Asia to a mutually beneficial intercourse." "The history of the world," added Buchanan, "proves that the nation which has gained possession of the trade with eastern Asia has always become wealthy and powerful." Soon the Far East fell into the orbit of American diplomacy.

As for the United States itself, Madison in 1816 had identified as the "peculiar felicity" of the Constitution that it was capable, "without losing its vital energies, of expanding itself over a spacious territory." Such sentiments forecast the age of "manifest destiny." By the Fifties, Pierce could reflect comfortably how the nation had "continued gradually and steadily to expand through acquisitions of territory, which how much soever some of them may have been questioned, are now universally seen and admitted to have been wise." Soon Buchanan called for the purchase of Cuba, and Johnson and Grant for the annexation of San Domingo (which Grant wanted as a home for the ex-slaves "where their civil rights would not be disputed").

But there were voices of caution. "Maintaining as I do," said Cleveland in his First Message, "the tenets of a line of precedents from Washington's day, which proscribe entangling alliances with foreign states, I do not favor a policy of acquisition of new and distant territory or the incorporation of remote interests with our own" or, indeed, even the assertion of national interest "outside of our own territory, when coupled with absolute and unlimited engagements to defend the territorial integrity of the state where such interests lie."

Yet the world swept on. In 1899 McKinley justified the annexation of the Philippines ("They are ours by every title of law and equity. They cannot be abandoned. If we desert them we leave them at once to anarchy and finally to barbarism"). Soon Theodore Roosevelt was explaining that "wars with barbarous or semi-barbarous peoples come in a different category [from wars between civilized powers], being merely a most regrettable but necessary international police duty which must be performed for the sake of the welfare of mankind." Recent events, Roosevelt declared, had "definitely decided that, for woe or for weal, our place must be great among the nations. We may either fail greatly or succeed greatly; but we cannot avoid the endeavor from which either great failure or great success must come."

The old isolationism thus gave way, in the first instance, to the new imperialism. "The diplomacy of the present administration," said Taft in his Fourth Message, ". . . is an effort frankly directed to the increase of American trade upon the axiomatic principle that the Government of the United States shall extend all proper support to every legitimate and beneficial American enterprise abroad." But the old isolationism was also beginning to be challenged by the new internationalism. The First World War led Wilson to his crusade for "a peace secure against the violence of irresponsible monarchs and ambitious military coteries and made ready for a new order, for new foundations of justice and fair dealing." "No policy of isolation," he said in his 1919 Message, "will satisfy the growing needs and opportunities of America. . . . The recent war has ended our isolation and thrown upon us a great duty and responsibility."

The debate nevertheless continued. "Our country," Coolidge announced in his First Message, "has one cardinal principle to maintain in its foreign policy. . . . We attend to our own affairs." But would this be enough? In a prescient Message thirteen years later Franklin Roosevelt begged "the people of the Americas" to "take cognizance of growing ill will, of marked trends toward aggression of increasing armaments, of shortening tempers—a situation which has in it many of the elements that lead to the tragedy of general war." What he then called the "twin spirits of autocracy and aggression" brought on war soon enough. In 1941, noting that "at no previous time has American security been as seriously threatened from without as it is today," Roosevelt set forth his Four Freedoms. Three years later, warning against the "tragic errors of ostrich isolationism," he called on the freedom-loving nations to join "in a just and durable system of peace."

The atomic age gave the quest for peace new urgency. "Lenin," said Truman in his great Message of 1953, "was a pre-atomic man, who viewed society and history with pre-atomic eyes. Something profound has happened since he wrote. War has changed its shape and its dimension." Atomic war, he continued, "is not a possible policy for rational man." (Eisenhower seven years later called it "the ultimate insanity.") "I do not know how much time may elapse before the Communist rulers bring themselves to recognize this truth," Truman added; but he held out the hope that "as we continue to confound Soviet expectations, as our world grows stronger, more united, more attractive to men on both sides of the iron curtain, then inevitably there will come a time of change within the Communist world. . . . It is not too much to expect their world to change its character, moderate its aims, become more realistic and less implacable, and recede from the cold war." A decade later Kennedy, noting that "the forces of diversity are at work inside the Communist camp," could conclude that it was "the closed Communist societies, not the free and open societies, which carry within themselves the seeds of internal disintegration." If communism would indeed moderate its aims, Kennedy suggested, "then, surely, the areas of agreement can be very wide indeed."

Time and space had long since obliterated "the singular blessings of the position in which nature has placed us." America was in the great world to stay: it could not escape its destiny. "We seek," said Kennedy, "not the worldwide victory of one nation or system but a worldwide victory of men."

4

Internal development. "It will not be doubted," said Washington in his Message of 1796, "that with reference either to individual or national welfare agriculture is of primary importance." More than a century later Theodore Roosevelt could note that "nearly half the people of this country devote their energies to growing things from the soil." Yet Washington in his First Message also stressed the importance of "new and useful inventions," and the history of the next century was the story of the cascading evolution of the United States from a rural republic into an industrial as well as a continental society.

National growth required the settlement of the public lands and the development of internal communications; it required the encouragement of manufactures; it required the promotion of education; and for all such purposes it seemed to require an active national government. One is particularly impressed by the immediate recognition by Presidents of the need for government support for the educational system. Thus Washington called for the "promotion of science and literature" and the establishment of a national university. Jefferson, Madison and John Quincy Adams repeated this recommendation. After the Civil War, Grant, pointing out that an ignorant electorate would inevitably be governed "by the demagogue or by priestcraft," declared, "The education of the masses becomes of the first necessity for the preservation of our institutions." In this spirit Hayes asked Congress for programs which would supplement "with national aid the local systems of education . . . in all the States"—a proposal renewed by Arthur and Benjamin Harrison. It was only in the 20th century in one of those curious moments of constitutional regression, that aid for education seemed for a season an improper policy for the general government.

This spacious view of the role of government received its classic statement from John Quincy Adams in his First Message. "The great object of the institution of civil government," Adams wrote

> is the improvement of the condition of those who are parties to the social compact, and no government, in whatever form constituted, can accomplish the lawful ends of its institution but in proportion as it improves the condition of those over whom it is established. . . . For the fulfillment of those duties governments are invested with power, and to the attainment of the end—the progressive improvement of the condition of the governed—the exercise of delegated powers is a duty as sacred and indispensable as the usurpation of powers not granted is criminal and odious.

The conception of affirmative national action commanded increasing support, even among those who had begun as opponents of a strong central government. Though Jefferson had said in his First Message, "Agriculture, manufactures, commerce, and navigation, the four pillars of our prosperity, are then most thriving when left most free to individual enterprise," he had quickly added, "Protection from casual embarrassments, however, may sometimes be seasonably interposed." By his Sixth Message he was urging that the budgetary surplus be applied "to the great purposes of the public education, roads, rivers, canals and such other objects of public improvement as it may be thought proper to add to the constitutional enumeration of Federal powers." The Virginia Presidents did not appear to doubt the wisdom of the policy of national development; they doubted only that the Constitution gave the central government the power to carry the policy out, and wished to clear up the doubt by constitutional amendment.

In the meantime, the country grew. It built cities, it began the process of industrialization, it spilled over into the vacant west. In 1801 Jefferson predicted that the population would double in another twenty-two years (he was off by a single year). "Within the last half century," Fillmore could write in 1852, "the number of States in this Union has nearly doubled, the population has almost quadrupled, and our boundaries have been extended from the Mississippi to the Pacific. Our territory is checkered over with railroads and furrowed with canals." A year later Pierce forecast a population of 100,000,000 in another half century (he was off by fifteen years). Lincoln was even more extravagant in his Message of 1861: "There are already among us those who if the Union be preserved will live to see it contain 250,000,000." The next year he announced 1930 as the date at which we would arrive at this state of beatitude (he was off by 127,000,000).

But the country grew in the main without the guiding national hand envisaged by John Quincy Adams: the constitutional doubts were still unresolved. So Jackson, coming to office as a champion of strict economy and strict construction, argued in his First Message that "the great mass of legislation relating to our internal affairs was intended to be left where the Federal Convention found it—in the State governments." Van Buren, confronted by a grave national depression, could only say bleakly in a message to a special session of Congress, "Those who look to the action of this Government for specific aid to the citizen to relieve embarrassments arising from losses by revulsions in commerce and credit lose sight of the ends for which it was created and the powers with which it was clothed. . . . All communities are apt to look to government for too much." Buchanan repeated the point in the midst of the Panic of 1857 twenty years later: "The Federal Government can not do much to provide against a recurrence of existing evils."

The argument about the role of government swayed back and forth through the century with the tariff and the currency as focal points. But in the meantime the economy itself began to acquire a new structure. Jackson, for all his presumed ideological opposition to centralized power, had made the national government stronger than ever before by asserting the national authority both against the states and against the United States Bank, the symbol of a corporate system tending, as he said in 1832, "to concentrate wealth into a few hands." By 1835 he was calling for "an effectual stand against this spirit of monopoly." Van Buren in 1837 condemned "the already overgrown influence of corporate authorities," and in 1840 the rise of "a concentrated money power." Polk, another faithful Jacksonian, rejected the American System in 1848 as a program "to advance the interests of large capitalists and monopolists at the expense of the great mass of the people . . . [tending] to build up an aristocracy of wealth, to control the masses of society, and monopolize the political power of the country. . . . Its effect was 'to make the rich richer and the poor poorer.' . . . It was an organized money power, which resisted the popular will and sought to shape and control the public policy."

Andrew Johnson, still another old Jacksonian, resuscitated the theme after the Civil War: "Monopolies, perpetuities and class legislation are contrary to the genius of free government." By 1888 Cleveland was talking in agitated language about "the existence of trusts, combinations, and monopolies, while the citizen is struggling far in the rear or is trampled to death beneath an iron heel. Corporations, which should be the carefully restrained creatures of the law and the servants of the people, are fast becoming the people's masters." He turned a familiar epithet to unfamiliar use:

> *Communism is a hateful thing and a menace to peace and organized government; but the communism of combined wealth and capital, the outgrowth of overweening cupidity and selfishness, which insidiously undermines the justice and integrity of free institutions, is not less dangerous than the communism of oppressed poverty and toil, which, exasperated by injustice and discontent, attacks with wild disorder the citadel of rule.*

Yet, like the old Jeffersonians and Jacksonians, Cleveland was caught in the dilemma between his social fears and his constitutional scruples. Ideology blocked him from acting against the situation he perceived with such vividness. "It is quite doubtful," he said in his final Message in 1896, "whether the evils of trusts and monopolies can be adequately treated through Federal action." He stuck to the same view of the limited federal role through the hard times of the Eighties and Nineties, brusquely dismissing the notion "that the General Government is the fountain of individual and private aid; that it may be expected to relieve with paternal care the distress of citizens and communities, and that from the fullness of its Treasury it should, upon the slightest possible pretext of promoting the general good, apply public funds to the benefit of localities and individuals." So too McKinley in his Third Message reinforced Adam Smith by Charles Darwin: "The doctrine of evolution and the rule of the survival of the fittest are as inexorable in their operation as they are positive in the results they bring about."

But, as Cleveland himself had said in another connection in his 1887 Message, "It is a *condition* which confronts us, not a theory." In the end, it was Theodore Roosevelt who closed the gap between 18th century dogma and 20th century reality by combining the social ends of Jefferson with the constitutional means of John Quincy Adams. The old laws and customs, T. R. claimed in his First Message, were no longer sufficient to regulate the accumulation and distribution of wealth. "The tremendous and highly complex industrial development . . . brings us face to face . . . with very serious social problems" . . . the great corporations, the relationship between capital and labor, the conditions of life of the working class, the exploitation of women and children, the overcrowding of cities, the waste and depletion of natural resources ("the fundamental problem which underlies almost every other problem of our National life"). There seemed only one way to meet such problems, and Roosevelt expounded it again and again in his Messages:

> In order to insure a healthy social and industrial life, every big corporation should be held responsible by, and account- able to, some sovereign strong enough to control its conduct. . . . Only the National Government can in thoroughgoing fashion exercise the needed control. . . .
>
> This does not represent centralization. It represents merely the acknowledgment of the patent fact that centralization has already come in business. If this irresponsible outside business power is to be controlled in the interest of the gen- eral public it can only be controlled in one way—by giving adequate power of control to the one sovereignty capable of exercising such power—the National Government.

What Theodore Roosevelt called "the enlargement of scope of the functions of the National Government required by our development as a nation" became the dominating tendency of the domestic policies of the 20th century. "My point," said Wilson in his Second Message, "is that the people of the United States do not wish to curtail the activities of this Government; they wish, rather, to enlarge them; and with every enlargement, with the mere growth, indeed, of the country itself, there must come, of course, the inevitable increase of expense. . . . It is not expenditure but extravagance that we should fear being criticized for." Going even farther, Wilson in 1919 called for "a genuine democratiza- tion of industry, based upon the full recognition of the right of those who work, in whatever rank, to participate in some organic way in every decision which directly affects their welfare."
Conservative Presidents tried in the next decade to revive the

past. "In my opinion," said Coolidge in 1924, "the Government can do more to remedy the economic ills of the people by a system of rigid economy in public expenditure than can be accomplished through any other action." Confronted by the worst depression in the nation's history, Hoover in 1930 issued a declaration of governmental impotence: "Economic depression cannot be cured by legislative action or executive pronouncement. Economic wounds must be healed by the action of the cells of the economic body—the producers and consumers themselves." But Franklin Roosevelt, carrying forward the New Nationalism of Theodore Roosevelt and the New Freedom of Wilson, held out in his First Message the prospect of building "on the ruins of the past a new structure designed better to meet the present problems of modern civilization." In his next to last Message in 1944, reflecting on the inalienable political rights of the American people, "our rights to life and liberty," he said:

> As our Nation has grown in size and stature . . . —as our industrial economy expanded—these political rights have proved inadequate to assure us equality in the pursuit of happiness.
> We have come to a clear realization of the fact that true individual freedom cannot exist without economic security and independence. 'Necessitous men are not free men.'

He then set forth an "economic bill of rights," thereby preparing a great part of the agenda for Truman's Fair Deal, Kennedy's New Frontier and Johnson's Great Society.

To the economic bill of rights Kennedy added a new concern with "the quality of American life"—"This country cannot afford to be materially rich and spiritually desperately poor"—and restated the national interest declared by Washington and Jefferson in the promotions of the arts and sciences. "The Great Society," said Johnson in his Second Message, "asks not only how much, but how good; not only how to create wealth, but how to use it; not only how fast we are going but where we are headed. It proposes as the first test for a nation: the quality of its people." And so the National Government continued in a changing world to discharge its responsibility to what John Quincy Adams had described as its "great object"—"the progressive improvement of the condition of the governed."

5

The place of ethnic minorities. The Constitution was written, in the main, *by* a group of white Anglo-Saxon Protestants. But it was written *for* all American citizens. The national consciousness has ever since been haunted by ethnic minorities—by Uncas and Chingachgook, by Queequeg and Nigger Jim—and the gap between the constitutional promise to all men and the practical exclusion of certain minorities has been an abiding problem for American Presidents.

Through the early years of American history the Indians were the focus of concern. "A system corresponding with the mild principles of religion and philanthropy toward an unenlightened race of men whose happiness depends on the conduct of the United States," as Washington put it, "would be as honorable to the national character as conformable to the dictates of sound policy." But some "deluded tribes," he remarked, were engaged in warfare against the white man; and it was "necessary to convince the refractory of the power of the United States to punish their depredations." Yet Washington also noted the need for "the protection of the Indians from the violences of the lawless part of our frontier inhabitants." Jefferson urged that by pursuing a uniform course of justice toward them and aiding them in all the improvements which may better their condition,

> *we may render ourselves so necessary to their comfort and prosperity that the protection of our citizens from their disorderly members will become their interest and their voluntary care. Instead, therefore, of the augmentation of military force proportioned to our extension of frontier, I propose a moderate enlargement of the capital employed in that commerce as a more effectual, economical, and humane instrument for preserving peace and good neighborhood with them.*

This early experiment in a "good neighbor" policy was not, alas, that easy. By 1812, various tribes, stimulated by the British, were on the warpath again—"that wretched portion of the human race," said Madison angrily, ". . . armed with the horrors of those instruments of carnage and torture which are known to spare neither age nor sex." Monroe offered a stark statement of the white man's philosophy: "To civilize them, and even to prevent their extinction, it seems to be indispensable that their independence as communities should cease, and that the control of the United States over them should be complete and undisputed. . . . Left to themselves, their extirpation is inevitable." Later he proposed that they be induced to migrate to the west, though to "remove them" from their present lands "by force, even with a view to their own security and happiness, would be revolting to humanity and utterly unjustifiable."

The white man was not wholly devoid of shame in his treatment of the Indians. "Professing a desire to civilize and settle them," as Jackson said, "we have at the same time lost no opportunity to purchase their lands and thrust them farther into the wilderness. By this means they have not only been kept in a wandering state, but been led to look upon us as unjust and indifferent to their fate. Thus, though lavish in its expenditures upon the subject, Government has constantly defeated its own policy." They were a "much-injured race." "One by one have many powerful tribes disappeared from the earth. . . . The fate of the Mohegan, the Narragansett, and the Delaware is fast overtaking the Choctaw, the Cherokee and the Creek." Yet Jackson, a son of the frontier, was philosophical about this prospect: "True philanthropy reconciles the mind to these vicissitudes as it does to the extinction of one generation to make room for another." Their only hope for survival, as he saw it, was to set apart territory west of the Mississippi, "to be guaranteed to the Indian tribes" under "governments of their own choice," and "to send them to a land where their existence may be prolonged and perhaps made perpetual."

And so, as the white man moved inexorably to the west, he drove the Indians before him. "From the foundation of the Government to the present," said Grant forty years after Jackson, "the management of the original inhabitants of this continent—the Indians—has been a subject of embarrassment and expense, and has been attended with continuous robberies, murders and wars." The white man was partly at fault; "the past, however, cannot be undone, and the question must be met as we now find it." In 1877 Hayes strengthened the indictment of the whites:

> *Many, if not most, of our Indian wars have had their origin in broken promises and acts of injustice upon our part, and the advance of the Indians in civilization has been slow because the treatment they received did not permit it to be faster and more general. We cannot expect them to improve and to follow our guidance unless we keep faith with them in respecting the rights they possess. . . . We owe it to them as a moral duty to help them in attaining at least that degree of civilization which they may be able to reach.*

To this day the debt remains unredeemed.

The Constitution, while avoiding all mention of Negro slavery, tacitly acquiesced in its existence where sanctioned by state law. It did, however, require the abolition of the slave trade by 1808, withdrawing, as Jefferson said in his Sixth Message, American citizens "from all further participation in those violations of human rights which have been so long continued on the unoffending inhabitants of Africa, and which the morality, the reputation, and the best interests of our country have long been eager to proscribe." With this exception, the early Presidents omitted discussion of slavery, and the rising sectional tension found only fitful reflection in the Annual Messages—as, for example, in 1835 when Jackson urged Congress to pass a law prohibiting the circulation in the south through the mail of "inflammatory appeals addressed to the passions of the slaves . . . calculated to stimulate them to insurrection and to produce all the horrors of a servile war."

But the question could not be kept down. In 1847 Polk, in an effort to hold together the compromises on which the republic rested, warned that the intensification of sectional politics was threatening the Union: "How unimportant," he hopefully said, "are all our differences of opinion upon minor questions of public policy compared with its preservation." Yet what he called "the only dangerous question which lies in our path" continued to defy resolution. In 1855 Pierce expressed indignation that a "considerable portion of the people of this enlightened country could have so surrendered themselves to the supposed interests of the relatively few Africans in the United States as totally to abandon and disregard the interests of the 25,000,000 Americans." The next year he inveighed against the abolitionists for seeking a "revolutionary" goal, which could be accomplished only "through burning cities, and ravaged fields, and slaughtered populations, and all there is most terrible and foreign complicated with civil and servile war," driving the nation "into mutual devastation and fratricidal carnage, transforming the now peaceful and felicitous brotherhood into a vast permanent camp of armed men like the rival monarchies of Europe and Asia."

But the moral sense of the nation could no longer tolerate a system by which one man owned another as his personal property. "Without slavery," said Lincoln in his Second Message, "the rebellion could never have existed; without slavery it could not continue." Then, when the Civil War at last ended slavery as a legal system, the problem remained of the national responsibility to the freedmen. Johnson, urging in his First Message (written by George Bancroft) a constitutional amendment abolishing slavery forever, said, "This is the measure which will efface the sad memory of the past. . . . [It] reunites us beyond all powers of disruption." As for the ex-slaves, "the career of free industry must be fairly opened to them, and then their future prosperity and condition must, after all, rest mainly on themselves. If they fail, and so perish away, let us be careful that the failure shall not be attributable to any denial of justice." Still, though a Unionist, Johnson was a Southerner, and two years later he was denouncing "the subjugation of the [southern] states to negro domination" and "the effort now making to Africanize the half of our country," claiming that "negroes have shown less capacity for government than any other race of persons . . .

Wherever they have been left to their own devices they have shown a constant tendency to relapse into barbarism."

Johnson was unquestionably speaking the mood of the white South. By 1874 Grant noted "decided indications" of a "determination, by acts of violence and intimidation, to deprive citizens of the freedom of the ballot." Without federal intervention, he said, "the whole scheme of colored enfranchisement is worse than a mockery and little better than a crime." He appealed to the South: "Treat the negro as a citizen and a voter, as he is and must remain, and soon parties will be divided, not on the color line, but on principle." Two years later, Hayes, announcing the end of military occupation, urged southern whites to respect "the civil and political rights of the colored people." But only a year after he was obliged to say that, in certain southern states, "the records of the elections seem to compel the conclusion that the rights of the colored voters have been overridden and their participation in the elections not permitted to be either general or free." It was the executive duty, Hayes went on, "to inquire into and punish violations" of the law: "It is the right of every citizen possessing the qualifications prescribed by law to cast one unintimidated ballot and to have his ballot honestly counted." In another year he called for "a more general and complete establishment, at whatever cost, of universal security and freedom in the exercise of the elective franchise" so that "all over our wide territory the name and character of citizen of the United States shall mean one and the same thing." In his Fourth Message Hayes once again condemned the southern states for their success "in defeating the exercise of the right preservative of all rights—the right of suffrage—which the Constitution expressly confers upon our enfranchised citizens."

But the question was receding from the national conscience and consciousness. Arthur hardly mentioned it; Cleveland ignored it; and it was not till a decade after Hayes when Benjamin Harrison reopened the issue with striking moral fervor.

> *The colored people did not intrude themselves upon us. They were brought here in chains and held in the communities where they are now chiefly found by a cruel slave code. Happily for both races, they are now free. They have from a standpoint of ignorance and poverty—which was our shame, not theirs—made remarkable advances in education and in the acquisition of property. . . .*
>
> *But notwithstanding all this, in many parts of our country where the colored population is large the people of that race are by various devices deprived of any effective exercise of their political rights and of many of their civil*

rights. The wrong does not expend itself upon those whose votes are suppressed. Every constituency in the Union is wronged.

Harrison took note of the southern arguments. "If it is said that these communities must work out this problem for themselves, we have a right to ask whether they are at work upon it. Do they suggest any solution? When and under what conditions is the black man to have a free ballot? When is he in fact to have those full civil rights which have so long been his in law? . . . This generation should courageously face these grave questions, and not leave them as a heritage of woe to the next."

For himself, Harrison recommended enlarged federal intervention. "The colored man should be protected in all of his relations to the Federal Government, whether as litigant, juror, or witness in our courts, as an elector for members of Congress, or as a peaceful traveler upon our interstate railways." In subsequent Messages he renewed his appeal for federal supervision of congressional elections, rejecting the idea that the conciliation of the south required "connivance at election practices that not only disturb local results, but rob the electors of other States and sections of their most priceless political rights." But Harrison's campaign had no effect on a complacent people. The nation became increasingly faithless to what he called the "first condition" of the government's trust—"the defense of the free and equal influence of the people in the choice of public officers and in the control of public affairs." The result was the passing on of the "heritage of woe" to future generations.

After Harrison the question of Negro rights—excepting only the right not to be lynched—disappeared from Annual Messages for many years; and even Theodore Roosevelt, in a passionate condemnation of lynching, was moved to add, "Every colored man should realize that the worst enemy of his race is the negro criminal, and above all the negro criminal who commits the dreadful crime of rape." Forty years passed before Truman revived the issue of civil rights in 1948: "Our first goal is to secure fully the essential human rights of our citizens. . . . Whether discrimination is based on race, or creed, or color, it is utterly contrary to American ideals of democracy." But what Truman in his last Message called "a great awakening of the American conscience on the issue of civil rights" was still shamefully slow to take effect. Eisenhower, while urging further progress, could as late as 1956 describe statements that "Negro citizens are being deprived of their right to vote" as "allegations." With Kennedy and his successor, the Presidency began at last to catch up with the problem. "As far as the writ of Federal law will run," said Lyndon Johnson in his First Message, "we must abolish not some but all racial discrimination. For this is not merely an economic issue—or a social, political, or international issue. It is a moral issue."

If Indians and Negroes were people of a different color, the course of immigration in the 19th century, bringing in members of white ethnic minorities created another range of problems. "Shall oppressed humanity find no asylum on this globe?" Jefferson had asked in his First Message in recommending a shortening of the time required for naturalization. As the rate of entry increased, Polk could say proudly in his Third Message in 1847:

> Numerous emigrants, of every lineage and language, attracted by the civil and religious freedom we enjoy and by our happy condition, annually crowd to our shores, and transfer their heart, not less than their allegiance, to the country whose dominion belong alone to the people.

"I regard our immigrants" said Lincoln, urging new measures for the "encouragement" of immigration in his last Message, "as one of the principal replenishing streams which are appointed by Providence to repair the ravages of internal war and its wastes of national strength and health."

But the national mood was beginning to change. The first casualties were the Chinese streaming into the Pacific states. In 1874 Grant asked for legislation against the import of Chinese contract labor. In his Third Message Benjamin Harrison, noting the rush of Russian Jews into the United States because of anti-Semitism in their homeland, observed, "The sudden transfer of such a multitude under conditions that tend to strip them of their small accumulations and to depress their energies and courage is neither good for them nor for us." A year later he suggested that "admission to our country and to the high privilege of its citizenship should be more restricted and more careful"; we have a duty "not only to keep out the vicious, the ignorant, the civil disturber, the pauper, and the contract laborer, but to check the too great flow of immigration now coming by further limitations." Theodore Roosevelt proposed educational and economic tests as well as the absolute exclusion of anarchists: "We cannot have too much immigration of the right kind, and we should have none at all of the wrong kind." (He added, however, "Let us remember that the question of being a good American has nothing whatever to do with a man's birthplace any more than it has to do with his creed," and he wanted to change the Chinese exclusion laws to "admit all Chinese, except Chinese of the coolie class.")

Wilson stood against the campaign for restriction. But by the

Twenties the struggle appeared lost. Harding called for alien registration, and Coolidge in his First Message crisply summed up the postwar attitude: "New arrivals should be limited to our capacity to absorb them into the ranks of good citizenship. America must be kept American." It took the Second World War to bring back the views of Jefferson and Lincoln. "Our democratic ideals," said Truman in his Fifth Message, "as well as our own best interests, require that we do our fair share in providing homes for the unfortunate victims of war and tyranny." Eisenhower and Kennedy moved steadily to reaffirm the earlier traditions of the republic—the policy defined by Lyndon Johnson in his Second Message as "an immigration law based on the work a man can do and not where he was born or how he spells his name."

6

The evolution of presidential power. The Annual Message, as an appointed medium of communication from President to Congress, became both an instrument and an index of presidential leadership. When Jefferson ended the practice of personal delivery of the Message, he was making a symbolic demonstration of his party's distrust of a strong executive. "Nothing shall be wanting on my part," he assured Congress in his own First Message, "to inform as far as in my power the legislative judgment, nor to carry that judgment into faithful execution." This deferential language actually concealed an astute executive purpose, but Jefferson's Virginia successors soon subsided into a more passive conception of the presidential responsibility.

Then with Jackson the Presidency suddenly acquired new vigor; and the Jacksonian theory of the Presidency as the tribune of the people received its ablest contemporary vindication by Polk in his last Message. Defending the most conspicuous form of Executive aggression against the congressional will—the veto power—Polk wrote:

> *If at any time Congress shall, after apparently full deliberation, resolve on measures which he deems subversive of the Constitution or of the vital interests of the country, it is his solemn duty to stand in the breach and resist them. . . . Any attempt to coerce the President to yield his sanction to measures which he cannot approve would be a violation of the spirit of the Constitution, palpable and flagrant, and if successful would break down the independence of the executive department and make the President, elected by the people and clothed by the Constitution with power to defend their rights, the mere instrument of a majority of Congress.*

Polk had no patience for the argument that Congress was more representative of the people than the President. "The President," he replied briskly, "represents in the executive department the whole people of the United States, as each member of the legislative department represents portions of them." Indeed, "the mere passage of a bill by Congress is no conclusive evidence that those who passed it represent the majority of the people of the United States or truly reflect their will."

Such statements could not, of course, settle the issue; and the cold war between the President and the Congress has remained a central (and wholesome) feature of American political history. It only rarely, however, reached the point it did in 1855 when Pierce waited a month for notification from Congress that it was ready to hear from him and, when no signal was forthcoming, sent his Message over anyway. The Presidency reached its nadir a few years later with Buchanan. "Without the authority of Congress," Buchanan said in his Third Message, "the President cannot fire a hostile gun in any case except to repel the attacks of an enemy." "After all," he added the next year, with the country on the verge of civil war, "he is no more than the chief executive officer of the Government. His province is not to make but to execute the laws." And, while he agreed that the southern states had no constitutional right to secede from the Union ("secession is neither more nor less than revolution"), he saw nothing that the President could do about it:

> Apart from the execution of the laws, so far as this may be practicable, the Executive has no authority to decide what shall be the relations between the Federal Government and South Carolina. . . . It is therefore my duty to submit to Congress the whole question in all its bearings.

Buchanan's successor, recoiling from this theory of executive and national impotence, returned to the Jacksonian theory of the Presidency. Lincoln, indeed, found in the idea of "the war power," as invoked in his Third Message, an apparently inexhaustible excuse for enlarging the presidential authority. After the war Congress struck back by passing the tenure-of-office act, requiring senatorial consent to the removal of all appointees who had senatorial confirmation—an act of legislative aggression against which Andrew Johnson vainly protested in his Third Message. Accepting the new mood, Grant told the Congress in the midst of the Depression of 1873, "It is the duty of Congress to devise the method of correcting the evils which are acknowledged to exist, and not mine."

The Buchanan-Grant conception of the Presidency could not easily survive the challenges placed on national leadership by the country's growth into an industrial society and a world power. In the 20th century, Theodore Roosevelt, Wilson and Franklin Roosevelt resumed the path of Jackson and Lincoln. Truman, admonishing his successor in his last Message, summed up this evolution:

> *The President-elect is about to take up the greatest burdens, the most compelling responsibilities, given to any man. . . .*
>
> *What are these tasks? The President is Chief of State, elected representative of all the people. He is Commander in Chief of our Armed Forces. He is charged with the conduct of our foreign relations. He is Chief Executive of the Nation's largest civilian organization. He must select and nominate all top officials of the executive branch and all Federal judges. And, on the legislative side, he has the obligation and the opportunity to recommend and to approve or veto legislation. Besides all this, it is to him that a great political party turns naturally for leadership, and that, too, he must provide as President.*
>
> *This bundle of burdens is unique; there is nothing like it on the face of the earth.*

Eisenhower, more attracted by the Buchanan-Grant thesis, responded in his own last Message: "Earnest and persistent attempts have been made to strengthen the position of State and local governments and thereby to stop the dangerous drift toward centralization of governmental power in Washington." His successors, however, restored the presidential tradition of Jackson and Lincoln.

Though the Message remained formally an epistle from the President to Congress, it was a communication which the rest of the nation was bound to overhear, and this, of course, was one of its points. Washington in his Second Message thus stressed the proposition that the Chief Executive must give "the fullest evidence of a disposition as far as may be practicable to consult the wishes of every part of the community and to lay the foundations of the public administration in the affections of the people." To do this, as Monroe argued thirty years later,

> *the people being with us exclusively the sovereign, it is indispensable that full information be laid before them on all important subjects, to enable them to exercise that high power with complete effect. If kept in the dark, they must be incompetent to it. We are all liable to error, and those who are engaged in the management of public affairs are more subject to excitement and to be led astray by their par-*

ticular interests and passions than the great body of our con-
stituents, who, living at home in the pursuit of their ordinary
avocations, are calm but deeply interested spectators of
events and of the conduct of those who are parties to them.
To the people every department of the Government and
every individual in each are responsible, and the more full
their information the better they can judge of the wisdom
of the policy pursued and of the conduct of each in regard
to it.

This act of presidential communication was not to be exercised lightly. "In times like the present," said Lincoln in his Second Message, "men should utter nothing for which they would not willingly be responsible through time and in eternity."

Nor, in a democracy, could it be a one-way process. The people through their representatives, their newspapers and their right of petition had to be free to send back their own state-of-the-union messages to the President. Thus Washington, noting that provisions in the postal law might hold up the transmission of newspapers, observed, "A full conviction of the importance of facilitating the circulation of political intelligence and information will, I doubt not, lead to the application of a remedy." In spite of this early presidential concern, it must be conceded, the Bill of Rights as such came in for surprisingly perfunctory attention in Annual Messages until recent times. Some Presidents even seemed to feel that liberty might too easily become license—not only Jackson trying to suppress abolitionist propaganda in the South, but even the great libertarian Jefferson himself. The law, Jefferson said in his Sixth Message, provided for the punishment of crimes against the public peace or authority once they were committed.

But would it not be salutary to give also the means of pre-
venting their commission? Where an enterprise is meditated
by private individuals against a foreign nation in amity with
the United States, powers of prevention to a certain extent
are given by the laws. Would they not be as reasonable and
useful where the enterprise preparing is against the United
States?

He had in mind, of course, the Burr conspiracy; but he seemed to be calling for the prosecution of thoughts, in advance of overt acts. The next year he returned to the theme: "The framers of our Constitution certainly supposed they had guarded as well their Government against destruction by treason as their citizens against oppression under pretense of it, and if these ends are not attained it is of importance to inquire by what means more effectual they may be secured."

Still another progressive President, Wilson, could in 1919 blame "the widespread condition of political restlessness in our body politic" in part on "the transfusion of radical theories from seething European centers" and "the machinations of passionate and malevolent agitators." Yet, except for wartime, Presidents have been on the whole reluctant to abridge the freedoms of expression and conscience pledged in the First Amendment. And the crusade waged by modern totalitarianism against individual freedom in the 20th century compelled an increasing recognition of the place of the Bill of Rights in the American system. So Franklin Roosevelt made "freedom of speech and expression everywhere in the world" the first of his Four Freedoms. "We must take our stand on the Bill of Rights," said Truman in his last Message. "The inquisition, the star chamber, have no place in a free society." Eisenhower saw the problem differently. "Our national security demands that the investigation of new employees and the evaluation of derogatory information respecting present employees be expedited," he said in his Second Message. ". . . We are dealing here with actions akin to treason." Like Jefferson, he sought "additional legal weapons with which to combat subversion." Kennedy, on the other hand, in his First Message returned to the spirit of the Bill of Rights: "Let it be clear that this Administration recognizes the value of dissent and daring—that we greet healthy controversy as the hallmark of healthy change."

7

The national experiment. "The preservation of the sacred fire of liberty and the destiny of the republican model of government," Washington said in his Inaugural Address, "are justly considered, perhaps, as *deeply,* as *finally* staked on the experiment intrusted to the hands of the American people."

His successors watched the progress of this experiment with anxiety and hope. In his last Message Madison permitted himself to "indulge the proud reflection that the American people have reached in safety and success their fortieth year as an independent nation." This, the Presidents knew, had more than local significance. "Our institutions," said Monroe in his own last Message, "form an important epoch in the history of the civilized world. On their preservation and in their utmost purity everything will depend." "The present year," added Van Buren in 1838, "closes the first half century of our Federal institutions. . . . It was reserved for the American Union to test the advantages of a government entirely dependent on the continual exercise of the popu-

lar will, and our experience has shown that it is as beneficent in practice as it is just in theory." Polk made the point even more strongly in
his Third Message:

> *After an existence of near three-fourths of a century as a free
> and independent Republic, the problem no longer remains
> to be solved whether man is capable of self-government. The
> success of our admirable system is a conclusive refutation of
> the theories of those in other countries who maintain that a
> 'favored few' are born to rule and that the mass of mankind
> must be governed by force.*

The successful prosecution of the Mexican War, Polk added in his last
Message, "evinces beyond all doubt that a popular representative government is equal to any emergency which is likely to arise in the affairs
of a nation." Sixty years after the Constitution, Taylor in his First Message pronounced the United States of America "the most stable and
permanent Government on earth."

Stability hardly seemed the most prominent feature of the American polity in the next years. But the nation survived the test of civil
war; and Andrew Johnson could say of the American form of government after the three-quarter of a century mark, "Experience has proved
its sufficiency in peace and in war; it has vindicated its authority
through dangers and afflictions, and sudden and terrible emergencies.
. . . The experience of centuries has been crowded into a few generations, and has created an intense, indestructible nationality. . . . The
latent conviction that our form of government is the best ever known
to the world has enabled us to emerge from civil war within four years
with a complete vindication of the constitutional authority of the General Government and with our local liberties and State institutions
unimpaired."

"Where in past history," Johnson concluded, "does a parallel exist
to the public happiness which is within the reach of the people of the
United States?" Still, the quest for national contentment remained
elusive. A century after the Constitution, Cleveland expressed gloomy
forebodings, reminiscent of nothing so much as Walt Whitman in
Democratic Vistas. The early years of the republic, Cleveland said, had
been marked by the sobriety of "the plain people who, side by side, in
friendly competition wrought for the ennoblement and dignity of man,
for the solution of the problem of free government, and for the achievement of the grand destiny awaiting the land which God had given
them." Now a century had passed.

> *Our cities are the abiding places of wealth and luxury; our
> manufactories yield fortunes never dreamed of by the fathers*

*of the Republic; our business men are madly striving in the
race for riches, and immense aggregations of capital outrun
the imagination in the magnitude of their undertakings.*

*We view with pride and satisfaction this bright picture
of our country's growth and prosperity, while only a closer
scrutiny develops a somber shading. Upon more careful inspection we find the wealth and luxury of our cities mingled
with poverty and wretchedness and unremunerative toil. A
crowded and constantly increasing urban population suggests the impoverishment of rural sections and discontent
with agricultural pursuits. The farmer's son, not satisfied
with his father's simple and laborious life, joins the eager
chase for easily acquired wealth. . . . The gulf between em-
ployers and the employed is constantly widening, the classes
are rapidly forming, one comprising the very rich and powerful, while in another are found the toiling poor. . . . The
existing situation is injurious to the health of our entire
body politic. . . . It appears in the sordid disregard of all
but personal interests, in the refusal to abate for the benefit
of others one iota of selfish advantage, and in combinations
to perpetuate such advantages through efforts to control
legislation and improperly influence the suffrages of the
people. . . . The beneficent purposes of our Government,
dependent upon the patriotism and contentment of our people, are endangered.*

Not everyone shared Cleveland's pessimism. "Popular government," said McKinley in his last Message, "has demonstrated in its one
hundred and twenty-four years of trial here its stability and security,
and its efficiency as the best instrument of national development and
the best safeguard to human rights. . . . Education, religion, and
morality have kept pace with our advancement in other directions.
. . . A nation so preserved and blessed gives reverent thanks to God."
But Theodore Roosevelt, less complacent, urged his countrymen to
strive for moral betterment.

*We have plenty of sins of our own to war against, and under
ordinary circumstances we can do more for the general
uplifting of humanity by striving with heart and soul to put
a stop to civic corruption, to brutal lawlessness and violent
race prejudices here at home than by passing resolutions
about wrongdoing elsewhere.*

The great Presidents of the 20th century agreed much more with
Theodore Roosevelt than with McKinley. As Franklin Roosevelt put

it in his Fourth Message, the Depression of 1929 meant something more than the breakdown of the visible economic mechanism. It was a supreme test of the democratic system. It meant that

> *long neglect of the needs of the underprivileged had brought too many of our people to the verge of doubt as to the successful adaptation of our historic traditions to the complex modern world. In that lay a challenge to our democratic form of government itself. Ours was the task to prove that democracy could be made to function in the world of today as effectively as in the simpler world of a hundred years ago.*

Nor was this simply a domestic challenge. "Dictatorships—and the philosophy of force which justifies and accompanies dictatorships—," Roosevelt said three years later, "have originated in almost every case in the necessity for drastic action to improve internal conditions where democratic action for one reason or another has failed to respond to modern needs and modern demands." The republic now faced "a set of world-wide forces of disintegration." Survival required purpose. "We have learned by bitter experience," said Truman, combating McKinley's Darwinism in his Fifth Message, "that progress is not automatic —that wrong policies lead to depression and disaster." Truman's last Message stated the issue with quiet eloquence:

> *Let all of us pause now, think back, consider carefully the meaning of our national experience. Let us draw comfort from it and faith and confidence in our future as Americans.*
>
> *The Nation's business is never finished. The basic questions we have been dealing with, these eight years past, present themselves anew. That is the way of our society. Circumstances change and current questions take on different forms, new complications, year by year. But underneath the great issues remain the same—prosperity, welfare, human rights, effective democracy, and, above all, peace.*

So the long labor of liberty continued. Kennedy in his First Message asked "whether a nation organized and governed such as ours can endure" and replied: "The outcome is by no means certain." And in his Second Message Lyndon Johnson pointed out that the American people were entering their third century in pursuit of union. In 1765 nine British colonies first joined together to affirm the first continental union of democracy. In 1865, "following a terrible test of blood and fire, the compact of union was finally sealed." In the second century Americans labored to establish a unity of interest and purpose among the diverse groups making up the national community.

Now, in 1965, we begin a new quest for union. We seek the unity of man with the world he has built—with the knowledge that can save or destroy him—with the cities which can stimulate or stifle him—with the wealth and machines which can enrich or menace his spirit. We seek to establish a harmony between man and society which will allow each of us to enlarge the meaning of his life and all of us to elevate the quality of our civilization.

The nation's business, as Truman said, is never finished. And in the unending quest Americans will always be guided by the most profound and beautiful passage in all the Annual Messages—the conclusion of Lincoln's Second Message in 1862:

The dogma of the quiet past are inadequate to the stormy present. The occasion is piled high with difficulty, and we must rise to the occasion. As our case is new, so we must think anew and act anew. We must disenthrall ourselves, and then we shall save our country.

Fellow-citizens, we cannot escape history. . . . The fiery trial through which we pass will light us down in honor or dishonor to the latest generation. In giving freedom to the slave we assure freedom to the free—honorable alike in what we give and what we preserve. We shall nobly save or meanly lose the last best hope of earth. Other means may succeed; this could not fail. The way is plain, peaceful, generous, just—a way which if followed the world will forever applaud and God must forever bless.

PRINCETON, NEW JERSEY
APRIL, 1966

George Washington

April 30, 1789 to March 4, 1797

FIRST ANNUAL ADDRESS.

UNITED STATES, *January 8, 1790.*

Fellow-Citizens of the Senate and House of Representatives:

I embrace with great satisfaction the opportunity which now presents itself of congratulating you on the present favorable prospects of our public affairs. The recent accession of the important State of North Carolina to the Constitution of the United States (of which official information has been received), the rising credit and respectability of our country, the general and increasing good will toward the Government of the Union, and the concord, peace, and plenty with which we are blessed are circumstances auspicious in an eminent degree to our national prosperity.

In resuming your consultations for the general good you can not but derive encouragement from the reflection that the measures of the last session have been as satisfactory to your constituents as the novelty and difficulty of the work allowed you to hope. Still further to realize their expectations and to secure the blessings which a gracious Providence has placed within our reach will in the course of the present important session call for the cool and deliberate exertion of your patriotism, firmness, and wisdom.

Among the many interesting objects which will engage your attention that of providing for the common defense will merit particular regard. To be prepared for war is one of the most effectual means of preserving peace.

A free people ought not only to be armed, but disciplined; to which end a uniform and well-digested plan is requisite; and their safety and interest require that they should promote such manufactories as tend to render them independent of others for essential, particularly military, supplies.

The proper establishment of the troops which may be deemed indispensable will be entitled to mature consideration. In the arrangements which may be made respecting it it will be of importance to conciliate the comfortable support of the officers and soldiers with a due regard to economy.

There was reason to hope that the pacific measures adopted with regard to certain hostile tribes of Indians would have relieved the inhabitants of our Southern and Western frontiers from their depredations, but you will perceive from the information contained in the papers which I shall direct to be laid before you (comprehending a communication from the Commonwealth of Virginia) that we ought to be prepared to afford protection to those parts of the Union, and, if necessary, to punish aggressors.

The interests of the United States require that our intercourse with other nations should be facilitated by such provisions as will enable me to fulfill my duty in that respect in the manner which circumstances may render most conducive to the public good, and to this end that the compensations to be made to the persons who may be employed should, according to the nature of their appointments, be defined by law, and a competent fund designated for defraying the expenses incident to the conduct of our foreign affairs.

Various considerations also render it expedient that the terms on which foreigners may be admitted to the rights of citizens should be speedily ascertained by a uniform rule of naturalization.

Uniformity in the currency, weights, and measures of the United States is an object of great importance, and will, I am persuaded, be duly attended to.

The advancement of agriculture, commerce, and manufactures by all proper means will not, I trust, need recommendation; but I can not forbear intimating to you the expediency of giving effectual encouragement as well to the introduction of new and useful inventions from abroad as to the exertions of skill and genius in producing them at home, and of facilitating the intercourse between the distant parts of our country by a due attention to the post-office and post-roads.

Nor am I less persuaded that you will agree with me in opinion that there is nothing which can better deserve your patronage than the promotion of science and literature. Knowledge is in every country the surest basis of public happiness. In one in which the measures of government receive their impressions so immediately from the sense of the community as in ours it is proportionably essential. To the security of a free constitution it contributes in various ways—by convincing those who are intrusted with the public administration that every valuable end of government is best answered by the enlightened confidence of the people, and by teaching the people themselves to know and to value their own rights; to discern and provide against invasions of them; to distinguish between oppression and the necessary exercise of lawful authority; between burthens proceeding from a disregard to their convenience and those resulting from the inevitable exigencies of society; to discriminate the spirit of liberty from that of licentiousness—cherishing the first, avoiding the last—and uniting a speedy but temperate vigilance against encroachments, with an inviolable respect to the laws.

Whether this desirable object will be best promoted by affording aids to seminaries of learning already established, by the institution of a national university, or by any other expedients will be well worthy of a place in the deliberations of the Legislature.

Gentlemen of the House of Representatives:

I saw with peculiar pleasure at the close of the last session the resolution entered into by you expressive of your opinion that an adequate provision for the support of the public credit is a matter of high importance to the national honor and prosperity. In this sentiment I entirely concur; and to a perfect confidence in your best endeavors to devise such a provision as will be truly consistent with the end I add an equal reliance on the cheerful cooperation of the other branch of the Legislature. It would be superfluous to specify inducements to a measure in which the character and permanent interests of the United States are so obviously and so deeply concerned, and which has received so explicit a sanction from your declaration.

Gentlemen of the Senate and House of Representatives:

I have directed the proper officers to lay before you, respectively, such papers and estimates as regard the affairs particularly recommended to your consideration, and necessary to convey to you that information of the state of the Union which it is my duty to afford.

The welfare of our country is the great object to which our cares and efforts ought to be directed, and I shall derive great satisfaction from a cooperation with you in the pleasing though arduous task of insuring to our fellow-citizens the blessings which they have a right to expect from a free, efficient, and equal government.

SECOND ANNUAL ADDRESS.

UNITED STATES, *December 8, 1790.*

Fellow-Citizens of the Senate and House of Representatives:

In meeting you again I feel much satisfaction in being able to repeat my congratulations on the favorable prospects which continue to distinguish our public affairs. The abundant fruits of another year have blessed our country with plenty and with the means of a flourishing commerce. The progress of public credit is witnessed by a considerable rise of American stock abroad as well as at home, and the revenues allotted for this and other national purposes have been productive beyond the calculations by which they were regulated. This latter circumstance is the more pleasing, as it is not only a proof of the fertility of our resources, but as it assures us of a further increase of the national respectability and credit, and, let me add, as it bears an honorable testimony to the patriotism and integrity of the mercantile and marine part of our citizens. The punctuality of the former in discharging their engagements has been exemplary.

In conformity to the powers vested in me by acts of the last session, a loan of 3,000,000 florins, toward which some provisional measures had previously taken place, has been completed in Holland. As well the celerity with which it has been filled as the nature of the terms (considering the more than ordinary demand for borrowing created by the situation of Europe) give a reasonable hope that the further execution of those powers may proceed with advantage and success. The Secretary of the Treasury has my directions to communicate such further particulars as may be requisite for more precise information.

Since your last sessions I have received communications by which it appears that the district of Kentucky, at present a part of Virginia, has concurred in certain propositions contained in a law of that State, in consequence of which the district is to become a distinct member of the Union, in case the requisite sanction of Congress be added. For this sanction application is now made. I shall cause the papers on this very important transaction to be laid before you. The liberality and harmony with which it has been conducted will be found to do great honor to both the parties, and the sentiments of warm attachment to the Union and its present Government expressed by our fellow-citizens of Kentucky can not fail to add an affectionate concern for their particular welfare to the great national impressions under which you will decide on the case submitted to you.

It has been heretofore known to Congress that frequent incursions have been made on our frontier settlements by certain banditti of Indians from the northwest side of the Ohio. These, with some of the tribes dwelling on and near the Wabash, have of late been particularly active in their depredations, and being emboldened by the impunity of their crimes and aided by such parts of the neighboring tribes as could be seduced to join in their hostilities or afford them a retreat for their prisoners and plunder, they have, instead of listening to the humane invitations and overtures made on the part of the United States, renewed their violences with fresh alacrity and greater effect. The lives of a number of valuable citizens have thus been sacrificed, and some of them under circumstances peculiarly shocking, whilst others have been carried into a deplorable captivity.

These aggravated provocations rendered it essential to the safety of the Western settlements that the aggressors should be made sensible that the Government of the Union is not less capable of punishing their crimes than it is disposed to respect their rights and reward their attachments. As this object could not be effected by defensive measures, it became necessary to put in force the act which empowers the President to call out the militia for the protection of the frontiers, and I have accordingly authorized an expedition in which the regular troops in that quarter are combined with such drafts of militia as were deemed sufficient. The event of the measure is yet unknown to me. The Secretary of War is directed to lay before you a statement of the information on which it is founded, as well as an estimate of the expense with which it will be attended.

The disturbed situation of Europe, and particularly the critical posture of the great maritime powers, whilst it ought to make us the more thankful for the general peace and security enjoyed by the United States, reminds us at the same time of the circumspection with which it becomes us to preserve these blessings. It requires also that we should not over-look the tendency of a war, and even of preparations for a war, among the nations most concerned in active commerce with this country to abridge the means, and thereby at least enhance the price, of transport-ing its valuable productions to their proper markets I recommend it to your serious reflections how far and in what mode it may be expedient to guard against embarrassments from these contingencies by such encouragements to our own navigation as will render our commerce and agriculture less dependent on foreign bottoms, which may fail us in the very moments most interesting to both of these great objects. Our fish-eries and the transportation of our own produce offer us abundant means for guarding ourselves against this evil.

Your attention seems to be not less due to that particular branch of our trade which belongs to the Mediterranean. So many circumstances unite in rendering the present state of it distressful to us that you will not think any deliberations misemployed which may lead to its relief and protection.

The laws you have already passed for the establishment of a judiciary system have opened the doors of justice to all descriptions of persons. You will consider in your wisdom whether improvements in that system may yet be made, and particularly whether an uniform process of execu-tion on sentences issuing from the Federal courts be not desirable through all the States.

The patronage of our commerce, of our merchants and seamen, has called for the appointment of consuls in foreign countries. It seems expedient to regulate by law the exercise of that jurisdiction and those functions which are permitted them, either by express convention or by a friendly indulgence, in the places of their residence. The consular convention, too, with His Most Christian Majesty has stipulated in certain cases the aid of the national authority to his consuls established here. Some legislative provision is requisite to carry these stipulations into full effect.

The establishment of the militia, of a mint, of standards of weights and measures, of the post-office and post-roads are subjects which I presume you will resume of course, and which are abundantly urged by their own importance.

Gentlemen of the House of Representatives:

The sufficiency of the revenues you have established for the objects to which they are appropriated leaves no doubt that the residuary provisions will be commensurate to the other objects for which the public faith stands now pledged. Allow me, moreover, to hope that it will be a favorite policy with you, not merely to secure a payment of the interest of the debt funded, but as far and as fast as the growing resources of the country will permit to exonerate it of the principal itself. The appropriation you have made of the Western land explains your dispositions on this subject, and I am persuaded that the sooner that valuable fund can be made to contribute, along with other means, to the actual reduction of the public debt the more salutary will the measure be to every public interest, as well as the more satisfactory to our constituents.

Gentlemen of the Senate and House of Representatives:

In pursuing the various and weighty business of the present session I indulge the fullest persuasion that your consultations will be equally marked with wisdom and animated by the love of your country. In whatever belongs to my duty you shall have all the cooperation which an undiminished zeal for its welfare can inspire. It will be happy for us both, and our best reward, if, by a successful administration of our respective trusts, we can make the established Government more and more instrumental in promoting the good of our fellow-citizens, and more and more the object of their attachment and confidence.

THIRD ANNUAL ADDRESS.

UNITED STATES, *October 25, 1791.*

Fellow-Citizens of the Senate and of the House of Representatives:

I meet you upon the present occasion with the feelings which are naturally inspired by a strong impression of the prosperous situation of our common country, and by a persuasion equally strong that the labors of the session which has just commenced will, under the guidance of a spirit no less prudent than patriotic, issue in measures conducive to the stability and increase of national prosperity.

Numerous as are the providential blessings which demand our grateful acknowledgments, the abundance with which another year has again rewarded the industry of the husbandman is too important to escape recollection.

Your own observations in your respective situations will have satisfied you of the progressive state of agriculture, manufactures, commerce, and navigation. In tracing their causes you will have remarked with particular pleasure the happy effects of that revival of confidence, public as well as private, to which the Constitution and laws of the United States have so eminently contributed; and you will have observed with no less interest new and decisive proofs of the increasing reputation and credit of the nation. But you nevertheless can not fail to derive satisfaction from the confirmation of these circumstances which will be disclosed in the several official communications that will be made to you in the course of your deliberations.

The rapid subscriptions to the Bank of the United States, which completed the sum allowed to be subscribed in a single day, is among the striking and pleasing evidences which present themselves, not only of confidence in the Government, but of resource in the community.

In the interval of your recess due attention has been paid to the execution of the different objects which were specially provided for by the laws and resolutions of the last session.

Among the most important of these is the defense and security of the Western frontiers. To accomplish it on the most humane principles was a primary wish.

Accordingly, at the same time that treaties have been provisionally concluded and other proper means used to attach the wavering and to confirm in their friendship the well-disposed tribes of Indians, effectual measures have been adopted to make those of a hostile description sensible that a pacification was desired upon terms of moderation and justice.

Those measures having proved unsuccessful, it became necessary to convince the refractory of the power of the United States to punish their depredations. Offensive operations have therefore been directed, to be conducted, however, as consistently as possible with the dictates of humanity. Some of these have been crowned with full success and others are yet depending. The expeditions which have been completed were carried on under the authority and at the expense of the United States by the militia of Kentucky, whose enterprise, intrepidity, and good conduct are entitled to peculiar commendation.

Overtures of peace are still continued to the deluded tribes, and considerable numbers of individuals belonging to them have lately renounced all further opposition, removed from their former situations, and placed themselves under the immediate protection of the United States.

It is sincerely to be desired that all need of coercion in future may cease and that an intimate intercourse may succeed, calculated to advance the happiness of the Indians and to attach them firmly to the United States.

In order to this it seems necessary—

That they should experience the benefits of an impartial dispensation of justice.

That the mode of alienating their lands, the main source of discontent and war, should be so defined and regulated as to obviate imposition and as far as may be practicable controversy concerning the reality and extent of the alienations which are made.

That commerce with them should be promoted under regulations tending to secure an equitable deportment toward them, and that such rational experiments should be made for imparting to them the blessings of civilization as may from time to time suit their condition.

That the Executive of the United States should be enabled to employ the means to which the Indians have been long accustomed for uniting their immediate interests with the preservation of peace.

And that efficacious provision should be made for inflicting adequate penalties upon all those who, by violating their rights, shall infringe the treaties and endanger the peace of the Union.

A system corresponding with the mild principles of religion and philanthropy toward an unenlightened race of men, whose happiness materially depends on the conduct of the United States, would be as honorable to the national character as conformable to the dictates of sound policy.

The powers specially vested in me by the act laying certain duties on distilled spirits, which respect the subdivisions of the districts into surveys, the appointment of officers, and the assignment of compensations, have likewise been carried into effect. In a matter in which both materials and experience were wanting to guide the calculation it will be readily conceived that there must have been difficulty in such an adjustment of the rates of compensation as would conciliate a reasonable competency with a proper regard to the limits prescribed by the law. It is hoped that the circumspection which has been used will be found in the result to have secured the last of the two objects; but it is probable that with a view to the first in some instances a revision of the provision will be found advisable.

The impressions with which this law has been received by the community have been upon the whole such as were to be expected among enlightened and well-disposed citizens from the propriety and necessity of the measure. The novelty, however, of the tax in a considerable part of the United States and a misconception of some of its provisions have given occasion in particular places to some degree of discontent; but it is satisfactory to know that this disposition yields to proper explanations and more just apprehensions of the true nature of the law, and I entertain a full confidence that it will in all give way to motives which arise out of a just sense of duty and a virtuous regard to the public welfare.

If there are any circumstances in the law which consistently with its main design may be so varied as to remove any well-intentioned objections that may happen to exist, it will consist with a wise moderation to make the proper variations. It is desirable on all occasions to unite with a steady and firm adherence to constitutional and necessary acts of

Government the fullest evidence of a disposition as far as may be practicable to consult the wishes of every part of the community and to lay the foundations of the public administration in the affections of the people.

Pursuant to the authority contained in the several acts on that subject, a district of 10 miles square for the permanent seat of the Government of the United States has been fixed and announced by proclamation, which district will comprehend lands on both sides of the river Potomac and the towns of Alexandria and Georgetown. A city has also been laid out agreeably to a plan which will be placed before Congress, and as there is a prospect, favored by the rate of sales which have already taken place, of ample funds for carrying on the necessary public buildings, there is every expectation of their due progress.

The completion of the census of the inhabitants, for which provision was made by law, has been duly notified (excepting one instance in which the return has been informal, and another in which it has been omitted or miscarried), and the returns of the officers who were charged with this duty, which will be laid before you, will give you the pleasing assurance that the present population of the United States borders on 4,000,000 persons.

It is proper also to inform you that a further loan of 2,500,000 florins has been completed in Holland, the terms of which are similar to those of the one last announced, except as to a small reduction of charges. Another, on like terms, for 6,000,000 florins, had been set on foot under circumstances that assured an immediate completion.

Gentlemen of the Senate:

Two treaties which have been provisionally concluded with the Cherokees and Six Nations of Indians will be laid before you for your consideration and ratification.

Gentlemen of the House of Representatives:

In entering upon the discharge of your legislative trust you must anticipate with pleasure that many of the difficulties necessarily incident to the first arrangements of a new government for an extensive country have been happily surmounted by the zealous and judicious exertions of your predecessors in cooperation with the other branch of the Legislature. The important objects which remain to be accomplished will, I am persuaded, be conducted upon principles equally comprehensive and equally well calculated for the advancement of the general weal.

The time limited for receiving subscriptions to the loans proposed by the act making provision for the debt of the United States having expired, statements from the proper department will as soon as possible apprise you of the exact result. Enough, however, is known already to afford an assurance that the views of that act have been substantially fulfilled. The subscription in the domestic debt of the United States has embraced by far the greatest proportion of that debt, affording at the same time proof of the general satisfaction of the public creditors with the system which has been proposed to their acceptance and of the spirit of accommodation to the convenience of the Government with which they are actuated. The subscriptions in the debts of the respective States as far as the provisions of the law have permitted may be said to be yet more general. The part of the debt of the United States which remains unsubscribed will naturally engage your further deliberations.

It is particularly pleasing to me to be able to announce to you that the revenues which have been established promise to be adequate to their objects, and may be permitted, if no unforeseen exigency occurs, to supersede for the present the necessity of any new burthens upon our constituents.

An object which will claim your early attention is a provision for the current service of the ensuing year, together with such ascertained demands upon the Treasury as require to be immediately discharged, and such casualties as may have arisen in the execution of the public business, for which no specific appropriation may have yet been made; of all which a proper estimate will be laid before you.

Gentlemen of the Senate and of the House of Representatives:

I shall content myself with a general reference to former communications for several objects upon which the urgency of other affairs has hitherto postponed any definitive resolution. Their importance will recall them to your attention, and I trust that the progress already made in the most arduous arrangements of the Government will afford you leisure to resume them with advantage.

There are, however, some of them of which I can not forbear a more particular mention. These are the militia, the post-office and post-roads, the mint, weights and measures, a provision for the sale of the vacant lands of the United States.

The first is certainly an object of primary importance whether viewed in reference to the national security to the satisfaction of the community or to the preservation of order. In connection with this the establishment of competent magazines and arsenals and the fortification of such places as are peculiarly important and vulnerable naturally present themselves to consideration. The safety of the United States under divine protection ought to rest on the basis of systematic and solid arrangements, exposed as little as possible to the hazards of fortuitous circumstances.

The importance of the post-office and post-roads on a plan sufficiently liberal and comprehensive, as they respect the expedition, safety, and facility of communication, is increased by their instrumentality in diffusing a knowledge of the laws and proceedings of the Government, which, while it contributes to the security of the people, serves also to guard them against the effects of misrepresentation and misconception.   The establishment of additional cross posts, especially to some of the important points in the Western and Northern parts of the Union, can not fail to be of material utility.

The disorders in the existing currency, and especially the scarcity of small change, a scarcity so peculiarly distressing to the poorer classes, strongly recommend the carrying into immediate effect the resolution already entered into concerning the establishment of a mint.   Measures have been taken pursuant to that resolution for procuring some of the most necessary artists, together with the requisite apparatus.

An uniformity in the weights and measures of the country is among the important objects submitted to you by the Constitution, and if it can be derived from a standard at once invariable and universal, must be no less honorable to the public councils than conducive to the public convenience.

A provision for the sale of the vacant lands of the United States is particularly urged, among other reasons, by the important considerations that they are pledged as a fund for reimbursing the public debt; that if timely and judiciously applied they may save the necessity of burthening our citizens with new taxes for the extinguishment of the principal; and that being free to discharge the principal but in a limited proportion, no opportunity ought to be lost for availing the public of its right.

FOURTH ANNUAL ADDRESS.

UNITED STATES, *November 6, 1792.*

Fellow-Citizens of the Senate and of the House of Representatives:

It is some abatement of the satisfaction with which I meet you on the present occasion that, in felicitating you on a continuance of the national prosperity generally, I am not able to add to it information that the Indian hostilities which have for some time past distressed our Northwestern frontier have terminated.

You will, I am persuaded, learn with no less concern than I communicate it that reiterated endeavors toward effecting a pacification have hitherto issued only in new and outrageous proofs of persevering hostility on the part of the tribes with whom we are in contest.   An earnest desire to procure tranquillity to the frontier, to stop the further effusion of blood, to arrest the progress of expense, to forward the prevalent wish of the nation for peace has led to strenuous efforts through various channels to accomplish these desirable purposes; in making which efforts I consulted less my own anticipations of the event, or the scruples which some considerations were calculated to inspire, than the wish to find the object attainable, or if not attainable, to ascertain unequivocally that such is the case.

A detail of the measures which have been pursued and of their consequences, which will be laid before you, while it will confirm to you the want of success thus far, will, I trust, evince that means as proper and as efficacious as could have been devised have been employed. The issue of some of them, indeed, is still depending, but a favorable one, though not to be despaired of, is not promised by anything that has yet happened.

In the course of the attempts which have been made some valuable citizens have fallen victims to their zeal for the public service. A sanction commonly respected even among savages has been found in this instance insufficient to protect from massacre the emissaries of peace. It will, I presume, be duly considered whether the occasion does not call for an exercise of liberality toward the families of the deceased.

It must add to your concern to be informed that, besides the continuation of hostile appearances among the tribes north of the Ohio, some threatening symptoms have of late been revived among some of those south of it.

A part of the Cherokees, known by the name of Chickamaugas, inhabiting five villages on the Tennessee River, have long been in the practice of committing depredations on the neighboring settlements.

It was hoped that the treaty of Holston, made with the Cherokee Nation in July, 1791, would have prevented a repetition of such depredations; but the event has not answered this hope. The Chickamaugas, aided by some banditti of another tribe in their vicinity, have recently perpetrated wanton and unprovoked hostilities upon the citizens of the United States in that quarter. The information which has been received on this subject will be laid before you. Hitherto defensive precautions only have been strictly enjoined and observed.

It is not understood that any breach of treaty or aggression whatsoever on the part of the United States or their citizens is even alleged as a pretext for the spirit of hostility in this quarter.

I have reason to believe that every practicable exertion has been made (pursuant to the provision by law for that purpose) to be prepared for the alternative of a prosecution of the war in the event of a failure of pacific overtures. A large proportion of the troops authorized to be raised have been recruited, though the number is still incomplete, and pains have been taken to discipline and put them in condition for the particular kind of service to be performed. A delay of operations (besides being dictated by the measures which were pursuing toward a pacific termination of the war) has been in itself deemed preferable to immature efforts. A statement from the proper department with regard to the number of troops raised, and some other points which have been suggested, will afford more precise information as a guide to the legislative consultations, and among other things will enable Congress to judge whether some additional stimulus to the recruiting service may not be advisable.

In looking forward to the future expense of the operations which may be found inevitable I derive consolation from the information I receive that the product of the revenues for the present year is likely to supersede the necessity of additional burthens on the community for the service of the ensuing year. This, however, will be better ascertained in the course of the session, and it is proper to add that the information alluded to proceeds upon the supposition of no material extension of the spirit of hostility.

I can not dismiss the subject of Indian affairs without again recommending to your consideration the expediency of more adequate provision for giving energy to the laws throughout our interior frontier and for restraining the commission of outrages upon the Indians, without which all pacific plans must prove nugatory. To enable, by competent rewards, the employment of qualified and trusty persons to reside among them as agents would also contribute to the preservation of peace and good neighborhood. If in addition to these expedients an eligible plan could be devised for promoting civilization among the friendly tribes and for carrying on trade with them upon a scale equal to their wants and under regulations calculated to protect them from imposition and extortion, its influence in cementing their interest with ours could not but be considerable.

The prosperous state of our revenue has been intimated. This would be still more the case were it not for the impediments which in some places continue to embarrass the collection of the duties on spirits distilled within the United States. These impediments have lessened and are lessening in local extent, and, as applied to the community at large, the contentment with the law appears to be progressive.

But symptoms of increased opposition having lately manifested themselves in certain quarters, I judged a special interposition on my part proper and advisable, and under this impression have issued a proclamation warning against all unlawful combinations and proceedings having for their object or tending to obstruct the operation of the law in question, and announcing that all lawful ways and means would be strictly put in execution for bringing to justice the infractors thereof and securing obedience thereto.

Measures have also been taken for the prosecution of offenders, and Congress may be assured that nothing within constitutional and legal limits which may depend upon me shall be wanting to assert and maintain the just authority of the laws. In fulfilling this trust I shall count entirely upon the full cooperation of the other departments of the Government and upon the zealous support of all good citizens.

I can not forbear to bring again into the view of the Legislature the subject of a revision of the judiciary system. A representation from the judges of the Supreme Court, which will be laid before you, points out some of the inconveniences that are experienced. In the course of the execution of the laws considerations arise out of the structure of that system which in some cases tend to relax their efficacy. As connected with this subject, provisions to facilitate the taking of bail upon processes out of the courts of the United States and a supplementary definition of offenses against the Constitution and laws of the Union and of the punishment for such offenses will, it is presumed, be found worthy of particular attention.

Observations on the value of peace with other nations are unnecessary. It would be wise, however, by timely provisions to guard against those acts of our own citizens which might tend to disturb it, and to put ourselves in a condition to give that satisfaction to foreign nations which we may sometimes have occasion to require from them. I particularly recommend to your consideration the means of preventing those aggressions by our citizens on the territory of other nations, and other infractions of the law of nations, which, furnishing just subject of complaint, might endanger our peace with them; and, in general, the maintenance of a friendly intercourse with foreign powers will be presented to your attention by the expiration of the law for that purpose, which takes place, if not renewed, at the close of the present session.

In execution of the authority given by the Legislature measures have been taken for engaging some artists from abroad to aid in the establishment of our mint. Others have been employed at home. Provision has been made of the requisite buildings, and these are now putting into proper condition for the purposes of the establishment. There has also been a small beginning in the coinage of half dimes, the want of small coins in circulation calling the first attention to them.

The regulation of foreign coins in correspondency with the principles of our national coinage, as being essential to their due operation and to order in our money concerns, will, I doubt not, be resumed and completed.

It is represented that some provisions in the law which establishes the post-office operate, in experiment, against the transmission of newspapers to distant parts of the country. Should this, upon due inquiry, be found to be the fact, a full conviction of the importance of facilitating the circulation of political intelligence and information will, I doubt not, lead to the application of a remedy.

The adoption of a constitution for the State of Kentucky has been notified to me. The Legislature will share with me in the satisfaction which arises from an event interesting to the happiness of the part of the nation to which it relates and conducive to the general order.

It is proper likewise to inform you that since my last communication on the subject, and in further execution of the acts severally making provision for the public debt and for the reduction thereof, three new loans have been effected, each for 3,000,000 florins—one at Antwerp, at the annual interest of 4½ per cent, with an allowance of 4 per cent in lieu of all charges, and the other two at Amsterdam, at the annual interest of 4 per cent, with an allowance of 5½ per cent in one case and of 5 per cent in the other in lieu of all charges. The rates of these loans and the circumstances under which they have been made are confirmations of the high state of our credit abroad.

Among the objects to which these funds have been directed to be applied, the payment of the debts due to certain foreign officers, according to the provision made during the last session, has been embraced.

Gentlemen of the House of Representatives:

I entertain a strong hope that the state of the national finances is now sufficiently matured to enable you to enter upon a systematic and effectual arrangement for the regular redemption and discharge of the public debt, according to the right which has been reserved to the Government. No measure can be more desirable, whether viewed with an eye to its intrinsic importance or to the general sentiment and wish of the nation.

Provision is likewise requisite for the reimbursement of the loan which has been made of the Bank of the United States, pursuant to the eleventh section of the act by which it is incorporated. In fulfilling the public stipulations in this particular it is expected a valuable saving will be made.

Appropriations for the current service of the ensuing year and for such extraordinaries as may require provision will demand, and I doubt not will engage, your early attention.

Gentlemen of the Senate and of the House of Representatives:

I content myself with recalling your attention generally to such objects, not particularized in my present, as have been suggested in my former communications to you.

Various temporary laws will expire during the present session. Among these, that which regulates trade and intercourse with the Indian tribes will merit particular notice.

The results of your common deliberations hitherto will, I trust, be productive of solid and durable advantages to our constituents, such as, by conciliating more and more their ultimate suffrage, will tend to strengthen and confirm their attachment to that Constitution of Government upon which, under Divine Providence, materially depend their union, their safety, and their happiness.

Still further to promote and secure these inestimable ends there is

nothing which can have a more powerful tendency than the careful cultivation of harmony, combined with a due regard to stability, in the public
councils.

FIFTH ANNUAL ADDRESS.

PHILADELPHIA, *December 3, 1793.*
Fellow-Citizens of the Senate and of the House of Representatives:

Since the commencement of the term for which I have been again
called into office no fit occasion has arisen for expressing to my fellow-
citizens at large the deep and respectful sense which I feel of the renewed
testimony of public approbation. While on the one hand it awakened
my gratitude for all those instances of affectionate partiality with which
I have been honored by my country, on the other it could not prevent
an earnest wish for that retirement from which no private consideration
should ever have torn me. But influenced by the belief that my conduct
would be estimated according to its real motives, and that the people,
and the authorities derived from them, would support exertions having
nothing personal for their object, I have obeyed the suffrage which commanded me to resume the Executive power; and I humbly implore that
Being on whose will the fate of nations depends to crown with success
our mutual endeavors for the general happiness.

As soon as the war in Europe had embraced those powers with whom
the United States have the most extensive relations there was reason to
apprehend that our intercourse with them might be interrupted and our
disposition for peace drawn into question by the suspicions too often
entertained by belligerent nations. It seemed, therefore, to be my duty
to admonish our citizens of the consequences of a contraband trade and
of hostile acts to any of the parties, and to obtain by a declaration of
the existing legal state of things an easier admission of our right to
the immunities belonging to our situation. Under these impressions
the proclamation which will be laid before you was issued.

In this posture of affairs, both new and delicate, I resolved to adopt
general rules which should conform to the treaties and assert the privileges of the United States. These were reduced into a system, which
will be communicated to you. Although I have not thought myself at
liberty to forbid the sale of the prizes permitted by our treaty of commerce with France to be brought into our ports, I have not refused to
cause them to be restored when they were taken within the protection
of our territory, or by vessels commissioned or equipped in a warlike
form within the limits of the United States.

It rests with the wisdom of Congress to correct, improve, or enforce this plan of procedure; and it will probably be found expedient to extend the legal code and the jurisdiction of the courts of the United States to many cases which, though dependent on principles already recognized, demand some further provisions.

Where individuals shall, within the United States, array themselves in hostility against any of the powers at war, or enter upon military expeditions or enterprises within the jurisdiction of the United States, or usurp and exercise judicial authority within the United States, or where the penalties on violations of the law of nations may have been indistinctly marked, or are inadequate—these offenses can not receive too early and close an attention, and require prompt and decisive remedies.

Whatsoever those remedies may be, they will be well administered by the judiciary, who possess a long-established course of investigation, effectual process, and officers in the habit of executing it.

In like manner, as several of the courts have doubted, under particular circumstances, their power to liberate the vessels of a nation at peace, and even of a citizen of the United States, although seized under a false color of being hostile property, and have denied their power to liberate certain captures within the protection of our territory, it would seem proper to regulate their jurisdiction in these points. But if the Executive is to be the resort in either of the two last-mentioned cases, it is hoped that he will be authorized by law to have facts ascertained by the courts when for his own information he shall request it.

I can not recommend to your notice measures for the fulfillment of our duties to the rest of the world without again pressing upon you the necessity of placing ourselves in a condition of complete defense and of exacting from them the fulfillment of their duties toward us. The United States ought not to indulge a persuasion that, contrary to the order of human events, they will forever keep at a distance those painful appeals to arms with which the history of every other nation abounds. There is a rank due to the United States among nations which will be withheld, if not absolutely lost, by the reputation of weakness. If we desire to avoid insult, we must be able to repel it; if we desire to secure peace, one of the most powerful instruments of our rising prosperity, it must be known that we are at all times ready for war. The documents which will be presented to you will shew the amount and kinds of arms and military stores now in our magazines and arsenals; and yet an addition even to these supplies can not with prudence be neglected, as it would leave nothing to the uncertainty of procuring of warlike apparatus in the moment of public danger.

Nor can such arrangements, with such objects, be exposed to the censure or jealousy of the warmest friends of republican government. They are incapable of abuse in the hands of the militia, who ought to possess a pride in being the depository of the force of the Republic, and may be trained to a degree of energy equal to every military exigency of the United States. But it is an inquiry which can not be too solemnly pursued, whether the act "more effectually to provide for the national defense by establishing an uniform militia throughout the United States" has organized them so as to produce their full effect; whether your own experience in the several States has not detected some imperfections in the scheme, and whether a material feature in an improvement of it ought not to be to afford an opportunity for the study of those branches of the military art which can scarcely ever be attained by practice alone.

The connection of the United States with Europe has become extremely interesting. The occurrences which relate to it and have passed under the knowledge of the Executive will be exhibited to Congress in a subsequent communication.

When we contemplate the war on our frontiers, it may be truly affirmed that every reasonable effort has been made to adjust the causes of dissension with the Indians north of the Ohio. The instructions given to the commissioners evince a moderation and equity proceeding from a sincere love of peace, and a liberality having no restriction but the essential interests and dignity of the United States. The attempt, however, of an amicable negotiation having been frustrated, the troops have marched to act offensively. Although the proposed treaty did not arrest the progress of military preparation, it is doubtful how far the advance of the season, before good faith justified active movements, may retard them during the remainder of the year. From the papers and intelligence which relate to this important subject you will determine whether the deficiency in the number of troops granted by law shall be compensated by succors of militia, or additional encouragements shall be proposed to recruits.

An anxiety has been also demonstrated by the Executive for peace with the Creeks and the Cherokees. The former have been relieved with corn and with clothing, and offensive measures against them prohibited during the recess of Congress. To satisfy the complaints of the latter, prosecutions have been instituted for the violences committed upon them. But the papers which will be delivered to you disclose the critical footing on which we stand in regard to both those tribes, and it is with Congress to pronounce what shall be done.

After they shall have provided for the present emergency, it will merit their most serious labors to render tranquillity with the savages permanent by creating ties of interest. Next to a rigorous execution of justice on the violators of peace, the establishment of commerce with the Indian nations in behalf of the United States is most likely to conciliate their attachment. But it ought to be conducted without fraud, without extortion, with constant and plentiful supplies, with a ready market for the commodities of the Indians and a stated price for what they give in payment and receive in exchange. Individuals will not pursue such a traffic unless they be allured by the hope of profit; but it will be enough for the United States to be reimbursed only. Should this recommendation accord with the opinion of Congress, they will recollect that it can not be accomplished by any means yet in the hands of the Executive.

Gentlemen of the House of Representatives:

The commissioners charged with the settlement of accounts between the United States and individual States concluded their important functions within the time limited by law, and the balances struck in their report, which will be laid before Congress, have been placed on the books of the Treasury.

On the 1st day of June last an installment of 1,000,000 florins became payable on the loans of the United States in Holland. This was adjusted by a prolongation of the period of reimbursement in nature of a new loan at an interest of 5 per cent for the term of ten years, and the expenses of this operation were a commission of 3 per cent.

The first installment of the loan of $2,000,000 from the Bank of the United States has been paid, as was directed by law. For the second it is necessary that provision should be made.

No pecuniary consideration is more urgent than the regular redemption and discharge of the public debt. On none can delay be more injurious or an economy of time more valuable.

The productiveness of the public revenues hitherto has continued to equal the anticipations which were formed of it, but it is not expected to prove commensurate with all the objects which have been suggested. Some auxiliary provisions will therefore, it is presumed, be requisite, and it is hoped that these may be made consistently with a due regard to the convenience of our citizens, who can not but be sensible of the true wisdom of encountering a small present addition to their contributions to obviate a future accumulation of burthens.

But here I can not forbear to recommend a repeal of the tax on the transportation of public prints. There is no resource so firm for the Government of the United States as the affections of the people, guided by an enlightened policy; and to this primary good nothing can conduce more than a faithful representation of public proceedings, diffused without restraint throughout the United States.

An estimate of the appropriations necessary for the current service of the ensuing year and a statement of a purchase of arms and military stores made during the recess will be presented to Congress.

Gentlemen of the Senate and of the House of Representatives:

The several subjects to which I have now referred open a wide range to your deliberations and involve some of the choicest interests of our common country. Permit me to bring to your remembrance the magnitude of your task. Without an unprejudiced coolness the welfare of the Government may be hazarded; without harmony as far as consists with freedom of sentiment its dignity may be lost. But as the legislative proceedings of the United States will never, I trust, be reproached for the want of temper or of candor, so shall not the public happiness languish from the want of my strenuous and warmest cooperation.

SIXTH ANNUAL ADDRESS.

UNITED STATES, *November 19, 1794.*

Fellow-Citizens of the Senate and of the House of Representatives:

When we call to mind the gracious indulgence of Heaven by which the American people became a nation; when we survey the general prosperity of our country, and look forward to the riches, power, and happiness to which it seems destined, with the deepest regret do I announce to you that during your recess some of the citizens of the United States have been found capable of an insurrection. It is due, however, to the character of our Government and to its stability, which can not be shaken by the enemies of order, freely to unfold the course of this event.

During the session of the year 1790 it was expedient to exercise the legislative power granted by the Constitution of the United States "to lay and collect excises." In a majority of the States scarcely an objection was heard to this mode of taxation. In some, indeed, alarms were at first conceived, until they were banished by reason and patriotism. In the four western counties of Pennsylvania a prejudice, fostered and imbittered by the artifice of men who labored for an ascendency over the will of others by the guidance of their passions, produced symptoms of riot and violence. It is well known that Congress did not hesitate to examine the complaints which were presented, and to relieve them as far as justice dictated or general convenience would permit. But the impression which this moderation made on the discontented did not correspond with what it deserved. The arts of delusion were no longer confined to the efforts of designing individuals. The very forbearance to press prosecutions was misinterpreted into a fear of urging the execution of the laws, and associations of men began to denounce threats against the officers employed. From a belief that by a more formal concert their operation might be defeated, certain self-created societies assumed the tone of condemnation. Hence, while the greater part of Pennsylvania itself were conforming themselves to the acts of excise, a few counties were resolved to frustrate them. It was now perceived that every expectation from the tenderness which had been hitherto pursued was unavailing, and that further delay could only create an opinion of impotency or irresolution in the Government. Legal process was therefore delivered to the marshal against the rioters and delinquent distillers.

No sooner was he understood to be engaged in this duty than the vengeance of armed men was aimed at *his* person and the person and property of the inspector of the revenue. They fired upon the marshal, arrested him, and detained him for some time as a prisoner. He was obliged, by the jeopardy of his life, to renounce the service of other process on the west side of the Allegheny Mountain, and a deputation was afterwards sent to him to demand a surrender of that which he *had* served. A numerous body repeatedly attacked the house of the inspector, seized his papers of office, and finally destroyed by fire his buildings and whatsoever they contained. Both of these officers, from a just regard to their safety, fled to the seat of Government, it being avowed that the motives to such outrages were to compel the resignation of the inspector, to withstand by force of arms the authority of the United States, and thereby to extort a repeal of the laws of excise and an alteration in the conduct of Government.

Upon the testimony of these facts an associate justice of the Supreme Court of the United States notified to me that " in the counties of Washington and Allegheny, in Pennsylvania, laws of the United States were opposed, and the execution thereof obstructed, by combinations too powerful to be suppressed by the ordinary course of judicial proceedings or by the powers vested in the marshal of that district.'' On this call, momentous in the extreme, I sought and weighed what might best subdue the crisis. On the one hand the judiciary was pronounced to be stripped of its capacity to enforce the laws; crimes which reached the very existence of social order were perpetrated without control; the friends of Government were insulted, abused, and overawed into silence or an apparent acquiescence; and to yield to the treasonable fury of so small a portion of the United States would be to violate the fundamental principle of our Constitution, which enjoins that the will of the majority shall prevail. On the other, to array citizen against citizen, to publish the dishonor of such excesses, to encounter the expense and other embarrassments of so distant an expedition, were steps too delicate, too closely interwoven with many affecting considerations, to be lightly adopted. I postponed, therefore, the summoning the militia immediately into the field, but I required them to be held in readiness, that if my anxious endeavors to reclaim the deluded and to convince the malignant of their danger should be fruitless, military force might be prepared to act before the season should be too far advanced.

My proclamation of the 7th of August last was accordingly issued, and accompanied by the appointment of commissioners, who were charged to repair to the scene of insurrection. They were authorized to confer with any bodies of men or individuals. They were instructed to be candid and explicit in stating the sensations which had been excited in the Executive, and his earnest wish to avoid a resort to coercion; to represent, however, that, without submission, coercion *must* be the resort; but to invite them, at the same time, to return to the demeanor of faithful citizens, by such accommodations as lay within the sphere of Executive power. Pardon, too, was tendered to them by the Government of the United States and that of Pennsylvania, upon no other condition than a satisfactory assurance of obedience to the laws.

Although the report of the commissioners marks their firmness and abilities, and must unite all virtuous men, by shewing that the means of conciliation have been exhausted, all of those who had committed or abetted the tumults did not subscribe the mild form which was proposed as the atonement, and the indications of a peaceable temper were neither sufficiently general nor conclusive to recommend or warrant the further suspension of the march of the militia.

Thus the painful alternative could not be discarded. I ordered the militia to march, after once more admonishing the insurgents in my proclamation of the 25th of September last.

It was a task too difficult to ascertain with precision the lowest degree of force competent to the quelling of the insurrection. From a respect, indeed, to economy and the ease of my fellow-citizens belonging to the militia, it would have gratified me to accomplish such an estimate. My very reluctance to ascribe too much importance to the opposition, had its extent been accurately seen, would have been a decided inducement to the smallest efficient numbers. In this uncertainty, therefore, I put into motion 15,000 men, as being an army which, according to all human calculation, would be prompt and adequate in every view, and might, perhaps, by rendering resistance desperate, prevent the effusion of blood. Quotas had been assigned to the States of New Jersey, Pennsylvania, Maryland, and Virginia, the governor of Pennsylvania having declared on this occasion an opinion which justified a requisition to the other States.

As commander in chief of the militia when called into the actual service of the United States, I have visited the places of general rendezvous to obtain more exact information and to direct a plan for ulterior movements. Had there been room for a persuasion that the laws were secure from obstruction; that the civil magistrate was able to bring to justice such of the most culpable as have not embraced the proffered terms of amnesty, and may be deemed fit objects of example; that the friends to peace and good government were not in need of that aid and countenance which they ought always to receive, and, I trust, ever will receive, against the vicious and turbulent, I should have caught with avidity the opportunity of restoring the militia to their families and homes. But succeeding intelligence has tended to manifest the necessity of what has been done, it being now confessed by those who were not inclined to exaggerate the ill conduct of the insurgents that their malevolence was not pointed merely to a particular law, but that a spirit inimical to all order has actuated many of the offenders.   If the state of things had afforded reason for the continuance of my presence with the army, it would not have been withholden.   But every appearance assuring such an issue as will redound to the reputation and strength of the United States, I have judged it most proper to resume my duties at the seat of Government, leaving the chief command with the governor of Virginia.

Still, however, as it is probable that in a commotion like the present, whatsoever may be the pretense, the purposes of mischief and revenge may not be laid aside, the stationing of a small force for a certain period in the four western counties of Pennsylvania will be indispensable, whether we contemplate the situation of those who are connected with the execution of the laws or of others who may have exposed themselves by an honorable attachment to them.   Thirty days from the commencement of this session being the legal limitation of the employment of the militia, Congress can not be too early occupied with this subject.

Among the discussions which may arise from this aspect of our affairs, and from the documents which will be submitted to Congress, it will not escape their observation that not only the inspector of the revenue, but other officers of the United States in Pennsylvania have, from their fidelity in the discharge of their functions, sustained material injuries to their property.   The obligation and policy of idemnifying them are strong and obvious.   It may also merit attention whether policy will not enlarge this provision to the retribution of other citizens who, though not under the ties of office, may have suffered damage by their generous exertions for upholding the Constitution and the laws.   The amount, even if all the injured were included, would not be great, and on future emergencies the Government would be amply repaid by the influence of an example that he who incurs a loss in its defense shall find a recompense in its liberality.

While there is cause to lament that occurrences of this nature should have disgraced the name or interrupted the tranquillity of any part of our community, or should have diverted to a new application any portion of the public resources, there are not wanting real and substantial consolations for the misfortune.   It has demonstrated that our prosperity rests on solid foundations, by furnishing an additional proof that my fellow-citizens understand the true principles of government and liberty; that they feel their inseparable union; that notwithstanding all the devices which have been used to sway them from their interest and duty, they are now as ready to maintain the authority of the laws against licentious invasions as they were to defend their rights against usurpation.   It has been a spectacle displaying to the highest advantage the value of republican government to behold the most and the least wealthy of our citizens standing in the same ranks as private soldiers, preeminently distinguished by being the army of the Constitution—undeterred by a march of 300 miles over rugged mountains, by the approach of an inclement season, or by any other discouragement. Nor ought I to omit to acknowledge the efficacious and patriotic cooperation which I have experienced from the chief magistrates of the States to which my requisitions have been addressed.

To every description of citizens, indeed, let praise be given. But let them persevere in their affectionate vigilance over that precious depository of American happiness, the Constitution of the United States. Let them cherish it, too, for the sake of those who, from every clime, are daily seeking a dwelling in our land. And when in the calm moments of reflection they shall have retraced the origin and progress of the insurrection, let them determine whether it has not been fomented by combinations of men who, careless of consequences and disregarding the unerring truth that those who rouse can not always appease a civil convulsion, have disseminated, from an ignorance or perversion of facts, suspicions, jealousies, and accusations of the whole Government.

Having thus fulfilled the engagement which I took when I entered into office, "to the best of my ability to preserve, protect, and defend the Constitution of the United States," on you, gentlemen, and the people by whom you are deputed, I rely for support.

In the arrangements to which the possibility of a similar contingency will naturally draw your attention it ought not to be forgotten that the militia laws have exhibited such striking defects as could not have been supplied but by the zeal of our citizens. Besides the extraordinary expense and waste, which are not the least of the defects, every appeal to those laws is attended with a doubt on its success.

The devising and establishing of a well-regulated militia would be a genuine source of legislative honor and a perfect title to public gratitude. I therefore entertain a hope that the present session will not pass without carrying to its full energy the power of organizing, arming, and disciplining the militia, and thus providing, in the language of the Constitution, for calling them forth to execute the laws of the Union, suppress insurrections, and repel invasions.

As auxiliary to the state of our defense, to which Congress can never too frequently recur, they will not omit to inquire whether the fortifications which have been already licensed by law be commensurate with our exigencies.

The intelligence from the army under the command of General Wayne is a happy presage to our military operations against the hostile Indians north of the Ohio. From the advices which have been forwarded, the advance which he has made must have damped the ardor of the savages and weakened their obstinacy in waging war against the United States. And yet, even at this late hour, when our power to punish them can not be questioned, we shall not be unwilling to cement a lasting peace upon terms of candor, equity, and good neighborhood.

Toward none of the Indian tribes have overtures of friendship been spared. The Creeks in particular are covered from encroachment by the interposition of the General Government and that of Georgia. From a desire also to remove the discontents of the Six Nations, a settlement meditated at Presque Isle, on Lake Erie, has been suspended, and an agent is now endeavoring to rectify any misconception into which they may have fallen. But I can not refrain from again pressing upon your deliberations the plan which I recommended at the last session for the improvement of harmony with all the Indians within our limits by the fixing and conducting of trading houses upon the principles then expressed.

Gentlemen of the House of Representatives:

The time which has elapsed since the commencement of our fiscal measures has developed our pecuniary resources so as to open the way for a definite plan for the redemption of the public debt. It is believed that the result is such as to encourage Congress to consummate this work without delay. Nothing can more promote the permanent welfare of the nation and nothing would be more grateful to our constituents. Indeed, whatsoever is unfinished of our system of public credit can not be benefited by procrastination; and as far as may be practicable we ought to place that credit on grounds which can not be disturbed, and to prevent that progressive accumulation of debt which must ultimately endanger all governments.

An estimate of the necessary appropriations, including the expenditures into which we have been driven by the insurrection, will be submitted to Congress.

Gentlemen of the Senate and of the House of Representatives.

The Mint of the United States has entered upon the coinage of the precious metals, and considerable sums of defective coins and bullion have been lodged with the Director by individuals. There is a pleasing prospect that the institution will at no remote day realize the expectation which was originally formed of its utility.

In subsequent communications certain circumstances of our intercourse with foreign nations will be transmitted to Congress. However, it may not be unseasonable to announce that my policy in our foreign transactions has been to cultivate peace with all the world; to observe treaties with pure and absolute faith; to check every deviation from the line of impartiality; to explain what may have been misapprehended and correct what may have been injurious to any nation, and having thus acquired the right, to lose no time in acquiring the ability to insist upon justice being done to ourselves.

Let us unite, therefore, in imploring the Supreme Ruler of Nations to spread his holy protection over these United States; to turn the machinations of the wicked to the confirming of our Constitution; to enable us at all times to root out internal sedition and put invasion to flight; to perpetuate to our country that prosperity which His goodness has already conferred, and to verify the anticipations of this Government being a safeguard to human rights.

SEVENTH ANNUAL ADDRESS.

UNITED STATES, *December 8, 1795.*

Fellow-Citizens of the Senate and of the House of Representatives:

I trust I do not deceive myself when I indulge the persuasion that I have never met you at any period when more than at the present the situation of our public affairs has afforded just cause for mutual congratulation, and for inviting you to join with me in profound gratitude to the Author of all Good for the numerous and extraordinary blessings we enjoy.

The termination of the long, expensive, and distressing war in which we have been engaged with certain Indians northwest of the Ohio is placed in the option of the United States by a treaty which the commander of our army has concluded provisionally with the hostile tribes in that region.

In the adjustment of the terms the satisfaction of the Indians was deemed an object worthy no less of the policy than of the liberality of the United States as the necessary basis of durable tranquillity. The object, it is believed, has been fully attained. The articles agreed upon will immediately be laid before the Senate for their consideration.

The Creek and Cherokee Indians, who alone of the Southern tribes had annoyed our frontiers, have lately confirmed their preexisting treaties with us, and were giving evidence of a sincere disposition to carry them into effect by the surrender of the prisoners and property they had taken. But we have to lament that the fair prospect in this quarter has been once more clouded by wanton murders, which some citizens of Georgia are represented to have recently perpetrated on hunting parties of the Creeks, which have again subjected that frontier to disquietude and danger, which will be productive of further expense, and may occasion more effusion of blood. Measures are pursuing to prevent or mitigate the usual consequences of such outrages, and with the hope of their succeeding at least to avert general hostility.

A letter from the Emperor of Morocco announces to me his recognition of our treaty made with his father, the late Emperor, and consequently the continuance of peace with that power. With peculiar satisfaction I add that information has been received from an agent deputed on our part to Algiers importing that the terms of the treaty with the Dey and Regency of that country had been adjusted in such a manner as to authorize the expectation of a speedy peace and the restoration of our unfortunate fellow-citizens from a grievous captivity.

The latest advices from our envoy at the Court of Madrid give, more-over, the pleasing information that he had received assurances of a speedy and satisfactory conclusion of his negotiation. While the event depending upon unadjusted particulars can not be regarded as ascertained, it is agreeable to cherish the expectation of an issue which, securing amicably very essential interests of the United States, will at the same time lay the foundation of lasting harmony with a power whose friendship we have uniformly and sincerely desired to cultivate.

Though not before officially disclosed to the House of Representatives, you, gentlemen, are all apprised that a treaty of amity, commerce, and navigation has been negotiated with Great Britain, and that the Senate have advised and consented to its ratification upon a condition which excepts part of one article. Agreeably thereto, and to the best judgment I was able to form of the public interest after full and mature deliberation, I have added my sanction. The result on the part of His Britannic Majesty is unknown. When received, the subject will without delay be placed before Congress.

This interesting summary of our affairs with regard to the foreign powers between whom and the United States controversies have subsisted, and with regard also to those of our Indian neighbors with whom we have been in a state of enmity or misunderstanding, opens a wide field for consoling and gratifying reflections. If by prudence and moderation on every side the extinguishment of all the causes of external discord which have heretofore menaced our tranquillity, on terms compatible with our national rights and honor, shall be the happy result, how firm and how precious a foundation will have been laid for accelerating, maturing, and establishing the prosperity of our country.

Contemplating the internal situation as well as the external relations of the United States, we discover equal cause for contentment and satisfaction. While many of the nations of Europe, with their American dependencies, have been involved in a contest unusually bloody, exhausting, and calamitous, in which the evils of foreign war have been aggravated by domestic convulsion and insurrection; in which many of the arts most useful to society have been exposed to discouragement and decay; in which scarcity of subsistence has imbittered other sufferings; while even the anticipations of a return of the blessings of peace and repose are alloyed by the sense of heavy and accumulating burthens, which press upon all the departments of industry and threaten to clog the future springs of government, our favored country, happy in a striking contrast, has enjoyed general tranquillity—a tranquillity the more satisfactory because maintained at the expense of no duty. Faithful to ourselves, we have violated no obligation to others. Our agriculture, commerce, and manufactures prosper beyond former example, the molestations of our trade (to prevent a continuance of which, however, very pointed remonstrances have been made) being overbalanced by the aggregate benefits which it derives from a neutral position. Our population advances with a celerity which, exceeding the most sanguine calculations, proportionally augments our strength and resources, and guarantees our future security. Every part of the Union displays indications of rapid and various improvement; and with burthens so light as scarcely to be perceived, with resources fully adequate to our present exigencies, with governments founded on the genuine principles of rational liberty, and with mild and wholesome laws, is it too much to say that our country exhibits a spectacle of national happiness never surpassed, if ever before equaled?

Placed in a situation every way so auspicious, motives of commanding force impel us, with sincere acknowledgment to Heaven and pure love to our country, to unite our efforts to preserve, prolong, and improve our immense advantages. To cooperate with you in this desirable work is a fervent and favorite wish of my heart.

It is a valuable ingredient in the general estimate of our welfare that the part of our country which was lately the scene of disorder and insurrection now enjoys the blessings of quiet and order. The misled have abandoned their errors, and pay the respect to our Constitution and laws which is due from good citizens to the public authorities of the society. These circumstances have induced me to pardon generally the offenders here referred to, and to extend forgiveness to those who had been adjudged to capital punishment. For though I shall always think it a sacred duty to exercise with firmness and energy the constitutional powers with which I am vested, yet it appears to me no less consistent with the public good than it is with my personal feelings to mingle in the operations of Government every degree of moderation and tenderness which the national justice, dignity, and safety may permit.

GENTLEMEN: Among the objects which will claim your attention in the course of the session, a review of our military establishment is not the least important. It is called for by the events which have changed, and may be expected still further to change, the relative situation of our frontiers. In this review you will doubtless allow due weight to the considerations that the questions between us and certain foreign powers are not yet finally adjusted, that the war in Europe is not yet terminated, and that our Western posts, when recovered, will demand provision for garrisoning and securing them.   A statement of our present military force will be laid before you by the Department of War.

With the review of our Army establishment is naturally connected that of the militia.   It will merit inquiry what imperfections 'n the existing plan further experience may have unfolded.   The subject is of so much moment in my estimation as to excite a constant solicitude that the consideration of it may be renewed until the greatest attainable perfection shall be accomplished.   Time is wearing away some advantages for forwarding the object, while none better deserves the persevering attention of the public councils.

While we indulge the satisfaction which the actual condition of our Western borders so well authorizes, it is necessary that we should not lose sight of an important truth which continually receives new confirmations, namely, that the provisions heretofore made with a view to the protection of the Indians from the violences of the lawless part of our frontier inhabitants are insufficient.   It is demonstrated that these violences can now be perpetrated with impunity, and it can need no argument to prove that unless the murdering of Indians can be restrained by bringing the murderers to condign punishment, all the exertions of the Government to prevent destructive retaliations by the Indians will prove fruitless and all our present agreeable prospects illusory.   The frequent destruction of innocent women and children, who are chiefly the victims of retaliation, must continue to shock humanity, and an enormous expense to drain the Treasury of the Union.

To enforce upon the Indians the observance of justice it is indispensable that there shall be competent means of rendering justice to them.   If these means can be devised by the wisdom of Congress, and especially if there can be added an adequate provision for supplying the necessities of the Indians on reasonable terms (a measure the mention of which I the more readily repeat, as in all the conferences with them they urge it with solicitude), I should not hesitate to entertain a strong hope of rendering our tranquillity permanent.   I add with pleasure that the probability even of their civilization is not diminished by the experiments which have been thus far made under the auspices of Government.   The accomplishment of this work, if practicable, will reflect undecaying luster on our national character and administer the most grateful consolations that virtuous minds can know.

Gentlemen of the House of Representatives:

The state of our revenue, with the sums which have been borrowed and reimbursed pursuant to different acts of Congress, will be submitted from the proper Department, together with an estimate of the appropriations necessary to be made for the service of the ensuing year.

Whether measures may not be advisable to reenforce the provision for the redemption of the public debt will naturally engage your examination.

Congress have demonstrated their sense to be, and it were superfluous to repeat mine, that whatsoever will tend to accelerate the honorable extinction of our public debt accords as much with the true interest of our country as with the general sense of our constituents.

Gentlemen of the Senate and of the House of Representatives:

The statements which will be laid before you relative to the Mint will shew the situation of that institution and the necessity of some further legislative provisions for carrying the business of it more completely into effect, and for checking abuses which appear to be arising in particular quarters.

The progress in providing materials for the frigates and in building them, the state of the fortifications of our harbors, the measures which have been pursued for obtaining proper sites for arsenals and for replenishing our magazines with military stores, and the steps which have been taken toward the execution of the law for opening a trade with the Indians will likewise be presented for the information of Congress.

Temperate discussion of the important subjects which may arise in the course of the session and mutual forbearance where there is a difference of opinion are too obvious and necessary for the peace, happiness, and welfare of our country to need any recommendation of mine.

EIGHTH ANNUAL ADDRESS.

UNITED STATES, *December 7, 1796.*

Fellow-Citizens of the Senate and of the House of Representatives:

In recurring to the internal situation of our country since I had last the pleasure to address you, I find ample reason for a renewed expression of that gratitude to the Ruler of the Universe which a continued series of prosperity has so often and so justly called forth.

The acts of the last session which required special arrangements have been as far as circumstances would admit carried into operation.

Measures calculated to insure a continuance of the friendship of the Indians and to preserve peace along the extent of our interior frontier have been digested and adopted. In the framing of these care has been taken to guard on the one hand our advanced settlements from the predatory incursions of those unruly individuals who can not be restrained by their tribes, and on the other hand to protect the rights secured to the Indians by treaty—to draw them nearer to the civilized state and inspire them with correct conceptions of the power as well as justice of the Government.

The meeting of the deputies from the Creek Nation at Colerain, in the State of Georgia, which had for a principal object the purchase of a parcel of their land by that State, broke up without its being accomplished, the nation having previous to their departure instructed them against making any sale. The occasion, however, has been improved to confirm by a new treaty with the Creeks their preexisting engagements with the United States, and to obtain their consent to the establishment of trading houses and military posts within their boundary, by means of which their friendship and the general peace may be more effectually secured.

The period during the late session at which the appropriation was passed for carrying into effect the treaty of amity, commerce, and navigation between the United States and His Britannic Majesty necessarily procrastinated the reception of the posts stipulated to be delivered beyond the date assigned for that event. As soon, however, as the Governor-General of Canada could be addressed with propriety on the subject, arrangements were cordially and promptly concluded for their evacuation, and the United States took possession of the principal of them, comprehending Oswego, Niagara, Detroit, Michilimackinac, and Fort Miami, where such repairs and additions have been ordered to be made as appeared indispensable.

The commissioners appointed on the part of the United States and of Great Britain to determine which is the river St. Croix mentioned in the treaty of peace of 1783, agreed in the choice of Egbert Benson, esq., of New York, for the third commissioner. The whole met at St. Andrew's, in Passamaquoddy Bay, in the beginning of October, and directed surveys to be made of the rivers in dispute; but deeming it impracticable to have these surveys completed before the next year, they adjourned to meet at Boston in August, 1797, for the final decision of the question.

Other commissioners appointed on the part of the United States, agreeably to the seventh article of the treaty with Great Britain, relative to captures and condemnation of vessels and other property, met the commissioners of His Britannic Majesty in London in August last, when John Trumbull, esq., was chosen by lot for the fifth commissioner. In October following the board were to proceed to business. As yet there has been no communication of commissioners on the part of Great Britain to unite with those who have been appointed on the part of the United States for carrying into effect the sixth article of the treaty.

The treaty with Spain required that the commissioners for running the boundary line between the territory of the United States and His Catholic Majesty's provinces of East and West Florida should meet at the Natchez before the expiration of six months after the exchange of the ratifications, which was effected at Aranjuez on the 25th day of April; and the troops of His Catholic Majesty occupying any posts within the limits of the United States were within the same period to be withdrawn. The commissioner of the United States therefore commenced his journey for the Natchez in September, and troops were ordered to occupy the posts from which the Spanish garrisons should be withdrawn. Information has been recently received of the appointment of a commissioner on the part of His Catholic Majesty for running the boundary line, but none of any appointment for the adjustment of the claims of our citizens whose vessels were captured by the armed vessels of Spain.

In pursuance of the act of Congress passed in the last session for the protection and relief of American seamen, agents were appointed, one to reside in Great Britain and the other in the West Indies. The effects of the agency in the West Indies are not yet fully ascertained, but those which have been communicated afford grounds to believe the measure will be beneficial. The agent destined to reside in Great Britain declining to accept the appointment, the business has consequently devolved on the minister of the United States in London, and will command his attention until a new agent shall be appointed.

After many delays and disappointments arising out of the European war, the final arrangements for fulfilling the engagements made to the Dey and Regency of Algiers will in all present appearance be crowned with success, but under great, though inevitable, disadvantages in the pecuniary transactions occasioned by that war, which will render further provision necessary. The actual liberation of all our citizens who were prisoners in Algiers, while it gratifies every feeling heart, is itself an earnest of a satisfactory termination of the whole negotiation. Measures are in operation for effecting treaties with the Regencies of Tunis and Tripoli.

To an active external commerce the protection of a naval force is indispensable. This is manifest with regard to wars in which a State is itself a party. But besides this, it is in our own experience that the most sincere neutrality is not a sufficient guard against the depredations of nations at war. To secure respect to a neutral flag requires a naval force organized and ready to vindicate it from insult or aggression. This may even prevent the necessity of going to war by discouraging belligerent powers from committing such violations of the rights of the neutral party as may, first or last, leave no other option. From the best information I have been able to obtain it would seem as if our trade to the Mediterranean without a protecting force will always be insecure and our citizens exposed to the calamities from which numbers of them have but just been relieved.

These considerations invite the United States to look to the means, and to set about the gradual creation of a navy. The increasing progress of their navigation promises them at no distant period the requisite supply of seamen, and their means in other respects favor the undertaking. It is an encouragement, likewise, that their particular situation will give weight and influence to a moderate naval force in their hands. Will it not, then, be advisable to begin without delay to provide and lay up the materials for the building and equipping of ships of war, and to proceed in the work by degrees, in proportion as our resources shall render it practicable without inconvenience, so that a future war of Europe may not find our commerce in the same unprotected state in which it was found by the present?

Congress have repeatedly, and not without success, directed their attention to the encouragement of manufactures. The object is of too much consequence not to insure a continuance of their efforts in every way which shall appear eligible. As a general rule, manufactures on public account are inexpedient; but where the state of things in a country leaves little hope that certain branches of manufacture will for a great length of time obtain, when these are of a nature essential to the furnishing and equipping of the public force in time of war, are not establishments for procuring them on public account to the extent of the ordinary demand for the public service recommended by strong considerations of national policy as an exception to the general rule? Ought our country to remain in such cases dependent on foreign supply, precarious because liable to be interrupted? If the necessary article should in this mode cost more in time of peace, will not the security and independence thence arising form an ample compensation? Establishments of this sort, commensurate only with the calls of the public service in time of peace, will in time of war easily be extended in proportion to the exigencies of the Government, and may even perhaps be made to yield a surplus for the supply of our citizens at large, so as to mitigate the privations from the interruption of their trade. If adopted, the plan ought to exclude all those branches which are already, or likely soon to be, established in the country, in order that there may be no danger of interference with pursuits of individual industry.

It will not be doubted that with reference either to individual or national welfare agriculture is of primary importance. In proportion as nations advance in population and other circumstances of maturity this truth becomes more apparent, and renders the cultivation of the soil more and more an object of public patronage. Institutions for promoting it grow up, supported by the public purse; and to what object can it be dedicated with greater propriety? Among the means which have been employed to this end none have been attended with greater success than the establishment of boards (composed of proper characters) charged with collecting and diffusing information, and enabled by premiums and small pecuniary aids to encourage and assist a spirit of discovery and improvement. This species of establishment contributes doubly to the increase of improvement by stimulating to enterprise and experiment, and by drawing to a common center the results everywhere of individual skill and observation, and spreading them thence over the whole nation. Experience accordingly has shewn that they are very cheap instruments of immense national benefits.

I have heretofore proposed to the consideration of Congress the expediency of establishing a national university and also a military academy. The desirableness of both these institutions has so constantly increased with every new view I have taken of the subject that I can not omit the opportunity of once for all recalling your attention to them.

The assembly to which I address myself is too enlightened not to be fully sensible how much a flourishing state of the arts and sciences contributes to national prosperity and reputation.

True it is that our country, much to its honor, contains many seminaries of learning highly respectable and useful; but the funds upon which they rest are too narrow to command the ablest professors in the different departments of liberal knowledge for the institution contemplated, though they would be excellent auxiliaries.

Amongst the motives to such an institution, the assimilation of the principles, opinions, and manners of our countrymen by the common education of a portion of our youth from every quarter well deserves attention. The more homogeneous our citizens can be made in these particulars the greater will be our prospect of permanent union; and a primary object of such a national institution should be the education of our youth in the science of *government*. In a republic what species of knowledge can be equally important and what duty more pressing on its legislature than to patronize a plan for communicating it to those who are to be the future guardians of the liberties of the country?

The institution of a military academy is also recommended by cogent reasons. However pacific the general policy of a nation may be, it ought never to be without an adequate stock of military knowledge for emergencies. The first would impair the energy of its character, and both would hazard its safety or expose it to greater evils when war could not be avoided ; besides that, war might often not depend upon its own choice. In proportion as the observance of pacific maxims might exempt a nation from the necessity of practicing the rules of the military art ought to be its care in preserving and transmitting, by proper establishments, the knowledge of that art. Whatever argument may be drawn from particular examples superficially viewed, a thorough examination of the subject will evince that the art of war is at once comprehensive and complicated, that it demands much previous study, and that the possession of it in its most improved and perfect state is always of great moment to the security of a nation. This, therefore, ought to be a serious care of every government, and for this purpose an academy where a regular course of instruction is given is an obvious expedient which different nations have successfully employed.

The compensations to the officers of the United States in various instances, and in none more than in respect to the most important stations, appear to call for legislative revision. The consequences of a defective provision are of serious import to the Government.   If private wealth is to supply the defect of public retribution, it will greatly contract the sphere within which the selection of character for office is to be made, and will proportionally diminish the probability of a choice of men able as well as upright.   Besides that, it would be repugnant to the vital principles of our Government virtually to exclude from public trusts talents and virtue unless accompanied by wealth.

While in our external relations some serious inconveniences and embarrassments have been overcome and others lessened, it is with much pain and deep regret I mention that circumstances of a very unwelcome nature have lately occurred.   Our trade has suffered and is suffering extensive injuries in the West Indies from the cruisers and agents of the French Republic, and communications have been received from its minister here which indicate the danger of a further disturbance of our commerce by its authority, and which are in other respects far from agreeable.

It has been my constant, sincere, and earnest wish, in conformity with that of our nation, to maintain cordial harmony and a perfectly friendly understanding with that Republic.   This wish remains unabated, and I shall persevere in the endeavor to fulfill it to the utmost extent of what shall be consistent with a just and indispensable regard to the rights and honor of our country; nor will I easily cease to cherish the expectation that a spirit of justice, candor, and friendship on the part of the Republic will eventually insure success.

In pursuing this course, however, I can not forget what is due to the character of our Government and nation, or to a full and entire confidence in the good sense, patriotism, self-respect, and fortitude of my countrymen.

I reserve for a special message a more particular communication on this interesting subject.

Gentlemen of the House of Representatives:

I have directed an estimate of the appropriations necessary for the service of the ensuing year to be submitted from the proper Department, with a view of the public receipts and expenditures to the latest period to which an account can be prepared.

It is with satisfaction I am able to inform you that the revenues of the United States continue in a state of progressive improvement.

A reenforcement of the existing provisions for discharging our public debt was mentioned in my address at the opening of the last session. Some preliminary steps were taken toward it, the maturing of which will no doubt engage your zealous attention during the present.   I will only add that it will afford me a heartfelt satisfaction to concur in such further measures as will ascertain to our country the prospect of a speedy extinguishment of the debt.   Posterity may have cause to regret if from any motive intervals of tranquillity are left unimproved for accelerating this valuable end.

Gentlemen of the Senate and of the House of Representatives:

My solicitude to see the militia of the United States placed on an efficient establishment has been so often and so ardently expressed that I shall but barely recall the subject to your view on the present occasion, at the same time that I shall submit to your inquiry whether our harbors are yet sufficiently secured.

The situation in which I now stand for the last time, in the midst of the representatives of the people of the United States, naturally recalls the period when the administration of the present form of government commenced, and I can not omit the occasion to congratulate you and my country on the success of the experiment, nor to repeat my fervent supplications to the Supreme Ruler of the Universe and Sovereign Arbiter of Nations that His providential care may still be extended to the United States, that the virtue and happiness of the people may be preserved, and that the Government which they have instituted for the protection of their liberties may be perpetual.

John Adams

March 4, 1797 to March 4, 1801

FIRST ANNUAL ADDRESS.

UNITED STATES, *November 22, 1797.*

Gentlemen of the Senate and Gentlemen of the House of Representatives:

I was for some time apprehensive that it would be necessary, on account of the contagious sickness which afflicted the city of Philadelphia, to convene the National Legislature at some other place. This measure it was desirable to avoid, because it would occasion much public inconvenience and a considerable public expense and add to the calamities of the inhabitants of this city, whose sufferings must have excited the sympathy of all their fellow-citizens. Therefore, after taking measures to ascertain the state and decline of the sickness, I postponed my determination, having hopes, now happily realized, that, without hazard to the lives or health of the members, Congress might assemble at this place, where it was next by law to meet. I submit, however, to your consideration whether a power to postpone the meeting of Congress, without passing the time fixed by the Constitution upon such occasions, would not be a useful amendment to the law of 1794.

Although I can not yet congratulate you on the reestablishment of peace in Europe and the restoration of security to the persons and properties of our citizens from injustice and violence at sea, we have, nevertheless, abundant cause of gratitude to the source of benevolence and influence for interior tranquillity and personal security, for propitious seasons, prosperous agriculture, productive fisheries, and general improvements, and, above all, for a rational spirit of civil and religious liberty and a calm but steady determination to support our sovereignty, as well as our moral and our religious principles, against all open and secret attacks.

Our envoys extraordinary to the French Republic embarked—one in July, the other early in August—to join their colleague in Holland. I have received intelligence of the arrival of both of them in Holland, from whence they all proceeded on their journeys to Paris within a few days of the 19th of September. Whatever may be the result of this mission, I trust that nothing will have been omitted on my part to conduct the negotiation to a successful conclusion, on such equitable terms as may be compatible with the safety, honor, and interest of the United States. Nothing, in the meantime, will contribute so much to the preservation of peace and the attainment of justice as a manifestation of that energy and unanimity of which on many former occasions the people of the United States have given such memorable proofs, and the exertion of those resources for national defense which a beneficent Providence has kindly placed within their power.

It may be confidently asserted that nothing has occurred since the adjournment of Congress which renders inexpedient those precautionary measures recommended by me to the consideration of the two Houses at the opening of your late extraordinary session. If that system was then prudent, it is more so now, as increasing depredations strengthen the reasons for its adoption.

Indeed, whatever may be the issue of the negotiation with France, and whether the war in Europe is or is not to continue, I hold it most certain that permanent tranquillity and order will not soon be obtained. The state of society has so long been disturbed, the sense of moral and religious obligations so much weakened, public faith and national honor have been so impaired, respect to treaties has been so diminished, and the law of nations has lost so much of its force, while pride, ambition, avarice, and violence have been so long unrestrained, there remains no reasonable ground on which to raise an expectation that a commerce without protection or defense will not be plundered.

The commerce of the United States is essential, if not to their existence, at least to their comfort, their growth, prosperity, and happiness. The genius, character, and habits of the people are highly commercial. Their cities have been formed and exist upon commerce. Our agriculture, fisheries, arts, and manufactures are connected with and depend upon it. In short, commerce has made this country what it is, and it can not be destroyed or neglected without involving the people in poverty and distress. Great numbers are directly and solely supported by navigation. The faith of society is pledged for the preservation of the rights of commercial and seafaring no less than of the other citizens. Under this view of our affairs, I should hold myself guilty of a neglect of duty if I forbore to recommend that we should make every exertion to protect our commerce and to place our country in a suitable posture of defense as the only sure means of preserving both.

I have entertained an expectation that it would have been in my power at the opening of this session to have communicated to you the agreeable information of the due execution of our treaty with His Catholic Majesty respecting the withdrawing of his troops from our territory and the demarcation of the line of limits, but by the latest authentic intelligence Spanish garrisons were still continued within our country, and the running of the boundary line had not been commenced. These circumstances are the more to be regretted as they can not fail to affect the Indians in a manner injurious to the United States. Still, however, indulging the hope that the answers which have been given will remove the objections offered by the Spanish officers to the immediate execution of the treaty, I have judged it proper that we should continue in readiness to receive the posts and to run the line of limits. Further information on this subject will be communicated in the course of the session.

In connection with this unpleasant state of things on our western frontier it is proper for me to mention the attempts of foreign agents to alienate the affections of the Indian nations and to excite them to actual hostilities against the United States. Great activity has been exerted by those persons who have insinuated themselves among the Indian tribes residing within the territory of the United States to influence them to transfer their affections and force to a foreign nation, to form them into a confederacy, and prepare them for war against the United States. Although measures have been taken to counteract these infractions of our rights, to prevent Indian hostilities, and to preserve entire their attachment to the United States, it is my duty to observe that to give a better effect to these measures and to obviate the consequences of a repetition of such practices a law providing adequate punishment for such offenses may be necessary.

The commissioners appointed under the fifth article of the treaty of amity, commerce, and navigation between the United States and Great Britain to ascertain the river which was truly intended under the name of the river St. Croix mentioned in the treaty of peace, met at Passamaquoddy Bay in October, 1796, and viewed the mouths of the rivers in question and the adjacent shores and islands, and, being of opinion that actual surveys of both rivers to their sources were necessary, gave to the agents of the two nations instructions for that purpose, and adjourned to meet at Boston in August. They met, but the surveys requiring more time than had been supposed, and not being then completed, the commissioners again adjourned, to meet at Providence, in the State of Rhode Island, in June next, when we may expect a final examination and decision.

The commissioners appointed in pursuance of the sixth article of the treaty met at Philadelphia in May last to examine the claims of British subjects for debts contracted before the peace and still remaining due to them from citizens or inhabitants of the United States. Various causes have hitherto prevented any determinations, but the business is now resumed, and doubtless will be prosecuted without interruption.

Several decisions on the claims of citizens of the United States for losses and damages sustained by reason of irregular and illegal captures or condemnations of their vessels or other property have been made by the commissioners in London comformably to the seventh article of the treaty. The sums awarded by the commissioners have been paid by the British Government. A considerable number of other claims, where costs and damages, and not captured property, were the only objects in question, have been decided by arbitration, and the sums awarded to the citizens of the United States have also been paid.

The commissioners appointed agreeably to the twenty-first article of our treaty with Spain met at Philadelphia in the summer past to examine and decide on the claims of our citizens for losses they have sustained in consequence of their vessels and cargoes having been taken by the subjects of His Catholic Majesty during the late war between

Spain and France. Their sittings have been interrupted, but are now resumed.

The United States being obligated to make compensation for the losses and damages sustained by British subjects, upon the award of the commissioners acting under the sixth article of the treaty with Great Britain, and for the losses and damages sustained by British subjects by reason of the capture of their vessels and merchandise taken within the limits and jurisdiction of the United States and brought into their ports, or taken by vessels originally armed in ports of the United States, upon the awards of the commissioners acting under the seventh article of the same treaty, it is necessary that provision be made for fulfilling these obligations.

The numerous captures of American vessels by the cruisers of the French Republic and of some by those of Spain have occasioned considerable expenses in making and supporting the claims of our citizens before their tribunals. The sums required for this purpose have in divers instances been disbursed by the consuls of the United States. By means of the same captures great numbers of our seamen have been thrown ashore in foreign countries, destitute of all means of subsistence, and the sick in particular have been exposed to grievous sufferings. The consuls have in these cases also advanced moneys for their relief. For these advances they reasonably expect reimbursements from the United States.

The consular act relative to seamen requires revision and amendment. The provisions for their support in foreign countries and for their return are found to be inadequate and ineffectual. Another provision seems necessary to be added to the consular act. Some foreign vessels have been discovered sailing under the flag of the United States and with forged papers. It seldom happens that the consuls can detect this deception, because they have no authority to demand an inspection of the registers and sea letters.

Gentlemen of the House of Representatives:

It is my duty to recommend to your serious consideration those objects which by the Constitution are placed particularly within your sphere— the national debts and taxes.

Since the decay of the feudal system, by which the public defense was provided for chiefly at the expense of individuals, the system of loans has been introduced, and as no nation can raise within the year by taxes sufficient sums for its defense and military operations in time of war the sums loaned and debts contracted have necessarily become the subjects of what have been called funding systems. The consequences arising from the continual accumulation of public debts in other countries ought to admonish us to be careful to prevent their growth in our own. The national defense must be provided for as well as the support of

Government; but both should be accomplished as much as possible by immediate taxes, and as little as possible by loans.

The estimates for the service of the ensuing year will by my direction be laid before you.

Gentlemen of the Senate and Gentlemen of the House of Representatives:

We are met together at a most interesting period. The situations of the principal powers of Europe are singular and portentous. Connected with some by treaties and with all by commerce, no important event there can be indifferent to us. Such circumstances call with peculiar importunity not less for a disposition to unite in all those measures on which the honor, safety, and prosperity of our country depend than for all the exertions of wisdom and firmness.

In all such measures you may rely on my zealous and hearty concurrence.

SECOND ANNUAL ADDRESS.

UNITED STATES, *December 8, 1798.*

Gentlemen of the Senate and Gentlemen of the House of Representatives:

While with reverence and resignation we contemplate the dispensations of Divine Providence in the alarming and destructive pestilence with which several of our cities and towns have been visited, there is cause for gratitude and mutual congratulations that the malady has disappeared and that we are again permitted to assemble in safety at the seat of Government for the discharge of our important duties. But when we reflect that this fatal disorder has within a few years made repeated ravages in some of our principal seaports, and with increased malignancy, and when we consider the magnitude of the evils arising from the interruption of public and private business, whereby the national interests are deeply affected, I think it my duty to invite the Legislature of the Union to examine the expediency of establishing suitable regulations in aid of the health laws of the respective States; for these being formed on the idea that contagious sickness may be communicated through the channels of commerce, there seems to be a necessity that Congress, who alone can regulate trade, should frame a system which, while it may tend to preserve the general health, may be compatible with the interests of commerce and the safety of the revenue.

While we think on this calamity and sympathize with the immediate sufferers, we have abundant reason to present to the Supreme Being our annual oblations of gratitude for a liberal participation in the ordinary blessings of His providence. To the usual subjects of gratitude I can not omit to add one of the first importance to our well-being and safety; I mean that spirit which has arisen in our country against the menaces and aggression of a foreign nation. A manly sense of national honor, dignity, and independence has appeared which, if encouraged and invigorated by every branch of the Government, will enable us to view undismayed the enterprises of any foreign power and become the sure foundation of national prosperity and glory.

The course of the transactions in relation to the United States and France which have come to my knowledge during your recess will be made the subject of a future communication. That communication will confirm the ultimate failure of the measures which have been taken by the Government of the United States toward an amicable adjustment of differences with that power. You will at the same time perceive that the French Government appears solicitous to impress the opinion that it is averse to a rupture with this country, and that it has in a qualified manner declared itself willing to receive a minister from the United States for the purpose of restoring a good understanding. It is unfortunate for professions of this kind that they should be expressed in terms which may countenance the inadmissible pretension of a right to prescribe the qualifications which a minister from the United States should possess, and that while France is asserting the existence of a disposition on her part to conciliate with sincerity the differences which have arisen, the sincerity of a like disposition on the part of the United States, of which so many demonstrative proofs have been given, should even be indirectly questioned. It is also worthy of observation that the decree of the Directory alleged to be intended to restrain the depredations of French cruisers on our commerce has not given, and can not give, any relief. It enjoins them to conform to all the laws of France relative to cruising and prizes, while these laws are themselves the sources of the depredations of which we have so long, so justly, and so fruitlessly complained.

The law of France enacted in January last, which subjects to capture and condemnation neutral vessels and their cargoes if any portion of the latter are of British fabric or produce, although the entire property belong to neutrals, instead of being rescinded has lately received a confirmation by the failure of a proposition for its repeal. While this law, which is an unequivocal act of war on the commerce of the nations it attacks, continues in force those nations can see in the French Government only a power regardless of their essential rights, of their independence and sovereignty; and if they possess the means they can reconcile nothing with their interest and honor but a firm resistance.

Hitherto, therefore, nothing is discoverable in the conduct of France which ought to change or relax our measures of defense. On the contrary, to extend and invigorate them is our true policy. We have no reason to regret that these measures have been thus far adopted and pursued, and in proportion as we enlarge our view of the portentous and incalculable situation of Europe we'shall discover new and cogent motives for the full development of our energies and resources.

But in demonstrating by our conduct that we do not fear war in the necessary protection of our rights and honor we shall give no room to infer that we abandon the desire of peace. An efficient preparation for war can alone insure peace. It is peace that we have uniformly and perseveringly cultivated, and harmony between us and France may be restored at her option. But to send another minister without more determinate assurances that he would be received would be an act of humiliation to which the United States ought not to submit. It must therefore be left with France (if she is indeed desirous of accommodation) to take the requisite steps. The United States will steadily observe the maxims by which they have hitherto been governed. They will respect the sacred rights of embassy; and with a sincere disposition on the part of France to desist from hostility, to make reparation for the injuries heretofore inflicted on our commerce, and to do justice in future, there will be no obstacle to the restoration of a friendly intercourse. In making to you this declaration I give a pledge to France and the world that the Executive authority of this country still adheres to the humane and pacific policy which has invariably governed its proceedings, in conformity with the wishes of the other branches of the Government and of the people of the United States. But considering the late manifestations of her policy toward foreign nations, I deem it a duty deliberately and solemnly to declare my opinion that whether we negotiate with her or not, vigorous preparations for war will be alike indispensable. These alone will give to us an equal treaty and insure its observance.

Among the measures of preparation which appear expedient, I take the liberty to recall your attention to the naval establishment. The beneficial effects of the small naval armament provided under the acts of the last session are known and acknowledged. Perhaps no country ever experienced more sudden and remarkable advantages from any measure of policy than we have derived from the arming for our maritime protection and defense. We ought without loss of time to lay the foundation for an increase of our Navy to a size sufficient to guard our coast and protect our trade. Such a naval force as it is doubtless in the power of the United States to create and maintain would also afford to them the best means of general defense by facilitating the safe transportation of troops and stores to every part of our extensive coast. To accomplish this important object, a prudent foresight requires that systematical measures be adopted for procuring at all times the requisite timber and other supplies. In what manner this shall be done I leave to your consideration.

I will now advert, gentlemen, to some matters of less moment, but proper to be communicated to the National Legislature.

After the Spanish garrisons had evacuated the posts they occupied at the Natchez and Walnut Hills the commissioner of the United States commenced his observations to ascertain the point near the Mississippi which terminated the northernmost part of the thirty-first degree of north latitude. From thence he proceeded to run the boundary line between the United States and Spain. He was afterwards joined by the Spanish commissioner, when the work of the former was confirmed, and they proceeded together to the demarcation of the line. Recent information renders it probable that the Southern Indians, either instigated to oppose the demarcation or jealous of the consequences of suffering white people to run a line over lands to which the Indian title had not been extinguished, have ere this time stopped the progress of the commissioners; and considering the mischiefs which may result from continuing the demarcation in opposition to the will of the Indian tribes, the great expense attending it, and that the boundaries which the commissioners have actually established probably extend at least as far as the Indian title has been extinguished, it will perhaps become expedient and necessary to suspend further proceedings by recalling our commissioner.

The commissioners appointed in pursuance of the fifth article of the treaty of amity, commerce, and navigation between the United States and His Britannic Majesty to determine what river was truly intended under the name of the river St. Croix mentioned in the treaty of peace, and forming a part of the boundary therein described, have finally decided that question. On the 25th of October they made their declaration that a river called Scoodiac, which falls into Passamaquoddy Bay at its northwestern quarter, was the true St. Croix intended in the treaty of peace, as far as its great fork, where one of its streams comes from the westward and the other from the northward, and that the latter stream is the continuation of the St. Croix to its source. This decision, it is understood, will preclude all contention among individual claimants, as it seems that the Scoodiac and its northern branch bound the grants of land which have been made by the respective adjoining Governments. A subordinate question, however, it has been suggested, still remains to be determined. Between the mouth of the St. Croix as now settled and what is usually called the Bay of Fundy lie a number of valuable islands. The commissioners have not continued the boundary line through any channel of these islands, and unless the bay of Passamaquoddy be a part of the Bay of Fundy this further adjustment of boundary will be necessary. But it is apprehended that this will not be a matter of any difficulty.

Such progress has been made in the examination and decision of cases of captures and condemnations of American vessels which were the subject of the seventh article of the treaty of amity, commerce, and navigation between the United States and Great Britain that it is supposed the commissioners will be able to bring their business to a conclusion in August of the ensuing year.

The commissioners acting under the twenty-fifth article of the treaty between the United States and Spain have adjusted most of the claims of our citizens for losses sustained in consequence of their vessels and cargoes having been taken by the subjects of His Catholic Majesty during the late war between France and Spain.

Various circumstances have concurred to delay the execution of the law for augmenting the military establishment, among these the desire of obtaining the fullest information to direct the best selection of officers. As this object will now be speedily accomplished, it is expected that the raising and organizing of the troops will proceed without obstacle and with effect.

Gentlemen of the House of Representatives:

I have directed an estimate of the appropriations which will be necessary for the service of the ensuing year to be laid before you, accompanied with a view of the public receipts and expenditures to a recent period. It will afford you satisfaction to infer the great extent and solidity of the public resources from the prosperous state of the finances, notwithstanding the unexampled embarrassments which have attended commerce. When you reflect on the conspicuous examples of patriotism and liberality which have been exhibited by our mercantile fellow-citizens, and how great a proportion of the public resources depends on their enterprise, you will naturally consider whether their convenience can not be promoted and reconciled with the security of the revenue by a revision of the system by which the collection is at present regulated.

During your recess measures have been steadily pursued for effecting the valuations and returns directed by the act of the last session, preliminary to the assessment and collection of a direct tax. No other delays or obstacles have been experienced except such as were expected to arise from the great extent of our country and the magnitude and novelty of the operation, and enough has been accomplished to assure a fulfillment of the views of the Legislature.

Gentlemen of the Senate and Gentlemen of the House of Representatives:

I can not close this address without once more adverting to our political situation and inculcating the essential importance of uniting in the maintenance of our dearest interests; and I trust that by the temper and wisdom of your proceedings and by a harmony of measures we shall secure to our country that weight and respect to which it is so justly entitled.

THIRD ANNUAL ADDRESS.

UNITED STATES, *December 3, 1799.*

Gentlemen of the Senate and Gentlemen of the House of Representatives:

It is with peculiar satisfaction that I meet the Sixth Congress of the United States of America. Coming from all parts of the Union at this critical and interesting period, the members must be fully possessed of the sentiments and wishes of our constituents.

The flattering prospects of abundance from the labors of the people by land and by sea; the prosperity of our extended commerce, notwithstanding interruptions occasioned by the belligerent state of a great part of the world; the return of health, industry, and trade to those cities which have lately been afflicted with disease, and the various and inestimable advantages, civil and religious, which, secured under our happy frame of government, are continued to us unimpaired, demand of the whole American people sincere thanks to a benevolent Deity for the merciful dispensations of His providence.

But while these numerous blessings are recollected, it is a painful duty to advert to the ungrateful return which has been made for them by some of the people in certain counties of Pennsylvania, where, seduced by the arts and misrepresentations of designing men, they have openly resisted the law directing the valuation of houses and lands. Such defiance was given to the civil authority as rendered hopeless all further attempts by judicial process to enforce the execution of the law, and it became necessary to direct a military force to be employed, consisting of some companies of regular troops, volunteers, and militia, by whose zeal and activity, in cooperation with the judicial power, order and submission were restored and many of the offenders arrested. Of these, some have been convicted of misdemeanors, and others, charged with various crimes, remain to be tried.

To give due effect to the civil administration of Government and to insure a just execution of the laws, a revision and amendment of the judiciary system is indispensably necessary. In this extensive country it can not but happen that numerous questions respecting the interpretation of the laws and the rights and duties of officers and citizens must arise. On the one hand, the laws should be executed; on the other, individuals should be guarded from oppression. Neither of these objects is sufficiently assured under the present organization of the judicial department. I therefore earnestly recommend the subject to your serious consideration.

Persevering in the pacific and humane policy which had been invariably professed and sincerely pursued by the Executive authority of the United States, when indications were made on the part of the French

Republic of a disposition to accommodate the existing differences between the two countries, I felt it to be my duty to prepare for meeting their advances by a nomination of ministers upon certain conditions which the honor of our country dictated, and which its moderation had given it a right to prescribe. The assurances which were required of the French Government previous to the departure of our envoys have been given through their minister of foreign relations, and I have directed them to proceed on their mission to Paris. They have full power to conclude a treaty, subject to the constitutional advice and consent of the Senate. The characters of these gentlemen are sure pledges to their country that nothing incompatible with its honor or interest, nothing inconsistent with our obligations of good faith or friendship to any other nation, will be stipulated.

It appearing probable from the information I received that our commercial intercourse with some ports in the island of St. Domingo might safely be renewed, I took such steps as seemed to me expedient to ascertain that point. The result being satisfactory, I then, in conformity with the act of Congress on the subject, directed the restraints and prohibitions of that intercourse to be discontinued on terms which were made known by proclamation. Since the renewal of this intercourse our citizens trading to those ports, with their property, have been duly respected, and privateering from those ports has ceased.

In examining the claims of British subjects by the commissioners at Philadelphia, acting under the sixth article of the treaty of amity, commerce, and navigation with Great Britain, a difference of opinion on points deemed essential in the interpretation of that article has arisen between the commissioners appointed by the United States and the other members of that board, from which the former have thought it their duty to withdraw. It is sincerely to be regretted that the execution of an article produced by a mutual spirit of amity and justice should have been thus unavoidably interrupted. It is, however, confidently expected that the same spirit of amity and the same sense of justice in which it originated will lead to satisfactory explanations. In consequence of the obstacles to the progress of the commission in Philadelphia, His Britannic Majesty has directed the commissioners appointed by him under the seventh article of the treaty relating to the British captures of American vessels to withdraw from the board sitting in London, but with the express declaration of his determination to fulfill with punctuality and good faith the engagements which His Majesty has contracted by his treaty with the United States, and that they will be instructed to resume their functions whenever the obstacles which impede the progress of the commission at Philadelphia shall be removed. It being in like manner my sincere determination, so far as the same depends on me, that with equal punctuality and good faith the engagements contracted by the United States in their treaties with His Britannic Majesty shall be fulfilled, I shall immediately instruct our minister at London to endeavor to obtain the explanations necessary to a just performance of those engagements on the part of the United States. With such dispositions on both sides, I can not entertain a doubt that all difficulties will soon be removed and that the two boards will then proceed and bring the business committed to them respectively to a satisfactory conclusion.

The act of Congress relative to the seat of the Government of the United States requiring that on the first Monday of December next it should be transferred from Philadelphia to the District chosen for its permanent seat, it is proper for me to inform you that the commissioners appointed to provide suitable buildings for the accommodation of Congress and of the President and of the public offices of the Government have made a report of the state of the buildings designed for those purposes in the city of Washington, from which they conclude that the removal of the seat of Government to that place at the time required will be practicable and the accommodation satisfactory. Their report will be laid before you.

Gentlemen of the House of Representatives:

I shall direct the estimates of the appropriations necessary for the service of the ensuing year, together with an account of the revenue and expenditure, to be laid before you. During a period in which a great portion of the civilized world has been involved in a war unusually calamitous and destructive, it was not to be expected that the United States could be exempted from extraordinary burthens. Although the period is not arrived when the measures adopted to secure our country against foreign attacks can be renounced, yet it is alike necessary for the honor of the Government and the satisfaction of the community that an exact economy should be maintained. I invite you, gentlemen, to investigate the different branches of the public expenditure. The examination will lead to beneficial retrenchments or produce a conviction of the wisdom of the measures to which the expenditure relates.

Gentlemen of the Senate and Gentlemen of the House of Representatives:

At a period like the present, when momentous changes are occurring and every hour is preparing new and great events in the political world, when a spirit of war is prevalent in almost every nation with whose affairs the interests of the United States have any connection, unsafe and precarious would be our situation were we to neglect the means of maintaining our just rights. The result of the mission to France is uncertain; but however it may terminate, a steady perseverance in a system of national defense commensurate with our resources and the situation of our country is an obvious dictate of wisdom; for, remotely as we are placed from the belligerent nations, and desirous as we are, by doing justice to all, to avoid offense to any, nothing short of the power of repelling aggressions will secure to our country a rational prospect of escaping the calamities of war or national degradation.   As to myself, it is my anxious desire so to execute the trust reposed in me as to render the people of the United States prosperous and happy.   I rely with entire confidence on your cooperation in objects equally your care, and that our mutual labors will serve to increase and confirm union among our fellow-citizens and an unshaken attachment to our Government.

FOURTH ANNUAL ADDRESS.

UNITED STATES, *November 22, 1800.*

Gentlemen of the Senate and Gentlemen of the House of Representatives:

Immediately after the adjournment of Congress at their last session in Philadelphia I gave directions, in compliance with the laws, for the removal of the public offices, records, and property.   These directions have been executed, and the public officers have since resided and conducted the ordinary business of the Government in this place.

I congratulate the people of the United States on the assembling of Congress at the permanent seat of their Government, and I congratulate you, gentlemen, on the prospect of a residence not to be changed. Although there is cause to apprehend that accommodations are not now so complete as might be wished, yet there is great reason to believe that this inconvenience will cease with the present session.

It would be unbecoming the representatives of this nation to assemble for the first time in this solemn temple without looking up to the Supreme Ruler of the Universe and imploring His blessing.

May this territory be the residence of virtue and happiness!   In this city may that piety and virtue, that wisdom and magnanimity, that constancy and self-government, which adorned the great character whose name it bears be forever held in veneration!   Here and throughout our country may simple manners, pure morals, and true religion flourish forever!

It is with you, gentlemen, to consider whether the local powers over the District of Columbia vested by the Constitution in the Congress of the United States shall be immediately exercised.   If in your opinion this important trust ought now to be executed, you can not fail while performing it to take into view the future probable situation of the territory for the happiness of which you are about to provide.   You will consider it as the capital of a great nation advancing with unexampled rapidity in arts, in commerce, in wealth, and in population, and possessing within itself those energies and resources which, if not thrown away or lamentably misdirected, will secure to it a long course of prosperity and self-government.

In compliance with a law of the last session of Congress, the officers and soldiers of the temporary army have been discharged. It affords real pleasure to recollect the honorable testimony they gave of the patriotic motives which brought them into the service of their country, by the readiness and regularity with which they returned to the station of private citizens.

It is in every point of view of such primary importance to carry the laws into prompt and faithful execution, and to render that part of the administration of justice which the Constitution and laws devolve on the Federal courts as convenient to the people as may consist with their present circumstances, that I can not omit once more to recommend to your serious consideration the judiciary system of the United States. No subject is more interesting than this to the public happiness, and to none can those improvements which may have been suggested by experience be more beneficially applied.

A treaty of amity and commerce with the King of Prussia has been concluded and ratified. The ratifications have been exchanged, and I have directed the treaty to be promulgated by proclamation.

The difficulties which suspended the execution of the sixth article of our treaty of amity, commerce, and navigation with Great Britain have not yet been removed. The negotiation on this subject is still depending. As it must be for the interest and honor of both nations to adjust this difference with good faith, I indulge confidently the expectation that the sincere endeavors of the Government of the United States to bring it to an amicable termination will not be disappointed.

The envoys extraordinary and ministers plenipotentiary from the United States to France were received by the First Consul with the respect due to their character, and three persons with equal powers were appointed to treat with them. Although at the date of the last official intelligence the negotiation had not terminated, yet it is to be hoped that our efforts to effect an accommodation will at length meet with a success proportioned to the sincerity with which they have been so often repeated.

While our best endeavors for the preservation of harmony with all nations will continue to be used, the experience of the world and our own experience admonish us of the insecurity of trusting too confidently to their success. We can not, without committing a dangerous imprudence, abandon those measures of self-protection which are adapted to our situation and to which, notwithstanding our pacific policy, the violence and injustice of others may again compel us to resort While our vast extent of seacoast, the commercial and agricultural habits of our people, the great capital they will continue to trust on the ocean, suggest the system of defense which will be most beneficial to ourselves, our distance

from Europe and our resources for maritime strength will enable us to
employ it with effect.   Seasonable and systematic arrangements, so far
as our resources will justify, for a navy adapted to defensive war, and
which may in case of necessity be quickly brought into use, seem to be
as much recommended by a wise and true economy as by a just regard
for our future tranquillity, for the safety of our shores, and for the protection of our property committed to the ocean.

The present Navy of the United States, called suddenly into existence
by a great national exigency, has raised us in our own esteem, and by the
protection afforded to our commerce has effected to the extent of our
expectations the objects for which it was created.

In connection with a navy ought to be contemplated the fortification
of some of our principal seaports and harbors.   A variety of considerations, which will readily suggest themselves, urge an attention to this
measure of precaution.   To give security to our principal ports considerable sums have already been expended, but the works remain incomplete.
It is for Congress to determine whether additional appropriations shall
be made in order to render competent to the intended purposes the fortifications which have been commenced.

The manufacture of arms within the United States still invites the
attention of the National Legislature.   At a considerable expense to the
public this manufacture has been brought to such a state of maturity as,
with continued encouragement, will supersede the necessity of future
importations from foreign countries.

Gentlemen of the House of Representatives:

I shall direct the estimates of the appropriations necessary for the
ensuing year, together with an account of the public revenue and expenditure to a late period, to be laid before you.   I observe with much satisfaction that the product of the revenue during the present year has been
more considerable than during any former equal period.   This result
affords conclusive evidence of the great resources of this country and of
the wisdom and efficiency of the measures which have been adopted by
Congress for the protection of commerce and preservation of public credit.

Gentlemen of the Senate and Gentlemen of the House of Representatives:

As one of the grand community of nations, our attention is irresistibly
drawn to the important scenes which surround us.   If they have exhibited an uncommon portion of calamity, it is the province of humanity to
deplore and of wisdom to avoid the causes which may have produced
it.   If, turning our eyes homeward, we find reason to rejoice at the
prospect which presents itself; if we perceive the interior of our country
prosperous, free, and happy; if all enjoy in safety, under the protection of
laws emanating only from the general will, the fruits of their own labor,
we ought to fortify and cling to those institutions which have been the

source of such real felicity and resist with unabating perseverance the progress of those dangerous innovations which may diminish their influence.

To your patriotism, gentlemen, has been confided the honorable duty of guarding the public interests; and while the past is to your country a sure pledge that it will be faithfully discharged, permit me to assure you that your labors to promote the general happiness will receive from me the most zealous cooperation.

Thomas Jefferson

March 4, 1801 to March 4, 1809

FIRST ANNUAL MESSAGE.

DECEMBER 8, 1801.

Fellow-Citizens of the Senate and House of Representatives:

It is a circumstance of sincere gratification to me that on meeting the great council of our nation I am able to announce to them on grounds of reasonable certainty that the wars and troubles which have for so many years afflicted our sister nations have at length come to an end, and that the communications of peace and commerce are once more opening among them. Whilst we devoutly return thanks to the beneficent Being who has been pleased to breathe into them the spirit of conciliation and forgiveness, we are bound with peculiar gratitude to be thankful to Him that our own peace has been preserved through so perilous a season, and ourselves permitted quietly to cultivate the earth and to practice and improve those arts which tend to increase our comforts. The assurances, indeed, of friendly disposition received from all the powers with whom we have principal relations had inspired a confidence that our peace with them would not have been disturbed. But a cessation of irregularities which had affected the commerce of neutral nations and of the irritations and injuries produced by them can not but add to this confidence, and strengthens at the same time the hope that wrongs committed on unoffending friends under a pressure of circumstances will now be reviewed with candor, and will be considered as founding just claims of retribution for the past and new assurance for the future.

Among our Indian neighbors also a spirit of peace and friendship generally prevails, and I am happy to inform you that the continued efforts to introduce among them the implements and the practice of husbandry and of the household arts have not been without success; that they are becoming more and more sensible of the superiority of this dependence for clothing and subsistence over the precarious resources of hunting and fishing, and already we are able to announce that instead of that constant diminution of their numbers produced by their wars and their wants, some of them begin to experience an increase of population.

To this state of general peace with which we have been blessed, one only exception exists. Tripoli, the least considerable of the Barbary States, had come forward with demands unfounded either in right or in compact, and had permitted itself to denounce war on our failure to comply before a given day. The style of the demand admitted but one answer. I sent a small squadron of frigates into the Mediterranean, with assurances to that power of our sincere desire to remain in peace, but with orders to protect our commerce against the threatened attack. The measure was seasonable and salutary. The Bey had already declared war. His cruisers were out. Two had arrived at Gibraltar.

Our commerce in the Mediterranean was blockaded and that of the Atlantic in peril. The arrival of our squadron dispelled the danger. One of the Tripolitan cruisers having fallen in with and engaged the small schooner *Enterprise*, commanded by Lieutenant Sterret, which had gone as a tender to our larger vessels, was captured, after a heavy slaughter of her men, without the loss of a single one on our part. The bravery exhibited by our citizens on that element will, I trust, be a testimony to the world that it is not the want of that virtue which makes us seek their peace, but a conscientious desire to direct the energies of our nation to the multiplication of the human race, and not to its destruction. Unauthorized by the Constitution, without the sanction of Congress, to go beyond the line of defense, the vessel, being disabled from committing further hostilities, was liberated with its crew. The Legislature will doubtless consider whether, by authorizing measures of offense also, they will place our force on an equal footing with that of its adversaries. I communicate all material information on this subject, that in the exercise of this important function confided by the Constitution to the Legislature exclusively their judgment may form itself on a knowledge and consideration of every circumstance of weight.

I wish I could say that our situation with all the other Barbary States was entirely satisfactory. Discovering that some delays had taken place in the performance of certain articles stipulated by us, I thought it my duty, by immediate measures for fulfilling them, to vindicate to ourselves the right of considering the effect of departure from stipulation on their side. From the papers which will be laid before you you will be enabled to judge whether our treaties are regarded by them as fixing at all the measure of their demands or as guarding from the exercise of force our vessels within their power, and to consider how far it will be safe and expedient to leave our affairs with them in their present posture.

I lay before you the result of the census lately taken of our inhabitants, to a conformity with which we are now to reduce the ensuing ratio of representation and taxation. You will perceive that the increase of numbers during the last ten years, proceeding in geometrical ratio, promises a duplication in little more than twenty-two years. We contemplate this rapid growth and the prospect it holds up to us, not with a view to the injuries it may enable us to do others in some future day, but to the settlement of the extensive country still remaining vacant within our limits to the multiplication of men susceptible of happiness, educated in the love of order, habituated to self-government, and valuing its blessings above all price.

Other circumstances, combined with the increase of numbers, have produced an augmentation of revenue arising from consumption in a ratio far beyond that of population alone; and though the changes in foreign relations now taking place so desirably for the whole world may for a season affect this branch of revenue, yet weighing all probabilities of expense as well as of income, there is reasonable ground of confidence that we may now safely dispense with all the internal taxes, comprehending excise, stamps, auctions, licenses, carriages, and refined sugars, to which the postage on newspapers may be added to facilitate the progress of information, and that the remaining sources of revenue will be sufficient to provide for the support of Government, to pay the interest of the public debts, and to discharge the principals within shorter periods than the laws or the general expectation had contemplated. War, indeed, and untoward events may change this prospect of things and call for expenses which the imposts could not meet; but sound principles will not justify our taxing the industry of our fellow-citizens to accumulate treasure for wars to happen we know not when, and which might not, perhaps, happen but from the temptations offered by that treasure.

These views, however, of reducing our burthens are formed on the expectation that a sensible and at the same time a salutary reduction may take place in our habitual expenditures. For this purpose those of the civil Government, the Army, and Navy will need revisal.

When we consider that this Government is charged with the external and mutual relations only of these States; that the States themselves have principal care of our persons, our property, and our reputation, constituting the great field of human concerns, we may well doubt whether our organization is not too complicated, too expensive; whether offices and officers have not been multiplied unnecessarily and sometimes injuriously to the service they were meant to promote. I will cause to be laid before you an essay toward a statement of those who, under public employment of various kinds, draw money from the Treasury or from our citizens. Time has not permitted a perfect enumeration, the ramifications of office being too multiplied and remote to be completely traced in a first trial. Among those who are dependent on Executive discretion I have begun the reduction of what was deemed unnecessary. The expenses of diplomatic agency have been considerably diminished. The inspectors of internal revenue who were found to obstruct the accountability of the institution have been discontinued. Several agencies created by Executive authority, on salaries fixed by that also, have been suppressed, and should suggest the expediency of regulating that power by law, so as to subject its exercises to legislative inspection and sanction. Other reformations of the same kind will be pursued with that caution which is requisite in removing useless things, not to injure what is retained. But the great mass of public offices is established by law, and therefore by law alone can be abolished. Should the Legislature think it expedient to pass this roll in review and try all its parts by the test of public utility, they may be assured of every aid and light which Executive information can yield. Considering the general tendency to multiply offices and dependencies and to increase expense to the ultimate term of burthen which the citizen can bear, it behooves us to avail ourselves of every occasion which presents itself for taking off the surcharge, that it never may be seen here that after leaving to labor the smallest portion of its earnings on which it can subsist, Government shall itself consume the whole residue of what it was instituted to guard.

In our care, too, of the public contributions intrusted to our direction it would be prudent to multiply barriers against their dissipation by appropriating specific sums to every specific purpose susceptible of definition; by disallowing all applications of money varying from the appropriation in object or transcending it in amount; by reducing the undefined field of contingencies and thereby circumscribing discretionary powers over money, and by bringing back to a single department all accountabilities for money, where the examinations may be prompt, efficacious, and uniform.

An account of the receipts and expenditures of the last year, as prepared by the Secretary of the Treasury, will, as usual, be laid before you. The success which has attended the late sales of the public lands shews that with attention they may be made an important source of receipt. Among the payments those made in discharge of the principal and interest of the national debt will shew that the public faith has been exactly maintained. To these will be added an estimate of appropriations necessary for the ensuing year. This last will, of course, be affected by such modifications of the system of expense as you shall think proper to adopt.

A statement has been formed by the Secretary of War, on mature consideration, of all the posts and stations where garrisons will be expedient and of the number of men requisite for each garrison. The whole amount is considerably short of the present military establishment. For the surplus no particular use can be pointed out. For defense against invasion their number is as nothing, nor is it conceived needful or safe that a standing army should be kept up in time of peace for that purpose. Uncertain as we must ever be of the particular point in our circumference where an enemy may choose to invade us, the only force which can be ready at every point and competent to oppose them is the body of neighboring citizens as formed into a militia. On these, collected from the parts most convenient in numbers proportioned to the invading force, it is best to rely not only to meet the first attack, but if it threatens to be permanent to maintain the defense until regulars may be engaged to relieve them. These considerations render it important that we should at every session continue to amend the defects which from time to time shew themselves in the laws for regulating the militia until they are sufficiently perfect. Nor should we now or at any time separate until we can say we have done everything for the militia which we could do were an enemy at our door.

The provision of military stores on hand will be laid before you, that you may judge of the additions still requisite.

With respect to the extent to which our naval preparations should be carried some difference of opinion may be expected to appear, but just attention to the circumstances of every part of the Union will doubtless reconcile all. A small force will probably continue to be wanted for actual service in the Mediterranean. Whatever annual sum beyond that you may think proper to appropriate to naval preparations would perhaps be better employed in providing those articles which may be kept without waste or consumption, and be in readiness when any exigence calls them into use. Progress has been made, as will appear by papers now communicated, in providing materials for 74-gun ships as directed by law.

How far the authority given by the Legislature for procuring and establishing sites for naval purposes has been perfectly understood and pursued in the execution admits of some doubt. A statement of the expenses already incurred on that subject is now laid before you. I have in certain cases suspended or slackened these expenditures, that the Legislature might determine whether so many yards are necessary as have been contemplated. The works at this place are among those permitted to go on, and five of the seven frigates directed to be laid up have been brought and laid up here, where, besides the safety of their position, they are under the eye of the Executive Administration, as well as of its agents, and where yourselves also will be guided by your own view in the legislative provisions respecting them which may from time to time be necessary. They are preserved in such condition, as well the vessels as whatever belongs to them, as to be at all times ready for sea on a short warning. Two others are yet to be laid up so soon as they shall have received the repairs requisite to put them also into sound condition. As a superintending officer will be necessary at each yard, his duties and emoluments, hitherto fixed by the Executive, will be a more proper subject for legislation. A communication will also be made of our progress in the execution of the law respecting the vessels directed to be sold.

The fortifications of our harbors, more or less advanced, present considerations of great difficulty. While some of them are on a scale sufficiently proportioned to the advantages of their position, to the efficacy of their protection, and the importance of the points within it, others are so extensive, will cost so much in their first erection, so much in their maintenance, and require such a force to garrison them as to make it questionable what is best now to be done. A statement of those commenced or projected, of the expenses already incurred, and estimates of their future cost, as far as can be foreseen, shall be laid before you, that you may be enabled to judge whether any alteration is necessary in the laws respecting this subject.

Agriculture, manufactures, commerce, and navigation, the four pillars of our prosperity, are then most thriving when left most free to individual enterprise. Protection from casual embarrassments, however, may sometimes be seasonably interposed. If in the course of your observations or inquiries they should appear to need any aid within the limits of our constitutional powers, your sense of their importance is a sufficient assurance they will occupy your attention. We can not, indeed, but all feel an anxious solicitude for the difficulties under which our carrying trade will soon be placed. How far it can be relieved, otherwise than by time, is a subject of important consideration.

The judiciary system of the United States, and especially that portion of it recently erected, will of course present itself to the contemplation of Congress, and, that they may be able to judge of the proportion which the institution bears to the business it has to perform, I have caused to be procured from the several States and now lay before Congress an exact statement of all the causes decided since the first establishment of the courts, and of those which were depending when additional courts and judges were brought in to their aid.

And while on the judiciary organization it will be worthy your consideration whether the protection of the inestimable institution of juries has been extended to all the cases involving the security of our persons and property. Their impartial selection also being essential to their value, we ought further to consider whether that is sufficiently secured in those States where they are named by a marshal depending on Executive will or designated by the court or by officers dependent on them.

I can not omit recommending a revisal of the laws on the subject of naturalization. Considering the ordinary chances of human life, a denial of citizenship under a residence of fourteen years is a denial to a great proportion of those who ask it, and controls a policy pursued from their first settlement by many of these States, and still believed of consequence to their prosperity; and shall we refuse to the unhappy fugitives from distress that hospitality which the savages of the wilderness extended to our fathers arriving in this land? Shall oppressed humanity find no asylum on this globe? The Constitution indeed has wisely provided that for admission to certain offices of important trust a residence shall be required sufficient to develop character and design. But might not the general character and capabilities of a citizen be safely communicated to everyone manifesting a bona fide purpose of embarking his life and fortunes permanently with us, with restrictions, perhaps, to guard against the fraudulent usurpation of our flag, an abuse which brings so much embarrassment and loss on the genuine citizen and so much danger to the nation of being involved in war that no endeavor should be spared to detect and suppress it?

These, fellow-citizens, are the matters respecting the state of the nation which I have thought of importance to be submitted to your consideration at this time. Some others of less moment or not yet ready for communication will be the subject of separate messages. I am happy in this opportunity of committing the arduous affairs of our Government to the collected wisdom of the Union. Nothing shall be wanting on my part to inform as far as in my power the legislative judgment, nor to carry that judgment into faithful execution.　The prudence and temperance of your discussions will promote within your own walls that conciliation which so much befriends rational conclusion, and by its example will encourage among our constituents that progress of opinion which is tending to unite them in object and in will.　That all should be satisfied with any one order of things is not to be expected; but I indulge the pleasing persuasion that the great body of our citizens will cordially concur in honest and disinterested efforts which have for their object to preserve the General and State Governments in their constitutional form and equilibrium; to maintain peace abroad, and order and obedience to the laws at home; to establish principles and practices of administration favorable to the security of liberty and property, and to reduce expenses to what is necessary for the useful purposes of Government.

SECOND ANNUAL MESSAGE.

DECEMBER 15, 1802.

To the Senate and House of Representatives of the United States:

When we assemble together, fellow-citizens, to consider the state of our beloved country, our just attentions are first drawn to those pleasing circumstances which mark the goodness of that Being from whose favor they flow and the large measure of thankfulness we owe for His bounty. Another year has come around, and finds us still blessed with peace and friendship abroad; law, order, and religion at home; good affection and harmony with our Indian neighbors; our burthens lightened, yet our income sufficient for the public wants, and the produce of the year great beyond example.　These, fellow-citizens, are the circumstances under which we meet, and we remark with special satisfaction those which under the smiles of Providence result from the skill, industry, and order of our citizens, managing their own affairs in their own way and for their own use, unembarrassed by too much regulation, unoppressed by fiscal exactions.

On the restoration of peace in Europe that portion of the general carrying trade which had fallen to our share during the war was abridged by the returning competition of the belligerent powers.　This was to be expected, and was just.　But in addition we find in some parts of Europe monopolizing discriminations, which in the form of duties tend effectually to prohibit the carrying thither our own produce in our own vessels.

From existing amities and a spirit of justice it is hoped that friendly discussion will produce a fair and adequate reciprocity. But should false calculations of interest defeat our hope, it rests with the Legislature to decide whether they will meet inequalities abroad with countervailing inequalities at home, or provide for the evil in any other way.

It is with satisfaction I lay before you an act of the British Parliament anticipating this subject so far as to authorize a mutual abolition of the duties and countervailing duties permitted under the treaty of 1794. It shows on their part a spirit of justice and friendly accommodation which it is our duty and our interest to cultivate with all nations. Whether this would produce a due equality in the navigation between the two countries is a subject for your consideration.

Another circumstance which claims attention as directly affecting the very source of our navigation is the defect or the evasion of the law providing for the return of seamen, and particularly of those belonging to vessels sold abroad. Numbers of them, discharged in foreign ports, have been thrown on the hands of our consuls, who, to rescue them from the dangers into which their distresses might plunge them and save them to their country, have found it necessary in some cases to return them at the public charge.

The cession of the Spanish Province of Louisiana to France, which took place in the course of the late war, will, if carried into effect, make a change in the aspect of our foreign relations which will doubtless have just weight in any deliberations of the Legislature connected with that subject.

There was reason not long since to apprehend that the warfare in which we were engaged with Tripoli might be taken up by some other of the Barbary Powers. A reenforcement, therefore, was immediately ordered to the vessels already there. Subsequent information, however, has removed these apprehensions for the present. To secure our commerce in that sea with the smallest force competent, we have supposed it best to watch strictly the harbor of Tripoli. Still, however, the shallowness of their coast and the want of smaller vessels on our part has permitted some cruisers to escape unobserved, and to one of these an American vessel unfortunately fell a prey. The captain, one American seaman, and two others of color remain prisoners with them unless exchanged under an agreement formerly made with the Bashaw, to whom, on the faith of that, some of his captive subjects had been restored.

The convention with the State of Georgia has been ratified by their legislature, and a repurchase from the Creeks has been consequently made of a part of the Talasscee country. In this purchase has been also comprehended a part of the lands within the fork of Oconee and Oakmulgee rivers. The particulars of the contract will be laid before Congress so soon as they shall be in a state for communication.

In order to remove every ground of difference possible with our Indian

neighbors, I have proceeded in the work of settling with them and marking the boundaries between us. That with the Choctaw Nation is fixed
in one part and will be through the whole within a short time. The
country to which their title had been extinguished before the Revolution
is sufficient to receive a very respectable population, which Congress will
probably see the expediency of encouraging so soon as the limits shall be
declared. We are to view this position as an outpost of the United States,
surrounded by strong neighbors and distant from its support; and how
far that monopoly which prevents population should here be guarded
against and actual habitation made a condition of the continuance of title
will be for your consideration. A prompt settlement, too, of all existing
rights and claims within this territory presents itself as a preliminary
operation.

In that part of the Indiana Territory which includes Vincennes the lines
settled with the neighboring tribes fix the extinction of their title at a
breadth of 24 leagues from east to west and about the same length parallel with and including the Wabash. They have also ceded a tract of
4 miles square, including the salt springs near the mouth of that river.

In the Department of Finance it is with pleasure I inform you that the
receipts of external duties for the last twelve months have exceeded those
of any former year, and that the ratio of increase has been also greater
than usual. This has enabled us to answer all the regular exigencies
of Government, to pay from the Treasury within one year upward of
$8,000,000, principal and interest, of the public debt, exclusive of upward
of one million paid by the sale of bank stock, and making in the whole
a reduction of nearly five millions and a half of principal, and to have
now in the Treasury $4,500,000, which are in a course of application to
the further discharge of debt and current demands. Experience, too, so
far, authorizes us to believe, if no extraordinary event supervenes, and
the expenses which will be actually incurred shall not be greater than
were contemplated by Congress at their last session, that we shall not be
disappointed in the expectations then formed. But nevertheless, as the
effect of peace on the amount of duties is not yet fully ascertained, it is
the more necessary to practice every useful economy and to incur no
expense which may be avoided without prejudice.

The collection of the internal taxes having been completed in some of
the States, the officers employed in it are of course out of commission.
In others they will be so shortly. But in a few, where the arrangements
for the direct tax had been retarded, it will be some time before the
system is closed. It has not yet been thought necessary to employ the
agent authorized by an act of the last session for transacting business in
Europe relative to debts and loans. Nor have we used the power confided by the same act of prolonging the foreign debt by reloans, and of
redeeming instead thereof an equal sum of the domestic debt. Should,
however, the difficulties of remittance on so large a scale render it neces-

sary at any time, the power shall be executed and the money thus unemployed abroad shall, in conformity with that law, be faithfully applied here in an equivalent extinction of domestic debt. When effects so salutary result from the plans you have already sanctioned; when merely by avoiding false objects of expense we are able, without a direct tax, without internal taxes, and without borrowing to make large and effectual payments toward the discharge of our public debt and the emancipation of our posterity from that mortal canker, it is an encouragement, fellow-citizens, of the highest order to proceed as we have begun in substituting economy for taxation, and in pursuing what is useful for a nation placed as we are, rather than what is practiced by others under different circumstances. And whensoever we are destined to meet events which shall call forth all the energies of our countrymen, we have the firmest reliance on those energies and the comfort of leaving for calls like these the extraordinary resources of loans and internal taxes. In the meantime, by payments of the principal of our debt, we are liberating annually portions of the external taxes and forming from them a growing fund still further to lessen the necessity of recurring to extraordinary resources.

The usual account of receipts and expenditures for the last year, with an estimate of the expenses of the ensuing one, will be laid before you by the Secretary of the Treasury.

No change being deemed necessary in our military establishment, an estimate of its expenses for the ensuing year on its present footing, as also of the sums to be employed in fortifications and other objects within that department, has been prepared by the Secretary of War, and will make a part of the general estimates which will be presented you.

Considering that our regular troops are employed for local purposes, and that the militia is our general reliance for great and sudden emergencies, you will doubtless think this institution worthy of a review, and give it those improvements of which you find it susceptible.

Estimates for the Naval Department, prepared by the Secretary of the Navy, for another year will in like manner be communicated with the general estimates. A small force in the Mediterranean will still be necessary to restrain the Tripoline cruisers, and the uncertain tenure of peace with some other of the Barbary Powers may eventually require that force to be augmented. The necessity of procuring some smaller vessels for that service will raise the estimate, but the difference in their maintenance will soon make it a measure of economy.

Presuming it will be deemed expedient to expend annually a convenient sum toward providing the naval defense which our situation may require, I can not but recommend that the first appropriations for that purpose may go to the saving what we already possess. No cares, no attentions, can preserve vessels from rapid decay which lie in water and exposed to the sun. These decays require great and constant repairs, and will consume, if continued, a great portion of the moneys destined to naval purposes. To avoid this waste of our resources it is proposed to add to our navy-yard here a dock within which our present vessels may be laid up dry and under cover from the sun. Under these circumstances experience proves that works of wood will remain scarcely at all affected by time. The great abundance of running water which this situation possesses, at heights far above the level of the tide, if employed as is practiced for lock navigation, furnishes the means for raising and laying up our vessels on a dry and sheltered bed. And should the measure be found useful here, similar depositories for laying up as well as for building and repairing vessels may hereafter be undertaken at other navy-yards offering the same means. The plans and estimates of the work, prepared by a person of skill and experience, will be presented to you without delay, and from this it will be seen that scarcely more than has been the cost of one vessel is necessary to save the whole, and that the annual sum to be employed toward its completion may be adapted to the views of the Legislature as to naval expenditure.

To cultivate peace and maintain commerce and navigation in all their lawful enterprises; to foster our fisheries as nurseries of navigation and for the nurture of man, and protect the manufactures adapted to our circumstances; to preserve the faith of the nation by an exact discharge of its debts and contracts, expend the public money with the same care and economy we would practice with our own, and impose on our citizens no unnecessary burthens; to keep in all things within the pale of our constitutional powers, and cherish the federal union as the only rock of safety—these, fellow-citizens, are the landmarks by which we are to guide ourselves in all our proceedings. By continuing to make these the rule of our action we shall endear to our countrymen the true principles of their Constitution and promote an union of sentiment and of action equally auspicious to their happiness and safety. On my part, you may count on a cordial concurrence in every measure for the public good and on all the information I possess which may enable you to discharge to advantage the high functions with which you are invested by your country.

THIRD ANNUAL MESSAGE.

OCTOBER 17, 1803.

To the Senate and House of Representatives of the United States:

In calling you together, fellow-citizens, at an earlier day than was contemplated by the act of the last session of Congress, I have not been insensible to the personal inconveniences necessarily resulting from an unexpected change in your arrangements. But matters of great public concernment have rendered this call necessary, and the interests you feel in these will supersede in your minds all private considerations.

Congress witnessed at their late session the extraordinary agitation produced in the public mind by the suspension of our right of deposit at the port of New Orleans, no assignment of another place having been made according to treaty. They were sensible that the continuance of that privation would be more injurious to our nation than any consequences which could flow from any mode of redress, but reposing just confidence in the good faith of the Government whose officer had committed the wrong, friendly and reasonable representations were resorted to, and the right of deposit was restored.

Previous, however, to this period we had not been unaware of the danger to which our peace would be perpetually exposed whilst so important a key to the commerce of the Western country remained under foreign power. Difficulties, too, were presenting themselves as to the navigation of other streams which, arising within our territories, pass through those adjacent. Propositions had therefore been authorized for obtaining on fair conditions the sovereignty of New Orleans and of other possessions in that quarter interesting to our quiet to such extent as was deemed practicable, and the provisional appropriation of $2,000,000 to be applied and accounted for by the President of the United States, intended as part of the price, was considered as conveying the sanction of Congress to the acquisition proposed. The enlightened Government of France saw with just discernment the importance to both nations of such liberal arrangements as might best and permanently promote the peace, friendship, and interests of both, and the property and sovereignty of all Louisiana which had been restored to them have on certain conditions been transferred to the United States by instruments bearing date the 30th of April last. When these shall have received the constitutional sanction of the Senate, they will without delay be communicated to the Representatives also for the exercise of their functions as to those conditions which are within the powers vested by the Constitution in Congress.

Whilst the property and sovereignty of the Mississippi and its waters secure an independent outlet for the produce of the Western States and an uncontrolled navigation through their whole course, free from collision with other powers and the dangers to our peace from that source, the fertility of the country, its climate and extent, promise in due season important aids to our Treasury, an ample provision for our posterity, and a wide spread for the blessings of freedom and equal laws.

With the wisdom of Congress it will rest to take those ulterior measures which may be necessary for the immediate occupation and temporary government of the country; for its incorporation into our Union; for rendering the change of government a blessing to our newly adopted brethren; for securing to them the rights of conscience and of property; for confirming to the Indian inhabitants their occupancy and self-government, establishing friendly and commercial relations with them, and for ascertaining the geography of the country acquired. Such materials, for your information, relative to its affairs in general as the short space of time has permitted me to collect will be laid before you when the subject shall be in a state for your consideration.

Another important acquisition of territory has also been made since the last session of Congress. The friendly tribe of Kaskaskia Indians, with which we have never had a difference, reduced by the wars and wants of savage life to a few individuals unable to defend themselves against the neighboring tribes, has transferred its country to the United States, reserving only for its members what is sufficient to maintain them in an agricultural way. The considerations stipulated are that we shall extend to them our patronage and protection and give them certain annual aids in money, in implements of agriculture, and other articles of their choice. This country, among the most fertile within our limits, extending along the Mississippi from the mouth of the Illinois to and up the Ohio, though not so necessary as a barrier since the acquisition of the other bank, may yet be well worthy of being laid open to immediate settlement, as its inhabitants may descend with rapidity in support of the lower country should future circumstances expose that to foreign enterprise. As the stipulations in this treaty also involve matters within the competence of both Houses only, it will be laid before Congress as soon as the Senate shall have advised its ratification.

With many of the other Indian tribes improvements in agriculture and household manufacture are advancing, and with all our peace and friendship are established on grounds much firmer than heretofore. The measure adopted of establishing trading houses among them and of furnishing them necessaries in exchange for their commodities at such moderate prices as leave no gain, but cover us from loss, has the most conciliatory and useful effect on them, and is that which will best secure their peace and good will.

The small vessels authorized by Congress with a view to the Mediterranean service have been sent into that sea, and will be able more effectually to confine the Tripoline cruisers within their harbors and supersede the necessity of convoy to our commerce in that quarter. They will sensibly lessen the expenses of that service the ensuing year.

A further knowledge of the ground in the northeastern and northwestern angles of the United States has evinced that the boundaries established by the treaty of Paris between the British territories and ours in those parts were too imperfectly described to be susceptible of execution. It has therefore been thought worthy of attention for preserving and cherishing the harmony and useful intercourse subsisting between the two nations to remove by timely arrangements what unfavorable incidents might otherwise render a ground of future misunderstanding. A convention has therefore been entered into which provides for a practicable demarcation of those limits to the satisfaction of both parties.

An account of the receipts and expenditures of the year ending the 30th of September last, with the estimates for the service of the ensuing year, will be laid before you by the Secretary of the Treasury so soon as the receipts of the last quarter shall be returned from the more distant States. It is already ascertained that the amount paid into the Treasury for that year has been between $11,000,000 and $12,000,000, and that the revenue accrued during the same term exceeds the sum counted on as sufficient for our current expenses and to extinguish the public debt within the period heretofore proposed.

The amount of debt paid for the same year is about $3,100,000, exclusive of interest, and making, with the payment of the preceding year, a discharge of more than $8,500,000 of the principal of that debt, besides the accruing interest; and there remain in the Treasury nearly $6,000,000. Of these, $880,000 have been reserved for payment of the first installment due under the British convention of January 8, 1802, and two millions are what have been before mentioned as placed by Congress under the power and accountability of the President toward the price of New Orleans and other territories acquired, which, remaining untouched, are still applicable to that object and go in diminution of the sum to be funded for it.

Should the acquisition of Louisiana be constitutionally confirmed and carried into effect, a sum of nearly $13,000,000 will then be added to our public debt, most of which is payable after fifteen years, before which term the present existing debts will all be discharged by the established operation of the sinking fund. When we contemplate the ordinary annual augmentation of impost from increasing population and wealth, the augmentation of the same revenue by its extension to the new acquisition, and the economies which may still be introduced into our public expenditures, I can not but hope that Congress in reviewing their resources will find means to meet the intermediate interest of this additional debt without recurring to new taxes, and applying to this object only the ordinary progression of our revenue. Its extraordinary increase in times of foreign war will be the proper and sufficient fund for any measures of safety or precaution which that state of things may render necessary in our neutral position.

Remittances for the installments of our foreign debt having been found practicable without loss, it has not been thought expedient to use the power given by a former act of Congress of continuing them by reloans, and of redeeming instead thereof equal sums of domestic debt, although no difficulty was found in obtaining that accommodation.

The sum of $50,000 appropriated by Congress for providing gunboats remains unexpended. The favorable and peaceable turn of affairs on the Mississippi rendered an immediate execution of that law unnecessary, and time was desirable in order that the institution of that branch of our force might begin on models the most approved by experience. The same issue of events dispensed with a resort to the appropriation of $1,500,000, contemplated for purposes which were effected by happier means.

We have seen with sincere concern the flames of war lighted up again in Europe, and nations with which we have the most friendly and useful relations engaged in mutual destruction. While we regret the miseries in which we see others involved, let us bow with gratitude to that kind Providence which, inspiring with wisdom and moderation our late legislative councils while placed under the urgency of the greatest wrongs guarded us from hastily entering into the sanguinary contest and left us only to look on and to pity its ravages. These will be heaviest on those immediately engaged. Yet the nations pursuing peace will not be exempt from all evil. In the course of this conflict let it be our endeavor, as it is our interest and desire, to cultivate the friendship of the belligerent nations by every act of justice and of innocent kindness; to receive their armed vessels with hospitality from the distresses of the sea, but to administer the means of annoyance to none; to establish in our harbors such a police as may maintain law and order; to restrain our citizens from embarking individually in a war in which their country takes no part; to punish severely those persons, citizen or alien, who shall usurp the cover of our flag for vessels not entitled to it, infecting thereby with suspicion those of real Americans and committing us into controversies for the redress of wrongs not our own; to exact from every nation the observance toward our vessels and citizens of those principles and practices which all civilized people acknowledge; to merit the character of a just nation, and maintain that of an independent one, preferring every consequence to insult and habitual wrong. Congress will consider whether the existing laws enable us efficaciously to maintain this course with our citizens in all places and with others while within the limits of our jurisdiction, and will give them the new modifications necessary for these objects. Some contraventions of right have already taken place, both within our jurisdictional limits and on the high seas. The friendly disposition of the Governments from whose agents they have proceeded, as well as their wisdom and regard for justice, leave us in reasonable expectation that they will be rectified and prevented in future, and that no act will be countenanced by them which threatens to disturb our friendly intercourse. Separated by a wide ocean from the nations of Europe and from the political interests which entangle them together, with productions and wants which render our commerce and friendship useful to them and theirs to us, it can not be the interest of any to assail us, nor ours to disturb them. We should be most unwise, indeed, were we to cast away the singular blessings of the position in which nature has placed us, the opportunity she has endowed us with of pursuing, at a distance from foreign contentions, the paths of industry, peace, and happiness, of cultivating general friendship, and of bringing collisions of interest to the umpirage of reason rather than of force. How desirable, then, must it be in a Government like ours to see its citizens adopt individually the views, the interests, and the conduct which their country should pursue, divesting themselves of those passions and partialities which tend to lessen useful friendships and to embarrass and embroil us in the calamitous scenes of Europe. Confident, fellow-citizens, that you will duly estimate the importance of neutral dispositions toward the observance of neutral conduct, that you will be sensible how much it is our duty to look on the bloody arena spread before us with commiseration indeed, but with no other wish than to see it closed, I am persuaded you will cordially cherish these dispositions in all discussions among yourselves and in all communications with your constituents; and I anticipate with satisfaction the measures of wisdom which the great interests now committed to you will give *you* an opportunity of providing, and *myself* that of approving and of carrying into execution with the fidelity I owe to my country.

FOURTH ANNUAL MESSAGE.

NOVEMBER 8, 1804.

To the Senate and House of Representatives of the United States:

To a people, fellow-citizens, who sincerely desire the happiness and prosperity of other nations; to those who justly calculate that their own well-being is advanced by that of the nations with which they have intercourse, it will be a satisfaction to observe that the war which was lighted up in Europe a little before our last meeting has not yet extended its flames to other nations, nor been marked by the calamities which sometimes stain the footsteps of war. The irregularities, too, on the ocean, which generally harass the commerce of neutral nations, have, in distant parts, disturbed ours less than on former occasions; but in the American seas they have been greater from peculiar causes, and even within our harbors and jurisdiction infringements on the authority of the laws have been committed which have called for serious attention.

The friendly conduct of the Governments from whose officers and subjects these acts have proceeded, in other respects and in places more under their observation and control, gives us confidence that our representations on this subject will have been properly regarded.

While noticing the irregularities committed on the ocean by others, those on our own part should not be omitted nor left unprovided for. Complaints have been received that persons residing within the United States have taken on themselves to arm merchant vessels and to force a commerce into certain ports and countries in defiance of the laws of those countries. That individuals should undertake to wage private war, independently of the authority of their country, can not be permitted in a well-ordered society. Its tendency to produce aggression on the laws and rights of other nations and to endanger the peace of our own is so obvious that I doubt not you will adopt measures for restraining it effectually in future.

Soon after the passage of the act of the last session authorizing the establishment of a district and port of entry on the waters of the Mobile we learnt that its object was misunderstood on the part of Spain. Candid explanations were immediately given and assurances that, reserving our claims in that quarter as a subject of discussion and arrangement with Spain, no act was meditated in the meantime inconsistent with the peace and friendship existing between the two nations, and that conformably to these intentions would be the execution of the law. That Government had, however, thought proper to suspend the ratification of the convention of 1802; but the explanations which would reach them soon after, and still more the confirmation of them by the tenor of the instrument establishing the port and district, may reasonably be expected to replace them in the dispositions and views of the whole subject which originally dictated the convention.

I have the satisfaction to inform you that the objections which had been urged by that Government against the validity of our title to the country of Louisiana have been withdrawn, its exact limits, however, remaining still to be settled between us; and to this is to be added that, having prepared and delivered the stock created in execution of the convention of Paris of April 30, 1803, in consideration of the cession of that country, we have received from the Government of France an acknowledgment, in due form, of the fulfillment of that stipulation.

With the nations of Europe in general our friendship and intercourse are undisturbed, and from the Governments of the belligerent powers especially we continue to receive those friendly manifestations which are justly due to an honest neutrality and to such good offices consistent with that as we have opportunities of rendering.

The activity and success of the small force employed in the Mediterranean in the early part of the present year, the reenforcements sent into that sea, and the energy of the officers having command in the several vessels will, I trust, by the sufferings of war, reduce the barbarians of Tripoli to the desire of peace on proper terms. Great injury, however, ensues to ourselves, as well as to others interested, from the distance to which prizes must be brought for adjudication and from the impracticability of bringing hither such as are not seaworthy.

The Bey of Tunis having made requisitions unauthorized by our treaty, their rejection has produced from him some expressions of discontent. But to those who expect us to calculate whether a compliance with unjust demands will not cost us less than a war we must leave as a question of calculation for them also whether to retire from unjust demands will not cost them less than a war. We can do to each other very sensible injuries by war, but the mutual advantages of peace make that the best interest of both.

Peace and intercourse with the other powers on the same coast continue on the footing on which they are established by treaty.

In pursuance of the act providing for the temporary government of Louisiana, the necessary officers for the Territory of Orleans were appointed in due time to commence the exercise of their functions on the 1st day of October. The distance, however, of some of them and indispensable previous arrangements may have retarded its commencement in some of its parts. The form of government thus provided having been considered but as temporary, and open to such future improvements as further information of the circumstances of our brethren there might suggest, it will of course be subject to your consideration.

In the district of Louisiana it has been thought best to adopt the division into subordinate districts which had been established under its former government. These being five in number, a commanding officer has been appointed to each, according to the provisions of the law, and so soon as they can be at their stations that district will also be in its due state of organization. In the meantime their places are supplied by the officers before commanding there. And the functions of the governor and judges of Indiana having commenced, the government, we presume, is proceeding in its new form. The lead mines in that district offer so rich a supply of that metal as to merit attention. The report now communicated will inform you of their state and of the necessity of immediate inquiry into their occupation and titles.

With the Indian tribes established within our newly acquired limits, I have deemed it necessary to open conferences for the purpose of establishing a good understanding and neighborly relations between us. So far as we have yet learned, we have reason to believe that their dispositions are generally favorable and friendly; and with these dispositions on their part, we have in our own hands means which can not fail us for preserving their peace and friendship. By pursuing an uniform course of justice toward them, by aiding them in all the improvements which may better their condition, and especially by establishing a commerce on terms which shall be advantageous to them and only not losing to us, and so regulated as that no incendiaries of our own or any other nation may be permitted to disturb the natural effects of our just and friendly offices, we may render ourselves so necessary to their comfort and prosperity that the protection of our citizens from their disorderly members will become their interest and their voluntary care. Instead, therefore, of an augmentation of military force proportioned to our extension of frontier, I propose a moderate enlargement of the capital employed in that commerce as a more effectual, economical, and humane instrument for preserving peace and good neighborhood with them.

On this side the Mississippi an important relinquishment of native title has been received from the Delawares. That tribe, desiring to extinguish in their people the spirit of hunting and to convert superfluous lands into the means of improving what they retain, has ceded to us all the country between the Wabash and Ohio south of and including the road from the rapids toward Vincennes, for which they are to receive annuities in animals and implements for agriculture and in other necessaries. This acquisition is important, not only for its extent and fertility, but as fronting 300 miles on the Ohio, and near half that on the Wabash. The produce of the settled country descending those rivers will no longer pass in review of the Indian frontier but in a small portion, and, with the cession heretofore made by the Kaskaskias, nearly consolidates our possessions north of the Ohio, in a very respectable breadth—from Lake Erie to the Mississippi. The Piankeshaws having some claim to the country ceded by the Delawares, it has been thought best to quiet that by fair purchase also. So soon as the treaties on this subject shall have received their constitutional sanctions they shall be laid before both Houses.

The act of Congress of February 28, 1803, for building and employing a number of gunboats, is now in a course of execution to the extent there provided for. The obstacle to naval enterprise which vessels of this construction offer for our seaport towns, their utility toward supporting within our waters the authority of the laws, the promptness with which they will be manned by the seamen and militia of the place in the moment they are wanting, the facility of their assembling from different parts of the coast to any point where they are required in greater force than ordinary, the economy of their maintenance and preservation from decay when not in actual service, and the competence of our finances to this defensive provision without any new burthen are considerations which will have due weight with Congress in deciding on the expediency of adding to their number from year to year, as experience shall test their utility, until all our important harbors, by these and auxiliary means, shall be secured against insult and opposition to the laws.

No circumstance has arisen since your last session which calls for any augmentation of our regular military force. Should any improvement occur in the militia system, that will be always seasonable.

Accounts of the receipts and expenditures of the last year, with estimates for the ensuing one, will as usual be laid before you.

The state of our finances continues to fulfill our expectations. Eleven millions and a half of dollars, received in the course of the year ending the 30th of September last, have enabled us, after meeting all the ordinary expenses of the year, to pay upward of $3,600,000 of the public debt, exclusive of interest. This payment, with those of the two preceding years, has extinguished upward of twelve millions of the principal and a greater sum of interest within that period, and by a proportionate diminution of interest renders already sensible the effect of the growing sum yearly applicable to the discharge of the principal.

It is also ascertained that the revenue accrued during the last year exceeds that of the preceding, and the probable receipts of the ensuing year may safely be relied on as sufficient, with the sum already in the Treasury, to meet all the current demands of the year, to discharge upward of three millions and a half of the engagements incurred under the British and French conventions, and to advance in the further redemption of the funded debt as rapidly as had been contemplated. These, fellow-citizens, are the principal matters which I have thought it necessary at this time to communicate for your consideration and attention. Some others will be laid before you in the course of the session; but in the discharge of the great duties confided to you by our country you will take a broader view of the field of legislation. Whether the great interests of agriculture, manufactures, commerce, or navigation can within the pale of your constitutional powers be aided in any of their relations; whether laws are provided in all cases where they are wanting; whether those provided are exactly what they should be; whether any abuses take place in their administration, or in that of the public revenues; whether the organization of the public agents or of the public force is perfect in all its parts; in fine, whether anything can be done to advance the general good, are questions within the limits of your functions which will necessarily occupy your attention. In these and all other matters which you in your wisdom may propose for the good of our country you may count with assurance on my hearty cooperation and faithful execution.

FIFTH ANNUAL MESSAGE.

DECEMBER 3, 1805.

To the Senate and House of Representatives of the United States:

At a moment when the nations of Europe are in commotion and arming against each other, and when those with whom we have principal intercourse are engaged in the general contest, and when the countenance of some of them toward our peaceable country threatens that even that may not be unaffected by what is passing on the general theater, a meeting of the representatives of the nation in both Houses of Congress has become more than usually desirable. Coming from every section of our country, they bring with them the sentiments and the information of the whole, and will be enabled to give a direction to the public affairs which the will and the wisdom of the whole will approve and support.

In taking a view of the state of our country we in the first place notice the late affliction of two of our cities under the fatal fever which in latter times has occasionally visited our shores. Providence in His goodness gave it an early termination on this occasion and lessened the number of victims which have usually fallen before it. In the course of the several visitations by this disease it has appeared that it is strictly local, incident to cities and on the tide waters only, incommunicable in the country either by persons under the disease or by goods carried from diseased places; that its access is with the autumn and it disappears with the early frosts. These restrictions within narrow limits of time and space give security even to our maritime cities during three-fourths of the year, and to the country always. Although from these facts it appears unnecessary, yet to satisfy the fears of foreign nations and cautions on their part not to be complained of in a danger whose limits are yet unknown to them I have strictly enjoined on the officers at the head of the customs to certify with exact truth for every vessel sailing for a foreign port the state of health respecting this fever which prevails at the place from which she sails. Under every motive from character and duty to certify the truth, I have no doubt they have faithfully executed this injunction. Much real injury has, however, been sustained from a propensity to identify with this endemic and to call by the same name fevers of very different kinds, which have been known at all times and in all countries, and never have been placed among those deemed contagious. As we advance in our knowledge of this disease, as facts develop the source from which individuals receive it, the State authorities charged with the care of the public health, and Congress with that of the general commerce, will become able to regulate with effect their respective functions in these departments. The burthen of quarantines is felt at home as well as abroad; their efficacy merits examination. Although the health laws of the States should be found to need no present revisal by Congress, yet commerce claims that their attention be ever awake to them.

Since our last meeting the aspect of our foreign relations has considerably changed. Our coasts have been infested and our harbors watched by private armed vessels, some of them without commissions, some with illegal commissions, others with those of legal form, but committing piratical acts beyond the authority of their commissions. They have captured in the very entrance of our harbors, as well as on the high seas, not only the vessels of our friends coming to trade with us, but our own also. They have carried them off under pretense of legal adjudication, but not daring to approach a court of justice, they have plundered and sunk them by the way or in obscure places where no evidence could arise against them, maltreated the crews, and abandoned them in boats in the open sea or on desert shores without food or covering. These enormities appearing to be unreached by any control of their sovereigns, I found it necessary to equip a force to cruise within our own seas, to arrest all vessels of these descriptions found hovering on our coasts within the limits of the Gulf Stream and to bring the offenders in for trial as pirates.

The same system of hovering on our coasts and harbors under color of seeking enemies has been also carried on by public armed ships to the great annoyance and oppression of our commerce. New principles, too, have been interpolated into the law of nations, founded neither in justice nor the usage or acknowledgment of nations. According to these a belligerent takes to itself a commerce with its own enemy which it denies to a neutral on the ground of its aiding that enemy in the war; but reason revolts at such an inconsistency, and the neutral having equal right with the belligerent to decide the question, the interests of our constituents and the duty of maintaining the authority of reason, the only umpire between just nations, impose on us the obligation of providing an effectual and determined opposition to a doctrine so injurious to the rights of peaceable nations. Indeed, the confidence we ought to have in the justice of others still countenances the hope that a sounder view of those rights will of itself induce from every belligerent a more correct observance of them.

With Spain our negotiations for a settlement of differences have not had a satisfactory issue. Spoliations during a former war, for which she had formally acknowledged herself responsible, have been refused to be compensated but on conditions affecting other claims in no wise connected with them. Yet the same practices are renewed in the present war and are already of great amount. On the Mobile, our commerce passing through that river continues to be obstructed by arbitrary duties and vexatious searches. Propositions for adjusting amicably the boundaries of Louisiana have not been acceded to. While, however, the right is unsettled, we have avoided changing the state of things by taking new posts or strengthening ourselves in the disputed territories, in the hope that the other power would not by a contrary conduct oblige us to meet their example and endanger conflicts of authority the issue of which may not be easily controlled. But in this hope we have now reason to lessen our confidence. Inroads have been recently made into the Territories of Orleans and the Mississippi, our citizens have been seized and their property plundered in the very parts of the former which had been actually delivered up by Spain, and this by the regular officers and soldiers of that Government. I have therefore found it necessary at length to give orders to our troops on that frontier to be in readiness to protect our citizens, and to repel by arms any similar aggressions in future. Other details necessary for your full information of the state of things between this country and that shall be the subject of another communication.

In reviewing these injuries from some of the belligerent powers the moderation, the firmness, and the wisdom of the Legislature will all be called into action. We ought still to hope that time and a more correct estimate of interest as well as of character will produce the justice we are bound to expect. But should any nation deceive itself by false calculations, and disappoint that expectation, we must join in the unprofitable contest of trying which party can do the other the most harm. Some of these injuries may perhaps admit a peaceable remedy. Where that is competent it is always the most desirable. But some of them are of a nature to be met by force only, and all of them may lead to it. I can not, therefore, but recommend such preparations as circumstances call for. The first object is to place our seaport towns out of the danger of insult. Measures have been already taken for furnishing them with heavy cannon for the service of such land batteries as may make a part of their defense against armed vessels approaching them. In aid of these it is desirable we should have a competent number of gunboats, and the number, to be competent, must be considerable. If immediately begun, they may be in readiness for service at the opening of the next season. Whether it will be necessary to augment our land forces will be decided by occurrences probably in the course of your session. In the meantime you will consider whether it would not be expedient for a state of peace as well as of war so to organize or class the militia as would enable us on any sudden emergency to call for the services of the younger portions, unencumbered with the old and those having families. Upward of 300,000 able-bodied men between the ages of 18 and 26 years, which the last census shews we may now count within our limits, will furnish a competent number for offense or defense in any point where they may be wanted, and will give time for raising regular forces after the necessity of them shall become certain; and the reducing to the early period of life all its active service can not but be desirable to our younger citizens of the present as well as future times, inasmuch as it engages to them in more advanced age a quiet and undisturbed repose in the bosom of their families. I can not, then, but earnestly recommend to your early consideration the expediency of so modifying our militia system as, by a separation of the more active part from that which is less so, we may draw from it when necessary an efficient corps fit for real and active service, and to be called to it in regular rotation.

Considerable provision has been made under former authorities from

Congress of materials for the construction of ships of war of 74 guns. These materials are on hand subject to the further will of the Legislature.

An immediate prohibition of the exportation of arms and ammunition is also submitted to your determination.

Turning from these unpleasant views of violence and wrong, I congratulate you on the liberation of our fellow-citizens who were stranded on the coast of Tripoli and made prisoners of war. In a government bottomed on the will of all the life and liberty of every individual citizen become interesting to all. In the treaty, therefore, which has concluded our warfare with that State an article for the ransom of our citizens has been agreed to. An operation by land by a small band of our countrymen and others, engaged for the occasion in conjunction with the troops of the ex-Bashaw of that country, gallantly conducted by our late consul, Eaton, and their successful enterprise on the city of Derne, contributed doubtless to the impression which produced peace, and the conclusion of this prevented opportunities of which the officers and men of our squadron destined for Tripoli would have availed themselves to emulate the acts of valor exhibited by their brethren in the attack of the last year. Reflecting with high satisfaction on the distinguished bravery displayed whenever occasions permitted in the late Mediterranean service, I think it would be an useful encouragement as well as a just reward to make an opening for some present promotion by enlarging our peace establishment of captains and lieutenants.

With Tunis some misunderstandings have arisen not yet sufficiently explained, but friendly discussions with their ambassador recently arrived and a mutual disposition to do whatever is just and reasonable can not fail of dissipating these, so that we may consider our peace on that coast, generally, to be on as sound a footing as it has been at any preceding time. Still, it will not be expedient to withdraw immediately the whole of our force from that sea.

The law providing for a naval peace establishment fixes the number of frigates which shall be kept in constant service in time of peace, and prescribes that they shall be manned by not more than two-thirds of their complement of seamen and ordinary seamen. Whether a frigate may be trusted to two-thirds only of her proper complement of men must depend on the nature of the service on which she is ordered; that may sometimes, for her safety as well as to insure her object, require her fullest complement. In adverting to this subject Congress will perhaps consider whether the best limitation on the Executive discretion in this case would not be by the number of seamen which may be employed in the whole service rather than by the number of the vessels. Occasions oftener arise for the employment of small than of large vessels, and it would lessen risk as well as expense to be authorized to employ them of preference. The limitation suggested by the number of seamen would admit a selection of vessels best adapted to the service.

Our Indian neighbors are advancing, many of them with spirit, and others beginning to engage in the pursuits of agriculture and household manufacture. They are becoming sensible that the earth yields subsistence with less labor and more certainty than the forest, and find it their interest from time to time to dispose of parts of their surplus and waste lands for the means of improving those they occupy and of subsisting their families while they are preparing their farms. Since your last session the Northern tribes have sold to us the lands between the Connecticut Reserve and the former Indian boundary and those on the Ohio from the same boundary to the rapids and for a considerable depth inland. The Chickasaws and Cherokees have sold us the country between and adjacent to the two districts of Tennessee, and the Creeks the residue of their lands in the fork of Ocmulgee up to the Ulcofauhatche. The three former purchases are important, inasmuch as they consolidate disjoined parts of our settled country and render their intercourse secure; and the second particularly so, as, with the small point on the river which we expect is by this time ceded by the Piankeshaws, it completes our possession of the whole of both banks of the Ohio from its source to near its mouth, and the navigation of that river is thereby rendered forever safe to our citizens settled and settling on its extensive waters. The purchase from the Creeks, too, has been for some time particularly interesting to the State of Georgia.

The several treaties which have been mentioned will be submitted to both Houses of Congress for the exercise of their respective functions.

Deputations now on their way to the seat of Government from various nations of Indians inhabiting the Missouri and other parts beyond the Mississippi come charged with assurances of their satisfaction with the new relations in which they are placed with us, of their dispositions to cultivate our peace and friendship, and their desire to enter into commercial intercourse with us. A state of our progress in exploring the principal rivers of that country, and of the information respecting them hitherto obtained, will be communicated so soon as we shall receive some further relations which we have reason shortly to expect.

The receipts at the Treasury during the year ending on the 30th day of September last have exceeded the sum of $13,000,000, which, with not quite five millions in the Treasury at the beginning of the year, have enabled us after meeting other demands to pay nearly two millions of the debt contracted under the British treaty and convention, upward of four millions of principal of the public debt, and four millions of interest. These payments, with those which had been made in three years and a half preceding, have extinguished of the funded debt nearly eighteen millions of principal. Congress by their act of November 10, 1803, authorized us to borrow $1,750,000 toward meeting the claims of our citizens assumed by the convention with France. We have not, however, made use of this authority, because the sum of four millions and a half, which remained in the Treasury on the same 30th day of September last, with the receipts which we may calculate on for the ensuing year, besides paying the annual sum of $8,000,000 appropriated to the funded debt and meeting all the current demands which may be expected, will enable us to pay the whole sum of $3,750,000 assumed by the French convention and still leave us a surplus of nearly $1,000,000 at our free disposal. Should you concur in the provisions of arms and armed vessels recommended by the circumstances of the times, this surplus will furnish the means of doing so.

On this first occasion of addressing Congress since, by the choice of my constituents, I have entered on a second term of administration, I embrace the opportunity to give this public assurance that I will exert my best endeavors to administer faithfully the executive department, and will zealously cooperate with you in every measure which may tend to secure the liberty, property, and personal safety of our fellow-citizens, and to consolidate the republican forms and principles of our Government.

In the course of your session you shall receive all the aid which I can give for the dispatch of public business, and all the information necessary for your deliberations, of which the interests of our own country and the confidence reposed in us by others will admit a communication.

SIXTH ANNUAL MESSAGE.

DECEMBER 2, 1806.

To the Senate and House of Representatives of the United States of America in Congress assembled:

It would have given me, fellow-citizens, great satisfaction to announce in the moment of your meeting that the difficulties in our foreign relations existing at the time of your last separation had been amicably and justly terminated. I lost no time in taking those measures which were most likely to bring them to such a termination—by special missions charged with such powers and instructions as in the event of failure could leave no imputation on either our moderation or forbearance. The delays which have since taken place in our negotiations with the British Government appear to have proceeded from causes which do not forbid the expectation that during the course of the session I may be enabled to lay before you their final issue. What will be that of the negotiations for settling our differences with Spain nothing which had taken place at the date of the last dispatches enables us to pronounce. On the western side of the Mississippi she advanced in considerable force, and took post at the settlement of Bayou Pierre, on the Red River. This village was originally settled by France, was held by her as long as she held Louisiana, and was delivered to Spain only as a part of Louisiana. Being small, insulated, and distant, it was not observed at the moment of redelivery to France and the United States that she continued a guard of half a dozen men which had been stationed there. A proposition, however, having been lately made by our commander in chief to assume the Sabine River as a temporary line of separation between the troops of the two nations until the issue of our negotiations shall be known, this has been referred by the Spanish commandant to his superior, and in the meantime he has withdrawn his force to the western side of the Sabine River. The correspondence on this subject now communicated will exhibit more particularly the present state of things in that quarter.

The nature of that country requires indispensably that an unusual proportion of the force employed there should be cavalry or mounted infantry. In order, therefore, that the commanding officer might be enabled to act with effect, I had authorized him to call on the governors of Orleans and Mississippi for a corps of 500 volunteer cavalry. The temporary arrangement he has proposed may perhaps render this unnecessary; but I inform you with great pleasure of the promptitude with which the inhabitants of those Territories have tendered their services in defense of their country. It has done honor to themselves, entitled them to the confidence of their fellow-citizens in every part of the Union, and must strengthen the general determination to protect them efficaciously under all circumstances which may occur.

Having received information that in another part of the United States a great number of private individuals were combining together, arming and organizing themselves contrary to law, to carry on a military expedition against the territories of Spain, I thought it necessary, by proclamation as well as by special orders, to take measures for preventing and suppressing this enterprise, for seizing the vessels, arms, and other means provided for it, and for arresting and bringing to justice its authors and abettors. It was due to that good faith which ought ever to be the rule of action in public as well as in private transactions, it was due to good order and regular government, that while the public force was acting strictly on the defensive and merely to protect our citizens from aggression the criminal attempts of private individuals to decide for their country the question of peace or war by commencing active and unauthorized hostilities should be promptly and efficaciously suppressed.

Whether it will be necessary to enlarge our regular force will depend on the result of our negotiations with Spain; but as it is uncertain when that result will be known, the provisional measures requisite for that, and to meet any pressure intervening in that quarter, will be a subject for your early consideration.

The possession of both banks of the Mississippi reducing to a single point the defense of that river, its waters, and the country adjacent, it becomes highly necessary to provide for that point a more adequate security. Some position above its mouth, commanding the passage of the river, should be rendered sufficiently strong to cover the armed vessels which may be stationed there for defense, and in conjunction with them to present an insuperable obstacle to any force attempting to pass. The approaches to the city of New Orleans from the eastern quarter also will require to be examined and more effectually guarded. For the internal support of the country the encouragement of a strong settlement on the western side of the Mississippi, within reach of New Orleans, will be worthy the consideration of the Legislature.

The gunboats authorized by an act of the last session are so advanced that they will be ready for service in the ensuing spring. Circumstances permitted us to allow the time necessary for their more solid construction. As a much larger number will still be wanting to place our seaport towns and waters in that state of defense to which we are competent and they entitled, a similar appropriation for a further provision for them is recommended for the ensuing year.

A further appropriation will also be necessary for repairing fortifications already established and the erection of such other works as may have real effect in obstructing the approach of an enemy to our seaport towns, or their remaining before them.

In a country whose constitution is derived from the will of the people, directly expressed by their free suffrages; where the principal executive functionaries and those of the legislature are renewed by them at short periods; where under the character of jurors they exercise in person the greatest portion of the judiciary powers; where the laws are consequently so formed and administered as to bear with equal weight and favor on all, restraining no man in the pursuits of honest industry and securing to everyone the property which that acquires, it would not be supposed that any safeguards could be needed against insurrection or enterprise on the public peace or authority. The laws, however, aware that these should not be trusted to moral restraints only, have wisely provided punishment for these crimes when committed. But would it not be salutary to give also the means of preventing their commission? Where an enterprise is meditated by private individuals against a foreign nation in amity with the United States, powers of prevention to a certain extent are given by the laws. Would they not be as reasonable and useful where the enterprise preparing is against the United States? While adverting to this branch of law it is proper to observe that in enterprises meditated against foreign nations the ordinary process of binding to the observance of the peace and good behavior, could it be extended to acts to be done out of the jurisdiction of the United States, would be effectual in some cases where the offender is able to keep out of sight every indication of his purpose which could draw on him the exercise of the powers now given by law.

The States on the coast of Barbary seem generally disposed at present to respect our peace and friendship; with Tunis alone some uncertainty remains. Persuaded that it is our interest to maintain our peace with them on equal terms or not at all, I propose to send in due time a reenforcement into the Mediterranean unless previous information shall shew it to be unnecessary.

We continue to receive proofs of the growing attachment of our Indian neighbors and of their disposition to place all their interests under the patronage of the United States. These dispositions are inspired by their confidence in our justice and in the sincere concern we feel for their welfare; and as long as we discharge these high and honorable functions with the integrity and good faith which alone can entitle us to their continuance we may expect to reap the just reward in their peace and friendship.

The expedition of Messrs. Lewis and Clarke for exploring the river Missouri and the best communication from that to the Pacific Ocean has had all the success which could have been expected. They have traced the Missouri nearly to its source, descended the Columbia to the Pacific Ocean, ascertained with accuracy the geography of that interesting communication across our continent, learnt the character of the country, of its commerce and inhabitants; and it is but justice to say that Messrs. Lewis and Clarke and their brave companions have by this arduous service deserved well of their country.

The attempt to explore the Red River, under the direction of Mr. Freeman, though conducted with a zeal and prudence meriting entire approbation, has not been equally successful. After proceeding up it about 600 miles, nearly as far as the French settlements had extended while the country was in their possession, our geographers were obliged to return without completing their work.

Very useful additions have also been made to our knowledge of the Mississippi by Lieutenant Pike, who has ascended it to its source, and whose journal and map, giving the details of his journey, will shortly be ready for communication to both Houses of Congress. Those of Messrs. Lewis, Clarke, and Freeman will require further time to be digested and prepared. These important surveys, in addition to those before possessed, furnish materials for commencing an accurate map of the Mississippi and its western waters. Some principal rivers, however, remain still to be explored, toward which the authorization of Congress by moderate appropriations will be requisite.

I congratulate you, fellow-citizens, on the approach of the period at which you may interpose your authority constitutionally to withdraw the citizens of the United States from all further participation in those violations of human rights which have been so long continued on the unoffending inhabitants of Africa, and which the morality, the reputation, and the best interests of our country have long been eager to proscribe. Although no law you may pass can take prohibitory effect till the first day of the year 1808, yet the intervening period is not too long to prevent by timely notice expeditions which can not be completed before that day.

The receipts at the Treasury during the year ending on the 30th day of September last have amounted to near $15,000,000, which have enabled us, after meeting the current demands, to pay $2,700,000 of the American claims in part of the price of Louisiana; to pay of the funded debt upward of three millions of principal and nearly four of interest, and, in addition, to reimburse in the course of the present month near two millions of 5½ per cent stock. These payments and reimbursements of the funded debt, with those which had been made in the four years and a half preceding, will at the close of the present year have extinguished upward of twenty-three millions of principal.

The duties composing the Mediterranean fund will cease by law at the end of the present session. Considering, however, that they are levied chiefly on luxuries and that we have an impost on salt, a necessary of life, the free use of which otherwise is so important, I recommend to your consideration the suppression of the duties on salt and the continuation of the Mediterranean fund instead thereof for a short time, after which that also will become unnecessary for any purpose now within contemplation.

When both of these branches of revenue shall in this way be relinquished there will still ere long be an accumulation of moneys in the Treasury beyond the installments of public debt which we are permitted by contract to pay. They can not then, without a modification assented to by the public creditors, be applied to the extinguishment of this debt and the complete liberation of our revenues, the most desirable of all objects. Nor, if our peace continues, will they be wanting for any other existing purpose. The question therefore now comes forward, To what other objects shall these surpluses be appropriated, and the whole surplus of impost, after the entire discharge of the public debt, and during those intervals when the purposes of war shall not call for them? Shall we suppress the impost and give that advantage to foreign over domestic manufactures? On a few articles of more general and necessary use the suppression in due season will doubtless be right, but the great mass of the articles on which impost is paid are foreign luxuries, purchased by those only who are rich enough to afford themselves the use of them. Their patriotism would certainly prefer its continuance and application to the great purposes of the public education, roads, rivers, canals, and such other objects of public improvement as it may be thought proper to add to the constitutional enumeration of Federal powers. By these operations new channels of communication will be opened between the States, the lines of separation will disappear, their interests will be identified, and their union cemented by new and indissoluble ties. Education is here placed among the articles of public care, not that it would be proposed to take its ordinary branches out of the hands of private enterprise, which manages so much better all the concerns to which it is equal, but a public institution can alone supply those sciences which though rarely called for are yet necessary to complete the circle, all the parts of which contribute to the improvement of the country and some of them to its preservation. The subject is now proposed for the consideration of Congress, because if approved by the time the State legislatures shall have deliberated on this extension of the Federal trusts, and the laws shall be passed and other arrangements made for their execution, the necessary funds will be on hand and without employment. I suppose an amendment to the Constitution, by consent of the States, necessary, because the objects now recommended are not among those enumerated in the Constitution, and to which it permits the public moneys to be applied.

The present consideration of a national establishment for education particularly is rendered proper by this circumstance also, that if Congress, approving the proposition, shall yet think it more eligible to found it on a donation of lands, they have it now in their power to endow it with those which will be among the earliest to produce the necessary income. This foundation would have the advantage of being independent of war, which may suspend other improvements by requiring for its own purposes the resources destined for them.

This, fellow-citizens, is the state of the public interests at the present moment and according to the information now possessed. But such is the situation of the nations of Europe and such, too, the predicament in which we stand with some of them that we can not rely with certainty on the present aspect of our affairs, that may change from moment to moment during the course of your session or after you shall have separated. Our duty is, therefore, to act upon things as they are and to make a reasonable provision for whatever they may be. Were armies to be raised whenever a speck of war is visible in our horizon, we never should have been without them. Our resources would have been exhausted on dangers which have never happened, instead of being reserved for what is really to take place. A steady, perhaps a quickened, pace in preparations for the defense of our seaport towns and waters; an early settlement of the most exposed and vulnerable parts of our country; a militia so organized that its effective portions can be called to any point in the Union, or volunteers instead of them to serve a sufficient time, are means which may always be ready, yet never preying on our resources until actually called into use. They will maintain the public interests while a more permanent force shall be in course of preparation. But much will depend on the promptitude with which these means can be brought into activity. If war be forced upon us, in spite of our long and vain appeals to the justice of nations, rapid and vigorous movements in its outset will go far toward securing us in its course and issue, and toward throwing its burthens on those who render necessary the resort from reason to force.

The result of our negotiations, or such incidents in their course as may enable us to infer their probable issue; such further movements also on our western frontiers as may shew whether war is to be pressed there while negotiation is protracted elsewhere, shall be communicated to you from time to time as they become known to me, with whatever other information I possess or may receive, which may aid your deliberations on the great national interests committed to your charge.

SEVENTH ANNUAL MESSAGE.

OCTOBER 27, 1807.

To the Senate and House of Representatives of the United States:

Circumstances, fellow-citizens, which seriously threatened the peace of our country have made it a duty to convene you at an earlier period than usual. The love of peace so much cherished in the bosoms of our citizens, which has so long guided the proceedings of their public councils and induced forbearance under so many wrongs, may not insure our continuance in the quiet pursuits of industry. The many injuries and depredations committed on our commerce and navigation upon the high seas for years past, the successive innovations on those principles of public law which have been established by the reason and usage of nations as the rule of their intercourse and the umpire and security of their rights and peace, and all the circumstances which induced the extraordinary mission to London are already known to you. The instructions given to our ministers were framed in the sincerest spirit of amity and moderation. They accordingly proceeded, in conformity therewith, to propose arrangements which might embrace and settle all the points in difference between us, which might bring us to a mutual understanding on our neutral and national rights and provide for a commercial intercourse on conditions of some equality. After long and fruitless endeavors to effect the purposes of their mission and to obtain arrangements within the limits of their instructions, they concluded to sign such as could be obtained and to send them for consideration, candidly declaring to the other negotiators at the same time that they were acting against their instructions, and that their Government, therefore, could not be pledged for ratification.   Some of the articles proposed might have been admitted on a principle of compromise, but others were too highly disadvantageous, and no sufficient provision was made against the principal source of the irritations and collisions which were constantly endangering the peace of the two nations.   The question, therefore, whether a treaty should be accepted in that form could have admitted but of one decision, even had no declarations of the other party impaired our confidence in it.   Still anxious not to close the door against friendly adjustment, new modifications were framed and further concessions authorized than could before have been supposed necessary; and our ministers were instructed to resume their negotiations on these grounds.   On this new reference to amicable discussion we were reposing in confidence, when on the 22d day of June last by a formal order from a British admiral the frigate *Chesapeake*, leaving her port for a distant service, was attacked by one of those vessels which had been lying in our harbors under the indulgences of hospitality, was disabled from proceeding, had several of her crew killed and four taken away.   On this outrage no commentaries are necessary.   Its character has been pronounced by the indignant voice of our citizens with an emphasis and unanimity never exceeded.   I immediately, by proclamation, interdicted our harbors and waters to all British armed vessels, forbade intercourse with them, and uncertain how far hostilities were intended, and the town of Norfolk, indeed, being threatened with immediate attack, a sufficient force was ordered for the protection of that place, and such other preparations commenced and pursued as the prospect rendered proper.   An armed vessel of the United States was dispatched with instructions to our ministers at London to call on that Government for the satisfaction and security required by the outrage. A very short interval ought now to bring the answer, which shall be communicated to you as soon as received; then also, or as soon after as the public interests shall be found to admit, the unratified treaty and proceedings relative to it shall be made known to you.

The aggression thus begun has been continued on the part of the British commanders by remaining within our waters in defiance of the authority of the country, by habitual violations of its jurisdiction, and at length by putting to death one of the persons whom they had forcibly taken from on board the *Chesapeake*. These aggravations necessarily lead to the policy either of never admitting an armed vessel into our harbors or of maintaining in every harbor such an armed force as may constrain obedience to the laws and protect the lives and property of our citizens against their armed guests; but the expense of such a standing force and its inconsistence with our principles dispense with those courtesies which would necessarily call for it, and leave us equally free to exclude the navy, as we are the army, of a foreign power from entering our limits.

To former violations of maritime rights another is now added of very extensive effect. The Government of that nation has issued an order interdicting all trade by neutrals between ports not in amity with them; and being now at war with nearly every nation on the Atlantic and Mediterranean seas, our vessels are required to sacrifice their cargoes at the first port they touch or to return home without the benefit of going to any other market. Under this new law of the ocean our trade on the Mediterranean has been swept away by seizures and condemnations, and that in other seas is threatened with the same fate.

Our differences with Spain remain still unsettled, no measure having been taken on her part since my last communications to Congress to bring them to a close. But under a state of things which may favor reconsideration they have been recently pressed, and an expectation is entertained that they may now soon be brought to an issue of some sort. With their subjects on our borders no new collisions have taken place nor seem immediately to be apprehended. To our former grounds of complaint has been added a very serious one, as you will see by the decree a copy of which is now communicated. Whether this decree, which professes to be conformable to that of the French Government of November 21, 1806, heretofore communicated to Congress, will also be conformed to that in its construction and application in relation to the United States had not been ascertained at the date of our last communications. These, however, gave reason to expect such a conformity.

With the other nations of Europe our harmony has been uninterrupted, and commerce and friendly intercourse have been maintained on their usual footing.

Our peace with the several states on the coast of Barbary appears as firm as at any former period and as likely to continue as that of any other nation.

Among our Indian neighbors in the northwestern quarter some fermentation was observed soon after the late occurrences, threatening the continuance of our peace. Messages were said to be interchanged and tokens to be passing, which usually denote a state of restlessness among them, and the character of the agitators pointed to the sources of excitement. Measures were immediately taken for providing against that danger; instructions were given to require explanations, and, with assurances of our continued friendship, to admonish the tribes to remain quiet at home, taking no part in quarrels not belonging to them. As far as we are yet informed, the tribes in our vicinity, who are most advanced in the pursuits of industry, are sincerely disposed to adhere to their friendship with us and to their peace with all others, while those more remote do not present appearances sufficiently quiet to justify the intermission of military precaution on our part.

The great tribes on our southwestern quarter, much advanced beyond

the others in agriculture and household arts, appear tranquil and identi-
fying their views with ours in proportion to their advancement.   With
the whole of these people, in every quarter, I shall continue to inculcate
peace and friendship with all their neighbors and perseverance in those
occupations and pursuits which will best promote their own well-being.

The appropriations of the last session for the defense of our seaport
towns and harbors were made under expectation that a continuance of
our peace would permit us to proceed in that work according to our convenience.   It has been thought better to apply the sums then given
toward the defense of New York, Charleston, and New Orleans chiefly,
as most open and most likely first to need protection, and to leave places
less immediately in danger to the provisions of the present session.

The gunboats, too, already provided have on a like principle been
chiefly assigned to New York, New Orleans, and the Chesapeake.
Whether our movable force on the water, so material in aid of the
defensive works on the land, should be augmented in this or any other
form is left to the wisdom of the Legislature.   For the purpose of man-
ning these vessels in sudden attacks on our harbors it is a matter for
consideration whether the seamen of the United States may not justly
be formed into a special militia, to be called on for tours of duty in defense of the harbors where they shall happen to be, the ordinary militia
of the place furnishing that portion which may consist of landsmen.

The moment our peace was threatened I deemed it indispensable to
secure a greater provision of those articles of military stores with which
our magazines were not sufficiently furnished.   To have awaited a previous and special sanction by law would have lost occasions which might
not be retrieved.   I did not hesitate, therefore, to authorize engagements for such supplements to our existing stock as would render it
adequate to the emergencies threatening us, and I trust that the Legislature, feeling the same anxiety for the safety of our country, so materially advanced by this precaution, will approve, when done, what they
would have seen so important to be done if then assembled.   Expenses,
also unprovided for, arose out of the necessity of calling all our gunboats
into actual service for the defense of our harbors; of all which accounts
will be laid before you.

Whether a regular army is to be raised, and to what extent, must depend on the information so shortly expected.   In the meantime I have
called on the States for quotas of militia, to be in readiness for present
defense, and have, moreover, encouraged the acceptance of volunteers;
and I am happy to inform you that these have offered themselves with
great alacrity in every part of the Union.   They are ordered to be organized and ready at a moment's warning to proceed on any service to
which they may be called, and every preparation within the Executive
powers has been made to insure us the benefit of early exertions.

I informed Congress at their last session of the enterprises against the public peace which were believed to be in preparation by Aaron Burr and his associates, of the measures taken to defeat them and to bring the offenders to justice. Their enterprises were happily defeated by the patriotic exertions of the militia whenever called into action, by the fidelity of the Army, and energy of the commander in chief in promptly arranging the difficulties presenting themselves on the Sabine, repairing to meet those arising on the Mississippi, and dissipating before their explosion plots engendering there. I shall think it my duty to lay before you the proceedings and the evidence publicly exhibited on the arraignment of the principal offenders before the circuit court of Virginia. You will be enabled to judge whether the defect was in the testimony, in the law, or in the administration of the law; and wherever it shall be found, the Legislature alone can apply or originate the remedy. The framers of our Constitution certainly supposed they had guarded as well their Government against destruction by treason as their citizens against oppression under pretense of it, and if these ends are not attained it is of importance to inquire by what means more effectual they may be secured.

The accounts of the receipts of revenue during the year ending on the 30th day of September last being not yet made up, a correct statement will be hereafter transmitted from the Treasury. In the meantime, it is ascertained that the receipts have amounted to near $16,000,000, which, with the five millions and a half in the Treasury at the beginning of the year, have enabled us, after meeting the current demands and interest incurred, to pay more than four millions of the principal of our funded debt. These payments, with those of the preceding five and a half years, have extinguished of the funded debt $25,500,000, being the whole which could be paid or purchased within the limits of the law and of our contracts, and have left us in the Treasury $8,500,000. A portion of this sum may be considered as a commencement of accumulation of the surpluses of revenue which, after paying the installments of debt as they shall become payable, will remain without any specific object. It may partly, indeed, be applied toward completing the defense of the exposed points of our country, on such a scale as shall be adapted to our principles and circumstances. This object is doubtless among the first entitled to attention in such a state of our finances, and it is one which, whether we have peace or war, will provide security where it is due. Whether what shall remain of this, with the future surpluses, may be usefully applied to purposes already authorized or more usefully to others requiring new authorities, or how otherwise they shall be disposed of, are questions calling for the notice of Congress, unless, indeed, they shall be superseded by a change in our public relations now awaiting the determination of others. Whatever be that determination, it is a great consolation that it will become known at a moment when the supreme council of the nation is assembled at its post, and ready to give the aids of its wisdom and authority to whatever course the good of our country shall then call us to pursue.

Matters of minor importance will be the subjects of future communications, and nothing shall be wanting on my part which may give information or dispatch to the proceedings of the Legislature in the exercise of their high duties, and at a moment so interesting to the public welfare.

EIGHTH ANNUAL MESSAGE.

NOVEMBER 8, 1808.

To the Senate and House of Representatives of the United States:

It would have been a source, fellow-citizens, of much gratification if our last communications from Europe had enabled me to inform you that the belligerent nations, whose disregard of neutral rights has been so destructive to our commerce, had become awakened to the duty and true policy of revoking their unrighteous edicts. That no means might be omitted to produce this salutary effect, I lost no time in availing myself of the act authorizing a suspension, in whole or in part, of the several embargo laws. Our ministers at London and Paris were instructed to explain to the respective Governments there our disposition to exercise the authority in such manner as would withdraw the pretext on which the aggressions were originally founded and open the way for a renewal of that commercial intercourse which it was alleged on all sides had been reluctantly obstructed. As each of those Governments had pledged its readiness to concur in renouncing a measure which reached its adversary through the incontestable rights of neutrals only, and as the measure had been assumed by each as a retaliation for an asserted acquiescence in the aggressions of the other, it was reasonably expected that the occasion would have been seized by both for evincing the sincerity of their professions, and for restoring to the commerce of the United States its legitimate freedom. The instructions to our ministers with respect to the different belligerents were necessarily modified with a reference to their different circumstances, and to the condition annexed by law to the Executive power of suspension, requiring a decree of security to our commerce which would not result from a repeal of the decrees of France. Instead of a pledge, therefore, of a suspension of the embargo as to her in case of such a repeal, it was presumed that a sufficient inducement might be found in other considerations, and particularly in the change produced by a compliance with our just demands by one belligerent and a refusal by the other in the relations between the other and the United States. To Great Britain, whose power on the ocean is so ascendant, it was deemed not inconsistent with that condition to state explicitly that on her rescinding her orders in relation to the United States their trade would be opened with her, and remain shut to her enemy in case of his failure to rescind his decrees also. From France no answer has been received, nor any indication that the requisite change in her decrees is contemplated. The favorable reception of the proposition to Great Britain was the less to be doubted, as her orders of council had not only been referred for their vindication to an acquiescence on the part of the United States no longer to be pretended, but as the arrangement proposed, whilst it resisted the illegal decrees of France, involved, moreover, substantially the precise advantages professedly aimed at by the British orders. The arrangement has nevertheless been rejected.

This candid and liberal experiment having thus failed, and no other event having occurred on which a suspension of the embargo by the Executive was authorized, it necessarily remains in the extent originally given to it. We have the satisfaction, however, to reflect that in return for the privations imposed by the measure, and which our fellow-citizens in general have borne with patriotism, it has had the important effects of saving our mariners and our vast mercantile property, as well as of affording time for prosecuting the defensive and provisional measures called for by the occasion. It has demonstrated to foreign nations the moderation and firmness which govern our councils, and to our citizens the necessity of uniting in support of the laws and the rights of their country, and has thus long frustrated those usurpations and spoliations which, if resisted, involved war; if submitted to, sacrificed a vital principle of our national independence.

Under a continuance of the belligerent measures which, in defiance of laws which consecrate the rights of neutrals, overspread the ocean with danger, it will rest with the wisdom of Congress to decide on the course best adapted to such a state of things; and bringing with them, as they do, from every part of the Union the sentiments of our constituents, my confidence is strengthened that in forming this decision they will, with an unerring regard to the essential rights and interests of the nation, weigh and compare the painful alternatives out of which a choice is to be made. Nor should I do justice to the virtues which on other occasions have marked the character of our fellow-citizens if I did not cherish an equal confidence that the alternative chosen, whatever it may be, will be maintained with all the fortitude and patriotism which the crisis ought to inspire.

The documents containing the correspondences on the subject of the foreign edicts against our commerce, with the instructions given to our ministers at London and Paris, are now laid before you.

The communications made to Congress at their last session explained

the posture in which the close of the discussions relating to the attack by
a British ship of war on the frigate *Chesapeake* left a subject on which
the nation had manifested so honorable a sensibility.   Every view of what
had passed authorized a belief that immediate steps would be taken by
the British Government for redressing a wrong which the more it was
investigated appeared the more clearly to require what had not been
provided for in the special mission.   It is found that no steps have been
taken for the purpose.   On the contrary, it will be seen in the documents
laid before you that the inadmissible preliminary which obstructed the
adjustment is still adhered to, and, moreover, that it is now brought into
connection with the distinct and irrelative case of the orders in council.
The instructions which had been given to our minister at London with
a view to facilitate, if necessary, the reparation claimed by the United
States are included in the documents communicated.

Our relations with the other powers of Europe have undergone no
material changes since your last session.   The important negotiations
with Spain which had been alternately suspended and resumed necessarily experience a pause under the extraordinary and interesting crisis
which distinguishes her internal situation.

With the Barbary Powers we continue in harmony, with the exception
of an unjustifiable proceeding of the Dey of Algiers toward our consul to
that Regency.   Its character and circumstances are now laid before you,
and will enable you to decide how far it may, either now or hereafter,
call for any measures not within the limits of the Executive authority.

With our Indian neighbors the public peace has been steadily maintained.   Some instances of individual wrong have, as at other times,
taken place, but in no wise implicating the will of the nation.   Beyond
the Mississippi the Ioways, the Sacs, and the Alabamas have delivered up
for trial and punishment individuals from among themselves accused of
murdering citizens of the United States.   On this side of the Mississippi
the Creeks are exerting themselves to arrest offenders of the same kind,
and the Choctaws have manifested their readiness and desire for amicable
and just arrangements respecting depredations committed by disorderly
persons of their tribe.   And, generally, from a conviction that we consider them as a part of ourselves, and cherish with sincerity their rights
and interests, the attachment of the Indian tribes is gaining strength
daily—is extending from the nearer to the more remote, and will amply
requite us for the justice and friendship practiced toward them.   Husbandry and household manufacture are advancing among them more rapidly with the Southern than Northern tribes, from circumstances of soil
and climate, and one of the two great divisions of the Cherokee Nation
have now under consideration to solicit the citizenship of the United
States, and to be identified with us in laws and government in such progressive manner as we shall think best.

In consequence of the appropriations of the last session of Congress for the security of our seaport towns and harbors, such works of defense have been erected as seemed to be called for by the situation of the several places, their relative importance, and the scale of expense indicated by the amount of the appropriation. These works will chiefly be finished in the course of the present season, except at New York and New Orleans, where most was to be done; and although a great proportion of the last appropriation has been expended on the former place, yet some further views will be submitted to Congress for rendering its security entirely adequate against naval enterprise. A view of what has been done at the several places, and of what is proposed to be done, shall be communicated as soon as the several reports are received.

Of the gunboats authorized by the act of December last, it has been thought necessary to build only 103 in the present year. These, with those before possessed, are sufficient for the harbors and waters most exposed, and the residue will require little time for their construction when it shall be deemed necessary.

Under the act of the last session for raising an additional military force so many officers were immediately appointed as were necessary for carrying on the business of recruiting, and in proportion as it advanced others have been added. We have reason to believe their success has been satisfactory, although such returns have not yet been received as enable me to present you a statement of the numbers engaged.

I have not thought it necessary in the course of the last season to call for any general detachments of militia or of volunteers under the laws passed for that purpose. For the ensuing season, however, they will be required to be in readiness should their service be wanted. Some small and special detachments have been necessary to maintain the laws of embargo on that portion of our northern frontier which offered peculiar facilities for evasion, but these were replaced as soon as it could be done by bodies of new recruits. By the aid of these and of the armed vessels called into service in other quarters the spirit of disobedience and abuse, which manifested itself early and with sensible effect while we were unprepared to meet it, has been considerably repressed.

Considering the extraordinary character of the times in which we live, our attention should unremittingly be fixed on the safety of our country. For a people who are free, and who mean to remain so, a well organized and armed militia is their best security. It is therefore incumbent on us at every meeting to revise the condition of the militia, and to ask ourselves if it is prepared to repel a powerful enemy at every point of our territories exposed to invasion. Some of the States have paid a laudable attention to this object, but every degree of neglect is to be found among others. Congress alone having the power to produce an uniform state of preparation in this great organ of defense, the interests which they so deeply feel in their own and their country's security will present this as among the most important objects of their deliberation.

Under the acts of March 11 and April 23 respecting arms, the difficulty of procuring them from abroad during the present situation and dispositions of Europe induced us to direct our whole efforts to the means of internal supply. The public factories have therefore been enlarged, additional machineries erected, and, in proportion as artificers can be found or formed, their effect, already more than doubled, may be increased so as to keep pace with the yearly increase of the militia. The annual sums appropriated by the latter act have been directed to the encouragement of private factories of arms, and contracts have been entered into with individual undertakers to nearly the amount of the first year's appropriation.

The suspension of our foreign commerce, produced by the injustice of the belligerent powers and the consequent losses and sacrifices of our citizens are subjects of just concern. The situation into which we have thus been forced has impelled us to apply a portion of our industry and capital to internal manufactures and improvements. The extent of this conversion is daily increasing, and little doubt remains that the establishments formed and forming will, under the auspices of cheaper materials and subsistence, the freedom of labor from taxation with us, and of protecting duties and prohibitions, become permanent. The commerce with the Indians, too, within our own boundaries is likely to receive abundant aliment from the same internal source, and will secure to them peace and the progress of civilization, undisturbed by practices hostile to both.

The accounts of the receipts and expenditures during the year ending the 30th of September last being not yet made up, a correct statement will hereafter be transmitted from the Treasury. In the meantime it is ascertained that the receipts have amounted to near $18,000,000, which, with the eight millions and a half in the Treasury at the beginning of the year, have enabled us, after meeting the current demands and interest incurred, to pay $2,300,000 of the principal of our funded debt, and left us in the Treasury on that day near $14,000,000. Of these, $5,350,000 will be necessary to pay what will be due on the 1st day of January next, which will complete the reimbursement of the 8 per cent stock. These payments, with those made in the six years and a half preceding, will have extinguished $33,580,000 of the principal of the funded debt, being the whole which could be paid or purchased within the limits of the law and of our contracts, and the amount of principal thus discharged will have liberated the revenue from about $2,000,000 of interest and added that sum annually to the disposable surplus. The probable accumulation of the surpluses of revenue beyond what can be applied to the payment of the public debt whenever the freedom and safety of our commerce shall be restored merits the consideration of Congress. Shall it lie unproductive in the public vaults? Shall the revenue be reduced? Or shall it not rather be appropriated to the improvements of roads, canals, rivers, education, and other great foundations of prosperity and union under the powers which Congress may already possess or such amendment of the Constitution as may be approved by the States? While uncertain of the course of things, the time may be advantageously employed in obtaining the powers necessary for a system of improvement, should that be thought best.

Availing myself of this the last occasion which will occur of addressing the two Houses of the Legislature at their meeting, I can not omit the expression of my sincere gratitude for the repeated proofs of confidence manifested to me by themselves and their predecessors since my call to the administration and the many indulgences experienced at their hands. The same grateful acknowledgments are due to my fellow-citizens generally, whose support has been my great encouragement under all embarrassments. In the transaction of their business I can not have escaped error. It is incident to our imperfect nature. But I may say with truth my errors have been of the understanding, not of intention, and that the advancement of their rights and interests has been the constant motive for every measure. On these considerations I solicit their indulgence Looking forward with anxiety to their future destinies, I trust that in their steady character, unshaken by difficulties, in their love of liberty, obedience to law, and support of the public authorities I see a sure guaranty of the permanence of our Republic; and, retiring from the charge of their affairs, I carry with me the consolation of a firm persuasion that Heaven has in store for our beloved country long ages to come of prosperity and happiness.

James Madison

March 4, 1809 to March 4, 1817

FIRST ANNUAL MESSAGE.

NOVEMBER 29, 1809.

Fellow-Citizens of the Senate and of the House of Representatives:

At the period of our last meeting I had the satisfaction of communicating an adjustment with one of the principal belligerent nations, highly important in itself, and still more so as presaging a more extended accommodation. It is with deep concern I am now to inform you that the favorable prospect has been overclouded by a refusal of the British Government to abide by the act of its minister plenipotentiary, and by its ensuing policy toward the United States as seen through the communications of the minister sent to replace him.

Whatever pleas may be urged for a disavowal of engagements formed by diplomatic functionaries in cases where by the terms of the engagements a mutual ratification is reserved, or where notice at the time may have been given of a departure from instructions, or in extraordinary cases essentially violating the principles of equity, a disavowal could not have been apprehended in a case where no such notice or violation existed. where no such ratification was reserved, and more especially where, as is now in proof, an engagement to be executed without any such ratification was contemplated by the instructions given, and where it had with good faith been carried into immediate execution on the part of the United States.

These considerations not having restrained the British Government from disavowing the arrangement by virtue of which its orders in council were to be revoked, and the event authorizing the renewal of commercial intercourse having thus not taken place, it necessarily became a question of equal urgency and importance whether the act prohibiting that intercourse was not to be considered as remaining in legal force. This question being, after due deliberation, determined in the affirmative, a proclamation to that effect was issued. It could not but happen, however, that a return to this state of things from that which had followed an execution of the arrangement by the United States would involve difficulties. With a view to diminish these as much as possible, the instructions from the Secretary of the Treasury now laid before you were transmitted to the collectors of the several ports. If in permitting British vessels to depart without giving bonds not to proceed to their own ports it should appear that the tenor of legal authority has not been strictly pursued, it is to be ascribed to the anxious desire which was felt that no individuals should be injured by so unforeseen an occurrence; and I rely on the regard of Congress for the equitable interests of our own citizens to adopt whatever further provisions may be found requisite for a general remission of penalties involuntarily incurred.

The recall of the disavowed minister having been followed by the appointment of a successor, hopes were indulged that the new mission would contribute to alleviate the disappointment which had been produced, and to remove the causes which had so long embarrassed the good understanding of the two nations. It could not be doubted that it would at least be charged with conciliatory explanations of the step which had been taken and with proposals to be substituted for the rejected arrangement. Reasonable and universal as this expectation was, it also has not been fulfilled. From the first official disclosures of the new minister it was found that he had received no authority to enter into explanations relative to either branch of the arrangement disavowed nor any authority to substitute proposals as to that branch which concerned the British orders in council, and, finally, that his proposals with respect to the other branch, the attack on the frigate *Chesapeake*, were founded on a presumption repeatedly declared to be inadmissible by the United States, that the first step toward adjustment was due from them, the proposals at the same time omitting even a reference to the officer answerable for the murderous aggression, and asserting a claim not less contrary to the British laws and British practice than to the principles and obligations of the United States.

The correspondence between the Department of State and this minister will show how unessentially the features presented in its commencement have been varied in its progress. It will show also that, forgetting the respect due to all governments, he did not refrain from imputations on this, which required that no further communications should be received from him. The necessity of this step will be made known to His Britannic Majesty through the minister plenipotentiary of the United States in London; and it would indicate a want of the confidence due to a Government which so well understands and exacts what becomes foreign ministers near it not to infer that the misconduct of its own representative will be viewed in the same light in which it has been regarded here. The British Government will learn at the same time that a ready attention will be given to communications through any channel which may be substituted. It will be happy if the change in this respect should be accompanied by a favorable revision of the unfriendly policy which has been so long pursued toward the United States.

With France, the other belligerent, whose trespasses on our commercial rights have long been the subject of our just remonstrances, the posture of our relations does not correspond with the measures taken on the part of the United States to effect a favorable change. The result of the several communications made to her Government, in pursuance of the authorities vested by Congress in the Executive, is contained in the correspondence of our minister at Paris now laid before you.

By some of the other belligerents, although professing just and amicable dispositions, injuries materially affecting our commerce have not been duly controlled or repressed. In these cases the interpositions deemed proper on our part have not been omitted.   But it well deserves the consideration of the Legislature how far both the safety and the honor of the American flag may be consulted, by adequate provisions against that collusive prostitution of it by individuals unworthy of the American name which has so much favored the real or pretended suspicions under which the honest commerce of their fellow-citizens has suffered.

In relation to the powers on the coast of Barbary, nothing has occurred which is not of a nature rather to inspire confidence than distrust as to the continuance of the existing amity.   With our Indian neighbors, the just and benevolent system continued toward them has also preserved peace, and is more and more advancing habits favorable to their civilization and happiness.

From a statement which will be made by the Secretary of War it will be seen that the fortifications on our maritime frontier are in many of the ports completed, affording the defense which was contemplated, and that a further time will be required to render complete the works in the harbor of New York and in some other places.   By the enlargement of the works and the employment of a greater number of hands at the public armories the supply of small arms of an improving quality appears to be annually increasing at a rate that, with those made on private contract, may be expected to go far toward providing for the public exigency.

The act of Congress providing for the equipment of our vessels of war having been fully carried into execution, I refer to the statement of the Secretary of the Navy for the information which may be proper on that subject.   To that statement is added a view of the transfers of appropriations authorized by the act of the session preceding the last and of the grounds on which the transfers were made.

Whatever may be the course of your deliberations on the subject of our military establishments, I should fail in my duty in not recommending to your serious attention the importance of giving to our militia, the great bulwark of our security and resource of our power, an organization the best adapted to eventual situations for which the United States ought to be prepared.

The sums which had been previously accumulated in the Treasury, together with the receipts during the year ending on the 30th of September last (and amounting to more than $9,000,000), have enabled us to fulfill all our engagements and to defray the current expenses of Government without recurring to any loan.   But the insecurity of our commerce and the consequent diminution of the public revenue will probably produce a deficiency in the receipts of the ensuing year, for which and for other details I refer to the statements which will be transmitted from the Treasury.

In the state which has been presented of our affairs with the great parties to a disastrous and protracted war, carried on in a mode equally injurious and unjust to the United States as a neutral nation, the wisdom of the National Legislature will be again summoned to the important decision on the alternatives before them. That these will be met in a spirit worthy the councils of a nation conscious both of its rectitude and of its rights, and careful as well of its honor as of its peace, I have an entire confidence; and that the result will be stamped by a unanimity becoming the occasion, and be supported by every portion of our citizens with a patriotism enlightened and invigorated by experience, ought as little to be doubted.

In the midst of the wrongs and vexations experienced from external causes there is much room for congratulation on the prosperity and happiness flowing from our situation at home. The blessing of health has never been more universal. The fruits of the seasons, though in particular articles and districts short of their usual redundancy, are more than sufficient for our wants and our comforts. The face of our country everywhere presents the evidence of laudable enterprise, of extensive capital, and of durable improvement. In a cultivation of the materials and the extension of useful manufactures, more especially in the general application to household fabrics, we behold a rapid diminution of our dependence on foreign supplies. Nor is it unworthy of reflection that this revolution in our pursuits and habits is in no slight degree a consequence of those impolitic and arbitrary edicts by which the contending nations, in endeavoring each of them to obstruct our trade with the other, have so far abridged our means of procuring the productions and manufactures of which our own are now taking the place.

Recollecting always that for every advantage which may contribute to distinguish our lot from that to which others are doomed by the unhappy spirit of the times we are indebted to that Divine Providence whose goodness has been so remarkably extended to this rising nation, it becomes us to cherish a devout gratitude, and to implore from the same omnipotent source a blessing on the consultations and measures about to be undertaken for the welfare of our beloved country.

SECOND ANNUAL MESSAGE.

WASHINGTON, *December 5, 1810.*

Fellow-Citizens of the Senate and of the House of Representatives:

The embarrassments which have prevailed in our foreign relations, and so much employed the deliberations of Congress, make it a primary duty in meeting you to communicate whatever may have occurred in that branch of our national affairs.

The act of the last session of Congress concerning the commercial intercourse between the United States and Great Britain and France and their dependencies having invited in a new form a termination of their edicts against our neutral commerce, copies of the act were immediately forwarded to our ministers at London and Paris, with a view that its object might be within the early attention of the French and British Governments.

By the communication received through our minister at Paris it appeared that a knowledge of the act by the French Government was followed by a declaration that the Berlin and Milan decrees were revoked, and would cease to have effect on the 1st day of November ensuing. These being the only known edicts of France within the description of the act, and the revocation of them being such that they ceased at that date to violate our neutral commerce, the fact, as prescribed by law, was announced by a proclamation bearing date the 2d day of November.

It would have well accorded with the conciliatory views indicated by this proceeding on the part of France to have extended them to all the grounds of just complaint which now remain unadjusted with the United States. It was particularly anticipated that, as a further evidence of just dispositions toward them, restoration would have been immediately made of the property of our citizens seized under a misapplication of the principle of reprisals combined with a misconstruction of a law of the United States. This expectation has not been fulfilled.

From the British Government no communication on the subject of the act has been received. To a communication from our minister at London of a revocation by the French Government of its Berlin and Milan decrees it was answered that the British system would be relinquished as soon as the repeal of the French decrees should have actually taken effect and the commerce of neutral nations have been restored to the condition in which it stood previously to the promulgation of those decrees. This pledge, although it does not necessarily import, does not exclude the intention of relinquishing, along with the orders in council, the practice of those novel blockades which have a like effect of interrupting our neutral commerce, and this further justice to the United States is the rather to be looked for, inasmuch as the blockades in question, being not more contrary to the established law of nations than inconsistent with the rules of blockade formally recognized by Great Britain herself, could have no alleged basis other than the plea of retaliation alleged as the basis of the orders in council. Under the modification of the original orders of November, 1807, into the orders of April, 1809, there is, indeed, scarcely a nominal distinction between the orders and the blockades. One of those illegitimate blockades, bearing date in May, 1806, having been expressly avowed to be still unrescinded, and to be in effect comprehended in the orders in council, was too distinctly brought within the purview of the act of Congress not to be comprehended in the explanation of the requisites to a compliance with it. The British Government was accordingly apprised by our minister near it that such was the light in which the subject was to be regarded.

On the other important subjects depending between the United States and that Government no progress has been made from which an early and satisfactory result can be relied on.

In this new posture of our relations with those powers the consideration of Congress will be properly turned to a removal of doubts which may occur in the exposition and of difficulties in the execution of the act above cited.

The commerce of the United States with the north of Europe, heretofore much vexed by licentious cruisers, particularly under the Danish flag, has latterly been visited with fresh and extensive depredations. The measures pursued in behalf of our injured citizens not having obtained justice for them, a further and more formal interposition with the Danish Government is contemplated. The principles which have been maintained by that Government in relation to neutral commerce, and the friendly professions of His Danish Majesty toward the United States, are valuable pledges in favor of a successful issue.

Among the events growing out of the state of the Spanish Monarchy, our attention was imperiously attracted to the change developing itself in that portion of West Florida which, though of right appertaining to the United States, had remained in the possession of Spain awaiting the result of negotiations for its actual delivery to them. The Spanish authority was subverted and a situation produced exposing the country to ulterior events which might essentially affect the rights and welfare of the Union. In such a conjuncture I did not delay the interposition required for the occupancy of the territory west of the river Perdido, to which the title of the United States extends, and to which the laws provided for the Territory of Orleans are applicable. With this view, the proclamation of which a copy is laid before you was confided to the governor of that Territory to be carried into effect. The legality and necessity of the course pursued assure me of the favorable light in which it will present itself to the Legislature, and of the promptitude with which they will supply whatever provisions may be due to the essential rights and equitable interests of the people thus brought into the bosom of the American family.

Our amity with the powers of Barbary, with the exception of a recent occurrence at Tunis, of which an explanation is just received, appears to have been uninterrupted and to have become more firmly established.

With the Indian tribes also the peace and friendship of the United States are found to be so eligible that the general disposition to preserve both continues to gain strength.

I feel particular satisfaction in remarking that an interior view of our country presents us with grateful proofs of its substantial and increasing prosperity. To a thriving agriculture and the improvements related to it is added a highly interesting extension of useful manufactures, the combined product of professional occupations and of household industry. Such indeed is the experience of economy as well as of policy in these substitutes for supplies heretofore obtained by foreign commerce that in a national view the change is justly regarded as of itself more than a recompense for those privations and losses resulting from foreign injustice which furnished the general impulse required for its accomplishment. How far it may be expedient to guard the infancy of this improvement in the distribution of labor by regulations of the commercial tariff is a subject which can not fail to suggest itself to your patriotic reflections.

It will rest with the consideration of Congress also whether a provident as well as fair encouragement would not be given to our navigation by such regulations as would place it on a level of competition with foreign vessels, particularly in transporting the important and bulky productions of our own soil. The failure of equality and reciprocity in the existing regulations on this subject operates in our ports as a premium to foreign competitors, and the inconvenience must increase as these may be multiplied under more favorable circumstances by the more than countervailing encouragements now given them by the laws of their respective countries.

Whilst it is universally admitted that a well-instructed people alone can be permanently a free people, and whilst it is evident that the means of diffusing and improving useful knowledge form so small a proportion of the expenditures for national purposes, I can not presume it to be unseasonable to invite your attention to the advantages of superadding to the means of education provided by the several States a seminary of learning instituted by the National Legislature within the limits of their exclusive jurisdiction, the expense of which might be defrayed or reimbursed out of the vacant grounds which have accrued to the nation within those limits.

Such an institution, though local in its legal character, would be universal in its beneficial effects. By enlightening the opinions, by expanding the patriotism, and by assimilating the principles, the sentiments, and the manners of those who might resort to this temple of science, to be redistributed in due time through every part of the community, sources of jealousy and prejudice would be diminished, the features of national character would be multiplied, and greater extent given to social harmony. But, above all, a well-constituted seminary in the center of the nation is recommended by the consideration that the additional instruction emanating from it would contribute not less to strengthen the foundations than to adorn the structure of our free and happy system of government.

Among the commercial abuses still committed under the American flag, and leaving in force my former reference to that subject, it appears

that American citizens are instrumental in carrying on a traffic in enslaved Africans, equally in violation of the laws of humanity and in
defiance of those of their own country. The same just and benevolent
motives which produced the interdiction in force against this criminal
conduct will doubtless be felt by Congress in devising further means of
suppressing the evil.

In the midst of uncertainties necessarily connected with the great
interests of the United States, prudence requires a continuance of our
defensive and precautionary arrangement. The Secretary of War and
Secretary of the Navy will submit the statements and estimates which
may aid Congress in their ensuing provisions for the land and naval
forces. The statements of the latter will include a view of the transfers
of appropriations in the naval expenditures and the grounds on which
they were made.

The fortifications for the defense of our maritime frontier have been
prosecuted according to the plan laid down in 1808. The works, with
some exceptions, are completed and furnished with ordnance. Those for
the security of the city of New York, though far advanced toward completion, will require a further time and appropriation. This is the case
with a few others, either not completed or in need of repairs.

The improvements in quality and quantity made in the manufacture
of cannon and small arms, both at the public armories and private factories, warrant additional confidence in the competency of these resources
for supplying the public exigencies.

These preparations for arming the militia having thus far provided for
one of the objects contemplated by the power vested in Congress with
respect to that great bulwark of the public safety, it is for their consideration whether further provisions are not requisite for the other
contemplated objects of organization and discipline. To give to this
great mass of physical and moral force the efficiency which it merits,
and is capable of receiving, it is indispensable that they should be instructed and practiced in the rules by which they are to be governed.
Toward an accomplishment of this important work I recommend for the
consideration of Congress the expediency of instituting a system which
shall in the first instance call into the field at the public expense and for
a given time certain portions of the commissioned and noncommissioned
officers. The instruction and discipline thus acquired would gradually
diffuse through the entire body of the militia that practical knowledge
and promptitude for active service which are the great ends to be pursued. Experience has left no doubt either of the necessity or of the
efficacy of competent military skill in those portions of an army in fitting
it for the final duties which it may have to perform.

The Corps of Engineers, with the Military Academy, are entitled to
the early attention of Congress. The buildings at the seat fixed by law
for the present Academy are so far in decay as not to afford the necessary

accommodation.   But a revision of the law is recommended, principally with a view to a more enlarged cultivation and diffusion of the advantages of such institutions, by providing professorships for all the necessary branches of military instruction, and by the establishment of an additional academy at the seat of Government or elsewhere.   The means by which war, as well for defense as for offense, are now carried on render these schools of the more scientific operations an indispensable part of every adequate system.   Even among nations whose large standing armies and frequent wars afford every other opportunity of instruction these establishments are found to be indispensable for the due attainment of the branches of military science which require a regular course of study and experiment.   In a government happily without the other opportunities seminaries where the elementary principles of the art of war can be taught without actual war, and without the expense of extensive and standing armies, have the precious advantage of uniting an essential preparation against external danger with a scrupulous regard to internal safety.   In no other way, probably, can a provision of equal efficacy for the public defense be made at so little expense or more consistently with the public liberty.

The receipts into the Treasury during the year ending on the 30th of September last (and amounting to more than $8,500,000) have exceeded the current expenses of the Government, including the interest on the public debt.   For the purpose of reimbursing at the end of the year $3,750,000 of the principal, a loan, as authorized by law, had been negotiated to that amount, but has since been reduced to $2,750,000, the reduction being permitted by the state of the Treasury, in which there will be a balance remaining at the end of the year estimated at $2,000,000. For the probable receipts of the next year and other details I refer to statements which will be transmitted from the Treasury, and which will enable you to judge what further provisions may be necessary for the ensuing years.

Reserving for future occasions in the course of the session whatever other communications may claim your attention, I close the present by expressing my reliance, under the blessing of Divine Providence, on the judgment and patriotism which will guide your measures at a period particularly calling for united councils and inflexible exertions for the welfare of our country, and by assuring you of the fidelity and alacrity with which my cooperation will be afforded.

THIRD ANNUAL MESSAGE.

WASHINGTON, *November 5, 1811.*

Fellow-Citizens of the Senate and of the House of Representatives:

In calling you together sooner than a separation from your homes would otherwise have been required I yielded to considerations drawn from the posture of our foreign affairs, and in fixing the present for the time of your meeting regard was had to the probability of further developments of the policy of the belligerent powers toward this country which might the more unite the national councils in the measures to be pursued.

At the close of the last session of Congress it was hoped that the successive confirmations of the extinction of the French decrees, so far as they violated our neutral commerce, would have induced the Government of Great Britain to repeal its orders in council, and thereby authorize a removal of the existing obstructions to her commerce with the United States.

Instead of this reasonable step toward satisfaction and friendship between the two nations, the orders were, at a moment when least to have been expected, put into more rigorous execution; and it was communicated through the British envoy just arrived that whilst the revocation of the edicts of France, as officially made known to the British Government, was denied to have taken place, it was an indispensable condition of the repeal of the British orders that commerce should be restored to a footing that would admit the productions and manufactures of Great Britain, when owned by neutrals, into markets shut against them by her enemy, the United States being given to understand that in the meantime a continuance of their nonimportation act would lead to measures of retaliation.

At a later date it has indeed appeared that a communication to the British Government of fresh evidence of the repeal of the French decrees against our neutral trade was followed by an intimation that it had been transmitted to the British plenipotentiary here in order that it might receive full consideration in the depending discussions. This communication appears not to have been received; but the transmission of it hither, instead of founding on it an actual repeal of the orders or assurances that the repeal would ensue, will not permit us to rely on any effective change in the British cabinet. To be ready to meet with cordiality satisfactory proofs of such a change, and to proceed in the meantime in adapting our measures to the views which have been disclosed through that minister will best consult our whole duty.

In the unfriendly spirit of those disclosures indemnity and redress for other wrongs have continued to be withheld, and our coasts and the mouths of our harbors have again witnessed scenes not less derogatory to the dearest of our national rights than vexatious to the regular course of our trade.

Among the occurrences produced by the conduct of British ships of war hovering on our coasts was an encounter between one of them and the American frigate commanded by Captain Rodgers, rendered unavoidable on the part of the latter by a fire commenced without cause by the former, whose commander is therefore alone chargeable with the blood unfortunately shed in maintaining the honor of the American flag. The proceedings of a court of inquiry requested by Captain Rodgers are communicated, together with the correspondence relating to the occurrence, between the Secretary of State and His Britannic Majesty's envoy. To these are added the several correspondences which have passed on the subject of the British orders in council, and to both the correspondence relating to the Floridas, in which Congress will be made acquainted with the interposition which the Government of Great Britain has thought proper to make against the proceeding of the United States.

The justice and fairness which have been evinced on the part of the United States toward France, both before and since the revocation of her decrees, authorized an expectation that her Government would have followed up that measure by all such others as were due to our reasonable claims, as well as dictated by its amicable professions. No proof, however, is yet given of an intention to repair the other wrongs done to the United States, and particularly to restore the great amount of American property seized and condemned under edicts which, though not affecting our neutral relations, and therefore not entering into questions between the United States and other belligerents, were nevertheless founded in such unjust principles that the reparation ought to have been prompt and ample.

In addition to this and other demands of strict right on that nation, the United States have much reason to be dissatisfied with the rigorous and unexpected restrictions to which their trade with the French dominions has been subjected, and which, if not discontinued, will require at least corresponding restrictions on importations from France into the United States.

On all those subjects our minister plenipotentiary lately sent to Paris has carried with him the necessary instructions, the result of which will be communicated to you, and, by ascertaining the ulterior policy of the French Government toward the United States, will enable you to adapt to it that of the United States toward France.

Our other foreign relations remain without unfavorable changes. With Russia they are on the best footing of friendship. The ports of Sweden have afforded proofs of friendly dispositions toward our commerce in the councils of that nation also, and the information from our special minister to Denmark shews that the mission had been attended with valuable effects to our citizens, whose property had been so extensively violated and endangered by cruisers under the Danish flag.

Under the ominous indications which commanded attention it became a duty to exert the means committed to the executive department in providing for the general security. The works of defense on our maritime frontier have accordingly been prosecuted with an activity leaving little to be added for the completion of the most important ones, and, as particularly suited for cooperation in emergencies, a portion of the gunboats have in particular harbors been ordered into use. The ships of war before in commission, with the addition of a frigate, have been chiefly employed as a cruising guard to the rights of our coast, and such a disposition has been made of our land forces as was thought to promise the services most appropriate and important. In this disposition is included a force consisting of regulars and militia, embodied in the Indiana Territory and marched toward our northwestern frontier. This measure was made requisite by several murders and depredations committed by Indians, but more especially by the menacing preparations and aspect of a combination of them on the Wabash, under the influence and direction of a fanatic of the Shawanese tribe. With these exceptions the Indian tribes retain their peaceable dispositions toward us, and their usual pursuits.

I must now add that the period is arrived which claims from the legislative guardians of the national rights a system of more ample provisions for maintaining them. Notwithstanding the scrupulous justice, the protracted moderation, and the multiplied efforts on the part of the United States to substitute for the accumulating dangers to the peace of the two countries all the mutual advantages of reestablished friendship and confidence, we have seen that the British cabinet perseveres not only in withholding a remedy for other wrongs, so long and so loudly calling for it, but in the execution, brought home to the threshold of our territory, of measures which under existing circumstances have the character as well as the effect of war on our lawful commerce.

With this evidence of hostile inflexibility in trampling on rights which no independent nation can relinquish, Congress will feel the duty of putting the United States into an armor and an attitude demanded by the crisis, and corresponding with the national spirit and expectations.

I recommend, accordingly, that adequate provision be made for filling the ranks and prolonging the enlistments of the regular troops; for an auxiliary force to be engaged for a more limited term; for the acceptance of volunteer corps, whose patriotic ardor may court a participation in urgent services; for detachments as they may be wanted of other portions of the militia, and for such a preparation of the great body as will proportion its usefulness to its intrinsic capacities. Nor can the occasion fail to remind you of the importance of those military seminaries which in every event will form a valuable and frugal part of our military establishment.

The manufacture of cannon and small arms has proceeded with due success, and the stock and resources of all the necessary munitions are adequate to emergencies. It will not be inexpedient, however, for Congress to authorize an enlargement of them.

Your attention will of course be drawn to such provisions on the subject of our naval force as may be required for the services to which it may be best adapted. I submit to Congress the seasonableness also of an authority to augment the stock of such materials as are imperishable in their nature, or may not at once be attainable.

In contemplating the scenes which distinguish this momentous epoch, and estimating their claims to our attention, it is impossible to overlook those developing themselves among the great communities which occupy the southern portion of our own hemisphere and extend into our neighborhood. An enlarged philanthropy and an enlightened forecast concur in imposing on the national councils an obligation to take a deep interest in their destinies, to cherish reciprocal sentiments of good will, to regard the progress of events, and not to be unprepared for whatever order of things may be ultimately established.

Under another aspect of our situation the early attention of Congress will be due to the expediency of further guards against evasions and infractions of our commercial laws. The practice of smuggling, which is odious everywhere, and particularly criminal in free governments, where, the laws being made by all for the good of all, a fraud is committed on every individual as well as on the state, attains its utmost guilt when it blends with a pursuit of ignominious gain a treacherous subserviency, in the transgressors, to a foreign policy adverse to that of their own country. It is then that the virtuous indignation of the public should be enabled to manifest itself through the regular animadversions of the most competent laws.

To secure greater respect to our mercantile flag, and to the honest interests which it covers, it is expedient also that it be made punishable in our citizens to accept licenses from foreign governments for a trade unlawfully interdicted by them to other American citizens, or to trade under false colors or papers of any sort.

A prohibition is equally called for against the acceptance by our citizens of special licenses to be used in a trade with the United States, and against the admission into particular ports of the United States of vessels from foreign countries authorized to trade with particular ports only.

Although other subjects will press more immediately on your deliberations, a portion of them can not but be well bestowed on the just and sound policy of securing to our manufactures the success they have attained, and are still attaining, in some degree, under the impulse of causes not permanent, and to our navigation, the fair extent of which is at present abridged by the unequal regulations of foreign governments.

Besides the reasonableness of saving our manufactures from sacrifices which a change of circumstances might bring on them, the national interest requires that, with respect to such articles at least as belong to our defense and our primary wants, we should not be left in unnecessary dependence on external supplies. And whilst foreign governments adhere to the existing discriminations in their ports against our navigation, and an equality or lesser discrimination is enjoyed by their navigation in our ports, the effect can not be mistaken, because it has been seriously felt by our shipping interests; and in proportion as this takes place the advantages of an independent conveyance of our products to foreign markets and of a growing body of mariners trained by their occupations for the service of their country in times of danger must be diminished.

The receipts into the Treasury during the year ending on the 30th of September last have exceeded $13,500,000, and have enabled us to defray the current expenses, including the interest on the public debt, and to reimburse more than $5,000,000 of the principal without recurring to the loan authorized by the act of the last session. The temporary loan obtained in the latter end of the year 1810 has also been reimbursed, and is not included in that amount.

The decrease of revenue arising from the situation of our commerce, and the extraordinary expenses which have and may become necessary, must be taken into view in making commensurate provisions for the ensuing year; and I recommend to your consideration the propriety of insuring a sufficiency of annual revenue at least to defray the ordinary expenses of Government, and to pay the interest on the public debt, including that on new loans which may be authorized.

I can not close this communication without expressing my deep sense of the crisis in which you are assembled, my confidence in a wise and honorable result to your deliberations, and assurances of the faithful zeal with which my cooperating duties will be discharged, invoking at the same time the blessing of Heaven on our beloved country and on all the means that may be employed in vindicating its rights and advancing its welfare.

FOURTH ANNUAL MESSAGE.

WASHINGTON, *November 4, 1812.*

Fellow-Citizens of the Senate and of the House of Representatives:

On our present meeting it is my first duty to invite your attention to the providential favors which our country has experienced in the unusual

degree of health dispensed to its inhabitants, and in the rich abundance
with which the earth has rewarded the labors bestowed on it.   In the
successful cultivation of other branches of industry, and in the progress
of general improvement favorable to the national prosperity, there is just
occasion also for our mutual congratulations and thankfulness.

With these blessings are necessarily mingled the pressures and vicissitudes incident to the state of war into which the United States have
been forced by the perseverance of a foreign power in its system of injustice and aggression.

Previous to its declaration it was deemed proper, as a measure of
precaution and forecast, that a considerable force should be placed in
the Michigan Territory with a general view to its security, and, in the
event of war, to such operations in the uppermost Canada as would in-
tercept the hostile influence of Great Britain over the savages, obtain
the command of the lake on which that part of Canada borders, and
maintain cooperating relations with such forces as might be most conveniently employed against other parts.   Brigadier-General Hull was
charged with this provisional service, having under his command a body
of troops composed of regulars and of volunteers from the State of Ohio.
Having reached his destination after his knowledge of the war, and
possessing discretionary authority to act offensively, he passed into the
neighboring territory of the enemy with a prospect of easy and victorious progress.   The expedition, nevertheless, terminated unfortunately,
not only in a retreat to the town and fort of Detroit, but in the surrender
of both and of the gallant corps commanded by that officer.   The causes
of this painful reverse will be investigated by a military tribunal.

A distinguishing feature in the operations which preceded and followed
this adverse event is the use made by the enemy of the merciless savages
under their influence.   Whilst the benevolent policy of the United States
invariably recommended peace and promoted civilization among that
wretched portion of the human race, and was making exertions to dissuade them from taking either side in the war, the enemy has not scru-
pled to call to his aid their ruthless ferocity, armed with the horrors of
those instruments of carnage and torture which are known to spare neither
age nor sex.   In this outrage against the laws of honorable war and
against the feelings sacred to humanity the British commanders can not
resort to a plea of retaliation, for it is committed in the face of our example.   They can not mitigate it by calling it a self-defense against men in
arms, for it embraces the most shocking butcheries of defenseless families.   Nor can it be pretended that they are not answerable for the atrocities perpetrated, since the savages are employed with a knowledge, and
even with menaces, that their fury could not be controlled.   Such is the
spectacle which the deputed authorities of a nation boasting its religion
and morality have not been restrained from presenting to an enlightened
age.

The misfortune at Detroit was not, however, without a consoling effect. It was followed by signal proofs that the national spirit rises according to the pressure on it. The loss of an important post and of the brave men surrendered with it inspired everywhere new ardor and determination. In the States and districts least remote it was no sooner known than every citizen was ready to fly with his arms at once to protect his brethren against the bloodthirsty savages let loose by the enemy on an extensive frontier, and to convert a partial calamity into a source of invigorated efforts. This patriotic zeal, which it was necessary rather to limit than excite, has embodied an ample force from the States of Kentucky and Ohio and from parts of Pennsylvania and Virginia. It is placed, with the addition of a few regulars, under the command of Brigadier-General Harrison, who possesses the entire confidence of his fellow-soldiers, among whom are citizens, some of them volunteers in the ranks, not less distinguished by their political stations than by their personal merits. The greater portion of this force is proceeding on its destination toward the Michigan Territory, having succeeded in relieving an important frontier post, and in several incidental operations against hostile tribes of savages, rendered indispensable by the subserviency into which they had been seduced by the enemy—a seduction the more cruel as it could not fail to impose a necessity of precautionary severities against those who yielded to it.

At a recent date an attack was made on a post of the enemy near Niagara by a detachment of the regular and other forces under the command of Major-General Van Rensselaer, of the militia of the State of New York. The attack, it appears, was ordered in compliance with the ardor of the troops, who executed it with distinguished gallantry, and were for a time victorious; but not receiving the expected support, they were compelled to yield to reenforcements of British regulars and savages. Our loss has been considerable, and is deeply to be lamented. That of the enemy, less ascertained, will be the more felt, as it includes among the killed the commanding general, who was also the governor of the Province, and was sustained by veteran troops from unexperienced soldiers, who must daily improve in the duties of the field.

Our expectation of gaining the command of the Lakes by the invasion of Canada from Detroit having been disappointed, measures were instantly taken to provide on them a naval force superior to that of the enemy. From the talents and activity of the officer charged with this object everything that can be done may be expected. Should the present season not admit of complete success, the progress made will insure for the next a naval ascendency where it is essential to our permanent peace with and control over the savages.

Among the incidents to the measures of the war I am constrained to advert to the refusal of the governors of Massachusetts and Connecticut to furnish the required detachments of militia toward the defense of the maritime frontier. The refusal was founded on a novel and unfortunate exposition of the provisions of the Constitution relating to the militia. The correspondences which will be laid before you contain the requisite information on the subject. It is obvious that if the authority of the United States to call into service and command the militia for the public defense can be thus frustrated, even in a state of declared war and of course under apprehensions of invasion preceding war, they are not one nation for the purpose most of all requiring it, and that the public safety may have no other resource than in those large and permanent military establishments which are forbidden by the principles of our free government, and against the necessity of which the militia were meant to be a constitutional bulwark.

On the coasts and on the ocean the war has been as successful as circumstances inseparable from its early stages could promise. Our public ships and private cruisers, by their activity, and, where there was occasion, by their intrepidity, have made the enemy sensible of the difference between a reciprocity of captures and the long confinement of them to their side. Our trade, with little exception, has safely reached our ports, having been much favored in it by the course pursued by a squadron of our frigates under the command of Commodore Rodgers, and in the instance in which skill and bravery were more particularly tried with those of the enemy the American flag had an auspicious triumph. The frigate *Constitution*, commanded by Captain Hull, after a close and short engagement completely disabled and captured a British frigate, gaining for that officer and all on board a praise which can not be too liberally bestowed, not merely for the victory actually achieved, but for that prompt and cool exertion of commanding talents which, giving to courage its highest character, and to the force applied its full effect, proved that more could have been done in a contest requiring more.

Anxious to abridge the evils from which a state of war can not be exempt, I lost no time after it was declared in conveying to the British Government the terms on which its progress might be arrested, without awaiting the delays of a formal and final pacification, and our chargé d'affaires at London was at the same time authorized to agree to an armistice founded upon them. These terms required that the orders in council should be repealed as they affected the United States, without a revival of blockades violating acknowledged rules, and that there should be an immediate discharge of American seamen from British ships, and a stop to impressment from American ships, with an understanding that an exclusion of the seamen of each nation from the ships of the other should be stipulated, and that the armistice should be improved into a definitive and comprehensive adjustment of depending controversies. Although a repeal of the orders susceptible of explanations meeting the views of this Government had taken place before this pacific advance was communicated to that of Great Britain, the advance was declined from an avowed repugnance to a suspension of the practice of impressments during the armistice, and without any intimation that the arrangement proposed with respect to seamen would be accepted. Whether the subsequent communications from this Government, affording an occasion for reconsidering the subject on the part of Great Britain, will be viewed in a more favorable light or received in a more accommodating spirit remains to be known. It would be unwise to relax our measures in any respect on a presumption of such a result.

The documents from the Department of State which relate to this subject will give a view also of the propositions for an armistice which have been received here, one of them from the authorities at Halifax and in Canada, the other from the British Government itself through Admiral Warren, and of the grounds on which neither of them could be accepted.

Our affairs with France retain the posture which they held at my last communications to you. Notwithstanding the authorized expectations of an early as well as favorable issue to the discussions on foot, these have been procrastinated to the latest date. The only intervening occurrence meriting attention is the promulgation of a French decree purporting to be a definitive repeal of the Berlin and Milan decrees. This proceeding, although made the ground of the repeal of the British orders in council, is rendered by the time and manner of it liable to many objections.

The final communications from our special minister to Denmark afford further proofs of the good effects of his mission, and of the amicable disposition of the Danish Government. From Russia we have the satisfaction to receive assurances of continued friendship, and that it will not be affected by the rupture between the United States and Great Britain. Sweden also professes sentiments favorable to the subsisting harmony.

With the Barbary Powers, excepting that of Algiers, our affairs remain on the ordinary footing. The consul-general residing with that Regency has suddenly and without cause been banished, together with all the American citizens found there. Whether this was the transitory effect of capricious despotism or the first act of predetermined hostility is not ascertained. Precautions were taken by the consul on the latter supposition.

The Indian tribes not under foreign instigations remain at peace, and receive the civilizing attentions which have proved so beneficial to them.

With a view to that vigorous prosecution of the war to which our national faculties are adequate, the attention of Congress will be particularly drawn to the insufficiency of existing provisions for filling up the military establishment. Such is the happy condition of our country, arising from the facility of subsistence and the high wages for every species of occupation, that notwithstanding the augmented inducements provided at the last session, a partial success only has attended the recruiting service. The deficiency has been necessarily supplied during the campaign by other than regular troops, with all the inconveniences and expense incident to them. The remedy lies in establishing more favorably for the private soldier the proportion between his recompense and the term of his enlistment, and it is a subject which can not too soon or too seriously be taken into consideration.

The same insufficiency has been experienced in the provisions for volunteers made by an act of the last session. The recompense for the service required in this case is still less attractive than in the other, and although patriotism alone has sent into the field some valuable corps of that description, those alone who can afford the sacrifice can be reasonably expected to yield to that impulse.

It will merit consideration also whether as auxiliary to the security of our frontiers corps may not be advantageously organized with a restriction of their services to particular districts convenient to them, and whether the local and occasional services of mariners and others in the seaport towns under a similar organization would not be a provident addition to the means of their defense.

I recommend a provision for an increase of the general officers of the Army, the deficiency of which has been illustrated by the number and distance of separate commands which the course of the war and the advantage of the service have required.

And I can not press too strongly on the earliest attention of the Legislature the importance of the reorganization of the staff establishment with a view to render more distinct and definite the relations and responsibilities of its several departments. That there is room for improvements which will materially promote both economy and success in what appertains to the Army and the war is equally inculcated by the examples of other countries and by the experience of our own.

A revision of the militia laws for the purpose of rendering them more systematic and better adapting them to emergencies of the war is at this time particularly desirable.

Of the additional ships authorized to be fitted for service, two will be shortly ready to sail, a third is under repair, and delay will be avoided in the repair of the residue. Of the appropriations for the purchase of materials for shipbuilding, the greater part has been applied to that object and the purchase will be continued with the balance.

The enterprising spirit which has characterized our naval force and its success, both in restraining insults and depredations on our coasts and in reprisals on the enemy, will not fail to recommend an enlargement of it.

There being reason to believe that the act prohibiting the acceptance of British licenses is not a sufficient guard against the use of them, for purposes favorable to the interests and views of the enemy, further provisions on that subject are highly important. Nor is it less so that penal enactments should be provided for cases of corrupt and perfidious intercourse with the enemy, not amounting to treason nor yet embraced by any statutory provisions.

A considerable number of American vessels which were in England when the revocation of the orders in council took place were laden with British manufactures under an erroneous impression that the nonimportation act would immediately cease to operate, and have arrived in the United States. It did not appear proper to exercise on unforeseen cases of such magnitude the ordinary powers vested in the Treasury Department to mitigate forfeitures without previously affording to Congress an opportunity of making on the subject such provision as they may think proper. In their decision they will doubtless equally consult what is due to equitable considerations and to the public interest.

The receipts into the Treasury during the year ending on the 30th of September last have exceeded $16,500,000, which have been sufficient to defray all the demands on the Treasury to that day, including a necessary reimbursement of near three millions of the principal of the public debt. In these receipts is included a sum of near $5,850,000, received on account of the loans authorized by the acts of the last session; the whole sum actually obtained on loan amounts to $11,000,000, the residue of which, being receivable subsequent to the 30th of September last, will, together with the current revenue, enable us to defray all the expenses of this year.

The duties on the late unexpected importations of British manufactures will render the revenue of the ensuing year more productive than could have been anticipated.

The situation of our country, fellow-citizens, is not without its difficulties, though it abounds in animating considerations, of which the view here presented of our pecuniary resources is an example. With more than one nation we have serious and unsettled controversies, and with one, powerful in the means and habits of war, we are at war. The spirit and strength of the nation are nevertheless equal to the support of all its rights, and to carry it through all its trials. They can be met in that confidence. Above all, we have the inestimable consolation of knowing that the war in which we are actually engaged is a war neither of ambition nor of vainglory; that it is waged not in violation of the rights of others, but in the maintenance of our own; that it was preceded by a patience without example under wrongs accumulating without end, and that it was finally not declared until every hope of averting it was extinguished by the transfer of the British scepter into new hands clinging to former councils, and until declarations were reiterated to the last hour, through the British envoy here, that the hostile edicts against our commercial rights and our maritime independence would not be revoked; nay, that they could not be revoked without violating the obligations of

Great Britain to other powers, as well as to her own interests. To have shrunk under such circumstances from manly resistance would have been a degradation blasting our best and proudest hopes; it would have struck us from the high rank where the virtuous struggles of our fathers had placed us, and have betrayed the magnificent legacy which we hold in trust for future generations. It would have acknowledged that on the element which forms three-fourths of the globe we inhabit, and where all independent nations have equal and common rights, the American people were not an independent people, but colonists and vassals. It was at this moment and with such an alternative that war was chosen. The nation felt the necessity of it, and called for it. The appeal was accordingly made, in a just cause, to the Just and All-powerful Being who holds in His hand the chain of events and the destiny of nations. It remains only that, faithful to ourselves, entangled in no connections with the views of other powers, and ever ready to accept peace from the hand of justice, we prosecute the war with united counsels and with the ample faculties of the nation until peace be so obtained and as the only means under the Divine blessing of speedily obtaining it.

FIFTH ANNUAL MESSAGE.

WASHINGTON, *December 7, 1813.*

Fellow-Citizens of the Senate and of the House of Representatives:

In meeting you at the present interesting conjuncture it would have been highly satisfactory if I could have communicated a favorable result to the mission charged with negotiations for restoring peace. It was a just expectation, from the respect due to the distinguished Sovereign who had invited them by his offer of mediation, from the readiness with which the invitation was accepted on the part of the United States, and from the pledge to be found in an act of their Legislature for the liberality which their plenipotentiaries would carry into the negotiations, that no time would be lost by the British Government in embracing the experiment for hastening a stop to the effusion of blood. A prompt and cordial acceptance of the mediation on that side was the less to be doubted, as it was of a nature not to submit rights or pretensions on either side to the decision of an umpire, but to afford merely an opportunity, honorable and desirable to both, for discussing and, if possible, adjusting them for the interest of both.

The British cabinet, either mistaking our desire of peace for a dread of British power or misled by other fallacious calculations, has disappointed this reasonable anticipation. No communications from our envoys having reached us, no information on the subject has been received from that source; but it is known that the mediation was declined in the first instance, and there is no evidence, notwithstanding the lapse of time, that a change of disposition in the British councils has taken place or is to be expected.

Under such circumstances a nation proud of its rights and conscious of its strength has no choice but an exertion of the one in support of the other.

To this determination the best encouragement is derived from the success with which it has pleased the Almighty to bless our arms both on the land and on the water.

Whilst proofs have been continued of the enterprise and skill of our cruisers, public and private, on the ocean, and a new trophy gained in the capture of a British by an American vessel of war, after an action giving celebrity to the name of the victorious commander, the great inland waters on which the enemy were also to be encountered have presented achievements of our naval arms as brilliant in their character as they have been important in their consequences.

On Lake Erie, the squadron under command of Captain Perry having met the British squadron of superior force, a sanguinary conflict ended in the capture of the whole. The conduct of that officer, adroit as it was daring, and which was so well seconded by his comrades, justly entitles them to the admiration and gratitude of their country, and will fill an early page in its naval annals with a victory never surpassed in luster, however much it may have been in magnitude.

On Lake Ontario the caution of the British commander, favored by contingencies, frustrated the efforts of the American commander to bring on a decisive action. Captain Chauncey was able, however, to establish an ascendency on that important theater, and to prove by the manner in which he effected everything possible that opportunities only were wanted for a more shining display of his own talents and the gallantry of those under his command.

The success on Lake Erie having opened a passage to the territory of the enemy, the officer commanding the Northwestern army transferred the war thither, and rapidly pursuing the hostile troops, fleeing with their savage associates, forced a general action, which quickly terminated in the capture of the British and dispersion of the savage force.

This result is signally honorable to Major-General Harrison, by whose military talents it was prepared; to Colonel Johnson and his mounted volunteers, whose impetuous onset gave a decisive blow to the ranks of the enemy, and to the spirit of the volunteer militia, equally brave and patriotic, who bore an interesting part in the scene; more especially to the chief magistrate of Kentucky, at the head of them, whose heroism signalized in the war which established the independence of his country, sought at an advanced age a share in hardships and battles for maintaining its rights and its safety.

The effect of these successes has been to rescue the inhabitants of Michigan from their oppressions, aggravated by gross infractions of the capitulation which subjected them to a foreign power; to alienate the savages of numerous tribes from the enemy, by whom they were disappointed and abandoned, and to relieve an extensive region of country from a merciless warfare which desolated its frontiers and imposed on its citizens the most harassing services.

In consequence of our naval superiority on Lake Ontario and the opportunity afforded by it for concentrating our forces by water, operations which had been provisionally planned were set on foot against the possessions of the enemy on the St. Lawrence. Such, however, was the delay produced in the first instance by adverse weather of unusual violence and continuance and such the circumstances attending the final movements of the army, that the prospect, at one time so favorable, was not realized.

The cruelty of the enemy in enlisting the savages into a war with a nation desirous of mutual emulation in mitigating its calamities has not been confined to any one quarter. Wherever they could be turned against us no exertions to effect it have been spared. On our southwestern border the Creek tribes, who, yielding to our persevering endeavors, were gradually acquiring more civilized habits, became the unfortunate victims of seduction. A war in that quarter has been the consequence, infuriated by a bloody fanaticism recently propagated among them. It was necessary to crush such a war before it could spread among the contiguous tribes and before it could favor enterprises of the enemy into that vicinity. With this view a force was called into the service of the United States from the States of Georgia and Tennessee, which, with the nearest regular troops and other corps from the Mississippi Territory, might not only chastise the savages into present peace but make a lasting impression on their fears.

The progress of the expedition, as far as is yet known, corresponds with the martial zeal with which it was espoused, and the best hopes of a satisfactory issue are authorized by the complete success with which a well-planned enterprise was executed against a body of hostile savages by a detachment of the volunteer militia of Tennessee, under the gallant command of General Coffee, and by a still more important victory over a larger body of them, gained under the immediate command of Major-General Jackson, an officer equally distinguished for his patriotism and his military talents.

The systematic perseverance of the enemy in courting the aid of the savages in all quarters had the natural effect of kindling their ordinary propensity to war into a passion, which, even among those best disposed toward the United States, was ready, if not employed on our side, to be turned against us. A departure from our protracted forbearance to accept the services tendered by them has thus been forced upon us. But in yielding to it the retaliation has been mitigated as much as possible, both in its extent and in its character, stopping far short of the example of the enemy, who owe the advantages they have occasionally gained in battle chiefly to the number of their savage associates, and who have not controlled them either from their usual practice of indiscriminate massacre on defenseless inhabitants or from scenes of carnage without a parallel on prisoners to the British arms, guarded by all the laws of humanity and of honorable war. For these enormities the enemy are equally responsible, whether with the power to prevent them they want the will or with the knowledge of a want of power they still avail themselves of such instruments.

In other respects the enemy are pursuing a course which threatens consequences most afflicting to humanity.

A standing law of Great Britain naturalizes, as is well known, all aliens complying with conditions limited to a shorter period than those required by the United States, and naturalized subjects are in war employed by her Government in common with native subjects. In a contiguous British Province regulations promulgated since the commencement of the war compel citizens of the United States being there under certain circumstances to bear arms, whilst of the native emigrants from the United States, who compose much of the population of the Province, a number have actually borne arms against the United States within their limits, some of whom, after having done so, have become prisoners of war, and are now in our possession. The British commander in that Province, nevertheless, with the sanction, as appears, of his Government, thought proper to select from American prisoners of war and send to Great Britain for trial as criminals a number of individuals who had emigrated from the British dominions long prior to the state of war between the two nations, who had incorporated themselves into our political society in the modes recognized by the law and the practice of Great Britain, and who were made prisoners of war under the banners of their adopted country, fighting for its rights and its safety.

The protection due to these citizens requiring an effectual interposition in their behalf, a like number of British prisoners of war were put into confinement, with a notification that they would experience whatever violence might be committed on the American prisoners of war sent to Great Britain.

It was hoped that this necessary consequence of the step unadvisedly taken on the part of Great Britain would have led her Government to reflect on the inconsistencies of its conduct, and that a sympathy with the British, if not with the American, sufferers would have arrested the cruel career opened by its example.

This was unhappily not the case.   In violation both of consistency and of humanity, American officers and noncommissioned officers in double the number of the British soldiers confined here were ordered into close confinement, with formal notice that in the event of a retaliation for the death which might be inflicted on the prisoners of war sent to Great Britain for trial the officers so confined would be put to death also.   It was notified at the same time that the commanders of the British fleets and armies on our coasts are instructed in the same event to proceed with a destructive severity against our towns and their inhabitants.

That no doubt might be left with the enemy of our adherence to the retaliatory resort imposed on us, a correspondent number of British officers, prisoners of war in our hands, were immediately put into close confinement to abide the fate of those confined by the enemy, and the British Government has been apprised of the determination of this Government to retaliate any other proceedings against us contrary to the legitimate modes of warfare.

It is as fortunate for the United States that they have it in their power to meet the enemy in this deplorable contest as it is honorable to them that they do not join in it but under the most imperious obligations, and with the humane purpose of effectuating a return to the established usages of war.

The views of the French Government on the subjects which have been so long committed to negotiation have received no elucidation since the close of your late session.   The minister plenipotentiary of the United States at Paris had not been enabled by proper opportunities to press the objects of his mission as prescribed by his instructions.

The militia being always to be regarded as the great bulwark of defense and security for free states, and the Constitution having wisely committed to the national authority a use of that force as the best provision against an unsafe military establishment, as well as a resource peculiarly adapted to a country having the extent and the exposure of the United States, I recommend to Congress a revision of the militia laws for the purpose of securing more effectually the services of all detachments called into the employment and placed under the Government of the United States.

It will deserve the consideration of Congress also whether among other improvements in the militia laws justice does not require a regulation, under due precautions, for defraying the expense incident to the first assembling as well as the subsequent movements of detachments called into the national service.

To give to our vessels of war, public and private, the requisite advantage in their cruises, it is of much importance that they should have, both for themselves and their prizes, the use of the ports and markets of friendly powers.   With this view, I recommend to Congress the expediency of such legal provisions as may supply the defects or remove the doubts of the Executive authority, to allow to the cruisers of other powers at war with enemies of the United States such use of the American ports as may correspond with the privileges allowed by such powers to American cruisers.

During the year ending on the 30th of September last the receipts into the Treasury have exceeded $37,500,000, of which near twenty-four millions were the produce of loans. After meeting all demands for the public service there remained in the Treasury on that day near $7,000,000. Under the authority contained in the act of the 2d of August last for borrowing $7,500,000, that sum has been obtained on terms more favorable to the United States than those of the preceding loan made during the present year. Further sums to a considerable amount will be necessary to be obtained in the same way during the ensuing year, and from the increased capital of the country, from the fidelity with which the public engagements have been kept and the public credit maintained, it may be expected on good grounds that the necessary pecuniary supplies will not be wanting.

The expenses of the current year, from the multiplied operations falling within it, have necessarily been extensive; but on a just estimate of the campaign in which the mass of them has been incurred the cost will not be found disproportionate to the advantages which have been gained. The campaign has, indeed, in its latter stages in one quarter been less favorable than was expected, but in addition to the importance of our naval success the progress of the campaign has been filled with incidents highly honorable to the American arms.

The attacks of the enemy on Craney Island, on Fort Meigs, on Sacketts Harbor, and on Sandusky have been vigorously and successfully repulsed; nor have they in any case succeeded on either frontier excepting when directed against the peaceable dwellings of individuals or villages unprepared or undefended.

On the other hand, the movements of the American Army have been followed by the reduction of York, and of Forts George, Erie, and Malden; by the recovery of Detroit and the extinction of the Indian war in the West, and by the occupancy or command of a large portion of Upper Canada. Battles have also been fought on the borders of the St. Lawrence, which, though not accomplishing their entire objects, reflect honor on the discipline and prowess of our soldiery, the best auguries of eventual victory. In the same scale are to be placed the late successes in the South over one of the most powerful, which had become one of the most hostile also, of the Indian tribes.

It would be improper to close this communication without expressing a thankfulness in which all ought to unite for the numerous blessings with which our beloved country continues to be favored; for the abundance which overspreads our land, and the prevailing health of its inhabitants; for the preservation of our internal tranquillity, and the stability

of our free institutions, and, above all, for the light of divine truth and
the protection of every man's conscience in 'the enjoyment of it.   And
although among our blessings we can not number an exemption from the
evils of war, yet these will never be regarded as the greatest of evils by
the friends of liberty and of the rights of nations.   Our country has before
preferred them to the degraded condition which was the alternative when
the sword was drawn in the cause which gave birth to our national independence, and none who contemplate the magnitude and feel the value
of that glorious event will shrink from a struggle to maintain the high
and happy ground on which it placed the American people.

With all good citizens the justice and necessity of resisting wrongs
and usurpations no longer to be borne will sufficiently outweigh the
privations and sacrifices inseparable from a state of war.   But it is a
reflection, moreover, peculiarly consoling, that, whilst wars are generally
aggravated by their baneful effects on the internal improvements and
permanent prosperity of the nations engaged in them, such is the favored
situation of the United States that the calamities of the contest into
which they have been compelled to enter are mitigated by improvements
and advantages of which the contest itself is the source.

If the war has increased the interruptions of our commerce, it has at
the same time cherished and multiplied our manufactures so as to make
us independent of all other countries for the more essential branches for
which we ought to be dependent on none, and is even rapidly giving
them an extent which will create additional staples in our future intercourse with foreign markets.

If much treasure has been expended, no inconsiderable portion of it
has been applied to objects durable in their value and necessary to our
permanent safety.

If the war has exposed us to increased spoliations on the ocean and to
predatory incursions on the land, it has developed the national means of
retaliating the former and of providing protection against the latter,
demonstrating to all that every blow aimed at our maritime independence
is an impulse accelerating the growth of our maritime power.

By diffusing through the mass of the nation the elements of military
discipline and instruction; by augmenting and distributing warlike preparations applicable to future use; by evincing the zeal and valor with
which they will be employed and the cheerfulness with which every
necessary burden will be borne, a greater respect for our rights and a
longer duration of our future peace are promised than could be expected
without these proofs of the national character and resources.

The war has proved moreover that our free Government, like other
free governments, though slow in its early movements, acquires in its
progress a force proportioned to its freedom, and that the union of these
States, the guardian of the freedom and safety of all and of each, is
strengthened by every occasion that puts it to the test.

In fine, the war, with all its vicissitudes, is illustrating the capacity and the destiny of the United States to be a great, a flourishing, and a powerful nation, worthy of the friendship which it is disposed to cultivate with all others, and authorized by its own example to require from all an observance of the laws of justice and reciprocity. Beyond these their claims have never extended, and in contending for these we behold a subject for our congratulations in the daily testimonies of increasing harmony throughout the nation, and may humbly repose our trust in the smiles of Heaven on so righteous a cause.

SIXTH ANNUAL MESSAGE.

WASHINGTON, *September 20, 1814.*
Fellow-Citizens of the Senate and of the House of Representatives:

Notwithstanding the early day which had been fixed for your session of the present year, I was induced to call you together still sooner, as well that any inadequacy in the existing provisions for the wants of the Treasury might be supplied as that no delay might happen in providing for the result of the negotiations on foot with Great Britain, whether it should require arrangements adapted to a return of peace or further and more effective provisions for prosecuting the war.

That result is not yet known. If, on the one hand, the repeal of the orders in council and the general pacification in Europe, which withdrew the occasion on which impressments from American vessels were practiced, suggest expectations that peace and amity may be reestablished, we are compelled, on the other hand, by the refusal of the British Government to accept the offered mediation of the Emperor of Russia, by the delays in giving effect to its own proposal of a direct negotiation, and, above all, by the principles and manner in which the war is now avowedly carried on to infer that a spirit of hostility is indulged more violent than ever against the rights and prosperity of this country.

This increased violence is best explained by the two important circumstances that the great contest in Europe for an equilibrium guaranteeing all its States against the ambition of any has been closed without any check on the overbearing power of Great Britain on the ocean, and it has left in her hands disposable armaments, with which, forgetting the difficulties of a remote war with a free people, and yielding to the intoxication of success, with the example of a great victim to it before her eyes, she cherishes hopes of still further aggrandizing a power already formidable in its abuses to the tranquillity of the civilized and commercial world.

But whatever may have inspired the enemy with these more violent purposes, the public councils of a nation more able to maintain than it was to acquire its independence, and with a devotion to it rendered more ardent by the experience of its blessings, can never deliberate but on the means most effectual for defeating the extravagant views or unwarrantable passions with which alone the war can now be pursued against us.

In the events of the present campaign the enemy, with all his augmented means and wanton use of them, has little ground for exultation, unless he can feel it in the success of his recent enterprises against this metropolis and the neighboring town of Alexandria, from both of which his retreats were as precipitate as his attempts were bold and fortunate. In his other incursions on our Atlantic frontier his progress, often checked and chastised by the martial spirit of the neighboring citizens, has had more effect in distressing individuals and in dishonoring his arms than in promoting any object of legitimate warfare; and in the two instances mentioned, however deeply to be regretted on our part, he will find in his transient success, which interrupted for a moment only the ordinary public business at the seat of Government, no compensation for the loss of character with the world by his violations of private property and by his destruction of public edifices protected as monuments of the arts by the laws of civilized warfare.

On our side we can appeal to a series of achievements which have given new luster to the American arms. Besides the brilliant incidents in the minor operations of the campaign, the splendid victories gained on the Canadian side of the Niagara by the American forces under Major-General Brown and Brigadiers Scott and Gaines have gained for these heroes and their emulating companions the most unfading laurels, and, having triumphantly tested the progressive discipline of the American soldiery, have taught the enemy that the longer he protracts his hostile efforts the more certain and decisive will be his final discomfiture.

On our southern border victory has continued also to follow the American standard. The bold and skillful operations of Major-General Jackson, conducting troops drawn from the militia of the States least distant, particularly of Tennessee, have subdued the principal tribes of hostile savages, and, by establishing a peace with them, preceded by recent and exemplary chastisement, has best guarded against the mischief of their cooperation with the British enterprises which may be planned against that quarter of our country. Important tribes of Indians on our northwestern frontier have also acceded to stipulations which bind them to the interests of the United States and to consider our enemy as theirs also.

In the recent attempt of the enemy on the city of Baltimore, defended by militia and volunteers, aided by a small body of regulars and seamen, he was received with a spirit which produced a rapid retreat to his ships, whilst a concurrent attack by a large fleet was successfully resisted by the steady and well-directed fire of the fort and batteries opposed to it.

In another recent attack by a powerful force on our troops at Plattsburg, of which regulars made a part only, the enemy, after a perseverance for many hours, was finally compelled to seek safety in a hasty retreat, with our gallant bands pressing upon him.

On the Lakes, so much contested throughout the war, the great exertions for the command made on our part have been well repaid. On Lake Ontario our squadron is now and has been for some time in a condition to confine that of the enemy to his own port, and to favor the operations of our land forces on that frontier.

A part of the squadron on Lake Erie has been extended into Lake Huron, and has produced the advantage of displaying our command on that lake also. One object of the expedition was the reduction of Mackinaw, which failed with the loss of a few brave men, among whom was an officer justly distinguished for his gallant exploits. The expedition, ably conducted by both the land and the naval commanders, was otherwise highly valuable in its effects.

On Lake Champlain, where our superiority had for some time been undisputed, the British squadron lately came into action with the American, commanded by Captain Macdonough. It issued in the capture of the whole of the enemy's ships. The best praise for this officer and his intrepid comrades is in the likeness of his triumph to the illustrious victory which immortalized another officer and established at a critical moment our command of another lake.

On the ocean the pride of our naval arms had been amply supported. A second frigate has indeed fallen into the hands of the enemy, but the loss is hidden in the blaze of heroism with which she was defended. Captain Porter, who commanded her, and whose previous career had been distinguished by daring enterprise and by fertility of genius, maintained a sanguinary contest against two ships, one of them superior to his own, and under other severe disadvantages, till humanity tore down the colors which valor had nailed to the mast. This officer and his brave comrades have added much to the rising glory of the American flag, and have merited all the effusions of gratitude which their country is ever ready to bestow on the champions of its rights and of its safety.

Two smaller vessels of war have also become prizes to the enemy, but by a superiority of force which sufficiently vindicates the reputation of their commanders, whilst two others, one commanded by Captain Warrington, the other by Captain Blakely, have captured British ships of the same class with a gallantry and good conduct which entitle them and their companions to a just share in the praise of their country.

In spite of the naval force of the enemy accumulated on our coasts, our private cruisers also have not ceased to annoy his commerce and to bring their rich prizes into our ports, contributing thus, with other proofs, to demonstrate the incompetency and illegality of a blockade the proclamation of which is made the pretext for vexing and discouraging the commerce of neutral powers with the United States.

To meet the extended and diversified warfare adopted by the enemy, great bodies of militia have been taken into service for the public defense, and great expenses incurred. That the defense everywhere may be both more convenient and more economical, Congress will see the necessity of immediate measures for filling the ranks of the Regular Army and of enlarging the provision for special corps, mounted and unmounted, to be engaged for longer periods of service than are due from the militia. I earnestly renew, at the same time, a recommendation of such changes in the system of the militia as, by classing and disciplining for the most prompt and active service the portions most capable of it, will give to that great resource for the public safety all the requisite energy and efficiency.

The moneys received into the Treasury during the nine months ending on the 30th day of June last amounted to $32,000,000, of which near eleven millions were the proceeds of the public revenue and the remainder derived from loans. The disbursements for public expenditures during the same period exceeded $34,000,000, and left in the Treasury on the 1st day of July near $5,000,000. The demands during the remainder of the present year already authorized by Congress and the expenses incident to an extension of the operations of the war will render it necessary that large sums should be provided to meet them.

From this view of the national affairs Congress will be urged to take up without delay as well the subject of pecuniary supplies as that of military force, and on a scale commensurate with the extent and the character which the war has assumed. It is not to be disguised that the situation of our country calls for its greatest efforts. Our enemy is powerful in men and in money, on the land and on the water. Availing himself of fortuitous advantages, he is aiming with his undivided force a deadly blow at our growing prosperity, perhaps at our national existence. He has avowed his purpose of trampling on the usages of civilized warfare, and given earnests of it in the plunder and wanton destruction of private property. In his pride of maritime dominion and in his thirst of commercial monopoly he strikes with peculiar animosity at the progress of our navigation and of our manufactures. His barbarous policy has not even spared those monuments of the arts and models of taste with which our country had enriched and embellished its infant metropolis. From such an adversary hostility in its greatest force and in its worst forms may be looked for. The American people will face it with the undaunted spirit which in their revolutionary struggle defeated his unrighteous projects. His threats and his barbarities, instead of dismay, will kindle in every bosom an indignation not to be extinguished but in the disaster and expulsion of such cruel invaders. In providing the means necessary the National Legislature will not distrust the heroic and enlightened patriotism of its constituents. They will cheerfully and proudly bear every burden of every kind which the safety and honor of the nation demand. We have seen them everywhere paying their taxes, direct and indirect, with the greatest promptness and alacrity. We see them rushing with enthusiasm to the scenes where danger and duty call. In offering their blood they give the surest pledge that no other tribute will be withheld.

Having forborne to declare war until to other aggressions had been added the capture of nearly a thousand American vessels and the impressment of thousands of American seafaring citizens, and until a final declaration had been made by the Government of Great Britain that her hostile orders against our commerce would not be revoked but on conditions as impossible as unjust, whilst it was known that these orders would not otherwise cease but with a war which had lasted nearly twenty years, and which, according to appearances at that time, might last as many more; having manifested on every occasion and in every proper mode a sincere desire to arrest the effusion of blood and meet our enemy on the ground of justice and reconciliation, our beloved country, in still opposing to his persevering hostility all its energies, with an undiminished disposition toward peace and friendship on honorable terms, must carry with it the good wishes of the impartial world and the best hopes of support from an omnipotent and kind Providence.

SEVENTH ANNUAL MESSAGE.

WASHINGTON, *December 5, 1815.*

Fellow-Citizens of the Senate and of the House of Representatives:

I have the satisfaction on our present meeting of being able to communicate to you the successful termination of the war which had been commenced against the United States by the Regency of Algiers. The squadron in advance on that service, under Commodore Decatur, lost not a moment after its arrival in the Mediterranean in seeking the naval force of the enemy then cruising in that sea, and succeeded in capturing two of his ships, one of them the principal ship, commanded by the Algerine admiral. The high character of the American commander was brilliantly sustained on the occasion which brought his own ship into close action with that of his adversary, as was the accustomed gallantry of all the officers and men actually engaged.   Having prepared the way by this demonstration of American skill and prowess, he hastened to the port of Algiers, where peace was promptly yielded to his victorious force. In the terms stipulated the rights and honor of the United States were particularly consulted by a perpetual relinquishment on the part of the Dey of all pretensions to tribute from them.   The impressions which have thus been made, strengthened as they will have been by subsequent transactions with the Regencies of Tunis and of Tripoli by the appearance of the larger force which followed under Commodore Bainbridge, the chief in command of the expedition, and by the judicious precautionary arrangements left by him in that quarter, afford a reasonable prospect of future security for the valuable portion of our commerce which passes within reach of the Barbary cruisers.

It is another source of satisfaction that the treaty of peace with Great Britain has been succeeded by a convention on the subject of commerce concluded by the plenipotentiaries of the two countries.   In this result a disposition is manifested on the part of that nation corresponding with the disposition of the United States, which it may be hoped will be improved into liberal arrangements on other subjects on which the parties have mutual interests, or which might endanger their future harmony. Congress will decide on the expediency of promoting such a sequel by giving effect to the measure of confining the American navigation to American seamen—a measure which, at the same time that it might have that conciliatory tendency, would have the further advantage of increasing the independence of our navigation and the resources for our maritime defense.

In conformity with the articles in the treaty of Ghent relating to the Indians, as well as with a view to the tranquillity of our western and northwestern frontiers, measures were taken to establish an immediate peace with the several tribes who had been engaged in hostilities against the United States.   Such of them as were invited to Detroit acceded readily to a renewal of the former treaties of friendship.   Of the other tribes who were invited to a station on the Mississippi the greater number have also accepted the peace offered to them.   The residue, consisting of the more distant tribes or parts of tribes, remain to be brought over by further explanations, or by such other means as may be adapted to the dispositions they may finally disclose.

The Indian tribes within and bordering on the southern frontier, whom a cruel war on their part had compelled us to chastise into peace, have latterly shown a restlessness which has called for preparatory measures for repressing it, and for protecting the commissioners engaged in carrying the terms of the peace into execution.

The execution of the act for fixing the military peace establishment has been attended with difficulties which even now can only be overcome by legislative aid.   The selection of officers, the payment and discharge of the troops enlisted for the war, the payment of the retained troops and their reunion from detached and distant stations, the collection and security of the public property in the Quartermaster, Commissary, and Ordnance departments, and the constant medical assistance required in hospitals and garrisons rendered a complete execution of the act impracticable on the 1st of May, the period more immediately contemplated. As soon, however, as circumstances would permit, and as far as it has been practicable consistently with the public interests, the reduction of the Army has been accomplished; but the appropriations for its pay and for other branches of the military service having proved inadequate, the earliest attention to that subject will be necessary; and the expediency of continuing upon the peace establishment the staff officers who have hitherto been provisionally retained is also recommended to the consideration of Congress.

In the performance of the Executive duty upon this occasion there has not been wanting a just sensibility to the merits of the American Army during the late war; but the obvious policy and design in fixing an efficient military peace establishment did not afford an opportunity to distinguish the aged and infirm on account of their past services nor the wounded and disabled on account of their present sufferings. The extent of the reduction, indeed, unavoidably involved the exclusion of many meritorious officers of every rank from the service of their country; and so equal as well as so numerous were the claims to attention that a decision by the standard of comparative merit could seldom be attained. Judged, however, in candor by a general standard of positive merit, the Army Register will, it is believed, do honor to the establishment, while the case of those officers whose names are not included in it devolves with the strongest interest upon the legislative authority for such provision as shall be deemed the best calculated to give support and solace to the veteran and the invalid, to display the beneficence as well as the justice of the Government, and to inspire a martial zeal for the public service upon every future emergency.

Although the embarrassments arising from the want of an uniform national currency have not been diminished since the adjournment of Congress, great satisfaction has been derived in contemplating the revival of the public credit and the efficiency of the public resources. The receipts into the Treasury from the various branches of revenue during the nine months ending on the 30th of September last have been estimated at $12,500,000; the issues of Treasury notes of every denomination during the same period amounted to the sum of $14,000,000, and there was also obtained upon loan during the same period a sum of $9,000,000, of which the sum of $6,000,000 was subscribed in cash and the sum of $3,000,000 in Treasury notes. With these means, added to the sum of $1,500,000, being the balance of money in the Treasury on the 1st day of January, there has been paid between the 1st of January and the 1st of October on account of the appropriations of the preceding and of the present year (exclusively of the amount of the Treasury notes subscribed to the loan and of the amount redeemed in the payment of duties and taxes) the aggregate sum of $33,500,000, leaving a balance then in the Treasury estimated at the sum of $3,000,000. Independent, however, of the arrearages due for military services and supplies, it is presumed that a further sum of $5,000,000, including the interest on the public debt payable on the 1st of January next, will be demanded at the Treasury to complete the expenditures of the present year, and for which the existing ways and means will sufficiently provide.

The national debt, as it was ascertained on the 1st of October last, amounted in the whole to the sum of $120,000,000, consisting of the unredeemed balance of the debt contracted before the late war ($39,000,000), the amount of the funded debt contracted in consequence of the war ($64,000,000), and the amount of the unfunded and floating debt, including the various issues of Treasury notes, $17,000,000, which is in a gradual course of payment. There will probably be some addition to the public debt upon the liquidation of various claims which are depending, and a conciliatory disposition on the part of Congress may lead honorably and advantageously to an equitable arrangement of the militia expenses incurred by the several States without the previous sanction or authority of the Government of the United States; but when it is considered that the new as well as the old portion of the debt has been contracted in the assertion of the national rights and independence, and when it is recollected that the public expenditures, not being exclusively bestowed upon subjects of a transient nature, will long be visible in the number and equipments of the American Navy, in the military works for the defense of our harbors and our frontiers, and in the supplies of our arsenals and magazines the amount will bear a gratifying comparison with the objects which have been attained, as well as with the resources of the country.

The arrangements of the finances with a view to the receipts and expenditures of a permanent peace establishment will necessarily enter into the deliberations of Congress during the present session. It is true that the improved condition of the public revenue will not only afford the means of maintaining the faith of the Government with its creditors inviolate, and of prosecuting successfully the measures of the most liberal policy, but will also justify an immediate alleviation of the burdens imposed by the necessities of the war. It is, however, essential to every modification of the finances that the benefits of an uniform national currency should be restored to the community. The absence of the precious metals will, it is believed, be a temporary evil, but until they can again be rendered the general medium of exchange it devolves on the wisdom of Congress to provide a substitute which shall equally engage the confidence and accommodate the wants of the citizens throughout the Union. If the operation of the State banks can not produce this result, the probable operation of a national bank will merit consideration; and if neither of these expedients be deemed effectual it may become necessary to ascertain the terms upon which the notes of the Government (no longer required as an instrument of credit) shall be issued upon motives of general policy as a common medium of circulation.

Notwithstanding the security for future repose which the United States ought to find in their love of peace and their constant respect for the rights of other nations, the character of the times particularly inculcates the lesson that, whether to prevent or repel danger, we ought not to be unprepared for it. This consideration will sufficiently recommend to Congress a liberal provision for the immediate extension and gradual completion of the works of defense, both fixed and floating, on our maritime frontier, and an adequate provision for guarding our inland frontier against dangers to which certain portions of it may continue to be exposed.

As an improvement in our military establishment, it will deserve the consideration of Congress whether a corps of invalids might not be so organized and employed as at once to aid in the support of meritorious individuals excluded by age or infirmities from the existing establishment, and to procure to the public the benefit of their stationary services and of their exemplary discipline. I recommend also an enlargement of the Military Academy already established, and the establishment of others in other sections of the Union; and I can not press too much on the attention of Congress such a classification and organization of the militia as will most effectually render it the safeguard of a free state. If experience has shewn in the recent splendid achievements of militia the value of this resource for the public defense, it has shewn also the importance of that skill in the use of arms and that familiarity with the essential rules of discipline which can not be expected from the regulations now in force. With this subject is intimately connected the necessity of accommodating the laws in every respect to the great object of enabling the political authority of the Union to employ promptly and effectually the physical power of the Union in the cases designated by the Constitution.

The signal services which have been rendered by our Navy and the capacities it has developed for successful cooperation in the national defense will give to that portion of the public force its full value in the eyes of Congress, at an epoch which calls for the constant vigilance of all governments. To preserve the ships now in a sound state, to complete those already contemplated, to provide amply the imperishable materials for prompt augmentations, and to improve the existing arrangements into more advantageous establishments for the construction, the repairs, and the security of vessels of war is dictated by the soundest policy.

In adjusting the duties on imports to the object of revenue the influence of the tariff on manufactures will necessarily present itself for consideration. However wise the theory may be which leaves to the sagacity and interest of individuals the application of their industry and resources, there are in this as in other cases exceptions to the general rule. Besides the condition which the theory itself implies of a reciprocal adoption by other nations, experience teaches that so many circumstances must concur in introducing and maturing manufacturing establishments, especially of the more complicated kinds, that a country may remain long without them, although sufficiently advanced and in some respects even peculiarly fitted for carrying them on with success. Under circumstances giving a powerful impulse to manufacturing industry it has made among us a progress and exhibited an efficiency which justify the belief that with a protection not more than is due to the enterprising citizens whose interests are now at stake it will become at an early day not only safe against occasional competitions from abroad, but a source of domestic wealth and even of external commerce. In selecting the branches more especially entitled to the public patronage a preference is obviously claimed by such as will relieve the United States from a dependence on foreign supplies, ever subject to casual failures, for articles necessary for the public defense or connected with the primary wants of individuals. It will be an additional recommendation of particular manufactures where the materials for them are extensively drawn from our agriculture, and consequently impart and insure to that great fund of national prosperity and independence an encouragement which can not fail to be rewarded.

Among the means of advancing the public interest the occasion is a proper one for recalling the attention of Congress to the great importance of establishing throughout our country the roads and canals which can best be executed under the national authority. No objects within the circle of political economy so richly repay the expense bestowed on them; there are none the utility of which is more universally ascertained and acknowledged; none that do more honor to the governments whose wise and enlarged patriotism duly appreciates them. Nor is there any country which presents a field where nature invites more the art of man to complete her own work for his accommodation and benefit. These considerations are strengthened, moreover, by the political effect of these facilities for intercommunication in bringing and binding more closely together the various parts of our extended confederacy. Whilst the States individually, with a laudable enterprise and emulation, avail themselves of their local advantages by new roads, by navigable canals, and by improving the streams susceptible of navigation, the General Government is the more urged to similar undertakings, requiring a national jurisdiction and national means, by the prospect of thus systematically completing so inestimable a work; and it is a happy reflection that any defect of constitutional authority which may be encountered can be supplied in a mode which the Constitution itself has providently pointed out.

The present is a favorable season also for bringing again into view the establishment of a national seminary of learning within the District of Columbia, and with means drawn from the property therein, subject to the authority of the General Government. Such an institution claims the patronage of Congress as a monument of their solicitude for the advancement of knowledge, without which the blessings of liberty can not be fully enjoyed or long preserved; as a model instructive in the formation of other seminaries; as a nursery of enlightened preceptors, and as a central resort of youth and genius from every part of their country, diffusing on their return examples of those national feelings, those liberal sentiments, and those congenial manners which contribute cement to our Union and strength to the great political fabric of which that is the foundation.

In closing this communication I ought not to repress a sensibility, in which you will unite, to the happy lot of our country and to the goodness of a superintending Providence, to which we are indebted for it. Whilst other portions of mankind are laboring under the distresses of war or struggling with adversity in other forms, the United States are in the tranquil enjoyment of prosperous and honorable peace. In reviewing the scenes through which it has been attained we can rejoice in the proofs given that our political institutions, founded in human rights and framed for their preservation, are equal to the severest trials of war, as well as adapted to the ordinary periods of repose. As fruits of this experience and of the reputation acquired by the American arms on the land and on the water, the nation finds itself possessed of a growing respect abroad and of a just confidence in itself, which are among the best pledges for its peaceful career. Under other aspects of our country the strongest features of its flourishing condition are seen in a population rapidly increasing on a territory as productive as it is extensive; in a general industry and fertile ingenuity which find their ample rewards, and in an affluent revenue which admits a reduction of the public burdens without withdrawing the means of sustaining the public credit, of gradually discharging the public debt, of providing for the necessary defensive and precautionary establishments, and of patronizing in every authorized mode undertakings conducive to the aggregate wealth and individual comfort of our citizens.

It remains for the guardians of the public welfare to persevere in that justice and good will toward other nations which invite a return of these sentiments toward the United States; to cherish institutions which guarantee their safety and their liberties, civil and religious; and to combine with a liberal system of foreign commerce an improvement of the national advantages and a protection and extension of the independent resources of our highly favored and happy country.

In all measures having such objects my faithful cooperation will be afforded.

EIGHTH ANNUAL MESSAGE.

DECEMBER 3, 1816.

Fellow-Citizens of the Senate and of the House of Representatives:

In reviewing the present state of our country, our attention can not be withheld from the effect produced by peculiar seasons which have very generally impaired the annual gifts of the earth and threatened scarcity in particular districts. Such, however, is the variety of soils, of climates, and of products within our extensive limits that the aggregate resources for subsistence are more than sufficient for the aggregate wants. And as far as an economy of consumption, more than usual, may be necessary, our thankfulness is due to Providence for what is far more than a compensation, in the remarkable health which has distinguished the present year.

Amidst the advantages which have succeeded the peace of Europe, and that of the United States with Great Britain, in a general invigoration of industry among us and in the extension of our commerce, the value of which is more and more disclosing itself to commercial nations, it is to be regretted that a depression is experienced by particular branches of our manufactures and by a portion of our navigation. As the first proceeds in an essential degree from an excess of imported merchandise, which carries a check in its own tendency, the cause in its present extent can not be of very long duration. The evil will not, however, be viewed by Congress without a recollection that manufacturing establishments, if suffered to sink too low or languish too long, may not revive after the causes shall have ceased, and that in the vicissitudes of human affairs situations may recur in which a dependence on foreign sources for indispensable supplies may be among the most serious embarrassments.

The depressed state of our navigation is to be ascribed in a material degree to its exclusion from the colonial ports of the nation most extensively connected with us in commerce, and from the indirect operation of that exclusion.

Previous to the late convention at London between the United States and Great Britain the relative state of the navigation laws of the two countries, growing out of the treaty of 1794, had given to the British navigation a material advantage over the American in the intercourse between the American ports and British ports in Europe. The convention of London equalized the laws of the two countries relating to those ports, leaving the intercourse between our ports and the ports of the British colonies subject, as before, to the respective regulations of the parties. The British Government enforcing now regulations which prohibit a trade between its colonies and the United States in American vessels, whilst they permit a trade in British vessels, the American navigation loses accordingly, and the loss is augmented by the advantage which is given to the British competition over the American in the navigation between our ports and British ports in Europe by the circuitous voyages enjoyed by the one and not enjoyed by the other.

The reasonableness of the rule of reciprocity applied to one branch of the commercial intercourse has been pressed on our part as equally applicable to both branches; but it is ascertained that the British cabinet **declines all negotiation on the subject, with a disavowal, however, of any** disposition to view in an unfriendly light whatever countervailing regulations the United States may oppose to the regulations of which they complain. The wisdom of the Legislature will decide on the course which, under these circumstances, is prescribed by a joint regard to the amicable relations between the two nations and to the just interests of the United States.

I have the satisfaction to state, generally, that we remain in amity with foreign powers.

An occurrence has indeed taken place in the Gulf of Mexico which, if sanctioned by the Spanish Government, may make an exception as to that power. According to the report of our naval commander on that station, one of our public armed vessels was attacked by an overpowering force under a Spanish commander, and the American flag, with the officers and crew, insulted in a manner calling for prompt reparation. This has been demanded. In the meantime a frigate and a smaller vessel of war have been ordered into that Gulf for the protection of our commerce. It would be improper to omit that the representative of His Catholic Majesty in the United States lost no time in giving the strongest assurances that no hostile order could have emanated from his Government, and that it will be as ready to do as to expect whatever the nature of the case and the friendly relations of the two countries shall be found to require.

The posture of our affairs with Algiers at the present moment is not known. The Dey, drawing pretexts from circumstances for which the United States were not answerable, addressed a letter to this Government declaring the treaty last concluded with him to have been annulled by our violation of it, and presenting as the alternative war or a renewal of the former treaty, which stipulated, among other things, an annual tribute. The answer, with an explicit declaration that the United States preferred war to tribute, required his recognition and observance of the treaty last made, which abolishes tribute and the slavery of our captured citizens. The result of the answer has not been received. Should he renew his warfare on our commerce, we rely on the protection it will find in our naval force actually in the Mediterranean.

With the other Barbary States our affairs have undergone no change.

The Indian tribes within our limits appear also disposed to remain at peace. From several of them purchases of lands have been made particularly favorable to the wishes and security of our frontier settlements, as well as to the general interests of the nation. In some instances the titles, though not supported by due proof, and clashing those of one tribe with the claims of another, have been extinguished by double purchases, the benevolent policy of the United States preferring the augmented expense to the hazard of doing injustice or to the enforcement of justice against a feeble and untutored people by means involving or threatening an effusion of blood. I am happy to add that the tranquillity which has been restored among the tribes themselves, as well as between them and our own population, will favor the resumption of the work of civilization which had made an encouraging progress among some tribes, and that the facility is increasing for extending that divided and individual ownership, which exists now in movable property only, to the soil itself, and of thus establishing in the culture and improvement of it the true foundation for a transit from the habits of the savage to the arts and comforts of social life.

As a subject of the highest importance to the national welfare, I must again earnestly recommend to the consideration of Congress a reorganization of the militia on a plan which will form it into classes according to the periods of life more or less adapted to military services. An efficient militia is authorized and contemplated by the Constitution and required by the spirit and safety of free government. The present organization of our militia is universally regarded as less efficient than it ought to be made, and no organization can be better calculated to give to it its due force than a classification which will assign the foremost place in the defense of the country to that portion of its citizens whose activity and animation best enable them to rally to its standard. Besides the consideration that a time of peace is the time when the change can be made with most convenience and equity, it will now be aided by the experience of a recent war in which the militia bore so interesting a part.

Congress will call to mind that no adequate provision has yet been made for the uniformity of weights and measures also contemplated by the Constitution. The great utility of a standard fixed in its nature and founded on the easy rule of decimal proportions is sufficiently obvious. It led the Government at an early stage to preparatory steps for introducing it, and a completion of the work will be a just title to the public gratitude.

The importance which I have attached to the establishment of a university within this District on a scale and for objects worthy of the American nation induces me to renew my recommendation of it to the favorable consideration of Congress. And I particularly invite again their attention to the expediency of exercising their existing powers, and, where necessary, of resorting to the prescribed mode of enlarging them, in order to effectuate a comprehensive system of roads and canals, such as will have the effect of drawing more closely together every part of our country by promoting intercourse and improvements and by increasing the share of every part in the common stock of national prosperity.

Occurrences having taken place which shew that the statutory provisions for the dispensation of criminal justice are deficient in relation both to places and to persons under the exclusive cognizance of the national authority, an amendment of the law embracing such cases will merit the earliest attention of the Legislature. It will be a seasonable occasion also for inquiring how far legislative interposition may be further requisite in providing penalties for offenses designated in the Constitution or in the statutes, and to which either no penalties are annexed or none with sufficient certainty. And I submit to the wisdom of Congress whether a more enlarged revisal of the criminal code be not expedient for the purpose of mitigating in certain cases penalties which were adopted into it antecedent to experiment and examples which justify and recommend a more lenient policy.

The United States, having been the first to abolish within the extent of their authority the transportation of the natives of Africa into slavery, by prohibiting the introduction of slaves and by punishing their citizens participating in the traffic, can not but be gratified at the progress made by concurrent efforts of other nations toward a general suppression of so great an evil. They must feel at the same time the greater solicitude to give the fullest efficacy to their own regulations. With that view, the interposition of Congress appears to be required by the violations and evasions which it is suggested are chargeable on unworthy citizens who mingle in the slave trade under foreign flags and with foreign ports, and by collusive importations of slaves into the United States through adjoining ports and territories. I present the subject to Congress with a full assurance of their disposition to apply all the remedy which can be afforded by an amendment of the law. The regulations which were intended to guard against abuses of a kindred character in the trade between the several States ought also to be rendered more effectual for their humane object.

To these recommendations I add, for the consideration of Congress, the expediency of a remodification of the judiciary establishment, and of an additional department in the executive branch of the Government.

The first is called for by the accruing business which necessarily swells the duties of the Federal courts, and by the great and widening space within which justice is to be dispensed by them. The time seems to have arrived which claims for members of the Supreme Court a relief from itinerary fatigues, incompatible as well with the age which a portion of them will always have attained as with the researches and preparations which are due to their stations and to the juridical reputation of their country. And considerations equally cogent require a more convenient organization of the subordinate tribunals, which may be accomplished without an objectionable increase of the number or expense of the judges.

The extent and variety of executive business also accumulating with the progress of our country and its growing population call for an additional department, to be charged with duties now overburdening other departments and with such as have not been annexed to any department

The course of experience recommends, as another improvement in the executive establishment, that the provision for the station of Attorney-General, whose residence at the seat of Government, official connections with it, and the management of the public business before the judiciary preclude an extensive participation in professional emoluments, be made more adequate to his services and his relinquishments, and that, with a view to his reasonable accommodation and to a proper depository of his official opinions and proceedings, there be included in the provision the usual appurtenances to a public office.

In directing the legislative attention to the state of the finances it is a subject of great gratification to find that even within the short period which has elapsed since the return of peace the revenue has far exceeded all the current demands upon the Treasury, and that under any probable diminution of its future annual products which the vicissitudes of commerce may occasion it will afford an ample fund for the effectual and early extinguishment of the public debt. It has been estimated that during the year 1816 the actual receipts of revenue at the Treasury, including the balance at the commencement of the year, and excluding the proceeds of loans and Treasury notes, will amount to about the sum of $47,000,000; that during the same year the actual payments at the Treasury, including the payment of the arrearages of the War Department as well as the payment of a considerable excess beyond the annual appropriations, will amount to about the sum of $38,000,000, and that consequently at the close of the year there will be a surplus in the Treasury of about the sum of $9,000,000.

The operations of the Treasury continued to be obstructed by difficulties arising from the condition of the national currency, but they have nevertheless been effectual to a beneficial extent in the reduction of the public debt and the establishment of the public credit. The floating debt of Treasury notes and temporary loans will soon be entirely discharged. The aggregate of the funded debt, composed of debts incurred during the wars of 1776 and 1812, has been estimated with reference to the 1st of January next at a sum not exceeding $110,000,000. The ordinary annual expenses of the Government for the maintenance of all its institutions, civil, military, and naval, have been estimated at a sum less than $20,000,000, and the permanent revenue to be derived from all the existing sources has been estimated at a sum of about $25,000,000.

Upon this general view of the subject it is obvious that there is only wanting to the fiscal prosperity of the Government the restoration of an uniform medium of exchange. The resources and the faith of the nation, displayed in the system which Congress has established, insure respect and confidence both at home and abroad. The local accumulations of the revenue have already enabled the Treasury to meet the public engagements in the local currency of most of the States, and it is expected that the same cause will produce the same effect throughout the Union; but for the interests of the community at large, as well as for the purposes of the Treasury, it is essential that the nation should possess a currency of equal value, credit, and use wherever it may circulate. The Constitution has intrusted Congress exclusively with the power of creating and regulating a currency of that description, and the measures which were taken during the last session in execution of the power give every promise of success. The Bank of the United States has been organized under auspices the most favorable, and can not fail to be an important auxiliary to those measures.

For a more enlarged view of the public finances, with a view o. the measures pursued by the Treasury Department previous to the resignation of the late Secretary, I transmit an extract from the last report of that officer. Congress will perceive in it ample proofs of the solid foundation on which the financial prosperity of the nation rests, and will do justice to the distinguished ability and successful exertions with which the duties of the Department were executed during a period remarkable for its difficulties and its peculiar perplexities.

The period of my retiring from the public service being at little distance, I shall find no occasion more proper than the present for expressing to my fellow-citizens my deep sense of the continued confidence and kind support which I have received from them. My grateful recollection of these distinguished marks of their favorable regard can never cease, and with the consciousness that, if I have not served my country with greater ability, I have served it with a sincere devotion will accompany me as a source of unfailing gratification.

Happily, I shall carry with me from the public theater other sources, which those who love their country most will best appreciate. I shall behold it blessed with tranquillity and prosperity at home and with peace and respect abroad. I can indulge the proud reflection that the American people have reached in safety and success their fortieth year as an independent nation; that for nearly an entire generation they have had experience of their present Constitution, the offspring of their undisturbed deliberations and of their free choice; that they have found it to bear the trials of adverse as well as prosperous circumstances; to contain in its combination of the federate and elective principles a reconcilement of public strength with individual liberty, of national power for the defense of national rights with a security against wars of injustice, of ambition, and of vainglory in the fundamental provision which subjects all questions of war to the will of the nation itself, which is to pay its costs and feel its calamities. Nor is it less a peculiar felicity of this Constitution, so dear to us all, that it is found to be capable, without losing its vital energies, of expanding itself over a spacious territory with the increase and expansion of the community for whose benefit it was established.

And may I not be allowed to add to this gratifying spectacle that I shall read in the character of the American people, in their devotion to true liberty and to the Constitution which is its palladium, sure presages that the destined career of my country will exhibit a Government pursuing the public good as its sole object, and regulating its means by the great principles consecrated in its charter and by those moral principles to which they are so well allied; a Government which watches over the purity of elections, the freedom of speech and of the press, the trial by jury, and the equal interdict against encroachments and compacts between religion and the state; which maintains inviolably the maxims of public faith, the security of persons and property, and encourages in every authorized mode that general diffusion of knowledge which guarantees to public liberty its permanency and to those who possess the blessing the true enjoyment of it; a Government which avoids intrusions on the internal repose of other nations, and repels them from its own; which does justice to all nations with a readiness equal to the firmness with which it requires justice from them; and which, whilst it refines its domestic code from every ingredient not congenial with the precepts of an enlightened age and the sentiments of a virtuous people, seeks by appeals to reason and by its liberal examples to infuse into the law which governs the civilized world a spirit which may diminish the frequency or circumscribe the calamities of war, and meliorate the social and beneficent relations of peace; a Government, in a word, whose conduct within and without may bespeak the most noble of all ambitions—that of promoting peace on earth and good will to man.

These contemplations, sweetening the remnant of my days, will animate my prayers for the happiness of my beloved country, and a perpetuity of the institutions under which it is enjoyed.

James Monroe

March 4, 1817 to March 4, 1825

FIRST ANNUAL MESSAGE.

Fellow-Citizens of the Senate and of the House of Representatives:

At no period of our political existence had we so much cause to felicitate ourselves at the prosperous and happy condition of our country.
The abundant fruits of the earth have filled it with plenty.   An extensive and profitable commerce has greatly augmented our revenue.   The
public credit has attained an extraordinary elevation.   Our preparations
for defense in case of future wars, from which, by the experience of all
nations, we ought not to expect to be exempted, are advancing under a
well-digested system with all the dispatch which so important a work
will admit.   Our free Government, founded on the interest and affections
of the people, has gained and is daily gaining strength.   Local jealousies
are rapidly yielding to more generous, enlarged, and enlightened views
of national policy.   For advantages so numerous and highly important
it is our duty to unite in grateful acknowledgments to that Omnipotent
Being from whom they are derived, and in unceasing prayer that He will
endow us with virtue and strength to maintain and hand them down in
their utmost purity to our latest posterity.

I have the satisfaction to inform you that an arrangement which had
been commenced by my predecessor with the British Government for the
reduction of the naval force by Great Britain and the United States on
the Lakes has been concluded, by which it is provided that neither party
shall keep in service on Lake Champlain more than one vessel, on Lake
Ontario more than one, and on Lake Erie and the upper lakes more than
two, to be armed each with one cannon only, and that all the other armed
vessels of both parties, of which an exact list is interchanged, shall be
dismantled.   It is also agreed that the force retained shall be restricted
in its duty to the internal purposes of each party, and that the arrangement shall remain in force until six months shall have expired after notice given by one of the parties to the other of its desire that it should
terminate.   By this arrangement useless expense on both sides and, what
is of still greater importance, the danger of collision between armed vessels in those inland waters, which was great, is prevented.

I have the satisfaction also to state that the commissioners under the
fourth article of the treaty of Ghent, to whom it was referred to decide
to which party the several islands in the bay of Passamaquoddy belonged
under the treaty of 1783, have agreed in a report, by which all the islands
in the possession of each party before the late war have been decreed to it.
The commissioners acting under the other articles of the treaty of Ghent
for the settlement of boundaries have also been engaged in the discharge
of their respective duties, but have not yet completed them.   The difference which arose between the two Governments under that treaty respecting the right of the United States to take and cure fish on the coast of
the British provinces north of our limits, which had been secured by the

treaty of 1783, is still in negotiation. The proposition made by this Government to extend to the colonies of Great Britain the principle of the convention of London, by which the commerce between the ports of the United States and British ports in Europe had been placed on a footing of equality, has been declined by the British Government. This subject having been thus amicably discussed between the two Governments, and it appearing that the British Government is unwilling to depart from its present regulations, it remains for Congress to decide whether they will make any other regulations in consequence thereof for the protection and improvement of our navigation.

The negotiation with Spain for spoliations on our commerce and the settlement of boundaries remains essentially in the state it held by the communications that were made to Congress by my predecessor. It has been evidently the policy of the Spanish Government to keep the negotiation suspended, and in this the United States have acquiesced, from an amicable disposition toward Spain and in the expectation that her Government would, from a sense of justice, finally accede to such an arrangement as would be equal between the parties. A disposition has been lately shown by the Spanish Government to move in the negotiation, which has been met by this Government, and should the conciliatory and friendly policy which has invariably guided our councils be reciprocated, a just and satisfactory arrangement may be expected. It is proper, however, to remark that no proposition has yet been made from which such a result can be presumed.

It was anticipated at an early stage that the contest between Spain and the colonies would become highly interesting to the United States. It was natural that our citizens should sympathize in events which affected their neighbors. It seemed probable also that the prosecution of the conflict along our coast and in contiguous countries would occasionally interrupt our commerce and otherwise affect the persons and property of our citizens. These anticipations have been realized. Such injuries have been received from persons acting under authority of both the parties, and for which redress has in most instances been withheld. Through every stage of the conflict the United States have maintained an impartial neutrality, giving aid to neither of the parties in men, money, ships, or munitions of war. They have regarded the contest not in the light of an ordinary insurrection or rebellion, but as a civil war between parties nearly equal, having as to neutral powers equal rights. Our ports have been open to both, and every article the fruit of our soil or of the industry of our citizens which either was permitted to take has been equally free to the other. Should the colonies establish their independence, it is proper now to state that this Government neither seeks nor would accept from them any advantage in commerce or otherwise which will not be equally open to all other nations. The colonies will in that event become independent states, free from any obligation to or connection with us

which it may not then be their interest to form on the basis of a fair reciprocity.

In the summer of the present year an expedition was set on foot against
East Florida by persons claiming to act under the authority of some of
the colonies, who took possession of Amelia Island, at the mouth of the
St. Marys River, near the boundary of the State of Georgia. As this
Province lies eastward of the Mississippi, and is bounded by the United
States and the ocean on every side, and has been a subject of negotiation
with the Government of Spain as an indemnity for losses by spoliation
or in exchange for territory of equal value westward of the Mississippi,
a fact well known to the world, it excited surprise that any countenance
should be given to this measure by any of the colonies. As it would
be difficult to reconcile it with the friendly relations existing between
the United States and the colonies, a doubt was entertained whether it
had been authorized by them, or any of them. This doubt has gained
strength by the circumstances which have unfolded themselves in the
prosecution of the enterprise, which have marked it as a mere private,
unauthorized adventure. Projected and commenced with an incompetent
force, reliance seems to have been placed on what might be drawn, in defiance of our laws, from within our limits; and of late, as their resources
have failed, it has assumed a more marked character of unfriendliness to
us, the island being made a channel for the illicit introduction of slaves
from Africa into the United States, an asylum for fugitive slaves from
the neighboring States, and a port for smuggling of every kind.

A similar establishment was made at an earlier period by persons of
the same description in the Gulf of Mexico at a place called Galvezton,
within the limits of the United States, as we contend, under the cession
of Louisiana. This enterprise has been marked in a more signal manner
by all the objectionable circumstances which characterized the other, and
more particularly by the equipment of privateers which have annoyed our
commerce, and by smuggling. These establishments, if ever sanctioned
by any authority whatever, which is not believed, have abused their trust
and forfeited all claim to consideration. A just regard for the rights
and interests of the United States required that they should be suppressed,
and orders have been accordingly issued to that effect. The imperious
considerations which produced this measure will be explained to the parties whom it may in any degree concern.

To obtain correct information on every subject in which the United
States are interested; to inspire just sentiments in all persons in authority,
on either side, of our friendly disposition so far as it may comport with
an impartial neutrality, and to secure proper respect to our commerce in
every port and from every flag, it has been thought proper to send a ship
of war with three distinguished citizens along the southern coast with
instruction to touch at such ports as they may find most expedient for
these purposes. With the existing authorities, with those in the posses-

sion of and exercising the sovereignty, must the communication be held; from them alone can redress for past injuries committed by persons acting under them be obtained; by them alone can the commission of the like in future be prevented.

Our relations with the other powers of Europe have experienced no essential change since the last session. In our intercourse with each due attention continues to be paid to the protection of our commerce, and to every other object in which the United States are interested. A strong hope is entertained that, by adhering to the maxims of a just, a candid, and friendly policy, we may long preserve amicable relations with all the powers of Europe on conditions advantageous and honorable to our country.

With the Barbary States and the Indian tribes our pacific relations have been preserved.

In calling your attention to the internal concerns of our country the view which they exhibit is peculiarly gratifying. The payments which have been made into the Treasury show the very productive state of the public revenue. After satisfying the appropriations made by law for the support of the civil Government and of the military and naval establishments, embracing suitable provision for fortifications and for the gradual increase of the Navy, paying the interest of the public debt, and extinguishing more than eighteen millions of the principal, within the present year, it is estimated that a balance of more than $6,000,000 will remain in the Treasury on the 1st day of January applicable to the current service of the ensuing year.

The payments into the Treasury during the year 1818 on account of imposts and tonnage, resulting principally from duties which have accrued in the present year, may be fairly estimated at $20,000,000; the internal revenues at $2,500,000; the public lands at $1,500,000; bank dividends and incidental receipts at $500,000; making in the whole $24,500,000.

The annual permanent expenditure for the support of the civil Government and of the Army and Navy, as now established by law, amounts to $11,800,000, and for the sinking fund to $10,000,000, making in the whole $21,800,000, leaving an annual excess of revenue beyond the expenditure of $2,700,000, exclusive of the balance estimated to be in the Treasury on the 1st day of January, 1818.

In the present state of the Treasury the whole of the Louisiana debt may be redeemed in the year 1819, after which, if the public debt continues as it now is, above par, there will be annually about five millions of the sinking fund unexpended until the year 1825, when the loan of 1812 and the stock created by funding Treasury notes will be redeemable.

It is also estimated that the Mississippi stock will be discharged during the year 1819 from the proceeds of the public lands assigned to that object, after which the receipts from those lands will annually add to the public revenue the sum of one million and a half, making the permanent annual revenue amount to $26,000,000, and leaving an annual excess of revenue after the year 1819 beyond the permanent authorized expenditure of more than $4,000,000.

By the last returns to the Department of War the militia force of the several States may be estimated at 800,000 men—infantry, artillery, and cavalry. Great part of this force is armed, and measures are taken to arm the whole. An improvement in the organization and discipline of the militia is one of the great objects which claims the unremitted attention of Congress.

The regular force amounts nearly to the number required by law, and is stationed along the Atlantic and inland frontiers.

Of the naval force it has been necessary to maintain strong squadrons in the Mediterranean and in the Gulf of Mexico.

From several of the Indian tribes inhabiting the country bordering on Lake Erie purchases have been made of lands on conditions very favorable to the United States, and, as it is presumed, not less so to the tribes themselves.

By these purchases the Indian title, with moderate reservations, has been extinguished to the whole of the land within the limits of the State of Ohio, and to a part of that in the Michigan Territory and of the State of Indiana. From the Cherokee tribe a tract has been purchased in the State of Georgia and an arrangement made by which, in exchange for lands beyond the Mississippi, a great part, if not the whole, of the land belonging to that tribe eastward of that river in the States of North Carolina, Georgia, and Tennessee, and in the Alabama Territory will soon be acquired. By these acquisitions, and others that may reasonably be expected soon to follow, we shall be enabled to extend our settlements from the inhabited parts of the State of Ohio along Lake Erie into the Michigan Territory, and to connect our settlements by degrees through the State of Indiana and the Illinois Territory to that of Missouri. A similar and equally advantageous effect will soon be produced to the south, through the whole extent of the States and territory which border on the waters emptying into the Mississippi and the Mobile. In this progress, which the rights of nature demand and nothing can prevent, marking a growth rapid and gigantic, it is our duty to make new efforts for the preservation, improvement, and civilization of the native inhabitants. The hunter state can exist only in the vast uncultivated desert. It yields to the more dense and compact form and greater force of civilized population; and of right it ought to yield, for the earth was given to mankind to support the greatest number of which it is capable, and no tribe or people have a right to withhold from the wants of others more than is necessary for their own support and comfort. It is gratifying to know that the reservations of land made by the treaties with the tribes on Lake Erie were made with a view to individual ownership among them and to the cultivation of the soil by all, and that an annual stipend has been pledged to supply their other wants. It will merit the consideration of Congress whether other provision not stipulated by treaty ought to be made for these tribes and for the advancement of the liberal and humane policy of the United States toward all the tribes within our limits, and more particularly for their improvement in the arts of civilized life.

Among the advantages incident to these purchases, and to those which have preceded, the security which may thereby be afforded to our inland frontiers is peculiarly important. With a strong barrier, consisting of our own people, thus planted on the Lakes, the Mississippi, and the Mobile, with the protection to be derived from the regular force, Indian hostilities, if they do not altogether cease, will henceforth lose their terror. Fortifications in those quarters to any extent will not be necessary, and the expense attending them may be saved. A people accustomed to the use of firearms only, as the Indian tribes are, will shun even moderate works which are defended by cannon. Great fortifications will therefore be requisite only in future along the coast and at some points in the interior connected with it. On these will the safety of our towns and the commerce of our great rivers, from the Bay of Fundy to the Mississippi, depend. On these, therefore, should the utmost attention, skill, and labor be bestowed.

A considerable and rapid augmentation in the value of all the public lands, proceeding from these and other obvious causes, may henceforward be expected. The difficulties attending early emigrations will be dissipated even in the most remote parts. Several new States have been admitted into our Union to the west and south, and Territorial governments, happily organized, established over every other portion in which there is vacant land for sale. In terminating Indian hostilities, as must soon be done, in a formidable shape at least, the emigration, which has heretofore been great, will probably increase, and the demand for land and the augmentation in its value be in like proportion. The great increase of our population throughout the Union will alone produce an important effect, and in no quarter will it be so sensibly felt as in those in contemplation. The public lands are a public stock, which ought to be disposed of to the best advantage for the nation. The nation should therefore derive the profit proceeding from the continual rise in their value. Every encouragement should be given to the emigrants consistent with a fair competition between them, but that competition should operate in the first sale to the advantage of the nation rather than of individuals. Great capitalists will derive all the benefit incident to their superior wealth under any mode of sale which may be adopted. But if, looking forward to the rise in the value of the public lands, they should have the opportunity of amassing at a low price vast bodies in their hands, the profit will accrue to them and not to the public. They would also have the power in that degree to control the emigration and settlement in such a manner as their opinion of their respective interests might dictate. I submit this subject to the consideration of Congress, that such further provision may be made in the sale of the public lands, with a view to the public interest, should any be deemed expedient, as in their judgment may be best adapted to the object.

When we consider the vast extent of territory within the United States, the great amount and value of its productions, the connection of its parts, and other circumstances on which their prosperity and happiness depend, we can not fail to entertain a high sense of the advantage to be derived from the facility which may be afforded in the intercourse between them by means of good roads and canals. Never did a country of such vast extent offer equal inducements to improvements of this kind, nor ever were consequences of such magnitude involved in them. As this subject was acted on by Congress at the last session, and there may be a disposition to revive it at the present, I have brought it into view for the purpose of communicating my sentiments on a very important circumstance connected with it with that freedom and candor which a regard for the public interest and a proper respect for Congress require. A difference of opinion has existed from the first formation of our Constitution to the present time among our most enlightened and virtuous citizens respecting the right of Congress to establish such a system of improvement. Taking into view the trust with which I am now honored, it would be improper after what has passed that this discussion should be revived with an uncertainty of my opinion respecting the right. Disregarding early impressions I have bestowed on the subject all the deliberation which its great importance and a just sense of my duty required, and the result is a settled conviction in my mind that Congress do not possess the right. It is not contained in any of the specified powers granted to Congress, nor can I consider it incidental to or a necessary means, viewed on the most liberal scale, for carrying into effect any of the powers which are specifically granted. In communicating this result I can not resist the obligation which I feel to suggest to Congress the propriety of recommending to the States the adoption of an amendment to the Constitution which shall give to Congress the right in question. In cases of doubtful construction, especially of such vital interest, it comports with the nature and origin of our institutions, and will contribute much to preserve them, to apply to our constituents for an explicit grant of the power. We may confidently rely that if it appears to their satisfaction that the power is necessary, it will always be granted.

In this case I am happy to observe that experience has afforded the most ample proof of its utility, and that the benign spirit of conciliation and harmony which now manifests itself throughout our Union promises to such a recommendation the most prompt and favorable result. I think proper to suggest also, in case this measure is adopted, that it be recommended to the States to include in the amendment sought a right in Congress to institute likewise seminaries of learning, for the all-important purpose of diffusing knowledge among our fellow-citizens throughout the United States.

Our manufactories will require the continued attention of Congress. The capital employed in them is considerable, and the knowledge acquired in the machinery and fabric of all the most useful manufactures is of great value. Their preservation, which depends on due encouragement, is connected with the high interests of the nation.

Although the progress of the public buildings has been as favorable as circumstances have permitted, it is to be regretted that the Capitol is not yet in a state to receive you. There is good cause to presume that the two wings, the only parts as yet commenced, will be prepared for that purpose at the next session. The time seems now to have arrived when this subject may be deemed worthy the attention of Congress on a scale adequate to national purposes. The completion of the middle building will be necessary to the convenient accommodation of Congress, of the committees, and various offices belonging to it. It is evident that the other public buildings are altogether insufficient for the accommodation of the several Executive Departments, some of whom are much crowded and even subjected to the necessity of obtaining it in private buildings at some distance from the head of the Department, and with inconvenience to the management of the public business. Most nations have taken an interest and a pride in the improvement and ornament of their metropolis, and none were more conspicuous in that respect than the ancient republics. The policy which dictated the establishment of a permanent residence for the National Government and the spirit in which it was commenced and has been prosecuted show that such improvement was thought worthy the attention of this nation. Its central position, between the northern and southern extremes of our Union, and its approach to the west at the head of a great navigable river which interlocks with the Western waters, prove the wisdom of the councils which established it.

Nothing appears to be more reasonable and proper than that convenient accommodation should be provided on a well-digested plan for the heads of the several Departments and for the Attorney-General, and it is believed that the public ground in the city applied to these objects will be found amply sufficient. I submit this subject to the consideration of Congress, that such further provision may be made in it as to them may seem proper.

In contemplating the happy situation of the United States, our attention is drawn with peculiar interest to the surviving officers and soldiers of our Revolutionary army, who so eminently contributed by their services to lay its foundation. Most of those very meritorious citizens have paid the debt of nature and gone to repose. It is believed that among the survivors there are some not provided for by existing laws, who are reduced to indigence and even to real distress. These men have a claim on the gratitude of their country, and it will do honor to their country to provide for them. The lapse of a few years more and the opportunity will be forever lost; indeed, so long already has been the interval that the number to be benefited by any provision which may be made will not be great.

It appearing in a satisfactory manner that the revenue arising from imposts and tonnage and from the sale of the public lands will be fully adequate to the support of the civil Government, of the present military and naval establishments, including the annual augmentation of the latter to the extent provided for, to the payment of the interest of the public debt, and to the extinguishment of it at the times authorized, without the aid of the internal taxes, I consider it my duty to recommend to Congress their repeal. To impose taxes when the public exigencies require them is an obligation of the most sacred character, especially with a free people. The faithful fulfillment of it is among the highest proofs of their virtue and capacity for self-government. To dispense with taxes when it may be done with perfect safety is equally the duty of their representatives. In this instance we have the satisfaction to know that they were imposed when the demand was imperious, and have been sustained with exemplary fidelity. I have to add that however gratifying it may be to me regarding the prosperous and happy condition of our country to recommend the repeal of these taxes at this time, I shall nevertheless be attentive to events, and, should any future emergency occur, be not less prompt to suggest such measures and burdens as may then be requisite and proper.

SECOND ANNUAL MESSAGE.

NOVEMBER 16, 1818.

Fellow-Citizens of the Senate and of the House of Representatives:

The auspicious circumstances under which you will commence the duties of the present session will lighten the burdens inseparable from the high trust committed to you. The fruits of the earth have been unusually abundant, commerce has flourished, the revenue has exceeded the most favorable anticipation, and peace and amity are preserved with foreign nations on conditions just and honorable to our country. For these inestimable blessings we can not but be grateful to that Providence which watches over the destiny of nations.

As the term limited for the operation of the commercial convention with Great Britain will expire early in the month of July next, and it was deemed important that there should be no interval during which that portion of our commerce which was provided for by that convention should not be regulated, either by arrangement between the two Governments or by the authority of Congress, the minister of the United States at London was instructed early in the last summer to invite the attention of the British Government to the subject, with a view to that object. He was instructed to propose also that the negotiation which it was wished to open might extend to the general commerce of the two countries, and to every other interest and unsettled difference between them particularly those relating to impressment, the fisheries, and boundaries, in the hope that an arrangement might be made on principles of reciprocal advantage which might comprehend and provide in a satisfactory manner for all these high concerns. I have the satisfaction to state that the proposal was received by the British Government in the spirit which prompted it, and that a negotiation has been opened at London embracing all these objects. On full consideration of the great extent and magnitude of the trust it was thought proper to commit it to not less than two of our distinguished citizens, and in consequence the envoy extraordinary and minister plenipotentiary of the United States at Paris has been associated with our envoy extraordinary and minister plenipotentiary at London, to both of whom corresponding instructions have been given, and they are now engaged in the discharge of its duties. It is proper to add that to prevent any inconvenience resulting from the delay incident to a negotiation on so many important subjects it was agreed before entering on it that the existing convention should be continued for a term not less than eight years.

Our relations with Spain remain nearly in the state in which they were at the close of the last session. The convention of 1802, providing for the adjustment of a certain portion of the claims of our citizens for injuries sustained by spoliation, and so long suspended by the Spanish Government, has at length been ratified by it, but no arrangement has yet been made for the payment of another portion of like claims, not less extensive or well founded, or for other classes of claims, or for the settlement of boundaries. These subjects have again been brought under consideration in both countries, but no agreement has been entered into respecting them. In the meantime events have occurred which clearly prove the ill effect of the policy which that Government has so long pursued on the friendly relations of the two countries, which it is presumed is at least of as much importance to Spain as to the United States to maintain. A state of things has existed in the Floridas the tendency of which has been obvious to all who have paid the slightest attention to the progress of affairs in that quarter. Throughout the whole of those Provinces to which the Spanish title extends the Government of Spain has scarcely been felt. Its authority has been confined almost exclusively to the walls of Pensacola and St. Augustine, within which only small garrisons have been maintained.   Adventurers from every country, fugitives from justice, and absconding slaves have found an asylum there.   Several tribes of Indians, strong in the number of their warriors, remarkable for their ferocity, and whose settlements extend to our limits, inhabit those Provinces.   These different hordes of people, connected together, disregarding on the one side the authority of Spain, and protected on the other by an imaginary line which separates Florida from the United States, have violated our laws prohibiting the introduction of slaves, have practiced various frauds on our revenue, and committed every kind of outrage on our peaceable citizens which their proximity to us enabled them to perpetrate.   The invasion of Amelia Island last year by a small band of adventurers, not exceeding 150 in number, who wrested it from the inconsiderable Spanish force stationed there, and held it several months, during which a single feeble effort only was made to recover it, which failed, clearly proves how completely extinct the Spanish authority had become, as the conduct of those adventurers while in possession of the island as distinctly shows the pernicious purposes for which their combination had been formed.

This country had, in fact, become the theater of every species of lawless adventure.   With little population of its own, the Spanish authority almost extinct, and the colonial governments in a state of revolution, having no pretension to it, and sufficiently employed in their own concerns, it was in a great measure derelict, and the object of cupidity to every adventurer.   A system of buccaneering was rapidly organizing over it which menaced in its consequences the lawful commerce of every nation, and particularly of the United States, while it presented a temptation to every people, on whose seduction its success principally depended.   In regard to the United States, the pernicious effect of this unlawful combination was not confined to the ocean; the Indian tribes have constituted the effective force in Florida.   With these tribes these adventurers had formed at an early period a connection with a view to avail themselves of that force to promote their own projects of accumulation and aggrandizement.   It is to the interference of some of these adventurers, in misrepresenting the claims and titles of the Indians to land and in practicing on their savage propensities, that the Seminole war is principally to be traced.   Men who thus connect themselves with savage communities and stimulate them to war, which is always attended on their part with acts of barbarity the most shocking, deserve to be viewed in a worse light than the savages. They would certainly have no claim to an immunity from the punishment which, according to the rules of warfare practiced by the savages, might justly be inflicted on the savages themselves.

If the embarrassments of Spain prevented her from making an indemnity to our citizens for so long a time from her treasury for their losses by spoliation and otherwise, it was always in her power to have provided it by the cession of this territory.   Of this her Government has been repeatedly apprised, and the cession was the more to have been anticipated as Spain must have known that in ceding it she would in effect cede what had become of little value to her, and would likewise relieve herself from the important obligation secured by the treaty of 1795 and all other compromitments respecting it.   If the United States, from consideration of these embarrassments, declined pressing their claims in a spirit of hostility, the motive ought at least to have been duly appreciated by the Government of Spain.   It is well known to her Government that other powers have made to the United States an indemnity for like losses sustained by their citizens at the same epoch.

There is nevertheless a limit beyond which this spirit of amity and forbearance can in no instance be justified.   If it was proper to rely on amicable negotiation for an indemnity for losses, it would not have been so to have permitted the inability of Spain to fulfill her engagements and to sustain her authority in the Floridas to be perverted by foreign adventurers and savages to purposes so destructive to the lives of our fellow-citizens and the highest interests of the United States.   The right of self-defense never ceases.   It is among the most sacred, and alike necessary to nations and to individuals, and whether the attack be made by Spain herself or by those who abuse her power, its obligation is not the less strong.   The invaders of Amelia Island had assumed a popular and respected title under which they might approach and wound us.   As their object was distinctly seen, and the duty imposed on the Executive by an existing law was profoundly felt, that mask was not permitted to protect them.   It was thought incumbent on the United States to suppress the establishment, and it was accordingly done.   The combination in Florida for the unlawful purposes stated, the acts perpetrated by that combination, and, above all, the incitement of the Indians to massacre our fellow-citizens of every age and of both sexes, merited a like treatment and received it.   In pursuing these savages to an imaginary line in the woods it would have been the height of folly to have suffered that line to protect them.   Had that been done the war could never cease.   Even if the territory had been exclusively that of Spain and her power complete over it, we had a right by the law of nations to follow the enemy on it and to subdue him there.   But the territory belonged, in a certain sense at least, to the savage enemy who inhabited it; the power of Spain had ceased to exist over it, and protection was sought under her title by those who had committed on our citizens hostilities which she was bound by treaty to have prevented, but had not the power to prevent.   To have stopped at that line would have given new encouragement to these savages and new vigor to the whole combination existing there in the prosecution of all its pernicious purposes.

In suppressing the establishment at Amelia Island no unfriendliness was manifested toward Spain, because the post was taken from a force which had wrested it from her.   The measure, it is true, was not adopted in concert with the Spanish Government or those in authority under it, because in transactions connected with the war in which Spain and the colonies are engaged it was thought proper in doing justice to the United States to maintain a strict impartiality toward both the belligerent parties without consulting or acting in concert with either. It gives me pleasure to state that the Governments of Buenos Ayres and Venezuela, whose names were assumed, have explicitly disclaimed all participation in those measures, and even the knowledge of them until communicated by this Government, and have also expressed their satisfaction that a course of proceedings had been suppressed which if justly imputable to them would dishonor their cause.

In authorizing Major-General Jackson to enter Florida in pursuit of the Seminoles care was taken not to encroach on the rights of Spain. I regret to have to add that in executing this order facts were disclosed respecting the conduct of the officers of Spain in authority there in encouraging the war, furnishing munitions of war and other supplies to carry it on, and in other acts not less marked which evinced their participation in the hostile purposes of that combination and justified the confidence with which it inspired the savages that by those officers they would be protected. A conduct so incompatible with the friendly relations existing between the two countries, particularly with the positive obligation of the fifth article of the treaty of 1795, by which Spain was bound to restrain, even by force, those savages from acts of hostility against the United States, could not fail to excite surprise. The commanding general was convinced that he should fail in his object, that he should in effect accomplish nothing, if he did not deprive those savages of the resource on which they had calculated and of the protection on which they had relied in making the war. As all the documents relating to this occurrence will be laid before Congress, it is not necessary to enter into further detail respecting it.

Although the reasons which induced Major-General Jackson to take these posts were duly appreciated, there was nevertheless no hesitation in deciding on the course which it became the Government to pursue. As there was reason to believe that the commanders of these posts had violated their instructions, there was no disposition to impute to their Government a conduct so unprovoked and hostile. An order was in consequence issued to the general in command there to deliver the posts— Pensacola unconditionally to any person duly authorized to receive it, and St. Marks, which is in the heart of the Indian country, on the arrival of competent force to defend it against those savages and their associates.

In entering Florida to suppress this combination no idea was entertained of hostility to Spain, and however justifiable the commanding general was, in consequence of the misconduct of the Spanish officers, in entering St. Marks and Pensacola to terminate it by proving to the savages and their associates that they should not be protected even there, yet the amicable relations existing between the United States and Spain could not be altered by that act alone. By ordering the restitution of the posts those relations were preserved. To a change of them the power of the Executive is deemed incompetent; it is vested in Congress only.

By this measure, so promptly taken, due respect was shown to the Government of Spain. The misconduct of her officers has not been imputed to her. She was enabled to review with candor her relations with the United States and her own situation, particularly in respect to the territory in question, with the dangers inseparable from it, and regarding the losses we have sustained for which indemnity has been so long withheld, and the injuries we have suffered through that territory, and her means of redress, she was likewise enabled to take with honor the course best calculated to do justice to the United States and to promote her own welfare.

Copies of the instructions to the commanding general, of his correspondence with the Secretary of War, explaining his motives and justifying his conduct, with a copy of the proceedings of the courts-martial in the trial of Arbuthnot and Ambristie, and of the correspondence between the Secretary of State and the minister plenipotentiary of Spain near this Government, and of the minister plenipotentiary of the United States at Madrid with the Government of Spain, will be laid before Congress.

The civil war which has so long prevailed between Spain and the Provinces in South America still continues, without any prospect of its speedy termination. The information respecting the condition of those countries which has been collected by the commissioners recently returned from thence will be laid before Congress in copies of their reports, with such other information as has been received from other agents of the United States.

It appears from these communications that the Government at Buenos Ayres declared itself independent in July, 1816, having previously exercised the power of an independent government, though in the name of the King of Spain, from the year 1810; that the Banda Oriental, Entre Rios, and Paraguay, with the city of Santa Fee, all of which are also independent, are unconnected with the present Government of Buenos Ayres; that Chili has declared itself independent and is closely connected with Buenos Ayres; that Venezuela has also declared itself independent, and now maintains the conflict with various success; and that the remaining parts of South America, except Monte Video and such other portions of the eastern bank of the La Plata as are held by Portugal, are still in the possession of Spain or in a certain degree under her influence.

By a circular note addressed by the ministers of Spain to the allied powers, with whom they are respectively accredited, it appears that the allies have undertaken to mediate between Spain and the South American Provinces, and that the manner and extent of their interposition would be settled by a congress which was to have met at Aix-la-Chapelle in September last. From the general policy and course of proceeding observed by the allied powers in regard to this contest it is inferred that they will confine their interposition to the expression of their sentiments, abstaining from the application of force. I state this impression that force will not be applied with the greater satisfaction because it is a course more consistent with justice and likewise authorizes a hope that the calamities of the war will be confined to the parties only, and will be of shorter duration.

From the view taken of this subject, founded on all the information that we have been able to obtain, there is good cause to be satisfied with the course heretofore pursued by the United States in regard to this contest, and to conclude that it is proper to adhere to it, especially in the present state of affairs.

I have great satisfaction in stating that our relations with France, Russia, and other powers continue on the most friendly basis.

In our domestic concerns we have ample cause of satisfaction. The receipts into the Treasury during the three first quarters of the year have exceeded $17,000,000.

After satisfying all the demands which have been made under existing appropriations, including the final extinction of the old 6 per cent stock and the redemption of a moiety of the Louisiana debt, it is estimated that there will remain in the Treasury on the 1st day of January next more than $2,000,000.

It is ascertained that the gross revenue which has accrued from the customs during the same period amounts to $21,000,000, and that the revenue of the whole year may be estimated at not less than $26,000,000. The sale of the public lands during the year has also greatly exceeded, both in quantity and price, that of any former year, and there is just reason to expect a progressive improvement in that source of revenue.

It is gratifying to know that although the annual expenditure has been increased by the act of the last session of Congress providing for Revolutionary pensions to an amount about equal to the proceeds of the internal duties which were then repealed, the revenue for the ensuing year will be proportionally augmented, and that whilst the public expenditure will probably remain stationary, each successive year will add to the national resources by the ordinary increase of our population and by the gradual development of our latent sources of national prosperity.

The strict execution of the revenue laws, resulting principally from the salutary provisions of the act of the 20th of April last amending the several collection laws, has, it is presumed, secured to domestic manufactures all the relief that can be derived from the duties which have been imposed upon foreign merchandise for their protection. Under the influence of this relief several branches of this important national interest have assumed greater activity, and although it is hoped that others will gradually revive and ultimately triumph over every obstacle, yet the expediency of granting further protection is submitted to your consideration.

The measures of defense authorized by existing laws have been pursued with the zeal and activity due to so important an object, and with all the dispatch practicable in so extensive and great an undertaking. The survey of our maritime and inland frontiers has been continued, and at the points where it was decided to erect fortifications the work has been commenced, and in some instances considerable progress has been made. In compliance with resolutions of the last session, the Board of Commissioners were directed to examine in a particular manner the parts of the coast therein designated and to report their opinion of the most suitable sites for two naval depots. This work is in a train of execution. The opinion of the Board on this subject, with a plan of all the works necessary to a general system of defense so far as it has been formed, will be laid before Congress in a report from the proper department as soon as it can be prepared.

In conformity with the appropriations of the last session, treaties have been formed with the Quapaw tribe of Indians, inhabiting the country on the Arkansaw, and with the Great and Little Osages north of the White River; with the tribes in the State of Indiana; with the several tribes within the State of Ohio and the Michigan Territory, and with the Chickasaws, by which very extensive cessions of territory have been made to the United States. Negotiations are now depending with the tribes in the Illinois Territory and with the Choctaws, by which it is expected that other extensive cessions will be made. I take great interest in stating that the cessions already made, which are considered so important to the United States, have been obtained on conditions very satisfactory to the Indians.

With a view to the security of our inland frontiers, it has been thought expedient to establish strong posts at the mouth of Yellow Stone River and at the Mandan village on the Missouri, and at the mouth of St. Peters on the Mississippi, at no great distance from our northern boundaries. It can hardly be presumed while such posts are maintained in the rear of the Indian tribes that they will venture to attack our peaceable inhabitants. A strong hope is entertained that this measure will likewise be productive of much good to the tribes themselves, especially in promoting the great object of their civilization. Experience has clearly demonstrated that independent savage communities can not long exist within the limits of a civilized population. The progress of the latter has almost invariably terminated in the extinction of the former, especially of the tribes belonging to our portion of this hemisphere, among whom loftiness of sentiment and gallantry in action have been conspicuous. To civilize them, and even to prevent their extinction, it seems to be indispensable that their independence as communities should cease, and that the control of the United States over them should be complete and undisputed. The hunter state will then be more easily abandoned, and recourse will be had to the acquisition and culture of land and to other pursuits tending to dissolve the ties which connect them together as a savage community and to give a new character to every individual. I present this subject to the consideration of Congress on the presumption that it may be found expedient and practicable to adopt some benevolent provisions, having these objects in view, relative to the tribes within our settlements.

It has been necessary during the present year to maintain a strong naval force in the Mediterranean and in the Gulf of Mexico, and to send some public ships along the southern coast and to the Pacific Ocean. By these means amicable relations with the Barbary Powers have been preserved, our commerce has been protected, and our rights respected. The augmentation of our Navy is advancing with a steady progress toward the limit contemplated by law.

I communicate with great satisfaction the accession of another State (Illinois) to our Union, because I perceive from the proof afforded by the additions already made the regular progress and sure consummation of a policy of which history affords no example, and of which the good effect can not be too highly estimated. By extending our Government on the principles of our Constitution over the vast territory within our limits, on the Lakes and the Mississippi and its numerous streams, new life and vigor are infused into every part of our system. By increasing the number of the States the confidence of the State governments in their own security is increased and their jealousy of the National Government proportionally diminished. The impracticability of one consolidated government for this great and growing nation will be more apparent and will be universally admitted. Incapable of exercising local authority except for general purposes, the General Government will no longer be dreaded. In those cases of a local nature and for all the great purposes for which it was instituted its authority will be cherished. Each government will acquire new force and a greater freedom of action within its proper sphere. Other inestimable advantages will follow. Our produce will be augmented to an incalculable amount in articles of the greatest value for domestic use and foreign commerce. Our navigation will in like degree be increased, and as the shipping of the Atlantic States will be employed in the transportation of the vast produce of the Western country, even those parts of the United States which are most remote from each other will be further bound together by the strongest ties which mutual interest can create.

The situation of this District, it is thought, requires the attention of Congress. By the Constitution the power of legislation is exclusively vested in the Congress of the United States. In the exercise of this power, in which the people have no participation, Congress legislate in all cases directly on the local concerns of the District. As this is a departure, for a special purpose, from the general principles of our system, it may merit consideration whether an arrangement better adapted to the principles of our Government and to the particular interests of the people may not be devised which will neither infringe the Constitution nor affect the object which the provision in question was intended to secure. The growing population, already considerable, and the increasing business of the District, which it is believed already interferes with the deliberations of Congress on great national concerns, furnish additional motives for recommending this subject to your consideration.

When we view the great blessings with which our country has been favored, those which we now enjoy, and the means which we possess of handing them down unimpaired to our latest posterity, our attention is irresistibly drawn to the source from whence they flow. Let us, then, unite in offering our most grateful acknowledgments for these blessings to the Divine Author of All Good.

THIRD ANNUAL MESSAGE.

WASHINGTON, *December 7, 1819.*

Fellow-Citizens of the Senate and of the House of Representatives:

The public buildings being advanced to a stage to afford accommodation for Congress, I offer you my sincere congratulations on the recommencement of your duties in the Capitol.

In bringing to view the incidents most deserving attention which have occurred since your last session, I regret to have to state that several of our principal cities have suffered by sickness, that an unusual drought has prevailed in the Middle and Western States, and that a derangement has been felt in some of our moneyed institutions which has proportionably affected their credit. I am happy, however, to have it in my power to assure you that the health of our cities is now completely restored; that the produce of the year, though less abundant than usual, will not only be amply sufficient for home consumption, but afford a large surplus for the supply of the wants of other nations, and that the derangement in the circulating paper medium, by being left to those remedies which its obvious causes suggested and the good sense and virtue of our fellow-citizens supplied, has diminished.

Having informed Congress, on the 27th of February last, that a treaty of amity, settlement, and limits had been concluded in this city between the United States and Spain, and ratified by the competent authorities of the former, full confidence was entertained that it would have been ratified by His Catholic Majesty with equal promptitude and a like earnest desire to terminate on the conditions of that treaty the differences

which had so long existed between the two countries. Every view which
the subject admitted of was thought to have justified this conclusion.
Great losses had been sustained by citizens of the United States from
Spanish cruisers more than twenty years before, which had not been redressed. These losses had been acknowledged and provided for by a
treaty as far back as the year 1802, which, although concluded at Madrid,
was not then ratified by the Government of Spain, nor since, until the
last year, when it was suspended by the late treaty, a more satisfactory
provision to both parties, as was presumed, having been made for them.
Other differences had arisen in this long interval, affecting their highest interests, which were likewise provided for by this last treaty. The
treaty itself was formed on great consideration and a thorough knowledge
of all circumstances, the subject-matter of every article having been for
years under discussion and repeated references having been made by
the minister of Spain to his Government on the points respecting which
the greatest difference of opinion prevailed. It was formed by a minister
duly authorized for the purpose, who had represented his Government in
the United States and been employed in this long-protracted negotiation
several years, and who, it is not denied, kept strictly within the letter of
his instructions. The faith of Spain was therefore pledged, under circumstances of peculiar force and solemnity, for its ratification. On the
part of the United States this treaty was evidently acceded to in a spirit
of conciliation and concession. The indemnity for injuries and losses so
long before sustained, and now again acknowledged and provided for,
was to be paid by them without becoming a charge on the treasury of
Spain. For territory ceded by Spain other territory of great value, to
which our claim was believed to be well founded, was ceded by the United
States, and in a quarter more interesting to her. This cession was nevertheless received as the means of indemnifying our citizens in a considerable sum, the presumed amount of their losses. Other considerations of
great weight urged the cession of this territory by Spain. It was surrounded by the Territories of the United States on every side except on
that of the ocean. Spain had lost her authority over it, and, falling into
the hands of adventurers connected with the savages, it was made the
means of unceasing annoyance and injury to our Union in many of its
most essential interests. By this cession, then, Spain ceded a territory in
reality of no value to her and obtained concessions of the highest importance by the settlement of long-standing differences with the United
States affecting their respective claims and limits, and likewise relieved
herself from the obligation of a treaty relating to it which she had failed
to fulfill, and also from the responsibility incident to the most flagrant
and pernicious abuses of her rights where she could not support her
authority.

It being known that the treaty was formed under these circumstances,
not a doubt was entertained that His Catholic Majesty would have rati-

fied it without delay. I regret to have to state that this reasonable expectation has been disappointed; that the treaty was not ratified within the time stipulated and has not since been ratified. As it is important that the nature and character of this unexpected occurrence should be distinctly understood, I think it my duty to communicate to you all the facts and circumstances in my possession relating to it.

Anxious to prevent all future disagreement with Spain by giving the most prompt effect to the treaty which had been thus concluded, and particularly by the establishment of a government in Florida which should preserve order there, the minister of the United States who had been recently appointed to His Catholic Majesty, and to whom the ratification by his Government had been committed to be exchanged for that of Spain, was instructed to transmit the latter to the Department of State as soon as obtained, by a public ship subjected to his order for the purpose. Unexpected delay occurring in the ratification by Spain, he requested to be informed of the cause. It was stated in reply that the great importance of the subject, and a desire to obtain explanations on certain points which were not specified, had produced the delay, and that an envoy would be dispatched to the United States to obtain such explanations of this Government. The minister of the United States offered to give full explanation on any point on which it might be desired, which proposal was declined. Having communicated this result to the Department of State in August last, he was instructed, notwithstanding the disappointment and surprise which it produced, to inform the Government of Spain that if the treaty should be ratified and transmitted here at any time before the meeting of Congress it would be received and have the same effect as if it had been ratified in due time. This order was executed, the authorized communication was made to the Government of Spain, and by its answer, which has just been received, we are officially made acquainted for the first time with the causes which have prevented the ratification of the treaty by His Catholic Majesty. It is alleged by the minister of Spain that this Government had attempted to alter one of the principal articles of the treaty by a declaration which the minister of the United States had been ordered to present when he should deliver the ratification by his Government in exchange for that of Spain, and of which he gave notice, explanatory of the sense in which that article was understood. It is further alleged that this Government had recently tolerated or protected an expedition from the United States against the Province of Texas. These two imputed acts are stated as the reasons which have induced His Catholic Majesty to withhold his ratification from the treaty, to obtain explanations respecting which it is repeated that an envoy would be forthwith dispatched to the United States. How far these allegations will justify the conduct of the Government of Spain will appear on a view of the following facts and the evidence which supports them:

It will be seen by the documents transmitted herewith that the declaration mentioned relates to a clause in the eighth article concerning certain grants of land recently made by His Catholic Majesty in Florida, which it was understood had conveyed all the lands which till then had been ungranted; it was the intention of the parties to annul these latter grants, and that clause was drawn for that express purpose and for none other. The date of these grants was unknown, but it was understood to be posterior to that inserted in the article; indeed, it must be obvious to all that if that provision in the treaty had not the effect of annulling these grants, it would be altogether nugatory. Immediately after the treaty was concluded and ratified by this Government an intimation was received that these grants were of anterior date to that fixed on by the treaty and that they would not, of course, be affected by it. The mere possibility of such a case, so inconsistent with the intention of the parties and the meaning of the article, induced this Government to demand an explanation on the subject, which was immediately granted, and which corresponds with this statement. With respect to the other act alleged, that this Government had tolerated or protected an expedition against Texas, it is utterly without foundation. Every discountenance has invariably been given to any such attempt from within the limits of the United States, as is fully evinced by the acts of the Government and the proceedings of the courts. There being cause, however, to apprehend, in the course of the last summer, that some adventurers entertained views of the kind suggested, the attention of the constituted authorities in that quarter was immediately drawn to them, and it is known that the project, whatever it might be, has utterly failed.

These facts will, it is presumed, satisfy every impartial mind that the Government of Spain had no justifiable cause for declining to ratify the treaty. A treaty concluded in conformity with instructions is obligatory, in good faith, in all its stipulations, according to the true intent and meaning of the parties. Each party is bound to ratify it. If either could set it aside without the consent of the other, there would be no longer any rules applicable to such transactions between nations. By this proceeding the Government of Spain has rendered to the United States a new and very serious injury. It has been stated that a minister would be sent to ask certain explanations of this Government; but if such were desired, why were they not asked within the time limited for the ratification? Is it contemplated to open a new negotiation respecting any of the articles or conditions of the treaty? If that were done, to what consequences might it not lead? At what time and in what manner would a new negotiation terminate? By this proceeding Spain has formed a relation between the two countries which will justify any measures on the part of the United States which a strong sense of injury and a proper regard for the rights and interests of the nation may dictate.

In the course to be pursued these objects should be constantly held in view and have their due weight. Our national honor must be maintained, and a new and a distinguished proof be afforded of that regard for justice and moderation which has invariably governed the councils of this free people. It must be obvious to all that if the United States had been desirous of making conquests, or had been even willing to aggrandize themselves in that way, they could have had no inducement to form this treaty. They would have much cause for gratulation at the course which has been pursued by Spain. An ample field for ambition is open before them, but such a career is not consistent with the principles of their Government nor the interests of the nation.

From a full view of all circumstances, it is submitted to the consideration of Congress whether it will not be proper for the United States to carry the conditions of the treaty into effect in the same manner as if it had been ratified by Spain, claiming on their part all its advantages and yielding to Spain those secured to her. By pursuing this course we shall rest on the sacred ground of right, sanctioned in the most solemn manner by Spain herself by a treaty which she was bound to ratify, for refusing to do which she must incur the censure of other nations, even those most friendly to her, while by confining ourselves within that limit we can not fail to obtain their well-merited approbation. We must have peace on a frontier where we have been so long disturbed; our citizens must be indemnified for losses so long since sustained, and for which indemnity has been so unjustly withheld from them. Accomplishing these great objects, we obtain all that is desirable.

But His Catholic Majesty has twice declared his determination to send a minister to the United States to ask explanations on certain points and to give them respecting his delay to ratify the treaty. Shall we act by taking the ceded territory and proceeding to execute the other conditions of the treaty before this minister arrives and is heard? This is a case which forms a strong appeal to the candor, the magnanimity, and the honor of this people. Much is due to courtesy between nations. By a short delay we shall lose nothing, for, resting on the ground of immutable truth and justice, we can not be diverted from our purpose. It ought to be presumed that the explanations which may be given to the minister of Spain will be satisfactory, and produce the desired result. In any event, the delay for the purpose mentioned, being a further manifestation of the sincere desire to terminate in the most friendly manner all differences with Spain, can not fail to be duly appreciated by His Catholic Majesty as well as by other powers. It is submitted, therefore, whether it will not be proper to make the law proposed for carrying the conditions of the treaty into effect, should it be adopted, contingent; to suspend its operation, upon the responsibility of the Executive, in such manner as to afford an opportunity for such friendly explanations as may be desired during the present session of Congress.

I communicate to Congress a copy of the treaty and of the instructions to the minister of the United States at Madrid respecting it; of his correspondence with the minister of Spain, and of such other documents as may be necessary to give a full view of the subject.

In the course which the Spanish Government have on this occasion thought proper to pursue it is satisfactory to know that they have not been countenanced by any other European power. On the contrary, the opinion and wishes both of France and Great Britain have not been withheld either from the United States or from Spain, and have been unequivocal in favor of the ratification. There is also reason to believe that the sentiments of the Imperial Government of Russia have been the same, and that they have also been made known to the cabinet of Madrid.

In the civil war existing between Spain and the Spanish Provinces in this hemisphere the greatest care has been taken to enforce the laws intended to preserve an impartial neutrality. Our ports have continued to be equally open to both parties and on the same conditions, and our citizens have been equally restrained from interfering in favor of either to the prejudice of the other. The progress of the war, however, has operated manifestly in favor of the colonies. Buenos Ayres still maintains unshaken the independence which it declared in 1816, and has enjoyed since 1810. Like success has also lately attended Chili and the Provinces north of the La Plata bordering on it, and likewise Venezuela.

This contest has from its commencement been very interesting to other powers, and to none more so than to the United States. A virtuous people may and will confine themselves within the limit of a strict neutrality; but it is not in their power to behold a conflict so vitally important to their neighbors without the sensibility and sympathy which naturally belong to such a case. It has been the steady purpose of this Government to prevent that feeling leading to excess, and it is very gratifying to have it in my power to state that so strong has been the sense throughout the whole community of what was due to the character and obligations of the nation that very few examples of a contrary kind have occurred.

The distance of the colonies from the parent country and the great extent of their population and resources gave them advantages which it was anticipated at a very early period would be difficult for Spain to surmount. The steadiness, consistency, and success with which they have pursued their object, as evinced more particularly by the undisturbed sovereignty which Buenos Ayres has so long enjoyed, evidently give them a strong claim to the favorable consideration of other nations. These sentiments on the part of the United States have not been withheld from other powers, with whom it is desirable to act in concert. Should it become manifest to the world that the efforts of Spain to subdue these Provinces will be fruitless, it may be presumed that the Spanish Government itself will give up the contest. In producing such a determination it can not be doubted that the opinion of friendly powers who have taken no part in the controversy will have their merited influence.

It is of the highest importance to our national character and indispensable to the morality of our citizens that all violations of our neutrality should be prevented. No door should be left open for the evasion of our laws, no opportunity afforded to any who may be disposed to take advantage of it to compromit the interest or the honor of the nation. It is submitted, therefore, to the consideration of Congress whether it may not be advisable to revise the laws with a view to this desirable result.

It is submitted also whether it may not be proper to designate by law the several ports or places along the coast at which only foreign ships of war and privateers may be admitted. The difficulty of sustaining the regulations of our commerce and of other important interests from abuse without such designation furnishes a strong motive for this measure.

At the time of the negotiation for the renewal of the commercial convention between the United States and Great Britain a hope had been entertained that an article might have been agreed upon mutually satisfactory to both countries, regulating upon principles of justice and reciprocity the commercial intercourse between the United States and the British possessions as well in the West Indies as upon the continent of North America. The plenipotentiaries of the two Governments not having been able to come to an agreement on this important interest, those of the United States reserved for the consideration of this Government the proposals which had been presented to them as the ultimate offer on the part of the British Government, and which they were not authorized to accept. On their transmission here they were examined with due deliberation, the result of which was a new effort to meet the views of the British Government. The minister of the United States was instructed to make a further proposal, which has not been accepted. It was, however, declined in an amicable manner. I recommend to the consideration of Congress whether further prohibitory provisions in the laws relating to this intercourse may not be expedient. It is seen with interest that although it has not been practicable as yet to agree in any arrangement of this important branch of their commerce, such is the disposition of the parties that each will view any regulations which the other may make respecting it in the most friendly light.

By the fifth article of the convention concluded on the 20th of October, 1818, it was stipulated that the differences which have arisen between the two Governments with regard to the true intent and meaning of the fifth article of the treaty of Ghent, in relation to the carrying away by British officers of slaves from the United States after the exchange of the ratifications of the treaty of peace, should be referred to the decision of some friendly sovereign or state to be named for that purpose. The minister of the United States has been instructed to name to the British Government a foreign sovereign, the common friend to both parties, for the decision of this question. The answer of that Government to the proposal when received will indicate the further measures to be pursued on the part of the United States.

Although the pecuniary embarrassments which affected various parts of the Union during the latter part of the preceding year have during the present been considerably augmented, and still continue to exist, the receipts into the Treasury to the 30th of September last have amounted to $19,000,000. After defraying the current expenses of the Government, including the interest and reimbursement of the public debt payable to that period, amounting to $18,200,000, there remained in the Treasury on that day more than $2,500,000, which, with the sums receivable during the remainder of the year, will exceed the current demands upon the Treasury for the same period.

The causes which have tended to diminish the public receipts could not fail to have a corresponding effect upon the revenue which has accrued upon imposts and tonnage during the three first quarters of the present year. It is, however, ascertained that the duties which have been secured during that period exceed $18,000,000, and those of the whole year will probably amount to $23,000,000.

For the probable receipts of the next year I refer you to the statements which will be transmitted from the Treasury, which will enable you to judge whether further provision be necessary.

The great reduction in the price of the principal articles of domestic growth which has occurred during the present year, and the consequent fall in the price of labor, apparently so favorable to the success of domestic manufactures, have not shielded them against other causes adverse to their prosperity. The pecuniary embarrassments which have so deeply affected the commercial interests of the nation have been no less adverse to our manufacturing establishments in several sections of the Union.

The great reduction of the currency which the banks have been constrained to make in order to continue specie payments, and the vitiated character of it where such reductions have not been attempted, instead of placing within the reach of these establishments the pecuniary aid necessary to avail themselves of the advantages resulting from the reduction in the prices of the raw materials and of labor, have compelled the banks to withdraw from them a portion of the capital heretofore advanced to them. That aid which has been refused by the banks has not been obtained from other sources, owing to the loss of individual confidence from the frequent failures which have recently occurred in some of our principal commercial cities.

An additional cause for the depression of these establishments may probably be found in the pecuniary embarrassments which have recently affected those countries with which our commerce has been principally prosecuted. Their manufactures, for the want of a ready or profitable market at home, have been shipped by the manufacturers to the United States, and in many instances sold at a price below their current value at the place of manufacture. Although this practice may from its nature be considered temporary or contingent, it is not on that account less injurious in its effects. Uniformity in the demand and price of an article is highly desirable to the domestic manufacturer.

It is deemed of great importance to give encouragement to our domestic manufacturers. In what manner the evils which have been adverted to may be remedied, and how far it may be practicable in other respects to afford to them further encouragement, paying due regard to the other great interests of the nation, is submitted to the wisdom of Congress.

The survey of the coast for the establishment of fortifications is now nearly completed, and considerable progress has been made in the collection of materials for the construction of fortifications in the Gulf of Mexico and in the Chesapeake Bay. The works on the eastern bank of the Potomac below Alexandria and on the Pea Patch, in the Delaware, are much advanced, and it is expected that the fortifications at the Narrows, in the harbor of New York, will be completed the present year. To derive all the advantages contemplated from these fortifications it was necessary that they should be judiciously posted, and constructed with a view to permanence. The progress hitherto has therefore been slow; but as the difficulties in parts heretofore the least explored and known are surmounted, it will in future be more rapid. As soon as the survey of the coast is completed, which it is expected will be done early in the next spring, the engineers employed in it will proceed to examine for like purposes the northern and northwestern frontiers.

The troops intended to occupy a station at the mouth of the St. Peters, on the Mississippi, have established themselves there, and those who were ordered to the mouth of the Yellow Stone, on the Missouri, have ascended that river to the Council Bluff, where they will remain until the next spring, when they will proceed to the place of their destination. I have the satisfaction to state that this measure has been executed in amity with the Indian tribes, and that it promises to produce, in regard to them, all the advantages which were contemplated by it.

Much progress has likewise been made in the construction of ships of war and in the collection of timber and other materials for shipbuilding. It is not doubted that our Navy will soon be augmented to the number and placed in all respects on the footing provided for by law.

The Board, consisting of engineers and naval officers, have not yet made their final report of sites for two naval depots, as instructed according to the resolutions of March 18 and April 20, 1818, but they have examined the coast therein designated, and their report is expected in the next month.

For the protection of our commerce in the Mediterranean, along the southern Atlantic coast, in the Pacific and Indian oceans, it has been found necessary to maintain a strong naval force, which it seems proper for the present to continue. There is much reason to believe that if any portion of the squadron heretofore stationed in the Mediterranean should be withdrawn our intercourse with the powers bordering on that sea would be much interrupted, if not altogether destroyed. Such, too, has been the growth of a spirit of piracy in the other quarters mentioned, by adventurers from every country, in abuse of the friendly flags which they have assumed, that not to protect our commerce there would be to abandon it as a prey to their rapacity. Due attention has likewise been paid to the suppression of the slave trade, in compliance with a law of the last session. Orders have been given to the commanders of all our public ships to seize all vessels navigated under our flag engaged in that trade, and to bring them in to be proceeded against in the manner prescribed by that law. It is hoped that these vigorous measures, supported by like acts by other nations, will soon terminate a commerce so disgraceful to the civilized world.

In the execution of the duty imposed by these acts, and of a high trust connected with it, it is with deep regret I have to state the loss which has been sustained by the death of Commodore Perry. His gallantry in a brilliant exploit in the late war added to the renown of his country. His death is deplored as a national misfortune.

FOURTH ANNUAL MESSAGE.

WASHINGTON, *November 14, 1820.*
Fellow-Citizens of the Senate and of the House of Representatives:

In communicating to you a just view of public affairs at the commencement of your present labors, I do it with great satisfaction, because, taking all circumstances into consideration which claim attention, I see much cause to rejoice in the felicity of our situation. In making this remark I do not wish to be understood to imply that an unvaried prosperity is to be seen in every interest of this great community. In the progress of a nation inhabiting a territory of such vast extent and great variety of climate, every portion of which is engaged in foreign commerce and liable to be affected in some degree by the changes which occur in the condition and regulations of foreign countries, it would be strange if the produce of our soil and the industry and enterprise of our fellow-citizens received at all times and in every quarter an uniform and equal encouragement. This would be more than we would have a right to expect under circumstances the most favorable. Pressures on certain interests, it is admitted, have been felt; but allowing to these their greatest extent, they detract but little from the force of the remarks already made. In forming a just estimate of our present situation it is proper to look at the whole in the outline as well as in the detail. A free, virtuous, and enlightened people know well the great principles and causes on which their happiness depends, and even those who suffer most occasionally in their transitory concerns find great relief under their sufferings from the blessings which they otherwise enjoy and in the consoling and animating hope which they administer. From whence do these pressures come? Not from a government which is founded by, administered for, and supported by the people. We trace them to the peculiar character of the epoch in which we live, and to the extraordinary occurrences which have signalized it. The convulsions with which several of the powers of Europe have been shaken and the long and destructive wars in which all were engaged, with their sudden transition to a state of peace, presenting in the first instance unusual encouragement to our commerce and withdrawing it in the second even within its wonted limit, could not fail to be sensibly felt here. The station, too, which we had to support through this long conflict, compelled as we were finally to become a party to it with a principal power, and to make great exertions, suffer heavy losses, and to contract considerable debts, disturbing the ordinary course of affairs by augmenting to a vast amount the circulating medium, and thereby elevating at one time the price of every article above a just standard and depressing it at another below it, had likewise its due effect.

It is manifest that the pressures of which we complain have proceeded in a great measure from these causes. When, then, we take into view the prosperous and happy condition of our country in all the great circumstances which constitute the felicity of a nation—every individual in the full enjoyment of all his rights, the Union blessed with plenty and rapidly rising to greatness under a National Government which operates with complete effect in every part without being felt in any except by the ample protection which it affords, and under State governments which perform their equal share, according to a wise distribution of power between them, in promoting the public happiness—it is impossible to behold so gratifying, so glorious a spectacle without being penetrated with the most profound and grateful acknowledgments to the Supreme Author of All Good for such manifold and inestimable blessings. Deeply impressed with these sentiments, I can not regard the pressures to which I have adverted otherwise than in the light of mild and instructive admonitions, warning us of dangers to be shunned in future, teaching us lessons of economy corresponding with the simplicity and purity of our institutions and best adapted to their support, evincing the connection and dependence which the various parts of our happy Union have on each other, thereby augmenting daily our social incorporation and adding by its strong ties new strength and vigor to the political; opening a wider range, and with new encouragement, to the industry and enterprise of our fellow-citizens at home and abroad, and more especially by the multiplied proofs which it has accumulated of the great perfection of our most excellent system of government, the powerful instrument in the hands of our All-merciful Creator in securing to us these blessings.

Happy as our situation is, it does not exempt us from solicitude and care for the future.   On the contrary, as the blessings which we enjoy are great, proportionably great should be our vigilance, zeal, and activity to preserve them.   Foreign wars may again expose us to new wrongs, which would impose on us new duties for which we ought to be prepared. The state of Europe is unsettled, and how long peace may be preserved is altogether uncertain; in addition to which we have interests of our own to adjust which will require particular attention.   A correct view of our relations with each power will enable you to form a just idea of existing difficulties, and of the measures of precaution best adapted to them.

Respecting our relations with Spain nothing explicit can now be communicated.   On the adjournment of Congress in May last the minister plenipotentiary of the United States at Madrid was instructed to inform the Government of Spain that if His Catholic Majesty should then ratify the treaty this Government would accept the ratification so far as to submit to the decision of the Senate the question whether such ratification should be received in exchange for that of the United States heretofore given.   By letters from the minister of the United States to the Secretary of State it appears that a communication in conformity with his instructions had been made to the Government of Spain, and that the Cortes had the subject under consideration.   The result of the deliberations of that body, which is daily expected, will be made known to Congress as soon as it is received.   The friendly sentiment which was expressed on the part of the United States in the message of the 9th of May last is still entertained for Spain.   Among the causes of regret, however, which are inseparable from the delay attending this transaction it is proper to state that satisfactory information has been received that measures have been recently adopted by designing persons to convert certain parts of the Province of East Florida into depots for the reception of foreign goods, from whence to smuggle them into the United States. By opening a port within the limits of Florida, immediately on our boundary where there was no settlement, the object could not be misunderstood. An early accommodation of differences will, it is hoped, prevent all such fraudulent and pernicious practices, and place the relations of the two countries on a very amicable and permanent basis.

The commercial relations between the United States and the British colonies in the West Indies and on this continent have undergone no change, the British Government still preferring to leave that commerce under the restriction heretofore imposed on it on each side.   It is satisfactory to recollect that the restraints resorted to by the United States were defensive only, intended to prevent a monopoly under British regulations in favor of Great Britain, as it likewise is to know that the experiment is advancing in a spirit of amity between the parties.

The question depending between the United States and Great Britain respecting the construction of the first article of the treaty of Ghent has been referred by both Governments to the decision of the Emperor of Russia, who has accepted the umpirage.

An attempt has been made with the Government of France to regulate by treaty the commerce between the two countries on the principle of reciprocity and equality. By the last communication from the minister plenipotentiary of the United States at Paris, to whom full power had been given, we learn that the negotiation had been commenced there; but serious difficulties having occurred, the French Government had resolved to transfer it to the United States, for which purpose the minister plenipotentiary of France had been ordered to repair to this city, and whose arrival might soon be expected. It is hoped that this important interest may be arranged on just conditions and in a manner equally satisfactory to both parties. It is submitted to Congress to decide, until such arrangement is made, how far it may be proper, on the principle of the act of the last session which augmented the tonnage duty on French vessels, to adopt other measures for carrying more completely into effect the policy of that act.

The act referred to, which imposed new tonnage on French vessels, having been in force from and after the 1st day of July, it has happened that several vessels of that nation which had been dispatched from France before its existence was known have entered the ports of the United States, and been subject to its operation, without that previous notice which the general spirit of our laws gives to individuals in similar cases. The object of that law having been merely to countervail the inequalities which existed to the disadvantage of the United States in their commercial intercourse with France, it is submitted also to the consideration of Congress whether, in the spirit of amity and conciliation which it is no less the inclination than the policy of the United States to preserve in their intercourse with other powers, it may not be proper to extend relief to the individuals interested in those cases by exempting from the operation of the law all those vessels which have entered our ports without having had the means of previously knowing the existence of the additional duty.

The contest between Spain and the colonies, according to the most authentic information, is maintained by the latter with improved success. The unfortunate divisions which were known to exist some time since at Buenos Ayres it is understood still prevail. In no part of South America has Spain made any impression on the colonies, while in many parts, and particularly in Venezuela and New Grenada, the colonies have gained strength and acquired reputation, both for the management of the war in which they have been successful and for the order of the internal administration. The late change in the Government of Spain, by the reestablishment of the constitution of 1812, is an event which promises to be favorable to the revolution.   Under the authority of the Cortes the Congress of Angostura was invited to open a negotiation for the settlement of differences between the parties, to which it was replied that they would willingly open the negotiation provided the acknowledgment of their independence was made its basis, but not otherwise.   Of further proceedings between them we are uninformed.   No facts are known to this Government to warrant the belief that any of the powers of Europe will take part in the contest, whence it may be inferred, considering all circumstances which must have weight in producing the result, that an adjustment will finally take place on the basis proposed by the colonies. To promote that result by friendly counsels with other powers, including Spain herself, has been the uniform policy of this Government.

In looking to the internal concerns of our country you will, I am persuaded, derive much satisfaction from a view of the several objects to which, in the discharge of your official duties, your attention will be drawn.   Among these none holds a more important place than the public revenue, from the direct operation of the power by which it is raised on the people, and by its influence in giving effect to every other power of the Government.   The revenue depends on the resources of the country, and the facility by which the amount required is raised is a strong proof of the extent of the resources and of the efficiency of the Government. A few prominent facts will place this great interest in a just light before you.   On the 30th of September, 1815, the funded and floating debt of the United States was estimated at $119,635,558.   If to this sum be added the amount of 5 per cent stock subscribed to the Bank of the United States, the amount of Mississippi stock and of the stock which was issued subsequently to that date, the balances ascertained to be due to certain States for military services and to individuals for supplies furnished and services rendered during the late war, the public debt may be estimated as amounting at that date, and as afterwards liquidated, to $158,713,049. On the 30th of September, 1820, it amounted to $91,993,883, having been reduced in that interval by payments $66,879,165.   During this term the expenses of the Government of the United States were likewise defrayed in every branch of the civil, military, and naval establishments; the public edifices in this city have been rebuilt with considerable additions; extensive fortifications have been commenced, and are in a train of execution; permanent arsenals and magazines have been erected in various parts of the Union; our Navy has been considerably augmented, and the ordnance, munitions of war, and stores of the Army and Navy, which were much exhausted during the war, have been replenished.

By the discharge of so large a proportion of the public debt and the execution of such extensive and important operations in so short a time a just estimate may be formed of the great extent of our national resources.   The demonstration is the more complete and gratifying when it is recollected that the direct tax and excise were repealed soon after the termination of the late war, and that the revenue applied to these purposes has been derived almost wholly from other sources.

The receipts into the Treasury from every source to the 30th of September last have amounted to $16,794,107.66, whilst the public expenditures to the same period amounted to $16,871,534.72, leaving in the Treasury on that day a sum estimated at $1,950,000. For the probable receipts of the following year I refer you to the statement which will be transmitted from the Treasury.

The sum of $3,000,000 authorized to be raised by loan by an act of the last session of Congress has been obtained upon terms advantageous to the Government, indicating not only an increased confidence in the faith of the nation, but the existence of a large amount of capital seeking that mode of investment at a rate of interest not exceeding 5 per cent per annum.

It is proper to add that there is now due to the Treasury for the sale of public lands $22,996,545. In bringing this subject to view I consider it my duty to submit to Congress whether it may not be advisable to extend to the purchasers of these lands, in consideration of the unfavorable change which has occurred since the sales, a reasonable indulgence. It is known that the purchases were made when the price of every article had risen to its greatest height, and that the installments are becoming due at a period of great depression. It is presumed that some plan may be devised by the wisdom of Congress, compatible with the public interest, which would afford great relief to these purchasers.

Considerable progress has been made during the present season in ex amining the coast and its various bays and other inlets, in the collectiou of materials, and in the construction of fortifications for the defense of the Union at several of the positions at which it has been decided to erect such works. At Mobile Point and Dauphin Island, and at the Rigolets, leading to Lake Pontchartrain, materials to a considerable amount have been collected, and all the necessary preparations made for the commencement of the works. At Old Point Comfort, at the mouth of James River, and at the Rip-Rap, on the opposite shore in the Chesapeake Bay, materials to a vast amount have been collected; and at the Old Point some progress has been made in the construction of the fortification, which is on a very extensive scale. The work at Fort Washington, on this river, will be completed early in the next spring, and that on the Pea Patch, in the Delaware, in the course of the next season. Fort Diamond, at the Narrows, in the harbor of New York, will be finished this year. The works at Boston, New York, Baltimore, Norfolk, Charleston, and Niagara have been in part repaired, and the coast of North Carolina, extending south to Cape Fear, has been examined, as have likewise other parts of the coast eastward of Boston. Great exertions have been made to push forward these works with the utmost dispatch possible; but when their extent is considered, with the important purposes for which they are intended—the defense of the whole coast, and, in consequence, of the whole interior—and that they are to last for ages, it will be manifest that a well-digested plan, founded on military principles, connecting the whole together, combining security with economy, could not be prepared without repeated examinations of the most exposed and difficult parts, and that it would also take considerable time to collect the materials at the several points where they would be required. From all the light that has been shed on this subject I am satisfied that every favorable anticipation which has been formed of this great undertaking will be verified, and that when completed it will afford very great if not complete protection to our Atlantic frontier in the event of another war—a protection sufficient to counterbalance in a single campaign with an enemy powerful at sea the expense of all these works, without taking into the estimate the saving of the lives of so many of our citizens, the protection of our towns and other property, or the tendency of such works to prevent war.

Our military positions have been maintained at Belle Point, on the Arkansas, at Council Bluffs, on the Missouri, at St. Peters, on the Mississippi, and at Green Bay, on the upper Lakes. Commodious barracks have already been erected at most of these posts, with such works as were necessary for their defense. Progress has also been made in opening communications between them and in raising supplies at each for the support of the troops by their own labor, particularly those most remote.

With the Indians peace has been preserved and a progress made in carrying into effect the act of Congress making an appropriation for their civilization, with the prospect of favorable results. As connected equally with both these objects, our trade with those tribes is thought to merit the attention of Congress. In their original state game is their sustenance and war their occupation, and if they find no employment from civilized powers they destroy each other. Left to themselves their extirpation is inevitable. By a judicious regulation of our trade with them we supply their wants, administer to their comforts, and gradually, as the game retires, draw them to us. By maintaining posts far in the interior we acquire a more thorough and direct control over them, without which it is confidently believed that a complete change in their manners can never be accomplished. By such posts, aided by a proper regulation of our trade with them and a judicious civil administration over them, to be provided for by law, we shall, it is presumed, be enabled not only to protect our own settlements from their savage incursions and preserve peace among the several tribes, but accomplish also the great purpose of their civilization.

Considerable progress has also been made in the construction of ships of war, some of which have been launched in the course of the present year.

Our peace with the powers on the coast of Barbary has been preserved, but we owe it altogether to the presence of our squadron in the Mediterranean. It has been found equally necessary to employ some of our vessels for the protection of our commerce in the Indian Sea, the Pacific, and along the Atlantic coast. The interests which we have depending in those quarters, which have been much improved of late, are of great extent and of high importance to the nation as well as to the parties concerned, and would undoubtedly suffer if such protection was not extended to them. In execution of the law of the last session for the suppression of the slave trade some of our public ships have also been employed on the coast of Africa, where several captures have already been made of vessels engaged in that disgraceful traffic.

FIFTH ANNUAL MESSAGE.

WASHINGTON, *December 3, 1821.*

Fellow-Citizens of the Senate and of the House of Representatives:

The progress of our affairs since the last session has been such as may justly be claimed and expected under a Government deriving all its powers from an enlightened people, and under laws formed by their representatives, on great consideration, for the sole purpose of promoting the welfare and happiness of their constituents. In the execution of those laws and of the powers vested by the Constitution in the Executive, unremitted attention has been paid to the great objects to which they extend. In the concerns which are exclusively internal there is good cause to be satisfied with the result. The laws have had their due operation and effect. In those relating to foreign powers, I am happy to state that peace and amity are preserved with all by a strict observance on both sides of the rights of each. In matters touching our commercial intercourse, where a difference of opinion has existed as to the conditions on which it should be placed, each party has pursued its own policy without giving just cause of offense to the other. In this annual communication, especially when it is addressed to a new Congress, the whole scope of our political concerns naturally comes into view, that errors, if such have been committed, may be corrected; that defects which have become manifest may be remedied; and, on the other hand, that measures which were adopted on due deliberation, and which experience has shewn are just in themselves and essential to the public welfare, should be persevered in and supported. In performing this necessary and very important duty I shall endeavor to place before you on its merits every subject that is thought to be entitled to your particular attention in as distinct and clear a light as I may be able.

By an act of the 3d of March, 1815, so much of the several acts as imposed higher duties on the tonnage of foreign vessels and on the manufactures and productions of foreign nations when imported into the United States in foreign vessels than when imported in vessels of the United States were repealed so far as respected the manufactures and productions of the nation to which such vessels belonged, on the condition that the repeal should take effect only in favor of any foreign nation when the Executive should be satisfied that such discriminating duties to the disadvantage of the United States had likewise been repealed by such nation. By this act a proposition was made to all nations to place our commerce with each on a basis which it was presumed would be acceptable to all. Every nation was allowed to bring its manufactures and productions into our ports and to take the manufactures and productions of the United States back to their ports in their own vessels on the same conditions that they might be transported in vessels of the United States, and in return it was required that a like accommodation should be granted to the vessels of the United States in the ports of other powers. The articles to be admitted or prohibited on either side formed no part of the proposed arrangement. Each party would retain the right to admit or prohibit such articles from the other as it thought proper, and on its own conditions.

When the nature of the commerce between the United States and every other country was taken into view, it was thought that this proposition would be considered fair, and even liberal, by every power. The exports of the United States consist generally of articles of the first necessity and of rude materials in demand for foreign manufactories, of great bulk, requiring for their transportation many vessels, the return for which in the manufactures and productions of any foreign country, even when disposed of there to advantage, may be brought in a single vessel. This observation is the more especially applicable to those countries from which manufactures alone are imported, but it applies in a great extent to the European dominions of every European power and in a certain extent to all the colonies of those powers. By placing, then, the navigation precisely on the same ground in the transportation of exports and imports between the United States and other countries it was presumed that all was offered which could be desired. It seemed to be the only proposition which could be devised which would retain even the semblance of equality in our favor.

Many considerations of great weight gave us a right to expect that this commerce should be extended to the colonies as well as to the European dominions of other powers. With the latter, especially with countries exclusively manufacturing, the advantage was manifestly on their side. An indemnity for that loss was expected from a trade with the colonies, and with the greater reason as it was known that the supplies which the colonies derived from us were of the highest importance to them, their labor being bestowed with so much greater profit in the culture of other articles; and because, likewise, the articles of which those supplies consisted, forming so large a proportion of the exports of the United States, were never admitted into any of the ports of Europe except in cases of great emergency to avert a serious calamity. When no article is admitted which is not required to supply the wants of the party admitting it, and admitted then not in favor of any particular country to the disadvantage of others, but on conditions equally applicable to all, it seems just that the articles thus admitted and invited should be carried thither in the vessels of the country affording such supply and that the reciprocity should be found in a corresponding accommodation on the other side. By allowing each party to participate in the transportation of such supplies on the payment of equal tonnage a strong proof was afforded of an accommodating spirit. To abandon to it the transportation of the whole would be a sacrifice which ought not to be expected. The demand in the present instance would be the more unreasonable in consideration of the great inequality existing in the trade with the parent country.

Such was the basis of our system as established by the act of 1815 and such its true character. In the year in which this act was passed a treaty was concluded with Great Britain, in strict conformity with its principles, in regard to her European dominions. To her colonies, however, in the West Indies and on this continent it was not extended, the British Government claiming the exclusive supply of those colonies, and from our own ports, and of the productions of the colonies in return in her own vessels. To this claim the United States could not assent, and in consequence each party suspended the intercourse in the vessels of the other by a prohibition which still exists.

The same conditions were offered to France, but not accepted. Her Government has demanded other conditions more favorable to her navigation, and which should also give extraordinary encouragement to her manufactures and productions in ports of the United States. To these it was thought improper to accede, and in consequence the restrictive regulations which had been adopted on her part, being countervailed on the part of the United States, the direct commerce between the two countries in the vessels of each party has been in a great measure suspended. It is much to be regretted that, although a negotiation has been long pending, such is the diversity of views entertained on the various points which have been brought into discussion that there does not appear to be any reasonable prospect of its early conclusion.

It is my duty to state, as a cause of very great regret, that very serious differences have occurred in this negotiation respecting the construction of the eighth article of the treaty of 1803, by which Louisiana was ceded to the United States, and likewise respecting the seizure of the *Apollo*, in 1820, for a violation of our revenue laws. The claim of the Government of France has excited not less surprise than concern, because there does not appear to be a just foundation for it in either instance. By the eighth article of the treaty referred to it is stipulated that after the expiration of twelve years, during which time it was provided by the seventh or preceding article that the vessels of France and Spain should be admitted into the ports of the ceded territory without paying higher duties on merchandise or tonnage on the vessels than such as were paid by citizens of the United States, the ships of France should forever afterwards be placed on the footing of the most favored nation. By the obvious construction of this article it is presumed that it was intended that no favor should be granted to any power in those ports to which France should not be forthwith entitled, nor should any accommodation be allowed to another power on conditions to which she would not also be entitled on the same conditions. Under this construction no favor or accommodation could be granted to any power to the prejudice of France. By allowing the equivalent allowed by those powers she would always stand in those ports on the footing of the most favored nation. But if this article should be so construed as that France should enjoy, of right, and without paying the equivalent, all the advantages of such conditions as might be allowed to other powers in return for important concessions made by them, then the whole character of the stipulation would be changed. She would not be placed on the footing of the most favored nation, but on a footing held by no other nation. She would enjoy all advantages allowed to them in consideration of like advantages allowed to us, free from every and any condition whatever.

As little cause has the Government of France to complain of the seizure of the *Apollo* and the removal of other vessels from the waters of the St. Marys. It will not be denied that every nation has a right to regulate its commercial system as it thinks fit and to enforce the collection of its revenue, provided it be done without an invasion of the rights of other powers. The violation of its revenue laws is an offense which all nations punish, the punishment of which gives no just cause of complaint to the power to which the offenders belong, provided it be extended to all equally. In this case every circumstance which occurred indicated a fixed purpose to violate our revenue laws. Had the party intended to have pursued a fair trade he would have entered our ports and paid the duties; or had he intended to carry on a legitimate circuitous commerce with the United States he would have entered the port of some other power, landed his goods at the custom-house according to law, and reshipped and sent them in the vessel of such power, or of some other power which might lawfully bring them, free from such duties, to a port of the United States. But the conduct of the party in this case was altogether different. He entered the river St. Marys, the boundary line between the United States and Florida, and took his position on the Spanish side, on which in the whole extent of the river there was no town, no port or custom-house, and scarcely any settlement. His purpose, therefore, was not to sell his goods to the inhabitants of Florida, but to citizens of the United States, in exchange for their productions, which could not be done without a direct and palpable breach of our laws. It is known that a regular systematic plan had been formed by certain persons for the violation of our revenue system, which made it the more necessary to check the proceeding in its commencement.

That the unsettled bank of a river so remote from the Spanish garrisons and population could give no protection to any party in such a practice is believed to be in strict accord with the law of nations. It would not have comported with a friendly policy in Spain herself to have established a custom-house there, since it could have subserved no other purpose than to elude our revenue law. But the Government of Spain did not adopt that measure. On the contrary, it is understood that the Captain-General of Cuba, to whom an application to that effect was made by these adventurers, had not acceded to it. The condition of those Provinces for many years before they were ceded to the United States need not now be dwelt on. Inhabited by different tribes of Indians and an inroad for every kind of adventurer, the jurisdiction of Spain may be said to have been almost exclusively confined to her garrisons. It certainly could not extend to places where she had no authority. The rules, therefore, applicable to settled countries governed by laws could not be deemed so to the deserts of Florida and to the occurrences there. It merits attention also that the territory had then been ceded to the United States by a treaty the ratification of which had not been refused, and which has since been performed. Under any circumstances, therefore, Spain became less responsible for such acts committed there, and the United States more at liberty to exercise authority to prevent so great a mischief. The conduct of this Government has in every instance been conciliatory and friendly to France. The construction of our revenue law in its application to the cases which have formed the ground of such serious complaint on her part and the order to the collector of St. Marys, in accord with it, were given two years before these cases occurred, and in reference to a breach which was attempted by the subjects of another power. The application, therefore, to the cases in question was inevitable. As soon as the treaty by which these Provinces were ceded to the United States was ratified, and all danger of further breach of our revenue laws ceased, an order was given for the release of the vessel which had been seized and for the dismission of the libel which had been instituted against her.

The principles of this system of reciprocity, founded on the law of the 3d of March, 1815, have been since carried into effect with the Kingdoms of the Netherlands, Sweden, Prussia, and with Hamburg, Bremen, Lubeck, and Oldenburg, with a provision made by subsequent laws in regard to the Netherlands, Prussia, Hamburg, and Bremen that such produce and manufactures as could only be, or most usually were, first shipped from the ports of those countries, the same being imported in vessels wholly belonging to their subjects, should be considered and admitted as their own manufactures and productions.

The Government of Norway has by an ordinance opened the ports of that part of the dominions of the King of Sweden to the vessels of the United States upon the payment of no other or higher duties than are paid by Norwegian vessels, from whatever place arriving and with whatever articles laden. They have requested the reciprocal allowance for the vessels of Norway in the ports of the United States. As this privilege is not within the scope of the act of the 3d of March, 1815, and can only be granted by Congress, and as it may involve the commercial relations of the United States with other nations, the subject is submitted to the wisdom of Congress.

I have presented thus fully to your view our commercial relations with other powers, that, seeing them in detail with each power, and knowing the basis on which they rest, Congress may in its wisdom decide whether any change ought to be made, and, if any, in what respect. If this basis is unjust or unreasonable, surely it ought to be abandoned; but if it be just and reasonable, and any change in it will make concessions subversive of equality and tending in its consequences to sap the foundations of our prosperity, then the reasons are equally strong for adhering to the ground already taken, and supporting it by such further regulations as may appear to be proper, should any additional support be found necessary.

The question concerning the construction of the first article of the treaty of Ghent has been, by a joint act of the representatives of the United States and of Great Britain at the Court of St. Petersburg, submitted to the decision of His Imperial Majesty the Emperor of Russia. The result of that submission has not yet been received. The commissioners under the fifth article of that treaty not having been able to agree upon their decision, their reports to the two Governments, according to the provisions of the treaty, may be expected at an early day.

With Spain the treaty of February 22, 1819, has been partly carried into execution. Possession of East and West Florida has been given to the United States, but the officers charged with that service by an order from His Catholic Majesty, delivered by his minister to the Secretary of State, and transmitted by a special agent to the Captain-General of Cuba, to whom it was directed and in whom the government of those Provinces was vested, have not only omitted, in contravention of the order of their Sovereign, the performance of the express stipulation to deliver over the archives and documents relating to the property and sovereignty of those Provinces, all of which it was expected would have been delivered either before or when the troops were withdrawn, but defeated since every effort of the United States to obtain them, especially those of the greatest importance. This omission has given rise to several incidents of a painful nature, the character of which will be fully disclosed by the documents which will be hereafter communicated.

In every other circumstance the law of the 3d of March last, for carrying into effect that treaty, has been duly attended to. For the execution of that part which preserved in force, for the government of the inhabitants for the term specified, all the civil, military, and judicial powers exercised by the existing government of those Provinces an adequate number of officers, as was presumed, were appointed, and ordered to their respective stations. Both Provinces were formed into one Territory, and a governor appointed for it; but in consideration of the pre-existing division and of the distance and difficulty of communication between Pensacola, the residence of the governor of West Florida, and St. Augustine, that of the governor of East Florida, at which places the inconsiderable population of each Province was principally collected, two secretaries were appointed, the one to reside at Pensacola and the other at St. Augustine. Due attention was likewise paid to the execution of the laws of the United States relating to the revenue and the slave trade, which were extended to these Provinces. The whole Territory was divided into three collection districts, that part lying between the river St. Marys and Cape Florida forming one, that from the Cape to the Apalachicola another, and that from the Apalachicola to the Perdido the third. To these districts the usual number of revenue officers were appointed; and to secure the due operation of these laws one judge and a district attorney were appointed to reside at Pensacola, and likewise one judge and a district attorney to reside at St. Augustine, with a specified boundary between them; and one marshal for the whole, with authority to appoint a deputy. In carrying this law into effect, and especially that part relating to the powers of the existing government of those Provinces, it was thought important, in consideration of the short term for which it was to operate and the radical change which would be made at the approaching session of Congress, to avoid expense, to make no appointment which should not be absolutely necessary to give effect to those powers, to withdraw none of our citizens from their pursuits, whereby to subject the Government to claims which could not be gratified and the parties to losses which it would be painful to witness.

It has been seen with much concern that in the performance of these duties a collision arose between the governor of the Territory and the judge appointed for the western district. It was presumed that the law under which this transitory government was organized, and the commissions which were granted to the officers who were appointed to execute each branch of the system, and to which the commissions were adapted, would have been understood in the same sense by them in which they were understood by the Executive. Much allowance is due to officers employed in each branch of this system, and the more so as there is good cause to believe that each acted under the conviction that he possessed the power which he undertook to exercise. Of the officer holding the principal station, I think it proper to observe that he accepted it with reluctance, in compliance with the invitation given him, and from a high sense of duty to his country, being willing to contribute to the consummation of an event which would insure complete protection to an important part of our Union, which had suffered much from incursion and invasion, and to the defense of which his very gallant and patriotic services had been so signally and usefully devoted.

From the intrinsic difficulty of executing laws deriving their origin from different sources, and so essentially different in many important circumstances, the advantage, and indeed the necessity, of establishing as soon as may be practicable a well-organized government over that Territory on the principles of our system is apparent. This subject is therefore recommended to the early consideration of Congress.

In compliance with an injunction of the law of the 3d of March last, three commissioners have also been appointed and a board organized for carrying into effect the eleventh article of the treaty above recited, making provision for the payment of such of our citizens as have well-founded claims on Spain of the character specified by that treaty. This board has entered on its duties and made some progress therein. The commissioner and surveyor of His Catholic Majesty, provided for by the fourth article of the treaty, have not yet arrived in the United States, but are soon expected. As soon as they do arrive corresponding appointments will be made and every facility be afforded for the due execution of this service.

The Government of His Most Faithful Majesty since the termination of the last session of Congress has been removed from Rio de Janeiro to Lisbon, where a revolution similar to that which had occurred in the neighboring Kingdom of Spain had in like manner been sanctioned by the accepted and pledged faith of the reigning monarch. The diplomatic intercourse between the United States and the Portuguese dominions, interrupted by this important event, has not yet been resumed, but the change of internal administration having already materially affected the commercial intercourse of the United States with the Portuguese dominions, the renewal of the public missions between the two countries appears to be desirable at an early day.

It is understood that the colonies in South America have had great success during the present year in the struggle for their independence. The new Government of Colombia has extended its territories and considerably augmented its strength, and at Buenos Ayres, where civil dissensions had for some time before prevailed, greater harmony and better order appear to have been established. Equal success has attended their efforts in the Provinces on the Pacific. It has long been manifest that it would be impossible for Spain to reduce these colonies by force, and equally so that no conditions short of their independence would be satisfactory to them. It may therefore be presumed, and it is earnestly hoped, that the Government of Spain, guided by enlightened and liberal councils, will find it to comport with its interests and due to its magnanimity to terminate this exhausting controversy on that basis. To promote this result by friendly counsel with the Government of Spain will be the object of the Government of the United States.

In conducting the fiscal operations of the year it has been found necessary to carry into full effect the act of the last session of Congress authorizing a loan of $5,000,000. This sum has been raised at an average premium of $5.59 per centum upon stock bearing an interest at the rate of 5 per cent per annum, redeemable at the option of the Government after the 1st day of January, 1835.

There has been issued under the provisions of this act $4,735,296.30 of 5 per cent stock, and there has been or will be redeemed during the year $3,197,030.71 of Louisiana 6 per cent deferred stock and Mississippi stock. There has therefore been an actual increase of the public debt contracted during the year of $1,538,266.69.

The receipts into the Treasury from the 1st of January to the 30th of September last have amounted to $16,219,197.70, which, with the balance of $1,198,461.21 in the Treasury on the former day, make the aggregate sum of $17,417,658.91. The payments from the Treasury during the same period have amounted to $15,655,288.47, leaving in the Treasury on the last-mentioned day the sum of $1,762,370.44. It is estimated that the receipts of the fourth quarter of the year will exceed the demands which will be made on the Treasury during the same period, and that the amount in the Treasury on the 30th of September last will be increased on the 1st day of January next.

At the close of the last session it was anticipated that the progressive diminution of the public revenue in 1819 and 1820, which had been the result of the languid state of our foreign commerce in those years, had in the latter year reached its extreme point of depression. It has, however, been ascertained that that point was reached only at the termination of the first quarter of the present year. From that time until the 30th of September last the duties secured have exceeded those of the corresponding quarters of the last year $1,172,000, whilst the amount of debentures issued during the three first quarters of this year is $952,000 less than that of the same quarters of the last year.

There are just grounds to believe that the improvement which has occurred in the revenue during the last-mentioned period will not only be maintained, but that it will progressively increase through the next and several succeeding years, so as to realize the results which were presented upon that subject by the official reports of the Treasury at the commencement of the last session of Congress.

Under the influence of the most unfavorable circumstances the revenue for the next and subsequent years to the year 1825 will exceed the demands at present authorized by law.

It may fairly be presumed that under the protection given to domestic manufactures by the existing laws we shall become at no distant period a manufacturing country on an extensive scale. Possessing as we do the raw materials in such vast amount, with a capacity to augment them to an indefinite extent; raising within the country aliment of every kind to an amount far exceeding the demand for home consumption, even in the most unfavorable years, and to be obtained always at a very moderate price; skilled also, as our people are, in the mechanic arts and in every improvement calculated to lessen the demand for and the price of labor, it is manifest that their success in every branch of domestic industry may and will be carried, under the encouragement given by the present duties, to an extent to meet any demand which under a fair competition may be made upon it.

A considerable increase of domestic manufactures, by diminishing the importation of foreign, will probably tend to lessen the amount of the public revenue. As, however, a large proportion of the revenue which is derived from duties is raised from other articles than manufactures, the demand for which will increase with our population, it is believed that a fund will still be raised from that source adequate to the greater part of the public expenditures, especially as those expenditures, should we continue to be blessed with peace, will be diminished by the completion of the fortifications, dockyards, and other public works, by the augmentation of the Navy to the point to which it is proposed to carry it, and by the payment of the public debt, including pensions for military services.

It can not be doubted that the more complete our internal resources and the less dependent we are on foreign powers for every national as well as domestic purpose the greater and more stable will be the public felicity. By the increase of domestic manufactures will the demand for the rude materials at home be increased, and thus will the dependence of the several parts of our Union on each other and the strength of the Union itself be proportionably augmented. In this process, which is very desirable, and inevitable under the existing duties, the resources which obviously present themselves to supply a deficiency in the revenue, should it occur, are the interests which may derive the principal benefit from the change. If domestic manufactures are raised by duties on foreign, the deficiency in the fund necessary for public purposes should be supplied by duties on the former. At the last session it seemed doubtful whether the revenue derived from the present sources would be adequate to all the great purposes of our Union, including the construction of our fortifications, the augmentation of the Navy, and the protection of our commerce against the dangers to which it is exposed. Had the deficiency been such as to subject us to the necessity either to abandon those measures of defense or to resort to other means for adequate funds, the course presented to the adoption of a virtuous and enlightened people appeared to be a plain one. It must be gratifying to all to know that this necessity does not exist. Nothing, however, in contemplation of such important objects, which can be easily provided for, should be left to hazard. It is thought that the revenue may receive an augmentation from the existing sources, and in a manner to aid our manufactures, without hastening prematurely the result which has been suggested. It is believed that a moderate additional duty on certain articles would have that effect, without being liable to any serious objection.

The examination of the whole coast, for the construction of permanent fortifications, from St. Croix to the Sabine, with the exception of part of the territory lately acquired, will be completed in the present year, as will be the survey of the Mississippi, under the resolution of the House of Representatives, from the mouth of the Ohio to the ocean, and likewise of the Ohio from Louisville to the Mississippi. A progress corresponding with the sums appropriated has also been made in the construction of these fortifications at the points designated. As they will form a system of defense for the whole maritime frontier, and in consequence for the interior, and are to last for ages, the greatest care has been taken to fix the position of each work and to form it on such a scale as will be adequate to the purpose intended by it. All the inlets and assailable parts of our Union have been minutely examined, and positions taken with a view to the best effect, observing in every instance a just regard for economy. Doubts, however, being entertained as to the propriety of the position and extent of the work at Dauphine Island, further progress in it was suspended soon after the last session of Congress, and an order given to the Board of Engineers and Naval Commissioners to make a further and more minute examination of it in both respects, and to report the result without delay.

Due progress has been made in the construction of vessels of war according to the law providing for the gradual augmentation of the Navy, and to the extent of existing appropriations. The vessels authorized by the act of 1820 have all been completed and are now in actual service. None of the larger ships have been or will be launched for the present, the object being to protect all which may not be required for immediate service from decay by suitable buildings erected over them. A squadron has been maintained, as heretofore, in the Mediterranean, by means whereof peace has been preserved with the Barbary Powers. This squadron has been reduced the present year to as small a force as is compatible with the fulfillment of the object intended by it. From past experience and the best information respecting the views of those powers it is distinctly understood that should our squadron be withdrawn they would soon recommence their hostilities and depredations upon our commerce. Their fortifications have lately been rebuilt and their maritime force increased. It has also been found necessary to maintain a naval force on the Pacific for the protection of the very important interests of our citizens engaged in commerce and the fisheries in that sea. Vessels have likewise been employed in cruising along the Atlantic coast, in the Gulf of Mexico, on the coast of Africa, and in the neighboring seas. In the latter many piracies have been committed on our commerce, and so extensive was becoming the range of those unprincipled adventurers that there was cause to apprehend, without a timely and decisive effort to suppress them, the worst consequences would ensue. Fortunately, a considerable check has been given to that spirit by our cruisers, who have succeeded in capturing and destroying several of their vessels. Nevertheless, it is considered an object of high importance to continue these cruises until the practice is entirely suppressed. Like success has attended our efforts to suppress the slave trade. Under the flag of the United States and the sanction of their papers the trade may be considered as entirely suppressed, and if any of our citizens are engaged in it under the flags and papers of other powers, it is only from a respect to the rights of those powers that these offenders are not seized and brought home to receive the punishment which the laws inflict. If every other power should adopt the same policy and pursue the same vigorous means for carrying it into effect, the trade could no longer exist.

Deeply impressed with the blessings which we enjoy, and of which we have such manifold proofs, my mind is irresistibly drawn to that Almighty Being, the great source from whence they proceed and to whom our most grateful acknowledgments are due.

SIXTH ANNUAL MESSAGE.

WASHINGTON, *December 3, 1822.*

Fellow-Citizens of the Senate and House of Representatives:

Many causes unite to make your present meeting peculiarly interesting to our constituents. The operation of our laws on the various subjects to which they apply, with the amendments which they occasionally require, imposes annually an important duty on the representatives of a free people. Our system has happily advanced to such maturity that I am not aware that your cares in that respect will be augmented. Other causes exist which are highly interesting to the whole civilized world, and to no portion of it more so, in certain views, than to the United States. Of these causes and of their bearing on the interests of our Union I shall communicate the sentiments which I have formed with that freedom which a sense of duty dictates. It is proper, however, to invite your attention in the first instance to those concerns respecting which legislative provision is thought to be particularly urgent.

On the 24th of June last a convention of navigation and commerce was concluded in this city between the United States and France by ministers duly authorized for the purpose. The sanction of the Executive having been given to this convention under a conviction that, taking all its stipulations into view, it rested essentially on a basis of reciprocal and equal advantage, I deemed it my duty, in compliance with the authority vested in the Executive by the second section of the act of the last session of the 6th of May, concerning navigation, to suspend by proclamation until the end of the next session of Congress the operation of the act entitled "An act to impose a new tonnage duty on French ships and vessels, and for other purposes," and to suspend likewise all other duties on French vessels or the goods imported in them which exceeded the duties on American vessels and on similar goods imported in them. I shall submit this convention forthwith to the Senate for its advice and consent as to the ratification.

Since your last session the prohibition which had been imposed on the commerce between the United States and the British colonies in the West Indies and on this continent has likewise been removed. Satisfactory evidence having been adduced that the ports of those colonies had been opened to the vessels of the United States by an act of the British Parliament bearing date on the 24th of June last, on the conditions specified therein, I deemed it proper, in compliance with the provision of the first section of the act of the last session above recited, to declare, by proclamation bearing date on the 24th of August last, that the ports of the United States should thenceforward and until the end of the next session of Congress be opened to the vessels of Great Britain employed in that trade, under the limitation specified in that proclamation.

A doubt was entertained whether the act of Congress applied to the British colonies on this continent as well as to those in the West Indies, but as the act of Parliament opened the intercourse equally with both, and it was the manifest intention of Congress, as well as the obvious policy of the United States, that the provisions of the act of Parliament should be met in equal extent on the part of the United States, and as also the act of Congress was supposed to vest in the President some discretion in the execution of it, I thought it advisable to give it a corresponding construction.

Should the constitutional sanction of the Senate be given to the ratification of the convention with France, legislative provisions will be necessary to carry it fully into effect, as it likewise will be to continue in force, on such conditions as may be deemed just and proper, the intercourse which has been opened between the United States and the British colonies. Every light in the possession of the Executive will in due time be communicated on both subjects.

Resting essentially on a basis of reciprocal and equal advantage, it has been the object of the Executive in transactions with other powers to meet the propositions of each with a liberal spirit, believing that thereby the interest of our country would be most effectually promoted. This course has been systematically pursued in the late occurrences with France and Great Britain, and in strict accord with the views of the Legislature. A confident hope is entertained that by the arrangement thus commenced with each all differences respecting navigation and commerce with the dominions in question will be adjusted, and a solid foundation be laid for an active and permanent intercourse which will prove equally advantageous to both parties.

The decision of His Imperial Majesty the Emperor of Russia on the question submitted to him by the United States and Great Britain, concerning the construction of the first article of the treaty of Ghent, has been received. A convention has since been concluded between the parties, under the mediation of His Imperial Majesty, to prescribe the mode by which that article shall be carried into effect in conformity with that decision. I shall submit this convention to the Senate for its advice and consent as to the ratification, and, if obtained, shall immediately bring the subject before Congress for such provisions as may require the interposition of the Legislature.

In compliance with an act of the last session a Territorial government has been established in Florida on the principles of our system. By this act the inhabitants are secured in the full enjoyment of their rights and liberties, and to admission into the Union, with equal participation in the Government with the original States on the conditions heretofore prescribed to other Territories. By a clause in the ninth article of the treaty with Spain, by which that Territory was ceded to the United States, it is stipulated that satisfaction shall be made for the injuries, if any, which by process of law shall be established to have been suffered by the Spanish officers and individual Spanish inhabitants by the late operations of our troops in Florida. No provision having yet been made to carry that stipulation into effect, it is submitted to the consideration of Congress whether it will not be proper to vest the competent power in the district court at Pensacola, or in some tribunal to be specially organized for the purpose.

The fiscal operations of the year have been more successful than had been anticipated at the commencement of the last session of Congress.

The receipts into the Treasury during the three first quarters of the year have exceeded the sum of $14,745,000. The payments made at the Treasury during the same period have exceeded $12,279,000, leaving in the Treasury on the 30th day of September last, including $1,168,592.24 which were in the Treasury on the 1st day of January last, a sum exceeding $4,128,000.

Besides discharging all demands for the current service of the year, including the interest and reimbursement of the public debt, the 6 per cent stock of 1796, amounting to $80,000, has been redeemed. It is esti-mated that, after defraying the current expenses of the present quarter and redeeming the two millions of 6 per cent stock of 1820, there will remain in the Treasury on the 1st of January next nearly $3,000,000. It is estimated that the gross amount of duties which have been secured from the 1st of January to the 30th of September last has exceeded $19,500,000, and the amount for the whole year will probably not fall short of $23,000,000.

Of the actual force in service under the present military establishment, the posts at which it is stationed, and the condition of each post, a report from the Secretary of War which is now communicated will give a dis-tinct idea. By like reports the state of the Academy at West Point will be seen, as will be the progress which has been made on the fortifications along the coast and at the national armories and arsenals.

The position on the Red River and that at the Sault of St. Marie are the only new posts that have been taken. These posts, with those already occupied in the interior, are thought to be well adapted to the protection of our frontiers. All the force not placed in the garrisons along the coast and in the ordnance depots, and indispensably necessary there, is placed on the frontiers.

The organization of the several corps composing the Army is such as to admit its expansion to a great extent in case of emergency, the officers carrying with them all the light which they possess to the new corps to which they might be appointed.

With the organization of the staff there is equal cause to be satisfied. By the concentration of every branch with its chief in this city, in the presence of the Department, and with a grade in the chief military station to keep alive and cherish a military spirit, the greatest promptitude in the execution of orders, with the greatest economy and efficiency, are secured. The same view is taken of the Military Academy. Good order is preserved in it, and the youth are well instructed in every science con-nected with the great objects of the institution. They are also well trained and disciplined in the practical parts of the profession. It has been always found difficult to control the ardor inseparable from that early age in such manner as to give it a proper direction. The rights of manhood are too often claimed prematurely, in pressing which too far the respect which is due to age and the obedience necessary to a course of study and instruction in every such institution are sometimes lost sight of. The great object to be accomplished is the restraint of that ardor by such wise regulations and government as, by directing all the energies of the youthful mind to the attainment of useful knowledge, will keep it within a just subordination and at the same time elevate it to the highest purposes. This object seems to be essentially obtained in this institution, and with great advantage to the Union.

The Military Academy forms the basis, in regard to science, on which the military establishment rests. It furnishes annually, after due examination and on the report of the academic staff, many well-informed youths to fill the vacancies which occur in the several corps of the Army, while others who retire to private life carry with them such attainments as, under the right reserved to the several States to appoint the officers and to train the militia, will enable them, by affording a wider field for selection, to promote the great object of the power vested in Congress of providing for the organizing, arming, and disciplining the militia. Thus by the mutual and harmonious cooperation of the two governments in the execution of a power divided between them, an object always to be cherished, the attainment of a great result, on which our liberties may depend, can not fail to be secured. I have to add that in proportion as our regular force is small should the instruction and discipline of the militia, the great resource on which we rely, be pushed to the utmost extent that circumstances will admit.

A report from the Secretary of the Navy will communicate the progress which has been made in the construction of vessels of war, with other interesting details respecting the actual state of the affairs of that Department. It has been found necessary for the protection of our commerce to maintain the usual squadrons on the Mediterranean, the Pacific, and along the Atlantic coast, extending the cruises of the latter into the West Indies, where piracy, organized into a system, has preyed on the commerce of every country trading thither. A cruise has also been maintained on the coast of Africa, when the season would permit, for the suppression of the slave trade, and orders have been given to the commanders of all our public ships to seize our own vessels, should they find any engaged in that trade, and to bring them in for adjudication.

In the West Indies piracy is of recent date, which may explain the cause why other powers have not combined against it. By the documents communicated it will be seen that the efforts of the United States to suppress it have had a very salutary effect. The benevolent provision of the act under which the protection has been extended alike to the commerce of other nations can not fail to be duly appreciated by them.

In compliance with the act of the last session entitled "An act to abolish the United States trading establishments," agents were immediately appointed and instructed, under the direction of the Secretary of the Treasury, to close the business of the trading houses among the Indian tribes and to settle the accounts of the factors and subfactors engaged in that trade, and to execute in all other respects the injunctions of that act in the mode prescribed therein. A final report of their proceedings shall be communicated to Congress as soon as it is received.

It is with great regret I have to state that a serious malady has deprived us of many valuable citizens at Pensacola and checked the progress of some of those arrangements which are important to the Territory. This effect has been sensibly felt in respect to the Indians who inhabit that Territory, consisting of the remnants of several tribes who occupy the middle ground between St. Augustine and Pensacola, with extensive claims but undefined boundaries. Although peace is preserved with those Indians, yet their position and claims tend essentially to interrupt the intercourse between the eastern and western parts of the Territory, on which our inhabitants are principally settled. It is essential to the growth and prosperity of the Territory, as well as to the interests of the Union, that these Indians should be removed, by special compact with them, to some other position or concentrated within narrower limits where they are. With the limited means in the power of the Executive, instructions were given to the governor to accomplish this object so far as it might be practicable, which was prevented by the distressing malady referred to. To carry it fully into effect in either mode additional funds will be necessary, to the provision of which the powers of Congress alone are competent. With a view to such provision as may be deemed proper, the subject is submitted to your consideration, and in the interim further proceedings are suspended.

It appearing that so much of the act entitled "An act regulating the staff of the Army," which passed on the 14th April, 1818, as relates to the commissariat will expire in April next, and the practical operation of that department having evinced its great utility, the propriety of its renewal is submitted to your consideration.

The view which has been taken of the probable productiveness of the lead mines, connected with the importance of the material to the public defense, makes it expedient that they should be managed with peculiar care. It is therefore suggested whether it will not comport with the public interest to provide by law for the appointment of an agent skilled in mineralogy to superintend them, under the direction of the proper department.

It is understood that the Cumberland road, which was constructed at a great expense, has already suffered from the want of that regular superintendence and of those repairs which are indispensable to the preservation of such a work. This road is of incalculable advantage in facilitating the intercourse between the Western and the Atlantic States. Through it the whole country from the northern extremity of Lake Erie to the Mississippi, and from all the waters which empty into each, finds an easy and direct communication to the seat of Government, and thence to the Atlantic. The facility which it affords to all military and commercial operations, and also to those of the Post-Office Department, can not be estimated too highly. This great work is likewise an ornament and an honor to the nation. Believing that a competent power to adopt and execute a system of internal improvement has not been granted to Congress, but that such a power, confined to great national purposes and with proper limitations, would be productive of eminent advantage to our Union, I have thought it advisable that an amendment of the Constitution to that effect should be recommended to the several States.   A bill which assumed the right to adopt and execute such a system having been presented for my signature at the last session, I was compelled, from the view which I had taken of the powers of the General Government, to negative it, on which occasion I thought it proper to communicate the sentiments which I had formed, on mature consideration, on the whole subject.   To that communication, in all the views in which the great interest to which it relates may be supposed to merit your attention, I have now to refer.   Should Congress, however, deem it improper to recommend such an amendment, they have, according to my judgment, the right to keep the road in repair by providing for the superintendence of it and appropriating the money necessary for repairs.   Surely if they had the right to appropriate money to make the road they have a right to appropriate it to preserve the road from ruin.   From the exercise of this power no danger is to be apprehended.   Under our happy system the people are the sole and exclusive fountain of power.   Each government originates from them, and to them alone, each to its proper constituents, are they respectively and solely responsible for the faithful discharge of their duties within their constitutional limits; and that the people will confine their public agents of every station to the strict line of their constitutional duties there is no cause to doubt.   Having, however, communicated my sentiments to Congress at the last session fully in the document to which I have referred, respecting the right of appropriation as distinct from the right of jurisdiction and sovereignty over the territory in question, I deem it improper to enlarge on the subject here.

From the best information that I have been able to obtain it appears that our manufactures, though depressed immediately after the peace, have considerably increased, and are still increasing, under the encouragement given them by the tariff of 1816 and by subsequent laws.   Satisfied I am, whatever may be the abstract doctrine in favor of unrestricted commerce, provided all nations would concur in it and it was not liable to be interrupted by war, which has never occurred and can not be expected, that there are other strong reasons applicable to our situation and relations with other countries which impose on us the obligation to cherish and sustain our manufactures.   Satisfied, however, I likewise am that the interest of every part of our Union, even of those most benefited by manufactures, requires that this subject should be touched with the greatest caution, and a critical knowledge of the effect to be produced by the slightest change.   On full consideration of the subject in all its relations I am persuaded that a further augmentation may now be made of the duties on certain foreign articles in favor of our own and without affecting injuriously any other interest.   For more precise details I refer you to the communications which were made to Congress during the last session.

So great was the amount of accounts for moneys advanced during the late war, in addition to others of a previous date which in the regular operations of the Government necessarily remained unsettled, that it required a considerable length of time for their adjustment. By a report from the First Comptroller of the Treasury it appears that on the 4th of March, 1817, the accounts then unsettled amounted to $103,068,876.41, of which, on the 30th of September of the present year, $93,175,396.56 had been settled, leaving on that day a balance unsettled of $9,893,479.85. That there have been drawn from the Treasury, in paying the public debt and sustaining the Government in all its operations and disbursements, since the 4th of March, 1817, $157,199,380.96, the accounts for which have been settled to the amount of $137,501,451.12, leaving a balance unsettled of $19,697,929.84. For precise details respecting each of these balances I refer to the report of the Comptroller and the documents which accompany it.

From this view it appears that our commercial differences with France and Great Britain have been placed in a train of amicable arrangement on conditions fair and honorable in both instances to each party; that our finances are in a very productive state, our revenue being at present fully competent to all the demands upon it; that our military force is well organized in all its branches and capable of rendering the most important service in case of emergency that its number will admit of; that due progress has been made, under existing appropriations, in the construction of fortifications and in the operations of the Ordnance Department; that due progress has in like manner been made in the construction of ships of war; that our Navy is in the best condition, felt and respected in every sea in which it is employed for the protection of our commerce; that our manufactures have augmented in amount and improved in quality; that great progress has been made in the settlement of accounts and in the recovery of the balances due by individuals, and that the utmost economy is secured and observed in every Department of the Administration.

Other objects will likewise claim your attention, because from the station which the United States hold as a member of the great community of nations they have rights to maintain, duties to perform, and dangers to encounter.

A strong hope was entertained that peace would ere this have been concluded between Spain and the independent governments south of the United States in this hemisphere. Long experience having evinced the competency of those governments to maintain the independence which they had declared, it was presumed that the considerations which induced their recognition by the United States would have had equal weight with other powers, and that Spain herself, yielding to those magnanimous feelings of which her history furnishes so many examples, would have terminated on that basis a controversy so unavailing and at the same time so destructive. We still cherish the hope that this result will not long be postponed.

Sustaining our neutral position and allowing to each party while the war continues equal rights, it is incumbent on the United States to claim of each with equal rigor the faithful observance of our rights according to the well-known law of nations. From each, therefore, a like cooperation is expected in the suppression of the piratical practice which has grown out of this war and of blockades of extensive coasts on both seas, which, considering the small force employed to sustain them, have not the slightest foundation to rest on.

Europe is still unsettled, and although the war long menaced between Russia and Turkey has not broken out, there is no certainty that the differences between those powers will be amicably adjusted. It is impossible to look to the oppressions of the country respecting which those differences arose without being deeply affected. The mention of Greece fills the mind with the most exalted sentiments and arouses in our bosoms the best feelings of which our nature is susceptible. Superior skill and refinement in the arts, heroic gallantry in action, disinterested patriotism, enthusiastic zeal and devotion in favor of public and personal liberty are associated with our recollections of ancient Greece. That such a country should have been overwhelmed and so long hidden, as it were, from the world under a gloomy despotism has been a cause of unceasing and deep regret to generous minds for ages past. It was natural, therefore, that the reappearance of those people in their original character, contending in favor of their liberties, should produce that great excitement and sympathy in their favor which have been so signally displayed throughout the United States. A strong hope is entertained that these people will recover their independence and resume their equal station among the nations of the earth.

A great effort has been made in Spain and Portugal to improve the condition of the people, and it must be very consoling to all benevolent minds to see the extraordinary moderation with which it has been conducted. That it may promote the happiness of both nations is the ardent wish of this whole people, to the expression of which we confine ourselves; for whatever may be the feelings or sentiments which every individual under our Government has a right to indulge and express, it is nevertheless a sacred maxim, equally with the Government and people, that the destiny of every independent nation in what relates to such improvements of right belongs and ought to be left exclusively to themselves.

Whether we reason from the late wars or from those menacing symptoms which now appear in Europe, it is manifest that if a convulsion should take place in any of those countries it will proceed from causes which have no existence and are utterly unknown in these States, in which there is but one order, that of the people, to whom the sovereignty exclusively belongs. Should war break out in any of those countries, who can foretell the extent to which it may be carried or the desolation which it may spread? Exempt as we are from these causes, our internal tranquillity is secure; and distant as we are from the troubled scene, and faithful to first principles in regard to other powers, we might reasonably presume that we should not be molested by them. This, however, ought not to be calculated on as certain. Unprovoked injuries are often inflicted, and even the peculiar felicity of our situation might with some be a cause for excitement and aggression. The history of the late wars in Europe furnishes a complete demonstration that no system of conduct, however correct in principle, can protect neutral powers from injury from any party; that a defenseless position and distinguished love of peace are the surest invitations to war, and that there is no way to avoid it other than by being always prepared and willing for just cause to meet it. If there be a people on earth whose more especial duty it is to be at all times prepared to defend the rights with which they are blessed, and to surpass all others in sustaining the necessary burthens, and in submitting to sacrifices to make such preparations, it is undoubtedly the people of these States.

When we see that a civil war of the most frightful character rages from the Adriatic to the Black Sea; that strong symptoms of war appear in other parts, proceeding from causes which, should it break out, may become general and be of long duration; that the war still continues between Spain and the independent governments, her late Provinces, in this hemisphere; that it is likewise menaced between Portugal and Brazil, in consequence of the attempt of the latter to dismember itself from the former, and that a system of piracy of great extent is maintained in the neighboring seas, which will require equal vigilance and decision to suppress it, the reasons for sustaining the attitude which we now hold and for pushing forward all our measures of defense with the utmost vigor appear to me to acquire new force.

The United States owe to the world a great example, and, by means thereof, to the cause of liberty and humanity a generous support. They have so far succeeded to the satisfaction of the virtuous and enlightened of every country. There is no reason to doubt that their whole movement will be regulated by a sacred regard to principle, all our institutions being founded on that basis. The ability to support our own cause under any trial to which it may be exposed is the great point on which the public solicitude rests. It has been often charged against free governments that they have neither the foresight nor the virtue to provide at the proper season for great emergencies; that their course is improvident and expensive; that war will always find them unprepared, and, whatever may be its calamities, that its terrible warnings will be disregarded and forgotten as soon as peace returns. I have full confidence that this charge so far as relates to the United States will be shewn to be utterly destitute of truth.

SEVENTH ANNUAL MESSAGE.

WASHINGTON, *December 2, 1823.*

Fellow-Citizens of the Senate and House of Representatives:

Many important subjects will claim your attention during the present session, of which I shall endeavor to give, in aid of your deliberations, a just idea in this communication. I undertake this duty with diffidence, from the vast extent of the interests on which I have to treat and of their great importance to every portion of our Union. I enter on it with zeal from a thorough conviction that there never was a period since the establishment of our Revolution when, regarding the condition of the civilized world and its bearing on us, there was greater necessity for devotion in the public servants to their respective duties, or for virtue, patriotism, and union in our constituents.

Meeting in you a new Congress, I deem it proper to present this view of public affairs in greater detail than might otherwise be necessary. I do it, however, with peculiar satisfaction, from a knowledge that in this respect I shall comply more fully with the sound principles of our Government. The people being with us exclusively the sovereign, it is indispensable that full information be laid before them on all important subjects, to enable them to exercise that high power with complete effect. If kept in the dark, they must be incompetent to it. We are all liable to error, and those who are engaged in the management of public affairs are more subject to exciten_ent and to be led astray by their particular interests and passions than the great body of our constituents, who, living at home in the pursuit of their ordinary avocations, are calm but deeply interested spectators of events and of the conduct of those who are parties to them. To the people every department of the Government and every individual in each are responsible, and the more full their information the better they can judge of the wisdom of the policy pursued and of the conduct of each in regard to it. From their dispassionate judgment much aid may always be obtained, while their approbation will form the greatest incentive and most gratifying reward for virtuous actions, and the dread of their censure the best security against the abuse of their confidence. Their interests in all vital questions are the same, and the bond, by sentiment as well as by interest, will be proportionably strengthened as they are better informed of the real state of public affairs, especially in difficult conjunctures. It is by such knowledge that local prejudices and jealousies are surmounted, and that a national policy, extending its fostering care and protection to all the great interests of our Union, is formed and steadily adhered to.

A precise knowledge of our relations with foreign powers as respects our negotiations and transactions with each is thought to be particularly necessary. Equally necessary is it that we should form a just estimate of our resources, revenue, and progress in every kind of improvement connected with the national prosperity and public defense. It is by rendering justice to other nations that we may expect it from them. It is by our ability to resent injuries and redress wrongs that we may avoid them.

The commissioners under the fifth article of the treaty of Ghent, having disagreed in their opinions respecting that portion of the boundary between the Territories of the United States and of Great Britain the establishment of which had been submitted to them, have made their respective reports in compliance with that article, that the same might be referred to the decision of a friendly power. It being manifest, however, that it would be difficult, if not impossible, for any power to perform that office without great delay and much inconvenience to itself, a proposal has been made by this Government, and acceded to by that of Great Britain, to endeavor to establish that boundary by amicable negotiation. It appearing from long experience that no satisfactory arrangement could be formed of the commercial intercourse between the United States and the British colonies in this hemisphere by legislative acts while each party pursued its own course without agreement or concert with the other, a proposal has been made to the British Government to regulate this commerce by treaty, as it has been to arrange in like manner the just claim of the citizens of the United States inhabiting the States and Territories bordering on the lakes and rivers which empty into the St. Lawrence to the navigation of that river to the ocean. For these and other objects of high importance to the interests of both parties a negotiation has been opened with the British Government which it is hoped will have a satisfactory result.

The commissioners under the sixth and seventh articles of the treaty of Ghent having successfully closed their labors in relation to the sixth, have proceeded to the discharge of those relating to the seventh. Their progress in the extensive survey required for the performance of their duties justifies the presumption that it will be completed in the ensuing year.

The negotiation which had been long depending with the French Government on several important subjects, and particularly for a just indemnity for losses sustained in the late wars by the citizens of the United States under unjustifiable seizures and confiscations of their property, has not as yet had the desired effect. As this claim rests on the same principle with others which have been admitted by the French Government, it is not perceived on what just ground it can be rejected. A minister will be immediately appointed to proceed to France and resume the negotiation on this and other subjects which may arise between the two nations.

At the proposal of the Russian Imperial Government, made through the minister of the Emperor residing here, a full power and instructions have been transmitted to the minister of the United States at St. Petersburg to arrange by amicable negotiation the respective rights and interests of the two nations on the northwest coast of this continent. A similar proposal had been made by His Imperial Majesty to the Government of Great Britain, which has likewise been acceded to. The Government of the United States has been desirous by this friendly proceeding of manifesting the great value which they have invariably attached to the friendship of the Emperor and their solicitude to cultivate the best understanding with his Government. In the discussions to which this interest has given rise and in the arrangements by which they may terminate the occasion has been judged proper for asserting, as a principle in which the rights and interests of the United States are involved, that the American continents, by the free and independent condition which they have assumed and maintain, are henceforth not to be considered as subjects for future colonization by any European powers.

Since the close of the last session of Congress the commissioners and arbitrators for ascertaining and determining the amount of indemnification which may be due to citizens of the United States under the decision of His Imperial Majesty the Emperor of Russia, in conformity to the convention concluded at St. Petersburg on the 12th of July, 1822, have assembled in this city, and organized themselves as a board for the performance of the duties assigned to them by that treaty. The commission constituted under the eleventh article of the treaty of the 22d of February, 1819, between the United States and Spain is also in session here, and as the term of three years limited by the treaty for the execution of the trust will expire before the period of the next regular meeting of Congress, the attention of the Legislature will be drawn to the measures which may be necessary to accomplish the objects for which the commission was instituted.

In compliance with a resolution of the House of Representatives adopted at their last session, instructions have been given to all the ministers of the United States accredited to the powers of Europe and America to propose the proscription of the African slave trade by classing it under the denomination, and inflicting on its perpetrators the punishment, of piracy. Should this proposal be acceded to, it is not doubted that this odious and criminal practice will be promptly and entirely suppressed. It is earnestly hoped that it will be acceded to, from the firm belief that it is the most effectual expedient that can be adopted for the purpose.

At the commencement of the recent war between France and Spain it was declared by the French Government that it would grant no commissions to privateers, and that neither the commerce of Spain herself nor of neutral nations should be molested by the naval force of France, except in the breach of a lawful blockade. This declaration, which appears to have been faithfully carried into effect, concurring with principles proclaimed and cherished by the United States from the first establishment of their independence, suggested the hope that the time had arrived when the proposal for adopting it as a permanent and invariable rule in all future maritime wars might meet the favorable consideration of the great European powers. Instructions have accordingly been given to our ministers with France, Russia, and Great Britain to make those proposals to their respective Governments, and when the friends of humanity reflect on the essential amelioration to the condition of the human race which would result from the abolition of private war on the sea and on the great facility by which it might be accomplished, requiring only the consent of a few sovereigns, an earnest hope is indulged that these overtures will meet with an attention animated by the spirit in which they were made, and that they will ultimately be successful.

The ministers who were appointed to the Republics of Colombia and Buenos Ayres during the last session of Congress proceeded shortly afterwards to their destinations. Of their arrival there official intelligence has not yet been received. The minister appointed to the Republic of Chile will sail in a few days. An early appointment will also be made to Mexico. A minister has been received from Colombia, and the other Governments have been informed that ministers, or diplomatic agents of inferior grade, would be received from each, accordingly as they might prefer the one or the other.

The minister appointed to Spain proceeded soon after his appointment for Cadiz, the residence of the Sovereign to whom he was accredited. In approaching that port the frigate which conveyed him was warned off by the commander of the French squadron by which it was blockaded and not permitted to enter, although apprised by the captain of the frigate of the public character of the person whom he had on board, the landing of whom was the sole object of his proposed entry. This act, being considered an infringement of the rights of ambassadors and of nations, will form a just cause of complaint to the Government of France against the officer by whom it was committed.

The actual condition of the public finances more than realizes the favorable anticipations that were entertained of it at the opening of the last session of Congress. On the 1st of January there was a balance in the Treasury of $4,237,427.55. From that time to the 30th September the receipts amounted to upward of $16,100,000, and the expenditures to $11,400,000. During the fourth quarter of the year it is estimated that the receipts will at least equal the expenditures, and that there will remain in the Treasury on the 1st day of January next a surplus of nearly $9,000,000.

On the 1st of January, 1825, a large amount of the war debt and a part of the Revolutionary debt become redeemable. Additional portions of the former will continue to become redeemable annually until the year 1835. It is believed, however, that if the United States remain at peace the whole of that debt may be redeemed by the ordinary revenue of those years during that period under the provision of the act of March 3, 1817, creating the sinking fund, and in that case the only part of the debt that will remain after the year 1835 will be the $7,000,000 of 5 per cent stock subscribed to the Bank of the United States, and the 3 per cent Revolutionary debt, amounting to $13,296,099.06, both of which are redeemable at the pleasure of the Government.

The state of the Army in its organization and discipline has been gradually improving for several years, and has now attained a high degree of perfection. The military disbursements have been regularly made and the accounts regularly and promptly rendered for settlement. The supplies of various descriptions have been of good quality, and regularly issued at all of the posts. A system of economy and accountability has been introduced into every branch of the service which admits of little additional improvement. This desirable state has been attained by the act reorganizing the staff of the Army, passed on the 14th of April, 1818.

The moneys appropriated for fortifications have been regularly and economically applied, and all the works advanced as rapidly as the amount appropriated would admit. Three important works will be completed in the course of this year—that is, Fort Washington, Fort Delaware, and the fort at the Rigolets, in Louisiana.

The Board of Engineers and the Topographical Corps have been in constant and active service in surveying the coast and projecting the works necessary for its defense.

The Military Academy has attained a degree of perfection in its discipline and instruction equal, as is believed, to any institution of its kind in any country.

The money appropriated for the use of the Ordnance Department has been regularly and economically applied. The fabrication of arms at the national armories and by contract with the Department has been gradually improving in quality and cheapness. It is believed that their quality is now such as to admit of but little improvement.

The completion of the fortifications renders it necessary that there should be a suitable appropriation for the purpose of fabricating the cannon and carriages necessary for those works.

Under the appropriation of $5,000 for exploring the Western waters for the location of a site for a Western armory, a commission was constituted, consisting of Colonel McRee, Colonel Lee, and Captain Talcott, who have been engaged in exploring the country. They have not yet reported the result of their labors, but it is believed that they will be prepared to do it at an early part of the session of Congress.

During the month of June last General Ashley and his party, who were trading under a license from the Government, were attacked by the Ricarees while peaceably trading with the Indians at their request. Several of the party were killed and wounded and their property taken or destroyed.

Colonel Leavenworth, who commanded Fort Atkinson, at the Council

Bluffs, the most western post, apprehending that the hostile spirit of the Ricarees would extend to other tribes in that quarter, and that thereby the lives of the traders on the Missouri and the peace of the frontier would be endangered, took immediate measures to check the evil.

With a detachment of the regiment stationed at the Bluffs he successfully attacked the Ricaree village, and it is hoped that such an impression has been made on them as well as on the other tribes on the Missouri as will prevent a recurrence of future hostility.

The report of the Secretary of War, which is herewith transmitted, will exhibit in greater detail the condition of the Department in its various branches, and the progress which has been made in its administration during the three first quarters of the year.

I transmit a return of the militia of the several States according to the last reports which have been made by the proper officers in each to the Department of War. By reference to this return it will be seen that it is not complete, although great exertions have been made to make it so. As the defense and even the liberties of the country must depend in times of imminent danger on the militia, it is of the highest importance that it be well organized, armed, and disciplined throughout the Union. The report of the Secretary of War shews the progress made during the three first quarters of the present year by the application of the fund appropriated for arming the militia. Much difficulty is found in distributing the arms according to the act of Congress providing for it from the failure of the proper departments in many of the States to make regular returns. The act of May 12, 1820, provides that the system of tactics and regulations of the various corps of the Regular Army shall be extended to the militia. This act has been very imperfectly executed from the want of uniformity in the organization of the militia, proceeding from the defects of the system itself, and especially in its application to that main arm of the public defense. It is thought that this important subject in all its branches merits the attention of Congress.

The report of the Secretary of the Navy, which is now communicated, furnishes an account of the administration of that Department for the three first quarters of the present year, with the progress made in augmenting the Navy, and the manner in which the vessels in commission have been employed.

The usual force has been maintained in the Mediterranean Sea, the Pacific Ocean, and along the Atlantic coast, and has afforded the necessary protection to our commerce in those seas.

In the West Indies and the Gulf of Mexico our naval force has been augmented by the addition of several small vessels provided for by the "act authorizing an additional naval force for the suppression of piracy," passed by Congress at their last session. That armament has been eminently successful in the accomplishment of its object. The piracies by which our commerce in the neighborhood of the island of Cuba had been afflicted have been repressed and the confidence of our merchants in a great measure restored.

The patriotic zeal and enterprise of Commodore Porter, to whom the command of the expedition was confided, has been fully seconded by the officers and men under his command. And in reflecting with high satisfaction on the honorable manner in which they have sustained the reputation of their country and its Navy, the sentiment is alloyed only by a concern that in the fulfillment of that arduous service the diseases incident to the season and to the climate in which it was discharged have deprived the nation of many useful lives, and among them of several officers of great promise.

In the month of August a very malignant fever made its appearance at Thompsons Island, which threatened the destruction of our station there. Many perished, and the commanding officer was severely attacked. Uncertain as to his fate and knowing that most of the medical officers had been rendered incapable of discharging their duties, it was thought expedient to send to that post an officer of rank and experience, with several skillful surgeons, to ascertain the origin of the fever and the probability of its recurrence there in future seasons; to furnish every assistance to those who were suffering, and, if practicable, to avoid the necessity of abandoning so important a station. Commodore Rodgers, with a promptitude which did him honor, cheerfully accepted that trust, and has discharged it in the manner anticipated from his skill and patriotism. Before his arrival Commodore Porter, with the greater part of the squadron, had removed from the island and returned to the United States in consequence of the prevailing sickness. Much useful information has, however, been obtained as to the state of the island and great relief afforded to those who had been necessarily left there.

Although our expedition, cooperating with an invigorated administration of the government of the island of Cuba, and with the corresponding active exertions of a British naval force in the same seas, have almost entirely destroyed the unlicensed piracies from that island, the success of our exertions has not been equally effectual to suppress the same crime, under other pretenses and colors, in the neighboring island of Porto Rico. They have been committed there under the abusive issue of Spanish commissions. At an early period of the present year remonstrances were made to the governor of that island, by an agent who was sent for the purpose, against those outrages on the peaceful commerce of the United States, of which many had occurred. That officer, professing his own want of authority to make satisfaction for our just complaints, answered only by a reference of them to the Government of Spain. The minister of the United States to that court was specially instructed to urge the necessity of the immediate and effectual interposition of that Government, directing restitution and indemnity for wrongs already committed and interdicting the repetition of them. The minister, as has been seen, was debarred access to the Spanish Government, and in the meantime several new cases of flagrant outrage have occurred, and citizens of the United States in the island of Porto Rico have suffered, and others been threatened with assassination for asserting their unquestionable rights even before the lawful tribunals of the country.

The usual orders have been given to all our public ships to seize American vessels engaged in the slave trade and bring them in for adjudication, and I have the gratification to state that not one so employed has been discovered, and there is good reason to believe that our flag is now seldom, if at all, disgraced by that traffic.

It is a source of great satisfaction that we are always enabled to recur to the conduct of our Navy with pride and commendation. As a means of national defense it enjoys the public confidence, and is steadily assuming additional importance. It is submitted whether a more efficient and equally economical organization of it might not in several respects be effected. It is supposed that higher grades than now exist by law would be useful. They would afford well-merited rewards to those who have long and faithfully served their country, present the best incentives to good conduct, and the best means of insuring a proper discipline; destroy the inequality in that respect between military and naval services, and relieve our officers from many inconveniences and mortifications which occur when our vessels meet those of other nations, ours being the only service in which such grades do not exist.

A report of the Postmaster-General, which accompanies this communication, will shew the present state of the Post-Office Department and its general operations for some years past.

There is established by law 88,600 miles of post-roads, on which the mail is now transported 85,700 miles, and contracts have been made for its transportation on all the established routes, with one or two exceptions. There are 5,240 post-offices in the Union, and as many postmasters. The gross amount of postage which accrued from the 1st July, 1822, to the 1st July, 1823, was $1,114,345.12. During the same period the expenditures of the Post-Office Department amounted to $1,169,885.51, and consisted of the following items, viz: Compensation to postmasters, $353,995.98; incidental expenses, $30,866.37; transportation of the mail, $784,600.08; payments into the Treasury, $423.08. On the 1st of July last there was due to the Department from postmasters $135,245.28; from *late* postmasters and contractors, $256,749.31; making a total amount of balances due to the Department of $391,994.59. These balances embrace all delinquencies of postmasters and contractors which have taken place since the organization of the Department. There was due by the Department to contractors on the 1st of July last $26,548.64.

The transportation of the mail within five years past has been greatly extended, and the expenditures of the Department proportionably increased. Although the postage which has accrued within the last three years has fallen short of the expenditures $262,821.46, it appears that collections have been made from the outstanding balances to meet the principal part of the current demands.

It is estimated that not more than $250,000 of the above balances can be collected, and that a considerable part of this sum can only be realized by a resort to legal process.   Some improvement in the receipts for postage is expected.   A prompt attention to the collection of moneys received by postmasters, it is believed, will enable the Department to continue its operations without aid from the Treasury, unless the expenditures shall be increased by the establishment of new mail routes.

A revision of some parts of the post-office law may be necessary; and it is submitted whether it would not be proper to provide for the appointment of postmasters, where the compensation exceeds a certain amount, by nomination to the Senate, as other officers of the General Government are appointed.

Having communicated my views to Congress at the commencement of the last session respecting the encouragement which ought to be given to our manufactures and the principle on which it should be founded, I have only to add that those views remain unchanged, and that the present state of those countries with which we have the most immediate political relations and greatest commercial intercourse tends to confirm them. Under this impression I recommend a review of the tariff for the purpose of affording such additional protection to those articles which we are prepared to manufacture, or which are more immediately connected with the defense and independence of the country.

The actual state of the public accounts furnishes additional evidence of the efficiency of the present system of accountability in relation to the public expenditure.   Of the moneys drawn from the Treasury since the 4th March, 1817, the sum remaining unaccounted for on the 30th of September last is more than a million and a half of dollars less than on the 30th of September preceding; and during the same period a reduction of nearly a million of dollars has been made in the amount of the unsettled accounts for moneys advanced previously to the 4th of March, 1817.   It will be obvious that in proportion as the mass of accounts of the latter description is diminished by settlement the difficulty of settling the residue is increased from the consideration that in many instances it can be obtained only by legal process.   For more precise details on this subject I refer to a report from the First Comptroller of the Treasury.

The sum which was appropriated at the last session for the repairs of the Cumberland road has been applied with good effect to that object. A final report has not yet been received from the agent who was appointed to superintend it.   As soon as it is received it shall be communicated to Congress.

Many patriotic and enlightened citizens who have made the subject an object of particular investigation have suggested an improvement of still greater importance. They are of opinion that the waters of the Chesapeake and Ohio may be connected together by one continued canal, and at an expense far short of the value and importance of the object to be obtained. If this could be accomplished it is impossible to calculate the beneficial consequences which would result from it. A great portion of the produce of the very fertile country through which it would pass would find a market through that channel. Troops might be moved with great facility in war, with cannon and every kind of munition, and in either direction. Connecting the Atlantic with the Western country in a line passing through the seat of the National Government, it would contribute essentially to strengthen the bond of union itself. Believing as I do that Congress possess the right to appropriate money for such a national object (the jurisdiction remaining to the States through which the canal would pass), I submit it to your consideration whether it may not be advisable to authorize by an adequate appropriation the employment of a suitable number of the officers of the Corps of Engineers to examine the unexplored ground during the next season and to report their opinion thereon. It will likewise be proper to extend their examination to the several routes through which the waters of the Ohio may be connected by canals with those of Lake Erie.

As the Cumberland road will require annual repairs, and Congress have not thought it expedient to recommend to the States an amendment to the Constitution for the purpose of vesting in the United States a power to adopt and execute a system of internal improvement, it is also submitted to your consideration whether it may not be expedient to authorize the Executive to enter into an arrangement with the several States through which the road passes to establish tolls, each within its limits, for the purpose of defraying the expense of future repairs and of providing also by suitable penalties for its protection against future injuries.

The act of Congress of the 7th of May, 1822, appropriated the sum of $22,700 for the purpose of erecting two piers as a shelter for vessels from ice near Cape Henlopen, Delaware Bay. To effect the object of the act the officers of the Board of Engineers, with Commodore Bainbridge, were directed to prepare plans and estimates of piers sufficient to answer the purpose intended by the act. It appears by their report, which accompanies the documents from the War Department, that the appropriation is not adequate to the purpose intended; and as the piers would be of great service both to the navigation of the Delaware Bay and the protection of vessels on the adjacent parts of the coast, I submit for the consideration of Congress whether additional and sufficient appropriation should not be made.

The Board of Engineers were also directed to examine and survey the entrance of the harbor of the port of Presquille, in Pennsylvania, in order to make an estimate of the expense of removing the obstructions to the entrance, with a plan of the best mode of effecting the same, under the appropriation for that purpose by act of Congress passed 3d of March last. The report of the Board accompanies the papers from the War Department, and is submitted for the consideration of Congress.

A strong hope has been long entertained, founded on the heroic struggle of the Greeks, that they would succeed in their contest and resume their equal station among the nations of the earth. It is believed that the whole civilized world take a deep interest in their welfare. Although no power has declared in their favor, yet none according to our information, has taken part against them. Their cause and their name have protected them from dangers which might ere this have overwhelmed any other people. The ordinary calculations of interest and of acquisition with a view to aggrandizement, which mingles so much in the transactions of nations, seem to have had no effect in regard to them. From the facts which have come to our knowledge there is good cause to believe that their enemy has lost forever all dominion over them; that Greece will become again an independent nation. That she may obtain that rank is the object of our most ardent wishes.

It was stated at the commencement of the last session that a great effort was then making in Spain and Portugal to improve the condition of the people of those countries, and that it appeared to be conducted with extraordinary moderation. It need scarcely be remarked that the result has been so far very different from what was then anticipated. Of events in that quarter of the globe, with which we have so much intercourse and from which we derive our origin, we have always been anxious and interested spectators. The citizens of the United States cherish sentiments the most friendly in favor of the liberty and happiness of their fellow-men on that side of the Atlantic. In the wars of the European powers in matters relating to themselves we have never taken any part, nor does it comport with our policy so to do. It is only when our rights are invaded or seriously menaced that we resent injuries or make preparation for our defense. With the movements in this hemisphere we are of necessity more immediately connected, and by causes which must be obvious to all enlightened and impartial observers. The political system of the allied powers is essentially different in this respect from that of America. This difference proceeds from that which exists in their respective Governments; and to the defense of our own, which has been achieved by the loss of so much blood and treasure, and matured by the wisdom of their most enlightened citizens, and under which we have enjoyed unexampled felicity, this whole nation is devoted. We owe it, therefore, to candor and to the amicable relations existing between the United States and those powers to declare that we should consider any attempt on their part to extend their system to any portion of this hemisphere as dangerous to our peace and safety. With the existing colonies or dependencies of any European power we have not interfered and shall not interfere. But with the Governments who have declared their independence and maintained it, and whose independence we have, on great consideration and on just principles, acknowledged, we could not view any interposition for the purpose of oppressing them, or controlling in any other manner their destiny, by any European power in any other light than as the manifestation of an unfriendly disposition toward the United States. In the war between those new Governments and Spain we declared our neutrality at the time of their recognition, and to this we have adhered, and shall continue to adhere, provided no change shall occur which, in the judgment of the competent authorities of this Government, shall make a corresponding change on the part of the United States indispensable to their security.

The late events in Spain and Portugal shew that Europe is still unsettled. Of this important fact no stronger proof can be adduced than that the allied powers should have thought it proper, on any principle satisfactory to themselves, to have interposed by force in the internal concerns of Spain. To what extent such interposition may be carried, on the same principle, is a question in which all independent powers whose governments differ from theirs are interested, even those most remote, and surely none more so than the United States. Our policy in regard to Europe, which was adopted at an early stage of the wars which have so long agitated that quarter of the globe, nevertheless remains the same, which is, not to interfere in the internal concerns of any of its powers; to consider the government *de facto* as the legitimate government for us; to cultivate friendly relations with it, and to preserve those relations by a frank, firm, and manly policy, meeting in all instances the just claims of every power, submitting to injuries from none. But in regard to those continents circumstances are eminently and conspicuously different. It is impossible that the allied powers should extend their political system to any portion of either continent without endangering our peace and happiness; nor can anyone believe that our southern brethren, if left to themselves, would adopt it of their own accord. It is equally impossible, therefore, that we should behold such interposition in any form with indifference. If we look to the comparative strength and resources of Spain and those new Governments, and their distance from each other, it must be obvious that she can never subdue them. It is still the true policy of the United States to leave the parties to themselves, in the hope that other powers will pursue the same course.

If we compare the present condition of our Union with its actual state at the close of our Revolution, the history of the world furnishes no example of a progress in improvement in all the important circumstances which constitute the happiness of a nation which bears any resemblance to it. At the first epoch our population did not exceed 3,000,000. By the last census it amounted to about 10,000,000, and, what is more extraordinary, it is almost altogether native, for the immigration from other countries has been inconsiderable At the first epoch half the territory within our acknowledged limits was uninhabited and a wilderness. Since then new territory has been acquired of vast extent, comprising within it many rivers, particularly the Mississippi, the navigation of which to the ocean was of the highest importance to the original States. Over this territory our population has expanded in every direction, and new States have been established almost equal in number to those which formed the first bond of our Union. This expansion of our population and accession of new States to our Union have had the happiest effect on all its highest interests. That it has eminently augmented our resources and added to our strength and respectability as a power is admitted by all. But it is not in these important circumstances only that this happy effect is felt. It is manifest that by enlarging the basis of our system and increasing the number of States the system itself has been greatly strengthened in both its branches. Consolidation and disunion have thereby been rendered equally impracticable. Each Government, confiding in its own strength, has less to apprehend from the other, and in consequence each, enjoying a greater freedom of action, is rendered more efficient for all the purposes for which it was instituted. It is unnecessary to treat here of the vast improvement made in the system itself by the adoption of this Constitution and of its happy effect in elevating the character and in protecting the rights of the nation as well as of individuals. To what, then, do we owe these blessings? It is known to all that we derive them from the excellence of our institutions. Ought we not, then, to adopt every measure which may be necessary to perpetuate them?

EIGHTH ANNUAL MESSAGE.

WASHINGTON, *December 7, 1824.*

Fellow-Citizens of the Senate and of the House of Representatives:

The view which I have now to present to you of our affairs, foreign and domestic, realizes the most sanguine anticipations which have been entertained of the public prosperity. If we look to the whole, our growth as a nation continues to be rapid beyond example; if to the States which compose it, the same gratifying spectacle is exhibited. Our expansion over the vast territory within our limits has been great, without indicating any decline in those sections from which the emigration has been most conspicuous. We have daily gained strength by a native population in every quarter—a population devoted to our happy system of government and cherishing the bond of union with fraternal affection. Experience has already shewn that the difference of climate and of industry, proceeding from that cause, inseparable from such vast domains, and which under other systems might have a repulsive tendency, can not fail to produce with us under wise regulations the opposite effect. What one portion wants the other may supply; and this will be most sensibly felt by the parts most distant from each other, forming thereby a domestic market and an active intercourse between the extremes and throughout every portion of our Union. Thus by a happy distribution of power between the National and State Governments, Governments which rest exclusively on the sovereignty of the people and are fully adequate to the great purposes for which they were respectively instituted, causes which might otherwise lead to dismemberment operate powerfully to draw us closer together. In every other circumstance a correct view of the actual state of our Union must be equally gratifying to our constituents. Our relations with foreign powers are of a friendly character, although certain interesting differences remain unsettled with some. Our revenue under the mild system of impost and tonnage continues to be adequate to all the purposes of the Government Our agriculture, commerce, manufactures, and navigation flourish. Our fortifications are advancing in the degree authorized by existing appropriations to maturity, and due progress is made in the augmentation of the Navy to the limit prescribed for it by law. For these blessings we owe to Almighty God, from whom we derive them, and with profound reverence, our most grateful and unceasing acknowledgments.

In adverting to our relations with foreign powers, which are always an object of the highest importance, I have to remark that of the subjects which have been brought into discussion with them during the present Administration some have been satisfactorily terminated, others have been suspended, to be resumed hereafter under circumstances more favorable to success, and others are still in negotiation, with the hope that they may be adjusted with mutual accommodation to the interests and to the satisfaction of the respective parties. It has been the invariable object of this Government to cherish the most friendly relations with every power, and on principles and conditions which might make them permanent. A systematic effort has been made to place our commerce with each power on a footing of perfect reciprocity, to settle with each in a spirit of candor and liberality all existing differences, and to anticipate and remove so far as it might be practicable all causes of future variance.

It having been stipulated by the seventh article of the convention of navigation and commerce which was concluded on the 24th of June, 1822, between the United States and France, that the said convention should continue in force for two years from the 1st of October of that year, and for an indefinite term afterwards, unless one of the parties should declare its intention to renounce it, in which event it should cease to operate at the end of six months from such declaration, and no such intention having been announced, the convention having been found advantageous to both parties, it has since remained, and still remains, in force. At the time when that convention was concluded many interesting subjects were left unsettled, and particularly our claim to indemnity for spoliations which were committed on our commerce in the late wars. For these interests and claims it was in the contemplation of the parties to make provision at a subsequent day by a more comprehensive and definitive treaty. The object has been duly attended to since by the Executive, but as yet it has not been accomplished. It is hoped that a favorable opportunity will present itself for opening a negotiation which may embrace and arrange all existing differences and every other concern in which they have a common interest upon the accession of the present King of France, an event which has occurred since the close of the last session of Congress.

With Great Britain our commercial intercourse rests on the same footing that it did at the last session. By the convention of 1815 the commerce between the United States and the British dominions in Europe and the East Indies was arranged on a principle of reciprocity. That convention was confirmed and continued in force, with slight exceptions, by a subsequent treaty for the term of ten years from the 20th of October, 1818, the date of the latter. The trade with the British colonies in the West Indies has not as yet been arranged, by treaty or otherwise, to our satisfaction. An approach to that result has been made by legislative acts, whereby many serious impediments which had been raised by the parties in defense of their respective claims were removed. An earnest desire exists, and has been manifested on the part of this Government, to place the commerce with the colonies, likewise, on a footing of reciprocal advantage, and it is hoped that the British Government, seeing the justice of the proposal and its importance to the colonies, will ere long accede to it.

The commissioners who were appointed for the adjustment of the boundary between the territories of the United States and those of Great Britain, specified in the fifth article of the treaty of Ghent, having disagreed in their decision, and both Governments having agreed to establish that boundary by amicable negotiation between them, it is hoped that it may be satisfactorily adjusted in that mode. The boundary specified by the sixth article has been established by the decision of the commissioners. From the progress made in that provided for by the seventh, according to a report recently received, there is good cause to presume that it will be settled in the course of the ensuing year.

It is a cause of serious regret that no arrangement has yet been finally concluded between the two Governments to secure by joint cooperation the suppression of the slave trade. It was the object of the British Government in the early stages of the negotiation to adopt a plan for the suppression which should include the concession of the mutual right of search by the ships of war of each party of the vessels of the other for suspected offenders. This was objected to by this Government on the principle that as the right of search was a right of war of a belligerent toward a neutral power it might have an ill effect to extend it by treaty, to an offense which had been made comparatively mild, to a time of peace. Anxious, however, for the suppression of this trade, it was thought advisable, in compliance with a resolution of the House of Representatives, founded on an act of Congress, to propose to the British Government an expedient which should be free from that objection and more effectual for the object, by making it piratical. In that mode the enormity of the crime would place the offenders out of the protection of their Government, and involve no question of search or other question between the parties touching their respective rights. It was believed, also, that it would completely suppress the trade in the vessels of both parties, and by their respective citizens and subjects in those of other powers, with whom it was hoped that the odium which would thereby be attached to it would produce a corresponding arrangement, and by means thereof its entire extirpation forever. A convention to this effect was concluded and signed in London on the 13th day of March, 1824, by plenipotentiaries duly authorized by both Governments, to the ratification of which certain obstacles have arisen which are not yet entirely removed. The difference between the parties still remaining has been reduced to a point not of sufficient magnitude, as is presumed, to be permitted to defeat an object so near to the heart of both nations and so desirable to the friends of humanity throughout the world. As objections, however, to the principle recommended by the House of Representatives, or at least to the consequences inseparable from it, and which are understood to apply to the law, have been raised, which may deserve a reconsideration of the whole subject, I have thought it proper to suspend the conclusion of a new convention until the definitive sentiments of Congress may be ascertained. The documents relating to the negotiation are with that intent submitted to your consideration.

Our commerce with Sweden has been placed on a footing of perfect reciprocity by treaty, and with Russia, the Netherlands, Prussia, the free Hanseatic cities, the Dukedom of Oldenburg, and Sardinia by internal regulations on each side, founded on mutual agreement between the respective Governments.

The principles upon which the commercial policy of the United States is founded are to be traced to an early period. They are essentially connected with those upon which their independence was declared, and owe their origin to the enlightened men who took the lead in our affairs at that important epoch. They are developed in their first treaty of commerce with France of 6th February, 1778, and by a formal commission which was instituted immediately after the conclusion of their Revolutionary struggle, for the purpose of negotiating treaties of commerce with every

European power.   The first treaty of the United States with Prussia, which was negotiated by that commission, affords a signal illustration of those principles.   The act of Congress of the 3d March, 1815, adopted immediately after the return of a general peace, was a new overture to foreign nations to establish our commercial relations with them on the basis of free and equal reciprocity.   That principle has pervaded all the acts of Congress and all the negotiations of the Executive on the subject.

A convention for the settlement of important questions in relation to the northwest coast of this continent and its adjoining seas was concluded and signed at St. Petersburg on the 5th day of April last by the minister plenipotentiary of the United States and plenipotentiaries of the Imperial Government of Russia.   It will immediately be laid before the Senate for the exercise of the constitutional authority of that body with reference to its ratification.   It is proper to add that the manner in which this negotiation was invited and conducted on the part of the Emperor has been very satisfactory.

The great and extraordinary changes which have happened in the Governments of Spain and Portugal within the last two years, without seriously affecting the friendly relations which under all of them have been maintained with those powers by the United States, have been obstacles to the adjustment of the particular subjects of discussion which have arisen with each.   A resolution of the Senate adopted at their last session called for information as to the effect produced upon our relations with Spain by the recognition on the part of the United States of the independent South American Governments.   The papers containing that information are now communicated to Congress.

A chargé d'affaires has been received from the independent Government of Brazil.   That country, heretofore a colonial possession of Portugal, had some years since been proclaimed by the Sovereign of Portugal himself an independent Kingdom.   Since his return to Lisbon a revolution in Brazil has established a new Government there with an imperial title, at the head of which is placed a prince, in whom the regency had been vested by the King at the time of his departure.   There is reason to expect that by amicable negotiation the independence of Brazil will ere long be recognized by Portugal herself.

With the remaining powers of Europe, with those on the coast of Barbary, and with all the new South American States our relations are of a friendly character.   We have ministers plenipotentiary residing with the Republics of Colombia and Chile, and have received ministers of the same rank from Colombia, Guatemala, Buenos Ayres, and Mexico.   Our commercial relations with all those States are mutually beneficial and increasing.   With the Republic of Colombia a treaty of commerce has been formed, of which a copy is received and the original daily expected.   A negotiation for a like treaty would have been commenced with Buenos Ayres had it not been prevented by the indisposition and lamented decease of Mr. Rodney, our minister there, and to whose memory the most respectful attention has been shewn by the Government of that Republic. An advantageous alteration in our treaty with Tunis has been obtained by our consular agent residing there, the official document of which when received will be laid before the Senate.

The attention of the Government has been drawn with great solicitude to other subjects, and particularly to that relating to a state of maritime war, involving the relative rights of neutral and belligerent in such wars. Most of the difficulties which we have experienced and of the losses which we have sustained since the establishment of our independence have proceeded from the unsettled state of those rights and the extent to which the belligerent claim has been carried against the neutral party. It is impossible to look back on the occurrences of the late wars in Europe, and to behold the disregard which was paid to our rights as a neutral power, and the waste which was made of our commerce by the parties to those wars by various acts of their respective Governments, and under the pretext by each that the other had set the example, without great mortification and a fixed purpose never to submit to the like in future. An attempt to remove those causes of possible variance by friendly negotiation and on just principles which should be applicable to all parties could, it was presumed, be viewed by none other than as a proof of an earnest desire to preserve those relations with every power. In the late war between France and Spain a crisis occurred in which it seemed probable that all the controvertible principles involved in such wars might be brought into discussion and settled to the satisfaction of all parties. Propositions having this object in view have been made to the Governments of Great Britain, France, Russia, and of other powers, which have been received in a friendly manner by all, but as yet no treaty has been formed with either for its accomplishment. The policy will, it is presumed, be persevered in, and in the hope that it may be successful.

It will always be recollected that with one of the parties to those wars, and from whom we received those injuries, we sought redress by war. From the other, by whose then reigning Government our vessels were seized in port as well as at sea and their cargoes confiscated, indemnity has been expected, but has not yet been rendered. It was under the influence of the latter that our vessels were likewise seized by the Governments of Spain, Holland, Denmark, Sweden, and Naples, and from whom indemnity has been claimed and is still expected, with the exception of Spain, by whom it has been rendered. With both parties we had abundant cause of war, but we had no alternative but to resist that which was most powerful at sea and pressed us nearest at home. With this all differences were settled by a treaty, founded on conditions fair and honorable to both, and which has been so far executed with perfect good faith. It has been earnestly hoped that the other would of its own accord, and from a sentiment of justice and conciliation, make to our citizens the indemnity to which they are entitled, and thereby remove from our relations any just cause of discontent on our side.

It is estimated that the receipts into the Treasury during the current year, exclusive of loans, will exceed $18,500,000, which, with the sum remaining in the Treasury at the end of the last year, amounting to $9,463,922.81, will, after discharging the current disbursements of the year, the interest on the public debt, and upward of $11,633,011.52 of the principal, leave a balance of more than $3,000,000 in the Treasury on the 1st day of January next.

A larger amount of the debt contracted during the late war, bearing an interest of 6 per cent, becoming redeemable in the course of the ensuing year than could be discharged by the ordinary revenue, the act of the 26th of May authorized a loan of $5,000,000 at 4½ per cent to meet the same. By this arrangement an annual saving will accrue to the public of $75,000.

Under the act of the 24th of May last a loan of $5,000,000 was authorized, in order to meet the awards under the Florida treaty, which was negotiated at par with the Bank of the United States at 4½ per cent, the limit of interest fixed by the act. By this provision the claims of our citizens who had sustained so great a loss by spoliations, and from whom indemnity had been so long withheld, were promptly paid. For these advances the public will be amply repaid at no distant day by the sale of the lands in Florida. Of the great advantages resulting from the acquisition of the Territory in other respects too high an estimate can not be formed.

It is estimated that the receipts into the Treasury during the year 1825 will be sufficient to meet the disbursements of the year, including the sum of $10,000,000, which is annually appropriated by the act constituting the sinking fund to the payment of the principal and interest of the public debt.

The whole amount of the public debt on the 1st of January next may be estimated at $86,000,000, inclusive of $2,500,000 of the loan authorized by the act of the 26th of May last. In this estimate is included a stock of $7,000,000, issued for the purchase of that amount of the capital stock of the Bank of the United States, and which, as the stock of the bank still held by the Government will at least be fully equal to its reimbursement, ought not to be considered as constituting a part of the public debt. Estimating, then, the whole amount of the public debt at $79,000,000 and regarding the annual receipts and expenditures of the Government, a well-founded hope may be entertained that, should no unexpected event occur, the whole of the public debt may be discharged in the course of ten years, and the Government be left at liberty thereafter to apply such portion of the revenue as may not be necessary for current expenses to such other objects as may be most conducive to the public security and welfare. That the sums applicable to these objects will be very considerable may be fairly concluded when it is recollected that a large amount of the public revenue has been applied since the late war to the construction of the public buildings in this city; to the erection of fortifications along the coast and of arsenals in different parts of the Union; to the augmentation of the Navy; to the extinguishment of the Indian title to large tracts of fertile territory; to the acquisition of Florida; to pensions to Revolutionary officers and soldiers, and to invalids of the late war. On many of these objects the expense will annually be diminished and cease at no distant period on most of them. On the 1st of January, 1817, the public debt amounted to $123,491,965.16, and, notwithstanding the large sums which have been applied to these objects, it has been reduced since that period $37,446,961.78. The last portion of the public debt will be redeemable on the 1st of January, 1835, and while there is the best reason to believe that the resources of the Government will be continually adequate to such portions of it as may become due in the interval, it is recommended to Congress to seize every opportunity which may present itself to reduce the rate of interest on every part thereof. The high state of the public credit and the great abundance of money are at this time very favorable to such a result. It must be very gratifying to our fellow-citizens to witness this flourishing state of the public finances when it is recollected that no burthen whatever has been imposed upon them.

The military establishment in all its branches, in the performance of the various duties assigned to each, justifies the favorable view which was presented of the efficiency of its organization at the last session. All the appropriations have been regularly applied to the objects intended by Congress, and so far as the disbursements have been made the accounts have been rendered and settled without loss to the public. The condition of the Army itself, as relates to the officers and men, in science and discipline is highly respectable. The Military Academy, on which the Army essentially rests, and to which it is much indebted for this state of improvement, has attained, in comparison with any other institution of a like kind, a high degree of perfection. Experience, however, has shewn that the dispersed condition of the corps of artillery is unfavorable to the discipline of that important branch of the military establishment. To remedy this inconvenience, eleven companies have been assembled at the fortification erected at Old Point Comfort as a school for artillery instruction, with intention as they shall be perfected in the various duties of that service to order them to other posts, and to supply their places with other companies for instruction in like manner. In this mode a complete knowledge of the science and duties of this arm will be extended throughout the whole corps of artillery. But to carry this object fully into effect will require the aid of Congress, to obtain which the subject is now submitted to your consideration.

Of the progress which has been made in the construction of fortifications for the permanent defense of our maritime frontier, according to the plan decided on and to the extent of the existing appropriations, the report of the Secretary of War, which is herewith communicated, will give a detailed account. Their final completion can not fail to give great additional security to that frontier, and to diminish proportionably the expense of defending it in the event of war.

The provisions in the several acts of Congress of the last session for the improvement of the navigation of the Mississippi and the Ohio, of the harbor of Presqu'isle, on Lake Erie, and the repair of the Plymouth beach are in a course of regular execution; and there is reason to believe that the appropriation in each instance will be adequate to the object. To carry these improvements fully into effect, the superintendence of them has been assigned to officers of the Corps of Engineers.

Under the act of 30th April last, authorizing the President to cause a survey to be made, with the necessary plans and estimates, of such roads and canals as he might deem of national importance in a commercial or military point of view, or for the transportation of the mail, a board has been instituted, consisting of two distinguished officers of the Corps of Engineers and a distinguished civil engineer, with assistants, who have been actively employed in carrying into effect the object of the act. They have carefully examined the route between the Potomac and the Ohio rivers; between the latter and Lake Erie; between the Alleghany and the Susquehannah; and the routes between the Delaware and the Raritan, Barnstable and Buzzards Bay, and between Boston Harbor and Narraganset Bay. Such portion of the Corps of Topographical Engineers as could be spared from the survey of the coast has been employed in surveying the very important route between the Potomac and the Ohio. Considerable progress has been made in it, but the survey can not be completed until the next season. It is gratifying to add, from the view already taken, that there is good cause to believe that this great national object may be fully accomplished.

It is contemplated to commence early in the next season the execution of the other branch of the act—that which relates to roads—and with the survey of a route from this city, through the Southern States, to New Orleans, the importance of which can not be too highly estimated. All the officers of both the corps of engineers who could be spared from other services have been employed in exploring and surveying the routes for canals. To digest a plan for both objects for the great purposes specified will require a thorough knowledge of every part of our Union and of the relation of each part to the others and of all to the seat of the General Government. For such a digest it will be necessary that the information be full, minute, and precise. With a view to these important objects, I submit to the consideration of the Congress the propriety of enlarging both the corps of engineers—the military and topographical. It need scarcely be remarked that the more extensively these corps are engaged in the improvement of their country, in the execution of the powers of Congress, and in aid of the States in such improvements as lie beyond that limit, when such aid is desired, the happier the effect will be in many views of which the subject is susceptible. By profiting of their science the works will always be well executed, and by giving to the officers such employment our Union will derive all the advantage, in peace as well as in war, from their talents and services which they can afford. In this mode, also, the military will be incorporated with the civil, and unfounded and injurious distinctions and prejudices of every kind be done away. To the corps themselves this service can not fail to be equally useful, since by the knowledge they would thus acquire they would be eminently better qualified in the event of war for the great purposes for which they were instituted.

Our relations with the Indian tribes within our limits have not been materially changed during the year. The hostile disposition evinced by certain tribes on the Missouri during the last year still continues, and has extended in some degree to those on the Upper Mississippi and the Upper Lakes. Several parties of our citizens have been plundered and murdered by those tribes. In order to establish relations of friendship with them, Congress at the last session made an appropriation for treaties with them and for the employment of a suitable military escort to accompany and attend the commissioners at the places appointed for the negotiations. This object has not been effected. The season was too far advanced when the appropriation was made and the distance too great to permit it, but measures have been taken, and all the preparations will be completed to accomplish it at an early period in the next season.

Believing that the hostility of the tribes, particularly on the Upper Mississippi and the Lakes, is in no small degree owing to the wars which are carried on between the tribes residing in that quarter, measures have been taken to bring about a general peace among them, which, if successful, will not only tend to the security of our citizens, but be of great advantage to the Indians themselves.

With the exception of the tribes referred to, our relations with all the others are on the same friendly footing, and it affords me great satisfaction to add that they are making steady advances in civilization and the improvement of their condition. Many of the tribes have already made great progress in the arts of civilized life. This desirable result has been brought about by the humane and persevering policy of the Government, and particularly by means of the appropriation for the civilization of the Indians. There have been established under the provisions of this act 32 schools, containing 916 scholars, who are well instructed in several branches of literature, and likewise in agriculture and the ordinary arts of life.

Under the appropriation to authorize treaties with the Creeks and Quaupaw Indians commissioners have been appointed and negotiations are now pending, but the result is not yet known.

For more full information respecting the principle which has been adopted for carrying into effect the act of Congress authorizing surveys, with plans and estimates for canals and roads, and on every other branch of duty incident to the Department of War, I refer you to the report of the Secretary.

The squadron in the Mediterranean has been maintained in the extent which was proposed in the report of the Secretary of the Navy of the last year, and has afforded to our commerce the necessary protection in that sea.   Apprehending, however, that the unfriendly relations which have existed between Algiers and some of the powers of Europe might be extended to us, it has been thought expedient to augment the force there, and in consequence the *North Carolina*, a ship of the line, has been prepared, and will sail in a few days to join it.

The force employed in the Gulf of Mexico and in the neighboring seas for the suppression of piracy has likewise been preserved essentially in the state in which it was during the last year.   A persevering effort has been made for the accomplishment of that object, and much protection has thereby been afforded to our commerce, but still the practice is far from being suppressed.   From every view which has been taken of the subject it is thought that it will be necessary rather to augment than to diminish our force in that quarter.   There is reason to believe that the piracies now complained of are committed by bands of robbers who inhabit the land, and who, by preserving good intelligence with the towns and seizing favorable opportunities, rush forth and fall on unprotected merchant vessels, of which they make an easy prey.   The pillage thus taken they carry to their lurking places, and dispose of afterwards at prices tending to seduce the neighboring population.   This combination is understood to be of great extent, and is the more to be deprecated because the crime of piracy is often attended with the murder of the crews, these robbers knowing if any survived their lurking places would be exposed and they be caught and punished.   That this atrocious practice should be carried to such extent is cause of equal surprise and regret.   It is presumed that it must be attributed to the relaxed and feeble state of the local governments, since it is not doubted, from the high character of the governor of Cuba, who is well known and much respected here, that if he had the power he would promptly suppress it.   Whether those robbers should be pursued on the land, the local authorities be made responsible for these atrocities, or any other measure be resorted to to suppress them, is submitted to the consideration of Congress.

In execution of the laws for the suppression of the slave trade a vessel has been occasionally sent from that squadron to the coast of Africa with orders to return thence by the usual track of the slave ships, and to seize any of our vessels which might be engaged in that trade.   None have been found, and it is believed that none are thus employed.   It is well known, however, that the trade still exists under other flags.

The health of our squadron while at Thompsons Island has been much better during the present than it was the last season.   Some improvements have been made and others are contemplated there which, it is believed, will have a very salutary effect.

On the Pacific our commerce has much increased, and on that coast, as well as on that sea, the United States have many important interests which require attention and protection. It is thought that all the considerations which suggested the expediency of placing a squadron on that sea operate with augmented force for maintaining it there, at least in equal extent.

For detailed information respecting the state of our maritime force on each sea, the improvement necessary to be made on either in the organization of the naval establishment generally, and of the laws for its better government I refer you to the report of the Secretary of the Navy, which is herewith communicated.

The revenue of the Post-Office Department has received a considerable augmentation in the present year. The current receipts will exceed the expenditures, although the transportation of the mail within the year has been much increased. A report of the Postmaster-General, which is transmitted, will furnish in detail the necessary information respecting the administration and present state of this Department.

In conformity with a resolution of Congress of the last session, an invitation was given to General Lafayette to visit the United States, with an assurance that a ship of war should attend at any port of France which he might designate, to receive and convey him across the Atlantic, whenever it might be convenient for him to sail. He declined the offer of the public ship from motives of delicacy, but assured me that he had long intended and would certainly visit our Union in the course of the present year. In August last he arrived at New York, where he was received with the warmth of affection and gratitude to which his very important and disinterested services and sacrifices in our Revolutionary struggle so eminently entitled him. A corresponding sentiment has since been manifested in his favor throughout every portion of our Union, and affectionate invitations have been given him to extend his visits to them. To these he has yielded all the accommodation in his power. At every designated point of rendezvous the whole population of the neighboring country has been assembled to greet him, among whom it has excited in a peculiar manner the sensibility of all to behold the surviving members of our Revolutionary contest, civil and military, who had shared with him in the toils and dangers of the war, many of them in a decrepit state. A more interesting spectacle, it is believed, was never witnessed, because none could be founded on purer principles, none proceed from higher or more disinterested motives. That the feelings of those who had fought and bled with him in a common cause should have been much excited was natural. There are, however, circumstances attending these interviews which pervaded the whole community and touched the breasts of every age, even the youngest among us. There was not an individual present who had not some relative who had not partaken in those scenes, nor an infant who had not heard the relation of them.   But the circumstance which was most sensibly felt, and which his presence brought forcibly to the recollection of all, was the great cause in which we were engaged and the blessings which we have derived from our success in it.   The struggle was for independence and liberty, public and personal, and in this we suc-ceeded.   The meeting with one who had borne so distinguished a part in that great struggle, and from such lofty and disinterested motives, could not fail to affect profoundly every individual and of every age.   It is natural that we should all take a deep interest in his future welfare, as we do.   His high claims on our Union are felt, and the sentiment universal that they should be met in a generous spirit.   Under these impressions I invite your attention to the subject, with a view that, regard-ing his very important services, losses, and sacrifices, a provision may be made and tendered to him which shall correspond with the sentiments and be worthy the character of the American people.

In turning our attention to the condition of the civilized world, in which the United States have always taken a deep interest, it is gratifying to see how large a portion of it is blessed with peace.   The only wars which now exist within that limit are those between Turkey and Greece, in Europe, and between Spain and the new Governments, our neighbors, in this hemisphere.   In both these wars the cause of independence, of lib-erty and humanity, continues to prevail.   The success of Greece, when the relative population of the contending parties is considered, commands our admiration and applause, and that it has had a similar effect with the neighboring powers is obvious.   The feeling of the whole civilized world is excited in a high degree in their favor.   May we not hope that these sentiments, winning on the hearts of their respective Governments, may lead to a more decisive result; that they may produce an accord among them to replace Greece on the ground which she formerly held, and to which her heroic exertions at this day so eminently entitle her?

With respect to the contest to which our neighbors are a party, it is evident that Spain as a power is scarcely felt in it.   These new States had completely achieved their independence before it was acknowledged by the United States, and they have since maintained it with little foreign pressure.   The disturbances which have appeared in certain portions of that vast territory have proceeded from internal causes, which had their origin in their former Governments and have not yet been thoroughly removed.   It is manifest that these causes are daily losing their effect, and that these new States are settling down under Governments elective and representative in every branch, similar to our own.   In this course we ardently wish them to persevere, under a firm conviction that it will promote their happiness.   In this, their career, however, we have not interfered, believing that every people have a right to institute for them-selves the government which, in their judgment, may suit them best.

Our example is before them, of the good effect of which, being our neighbors, they are competent judges, and to their judgment we leave it, in the expectation that other powers will pursue the same policy. The deep interest which we take in their independence, which we have acknowledged, and in their enjoyment of all the rights incident thereto, especially in the very important one of instituting their own Governments, has been declared, and is known to the world. Separated as we are from Europe by the great Atlantic Ocean, we can have no concern in the wars of the European Governments nor in the causes which produce them. The balance of power between them, into whichever scale it may turn in its various vibrations, can not affect us. It is the interest of the United States to preserve the most friendly relations with every power and on conditions fair, equal, and applicable to all. But in regard to our neighbors our situation is different. It is impossible for the European Governments to interfere in their concerns, especially in those alluded to, which are vital, without affecting us; indeed, the motive which might induce such interference in the present state of the war between the parties, if a war it may be called, would appear to be equally applicable to us. It is gratifying to know that some of the powers with whom we enjoy a very friendly intercourse, and to whom these views have been communicated, have appeared to acquiesce in them.

The augmentation of our population with the expansion of our Union and increased number of States have produced effects in certain branches of our system which merit the attention of Congress. Some of our arrangements, and particularly the judiciary establishment, were made with a view to the original thirteen States only. Since then the United States have acquired a vast extent of territory; eleven new States have been admitted into the Union, and Territories have been laid off for three others, which will likewise be admitted at no distant day. An organization of the Supreme Court which assigns to the judges any portion of the duties which belong to the inferior, requiring their passage over so vast a space under any distribution of the States that may now be made, if not impracticable in the execution, must render it impossible for them to discharge the duties of either branch with advantage to the Union. The duties of the Supreme Court would be of great importance if its decisions were confined to the ordinary limits of other tribunals, but when it is considered that this court decides, and in the last resort, on all the great questions which arise under our Constitution, involving those between the United States individually, between the States and the United States, and between the latter and foreign powers, too high an estimate of their importance can not be formed. The great interests of the nation seem to require that the judges of the Supreme Court should be exempted from every other duty than those which are incident to that high trust. The organization of the inferior courts would of course be adapted to circumstances. It is presumed that such an one might be formed as would secure an able and faithful discharge of their duties, and without any material augmentation of expense.

The condition of the aborigines within our limits, and especially those who are within the limits of any of the States, merits likewise particular attention. Experience has shown that unless the tribes be civilized they can never be incorporated into our system in any form whatever. It has likewise shown that in the regular augmentation of our population with the extension of our settlements their situation will become deplorable, if their extinction is not menaced. Some well-digested plan which will rescue them from such calamities is due to their rights, to the rights of humanity, and to the honor of the nation. Their civilization is indispensable to their safety, and this can be accomplished only by degrees. The process must commence with the infant state, through whom some effect may be wrought on the parental. Difficulties of the most serious character present themselves to the attainment of this very desirable result on the territory on which they now reside. To remove them from it by force, even with a view to their own security and happiness, would be revolting to humanity and utterly unjustifiable. Between the limits of our present States and Territories and the Rocky Mountains and Mexico there is a vast territory to which they might be invited with inducements which might be successful. It is thought if that territory should be divided into districts by previous agreement with the tribes now residing there and civil governments be established in each, with schools for every branch of instruction in literature and the arts of civilized life, that all the tribes now within our limits might gradually be drawn there. The execution of this plan would necessarily be attended with expense, and that not inconsiderable, but it is doubted whether any other can be devised which would be less liable to that objection or more likely to succeed.

In looking to the interests which the United States have on the Pacific Ocean and on the western coast of this continent, the propriety of establishing a military post at the mouth of Columbia River, or at some other point in that quarter within our acknowledged limits, is submitted to the consideration of Congress. Our commerce and fisheries on that sea and along the coast have much increased and are increasing. It is thought that a military post, to which our ships of war might resort, would afford protection to every interest, and have a tendency to conciliate the tribes to the northwest, with whom our trade is extensive. It is thought also that by the establishment of such a post the intercourse between our Western States and Territories and the Pacific and our trade with the tribes residing in the interior on each side of the Rocky Mountains would be essentially promoted. To carry this object into effect the appropriation of an adequate sum to authorize the employment of a frigate, with an officer of the Corps of Engineers, to explore the mouth of the Columbia River and the coast contiguous thereto, to enable the Executive to make such establishment at the most suitable point, is recommended to Congress.

It is thought that attention is also due to the improvement of this city. The communication between the public buildings and in various other parts and the grounds around those buildings require it. It is presumed also that the completion of the canal from the Tiber to the Eastern Branch would have a very salutary effect. Great exertions have been made and expenses incurred by the citizens in improvements of various kinds; but those which are suggested belong exclusively to the Government, or are of a nature to require expenditures beyond their resources. The public lots which are still for sale would, it is not doubted, be more than adequate to these purposes.

From the view above presented it is manifest that the situation of the United States is in the highest degree prosperous and happy. There is no object which as a people we can desire which we do not possess or which is not within our reach. Blessed with governments the happiest which the world ever knew, with no distinct orders in society or divided interests in any portion of the vast territory over which their dominion extends, we have every motive to cling together which can animate a virtuous and enlightened people. The great object is to preserve these blessings, and to hand them down to the latest posterity. Our experience ought to satisfy us that our progress under the most correct and provident policy will not be exempt from danger. Our institutions form an important epoch in the history of the civilized world. On their preservation and in their utmost purity everything will depend. Extending as our interests do to every part of the inhabited globe and to every sea to which our citizens are carried by their industry and enterprise, to which they are invited by the wants of others, and have a right to go, we must either protect them in the enjoyment of their rights or abandon them in certain events to waste and desolation. Our attitude is highly interesting as relates to other powers, and particularly to our southern neighbors. We have duties to perform with respect to all to which we must be faithful. To every kind of danger we should pay the most vigilant and unceasing attention, remove the cause where it may be practicable, and be prepared to meet it when inevitable.

Against foreign danger the policy of the Government seems to be already settled. The events of the late war admonished us to make our maritime frontier impregnable by a well-digested chain of fortifications, and to give efficient protection to our commerce by augmenting our Navy to a certain extent, which has been steadily pursued, and which it is incumbent upon us to complete as soon as circumstances will permit. In the event of war it is on the maritime frontier that we shall be assailed. It is in that quarter, therefore, that we should be prepared to meet the attack. It is there that our whole force will be called into action to prevent the destruction of our towns and the desolation and pillage of the interior. To give full effect to this policy great improvements will be indispensable. Access to those works by every practicable communication should be made easy and in every direction. The intercourse between every part of our Union should also be promoted and facilitated by the exercise of those powers which may comport with a faithful regard to the great principles of our Constitution. With respect to internal causes, those great principles point out with equal certainty the policy to be pursued. Resting on the people as our Governments do, State and National, with well-defined powers, it is of the highest importance that they severally keep within the limits prescribed to them. Fulfilling that sacred duty, it is of equal importance that the movement between them be harmonious, and in case of any disagreement, should any such occur, a calm appeal be made to the people, and that their voice be heard and promptly obeyed. Both Governments being instituted for the common good, we can not fail to prosper while those who made them are attentive to the conduct of their representatives and control their measures. In the pursuit of these great objects let a generous spirit and national views and feelings be indulged, and let every part recollect that by cherishing that spirit and improving the condition of the others in what relates to their welfare the general interest will not only be promoted, but the local advantage be reciprocated by all.

I can not conclude this communication, the last of the kind which I shall have to make, without recollecting with great sensibility and heartfelt gratitude the many instances of the public confidence and the generous support which I have received from my fellow-citizens in the various trusts with which I have been honored. Having commenced my service in early youth, and continued it since with few and short intervals, I have witnessed the great difficulties to which our Union has been exposed, and admired the virtue and intelligence with which they have been surmounted. From the present prosperous and happy state I derive a gratification which I can not express. That these blessings may be preserved and perpetuated will be the object of my fervent and unceasing prayers to the Supreme Ruler of the Universe.

John Quincy Adams

March 4, 1825 to March 4, 1829

FIRST ANNUAL MESSAGE.

WASHINGTON, *December 6, 1825.*

Fellow-Citizens of the Senate and of the House of Representatives:

In taking a general survey of the concerns of our beloved country, with reference to subjects interesting to the common welfare, the first sentiment which impresses itself upon the mind is of gratitude to the Omnipotent Disposer of All Good for the continuance of the signal blessings of His providence, and especially for that health which to an unusual extent has prevailed within our borders, and for that abundance which in the vicissitudes of the seasons has been scattered with profusion over our land. Nor ought we less to ascribe to Him the glory that we are permitted to enjoy the bounties of His hand in peace and tranquillity—in peace with all the other nations of the earth, in tranquillity among ourselves. There has, indeed, rarely been a period in the history of civilized man in which the general condition of the Christian nations has been marked so extensively by peace and prosperity.

Europe, with a few partial and unhappy exceptions, has enjoyed ten years of peace, during which all her Governments, whatever the theory of their constitutions may have been, are successively taught to feel that the end of their institution is the happiness of the people, and that the exercise of power among men can be justified only by the blessings it confers upon those over whom it is extended.

During the same period our intercourse with all those nations has been pacific and friendly; it so continues. Since the close of your last session no material variation has occurred in our relations with any one of them. In the commercial and navigation system of Great Britain important changes of municipal regulation have recently been sanctioned by acts of Parliament, the effect of which upon the interests of other nations, and particularly upon ours, has not yet been fully developed. In the recent renewal of the diplomatic missions on both sides between the two Governments assurances have been given and received of the continuance and increase of the mutual confidence and cordiality by which the adjustment of many points of difference had already been effected, and which affords the surest pledge for the ultimate satisfactory adjustment of those which still remain open or may hereafter arise.

The policy of the United States in their commercial intercourse with other nations has always been of the most liberal character. In the mutual exchange of their respective productions they have abstained altogether from prohibitions; they have interdicted themselves the power of laying taxes upon exports, and whenever they have favored their own shipping by special preferences or exclusive privileges in their own ports it has been only with a view to countervail similar favors and exclusions granted by the nations with whom we have been engaged in traffic to their own people or shipping, and to the disadvantage of ours. Immediately after the close of the last war a proposal was fairly made by the act of Congress of the 3d of March, 1815, to all the maritime nations to lay aside the system of retaliating restrictions and exclusions, and to place the shipping of both parties to the common trade on a footing of equality in respect to the duties of tonnage and impost. This offer was partially and successively accepted by Great Britain, Sweden, the Netherlands, the Hanseatic cities, Prussia, Sardinia, the Duke of Oldenburg, and Russia. It was also adopted, under certain modifications, in our late commercial convention with France, and by the act of Congress of the 8th January, 1824, it has received a new confirmation with all the nations who had acceded to it, and has been offered again to all those who are or may hereafter be willing to abide in reciprocity by it. But all these regulations, whether established by treaty or by municipal enactments, are still subject to one important restriction.

The removal of discriminating duties of tonnage and of impost is limited to articles of the growth, produce, or manufacture of the country to which the vessel belongs or to such articles as are most usually first shipped from her ports. It will deserve the serious consideration of Congress whether even this remnant of restriction may not be safely abandoned, and whether the general tender of equal competition made in the act of 8th January, 1824, may not be extended to include all articles of merchandise not prohibited, of what country soever they may be the produce or manufacture. Propositions to this effect have already been made to us by more than one European Government, and it is probable that if once established by legislation or compact with any distinguished maritime state it would recommend itself by the experience of its advantages to the general accession of all.

The convention of commerce and navigation between the United States and France, concluded on the 24th of June, 1822, was, in the understanding and intent of both parties, as appears upon its face, only a temporary arrangement of the points of difference between them of the most immediate and pressing urgency. It was limited in the first instance to two years from the 1st of October, 1822, but with a proviso that it should further continue in force till the conclusion of a general and definitive treaty of commerce, unless terminated by a notice, six months in advance, of either of the parties to the other. Its operation so far as it extended has been mutually advantageous, and it still continues in force by common consent. But it left unadjusted several objects of great interest to the citizens and subjects of both countries, and particularly a mass of claims to considerable amount of citizens of the United States upon the Government of France of indemnity for property taken or destroyed under circumstances of the most aggravated and outrageous character. In the long period during which continual and earnest appeals have been made to the equity and magnanimity of France in behalf of these claims their justice has not been, as it could not be, denied. It was hoped that the accession of a new Sovereign to the throne would have afforded a favorable opportunity for presenting them to the consideration of his Government. They have been presented and urged hitherto without effect. The repeated and earnest representations of our minister at the Court of France remain as yet even without an answer. Were the demands of nations upon the justice of each other susceptible of adjudication by the sentence of an impartial tribunal, those to which I now refer would long since have been settled and adequate indemnity would have been obtained. There are large amounts of similar claims upon the Netherlands, Naples, and Denmark. For those upon Spain prior to 1819 indemnity was, after many years of patient forbearance, obtained; and those upon Sweden have been lately compromised by a private settlement, in which the claimants themselves have acquiesced. The Governments of Denmark and of Naples have been recently reminded of those yet existing against them, nor will any of them be forgotten while a hope may be indulged of obtaining justice by the means within the constitutional power of the Executive, and without resorting to those means of self-redress which, as well as the time, circumstances, and occasion which may require them, are within the exclusive competency of the Legislature.

It is with great satisfaction that I am enabled to bear witness to the liberal spirit with which the Republic of Colombia has made satisfaction for well-established claims of a similar character, and among the documents now communicated to Congress will be distinguished a treaty of commerce and navigation with that Republic, the ratifications of which have been exchanged since the last recess of the Legislature. The negotiation of similar treaties with all the independent South American States has been contemplated and may yet be accomplished. The basis of them all, as proposed by the United States, has been laid in two principles—the one of entire and unqualified reciprocity, the other the mutual obligation of the parties to place each other permanently upon the footing of the most favored nation. These principles are, indeed, indispensable to the effectual emancipation of the American hemisphere from the thraldom of colonizing monopolies and exclusions, an event rapidly realizing in the progress of human affairs, and which the resistance still opposed in certain parts of Europe to the acknowledgment of the Southern American Republics as independent States will, it is believed, contribute more effectually to accomplish. The time has been, and that not remote, when some of those States might, in their anxious desire to obtain a nominal recognition, have accepted of a nominal independence, clogged with burdensome conditions, and exclusive commercial privileges granted to the nation from which they have separated to the disadvantage of all others. They are all now aware that such concessions to any European nation would be incompatible with that independence which they have declared and maintained.

Among the measures which have been suggested to them by the new relations with one another, resulting from the recent changes in their condition, is that of assembling at the Isthmus of Panama a congress, at which each of them should be represented, to deliberate upon objects important to the welfare of all. The Republics of Colombia, of Mexico, and of Central America have already deputed plenipotentiaries to such a meeting, and they have invited the United States to be also represented there by their ministers. The invitation has been accepted, and ministers on the part of the United States will be commissioned to attend at those deliberations, and to take part in them so far as may be compatible with that neutrality from which it is neither our intention nor the desire of the other American States that we should depart.

The commissioners under the seventh article of the treaty of Ghent have so nearly completed their arduous labors that, by the report recently received from the agent on the part of the United States, there is reason to expect that the commission will be closed at their next session, appointed for the 22d of May of the ensuing year.

The other commission, appointed to ascertain the indemnities due for slaves carried away from the United States after the close of the late war, have met with some difficulty, which has delayed their progress in the inquiry. A reference has been made to the British Government on the subject, which, it may be hoped, will tend to hasten the decision of the commissioners, or serve as a substitute for it.

Among the powers specifically granted to Congress by the Constitution are those of establishing uniform laws on the subject of bankruptcies throughout the United States and of providing for organizing, arming, and disciplining the militia and for governing such part of them as may be employed in the service of the United States. The magnitude and complexity of the interests affected by legislation upon these subjects may account for the fact that, long and often as both of them have occupied the attention and animated the debates of Congress, no systems have yet been devised for fulfilling to the satisfaction of the community the duties prescribed by these grants of power. To conciliate the claim of the individual citizen to the enjoyment of personal liberty, with the effective obligation of private contracts, is the difficult problem to be solved by a law of bankruptcy. These are objects of the deepest interest to society, affecting all that is precious in the existence of multitudes of persons, many of them in the classes essentially dependent and helpless, of the age requiring nurture, and of the sex entitled to protection from the free agency of the parent and the husband. The organization of the militia is yet more indispensable to the liberties of the country. It is only by an effective militia that we can at once enjoy the repose of peace and bid defiance to foreign aggression; it is by the militia that we are constituted an armed nation, standing in perpetual panoply of defense in the presence of all the other nations of the earth. To this end it would be necessary, if possible, so to shape its organization as to give it a more

united and active energy.   There are laws for establishing an uniform
militia throughout the United States and for arming and equipping its
whole body.   But it is a body of dislocated members, without the vigor
of unity and having little of uniformity but the name.   To infuse into
this most important institution the power of which it is susceptible and
to make it available for the defense of the Union at the shortest notice
and at the smallest expense possible of time, of life, and of treasure are
among the benefits to be expected from the persevering deliberations of
Congress.

Among the unequivocal indications of our national prosperity is the
flourishing state of our finances.   The revenues of the present year, from
all their principal sources, will exceed the anticipations of the last.   The
balance in the Treasury on the 1st of January last was a little short of
$2,000,000, exclusive of two millions and a half, being the moiety of the
loan of five millions authorized by the act of 26th of May, 1824.   The
receipts into the Treasury from the 1st of January to the 30th of September, exclusive of the other moiety of the same loan, are estimated
at $16,500,000, and it is expected that those of the current quarter will
exceed $5,000,000, forming an aggregate of receipts of nearly twenty-two
millions, independent of the loan.   The expenditures of the year will not
exceed that sum more than two millions.   By those expenditures nearly
eight millions of the principal of the public debt have been discharged.
More than a million and a half has been devoted to the debt of gratitude
to the warriors of the Revolution; a nearly equal sum to the construction
of fortifications and the acquisition of ordnance and other permanent
preparations of national defense; half a million to the gradual increase of
the Navy; an equal sum for purchases of territory from the Indians and
payment of annuities to them; and upward of a million for objects of
internal improvement authorized by special acts of the last Congress.   If
we add to these $4,000,000 for payment of interest upon the public debt,
there remains a sum of about seven millions, which have defrayed the
whole expense of the administration of Government in its legislative,
executive, and judiciary departments, including the support of the military and naval establishments and all the occasional contingencies of a
government coextensive with the Union.

The amount of duties secured on merchandise imported since the commencement of the year is about twenty-five millions and a half, and that
which will accrue during the current quarter is estimated at five millions
and a half; from these thirty-one millions, deducting the drawbacks, estimated at less than seven millions, a sum exceeding twenty-four millions
will constitute the revenue of the year, and will exceed the whole expenditures of the year.   The entire amount of the public debt remaining due
on the 1st of January next will be short of $81,000,000.

By an act of Congress of the 3d of March last a loan of $12,000,000
was authorized at 4½ per cent, or an exchange of stock to that amount

of 4½ per cent for a stock of 6 per cent, to create a fund for extinguishing an equal amount of the public debt, bearing an interest of 6 per cent, redeemable in 1826. An account of the measures taken to give effect to this act will be laid before you by the Secretary of the Treasury. As the object which it had in view has been but partially accomplished, it will be for the consideration of Congress whether the power with which it clothed the Executive should not be renewed at an early day of the present session, and under what modifications.

The act of Congress of the 3d of March last, directing the Secretary of the Treasury to subscribe, in the name and for the use of the United States, for 1,500 shares of the capital stock of the Chesapeake and Delaware Canal Company, has been executed by the actual subscription for the amount specified; and such other measures have been adopted by that officer, under the act, as the fulfillment of its intentions requires. The latest accounts received of this important undertaking authorize the belief that it is in successful progress.

The payments into the Treasury from the proceeds of the sales of the public lands during the present year were estimated at $1,000,000. The actual receipts of the first two quarters have fallen very little short of that sum; it is not expected that the second half of the year will be equally productive, but the income of the year from that source may now be safely estimated at a million and a half. The act of Congress of 18th May, 1824, to provide for the extinguishment of the debt due to the United States by the purchasers of public lands, was limited in its operation of relief to the purchaser to the 10th of April last. Its effect at the end of the quarter during which it expired was to reduce that debt from ten to seven millions. By the operation of similar prior laws of relief, from and since that of 2d March, 1821, the debt had been reduced from upward of twenty-two millions to ten. It is exceedingly desirable that it should be extinguished altogether; and to facilitate that consummation I recommend to Congress the revival for one year more of the act of 18th May, 1824, with such provisional modification as may be necessary to guard the public interests against fraudulent practices in the resale of the relinquished land. The purchasers of public lands are among the most useful of our fellow-citizens, and since the system of sales for cash alone has been introduced great indulgence has been justly extended to those who had previously purchased upon credit. The debt which had been contracted under the credit sales had become unwieldy, and its extinction was alike advantageous to the purchaser and to the public. Under the system of sales, matured as it has been by experience, and adapted to the exigencies of the times, the lands will continue as they have become, an abundant source of revenue; and when the pledge of them to the public creditor shall have been redeemed by the entire discharge of the national debt, the swelling tide of wealth with which they replenish the common Treasury may be made to reflow in unfailing streams of improvement from the

Atlantic to the Pacific Ocean.

The condition of the various branches of the public service resorting from the Department of War, and their administration during the current year, will be exhibited in the report of the Secretary of War and the accompanying documents herewith communicated. The organization and discipline of the Army are effective and satisfactory. To counteract the prevalence of desertion among the troops it has been suggested to withhold from the men a small portion of their monthly pay until the period of their discharge; and some expedient appears to be necessary to preserve and maintain among the officers so much of the art of horsemanship as could scarcely fail to be found wanting on the possible sudden eruption of a war, which should take us unprovided with a single corps of cavalry. The Military Academy at West Point, under the restrictions of a severe but paternal superintendence, recommends itself more and more to the patronage of the nation, and the numbers of meritorious officers which it forms and introduces to the public service furnishes the means of multiplying the undertakings of public improvements to which their acquirements at that institution are peculiarly adapted. The school of artillery practice established at Fortress Monroe is well suited to the same purpose, and may need the aid of further legislative provision to the same end. The reports of the various officers at the head of the administrative branches of the military service, connected with the quartering, clothing, subsistence, health, and pay of the Army, exhibit the assiduous vigilance of those officers in the performance of their respective duties, and the faithful accountability which has pervaded every part of the system.

Our relations with the numerous tribes of aboriginal natives of this country, scattered over its extensive surface and so dependent even for their existence upon our power, have been during the present year highly interesting. An act of Congress of 25th of May, 1824, made an appropriation to defray the expenses of making treaties of trade and friendship with the Indian tribes beyond the Mississippi. An act of 3d of March, 1825, authorized treaties to be made with the Indians for their consent to the making of a road from the frontier of Missouri to that of New Mexico, and another act of the same date provided for defraying the expenses of holding treaties with the Sioux, Chippeways, Menomenees, Sauks, Foxes, etc., for the purpose of establishing boundaries and promoting peace between said tribes. The first and the last objects of these acts have been accomplished, and the second is yet in a process of execution. The treaties which since the last session of Congress have been concluded with the several tribes will be laid before the Senate for their consideration conformably to the Constitution. They comprise large and valuable acquisitions of territory, and they secure an adjustment of boundaries and give pledges of permanent peace between several tribes which had been long waging bloody wars against each other.

On the 12th of February last a treaty was signed at the Indian Springs between commissioners appointed on the part of the United States and certain chiefs and individuals of the Creek Nation of Indians, which was received at the seat of Government only a very few days before the close of the last session of Congress and of the late Administration. The advice and consent of the Senate was given to it on the 3d of March, too late for it to receive the ratification of the then President of the United States; it was ratified on the 7th of March, under the unsuspecting impression that it had been negotiated in good faith and in the confidence inspired by the recommendation of the Senate. The subsequent transactions in relation to this treaty will form the subject of a separate communication.

The appropriations made by Congress for public works, as well in the construction of fortifications as for purposes of internal improvement, so far as they have been expended, have been faithfully applied. Their progress has been delayed by the want of suitable officers for superintending them. An increase of both the corps of engineers, military and topographical, was recommended by my predecessor at the last session of Congress. The reasons upon which that recommendation was founded subsist in all their force and have acquired additional urgency since that time. It may also be expedient to organize the topographical engineers into a corps similar to the present establishment of the Corps of Engineers. The Military Academy at West Point will furnish from the cadets there officers well qualified for carrying this measure into effect.

The Board of Engineers for Internal Improvement, appointed for carrying into execution the act of Congress of 30th of April, 1824, "to procure the necessary surveys, plans, and estimates on the subject of roads and canals," have been actively engaged in that service from the close of the last session of Congress. They have completed the surveys necessary for ascertaining the practicability of a canal from the Chesapeake Bay to the Ohio River, and are preparing a full report on that subject, which, when completed, will be laid before you. The same observation is to be made with regard to the two other objects of national importance upon which the Board have been occupied, namely, the accomplishment of a national road from this city to New Orleans, and the practicability of uniting the waters of Lake Memphramagog with Connecticut River and the improvement of the navigation of that river. The surveys have been made and are nearly completed. The report may be expected at an early period during the present session of Congress.

The acts of Congress of the last session relative to the surveying, marking, or laying out roads in the Territories of Florida, Arkansas, and Michigan, from Missouri to Mexico, and for the continuation of the Cumberland road, are, some of them, fully executed, and others in the process of execution. Those for completing or commencing fortifications have been delayed only so far as the Corps of Engineers has been inadequate to furnish officers for the necessary superintendence of the works. Under

the act confirming the statutes of Virginia and Maryland incorporating
the Chesapeake and Ohio Canal Company, three commissioners on the
part of the United States have been appointed for opening books and
receiving subscriptions, in concert with a like number of commissioners
appointed on the part of each of those States. A meeting of the commissioners has been postponed, to await the definitive report of the board of
engineers. The light-houses and monuments for the safety of our commerce and mariners, the works for the security of Plymouth Beach and
for the preservation of the islands in Boston Harbor, have received the
attention required by the laws relating to those objects respectively.
The continuation of the Cumberland road, the most important of them
all, after surmounting no inconsiderable difficulty in fixing upon the
direction of the road, has commenced under the most promising auspices,
with the improvements of recent invention in the mode of construction,
and with the advantage of a great reduction in the comparative cost of
the work.

The operation of the laws relating to the Revolutionary pensioners may
deserve the renewed consideration of Congress. The act of the 18th of
March, 1818, while it made provision for many meritorious and indigent
citizens who had served in the War of Independence, opened a door to
numerous abuses and impositions. To remedy this the act of 1st May,
1820, exacted proofs of absolute indigence, which many really in want
were unable and all susceptible of that delicacy which is allied to many
virtues must be deeply reluctant to give. The result has been that some
among the least deserving have been retained, and some in whom the
requisites both of worth and want were combined have been stricken
from the list. As the numbers of these venerable relics of an age gone
by diminish; as the decays of body, mind, and estate of those that survive
must in the common course of nature increase, should not a more liberal
portion of indulgence be dealt out to them? May not the want in most
instances be inferred from the demand when the service can be proved,
and may not the last days of human infirmity be spared the mortification
of purchasing a pittance of relief only by the exposure of its own necessities? I submit to Congress the expediency of providing for individual
cases of this description by special enactment, or of revising the act of
the 1st of May, 1820, with a view to mitigate the rigor of its exclusions in
favor of persons to whom charity now bestowed can scarcely discharge
the debt of justice.

The portion of the naval force of the Union in actual service has been
chiefly employed on three stations—the Mediterranean, the coasts of
South America bordering on the Pacific Ocean, and the West Indies. An
occasional cruiser has been sent to range along the African shores most
polluted by the traffic of slaves; one armed vessel has been stationed on
the coast of our eastern boundary, to cruise along the fishing grounds
in Hudsons Bay and on the coast of Labrador, and the first service of a

new frigate has been performed in restoring to his native soil and domestic enjoyments the veteran hero whose youthful blood and treasure had freely flowed in the cause of our country's independence, and whose whole life has been a series of services and sacrifices to the improvement of his fellow-men. The visit of General Lafayette, alike honorable to himself and to our country, closed, as it had commenced, with the most affecting testimonials of devoted attachment on his part, and of unbounded gratitude of this people to him in return. It will form hereafter a pleasing incident in the annals of our Union, giving to real history the intense interest of romance and signally marking the unpurchasable tribute of a great nation's social affections to the disinterested champion of the liberties of human-kind.

The constant maintenance of a small squadron in the Mediterranean is a necessary substitute for the humiliating alternative of paying tribute for the security of our commerce in that sea, and for a precarious peace, at the mercy of every caprice of four Barbary States, by whom it was liable to be violated. An additional motive for keeping a respectable force stationed there at this time is found in the maritime war raging between the Greeks and the Turks, and in which the neutral navigation of this Union is always in danger of outrage and depredation. A few instances have occurred of such depredations upon our merchant vessels by privateers or pirates wearing the Grecian flag, but without real authority from the Greek or any other Government. The heroic struggles of the Greeks themselves, in which our warmest sympathies as freemen and Christians have been engaged, have continued to be maintained with vicissitudes of success adverse and favorable.

Similar motives have rendered expedient the keeping of a like force on the coasts of Peru and Chile on the Pacific. The irregular and convulsive character of the war upon the shores has been extended to the conflicts upon the ocean. An active warfare has been kept up for years with alternate success, though generally to the advantage of the American patriots. But their naval forces have not always been under the control of their own Governments. Blockades, unjustifiable upon any acknowledged principles of international law, have been proclaimed by officers in command, and though disavowed by the supreme authorities, the protection of our own commerce against them has been made cause of complaint and erroneous imputations against some of the most gallant officers of our Navy. Complaints equally groundless have been made by the commanders of the Spanish royal forces in those seas; but the most effective protection to our commerce has been the flag and the firmness of our own commanding officers. The cessation of the war by the complete triumph of the patriot cause has removed, it is hoped, all cause of dissension with one party and all vestige of force of the other. But an unsettled coast of many degrees of latitude forming a part of our own territory and a flourishing commerce and fishery extending to the islands of the Pacific and to China still require that the protecting power of the Union should be displayed under its flag as well upon the ocean as upon the land.

The objects of the West India Squadron have been to carry into execution the laws for the suppression of the African slave trade; for the protection of our commerce against vessels of piratical character, though bearing commissions from either of the belligerent parties; for its protection against open and unequivocal pirates. These objects during the present year have been accomplished more effectually than at any former period. The African slave trade has long been excluded from the use of our flag, and if some few citizens of our country have continued to set the laws of the Union as well as those of nature and humanity at defiance by persevering in that abominable traffic, it has been only by sheltering themselves under the banners of other nations less earnest for the total extinction of the trade than ours. The irregular privateers have within the last year been in a great measure banished from those seas, and the pirates for months past appear to have been almost entirely swept away from the borders and the shores of the two Spanish islands in those regions. The active, persevering, and unremitted energy of Captain Warrington and of the officers and men under his command on that trying and perilous service have been crowned with signal success, and are entitled to the approbation of their country. But experience has shown that not even a temporary suspension or relaxation from assiduity can be indulged on that station without reproducing piracy and murder in all their horrors; nor is it probable that for years to come our immensely valuable commerce in those seas can navigate in security without the steady continuance of an armed force devoted to its protection.

It were, indeed, a vain and dangerous illusion to believe that in the present or probable condition of human society a commerce so extensive and so rich as ours could exist and be pursued in safety without the continual support of a military marine—the only arm by which the power of this Confederacy can be estimated or felt by foreign nations, and the only standing military force which can never be dangerous to our own liberties at home. A permanent naval peace establishment, therefore, adapted to our present condition, and adaptable to that gigantic growth with which the nation is advancing in its career, is among the subjects which have already occupied the foresight of the last Congress, and which will deserve your serious deliberations. Our Navy, commenced at an early period of our present political organization upon a scale commensurate with the incipient energies, the scanty resources, and the comparative indigence of our infancy, was even then found adequate to cope with all the powers of Barbary, save the first, and with one of the principal maritime powers of Europe.

At a period of further advancement, but with little accession of strength, it not only sustained with honor the most unequal of conflicts, but covered itself and our country with unfading glory. But it is only since the close of the late war that by the numbers and force of the ships of which it was composed it could deserve the name of a navy. Yet it retains nearly the same organization as when it consisted only of five frigates. The rules and regulations by which it is governed earnestly call for revision, and the want of a naval school of instruction, corresponding with the Military Academy at West Point, for the formation of scientific and accomplished officers, is felt with daily increasing aggravation.

The act of Congress of 26th of May, 1824, authorizing an examination and survey of the harbor of Charleston, in South Carolina, of St. Marys, in Georgia, and of the coast of Florida, and for other purposes, has been executed so far as the appropriation would admit. Those of the 3d of March last, authorizing the establishment of a navy-yard and depot on the coast of Florida, in the Gulf of Mexico, and authorizing the building of ten sloops of war, and for other purposes, are in the course of execution, for the particulars of which and other objects connected with this Department I refer to the report of the Secretary of the Navy, herewith communicated.

A report from the Postmaster-General is also submitted, exhibiting the present flourishing condition of that Department. For the first time for many years the receipts for the year ending on the 1st of July last exceeded the expenditures during the same period to the amount of more than $45,000. Other facts equally creditable to the administration of this Department are that in two years from the 1st of July, 1823, an improvement of more than $185,000 in its pecuniary affairs has been realized; that in the same interval the increase of the transportation of the mail has exceeded 1,500,000 miles annually, and that 1,040 new post-offices have been established. It hence appears that under judicious management the income from this establishment may be relied on as fully adequate to defray its expenses, and that by the discontinuance of post-roads altogether unproductive others of more useful character may be opened, till the circulation of the mail shall keep pace with the spread of our population, and the comforts of friendly correspondence, the exchanges of internal traffic, and the lights of the periodical press shall be distributed to the remotest corners of the Union, at a charge scarcely perceptible to any individual, and without the cost of a dollar to the public Treasury.

Upon this first occasion of addressing the Legislature of the Union, with which I have been honored, in presenting to their view the execution so far as it has been effected of the measures sanctioned by them for promoting the internal improvement of our country, I can not close the communication without recommending to their calm and persevering consideration the general principle in a more enlarged extent. The great object of the institution of civil government is the improvement of the condition of those who are parties to the social compact, and no government, in whatever form constituted, can accomplish the lawful ends of its institution but in proportion as it improves the condition of those over whom it is established. Roads and canals, by multiplying and facilitating the communications and intercourse between distant regions and multitudes of men, are among the most important means of improvement. But moral, political, intellectual improvement are duties assigned by the Author of Our Existence to social no less than to individual man. For the fulfillment of those duties governments are invested with power, and to the attainment of the end—the progressive improvement of the condition of the governed—the exercise of delegated powers is a duty as sacred and indispensable as the usurpation of powers not granted is criminal and odious. Among the first, perhaps the very first, instrument for the improvement of the condition of men is knowledge, and to the acquisition of much of the knowledge adapted to the wants, the comforts, and enjoyments of human life public institutions and seminaries of learning are essential. So convinced of this was the first of my predecessors in this office, now first in the memory, as, living, he was first in the hearts, of our countrymen, that once and again in his addresses to the Congresses with whom he cooperated in the public service he earnestly recommended the establishment of seminaries of learning, to prepare for all the emergencies of peace and war—a national university and a military academy. With respect to the latter, had he lived to the present day, in turning his eyes to the institution at West Point he would have enjoyed the gratification of his most earnest wishes; but in surveying the city which has been honored with his name he would have seen the spot of earth which he had destined and bequeathed to the use and benefit of his country as the site for an university still bare and barren.

In assuming her station among the civilized nations of the earth it would seem that our country had contracted the engagement to contribute her share of mind, of labor, and of expense to the improvement of those parts of knowledge which lie beyond the reach of individual acquisition, and particularly to geographical and astronomical science. Looking back to the history only of the half century since the declaration of our independence, and observing the generous emulation with which the Governments of France, Great Britain, and Russia have devoted the genius, the intelligence, the treasures of their respective nations to the common improvement of the species in these branches of science, is it not incumbent upon us to inquire whether we are not bound by obligations of a high and honorable character to contribute our portion of energy and exertion to the common stock? The voyages of discovery prosecuted in the course of that time at the expense of those nations have not only redounded to their glory, but to the improvement of human knowledge. We have been partakers of that improvement and owe for it a sacred debt, not only of gratitude, but of equal or proportional exertion in the same common cause. Of the cost of these undertakings, if the mere expenditures of outfit, equipment, and completion of the expeditions were to be considered the only charges, it would be unworthy of a great and generous nation to take a second thought. One hundred expeditions of circumnavigation like those of Cook and La Pérouse would not burden the exchequer of the nation fitting them out so much as the ways and means of defraying a single campaign in war. But if we take into the account the lives of those benefactors of mankind of which their services in the cause of their species were the purchase, how shall the cost of those heroic enterprises be estimated, and what compensation can be made to them or to their countries for them? Is it not by bearing them in affectionate remembrance? Is it not still more by imitating their example— by enabling countrymen of our own to pursue the same career and to hazard their lives in the same cause?

In inviting the attention of Congress to the subject of internal improvements upon a view thus enlarged it is not my design to recommend the equipment of an expedition for circumnavigating the globe for purposes of scientific research and inquiry. We have objects of useful investigation nearer home, and to which our cares may be more beneficially applied. The interior of our own territories has yet been very imperfectly explored. Our coasts along many degrees of latitude upon the shores of the Pacific Ocean, though much frequented by our spirited commercial navigators, have been barely visited by our public ships. The River of the West, first fully discovered and navigated by a countryman of our own, still bears the name of the ship in which he ascended its waters, and claims the protection of our armed national flag at its mouth. With the establishment of a military post there or at some other point of that coast, recommended by my predecessor and already matured in the deliberations of the last Congress, I would suggest the expediency of connecting the equipment of a public ship for the exploration of the whole northwest coast of this continent.

The establishment of an uniform standard of weights and measures was one of the specific objects contemplated in the formation of our Constitution, and to fix that standard was one of the powers delegated by express terms in that instrument to Congress. The Governments of Great Britain and France have scarcely ceased to be occupied with inquiries and speculations on the same subject since the existence of our Constitution, and with them it has expanded into profound, laborious, and expensive researches into the figure of the earth and the comparative length of the pendulum vibrating seconds in various latitudes from the equator to the pole. These researches have resulted in the composition and publication of several works highly interesting to the cause of science. The experiments are yet in the process of performance. Some of them have recently been made on our own shores, within the walls of one of our own colleges, and partly by one of our own fellow-citizens. It would be honorable to our country if the sequel of the same experiments should be countenanced by the patronage of our Government, as they have hitherto been by those of France and Britain.

Connected with the establishment of an university, or separate from it, might be undertaken the erection of an astronomical observatory, with provision for the support of an astronomer, to be in constant attendance of observation upon the phenomena of the heavens, and for the periodical publication of his observations.   It is with no feeling of pride as an American that the remark may be made that on the comparatively small territorial surface of Europe there are existing upward of 130 of these light-houses of the skies, while throughout the whole American hemisphere there is not one.   If we reflect a moment upon the discoveries which in the last four centuries have been made in the physical constitution of the universe by the means of these buildings and of observers stationed in them, shall we doubt of their usefulness to every nation? And while scarcely a year passes over our heads without bringing some new astronomical discovery to light, which we must fain receive at second hand from Europe, are we not cutting ourselves off from the means of returning light for light while we have neither observatory nor observer upon our half of the globe and the earth revolves in perpetual darkness to our unsearching eyes?

When, on the 25th of October, 1791, the first President of the United States announced to Congress the result of the first enumeration of the inhabitants of this Union, he informed them that the returns gave the pleasing assurance that the population of the United States bordered on 4,000,000 persons.   At the distance of thirty years from that time the last enumeration, five years since completed, presented a population bordering upon 10,000,000.   Perhaps of all the evidences of a prosperous and happy condition of human society the rapidity of the increase of population is the most unequivocal.   But the demonstration of our prosperity rests not alone upon this indication.   Our commerce, our wealth, and the extent of our territories have increased in corresponding proportions, and the number of independent communities associated in our Federal Union has since that time nearly doubled.   The legislative representation of the States and people in the two Houses of Congress has grown with the growth of their constituent bodies.   The House, which then consisted of 65 members, now numbers upward of 200.   The Senate, which consisted of 26 members, has now 48.   But the executive and, still more, the judiciary departments are yet in a great measure confined to their primitive organization, and are now not adequate to the urgent wants of a still growing community.

The naval armaments, which at an early period forced themselves upon the necessities of the Union, soon led to the establishment of a Department of the Navy.   But the Departments of Foreign Affairs and of the Interior, which early after the formation of the Government had been united in one, continue so united to this time, to the unquestionable detriment of the public service. The multiplication of our relations with the nations and Governments of the Old World has kept pace with that of our population and commerce, while within the last ten years a new family of nations in our own hemisphere has arisen among the inhabitants of the earth, with whom our intercourse, commercial and political, would of itself furnish occupation to an active and industrious department. The constitution of the judiciary, experimental and imperfect as it was even in the infancy of our existing Government, is yet more inadequate to the administration of national justice at our present maturity. Nine years have elapsed since a predecessor in this office, now not the last, the citizen who, perhaps, of all others throughout the Union contributed most to the formation and establishment of our Constitution, in his valedictory address to Congress, immediately preceding his retirement from public life, urgently recommended the revision of the judiciary and the establishment of an additional executive department. The exigencies of the public service and its unavoidable deficiencies, as now in exercise, have added yearly cumulative weight to the considerations presented by him as persuasive to the measure, and in recommending it to your deliberations I am happy to have the influence of his high authority in aid of the undoubting convictions of my own experience.

The laws relating to the administration of the Patent Office are deserving of much consideration and perhaps susceptible of some improvement. The grant of power to regulate the action of Congress upon this subject has specified both the end to be obtained and the means by which it is to be effected, "to promote the progress of science and useful arts by securing for limited times to authors and inventors the exclusive right to their respective writings and discoveries." If an honest pride might be indulged in the reflection that on the records of that office are already found inventions the usefulness of which has scarcely been transcended in the annals of human ingenuity, would not its exultation be allayed by the inquiry whether the laws have effectively insured to the inventors the reward destined to them by the Constitution—even a limited term of exclusive right to their discoveries?

On the 24th of December, 1799, it was resolved by Congress that a marble monument should be erected by the United States in the Capitol at the city of Washington; that the family of General Washington should be requested to permit his body to be deposited under it, and that the monument be so designed as to commemorate the great events of his military and political life. In reminding Congress of this resolution and that the monument contemplated by it remains yet without execution, I shall indulge only the remarks that the works at the Capitol are approaching to completion; that the consent of the family, desired by the resolution, was requested and obtained; that a monument has been recently erected in this city over the remains of another distinguished patriot of the Revolution, and that a spot has been reserved within the walls where you are deliberating for the benefit of this and future ages, in which the mortal remains may be deposited of him whose spirit hovers over you and listens with delight to every act of the representatives of his nation which can tend to exalt and adorn his and their country.

The Constitution under which you are assembled is a charter of limited powers. After full and solemn deliberation upon all or any of the objects which, urged by an irresistible sense of my own duty, I have recommended to your attention should you come to the conclusion that, however desirable in themselves, the enactment of laws for effecting them would transcend the powers committed to you by that venerable instrument which we are all bound to support, let no consideration induce you to assume the exercise of powers not granted to you by the people. But if the power to exercise exclusive legislation in all cases whatsoever over the District of Columbia; if the power to lay and collect taxes, duties, imposts, and excises, to pay the debts and provide for the common defense and general welfare of the United States; if the power to regulate commerce with foreign nations and among the several States and with the Indian tribes, to fix the standard of weights and measures, to establish post-offices and post-roads, to declare war, to raise and support armies, to provide and maintain a navy, to dispose of and make all needful rules and regulations respecting the territory or other property belonging to the United States, and to make all laws which shall be necessary and proper for carrying these powers into execution—if these powers and others enumerated in the Constitution may be effectually brought into action by laws promoting the improvement of agriculture, commerce, and manufactures, the cultivation and encouragement of the mechanic and of the elegant arts, the advancement of literature, and the progress of the sciences, ornamental and profound, to refrain from exercising them for the benefit of the people themselves would be to hide in the earth the talent committed to our charge—would be treachery to the most sacred of trusts.

The spirit of improvement is abroad upon the earth. It stimulates the hearts and sharpens the faculties not of our fellow-citizens alone, but of the nations of Europe and of their rulers. While dwelling with pleasing satisfaction upon the superior excellence of our political institutions, let us not be unmindful that liberty is power; that the nation blessed with the largest portion of liberty must in proportion to its numbers be the most powerful nation upon earth, and that the tenure of power by man is, in the moral purposes of his Creator, upon condition that it shall be exercised to ends of beneficence, to improve the condition of himself and his fellow-men. While foreign nations less blessed with that freedom which is power than ourselves are advancing with gigantic strides in the career of public improvement, were we to slumber in indolence or fold up our arms and proclaim to the world that we are palsied by the will of our constituents, would it not be to cast away the bounties of Providence and doom ourselves to perpetual inferiority? In the course of the year now drawing to its close we have beheld, under the auspices and at the expense of one State of this Union, a new university unfolding its portals to the sons of science and holding up the torch of human improvement to eyes that seek the light. We have seen under the persevering and enlightened enterprise of another State the waters of our Western lakes mingle with those of the ocean. If undertakings like these have been accomplished in the compass of a few years by the authority of single members of our Confederation, can we, the representative authorities of the whole Union, fall behind our fellow-servants in the exercise of the trust committed to us for the benefit of our common sovereign by the accomplishment of works important to the whole and to which neither the authority nor the resources of any one State can be adequate?

Finally, fellow-citizens, I shall await with cheering hope and faithful cooperation the result of your deliberations, assured that, without encroaching upon the powers reserved to the authorities of the respective States or to the people, you will, with a due sense of your obligations to your country and of the high responsibilities weighing upon yourselves, give efficacy to the means committed to you for the common good. And may He who searches the hearts of the children of men prosper your exertions to secure the blessings of peace and promote the highest welfare of our country.

SECOND ANNUAL MESSAGE.

WASHINGTON, *December 5, 1826.*

Fellow-Citizens of the Senate and of the House of Representatives:

The assemblage of the representatives of our Union in both Houses of the Congress at this time occurs under circumstances calling for the renewed homage of our grateful acknowledgments to the Giver of All Good. With the exceptions incidental to the most felicitous condition of human existence, we continue to be highly favored in all the elements which contribute to individual comfort and to national prosperity. In the survey of our extensive country we have generally to observe abodes of health and regions of plenty. In our civil and political relations we have peace without and tranquillity within our borders. We are, as a people, increasing with unabated rapidity in population, wealth, and national resources, and whatever differences of opinion exist among us with regard to the mode and the means by which we shall turn the beneficence of Heaven to the improvement of our own condition, there is yet a spirit animating us all which will not suffer the bounties of Providence to be showered upon us in vain, but will receive them with grateful hearts, and apply them with unwearied hands to the advancement of the general good.

Of the subjects recommended to Congress at their last session, some were then definitively acted upon. Others, left unfinished, but partly matured, will recur to your attention without needing a renewal of notice from me. The purpose of this communication will be to present to your view the general aspect of our public affairs at this moment and the measures which have been taken to carry into effect the intentions of the Legislature as signified by the laws then and heretofore enacted.

In our intercourse with the other nations of the earth we have still the happiness of enjoying peace and a general good understanding, qualified, however, in several important instances by collisions of interest and by unsatisfied claims of justice, to the settlement of which the constitutional interposition of the legislative authority may become ultimately indispensable.

By the decease of the Emperor Alexander, of Russia, which occurred cotemporaneously with the commencement of the last session of Congress, the United States have been deprived of a long-tried, steady, and faithful friend. Born to the inheritance of absolute power and trained in the school of adversity, from which no power on earth, however absolute, is exempt, that monarch from his youth had been taught to feel the force and value of public opinion and to be sensible that the interests of his own Government would best be promoted by a frank and friendly intercourse with this Republic, as those of his people would be advanced by a liberal commercial intercourse with our country. A candid and confidential interchange of sentiments between him and the Government of the United States upon the affairs of Southern America took place at a period not long preceding his demise, and contributed to fix that course of policy which left to the other Governments of Europe no alternative but that of sooner or later recognizing the independence of our southern neighbors, of which the example had by the United States already been set. The ordinary diplomatic communications between his successor, the Emperor Nicholas, and the United States have suffered some interruption by the illness, departure, and subsequent decease of his minister residing here, who enjoyed, as he merited, the entire confidence of his new sovereign, as he had eminently responded to that of his predecessor. But we have had the most satisfactory assurances that the sentiments of the reigning Emperor toward the United States are altogether conformable to those which had so long and constantly animated his imperial brother, and we have reason to hope that they will serve to cement that harmony and good understanding between the two nations which, founded in congenial interests, can not but result in the advancement of the welfare and prosperity of both.

Our relations of commerce and navigation with France are, by the operation of the convention of 24th of June, 1822, with that nation, in a state of gradual and progressive improvement. Convinced by all our experience, no less than by the principles of fair and liberal reciprocity which the United States have constantly tendered to all the nations of the earth as the rule of commercial intercourse which they would universally prefer, that fair and equal competition is most conducive to the interests of both parties, the United States in the negotiation of that convention earnestly contended for a mutual renunciation of discriminating duties and charges in the ports of the two countries. Unable to obtain the immediate recognition of this principle in its full extent, after reducing the duties of discrimination so far as was found attainable it was agreed that at the expiration of two years from the 1st of October, 1822, when the convention was to go into effect, unless a notice of six months on either side should be given to the other that the convention itself must terminate, those duties should be reduced one-fourth, and that this reduction should be yearly repeated, until all discrimination should cease, while the convention itself should continue in force. By the effect of this stipulation three-fourths of the discriminating duties which had been levied by each party upon the vessels of the other in its ports have already been removed; and on the 1st of next October, should the convention be still in force, the remaining fourth will be discontinued. French vessels laden with French produce will be received in our ports on the same terms as our own, and ours in return will enjoy the same advantages in the ports of France.

By these approximations to an equality of duties and of charges not only has the commerce between the two countries prospered, but friendly dispositions have been on both sides encouraged and promoted. They will continue to be cherished and cultivated on the part of the United States. It would have been gratifying to have had it in my power to add that the claims upon the justice of the French Government, involving the property and the comfortable subsistence of many of our fellow-citizens, and which have been so long and so earnestly urged, were in a more promising train of adjustment than at your last meeting; but their condition remains unaltered.

With the Government of the Netherlands the mutual abandonment of discriminating duties had been regulated by legislative acts on both sides. The act of Congress of the 20th of April, 1818, abolished all discriminating duties of impost and tonnage upon the vessels and produce of the Netherlands in the ports of the United States upon the assurance given by the Government of the Netherlands that all such duties operating against the shipping and commerce of the United States in that Kingdom had been abolished. These reciprocal regulations had continued in force several years when the discriminating principle was resumed by the Netherlands in a new and indirect form by a bounty of 10 per cent in the shape of a return of duties to their national vessels, and in which those of the United States are not permitted to participate. By the act of Congress of 7th January, 1824, all discriminating duties in the United States were again suspended, so far as related to the vessels and produce of the Netherlands, so long as the reciprocal exemption should be extended to the vessels and produce of the United States in the Netherlands. But the same act provides that in the event of a restoration of discriminating duties to operate against the shipping and commerce of the United States in any of the foreign countries referred to therein the suspension of discriminating duties in favor of the navigation of such foreign country should cease and all the provisions of the acts imposing discriminating foreign tonnage and impost duties in the United States should revive and be in full force with regard to that nation.

In the correspondence w.ᵉ 1 the Government of the Netherlands upon this subject they have contended that the favor shown to their own shipping by this bounty upon their tonnage is not to be considered as a discriminating duty; but it can not be denied that it produces all the same effects. Had the mutual abolition been stipulated by treaty, such a bounty upon the national vessels could scarcely have been granted consistently with good faith. Yet as the act of Congress of 7th January, 1824, has not expressly authorized the Executive authority to determine what shall be considered as a revival of discriminating duties by a foreign government to the disadvantage of the United States, and as the retaliatory measure on our part, however just and necessary, may tend rather to that conflict of legislation which we deprecate than to that concert to which we invite all commercial nations, as most conducive to their interest and our own, I have thought it more consistent with the spirit of our institutions to refer the subject again to the paramount authority of the Legislature to decide what measure the emergency may require than abruptly by proclamation to carry into effect the minatory provisions of the act of 1824.

During the last session of Congress treaties of amity, navigation, and commerce were negotiated and signed at this place with the Government of Denmark, in Europe, and with the Federation of Central America, in this hemisphere. These treaties then received the constitutional sanction of the Senate, by the advice and consent to their ratification. They were accordingly ratified on the part of the United States, and during the recess of Congress have been also ratified by the other respective contracting parties. The ratifications have been exchanged, and they have been published by proclamations, copies of which are herewith communicated to Congress.

These treaties have established between the contracting parties the principles of equality and reciprocity in their broadest and most liberal extent, each party admitting the vessels of the other into its ports, laden with cargoes the produce or manufacture of any quarter of the globe, upon the payment of the same duties of tonnage and impost that are chargeable upon their own. They have further stipulated that the parties shall hereafter grant no favor of navigation or commerce to any other nation which shall not upon the same terms be granted to each other, and that neither party will impose upon articles of merchandise the produce or manufacture of the other any other or higher duties than upon the like articles being the produce or manufacture of any other country. To these principles there is in the convention with Denmark an exception with regard to the colonies of that Kingdom in the arctic seas, but none with regard to her colonies in the West Indies.

In the course of the last summer the term to which our last commercial treaty with Sweden was limited has expired. A continuation of it is in the contemplation of the Swedish Government, and is believed to be desirable on the part of the United States. It has been proposed by the King of Sweden that pending the negotiation of renewal the expired treaty should be mutually considered as still in force, a measure which will require the sanction of Congress to be carried into effect on our part, and which I therefore recommend to your consideration.

With Prussia, Spain, Portugal, and, in general, all the European powers between whom and the United States relations of friendly intercourse have existed their condition has not materially varied since the last session of Congress. I regret not to be able to say the same of our commercial intercourse with the colonial possessions of Great Britain in America. Negotiations of the highest importance to our common interests have been for several years in discussion between the two Governments, and on the part of the United States have been invariably pursued in the spirit of candor and conciliation. Interests of great magnitude and delicacy had been adjusted by the conventions of 1815 and 1818, while that of 1822, mediated by the late Emperor Alexander, had promised a satisfactory compromise of claims which the Government of the United States, in justice to the rights of a numerous class of their citizens, was bound to sustain. But with regard to the commercial intercourse between the United States and the British colonies in America, it has been hitherto found impracticable to bring the parties to an understanding satisfactory to both. The relative geographical position and the respective products of nature cultivated by human industry had constituted the elements of a commercial intercourse between the United States and British America, insular and continental, important to the inhabitants of both countries; but it had been interdicted by Great Britain upon a principle heretofore practiced upon by the colonizing nations of Europe, of holding the trade of their colonies each in exclusive monopoly to herself. After the termination of the late war this interdiction had been revived, and the

British Government declined including this portion of our intercourse with her possessions in the negotiation of the convention of 1815. The trade was then carried on exclusively in British vessels till the act of Congress, concerning navigation, of 1818 and the supplemental act of 1820 met the interdict by a corresponding measure on the part of the United States. These measures, not of retaliation, but of necessary self-defense, were soon succeeded by an act of Parliament opening certain colonial ports to the vessels of the United States coming directly from them, and to the importation from them of certain articles of our produce burdened with heavy duties, and excluding some of the most valuable articles of our exports. The United States opened their ports to British vessels from the colonies upon terms as exactly corresponding with those of the act of Parliament as in the relative position of the parties could be made, and a negotiation was commenced by mutual consent, with the hope on our part that a reciprocal spirit of accommodation and a common sentiment of the importance of the trade to the interests of the inhabitants of the two countries between whom it must be carried on would ultimately bring the parties to a compromise with which both might be satisfied. With this view the Government of the United States had determined to sacrifice something of that entire reciprocity which in all commercial arrangements with foreign powers they are entitled to demand, and to acquiesce in some inequalities disadvantageous to ourselves rather than to forego the benefit of a final and permanent adjustment of this interest to the satisfaction of Great Britain herself. The negotiation, repeatedly suspended by accidental circumstances, was, however, by mutual agreement and express assent, considered as pending and to be speedily resumed. In the meantime another act of Parliament, so doubtful and ambiguous in its import as to have been misunderstood by the officers in the colonies who were to carry it into execution, opens again certain colonial ports upon new conditions and terms, with a threat to close them against any nation which may not accept those terms as prescribed by the British Government. This act, passed in July, 1825, not communicated to the Government of the United States, not understood by the British officers of the customs in the colonies where it was to be enforced, was nevertheless submitted to the consideration of Congress at their last session. With the knowledge that a negotiation upon the subject had long been in progress and pledges given of its resumption at an early day, it was deemed expedient to await the result of that negotiation rather than to subscribe implicitly to terms the import of which was not clear and which the British authorities themselves in this hemisphere were not prepared to explain.

Immediately after the close of the last session of Congress one of our most distinguished citizens was dispatched as envoy extraordinary and minister plenipotentiary to Great Britain, furnished with instructions which we could not doubt would lead to a conclusion of this long-controverted interest upon terms acceptable to Great Britain. Upon his arrival, and before he had delivered his letters of credence, he was met by an order of the British council excluding from and after the 1st of December now current the vessels of the United States from all the colonial British ports excepting those immediately bordering on our territories. In answer to his expostulations upon a measure thus unexpected he is informed that according to the ancient maxims of policy of European nations having colonies their trade is an exclusive possession of the mother country; that all participation in it by other nations is a boon or favor not forming a subject of negotiation, but to be regulated by the legislative acts of the power owning the colony; that the British Government therefore declines negotiating concerning it, and that as the United States did not forthwith accept purely and simply the terms offered by the act of Parliament of July, 1825, Great Britain would not now admit the vessels of the United States even upon the terms on which she has opened them to the navigation of other nations.

We have been accustomed to consider the trade which we have enjoyed with the British colonies rather as an interchange of mutual benefits than as a mere favor received; that under every circumstance we have given an ample equivalent. We have seen every other nation holding colonies negotiate with other nations and grant them freely admission to the colonies by treaty, and so far are the other colonizing nations of Europe now from refusing to negotiate for trade with their colonies that we ourselves have secured access to the colonies of more than one of them by treaty. The refusal, however, of Great Britain to negotiate leaves to the United States no other alternative than that of regulating or interdicting altogether the trade on their part, according as either measure may affect the interests of our own country, and with that exclusive object I would recommend the whole subject to your calm and candid deliberations.

It is hoped that our unavailing exertions to accomplish a cordial good understanding on this interest will not have an unpropitious effect upon the other great topics of discussion between the two Governments. Our northeastern and northwestern boundaries are still unadjusted. The commissioners under the seventh article of the treaty of Ghent have nearly come to the close of their labors; nor can we renounce the expectation, enfeebled as it is, that they may agree upon their report to the satisfaction or acquiescence of both parties. The commission for liquidating the claims for indemnity for slaves carried away after the close of the war has been sitting, with doubtful prospects of success. Propositions of compromise have, however, passed between the two Governments, the result of which we flatter ourselves may yet prove satisfactory. Our own dispositions and purposes toward Great Britain are all friendly and conciliatory; nor can we abandon but with strong reluctance the belief that they will ultimately meet a return, not of favors, which we neither ask nor desire, but of equal reciprocity and good will.

With the American Governments of this hemisphere we continue to maintain an intercourse altogether friendly, and between their nations and ours that commercial interchange of which mutual benefit is the source and mutual comfort and harmony the result is in a continual state of improvement.   The war between Spain and them since the total expulsion of the Spanish military force from their continental territories has been little more than nominal, and their internal tranquillity, though occasionally menaced by the agitations which civil wars never fail to leave behind them, has not been affected by any serious calamity.

The congress of ministers from several of those nations which assembled at Panama, after a short session there, adjourned to meet again at a more favorable season in the neighborhood of Mexico.   The decease of one of our ministers on his way to the Isthmus, and the impediments of the season, which delayed the departure of the other, deprived us of the advantage of being represented at the first meeting of the congress.   There is, however, no reason to believe that any of the transactions of the congress were of a nature to affect injuriously the interests of the United States or to require the interposition of our ministers had they been present.   Their absence has, indeed, deprived us of the opportunity of possessing precise and authentic information of the treaties which were concluded at Panama; and the whole result has confirmed me in the conviction of the expediency to the United States of being represented at the congress.   The surviving member of the mission, appointed during your last session, has accordingly proceeded to his destination, and a successor to his distinguished and lamented associate will be nominated to the Senate.   A treaty of amity, navigation, and commerce has in the course of the last summer been concluded by our minister plenipotentiary at Mexico with the united states of that Confederacy, which will also be laid before the Senate for their advice with regard to its ratification.

In adverting to the present condition of our fiscal concerns and to the prospects of our revenue the first remark that calls our attention is that they are less exuberantly prosperous than they were at the corresponding period of the last year.   The severe shock so extensively sustained by the commercial and manufacturing interests in Great Britain has not been without a perceptible recoil upon ourselves.   A reduced importation from abroad is necessarily succeeded by a reduced return to the Treasury at home.   The net revenue of the present year will not equal that of the last, and the receipts of that which is to come will fall short of those in the current year.   The diminution, however, is in part attributable to the flourishing condition of some of our domestic manufactures, and so far is compensated by an equivalent more profitable to the nation.   It is also highly gratifying to perceive that the deficiency in the revenue, while it scarcely exceeds the anticipations of the last year's estimate from the Treasury, has not interrupted the application of more than eleven millions during the present year to the discharge of the principal and interest of the debt, nor the reduction of upward of seven millions of the capital of the debt itself. The balance in the Treasury on the 1st of January last was $5,201,650.43; the receipts from that time to the 30th of September last were $19,585,932.50; the receipts of the current quarter, estimated at $6,000,000, yield, with the sums already received, a revenue of about twenty-five millions and a half for the year; the expenditures for the three first quarters of the year have amounted to $18,714,226.66; the expenditures of the current quarter are expected, including the two millions of the principal of the debt to be paid, to balance the receipts; so that the expenses of the year, amounting to upward of a million less than its income, will leave a proportionally increased balance in the Treasury on the 1st of January, 1827, over that of the 1st of January last; instead of $5,200,000 there will be $6,400,000.

The amount of duties secured on merchandise imported from the commencement of the year till September 30 is estimated at $21,250,000, and the amount that will probably accrue during the present quarter is estimated at $4,250,000, making for the whole year $25,500,000, from which the drawbacks being deducted will leave a clear revenue from the customs receivable in the year 1827 of about $20,400,000, which, with the sums to be received from the proceeds of public lands, the bank dividends, and other incidental receipts, will form an aggregate of about $23,000,000, a sum falling short of the whole expenses of the present year little more than the portion of those expenditures applied to the discharge of the public debt beyond the annual appropriation of $10,000,000 by the act of the 3d March, 1817. At the passage of that act the public debt amounted to $123,500,000. On the 1st of January next it will be short of $74,000,000. In the lapse of these ten years $50,000,000 of public debt, with the annual charge of upward of $3,000,000 of interest upon them, have been extinguished. At the passage of that act, of the annual appropriation of ten millions seven were absorbed in the payment of interest, and not more than three millions went to reduce the capital of the debt. Of the same ten millions, at this time scarcely four are applicable to the interest, and upward of six are effective in melting down the capital. Yet our experience has proved that a revenue consisting so largely of imposts and tonnage ebbs and flows to an extraordinary extent, with all the fluctuations incident to the general commerce of the world. It is within our recollection that even in the compass of the same last ten years the receipts of the Treasury were not adequate to the expenditures of the year, and that in two successive years it was found necessary to resort to loans to meet the engagements of the nation. The returning tides of the succeeding years replenished the public coffers until they have again begun to feel the vicissitude of a decline. To produce these alternations of fullness and exhaustion the relative operation of abundant or unfruitful seasons, the regulations of foreign governments, political revolutions, the prosperous or decaying condition of manufactures, commercial speculations, and many other causes, not always to be traced, variously combine. We have found the alternate swells and diminutions embracing periods of from two to three years. The last period of depression to us was from 1819 to 1822. The corresponding revival was from 1823 to the commencement of the present year. Still, we have no cause to apprehend a depression comparable to that of the former period, or even to anticipate a deficiency which will intrench upon the ability to apply the annual ten millions to the reduction of the debt. It is well for us, however, to be admonished of the necessity of abiding by the maxims of the most vigilant economy, and of resorting to all honorable and useful expedients for pursuing with steady and inflexible perseverance the total discharge of the debt.

Besides the seven millions of the loans of 1813 which will have been discharged in the course of the present year, there are nine millions which by the terms of the contracts would have been and are now redeemable. Thirteen millions more of the loan of 1814 will become redeemable from and after the expiration of the present month, and nine other millions from and after the close of the ensuing year. They constitute a mass of $31,000,000, all bearing an interest of 6 per cent, more than twenty millions of which will be immediately redeemable, and the rest within little more than a year. Leaving of this amount fifteen millions to continue at the interest of 6 per cent, but to be paid off as far as shall be found practicable in the years 1827 and 1828, there is scarcely a doubt that the remaining sixteen millions might within a few months be discharged by a loan at not exceeding 5 per cent, redeemable in the years 1829 and 1830. By this operation a sum of nearly half a million of dollars may be saved to the nation, and the discharge of the whole thirty-one millions within the four years may be greatly facilitated if not wholly accomplished.

By an act of Congress of 3d March, 1835, a loan for the purpose now referred to, or a subscription to stock, was authorized, at an interest not exceeding 4½ per cent. But at that time so large a portion of the floating capital of the country was absorbed in commercial speculations and so little was left for investment in the stocks that the measure was but partially successful. At the last session of Congress the condition of the funds was still unpropitious to the measure; but the change so soon afterwards occurred that, had the authority existed to redeem the nine millions now redeemable by an exchange of stocks or a loan at 5 per cent, it is morally certain that it might have been effected, and with it a yearly saving of $90,000.

With regard to the collection of the revenue of imposts, certain occurrences have within the last year been disclosed in one or two of our principal ports, which engaged the attention of Congress at their last session and may hereafter require further consideration. Until within a very few years the execution of the laws for raising the revenue, like that of all our other laws, has been insured more by the moral sense of the community than by the rigors of a jealous precaution or by penal sanctions. Confiding in the exemplary punctuality and unsullied integrity of our importing merchants, a gradual relaxation from the provisions of the collection laws, a close adherence to which would have caused inconvenience and expense to them, had long become habitual, and indulgences had been extended universally because they had never been abused. It may be worthy of your serious consideration whether some further legislative provision may not be necessary to come in aid of this state of unguarded security.

From the reports herewith communicated of the Secretaries of War and of the Navy, with the subsidiary documents annexed to them, will be discovered the present condition and administration of our military establishment on the land and on the sea. The organization of the Army having undergone no change since its reduction to the present peace establishment in 1821, it remains only to observe that it is yet found adequate to all the purposes for which a permanent armed force in time of peace can be needed or useful. It may be proper to add that, from a difference of opinion between the late President of the United States and the Senate with regard to the construction of the act of Congress of 2d March, 1821, to reduce and fix the military peace establishment of the United States, it remains hitherto so far without execution that no colonel has been appointed to command one of the regiments of artillery. A supplementary or explanatory act of the Legislature appears to be the only expedient practicable for removing the difficulty of this appointment.

In a period of profound peace the conduct of the mere military establishment forms but a very inconsiderable portion of the duties devolving upon the administration of the Department of War. It will be seen by the returns from the subordinate departments of the Army that every branch of the service is marked with order, regularity, and discipline; that from the commanding general through all the gradations of superintendence the officers feel themselves to have been citizens before they were soldiers, and that the glory of a republican army must consist in the spirit of freedom, by which it is animated, and of patriotism, by which it is impelled. It may be confidently stated that the moral character of the Army is in a state of continual improvement, and that all the arrangements for the disposal of its parts have a constant reference to that end.

But to the War Department are attributed other duties, having, indeed, relation to a future possible condition of war, but being purely defensive, and in their tendency contributing rather to the security and permanency of peace—the erection of the fortifications provided for by Congress, and adapted to secure our shores from hostile invasion; the distribution of the fund of public gratitude and justice to the pensioners of the Revolutionary war; the maintenance of our relations of peace and of protection with the Indian tribes, and the internal improvements and surveys for the location of roads and canals, which during the last three sessions of Congress have engaged so much of their attention, and may engross so large a share of their future benefactions to our country.

By the act of the 30th of April, 1824, suggested and approved by my predecessor, the sum of $30,000 was appropriated for the purpose of causing to be made the necessary surveys, plans, and estimates of the routes of such roads and canals as the President of the United States might deem of national importance in a commercial or military point of view, or necessary for the transportation of the public mail. The surveys, plans, and estimates for each, when completed, will be laid before Congress.

In execution of this act a board of engineers was immediately instituted, and have been since most assiduously and constantly occupied in carrying it into effect. The first object to which their labors were directed, by order of the late President, was the examination of the country between the tide waters of the Potomac, the Ohio, and Lake Erie, to ascertain the practicability of a communication between them, to designate the most suitable route for the same, and to form plans and estimates in detail of the expense of execution.

On the 3d of February, 1825, they made their first report, which was immediately communicated to Congress, and in which they declared that having maturely considered the circumstances observed by them personally, and carefully studied the results of such of the preliminary surveys as were then completed, they were decidedly of opinion that the communication was practicable.

At the last session of Congress, before the board of engineers were enabled to make up their second report containing a general plan and preparatory estimate for the work, the Committee of the House of Representatives upon Roads and Canals closed the session with a report expressing the hope that the plan and estimate of the board of engineers might at this time be prepared, and that the subject be referred to the early and favorable consideration of Congress at their present session. That expected report of the board of engineers is prepared, and will forthwith be laid before you.

Under the resolution of Congress authorizing the Secretary of War to have prepared a complete system of cavalry tactics, and a system of exercise and instruction of field artillery, for the use of the militia of the United States, to be reported to Congress at the present session, a board of distinguished officers of the Army and of the militia has been convened, whose report will be submitted to you with that of the Secretary of War. The occasion was thought favorable for consulting the same board, aided by the results of a correspondence with the governors of the several States and Territories and other citizens of intelligence and experience, upon the acknowledged defective condition of our militia system, and of the improvements of which it is susceptible. The report of the board upon this subject is also submitted for your consideration.

In the estimates of appropriations for the ensuing year upward of $5,000,000 will be submitted for the expenditures to be paid from the Department of War. Less than two-fifths of this will be applicable to the maintenance and support of the Army. A million and a half, in the form of pensions, goes as a scarcely adequate tribute to the services and sacrifices of a former age, and a more than equal sum invested in fortifications, or for the preparations of internal improvement, provides for the quiet, the comfort, and happier existence of the ages to come. The appropriations to indemnify those unfortunate remnants of another race unable alike to share in the enjoyments and to exist in the presence of civilization, though swelling in recent years to a magnitude burdensome to the Treasury, are generally not without their equivalents in profitable value, or serve to discharge the Union from engagements more burdensome than debt.

In like manner the estimate of appropriations for the Navy Department will present an aggregate sum of upward of $3,000,000. About one-half of these, however, covers the current expenditures of the Navy in actual service, and one-half constitutes a fund of national property, the pledge of our future glory and defense. It was scarcely one short year after the close of the late war, and when the burden of its expenses and charges was weighing heaviest upon the country, that Congress, by the act of 29th April, 1816, appropriated $1,000,000 annually for eight years to the *gradual increase of the Navy.* At a subsequent period this annual appropriation was reduced to half a million for six years, of which the present year is the last. A yet more recent appropriation the last two years, for building ten sloops of war, has nearly restored the original appropriation of 1816 of a million for every year. The result is before us all. We have twelve line-of-battle ships, twenty frigates, and sloops of war in proportion, which, with a few months of preparation, may present a line of floating fortifications along the whole range of our coast ready to meet any invader who might attempt to set foot upon our shores. Combining with a system of fortifications upon the shores themselves, commenced about the same time under the auspices of my immediate predecessor, and hitherto systematically pursued, it has placed in our possession the most effective sinews of war and has left us at once an example and a lesson from which our own duties may be inferred. The gradual increase of the Navy was the principle of which the act of 29th April, 1816, was the first development. It was the introduction of a system to act upon the character and history of our country for an indefinite series of ages. It was a declaration of that Congress to their constituents and to posterity that it was the destiny and the duty of these confederated States to become in regular process of time and by no petty advances a great naval power. That which they proposed to accomplish in eight years is rather to be considered as the measure of their means than the limitation of their design.

They looked forward for a term of years sufficient for the accomplishment of a definite portion of their purpose, and they left to their successors to fill up the canvas of which they had traced the large and prophetic outline. The ships of the line and frigates which they had in contemplation will be shortly completed. The time which they had allotted for the accomplishment of the work has more than elapsed. It remains for your consideration how their successors may contribute their portion of toil and of treasure for the benefit of the succeeding age in the gradual increase of our Navy. There is perhaps no part of the exercise of the constitutional powers of the Federal Government which has given more general satisfaction to the people of the Union than this. The system has not been thus vigorously introduced and hitherto sustained to be now departed from or abandoned. In continuing to provide for the gradual increase of the Navy it may not be necessary or expedient to add for the present any more to the number of our ships; but should you deem it advisable to continue the yearly appropriation of half a million to the same objects, it may be profitably expended in providing a supply of timber to be seasoned and other materials for future use in the construction of docks or in laying the foundations of a school for naval education, as to the wisdom of Congress either of those measures may appear to claim the preference.

Of the small portions of this Navy engaged in actual service during the peace, squadrons have continued to be maintained in the Pacific Ocean, in the West India seas, and in the Mediterranean, to which has been added a small armament to cruise on the eastern coast of South America. In all they have afforded protection to our commerce, have contributed to make our country advantageously known to foreign nations, have honorably employed multitudes of our seamen in the service of their country, and have inured numbers of youths of the rising generation to lives of manly hardihood and of nautical experience and skill. The piracies with which the West India seas were for several years infested have been totally suppressed, but in the Mediterranean they have increased in a manner afflictive to other nations, and but for the continued presence of our squadron would probably have been distressing to our own. The war which has unfortunately broken out between the Republic of Buenos Ayres and the Brazilian Government has given rise to very great irregularities among the naval officers of the latter, by whom principles in relation to blockades and to neutral navigation have been brought forward to which we can not subscribe and which our own commanders have found it necessary to resist. From the friendly disposition toward the United States constantly manifested by the Emperor of Brazil, and the very useful and friendly commercial intercourse between the United States and his dominions, we have reason to believe that the just reparation demanded for the injuries sustained by several of our citizens from some of his officers will not be withheld. Abstracts from the recent dispatches of the commanders

of our several squadrons are communicated with the report of the Secretary of the Navy to Congress.

A report from the Postmaster-General is likewise communicated, presenting in a highly satisfactory manner the result of a vigorous, efficient, and economical administration of that Department. The revenue of the office, even of the year including the latter half of 1824 and the first half of 1825, had exceeded its expenditures by a sum of more than $45,000. That of the succeeding year has been still more productive. The increase of the receipts in the year preceding the 1st of July last over that of the year before exceeds $136,000, and the excess of the receipts over the expenditures of the year has swollen from $45,000 to nearly $80,000. During the same period contracts for additional transportation of the mail in stages for about 260,000 miles have been made, and for 70,000 miles annually on horseback. Seven hundred and fourteen new post-offices have been established within the year, and the increase of revenue within the last three years, as well as the augmentation of the transportation by mail, is more than equal to the whole amount of receipts and of mail conveyance at the commencement of the present century, when the seat of the General Government was removed to this place. When we reflect that the objects effected by the transportation of the mail are among the choicest comforts and enjoyments of social life, it is pleasing to observe that the dissemination of them to every corner of our country has outstripped in their increase even the rapid march of our population.

By the treaties with France and Spain, respectively ceding Louisiana and the Floridas to the United States, provision was made for the security of land titles derived from the Governments of those nations. Some progress has been made under the authority of various acts of Congress in the ascertainment and establishment of those titles, but claims to a very large extent remain unadjusted. The public faith no less than the just rights of individuals and the interest of the community itself appears to require further provision for the speedy settlement of those claims, which I therefore recommend to the care and attention of the Legislature.

In conformity with the provisions of the act of 20th May last, to provide for erecting a penitentiary in the District of Columbia, and for other purposes, three commissioners were appointed to select a site for the erection of a penitentiary for the District, and also a site in the county of Alexandria for a county jail, both of which objects have been effected. The building of the penitentiary has been commenced, and is in such a degree of forwardness as to promise that it will be completed before the meeting of the next Congress. This consideration points to the expediency of maturing at the present session a system for the regulation and government of the penitentiary, and of defining the class of offenses which shall be punishable by confinement in this edifice.

In closing this communication I trust that it will not be deemed inappropriate to the occasion and purposes upon which we are here assembled to indulge a momentary retrospect, combining in a single glance the period of our origin as a national confederation with that of our present existence, at the precise interval of half a century from each other. Since your last meeting at this place the fiftieth anniversary of the day when our independence was declared has been celebrated throughout our land, and on that day, while every heart was bounding with joy and every voice was tuned to gratulation, amid the blessings of freedom and independence which the sires of a former age had handed down to their children, two of the principal actors in that solemn scene—the hand that penned the ever-memorable Declaration and the voice that sustained it in debate—were by one summons, at the distance of 700 miles from each other, called before the Judge of All to account for their deeds done upon earth. They departed cheered by the benedictions of their country, to whom they left the inheritance of their fame and the memory of their bright example. If we turn our thoughts to the condition of their country, in the contrast of the first and last day of that half century, how resplendent and sublime is the transition from gloom to glory! Then, glancing through the same lapse of time, in the condition of the individuals we see the first day marked with the fullness and vigor of youth, in the pledge of their lives, their fortunes, and their sacred honor to the cause of freedom and of mankind; and on the last, extended on the bed of death, with but sense and sensibility left to breathe a last aspiration to Heaven of blessing upon their country, may we not humbly hope that to them too it was a pledge of transition from gloom to glory, and that while their mortal vestments were sinking into the clod of the valley their emancipated spirits were ascending to the bosom of their God!

THIRD ANNUAL MESSAGE.

WASHINGTON, *December 4, 1827.*

Fellow-Citizens of the Senate and of the House of Representatives:

A revolution of the seasons has nearly been completed since the representatives of the people and States of this Union were last assembled at this place to deliberate and to act upon the common important interests of their constituents. In that interval the never-slumbering eye of a wise and beneficent Providence has continued its guardian care over the welfare of our beloved country; the blessing of health has continued generally to prevail throughout the land; the blessing of peace with our brethren of the human race has been enjoyed without interruption; internal quiet has left our fellow-citizens in the full enjoyment of all their rights and in the free exercise of all their faculties, to pursue the impulse

of their nature and the obligation of their duty in the improvement of their own condition; the productions of the soil, the exchanges of commerce, the vivifying labors of human industry, have combined to mingle in our cup a portion of enjoyment as large and liberal as the indulgence of Heaven has perhaps ever granted to the imperfect state of man upon earth; and as the purest of human felicity consists in its participation with others, it is no small addition to the sum of our national happiness at this time that peace and prosperity prevail to a degree seldom experienced over the whole habitable globe, presenting, though as yet with painful exceptions, a foretaste of that blessed period of promise when the lion shall lie down with the lamb and wars shall be no more. To preserve, to improve, and to perpetuate the sources and to direct in their most effective channels the streams which contribute to the public weal is the purpose for which Government was instituted. Objects of deep importance to the welfare of the Union are constantly recurring to demand the attention of the Federal Legislature, and they call with accumulated interest at the first meeting of the two Houses after their periodical renovation. To present to their consideration from time to time subjects in which the interests of the nation are most deeply involved, and for the regulation of which the legislative will is alone competent, is a duty prescribed by the Constitution, to the performance of which the first meeting of the new Congress is a period eminently appropriate, and which it is now my purpose to discharge.

Our relations of friendship with the other nations of the earth, political and commercial, have been preserved unimpaired, and the opportunities to improve them have been cultivated with anxious and unremitting attention. A negotiation upon subjects of high and delicate interest with the Government of Great Britain has terminated in the adjustment of some of the questions at issue upon satisfactory terms and the postponement of others for future discussion and agreement. The purposes of the convention concluded at St. Petersburg on the 12th day of July, 1822, under the mediation of the late Emperor Alexander, have been carried into effect by a subsequent convention, concluded at London on the 13th of November, 1826, the ratifications of which were exchanged at that place on the 6th day of February last. A copy of the proclamation issued on the 19th day of March last, publishing this convention, is herewith communicated to Congress. The sum of $1,204,960, therein stipulated to be paid to the claimants of indemnity under the first article of the treaty of Ghent, has been duly received, and the commission instituted, comformably to the act of Congress of the 2d of March last, for the distribution of the indemnity to the persons entitled to receive it are now in session and approaching the consummation of their labors. This final disposal of one of the most painful topics of collision between the United States and Great Britain not only affords an occasion of gratulation to ourselves, but has had the happiest effect in promoting a friendly disposition and in sof-

tening asperities upon other objects of discussion; nor ought it to pass without the tribute of a frank and cordial acknowledgment of the magnanimity with which an honorable nation, by the reparation of their own wrongs, achieves a triumph more glorious than any field of blood can ever bestow.

The conventions of 3d July, 1815, and of 20th October, 1818, will expire by their own limitation on the 20th of October, 1828. These have regulated the direct commercial intercourse between the United States and Great Britain upon terms of the most perfect reciprocity; and they effected a temporary compromise of the respective rights and claims to territory westward of the Rocky Mountains. These arrangements have been continued for an indefinite period of time after the expiration of the above-mentioned conventions, leaving each party the liberty of terminating them by giving twelve months' notice to the other. The radical principle of all commercial intercourse between independent nations is the mutual interest of both parties. It is the vital spirit of trade itself; nor can it be reconciled to the nature of man or to the primary laws of human society that any traffic should long be willingly pursued of which all the advantages are on one side and all the burdens on the other. Treaties of commerce have been found by experience to be among the most effective instruments for promoting peace and harmony between nations whose interests, exclusively considered on either side, are brought into frequent collisions by competition. In framing such treaties it is the duty of each party not simply to urge with unyielding pertinacity that which suits its own interest, but to concede liberally to that which is adapted to the interest of the other. To accomplish this, little more is generally required than a simple observance of the rule of reciprocity, and were it possible for the statesmen of one nation by stratagem and management to obtain from the weakness or ignorance of another an overreaching treaty, such a compact would prove an incentive to war rather than a bond of peace. Our conventions with Great Britain are founded upon the principles of reciprocity. The commercial intercourse between the two countries is greater in magnitude and amount than between any two other nations on the globe. It is for all purposes of benefit or advantage to both as precious, and in all probability far more extensive, than if the parties were still constituent parts of one and the same nation. Treaties between such States, regulating the intercourse of peace between them and adjusting interests of such transcendent importance to both, which have been found in a long experience of years mutually advantageous, should not be lightly canceled or discontinued. Two conventions for continuing in force those above mentioned have been concluded between the plenipotentiaries of the two Governments on the 6th of August last, and will be forthwith laid before the Senate for the exercise of their constitutional authority concerning them.

In the execution of the treaties of peace of November, 1782, and Sep-

tember, 1783, between the United States and Great Britain, and which terminated the war of our independence, a line of boundary was drawn as the demarcation of territory between the two countries, extending over near 20 degrees of latitude, and ranging over seas, lakes, and mountains, then very imperfectly explored and scarcely opened to the geographical knowledge of the age. In the progress of discovery and settlement by both parties since that time several questions of boundary between their respective territories have arisen, which have been found of exceedingly difficult adjustment. At the close of the last war with Great Britain four of these questions pressed themselves upon the consideration of the negotiators of the treaty of Ghent, but without the means of concluding a definitive arrangement concerning them. They were referred to three separate commissions consisting of two commissioners, one appointed by each party, to examine and decide upon their respective claims. In the event of a disagreement between the commissioners it was provided that they should make reports to their several Governments, and that the reports should finally be referred to the decision of a sovereign the common friend of both. Of these commissions two have already terminated their sessions and investigations, one by entire and the other by partial agreement. The commissioners of the fifth article of the treaty of Ghent have finally disagreed, and made their conflicting reports to their own Governments. But from these reports a great difficulty has occurred in making up a question to be decided by the arbitrator. This purpose has, however, been effected by a fourth convention, concluded at London by the plenipotentiaries of the two Governments on the 29th of September last. It will be submitted, together with the others, to the consideration of the Senate.

While these questions have been pending incidents have occurred of conflicting pretensions and of dangerous character upon the territory itself in dispute between the two nations. By a common understanding between the Governments it was agreed that no exercise of exclusive jurisdiction by either party while the negotiation was pending should change the state of the question of right to be definitively settled. Such collision has, nevertheless, recently taken place by occurrences the precise character of which has not yet been ascertained. A communication from the governor of the State of Maine, with accompanying documents, and a correspondence between the Secretary of State and the minister of Great Britain on this subject are now communicated. Measures have been taken to ascertain the state of the facts more correctly by the employment of a special agent to visit the spot where the alleged outrages have occurred, the result of whose inquiries, when received, will be transmitted to Congress.

While so many of the subjects of high interest to the friendly relations between the two countries have been so far adjusted, it is matter of regret that their views respecting the commercial intercourse between the United

States and the British colonial possessions have not equally approximated to a friendly agreement.

At the commencement of the last session of Congress they were informed of the sudden and unexpected exclusion by the British Government of access in vessels of the United States to all their colonial ports, except those immediately bordering upon our own territories. In the amicable discussions which have succeeded the adoption of this measure, which, as it affected harshly the interests of the United States, became a subject of expostulation on our part, the principles upon which its justification has been placed have been of a diversified character. It has been at once ascribed to a mere recurrence to the old, long-established principle of colonial monopoly and at the same time to a feeling of resentment because the offers of an act of Parliament opening the colonial ports upon certain conditions had not been grasped at with sufficient eagerness by an instantaneous conformity to them. At a subsequent period it has been intimated that the new exclusion was in resentment because a prior act of Parliament, of 1822, opening certain colonial ports, under heavy and burdensome restrictions, to vessels of the United States, had not been reciprocated by an admission of British vessels from the colonies, and their cargoes, without any restriction or discrimination whatever. But be the motive for the interdiction what it may, the British Government have manifested no disposition, either by negotiation or by corresponding legislative enactments, to recede from it, and we have been given distinctly to understand that neither of the bills which were under the consideration of Congress at their last session would have been deemed sufficient in their concessions to have been rewarded by any relaxation from the British interdict. It is one of the inconveniences inseparably connected with the attempt to adjust by reciprocal legislation interests of this nature that neither party can know what would be satisfactory to the other, and that after enacting a statute for the avowed and sincere purpose of conciliation it will generally be found utterly inadequate to the expectations of the other party, and will terminate in mutual disappointment.

The session of Congress having terminated without any act upon the subject, a proclamation was issued on the 17th of March last, conformably to the provisions of the sixth section of the act of 1st March, 1823, declaring the fact that the trade and intercourse authorized by the British act of Parliament of 24th June, 1822, between the United States and the British enumerated colonial ports had been by the subsequent acts of Parliament of 5th July, 1825, and the order of council of 27th July, 1826, prohibited. The effect of this proclamation, by the terms of the act under which it was issued, has been that each and every provision of the act concerning navigation of 18th April, 1818, and of the act supplementary thereto of 15th May, 1820, revived and is in full force. Such, then, is the present condition of the trade that, useful as it is to both parties, it can, with a single momentary exception, be carried on directly by the vessels of neither. That exception itself is found in a proclamation of the governor of the island of St. Christopher and of the Virgin Islands, inviting for three months from the 28th of August last the importation of the articles of the produce of the United States which constitute their export portion of this trade in the vessels of all nations. That period having already expired, the state of mutual interdiction has again taken place. The British Government have not only declined negotiation upon this subject, but by the principle they have assumed with reference to it have precluded even the means of negotiation. It becomes not the self-respect of the United States either to solicit gratuitous favors or to accept as the grant of a favor that for which an ample equivalent is exacted. It remains to be determined by the respective Governments whether the trade shall be opened by acts of reciprocal legislation. It is, in the meantime, satisfactory to know that apart from the inconveniences resulting from a disturbance of the usual channels of trade no loss has been sustained by the commerce, the navigation, or the revenue of the United States, and none of magnitude is to be apprehended from this existing state of mutual interdict.

With the other maritime and commercial nations of Europe our intercourse continues with little variation. Since the cessation by the convention of 24th June, 1822, of all discriminating duties upon the vessels of the United States and of France in either country our trade with that nation has increased and is increasing. A disposition on the part of France has been manifested to renew that negotiation, and in acceding to the proposal we have expressed the wish that it might be extended to other subjects upon which a good understanding between the parties would be beneficial to the interests of both. The origin of the political relations between the United States and France is coeval with the first years of our independence. The memory of it is interwoven with that of our arduous struggle for national existence. Weakened as it has occasionally been since that time, it can by us never be forgotten, and we should hail with exultation the moment which should indicate a recollection equally friendly in spirit on the part of France. A fresh effort has recently been made by the minister of the United States residing at Paris to obtain a consideration of the just claims of citizens of the United States to the reparation of wrongs long since committed, many of them frankly acknowledged and all of them entitled upon every principle of justice to a candid examination. The proposal last made to the French Government has been to refer the subject which has formed an obstacle to this consideration to the determination of a sovereign the common friend of both. To this offer no definitive answer has yet been received, but the gallant and honorable spirit which has at all times been the pride and glory of France will not ultimately permit the demands of innocent sufferers to be extinguished in the mere consciousness of the power to reject them.

A new treaty of amity, navigation, and commerce has been concluded with the Kingdom of Sweden, which will be submitted to the Senate for their advice with regard to its ratification. At a more recent date a minister plenipotentiary from the Hanseatic Republics of Hamburg, Lubeck, and Bremen has been received, charged with a special mission for the negotiation of a treaty of amity and commerce between that ancient and renowned league and the United States. This negotiation has accordingly been commenced, and is now in progress, the result of which will, if successful, be also submitted to the Senate for their consideration.

Since the accession of the Emperor Nicholas to the imperial throne of all the Russias the friendly dispositions toward the United States so constantly manifested by his predecessor have continued unabated, and have been recently testified by the appointment of a minister plenipotentiary to reside at this place. From the interest taken by this Sovereign in behalf of the suffering Greeks and from the spirit with which others of the great European powers are cooperating with him the friends of freedom and of humanity may indulge the hope that they will obtain relief from that most unequal of conflicts which they have so long and so gallantly sustained; that they will enjoy the blessing of self-government, which by their sufferings in the cause of liberty they have richly earned, and that their independence will be secured by those liberal institutions of which their country furnished the earliest examples in the history of mankind, and which have consecrated to immortal remembrance the very soil for which they are now again profusely pouring forth their blood. The sympathies which the people and Government of the United States have so warmly indulged with their cause have been acknowledged by their Government in a letter of thanks, which I have received from their illustrious President, a translation of which is now communicated to Congress, the representatives of that nation to whom this tribute of gratitude was intended to be paid, and to whom it was justly due.

In the American hemisphere the cause of freedom and independence has continued to prevail, and if signalized by none of those splendid triumphs which had crowned with glory some of the preceding years it has only been from the banishment of all external force against which the struggle had been maintained. The shout of victory has been superseded by the expulsion of the enemy over whom it could have been achieved. Our friendly wishes and cordial good will, which have constantly followed the southern nations of America in all the vicissitudes of their war of independence, are succeeded by a solicitude equally ardent and cordial that by the wisdom and purity of their institutions they may secure to themselves the choicest blessings of social order and the best rewards of virtuous liberty. Disclaiming alike all right and all intention of interfering in those concerns which it is the prerogative of their independence to regulate as to them shall seem fit, we hail with joy every indication of their prosperity, of their harmony, of their persevering and inflexible homage to those principles of freedom and of equal rights which are alone suited to the genius and temper of the American nations. It has been, therefore, with some concern that we have observed indications of intestine divisions in some of the Republics of the south, and appearances of less union with one another than we believe **to be the interest of all.** Among the results of this state of things has been that the treaties concluded at Panama do not appear to have been ratified by the contracting parties, and that the meeting of the congress at Tacubaya has been indefinitely postponed. In accepting the invitations to be represented at this congress, while a manifestation was intended on the part of the United States of the most friendly disposition toward the southern Republics by whom it had been proposed, it was hoped that it would furnish an opportunity for bringing all the nations of this hemisphere to the common acknowledgment and adoption of the principles in the regulation of their internal relations which would have secured a lasting peace and harmony between them and have promoted the cause of mutual benevolence throughout the globe. But as obstacles appear to have arisen to the reassembling of the congress, one of the two ministers commissioned on the part of the United States has returned to the bosom of his country, while the minister charged with the ordinary mission to Mexico remains authorized to attend at the conferences of the congress whenever they may be resumed.

A hope was for a short time entertained that a treaty of peace actually signed between the Governments of Buenos Ayres and of Brazil would supersede all further occasion for those collisions between belligerent pretensions and neutral rights which are so commonly the result of maritime war, and which have unfortunately disturbed the harmony of the relations between the United States and the Brazilian Governments. At their last session Congress were informed that some of the naval officers of that Empire had advanced and practiced upon principles in relation to blockades and to neutral navigation which we could not sanction, and which our commanders found it necessary to resist. It appears that they have not been sustained by the Government of Brazil itself. Some of the vessels captured under the assumed authority of these erroneous principles have been restored, and we trust that our just expectations will be realized that adequate indemnity will be made to all the citizens of the United States who have suffered by the unwarranted captures which the Brazilian tribunals themselves have pronounced unlawful.

In the diplomatic discussions at Rio de Janeiro of these wrongs sustained by citizens of the United States and of others which seemed as if emanating immediately from that Government itself the chargé d'affaires of the United States, under an impression that his representations in behalf of the rights and interests of his countrymen were totally disregarded and useless, deemed it his duty, without waiting for instructions, to terminate his official functions, to demand his passports, and return to the

United States. This movement, dictated by an honest zeal for the honor and interests of his country—motives which operated exclusively on the mind of the officer who resorted to it—has not been disapproved by me. The Brazilian Government, however, complained of it as a measure for which no adequate intentional cause had been given by them, and upon an explicit assurance through their chargé d'affaires residing here that a successor to the late representative of the United States near that Government, the appointment of whom they desired, should be received and treated with the respect due to his character, and that indemnity should be promptly made for all injuries inflicted on citizens of the United States or their property contrary to the laws of nations, a temporary commission as chargé d'affaires to that country has been issued, which it is hoped will entirely restore the ordinary diplomatic intercourse between the two Governments and the friendly relations between their respective nations.

Turning from the momentous concerns of our Union in its intercourse with foreign nations to those of the deepest interest in the administration of our internal affairs, we find the revenues of the present year corresponding as nearly as might be expected with the anticipations of the last, and presenting an aspect still more favorable in the promise of the next. The balance in the Treasury on January 1 last was $6,358,686.18. The receipts from that day to the 30th of September last, as near as the returns of them yet received can show, amount to $16,886,581.32. The receipts of the present quarter, estimated at $4,515,000, added to the above form an aggregate of $21,400,000 of receipts. The expenditures of the year may perhaps amount to $22,300,000, presenting a small excess over the receipts. But of these twenty-two millions, upward of six have been applied to the discharge of the principal of the public debt, the whole amount of which, approaching seventy-four millions on the 1st of January last, will on the first day of the next year fall short of sixty-seven millions and a half. The balance in the Treasury on the 1st of January next it is expected will exceed $5,450,000, a sum exceeding that of the 1st of January, 1825, though falling short of that exhibited on the 1st of January last.

It was foreseen that the revenue of the present year would not equal that of the last, which had itself been less than that of the next preceding year. But the hope has been realized which was entertained, that these deficiencies would in nowise interrupt the steady operation of the discharge of the public debt by the annual ten millions devoted to that object by the act of 3d March, 1817.

The amount of duties secured on merchandise imported from the commencement of the year until the 30th of September last is $21,226,000, and the probable amount of that which will be secured during the remainder of the year is $5,774,000, forming a sum total of $27,000,000. With the allowances for drawbacks and contingent deficiencies which may occur, though not specifically foreseen, we may safely estimate the receipts of the ensuing year at $22,300,000—a revenue for the next equal to the expenditure of the present year.

The deep solicitude felt by our citizens of all classes throughout the Union for the total discharge of the public debt will apologize for the earnestness with which I deem it my duty to urge this topic upon the consideration of Congress—of recommending to them again the observance of the strictest economy in the application of the public funds. The depression upon the receipts of the revenue which had commenced with the year 1826 continued with increased severity during the two first quarters of the present year. The returning tide began to flow with the third quarter, and, so far as we can judge from experience, may be expected to continue through the course of the ensuing year. In the meantime an alleviation from the burden of the public debt will in the three years have been effected to the amount of nearly sixteen millions, and the charge of annual interest will have been reduced upward of one million. But among the maxims of political economy which the stewards of the public moneys should never suffer without urgent necessity to be transcended is that of keeping the expenditures of the year within the limits of its receipts. The appropriations of the two last years, including the yearly ten millions of the sinking fund, have each equaled the promised revenue of the ensuing year. While we foresee with confidence that the public coffers will be replenished from the receipts as fast as they will be drained by the expenditures, equal in amount to those of the current year, it should not be forgotten that they could ill suffer the exhaustion of larger disbursements.

The condition of the Army and of all the branches of the public service under the superintendence of the Secretary of War will be seen by the report from that officer and the documents with which it is accompanied.

During the last summer a detachment of the Army has been usefully and successfully called to perform their appropriate duties. At the moment when the commissioners appointed for carrying into execution certain provisions of the treaty of August 19, 1825, with various tribes of the Northwestern Indians were about to arrive at the appointed place of meeting the unprovoked murder of several citizens and other acts of unequivocal hostility committed by a party of the Winnebago tribe, one of those associated in the treaty, followed by indications of a menacing character among other tribes of the same region, rendered necessary an immediate display of the defensive and protective force of the Union in that quarter. It was accordingly exhibited by the immediate and concerted movements of the governors of the State of Illinois and of the Territory of Michigan, and competent levies of militia, under their authority, with a corps of 700 men of United States troops, under the command of General Atkinson, who, at the call of Governor Cass, immediately repaired to the scene of danger from their station at St. Louis.

Their presence dispelled the alarms of our fellow-citizens on those borders, and overawed the hostile purposes of the Indians. The perpetrators of the murders were surrendered to the authority and operation of our laws, and every appearance of purposed hostility from those Indian tribes has subsided.

Although the present organization of the Army and the administration of its various branches of service are, upon the whole, satisfactory, they are yet susceptible of much improvement in particulars, some of which have been heretofore submitted to the consideration of Congress, and others are now first presented in the report of the Secretary of War.

The expediency of providing for additional numbers of officers in the two corps of engineers will in some degree depend upon the number and extent of the objects of national importance upon which Congress may think it proper that surveys should be made conformably to the act of the 30th of April, 1824. Of the surveys which before the last session of Congress had been made under the authority of that act, reports were made—

1. Of the Board of Internal Improvement, on the Chesapeake and Ohio Canal.

2. On the continuation of the national road from Cumberland to the tide waters within the District of Columbia.

3. On the continuation of the national road from Canton to Zanesville.

4. On the location of the national road from Zanesville to Columbus.

5. On the continuation of the same to the seat of government in Missouri.

6. On a post-road from Baltimore to Philadelphia.

7. Of a survey of Kennebec River (in part).

8. On a national road from Washington to Buffalo.

9. On the survey of Saugatuck Harbor and River.

10. On a canal from Lake Pontchartrain to the Mississippi River.

11. On surveys at Edgartown, Newburyport, and Hyannis Harbor.

12. On survey of La Plaisance Bay, in the Territory of Michigan.

And reports are now prepared and will be submitted to Congress—

On surveys of the peninsula of Florida, to ascertain the practicability of a canal to connect the waters of the Atlantic with the Gulf of Mexico across that peninsula; and also of the country between the bays of Mobile and of Pensacola, with the view of connecting them together by a canal.

On surveys of a route for a canal to connect the waters of James and Great Kenhawa rivers.

On the survey of the Swash, in Pamlico Sound, and that of Cape Fear, below the town of Wilmington, in North Carolina.

On the survey of the Muscle Shoals, in the Tennessee River, and for a route for a contemplated communication between the Hiwassee and Coosa rivers, in the State of Alabama.

Other reports of surveys upon objects pointed out by the several acts of Congress of the last and preceding sessions are in the progress of preparation, and most of them may be completed before the close of this session. All the officers of both corps of engineers, with several other persons duly qualified, have been constantly employed upon these services from the passage of the act of 30th April, 1824, to this time. Were no other advantage to accrue to the country from their labors than the fund of topographical knowledge which they have collected and communicated, that alone would have been a profit to the Union more than adequate to all the expenditures which have been devoted to the object; but the appropriations for the repair and continuation of the Cumberland road, for the construction of various other roads, for the removal of obstructions from the rivers and harbors, for the erection of light-houses, beacons, piers, and buoys, and for the completion of canals undertaken by individual associations, but needing the assistance of means and resources more comprehensive than individual enterprise can command, may be considered rather as treasures laid up from the contributions of the present age for the benefit of posterity than as unrequited applications of the accruing revenues of the nation. To such objects of permanent improvement to the condition of the country, of real addition to the wealth as well as to the comfort of the people by whose authority and resources they have been effected, from three to four millions of the annual income of the nation have, by laws enacted at the three most recent sessions of Congress, been applied, without intrenching upon the necessities of the Treasury, without adding a dollar to the taxes or debts of the community, without suspending even the steady and regular discharge of the debts contracted in former days, which within the same three years have been diminished by the amount of nearly $16,000,000.

The same observations are in a great degree applicable to the appropriations made for fortifications upon the coasts and harbors of the United States, for the maintenance of the Military Academy at West Point, and for the various objects under the superintendence of the Department of the Navy. The report from the Secretary of the Navy and those from the subordinate branches of both the military departments exhibit to Congress in minute detail the present condition of the public establishments dependent upon them, the execution of the acts of Congress relating to them, and the views of the officers engaged in the several branches of the service concerning the improvements which may tend to their perfection. The fortification of the coasts and the gradual increase and improvement of the Navy are parts of a great system of national defense which has been upward of ten years in progress, and which for a series of years to come will continue to claim the constant and persevering protection and superintendence of the legislative authority. Among the measures which have emanated from these principles the act of the last session of Congress for the gradual improvement of the Navy holds a conspicuous place.   The collection of timber for the future construction of vessels of war, the preservation and reproduction of the species of timber peculiarly adapted to that purpose, the construction of dry docks for the use of the Navy, the erection of a marine railway for the repair of the public ships, and the improvement of the navy-yards for the preservation of the public property deposited in them have all received from the Executive the attention required by that act, and will continue to receive it, steadily proceeding toward the execution of all its purposes.   The establishment of a naval academy, furnishing the means of theoretic instruction to the youths who devote their lives to the service of their country upon the ocean, still solicits the sanction of the Legislature. Practical seamanship and the art of navigation may be acquired on the cruises of the squadrons which from time to time are dispatched to distant seas, but a competent knowledge even of the art of shipbuilding, the higher mathematics, and astronomy; the literature which can place our officers on a level of polished education with the officers of other maritime nations; the knowledge of the laws, municipal and national, which in their intercourse with foreign states and their governments are continually called into operation, and, above all, that acquaintance with the principles of honor and justice, with the higher obligations of morals and of general laws, human and divine, which constitutes the great distinction between the warrior-patriot and the licensed robber and pirate— these can be systematically taught and eminently acquired only in a permanent school, stationed upon the shore and provided with the teachers, the instruments, and the books conversant with and adapted to the communication of the principles of these respective sciences to the youthful and inquiring mind.

The report from the Postmaster-General exhibits the condition of that Department as highly satisfactory for the present and still more promising for the future.   Its receipts for the year ending the 1st of July last amounted to $1,473,551, and exceeded its expenditures by upward of $100,000.   It can not be an oversanguine estimate to predict that in less than ten years, of which one-half have elapsed, the receipts will have been more than doubled.   In the meantime a reduced expenditure upon established routes has kept pace with increased facilities of public accommodation and additional services have been obtained at reduced rates of compensation.   Within the last year the transportation of the mail in stages has been greatly augmented.   The number of post-offices has been increased to 7,000, and it may be anticipated that while the facilities of intercourse between fellow-citizens in person or by correspondence will soon be carried to the door of every villager in the Union, a yearly surplus of revenue will accrue which may be applied as the wisdom of Congress under the exercise of their constitutional powers may devise for the further establishment and improvement of the public roads, or by adding still further to the facilities in the transportation of the mails.

Of the indications of the prosperous condition of our country, none can be more pleasing than those presented by the multiplying relations of personal and intimate intercourse between the citizens of the Union dwelling at the remotest distances from each other.

Among the subjects which have heretofore occupied the earnest solicitude and attention of Congress is the management and disposal of that portion of the property of the nation which consists of the public lands. The acquisition of them, made at the expense of the whole Union, not only in treasure but in blood, marks a right of property in them equally extensive. By the report and statements from the General Land Office now communicated it appears that under the present Government of the United States a sum little short of $33,000,000 has been paid from the common Treasury for that portion of this property which has been purchased from France and Spain, and for the extinction of the aboriginal titles. The amount of lands acquired is near 260,000,000 acres, of which on the 1st of January, 1826, about 139,000,000 acres had been surveyed, and little more than 19,000,000 acres had been sold. The amount paid into the Treasury by the purchasers of the public lands sold is not yet equal to the sums paid for the whole, but leaves a small balance to be refunded. The proceeds of the sales of the lands have long been pledged to the creditors of the nation, a pledge from which we have reason to hope that they will in a very few years be redeemed.

The system upon which this great national interest has been managed was the result of long, anxious, and persevering deliberation. Matured and modified by the progress of our population and the lessons of experience, it has been hitherto eminently successful. More than nine-tenths of the lands still remain the common property of the Union, the appropriation and disposal of which are sacred trusts in the hands of Congress. Of the lands sold, a considerable part were conveyed under extended credits, which in the vicissitudes and fluctuations in the value of lands and of their produce became oppressively burdensome to the purchasers. It can never be the interest or the policy of the nation to wring from its own citizens the reasonable profits of their industry and enterprise by holding them to the rigorous import of disastrous engagements. In March, 1821, a debt of $22,000,000, due by purchasers of the public lands, had accumulated, which they were unable to pay. An act of Congress of the 2d March, 1821, came to their relief, and has been succeeded by others, the latest being the act of the 4th of May, 1826, the indulgent provisions of which expired on the 4th July last. The effect of these laws has been to reduce the debt from the purchasers to a remaining balance of about $4,300,000 due, more than three-fifths of which are for lands within the State of Alabama. I recommend to Congress the revival and continuance for a further term of the beneficent accommodations to the public debtors of that statute, and submit to their consideration, in the same spirit of equity, the remission, under proper discriminations, of the forfeitures of partial payments on account of purchases of the public lands, so far as to allow of their application to other payments.

There are various other subjects of deep interest to the whole Union which have heretofore been recommended to the consideration of Congress, as well by my predecessors as, under the impression of the duties devolving upon me, by myself.   Among these are the debt, rather of justice than gratitude, to the surviving warriors of the Revolutionary war; the extension of the judicial administration of the Federal Government to those extensive and important members of the Union which, having risen into existence since the organization of the present judiciary establishment, now constitute at least one-third of its territory, power, and population; the formation of a more effective and uniform system for the government of the militia, and the amelioration in some form or modification of the diversified and often oppressive codes relating to insolvency.   Amidst the multiplicity of topics of great national concernment which may recommend themselves to the calm and patriotic deliberations of the Legislature, it may suffice to say that on these and all other measures which may receive their sanction my hearty cooperation will be given, conformably to the duties enjoined upon me and under the sense of all the obligations prescribed by the Constitution.

FOURTH ANNUAL MESSAGE.

WASHINGTON, *December 2, 1828.*

Fellow-Citizens of the Senate and of the House of Representatives:

If the enjoyment in profusion of the bounties of Providence forms a suitable subject of mutual gratulation and grateful acknowledgment, we are admonished at this return of the season when the representatives of the nation are assembled to deliberate upon their concerns to offer up the tribute of fervent and grateful hearts for the never-failing mercies of Him who ruleth over all.   He has again favored us with healthful seasons and abundant harvests; He has sustained us in peace with foreign countries and in tranquillity within our borders; He has preserved us in the quiet and undisturbed possession of civil and religious liberty; He has crowned the year with His goodness, imposing on us no other conditions than of improving for our own happiness the blessings bestowed by His hands, and, in the fruition of all His favors, of devoting the faculties with which we have been endowed by Him to His glory and to our own temporal and eternal welfare.

In the relations of our Federal Union with our brethren of the human race the changes which have occurred since the close of your last session have generally tended to the preservation of peace and to the cultivation of harmony. Before your last separation a war had unhappily been kindled between the Empire of Russia, one of those with which our intercourse has been no other than a constant exchange of good offices, and that of the Ottoman Porte, a nation from which geographical distance, religious opinions and maxims of government on their part little suited to the formation of those bonds of mutual benevolence which result from the benefits of commerce had kept us in a state, perhaps too much prolonged, of coldness and alienation. The extensive, fertile, and populous dominions of the Sultan belong rather to the Asiatic than the European division of the human family. They enter but partially into the system of Europe, nor have their wars with Russia and Austria, the European States upon which they border, for more than a century past disturbed the pacific relations of those States with the other great powers of Europe. Neither France nor Prussia nor Great Britain has ever taken part in them, nor is it to be expected that they will at this time. The declaration of war by Russia has received the approbation or acquiescence of her allies, and we may indulge the hope that its progress and termination will be signalized by the moderation and forbearance no less than by the energy of the Emperor Nicholas, and that it will afford the opportunity for such collateral agency in behalf of the suffering Greeks as will secure to them ultimately the triumph of humanity and of freedom.

The state of our particular relations with France has scarcely varied in the course of the present year. The commercial intercourse between the two countries has continued to increase for the mutual benefit of both. The claims of indemnity to numbers of our fellow-citizens for depredations upon their property, heretofore committed during the revolutionary governments, remain unadjusted, and still form the subject of earnest representation and remonstrance. Recent advices from the minister of the United States at Paris encourage the expectation that the appeal to the justice of the French Government will ere long receive a favorable consideration.

The last friendly expedient has been resorted to for the decision of the controversy with Great Britain relating to the northeastern boundary of the United States. By an agreement with the British Government, carrying into effect the provisions of the fifth article of the treaty of Ghent, and the convention of 29th September, 1827, His Majesty the King of the Netherlands has by common consent been selected as the umpire between the parties. The proposal to him to accept the designation for the performance of this friendly office will be made at an early day, and the United States, relying upon the justice of their cause, will cheerfully commit the arbitrament of it to a prince equally distinguished for the independence of his spirit, his indefatigable assiduity to the duties of his station, and his inflexible personal probity.

Our commercial relations with Great Britain will deserve the serious consideration of Congress and the exercise of a conciliatory and forbearing spirit in the policy of both Governments. The state of them has been materially changed by the act of Congress, passed at their last session, in alteration of the several acts imposing duties on imports, and by acts of more recent date of the British Parliament. The effect of the interdiction of direct trade, commenced by Great Britain and reciprocated by the United States, has been, as was to be foreseen, only to substitute different channels for an exchange of commodities indispensable to the colonies and profitable to a numerous class of our fellow-citizens. The exports, the revenue, the navigation of the United States have suffered no diminution by our exclusion from direct access to the British colonies. The colonies pay more dearly for the necessaries of life which their Government burdens with the charges of double voyages, freight, insurance, and commission, and the profits of our exports are somewhat impaired and more injuriously transferred from one portion of our citizens to another. The resumption of this old and otherwise exploded system of colonial exclusion has not secured to the shipping interest of Great Britain the relief which, at the expense of the distant colonies and of the United States, it was expected to afford. Other measures have been resorted to more pointedly bearing upon the navigation of the United States, and which, unless modified by the construction given to the recent acts of Parliament, will be manifestly incompatible with the positive stipulations of the commercial convention existing between the two countries. That convention, however, may be terminated with twelve months' notice, at the option of either party.

A treaty of amity, navigation, and commerce between the United States and His Majesty the Emperor of Austria, King of Hungary and Bohemia, has been prepared for signature by the Secretary of State and by the Baron de Lederer, intrusted with full powers of the Austrian Government. Independently of the new and friendly relations which may be thus commenced with one of the most eminent and powerful nations of the earth, the occasion has been taken in it, as in other recent treaties concluded by the United States, to extend those principles of liberal intercourse and of fair reciprocity which intertwine with the exchanges of commerce the principles of justice and the feelings of mutual benevolence. This system, first proclaimed to the world in the first commercial treaty ever concluded by the United States—that of 6th February, 1778, with France—has been invariably the cherished policy of our Union. It is by treaties of commerce alone that it can be made ultimately to prevail as the established system of all civilized nations. With this principle our fathers extended the hand of friendship to every nation of the globe, and to this policy our country has ever since adhered. Whatever of regulation in our laws has ever been adopted unfavorable to the interest of any foreign nation has been essentially defensive and counteracting to similar regulations of theirs operating against us.

Immediately after the close of the War of Independence commissioners were appointed by the Congress of the Confederation authorized to conclude treaties with every nation of Europe disposed to adopt them. Before the wars of the French Revolution such treaties had been consummated with the United Netherlands, Sweden, and Prussia. During those wars treaties with Great Britain and Spain had been effected, and those with Prussia and France renewed. In all these some concessions to the liberal principles of intercourse proposed by the United States had been obtained; but as in all the negotiations they came occasionally in collision with previous internal regulations or exclusive and excluding compacts of monopoly with which the other parties had been trammeled, the advances made in them toward the freedom of trade were partial and imperfect. Colonial establishments, chartered companies, and shipbuilding influence pervaded and encumbered the legislation of all the great commercial states; and the United States, in offering free trade and equal privilege to all, were compelled to acquiesce in many exceptions with each of the parties to their treaties, accommodated to their existing laws and anterior engagements.

The colonial system by which this whole hemisphere was bound has fallen into ruins, totally abolished by revolutions converting colonies into independent nations throughout the two American continents, excepting a portion of territory chiefly at the northern extremity of our own, and confined to the remnants of dominion retained by Great Britain over the insular archipelago, geographically the appendages of our part of the globe. With all the rest we have free trade, even with the insular colonies of all the European nations, except Great Britain. Her Government also had manifested approaches to the adoption of a free and liberal intercourse between her colonies and other nations, though by a sudden and scarcely explained revulsion the spirit of exclusion has been revived for operation upon the United States alone.

The conclusion of our last treaty of peace with Great Britain was shortly afterwards followed by a commercial convention, placing the direct intercourse between the two countries upon a footing of more equal reciprocity than had ever before been admitted. The same principle has since been much further extended by treaties with France, Sweden, Denmark, the Hanseatic cities, Prussia, in Europe, and with the Republics of Colombia and of Central America, in this hemisphere. The mutual abolition of discriminating duties and charges upon the navigation and commercial intercourse between the parties is the general maxim which characterizes them all. There is reason to expect that it will at no distant period be adopted by other nations, both of Europe and America, and to hope that by its universal prevalence one of the fruitful sources of wars of commercial competition will be extinguished.

Among the nations upon whose Governments many of our fellow-citizens have had long-pending claims of indemnity for depredations upon their property during a period when the rights of neutral commerce were disregarded was that of Denmark.   They were soon after the events occurred the subject of a special mission from the United States, at the close of which the assurance was given by His Danish Majesty that at a period of more tranquillity and of less distress they would be considered, examined, and decided upon in a spirit of determined purpose for the dispensation of justice.   I have much pleasure in informing Congress that the fulfillment of this honorable promise is now in progress; that a small portion of the claims has already been settled to the satisfaction of the claimants, and that we have reason to hope that the remainder will shortly be placed in a train of equitable adjustment.   This result has always been confidently expected, from the character of personal integrity and of benevolence which the Sovereign of the Danish domin-ions has through every vicissitude of fortune maintained.

The general aspect of the affairs of our neighboring American nations of the south has been rather of approaching than of settled tranquillity. Internal disturbances have been more frequent among them than their common friends would have desired.   Our intercourse with all has con-tinued to be that of friendship and of mutual good will.   Treaties of commerce and of boundaries with the United Mexican States have been negotiated, but, from various successive obstacles, not yet brought to a final conclusion.

The civil war which unfortunately still prevails in the Republics of Central America has been unpropitious to the cultivation of our commer-cial relations with them; and the dissensions and revolutionary changes in the Republics of Colombia and of Peru have been seen with cordial regret by us, who would gladly contribute to the happiness of both.   It is with great satisfaction, however, that we have witnessed the recent conclusion of a peace between the Governments of Buenos Ayres and of Brazil, and it is equally gratifying to observe that indemnity has been obtained for some of the injuries which our fellow-citizens had sustained in the latter of those countries.   The rest are in a train of negotiation, which we hope may terminate to mutual satisfaction, and that it may be succeeded by a treaty of commerce and navigation, upon liberal princi-ples, propitious to a great and growing commerce, already important to the interests of our country.

The condition and prospects of the revenue are more favorable than our most sanguine expectations had anticipated.   The balance in the Treasury on the 1st of January last, exclusive of the moneys received under the convention of 13th of November, 1826, with Great Britain, was $5,861,972.83.   The receipts into the Treasury from the 1st of Jan-uary to the 30th of September last, so far as they have been ascertained to form the basis of an estimate, amount to $18,633,580.27, which, with the receipts of the present quarter, estimated at $5,461,283.40, form an aggregate of receipts during the year of $24,094,863.67. The expenditures of the year may probably amount to $25,637,111.63, and leave in the Treasury on the 1st of January next the sum of $5,125,638.14.

The receipts of the present year have amounted to near two millions more than was anticipated at the commencement of the last session of Congress.

The amount of duties secured on importations from the 1st of January to the 30th of September was about $22,997,000, and that of the estimated accruing revenue is five millions, forming an aggregate for the year of near twenty-eight millions. This is one million more than the estimate made last December for the accruing revenue of the present year, which, with allowances for drawbacks and contingent deficiencies, was expected to produce an actual revenue of $22,300,000. Had these only been realized the expenditures of the year would have been also proportionally reduced, for of these twenty-four millions received upward of nine millions have been applied to the extinction of public debt, bearing an interest of 6 per cent a year, and of course reducing the burden of interest annually payable in future by the amount of more than half a million. The payments on account of interest during the current year exceed $3,000,000, presenting an aggregate of more than twelve millions applied during the year to the discharge of the public debt, the whole of which remaining due on the 1st of January next will amount only to $58,362,135.78.

That the revenue of the ensuing year will not fall short of that received in the one now expiring there are indications which can scarcely prove deceptive. In our country an uniform experience of forty years has shown that whatever the tariff of duties upon articles imported from abroad has been, the amount of importations has always borne an average value nearly approaching to that of the exports, though occasionally differing in the balance, sometimes being more and sometimes less. It is, indeed, a general law of prosperous commerce that the real value of exports should by a small, and only a small, balance exceed that of imports, that balance being a permanent addition to the wealth of the nation. The extent of the prosperous commerce of the nation must be regulated by the amount of its exports, and an important addition to the value of these will draw after it a corresponding increase of importations. It has happened in the vicissitudes of the seasons that the harvests of all Europe have in the late summer and autumn fallen short of their usual average. A relaxation of the interdict upon the importation of grain and flour from abroad has ensued, a propitious market has been opened to the granaries of our country, and a new prospect of reward presented to the labors of the husbandman, which for several years has been denied. This accession to the profits of agriculture in the middle and western portions of our Union is accidental and temporary. It may continue only for a single year. It may be, as has been often experienced in the revolutions of time, but the first of several scanty harvests in succession. We may consider it certain that for the approaching year it has added an item of large amount to the value of our exports and that it will produce a corresponding increase of importations. It may therefore confidently be foreseen that the revenue of 1829 will equal and probably exceed that of 1828, and will afford the means of extinguishing ten millions more of the principal of the public debt.

This new element of prosperity to that part of our agricultural indus- try which is occupied in producing the first article of human subsistence is of the most cheering character to the feelings of patriotism. Proceed- ing from a cause which humanity will view with concern, the sufferings of scarcity in distant lands, it yields a consolatory reflection that this scarcity is in no respect attributable to us; that it comes from the dis- pensation of Him who ordains all in wisdom and goodness, and who permits evil itself only as an instrument of good; that, far from contribu- ting to this scarcity, our agency will be applied only to the alleviation of its severity, and that in pouring forth from the abundance of our own garners the supplies which will partially restore plenty to those who are in need we shall ourselves reduce our stores and add to the price of our own bread, so as in some degree to participate in the wants which it will be the good fortune of our country to relieve.

The great interests of an agricultural, commercial, and manufacturing nation are so linked in union together that no permanent cause of pros- perity to one of them can operate without extending its influence to the others. All these interests are alike under the protecting power of the legislative authority, and the duties of the representative bodies are to conciliate them in harmony together. So far as the object of taxation is to raise a revenue for discharging the debts and defraying the expenses of the community, its operation should be adapted as much as possible to suit the burden with equal hand upon all in proportion with their abil- ity of bearing it without oppression. But the legislation of one nation is sometimes intentionally made to bear heavily upon the interests of another. That legislation, adapted, as it is meant to be, to the special interests of its own people, will often press most unequally upon the sev- eral component interests of its neighbors. Thus the legislation of Great Britain, when, as has recently been avowed, adapted to the depression of a rival nation, will naturally abound with regulations of interdict upon the productions of the soil or industry of the other which come in competi- tion with its own, and will present encouragement, perhaps even bounty, to the raw material of the other State which it can not produce itself, and which is essential for the use of its manufactures, competitors in the markets of the world with those of its commercial rival. Such is the state of the commercial legislation of Great Britain as it bears upon our interests. It excludes with interdicting duties all importation (except in time of approaching famine) of the great staple of productions of our

Middle and Western States; it proscribes with equal rigor the bulkier lumber and live stock of the same portion and also of the Northern and Eastern part of our Union. It refuses even the rice of the South unless aggravated with a charge of duty upon the Northern carrier who brings it to them. But the cotton, indispensable for their looms, they will receive almost duty free to weave it into a fabric for our own wear, to the destruction of our own manufactures, which they are enabled thus to undersell.

Is the self-protecting energy of this nation so helpless that there exists in the political institutions of our country no power to counteract the bias of this foreign legislation; that the growers of grain must submit to this exclusion from the foreign markets of their produce; that the shippers must dismantle their ships, the trade of the North stagnate at the wharves, and the manufacturers starve at their looms, while the whole people shall pay tribute to foreign industry to be clad in a foreign garb; that the Congress of the Union are impotent to restore the balance in favor of native industry destroyed by the statutes of another realm? **More just and more generous sentiments will, I trust, prevail.** If the tariff adopted at the last session of Congress shall be found by experience to bear oppressively upon the interests of any one section of the Union, it ought to be, and I can not doubt will be, so modified as to alleviate its burden. To the voice of just complaint from any portion of their constituents the representatives of the States and of the people will never turn away their ears. But so long as the duty of the foreign shall operate only as a bounty upon the domestic article; while the planter and the merchant and the shepherd and the husbandman shall be found thriving in their occupations under the duties imposed for the protection of domestic manufactures, they will not repine at the prosperity shared with themselves by their fellow-citizens of other professions, nor denounce as violations of the Constitution the deliberate acts of Congress to shield from the wrongs of foreign laws the native industry of the Union. While the tariff of the last session of Congress was a subject of legislative deliberation it was foretold by some of its opposers that one of its necessary consequences would be to impair the revenue. It is yet too soon to pronounce with confidence that this prediction was erroneous. The obstruction of one avenue of trade not unfrequently opens an issue to another. The consequence of the tariff will be to increase the exportation and to diminish the importation of some specific articles; but by the general law of trade the increase of exportation of one article will be followed by an increased importation of others, the duties upon which will supply the deficiencies which the diminished importation would otherwise occasion. The effect of taxation upon revenue can seldom be foreseen with certainty. It must abide the test of experience. As yet no symptoms of diminution are perceptible in the receipts of the Treasury. As yet little addition of cost has even been experienced upon the articles burdened with heavier duties by the last tariff. The domestic manufacturer supplies the same or a kindred article at a diminished price, and the consumer pays the same tribute to the labor of his own countryman which he must otherwise have paid to foreign industry and toil.

The tariff of the last session was in its details not acceptable to the great interests of any portion of the Union, not even to the interest which it was specially intended to subserve. Its object was to balance the burdens upon native industry imposed by the operation of foreign laws, but not to aggravate the burdens of one section of the Union by the relief afforded to another. To the great principle sanctioned by that act—one of those upon which the Constitution itself was formed—I hope and trust the authorities of the Union will adhere. But if any of the duties imposed by the act only relieve the manufacturer by aggravating the burden of the planter, let a careful revisal of its provisions, enlightened by the practical experience of its effects, be directed to retain those which impart protection to native industry and remove or supply the place of those which only alleviate one great national interest by the depression of another.

The United States of America and the people of every State of which they are composed are each of them sovereign powers. The legislative authority of the whole is exercised by Congress under authority granted them in the common Constitution. The legislative power of each State is exercised by assemblies deriving their authority from the constitution of the State. Each is sovereign within its own province. The distribution of power between them presupposes that these authorities will move in harmony with each other. The members of the State and General Governments are all under oath to support both, and allegiance is due to the one and to the other. The case of a conflict between these two powers has not been supposed, nor has any provision been made for it in our institutions; as a virtuous nation of ancient times existed more than five centuries without a law for the punishment of parricide.

More than once, however, in the progress of our history have the people and the legislatures of one or more States, in moments of excitement, been instigated to this conflict; and the means of effecting this impulse have been allegations that the acts of Congress to be resisted were *unconstitutional*. The people of no one State have ever delegated to their legislature the power of pronouncing an act of Congress unconstitutional, but they have delegated to them powers by the exercise of which the execution of the laws of Congress within the State may be resisted. If we suppose the case of such conflicting legislation sustained by the corresponding executive and judicial authorities, patriotism and philanthropy turn their eyes from the condition in which the parties would be placed, and from that of the people of both, which must be its victims.

The reports from the Secretary of War and the various subordinate offices of the resort of that Department present an exposition of the public administration of affairs connected with them through the course of the current year. The present state of the Army and the distribution of the force of which it is composed will be seen from the report of the Major-General. Several alterations in the disposal of the troops have been found expedient in the course of the year, and the discipline of the Army, though not entirely free from exception, has been generally good.

The attention of Congress is particularly invited to that part of the report of the Secretary of War which concerns the existing system of our relations with the Indian tribes. At the establishment of the Federal Government under the present Constitution of the United States the principle was adopted of considering them as foreign and independent powers and also as proprietors of lands. They were, moreover, considered as savages, whom it was our policy and our duty to use our influence in converting to Christianity and in bringing within the pale of civilization.

As independent powers, we negotiated with them by treaties; as proprietors, we purchased of them all the lands which we could prevail upon them to sell; as brethren of the human race, rude and ignorant, we endeavored to bring them to the knowledge of religion and of letters. The ultimate design was to incorporate in our own institutions that portion of them which could be converted to the state of civilization. In the practice of European States, before our Revolution, they had been considered *as children* to be governed; as tenants at discretion, to be dispossessed as occasion might require; as hunters to be indemnified by trifling concessions for removal from the grounds from which their game was extirpated. In changing the system it would seem as if a full contemplation of the consequences of the change had not been taken. We have been far more successful in the acquisition of their lands than in imparting to them the principles or inspiring them with the spirit of civilization. But in appropriating to ourselves their hunting grounds we have brought upon ourselves the obligation of providing them with subsistence; and when we have had the rare good fortune of teaching them the arts of civilization and the doctrines of Christianity we have unexpectedly found them forming in the midst of ourselves communities claiming to be independent of ours and rivals of sovereignty within the territories of the members of our Union. This state of things requires that a remedy should be provided—a remedy which, while it shall do justice to those unfortunate children of nature, may secure to the members of our confederation their rights of sovereignty and of soil. As the outline of a project to that effect, the views presented in the report of the Secretary of War are recommended to the consideration of Congress.

The report from the Engineer Department presents a comprehensive view of the progress which has been made in the great systems promotive of the public interest, commenced and organized under authority of Congress, and the effects of which have already contributed to the security, as they will hereafter largely contribute to the honor and dignity, of the nation.

The first of these great systems is that of fortifications, commenced immediately after the close of our last war, under the salutary experience which the events of that war had impressed upon our countrymen of its necessity. Introduced under the auspices of my immediate predecessor, it has been continued with the persevering and liberal encouragement of the Legislature, and, combined with corresponding exertions for the gradual increase and improvement of the Navy, prepares for our extensive country a condition of defense adapted to any critical emergency which the varying course of events may bring forth. Our advances in these concerted systems have for the last ten years been steady and progressive, and in a few years more will be so completed as to leave no cause for apprehension that our seacoast will ever again offer a theater of hostile invasion.

The next of these cardinal measures of policy is the preliminary to great and lasting works of public improvement in the surveys of roads, examination for the course of canals, and labors for the removal of the obstructions of rivers and harbors, first commenced by the act of Congress of 30th of April, 1824.

The report exhibits in one table the funds appropriated at the last and preceding sessions of Congress for all these fortifications, surveys, and works of public improvement, the manner in which these funds have been applied, the amount expended upon the several works under construction, and the further sums which may be necessary to complete them; in a second, the works projected by the Board of Engineers which have not been commenced, and the estimate of their cost; in a third, the report of the annual Board of Visitors at the Military Academy at West Point.

For thirteen fortifications erecting on various points of our Atlantic coast, from Rhode Island to Louisiana, the aggregate expenditure of the year has fallen little short of $1,000,000. For the preparation of five additional reports of reconnoissances and surveys since the last session of Congress, for the civil constructions upon thirty-seven different public works commenced, eight others for which specific appropriations have been made by acts of Congress, and twenty other incipient surveys under the authority given by the act of 30th April, 1824, about one million more of dollars has been drawn from the Treasury.

To these $2,000,000 is to be added the appropriation of $250,000 to commence the erection of a breakwater near the mouth of the Delaware River, the subscriptions to the Delaware and Chesapeake, the Louisville and Portland, the Dismal Swamp, and the Chesapeake and Ohio canals, the large donations of lands to the States of Ohio, Indiana, Illinois, and Alabama for objects of improvements within those States, and the sums appropriated for light-houses, buoys, and piers on the coast; and a full view will be taken of the munificence of the nation in the application of its resources to the improvement of its own condition.

Of these great national undertakings the Academy at West Point is among the most important in itself and the most comprehensive in its consequences. In that institution a part of the revenue of the nation is applied to defray the expense of educating a competent portion of her youth chiefly to the knowledge and the duties of military life. It is the living armory of the nation. While the other works of improvement enumerated in the reports now presented to the attention of Congress are destined to ameliorate the face of nature, to multiply the facilities of communication between the different parts of the Union, to assist the labors, increase the comforts, and enhance the enjoyments of individuals, the instruction acquired at West Point enlarges the dominion and expands the capacities of the mind. Its beneficial results are already experienced in the composition of the Army, and their influence is felt in the intellectual progress of society. The institution is susceptible still of great improvement from benefactions proposed by several successive Boards of Visitors, to whose earnest and repeated recommendations I cheerfully add my own.

With the usual annual reports from the Secretary of the Navy and the Board of Commissioners will be exhibited to the view of Congress the execution of the laws relating to that department of the public service. The repression of piracy in the West Indian and in the Grecian seas has been effectually maintained, with scarcely any exception. During the war between the Governments of Buenos Ayres and of Brazil frequent collisions between the belligerent acts of power and the rights of neutral commerce occurred. Licentious blockades, irregularly enlisted or impressed seamen, and the property of honest commerce seized with violence, and even plundered under legal pretenses, are disorders never separable from the conflicts of war upon the ocean. With a portion of them the correspondence of our commanders on the eastern aspect of the South American coast and among the islands of Greece discover how far we have been involved. In these the honor of our country and the rights of our citizens have been asserted and vindicated. The appearance of new squadrons in the Mediterranean and the blockade of the Dardanelles indicate the danger of other obstacles to the freedom of commerce and the necessity of keeping our naval force in those seas. To the suggestions repeated in the report of the Secretary of the Navy, and tending to the permanent improvement of this institution, I invite the favorable consideration of Congress.

A resolution of the House of Representatives requesting that one of our small public vessels should be sent to the Pacific Ocean and South Sea to examine the coasts, islands, harbors, shoals, and reefs in those seas, and to ascertain their true situation and description, has been put in a train of execution. The vessel is nearly ready to depart. The successful accomplishment of the expedition may be greatly facilitated by suitable legislative provisions, and particularly by an appropriation to defray its necessary expense. The addition of a second, and perhaps a third, vessel, with a slight aggravation of the cost, would contribute much to the safety of the citizens embarked on this undertaking, the results of which may be of the deepest interest to our country.

With the report of the Secretary of the Navy will be submitted, in conformity to the act of Congress of 3d March, 1827, for the gradual improvement of the Navy of the United States, statements of the expenditures under that act and of the measures taken for carrying the same into effect. Every section of that statute contains a distinct provision looking to the great object of the whole—the gradual improvement of the Navy. Under its salutary sanction stores of ship timber have been procured and are in process of seasoning and preservation for the future uses of the Navy. Arrangements have been made for the preservation of the live-oak timber growing on the lands of the United States, and for its reproduction, to supply at future and distant days the waste of that most valuable material for shipbuilding by the great consumption of it yearly for the commercial as well as for the military marine of our country. The construction of the two dry docks at Charlestown and at Norfolk is making satisfactory progress toward a durable establishment. The examinations and inquiries to ascertain the practicability and expediency of a marine railway at Pensacola, though not yet accomplished, have been postponed but to be more effectually made. The navy-yards of the United States have been examined, and plans for their improvement and the preservation of the public property therein at Portsmouth, Charlestown, Philadelphia, Washington, and Gosport, and to which two others are to be added, have been prepared and received my sanction; and no other portion of my public duties has been performed with a more intimate conviction of its importance to the future welfare and security of the Union.

With the report from the Postmaster-General is exhibited a comparative view of the gradual increase of that establishment, from five to five years, since 1792 till this time in the number of post-offices, which has grown from less than 200 to nearly 8,000; in the revenue yielded by them, which from $67,000 has swollen to upward of a million and a half, and in the number of miles of post-roads, which from 5,642 have multiplied to 114,536. While in the same period of time the population of the Union has about thrice doubled, the rate of increase of these offices is nearly 40, and of the revenue and of traveled miles from 20 to 25 for 1. The increase of revenue within the last five years has been nearly equal to the whole revenue of the Department in 1812.

The expenditures of the Department during the year which ended on the 1st of July last have exceeded the receipts by a sum of about $25,000. The excess has been occasioned by the increase of mail conveyances and facilities to the extent of near 800,000 miles. It has been supplied by collections from the postmasters of the arrearages of preceding years. While the correct principle seems to be that the income levied by the Department should defray all its expenses, it has never been the policy of this Government to raise from this establishment any revenue to be applied to any other purposes. The suggestion of the Postmaster-General that the insurance of the safe transmission of moneys by the mail might be assumed by the Department for a moderate and competent remuneration will deserve the consideration of Congress.

A report from the commissioner of the public buildings in this city exhibits the expenditures upon them in the course of the current year. It will be seen that the humane and benevolent intentions of Congress in providing, by the act of 20th May, 1826, for the erection of a penitentiary in this District have been accomplished. The authority of further legislation is now required for the removal to this tenement of the offenders against the laws sentenced to atone by personal confinement for their crimes, and to provide a code for their employment and government while thus confined.

The commissioners appointed, conformably to the act of 2d March, 1827, to provide for the adjustment of claims of persons entitled to indemnification under the first article of the treaty of Ghent, and for the distribution among such claimants of the sum paid by the Government of Great Britain under the convention of 13th of November, 1826, closed their labors on the 30th of August last by awarding to the claimants the sum of $1,197,422.18, leaving a balance of $7,537.82, which was distributed ratably amongst all the claimants to whom awards had been made, according to the directions of the act.

The exhibits appended to the report from the Commissioner of the General Land Office present the actual condition of that common property of the Union. The amount paid into the Treasury from the proceeds of lands during the year 1827 and the first half of 1828 falls little short of $2,000,000. The propriety of further extending the time for the extinguishment of the debt due to the United States by the purchasers of the public lands, limited by the act of 21st March last to the 4th of July next, will claim the consideration of Congress, to whose vigilance and careful attention the regulation, disposal, and preservation of this great national inheritance has by the people of the United States been intrusted.

Among the important subjects to which the attention of the present Congress has already been invited, and which may occupy their further and deliberate discussion, will be the provision to be made for taking the fifth census or enumeration of the inhabitants of the United States. The Constitution of the United States requires that this enumeration should be made within every term of ten years, and the date from which the last enumeration commenced was the first Monday of August of the year 1820. The laws under which the former enumerations were taken were enacted at the session of Congress immediately preceding the operation; but considerable inconveniences were experienced from the delay of legislation to so late a period. That law, like those of the preceding enumerations, directed that the census should be taken by the marshals of the several districts and Territories of the Union under instructions from the Secretary of State. The preparation and transmission to the marshals of those instructions required more time than was then allowed between the passage of the law and the day when the enumeration was to commence. The term of six months limited for the returns of the marshals was also found even then too short, and must be more so now, when an additional population of at least 3,000,000 must be presented upon the returns. As they are to be made at the short session of Congress, it would, as well as from other considerations, be more convenient to commence the enumeration from an earlier period of the year than the 1st of August. The most favorable season would be the spring. On a review of the former enumerations it will be found that the plan for taking every census has contained many improvements upon that of its predecessor. The last is still susceptible of much improvement. The Third Census was the first at which any account was taken of the manufactures of the country. It was repeated at the last enumeration, but the returns in both cases were necessarily very imperfect. They must always be so, resting, of course, only upon the communications voluntarily made by individuals interested in some of the manufacturing establishments. Yet they contained much valuable information, and may by some supplementary provision of the law be rendered more effective. The columns of age, commencing from infancy, have hitherto been confined to a few periods, all under the number of 45 years. Important knowledge would be obtained by extending these columns, in intervals of ten years, to the utmost boundaries of human life. The labor of taking them would be a trifling addition to that already prescribed, and the result would exhibit comparative tables of longevity highly interesting to the country. I deem it my duty further to observe that much of the imperfections in the returns of the last and perhaps of preceding enumerations proceeded from the inadequateness of the compensations allowed to the marshals and their assistants in taking them.

In closing this communication it only remains for me to assure the Legislature of my continued earnest wish for the adoption of measures recommended by me heretofore and yet to be acted on by them, and of the cordial concurrence on my part in every constitutional provision which may receive their sanction during the session tending to the general welfare.

Andrew Jackson

March 4, 1829 to March 4, 1837

FIRST ANNUAL MESSAGE.

Fellow-Citizens of the Senate and House of Representatives:

It affords me pleasure to tender my friendly greetings to you on the occasion of your assembling at the seat of Government to enter upon the important duties to which you have been called by the voice of our countrymen. The task devolves on me, under a provision of the Constitution, to present to you, as the Federal Legislature of twenty-four sovereign States and 12,000,000 happy people, a view of our affairs, and to propose such measures as in the discharge of my official functions have suggested themselves as necessary to promote the objects of our Union.

In communicating with you for the first time it is to me a source of unfeigned satisfaction, calling for mutual gratulation and devout thanks to a benign Providence, that we are at peace with all mankind, and that our country exhibits the most cheering evidence of general welfare and progressive improvement. Turning our eyes to other nations, our great desire is to see our brethren of the human race secured in the blessings enjoyed by ourselves, and advancing in knowledge, in freedom, and in social happiness.

Our foreign relations, although in their general character pacific and friendly, present subjects of difference between us and other powers of deep interest as well to the country at large as to many of our citizens. To effect an adjustment of these shall continue to be the object of my earnest endeavors, and notwithstanding the difficulties of the task, I do not allow myself to apprehend unfavorable results. Blessed as our country is with everything which constitutes national strength, she is fully adequate to the maintenance of all her interests. In discharging the responsible trust confided to the Executive in this respect it is my settled purpose to ask nothing that is not clearly right and to submit to nothing that is wrong; and I flatter myself that, supported by the other branches of the Government and by the intelligence and patriotism of the people, we shall be able, under the protection of Providence, to cause all our just rights to be respected.

Of the unsettled matters between the United States and other powers, the most prominent are those which have for years been the subject of negotiation with England, France, and Spain. The late periods at which our ministers to those Governments left the United States render it impossible at this early day to inform you of what has been done on the subjects with which they have been respectively charged. Relying upon the justice of our views in relation to the points committed to negotiation and the reciprocal good feeling which characterizes our intercourse with those nations, we have the best reason to hope for a satisfactory adjustment of existing differences.

With Great Britain, alike distinguished in peace and war, we may look forward to years of peaceful, honorable, and elevated competition. Everything in the condition and history of the two nations is calculated to inspire sentiments of mutual respect and to carry conviction to the minds of both that it is their policy to preserve the most cordial relations. Such are my own views, and it is not to be doubted that such are also the prevailing sentiments of our constituents. Although neither time nor opportunity has been afforded for a full development of the policy which the present cabinet of Great Britain designs to pursue toward this country, I indulge the hope that it will be of a just and pacific character; and if this anticipation be realized we may look with confidence to a speedy and acceptable adjustment of our affairs.

Under the convention for regulating the reference to arbitration of the disputed points of boundary under the fifth article of the treaty of Ghent, the proceedings have hitherto been conducted in that spirit of candor and liberality which ought ever to characterize the acts of sovereign States seeking to adjust by the most unexceptionable means important and delicate subjects of contention. The first statements of the parties have been exchanged, and the final replication on our part is in a course of preparation. This subject has received the attention demanded by its great and peculiar importance to a patriotic member of this Confederacy. The exposition of our rights already made is such as, from the high reputation of the commissioners by whom it has been prepared, we had a right to expect. Our interests at the Court of the Sovereign who has evinced his friendly disposition by assuming the delicate task of arbitration have been committed to a citizen of the State of Maine, whose character, talents, and intimate acquaintance with the subject eminently qualify him for so responsible a trust. With full confidence in the justice of our cause and in the probity, intelligence, and uncompromising independence of the illustrious arbitrator, we can have nothing to apprehend from the result.

From France, our ancient ally, we have a right to expect that justice which becomes the sovereign of a powerful, intelligent, and magnanimous people. The beneficial effects produced by the commercial convention of 1822, limited as are its provisions, are too obvious not to make a salutary impression upon the minds of those who are charged with the administration of her Government. Should this result induce a disposition to embrace to their full extent the wholesome principles which constitute our commercial policy, our minister to that Court will be found instructed to cherish such a disposition and to aid in conducting it to useful practical conclusions. The claims of our citizens for depredations upon their property, long since committed under the authority, and in many instances by the express direction, of the then existing Government of France, remain unsatisfied, and must therefore continue to furnish a subject of unpleasant discussion and possible collision between the two Governments. I cherish, however, a lively hope, founded as well on the validity of those claims and the established policy of all enlightened governments as on the known integrity of the French Monarch, that the injurious delays of the past will find redress in the equity of the future. Our minister has been instructed to press these demands on the French Government with all the earnestness which is called for by their importance and irrefutable justice, and in a spirit that will evince the respect which is due to the feelings of those from whom the satisfaction is required.

Our minister recently appointed to Spain has been authorized to assist in removing evils alike injurious to both countries, either by concluding a commercial convention upon liberal and reciprocal terms or by urging the acceptance in their full extent of the mutually beneficial provisions of our navigation acts. He has also been instructed to make a further appeal to the justice of Spain, in behalf of our citizens, for indemnity for spoliations upon our commerce committed under her authority—an appeal which the pacific and liberal course observed on our part and a due confidence in the honor of that Government authorize us to expect will not be made in vain.

With other European powers our intercourse is on the most friendly footing. In Russia, placed by her territorial limits, extensive population, and great power high in the rank of nations, the United States have always found a steadfast friend. Although her recent invasion of Turkey awakened a lively sympathy for those who were exposed to the desolations of war, we can not but anticipate that the result will prove favorable to the cause of civilization and to the progress of human happiness. The treaty of peace between these powers having been ratified, we can not be insensible to the great benefit to be derived by the commerce of the United States from unlocking the navigation of the Black Sea, a free passage into which is secured to all merchant vessels bound to ports of Russia under a flag at peace with the Porte. This advantage, enjoyed upon conditions by most of the powers of Europe, has hitherto been withheld from us. During the past summer an antecedent but unsuccessful attempt to obtain it was renewed under circumstances which promised the most favorable results. Although these results have fortunately been thus in part attained, further facilities to the enjoyment of this new field for the enterprise of our citizens are, in my opinion, sufficiently desirable to insure to them our most zealous attention.

Our trade with Austria, although of secondary importance, has been gradually increasing, and is now so extended as to deserve the fostering care of the Government. A negotiation, commenced and nearly completed with that power by the late Administration, has been consummated by a treaty of amity, navigation, and commerce, which will be laid before the Senate.

During the recess of Congress our diplomatic relations with Portugal have been resumed. The peculiar state of things in that country caused a suspension of the recognition of the representative who presented himself until an opportunity was had to obtain from our official organ there information regarding the actual and, as far as practicable, prospective condition of the authority by which the representative in question was appointed. This information being received, the application of the established rule of our Government in like cases was no longer withheld.

Considerable advances have been made during the present year in the adjustment of claims of our citizens upon Denmark for spoliations, but all that we have a right to demand from that Government in their behalf has not yet been conceded. From the liberal footing, however, upon which this subject has, with the approbation of the claimants, been placed by the Government, together with the uniformly just and friendly disposition which has been evinced by His Danish Majesty, there is a reasonable ground to hope that this single subject of difference will speedily be removed.

Our relations with the Barbary Powers continue, as they have long been, of the most favorable character. The policy of keeping an adequate force in the Mediterranean, as security for the continuance of this tranquillity, will be persevered in, as well as a similar one for the protection of our commerce and fisheries in the Pacific.

The southern Republics of our own hemisphere have not yet realized all the advantages for which they have been so long struggling. We trust, however, that the day is not distant when the restoration of peace and internal quiet, under permanent systems of government, securing the liberty and promoting the happiness of the citizens, will crown with complete success their long and arduous efforts in the cause of self-government, and enable us to salute them as friendly rivals in all that is truly great and glorious.

The recent invasion of Mexico, and the effect thereby produced upon her domestic policy, must have a controlling influence upon the great question of South American emancipation. We have seen the fell spirit of civil dissension rebuked, and perhaps forever stifled, in that Republic by the love of independence. If it be true, as appearances strongly indicate, that the spirit of independence is the master spirit, and if a corresponding sentiment prevails in the other States, this devotion to liberty can not be without a proper effect upon the counsels of the mother country. The adoption by Spain of a pacific policy toward her former colonies—an event consoling to humanity, and a blessing to the world, in which she herself can not fail largely to participate—may be most reasonably expected.

The claims of our citizens upon the South American Governments generally are in a train of settlement, while the principal part of those upon Brazil have been adjusted, and a decree in council ordering bonds to be issued by the minister of the treasury for their amount has received the sanction of His Imperial Majesty. This event, together with the exchange of the ratifications of the treaty negotiated and concluded in 1828, happily terminates all serious causes of difference with that power.

Measures have been taken to place our commercial relations with Peru upon a better footing than that upon which they have hitherto rested, and if met by a proper disposition on the part of that Government important benefits may be secured to both countries.

Deeply interested as we are in the prosperity of our sister Republics, and more particularly in that of our immediate neighbor, it would be most gratifying to me were I permitted to say that the treatment which we have received at her hands has been as universally friendly as the early and constant solicitude manifested by the United States for her success gave us a right to expect. But it becomes my duty to inform you that prejudices long indulged by a portion of the inhabitants of Mexico against the envoy extraordinary and minister plenipotentiary of the United States have had an unfortunate influence upon the affairs of the two countries, and have diminished that usefulness to his own which was justly to be expected from his talents and zeal. To this cause, in a great degree, is to be imputed the failure of several measures equally interesting to both parties, but particularly that of the Mexican Government to ratify a treaty negotiated and concluded in its own capital and under its own eye. Under these circumstances it appeared expedient to give to Mr. Poinsett the option either to return or not, as in his judgment the interest of his country might require, and instructions to that end were prepared; but before they could be dispatched a communication was received from the Government of Mexico, through its chargé d'affaires here, requesting the recall of our minister. This was promptly complied with, and a representative of a rank corresponding with that of the Mexican diplomatic agent near this Government was appointed. Our conduct toward that Republic has been uniformly of the most friendly character, and having thus removed the only alleged obstacle to harmonious intercourse, I can not but hope that an advantageous change will occur in our affairs.

In justice to Mr. Poinsett it is proper to say that my immediate compliance with the application for his recall and the appointment of a successor are not to be ascribed to any evidence that the imputation of an improper interference by him in the local politics of Mexico was well founded, nor to a want of confidence in his talents or integrity, and to add that the truth of that charge has never been affirmed by the federal Government of Mexico in its communications with this.

I consider it one of the most urgent of my duties to bring to your attention the propriety of amending that part of our Constitution which relates to the election of President and Vice-President. Our system of government was by its framers deemed an experiment, and they therefore consistently provided a mode of remedying its defects.

To the people belongs the right of electing their Chief Magistrate; it was never designed that their choice should in any case be defeated, either by the intervention of electoral colleges or by the agency confided, under certain contingencies, to the House of Representatives. Experience proves that in proportion as agents to execute the will of the people are multiplied there is danger of their wishes being frustrated. Some may be unfaithful; all are liable to err. So far, therefore, as the people can with convenience speak, it is safer for them to express their own will.

The number of aspirants to the Presidency and the diversity of the interests which may influence their claims leave little reason to expect a choice in the first instance, and in that event the election must devolve on the House of Representatives, where it is obvious the will of the people may not be always ascertained, or, if ascertained, may not be regarded. From the mode of voting by States the choice is to be made by 24 votes, and it may often occur that one of these will be controlled by an individual Representative. Honors and offices are at the disposal of the successful candidate. Repeated ballotings may make it apparent that a single individual holds the cast in his hand. May he not be tempted to name his reward? But even without corruption, supposing the probity of the Representative to be proof against the powerful motives by which it may be assailed, the will of the people is still constantly liable to be misrepresented. One may err from ignorance of the wishes of his constituents; another from a conviction that it is his duty to be governed by his own judgment of the fitness of the candidates; finally, although all were inflexibly honest, all accurately informed of the wishes of their constituents, yet under the present mode of election a minority may often elect a President, and when this happens it may reasonably be expected that efforts will be made on the part of the majority to rectify this injurious operation of their institutions. But although no evil of this character should result from such a perversion of the first principle of our system—*that the majority is to govern*—it must be very certain that a President elected by a minority can not enjoy the confidence necessary to the successful discharge of his duties.

In this as in all other matters of public concern policy requires that as few impediments as possible should exist to the free operation of the public will. Let us, then, endeavor so to amend our system that the office of Chief Magistrate may not be conferred upon any citizen but in pursuance of a fair expression of the will of the majority.

I would therefore recommend such an amendment of the Constitution as may remove all intermediate agency in the election of the President and Vice-President. The mode may be so regulated as to preserve to each State its present relative weight in the election, and a failure in the first attempt may be provided for by confining the second to a choice between the two highest candidates. In connection with such an amendment it would seem advisable to limit the service of the Chief Magistrate to a single term of either four or six years.   If, however, it should not be adopted, it is worthy of consideration whether a provision disqualifying for office the Representatives in Congress on whom such an election may have devolved would not be proper.

While members of Congress can be constitutionally appointed to offices of trust and profit it will be the practice, even under the most conscientious adherence to duty, to select them for such stations as they are believed to be better qualified to fill than other citizens; but the purity of our Government would doubtless be promoted by their exclusion from all appointments in the gift of the President, in whose election they may have been officially concerned.   The nature of the judicial office and the necessity of securing in the Cabinet and in diplomatic stations of the highest rank the best talents and political experience should, perhaps, except these from the exclusion.

There are, perhaps, few men who can for any great length of time enjoy office and power without being more or less under the influence of feelings unfavorable to the faithful discharge of their public duties. Their integrity may be proof against improper considerations immediately addressed to themselves, but they are apt to acquire a habit of looking with indifference upon the public interests and of tolerating conduct from which an unpracticed man would revolt.   Office is considered as a species of property, and government rather as a means of promoting individual interests than as an instrument created solely for the service of the people.   Corruption in some and in others a perversion of correct feelings and principles divert government from its legitimate ends and make it an engine for the support of the few at the expense of the many. The duties of all public officers are, or at least admit of being made, so plain and simple that men of intelligence may readily qualify themselves for their performance; and I can not but believe that more is lost by the long continuance of men in office than is generally to be gained by their experience.   I submit, therefore, to your consideration whether the efficiency of the Government would not be promoted and official industry and integrity better secured by a general extension of the law which limits appointments to four years.

In a country where offices are created solely for the benefit of the people no one man has any more intrinsic right to official station than another.   Offices were not established to give support to particular men at the public expense.   No individual wrong is, therefore, done by removal, since neither appointment to nor continuance in office is matter of right. The incumbent became an officer with a view to public benefits, and when these require his removal they are not to be sacrificed to private interests.   It is the people, and they alone, who have a right to complain when a bad officer is substituted for a good one.   He who is removed has the same means of obtaining a living that are enjoyed by the millions who never held office.   The proposed limitation would destroy the idea of property now so generally connected with official station, and although individual distress may be sometimes produced, it would, by promoting that rotation which constitutes a leading principle in the republican creed, give healthful action to the system.

No very considerable change has occurred during the recess of Congress in the condition of either our agriculture, commerce, or manufactures. The operation of the tariff has not proved so injurious to the two former or as beneficial to the latter as was anticipated. Importations of foreign goods have not been sensibly diminished, while domestic competition, under an illusive excitement, has increased the production much beyond the demand for home consumption. The consequences have been low prices, temporary embarrassment, and partial loss. That such of our manufacturing establishments as are based upon capital and are prudently managed will survive the shock and be ultimately profitable there is no good reason to doubt.

To regulate its conduct so as to promote equally the prosperity of these three cardinal interests is one of the most difficult tasks of Government; and it may be regretted that the complicated restrictions which now embarrass the intercourse of nations could not by common consent be abolished, and commerce allowed to flow in those channels to which individual enterprise, always its surest guide, might direct it. But we must ever expect selfish legislation in other nations, and are therefore compelled to adapt our own to their regulations in the manner best calculated to avoid serious injury and to harmonize the conflicting interests of our agriculture, our commerce, and our manufactures. Under these impressions I invite your attention to the existing tariff, believing that some of its provisions require modification.

The general rule to be applied in graduating the duties upon articles of foreign growth or manufacture is that which will place our own in fair competition with those of other countries; and the inducements to advance even a step beyond this point are controlling in regard to those articles which are of primary necessity in time of war. When we reflect upon the difficulty and delicacy of this operation, it is important that it should never be attempted but with the utmost caution. Frequent legislation in regard to any branch of industry, affecting its value, and by which its capital may be transferred to new channels, must always be productive of hazardous speculation and loss.

In deliberating, therefore, on these interesting subjects local feelings and prejudices should be merged in the patriotic determination to promote the great interests of the whole. All attempts to connect them with the party conflicts of the day are necessarily injurious, and should be discountenanced. Our action upon them should be under the control of higher and purer motives. Legislation subjected to such influences can never be just, and will not long retain the sanction of a people whose active patriotism is not bounded by sectional limits nor insensible to that

spirit of concession and forbearance which gave life to our political compact and still sustains it.   Discarding all calculations of political ascendency, the North, the South, the East, and the West should unite in
diminishing any burthen of which either may justly complain.

The agricultural interest of our country is so essentially connected
with every other and so superior in importance to them all that it is
scarcely necessary to invite to it your particular attention.   It is principally as manufactures and commerce tend to increase the value of agricultural productions and to extend their application to the wants and
comforts of society that they deserve the fostering care of Government.

Looking forward to the period, not far distant, when a sinking fund
will no longer be required, the duties on those articles of importation
which can not come in competition with our own productions are the
first that should engage the attention of Congress in the modification of
the tariff.   Of these, tea and coffee are the most prominent.   They enter
largely into the consumption of the country, and have become articles of
necessity to all classes.   A reduction, therefore, of the existing duties
will be felt as a common benefit, but like all other legislation connected
with commerce, to be efficacious and not injurious it should be gradual
and certain.

The public prosperity is evinced in the increased revenue arising from
the sales of the public lands and in the steady maintenance of that produced by imposts and tonnage, notwithstanding the additional duties
imposed by the act of 19th May, 1828, and the unusual importations in
the early part of that year.

The balance in the Treasury on January 1, 1829, was \$5,972,435.81.
The receipts of the current year are estimated at \$24,602,230 and the
expenditures for the same time at \$26,164,595, leaving a balance in
the Treasury on the 1st of January next of \$4,410,070.81.

There will have been paid on account of the public debt during the
present year the sum of \$12,405,005.80, reducing the whole debt of the
Government on the 1st of January next to \$48,565,406.50, including
seven millions of 5 per cent stock subscribed to the Bank of the United
States.   The payment on account of public debt made on the 1st of
July last was \$8,715,462.87.   It was apprehended that the sudden with-
drawal of so large a sum from the banks in which it was deposited, at a
time of unusual pressure in the money market, might cause much injury
to the interests dependent on bank accommodations.   But this evil was
wholly averted by an early anticipation of it at the Treasury, aided by
the judicious arrangements of the officers of the Bank of the United
States.

This state of the finances exhibits the resources of the nation in an
aspect highly flattering to its industry and auspicious of the ability of
Government in a very short time to extinguish the public debt.   When
this shall be done our population will be relieved from a considerable

portion of its present burthens, and will find not only new motives to patriotic affection, but additional means for the display of individual enterprise. The fiscal power of the States will also be increased, and may be more extensively exerted in favor of education and other public objects, while ample means will remain in the Federal Government to promote the general weal in all the modes permitted to its authority.

After the extinction of the public debt it is not probable that any adjustment of the tariff upon principles satisfactory to the people of the Union will until a remote period, if ever, leave the Government without a considerable surplus in the Treasury beyond what may be required for its current service. As, then, the period approaches when the application of the revenue to the payment of debt will cease, the disposition of the surplus will present a subject for the serious deliberation of Congress; and it may be fortunate for the country that it is yet to be decided. Considered in connection with the difficulties which have heretofore attended appropriations for purposes of internal improvement, and with those which this experience tells us will certainly arise whenever power over such subjects may be exercised by the General Government, it is hoped that it may lead to the adoption of some plan which will reconcile the diversified interests of the States and strengthen the bonds which unite them. Every member of the Union, in peace and in war, will be benefited by the improvement of inland navigation and the construction of highways in the several States. Let us, then, endeavor to attain this benefit in a mode which will be satisfactory to all. That hitherto adopted has by many of our fellow-citizens been deprecated as an infraction of the Constitution, while by others it has been viewed as inexpedient. All feel that it has been employed at the expense of harmony in the legislative councils.

To avoid these evils it appears to me that the most safe, just, and federal disposition which could be made of the surplus revenue would be its apportionment among the several States according to their ratio of representation, and should this measure not be found warranted by the Constitution that it would be expedient to propose to the States an amendment authorizing it. I regard an appeal to the source of power in cases of real doubt, and where its exercise is deemed indispensable to the general welfare, as among the most sacred of all our obligations. Upon this country more than any other has, in the providence of God, been cast the special guardianship of the great principle of adherence to written constitutions. If it fail here, all hope in regard to it will be extinguished. That this was intended to be a government of limited and specific, and not general, powers must be admitted by all, and it is our duty to preserve for it the character intended by its framers. If experience points out the necessity for an enlargement of these powers, let us apply for it to those for whose benefit it is to be exercised, and not undermine the whole system by a resort to overstrained constructions.

The scheme has worked well. It has exceeded the hopes of those who devised it, and become an object of admiration to the world. We are responsible to our country and to the glorious cause of self-government for the preservation of so great a good. The great mass of legislation relating to our internal affairs was intended to be left where the Federal Convention found it—in the State governments. Nothing is clearer, in my view, than that we are chiefly indebted for the success of the Constitution under which we are now acting to the watchful and auxiliary operation of the State authorities. This is not the reflection of a day, but belongs to the most deeply rooted convictions of my mind. I can not, therefore, too strongly or too earnestly, for my own sense of its importance, warn you against all encroachments upon the legitimate sphere of State sovereignty. Sustained by its healthful and invigorating influence the federal system can never fall.

In the collection of the revenue the long credits authorized on goods imported from beyond the Cape of Good Hope are the chief cause of the losses at present sustained. If these were shortened to six, nine, and twelve months, and warehouses provided by Government sufficient to receive the goods offered in deposit for security and for debenture, and if the right of the United States to a priority of payment out of the estates of its insolvent debtors were more effectually secured, this evil would in a great measure be obviated. An authority to construct such houses is therefore, with the proposed alteration of the credits, recommended to your attention.

It is worthy of notice that the laws for the collection and security of the revenue arising from imposts were chiefly framed when the rates of duties on imported goods presented much less temptation for illicit trade than at present exists. There is reason to believe that these laws are in some respects quite insufficient for the proper security of the revenue and the protection of the interests of those who are disposed to observe them. The injurious and demoralizing tendency of a successful system of smuggling is so obvious as not to require comment, and can not be too carefully guarded against. I therefore suggest to Congress the propriety of adopting efficient measures to prevent this evil, avoiding, however, as much as possible, every unnecessary infringement of individual liberty and embarrassment of fair and lawful business.

On an examination of the records of the Treasury I have been forcibly struck with the large amount of public money which appears to be outstanding. Of the sum thus due from individuals to the Government a considerable portion is undoubtedly desperate, and in many instances has probably been rendered so by remissness in the agents charged with its collection. By proper exertions a great part, however, may yet be recovered; and whatever may be the portions respectively belonging to these two classes, it behooves the Government to ascertain the real state of the fact. This can be done only by the prompt adoption of judicious measures for the collection of such as may be made available. It is believed that a very large amount has been lost through the inadequacy of the means provided for the collection of debts due to the public, and that this inadequacy lies chiefly in the want of legal skill habitually and constantly employed in the direction of the agents engaged in the service. It must, I think, be admitted that the supervisory power over suits brought by the public, which is now vested in an *accounting* officer of the Treasury, not selected with a view to his legal knowledge, and encumbered as he is with numerous other duties, operates unfavorably to the public interest.

It is important that this branch of the public service should be subjected to the supervision of such professional skill as will give it efficiency. The expense attendant upon such a modification of the executive department would be justified by the soundest principles of economy. I would recommend, therefore, that the duties now assigned to the agent of the Treasury, so far as they relate to the superintendence and management of legal proceedings on the part of the United States, be transferred to the Attorney-General, and that this officer be placed on the same footing in all respects as the heads of the other Departments, receiving like compensation and having such subordinate officers provided for his Department as may be requisite for the discharge of these additional duties. The professional skill of the Attorney-General, employed in directing the conduct of marshals and district attorneys, would hasten the collection of debts now in suit and hereafter save much to the Government. It might be further extended to the superintendence of all criminal proceedings for offenses against the United States. In making this transfer great care should be taken, however, that the power necessary to the Treasury Department be not impaired, one of its greatest securities consisting in a control over all accounts until they are audited or reported for suit.

In connection with the foregoing views I would suggest also an inquiry whether the provisions of the act of Congress authorizing the discharge of the persons of debtors to the Government from imprisonment may not, consistently with the public interest, be extended to the release of the debt where the conduct of the debtor is wholly exempt from the imputation of fraud. Some more liberal policy than that which now prevails in reference to this unfortunate class of citizens is certainly due to them, and would prove beneficial to the country. The continuance of the liability after the means to discharge it have been exhausted can only serve to dispirit the debtor; or, where his resources are but partial, the want of power in the Government to compromise and release the demand instigates to fraud as the only resource for securing a support to his family. He thus sinks into a state of apathy, and becomes a useless drone in society or a vicious member of it, if not a feeling witness of the rigor and inhumanity of his country. All experience proves that oppressive debt is the bane of enterprise, and it should be the care of a republic not to exert a grinding power over misfortune and poverty.

Since the last session of Congress numerous frauds on the Treasury have been discovered, which I thought it my duty to bring under the cognizance of the United States court for this district by a criminal prosecution. It was my opinion and that of able counsel who were consulted that the cases came within the penalties of the act of the Seventeenth Congress approved 3d March, 1823, providing for the punishment of frauds committed on the Government of the United States. Either from some defect in the law or in its administration every effort to bring the accused to trial under its provisions proved ineffectual, and the Government was driven to the necessity of resorting to the vague and inadequate provisions of the common law. It is therefore my duty to call your attention to the laws which have been passed for the protection of the Treasury. If, indeed, there be no provision by which those who may be unworthily intrusted with its guardianship can be punished for the most flagrant violation of duty, extending even to the most fraudulent appropriation of the public funds to their own use, it is time to remedy so dangerous an omission; or if the law has been perverted from its original purposes, and criminals deserving to be punished under its provisions have been rescued by legal subtleties, it ought to be made so plain by amendatory provisions as to baffle the arts of perversion and accomplish the ends of its original enactment.

In one of the most flagrant cases the court decided that the prosecution was barred by the statute which limits prosecutions for fraud to two years. In this case all the evidences of the fraud, and, indeed, all knowledge that a fraud had been committed, were in possession of the party accused until after the two years had elapsed. Surely the statute ought not to run in favor of any man while he retains all the evidences of his crime in his own possession, and least of all in favor of a public officer who continues to defraud the Treasury and conceal the transaction for the brief term of two years. I would therefore recommend such an alteration of the law as will give the injured party and the Government two years after the disclosure of the fraud or after the accused is out of office to commence their prosecution.

In connection with this subject I invite the attention of Congress to a general and minute inquiry into the condition of the Government, with a view to ascertain what offices can be dispensed with, what expenses retrenched, and what improvements may be made in the organization of its various parts to secure the proper responsibility of public agents and promote efficiency and justice in all its operations.

The report of the Secretary of War will make you acquainted with the condition of our Army, fortifications, arsenals, and Indian affairs. The proper discipline of the Army, the training and equipment of the militia, the education bestowed at West Point, and the accumulation of the means of defense applicable to the naval force will tend to prolong the peace we now enjoy, and which every good citizen, more especially those who have felt the miseries of even a successful warfare, must ardently desire to perpetuate.

The returns from the subordinate branches of this service exhibit a regularity and order highly creditable to its character. Both officers and soldiers seem imbued with a proper sense of duty, and conform to the restraints of exact discipline with that cheerfulness which becomes the profession of arms. There is need, however, of further legislation to obviate the inconveniences specified in the report under consideration, to some of which it is proper that I should call your particular attention.

The act of Congress of the 2d March, 1821, to reduce and fix the military establishment, remaining unexecuted as it regards the command of one of the regiments of artillery, can not now be deemed a guide to the Executive in making the proper appointment. An explanatory act, designating the class of officers out of which this grade is to be filled— whether from the military list as existing prior to the act of 1821 or from it as it has been fixed by that act—would remove this difficulty. It is also important that the laws regulating the pay and emoluments of officers generally should be more specific than they now are. Those, for example, in relation to the Paymaster and Surgeon General assign to them an annual salary of $2,500, but are silent as to allowances which in certain exigencies of the service may be deemed indispensable to the discharge of their duties. This circumstance has been the authority for extending to them various allowances at different times under former Administrations, but no uniform rule has been observed on the subject. Similar inconveniences exist in other cases, in which the construction put upon the laws by the public accountants may operate unequally, produce confusion, and expose officers to the odium of claiming what is not their due.

I recommend to your fostering care, as one of our safest means of national defense, the Military Academy. This institution has already exercised the happiest influence upon the moral and intellectual character of our Army; and such of the graduates as from various causes may not pursue the profession of arms will be scarcely less useful as citizens. Their knowledge of the military art will be advantageously employed in the militia service, and in a measure secure to that class of troops the advantages which in this respect belong to standing armies.

I would also suggest a review of the pension law, for the purpose of extending its benefits to every Revolutionary soldier who aided in establishing our liberties, and who is unable to maintain himself in comfort. These relics of the War of Independence have strong claims upon their country's gratitude and bounty. The law is defective in not embracing within its provisions all those who were during the last war disabled from supporting themselves by manual labor. Such an amendment would add but little to the amount of pensions, and is called for by the sympathies of the people as well as by considerations of sound policy. It will be perceived that a large addition to the list of pensioners has been occasioned by an order of the late Administration, departing materially from the rules which had previously prevailed. Considering it an act of legislation, I suspended its operation as soon as I was informed that it had commenced. Before this period, however, applications under the new regulation had been preferred to the number of 154, of which, on the 27th March, the date of its revocation, 87 were admitted. For the amount there was neither estimate nor appropriation; and besides this deficiency, the regular allowances, according to the rules which have heretofore governed the Department, exceed the estimate of its late Secretary by about $50,000, for which an appropriation is asked.

Your particular attention is requested to that part of the report of the Secretary of War which relates to the money held in trust for the Seneca tribe of Indians. It will be perceived that without legislative aid the Executive can not obviate the embarrassments occasioned by the diminution of the dividends on that fund, which originally amounted to $100,000, and has recently been invested in United States 3 per cent stock.

The condition and ulterior destiny of the Indian tribes within the limits of some of our States have become objects of much interest and importance. It has long been the policy of Government to introduce among them the arts of civilization, in the hope of gradually reclaiming them from a wandering life. This policy has, however, been coupled with another wholly incompatible with its success. Professing a desire to civilize and settle them, we have at the same time lost no opportunity to purchase their lands and thrust them farther into the wilderness. By this means they have not only been kept in a wandering state, but been led to look upon us as unjust and indifferent to their fate. Thus, though lavish in its expenditures upon the subject, Government has constantly defeated its own policy, and the Indians in general, receding farther and farther to the west, have retained their savage habits. A portion, however, of the Southern tribes, having mingled much with the whites and made some progress in the arts of civilized life, have lately attempted to erect an independent government within the limits of Georgia and Alabama. These States, claiming to be the only sovereigns within their territories, extended their laws over the Indians, which induced the latter to call upon the United States for protection.

Under these circumstances the question presented was whether the General Government had a right to sustain those people in their pretensions. The Constitution declares that "no new State shall be formed or erected within the jurisdiction of any other State" without the consent of its legislature. If the General Government is not permitted to tolerate the erection of a confederate State within the territory of one of the members of this Union against her consent, much less could it allow a foreign and independent government to establish itself there. Georgia became a member of the Confederacy which eventuated in our Federal Union as a sovereign State, always asserting her claim to certain limits, which, having been originally defined in her colonial charter and subsequently recognized in the treaty of peace, she has ever since continued to enjoy, except as they have been circumscribed by her own voluntary transfer of a portion of her territory to the United States in the articles of cession of 1802. Alabama was admitted into the Union on the same footing with the original States, with boundaries which were prescribed by Congress. There is no constitutional, conventional, or legal provision which allows them less power over the Indians within their borders than is possessed by Maine or New York. Would the people of Maine permit the Penobscot tribe to erect an independent government within their State? And unless they did would it not be the duty of the General Government to support them in resisting such a measure? Would the people of New York permit each remnant of the Six Nations within her borders to declare itself an independent people under the protection of the United States? Could the Indians establish a separate republic on each of their reservations in Ohio? And if they were so disposed would it be the duty of this Government to protect them in the attempt? If the principle involved in the obvious answer to these questions be abandoned, it will follow that the objects of this Government are reversed, and that it has become a part of its duty to aid in destroying the States which it was established to protect.

Actuated by this view of the subject, I informed the Indians inhabiting parts of Georgia and Alabama that their attempt to establish an independent government would not be countenanced by the Executive of the United States, and advised them to emigrate beyond the Mississippi or submit to the laws of those States.

Our conduct toward these people is deeply interesting to our national character. Their present condition, contrasted with what they once were, makes a most powerful appeal to our sympathies. Our ancestors found them the uncontrolled possessors of these vast regions. By persuasion and force they have been made to retire from river to river and from mountain to mountain, until some of the tribes have become extinct and others have left but remnants to preserve for awhile their once terrible names. Surrounded by the whites with their arts of civilization, which by destroying the resources of the savage doom him to weakness and decay, the fate of the Mohegan, the Narragansett, and the Delaware is fast overtaking the Choctaw, the Cherokee, and the Creek. That this fate surely awaits them if they remain within the limits of the States does not admit of a doubt. Humanity and national honor demand that every effort should be made to avert so great a calamity. It is too late to inquire whether it was just in the United States to include them and their territory within the bounds of new States, whose limits they could control. That step can not be retraced. A State can not be dismembered by Congress or restricted in the exercise of her constitutional power. But the people of those States and of every State, actuated by feelings of justice and a regard for our national honor, submit to you the interesting question whether something can not be done, consistently with the rights of the States, to preserve this much-injured race.

As a means of effecting this end I suggest for your consideration the propriety of setting apart an ample district west of the Mississippi, and without the limits of any State or Territory now formed, to be guaranteed to the Indian tribes as long as they shall occupy it, each tribe having a distinct control over the portion designated for its use. There they may be secured in the enjoyment of governments of their own choice, subject to no other control from the United States than such as may be necessary to preserve peace on the frontier and between the several tribes. There the benevolent may endeavor to teach them the arts of civilization, and, by promoting union and harmony among them, to raise up an interesting commonwealth, destined to perpetuate the race and to attest the humanity and justice of this Government.

This emigration should be voluntary, for it would be as cruel as unjust to compel the aborigines to abandon the graves of their fathers and seek a home in a distant land. But they should be distinctly informed that if they remain within the limits of the States they must be subject to their laws. In return for their obedience as individuals they will without doubt be protected in the enjoyment of those possessions which they have improved by their industry. But it seems to me visionary to suppose that in this state of things claims can be allowed on tracts of country on which they have neither dwelt nor made improvements, merely because they have seen them from the mountain or passed them in the chase. Submitting to the laws of the States, and receiving, like other citizens, protection in their persons and property, they will ere long become merged in the mass of our population.

The accompanying report of the Secretary of the Navy will make you acquainted with the condition and useful employment of that branch of our service during the present year. Constituting as it does the best standing security of this country against foreign aggression, it claims the especial attention of Government. In this spirit the measures which since the termination of the last war have been in operation for its gradual enlargement were adopted, and it should continue to be cherished as the offspring of our national experience. It will be seen, however, that notwithstanding the great solicitude which has been manifested for the perfect organization of this arm and the liberality of the appropriations which that solicitude has suggested, this object has in many important respects not been secured.

In time of peace we have need of no more ships of war than are requisite to the protection of our commerce. Those not wanted for this object must lay in the harbors, where without proper covering they rapidly decay, and even under the best precautions for their preservation must soon become useless. Such is already the case with many of our finest vessels, which, though unfinished, will now require immense sums of money to be restored to the condition in which they were when committed to their proper element. On this subject there can be but little doubt that our best policy would be to discontinue the building of ships of the first and second class, and look rather to the possession of ample materials, prepared for the emergencies of war, than to the number of vessels which we can float in a season of peace, as the index of our naval power. Judicious deposits in navy-yards of timber and other materials, fashioned under the hands of skillful workmen and fitted for prompt application to their various purposes, would enable us at all times to construct vessels as fast as they can be manned, and save the heavy expense of repairs, except to such vessels as must be employed in guarding our commerce. The proper points for the establishment of these yards are indicated with so much force in the report of the Navy Board that in recommending it to your attention I deem it unnecessary to do more than express my hearty concurrence in their views. The yard in this District, being already furnished with most of the machinery necessary for shipbuilding, will be competent to the supply of the two selected by the Board as the best for the concentration of materials, and, from the facility and certainty of communication between them, it will be useless to incur at those depots the expense of similar machinery, especially that used in preparing the usual metallic and wooden furniture of vessels.

Another improvement would be effected by dispensing altogether with the Navy Board as now constituted, and substituting in its stead bureaus similar to those already existing in the War Department. Each member of the Board, transferred to the head of a separate bureau charged with specific duties, would feel in its highest degree that wholesome responsibility which can not be divided without a far more than proportionate diminution of its force. Their valuable services would become still more so when separately appropriated to distinct portions of the great interests of the Navy, to the prosperity of which each would be impelled to devote himself by the strongest motives. Under such an arrangement every branch of this important service would assume a more simple and precise character, its efficiency would be increased, and scrupulous economy in the expenditure of public money promoted.

I would also recommend that the Marine Corps be merged in the artillery or infantry, as the best mode of curing the many defects in its organization. But little exceeding in number any of the regiments of infantry, that corps has, besides its lieutenant-colonel commandant, five brevet lieutenant-colonels, who receive the full pay and emoluments of their brevet rank, without rendering proportionate service. Details for marine service could as well be made from the artillery or infantry, there being no peculiar training requisite for it.

With these improvements, and such others as zealous watchfulness and mature consideration may suggest, there can be little doubt that under an energetic administration of its affairs the Navy may soon be made everything that the nation wishes it to be. Its efficiency in the suppression of piracy in the West India seas, and wherever its squadrons have been employed in securing the interests of the country, will appear from the report of the Secretary, to which I refer you for other interesting details. Among these I would bespeak the attention of Congress for the views presented in relation to the inequality between the Army and Navy as to the pay of officers. No such inequality should prevail between these brave defenders of their country, and where it does exist it is submitted to Congress whether it ought not to be rectified.

The report of the Postmaster-General is referred to as exhibiting a highly satisfactory administration of that Department. Abuses have been reformed, increased expedition in the transportation of the mail secured, and its revenue much improved. In a political point of view this Department is chiefly important as affording the means of diffusing knowledge. It is to the body politic what the veins and arteries are to the natural—conveying rapidly and regularly to the remotest parts of the system correct information of the operations of the Government, and bringing back to it the wishes and feelings of the people. Through its agency we have secured to ourselves the full enjoyment of the blessings of a free press.

In this general survey of our affairs a subject of high importance presents itself in the present organization of the judiciary. An uniform operation of the Federal Government in the different States is certainly desirable, and existing as they do in the Union on the basis of perfect equality, each State has a right to expect that the benefits conferred on the citizens of others should be extended to hers. The judicial system of the United States exists in all its efficiency in only fifteen members of the Union; to three others the circuit courts, which constitute an important part of that system, have been imperfectly extended, and to the remaining six altogether denied. The effect has been to withhold from the inhabitants of the latter the advantages afforded (by the Supreme Court) to their fellow-citizens in other States in the whole extent of the criminal and much of the civil authority of the Federal judiciary. That this state of things ought to be remedied, if it can be done consistently with the public welfare, is not to be doubted. Neither is it to be disguised that the organization of our judicial system is at once a difficult and delicate task. To extend the circuit courts equally throughout the different parts of the Union, and at the same time to avoid such a multiplication of members as would encumber the supreme appellate tribunal, is the object desired. Perhaps it might be accomplished by dividing the circuit judges into two classes, and providing that the Supreme Court should be held by these classes alternately, the Chief Justice always presiding.

If an extension of the circuit-court system to those States which do not now enjoy its benefits should be determined upon, it would of course be necessary to revise the present arrangement of the circuits; and even if that system should not be enlarged, such a revision is recommended.

A provision for taking the census of the people of the United States will, to insure the completion of that work within a convenient time, claim the early attention of Congress.

The great and constant increase of business in the Department of State forced itself at an early period upon the attention of the Executive. Thirteen years ago it was, in Mr. Madison's last message to Congress, made the subject of an earnest recommendation, which has been repeated by both of his successors; and my comparatively limited experience has satisfied me of its justness. It has arisen from many causes, not the least of which is the large addition that has been made to the family of independent nations and the proportionate extension of our foreign relations. The remedy proposed was the establishment of a home department—a measure which does not appear to have met the views of Congress on account of its supposed tendency to increase, gradually and imperceptibly, the already too strong bias of the federal system toward the exercise of authority not delegated to it. I am not, therefore, disposed to revive the recommendation, but am not the less impressed with the importance of so organizing that Department that its Secretary may devote more of his time to our foreign relations. Clearly satisfied that the public good would be promoted by some suitable provision on the subject, I respectfully invite your attention to it.

The charter of the Bank of the United States expires in 1836, and its stockholders will most probably apply for a renewal of their privileges. In order to avoid the evils resulting from precipitancy in a measure involving such important principles and such deep pecuniary interests, I feel that I can not, in justice to the parties interested, too soon present it to the deliberate consideration of the Legislature and the people. Both the constitutionality and the expediency of the law creating this bank are well questioned by a large portion of our fellow-citizens, and it must be admitted by all that it has failed in the great end of establishing a uniform and sound currency.

Under these circumstances, if such an institution is deemed essential to the fiscal operations of the Government, I submit to the wisdom of the Legislature whether a national one, founded upon the credit of the Government and its revenues, might not be devised which would avoid all constitutional difficulties and at the same time secure all the advantages to the Government and country that were expected to result from the present bank.

I can not close this communication without bringing to your view the just claim of the representatives of Commodore Decatur, his officers and crew, arising from the recapture of the frigate *Philadelphia* under the heavy batteries of Tripoli. Although sensible, as a general rule, of the impropriety of Executive interference under a Government like ours, where every individual enjoys the right of directly petitioning Congress, yet, viewing this case as one of very peculiar character, I deem it my duty to recommend it to your favorable consideration. Besides the justice of this claim, as corresponding to those which have been since recognized and satisfied, it is the fruit of a deed of patriotic and chivalrous daring which infused life and confidence into our infant Navy and contributed as much as any exploit in its history to elevate our national character. Public gratitude, therefore, stamps her seal upon it, and the meed should not be withheld which may hereafter operate as a stimulus to our gallant tars.

I now commend you, fellow-citizens, to the guidance of Almighty God, with a full reliance on His merciful providence for the maintenance of our free institutions, and with an earnest supplication that whatever errors it may be my lot to commit in discharging the arduous duties which have devolved on me will find a remedy in the harmony and wisdom of your counsels.

SECOND ANNUAL MESSAGE.

DECEMBER 6, 1830.

Fellow-Citizens of the Senate and House of Representatives:

The pleasure I have in congratulating you upon your return to your constitutional duties is much heightened by the satisfaction which the condition of our beloved country at this period justly inspires. The beneficent Author of All Good has granted to us during the present year health, peace, and plenty, and numerous causes for joy in the wonderful success which attends the progress of our free institutions.

With a population unparalleled in its increase, and possessing a character which combines the hardihood of enterprise with the considerateness of wisdom, we see in every section of our happy country a steady improvement in the means of social intercourse, and correspondent effects upon the genius and laws of our extended Republic.

The apparent exceptions to the harmony of the prospect are to be referred rather to inevitable diversities in the various interests which enter into the composition of so extensive a whole than to any want of attachment to the Union—interests whose collisions serve only in the end to foster the spirit of conciliation and patriotism so essential to the preservation of that Union which I most devoutly hope is destined to prove imperishable.

In the midst of these blessings we have recently witnessed changes in the condition of other nations which may in their consequences call for the utmost vigilance, wisdom, and unanimity in our councils, and the exercise of all the moderation and patriotism of our people.

The important modifications of their Government, effected with so much courage and wisdom by the people of France, afford a happy presage of their future course, and have naturally elicited from the kindred feelings of this nation that spontaneous and universal burst of applause in which you have participated. In congratulating you, my fellow-citizens, upon an event so auspicious to the dearest interests of mankind I do no more than respond to the voice of my country, without transcending in the slightest degree that salutary maxim of the illustrious Washington which enjoins an abstinence from all interference with the internal affairs of other nations. From a people exercising in the most unlimited degree the right of self-government, and enjoying, as derived from this proud characteristic, under the favor of Heaven, much of the happiness with which they are blessed; a people who can point in triumph to their free institutions and challenge comparison with the fruits they bear, as well as with the moderation, intelligence, and energy with which they are administered—from such a people the deepest sympathy was to be expected in a struggle for the sacred principles of liberty, conducted in a spirit every way worthy of the cause, and crowned by a heroic moderation which has disarmed revolution of its terrors. Notwithstanding the strong assurances which the man whom we so sincerely love and justly admire has given to the world of the high character of the present King of the French, and which if sustained to the end will secure to him the proud appellation of Patriot King, it is not in his success, but in that of the great principle which has borne him to the throne—the paramount authority of the public will—that the American people rejoice.

I am happy to inform you that the anticipations which were indulged at the date of my last communication on the subject of our foreign affairs have been fully realized in several important particulars.

An arrangement has been effected with Great Britain in relation to the trade between the United States and her West India and North American colonies which has settled a question that has for years afforded matter for contention and almost uninterrupted discussion, and has been the subject of no less than six negotiations, in a manner which promises results highly favorable to the parties.

The abstract right of Great Britain to monopolize the trade with her colonies or to exclude us from a participation therein has never been denied by the United States. But we have contended, and with reason,

that if at any time Great Britain may desire the productions of this country as necessary to her colonies they must be received upon principles
of just reciprocity, and, further, that it is making an invidious and
unfriendly distinction to open her colonial ports to the vessels of other
nations and close them against those of the United States.

Antecedently to 1794 a portion of our productions was admitted into
the colonial islands of Great Britain by particular concessions, limited to
the term of one year, but renewed from year to year. In the transportation of these productions, however, our vessels were not allowed to
engage, this being a privilege reserved to British shipping, by which
alone our produce could be taken to the islands and theirs brought to
us in return. From Newfoundland and her continental possessions all
our productions, as well as our vessels, were excluded, with occasional
relaxations, by which, in seasons of distress, the former were admitted
in British bottoms.

By the treaty of 1794 she offered to concede to us for a limited time the
right of carrying to her West India possessions in our vessels not exceeding 70 tons burthen, and upon the same terms as British vessels, any
productions of the United States which British vessels might import
therefrom. But this privilege was coupled with conditions which are
supposed to have led to its rejection by the Senate; that is, that American vessels should land their return cargoes in the United States only,
and, moreover, that they should during the continuance of the privilege be precluded from carrying molasses, sugar, coffee, cocoa, or cotton
either from those islands or from the United States to any other part
of the world. Great Britain readily consented to expunge this article
from the treaty, and subsequent attempts to arrange the terms of the
trade either by treaty stipulations or concerted legislation having failed,
it has been successively suspended and allowed according to the varying
legislation of the parties.

The following are the prominent points which have in later years separated the two Governments: Besides a restriction whereby all importations into her colonies in American vessels are confined to our own
products carried hence, a restriction to which it does not appear that
we have ever objected, a leading object on the part of Great Britain has
been to prevent us from becoming the carriers of British West India
commodities to any other country than our own. On the part of the
United States it has been contended, first, that the subject should be regulated by treaty stipulation in preference to separate legislation; second,
that our productions, when imported into the colonies in question, should
not be subject to higher duties than the productions of the mother country or of her other colonial possessions, and, third, that our vessels should
be allowed to participate in the circuitous trade between the United States
and different parts of the British dominions.

The first point, after having been for a long time strenuously insisted upon by Great Britain, was given up by the act of Parliament of July, 1825, all vessels suffered to trade with the colonies being permitted to clear from thence with any articles which British vessels might export and proceed to any part of the world, Great Britain and her dependencies alone excepted. On our part each of the above points had in succession been explicitly abandoned in negotiations preceding that of which the result is now announced.

This arrangement secures to the United States every advantage asked by them, and which the state of the negotiation allowed us to insist upon. The trade will be placed upon a footing decidedly more favorable to this country than any on which it ever stood, and our commerce and navigation will enjoy in the colonial ports of Great Britain every privilege allowed to other nations.

That the prosperity of the country so far as it depends on this trade will be greatly promoted by the new arrangement there can be no doubt. Independently of the more obvious advantages of an open and direct intercourse, its establishment will be attended with other consequences of a higher value. That which has been carried on since the mutual interdict under all the expense and inconvenience unavoidably incident to it would have been insupportably onerous had it not been in a great degree lightened by concerted evasions in the mode of making the transshipments at what are called the neutral ports. These indirections are inconsistent with the dignity of nations that have so many motives not only to cherish feelings of mutual friendship, but to maintain such relations as will stimulate their respective citizens and subjects to efforts of direct, open, and honorable competition only, and preserve them from the influence of seductive and vitiating circumstances.

When your preliminary interposition was asked at the close of the last session, a copy of the instructions under which Mr. McLane has acted, together with the communications which had at that time passed between him and the British Government, was laid before you. Although there has not been anything in the acts of the two Governments which requires secrecy, it was thought most proper in the then state of the negotiation to make that communication a confidential one. So soon, however, as the evidence of execution on the part of Great Britain is received the whole matter shall be laid before you, when it will be seen that the apprehension which appears to have suggested one of the provisions of the act passed at your last session, that the restoration of the trade in question might be connected with other subjects and was sought to be obtained at the sacrifice of the public interest in other particulars, was wholly unfounded, and that the change which has taken place in the views of the British Government has been induced by considerations as honorable to both parties as I trust the result will prove beneficial.

This desirable result was, it will be seen, greatly promoted by the liberal and confiding provisions of the act of Congress of the last session, by which our ports were upon the reception and annunciation by the President of the required assurance on the part of Great Britain forthwith opened to her vessels before the arrangement could be carried into effect on her part, pursuing in this act of prospective legislation a similar course to that adopted by Great Britain in abolishing, by her act of Parliament in 1825, a restriction then existing and permitting our vessels to clear from the colonies on their return voyages for any foreign country whatever before British vessels had been relieved from the restriction imposed by our law of returning directly from the United States to the colonies, a restriction which she required and expected that we should abolish. Upon each occasion a limited and temporary advantage has been given to the opposite party, but an advantage of no importance in comparison with the restoration of mutual confidence and good feeling, and the ultimate establishment of the trade upon fair principles.

It gives me unfeigned pleasure to assure you that this negotiation has been throughout characterized by the most frank and friendly spirit on the part of Great Britain, and concluded in a manner strongly indicative of a sincere desire to cultivate the best relations with the United States. To reciprocate this disposition to the fullest extent of my ability is a duty which I shall deem it a privilege to discharge.

Although the result is itself the best commentary on the services rendered to his country by our minister at the Court of St. James, it would be doing violence to my feelings were I to dismiss the subject without expressing the very high sense I entertain of the talent and exertion which have been displayed by him on the occasion.

The injury to the commerce of the United States resulting from the exclusion of our vessels from the Black Sea and the previous footing of mere sufferance upon which even the limited trade enjoyed by us with Turkey has hitherto been placed have for a long time been a source of much solicitude to this Government, and several endeavors have been made to obtain a better state of things. Sensible of the importance of the object, I felt it my duty to leave no proper means unemployed to acquire for our flag the same privileges that are enjoyed by the principal powers of Europe. Commissioners were consequently appointed to open a negotiation with the Sublime Porte. Not long after the member of the commission who went directly from the United States had sailed, the account of the treaty of Adrianople, by which one of the objects in view was supposed to be secured, reached this country. The Black Sea was understood to be opened to us. Under the supposition that this was the case, the additional facilities to be derived from the establishment of commercial regulations with the Porte were deemed of sufficient importance to require a prosecution of the negotiation as originally contemplated. It was therefore persevered in, and resulted in a treaty, which will be forthwith laid before the Senate.

By its provisions a free passage is secured, without limitation of time, to the vessels of the United States to and from the Black Sea, including the navigation thereof, and our trade with Turkey is placed on the footing of the most favored nation. The latter is an arrangement wholly independent of the treaty of Adrianople, and the former derives much value, not only from the increased security which under any circumstances it would give to the right in question, but from the fact, ascertained in the course of the negotiation, that by the construction put upon that treaty by Turkey the article relating to the passage of the Bosphorus is confined to nations having treaties with the Porte. The most friendly feelings appear to be entertained by the Sultan, and an enlightened disposition is evinced by him to foster the intercourse between the two countries by the most liberal arrangements. This disposition it will be our duty and interest to cherish.

Our relations with Russia are of the most stable character. Respect for that Empire and confidence in its friendship toward the United States have been so long entertained on our part and so carefully cherished by the present Emperor and his illustrious predecessor as to have become incorporated with the public sentiment of the United States. No means will be left unemployed on my part to promote these salutary feelings and those improvements of which the commercial intercourse between the two countries is susceptible, and which have derived increased importance from our treaty with the Sublime Porte.

I sincerely regret to inform you that our minister lately commissioned to that Court, on whose distinguished talents and great experience in public affairs I place great reliance, has been compelled by extreme indisposition to exercise a privilege which, in consideration of the extent to which his constitution had been impaired in the public service, was committed to his discretion—of leaving temporarily his post for the advantage of a more genial climate.

If, as it is to be hoped, the improvement of his health should be such as to justify him in doing so, he will repair to St. Petersburg and resume the discharge of his official duties. I have received the most satisfactory assurances that in the meantime the public interest in that quarter will be preserved from prejudice by the intercourse which he will continue through the secretary of legation with the Russian cabinet.

You are apprised, although the fact has not yet been officially announced to the House of Representatives, that a treaty was in the month of March last concluded between the United States and Denmark, by which $650,000 are secured to our citizens as an indemnity for spoliations upon their commerce in the years 1808, 1809, 1810, and 1811. This treaty was sanctioned by the Senate at the close of its last session, and it now becomes the duty of Congress to pass the necessary laws for the organization of the board of commissioners to distribute the indemnity among the claimants. It is an agreeable circumstance in this adjustment that the terms are in conformity with the previously ascertained views of the claimants themselves, thus removing all pretense for a future agitation of the subject in any form.

The negotiations in regard to such points in our foreign relations as remain to be adjusted have been actively prosecuted during the recess. Material advances have been made, which are of a character to promise favorable results. Our country, by the blessing of God, is not in a situation to invite aggression, and it will be our fault if she ever becomes so. Sincerely desirous to cultivate the most liberal and friendly relations with all; ever ready to fulfill our engagements with scrupulous fidelity; limiting our demands upon others to mere justice; holding ourselves ever ready to do unto them as we would wish to be done by, and avoiding even the appearance of undue partiality to any nation, it appears to me impossible that a simple and sincere application of our principles to our foreign relations can fail to place them ultimately upon the footing on which it is our wish they should rest.

Of the points referred to, the most prominent are our claims upon France for spoliations upon our commerce; similar claims upon Spain, together with embarrassments in the commercial intercourse between the two countries which ought to be removed; the conclusion of the treaty of commerce and navigation with Mexico, which has been so long in suspense, as well as the final settlement of limits between ourselves and that Republic, and, finally, the arbitrament of the question between the United States and Great Britain in regard to the northeastern boundary.

The negotiation with France has been conducted by our minister with zeal and ability, and in all respects to my entire satisfaction. Although the prospect of a favorable termination was occasionally dimmed by counter pretensions to which the United States could not assent, he yet had strong hopes of being able to arrive at a satisfactory settlement with the late Government. The negotiation has been renewed with the present authorities, and, sensible of the general and lively confidence of our citizens in the justice and magnanimity of regenerated France, I regret the more not to have it in my power yet to announce the result so confidently anticipated. No ground, however, inconsistent with this expectation has yet been taken, and I do not allow myself to doubt that justice will soon be done us. The amount of the claims, the length of time they have remained unsatisfied, and their incontrovertible justice make an earnest prosecution of them by this Government an urgent duty. The illegality of the seizures and confiscations out of which they have arisen is not disputed, and whatever distinctions may have heretofore been set up in regard to the liability of the existing Government it is quite clear that such considerations can not now be interposed.

The commercial intercourse between the two countries is susceptible of highly advantageous improvements, but the sense of this injury has had, and must continue to have, a very unfavorable influence upon them. From its satisfactory adjustment not only a firm and cordial friendship, but a progressive development of all their relations, may be expected. It is, therefore, my earnest hope that this old and vexatious subject of difference may be speedily removed.

I feel that my confidence in our appeal to the motives which should govern a just and magnanimous nation is alike warranted by the character of the French people and by the high voucher we possess for the enlarged views and pure integrity of the Monarch who now presides over their councils, and nothing shall be wanting on my part to meet any manifestation of the spirit we anticipate in one of corresponding frankness and liberality.

The subjects of difference with Spain have been brought to the view of that Government by our minister there with much force and propriety, and the strongest assurances have been received of their early and favorable consideration.

The steps which remained to place the matter in controversy between Great Britain and the United States fairly before the arbitrator have all been taken in the same liberal and friendly spirit which characterized those before announced. Recent events have doubtless served to delay the decision, but our minister at the Court of the distinguished arbitrator has been assured that it will be made within the time contemplated by the treaty.

I am particularly gratified in being able to state that a decidedly favorable, and, as I hope, lasting, change has been effected in our relations with the neighboring Republic of Mexico. The unfortunate and unfounded suspicions in regard to our disposition which it became my painful duty to advert to on a former occasion have been, I believe, entirely removed, and the Government of Mexico has been made to understand the real character of the wishes and views of this in regard to that country. The consequence is the establishment of friendship and mutual confidence. Such are the assurances I have received, and I see no cause to doubt their sincerity.

I had reason to expect the conclusion of a commercial treaty with Mexico in season for communication on the present occasion. Circumstances which are not explained, but which I am persuaded are not the result of an indisposition on her part to enter into it, have produced the delay.

There was reason to fear in the course of the last summer that the harmony of our relations might be disturbed by the acts of certain claimants, under Mexican grants, of territory which had hitherto been under our jurisdiction. The cooperation of the representative of Mexico near this Government was asked on the occasion and was readily afforded. Instructions and advice have been given to the governor of Arkansas and the officers in command in the adjoining Mexican State by which it is hoped the quiet of that frontier will be preserved until a final settlement of the dividing line shall have removed all ground of controversy.

The exchange of ratifications of the treaty concluded last year with Austria has not yet taken place. The delay has been occasioned by the nonarrival of the ratification of that Government within the time prescribed by the treaty. Renewed authority has been asked for by the representative of Austria, and in the meantime the rapidly increasing trade and navigation between the two countries have been placed upon the most liberal footing of our navigation acts.

Several alleged depredations have been recently committed on our commerce by the national vessels of Portugal. They have been made the subject of immediate remonstrance and reclamation. I am not yet possessed of sufficient information to express a definitive opinion of their character, but expect soon to receive it. No proper means shall be omitted to obtain for our citizens all the redress to which they may appear to be entitled.

Almost at the moment of the adjournment of your last session two bills—the one entitled "An act for making appropriations for building light-houses, light-boats, beacons, and monuments, placing buoys, and for improving harbors and directing surveys," and the other "An act to authorize a subscription for stock in the Louisville and Portland Canal Company"—were submitted for my approval. It was not possible within the time allowed me before the close of the session to give to these bills the consideration which was due to their character and importance, and I was compelled to retain them for that purpose. I now avail myself of this early opportunity to return them to the Houses in which they respectively originated with the reasons which, after mature deliberation, compel me to withhold my approval.

The practice of defraying out of the Treasury of the United States the expenses incurred by the establishment and support of light-houses, beacons, buoys, and public piers within the bays, inlets, harbors, and ports of the United States, to render the navigation thereof safe and easy, is coeval with the adoption of the Constitution, and has been continued without interruption or dispute.

As our foreign commerce increased and was extended into the interior of the country by the establishment of ports of entry and delivery upon our navigable rivers the sphere of those expenditures received a corresponding enlargement. Light-houses, beacons, buoys, public piers, and the removal of sand bars, sawyers, and other partial or temporary impediments in the navigable rivers and harbors which were embraced in the revenue districts from time to time established by law were authorized upon the same principle and the expense defrayed in the same manner. That these expenses have at times been extravagant and disproportionate is very probable. The circumstances under which they are incurred are well calculated to lead to such a result unless their application is subjected to the closest scrutiny. The local advantages arising from the disbursement of public money too frequently, it is to be feared, invite appropriations for objects of this character that are neither necessary nor useful.

The number of light-house keepers is already very large, and the bill before me proposes to add to it fifty-one more of various descriptions. From representations upon the subject which are understood to be entitled to respect I am induced to believe that there has not only been great improvidence in the past expenditures of the Government upon these objects, but that the security of navigation has in some instances been diminished by the multiplication of light-houses and consequent change of lights upon the coast. It is in this as in other respects our duty to avoid all unnecessary expense, as well as every increase of patronage not called for by the public service. But in the discharge of that duty in this particular it must not be forgotten that in relation to our foreign commerce the burden and benefit of protecting and accommodating it necessarily go together, and must do so as long as the public revenue is drawn from the people through the custom-house. It is indisputable that whatever gives facility and security to navigation cheapens imports, and all who consume them are-alike interested in whatever produces this effect. If they consume, they ought, as they now do, to pay; otherwise they do not pay. The consumer in the most inland State derives the same advantage from every necessary and prudent expenditure for the facility and security of our foreign commerce and navigation that he does who resides in a maritime State. Local expenditures have not of themselves a corresponding operation.

From a bill making *direct* appropriations for such objects I should not have withheld my assent. The one now returned does so in several particulars, but it also contains appropriations for surveys of a local character, which I can not approve. It gives me satisfaction to find that no serious inconvenience has arisen from withholding my approval from this bill; nor will it, I trust, be cause of regret that an opportunity will be thereby afforded for Congress to review its provisions under circumstances better calculated for full investigation than those under which it was passed.

In speaking of direct appropriations I mean not to include a practice which has obtained to some extent, and to which I have in one instance, in a different capacity, given my assent—that of subscribing to the stock of private associations. Positive experience and a more thorough consideration of the subject have convinced me of the impropriety as well as inexpediency of such investments. All improvements effected by the funds of the nation for general use should be open to the enjoyment of all our fellow-citizens, exempt from the payment of tolls or any imposition of that character. The practice of thus mingling the concerns of the Government with those of the States or of individuals is inconsistent with the object of its institution and highly impolitic. The successful operation of the federal system can only be preserved by confining it to the few and simple, but yet important, objects for which it was desigued.

A different practice, if allowed to progress, would ultimately change the character of this Government by consolidating into one the General and State Governments, which were intended to be kept forever distinct. I can not perceive how bills authorizing such subscriptions can be otherwise regarded than as bills for revenue, and consequently subject to the rule in that respect prescribed by the Constitution. If the interest of the Government in private companies is subordinate to that of individuals, the management and control of a portion of the public funds is delegated to an authority unknown to the Constitution and beyond the supervision of our constituents; if superior, its officers and agents will be constantly exposed to imputations of favoritism and oppression. Direct prejudice to the public interest or an alienation of the affections and respect of portions of the people may, therefore, in addition to the general discredit resulting to the Government from embarking with its constituents in pecuniary stipulations, be looked for as the probable fruit of such associations. It is no answer to this objection to say that the extent of consequences like these can not be great from a limited and small number of investments, because experience in other matters teaches us—and we are not at liberty to disregard its admonitions—that unless an entire stop be put to them it will soon be impossible to prevent their accumulation until they are spread over the whole country and made to embrace many of the private and appropriate concerns of individuals.

The power which the General Government would acquire within the several States by becoming the principal stockholder in corporations, controlling every canal and each 60 or 100 miles of every important road, and giving a proportionate vote in all their elections, is almost inconceivable, and in my view dangerous to the liberties of the people.

This mode of aiding such works is also in its nature deceptive, and in many cases conducive to improvidence in the administration of the national funds. Appropriations will be obtained with much greater facility and granted with less security to the public interest when the measure is thus disguised than when definite and direct expenditures of money are asked for. The interests of the nation would doubtless be better served by avoiding all such indirect modes of aiding particular objects. In a government like ours more especially should all public acts be, as far as practicable, simple, undisguised, and intelligible, that they may become fit subjects for the approbation or animadversion of the people. The bill authorizing a subscription to the Louisville and Portland Canal affords a striking illustration of the difficulty of withholding additional appropriations for the same object when the first erroneous step has been taken by instituting a partnership between the Government and private companies. It proposes a third subscription on the part of the United States, when each preceding one was at the time regarded as the extent of the aid which Government was to render to that work; and the accompanying bill for light-houses, etc., contains an appropriation for a survey of the bed of the river, with a view to its improvement by removing the obstruction which the canal is designed to avoid. This improvement, if successful, would afford a free passage of the river and render the canal entirely useless. To such improvidence is the course of legislation subject in relation to internal improvements on local matters, even with the best intentions on the part of Congress.

Although the motives which have influenced me in this matter may be already sufficiently stated, I am, nevertheless, induced by its importance to add a few observations of a general character.

In my objections to the bills authorizing subscriptions to the Maysville and Rockville road companies I expressed my views fully in regard to the power of Congress to construct roads and canals within a State or to appropriate money for improvements of a local character. I at the same time intimated my belief that the right to make appropriations for such as were of a national character had been so generally acted upon and so long acquiesced in by the Federal and State Governments and the constituents of each as to justify its exercise on the ground of continued and uninterrupted usage, but that it was, nevertheless, highly expedient that appropriations even of that character should, with the exception made at the time, be deferred until the national debt is paid, and that in the meanwhile some general rule for the action of the Government in that respect ought to be established.

These suggestions were not necessary to the decision of the question then before me, and were, I readily admit, intended to awake the attention and draw forth the opinions and observations of our constituents upon a subject of the highest importance to their interests, and one destined to exert a powerful influence upon the future operations of our political system. I know of no tribunal to which a public man in this country, in a case of doubt and difficulty, can appeal with greater advantage or more propriety than the judgment of the people; and although I must necessarily in the discharge of my official duties be governed by the dictates of my own judgment, I have no desire to conceal my anxious wish to conform as far as I can to the views of those for whom I act.

All irregular expressions of public opinion are of necessity attended with some doubt as to their accuracy, but making full allowances on that account I can not, I think, deceive myself in believing that the acts referred to, as well as the suggestions which I allowed myself to make in relation to their bearing upon the future operations of the Government, have been approved by the great body of the people. That those whose immediate pecuniary interests are to be affected by proposed expenditures should shrink from the application of a rule which prefers their more general and remote interests to those which are personal and immediate is to be expected. But even such objections must from the nature of our population be but temporary in their duration, and if it were otherwise our course should be the same, for the time is yet, I hope, far distant when those intrusted with power to be exercised for the good of the whole will consider it either honest or wise to purchase local favors at the sacrifice of principle and general good.

So understanding public sentiment, and thoroughly satisfied that the best interests of our common country imperiously require that the course which I have recommended in this regard should be adopted, I have, upon the most mature consideration, determined to pursue it.

It is due to candor, as well as to my own feelings, that I should express the reluctance and anxiety which I must at all times experience in exercising the undoubted right of the Executive to withhold his assent from bills on other grounds than their constitutionality. That this right should not be exercised on slight occasions all will admit. It is only in matters of deep interest, when the principle involved may be justly regarded as next in importance to infractions of the Constitution itself, that such a step can be expected to meet with the approbation of the people. Such an occasion do I conscientiously believe the present to be. In the discharge of this delicate and highly responsible duty I am sustained by the reflection that the exercise of this power has been deemed consist. ent with the obligation of official duty by several of my predecessors, and by the persuasion, too, that whatever liberal institutions may have to fear from the encroachments of Executive power, which has been everywhere the cause of so much strife and bloody contention, but little danger is to be apprehended from a precedent by which that authority denies to itself the exercise of powers that bring in their train influence and patronage of great extent, and thus excludes the operation of personal interests, everywhere the bane of official trust. I derive, too, no small degree of satisfaction from the reflection that if I have mistaken the interests and wishes of the people the Constitution affords the means of soon redressing the error by selecting for the place their favor has bestowed upon me a citizen whose opinions may accord with their own. I trust, in the meantime, the interests of the nation will be saved from prejudice by a rigid application of that portion of the public funds which might otherwise be applied to different objects to that highest of all our obligations, the payment of the public debt, and an opportunity be afforded for the adoption of some better rule for the operations of the Government in this matter than any which has hitherto been acted upon.

Profoundly impressed with the importance of the subject, not merely as relates to the general prosperity of the country, but to the safety of the federal system, I can not avoid repeating my earnest hope that all good citizens who take a proper interest in the success and harmony of our admirable political institutions, and who are incapable of desiring to convert an opposite state of things into means for the gratification of personal ambition, will, laying aside minor considerations and discarding local prejudices, unite their honest exertions to establish some fixed general principle which shall be calculated to effect the greatest extent of public good in regard to the subject of internal improvement, and afford the least ground for sectional discontent.

The general grounds of my objection to local appropriations have been heretofore expressed, and I shall endeavor to avoid a repetition of what has been already urged—the importance of sustaining the State sover- eignties as far as is consistent with the rightful action of the Federal Government, and of preserving the greatest attainable harmony between them. I will now only add an expression of my conviction—a convic- tion which every day's experience serves to confirm—that the political creed which inculcates the pursuit of those great objects as a paramount duty is the true faith, and one to which we are mainly indebted for the present success of the entire system, and to which we must alone look for its future stability.

That there are diversities in the interests of the different States which compose this extensive Confederacy must be admitted. Those diversi- ties arising from situation, climate, population, and pursuits are doubt- less, as it is natural they should be, greatly exaggerated by jealousies and that spirit of rivalry so inseparable from neighboring communities. These circumstances make it the duty of those who are intrusted with the management of its affairs to neutralize their effects as far as practi- cable by making the beneficial operation of the Federal Government as equal and equitable among the several States as can be done consistently with the great ends of its institution.

It is only necessary to refer to undoubted facts to see how far the past acts of the Government upon the subject under consideration have fallen short of this object. The expenditures heretofore made for internal im- provements amount to upward of $5,000,000, and have been distributed in very unequal proportions amongst the States. The estimated expense of works of which surveys have been made, together with that of others projected and partially surveyed, amounts to more than $96,000,000.

That such improvements, on account of particular circumstances, may be more advantageously and beneficially made in some States than in others is doubtless true, but that they are of a character which should prevent an equitable distribution of the funds amongst the several States is not to be conceded. The want of this equitable distribution can not fail to prove a prolific source of irritation among the States.

We have it constantly before our eyes that professions of superior zeal in the cause of internal improvement and a disposition to lavish the pub- lic funds upon objects of this character are daily and earnestly put forth by aspirants to power as constituting the highest claims to the confidence of the people. Would it be strange, under such circumstances, and in times of great excitement, that grants of this description should find their motives in objects which may not accord with the public good? Those who have not had occasion to see and regret the indication of a

sinister influence in these matters in past times have been more fortunate than myself in their observation of the course of public affairs.   If
to these evils be added the combinations and angry contentions to which
such a course of things gives rise, with their baleful influences upon the
legislation of Congress touching the leading and appropriate duties of
the Federal Government, it was but doing justice to the character of our
people to expect the severe condemnation of the past which the recent
exhibitions of public sentiment has evinced.

Nothing short of a radical change in the action of the Government upon
the subject can, in my opinion, remedy the evil.   If, as it would be natural to expect, the States which have been least favored in past appropriations should insist on being redressed in those hereafter to be made, at
the expense of the States which have so largely and disproportionately
participated, we have, as matters now stand, but little security that the
attempt would do more than change the inequality from one quarter to
another.

Thus viewing the subject, I have heretofore felt it my duty to recommend the adoption of some plan for the distribution of the surplus funds,
which may at any time remain in the Treasury after the national debt
shall have been paid, among the States, in proportion to the number
of their Representatives, to be applied by them to objects of internal
improvement.

Although this plan has met with favor in some portions of the Union,
it has also elicited objections which merit deliberate consideration.   A
brief notice of these objections here will not, therefore, I trust, be regarded as out of place.

They rest, as far as they have come to my knowledge, on the following grounds: First, an objection to the ratio of distribution; second, an
apprehension that the existence of such a regulation would produce
improvident and oppressive taxation to raise the funds for distribution;
third, that the mode proposed would lead to the construction of works of
a local nature, to the exclusion of such as are general and as would consequently be of a more useful character; and, last, that it would create a
discreditable and injurious dependence on the part of the State governments upon the Federal power.   Of those who object to the ratio of representation as the basis of distribution, some insist that the importations
of the respective States would constitute one that would be more equitable; and others again, that the extent of their respective territories
would furnish a standard which would be more expedient and sufficiently
equitable.   The ratio of representation presented itself to my mind,
and it still does, as one of obvious equity, because of its being the ratio
of contribution, whether the funds to be distributed be derived from
the customs or from direct taxation.   It does not follow, however, that
its adoption is indispensable to the establishment of the system proposed.   There may be considerations appertaining to the subject which

would render a departure, to some extent, from the rule of contribution proper. Nor is it absolutely necessary that the basis of distribution be confined to one ground. It may, if in the judgment of those whose right it is to fix it it be deemed politic and just to give it that character, have regard to several.

In my first message I stated it to be my opinion that "it is not probable that any adjustment of the tariff upon principles satisfactory to the people of the Union will until a remote period, if ever, leave the Government without a considerable surplus in the Treasury beyond what may be required for its current service." I have had no cause to change that opinion, but much to confirm it. Should these expectations be realized, a suitable fund would thus be produced for the plan under consideration to operate upon, and if there be no such fund its adoption will, in my opinion, work no injury to any interest; for I can not assent to the justness of the apprehension that the establishment of the proposed system would tend to the encouragement of improvident legislation of the character supposed. Whatever the proper authority in the exercise of constitutional power shall at any time hereafter decide to be for the general good will in that as in other respects deserve and receive the acquiescence and support of the whole country, and we have ample security that every abuse of power in that regard by agents of the people will receive a speedy and effectual corrective at their hands. The views which I take of the future, founded on the obvious and increasing improvement of all classes of our fellow-citizens in intelligence and in public and private virtue, leave me without much apprehension on that head.

I do not doubt that those who come after us will be as much alive as we are to the obligation upon all the trustees of political power to exempt those for whom they act from all unnecessary burthens, and as sensible of the great truth that the resources of the nation beyond those required for immediate and necessary purposes of Government can nowhere be so well deposited as in the pockets of the people.

It may sometimes happen that the interests of particular States would not be deemed to coincide with the general interest in relation to improvements within such States. But if the danger to be apprehended from this source is sufficient to require it, a discretion might be reserved to Congress to direct to such improvements of a general character as the States concerned might not be disposed to unite in, the application of the quotas of those States, under the restriction of confining to each State the expenditure of its appropriate quota. It may, however, be assumed as a safe general rule that such improvements as serve to increase the prosperity of the respective States in which they are made, by giving new facilities to trade, and thereby augmenting the wealth and comfort of their inhabitants, constitute the surest mode of conferring permanent and substantial advantages upon the whole. The strength as well as the true glory of the Confederacy is founded on the prosperity and power of the several independent sovereignties of which it is composed and the certainty with which they can be brought into successful active cooperation through the agency of the Federal Government.

It is, moreover, within the knowledge of such as are at all conversant with public affairs that schemes of internal improvement have from time to time been proposed which, from their extent and seeming magnificence, were readily regarded as of national concernment, but which upon fuller consideration and further experience would now be rejected with great unanimity.

That the plan under consideration would derive important advantages from its certainty, and that the moneys set apart for these purposes would be more judiciously applied and economically expended under the direction of the State legislatures, in which every part of each State is immediately represented, can not, I think, be doubted. In the new States particularly, where a comparatively small population is scattered over an extensive surface, and the representation in Congress consequently very limited, it is natural to expect that the appropriations made by the Federal Government would be more likely to be expended in the vicinity of those members through whose immediate agency they were obtained than if the funds were placed under the control of the legislature, in which every county of the State has its own representative. This supposition does not necessarily impugn the motives of such Congressional representatives, nor is it so intended. We are all sensible of the bias to which the strongest minds and purest hearts are, under such circumstances, liable. In respect to the last objection—its probable effect upon the dignity and independence of State governments—it appears to me only necessary to state the case as it is, and as it would be if the measure proposed were adopted, to show that the operation is most likely to be the very reverse of that which the objection supposes.

In the one case the State would receive its quota of the national revenue for domestic use upon a fixed principle as a matter of right, and from a fund to the creation of which it had itself contributed its fair proportion. Surely there could be nothing derogatory in that. As matters now stand the States themselves, in their sovereign character, are not unfrequently petitioners at the bar of the Federal Legislature for such allowances out of the National Treasury as it may comport with their pleasure or sense of duty to bestow upon them. It can not require argument to prove which of the two courses is most compatible with the efficiency or respectability of the State governments.

But all these are matters for discussion and dispassionate consideration. That the desired adjustment would be attended with difficulty affords no reason why it should not be attempted. The effective operation of such motives would have prevented the adoption of the Constitution under which we have so long lived and under the benign influence of which our beloved country has so signally prospered. The framers of that sacred instrument had greater difficulties to overcome, and they did overcome them. The patriotism of the people, directed by a deep conviction of the importance of the Union, produced mutual concession and reciprocal forbearance. Strict right was merged in a spirit of compromise, and the result has consecrated their disinterested devotion to the general weal. Unless the American people have degenerated, the same result can be again effected whenever experience points out the necessity of a resort to the same means to uphold the fabric which their fathers have reared. It is beyond the power of man to make a system of government like ours or any other operate with precise equality upon States situated like those which compose this Confederacy; nor is inequality always injustice. Every State can not expect to shape the measures of the General Government to suit its own particular interests. The causes which prevent it are seated in the nature of things, and can not be entirely counteracted by human means. Mutual forbearance becomes, therefore, a duty obligatory upon all, and we may, I am confident, count upon a cheerful compliance with this high injunction on the part of our constituents. It is not to be supposed that they will object to make such comparatively inconsiderable sacrifices for the preservation of rights and privileges which other less favored portions of the world have in vain waded through seas of blood to acquire.

Our course is a safe one if it be but faithfully adhered to. Acquiescence in the constitutionally expressed will of the majority, and the exercise of that will in a spirit of moderation, justice, and brotherly kindness, will constitute a cement which would forever preserve our Union. Those who cherish and inculcate sentiments like these render a most essential service to their country, while those who seek to weaken their influence are, however conscientious and praiseworthy their intentions, in effect its worst enemies.

If the intelligence and influence of the country, instead of laboring to foment sectional prejudices, to be made subservient to party warfare, were in good faith applied to the eradication of causes of local discontent, by the improvement of our institutions and by facilitating their adaptation to the condition of the times, this task would prove one of less difficulty. May we not hope that the obvious interests of our common country and the dictates of an enlightened patriotism will in the end lead the public mind in that direction?

After all, the nature of the subject does not admit of a plan wholly free from objection. That which has for some time been in operation is, perhaps, the worst that could exist, and every advance that can be made in its improvement is a matter eminently worthy of your most deliberate attention.

It is very possible that one better calculated to effect the objects in view may yet be devised. If so, it is to be hoped that those who disapprove the past and dissent from what is proposed for the future will feel it their duty to direct their attention to it, as they must be sensible that unless some fixed rule for the action of the Federal Government in this respect is established the course now attempted to be arrested will be again resorted to. Any mode which is calculated to give the greatest degree of effect and harmony to our legislation upon the subject, which shall best serve to keep the movements of the Federal Government within the sphere intended by those who modeled and those who adopted it, which shall lead to the extinguishment of the national debt in the shortest period and impose the lightest burthens upon our constituents, shall receive from me a cordial and firm support.

Among the objects of great national concern I can not omit to press again upon your attention that part of the Constitution which regulates the election of President and Vice-President. The necessity for its amendment is made so clear to my mind by observation of its evils and by the many able discussions which they have elicited on the floor of Congress and elsewhere that I should be wanting to my duty were I to withhold another expression of my deep solicitude on the subject. Our system fortunately contemplates a recurrence to first principles, differing in this respect from all that have preceded it, and securing it, I trust, equally against the decay and the commotions which have marked the progress of other governments. Our fellow-citizens, too, who in proportion to their love of liberty keep a steady eye upon the means of sustaining it, do not require to be reminded of the duty they owe to themselves to remedy all essential defects in so vital a part of their system. While they are sensible that every evil attendant upon its operation is not necessarily indicative of a bad organization, but may proceed from temporary causes, yet the habitual presence, or even a single instance, of evils which can be clearly traced to an organic defect will not, I trust, be overlooked through a too scrupulous veneration for the work of their ancestors. The Constitution was an experiment committed to the virtue and intelligence of the great mass of our countrymen, in whose ranks the framers of it themselves were to perform the part of patriotic observation and scrutiny, and if they have passed from the stage of existence with an increased confidence in its general adaptation to our condition we should learn from authority so high the duty of fortifying the points in it which time proves to be exposed rather than be deterred from approaching them by the suggestions of fear or the dictates of misplaced reverence.

A provision which does not secure to the people a direct choice of their Chief Magistrate, but has a tendency to defeat their will, presented to my mind such an inconsistency with the general spirit of our institutions that I was induced to suggest for your consideration the substitute which appeared to me at the same time the most likely to correct the evil and to meet the views of our constituents. The most mature reflection since has added strength to the belief that the best interests of our country require the speedy adoption of some plan calculated to effect this end. A contingency which sometimes places it in the power of a single member of the House of Representatives to decide an election of so high and solemn a character is unjust to the people, and becomes when it occurs a source of embarrassment to the individuals thus brought into power and a cause of distrust of the representative body. Liable as the Confederacy is, from its great extent, to parties founded upon sectional interests, and to a corresponding multiplication of candidates for the Presidency, the tendency of the constitutional reference to the House of Representatives is to devolve the election upon that body in almost every instance, and, whatever choice may then be made among the candidates thus presented to them, to swell the influence of particular interests to a degree inconsistent with the general good. The consequences of this feature of the Constitution appear far more threatening to the peace and integrity of the Union than any which I can conceive as likely to result from the simple legislative action of the Federal Government.

It was a leading object with the framers of the Constitution to keep as separate as possible the action of the legislative and executive branches of the Government. To secure this object nothing is more essential than to preserve the former from all temptations of private interest, and therefore so to direct the patronage of the latter as not to permit such temptations to be offered. Experience abundantly demonstrates that every precaution in this respect is a valuable safeguard of liberty, and one which my reflections upon the tendencies of our system incline me to think should be made still stronger. It was for this reason that, in connection with an amendment of the Constitution removing all intermediate agency in the choice of the President, I recommended some restrictions upon the reeligibility of that officer and upon the tenure of offices generally. The reason still exists, and I renew the recommendation with an increased confidence that its adoption will strengthen those checks by which the Constitution designed to secure the independence of each department of the Government and promote the healthful and equitable administration of all the trusts which it has created. The agent most likely to contravene this design of the Constitution is the Chief Magistrate. In order, particularly, that his appointment may as far as possible be placed beyond the reach of any improper influences; in order that he may approach the solemn responsibilities of the highest office in the gift of a free people uncommitted to any other course than the strict line of constitutional duty, and that the securities for this independence may be rendered as strong as the nature of power and the weakness of its possessor will admit, I can not too earnestly invite your attention to the propriety of promoting such an amendment of the Constitution as will render him ineligible after one term of service.

It gives me pleasure to announce to Congress that the benevolent policy of the Government, steadily pursued for nearly thirty years, in relation to the removal of the Indians beyond the white settlements

is approaching to a happy consummation.   Two important tribes have
accepted the provision made for their removal at the last session of
Congress, and it is believed that their example will induce the remaining
tribes also to seek the same obvious advantages.

The consequences of a speedy removal will be important to the United
States, to individual States, and to the Indians themselves.   The pecuniary advantages which it promises to the Government are the least of
its recommendations.   It puts an end to all possible danger of collision
between the authorities of the General and State Governments on account
of the Indians.   It will place a dense and civilized population in large
tracts of country now occupied by a few savage hunters.   By opening
the whole territory between Tennessee on the north and Louisiana on the
south to the settlement of the whites it will incalculably strengthen
the southwestern frontier and render the adjacent States strong enough
to repel future invasions without remote aid.   It will relieve the whole
State of Mississippi and the western part of Alabama of Indian occupancy, and enable those States to advance rapidly in population, wealth,
and power.   It will separate the Indians from immediate contact with
settlements of whites; free them from the power of the States; enable
them to pursue happiness in their own way and under their own rude
institutions; will retard the progress of decay, which is lessening their
numbers, and perhaps cause them gradually, under the protection of the
Government and through the influence of good counsels, to cast off their
savage habits and become an interesting, civilized, and Christian community.   These consequences, some of them so certain and the rest so
probable, make the complete execution of the plan sanctioned by Congress at their last session an object of much solicitude.

Toward the aborigines of the country no one can indulge a more friendly
feeling than myself, or would go further in attempting to reclaim them
from their wandering habits and make them a happy, prosperous people.
I have endeavored to impress upon them my own solemn convictions of
the duties and powers of the General Government in relation to the State
authorities.   For the justice of the laws passed by the States within the
scope of their reserved powers they are not responsible to this Government.   As individuals we may entertain and express our opinions of their
acts, but as a Government we have as little right to control them as we
have to prescribe laws for other nations.

With a full understanding of the subject, the Choctaw and the Chickasaw tribes have with great unanimity determined to avail themselves of
the liberal offers presented by the act of Congress, and have agreed to
remove beyond the Mississippi River.   Treaties have been made with
them, which in due season will be submitted for consideration.   In negotiating these treaties they were made to understand their true condition,
and they have preferred maintaining their independence in the Western
forests to submitting to the laws of the States in which they now reside.

These treaties, being probably the last which will ever be made with them, are characterized by great liberality on the part of the Government. They give the Indians a liberal sum in consideration of their removal, and comfortable subsistence on their arrival at their new homes. If it be their real interest to maintain a separate existence, they will there be at liberty to do so without the inconveniences and vexations to which they would unavoidably have been subject in Alabama and Mississippi.

Humanity has often wept over the fate of the aborigines of this country, and Philanthropy has been long busily employed in devising means to avert it, but its progress has never for a moment been arrested, and one by one have many powerful tribes disappeared from the earth. To follow to the tomb the last of his race and to tread on the graves of extinct nations excite melancholy reflections. But true philanthropy reconciles the mind to these vicissitudes as it does to the extinction of one generation to make room for another. In the monuments and fortresses of an unknown people, spread over the extensive regions of the West, we behold the memorials of a once powerful race, which was exterminated or has disappeared to make room for the existing savage tribes. Nor is there anything in this which, upon a comprehensive view of the general interests of the human race, is to be regretted. Philanthropy could not wish to see this continent restored to the condition in which it was found by our forefathers. What good man would prefer a country covered with forests and ranged by a few thousand savages to our extensive Republic, studded with cities, towns, and prosperous farms, embellished with all the improvements which art can devise or industry execute, occupied by more than 12,000,000 happy people, and filled with all the blessings of liberty, civilization, and religion?

The present policy of the Government is but a continuation of the same progressive change by a milder process. The tribes which occupied the countries now constituting the Eastern States were annihilated or have melted away to make room for the whites. The waves of population and civilization are rolling to the westward, and we now propose to acquire the countries occupied by the red men of the South and West by a fair exchange, and, at the expense of the United States, to send them to a land where their existence may be prolonged and perhaps made perpetual. Doubtless it will be painful to leave the graves of their fathers; but what do they more than our ancestors did or than our children are now doing? To better their condition in an unknown land our forefathers left all that was dear in earthly objects. Our children by thousands yearly leave the land of their birth to seek new homes in distant regions. Does Humanity weep at these painful separations from everything, animate and inanimate, with which the young heart has become entwined? Far from it. It is rather a source of joy that our country affords scope where our young population may range unconstrained in body or in mind, developing the power and faculties of man in their highest perfection.　These remove hundreds and almost thousands of miles at their own expense, purchase the lands they occupy, and support themselves at their new homes from the moment of their arrival. Can it be cruel in this Government when, by events which it can not control, the Indian is made discontented in his ancient home to purchase his lands, to give him a new and extensive territory, to pay the expense of his removal, and support him a year in his new abode?　How many thousands of our own people would gladly embrace the opportunity of removing to the West on such conditions!　If the offers made to the Indians were extended to them, they would be hailed with gratitude and joy.

And is it supposed that the wandering savage has a stronger attachment to his home than the settled, civilized Christian?　Is it more afflicting to him to leave the graves of his fathers than it is to our brothers and children?　Rightly considered, the policy of the General Government toward the red man is not only liberal, but generous.　He is unwilling to submit to the laws of the States and mingle with their population. To save him from this alternative, or perhaps utter annihilation, the General Government kindly offers him a new home, and proposes to pay the whole expense of his removal and settlement.

In the consummation of a policy originating at an early period, and steadily pursued by every Administration within the present century—so just to the States and so generous to the Indians—the Executive feels it has a right to expect the cooperation of Congress and of all good and disinterested men.　The States, moreover, have a right to demand it. It was substantially a part of the compact which made them members of our Confederacy.　With Georgia there is an express contract; with the new States an implied one of equal obligation.　Why, in authorizing Ohio, Indiana, Illinois, Missouri, Mississippi, and Alabama to form constitutions and become separate States, did Congress include within their limits extensive tracts of Indian lands, and, in some instances, powerful Indian tribes?　Was it not understood by both parties that the power of the States was to be coextensive with their limits, and that with all convenient dispatch the General Government should extinguish the Indian title and remove every obstruction to the complete jurisdiction of the State governments over the soil?　Probably not one of those States would have accepted a separate existence—certainly it would never have been granted by Congress—had it been understood that they were to be confined forever to those small portions of their nominal territory the Indian title to which had at the time been extinguished.

It is, therefore, a duty which this Government owes to the new States to extinguish as soon as possible the Indian title to all lands which Congress themselves have included within their limits.　When this is done the duties of the General Government in relation to the States and the Indians within their limits are at an end.　The Indians may leave the

State or not, as they choose. The purchase of their lands does not alter in the least their personal relations with the State government. No act of the General Government has ever been deemed necessary to give the States jurisdiction over the persons of the Indians. That they possess by virtue of their sovereign power within their own limits in as full a manner before as after the purchase of the Indian lands; nor can this Government add to or diminish it.

May we not hope, therefore, that all good citizens, and none more zealously than those who think the Indians oppressed by subjection to the laws of the States, will unite in attempting to open the eyes of those children of the forest to their true condition, and by a speedy removal to relieve them from all the evils, real or imaginary, present or prospective, with which they may be supposed to be threatened.

Among the numerous causes of congratulation the condition of our impost revenue deserves special mention, inasmuch as it promises the means of extinguishing the public debt sooner than was anticipated, and furnishes a strong illustration of the practical effects of the present tariff upon our commercial interests.

The object of the tariff is objected to by some as unconstitutional, and it is considered by almost all as defective in many of its parts.

The power to impose duties on imports originally belonged to the several States. The right to adjust those duties with a view to the encouragement of domestic branches of industry is so completely incidental to that power that it is difficult to suppose the existence of the one without the other. The States have delegated their whole authority over imports to the General Government without limitation or restriction, saving the very inconsiderable reservation relating to their inspection laws. This authority having thus entirely passed from the States, the right to exercise it for the purpose of protection does not exist in them, and consequently if it be not possessed by the General Government it must be extinct. Our political system would thus present the anomaly of a people stripped of the right to foster their own industry and to counteract the most selfish and destructive policy which might be adopted by foreign nations. This surely can not be the case. This indispensable power thus surrendered by the States must be within the scope of the authority on the subject expressly delegated to Congress.

In this conclusion I am confirmed as well by the opinions of Presidents Washington, Jefferson, Madison, and Monroe, who have each repeatedly recommended the exercise of this right under the Constitution, as by the uniform practice of Congress, the continued acquiescence of the States, and the general understanding of the people.

The difficulties of a more expedient adjustment of the present tariff, although great, are far from being insurmountable. Some are unwilling to improve any of its parts because they would destroy the whole; others fear to touch the objectionable parts lest those they approve should be

jeoparded.   I am persuaded that the advocates of these conflicting views
do injustice to the American people and to their representatives.   The
general interest is the interest of each, and my confidence is entire that to
insure the adoption of such modifications of the tariff as the general interest requires it is only necessary that that interest should be understood.

It is an infirmity of our nature to mingle our interests and prejudices
with the operation of our reasoning powers, and attribute to the objects
of our likes and dislikes qualities they do not possess and effects they can
not produce.   The effects of the present tariff are doubtless overrated,
both in its evils and in its advantages.   By one class of reasoners the
reduced price of cotton and other agricultural products is ascribed wholly
to its influence, and by another the reduced price of manufactured articles.   The probability is that neither opinion approaches the truth, and
that both are induced by that influence of interests and prejudices to
which I have referred.   The decrease of prices extends throughout the
commercial world, embracing not only the raw material and the manufactured article, but provisions and lands.   The cause must therefore
be deeper and more pervading than the tariff of the United States.   It
may in a measure be attributable to the increased value of the precious
metals, produced by a diminution of the supply and an increase in the
demand, while commerce has rapidly extended itself and population
has augmented.   The supply of gold and silver, the general medium of
exchange, has been greatly interrupted by civil convulsions in the countries from which they are principally drawn.   A part of the effect, too,
is doubtless owing to an increase of operatives and improvements in
machinery.   But on the whole it is questionable whether the reduction
in the price of lands, produce, and manufactures has been greater than
the appreciation of the standard of value.

While the chief object of duties should be revenue, they may be
so adjusted as to encourage manufactures.   In this adjustment, however, it is the duty of the Government to be guided by the general good.
Objects of national importance alone ought to be protected.   Of these
the productions of our soil, our mines, and our workshops, essential
to national defense, occupy the first rank.   Whatever other species of
domestic industry, having the importance to which I have referred, may
be expected, after temporary protection, to compete with foreign labor
on equal terms merit the same attention in a subordinate degree.

The present tariff taxes some of the comforts of life unnecessarily
high; it undertakes to protect interests too local and minute to justify a
general exaction, and it also attempts to force some kinds of manufactures for which the country is not ripe.   Much relief will be derived in
some of these respects from the measures of your last session.

The best as well as fairest mode of determining whether from any just
considerations a particular interest ought to receive protection would be
to submit the question singly for deliberation.   If after due examination

of its merits, unconnected with extraneous considerations—such as a desire to sustain a general system or to purchase support for a different interest—it should enlist in its favor a majority of the representatives of the people, there can be little danger of wrong or injury in adjusting the tariff with reference to its protective effect. If this obviously just principle were honestly adhered to, the branches of industry which deserve protection would be saved from the prejudice excited against them when that protection forms part of a system by which portions of the country feel or conceive themselves to be oppressed. What is incalculably more important, the vital principle of our system—that principle which requires acquiescence in the will of the majority—would be secure from the discredit and danger to which it is exposed by the acts of majorities founded not on identity of conviction, but on combinations of small minorities entered into for the purpose of mutual assistance in measures which, resting solely on their own merits, could never be carried.

I am well aware that this is a subject of so much delicacy, on account of the extended interests it involves, as to require that it should be touched with the utmost caution, and that while an abandonment of the policy in which it originated—a policy coeval with our Government, and pursued through successive Administrations—is neither to be expected or desired, the people have a right to demand, and have demanded, that it be so modified as to correct abuses and obviate injustice.

That our deliberations on this interesting subject should be uninfluenced by those partisan conflicts that are incident to free institutions is the fervent wish of my heart. To make this great question, which unhappily so much divides and excites the public mind, subservient to the short-sighted views of faction must destroy all hope of settling it satisfactorily to the great body of the people and for the general interest. I can not, therefore, in taking leave of the subject, too earnestly for my own feelings or the common good warn you against the blighting consequences of such a course.

According to the estimates at the Treasury Department, the receipts in the Treasury during the present year will amount to $24,161,018, which will exceed by about $300,000 the estimate presented in the last annual report of the Secretary of the Treasury. The total expenditure during the year, exclusive of public debt, is estimated at $13,742,311, and the payment on account of public debt for the same period will have been $11,354,630, leaving a balance in the Treasury on the 1st of January, 1831, of $4,819,781.

In connection with the condition of our finances, it affords me pleasure to remark that judicious and efficient arrangements have been made by the Treasury Department for securing the pecuniary responsibility of the public officers and the more punctual payment of the public dues. The Revenue-Cutter Service has been organized and placed on a good footing, and aided by an increase of inspectors at exposed points, and regulations adopted under the act of May, 1830, for the inspection and appraisement of merchandise, has produced much improvement in the execution of the laws and more security against the commission of frauds upon the revenue.   Abuses in the allowances for fishing bounties have also been corrected, and a material saving in that branch of the service thereby effected.   In addition to these improvements the system of expenditure for sick seamen belonging to the merchant service has been revised, and being rendered uniform and economical the benefits of the fund applicable to this object have been usefully extended.

The prosperity of our country is also further evinced by the increased revenue arising from the sale of public lands, as will appear from the report of the Commissioner of the General Land Office and the documents accompanying it, which are herewith transmitted.   I beg leave to draw your attention to this report, and to the propriety of making early appropriations for the objects which it specifies.

Your attention is again invited to the subjects connected with that portion of the public interests intrusted to the War Department.   Some of them were referred to in my former message, and they are presented in detail in the report of the Secretary of War herewith submitted.   I refer you also to the report of that officer for a knowledge of the state of the Army, fortifications, arsenals, and Indian affairs, all of which it will be perceived have been guarded with zealous attention and care.   It is worthy of your consideration whether the armaments necessary for the fortifications on our maritime frontier which are now or shortly will be completed should not be in readiness sooner than the customary appropriations will enable the Department to provide them.   This precaution seems to be due to the general system of fortification which has been sanctioned by Congress, and is recommended by that maxim of wisdom which tells us in peace to prepare for war.

I refer you to the report of the Secretary of the Navy for a highly satisfactory account of the manner in which the concerns of that Department have been conducted during the present year.   Our position in relation to the most powerful nations of the earth, and the present condition of Europe, admonish us to cherish this arm of our national defense with peculiar care.   Separated by wide seas from all those Governments whose power we might have reason to dread, we have nothing to apprehend from attempts at conquest.   It is chiefly attacks upon our commerce and harassing inroads upon our coast against which we have to guard.   A naval force adequate to the protection of our commerce, always afloat, with an accumulation of the means to give it a rapid extension in case of need, furnishes the power by which all such aggressions may be prevented or repelled.   The attention of the Government has therefore been recently directed more to preserving the public vessels already built and providing materials to be placed in depot for future use than to increasing their number.   With the aid of Congress, in a few years the Government will be prepared in case of emergency to put afloat a powerful navy of new ships almost as soon as old ones could be repaired.

The modifications in this part of the service suggested in my last annual message, which are noticed more in detail in the report of the Secretary of the Navy, are again recommended to your serious attention.

The report of the Postmaster-General in like manner exhibits a satisfactory view of the important branch of the Government under his charge. In addition to the benefits already secured by the operations of the Post-Office Department, considerable improvements within the present year have been made by an increase in the accommodation afforded by stage coaches, and in the frequency and celerity of the mail between some of the most important points of the Union.

Under the late contracts improvements have been provided for the southern section of the country, and at the same time an annual saving made of upward of $72,000. Notwithstanding the excess of expenditure beyond the current receipts for a few years past, necessarily incurred in the fulfillment of existing contracts and in the additional expenses between the periods of contracting to meet the demands created by the rapid growth and extension of our flourishing country, yet the satisfactory assurance is given that the future revenue of the Department will be sufficient to meet its extensive engagements. The system recently introduced that subjects its receipts and disbursements to strict regulation has entirely fulfilled its designs. It gives full assurance of the punctual transmission, as well as the security of the funds of the Department. The efficiency and industry of its officers and the ability and energy of contractors justify an increased confidence in its continued prosperity.

The attention of Congress was called on a former occasion to the necessity of such a modification in the office of Attorney-General of the United States as would render it more adequate to the wants of the public service. This resulted in the establishment of the office of Solicitor of the Treasury, and the earliest measures were taken to give effect to the provisions of the law which authorized the appointment of that officer and defined his duties. But it is not believed that this provision, however useful in itself, is calculated to supersede the necessity of extending the duties and powers of the Attorney-General's Office. On the contrary, I am convinced that the public interest would be greatly promoted by giving to that officer the general superintendence of the various law agents of the Government, and of all law proceedings, whether civil or criminal, in which the United States may be interested, allowing him at the same time such a compensation as would enable him to devote his undivided attention to the public business. I think such a provision is alike due to the public and to the officer.

Occasions of reference from the different Executive Departments to the Attorney-General are of frequent occurrence, and the prompt decision of the questions so referred tends much to facilitate the dispatch of business in those Departments.   The report of the Secretary of the Treasury hereto appended shows also a branch of the public service not specifically intrusted to any officer which might be advantageously committed to the Attorney-General.   But independently of those considerations this office is now one of daily duty.   It was originally organized and its compensation fixed with a view to occasional service, leaving to the incumbent time for the exercise of his profession in private practice.   The state of things which warranted such an organization no longer exists. The frequent claims upon the services of this officer would render his absence from the seat of Government in professional attendance upon the courts injurious to the public service, and the interests of the Government could not fail to be promoted by charging him with the general superintendence of all its legal concerns.

Under a strong conviction of the justness of these suggestions, I recommend it to Congress to make the necessary provisions for giving effect to them, and to place the Attorney-General in regard to compensation on the same footing with the heads of the several Executive Departments. To this officer might also be intrusted a cognizance of the cases of insolvency in public debtors, especially if the views which I submitted on this subject last year should meet the approbation of Congress—to which I again solicit your attention.

Your attention is respectfully invited to the situation of the District of Columbia.   Placed by the Constitution under the exclusive jurisdiction and control of Congress, this District is certainly entitled to a much greater share of its consideration than it has yet received.   There is a want of uniformity in its laws, particularly in those of a penal character, which increases the expense of their administration and subjects the people to all the inconveniences which result from the operation of different codes in so small a territory.   On different sides of the Potomac the same offense is punishable in unequal degrees, and the peculiarities of many of the early laws of Maryland and Virginia remain in force, notwithstanding their repugnance in some cases to the improvements which have superseded them in those States.

Besides a remedy for these evils, which is loudly called for, it is respectfully submitted whether a provision authorizing the election of a delegate to represent the wants of the citizens of this District on the floor of Congress is not due to them and to the character of our Government.   No portion of our citizens should be without a practical enjoyment of the principles of freedom, and there is none more important than that which cultivates a proper relation between the governors and the governed. Imperfect as this must be in this case, yet it is believed that it would be greatly improved by a representation in Congress with the same privileges that are allowed to the other Territories of the United States.

The penitentiary is ready for the reception of convicts, and only awaits the necessary legislation to put it into operation, as one object of which I beg leave to recall your attention to the propriety of providing suitable compensation for the officers charged with its inspection.

The importance of the principles involved in the inquiry whether it will be proper to recharter the Bank of the United States requires that I should again call the attention of Congress to the subject. Nothing has occurred to lessen in any degree the dangers which many of our citizens apprehend from that institution as at present organized. In the spirit of improvement and compromise which distinguishes our country and its institutions it becomes us to inquire whether it be not possible to secure the advantages afforded by the present bank through the agency of a Bank of the United States so modified in its principles and structure as to obviate constitutional and other objections.

It is thought practicable to organize such a bank with the necessary officers as a branch of the Treasury Department, based on the public and individual deposits, without power to make loans or purchase property, which shall remit the funds of the Government, and the expense of which may be paid, if thought advisable, by allowing its officers to sell bills of exchange to private individuals at a moderate premium. Not being a corporate body, having no stockholders, debtors, or property, and but few officers, it would not be obnoxious to the constitutional objections which are urged against the present bank; and having no means to operate on the hopes, fears, or interests of large masses of the community, it would be shorn of the influence which makes that bank formidable. The States would be strengthened by having in their hands the means of furnishing the local paper currency through their own banks, while the Bank of the United States, though issuing no paper, would check the issues of the State banks by taking their notes in deposit and for exchange only so long as they continue to be redeemed with specie. In times of public emergency the capacities of such an institution might be enlarged by legislative provisions.

These suggestions are made not so much as a recommendation as with a view of calling the attention of Congress to the possible modifications of a system which can not continue to exist in its present form without occasional collisions with the local authorities and perpetual apprehensions and discontent on the part of the States and the people.

In conclusion, fellow-citizens, allow me to invoke in behalf of your deliberations that spirit of conciliation and disinterestedness which is the gift of patriotism. Under an overruling and merciful Providence the agency of this spirit has thus far been signalized in the prosperity and glory of our beloved country. May its influence be eternal.

THIRD ANNUAL MESSAGE.

DECEMBER 6, 1831.

Fellow-Citizens of the Senate and House of Representatives:

The representation of the people has been renewed for the twenty-second time since the Constitution they formed has been in force. For near half a century the Chief Magistrates who have been successively chosen have made their annual communications of the state of the nation to its representatives. Generally these communications have been of the most gratifying nature, testifying an advance in all the improvements of social and all the securities of political life. But frequently and justly as you have been called on to be grateful for the bounties of Providence, at few periods have they been more abundantly or extensively bestowed than at the present; rarely, if ever, have we had greater reason to congratulate each other on the continued and increasing prosperity of our beloved country.

Agriculture, the first and most important occupation of man, has compensated the labors of the husbandman with plentiful crops of all the varied products of our extensive country. Manufactures have been established in which the funds of the capitalist find a profitable investment, and which give employment and subsistence to a numerous and increasing body of industrious and dexterous mechanics. The laborer is rewarded by high wages in the construction of works of internal improvement, which are extending with unprecedented rapidity. Science is steadily penetrating the recesses of nature and disclosing her secrets, while the ingenuity of free minds is subjecting the elements to the power of man and making each new conquest auxiliary to his comfort. By our mails, whose speed is regularly increased and whose routes are every year extended, the communication of public intelligence and private business is rendered frequent and safe; the intercourse between distant cities, which it formerly required weeks to accomplish, is now effected in a few days; and in the construction of railroads and the application of steam power we have a reasonable prospect that the extreme parts of our country will be so much approximated and those most isolated by the obstacles of nature rendered so accessible as to remove an apprehension sometimes entertained that the great extent of the Union would endanger its permanent existence.

If from the satisfactory view of our agriculture, manufactures, and internal improvements we turn to the state of our navigation and trade with foreign nations and between the States, we shall scarcely find less cause for gratulation. A beneficent Providence has provided for their exercise and encouragement an extensive coast, indented by capacious bays, noble rivers, inland seas; with a country productive of every material for shipbuilding and every commodity for gainful commerce, and filled with a population active, intelligent, well-informed, and fearless of danger. These advantages are not neglected, and an impulse has lately been given to commercial enterprise, which fills our shipyards with new constructions, encourages all the arts and branches of industry connected with them, crowds the wharves of our cities with vessels, and covers the most distant seas with our canvas.

Let us be grateful for these blessings to the beneficent Being who has conferred them, and who suffers us to indulge a reasonable hope of their continuance and extension, while we neglect not the means by which they may be preserved. If we may dare to judge of His future designs by the manner in which His past favors have been bestowed, He has made our national prosperity to depend on the preservation of our liberties, our national force on our Federal Union, and our individual happiness on the maintenance of our State rights and wise institutions. If we are prosperous at home and respected abroad, it is because we are free, united, industrious, and obedient to the laws. While we continue so we shall by the blessing of Heaven go on in the happy career we have begun, and which has brought us in the short period of our political existence from a population of three to thirteen millions; from thirteen separate colonies to twenty-four united States; from weakness to strength; from a rank scarcely marked in the scale of nations to a high place in their respect.

This last advantage is one that has resulted in a great degree from the principles which have guided our intercourse with foreign powers since we have assumed an equal station among them, and hence the annual account which the Executive renders to the country of the manner in which that branch of his duties has been fulfilled proves instructive and salutary.

The pacific and wise policy of our Government kept us in a state of neutrality during the wars that have at different periods since our political existence been carried on by other powers; but this policy, while it gave activity and extent to our commerce, exposed it in the same proportion to injuries from the belligerent nations. Hence have arisen claims of indemnity for those injuries. England, France, Spain, Holland, Sweden, Denmark, Naples, and lately Portugal had all in a greater or less degree infringed our neutral rights. Demands for reparation were made upon all. They have had in all, and continue to have in some, cases a leading influence on the nature of our relations with the powers on whom they were made.

Of the claims upon England it is unnecessary to speak further than to say that the state of things to which their prosecution and denial gave rise has been succeeded by arrangements productive of mutual good feeling and amicable relations between the two countries, which it is hoped will not be interrupted. One of these arrangements is that relating to the colonial trade which was communicated to Congress at the last session; and although the short period during which it has been in force will not enable me to form an accurate judgment of its operation, there is every reason to believe that it will prove highly beneficial. The trade thereby authorized has employed to the 30th September last upward of 30,000 tons of American and 15,000 tons of foreign shipping in the outward voyages, and in the inward nearly an equal amount of American and 20,000 only of foreign tonnage. Advantages, too, have resulted to our agricultural interests from the state of the trade between Canada and our Territories and States bordering or the St. Lawrence and the Lakes which may prove more than equivalent to the loss sustained by the discrimination made to favor the trade of the northern colonies with the West Indies.

After our transition from the state of colonies to that of an independent nation many points were found necessary to be settled between us and Great Britain. Among them was the demarcation of boundaries not described with sufficient precision in the treaty of peace. Some of the lines that divide the States and Territories of the United States from the British Provinces have been definitively fixed. That, however, which separates us from the Provinces of Canada and New Brunswick to the north and the east was still in dispute when I came into office, but I found arrangements made for its settlement over which I had no control. The commissioners who had been appointed under the provisions of the treaty of Ghent having been unable to agree, a convention was made with Great Britain by my immediate predecessor in office, with the advice and consent of the Senate, by which it was agreed "that the points of difference which have arisen in the settlement of the boundary line between the American and British dominions, as described in the fifth article of the treaty of Ghent, shall be referred, as therein provided, to some friendly sovereign or State, who shall be invited to investigate and make a decision upon such points of difference;" and the King of the Netherlands having by the late President and His Britannic Majesty been designated as such friendly sovereign, it became my duty to carry with good faith the agreement so made into full effect. To this end I caused all the measures to be taken which were necessary to a full exposition of our case to the sovereign arbiter, and nominated as minister plenipotentiary to his Court a distinguished citizen of the State most interested in the question, and who had been one of the agents previously employed for settling the controversy. On the 10th day of January last His Majesty the King of the Netherlands delivered to the plenipotentiaries of the United States and of Great Britain his written opinion on the case referred to him. The papers in relation to the subject will be communicated by a special message to the proper branch of the Government with the perfect confidence that its wisdom will adopt such measures as will secure an amicable settlement of the controversy without infringing any constitutional right of the States immediately interested.

It affords me satisfaction to inform you that suggestions made by my direction to the chargé d'affaires of His Britannic Majesty to this Government have had their desired effect in producing the release of certain American citizens who were imprisoned for setting up the authority of the State of Maine at a place in the disputed territory under the actual jurisdiction of His Britannic Majesty. From this and the assurances I have received of the desire of the local authorities to avoid any cause of collision I have the best hopes that a good understanding will be kept up until it is confirmed by the final disposition of the subject.

The amicable relations which now subsist between the United States and Great Britain, the increasing intercourse between their citizens, and the rapid obliteration of unfriendly prejudices to which former events naturally gave rise concurred to present this as a fit period for renewing our endeavors to provide against the recurrence of causes of irritation which in the event of war between Great Britain and any other power would inevitably endanger our peace. Animated by the sincerest desire to avoid such a state of things, and peacefully to secure under all possible circumstances the rights and honor of the country, I have given such instructions to the minister lately sent to the Court of London as will evince that desire, and if met by a correspondent disposition, which we can not doubt, will put an end to causes of collision which, without advantage to either, tend to estrange from each other two nations who have every motive to preserve not only peace, but an intercourse of the most amicable nature.

In my message at the opening of the last session of Congress I expressed a confident hope that the justice of our claims upon France, urged as they were with perseverance and signal ability by our minister there, would finally be acknowledged. This hope has been realized. A treaty has been signed which will immediately be laid before the Senate for its approbation, and which, containing stipulations that require legislative acts, must have the concurrence of both Houses before it can be carried into effect. By it the French Government engage to pay a sum which, if not quite equal to that which may be found due to our citizens, will yet, it is believed, under all circumstances, be deemed satisfactory by those interested. The offer of a gross sum instead of the satisfaction of each individual claim was accepted because the only alternatives were a rigorous exaction of the whole amount stated to be due on each claim, which might in some instances be exaggerated by design, in others overrated through error, and which, therefore, it would have been both ungracious and unjust to have insisted on; or a settlement by a mixed commission, to which the French negotiators were very averse, and which experience in other cases had shewn to be dilatory and often wholly inadequate to the end. A comparatively small sum is stipulated on our part to go to the extinction of all claims by French citizens on our Government, and a reduction of duties on our cotton and their wines has been agreed on as a consideration for the renunciation of an important claim for commercial privileges under the construction they gave to the treaty for the cession of Louisiana.

Should this treaty receive the proper sanction, a source of irritation will be stopped that has for so many years in some degree alienated from each other two nations who, from interest as well as the remembrance of early associations, ought to cherish the most friendly relations; an encouragement will be given for perseverance in the demands of justice by this new proof that if steadily pursued they will be listened to, and admonition will be offered to those powers, if any, which may be inclined to evade them that they will never be abandoned; above all, a just confidence will be inspired in our fellow-citizens that their Government will exert all the powers with which they have invested it in snpport of their just claims upon foreign nations; at the same time that the frank acknowledgment and provision for the payment of those which were addressed to our equity, although unsupported by legal proof, affords a practical illustration of our submission to the divine rule of doing to others what we desire they should do unto us.

Sweden and Denmark having made compensation for the irregularities committed by their vessels or in their ports to the perfect satisfaction of the parties concerned, and having renewed the treaties of commerce entered into with them, our political and commercial relations with those powers continue to be on the most friendly footing.

With Spain our differences up to the 22d of February, 1819, were settled by the treaty of Washington of that date, but at a subsequent period our commerce with the States formerly colonies of Spain on the continent of America was annoyed and frequently interrupted by her public and private armed ships. They captured many of our vessels prosecuting a lawful commerce and sold them and their cargoes, and at one time to our demands for restoration and indemnity opposed the allegation that they were taken in the violation of a blockade of all the ports of those States. This blockade was declaratory only, and the inadequacy of the force to maintain it was so manifest that this allegation was varied to a charge of trade in contraband of war. This, in its turn, was also found untenable, and the minister whom I sent with instructions to press for the reparation that was due to our injured fellow-citizens has transmitted an answer to his demand by which the captures are declared to have been legal, and are justified because the independence of the States of America never having been acknowledged by Spain she had a right to prohibit trade with them under her old colonial laws. This ground of defense was contradictory, not only to those which had been formerly alleged, but to the uniform practice and established laws of nations, and had been abandoned by Spain herself in the convention which granted indemnity to British subjects for captures made at the same time, under the same circumstances, and for the same allegations with those of which we complain.

I, however, indulge the hope that further reflection will lead to other views, and feel confident that when His Catholic Majesty shall be convinced of the justice of the claims his desire to preserve friendly relations between the two countries, which it is my earnest endeavor to maintain, will induce him to accede to our demand. I have therefore dispatched a special messenger with instructions to our minister to bring the case once more to his consideration, to the end that if (which I can not bring myself to believe) the same decision (that can not but be deemed an unfriendly denial of justice) should be persisted in the matter may before your adjournment be laid before you, the constitutional judges of what is proper to be done when negotiation for redress of injury fails.

The conclusion of a treaty for indemnity with France seemed to present a favorable opportunity to renew our claims of a similar nature on other powers, and particularly in the case of those upon Naples, more especially as in the course of former negotiations with that power our failure to induce France to render us justice was used as an argument against us. The desires of the merchants, who were the principal sufferers, have therefore been acceded to, and a mission has been instituted for the special purpose of obtaining for them a reparation already too long delayed. This measure having been resolved on, it was put in execution without waiting for the meeting of Congress, because the state of Europe created an apprehension of events that might have rendered our application ineffectual.

Our demands upon the Government of the Two Sicilies are of a peculiar nature. The injuries on which they are founded are not denied, nor are the atrocity and perfidy under which those injuries were perpetrated attempted to be extenuated. The sole ground on which indemnity has been refused is the alleged illegality of the tenure by which the monarch who made the seizures held his crown. This defense, always unfounded in any principle of the law of nations, now universally abandoned, even by those powers upon whom the responsibility for acts of past rulers bore the most heavily, will unquestionably be given up by His Sicilian Majesty, whose counsels will receive an impulse from that high sense of honor and regard to justice which are said to characterize him; and I feel the fullest confidence that the talents of the citizen commissioned for that purpose will place before him the just claims of our injured citizens in such a light as will enable me before your adjournment to announce that they have been adjusted and secured. Precise instructions to the effect of bringing the negotiation to a speedy issue have been given, and will be obeyed.

In the late blockade of Terceira some of the Portuguese fleet captured several of our vessels and committed other excesses, for which reparation was demanded, and I was on the point of dispatching an armed force to prevent any recurrence of a similar violence and protect our citizens in the prosecution of their lawful commerce when official assurances, on which I relied, made the sailing of the ships unnecessary. Since that period frequent promises have been made that full indemnity shall be given for the injuries inflicted and the losses sustained. In the performance there has been some, perhaps unavoidable, delay; but I have the fullest confidence that my earnest desire that this business may at once be closed, which our minister has been instructed strongly to express, will very soon be gratified. I have the better ground for this hope from the evidence of a friendly disposition which that Government has shown by an actual reduction in the duty on rice the produce of our Southern States, authorizing the anticipation that this important article of our export will soon be admitted on the same footing with that produced by the most favored nation.

With the other powers of Europe we have fortunately had no cause of discussions for the redress of injuries. With the Empire of the Russias our political connection is of the most friendly and our commercial of the most liberal kind. We enjoy the advantages of navigation and trade given to the most favored nation, but it has not yet suited their policy, or perhaps has not been found convenient from other considerations, to give stability and reciprocity to those privileges by a commercial treaty. The ill health of the minister last year charged with making a proposition for that arrangement did not permit him to remain at St. Petersburg, and the attention of that Government during the whole of the period since his departure having been occupied by the war in which it was engaged, we have been assured that nothing could have been effected by his presence. A minister will soon be nominated, as well to effect this important object as to keep up the relations of amity and good understanding of which we have received so many assurances and proofs from His Imperial Majesty and the Emperor his predecessor.

The treaty with Austria is opening to us an important trade with the hereditary dominions of the Emperor, the value of which has been hitherto little known, and of course not sufficiently appreciated. While our commerce finds an entrance into the south of Germany by means of this treaty, those we have formed with the Hanseatic towns and Prussia and others now in negotiation will open that vast country to the enterprising spirit of our merchants on the north—a country abounding in all the materials for a mutually beneficial commerce, filled with enlightened and industrious inhabitants, holding an important place in the politics of Europe, and to which we owe so many valuable citizens. The ratification of the treaty with the Porte was sent to be exchanged by the gentleman appointed our chargé d'affaires to that Court. Some difficulties occurred on his arrival, but at the date of his last official dispatch he supposed they had been obviated and that there was every prospect of the exchange being speedily effected.

This finishes the connected view I have thought it proper to give of our political and commercial relations in Europe. Every effort in my power will be continued to strengthen and extend them by treaties founded on principles of the most perfect reciprocity of interest, neither asking nor conceding any exclusive advantage, but liberating as far as it lies in my power the activity and industry of our fellow-citizens from the shackles which foreign restrictions may impose.

To China and the East Indies our commerce continues in its usual extent, and with increased facilities which the credit and capital of our merchants afford by substituting bills for payments in specie. A daring outrage having been committed in those seas by the plunder of one of our merchantmen engaged in the pepper trade at a port in Sumatra, and the piratical perpetrators belonging to tribes in such a state of society that the usual course of proceedings between civilized nations could not be pursued, I forthwith dispatched a frigate with orders to require immediate satisfaction for the injury and indemnity to the sufferers.

Few changes have taken place in our connections with the independent States of America since my last communication to Congress. The ratification of a commercial treaty with the United Republics of Mexico has been for some time under deliberation in their Congress, but was still undecided at the date of our last dispatches. The unhappy civil commotions that have prevailed there were undoubtedly the cause of the delay, but as the Government is now said to be tranquillized we may hope soon to receive the ratification of the treaty and an arrangement for the demarcation of the boundaries between us. In the meantime, an important trade has been opened with mutual benefit from St. Louis, in the State of Missouri, by caravans to the interior Provinces of Mexico. This commerce is protected in its progress through the Indian countries by the troops of the United States, which have been permitted to escort the caravans beyond our boundaries to the settled part of the Mexican territory.

From Central America I have received assurances of the most friendly kind and a gratifying application for our good offices to remove a supposed indisposition toward that Government in a neighboring State. This application was immediately and successfully complied with. They gave us also the pleasing intelligence that differences which had prevailed in their internal affairs had been peaceably adjusted. Our treaty with this Republic continues to be faithfully observed, and promises a great and beneficial commerce between the two countries—a commerce of the greatest importance if the magnificent project of a ship canal through the dominions of that State from the Atlantic to the Pacific Ocean, now in serious contemplation, shall be executed.

I have great satisfaction in communicating the success which has attended the exertions of our minister in Colombia to procure a very considerable reduction in the duties on our flour in that Republic. Indemnity also has been stipulated for injuries received by our merchants from illegal seizures, and renewed assurances are given that the treaty between the two countries shall be faithfully observed.

Chili and Peru seem to be still threatened with civil commotions, and until they shall be settled disorders may naturally be apprehended, requiring the constant presence of a naval force in the Pacific Ocean to protect our fisheries and guard our commerce.

The disturbances that took place in the Empire of Brazil previously to and immediately consequent upon the abdication of the late Emperor necessarily suspended any effectual application for the redress of some past injuries suffered by our citizens from that Government, while they have been the cause of others, in which all foreigners seem to have participated. Instructions have been given to our minister there to press for indemnity due for losses occasioned by these irregularities, and to take care that our fellow-citizens shall enjoy all the privileges stipulated in their favor by the treaty lately made between the two powers, all which the good intelligence that prevails between our minister at Rio Janeiro and the Regency gives us the best reason to expect.

I should have placed Buenos Ayres in the list of South American powers in respect to which nothing of importance affecting us was to be communicated but for occurrences which have lately taken place at the Falkland Islands, in which the name of that Republic has been used to cover with a show of authority acts injurious to our commerce and to the property and liberty of our fellow-citizens. In the course of the present year one of our vessels, engaged in the pursuit of a trade which we have always enjoyed without molestation, has been captured by a band acting, as they pretend, under the authority of the Government of Buenos Ayres. I have therefore given orders for the dispatch of an armed vessel to join our squadron in those seas and aid in affording all lawful protection to our trade which shall be necessary, and shall without delay send a minister to inquire into the nature of the circumstances and also of the claim, if any, that is set up by that Government to those islands. In the meantime, I submit the case to the consideration of Congress, to the end that they may clothe the Executive with such authority and means as they may deem necessary for providing a force adequate to the complete protection of our fellow-citizens fishing and trading in those seas.

This rapid sketch of our foreign relations, it is hoped, fellow-citizens, may be of some use in so much of your legislation as may bear on that important subject, while it affords to the country at large a source of high gratification in the contemplation of our political and commercial connection with the rest of the world. At peace with all; having subjects of future difference with few, and those susceptible of easy adjustment; extending our commerce gradually on all sides and on none by any but the most liberal and mutually beneficial means, we may, by the blessing of Providence, hope for all that national prosperity which can be derived from an intercourse with foreign nations, guided by those eternal principles of justice and reciprocal good will which are binding as well upon

States as the individuals of whom they are composed.

I have great satisfaction in making this statement of our affairs, because the course of our national policy enables me to do it without any indiscreet exposure of what in other governments is usually concealed from the people. Having none but a straightforward, open course to pursue, guided by a single principle that will bear the strongest light, we have happily no political combinations to form, no alliances to entangle us, no complicated interests to consult, and in subjecting all we have done to the consideration of our citizens and to the inspection of the world we give no advantage to other nations and lay ourselves open to no injury.

It may not be improper to add that to preserve this state of things and give confidence to the world in the integrity of our designs all our consular and diplomatic agents are strictly enjoined to examine well every cause of complaint preferred by our citizens, and while they urge with proper earnestness those that are well founded, to countenance none that are unreasonable or unjust, and to enjoin on our merchants and navigators the strictest obedience to the laws of the countries to which they resort, and a course of conduct in their dealings that may support the character of our nation and render us respected abroad.

Connected with this subject, I must recommend a revisal of our consular laws. Defects and omissions have been discovered in their operation that ought to be remedied and supplied. For your further information on this subject I have directed a report to be made by the Secretary of State, which I shall hereafter submit to your consideration.

The internal peace and security of our confederated States is the next principal object of the General Government. Time and experience have proved that the abode of the native Indian within their limits is dangerous to their peace and injurious to himself. In accordance with my recommendation at a former session of Congress, an appropriation of half a million of dollars was made to aid the voluntary removal of the various tribes beyond the limits of the States. At the last session I had the happiness to announce that the Chickasaws and Choctaws had accepted the generous offer of the Government and agreed to remove beyond the Mississippi River, by which the whole of the State of Mississippi and the western part of Alabama will be freed from Indian occupancy and opened to a civilized population. The treaties with these tribes are in a course of execution, and their removal, it is hoped, will be completed in the course of 1832.

At the request of the authorities of Georgia the registration of Cherokee Indians for emigration has been resumed, and it is confidently expected that one-half, if not two-thirds, of that tribe will follow the wise example of their more westerly brethren. Those who prefer remaining at their present homes will hereafter be governed by the laws of Georgia, as all her citizens are, and cease to be the objects of peculiar care on the part of the General Government.

During the present year the attention of the Government has been particularly directed to those tribes in the powerful and growing State of Ohio, where considerable tracts of the finest lands were still occupied by the aboriginal proprietors.   Treaties, either absolute or conditional, have been made extinguishing the whole Indian title to the reservations in that State, and the time is not distant, it is hoped, when Ohio will be no longer embarrassed with the Indian population.   The same measures will be extended to Indiana as soon as there is reason to anticipate success.   It is confidently believed that perseverance for a few years in the present policy of the Government will extinguish the Indian title to all lands lying within the States composing our Federal Union, and remove beyond their limits every Indian who is not willing to submit to their laws.   Thus will all conflicting claims to jurisdiction between the States and the Indian tribes be put to rest.   It is pleasing to reflect that results so beneficial, not only to the States immediately concerned, but to the harmony of the Union, will have been accomplished by measures equally advantageous to the Indians.   What the native savages become when surrounded by a dense population and by mixing with the whites may be seen in the miserable remnants of a few Eastern tribes, deprived of political and civil rights, forbidden to make contracts, and subjected to guardians, dragging out a wretched existence, without excitement, without hope, and almost without thought.

But the removal of the Indians beyond the limits and jurisdiction of the States does not place them beyond the reach of philanthropic aid and Christian instruction.   On the contrary, those whom philanthropy or religion may induce to live among them in their new abode will be more free in the exercise of their benevolent functions than if they had remained within the limits of the States, embarrassed by their internal regulations.   Now subject to no control but the superintending agency of the General Government, exercised with the sole view of preserving peace, they may proceed unmolested in the interesting experiment of gradually advancing a community of American Indians from barbarism to the habits and enjoyments of civilized life.

Among the happiest effects of the improved relations of our Republic has been an increase of trade, producing a corresponding increase of revenue beyond the most sanguine anticipations of the Treasury Department.

The state of the public finances will be fully shown by the Secretary of the Treasury in the report which he will presently lay before you.   I will here, however, congratulate you upon their prosperous condition.   The revenue received in the present year will not fall short of $27,700,000, and the expenditures for all objects other than the public debt will not exceed $14,700,000.   The payment on account of the principal and interest of the debt during the year will exceed $16,500,000, a greater sum than has been applied to that object out of the revenue in any year since the enlargement of the sinking fund except the two years following immediately thereafter. The amount which will have been applied to the public debt from the 4th of March, 1829, to the 1st of January next, which is less than three years since the Administration has been placed in my hands, will exceed $40,000,000.

From the large importations of the present year it may be safely estimated that the revenue which will be received into the Treasury from that source during the next year, with the aid of that received from the public lands, will considerably exceed the amount of the receipts of the present year; and it is believed that with the means which the Government will have at its disposal from various sources, which will be fully stated by the proper Department, the whole of the public debt may be extinguished, either by redemption or purchase, within the four years of my Administration. We shall then exhibit the rare example of a great nation, abounding in all the means of happiness and security, altogether free from debt.

The confidence with which the extinguishment of the public debt may be anticipated presents an opportunity for carrying into effect more fully the policy in relation to import duties which has been recommended in my former messages. A modification of the tariff which shall produce a reduction of our revenue to the wants of the Government and an adjustment of the duties on imports with a view to equal justice in relation to all our national interests and to the counteraction of foreign policy so far as it may be injurious to those interests, is deemed to be one of the principal objects which demand the consideration of the present Congress. Justice to the interests of the merchant as well as the manufacturer requires that material reductions in the import duties be prospective; and unless the present Congress shall dispose of the subject the proposed reductions can not properly be made to take effect at the period when the necessity for the revenue arising from present rates shall cease. It is therefore desirable that arrangements be adopted at your present session to relieve the people from unnecessary taxation after the extinguishment of the public debt. In the exercise of that spirit of concession and conciliation which has distinguished the friends of our Union in all great emergencies, it is believed that this object may be effected without injury to any national interest.

In my annual message of December, 1829, I had the honor to recommend the adoption of a more liberal policy than that which then prevailed toward unfortunate debtors to the Government, and I deem it my duty again to invite your attention to this subject.

Actuated by similar views, Congress at their last session passed an act for the relief of certain insolvent debtors of the United States, but the provisions of that law have not been deemed such as were adequate to that relief to this unfortunate class of our fellow-citizens which may be safely extended to them. The points in which the law appears to be defective will be particularly communicated by the Secretary of the Treasury, and I take pleasure in recommending such an extension of its provisions as will unfetter the enterprise of a valuable portion of our citizens and restore to them the means of usefulness to themselves and the community. While deliberating on this subject I would also recommend to your consideration the propriety of so modifying the laws for enforcing the payment of debts due either to the public or to individuals suing in the courts of the United States as to restrict the imprisonment of the person to cases of fraudulent concealment of property. The personal liberty of the citizen seems too sacred to be held, as in many cases it now is, at the will of a creditor to whom he is willing to surrender all the means he has of discharging his debt.

The reports from the Secretaries of the War and Navy Departments and from the Postmaster-General, which accompany this message, present satisfactory views of the operations of the Departments respectively under their charge, and suggest improvements which are worthy of and to which I invite the serious attention of Congress. Certain defects and omissions having been discovered in the operation of the laws respecting patents, they are pointed out in the accompanying report from the Secretary of State.

I have heretofore recommended amendments of the Federal Constitution giving the election of President and Vice-President to the people and limiting the service of the former to a single term. So important do I consider these changes in our fundamental law that I can not, in accordance with my sense of duty, omit to press them upon the consideration of a new Congress. For my views more at large, as well in relation to these points as to the disqualification of members of Congress to receive an office from a President in whose election they have had an official agency, which I proposed as a substitute, I refer you to my former messages.

Our system of public accounts is extremely complicated, and it is believed may be much improved. Much of the present machinery and a considerable portion of the expenditure of public money may be dispensed with, while greater facilities can be afforded to the liquidation of claims upon the Government and an examination into their justice and legality quite as efficient as the present secured. With a view to a general reform in the system, I recommend the subject to the attention of Congress.

I deem it my duty again to call your attention to the condition of the District of Columbia. It was doubtless wise in the framers of our Constitution to place the people of this District under the jurisdiction of the General Government, but to accomplish the objects they had in view it is not necessary that this people should be deprived of all the privileges of self-government. Independently of the difficulty of inducing the representatives of distant States to turn their attention to projects of laws which are not of the highest interest to their constituents, they are not individually, nor in Congress collectively, well qualified to legislate over the local concerns of this District. Consequently its interests are much neglected, and the people are almost afraid to present their grievances, lest a body in which they are not represented and which feels little sympathy in their local relations should in its attempt to make laws for them do more harm than good. Governed by the laws of the States whence they were severed, the two shores of the Potomac within the 10 miles square have different penal codes—not the present codes of Virginia and Maryland, but such as existed in those States at the time of the cession to the United States. As Congress will not form a new code, and as the people of the District can not make one for themselves, they are virtually under two governments. Is it not just to allow them at least a Delegate in Congress, if not a local legislature, to make laws for the District, subject to the approval or rejection of Congress? I earnestly recommend the extension to them of every political right which their interests require and which may be compatible with the Constitution.

The extension of the judiciary system of the United States is deemed to be one of the duties of Government. One-fourth of the States in the Union do not participate in the benefits of a circuit court. To the States of Indiana, Illinois, Missouri, Alabama, Mississippi, and Louisiana, admitted into the Union since the present judicial system was organized, only a district court has been allowed. If this be sufficient, then the circuit courts already existing in eighteen States ought to be abolished; if it be not sufficient, the defect ought to be remedied, and these States placed on the same footing with the other members of the Union. It was on this condition and on this footing that they entered the Union, and they may demand circuit courts as a matter not of concession, but of right. I trust that Congress will not adjourn leaving this anomaly in our system.

Entertaining the opinions heretofore expressed in relation to the Bank of the United States as at present organized, I felt it my duty in my former messages frankly to disclose them, in order that the attention of the Legislature and the people should be seasonably directed to that important subject, and that it might be considered and finally disposed of in a manner best calculated to promote the ends of the Constitution and subserve the public interests. Having thus conscientiously discharged a constitutional duty, I deem it proper on this occasion, without a more particular reference to the views of the subject then expressed, to leave it for the present to the investigation of an enlightened people and their representatives.

In conclusion permit me to invoke that Power which superintends all governments to infuse into your deliberations at this important crisis of our history a spirit of mutual forbearance and conciliation. In that spirit was our Union formed, and in that spirit must it be preserved.

FOURTH ANNUAL MESSAGE.

DECEMBER 4, 1832.

Fellow-Citizens of the Senate and House of Representatives:

It gives me pleasure to congratulate you upon your return to the seat of Government for the purpose of discharging your duties to the people of the United States. Although the pestilence which had traversed the Old World has entered our limits and extended its ravages over much of our land, it has pleased Almighty God to mitigate its severity and lessen the number of its victims compared with those who have fallen in most other countries over which it has spread its terrors. Notwithstanding this visitation, our country presents on every side marks of prosperity and happiness unequaled, perhaps, in any other portion of the world. If we fully appreciate our comparative condition, existing causes of discontent will appear unworthy of attention, and, with hearts of thankfulness to that divine Being who has filled our cup of prosperity, we shall feel our resolution strengthened to preserve and hand down to posterity that liberty and that union which we have received from our fathers, and which constitute the sources and the shield of all our blessings.

The relations of our country continue to present the same picture of amicable intercourse that I had the satisfaction to hold up to your view at the opening of your last session. The same friendly professions, the same desire to participate in our flourishing commerce, the same disposition to refrain from injuries unintentionally offered, are, with few exceptions, evinced by all nations with whom we have any intercourse. This desirable state of things may be mainly ascribed to our undeviating practice of the rule which has long guided our national policy, to require no exclusive privileges in commerce and to grant none. It is daily producing its beneficial effect in the respect shown to our flag, the protection of our citizens and their property abroad, and in the increase of our navigation and the extension of our mercantile operations. The returns which have been made out since we last met will show an increase during the last preceding year of more than 80,000 tons in our shipping and of near $40,000,000 in the aggregate of our imports and exports.

Nor have we less reason to felicitate ourselves on the position of our political than of our commercial concerns. They remain in the state in which they were when I last addressed you—a state of prosperity and peace, the effect of a wise attention to the parting advice of the revered Father of his Country on this subject, condensed into a maxim for the use of posterity by one of his most distinguished successors—to cultivate free commerce and honest friendship with all nations, but to make entangling alliances with none. A strict adherence to this policy has kept us aloof from the perplexing questions that now agitate the European world and have more than once deluged those countries with blood.

Should those scenes unfortunately recur, the parties to the contest may count on a faithful performance of the duties incumbent on us as a neutral nation, and our own citizens may equally rely on the firm assertion of their neutral rights.

With the nation that was our earliest friend and ally in the infancy of our political existence the most friendly relations have subsisted through the late revolutions of its Government, and, from the events of the last, promise a permanent duration. It has made an approximation in some of its political institutions to our own, and raised a monarch to the throne who preserves, it is said, a friendly recollection of the period during which he acquired among our citizens the high consideration that could then have been produced by his personal qualifications alone.

Our commerce with that nation is gradually assuming a mutually beneficial character, and the adjustment of the claims of our citizens has removed the only obstacle there was to an intercourse not only lucrative, but productive of literary and scientific improvement.

From Great Britain I have the satisfaction to inform you that I continue to receive assurances of the most amicable disposition, which have on my part on all proper occasions been promptly and sincerely reciprocated. The attention of that Government has latterly been so much engrossed by matters of a deeply interesting domestic character that we could not press upon it the renewal of negotiations which had been unfortunately broken off by the unexpected recall of our minister, who had commenced them with some hopes of success. My great object was the settlement of questions which, though now dormant, might hereafter be revived under circumstances that would endanger the good understanding which it is the interest of both parties to preserve inviolate, cemented as it is by a community of language, manners, and social habits, and by the high obligations we owe to our British ancestors for many of our most valuable institutions and for that system of representative government which has enabled us to preserve and improve them.

The question of our northeastern boundary still remains unsettled. In my last annual message I explained to you the situation in which I found that business on my coming into office, and the measures I thought it my duty to pursue for asserting the rights of the United States before the sovereign who had been chosen by my predecessor to determine the question, and also the manner in which he had disposed of it. A special message to the Senate in their executive capacity afterwards brought before them the question whether they would advise a submission to the opinion of the sovereign arbiter. That body having considered the award as not obligatory and advised me to open a further negotiation, the proposition was immediately made to the British Government, but the circumstances to which I have alluded have hitherto prevented any answer being given to the overture. Early attention, however, has been promised to the subject, and every effort on my part will be made for a satisfactory settlement of this question, interesting to the Union generally, and particularly so to one of its members.

The claims of our citizens on Spain are not yet acknowledged. On a closer investigation of them than appears to have heretofore taken place it was discovered that some of these demands, however strong they might be upon the equity of that Government, were not such as could be made the subject of national interference; and faithful to the principle of asking nothing but what was clearly right, additional instructions have been sent to modify our demands so as to embrace those only on which, according to the laws of nations, we had a strict right to insist. An inevitable delay in procuring the documents necessary for this review of the merits of these claims retarded this operation until an unfortunate malady which has afflicted His Catholic Majesty prevented an examination of them. Being now for the first time presented in an unexceptionable form, it is confidently hoped that the application will be successful.

I have the satisfaction to inform you that the application I directed to be made for the delivery of a part of the archives of Florida, which had been carried to The Havannah, has produced a royal order for their delivery, and that measures have been taken to procure its execution.

By the report of the Secretary of State communicated to you on the 25th June last you were informed of the conditional reduction obtained by the minister of the United States at Madrid of the duties on tonnage levied on American shipping in the ports of Spain. The condition of that reduction having been complied with on our part by the act passed the 13th of July last, I have the satisfaction to inform you that our ships now pay no higher nor other duties in the continental ports of Spain than are levied on their national vessels.

The demands against Portugal for illegal captures in the blockade of Terceira have been allowed to the full amount of the accounts presented by the claimants, and payment was promised to be made in three installments. The first of these has been paid; the second, although due, had not at the date of our last advices been received, owing, it was alleged, to embarrassments in the finances consequent on the civil war in which that nation is engaged.

The payments stipulated by the convention with Denmark have been punctually made, and the amount is ready for distribution among the claimants as soon as the board, now sitting, shall have performed their functions.

I regret that by the last advices from our chargé d'affaires at Naples that Government had still delayed the satisfaction due to our citizens, but at that date the effect of the last instructions was not known. Dispatches from thence are hourly expected, and the result will be communicated to you without delay.

With the rest of Europe our relations, political and commercial, remain unchanged. Negotiations are going on to put on a permanent basis the liberal system of commerce now carried on between us and the Empire of Russia. The treaty concluded with Austria is executed by His Imperial Majesty with the most perfect good faith, and as we have no diplomatic agent at his Court he personally inquired into and corrected a proceeding of some of his subaltern officers to the injury of our consul in one of his ports.

Our treaty with the Sublime Porte is producing its expected effects on our commerce. New markets are opening for our commodities and a more extensive range for the employment of our ships. A slight augmentation of the duties on our commerce, inconsistent with the spirit of the treaty, had been imposed, but on the representation of our chargé d'affaires it has been promptly withdrawn, and we now enjoy the trade and navigation of the Black Sea and of all the ports belonging to the Turkish Empire and Asia on the most perfect equality with all foreign nations.

I wish earnestly that in announcing to you the continuance of friendship and the increase of a profitable commercial intercourse with Mexico, with Central America, and the States of the South I could accompany it with the assurance that they all are blessed with that internal tranquillity and foreign peace which their heroic devotion to the cause of their independence merits. In Mexico a sanguinary struggle is now carried on, which has caused some embarrassment to our commerce, but both parties profess the most friendly disposition toward us. To the termination of this contest we look for the establishment of that secure intercourse so necessary to nations whose territories are contiguous. How important it will be to us we may calculate from the fact that even in this unfavorable state of things our maritime commerce has increased, and an internal trade by caravans from St. Louis to Santa Fe, under the protection of escorts furnished by the Government, is carried on to great advantage and is daily increasing. The agents provided for by the treaty, with this power to designate the boundaries which it established, have been named on our part, but one of the evils of the civil war now raging there has been that the appointment of those with whom they were to cooperate has not yet been announced to us.

The Government of Central America has expelled from its territory the party which some time since disturbed its peace. Desirous of fostering a favorable disposition toward us, which has on more than one occasion been evinced by this interesting country, I made a second attempt in this year to establish a diplomatic intercourse with them; but the death of the distinguished citizen whom I had appointed for that purpose has retarded the execution of measures from which I hoped much advantage to our commerce. The union of the three States which formed the Republic of Colombia has been dissolved, but they all, it is believed, consider themselves as separately bound by the treaty which was made in their federal capacity. The minister accredited to the federation continues in that character near the Government of New

Granada, and hopes were entertained that a new union would be formed between the separate States, at least for the purposes of foreign intercourse. Our minister has been instructed to use his good offices, whenever they shall be desired, to produce the reunion so much to be wished for, the domestic tranquillity of the parties, and the security and facility of foreign commerce.

Some agitations naturally attendant on an infant reign have prevailed in the Empire of Brazil, which have had the usual effect upon commercial operations, and while they suspended the consideration of claims created on similar occasions, they have given rise to new complaints on the part of our citizens. A proper consideration for calamities and difficulties of this nature has made us less urgent and peremptory in our demands for justice than duty to our fellow-citizens would under other circumstances have required. But their claims are not neglected, and will on all proper occasions be urged, and it is hoped with effect.

I refrain from making any communication on the subject of our affairs with Buenos Ayres, because the negotiation communicated to you in my last annual message was at the date of our last advices still pending and in a state that would render a publication of the details inexpedient.

A treaty of amity and commerce has been formed with the Republic of Chili, which, if approved by the Senate, will be laid before you. That Government seems to be established, and at peace with its neighbors; and its ports being the resorts of our ships which are employed in the highly important trade of the fisheries, this commercial convention can not but be of great advantage to our fellow-citizens engaged in that perilous but profitable business.

Our commerce with the neighboring State of Peru, owing to the onerous duties levied on our principal articles of export, has been on the decline, and all endeavors to procure an alteration have hitherto proved fruitless. With Bolivia we have yet no diplomatic intercourse, and the continual contests carried on between it and Peru have made me defer until a more favorable period the appointment of any agent for that purpose.

An act of atrocious piracy having been committed on one of our trading ships by the inhabitants of a settlement on the west coast of Sumatra, a frigate was dispatched with orders to demand satisfaction for the injury if those who committed it should be found to be members of a regular government, capable of maintaining the usual relations with foreign nations; but if, as it was supposed and as they proved to be, they were a band of lawless pirates, to inflict such a chastisement as would deter them and others from like aggressions. This last was done, and the effect has been an increased respect for our flag in those distant seas and additional security for our commerce.

In the view I have given of our connection with foreign powers allusions have been made to their domestic disturbances or foreign wars, to their revolutions or dissensions. It may be proper to observe that this is done solely in cases where those events affect our political relations with them, or to show their operation on our commerce. Further than this it is neither our policy nor our right to interfere. Our best wishes on all occasions, our good offices when required, will be afforded to promote the domestic tranquillity and foreign peace of all nations with whom we have any intercourse. Any intervention in their affairs further than this, even by the expression of an official opinion, is contrary to our principles of international policy, and will always be avoided.

The report which the Secretary of the Treasury will in due time lay before you will exhibit the national finances in a highly prosperous state. Owing to the continued success of our commercial enterprise, which has enabled the merchants to fulfill their engagements with the Government, the receipts from customs during the year will exceed the estimate presented at the last session, and with the other means of the Treasury will prove fully adequate not only to meet the increased expenditures resulting from the large appropriations made by Congress, but to provide for the payment of all the public debt which is at present redeemable. It is now estimated that the customs will yield to the Treasury during the present year upward of $28,000,000 The public lands, however, have proved less productive than was anticipated, and according to present information will not much exceed two millions. The expenditures for all objects other than the public debt are estimated to amount during the year to about sixteen millions and a half, while a still larger sum, viz, $18,000,000, will have been applied to the principal and interest of the public debt.

It is expected, however, that in consequence of the reduced rates of duty which will take effect after the 3d of March next there will be a considerable falling off in the revenue from customs in the year 1833. It will nevertheless be amply sufficient to provide for all the wants of the public service, estimated even upon a liberal scale, and for the redemption and purchase of the remainder of the public debt. On the 1st of January next the entire public debt of the United States, funded and unfunded, will be reduced to within a fraction of $7,000,000, of which $2,227,363 are not of right redeemable until the 1st of January, 1834, and $4,735,296 not until the 2d of January, 1835. The commissioners of the sinking funds, however, being invested with full authority to purchase the debt at the market price, and the means of the Treasury being ample, it may be hoped that the whole will be extinguished within the year 1833.

I can not too cordially congratulate Congress and my fellow-citizens on the near approach of that memorable and happy event—the extinction of the public debt of this great and free nation. Faithful to the wise and patriotic policy marked out by the legislation of the country for this object, the present Administration has devoted to it all the means which a flourishing commerce has supplied and a prudent economy preserved for the public Treasury. Within the four years for which the people have confided the Executive power to my charge $58,000,000 will have been applied to the payment of the public debt. That this has been accomplished without stinting the expenditures for all other proper objects will be seen by referring to the liberal provision made during the same period for the support and increase of our means of maritime and military defense, for internal improvements of a national character, for the removal and preservation of the Indians, and, lastly, for the gallant veterans of the Revolution.

The final removal of this great burthen from our resources affords the means of further provision for all the objects of general welfare and public defense which the Constitution authorizes, and presents the occasion for such further reduction in the revenue as may not be required for them. From the report of the Secretary of the Treasury it will be seen that after the present year such a reduction may be made to a considerable extent, and the subject is earnestly recommended to the consideration of Congress in the hope that the combined wisdom of the representatives of the people will devise such means of effecting that salutary object as may remove those burthens which shall be found to fall unequally upon any and as may promote all the great interests of the community.

Long and patient reflection has strengthened the opinions I have heretofore expressed to Congress on this subject, and I deem it my duty on the present occasion again to urge them upon the attention of the Legislature. The soundest maxims of public policy and the principals upon which our republican institutions are founded recommend a proper adaptation of the revenue to the expenditure, and they also require that the expenditure shall be limited to what, by an economical administration, shall be consistent with the simplicity of the Government and necessary to an efficient public service. In effecting this adjustment it is due, in justice to the interests of the different States, and even to the preservation of the Union itself, that the protection afforded by existing laws to any branches of the national industry should not exceed what may be necessary to counteract the regulations of foreign nations and to secure a supply of those articles of manufacture essential to the national independence and safety in time of war. If upon investigation it shall be found, as it is believed it will be, that the legislative protection granted to any particular interest is greater than is indispensably requisite for these objects, I recommend that it be gradually diminished, and that as far as may be consistent with these objects the whole scheme of duties be reduced to the revenue standard as soon as a just regard to the faith of the Government and to the preservation of the large capital invested in establishments of domestic industry will permit.

That manufactures adequate to the supply of our domestic consumption would in the abstract be beneficial to our country there is no reason to doubt, and to effect their establishment there is perhaps no American citizen who would not for awhile be willing to pay a higher price for them. But for this purpose it is presumed that a tariff of high duties, designed for perpetual protection, has entered into the minds of but few of our statesmen. The most they have anticipated is a temporary and, generally, incidental protection, which they maintain has the effect to reduce the price by domestic competition below that of the foreign article. Experience, however, our best guide on this as on other subjects, makes it doubtful whether the advantages of this system are not counterbalanced by many evils, and whether it does not tend to beget in the minds of a large portion of our countrymen a spirit of discontent and jealousy dangerous to the stability of the Union.

What, then, shall be done? Large interests have grown up under the implied pledge of our national legislation, which it would seem a violation of public faith suddenly to abandon. Nothing could justify it but the public safety, which is the supreme law. But those who have vested their capital in manufacturing establishments can not expect that the people will continue permanently to pay high taxes for their benefit, when the money is not required for any legitimate purpose in the administration of the Government. Is it not enough that the high duties have been paid as long as the money arising from them could be applied to the common benefit in the extinguishment of the public debt?

Those who take an enlarged view of the condition of our country must be satisfied that the policy of protection must be ultimately limited to those articles of domestic manufacture which are indispensable to our safety in time of war. Within this scope, on a reasonable scale, it is recommended by every consideration of patriotism and duty, which will doubtless always secure to it a liberal and efficient support. But beyond this object we have already seen the operation of the system productive of discontent. In some sections of the Republic its influence is deprecated as tending to concentrate wealth into a few hands, and as creating those germs of dependence and vice which in other countries have characterized the existence of monopolies and proved so destructive of liberty and the general good. A large portion of the people in one section of the Republic declares it not only inexpedient on these grounds, but as disturbing the equal relations of property by legislation, and therefore unconstitutional and unjust.

Doubtless these effects are in a great degree exaggerated, and may be ascribed to a mistaken view of the considerations which led to the adoption of the tariff system; but they are nevertheless important in enabling us to review the subject with a more thorough knowledge of all its bearings upon the great interests of the Republic, and with a determination to dispose of it so that none can with justice complain.

It is my painful duty to state that in one quarter of the United States opposition to the revenue laws has arisen to a height which threatens to thwart their execution, if not to endanger the integrity of the Union. Whatever obstructions may be thrown in the way of the judicial authorities of the General Government, it is hoped they will be able peaceably to overcome them by the prudence of their own officers and the patriotism of the people. But should this reasonable reliance on the moderation and good sense of all portions of our fellow-citizens be disappointed, it is believed that the laws themselves are fully adequate to the suppression of such attempts as may be immediately made. Should the exigency arise rendering the execution of the existing laws impracticable from any cause whatever, prompt notice of it will be given to Congress, with a suggestion of such views and measures as may be deemed necessary to meet it.

In conformity with principles heretofore explained, and with the hope of reducing the General Government to that simple machine which the Constitution created and of withdrawing from the States all other influence than that of its universal beneficence in preserving peace, affording an uniform currency, maintaining the inviolability of contracts, diffusing intelligence, and discharging unfelt its other superintending functions, I recommend that provision be made to dispose of all stocks now held by it in corporations, whether created by the General or State Governments, and placing the proceeds in the Treasury. As a source of profit these stocks are of little or no value; as a means of influence among the States they are adverse to the purity of our institutions. The whole principle on which they are based is deemed by many unconstitutional, and to persist in the policy which they indicate is considered wholly inexpedient.

It is my duty to acquaint you with an arrangement made by the Bank of the United States with a portion of the holders of the 3 per cent stock, by which the Government will be deprived of the use of the public funds longer than was anticipated. By this arrangement, which will be particularly explained by the Secretary of the Treasury, a surrender of the certificates of this stock may be postponed until October, 1833, and thus the liability of the Government, after its ability to discharge the debt, may be continued by the failure of the bank to perform its duties.

Such measures as are within the reach of the Secretary of the Treasury have been taken to enable him to judge whether the public deposits in that institution may be regarded as entirely safe; but as his limited power may prove inadequate to this object, I recommend the subject to the attention of Congress, under the firm belief that it is worthy of their serious investigation. An inquiry into the transactions of the institution, embracing the branches as well as the principal bank, seems called for by the credit which is given throughout the country to many serious charges impeaching its character, and which if true may justly excite the apprehension that it is no longer a safe depository of the money of the people.

Among the interests which merit the consideration of Congress after the payment of the public debt, one of the most important, in my view, is that of the public lands. Previous to the formation of our present Constitution it was recommended by Congress that a portion of the waste lands owned by the States should be ceded to the United States for the purposes of general harmony and as a fund to meet the expenses of the war. The recommendation was adopted, and at different periods of time the States of Massachusetts, New York, Virginia, North and South Carolina, and Georgia granted their vacant soil for the uses for which they had been asked. As the lands may now be considered as relieved from this pledge, the object for which they were ceded having been accomplished, it is in the discretion of Congress to dispose of them in such way as best to conduce to the quiet, harmony, and general interest of the American people. In examining this question all local and sectional feelings should be discarded and the whole United States regarded as one people, interested alike in the prosperity of their common country.

It can not be doubted that the speedy settlement of these lands constitutes the true interest of the Republic. The wealth and strength of a country are its population, and the best part of that population are the cultivators of the soil. Independent farmers are everywhere the basis of society and true friends of liberty.

In addition to these considerations questions have already arisen, and may be expected hereafter to grow out of the public lands, which involve the rights of the new States and the powers of the General Government, and unless a liberal policy be now adopted there is danger that these questions may speedily assume an importance not now generally anticipated. The influence of a great sectional interest, when brought into full action, will be found more dangerous to the harmony and union of the States than any other cause of discontent, and it is the part of wisdom and sound policy to foresee its approaches and endeavor if possible to counteract them.

Of the various schemes which have been hitherto proposed in regard to the disposal of the public lands, none has yet received the entire approbation of the National Legislature. Deeply impressed with the importance of a speedy and satisfactory arrangement of the subject, I deem it my duty on this occasion to urge it upon your consideration, and to the propositions which have been heretofore suggested by others to contribute those reflections which have occurred to me, in the hope that they may assist you in your future deliberations.

It seems to me to be our true policy that the public lands shall cease as soon as practicable to be a source of revenue, and that they be sold to settlers in limited parcels at a price barely sufficient to reimburse to the United States the expense of the present system and the cost arising under our Indian compacts. The advantages of accurate surveys and undoubted titles now secured to purchasers seem to forbid the abolition of the present system, because none can be substituted which will more perfectly accomplish these important ends. It is desirable, however, that in convenient time this machinery be withdrawn from the States, and that the right of soil and the future disposition of it be surrendered to the States respectively in which it lies.

The adventurous and hardy population of the West, besides contributing their equal share of taxation under our impost system, have in the progress of our Government, for the lands they occupy, paid into the Treasury a large proportion of $40,000,000, and of the revenue received therefrom but a small part has been expended amongst them. When to the disadvantage of their situation in this respect we add the consideration that it is their labor alone which gives real value to the lands, and that the proceeds arising from their sale are distributed chiefly among States which had not originally any claim to them, and which have enjoyed the undivided emolument arising from the sale of their own lands, it can not be expected that the new States will remain longer contented with the present policy after the payment of the public debt. To avert the consequences which may be apprehended from this cause, to put an end forever to all partial and interested legislation on the subject, and to afford to every American citizen of enterprise the opportunity of securing an independent freehold, it seems to me, therefore, best to abandon the idea of raising a future revenue out of the public lands.

In former messages I have expressed my conviction that the Constitution does not warrant the application of the funds of the General Government to objects of internal improvement which are not national in their character, and, both as a means of doing justice to all interests and putting an end to a course of legislation calculated to destroy the purity of the Government, have urged the necessity of reducing the whole subject to some fixed and certain rule. As there never will occur a period, perhaps, more propitious than the present to the accomplishment of this object, I beg leave to press the subject again upon your attention.

Without some general and well-defined principles ascertaining those objects of internal improvement to which the means of the nation may be constitutionally applied, it is obvious that the exercise of the power can never be satisfactory. Besides the danger to which it exposes Congress of making hasty appropriations to works of the character of which they may be frequently ignorant, it promotes a mischievous and corrupting influence upon elections by holding out to the people the fallacious hope that the success of a certain candidate will make navigable their neighboring creek or river, bring commerce to their doors, and increase the value of their property. It thus favors combinations to squander the treasure of the country upon a multitude of local objects, as fatal to just legislation as to the purity of public men.

If a system compatible with the Constitution can not be devised which is free from such tendencies, we should recollect that that instrument provides within itself the mode of its amendment, and that there is, therefore, no excuse for the assumption of doubtful powers by the General Government. If those which are clearly granted shall be found incompetent to the ends of its creation, it can at any time apply for their enlargement; and there is no probability that such an application, if founded on the public interest, will ever be refused. If the propriety of the proposed grant be not sufficiently apparent to command the assent of three-fourths of the States, the best possible reason why the power should not be assumed on doubtful authority is afforded; for if more than one-fourth of the States are unwilling to make the grant its exercise will be productive of discontents which will far overbalance any advantages that could be derived from it. All must admit that there is nothing so worthy of the constant solicitude of this Government as the harmony and union of the people.

Being solemnly impressed with the conviction that the extension of the power to make internal improvements beyond the limit I have suggested, even if it be deemed constitutional, is subversive of the best interests of our country, I earnestly recommend to Congress to refrain from its exercise in doubtful cases, except in relation to improvements already begun, unless they shall first procure from the States such an amendment of the Constitution as will define its character and prescribe its bounds. If the States feel themselves competent to these objects, why should this Government wish to assume the power? If they do not, then they will not hesitate to make the grant. Both Governments are the Governments of the people; improvements must be made with the money of the people, and if the money can be collected and applied by those more simple and economical political machines, the State governments, it will unquestionably be safer and better for the people than to add to the splendor, the patronage, and the power of the General Government. But if the people of the several States think otherwise they will amend the Constitution, and in their decision all ought cheerfully to acquiesce.

For a detailed and highly satisfactory view of the operations of the War Department I refer you to the accompanying report of the Secretary of War.

The hostile incursions of the Sac and Fox Indians necessarily led to the interposition of the Government. A portion of the troops, under Generals Scott and Atkinson, and of the militia of the State of Illinois were called into the field. After a harassing warfare, prolonged by the nature of the country and by the difficulty of procuring subsistence, the Indians were entirely defeated, and the disaffected band dispersed or destroyed. The result has been creditable to the troops engaged in the service. Severe as is the lesson to the Indians, it was rendered necessary by their unprovoked aggressions, and it is to be hoped that its impression will be permanent and salutary.

This campaign has evinced the efficient organization of the Army and its capacity for prompt and active service. Its several departments have performed their functions with energy and dispatch, and the general movement was satisfactory.

Our fellow-citizens upon the frontiers were ready, as they always are, in the tender of their services in the hour of danger. But a more efficient organization of our militia system is essential to that security which is one of the principal objects of all governments. Neither our situation nor our institutions require or permit the maintenance of a large regular force. History offers too many lessons of the fatal result of such a measure not to warn us against its adoption here. The expense which attends it, the obvious tendency to employ it because it exists and thus to engage in unnecessary wars, and its ultimate danger to public liberty will lead us, I trust, to place our principal dependence for protection upon the great body of the citizens of the Republic. If in asserting rights or in repelling wrongs war should come upon us, our regular force should be increased to an extent proportioned to the emergency, and our present small Army is a nucleus around which such force could be formed and embodied. But for the purposes of defense under ordinary circumstances we must rely upon the electors of the country. Those by whom and for whom the Government was instituted and is supported will constitute its protection in the hour of danger as they do its check in the hour of safety.

But it is obvious that the militia system is imperfect. Much time is lost, much unnecessary expense incurred, and much public property wasted under the present arrangement. Little useful knowledge is gained by the musters and drills as now established, and the whole subject evidently requires a thorough examination. Whether a plan of classification remedying these defects and providing for a system of instruction might not be adopted is submitted to the consideration of Congress. The Constitution has vested in the General Government an independent authority upon the subject of the militia which renders its action essential to the establishment or improvement of the system, and I recommend the matter to your consideration in the conviction that the state of this important arm of the public defense requires your attention.

I am happy to inform you that the wise and humane policy of transferring from the eastern to the western side of the Mississippi the remnants of our aboriginal tribes, with their own consent and upon just terms, has been steadily pursued, and is approaching, I trust, its consummation. By reference to the report of the Secretary of War and to the documents submitted with it you will see the progress which has been made since your last session in the arrangement of the various matters connected with our Indian relations. With one exception every subject involving any question of conflicting jurisdiction or of peculiar difficulty has been happily disposed of, and the conviction evidently gains ground among the Indians that their removal to the country assigned by the United States for their permanent residence furnishes the only hope of their ultimate prosperity.

With that portion of the Cherokees, however, living within the State of Georgia it has been found impracticable as yet to make a satisfactory adjustment. Such was my anxiety to remove all the grounds of complaint and to bring to a termination the difficulties in which they are involved that I directed the very liberal propositions to be made to them which accompany the documents herewith submitted. They can not but have seen in these offers the evidence of the strongest disposition on the part of the Government to deal justly and liberally with them. An ample indemnity was offered for their present possessions, a liberal provision for their future support and improvement, and full security for their private and political rights. Whatever difference of opinion may have prevailed respecting the just claims of these people, there will probably be none respecting the liberality of the propositions, and very little respecting the expediency of their immediate acceptance. They were, however, rejected, and thus the position of these Indians remains unchanged, as do the views communicated in my message to the Senate of February 22, 1831.

I refer you to the annual report of the Secretary of the Navy, which accompanies this message, for a detail of the operations of that branch of the service during the present year.

Besides the general remarks on some of the transactions of our Navy presented in the view which has been taken of our foreign relations, I seize this occasion to invite to your notice the increased protection which it has afforded to our commerce and citizens on distant seas without any augmentation of the force in commission. In the gradual improvement of its pecuniary concerns, in the constant progress in the collection of materials suitable for use during future emergencies, and in the construction of vessels and the buildings necessary to their preservation and repair, the present state of this branch of the service exhibits the fruits of that vigilance and care which are so indispensable to its efficiency. Various new suggestions, contained in the annexed report, as well as others heretofore submitted to Congress, are worthy of your attention, but none more so than that urging the renewal for another term of six years of the general appropriation for the gradual improvement of the Navy.

From the accompanying report of the Postmaster-General you will also perceive that that Department continues to extend its usefulness without impairing its resources or lessening the accommodations which it affords in the secure and rapid transportation of the mail.

I beg leave to call the attention of Congress to the views heretofore expressed in relation to the mode of choosing the President and Vice-President of the United States, and to those respecting the tenure of office generally. Still impressed with the justness of those views and with the belief that the modifications suggested on those subjects if adopted will contribute to the prosperity and harmony of the country, I earnestly recommend them to your consideration at this time.

I have heretofore pointed out defects in the law for punishing official frauds, especially within the District of Columbia. It has been found almost impossible to bring notorious culprits to punishment, and, according to a decision of the court for this District, a prosecution is barred by a lapse of two years after the fraud has been committed. It may happen again, as it has already happened, that during the whole two years all the evidences of the fraud may be in the possession of the culprit himself. However proper the limitation may be in relation to private citizens, it would seem that it ought not to commence running in favor of public officers until they go out of office.

The judiciary system of the United States remains imperfect. Of the nine Western and Southwestern States three only enjoy the benefits of a circuit court. Ohio, Kentucky, and Tennessee are embraced in the general system, but Indiana, Illinois, Missouri, Alabama, Mississippi, and Louisiana have only district courts. If the existing system be a good one, why should it not be extended? If it be a bad one, why is it suffered to exist? The new States were promised equal rights and privileges when they came into the Union, and such are the guaranties of the Constitution. Nothing can be more obvious than the obligation of the General Government to place all the States on the same footing in relation to the administration of justice, and I trust this duty will be neglected no longer.

On many of the subjects to which your attention is invited in this communication it is a source of gratification to reflect that the steps to be now adopted are uninfluenced by the embarrassments entailed upon the country by the wars through which it has passed. In regard to most of our great interests we may consider ourselves as just starting in our career, and after a salutary experience about to fix upon a permanent basis the policy best calculated to promote the happiness of the people and facilitate their progress toward the most complete enjoyment of civil liberty. On an occasion so interesting and important in our history, and of such anxious concern to the friends of freedom throughout the world, it is our imperious duty to lay aside all selfish and local considerations and be guided by a lofty spirit of devotion to the great principles on which our institutions are founded.

That this Government may be so administered as to preserve its efficiency in promoting and securing these general objects should be the only aim of our ambition, and we can not, therefore, too carefully examine its structure, in order that we may not mistake its powers or assume those which the people have reserved to themselves or have preferred to assign to other agents. We should bear constantly in mind the fact that the considerations which induced the framers of the Constitution to withhold from the General Government the power to regulate the great mass of the business and concerns of the people have been fully justified by experience, and that it can not now be doubted that the genius of all our institutions prescribes simplicity and economy as the characteristics of the reform which is yet to be effected in the present and future execution of the functions bestowed upon us by the Constitution.

Limited to a general superintending power to maintain peace at home and abroad, and to prescribe laws on a few subjects of general interest not calculated to restrict human liberty, but to enforce human rights, this Government will find its strength and its glory in the faithful discharge of these plain and simple duties. Relieved by its protecting shield from the fear of war and the apprehension of oppression, the free enterprise of our citizens, aided by the State sovereignties, will work out improvements and ameliorations which can not fail to demonstrate that the great truth that the people can govern themselves is not only realized in our example, but that it is done by a machinery in government so simple and economical as scarcely to be felt. That the Almighty Ruler of the Universe may so direct our deliberations and overrule our acts as to make us instrumental in securing a result so dear to mankind is my most earnest and sincere prayer.

FIFTH ANNUAL MESSAGE.

DECEMBER 3, 1833.

Fellow-Citizens of the Senate and House of Representatives:

On your assembling to perform the high trusts which the people of the United States have confided to you, of legislating for their common welfare, it gives me pleasure to congratulate you upon the happy condition of our beloved country. By the favor of Divine Providence health is again restored to us, peace reigns within our borders, abundance crowns the labors of our fields, commerce and domestic industry flourish and increase, and individual happiness rewards the private virtue and enterprise of our citizens.

Our condition abroad is no less honorable than it is prosperous at home. Seeking nothing that is not right and determined to submit to nothing that is wrong, but desiring honest friendships and liberal intercourse with all nations, the United States have gained throughout the world the confidence and respect which are due to a policy so just and so congenial to the character of the American people and to the spirit of their institutions.

In bringing to your notice the particular state of our foreign affairs, it affords me high gratification to inform you that they are in a condition which promises the continuance of friendship with all nations.

With Great Britain the interesting question of our northeastern boundary remains still undecided. A negotiation, however, upon that subject has been renewed since the close of the last Congress, and a proposition has been submitted to the British Government with the view of establishing, in conformity with the resolution of the Senate, the line designated by the treaty of 1783. Though no definitive answer has been received, it may be daily looked for, and I entertain a hope that the overture may ultimately lead to a satisfactory adjustment of this important matter.

I have the satisfaction to inform you that a negotiation which, by desire of the House of Representatives, was opened some years ago with the British Government, for the erection of light-houses on the Bahamas, has been successful. Those works, when completed, together with those which the United States have constructed on the western side of the Gulf of Florida, will contribute essentially to the safety of navigation in that sea. This joint participation in establishments interesting to humanity and beneficial to commerce is worthy of two enlightened nations, and indicates feelings which can not fail to have a happy influence upon their political relations. It is gratifying to the friends of both to perceive that the intercourse between the two people is becoming daily more extensive, and that sentiments of mutual good will have grown up befitting their common origin and justifying the hope that by wise counsels on each side not only unsettled questions may be satisfactorily terminated, but new causes of misunderstanding prevented.

Notwithstanding that I continue to receive the most amicable assurances from the Government of France, and that in all other respects the most friendly relations exist between the United States and that Government, it is to be regretted that the stipulations of the convention concluded on the 4th July, 1831, remain in some important parts unfulfilled.

By the second article of that convention it was stipulated that the sum payable to the United States should be paid at Paris, in six annual installments, into the hands of such person or persons as should be authorized by the Government of the United States to receive it, and by the same article the first installment was payable on the 2d day of February, 1833. By the act of Congress of the 13th July, 1832, it was made the duty of the Secretary of the Treasury to cause the several installments, with the interest thereon, to be received from the French Government and transferred to the United States in such manner as he may deem best; and by the same act of Congress the stipulations on the part of the United States in the convention were in all respects fulfilled. Not doubting that a treaty thus made and ratified by the two Governments, and faithfully executed by the United States, would be promptly complied with by the other party, and desiring to avoid the risk and expense of intermediate agencies, the Secretary of the Treasury deemed it advisable to receive and transfer the first installment by means of a draft upon the French minister of finance. A draft for this purpose was accordingly drawn in favor of the cashier of the Bank of the United States for the amount accruing to the United States out of the first installment, and the interest payable with it. This bill was not drawn at Washington until five days after the installment was payable at Paris, and was accompanied by a special authority from the President authorizing the cashier or his assigns to receive the amount. The mode thus adopted of receiving the installment was officially made known to the French Government by the American chargé d'affaires at Paris, pursuant to instructions from the Department of State. The bill, however, though not presented for payment until the 23d day of March, was not paid, and for the reason assigned by the French minister of finance that no appropriation had been made by the French Chambers. It is not known to me that up to that period any appropriation had been required of the Chambers, and although a communication was subsequently made to the Chambers by direction of the King, recommending that the necessary provision should be made for carrying the convention into effect, it was at an advanced period of the session, and the subject was finally postponed until the next meeting of the Chambers.

Notwithstanding it has been supposed by the French ministry that the financial stipulations of the treaty can not be carried into effect without an appropriation by the Chambers, it appears to me to be not only consistent with the character of France, but due to the character of both Governments, as well as to the rights of our citizens, to treat the convention, made and ratified in proper form, as pledging the good faith of the French Government for its execution, and as imposing upon each department an obligation to fulfill it; and I have received assurances through our chargé d'affaires at Paris and the French minister plenipotentiary at Washington, and more recently through the minister of the United States at Paris, that the delay has not proceeded from any indisposition on the part of the King and his ministers to fulfill the treaty, and that measures will be presented at the next meeting of the Chambers, and with a reasonable hope of success, to obtain the necessary appropriation.

It is necessary to state, however, that the documents, except certain lists of vessels captured, condemned, or burnt at sea, proper to facilitate the examination and liquidation of the reclamations comprised in the stipulations of the convention, and which by the sixth article France engaged to communicate to the United States by the intermediary of the legation, though repeatedly applied for by the American chargé d'affaires under instructions from this Government, have not yet been communicated; and this delay, it is apprehended, will necessarily prevent the completion of the duties assigned to the commissioners within the time at present prescribed by law.

The reasons for delaying to communicate these documents have not been explicitly stated, and this is the more to be regretted as it is not understood that the interposition of the Chambers is in any manner required for the delivery of those papers.

Under these circumstances, in a case so important to the interests of our citizens and to the character of our country, and under disappointments so unexpected, I deemed it my duty, however I might respect the general assurances to which I have adverted, no longer to delay the appointment of a minister plenipotentiary to Paris, but to dispatch him in season to communicate the result of his application to the French Government at an early period of your session. I accordingly appointed a distinguished citizen for this purpose, who proceeded on his mission in August last and was presented to the King early in the month of October. He is particularly instructed as to all matters connected with the present posture of affairs, and I indulge the hope that with the representations he is instructed to make, and from the disposition manifested by the King and his ministers in their recent assurances to our minister at Paris, the subject will be early considered, and satisfactorily disposed of at the next meeting of the Chambers.

As this subject involves important interests and has attracted a considerable share of the public attention, I have deemed it proper to make this explicit statement of its actual condition, and should I be disappointed in the hope now entertained the subject will be again brought to the notice of Congress in such manner as the occasion may require.

The friendly relations which have always been maintained between the United States and Russia have been further extended and strengthened by the treaty of navigation and commerce concluded on the 6th of December last, and sanctioned by the Senate before the close of its last session. The ratifications having been since exchanged, the liberal provisions of the treaty are now in full force, and under the encouragement which they have secured a flourishing and increasing commerce, yielding its benefits to the enterprise of both nations, affords to each the just recompense of wise measures, and adds new motives for that mutual friendship which the two countries have hitherto cherished toward each other.

It affords me peculiar satisfaction to state that the Government of Spain has at length yielded to the justice of the claims which have been so long urged in behalf of our citizens, and has expressed a willingness to provide an indemnification as soon as the proper amount can be agreed upon. Upon this latter point it is probable an understanding had taken place between the minister of the United States and the Spanish Government before the decease of the late King of Spain; and, unless that event may have delayed its completion, there is reason to hope that it may be in my power to announce to you early in your present session the conclusion of a convention upon terms not less favorable than those entered into for similar objects with other nations. That act of justice would well accord with the character of Spain, and is due to the United States from their ancient friend. It could not fail to strengthen the sentiments of amity and good will between the two nations which it is so much the wish of the United States to cherish and so truly the interest of both to maintain.

By the first section of an act of Congress passed on the 13th of July, 1832, the tonnage duty on Spanish ships arriving from the ports of Spain was limited to the duty payable on American vessels in the ports of Spain previous to the 20th of October, 1817, being 5 cents per ton. That act was intended to give effect on our side to an arrangement made with the Spanish Government by which discriminating duties of tonnage were to be abolished in the ports of the United States and Spain on the vessels of the two nations. Pursuant to that arrangement, which was carried into effect on the part of Spain on the 20th of May, 1832, by a royal order dated the 29th of April, 1832, American vessels in the ports of Spain have paid 5 cents per ton, which rate of duty is also paid in those ports by Spanish ships; but as American vessels pay no tonnage duty in the ports of the United States, the duty of 5 cents payable in our ports by Spanish vessels under the act above mentioned is really a discriminating duty, operating to the disadvantage of Spain. Though no complaint has yet been made on the part of Spain, we are not the less bound by the obligations of good faith to remove the discrimination, and I recommend that the act be amended accordingly. As the royal order above alluded to includes the ports of the Balearic and Canary islands as well as those of Spain, it would seem that the provisions of the act of Congress should be equally extensive, and that for the repayment of such duties as may have been improperly received an addition should be made to the sum appropriated at the last session of Congress for refunding discriminating duties.

As the arrangement referred to, however, did not embrace the islands of Cuba and Puerto Rico, discriminating duties to the prejudice of American shipping continue to be levied there. From the extent of the commerce carried on between the United States and those islands, particularly the former, this discrimination causes serious injury to one of those great national interests which it has been considered an essential part of our policy to cherish, and has given rise to complaints on the part of our merchants. Under instructions given to our minister at Madrid, earnest representations have been made by him to the Spanish Government upon this subject, and there is reason to expect, from the friendly disposition which is entertained toward this country, that a beneficial change will be produced. The disadvantage, however, to which our shipping is subjected by the operation of these discriminating duties requires that they be met by suitable countervailing duties during your present session, power being at the same time vested in the President to modify or discontinue them as the discriminating duties on American vessels or their cargoes may be modified or discontinued at those islands. Intimations have been given to the Spanish Government that the United States may be obliged to resort to such measures as are of necessary self-defense, and there is no reason to apprehend that it would be unfavorably received. The proposed proceeding if adopted would not be permitted, however, in any degree to induce a relaxation in the efforts of our minister to effect a repeal of this irregularity by friendly negotiation, and it might serve to give force to his representations by showing the dangers to which that valuable trade is exposed by the obstructions and burdens which a system of discriminating and countervailing duties necessarily produces.

The selection and preparation of the Florida archives for the purpose of being delivered over to the United States, in conformity with the royal order as mentioned in my last annual message, though in progress, has not yet been completed. This delay has been produced partly by causes which were unavoidable, particularly the prevalence of the cholera at Havana; but measures have been taken which it is believed will expedite the delivery of those important records.

Congress were informed at the opening of the last session that "owing, as was alleged, to embarrassments in the finances of Portugal, consequent upon the civil war in which that nation was engaged," payment had been made of only one installment of the amount which the Portuguese Government had stipulated to pay for indemnifying our citizens for property illegally captured in the blockade of Terceira. Since that time a postponement for two years, with interest, of the two remaining installments was requested by the Portuguese Government, and as a consideration it offered to stipulate that rice of the United States should be admitted into Portugal at the same duties as Brazilian rice. Being satisfied that no better arrangement could be made, my consent was given, and a royal order of the King of Portugal was accordingly issued on the 4th of February last for the reduction of the duty on rice of the United States. It would give me great pleasure if in speaking of that country, in whose prosperity the United States are so much interested, and with whom a long-subsisting, extensive, and mutually advantageous commercial intercourse has strengthened the relations of friendship, I could announce to you the restoration of its internal tranquillity.

Subsequently to the commencement of the last session of Congress the final installment payable by Denmark under the convention of the 28th day of March, 1830, was received. The commissioners for examining the claims have since terminated their labors, and their awards have been paid at the Treasury as they have been called for. The justice rendered to our citizens by that Government is thus completed, and a pledge is thereby afforded for the maintenance of that friendly intercourse becoming the relations that the two nations mutually bear to each other.

It is satisfactory to inform you that the Danish Government have recently issued an ordinance by which the commerce with the island of St. Croix is placed on a more liberal footing than heretofore. This change can not fail to prove beneficial to the trade between the United

States and that colony, and the advantages likely to flow from it may lead to greater relaxations in the colonial systems of other nations.

The ratifications of the convention with the King of the Two Sicilies have been duly exchanged, and the commissioners appointed for examining the claims under it have entered upon the duties assigned to them by law. The friendship that the interests of the two nations require of them being now established, it may be hoped that each will enjoy the benefits which a liberal commerce should yield to both.

A treaty of amity and commerce between the United States and Belgium was concluded during the last winter and received the sanction of the Senate, but the exchange of the ratifications has been hitherto delayed, in consequence, in the first instance, of some delay in the reception of the treaty at Brussels, and, subsequently, of the absence of the Belgian minister of foreign affairs at the important conferences in which his Government is engaged at London. That treaty does but embody those enlarged principles of friendly policy which it is sincerely hoped will always regulate the conduct of the two nations having such strong motives to maintain amicable relations toward each other and so sincerely desirous to cherish them.

With all the other European powers with whom the United States have formed diplomatic relations and with the Sublime Porte the best understanding prevails. From all I continue to receive assurances of good will toward the United States—assurances which it gives me no less pleasure to reciprocate than to receive. With all, the engagements which have been entered into are fulfilled with good faith on both sides. Measures have also been taken to enlarge our friendly relations and extend our commercial intercourse with other States. The system we have pursued of aiming at no exclusive advantages, of dealing with all on terms of fair and equal reciprocity, and of adhering scrupulously to all our engagements is well calculated to give success to efforts intended to be mutually beneficial.

The wars of which the southern part of this continent was so long the theater, and which were carried on either by the mother country against the States which had formerly been her colonies or by the States against each other, having terminated, and their civil dissensions having so far subsided as with few exceptions no longer to disturb the public tranquillity, it is earnestly hoped those States will be able to employ themselves without interruption in perfecting their institutions, cultivating the arts of peace, and promoting by wise councils and able exertions the public and private prosperity which their patriotic struggles so well entitle them to enjoy.

With those States our relations have undergone but little change during the present year. No reunion having yet taken place between the States which composed the Republic of Colombia, our chargé d'affaires at Bogota has been accredited to the Government of New Grenada, and we have, therefore, no diplomatic relations with Venezuela and Equator, except as they may be included in those heretofore formed with the Colombian Republic.

It is understood that representatives from the three States were about to assemble at Bogota to confer on the subject of their mutual interests, particularly that of their union, and if the result should render it necessary, measures will be taken on our part to preserve with each that friendship and those liberal commercial connections which it has been the constant desire of the United States to cultivate with their sister Republics of this hemisphere. Until the important question of reunion shall be settled, however, the different matters which have been under discussion between the United States and the Republic of Colombia, or either of the States which composed it, are not likely to be brought to a satisfactory issue.

In consequence of the illness of the chargé d'affaires appointed to Central America at the last session of Congress, he was prevented from proceeding on his mission until the month of October. It is hoped, however, that he is by this time at his post, and that the official intercourse, unfortunately so long interrupted, has been thus renewed on the part of the two nations so amicably and advantageously connected by engagements founded on the most enlarged principles of commercial reciprocity.

It is gratifying to state that since my last annual message some of the most important claims of our fellow-citizens upon the Government of Brazil have been satisfactorily adjusted, and a reliance is placed on the friendly dispositions manifested by it that justice will also be done in others. No new causes of complaint have arisen, and the trade between the two countries flourishes under the encouragement secured to it by the liberal provisions of the treaty.

It is cause of regret that, owing, probably, to the civil dissensions which have occupied the attention of the Mexican Government, the time fixed by the treaty of limits with the United States for the meeting of the commissioners to define the boundaries between the two nations has been suffered to expire without the apppointment of any commissioners on the part of that Government. While the true boundary remains in doubt by either party it is difficult to give effect to those measures which are necessary to the protection and quiet of our numerous citizens residing near that frontier. The subject is one of great solicitude to the United States, and will not fail to receive my earnest attention.

The treaty concluded with Chili and approved by the Senate at its last session was also ratified by the Chilian Government, but with certain additional and explanatory articles of a nature to have required it to be again submitted to the Senate. The time limited for the exchange of the ratifications, however, having since expired, the action of both Governments on the treaty will again become necessary.

The negotiations commenced with the Argentine Republic relative to the outrages committed on our vessels engaged in the fisheries at the Falkland Islands by persons acting under the color of its authority, as well as the other matters in controversy between the two Governments, have been suspended by the departure of the chargé d'affaires of the United States from Buenos Ayres. It is understood, however, that a minister was subsequently appointed by that Government to renew the negotiation in the United States, but though daily expected he has not yet arrived in this country.

With Peru no treaty has yet been formed, and with Bolivia no diplomatic intercourse has yet been established. It will be my endeavor to encourage those sentiments of amity and that liberal commerce which belong to the relations in which all the independent States of this continent stand toward each other.

I deem it proper to recommend to your notice the revision of our consular system. This has become an important branch of the public service, inasmuch as it is intimately connected with the preservation of our national character abroad, with the interest of our citizens in foreign countries, with the regulation and care of our commerce, and with the protection of our seamen. At the close of the last session of Congress I communicated a report from the Secretary of State upon the subject, to which I now refer, as containing information which may be useful in any inquiries that Congress may see fit to institute with a view to a salutary reform of the system.

It gives me great pleasure to congratulate you upon the prosperous condition of the finances of the country, as will appear from the report which the Secretary of the Treasury will in due time lay before you. The receipts into the Treasury during the present year will amount to more than $32,000,000. The revenue derived from customs will, it is believed, be more than $28,000,000, and the public lands will yield about $3,000,000. The expenditures within the year for all objects, including $2,572,240.99 on account of the public debt, will not amount to $25,000,000, and a large balance will remain in the Treasury after satisfying all the appropriations chargeable on the revenue for the present year.

The measures taken by the Secretary of the Treasury will probably enable him to pay off in the course of the present year the residue of the exchanged 4½ per cent stock. redeemable on the 1st of January next. It has therefore been included in the estimated expenditures of this year, and forms a part of the sum above stated to have been paid on account of the public debt. The payment of this stock will reduce the whole debt of the United States, funded and unfunded, to the sum of $4,760,082.08, and as provision has already been made for the 4½ percents above mentioned, and charged in the expenses of the present year, the sum last stated is all that now remains of the national debt; and the revenue of the coming year, together with the balance now in the Treasury, will be sufficient to discharge it, after meeting the current expenses of the Government. Under the power given to the commissioners of the sinking fund, it will, I have no doubt, be purchased on favorable terms within the year.

From this view of the state of the finances and the public engagements yet to be fulfilled you will perceive that if Providence permits me to meet you at another session I shall have the high gratification of announcing to you that the national debt is extinguished. I can not refrain from expressing the pleasure I feel at the near approach of that desirable event. The short period of time within which the public debt will have been discharged is strong evidence of the abundant resources of the country and of the prudence and economy with which the Government has heretofore been administered. We have waged two wars since we became a nation, with one of the most powerful kingdoms in the world, both of them undertaken in defense of our dearest rights, both successfully prosecuted and honorably terminated; and many of those who partook in the first struggle as well as in the second will have lived to see the last item of the debt incurred in these necessary but expensive conflicts faithfully and honestly discharged. And we shall have the proud satisfaction of bequeathing to the public servants who follow us in the administration of the Government the rare blessing of a revenue sufficiently abundant, raised without injustice or oppression to our citizens, and unencumbered with any burdens but what they themselves shall think proper to impose upon it.

The flourishing state of the finances ought not, however, to encourage us to indulge in a lavish expenditure of the public treasure. The receipts of the present year do not furnish the test by which we are to estimate the income of the next. The changes made in our revenue system by the acts of Congress of 1832 and 1833, and more especially by the former, have swelled the receipts of the present year far beyond the amount to be expected in future years upon the reduced tariff of duties. The shortened credits on revenue bonds and the cash duties on woolens which were introduced by the act of 1832, and took effect on the 4th of March last, have brought large sums into the Treasury in 1833, which, according to the credits formerly given, would not have been payable until 1834, and would have formed a part of the income of that year. These causes would of themselves produce a great diminution of the receipts in the year 1834 as compared with the present one, and they will be still more diminished by the reduced rates of duties which take place on the 1st of January next on some of the most important and productive articles. Upon the best estimates that can be made the receipts of the next year, with the aid of the unappropriated amount now in the Treasury, will not be much more than sufficient to meet the expenses of the year and pay the small remnant of the national debt which yet remains unsatisfied. I can not, therefore, recommend to you any alteration in the present tariff of duties. The rate as now fixed by law on the various articles was adopted at the last session of Congress, as a matter of compromise, with unusual unanimity, and unless it is found to produce more than the necessities of the Government call for there would seem to be no reason at this time to justify a change.

But while I forbear to recommend any further reduction of the duties beyond that already provided for by the existing laws, I must earnestly and respectfully press upon Congress the importance of abstaining from all appropriations which are not absolutely required for the public interest and authorized by the powers clearly delegated to the United States. We are beginning a new era in our Government. The national debt, which has so long been a burden on the Treasury, will be finally discharged in the course of the ensuing year. No more money will afterwards be needed than what may be necessary to meet the ordinary expenses of the Government. Now, then, is the proper moment to fix our system of expenditure on firm and durable principles, and I can not too strongly urge the necessity of a rigid economy and an inflexible determination not to enlarge the income beyond the real necessities of the Government and not to increase the wants of the Government by unnecessary and profuse expenditures. If a contrary course should be pursued, it may happen that the revenue of 1834 will fall short of the demands upon it, and after reducing the tariff in order to lighten the burdens of the people, and providing for a still further reduction to take effect hereafter, it would be much to be deplored if at the end of another year we should find ourselves obliged to retrace our steps and impose additional taxes to meet unnecessary expenditures.

It is my duty on this occasion to call your attention to the destruction of the public building occupied by the Treasury Department, which happened since the last adjournment of Congress. A thorough inquiry into the causes of this loss was directed and made at the time, the result of which will be duly communicated to you. I take pleasure, however, in stating here that by the laudable exertions of the officers of the Department and many of the citizens of the District but few papers were lost, and none that will materially affect the public interest.

The public convenience requires that another building should be erected as soon as practicable, and in providing for it it will be advisable to enlarge in some manner the accommodations for the public officers of the several Departments, and to authorize the erection of suitable depositories for the safe-keeping of the public documents and records.

Since the last adjournment of Congress the Secretary of the Treasury has directed the money of the United States to be deposited in certain State banks designated by him, and he will immediately lay before you his reasons for this direction. I concur with him entirely in the view he has taken of the subject, and some months before the removal I urged upon the Department the propriety of taking that step. The near approach of the day on which the charter will expire, as well as the conduct of the bank, appeared to me to call for this measure upon the high considerations of public interest and public duty.   The extent of its misconduct, however, although known to be great, was not at that time fully developed by proof.   It was not until late in the month of August that I received from the Government directors an official report establishing beyond question that this great and powerful institution had been actively engaged in attempting to influence the elections of the public officers by means of its money, and that, in violation of the express provisions of its charter, it had by a formal resolution placed its funds at the disposition of its president to be employed in sustaining the political power of the bank.   A copy of this resolution is contained in the report of the Government directors before referred to, and however the object may be disguised by cautious language, no one can doubt that this money was in truth intended for electioneering purposes, and the particular uses to which it was proved to have been applied abundantly show that it was so understood.   Not only was the evidence complete as to the past application of the money and power of the bank to electioneering purposes, but that the resolution of the board of directors authorized the same course to be pursued in future.

It being thus established by unquestionable proof that the Bank of the United States was converted into a permanent electioneering engine, it appeared to me that the path of duty which the executive department of the Government ought to pursue was not doubtful.   As by the terms of the bank charter no officer but the Secretary of the Treasury could remove the deposits, it seemed to me that this authority ought to be at once exerted to deprive that great corporation of the support and countenance of the Government in such an use of its funds and such an exertion of its power.   In this point of the case the question is distinctly presented whether the people of the United States are to govern through representatives chosen by their unbiased suffrages or whether the money and power of a great corporation are to be secretly exerted to influence their judgment and control their decisions.   It must now be determined whether the bank is to have its candidates for all offices in the country, from the highest to the lowest, or whether candidates on both sides of political questions shall be brought forward as heretofore and supported by the usual means.

At this time the efforts of the bank to control public opinion, through the distresses of some and the fears of others, are equally apparent, and, if possible, more objectionable.   By a curtailment of its accommodations more rapid than any emergency requires, and even while it retains specie to an almost unprecedented amount in its vaults, it is attempting to produce great embarrassment in one portion of the community, while through presses known to have been sustained by its money it attempts by unfounded alarms to create a panic in all.

These are the means by which it seems to expect that it can force a restoration of the deposits, and as a necessary consequence extort from Congress a renewal of its charter. I am happy to know that through the good sense of our people the effort to get up a panic has hitherto failed, and that through the increased accommodations which the State banks have been enabled to afford, no public distress has followed the exertions of the bank, and it can not be doubted that the exercise of its power and the expenditure of its money, as well as its efforts to spread groundless alarm, will be met and rebuked as they deserve. In my own sphere of duty I should feel myself called on by the facts disclosed to order a *scire facias* against the bank, with a view to put an end to the chartered rights it has so palpably violated, were it not that the charter itself will expire as soon as a decision would probably be obtained from the court of last resort.

I called the attention of Congress to this subject in my last annual message, and informed them that such measures as were within the reach of the Secretary of the Treasury had been taken to enable him to judge whether the public deposits in the Bank of the United States were entirely safe; but that as his single powers might be inadequate to the object, I recommended the subject to Congress as worthy of their serious investigation, declaring it as my opinion that an inquiry into the transactions of that institution, embracing the branches as well as the principal bank, was called for by the credit which was given throughout the country to many serious charges impeaching their character, and which, if true, might justly excite the apprehension that they were no longer a safe depository for the public money. The extent to which the examination thus recommended was gone into is spread upon your journals, and is too well known to require to be stated. Such as was made resulted in a report from a majority of the Committee of Ways and Means touching certain specified points only, concluding with a resolution that the Government deposits might safely be continued in the Bank of the United States. This resolution was adopted at the close of the session by the vote of a majority of the House of Representatives.

Although I may not always be able to concur in the views of the public interest or the duties of its agents which may be taken by the other departments of the Government or either of its branches, I am, notwithstanding, wholly incapable of receiving otherwise than with the most sincere respect all opinions or suggestions proceeding from such a source, and in respect to none am I more inclined to do so than to the House of Representatives. But it will be seen from the brief views at this time taken of the subject by myself, as well as the more ample ones presented by the Secretary of the Treasury, that the change in the deposits which has been ordered has been deemed to be called for by considerations which are not affected by the proceedings referred to, and which, if correctly viewed by that Department, rendered its act a matter of imperious duty.

Coming as you do, for the most part, immediately from the people and the States by election, and possessing the fullest opportunity to know their sentiments, the present Congress will be sincerely solicitous to carry into full and fair effect the will of their constituents in regard to this institution. It will be for those in whose behalf we all act to decide whether the executive department of the Government, in the steps which it has taken on this subject, has been found in the line of its duty.

The accompanying report of the Secretary of War, with the documents annexed to it, exhibits the operations of the War Department for the past year and the condition of the various subjects intrusted to its administration.

It will be seen from them that the Army maintains the character it has heretofore acquired for efficiency and military knowledge. Nothing has occurred since your last session to require its services beyond the ordinary routine of duties which upon the seaboard and the inland frontier devolve upon it in a time of peace. The system so wisely adopted and so long pursued of constructing fortifications at exposed points and of preparing and collecting the supplies necessary for the military defense of the country, and thus providently furnishing in peace the means of defense in war, has been continued with the usual results. I recommend to your consideration the various subjects suggested in the report of the Secretary of War. Their adoption would promote the public service and meliorate the condition of the Army.

Our relations with the various Indian tribes have been undisturbed since the termination of the difficulties growing out of the hostile aggressions of the Sac and Fox Indians. Several treaties have been formed for the relinquishment of territory to the United States and for the migration of the occupants of the region assigned for their residence west of the Mississippi. Should these treaties be ratified by the Senate, provision will have been made for the removal of almost all the tribes now remaining east of that river and for the termination of many difficult and embarrassing questions arising out of their anomalous political condition. It is to be hoped that those portions of two of the Southern tribes, which in that event will present the only remaining difficulties, will realize the necessity of emigration, and will speedily resort to it. My original convictions upon this subject have been confirmed by the course of events for several years, and experience is every day adding to their strength. That those tribes can not exist surrounded by our settlements and in continual contact with our citizens is certain. They have neither the intelligence, the industry, the moral habits, nor the desire of improvement which are essential to any favorable change in their condition. Established in the midst of another and a superior race, and without appreciating the causes of their inferiority or seeking to control them, they must necessarily yield to the force of circumstances and ere long disappear. Such has been their fate heretofore, and if it is to be averted— and it is—it can only be done by a general removal beyond our boundary and by the reorganization of their political system upon principles adapted to the new relations in which they will be placed. The experiment which has been recently made has so far proved successful. The emigrants generally are represented to be prosperous and contented, the country suitable to their wants and habits, and the essential articles of subsistence easily procured. When the report of the commissioners now engaged in investigating the condition and prospects of these Indians and in devising a plan for their intercourse and government is received, I trust ample means of information will be in possession of the Government for adjusting all the unsettled questions connected with this interesting subject.

The operations of the Navy during the year and its present condition are fully exhibited in the annual report from the Navy Department.

Suggestions are made by the Secretary of various improvements, which deserve careful consideration, and most of which, if adopted, bid fair to promote the efficiency of this important branch of the public service. Among these are the new organization of the Navy Board, the revision of the pay to officers, and a change in the period of time or in the manner of making the annual appropriations, to which I beg leave to call your particular attention.

The views which are presented on almost every portion of our naval concerns, and especially on the amount of force and the number of officers, and the general course of policy appropriate in the present state of our country for securing the great and useful purposes of naval protection in peace and due preparation for the contingencies of war, meet with my entire approbation.

It will be perceived from the report referred to that the fiscal concerns of the establishment are in an excellent condition, and it is hoped that Congress may feel disposed to make promptly every suitable provision desired either for preserving or improving the system.

The general Post-Office Department has continued, upon the strength of its own resources, to facilitate the means of communication between the various portions of the Union with increased activity. The method, however, in which the accounts of the transportation of the mail have always been kept appears to have presented an imperfect view of its expenses. It has recently been discovered that from the earliest records of the Department the annual statements have been calculated to exhibit an amount considerably short of the actual expense incurred for that service. These illusory statements, together with the expense of carrying into effect the law of the last session of Congress establishing new mail routes, and a disposition on the part of the head of the Department to gratify the wishes of the public in the extension of mail facilities, have induced him to incur responsibilities for their improvement beyond what the current resources of the Department would sustain. As soon as he had discovered the imperfection of the method he caused an investigation to be made of its results and applied the proper remedy to correct the evil. It became necessary for him to withdraw some of the improvements which he had made to bring the expenses of the Department within its own resources. These expenses were incurred for the public good, and the public have enjoyed their benefit. They are now but partially suspended, and that where they may be discontinued with the least inconvenience to the country.

The progressive increase in the income from postages has equaled the highest expectations, and it affords demonstrative evidence of the growing importance and great utility of this Department. The details are exhibited in the accompanying report of the Postmaster-General.

The many distressing accidents which have of late occurred in that portion of our navigation carried on by the use of steam power deserve the immediate and unremitting attention of the constituted authorities of the country. The fact that the number of those fatal disasters is constantly increasing, notwithstanding the great improvements which are everywhere made in the machinery employed and in the rapid advances which have been made in that branch of science, shows very clearly that they are in a great degree the result of criminal negligence on the part of those by whom the vessels are navigated and to whose care and attention the lives and property of our citizens are so extensively intrusted.

That these evils may be greatly lessened, if not substantially removed, by means of precautionary and penal legislation seems to be highly probable. So far, therefore, as the subject can be regarded as within the constitutional purview of Congress I earnestly recommend it to your prompt and serious consideration.

I would also call your attention to the views I have heretofore expressed of the propriety of amending the Constitution in relation to the mode of electing the President and the Vice-President of the United States. Regarding it as all important to the future quiet and harmony of the people that every intermediate agency in the election of these officers should be removed and that their eligibility should be limited to one term of either four or six years, I can not too earnestly invite your consideration of the subject.

Trusting that your deliberations on all the topics of general interest to which I have adverted, and such others as your more extensive knowledge of the wants of our beloved country may suggest, may be crowned with success, I tender you in conclusion the cooperation which it may be in my power to afford them,

SIXTH ANNUAL MESSAGE.

DECEMBER 1, 1834.

Fellow-Citizens of the Senate and House of Representatives:

In performing my duty at the opening of your present session it gives me pleasure to congratulate you again upon the prosperous condition of our beloved country. Divine Providence has favored us with general health, with rich rewards in the fields of agriculture and in every branch of labor, and with peace to cultivate and extend the various resources which employ the virtue and enterprise of our citizens. Let us trust that in surveying a scene so flattering to our free institutions our joint deliberations to preserve them may be crowned with success.

Our foreign relations continue, with but few exceptions, to maintain the favorable aspect which they bore in my last annual message, and promise to extend those advantages which the principles that regulate our intercourse with other nations are so well calculated to secure.

The question of the northeastern boundary is still pending with Great Britain, and the proposition made in accordance with the resolution of the Senate for the establishment of a line according to the treaty of 1783 has not been accepted by that Government. Believing that every disposition is felt on both sides to adjust this perplexing question to the satisfaction of all the parties interested in it, the hope is yet indulged that it may be effected on the basis of that proposition.

With the Governments of Austria, Russia, Prussia, Holland, Sweden, and Denmark the best understanding exists. Commerce with all is fostered and protected by reciprocal good will under the sanction of liberal conventional or legal provisions.

In the midst of her internal difficulties the Queen of Spain has ratified the convention for the payment of the claims of our citizens arising since 1819. It is in the course of execution on her part, and a copy of it is now laid before you for such legislation as may be found necessary to enable those interested to derive the benefits of it.

Yielding to the force of circumstances and to the wise counsels of time and experience, that power has finally resolved no longer to occupy the unnatural position in which she stood to the new Governments established in this hemisphere. I have the great satisfaction of stating to you that in preparing the way for the restoration of harmony between those who have sprung from the same ancestors, who are allied by common interests, profess the same religion, and speak the same language the United States have been actively instrumental. Our efforts to effect this good work will be persevered in while they are deemed useful to the parties and our entire disinterestedness continues to be felt and understood. The act of Congress to countervail the discriminating duties to the prejudice of our navigation levied in Cuba and Puerto Rico has been transmitted to the minister of the United States at Madrid, to be communicated to the Government of the Queen.   No intelligence of its receipt has yet reached the Department of State.   If the present condition of the country permits the Government to make a careful and enlarged examination of the true interests of these important portions of its dominions, no doubt is entertained that their future intercourse with the United States will be placed upon a more just and liberal basis.

The Florida archives have not yet been selected and delivered.   Recent orders have been sent to the agent of the United States at Havana to return with all that he can obtain, so that they may be in Washington before the session of the Supreme Court, to be used in the legal questions there pending to which the Government is a party.

Internal tranquillity is happily restored to Portugal.   The distracted state of the country rendered unavoidable the postponement of a final payment of the just claims of our citizens.   Our diplomatic relations will be soon resumed, and the long-subsisting friendship with that power affords the strongest guaranty that the balance due will receive prompt attention.

The first installment due under the convention of indemnity with the King of the Two Sicilies has been duly received, and an offer has been made to extinguish the whole by a prompt payment—an offer I did not consider myself authorized to accept, as the indemnification provided is the exclusive property of individual citizens of the United States.   The original adjustment of our claims and the anxiety displayed to fulfill at once the stipulations made for the payment of them are highly honorable to the Government of the Two Sicilies.   When it is recollected that they were the result of the injustice of an intrusive power temporarily dominant in its territory, a repugnance to acknowledge and to pay which would have been neither unnatural nor unexpected, the circumstances can not fail to exalt its character for justice and good faith in the eyes of all nations.

The treaty of amity and commerce between the United States and Belgium, brought to your notice in my last annual message as sanctioned by the Senate, but the ratifications of which had not been exchanged owing to a delay in its reception at Brussels and a subsequent absence of the Belgian minister of foreign affairs, has been, after mature deliberation, finally disavowed by that Government as inconsistent with the powers and instructions given to their minister who negotiated it.   This disavowal was entirely unexpected, as the liberal principles embodied in the convention, and which form the groundwork of the objections to it, were perfectly satisfactory to the Belgian representative, and were supposed to be not only within the powers granted, but expressly conformable to the instructions given to him.   An offer, not yet accepted, has been made by Belgium to renew negotiations for a treaty less liberal in its provisions on questions of general maritime law.

Our newly established relations with the Sublime Porte promise to be useful to our commerce and satisfactory in every respect to this Government. Our intercourse with the Barbary Powers continues without important change, except that the present political state of Algiers has induced me to terminate the residence there of a salaried consul and to substitute an ordinary consulate, to remain so long as the place continues in the possession of France. Our first treaty with one of these powers, the Emperor of Morocco, was formed in 1786, and was limited to fifty years. That period has almost expired. I shall take measures to renew it with the greater satisfaction as its stipulations are just and liberal and have been, with mutual fidelity and reciprocal advantage, scrupulously fulfilled.

Intestine dissensions have too frequently occurred to mar the prosperity, interrupt the commerce, and distract the governments of most of the nations of this hemisphere which have separated themselves from Spain. When a firm and permanent understanding with the parent country shall have produced a formal acknowledgment of their independence, and the idea of danger from that quarter can be no longer entertained, the friends of freedom expect that those countries, so favored by nature, will be distinguished for their love of justice and their devotion to those peaceful arts the assiduous cultivation of which confers honor upon nations and gives value to human life. In the meantime I confidently hope that the apprehensions entertained that some of the people of these luxuriant regions may be tempted, in a moment of unworthy distrust of their own capacity for the enjoyment of liberty, to commit the too common error of purchasing present repose by bestowing on some favorite leaders the fatal gift of irresponsible power will not be realized. With all these Governments and with that of Brazil no unexpected changes in our relations have occurred during the present year. Frequent causes of just complaint have arisen upon the part of the citizens of the United States, sometimes from the irregular action of the constituted subordinate authorities of the maritime regions and sometimes from the leaders or partisans of those in arms against the established Governments. In all cases representations have been or will be made, and as soon as their political affairs are in a settled position it is expected that our friendly remonstrances will be followed by adequate redress.

The Government of Mexico made known in December last the appointment of commissioners and a surveyor on its part to run, in conjunction with ours, the boundary line between its territories and the United States, and excused the delay for the reasons anticipated—the prevalence of civil war. The commissioners and surveyors not having met within the time stipulated by the treaty, a new arrangement became necessary, and our chargé d'affaires was instructed in January last to negotiate in Mexico an article additional to the preexisting treaty. This instruction was acknowledged, and no difficulty was apprehended in the accomplishment of that object. By information just received that additional article to the treaty will be obtained and transmitted to this country as soon as it can receive the ratification of the Mexican Congress.

The reunion of the three States of New Grenada, Venezuela, and Equador, forming the Republic of Colombia, seems every day to become more improbable. The commissioners of the two first are understood to be now negotiating a just division of the obligations contracted by them when united under one government. The civil war in Equador, it is believed, has prevented even the appointment of a commissioner on its part.

I propose at an early day to submit, in the proper form, the appointment of a diplomatic agent to Venezuela, the importance of the commerce of that country to the United States and the large claims of our citizens upon the Government arising before and since the division of Colombia rendering it, in my judgment, improper longer to delay this step.

Our representatives to Central America, Peru, and Brazil are either at or on their way to their respective posts.

From the Argentine Republic, from which a minister was expected to this Government, nothing further has been heard. Occasion has been taken on the departure of a new consul to Buenos Ayres to remind that Government that its long-delayed minister, whose appointment had been made known to us, had not arrived.

It becomes my unpleasant duty to inform you that this pacific and highly gratifying picture of our foreign relations does not include those with France at this time. It is not possible that any Government and people could be more sincerely desirous of conciliating a just and friendly intercourse with another nation than are those of the United States with their ancient ally and friend. This disposition is founded as well on the most grateful and honorable recollections associated with our struggle for independence as upon a well-grounded conviction that it is consonant with the true policy of both. The people of the United States could not, therefore, see without the deepest regret even a temporary interruption of the friendly relations between the two countries—a regret which would, I am sure, be greatly aggravated if there should turn out to be any reasonable ground for attributing such a result to any act of omission or commission on our part. I derive, therefore, the highest satisfaction from being able to assure you that the whole course of this Government has been characterized by a spirit so conciliatory and forbearing as to make it impossible that our justice and moderation should be questioned, whatever may be the consequences of a longer perseverance on the part of the French Government in her omission to satisfy the conceded claims of our citizens.

The history of the accumulated and unprovoked aggressions upon our commerce committed by authority of the existing Governments of France between the years 1800 and 1817 has been rendered too painfully familiar to Americans to make its repetition either necessary or desirable. It will be sufficient here to remark that there has for many years been scarcely a single administration of the French Government by whom the justice and legality of the claims of our citizens to indemnity were not to a very considerable extent admitted, and yet near a quarter of a century has been wasted in ineffectual negotiations to secure it.

Deeply sensible of the injurious effects resulting from this state of things upon the interests and character of both nations, I regarded it as among my first duties to cause one more effort to be made to satisfy France that a just and liberal settlement of our claims was as well due to her own honor as to their incontestable validity. The negotiation for this purpose was commenced with the late Government of France, and was prosecuted with such success as to leave no reasonable ground to doubt that a settlement of a character quite as liberal as that which was subsequently made would have been effected had not the revolution by which the negotiation was cut off taken place. The discussions were resumed with the present Government, and the result showed that we were not wrong in supposing that an event by which the two Governments were made to approach each other so much nearer in their political principles, and by which the motives for the most liberal and friendly intercourse were so greatly multiplied, could exercise no other than a salutary influence upon the negotiation. After the most deliberate and thorough examination of the whole subject a treaty between the two Governments was concluded and signed at Paris on the 4th of July, 1831, by which it was stipulated that ''the French Government, in order to liberate itself from all the reclamations preferred against it by citizens of the United States for unlawful seizures, captures, sequestrations, confiscations, or destruction of their vessels, cargoes, or other property, engages to pay a sum of 25,000,000 francs to the United States, who shall distribute it among those entitled in the manner and according to the rules it shall determine;'' and it was also stipulated on the part of the French Government that this 25,000,000 francs should ''be paid at Paris, in six annual installments of 4,166,666 francs and 66 centimes each, into the hands of such person or persons as shall be authorized by the Government of the United States to receive it,'' the first installment to be paid ''at the expiration of one year next following the exchange of the ratifications of this convention and the others at successive intervals of a year, one after another, till the whole shall be paid. To the amount of each of the said installments shall be added interest at 4 per cent thereupon, as upon the other installments then remaining unpaid, the said interest to be computed from the day of the exchange of the present convention.''

It was also stipulated on the part of the United States, for the purpose of being completely liberated from all the reclamations presented by France on behalf of its citizens, that the sum of 1,500,000 francs should be paid to the Government of France in six annual installments, to be deducted out of the annual sums which France had agreed to pay, interest thereupon being in like manner computed from the day of the exchange of the ratifications. In addition to this stipulation, important advantages were secured to France by the following article, viz:

The wines of France, from and after the exchange of the ratifications of the present convention, shall be admitted to consumption in the States of the Union at duties which shall not exceed the following rates by the gallon (such as it is used at present for wines in the United States), to wit: 6 cents for red wines in casks; 10 cents for white wines in casks, and 22 cents for wines of all sorts in bottles. The proportions existing between the duties on French wines thus reduced and the general rates of the tariff which went into operation the 1st January, 1829, shall be maintained in case the Government of the United States should think proper to diminish those general rates in a new tariff.

In consideration of this stipulation, which shall be binding on the United States for ten years, the French Government abandons the reclamations which it had formed in relation to the eighth article of the treaty of cession of Louisiana. It engages, moreover, to establish on the *long-staple* cottons of the United States which after the exchange of the ratifications of the present convention shall be brought directly thence to France by the vessels of the United States or by French vessels the same duties as on *short-staple* cottons.

This treaty was duly ratified in the manner prescribed by the constitutions of both countries, and the ratification was exchanged at the city of Washington on the 2d of February, 1832. On account of its commercial stipulations it was in five days thereafter laid before the Congress of the United States, which proceeded to enact such laws favorable to the commerce of France as were necessary to carry it into full execution, and France has from that period to the present been in the unrestricted enjoyment of the valuable privileges that were thus secured to her. The faith of the French nation having been thus solemnly pledged through its constitutional organ for the liquidation and ultimate payment of the long-deferred claims of our citizens, as also for the adjustment of other points of great and reciprocal benefits to both countries, and the United States having, with a fidelity and promptitude by which their conduct will, I trust, be always characterized, done everything that was necessary to carry the treaty into full and fair effect on their part, counted with the most perfect confidence on equal fidelity and promptitude on the part of the French Government. In this reasonable expectation we have been, I regret to inform you, wholly disappointed. No legislative provision has been made by France for the execution of the treaty, either as it respects the indemnity to be paid or the commercial benefits to be secured to the United States, and the relations between the United States and that power in consequence thereof are placed in a situation threatening to interrupt the good understanding which has so long and so happily existed between the two nations.

Not only has the French Government been thus wanting in the performance of the stipulations it has so solemnly entered into with the

United States, but its omissions have been marked by circumstances which would seem to leave us without satisfactory evidences that such performance will certainly take place at a future period. Advice of the exchange of ratifications reached Paris prior to the 8th April, 1832. The French Chambers were then sitting, and continued in session until the 21st of that month, and although one installment of the indemnity was payable on the 2d of February, 1833, one year after the exchange of ratifications, no application was made to the Chambers for the required appropriation, and in consequence of no appropriation having then been made the draft of the United States Government for that installment was dishonored by the minister of finance, and the United States thereby involved in much controversy. The next session of the Chambers commenced on the 19th November, 1832, and continued until the 25th April, 1833. Notwithstanding the omission to pay the first installment had been made the subject of earnest remonstrance on our part, the treaty with the United States and a bill making the necessary appropriations to execute it were not laid before the Chamber of Deputies until the 6th of April, nearly five months after its meeting, and only nineteen days before the close of the session. The bill was read and referred to a committee, but there was no further action upon it. The next session of the Chambers commenced on the 26th of April, 1833, and continued until the 26th of June following. A new bill was introduced on the 11th of June, but nothing important was done in relation to it during the session. In the month of April, 1834, nearly three years after the signature of the treaty, the final action of the French Chambers upon the bill to carry the treaty into effect was obtained, and resulted in a refusal of the necessary appropriations. The avowed grounds upon which the bill was rejected are to be found in the published debates of that body, and no observations of mine can be necessary to satisfy Congress of their utter insufficiency. Although the gross amount of the claims of our citizens is probably greater than will be ultimately allowed by the commissioners, sufficient is, nevertheless, shown to render it absolutely certain that the indemnity falls far short of the actual amount of our just claims, independently of the question of damages and interest for the detention. That the settlement involved a sacrifice in this respect was well known at the time—a sacrifice which was cheerfully acquiesced in by the different branches of the Federal Government, whose action upon the treaty was required from a sincere desire to avoid further collision upon this old and disturbing subject and in the confident expectation that the general relations between the two countries would be improved thereby.

The refusal to vote the appropriation, the news of which was received from our minister in Paris about the 15th day of May last, might have been considered the final determination of the French Government not to execute the stipulations of the treaty, and would have justified an immediate communication of the facts to Congress, with a recommendation of such ultimate measures as the interest and honor of the United States might seem to require. But with the news of the refusal of the Chambers to make the appropriation were conveyed the regrets of the King and a declaration that a national vessel should be forthwith sent out with instructions to the French minister to give the most ample explanations of the past and the strongest assurances for the future. After a long passage the promised dispatch vessel arrived. The pledges given by the French minister upon receipt of his instructions were that as soon after the election of the new members as the charter would permit the legislative Chambers of France should be called together and the proposition for an appropriation laid before them; that all the constitutional powers of the King and his cabinet should be exerted to accomplish the object, and that the result should be made known early enough to be communicated to Congress at the commencement of the present session. Relying upon these pledges, and not doubting that the acknowledged justice of our claims, the promised exertions of the King and his cabinet, and, above all, that sacred regard for the national faith and honor for which the French character has been so distinguished would secure an early execution of the treaty in all its parts, I did not deem it necessary to call the attention of Congress to the subject at the last session.

I regret to say that the pledges made through the minister of France have not been redeemed. The new Chambers met on the 31st July last, and although the subject of fulfilling treaties was alluded to in the speech from the throne, no attempt was made by the King or his cabinet to procure an appropriation to carry it into execution. The reasons given for this omission, although they might be considered sufficient in an ordinary case, are not consistent with the expectations founded upon the assurances given here, for there is no constitutional obstacle to entering into legislative business at the first meeting of the Chambers. This point, however, might have been overlooked had not the Chambers, instead of being called to meet at so early a day that the result of their deliberations might be communicated to me before the meeting of Congress, been prorogued to the 29th of the present month—a period so late that their decision can scarcely be made known to the present Congress prior to its dissolution. To avoid this delay our minister in Paris, in virtue of the assurance given by the French minister in the United States, strongly urged the convocation of the Chambers at an earlier day, but without success. It is proper to remark, however, that this refusal has been accompanied with the most positive assurances on the part of the executive government of France of their intention to press the appropriation at the ensuing session of the Chambers.

The executive branch of this Government has, as matters stand, exhausted all the authority upon the subject with which it is invested and which it had any reason to believe could be beneficially employed.

The idea of acquiescing in the refusal to execute the treaty will not, I am confident, be for a moment entertained by any branch of this Government, and further negotiation upon the subject is equally out of the question.

If it shall be the pleasure of Congress to await the further action of the French Chambers, no further consideration of the subject will at this session probably be required at your hands. But if from the original delay in asking for an appropriation, from the refusal of the Chambers to grant it when asked, from the omission to bring the subject before the Chambers at their last session, from the fact that, including that session, there have been five different occasions when the appropriation might have been made, and from the delay in convoking the Chambers until some weeks after the meeting of Congress, when it was well known that a communication of the whole subject to Congress at the last session was prevented by assurances that it should be disposed of before its present meeting, you should feel yourselves constrained to doubt whether it be the intention of the French Government, in all its branches, to carry the treaty into effect, and think that such measures as the occasion may be deemed to call for should be now adopted, the important question arises what those measures shall be.

Our institutions are essentially pacific. Peace and friendly intercourse with all nations are as much the desire of our Government as they are the interest of our people. But these objects are not to be permanently secured by surrendering the rights of our citizens or permitting solemn treaties for their indemnity, in cases of flagrant wrong, to be abrogated or set aside.

It is undoubtedly in the power of Congress seriously to affect the agricultural and manufacturing interests of France by the passage of laws relating to her trade with the United States. Her products, manufactures, and tonnage may be subjected to heavy duties in our ports, or all commercial intercourse with her may be suspended. But there are powerful and to my mind conclusive objections to this mode of proceeding. We can not embarrass or cut off the trade of France without at the same time in some degree embarrassing or cutting off our own trade. The injury of such a warfare must fall, though unequally, upon our own citizens, and could not but impair the means of the Government and weaken that united sentiment in support of the rights and honor of the nation which must now pervade every bosom. Nor is it impossible that such a course of legislation would introduce once more into our national councils those disturbing questions in relation to the tariff of duties which have been so recently put to rest. Besides, by every measure adopted by the Government of the United States with the view of injuring France the clear perception of right which will induce our own people and the rulers and people of all other nations, even of France herself, to pronounce our quarrel just will be obscured and the support rendered to us in a final resort to more decisive measures will be more limited and equivocal. There is but one point in the controversy, and upon that the whole civilized world must pronounce France to be in the wrong. We insist that she shall pay us a sum of money which she has acknowledged to be due, and of the justice of this demand there can be but one opinion among mankind. True policy would seem to dictate that the question at issue should be kept thus disencumbered and that not the slightest pretense should be given to France to persist in her refusal to make payment by any act on our part affecting the interests of her people. The question should be left, as it is now, in such an attitude that when France fulfills her treaty stipulations all controversy will be at an end.

It is my conviction that the United States ought to insist on a prompt execution of the treaty, and in case it be refused or longer delayed take redress into their own hands. After the delay on the part of France of a quarter of a century in acknowledging these claims by treaty, it is not to be tolerated that another quarter of a century is to be wasted in negotiating about the payment. The laws of nations provide a remedy for such occasions. It is a well-settled principle of the international code that where one nation owes another a liquidated debt which it refuses or neglects to pay the aggrieved party may seize on the property belonging to the other, its citizens or subjects, sufficient to pay the debt without giving just cause of war. This remedy has been repeatedly resorted to, and recently by France herself toward Portugal, under circumstances less unquestionable.

The time at which resort should be had to this or any other mode of redress is a point to be decided by Congress. If an appropriation shall not be made by the French Chambers at their next session, it may justly be concluded that the Government of France has finally determined to disregard its own solemn undertaking and refuse to pay an acknowledged debt. In that event every day's delay on our part will be a stain upon our national honor, as well as a denial of justice to our injured citizens. Prompt measures, when the refusal of France shall be comp'ete, will not only be most honorable and just, but will have the best effect upon our national character.

Since France, in violation of the pledges given through her minister here, has delayed her final action so long that her decision will not probably be known in time to be communicated to this Congress, I recommend that a law be passed authorizing reprisals upon French property in case provision shall not be made for the payment of the debt at the approaching session of the French Chambers. Such a measure ought not to be considered by France as a menace. Her pride and power are too well known to expect anything from her fears and preclude the necessity of a declaration that nothing partaking of the character of intimidation is intended by us. She ought to look upon it as the evidence only of an inflexible determination on the part of the United States to insist on their rights. That Government, by doing only what it has itself acknowledged to be just, will be able to spare the United States the necessity of taking redress into their own hands and save the property of French citizens from that seizure and sequestration which American citizens so long endured without retaliation or redress. If she should continue to refuse that act of acknowledged justice and, in violation of the law of nations, make reprisals on our part the occasion of hostilities against the United States, she would but add violence to injustice, and could not fail to expose herself to the just censure of civilized nations and to the retributive judgments of Heaven.

Collision with France is the more to be regretted on account of the position she occupies in Europe in relation to liberal institutions, but in maintaining our national rights and honor all governments are alike to us. If by a collision with France in a case where she is clearly in the wrong the march of liberal principles shall be impeded, the responsibility for that result as well as every other will rest on her own head.

Having submitted these considerations, it belongs to Congress to decide whether after what has taken place it will still await the further action of the French Chambers or now adopt such provisional measures as it may deem necessary and best adapted to protect the rights and maintain the honor of the country. Whatever that decision may be, it will be faithfully enforced by the Executive as far as he is authorized so to do.

According to the estimate of the Treasury Department, the revenue accruing from all sources during the present year will amount to $20,624,717, which, with the balance remaining in the Treasury on the 1st of January last of $11,702,905, produces an aggregate of $32,327,623. The total expenditure during the year for all objects, including the public debt, is estimated at $25,591,390, which will leave a balance in the Treasury on the 1st of January, 1835, of $6,736,232. In this balance, however, will be included about $1,150,000 of what was heretofore reported by the Department as not effective.

Of former appropriations it is estimated that there will remain unexpended at the close of the year $8,002,925, and that of this sum there will not be required more than $5,141,964 to accomplish the objects of all the current appropriations. Thus it appears that after satisfying all those appropriations and after discharging the last item of our public debt, which will be done on the 1st of January next, there will remain unexpended in the Treasury an effective balance of about $440,000. That such should be the aspect of our finances is highly flattering to the industry and enterprise of our population and auspicious of the wealth and prosperity which await the future cultivation of their growing resources. It is not deemed prudent, however, to recommend any change for the present in our impost rates, the effect of the gradual reduction now in progress in many of them not being sufficiently tested to guide us in determining the precise amount of revenue which they will produce.

Free from public debt, at peace with all the world, and with no complicated interests to consult in our intercourse with foreign powers, the present may be hailed as the epoch in our history the most favorable for the settlement of those principles in our domestic policy which shall be best calculated to give stability to our Republic and secure the blessings of freedom to our citizens.

Among these principles, from our past experience, it can not be doubted that simplicity in the character of the Federal Government and a rigid economy in its administration should be regarded as fundamental and sacred. All must be sensible that the existence of the public debt, by rendering taxation necessary for its extinguishment, has increased the difficulties which are inseparable from every exercise of the taxing power, and that it was in this respect a remote agent in producing those disturbing questions which grew out of the discussions relating to the tariff. If such has been the tendency of a debt incurred in the acquisition and maintenance of our national rights and liberties, the obligations of which all portions of the Union cheerfully acknowledged, it must be obvious that whatever is calculated to increase the burdens of Government without necessity must be fatal to all our hopes of preserving its true character. While we are felicitating ourselves, therefore, upon the extinguishment of the national debt and the prosperous state of our finances, let us not be tempted to depart from those sound maxims of public policy which enjoin a just adaptation of the revenue to the expenditures that are consistent with a rigid economy and an entire abstinence from all topics of legislation that are not clearly within the constitutional powers of the Government and suggested by the wants of the country. Properly regarded under such a policy, every diminution of the public burdens arising from taxation gives to individual enterprise increased power and furnishes to all the members of our happy Confederacy new motives for patriotic affection and support. But above all, its most important effect will be found in its influence upon the character of the Government by confining its action to those objects which will be sure to secure to it the attachment and support of our fellow-citizens.

Circumstances make it my duty to call the attention of Congress to the Bank of the United States. Created for the convenience of the Government, that institution has become the scourge of the people. Its interference to postpone the payment of a portion of the national debt that it might retain the public money appropriated for that purpose to strengthen it in a political contest, the extraordinary extension and contraction of its accommodations to the community, its corrupt and partisan loans, its exclusion of the public directors from a knowledge of its most important proceedings, the unlimited authority conferred on the president to expend its funds in hiring writers and procuring the execution of printing, and the use made of that authority, the retention of the pension money and books after the selection of new agents, the groundless claim to heavy damages in consequence of the protest of the bill drawn on the French Government, have through various channels been laid before Congress. Immediately after the close of the last session the bank, through its president, announced its ability and readiness to abandon the system of unparalleled curtailment and the interruption of domestic exchanges which it had practiced upon from the 1st of August, 1833, to the 30th of June, 1834, and to extend its accommodations to the community. The grounds assumed in this annunciation amounted to an acknowledgment that the curtailment, in the extent to which it had been carried, was not necessary to the safety of the bank, and had been persisted in merely to induce Congress to grant the prayer of the bank in its memorial relative to the removal of the deposits and to give it a new charter. They were substantially a confession that all the real distresses which individuals and the country had endured for the preceding six or eight months had been needlessly produced by it, with the view of affecting through the sufferings of the people the legislative action of Congress. It is a subject of congratulation that Congress and the country had the virtue and firmness to bear the infliction, that the energies of our people soon found relief from this wanton tyranny in vast importations of the precious metals from almost every part of the world, and that at the close of this tremendous effort to control our Government the bank found itself powerless and no longer able to loan out its surplus means. The community had learned to manage its affairs without its assistance, and trade had already found new auxiliaries, so that on the 1st of October last the extraordinary spectacle was presented of a national bank more than one-half of whose capital was either lying unproductive in its vaults or in the hands of foreign bankers.

To the needless distresses brought on the country during the last session of Congress has since been added the open seizure of the dividends on the public stock to the amount of $170,041, under pretense of paying damages, cost, and interest upon the protested French bill. This sum constituted a portion of the estimated revenues for the year 1834, upon which the appropriations made by Congress were based. It would as soon have been expected that our collectors would seize on the customs or the receivers of our land offices on the moneys arising from the sale of public lands under pretenses of claims against the United States as that the bank would have retained the dividends. Indeed, if the principle be established that anyone who chooses to set up a claim against the United States may without authority of law· seize on the public property or money wherever he can find it to pay such claim, there will remain no assurance that our revenue will reach the Treasury or that it will be applied after the appropriation to the purposes designated in the law. The paymasters of our Army and the pursers of our Navy may under like pretenses apply to their own use moneys appropriated to set in motion the public force, and in time of war leave the country without defense. This measure resorted to by the bank is disorganizing and revolutionary, and if generally resorted to by private citizens in like cases would fill the land with anarchy and violence.

It is a constitutional provision "that no money shall be drawn from the Treasury but in consequence of appropriations made by law." The palpable object of this provision is to prevent the expenditure of the public money for any purpose whatsoever which shall not have been first approved by the representatives of the people and the States in Congress assembled. It vests the power of declaring for what purposes the public money shall be expended in the legislative department of the Government, to the exclusion of the executive and judicial, and it is not within the constitutional authority of either of those departments to pay it away without law or to sanction its payment. According to this plain constitutional provision, the claim of the bank can never be paid without an appropriation by act of Congress. But the bank has never asked for an appropriation. It attempts to defeat the provision of the Constitution and obtain payment without an act of Congress. Instead of awaiting an appropriation passed by both Houses and approved by the President, it makes an appropriation for itself and invites an appeal to the judiciary to sanction it. That the money had not technically been paid into the Treasury does not affect the principle intended to be estab-lished by the Constitution. The Executive and the judiciary have as little right to appropriate and expend the public money without authority of law before it is placed to the credit of the Treasury as to take it from the Treasury. In the annual report of the Secretary of the Treasury, and in his correspondence with the president of the bank, and the opin-ions of the Attorney-General accompanying it, you will find a further examination of the claims of the bank and the course it has pursued.

It seems due to the safety of the public funds remaining in that bank and to the honor of the American people that measures be taken to separate the Government entirely from an institution so mischievous to the public prosperity and so regardless of the Constitution and laws. By transferring the public deposits, by appointing other pension agents as far as it had the power, by ordering the discontinuance of the receipt of bank checks in the payment of the public dues after the 1st day of January, the Executive has exerted all its lawful authority to sever the connection between the Government and this faithless corporation.

The high-handed career of this institution imposes upon the constitu-tional functionaries of this Government duties of the gravest and most imperative character—duties which they can not avoid and from which I trust there will be no inclination on the part of any of them to shrink. My own sense of them is most clear, as is also my readiness to discharge those which may rightfully fall on me. To continue any business relations with the Bank of the United States that may be avoided without a violation of the national faith after that institution has set at open defiance the conceded right of the Government to examine its affairs, after it has done all in its power to deride the public authority in other respects and to bring it into disrepute at home and abroad, after it has attempted to defeat the clearly expressed will of the people by turning against them the immense power intrusted to its hands and by involving a country otherwise peaceful, flourishing, and happy, in dissension, embarrassment, and distress, would make the nation itself a party to the degradation so sedulously prepared for its public agents and do much to destroy the confidence of mankind in popular governments and to bring into contempt their authority and efficiency. In guarding against an evil of such magnitude considerations of temporary convenience should be thrown out of the question, and we should be influenced by such motives only as look to the honor and preservation of the republican system. Deeply and solemnly impressed with the justice of these views, I feel it to be my duty to recommend to you that a law be passed authorizing the sale of the public stock; that the provision of the charter requiring the receipt of notes of the bank in payment of public dues shall, in accordance with the power reserved to Congress in the fourteenth section of the charter, be suspended until the bank pays to the Treasury the dividends withheld, and that all laws connecting the Government or its officers with the bank, directly or indirectly, be repealed, and that the institution be left hereafter to its own resources and means.

Events have satisfied my mind, and I think the minds of the American people, that the mischiefs and dangers which flow from a national bank far overbalance all its advantages. The bold effort the present bank has made to control the Government, the distresses it has wantonly produced, the violence of which it has been the occasion in one of our cities famed for its observance of law and order, are but premonitions of the fate which awaits the American people should they be deluded into a perpetuation of this institution or the establishment of another like it. It is fervently hoped that thus admonished those who have heretofore favored the establishment of a substitute for the present bank will be induced to abandon it, as it is evidently better to incur any inconvenience that may be reasonably expected than to concentrate the whole moneyed power of the Republic in any form whatsoever or under any restrictions.

Happily it is already illustrated that the agency of such an institution is not necessary to the fiscal operations of the Government. The State banks are found fully adequate to the performance of all services which were required of the Bank of the United States, quite as promptly and with the same cheapness. They have maintained themselves and discharged all these duties while the Bank of the United States was still powerful and in the field as an open enemy, and it is not possible to conceive that they will find greater difficulties in their operations when that enemy shall cease to exist.

The attention of Congress is earnestly invited to the regulation of the deposits in the State banks by law. Although the power now exercised by the executive department in this behalf is only such as was uniformly exerted through every Administration from the origin of the Government up to the establishment of the present bank, yet it is one which is susceptible of regulation by law, and therefore ought so to be regulated. The power of Congress to direct in what places the Treasurer shall keep the moneys in the Treasury and to impose restrictions upon the Executive authority in relation to their custody and removal is unlimited, and its exercise will rather be courted than discouraged by those public officers and agents on whom rests the responsibility for their safety. It is desirable that as little power as possible should be left to the President or the Secretary of the Treasury over those institutions, which, being thus freed from Executive influence, and without a common head to direct their operations, would have neither the temptation nor the ability to interfere in the political conflicts of the country. Not deriving their charters from the national authorities, they would never have those inducements to meddle in general elections which have led the Bank of the United States to agitate and convulse the country for upward of two years.

The progress of our gold coinage is creditable to the officers of the Mint, and promises in a short period to furnish the country with a sound and portable currency, which will much diminish the inconvenience to travelers of the want of a general paper currency should the State banks be incapable of furnishing it. Those institutions have already shown themselves competent to purchase and furnish domestic exchange for the convenience of trade at reasonable rates, and not a doubt is entertained that in a short period all the wants of the country in bank accommodations and exchange will be supplied as promptly and as cheaply as they have heretofore been by the Bank of the United States. If the several States shall be induced gradually to reform their banking systems and prohibit the issue of all small notes, we shall in a few years have a currency as sound and as little liable to fluctuations as any other commercial country.

The report of the Secretary of War, together with the accompanying documents from the several bureaus of that Department, will exhibit the situation of the various objects committed to its administration.

No event has occurred since your last session rendering necessary any movements of the Army, with the exception of the expedition of the regiment of dragoons into the territory of the wandering and predatory tribes inhabiting the western frontier and living adjacent to the Mexican boundary. These tribes have been heretofore known to us principally by their attacks upon our own citizens and upon other Indians entitled to the protection of the United States. It became necessary for the peace of the frontiers to check these habitual inroads, and I am happy to inform you that the object has been effected without the commission of any act of hostility. Colonel Dodge and the troops under his command have acted with equal firmness and humanity, and an arrangement has been made with those Indians which it is hoped will assure their permanent pacific relations with the United States and the other tribes of Indians upon that border. It is to be regretted that the prevalence of sickness in that quarter has deprived the country of a number of valuable lives, and particularly that General Leavenworth, an officer well known, and esteemed for his gallant services in the late war and for his subsequent good conduct, has fallen a victim to his zeal and exertions in the discharge of his duty.

The Army is in a high state of discipline. Its moral condition, so far as that is known here, is good, and the various branches of the public service are carefully attended to. It is amply sufficient under its present organization for providing the necessary garrisons for the seaboard and for the defense of the internal frontier, and also for preserving the elements of military knowledge and for keeping pace with those improvements which modern experience is continually making. And these objects appear to me to embrace all the legitimate purposes for which a permanent military force should be maintained in our country. The lessons of history teach us its danger and the tendency which exists to an increase. This can be best met and averted by a just caution on the part of the public itself, and of those who represent them in Congress.

From the duties which devolve on the Engineer Department and upon the topographical engineers, a different organization seems to be demanded by the public interest, and I recommend the subject to your consideration.

No important change has during this season taken place in the condition of the Indians. Arrangements are in progress for the removal of the Creeks, and will soon be for the removal of the Seminoles. I regret that the Cherokees east of the Mississippi have not yet determined as a community to remove. How long the personal causes which have heretofore retarded that ultimately inevitable measure will continue to operate I am unable to conjecture. It is certain, however, that delay will bring with it accumulated evils which will render their condition more and more unpleasant. The experience of every year adds to the conviction that emigration, and that alone, can preserve from destruction the remnant of the tribes yet living amongst us. The facility with which the necessaries of life are procured and the treaty stipulations providing aid for the emigrant Indians in their agricultural pursuits and in the important concern of education, and their removal from those causes which have heretofore depressed all and destroyed many of the tribes, can not fail to stimulate their exertions and to reward their industry.

The two laws passed at the last session of Congress on the subject of Indian affairs have been carried into effect, and detailed instructions

for their administration have been given.   It will be seen by the estimates for the present session that a great reduction will take place in
the expenditures of the Department in consequence of these laws, and
there is reason to believe that their operation will be salutary and that
the colonization of the Indians on the western frontier, together with a
judicious system of administration, will still further reduce the expenses
of this branch of the public service and at the same time promote its
usefulness and efficiency.

Circumstances have been recently developed showing the existence
of extensive frauds under the various laws granting pensions and gratuities for Revolutionary services.   It is impossible to estimate the amount
which may have been thus fraudulently obtained from the National
Treasury.   I am satisfied, however, it has been such as to justify a
reexamination of the system and the adoption of the necessary checks in
its administration.   All will agree that the services and sufferings of the
remnant of our Revolutionary band should be fully compensated; but
while this is done, every proper precaution should be taken to prevent
the admission of fabricated and fraudulent claims.   In the present mode
of proceeding the attestations and certificates of the judicial officers of
the various States form a considerable portion of the checks which are
interposed against the commission of frauds.   These, however, have
been and may be fabricated, and in such a way as to elude detection at
the examining offices.   And independently of this practical difficulty, it
is ascertained that these documents are often loosely granted; sometimes
even blank certificates have been issued;   sometimes prepared papers
have been signed without inquiry, and in one instance, at least, the
seal of the court has been within reach of a person most interested in its
improper application.   It is obvious that under such circumstances no
severity of administration can check the abuse of the law.   And information has from time to time been communicated to the Pension Office
questioning or denying the right of persons placed upon the pension list
to the bounty of the country.   Such cautions are always attended to and
examined, but a far more general investigation is called for, and I therefore recommend, in conformity with the suggestion of the Secretary of
War, that an actual inspection should be made in each State into the
circumstances and claims of every person now drawing a pension.   The
honest veteran has nothing to fear from such a scrutiny, while the fraudulent claimant will be detected and the public Treasury relieved to an
amount, I have reason to believe, far greater than has heretofore been
suspected.   The details of such a plan could be so regulated as to interpose the necessary checks without any burdensome operation upon the
pensioners.   The object should be twofold:

1. To look into the original justice of the claims, so far as this can be
done under a proper system of regulations, by an examination of the
claimants themselves and by inquiring in the vicinity of their residence

into their history and into the opinion entertained of their Revolutionary services.

2. To ascertain in all cases whether the original claimant is living and this by actual personal inspection.

This measure will, if adopted, be productive, I think, of the desired results, and I therefore recommend it to your consideration, with the further suggestion that all payments should be suspended till the necessary reports are received.

It will be seen by a tabular statement annexed to the documents transmitted to Congress that the appropriations for objects connected with the War Department, made at the last session, for the service of the year 1834, excluding the permanent appropriation for the payment of military gratuities under the act of June 7, 1832, the appropriation of $200,000 for arming and equipping the militia, and the appropriation of $10,000 for the civilization of the Indians, which are not annually renewed, amounted to the sum of $9,003,261, and that the estimates of appropriations necessary for the same branches of service for the year 1835 amount to the sum of $5,778,964, making a difference in the appropriations of the current year over the estimates of the appropriations for the next of $3,224,297.

The principal causes which have operated at this time to produce this great difference are shown in the reports and documents and in the detailed estimates. Some of these causes are accidental and temporary, while others are permanent, and, aided by a just course of administration, may continue to operate beneficially upon the public expenditures.

A just economy, expending where the public service requires and withholding where it does not, is among the indispensable duties of the Government.

I refer you to the accompanying report of the Secretary of the Navy and to the documents with it for a full view of the operations of that important branch of our service during the present year. It will be seen that the wisdom and liberality with which Congress has provided for the gradual increase of our navy material have been seconded by a corresponding zeal and fidelity on the part of those to whom has been confided the execution of the laws on the subject, and that but a short period would be now required to put in commission a force large enough for any exigency into which the country may be thrown.

When we reflect upon our position in relation to other nations, it must be apparent that in the event of conflicts with them we must look chiefly to our Navy for the protection of our national rights. The wide seas which separate us from other Governments must of necessity be the theater on which an enemy will aim to assail us, and unless we are prepared to meet him on this element we can not be said to possess the power requisite to repel or prevent aggressions. We can not, therefore, watch with too much attention this arm of our defense, or cherish with too much care the means by which it can possess the necessary efficiency and exten-sion. To this end our policy has been heretcfore wisely directed to the constant employment of a force sufficient to guard our commerce, and to the rapid accumulation of the materials which are necessary to repair our vessels and construct with ease such new ones as may be required in a state of war.

In accordance with this policy, I recommend to your consideration the erection of the additional dry dock described by the Secretary of the Navy, and also the construction of the steam batteries to which he has referred, for the purpose of testing their efficacy as auxiliaries to the system of defense now in use.

The report of the Postmaster-General herewith submitted exhibits the condition and prospects of that Department. From that document it appears that there was a deficit in the funds of the Department at the commencement of the present year beyond its available means of $315,599.98, which on the 1st July last had been reduced to $268,092.74. It appears also that the revenues for the coming year will exceed the expenditures about $270,000, which, with the excess of revenue whic will result from the operations of the current half year, may be expected, independently of any increase in the gross amount of postages, to supply the entire deficit before the end of 1835. But as this calculation is based on the gross amount of postages which had accrued within the period embraced by the times of striking the balances, it is obvious that without a progressive increase in the amount of postages the existing retrench-ments must be persevered in through the year 1836 that the Department may accumulate a surplus fund sufficient to place it in a condition of perfect ease.

It will be observed that the revenues of the Post-Office Department, though they have increased, and their amount is above that of any for-mer year, have yet fallen short of the estimates more than $100,000. This is attributed in a great degree to the increase of free letters growing out of the extension and abuse of the franking privilege. There has been a gradual increase in the number of executive offices to which it has been granted, and by an act passed in March, 1833, it was extended to members of Congress throughout the whole year. It is believed that a revision of the laws relative to the franking privilege, with some enact-ments to enforce more rigidly the restrictions under which it is granted, would operate beneficially to the country, by enabling the Department at an earlier period to restore the mail facilities that have been with-drawn, and to extend them more widely, as the growing settlements of the country may require.

To a measure so important to the Government and so just to our con-stituents, who ask no exclusive privileges for themselves and are not willing to concede them to others, I earnestly recommend the serious attention of Congress.

The importance of the Post-Office Department and the magnitude to which it has grown, both in its revenues and in its operations, seem to demand its reorganization by law. The whole of its receipts and disbursements have hitherto been left entirely to Executive control and individual discretion. The principle is as sound in relation to this as to any other Department of the Government, that as little discretion should be confided to the executive officer who controls it as is compatible with its efficiency. It is therefore earnestly recommended that it be organized with an auditor and treasurer of its own, appointed by the President and Senate, who shall be branches of the Treasury Department.

Your attention is again respectfully invited to the defect which exists in the judicial system of the United States. Nothing can be more desirable than the uniform operation of the Federal judiciary throughout the several States, all of which, standing on the same footing as members of the Union, have equal rights to the advantages and benefits resulting from its laws. This object is not attained by the judicial acts now in force, because they leave one-fourth of the States without circuit courts.

It is undoubtedly the duty of Congress to place all the States on the same footing in this respect, either by the creation of an additional number of associate judges or by an enlargement of the circuits assigned to those already appointed so as to include the new States. Whatever may be the difficulty in a proper organization of the judicial system so as to secure its efficiency and uniformity in all parts of the Union and at the same time to avoid such an increase of judges as would encumber the supreme appellate tribunal, it should not be allowed to weigh against the great injustice which the present operation of the system produces.

I trust that I may be also pardoned for renewing the recommendation I have so often submitted to your attention in regard to the mode of electing the President and Vice-President of the United States. All the reflection I have been able to bestow upon the subject increases my conviction that the best interests of the country will be promoted by the adoption of some plan which will secure in all contingencies that important right of sovereignty to the direct control of the people. Could this be attained, and the terms of those officers be limited to a single period of either four or six years, I think our liberties would possess an additional safeguard.

At your last session I called the attention of Congress to the destruction of the public building occupied by the Treasury Department. As the public interest requires that another building should be erected with as little delay as possible, it is hoped that the means will be seasonably provided and that they will be ample enough to authorize such an enlargement and improvement in the plan of the building as will more effectually accommodate the public officers and secure the public documents deposited in it from the casualties of fire.

I have not been able to satisfy myself that the bill entitled "An act to improve the navigation of the Wabash River,'' which was sent to me at the close of your last session, ought to pass, and I have therefore withheld from it my approval and now return it to the Senate, the body in which it originated.

There can be no question connected with the administration of public affairs more important or more difficult to be satisfactorily dealt with than that which relates to the rightful authority and proper action of the Federal Government upon the subject of internal improvements. To inherent embarrassments have been added others resulting from the course of our legislation concerning it.

I have heretofore communicated freely with Congress upon this subject, and in adverting to it again I can not refrain from expressing my increased conviction of its extreme importance as well in regard to its bearing upon the maintenance of the Constitution and the prudent management of the public revenue as on account of its disturbing effect upon the harmony of the Union.

We are in no danger from violations of the Constitution by which encroachments are made upon the personal rights of the citizen. The sentence of condemnation long since pronounced by the American people upon acts of that character will, I doubt not, continue to prove as salutary in its effects as it is irreversible in its nature. But against the dangers of unconstitutional acts which, instead of menacing the vengeance of offended authority, proffer local advantages and bring in their train the patronage of the Government, we are, I fear, not so safe. To suppose that because our Government has been instituted for the benefit of the people it must therefore have the power to do whatever may seem to conduce to the public good is an error into which even honest minds are too apt to fall. In yielding themselves to this fallacy they overlook the great considerations in which the Federal Constitution was founded. They forget that in consequence of the conceded diversities in the interest and condition of the different States it was foreseen at the period of its adoption that although a particular measure of the Government might be beneficial and proper in one State it might be the reverse in another; that it was for this reason the States would not consent to make a grant to the Federal Government of the general and usual powers of government, but of such only as were specifically enumerated, and the probable effects of which they could, as they thought, safely anticipate; and they forget also the paramount obligation upon all to abide by the compact then so solemnly and, as it was hoped, so firmly established. In addition to the dangers to the Constitution springing from the sources I have stated, there has been one which was perhaps greater than all. I allude to the materials which this subject has afforded for sinister appeals to selfish feelings, and the opinion heretofore so extensively entertained of its adaptation to the purposes of personal ambition. With such stimulants it is not surprising that the acts and pretensions of the Federal Government in this behalf should sometimes have been carried to an alarming extent. The questions which have arisen upon this subject have related—

First. To the power of making internal improvements within the limits of a State, with the right of territorial jurisdiction, sufficient at least for their preservation and use.

Second. To the right of appropriating money in aid of such works when carried on by a State or by a company in virtue of State authority, surrendering the claim of jurisdiction; and

Third. To the propriety of appropriation for improvements of a particular class, viz, for light-houses, beacons, buoys, public piers, and for the removal of sand bars, sawyers, and other temporary and partial impediments in our navigable rivers and harbors.

The claims of power for the General Government upon each of these points certainly present matter of the deepest interest. The first is, however, of much the greatest importance, inasmuch as, in addition to the dangers of unequal and improvident expenditures of public moneys common to all, there is superadded to that the conflicting jurisdictions of the respective governments. Federal jurisdiction, at least to the extent I have stated, has been justly regarded by its advocates as necessarily appurtenant to the power in question, if that exists by the Constitution. That the most injurious conflicts would unavoidably arise between the respective jurisdictions of the State and Federal Governments in the absence of a constitutional provision marking out their respective boundaries can not be doubted. The local advantages to be obtained would induce the States to overlook in the beginning the dangers and difficulties to which they might ultimately be exposed. The powers exercised by the Federal Government would soon be regarded with jealousy by the State authorities, and originating as they must from implication or assumption, it would be impossible to affix to them certain and safe limits. Opportunities and temptations to the assumption of power incompatible with State sovereignty would be increased and those barriers which resist the tendency of our system toward consolidation greatly weakened. The officers and agents of the General Government might not always have the discretion to abstain from intermeddling with State concerns, and if they did they would not always escape the suspicion of having done so. Collisions and consequent irritations would spring up; that harmony which should ever exist between the General Government and each member of the Confederacy would be frequently interrupted; a spirit of contention would be engendered and the dangers of disunion greatly multiplied.

Yet we all know that notwithstanding these grave objections this dangerous doctrine was at one time apparently proceeding to its final establishment with fearful rapidity. The desire to embark the Federal Government in works of internal improvement prevailed in the highest degree during the first session of the first Congress that I had the honor to meet in my present situation. When the bill authorizing a subscription on the part of the United States for stock in the Maysville and Lexington Turnpike Company passed the two Houses, there had been reported by the Committees of Internal Improvements bills containing appropriations for such objects, inclusive of those for the Cumberland road and for harbors and light-houses, to the amount of $106,000,000. In this amount was included authority to the Secretary of the Treasury to subscribe for the stock of different companies to a great extent, and the residue was principally for the direct construction of roads by this Government. In addition to these projects, which had been presented to the two Houses under the sanction and recommendation of their respective Committees on Internal Improvements, there were then still pending before the committees, and in memorials to Congress presented but not referred, different projects for works of a similar character, the expense of which can not be estimated with certainty, but must have exceeded $100,000,000.

Regarding the bill authorizing a subscription to the stock of the Maysville and Lexington Turnpike Company as the entering wedge of a system which, however weak at first, might soon become strong enough to rive the bands of the Union asunder, and believing that if its passage was acquiesced in by the Executive and the people there would no longer be any limitation upon the authority of the General Government in respect to the appropriation of money for such objects, I deemed it an imperative duty to withhold from it the Executive approval. Although from the obviously local character of that work I might well have contented myself with a refusal to approve the bill upon that ground, yet sensible of the vital importance of the subject, and anxious that my views and opinions in regard to the whole matter should be fully understood by Congress and by my constituents, I felt it my duty to go further. I therefore embraced that early occasion to apprise Congress that in my opinion the Constitution did not confer upon it the power to authorize the construction of ordinary roads and canals within the limits of a State and to say, respectfully, that no bill admitting such a power could receive my official sanction. I did so in the confident expectation that the speedy settlement of the public mind upon the whole subject would be greatly facilitated by the difference between the two Houses and myself, and that the harmonious action of the several departments of the Federal Government in regard to it would be ultimately secured.

So far, at least, as it regards this branch of the subject, my best hopes have been realized. Nearly four years have elapsed, and several sessions of Congress have intervened, and no attempt within my recollection has been made to induce Congress to exercise this power. The applications for the construction of roads and canals which were formerly multiplied upon your files are no longer presented, and we have good reason to infer that the current of public sentiment has become so decided against the pretension as effectually to discourage its reassertion. So thinking, I derive the greatest satisfaction from the conviction that thus much at least has been secured upon this important and embarrassing subject.

From attempts to appropriate the national funds to objects which are confessedly of a local character we can not, I trust, have anything further to apprehend. My views in regard to the expediency of making appropriations for works which are claimed to be of a national character and prosecuted under State authority—assuming that Congress have the right to do so—were stated in my annual message to Congress in 1830, and also in that containing my objections to the Maysville road bill.

So thoroughly convinced am I that no such appropriations ought to be made by Congress until a suitable constitutional provision is made upon the subject, and so essential do I regard the point to the highest interests of our country, that I could not consider myself as discharging my duty to my constituents in giving the Executive sanction to any bill containing such an appropriation. If the people of the United States desire that the public Treasury shall be resorted to for the means to prosecute such works, they will concur in an amendment of the Constitution prescribing a rule by which the national character of the works is to be tested, and by which the greatest practicable equality of benefits may be secured to each member of the Confederacy. The effects of such a regulation would be most salutary in preventing unprofitable expenditures, in securing our legislation from the pernicious consequences of a scramble for the favors of Government, and in repressing the spirit of discontent which must inevitably arise from an unequal distribution of treasures which belong alike to all.

There is another class of appropriations for what may be called, without impropriety, internal improvements, which have always been regarded as standing upon different grounds from those to which I have referred. I allude to such as have for their object the improvement of our harbors, the removal of partial and temporary obstructions in our navigable rivers, for the facility and security of our foreign commerce. The grounds upon which I distinguished appropriations of this character from others have already been stated to Congress. I will now only add that at the first session of Congress under the new Constitution it was provided by law that all expenses which should accrue from and after the 15th day of August, 1789, in the necessary support and maintenance and repairs of all light-houses, beacons. buoys, and public piers erected, placed, or sunk before the passage of the act within any bay, inlet, harbor, or port of the United States, for rendering the navigation thereof easy and safe, should be defrayed out of the Treasury of the United States, and, further, that it should be the duty of the Secretary of the Treasury to provide by contracts, with the approbation of the President, for rebuilding when necessary and keeping in good repair the light-houses, beacons, buoys, and public piers in the several States, and for furnishing them with supplies. Appropriations for similar objects have been continued from that time to the present without interruption or dispute. As a natural consequence of the increase and extension of our foreign commerce, ports of entry and delivery have been multiplied and established, not only upon our sea-board, but in the interior of the country upon our lakes and navigable rivers. The convenience and safety of this commerce have led to the gradual extension of these expenditures; to the erection of light-houses, the placing, planting, and sinking of buoys, beacons, and piers, and to the removal of partial and temporary obstructions in our navigable rivers and in the harbors upon our Great Lakes as well as on the seaboard. Although I have expressed to Congress my apprehension that these expenditures have sometimes been extravagant and disproportionate to the advantages to be derived from them, I have not felt it to be my duty to refuse my assent to bills containing them, and have contented myself to follow in this respect in the footsteps of all my predecessors. Sensible, however, from experience and observation of the great abuses to which the unrestricted exercise of this authority by Congress was exposed, I have prescribed a limitation for the government of my own conduct by which expenditures of this character are confined to places below the ports of entry or delivery established by law. I am very sensible that this restriction is not as satisfactory as could be desired, and that much embarrassment may be caused to the executive department in its execu-tion by appropriations for remote and not well-understood objects. But as neither my own reflections nor the lights which I may properly derive from other sources have supplied me with a better, I shall continue to apply my best exertions to a faithful application of the rule upon which it is founded. I sincerely regret that I could not give my assent to the bill entitled "An act to improve the navigation of the Wabash River;" but I could not have done so without receding from the ground which I have, upon the fullest consideration, taken upon this subject, and of which Congress has been heretofore apprised, and without throwing the subject again open to abuses which no good citizen entertaining my opinions could desire.

I rely upon the intelligence and candor of my fellow-citizens, in whose liberal indulgence I have already so largely participated, for a correct appreciation of my motives in interposing as I have done on this and other occasions checks to a course of legislation which, without in the slightest degree calling in question the motives of others, I consider as sanctioning improper and unconstitutional expenditures of public treasure.

I am not hostile to internal improvements, and wish to see them extended to every part of the country. But I am fully persuaded, if they are not commenced in a proper manner, confined to proper objects, and conducted under an authority generally conceded to be rightful, that a successful prosecution of them can not be reasonably expected. The attempt will meet with resistance where it might otherwise receive support, and instead of strengthening the bonds of our Confederacy it will only multiply and aggravate the causes of disunion.

SEVENTH ANNUAL MESSAGE.

WASHINGTON, *December 7, 1835*

Fellow-Citizens of the Senate and House of Representatives:

In the discharge of my official duty the task again devolves upon me of communicating with a new Congress. The reflection that the representation of the Union has been recently renewed, and that the constitutional term of its service will expire with my own, heightens the solicitude with which I shall attempt to lay before it the state of our national concerns and the devout hope which I cherish that its labors to improve them may be crowned with success.

You are assembled at a period of profound interest to the American patriot. The unexampled growth and prosperity of our country having given us a rank in the scale of nations which removes all apprehension of danger to our integrity and independence from external foes, the career of freedom is before us, with an earnest from the past that if true to ourselves there can be no formidable obstacle in the future to its peaceful and uninterrupted pursuit. Yet, in proportion to the disappearance of those apprehensions which attended our weakness, as once contrasted with the power of some of the States of the Old World, should we now be solicitous as to those which belong to the conviction that it is to our own conduct we must look for the preservation of those causes on which depend the excellence and the duration of our happy system of government.

In the example of other systems founded on the will of the people we trace to internal dissension the influences which have so often blasted the hopes of the friends of freedom. The social elements, which were strong and successful when united against external danger, failed in the more difficult task of properly adjusting their own internal organization, and thus gave way the great principle of self-government. Let us trust that this admonition will never be forgotten by the Government or the people of the United States, and that the testimony which our experience thus far holds out to the great human family of the practicability and the blessings of free government will be confirmed in all time to come.

We have but to look at the state of our agriculture, manufactures, and commerce and the unexampled increase of our population to feel the magnitude of the trust committed to us. Never in any former period of our history have we had greater reason than we now have to be thankful to Divine Providence for the blessings of health and general prosperity. Every branch of labor we see crowned with the most abundant rewards. In every element of national resources and wealth and of individual comfort we witness the most rapid and solid improvements. With no interruptions to this pleasing prospect at home which will not yield to the spirit of harmony and good will that so strikingly pervades the mass of the people in every quarter, amidst all the diversity of interest and pursuits to which they are attached, and with no cause of solicitude in regard to our external affairs which will not, it is hoped, disappear before the principles of simple justice and the forbearance that mark our intercourse with foreign powers, we have every reason to feel proud of our beloved country.

The general state of our foreign relations has not materially changed since my last annual message.

In the settlement of the question of the northeastern boundary little progress has been made. Great Britain has declined acceding to the proposition of the United States, presented in accordance with the resolution of the Senate, unless certain preliminary conditions were admitted, which I deemed incompatible with a satisfactory and rightful adjustment of the controversy. Waiting for some distinct proposal from the Government of Great Britain, which has been invited, I can only repeat the expression of my confidence that, with the strong mutual disposition which I believe exists to make a just arrangement, this perplexing question can be settled with a due regard to the well-founded pretensions and pacific policy of all the parties to it. Events are frequently occurring on the northeastern frontier of a character to impress upon all the necessity of a speedy and definitive termination of the dispute. This consideration, added to the desire common to both to relieve the liberal and friendly relations so happily existing between the two countries from all embarrassment, will no doubt have its just influence upon both.

Our diplomatic intercourse with Portugal has been renewed, and it is expected that the claims of our citizens, partially paid, will be fully satisfied as soon as the condition of the Queen's Government will permit the proper attention to the subject of them. That Government has, I am happy to inform you, manifested a determination to act upon the liberal principles which have marked our commercial policy. The happiest effects upon the future trade between the United States and Portugal are anticipated from it, and the time is not thought to be remote when a system of perfect reciprocity will be established.

The installments due under the convention with the King of the Two

Sicilies have been paid with that scrupulous fidelity by which his whole conduct has been characterized, and the hope is indulged that the adjustment of the vexed question of our claims will be followed by a more extended and mutually beneficial intercourse between the two countries.

The internal contest still continues in Spain. Distinguished as this struggle has unhappily been by incidents of the most sanguinary character, the obligations of the late treaty of indemnification with us have been, nevertheless, faithfully executed by the Spanish Government.

No provision having been made at the last session of Congress for the ascertainment of the claims to be paid and the apportionment of the funds under the convention made with Spain, I invite your early attention to the subject. The public evidences of the debt have, according to the terms of the convention and in the forms prescribed by it, been placed in the possession of the United States, and the interest as it fell due has been regularly paid upon them. Our commercial intercourse with Cuba stands as regulated by the act of Congress. No recent information has been received as to the disposition of the Government of Madrid on this subject, and the lamented death of our recently appointed minister on his way to Spain, with the pressure of their affairs at home, renders it scarcely probable that any change is to be looked for during the coming year. Further portions of the Florida archives have been sent to the United States, although the death of one of the commissioners at a critical moment embarrassed the progress of the delivery of them. The higher officers of the local government have recently shewn an anxious desire, in compliance with the orders from the parent Government, to facilitate the selection and delivery of all we have a right to claim.

Negotiations have been opened at Madrid for the establishment of a lasting peace between Spain and such of the Spanish American Governments of this hemisphere as have availed themselves of the intimation given to all of them of the disposition of Spain to treat upon the basis of their entire independence. It is to be regretted that simultaneous appointments by all of ministers to negotiate with Spain had not been made. The negotiation itself would have been simplified, and this long-standing dispute, spreading over a large portion of the world, would have been brought to a more speedy conclusion.

Our political and commercial relations with Austria, Prussia, Sweden, and Denmark stand on the usual favorable bases. One of the articles of our treaty with Russia in relation to the trade on the northwest coast of America having expired, instructions have been given to our minister at St. Petersburg to negotiate a renewal of it. The long and unbroken amity between the two Governments gives every reason for supposing the article will be renewed, if stronger motives do not exist to prevent it than with our view of the subject can be anticipated here.

I ask your attention to the message of my predecessor at the opening of the second session of the Nineteenth Congress, relative to our commercial intercourse with Holland, and to the documents connected with that subject, communicated to the House of Representatives on the 10th of January, 1825, and 18th of January, 1827. Coinciding in the opinion of my predecessor that Holland is not, under the regulations of her present system, entitled to have her vessels and their cargoes received into the United States on the footing of American vessels and cargoes as regards duties of tonnage and impost, a respect for his reference of it to the Legislature has alone prevented me from acting on the subject. I should still have waited without comment for the action of Congress, but recently a claim has been made by Belgian subjects to admission into our ports for their ships and cargoes on the same footing as American, with the allegation we could not dispute that our vessels received in their ports the identical treatment shewn to them in the ports of Holland, upon whose vessels no discrimination is made in the ports of the United States. Giving the same privileges the Belgians expected the same benefits— benefits that were, in fact, enjoyed when Belgium and Holland were united under one Government. Satisfied with the justice of their pretension to be placed on the same footing with Holland, I could not, nevertheless, without disregard to the principle of our laws, admit their claim to be treated as Americans, and at the same time a respect for Congress, to whom the subject had long since been referred, has prevented me from producing a just equality by taking from the vessels of Holland privileges conditionally granted by acts of Congress, although the condition upon which the grant was made has, in my judgment, failed since 1822. I recommend, therefore, a review of the act of 1824, and such a modification of it as will produce an equality on such terms as Congress shall think best comports with our settled policy and the obligations of justice to two friendly powers.

With the Sublime Porte and all the Governments on the coast of Barbary our relations continue to be friendly. The proper steps have been taken to renew our treaty with Morocco.

The Argentine Republic has again promised to send within the current year a minister to the United States.

A convention with Mexico for extending the time for the appointment of commissioners to run the boundary line has been concluded and will be submitted to the Senate. Recent events in that country have awakened the liveliest solicitude in the United States. Aware of the strong temptations existing and powerful inducements held out to the citizens of the United States to mingle in the dissensions of our immediate neighbors, instructions have been given to the district attorneys of the United States where indications warranted it to prosecute without respect to persons all who might attempt to violate the obligations of our neutrality, while at the same time it has been thought necessary to apprise the Government of Mexico that we should require the integrity of our territory to be scrupulously respected by both parties.

From our diplomatic agents in Brazil, Chile, Peru, Central America, Venezuela, and New Granada constant assurances are received of the continued good understanding with the Governments to which they are severally accredited. With those Governments upon which our citizens have valid and accumulating claims, scarcely an advance toward a settlement of them is made, owing mainly to their distracted state or to the pressure of imperative domestic questions. Our patience has been and will probably be still further severely tried, but our fellow-citizens whose interests are involved may confide in the determination of the Government to obtain for them eventually ample retribution.

Unfortunately, many of the nations of this hemisphere are still self-tormented by domestic dissensions. Revolution succeeds revolution; injuries are committed upon foreigners engaged in lawful pursuits; much time elapses before a government sufficiently stable is erected to justify expectation of redress; ministers are sent and received, and before the discussions of past injuries are fairly begun fresh troubles arise; but too frequently new injuries are added to the old, to be discussed together with the existing government after it has proved its ability to sustain the assaults made upon it, or with its successor if overthrown. If this unhappy condition of things continues much longer, other nations will be under the painful necessity of deciding whether justice to their suffering citizens does not require a prompt redress of injuries by their own power, without waiting for the establishment of a government competent and enduring enough to discuss and to make satisfaction for them.

Since the last session of Congress the validity of our claims upon France, as liquidated by the treaty of 1831, has been acknowledged by both branches of her legislature, and the money has been appropriated for their discharge; but the payment is, I regret to inform you, still withheld.

A brief recapitulation of the most important incidents in this protracted controversy will shew how utterly untenable are the grounds upon which this course is attempted to be justified.

On entering upon the duties of my station I found the United States an unsuccessful applicant to the justice of France for the satisfaction of claims the validity of which was never questionable, and has now been most solemnly admitted by France herself. The antiquity of these claims, their high justice, and the aggravating circumstances out of which they arose are too familiar to the American people to require description. It is sufficient to say that for a period of ten years and upward our commerce was, with but little interruption, the subject of constant aggressions on the part of France—aggressions the ordinary features of which were condemnations of vessels and cargoes under arbitrary decrees, adopted in contravention as well of the laws of nations as of treaty stipulations, burnings on the high seas, and seizures and confiscations under special imperial rescripts in the ports of other nations occupied by the armies or under the control of France. Such it is now conceded is the character of the wrongs we suffered—wrongs in many cases so flagrant that even their authors never denied our right to reparation. Of the extent of these injuries some conception may be formed from the fact that after the burning of a large amount at sea and the necessary deterioration in other cases by long detention the American property so seized and sacrificed at forced sales, excluding what was adjudged to privateers before or without condemnation, brought into the French treasury upward of 24,000,000 francs, besides large custom-house duties.

The subject had already been an affair of twenty years' uninterrupted negotiation, except for a short time when France was overwhelmed by the military power of united Europe. During this period, whilst other nations were extorting from her payment of their claims at the point of the bayonet, the United States intermitted their demand for justice out of respect to the oppressed condition of a gallant people to whom they felt under obligations for fraternal assistance in their own days of suffering and of peril. The bad effects of these protracted and unavailing discussions, as well upon our relations with France as upon our national character, were obvious, and the line of duty was to my mind equally so. This was either to insist upon the adjustment of our claims within a reasonable period or to abandon them altogether. I could not doubt that by this course the interests and honor of both countries would be best consulted. Instructions were therefore given in this spirit to the minister who was sent out once more to demand reparation. Upon the meeting of Congress in December, 1829, I felt it my duty to speak of these claims and the delays of France in terms calculated to call the serious attention of both countries to the subject. The then French ministry took exception to the message on the ground of its containing a menace, under which it was not agreeable to the French Government to negotiate. The American minister of his own accord refuted the construction which was attempted to be put upon the message and at the same time called to the recollection of the French ministry that the President's message was a communication addressed, not to foreign governments, but to the Congress of the United States, in which it was enjoined upon him by the Constitution to lay before that body information of the state of the Union, comprehending its foreign as well as its domestic relations, and that if in the discharge of this duty he felt it incumbent upon him to summon the attention of Congress in due time to what might be the possible consequences of existing difficulties with any foreign government, he might fairly be supposed to do so under a sense of what was due from him in a frank communication with another branch of his own Government, and not from any intention of holding a menace over a foreign power. The views taken by him received my approbation, the

French Government was satisfied, and the negotiation was continued. It terminated in the treaty of July 4, 1831, recognizing the justice of our claims in part and promising payment to the amount of 25,000,000 francs in six annual installments.

The ratifications of this treaty were exchanged at Washington on the 2d of February, 1832, and in five days thereafter it was laid before Congress, who immediately passed the acts necessary on our part to secure to France the commercial advantages conceded to her in the compact. The treaty had previously been solemnly ratified by the King of the French in terms which are certainly not mere matters of form, and of which the translation is as follows:

We, approving the above convention in all and each of the dispositions which are contained in it, do declare, by ourselves as well as by our heirs and successors, that it is accepted, approved, ratified, and confirmed, and by these presents, signed by our hand, we do accept, approve, ratify, and confirm it; promising, on the faith and word of a king, to observe it and to cause it to be observed inviolably, without ever contravening it or suffering it to be contravened, directly or indirectly, for any cause or under any pretense whatsoever.

Official information of the exchange of ratifications in the United States reached Paris whilst the Chambers were in session. The extraordinary and to us injurious delays of the French Government in their action upon the subject of its fulfillment have been heretofore stated to Congress, and I have no disposition to enlarge upon them here. It is sufficient to observe that the then pending session was allowed to expire without even an effort to obtain the necessary appropriations; that the two succeeding ones were also suffered to pass away without anything like a serious attempt to obtain a decision upon the subject, and that it was not until the fourth session, almost three years after the conclusion of the treaty and more than two years after the exchange of ratifications, that the bill for the execution of the treaty was pressed to a vote and rejected.

In the meantime the Government of the United States, having full confidence that a treaty entered into and so solemnly ratified by the French King would be executed in good faith, and not doubting that provision would be made for the payment of the first installment which was to become due on the 2d day of February, 1833, negotiated a draft for the amount through the Bank of the United States. When this draft was presented by the holder with the credentials required by the treaty to authorize him to receive the money, the Government of France allowed it to be protested. In addition to the injury in the nonpayment of the money by France, conformably to her engagement, the United States were exposed to a heavy claim on the part of the bank under pretense of damages, in satisfaction of which that institution seized upon and still retains an equal amount of the public money. Congress was in session when the decision of the Chambers reached Washington, and an immediate communication of this apparently final decision of France not to fulfill the stipulations of the treaty was the course naturally to be expected from the President. The deep tone of dissatisfaction which pervaded the public mind and the correspondent excitement produced in Congress by only a general knowledge of the result rendered it more than probable that a resort to immediate measures of redress would be the consequence of calling the attention of that body to the subject. Sincerely desirous of preserving the pacific relations which had so long existed between the two countries, I was anxious to avoid this course if I could be satisfied that by doing so neither the interests nor the honor of my country would be compromitted. Without the fullest assurances upon that point, I could not hope to acquit myself of the responsibility to be incurred in suffering Congress to adjourn without laying the subject before them. Those received by me were believed to be of that character.

That the feelings produced in the United States by the news of the rejection of the appropriation would be such as I have described them to have been was foreseen by the French Government, and prompt measures were taken by it to prevent the consequences. The King in person expressed through our minister at Paris his profound regret at the decision of the Chambers, and promised to send forthwith a national ship with dispatches to his minister here authorizing him to give such assurances as would satisfy the Government and people of the United States that the treaty would yet be faithfully executed by France. The national ship arrived, and the minister received his instructions. Claiming to act under the authority derived from them, he gave to this Government in the name of his the most solemn assurances that as soon after the new elections as the charter would permit the French Chambers would be convened and the attempt to procure the necessary appropriations renewed; that all the constitutional powers of the King and his ministers should be put in requisition to accomplish the object, and he was understood, and so expressly informed by this Government at the time, to engage that the question should be pressed to a decision at a period sufficiently early to permit information of the result to be communicated to Congress at the commencement of their next session. Relying upon these assurances, I incurred the responsibility, great as I regarded it to be, of suffering Congress to separate without communicating with them upon the subject.

The expectations justly founded upon the promises thus solemnly made to this Government by that of France were not realized. The French Chambers met on the 31st of July, 1834, soon after the election, and although our minister in Paris urged the French ministry to bring the subject before them, they declined doing so. He next insisted that the Chambers, if prorogued without acting on the subject, should be reassembled at a period so early that their action on the treaty might be known in Washington prior to the meeting of Congress. This reasonable request was not only declined, but the Chambers were prorogued to the 29th of December, a day so late that their decision, however urgently pressed, could not in all probability be obtained in time to reach Washington before the necessary adjournment of Congress by the Constitution. The reasons given by the ministry for refusing to convoke the Chambers at an earlier period were afterwards shewn not to be insuperable by their actual convocation on the 1st of December under a special call for domestic purposes, which fact, however, did not become known to this Government until after the commencement of the last session of Congress.

Thus disappointed in our just expectations, it became my imperative duty to consult with Congress in regard to the expediency of a resort to retaliatory measures in case the stipulations of the treaty should not be speedily complied with, and to recommend such as in my judgment the occasion called for. To this end an unreserved communication of the case in all its aspects became indispensable. To have shrunk in making it from saying all that was necessary to its correct understanding, and that the truth would justify, for fear of giving offense to others, would have been unworthy of us. To have gone, on the other hand, a single step further for the purpose of wounding the pride of a Government and people with whom we had so many motives for cultivating relations of amity and reciprocal advantage would have been unwise and improper. Admonished by the past of the difficulty of making even the simplest statement of our wrongs without disturbing the sensibilities of those who had by their position become responsible for their redress, and earnestly desirous of preventing further obstacles from that source, I went out of my way to preclude a construction of the message by which the recommendation that was made to Congress might be regarded as a menace to France in not only disavowing such a design, but in declaring that her pride and her power were too well known to expect anything from her fears. The message did not reach Paris until more than a month after the Chambers had been in session, and such was the insensibility of the ministry to our rightful claims and just expectations that our minister had been informed that the matter when introduced would not be pressed as a cabinet measure.

Although the message was not officially communicated to the French Government, and notwithstanding the declaration to the contrary which it contained, the French ministry decided to consider the conditional recommendation of reprisals a menace and an insult which the honor of the nation made it incumbent on them to resent. The measures resorted to by them to evince their sense of the supposed indignity were the immediate recall of their minister at Washington, the offer of passports to the American minister at Paris, and a public notice to the legislative Chambers that all diplomatic intercourse with the United States had been suspended. Having in this manner vindicated the dignity of France, they

next proceeded to illustrate her justice.   To this end a bill was immediately introduced into the Chamber of Deputies proposing to make the
appropriations necessary to carry into effect the treaty.   As this bill subsequently passed into a law, the provisions of which now constitute the
main subject of difficulty between the two nations, it becomes my duty, in
order to place the subject before you in a clear light, to trace the history
of its passage and to refer with some particularity to the proceedings and
discussions in regard to it.

The minister of finance in his opening speech alluded to the measures
which had been adopted to resent the supposed indignity, and recommended the execution of the treaty as a measure required by the honor
and justice of France.   He as the organ of the ministry declared the message, so long as it had not received the sanction of Congress, a mere
expression of the personal opinion of the President, for which neither the
Government nor people of the United States were responsible, and that
an engagement had been entered into for the fulfillment of which the
honor of France was pledged.   Entertaining these views, the single condition which the French ministry proposed to annex to the payment of
the money was that it should not be made until it was ascertained that
the Government of the United States had done nothing to injure the
interests of France, or, in other words, that no steps had been authorized
by Congress of a hostile character toward France.

What the disposition or action of Congress might be was then unknown
to the French cabinet; but on the 14th of January the Senate resolved
that it was at that time inexpedient to adopt any legislative measures in
regard to the state of affairs between the United States and France, and
no action on the subject had occurred in the House of Representatives.
These facts were known in Paris prior to the 28th of March, 1835, when
the committee to whom the bill of indemnification had been referred
reported it to the Chamber of Deputies.   That committee substantially
reechoed the sentiments of the ministry, declared that Congress had set
aside the proposition of the President, and recommended the passage
of the bill without any other restriction than that originally proposed.
Thus was it known to the French ministry and Chambers that if the
position assumed by them, and which had been so frequently and solemnly announced as the only one compatible with the honor of France,
was maintained and the bill passed as originally proposed, the money
would be paid and there would be an end of this unfortunate controversy.

But this cheering prospect was soon destroyed by an amendment
introduced into the bill at the moment of its passage, providing that the
money should not be paid until the French Government had received
satisfactory explanations of the President's message of the 2d December,
1834, and, what is still more extraordinary, the president of the council of
ministers adopted this amendment and consented to its incorporation
in the bill.   In regard to a supposed insult which had been formally

resented by the recall of their minister and the offer of passports to ours, they now for the first time proposed to ask explanations. Sentiments and propositions which they had declared could not justly be imputed to the Government or people of the United States are set up as obstacles to the performance of an act of conceded justice to that Government and people. They had declared that the honor of France required the fulfillment of the engagement into which the King had entered, unless Congress adopted the recommendations of the message. They ascertained that Congress did not adopt them, and yet that fulfillment is refused unless they first obtain from the President explanations of an opinion characterized by themselves as personal and inoperative.

The conception that it was my intention to menace or insult the Government of France is as unfounded as the attempt to extort from the fears of that nation what her sense of justice may deny would be vain and ridiculous. But the Constitution of the United States imposes on the President the duty of laying before Congress the condition of the country in its foreign and domestic relations, and of recommending such measures as may in his opinion be required by its interests. From the performance of this duty he can not be deterred by the fear of wounding the sensibilities of the people or government of whom it may become necessary to speak; and the American people are incapable of submitting to an interference by any government on earth, however powerful, with the free performance of the domestic duties which the Constitution has imposed on their public functionaries. The discussions which intervene between the several departments of our Government belong to ourselves, and for anything said in them our public servants are only responsible to their own constituents and to each other. If in the course of their consultations facts are erroneously stated or unjust deductions are made, they require no other inducement to correct them, however informed of their error, than their love of justice and what is due to their own character; but they can never submit to be interrogated upon the subject as a matter of right by a foreign power. When our discussions terminate in acts, our responsibility to foreign powers commences, not as individuals, but as a nation. The principle which calls in question the President for the language of his message would equally justify a foreign power in demanding explanation of the language used in the report of a committee or by a member in debate.

This is not the first time that the Government of France has taken exception to the messages of American Presidents. President Washington and the first President Adams in the performance of their duties to the American people fell under the animadversions of the French Directory. The objection taken by the ministry of Charles X, and removed by the explanations made by our minister upon the spot, has already been adverted to. When it was understood that the ministry of the present King took exception to my message of last year, putting a construction upon it which was disavowed on its face, our late minister at Paris, in answer to the note which first announced a dissatisfaction with the language used in the message, made a communication to the French Government under date of the 29th of January, 1835, calculated to remove all impressions which an unreasonable susceptibility had created. He repeated and called the attention of the French Government to the disavowal contained in the message itself of any intention to intimidate by menace; he truly declared that it contained and was intended to contain no charge of ill faith against the King of the French, and properly distinguished between the right to complain in unexceptionable terms of the omission to execute an agreement and an accusation of bad motives in withholding such execution, and demonstrated that the necessary use of that right ought not to be considered as an offensive imputation. Although this communication was made without instructions and entirely on the minister's own responsibility, yet it was afterwards made the act of this Government by my full approbation, and that approbation was officially made known on the 25th of April, 1835, to the French Government. It, however, failed to have any effect. The law, after this friendly explanation, passed with the obnoxious amendment, supported by the King's ministers, and was finally approved by the King.

The people of the United States are justly attached to a pacific system in their intercourse with foreign nations. It is proper, therefore, that they should know whether their Government has adhered to it. In the present instance it has been carried to the utmost extent that was consistent with a becoming self-respect. The note of the 29th of January, to which I have before alluded, was not the only one which our minister took upon himself the responsibility of presenting on the same subject and in the same spirit. Finding that it was intended to make the payment of a just debt dependent on the performance of a condition which he knew could never be complied with, he thought it a duty to make another attempt to convince the French Government that whilst self-respect and regard to the dignity of other nations would always prevent us from using any language that ought to give offense, yet we could never admit a right in any foreign government to ask explanations of or to interfere in any manner in the communications which one branch of our public councils made with another; that in the present case no such language had been used, and that this had in a former note been fully and voluntarily stated, before it was contemplated to make the explanation a condition; and that there might be no misapprehension he stated the terms used in that note, and he officially informed them that it had been approved by the President, and that therefore every explanation which could reasonably be asked or honorably given had been already made; that the contemplated measure had been anticipated by a voluntary and friendly declaration, and was therefore not only useless, but might be deemed offensive, and certainly would not be complied with if annexed as a condition.

When this latter communication, to which I especially invite the attention of Congress, was laid before me, I entertained the hope that the means it was obviously intended to afford of an honorable and speedy adjustment of the difficulties between the two nations would have been accepted, and I therefore did not hesitate to give it my sanction and full approbation. This was due to the minister who had made himself responsible for the act, and it was published to the people of the United States and is now laid before their representatives to shew how far their Executive has gone in its endeavors to restore a good understanding between the two countries. It would have been at any time communicated to the Government of France had it been officially requested.

.The French Government having received all the explanation which honor and principle permitted, and which could in reason be asked, it was hoped it would no longer hesitate to pay the installments now due. The agent authorized to receive the money was instructed to inform the French minister of his readiness to do so. In reply to this notice he was told that the money could not then be paid, because the formalities required by the act of the Chambers had not been arranged.

Not having received any official information of the intentions of the French Government, and anxious to bring, as far as practicable, this unpleasant affair to a close before the meeting of Congress, that you might have the whole subject before you, I caused our chargé d'affaires at Paris to be instructed to ask for the final determination of the French Government, and in the event of their refusal to pay the installments now due, without further explanations to return to the United States.

The result of this last application has not yet reached us, but is daily expected. That it may be favorable is my sincere wish. France having now, through all the branches of her Government, acknowledged the validity of our claims and the obligation of the treaty of 1831, and there really existing no adequate cause for further delay, will at length, it may be hoped, adopt the course which the interests of both nations, not less than the principles of justice, so imperiously require. The treaty being once executed on her part, little will remain to disturb the friendly relations of the two countries—nothing, indeed, which will not yield to the suggestions of a pacific and enlightened policy and to the influence of that mutual good will and of those generous recollections which we may confidently expect will then be revived in all their ancient force. In any event, however, the principle involved in the new aspect which has been given to the controversy is so vitally important to the independent administration of the Government that it can neither be surrendered nor compromitted without national degradation. I hope it is unnecessary for me to say that such a sacrifice will not be made through any agency of mine. The honor of my country shall never be stained by an apology from me for the statement of truth and the performance of duty; nor can I give any explanation of my official acts except such as is due to integ-

rity and justice and consistent with the principles on which our institutions have been framed. This determination will, I am confident, be
approved by my constituents. I have, indeed, studied their character to
but little purpose if the sum of 25,000,000 francs will have the weight
of a feather in the estimation of what appertains to their national independence, and if, unhappily, a different impression should at any time
obtain in any quarter, they will, I am sure, rally round the Government
of their choice with alacrity and unanimity, and silence forever the
degrading imputation.

Having thus frankly presented to you the circumstances which since
the last session of Congress have occurred in this interesting and important matter, with the views of the Executive in regard to them, it is at
this time only necessary to add that whenever the advices now daily
expected from our chargé d'affaires shall have been received they will
be made the subject of a special communication.

The condition of the public finances was never more flattering than at
the present period.

Since my last annual communication all the remains of the public debt
have been redeemed, or money has been placed in deposit for this purpose whenever the creditors choose to receive it. All the other pecuniary engagements of the Government have been honorably and promptly
fulfilled, and there will be a balance in the Treasury at the close of the
present year of about $19,000,000. It is believed that after meeting all
outstanding and unexpended appropriations there will remain near eleven
millions to be applied to any new objects which Congress may designate
or to the more rapid execution of the works already in progress. In aid
of these objects, and to satisfy the current expenditures of the ensuing
year, it is estimated that there will be received from various sources
twenty millions more in 1836.

Should Congress make new appropriations in conformity with the
estimates which will be submitted from the proper Departments, amounting to about twenty-four millions, still the available surplus at the close
of the next year, after deducting all unexpended appropriations, will
probably not be less than six millions. This sum can, in my judgment,
be now usefully applied to proposed improvements in our navy-yards,
and to new national works which are not enumerated in the present
estimates or to the more rapid completion of those already begun.
Either would be constitutional and useful, and would render unnecessary any attempt in our present peculiar condition to divide the surplus
revenue or to reduce it any faster than will be effected by the existing
laws. In any event, as the annual report from the Secretary of the
Treasury will enter into details, shewing the probability of some decrease
in the revenue during the next seven years and a very considerable
deduction in 1842, it is not recommended that Congress should undertake to modify the present tariff so as to disturb the principles on which

the compromise act was passed. Taxation on some of the articles of general consumption which are not in competition with our own productions may be no doubt so diminished as to lessen to some extent the source of this revenue, and the same object can also be assisted by more liberal provisions for the subjects of public defense, which in the present state of our prosperity and wealth may be expected to engage your attention. If, however, after satisfying all the demands which can arise from these sources the unexpended balance in the Treasury should still continue to increase, it would be better to bear with the evil until the great changes contemplated in our tariff laws have occurred and shall enable us to revise the system with that care and circumspection which are due to so delicate and important a subject.

It is certainly our duty to diminish as far as we can the burdens of taxation and to regard all the restrictions which are imposed on the trade and navigation of our citizens as evils which we shall mitigate whenever we are not prevented by the adverse legislation and policy of foreign nations or those primary duties which the defense and independence of our country enjoin upon us. That we have accomplished much toward the relief of our citizens by the changes which have accompanied the payment of the public debt and the adoption of the present revenue laws is manifest from the fact that compared with 1833 there is a diminution of near twenty-five millions in the last two years, and that our expenditures, independently of those for the public debt, have been reduced near nine millions during the same period. Let us trust that by the continued observance of economy and by harmonizing the great interests of agriculture, manufactures, and commerce much more may be accomplished to diminish the burdens of government and to increase still further the enterprise and the patriotic affection of all classes of our citizens and all the members of our happy Confederacy. As the data which the Secretary of the Treasury will lay before you in regard to our financial resources are full and extended, and will afford a safe guide in your future calculations, I think it unnecessary to offer any further observations on that subject here.

Among the evidences of the increasing prosperity of the country, not the least gratifying is that afforded by the receipts from the sales of the public lands, which amount in the present year to the unexpected sum of $11,000,000. This circumstance attests the rapidity with which agriculture, the first and most important occupation of man, advances and contributes to the wealth and power of our extended territory. Being still of the opinion that it is our best policy, as far as we can consistently with the obligations under which those lands were ceded to the United States, to promote their speedy settlement, I beg leave to call the attention of the present Congress to the suggestions I have offered respecting it in my former messages.

The extraordinary receipts from the sales of the public lands invite

you to consider what improvements the land system, and particularly the
condition of the General Land Office, may require. At the time this institution was organized, near a quarter of a century ago, it would probably
have been thought extravagant to anticipate for this period such an addition to its business as has been produced by the vast increase of those sales
during the past and present years. It may also be observed that since
the year 1812 the land offices and surveying districts have been greatly
multiplied, and that numerous legislative enactments from year to year
since that time have imposed a great amount of new and additional
duties upon that office, while the want of a timely application of force
commensurate with the care and labor required has caused the increasing embarrassment of accumulated arrears in the different branches of
the establishment.

These impediments to the expedition of much duty in the General
Land Office induce me to submit to your judgment whether some modification of the laws relating to its organization, or an organization of a
new character, be not called for at the present juncture, to enable the
office to accomplish all the ends of its institution with a greater degree
of facility and promptitude than experience has proved to be practicable
under existing regulations. The variety of the concerns and the magnitude and complexity of the details occupying and dividing the attention
of the Commissioner appear to render it difficult, if not impracticable, for
that officer by any possible assiduity to bestow on all the multifarious
subjects upon which he is called to act the ready and careful attention
due to their respective importance, unless the Legislature shall assist
him by a law providing, or enabling him to provide, for a more regular
and economical distribution of labor, with the incident responsibility
among those employed under his direction. The mere manual operation of affixing his signature to the vast number of documents issuing
from his office subtracts so largely from the time and attention claimed
by the weighty and complicated subjects daily accumulating in that
branch of the public service as to indicate the strong necessity of revising the organic law of the establishment. It will be easy for Congress
hereafter to proportion the expenditure on account of this branch of the
service to its real wants by abolishing from time to time the offices which
can be dispensed with.

The extinction of the public debt having taken place, there is no
longer any use for the offices of Commissioners of Loans and of the
Sinking Fund. I recommend, therefore, that they be abolished, and
that proper measures be taken for the transfer to the Treasury Department of any funds, books, and papers connected with the operations of
those offices, and that the proper power be given to that Department for
closing finally any portion of their business which may remain to be
settled.

It is also incumbent on Congress in guarding the pecuniary interests of the country to discontinue by such a law as was passed in 1812 the receipt of the bills of the Bank of the United States in payment of the public revenue, and to provide for the designation of an agent whose duty it shall be to take charge of the books and stock of the United States in that institution, and to close all connection with it after the 3d of March, 1836, when its charter expires. In making provision in regard to the disposition of this stock it will be essential to define clearly and strictly the duties and powers of the officer charged with that branch of the public service.

It will be seen from the correspondence which the Secretary of the Treasury will lay before you that notwithstanding the large amount of the stock which the United States hold in that institution no information has yet been communicated which will enable the Government to anticipate when it can receive any dividends or derive any benefit from it.

Connected with the condition of the finances and the flourishing state of the country in all its branches of industry, it is pleasing to witness the advantages which have been already derived from the recent laws regulating the value of the gold coinage. These advantages will be more apparent in the course of the next year, when the branch mints authorized to be established in North Carolina, Georgia, and Louisiana shall have gone into operation. Aided, as it is hoped they will be, by further reforms in the banking systems of the States and by judicious regulations on the part of Congress in relation to the custody of the public moneys, it may be confidently anticipated that the use of gold and silver as a circulating medium will become general in the ordinary transactions connected with the labor of the country. The great desideratum in modern times is an efficient check upon the power of banks, preventing that excessive issue of paper whence arise those fluctuations in the standard of value which render uncertain the rewards of labor. It was supposed by those who established the Bank of the United States that from the credit given to it by the custody of the public moneys and other privileges and the precautions taken to guard against the evils which the country had suffered in the bankruptcy of many of the State institutions of that period we should derive from that institution all the security and benefits of a sound currency and every good end that was attainable under that provision of the Constitution which authorizes Congress alone to coin money and regulate the value thereof. But it is scarcely necessary now to say that these anticipations have not been realized.

After the extensive embarrassment and distress recently produced by the Bank of the United States, from which the country is now recovering, aggravated as they were by pretensions to power which defied the public authority, and which if acquiesced in by the people would have changed the whole character of our Government, every candid and intelligent individual must admit that for the attainment of the great advantages of a sound currency we must look to a course of legislation radically different from that which created such an institution.

In considering the means of obtaining so important an end we must set aside all calculations of temporary convenience, and be influenced by those only which are in harmony with the true character and the permanent interests of the Republic. We must recur to first principles and see what it is that has prevented the legislation of Congress and the States on the subject of currency from satisfying the public expectation and realizing results corresponding to those which have attended the action of our system when truly consistent with the great principle of equality upon which it rests, and with that spirit of forbearance and mutual concession and generous patriotism which was originally, and must ever continue to be, the vital element of our Union.

On this subject I am sure that I can not be mistaken in ascribing our want of success to the undue countenance which has been afforded to the spirit of monopoly. All the serious dangers which our system has yet encountered may be traced to the resort to implied powers and the use of corporations clothed with privileges, the effect of which is to advance the interests of the few at the expense of the many. We have felt but one class of these dangers exhibited in the contest waged by the Bank of the United States against the Government for the last four years. Happily they have been obviated for the present by the indignant resistance of the people, but we should recollect that the principle whence they sprung is an ever-active one, which will not fail to renew its efforts in the same and in other forms so long as there is a hope of success, founded either on the inattention of the people or the treachery of their representatives to the subtle progress of its influence. The bank is, in fact, but one of the fruits of a system at war with the genius of all our institutions—a system founded upon a political creed the fundamental principle of which is a distrust of the popular will as a safe regulator of political power, and whose great ultimate object and inevitable result, should it prevail, is the consolidation of all power in our system in one central government. Lavish public disbursements and corporations with exclusive privileges would be its substitutes for the original and as yet sound checks and balances of the Constitution—the means by whose silent and secret operation a control would be exercised by the few over the political conduct of the many by first acquiring that control over the labor and earnings of the great body of the people. Wherever this spirit has effected an alliance with political power, tyranny and despotism have been the fruit. If it is ever used for the ends of government, it has to be incessantly watched, or it corrupts the sources of the public virtue and agitates the country with questions unfavorable to the harmonious and steady pursuit of its true interests.

We are now to see whether, in the present favorable condition of the country, we can not take an effectual stand against this spirit of monopoly, and practically prove in respect to the currency as well as other important interests that there is no necessity for so extensive a resort to it as that which has been heretofore practiced. The experience of another year has confirmed the utter fallacy of the idea that the Bank of the United States was necessary as a fiscal agent of the Government. Without its aid as such, indeed, in despite of all the embarrassment it was in its power to create, the revenue has been paid with punctuality by our citizens, the business of exchange, both foreign and domestic, has been conducted with convenience, and the circulating medium has been greatly improved. By the use of the State banks, which do not derive their charters from the General Government and are not controlled by its authority, it is ascertained that the moneys of the United States can be collected and disbursed without loss or inconvenience, and that all the wants of the community in relation to exchange and currency are supplied as well as they have ever been before. If under circumstances the most unfavorable to the steadiness of the money market it has been found that the considerations on which the Bank of the United States rested its claims to the public favor were imaginary and groundless, it can not be doubted that the experience of the future will be more decisive against them.

It has been seen that without the agency of a great moneyed monopoly the revenue can be collected and conveniently and safely applied to all the purposes of the public expenditure. It is also ascertained that instead of being necessarily made to promote the evils of an unchecked paper system, the management of the revenue can be made auxiliary to the reform which the legislatures of several of the States have already commenced in regard to the suppression of small bills, and which has only to be fostered by proper regulations on the part of Congress to secure a practical return to the extent required for the security of the currency to the constitutional medium. Severed from the Government as political engines, and not susceptible of dangerous extension and combination, the State banks will not be tempted, nor will they have the power, which we have seen exercised, to divert the public funds from the legitimate purposes of the Government. The collection and custody of the revenue, being, on the contrary, a source of credit to them, will increase the security which the States provide for a faithful execution of their trusts by multiplying the scrutinies to which their operations and accounts will be subjected. Thus disposed, as well from interest as the obligations of their charters, it can not be doubted that such conditions as Congress may see fit to adopt respecting the deposits in these institutions, with a view to the gradual disuse, of the small bills will be cheerfully complied with, and that we shall soon gain in place of the Bank of the United States a practical reform in the whole paper system of the country. If by this policy we can ultimately witness the suppression of all bank bills below $20, it is apparent that gold and silver will take their place and become the principal circulating medium in the common business of the farmers and mechanics of the country. The attainment of

such a result will form an era in the history of our country which will
be dwelt upon with delight by every true friend of its liberty and independence.   It will lighten the great tax which our paper system has so
long collected from the earnings of labor, and do more to revive and perpetuate those habits of economy and simplicity which are so congenial to
the character of republicans than all the legislation which has yet been
attempted.

To this subject I feel that I can not too earnestly invite the special
attention of Congress, without the exercise of whose authority the opportunity to accomplish so much public good must pass unimproved.
Deeply impressed with its vital importance, the Executive has taken all
the steps within his constitutional power to guard the public revenue
and defeat the expectation which the Bank of the United States indulged
of renewing and perpetuating its monopoly on the ground of its necessity as a fiscal agent and as affording a sounder currency than could be
obtained without such an institution.   In the performance of this duty
much responsibility was incurred which would have been gladly avoided
if the stake which the public had in the question could have been otherwise preserved.   Although clothed with the legal authority and supported
by precedent, I was aware that there was in the act of the removal of the
deposits a liability to excite that sensitiveness to Executive power which
it is the characteristic and the duty of freemen to indulge; but I relied
on this feeling also, directed by patriotism and intelligence, to vindicate
the conduct which in the end would appear to have been called for by the
best interests of my country.   The apprehensions natural to this feeling
that there may have been a desire, through the instrumentality of that
measure, to extend the Executive influence, or that it may have been
prompted by motives not sufficiently free from ambition, were not overlooked.   Under the operation of our institutions the public servant who
is called on to take a step of high responsibility should feel in the freedom which gives rise to such apprehensions his highest security.   When
unfounded the attention which they arouse and the discussions they
excite deprive those who indulge them of the power to do harm; when just
they but hasten the certainty with which the great body of our citizens
never fail to repel an attempt to procure their sanction to any exercise of
power inconsistent with the jealous maintenance of their rights.   Under
such convictions, and entertaining no doubt that my constitutional obligations demanded the steps which were taken in reference to the removal
of the deposits, it was impossible for me to be deterred from the path of
duty by a fear that my motives could be misjudged or that political prejudices could defeat the just consideration of the merits of my conduct.
The result has shewn how safe is this reliance upon the patriotic temper
and enlightened discernment of the people.   That measure has now been
before them and has stood the test of all the severe analysis which its
general importance, the interests it affected, and the apprehensions it

excited were calculated to produce, and it now remains for Congress to consider what legislation has become necessary in consequence.

I need only add to what I have on former occasions said on this subject generally that in the regulations which Congress may prescribe respecting the custody of the public moneys it is desirable that as little discretion as may be deemed consistent with their safe-keeping should be given to the executive agents. No one can be more deeply impressed than I am with the soundness of the doctrine which restrains and limits, by specific provisions, executive discretion, as far as it can be done consistently with the preservation of its constitutional character. In respect to the control over the public money this doctrine is peculiarly applicable, and is in harmony with the great principle which I felt I was sustaining in the controversy with the Bank of the United States, which has resulted in severing to some extent a dangerous connection between a moneyed and political power. The duty of the Legislature to define, by clear and positive enactments, the nature and extent of the action which it belongs to the Executive to superintend springs out of a policy analogous to that which enjoins upon all the branches of the Federal Government an abstinence from the exercise of powers not clearly granted.

In such a Government, possessing only limited and specific powers, the spirit of its general administration can not be wise or just when it opposes the reference of all doubtful points to the great source of authority, the States and the people, whose number and diversified relations securing them against the influences and excitements which may mislead their agents, make them the safest depository of power. In its application to the Executive, with reference to the legislative branch of the Government, the same rule of action should make the President ever anxious to avoid the exercise of any discretionary authority which can be regulated by Congress. The biases which may operate upon him will not be so likely to extend to the representatives of the people in that body.

In my former messages to Congress I have repeatedly urged the propriety of lessening the discretionary authority lodged in the various Departments, but it has produced no effect as yet, except the discontinuance of extra allowances in the Army and Navy and the substitution of fixed salaries in the latter. It is believed that the same principles could be advantageously applied in all cases, and would promote the efficiency and economy of the public service, at the same time that greater satisfaction and more equal justice would be secured to the public officers generally.

The accompanying report of the Secretary of War will put you in possession of the operations of the Department confided to his care in all its diversified relations during the past year.

I am gratified in being able to inform you that no occurrence has required any movement of the military force, except such as is common to a state of peace. The services of the Army have been limited to their usual duties at the various garrisons upon the Atlantic and inland frontier, with the exceptions stated by the Secretary of War. Our small military establishment appears to be adequate to the purposes for which it is maintained, and it forms a nucleus around which any additional force may be collected should the public exigencies unfortunately require any increase of our military means.

The various acts of Congress which have been recently passed in relation to the Army have improved its condition, and have rendered its organization more useful and efficient. It is at all times in a state for prompt and vigorous action, and it contains within itself the power of extension to any useful limit, while at the same time it preserves that knowledge, both theoretical and practical, which education and experience alone can give, and which, if not acquired and preserved in time of peace, must be sought under great disadvantages in time of war.

The duties of the Engineer Corps press heavily upon that branch of the service, and the public interest requires an addition to its strength. The nature of the works in which the officers are engaged renders necessary professional knowledge and experience, and there is no economy in committing to them more duties than they can perform or in assigning these to other persons temporarily employed, and too often of necessity without all the qualifications which such service demands. I recommend this subject to your attention, and also the proposition submitted at the last session of Congress and now renewed, for a reorganization of the Topographical Corps. This reorganization can be effected without any addition to the present expenditure and with much advantage to the public service. The branch of duties which devolves upon these officers is at all times interesting to the community, and the information furnished by them is useful in peace and war.

Much loss and inconvenience have been experienced in consequence of the failure of the bill containing the ordinary appropriations for fortifications which passed one branch of the National Legislature at the last session, but was lost in the other. This failure was the more regretted not only because it necessarily interrupted and delayed the progress of a system of national defense, projected immediately after the last war and since steadily pursued, but also because it contained a contingent appropriation, inserted in accordance with the views of the Executive, in aid of this important object and other branches of the national defense, some portions of which might have been most usefully applied during the past season. I invite your early attention to that part of the report of the Secretary of War which relates to this subject, and recommend an appropriation sufficiently liberal to accelerate the armament of the fortifications agreeably to the proposition submitted by him, and to place our whole Atlantic seaboard in a complete state of defense. A just regard to the permanent interests of the country evidently requires this measure, but there are also other reasons which at the present juncture give it peculiar force and make it my duty to call to the subject your special consideration.

The present system of military education has been in operation sufficiently long to test its usefulness, and it has given to the Army a valuable body of officers. It is not alone in the improvement, discipline, and operation of the troops that these officers are employed. They are also extensively engaged in the administrative and fiscal concerns of the various matters confided to the War Department; in the execution of the staff duties usually appertaining to military organization; in the removal of the Indians and in the disbursement of the various expenditures growing out of our Indian relations; in the formation of roads and in the improvement of harbors and rivers; in the construction of fortifications, in the fabrication of much of the *matériel* required for the public defense, and in the preservation, distribution, and accountability of the whole, and in other miscellaneous duties not admitting of classification.

These diversified functions embrace very heavy expenditures of public money, and require fidelity, science, and business habits in their execution, and a system which shall secure these qualifications is demanded by the public interest. That this object has been in a great measure obtained by the Military Academy is shewn by the state of the service and by the prompt accountability which has generally followed the necessary advances. Like all other political systems, the present mode of military education no doubt has its imperfections, both of principle and practice; but I trust these can be improved by rigid inspections and by legislative scrutiny without destroying the institution itself.

Occurrences to which we as well as all other nations are liable, both in our internal and external relations, point to the necessity of an efficient organization of the militia. I am again induced by the importance of the subject to bring it to your attention. To suppress domestic violence and to repel foreign invasion, should these calamities overtake us, we must rely in the first instance upon the great body of the community whose will has instituted and whose power must support the Government. A large standing military force is not consonant to the spirit of our institutions nor to the feelings of our countrymen, and the lessons of former days and those also of our own times shew the danger as well as the enormous expense of these permanent and extensive military organizations. That just medium which avoids an inadequate preparation on one hand and the danger and expense of a large force on the other is what our constituents have a right to expect from their Government. This object can be attained only by the maintenance of a small military force and by such an organization of the physical strength of the country as may bring this power into operation whenever its services are required. A classification of the population offers the most obvious means of effecting this organization.   Such a division may be made as will be just to all by transferring each at a proper period of life from one class to another and by calling first for the services of that class, whether for instruction or action, which from age is qualified for the duty and may be called to perform it with least injury to themselves or to the public.   Should the danger ever become so imminent as to require additional force, the other classes in succession would be ready for the call.   And if in addition to this organization voluntary associations were encouraged and inducements held out for their formation, our militia would be in a state of efficient service.   Now, when we are at peace, is the proper time to digest and establish a practicable system.   The object is certainly worth the experiment and worth the expense.   No one appreciating the blessings of a republican government can object to his share of the burden which such a plan may impose.   Indeed, a moderate portion of the national funds could scarcely be better applied than in carrying into effect and continuing such an arrangement, and in giving the necessary elementary instruction.   We are happily at peace with all the world.   A sincere desire to continue so and a fixed determination to give no just cause of offense to other nations furnish, unfortunately, no certain grounds of expectation that this relation will be uninterrupted.   With this determination to give no offense is associated a resolution, equally decided, tamely to submit to none.   The armor and the attitude of defense afford the best security against those collisions which the ambition, or interest, or some other passion of nations not more justifiable is liable to produce.   In many countries it is considered unsafe to put arms into the hands of the people and to instruct them in the elements of military knowledge.   That fear can have no place here when it is recollected that the people are the sovereign power.   Our Government was instituted and is supported by the ballot box, not by the musket.   Whatever changes await it, still greater changes must be made in our social institutions before our political system can yield to physical force.   In every aspect, therefore, in which I can view the subject I am impressed with the importance of a prompt and efficient organization of the militia.

The plan of removing the aboriginal people who yet remain within the settled portions of the United States to the country west of the Mississippi River approaches its consummation.   It was adopted on the most mature consideration of the condition of this race, and ought to be persisted in till the object is accomplished, and prosecuted with as much vigor as a just regard to their circumstances will permit, and as fast as their consent can be obtained.   All preceding experiments for the improvement of the Indians have failed.   It seems now to be an established fact that they can not live in contact with a civilized community and prosper.   Ages of fruitless endeavors have at length brought us to a knowledge of this principle of intercommunication with them.   The past we can not recall, but the future we can provide for.   Independently of the treaty stipulations into which we have entered with the various tribes for the usufructuary rights they have ceded to us, no one can doubt the moral duty of the Government of the United States to protect and if possible to preserve and perpetuate the scattered remnants of this race which are left within our borders. In the discharge of this duty an extensive region in the West has been assigned for their permanent residence. It has been divided into districts and allotted among them. Many have already removed and others are preparing to go, and with the exception of two small bands living in Ohio and Indiana, not exceeding 1,500 persons, and of the Cherokees, all the tribes on the east side of the Mississippi, and extending from Lake Michigan to Florida, have entered into engagements which will lead to their transplantation.

The plan for their removal and reestablishment is founded upon the knowledge we have gained of their character and habits, and has been dictated by a spirit of enlarged liberality. A territory exceeding in extent that relinquished has been granted to each tribe. Of its climate, fertility, and capacity to support an Indian population the representations are highly favorable. To these districts the Indians are removed at the expense of the United States, and with certain supplies of clothing, arms. ammunition, and other indispensable articles; they are also furnished gratuitously with provisions for the period of a year after their arrival at their new homes. In that time, from the nature of the country and of the products raised by them, they can subsist themselves by agricultural labor, if they choose to resort to that mode of life; if they do not they are upon the skirts of the great prairies, where countless herds of buffalo roam, and a short time suffices to adapt their own habits to the changes which a change of the animals destined for their food may require. Ample arrangements have also been made for the support of schools; in some instances council houses and churches are to be erected, dwellings constructed for the chiefs, and mills for common use. Funds have been set apart for the maintenance of the poor; the most necessary mechanical arts have been introduced, and blacksmiths, gunsmiths, wheelwrights, millwrights, etc., are supported among them. Steel and iron, and sometimes salt, are purchased for them, and plows and other farming utensils, domestic animals, looms, spinning wheels, cards, etc., are presented to them. And besides these beneficial arrangements, annuities are in all cases paid, amounting in some instances to more than $30 for each individual of the tribe, and in all cases sufficiently great, if justly divided and prudently expended, to enable them, in addition to their own exertions, to live comfortably. And as a stimulus for exertion, it is now provided by law that "in all cases of the appointment of interpreters or other persons employed for the benefit of the Indians a preference shall be given to persons of Indian descent, if such can be found who are properly qualified for the discharge of the duties."

Such are the arrangements for the physical comfort and for the moral improvement of the Indians. The necessary measures for their political advancement and for their separation from our citizens have not been neglected. The pledge of the United States has been given by Congress that the country destined for the residence of this people shall be forever "secured and guaranteed to them." A country west of Missouri and Arkansas has been assigned to them, into which the white settlements are not to be pushed. No political communities can be formed in that extensive region, except those which are established by the Indians themselves or by the United States for them and with their concurrence. A barrier has thus been raised for their protection against the encroachment of our citizens, and guarding the Indians as far as possible from those evils which have brought them to their present condition. Summary authority has been given by law to destroy all ardent spirits found in their country, without waiting the doubtful result and slow process of a legal seizure. I consider the absolute and unconditional interdiction of this article among these people as the first and great step in their melioration. Halfway measures will answer no purpose. These can not successfully contend against the cupidity of the seller and the overpowering appetite of the buyer. And the destructive effects of the traffic are marked in every page of the history of our Indian intercourse.

Some general legislation seems necessary for the regulation of the relations which will exist in this new state of things between the Government and people of the United States and these transplanted Indian tribes, and for the establishment among the latter, and with their own consent, of some principles of intercommunication which their juxtaposition will call for; that moral may be substituted for physical force, the authority of a few and simple laws for the tomahawk, and that an end may be put to those bloody wars whose prosecution seems to have made part of their social system.

After the further details of this arrangement are completed, with a very general supervision over them, they ought to be left to the progress of events. These, I indulge the hope, will secure their prosperity and improvement, and a large portion of the moral debt we owe them will then be paid.

The report from the Secretary of the Navy, shewing the condition of that branch of the public service, is recommended to your special attention. It appears from it that our naval force at present in commission, with all the activity which can be given to it, is inadequate to the protection of our rapidly increasing commerce. This consideration and the more general one which regards this arm of the national defense as our best security against foreign aggressions strongly urge the continuance of the measures which promote its gradual enlargement and a speedy increase of the force which has been heretofore employed abroad and at home. You will perceive from the estimates which appear in the report of the Secretary of the Navy that the expenditures necessary to this increase of its force, though of considerable amount, are small compared with the benefits which they will secure to the country.

As a means of strengthening this national arm I also recommend to your particular attention the propriety of the suggestion which attracted the consideration of Congress at its last session, respecting the enlistment of boys at a suitable age in the service. In this manner a nursery of skillful and able-bodied seamen can be established, which will be of the greatest importance. Next to the capacity to put afloat and arm the requisite number of ships is the possession of the means to man them efficiently, and nothing seems better calculated to aid this object than the measure proposed. As an auxiliary to the advantages derived from our extensive commercial marine, it would furnish us with a resource ample enough for all the exigencies which can be anticipated. Considering the state of our resources, it can not be doubted that whatever provision the liberality and wisdom of Congress may now adopt with a view to the perfect organization of this branch of our service will meet the approbation of all classes of our citizens.

By the report of the Postmaster-General it appears that the revenue of the Department during the year ending on the 30th day of June last exceeded its accruing responsibilities $236,206, and that the surplus of the present fiscal year is estimated at $476,227. It further appears that the debt of the Department on the 1st day of July last, including the amount due to contractors for the quarter then just expired, was about $1,064,381, exceeding the available means about $23,700; and that on the 1st instant about $597,077 of this debt had been paid—$409,991 out of postages accruing before July and $187,086 out of postages accruing since. In these payments are included $67,000 of the old debt due to banks. After making these payments the Department had $73,000 in bank on the 1st instant. The pleasing assurance is given that the Department is entirely free from embarrassment, and that by collection of outstanding balances and using the current surplus the remaining portion of the bank debt and most of the other debt will probably be paid in April next, leaving thereafter a heavy amount to be applied in extending the mail facilities of the country. Reserving a considerable sum for the improvement of existing mail routes, it is stated that the Department will be able to sustain with perfect convenience an annual charge of $300,000 for the support of new routes, to commence as soon as they can be established and put in operation.

The measures adopted by the Postmaster-General to bring the means of the Department into action and to effect a speedy extinguishment of its debt, as well as to produce an efficient administration of its affairs, will be found detailed at length in his able and luminous report. Aided by a reorganization on the principles suggested and such salutary provisions in the laws regulating its administrative duties as the wisdom of

Congress may devise or approve, that important Department will soon attain a degree of usefulness proportioned to the increase of our population and the extension of our settlements.

Particular attention is solicited to that portion of the report of the Postmaster-General which relates to the carriage of the mails of the United States upon railroads constructed by private corporations under the authority of the several States. The reliance which the General Government can place on those roads as a means of carrying on its operations and the principles on which the use of them is to be obtained can not too soon be considered and settled. Already does the spirit of monopoly begin to exhibit its natural propensities in attempts to exact from the public, for services which it supposes can not be obtained on other terms, the most extravagant compensation. If these claims be persisted in, the question may arise whether a combination of citizens, acting under charters of incorporation from the States, can, by a direct refusal or the demand of an exorbitant price, exclude the United States from the use of the established channels of communication between the different sections of the country, and whether the United States can not, without transcending their constitutional powers, secure to the Post-Office Department the use of those roads by an act of Congress which shall proviuc within itself some equitable mode of adjusting the amount of compensation. To obviate, if possible, the necessity of considering this question, it is suggested whether it be not expedient to fix by law the amounts which shall be offered to railroad companies for the conveyance of the mails, graduated according to their average weight, to be ascertained and declared by the Postmaster-General. It is probable that a liberal proposition of that sort would be accepted.

In connection with these provisions in relation to the Post-Office Department, I must also invite your attention to the painful excitement produced in the South by attempts to circulate through the mails inflammatory appeals addressed to the passions of the slaves, in prints and in various sorts of publications, calculated to stimulate them to insurrection and to produce all the horrors of a servile war. There is doubtless no respectable portion of our countrymen who can be so far misled as to feel any other sentiment than that of indignant regret at conduct so destructive of the harmony and peace of the country, and so repugnant to the principles of our national compact and to the dictates of humanity and religion. Our happiness and prosperity essentially depend upon peace within our borders, and peace depends upon the maintenance in good faith of those compromises of the Constitution upon which the Union is founded. It is fortunate for the country that the good sense, the generous feeling, and the deep-rooted attachment of the people of the non-slaveholding States to the Union and to their fellow-citizens of the same blood in the South have given so strong and impressive a tone to the sentiments entertained against the proceedings of the misguided persons who have engaged in these unconstitutional and wicked attempts, and especially against the emissaries from foreign parts who have dared to interfere in this matter, as to authorize the hope that those attempts will no longer be persisted in. But if these expressions of the public will shall not be sufficient to effect so desirable a result, not a doubt can be entertained that the nonslaveholding States, so far from countenancing the slightest interference with the constitutional rights of the South, will be prompt to exercise their authority in suppressing so far as in them lies whatever is calculated to produce this evil.

In leaving the care of other branches of this interesting subject to the State authorities, to whom they properly belong, it is nevertheless proper for Congress to take such measures as will prevent the Post-Office Department, which was designed to foster an amicable intercourse and correspondence between all the members of the Confederacy, from being used as an instrument of an opposite character. The General Government, to which the great trust is confided of preserving inviolate the relations created among the States by the Constitution, is especially bound to avoid in its own action anything that may disturb them. I would therefore call the special attention of Congress to the subject, and respectfully suggest the propriety of passing such a law as will prohibit, under severe penalties, the circulation in the Southern States, through the mail, of incendiary publications intended to instigate the slaves to insurrection.

I felt it to be my duty in the first message which I communicated to Congress to urge upon its attention the propriety of amending that part of the Constitution which provides for the election of the President and the Vice-President of the United States. The leading object which I had in view was the adoption of some new provisions which would secure to the people the performance of this high duty without any intermediate agency. In my annual communications since I have enforced the same views, from a sincere conviction that the best interests of the country would be promoted by their adoption. If the subject were an ordinary one, I should have regarded the failure of Congress to act upon it as an indication of their judgment that the disadvantages which belong to the present system were not so great as those which would result from any attainable substitute that had been submitted to their consideration. Recollecting, however, that propositions to introduce a new feature in our fundamental laws can not be too patiently examined, and ought not to be received with favor until the great body of the people are thoroughly impressed with their necessity and value as a remedy for real evils, I feel that in renewing the recommendation I have heretofore made on this subject I am not transcending the bounds of a just deference to the sense of Congress or to the disposition of the people. However much we may differ in the choice of the measures which should guide the administration of the Government, there can be but little doubt in the minds of those who are really friendly to the republican features of our system that one of its most important securities consists in the separation of the legislative and executive powers at the same time that each is held responsible to the great source of authority, which is acknowledged to be supreme, in the will of the people constitutionally expressed. My reflection and experience satisfy me that the framers of the Constitution, although they were anxious to mark this feature as a settled and fixed principle in the structure of the Government, did not adopt all the precautions that were necessary to secure its practical observance, and that we can not be said to have carried into complete effect their intentions until the evils which arise from this organic defect are remedied.

Considering the great extent of our Confederacy, the rapid increase of its population, and the diversity of their interests and pursuits, it can not be disguised that the contingency by which one branch of the Legislature is to form itself into an electoral college can not become one of ordinary occurrence without producing incalculable mischief. What was intended as the medicine of the Constitution in extreme cases can not be frequently used without changing its character and sooner or later producing incurable disorder.

Every election by the House of Representatives is calculated to lessen the force of that security which is derived from the distinct and separate character of the legislative and executive functions, and while it exposes each to temptations adverse to their efficiency as organs of the Constitution and laws, its tendency will be to unite both in resisting the will of the people, and thus give a direction to the Government antirepublican and dangerous. All history tells us that a free people should be watchful of delegated power, and should never acquiesce in a practice which will diminish their control over it. This obligation, so universal in its application to all the principles of a republic, is peculiarly so in ours, where the formation of parties founded on sectional interests is so much fostered by the extent of our territory. These interests, represented by candidates for the Presidency, are constantly prone, in the zeal of party and selfish objects, to generate influences unmindful of the general good and forgetful of the restraints which the great body of the people would enforce if they were in no contingency to lose the right of expressing their will. The experience of our country from the formation of the Government to the present day demonstrates that the people can not too soon adopt some stronger safeguard for their right to elect the highest officers known to the Constitution than is contained in that sacred instrument as it now stands.

It is my duty to call the particular attention of Congress to the present condition of the District of Columbia. From whatever cause the great depression has arisen which now exists in the pecuniary concerns of this District, it is proper that its situation should be fully understood and such relief or remedies provided as are consistent with the powers of Congress. I earnestly recommend the extension of every political right to the citizens of this District which their true interests require, and which does not conflict with the provisions of the Constitution. It is believed that the laws for the government of the District require revisal and amendment, and that much good may be done by modifying the penal code so as to give uniformity to its provisions.

Your attention is also invited to the defects which exist in the judicial system of the United States. As at present organized the States of the Union derive unequal advantages from the Federal judiciary, which have been so often pointed out that I deem it unnecessary to repeat them here. It is hoped that the present Congress will extend to all the States that equality in respect to the benefits of the laws of the Union which can only be secured by the uniformity and efficiency of the judicial system.

With these observations on the topics of general interest which are deemed worthy of your consideration, I leave them to your care, trusting that the legislative measures they call for will be met as the wants and the best interests of our beloved country demand.

EIGHTH ANNUAL MESSAGE.

WASHINGTON, *December 5, 1836.*

Fellow-Citizens of the Senate and House of Representatives:

Addressing to you the last annual message I shall ever present to the Congress of the United States, it is a source of the most heartfelt satisfaction to be able to congratulate you on the high state of prosperity which our beloved country has attained. With no causes at home or abroad to lessen the confidence with which we look to the future for continuing proofs of the capacity of our free institutions to produce all the fruits of good government, the general condition of our affairs may well excite our national pride.

I can not avoid congratulating you, and my country particularly, on the success of the efforts made during my Administration by the Executive and Legislature, in conformity with the sincere, constant, and earnest desire of the people, to maintain peace and establish cordial relations with all foreign powers. Our gratitude is due to the Supreme Ruler of the Universe, and I invite you to unite with me in offering to Him fervent supplications that His providential care may ever be extended to those who follow us, enabling them to avoid the dangers and the horrors of war consistently with a just and indispensable regard to the rights

and honor of our country. But although the present state of our foreign affairs, standing, without important change, as they did when you
separated in July last, is flattering in the extreme, I regret to say that
many questions of an interesting character, at issue with other powers,
are yet unadjusted. Amongst the most prominent of these is that of
our northeastern boundary. With an undiminished confidence in the
sincere desire of His Britannic Majesty's Government to adjust that
question, I am not yet in possession of the precise grounds upon which
it proposes a satisfactory adjustment.

With France our diplomatic relations have been resumed, and under
circumstances which attest the disposition of both Governments to preserve a mutually beneficial intercourse and foster those amicable feelings
which are so strongly required by the true interests of the two countries. With Russia, Austria, Prussia, Naples, Sweden, and Denmark the
best understanding exists, and our commercial intercourse is gradually
expanding itself with them. It is encouraged in all these countries,
except Naples, by their mutually advantageous and liberal treaty stipulations with us.

The claims of our citizens on Portugal are admitted to be just, but
provision for the payment of them has been unfortunately delayed by
frequent political changes in that Kingdom.

The blessings of peace have not been secured by Spain. Our connections with that country are on the best footing, with the exception of
the burdens still imposed upon our commerce with her possessions out
of Europe.

The claims of American citizens for losses sustained at the bombardment of Antwerp have been presented to the Governments of Holland
and Belgium, and will be pressed, in due season, to settlement.

With Brazil and all our neighbors of this continent we continue to
maintain relations of amity and concord, extending our commerce with
them as far as the resources of the people and the policy of their Governments will permit. The just and long-standing claims of our citizens upon some of them are yet sources of dissatisfaction and complaint.
No danger is apprehended, however, that they will not be peacefully,
although tardily, acknowledged and paid by all, unless the irritating
effect of her struggle with Texas should unfortunately make our immediate neighbor, Mexico, an exception.

It is already known to you, by the correspondence between the two
Governments communicated at your last session, that our conduct in relation to that struggle is regulated by the same principles that governed us
in the dispute between Spain and Mexico herself, and I trust that it will
be found on the most severe scrutiny that our acts have strictly corre-
sponded with our professions. That the inhabitants of the United States
should feel strong prepossessions for the one party is not surprising. But
this circumstance should of itself teach us great caution, lest it lead us

into the great error of suffering public policy to be regulated by partiality or prejudice; and there are considerations connected with the possible result of this contest between the two parties of so much delicacy and importance to the United States that our character requires that we should neither anticipate events nor attempt to control them. The known desire of the Texans to become a part of our system, although its gratification depends upon the reconcilement of various, and conflicting interests, necessarily a work of time and uncertain in itself, is calculated to expose our conduct to misconstruction in the eyes of the world. There are already those who, indifferent to principle themselves and prone to suspect the want of it in others, charge us with ambitious designs and insidious policy. You will perceive by the accompanying documents that the extraordinary mission from Mexico has been terminated on the sole ground that the obligations of this Government to itself and to Mexico, under treaty stipulations, have compelled me to trust a discretionary authority to a high officer of our Army to advance into territory claimed as part of Texas if necessary to protect our own or the neighboring frontier from Indian depredation. In the opinion of the Mexican functionary who has just left us, the honor of his country will be wounded by American soldiers entering, with the most amicable avowed purposes, upon ground from which the followers of his Government have been expelled, and over which there is at present no certainty of a serious effort on its part being made to reestablish its dominion. The departure of this minister was the more singular as he was apprised that the sufficiency of the causes assigned for the advance of our troops by the commanding general had been seriously doubted by me, and there was every reason to suppose that the troops of the United States, their commander having had time to ascertain the truth or falsehood of the information upon which they had been marched to Nacogdoches, would be either there in perfect accordance with the principles admitted to be just in his conference with the Secretary of State by the Mexican minister himself, or were already withdrawn in consequence of the impressive warnings their commanding officer had received from the Department of War. It is hoped and believed that his Government will take a more dispassionate and just view of this subject, and not be disposed to construe a measure of justifiable precaution, made necessary by its known inability in execution of the stipulations of our treaty to act upon the frontier, into an encroachment upon its rights or a stain upon its honor.

In the meantime the ancient complaints of injustice made on behalf of our citizens are disregarded, and new causes of dissatisfaction have arisen, some of them of a character requiring prompt remonstrance and ample and immediate redress. I trust, however, by tempering firmness with courtesy and acting with great forbearance upon every incident that has occurred or that may happen, to do and to obtain justice, and thus avoid the necessity of again bringing this subject to the view of

Congress.

It is my duty to remind you that no provision has been made to execute our treaty with Mexico for tracing the boundary line between the two countries. Whatever may be the prospect of Mexico's being soon able to execute the treaty on its part, it is proper that we should be in anticipation prepared at all times to perform our obligations, without regard to the probable condition of those with whom we have contracted them.

The result of the confidential inquiries made into the condition and prospects of the newly declared Texan Government will be communicated to you in the course of the session.

Commercial treaties promising great advantages to our enterprising merchants and navigators have been formed with the distant Governments of Muscat and Siam. The ratifications have been exchanged, but have not reached the Department of State. Copies of the treaties will be transmitted to you if received before, or published if arriving after, the close of the present session of Congress.

Nothing has occurred to interrupt the good understanding that has long existed with the Barbary Powers, nor to check the good will which is gradually growing up from our intercourse with the dominions of the Government of the distinguished chief of the Ottoman Empire.

Information has been received at the Department of State that a treaty with the Emperor of Morocco has just been negotiated, which, I hope, will be received in time to be laid before the Senate previous to the close of the session.

You will perceive from the report of the Secretary of the Treasury that the financial means of the country continue to keep pace with its improvement in all other respects. The receipts into the Treasury during the present year will amount to about $47,691,898; those from customs being estimated at $22,523,151, those from lands at about $24,000,000, and the residue from miscellaneous sources. The expenditures for all objects during the year are estimated not to exceed $32,000,000, which will leave a balance in the Treasury for public purposes on the 1st day of January next of about $41,723,959. This sum, with the exception of $5,000,000, will be transferred to the several States in accordance with the provisions of the act regulating the deposits of the public money.

The unexpended balances of appropriation on the 1st day of January next are estimated at $14,636,062, exceeding by $9,636,062 the amount which will be left in the deposit banks, subject to the draft of the Treasurer of the United States, after the contemplated transfers to the several States are made. If, therefore, the future receipts should not be sufficient to meet these outstanding and future appropriations, there may be soon a necessity to use a portion of the funds deposited with the States.

The consequences apprehended when the deposit act of the last session received a reluctant approval have been measurably realized. Though an act merely for the deposit of the surplus moneys of the United States in the State treasuries for safe-keeping until they may be wanted for the service of the General Government, it has been extensively spoken of as an act to give the money to the several States, and they have been advised to use it as a gift, without regard to the means of refunding it when called for. Such a suggestion has doubtless been made without a due consideration of the obligations of the deposit act, and without a proper attention to the various principles and interests which are affected by it. It is manifest that the law itself can not sanction such a suggestion, and that as it now stands the States have no more authority to receive and use these deposits without intending to return them than any deposit bank or any individual temporarily charged with the safe-keeping or application of the public money would now have for converting the same to their private use without the consent and against the will of the Government. But independently of the violation of public faith and moral obligation which are involved in this suggestion when examined in reference to the terms of the present deposit act, it is believed that the considerations which should govern the future legislation of Congress on this subject will be equally conclusive against the adoption of any measure recognizing the principles on which the suggestion has been made.

Considering the intimate connection of the subject with the financial interests of the country and its great importance in whatever aspect it can be viewed, I have bestowed upon it the most anxious reflection, and feel it to be my duty to state to Congress such thoughts as have occurred to me, to aid their deliberation in treating it in the manner best calculated to conduce to the common good.

The experience of other nations admonished us to hasten the extinguishment of the public debt; but it will be in vain that we have congratulated each other upon the disappearance of this evil if we do not guard against the equally great one of promoting the unnecessary accumulation of public revenue. No political maxim is better established than that which tells us that an improvident expenditure of money is the parent of profligacy, and that no people can hope to perpetuate their liberties who long acquiesce in a policy which taxes them for objects not necessary to the legitimate and real wants of their Government. Flattering as is the condition of our country at the present period, because of its unexampled advance in all the steps of social and political improvement, it can not be disguised that there is a lurking danger already apparent in the neglect of this warning truth, and that the time has arrived when the representatives of the people should be employed in devising some more appropriate remedy than now exists to avert it.

Under our present revenue system there is every probability that there will continue to be a surplus beyond the wants of the Government, and it has become our duty to decide whether such a result be consistent with the true objects of our Government.

Should a surplus be permitted to accumulate beyond the appropriations, it must be retained in the Treasu y, as it now is, or distributed among the people or the States.

To retain it in the Treasury unemployed in any way is impracticable; it is, besides, against the genius of our free institutions to lock up in vaults the treasure of the nation. To take from the people the right of bearing arms and put their weapons of defense in the hands of a standing army would be scarcely more dangerous to their liberties than to permit the Government to accumulate immense amounts of treasure beyond the supplies necessary to its legitimate wants. Such a treasure would doubtless be employed at some time, as it has been in other countries, when opportunity tempted ambition.

To collect it merely for distribution to the States would seem to be highly impolitic, if not as dangerous as the proposition to retain it in the Treasury. The shortest reflection must satisfy everyone that to require the people to pay taxes to the Government merely that they may be paid back again is sporting with the substantial interests of the country, and no system which produces such a result can be expected to receive the public countenance. Nothing could be gained by it even if each individual who contributed a portion of the tax could receive back promptly the same portion. But it is apparent that no system of the kind can ever be enforced which will not absorb a considerable portion of the money to be distributed in salaries and commissions to the agents employed in the process and in the various losses and depreciations which arise from other causes, and the practical effect of such an attempt must ever be to burden the people with taxes, not for purposes beneficial to them, but to swell the profits of deposit banks and support a band of useless public officers.

A distribution to the people is impracticable and unjust in other respects. It would be taking one man's property and giving it to another. Such would be the unavoidable result of a rule of equality (and none other is spoken of or would be likely to be adopted), inasmuch as there is no mode by which the amount of the individual contributions of our citizens to the public revenue can be ascertained. We know that they contribute *unequally*, and a rule, therefore, that would distribute to them *equally* would be liable to all the objections which apply to the principle of an equal division of property. To make the General Government the instrument of carrying this odious principle into effect would be at once to destroy the means of its usefulness and change the character designed for it by the framers of the Constitution.

But the more extended and injurious consequences likely to result from a policy which would collect a surplus revenue for the purpose of distributing it may be forcibly illustrated by an examination of the effects already produced by the present deposit act. This act, although certainly designed to secure the safe-keeping of the public revenue, is not entirely free in its tendencies from any of the objections which apply to this principle of distribution. The Government had without necessity received from the people a large surplus, which, instead of being employed as heretofore and returned to them by means of the public expenditure, was deposited with sundry banks. The banks proceeded to make loans upon this surplus, and thus converted it into banking capital, and in this manner it has tended to multiply bank charters and has had a great agency in producing a spirit of wild speculation. The possession and use of the property out of which this surplus was created belonged to the people, but the Government has transferred its possession to incorporated banks, whose interest and effort it is to make large profits out of its use. This process need only be stated to show its injustice and bad policy.

And the same observations apply to the influence which is produced by the steps necessary to collect as well as to distribute such a revenue. About three-fifths of all the duties on imports are paid in the city of New York, but it is obvious that the means to pay those duties are drawn from every quarter of the Union. Every citizen in every State who purchases and consumes an article which has paid a duty at that port contributes to the accumulating mass. The surplus collected there must therefore be made up of moneys or property withdrawn from other points and other States. Thus the wealth and business of every region from which these surplus funds proceed must be to some extent injured, while that of the place where the funds are concentrated and are employed in banking are proportionably extended. But both in making the transfer of the funds which are first necessary to pay the duties and collect the surplus and in making the retransfer which becomes necessary when the time arrives for the distribution of that surplus there is a considerable period when the funds can not be brought into use, and it is manifest that, besides the loss inevitable from such an operation, its tendency is to produce fluctuations in the business of the country, which are always productive of speculation and detrimental to the interests of regular trade. Argument can scarcely be necessary to show that a measure of this character ought not to receive further legislative encouragement.

By examining the practical operation of the ratio for distribution adopted in the deposit bill of the last session we shall discover other features that appear equally objectionable. Let it be assumed, for the sake of argument, that the surplus moneys to be deposited with the States have been collected and belong to them in the ratio of their federal representative population—an assumption founded upon the fact that any deficiencies in our future revenue from imposts and public lands must be made up by direct taxes collected from the States in that ratio. It is proposed to distribute this surplus—say $30,000,000—not according to the ratio in which it has been collected and belongs to the people of the States, but in that of their votes in the colleges of electors of President and Vice-President. The effect of a distribution upon that ratio is shown by the annexed table, marked A.

By an examination of that table it will be perceived that in the distribution of a surplus of $30,000,000 upon that basis there is a great departure from the principle which regards representation as the true measure of taxation, and it will be found that the tendency of that departure will be to increase whatever inequalities have been supposed to attend the operation of our federal system in respect to its bearings upon the different interests of the Union. In making the basis of representation the basis of taxation the framers of the Constitution intended to equalize the burdens which are necessary to support the Government, and the adoption of that ratio, while it accomplished this object, was also the means of adjusting other great topics arising out of the conflicting views respecting the political equality of the various members of the Confederacy. Whatever, therefore, disturbs the liberal spirit of the compromises which established a rule of taxation so just and equitable, and which experience has proved to be so well adapted to the genius and habits of our people, should be received with the greatest caution and distrust.

A bare inspection in the annexed table of the differences produced by the ratio used in the deposit act compared with the results of a distribution according to the ratio of direct taxation must satisfy every unprejudiced mind that the former ratio contravenes the spirit of the Constitution and produces a degree of injustice in the operations of the Federal Government which would be fatal to the hope of perpetuating it. By the ratio of direct taxation, for example, the State of Delaware in the collection of $30,000,000 of revenue would pay into the Treasury $188,716, and in a distribution of $30,000,000 she would receive back from the Government, according to the ratio of the deposit bill, the sum of $306,122; and similar results would follow the comparison between the small and the large States throughout the Union, thus realizing to the small States an advantage which would be doubtless as unacceptable to them as a motive for incorporating the principle in any system which would produce it as it would be inconsistent with the rights and expectations of the large States. It was certainly the intention of that provision of the Constitution which declares that "all duties, imposts, and excises" shall "be uniform throughout the United States" to make the burdens of taxation fall equally upon the people in whatever State of the Union they may reside. But what would be the value of such a uniform rule if the moneys raised by it could be immediately returned by a different one which will give to the people of some States much more and to those of others much less than their fair proportions? Were the Federal Government to exempt in express terms the imports, products, and manufactures of some portions of the country from all duties while it imposed heavy ones on others, the injustice could not be greater.

It would be easy to show how by the operation of such a principle the large States of the Union would not only have to contribute their just share toward the support of the Federal Government, but also have to bear in some degree the taxes necessary to support the governments of their smaller sisters; but it is deemed unnecessary to state the details where the general principle is so obvious.

A system liable to such objections can never be supposed to have been sanctioned by the framers of the Constitution when they conferred on Congress the taxing power, and I feel persuaded that a mature examination of the subject will satisfy everyone that there are insurmountable difficulties in the operation of any plan which can be devised of collecting revenue for the purpose of distributing it. Congress is only authorized to levy taxes *"to pay the debts and provide for the common defense and general welfare of the United States."* There is no such provision as would authorize Congress to collect together the property of the country, under the name of revenue, for the purpose of dividing it equally or unequally among the States or the people. Indeed, it is not probable that such an idea ever occurred to the States when they adopted the Constitution. But however this may be, the only safe rule for us in interpreting the powers granted to the Federal Government is to regard the absence of express authority to touch a subject so important and delicate as this is as equivalent to a prohibition.

Even if our powers were less doubtful in this respect as the Constitution now stands, there are considerations afforded by recent experience which would seem to make it our duty to avoid a resort to such a system.

All will admit that the simplicity and economy of the State governments mainly depend on the fact that money has to be supplied to support them by the same men, or their agents, who vote it away in appropriations. Hence when there are extravagant and wasteful appropriations there must be a corresponding increase of taxes, and the people, becoming awakened, will necessarily scrutinize the character of measures which thus increase their burdens. By the watchful eye of self-interest the agents of the people in the State governments are repressed and kept within the limits of a just economy. But if the necessity of levying the taxes be taken from those who make the appropriations and thrown upon a more distant and less responsible set of public agents, who have power to approach the people by an indirect and stealthy taxation, there is reason to fear that prodigality will soon supersede those characteristics which have thus far made us look with so much pride and confidence to the State governments as the mainstay of our Union and liberties. The State legislatures, instead of studying to restrict their State expenditures to the smallest possible sum, will claim credit for their profusion, and harass the General Government for increased supplies. Practically there would soon be but one taxing power, and that vested in a body of men far removed from the people, in which the farming and mechanic interests would scarcely be represented. The States would gradually lose their purity as well as their independence; they would not dare to murmur at the proceedings of the General Government, lest they should lose their supplies; all would be merged in a practical consolidation, cemented by widespread corruption, which could only be eradicated by one of those bloody revolutions which occasionally overthrow the despotic systems of the Old World. In all the other aspects in which I have been able to look at the effect of such a principle of distribution upon the best interests of the country I can see nothing to compensate for the disadvantages to which I have adverted. If we consider the protective duties, which are in a great degree the source of the surplus revenue, beneficial to one section of the Union and prejudicial to another, there is no corrective for the evil in such a plan of distribution. On the contrary, there is reason to fear that all the complaints which have sprung from this cause would be aggravated. Everyone must be sensible that a distribution of the surplus must beget a disposition to cherish the means which create it, and any system, therefore, into which it enters must have a powerful tendency to increase rather than diminish the tariff. If it were even admitted that the advantages of such a system could be made equal to all the sections of the Union, the reasons already so urgently calling for a reduction of the revenue would nevertheless lose none of their force, for it will always be improbable that an intelligent and virtuous community can consent to raise a surplus for the mere purpose of dividing it, diminished as it must inevitably be by the expenses of the various machinery necessary to the process.

The safest and simplest mode of obviating all the difficulties which have been mentioned is to collect only revenue enough to meet the wants of the Government, and let the people keep the balance of their property in their own hands, to be used for their own profit. Each State will then support its own government and contribute its due share toward the support of the General Government. There would be no surplus to cramp and lessen the resources of individual wealth and enterprise, and the banks would be left to their ordinary means. Whatever agitations and fluctuations might arise from our unfortunate paper system, they could never be attributed, justly or unjustly, to the action of the Federal Government. There would be some guaranty that the spirit of wild speculation which seeks to convert the surplus revenue into banking capital would be effectually checked, and that the scenes of demoralization which are now so prevalent through the land would disappear.

Without desiring to conceal that the experience and observation of the last two years have operated a partial change in my views upon this interesting subject, it is nevertheless regretted that the suggestions made by me in my annual messages of 1829 and 1830 have been greatly misunderstood. At that time the great struggle was begun against that latitudinarian construction of the Constitution which authorizes the unlimited appropriation of the revenues of the Union to internal improvements within the States, tending to invest in the hands and place under the control of the General Government all the principal roads and canals of the country, in violation of State rights and in derogation of State authority. At the same time the condition of the manufacturing interest was such as to create an apprehension that the duties on imports could not without extensive mischief be reduced in season to prevent the accumulation of a considerable surplus after the payment of the national debt. In view of the dangers of such a surplus, and in preference to its application to internal improvements in derogation of the rights and powers of the States, the suggestion of an amendment of the Constitution to authorize its distribution was made. It was an alternative for what were deemed greater evils—a temporary resort to relieve an overburdened treasury until the Government could, without a sudden and destructive revulsion in the business of the country, gradually return to the just principle of raising no more revenue from the people in taxes than is necessary for its economical support. Even that alternative was not spoken of but in connection with an amendment of the Constitution. No temporary inconvenience can justify the exercise of a prohibited power or a power not granted by that instrument, and it was from a conviction that the power to distribute even a temporary surplus of revenue is of that character that it was suggested only in connection with an appeal to the source of all legal power in the General Government, the States which have established it. No such appeal has been taken, and in my opinion a distribution of the surplus revenue by Congress either to the States or the people is to be considered as among the prohibitions of the Constitution. As already intimated, my views have undergone a change so far as to be convinced that no alteration of the Constitution in this respect is wise or expedient. The influence of an accumulating surplus upon the legislation of the General Government and the States, its effect upon the credit system of the country, producing dangerous extensions and ruinous contractions, fluctuations in the price of property, rash speculation, idleness, extravagance, and a deterioration of morals, have taught us the important lesson that any transient mischief which may attend the reduction of our revenue to the wants of our Government is to be borne in preference to an overflowing treasury.

I beg leave to call your attention to another subject intimately associated with the preceding one—the currency of the country.

It is apparent from the whole context of the Constitution, as well as the history of the times which gave birth to it, that it was the purpose of the Convention to establish a currency consisting of the precious metals. These, from their peculiar properties which rendered them the standard of value in all other countries, were adopted in this as well to establish its commercial standard in reference to foreign countries by a permanent rule as to exclude the use of a mutable medium of exchange, such as of certain agricultural commodities recognized by the statutes of some States as a tender for debts, or the still more pernicious expedient of a paper currency. The last, from the experience of the evils of the issues of paper during the Revolution, had become so justly obnoxious as not only to suggest the clause in the Constitution forbidding the emission of bills of credit by the States, but also to produce that vote in the Convention which negatived the proposition to grant power to Congress to charter corporations—a proposition well understood at the time as intended to authorize the establishment of a national bank, which was to issue a currency of bank notes on a capital to be created to some extent out of Government stocks. Although this proposition was refused by a direct vote of the Convention, the object was afterwards in effect obtained by its ingenious advocates through a strained construction of the Constitution. The debts of the Revolution were funded at prices which formed no equivalent compared with the nominal amount of the stock, and under circumstances which exposed the motives of some of those who participated in the passage of the act to distrust.

The facts that the value of the stock was greatly enhanced by the creation of the bank, that it was well understood that such would be the case, and that some of the advocates of the measure were largely benefited by it belong to the history of the times, and are well calculated to diminish the respect which might otherwise have been due to the action of the Congress which created the institution.

On the establishment of a national bank it became the interest of its creditors that gold should be superseded by the paper of the bank as a general currency. A value was soon attached to the gold coins which made their exportation to foreign countries as a mercantile commodity more profitable than their retention and use at home as money. It followed as a matter of course, if not designed by those who established the bank, that the bank became in effect a substitute for the Mint of the United States.

Such was the origin of a national-bank currency, and such the beginning of those difficulties which now appear in the excessive issues of the banks incorporated by the various States.

Although it may not be possible by any legislative means within our power to change at once the system which has thus been introduced, and has received the acquiescence of all portions of the country, it is certainly our duty to do all that is consistent with our constitutional obligations in preventing the mischiefs which are threatened by its undue extension. That the efforts of the fathers of our Government to guard against it by a constitutional provision were founded on an intimate knowledge of the subject has been frequently attested by the bitter experience of the country. The same causes which led them to refuse their sanction to a power authorizing the establishment of incorporations for banking purposes now exist in a much stronger degree to urge us to exert the utmost vigilance in calling into action the means necessary to correct the evils resulting from the unfortunate exercise of the power, and it is to be hoped that the opportunity for effecting this great good will be improved before the country witnesses new scenes of embarrassment and distress.

Variableness must ever be the characteristic of a currency of which the precious metals are not the chief ingredient, or which can be expanded or contracted without regard to the principles that regulate the value of those metals as a standard in the general trade of the world. With us bank issues constitute such a currency, and must ever do so until they are made dependent on those just proportions of gold and silver as a circulating medium which experience has proved to be necessary not only in this but in all other commercial countries. Where those proportions are not infused into the circulation and do not control it, it is manifest that prices must vary according to the tide of bank issues, and the value and stability of property must stand exposed to all the uncertainty which attends the administration of institutions that are constantly liable to the temptation of an interest distinct from that of the community in which they are established.

The progress of an expansion, or rather a depreciation, of the currency by excessive bank issues is always attended by a loss to the laboring classes. This portion of the community have neither time nor opportunity to watch the ebbs and flows of the money market. Engaged from day to day in their useful toils, they do not perceive that although their wages are nominally the same, or even somewhat higher, they are greatly reduced in fact by the rapid increase of a spurious currency, which, as it appears to make money abound, they are at first inclined to consider a blessing. It is not so with the speculator, by whom this operation is better understood, and is made to contribute to his advantage. It is not until the prices of the necessaries of life become so dear that the laboring classes can not supply their wants out of their wages that the wages rise and gradually reach a justly proportioned rate to that of the products of their labor. When thus, by the depreciation in consequence of the quantity of paper in circulation, wages as well as prices become exorbitant, it is soon found that the whole effect of the adulteration is a tariff on our home industry for the benefit of the countries where gold and silver circulate and maintain uniformity and moderation in prices. It is then perceived that the enhancement of the price of land and labor produces a corresponding increase in the price of products until these products do not sustain a competition with similar ones in other countries, and thus both manufactured and agricultural productions cease to bear exportation from the country of the spurious currency, because they can not be sold for cost. This is the process by which specie is banished by the paper of the banks. Their vaults are soon exhausted to pay for foreign commodities. The next step is a stoppage of specie payment—a total degradation of paper as a currency—unusual depression of prices, the ruin of debtors, and the accumulation of property in the hands of creditors and cautious capitalists.

It was in view of these evils, together with the dangerous power wielded by the Bank of the United States and its repugnance to our Constitution, that I was induced to exert the power conferred upon me by the American people to prevent the continuance of that institution. But although various dangers to our republican institutions have been obviated by the failure of that bank to extort from the Government a renewal of its charter, it is obvious that little has been accomplished except a salutary change of public opinion toward restoring to the country the sound currency provided for in the Constitution. In the acts of several of the States prohibiting the circulation of small notes, and the auxiliary enactments of Congress at the last session forbidding their reception or payment on public account, the true policy of the country has been advanced and a larger portion of the precious metals infused into our circulating medium. These measures will probably be followed up in due time by the enactment of State laws banishing from circulation bank notes of still higher denominations, and the object may be materially promoted by further acts of Congress forbidding the employment as fiscal agents of such banks as continue to issue notes of low denominations and throw impediments in the way of the circulation of gold and silver.

The effects of an extension of bank credits and overissues of bank paper have been strikingly illustrated in the sales of the public lands. From the returns made by the various registers and receivers in the early part of last summer it was perceived that the receipts arising from the sales of the public lands were increasing to an unprecedented amount. In effect, however, these receipts amounted to nothing more than credits in bank. The banks lent out their notes to speculators. They were paid to the receivers and immediately returned to the banks, to be lent out again and again, being mere instruments to transfer to speculators the most valuable public land and pay the Government by a credit on the books of the banks. Those credits on the books of some of the Western banks, usually called deposits, were already greatly beyond their immediate means of payment, and were rapidly increasing. Indeed, each speculation furnished means for another; for no sooner had one individual or company paid in the notes than they were immediately lent to another for a like purpose, and the banks were extending their business and their issues so largely as to alarm considerate men and render it doubtful whether these bank credits if permitted to accumulate would ultimately be of the least value to the Government. The spirit of expansion and speculation was not confined to the deposit banks, but pervaded the whole multitude of banks throughout the Union and was giving rise to new institutions to aggravate the evil.

The safety of the public funds and the interest of the people generally required that these operations should be checked; and it became the duty of every branch of the General and State Governments to adopt all legitimate and proper means to produce that salutary effect. Under this view of my duty I directed the issuing of the order which will be laid before you by the Secretary of the Treasury, requiring payment for the public lands sold to be made in specie, with an exception until the 15th of the present month in favor of actual settlers. This measure has produced many salutary consequences. It checked the career of the Western banks and gave them additional strength in anticipation of the pressure which has since pervaded our Eastern as well as the European commercial cities. By preventing the extension of the credit system it measurably cut off the means of speculation and retarded its progress in monopolizing the most valuable of the public lands. It has tended to save the new States from a nonresident proprietorship, one of the greatest obstacles to the advancement of a new country and the prosperity of an old one. It has tended to keep open the public lands for entry by emigrants at Government prices instead of their being compelled to purchase of speculators at double or triple prices. And it is conveying into the interior large sums in silver and gold, there to enter permanently into the currency of the country and place it on a firmer foundation. It is confidently believed that the country will find in the motives which induced that order and the happy consequences which will have ensued much to commend and nothing to condemn.

It remains for Congress if they approve the policy which dictated this order to follow it up in its various bearings. Much good, in my judgment, would be produced by prohibiting sales of the public lands except to actual settlers at a reasonable reduction of price, and to limit the quantity which shall be sold to them. Although it is believed the General Government never ought to receive anything but the constitutional currency in exchange for the public lands, that point would be of less importance if the lands were sold for immediate settlement and cultivation. Indeed, there is scarcely a mischief arising out of our present land system, including the accumulating surplus of revenues, which would not be remedied at once by a restriction on land sales to actual settlers; and it promises other advantages to the country in general and to the new States in particular which can not fail to receive the most profound consideration of Congress.

Experience continues to realize the expectations entertained as to the capacity of the State banks to perform the duties of fiscal agents for the Government at the time of the removal of the deposits. It was alleged by the advocates of the Bank of the United States that the State banks, whatever might be the regulations of the Treasury Department, could not make the transfers required by the Government or negotiate the domestic exchanges of the country. It is now well ascertained that the real domestic exchanges performed through discounts by the United States Bank and its twenty-five branches were at least one-third less than those of the deposit banks for an equal period of time; and if a comparison be instituted between the amounts of service rendered by these institutions on the broader basis which has been used by the advocates of the United States Bank in estimating what they consider the domestic exchanges transacted by it, the result will be still more favorable to the deposit banks.

The whole amount of public money transferred by the Bank of the United States in 1832 was $16,000,000. The amount transferred and actually paid by the deposit banks in the year ending the 1st of October last was $39,319,899; the amount transferred and paid between that period and the 6th of November was $5,399,000, and the amount of transfer warrants outstanding on that day was $14,450,000, making an aggregate of $59,168,894. These enormous sums of money first mentioned have been transferred with the greatest promptitude and regularity, and the rates at which the exchanges have been negotiated previously to the passage of the deposit act were generally below those charged by the Bank of the United States. Independently of these services, which are far greater than those rendered by the United States Bank and its twenty-five branches, a number of the deposit banks have, with a commendable zeal to aid in the improvement of the currency, imported from abroad, at their own expense, large sums of the precious metals for coinage and circulation.

In the same manner have nearly all the predictions turned out in respect to the effect of the removal of the deposits—a step unquestionably necessary to prevent the evils which it was foreseen the bank itself would endeavor to create in a final struggle to procure a renewal of its charter. It may be thus, too, in some degree with the further steps which may be taken to prevent the excessive issue of other bank paper, but it is to be hoped that nothing will now deter the Federal and State authorities from the firm and vigorous performance of their duties to themselves and to the people in this respect.

In reducing the revenue to the wants of the Government your particular attention is invited to those articles which constitute the necessaries of life. The duty on salt was laid as a war tax, and was no doubt continued to assist in providing for the payment of the war debt. There is no article the release of which from taxation would be felt so generally and so beneficially. To this may be added all kinds of fuel and provisions. Justice and benevolence unite in favor of releasing the poor of our cities from burdens which are not necessary to the support of our Government and tend only to increase the wants of the destitute.

It will be seen by the report of the Secretary of the Treasury and the accompanying documents that the Bank of the United States has made no payment on account of the stock held by the Government in that institution, although urged to pay any portion which might suit its convenience, and that it has given no information when payment may be expected. Nor, although repeatedly requested, has it furnished the information in relation to its condition which Congress authorized the Secretary to collect at their last session. Such measures as are within the power of the Executive have been taken to ascertain the value of the stock and procure the payment as early as possible.

The conduct and present condition of that bank and the great amount of capital vested in it by the United States require your careful attention. Its charter expired on the 3d day of March last, and it has now no power but that given in the twenty-first section, "to use the corporate name, style, and capacity for the purpose of suits for the final settlement and liquidation of the affairs and accounts of the corporation, and for the sale and disposition of their estate—real, personal, and mixed—but not for any other purpose or in any other manner whatsoever, nor for a period exceeding two years after the expiration of the said term of incorporation." Before the expiration of the charter the stockholders of the bank obtained an act of incorporation from the legislature of Pennsylvania, excluding only the United States. Instead of proceeding to wind up their concerns and pay over to the United States the amount due on account of the stock held by them, the president and directors of the old bank appear to have transferred the books, papers, notes, obligations, and most or all of its property to this new corporation, which entered upon business as a continuation of the old concern. Amongst other acts of questionable validity, the notes of the expired corporation are known to have been used as its own and again put in circulation. That the old bank had no right to issue or reissue its notes after the expiration of its charter can not be denied, and that it could not confer any such right on its substitute any more than exercise it itself is equally plain. In law and honesty the notes of the bank in circulation at the expiration of its charter should have been called in by public advertisement, paid up as presented, and, together with those on hand, canceled and destroyed. Their reissue is sanctioned by no law and warranted by no necessity. If the United States be responsible in their stock for the payment of these notes, their reissue by the new corporation for their own profit is a fraud on the Government. If the United States is not responsible, then there is no legal responsibility in any quarter, and it is a fraud on the country. They are the redeemed notes of a dissolved partnership, but, contrary to the wishes of the retiring partner and without his consent, are again reissued and circulated.

It is the high and peculiar duty of Congress to decide whether any further legislation be necessary for the security of the large amount of public property now held and in use by the new bank, and for vindicating the rights of the Government and compelling a speedy and honest settlement with all the creditors of the old bank, public and private, or whether the subject shall be left to the power now possessed by the Executive and judiciary.   It remains to be seen whether the persons who as managers of the old bank undertook to control the Government, retained the public dividends, shut their doors upon a committee of the House of Representatives, and filled the country with panic to accomplish their own sinister objects may now as managers of a new bank continue with impunity to flood the country with a spurious currency, use the seven millions of Government stock for their own profit, and refuse to the United States all information as to the present condition of their own property and the prospect of recovering it into their own possession.

The lessons taught by the Bank of the United States can not well be lost upon the American people.   They will take care never again to place so tremendous a power in irresponsible hands, and it will be fortunate if they seriously consider the consequences which are likely to result on a smaller scale from the facility with which corporate powers are granted by their State governments.

It is believed that the law of the last session regulating the deposit banks operates onerously and unjustly upon them in many respects, and it is hoped that Congress, on proper representations, will adopt the modifications which are necessary to prevent this consequence.

The report of the Secretary of War *ad interim* and the accompanying documents, all which are herewith laid before you, will give you a full view of the diversified and important operations of that Department during the past year.

The military movements rendered necessary by the aggressions of the hostile portions of the Seminole and Creek tribes of Indians, and by other circumstances, have required the active employment of nearly our whole regular force, including the Marine Corps, and of large bodies of militia and volunteers.   With all these events so far as they were known at the seat of Government before the termination of your last session you are already acquainted, and it is therefore only needful in this place to lay before you a brief summary of what has since occurred.

The war with the Seminoles during the summer was on our part chiefly confined to the protection of our frontier settlements from the incursions of the enemy, and, as a necessary and important means for the accomplishment of that end, to the maintenance of the posts previously established.   In the course of this duty several actions took place, in which the bravery and discipline of both officers and men were conspicuously displayed, and which I have deemed it proper to notice in respect to the former by the granting of brevet rank for gallant services in the field.   But as the force of the Indians was not so far weakened by these partial successes as to lead them to submit, and as their savage inroads were frequently repeated, early measures were taken for placing at the disposal of Governor Call, who as commander in chief of the Territorial militia had been temporarily invested with the command, an ample force for the purpose of resuming offensive operations in the most efficient manner so soon as the season should permit. Major-General Jesup was also directed, on the conclusion of his duties in the Creek country, to repair to Florida and assume the command.

The result of the first movement made by the forces under the direction of Governor Call in October last, as detailed in the accompanying papers, excited much surprise and disappointment. A full explanation has been required of the causes which led to the failure of that movement, but has not yet been received. In the meantime, as it was feared that the health of Governor Call, who was understood to have suffered much from sickness, might not be adequate to the crisis, and as Major-General Jesup was known to have reached Florida, that officer was directed to assume the command, and to prosecute all needful operations with the utmost promptitude and vigor. From the force at his disposal and the dispositions he has made and is instructed to make, and from the very efficient measures which it is since ascertained have been taken by Governor Call, there is reason to hope that they will soon be enabled to reduce the enemy to subjection. In the meantime, as you will perceive from the report of the Secretary, there is urgent necessity for further appropriations to suppress these hostilities.

Happily for the interests of humanity, the hostilities with the Creeks were brought to a close soon after your adjournment, without that effusion of blood which at one time was apprehended as inevitable. The unconditional submission of the hostile party was followed by their speedy removal to the country assigned them west of the Mississippi. The inquiry as to alleged frauds in the purchase of the reservations of these Indians and the causes of their hostilities, requested by the resolution of the House of Representatives of the 1st of July last to be made by the President, is now going on through the agency of commissioners appointed for that purpose. Their report may be expected during your present session.

The difficulties apprehended in the Cherokee country have been prevented, and the peace and safety of that region and its vicinity effectually secured, by the timely measures taken by the War Department, and still continued.

The discretionary authority given to General Gaines to cross the Sabine and to occupy a position as far west as Nacogdoches, in case he should deem such a step necessary to the protection of the frontier and to the fulfillment of the stipulations contained in our treaty with Mexico, and the movement subsequently made by that officer have been alluded to in a former part of this message. At the date of the latest intelligence from Nacogdoches our troops were yet at that station, but the officer who has succeeded General Gaines has recently been advised that from the facts known at the seat of Government there would seem to be no adequate cause for any longer maintaining that position, and he was accordingly instructed, in case the troops were not already withdrawn under the discretionary powers before possessed by him, to give the requisite orders for that purpose on the receipt of the instructions, unless he shall then have in his possession such information as shall satisfy him that the maintenance of the post is essential to the protection of our frontiers and to the due execution of our treaty stipulations, as previously explained to him.

Whilst the necessities existing during the present year for the service of militia and volunteers have furnished new proofs of the patriotism of our fellow-citizens, they have also strongly illustrated the importance of an increase in the rank and file of the Regular Army. The views of this subject submitted by the Secretary of War in his report meet my entire concurrence, and are earnestly commended to the deliberate attention of Congress. In this connection it is also proper to remind you that the defects in our present militia system are every day rendered more apparent. The duty of making further provision by law for organizing, arming, and disciplining this arm of defense has been so repeatedly presented to Congress by myself and my predecessors that I deem it sufficient on this occasion to refer to the last annual message and to former Executive communications in which the subject has been discussed.

It appears from the reports of the officers charged with mustering into service the volunteers called for under the act of Congress of the last session that more presented themselves at the place of rendezvous in Tennessee than were sufficient to meet the requisition which had been made by the Secretary of War upon the governor of that State. This was occasioned by the omission of the governor to apportion the requisition to the different regiments of militia so as to obtain the proper number of troops and no more. It seems but just to the patriotic citizens who repaired to the general rendezvous under circumstances authorizing them to believe that their services were needed and would be accepted that the expenses incurred by them while absent from their homes should be paid by the Government. I accordingly recommend that a law to this effect be passed by Congress, giving them a compensation which will cover their expenses on the march to and from the place of rendezvous and while there; in connection with which it will also be proper to make provision for such other equitable claims growing out of the service of the militia as may not be embraced in the existing laws.

On the unexpected breaking out of hostilities in Florida, Alabama, and Georgia it became necessary in some cases to take the property of individuals for public use. Provision should be made by law for indemnifying the owners; and I would also respectfully suggest whether some provision may not be made, consistently with the principles of our Government, for the relief of the sufferers by Indian depredations or by the operations of our own troops.

No time was lost after the making of the requisite appropriations in resuming the great national work of completing the unfinished fortifications on our seaboard and of placing them in a proper state of defense. In consequence, however, of the very late day at which those bills were passed, but little progress could be made during the season which has just closed. A very large amount of the moneys granted at your last session accordingly remains unexpended; but as the work will be again resumed at the earliest moment in the coming spring, the balance of the existing appropriations, and in several cases which will be laid before you, with the proper estimates, further sums for the like objects, may be usefully expended during the next year.

The recommendations of an increase in the Engineer Corps and for a reorganization of the Topographical Corps, submitted to you in my last annual message, derive additional strength from the great embarrassments experienced during the present year in those branches of the service, and under which they are now suffering. Several of the most important surveys and constructions directed by recent laws have been suspended in consequence of the want of adequate force in these corps.

The like observations may be applied to the Ordnance Corps and to the general staff, the operations of which as they are now organized must either be frequently interrupted or performed by officers taken from the line of the Army, to the great prejudice of the service.

For a general view of the condition of the Military Academy and of other branches of the military service not already noticed, as well as for fuller illustrations of those which have been mentioned, I refer you to the accompanying documents, and among the various proposals contained therein for legislative action I would particularly notice the suggestion of the Secretary of War for the revision of the pay of the Army as entitled to your favorable regard.

The national policy, founded alike in interest and in humanity, so long and so steadily pursued by this Government for the removal of the Indian tribes originally settled on this side of the Mississippi to the west of that river, may be said to have been consummated by the conclusion of the late treaty with the Cherokees. The measures taken in the execution of that treaty and in relation to our Indian affairs generally will fully appear by referring to the accompanying papers. Without dwelling on the numerous and important topics embraced in them, I again invite your attention to the importance of providing a well-digested and comprehensive system for the protection, supervision, and improvement of the various tribes now planted in the Indian country. The suggestions submitted by the Commissioner of Indian Affairs, and enforced by the Secretary, on this subject, and also in regard to the establishment of additional military posts in the Indian country, are entitled to your profound consideration. Both measures are necessary, for the double purpose of protecting the Indians from intestine war, and in other respects complying with our engagements to them, and of securing our western frontier against incursions which otherwise will assuredly be made on it. The best hopes of humanity in regard to the aboriginal race, the welfare of our rapidly extending settlements, and the honor of the United States are all deeply involved in the relations existing between this Government and the emigrating tribes. I trust, therefore, that the various matters submitted in the accompanying documents in respect to those relations will receive your early and mature deliberation, and that it may issue in the adoption of legislative measures adapted to the circumstances and duties of the present crisis.

You are referred to the report of the Secretary of the Navy for a satisfactory view of the operations of the Department under his charge during the present year. In the construction of vessels at the different navy-yards and in the employment of our ships and squadrons at sea that branch of the service has been actively and usefully employed. While the situation of our commercial interests in the West Indies required a greater number than usual of armed vessels to be kept on that station, it is gratifying to perceive that the protection due to our commerce in other quarters of the world has not proved insufficient. Every effort has been made to facilitate the equipment of the exploring expedition authorized by the act of the last session, but all the preparation necessary to enable it to sail has not yet been completed. No means will be spared by the Government to fit out the expedition on a scale corresponding with the liberal appropriations for the purpose and with the elevated character of the objects which are to be effected by it.

I beg leave to renew the recommendation made in my last annual message respecting the enlistment of boys in our naval service, and to urge upon your attention the necessity of further appropriations to increase the number of ships afloat and to enlarge generally the capacity and force of the Navy. The increase of our commerce and our position in regard to the other powers of the world will always make it our policy and interest to cherish the great naval resources of our country.

The report of the Postmaster-General presents a gratifying picture of the condition of the Post-Office Department. Its revenues for the year ending the 30th June last were $3,398,455.19, showing an increase of revenue over that of the preceding year of $404,878.53, or more than 13 per cent. The expenditures for the same year were $2,755,623.76, exhibiting a surplus of $642,831.43. The Department has been redeemed from embarrassment and debt, has accumulated a surplus exceeding half a million of dollars, has largely extended and is preparing still further to extend the mail service, and recommends a reduction of postages equal to about 20 per cent. It is practicing upon the great principle which should control every branch of our Government of rendering to the public the greatest good possible with the least possible taxation to the people.

The scale of postages suggested by the Postmaster-General recommends itself, not only by the reduction it proposes, but by the simplicity of its arrangement, its conformity with the Federal currency, and the improvement it will introduce into the accounts of the Department and its agents.

Your particular attention is invited to the subject of mail contracts with railroad companies. The present laws providing for the making of contracts are based upon the presumption that competition among bidders will secure the service at a fair price; but on most of the railroad lines there is no competition in that kind of transportation, and advertising is therefore useless. No contract can now be made with them except such as shall be negotiated before the time of offering or afterwards, and the power of the Postmaster-General to pay them high prices is practically without limitation. It would be a relief to him and no doubt would conduce to the public interest to prescribe by law some equitable basis upon which such contracts shall rest, and restrict him by a fixed rule of allowance. Under a liberal act of that sort he would undoubtedly be able to secure the services of most of the railroad companies, and the interest of the Department would be thus advanced.

The correspondence between the people of the United States and the European nations, and particularly with the British Islands, has become very extensive, and requires the interposition of Congress to give it security. No obstacle is perceived to an interchange of mails between New York and Liverpool or other foreign ports, as proposed by the Postmaster-General. On the contrary, it promises, by the security it will afford, to facilitate commercial transactions and give rise to an enlarged intercourse among the people of different nations, which can not but have a happy effect. Through the city of New York most of the correspondence between the Canadas and Europe is now carried on, and urgent representations have been received from the head of the provincial post-office asking the interposition of the United States to guard it from the accidents and losses to which it is now subjected. Some legislation appears to be called for as well by our own interest as by comity to the adjoining British provinces.

The expediency of providing a fireproof building for the important books and papers of the Post-Office Department is worthy of consideration. In the present condition of our Treasury it is neither necessary nor wise to leave essential public interests exposed to so much danger when they can so readily be made secure. There are weighty considerations in the location of a new building for that Department in favor of placing it near the other executive buildings.

The important subjects of a survey of the coast and the manufacture of a standard of weights and measures for the different custom-houses have been in progress for some years under the general direction of the

Executive and the immediate superintendence of a gentleman possessing high scientific attainments. At the last session of Congress the making of a set of weights and measures for each State in the Union was added to the others by a joint resolution.

The care and correspondence as to all these subjects have been devolved on the Treasury Department during the last year. A special report from the Secretary of the Treasury will soon be communicated to Congress, which will show what has been accomplished as to the whole, the number and compensation of the persons now employed in these duties, and the progress expected to be made during the ensuing year, with a copy of the various correspondence deemed necessary to throw light on the subjects which seem to require additional legislation. Claims have been made for retrospective allowances in behalf of the superintendent and some of his assistants, which I did not feel justified in granting. Other claims have been made for large increases in compensation, which, under all the circumstances of the several cases, I declined making without the express sanction of Congress. In order to obtain that sanction the subject was at the last session, on my suggestion and by request of the immediate superintendent, submitted by the Treasury Department to the Committee on Commerce of the House of Representatives. But no legislative action having taken place, the early attention of Congress is now invited to the enactment of some express and detailed provisions in relation to the various claims made for the past, and to the compensation and allowances deemed proper for the future.

It is further respectfully recommended that, such being the inconvenience of attention to these duties by the Chief Magistrate, and such the great pressure of business on the Treasury Department, the general supervision of the coast survey and the completion of the weights and measures, if the works are kept united, should be devolved on a board of officers organized specially for that purpose, or on the Navy Board attached to the Navy Department.

All my experience and reflection confirm the conviction I have so often expressed to Congress in favor of an amendment of the Constitution which will prevent in any event the election of the President and Vice-President of the United States devolving on the House of Representatives and the Senate, and I therefore beg leave again to solicit your attention to the subject. There were various other suggestions in my last annual message not acted upon, particularly that relating to the want of uniformity in the laws of the District of Columbia, that are deemed worthy of your favorable consideration.

Before concluding this paper I think it due to the various Executive Departments to bear testimony to their prosperous condition and to the ability and integrity with which they have been conducted. It has been my aim to enforce in all of them a vigilant and faithful discharge of the public business, and it is gratifying to me to believe that there is no just cause of complaint from any quarter at the manner in which they have fulfilled the objects of their creation.

Having now finished the observations deemed proper on this the last occasion I shall have of communicating with the two Houses of Congress at their meeting, I can not omit an expression of the gratitude which is due to the great body of my fellow-citizens, in whose partiality and indulgence I have found encouragement and support in the many difficult and trying scenes through which it has been my lot to pass during my public career. Though deeply sensible that my exertions have not been crowned with a success corresponding to the degree of favor bestowed upon me, I am sure that they will be considered as having been directed by an earnest desire to promote the good of my country, and I am consoled by the persuasion that whatever errors have been committed will find a corrective in the intelligence and patriotism of those who will succeed us. All that has occurred during my Administration is calculated to inspire me with increased confidence in the stability of our institutions; and should I be spared to enter upon that retirement which is so suitable to my age and infirm health and so much desired by me in other respects, I shall not cease to invoke that beneficent Being to whose providence we are already so signally indebted for the continuance of His blessings on our beloved country.

A.—*Statement of distribution of surplus revenue of $30,000,000 among the several States, agreeably to the number of electoral votes for President and according to the constitutional mode of direct taxation by representative population, and the difference arising from those two modes of distribution, as per census of 1830.*

State.	Representative population.	Electoral vote.	Share according to system of direct taxation.	Share according to electoral vote.	Difference in favor of direct-tax mode.	Difference in favor of electoral-vote mode.
Maine	399,454	10	$999,371	$1,020,408	....	$21,037
New Hampshire ..	269,327	7	673,813	714,286	....	40,473
Massachusetts	610,408	14	1,527,144	1,428,571	$98,573	....
Rhode Island	97,192	4	243,159	408,163	....	165,004
Connecticut	297,665	8	744,711	816,327	....	71,616
Vermont	280,652	7	702,147	714,286	....	12,139
New York.........	1,918,578	42	4,799,978	4,285,714	514,264	....
New Jersey	319,921	8	800,392	816,427	....	15,935
Pennsylvania	1,348,072	30	3,372,662	3,061,225	311,437	....
Delaware	75,431	3	188,716	306,122	....	117,406
Maryland	405,842	10	1,015,352	1,020,408	....	5,056
Virginia...........	1,023,502	23	2,560,640	2,346,939	213,701	....
North Carolina....	639,747	15	1,600,546	1,530,612	69,934	....
South Carolina....	455,025	11	1,138,400	1,122,449	15,951	....
Georgia	429,811	11	1,075,319	1,122,449	....	47,130
Alabama..........	262,507	7	656,751	714,286	....	57,535
Mississippi	110,357	4	276,096	408,163	....	132,067
Louisiana	171,904	5	430,076	510,204	....	80,128
Tennessee	625,263	15	1,564,309	1,530,612	33,697	....
Kentucky	621,832	15	1,555,725	1,530,612	25,113	....
Ohio..............	937,901	21	2,346,479	2,142,858	203,621	....
Indiana	343,030	9	858,206	918,368	....	60,162
Illinois...........	157,146	5	393,154	510,204	....	117,050
Missouri	130,419	4	326,288	408,163	....	81,875
Arkansas.........	28,557	3	71,445	306,122	....	234,677
Michigan	31,625	3	79,121	306,102	....	227,001
Total........	11,991,168	294	30,000,000	30,000,000	1,486,291	1,486,291

Martin Van Buren

March 4, 1837 to March 4, 1841

FIRST ANNUAL MESSAGE.

WASHINGTON, *December 5, 1837.*

Fellow-Citizens of the Senate and House of Representatives:

We have reason to renew the expression of our devout gratitude to the Giver of All Good for His benign protection. Our country presents on every side the evidences of that continued favor under whose auspices it has gradually risen from a few feeble and dependent colonies to a prosperous and powerful confederacy. We are blessed with domestic tranquillity and all the elements of national prosperity. The pestilence which, invading for a time some flourishing portions of the Union, interrupted the general prevalence of unusual health has happily been limited in extent and arrested in its fatal career. The industry and prudence of our citizens are gradually relieving them from the pecuniary embarrassments under which portions of them have labored; judicious legislation and the natural and boundless resources of the country have afforded wise and timely aid to private enterprise, and the activity always characteristic of our people has already in a great degree resumed its usual and profitable channels.

The condition of our foreign relations has not materially changed since the last annual message of my predecessor. We remain at peace with all nations, and no efforts on my part consistent with the preservation of our rights and the honor of the country shall be spared to maintain a position so consonant to our institutions. We have faithfully sustained the foreign policy with which the United States, under the guidance of their first President, took their stand in the family of nations—that of regulating their intercourse with other powers by the approved principles of private life; asking and according equal rights and equal privileges; rendering and demanding justice in all cases; advancing their own and discussing the pretensions of others with candor, directness, and sincerity; appealing at all times to reason, but never yielding to force nor seeking to acquire anything for themselves by its exercise.

A rigid adherence to this policy has left this Government with scarcely a claim upon its justice for injuries arising from acts committed by its authority. The most imposing and perplexing of those of the United States upon foreign governments for aggressions upon our citizens were disposed of by my predecessor. Independently of the benefits conferred upon our citizens by restoring to the mercantile community so many millions of which they had been wrongfully divested, a great service was also rendered to his country by the satisfactory adjustment of so many ancient and irritating subjects of contention; and it reflects no ordinary credit on his successful administration of public affairs that this great object was accomplished without compromising on any occasion either the honor or the peace of the nation.

With European powers no new subjects of difficulty have arisen, and those which were under discussion, although not terminated, do not present a more unfavorable aspect for the future preservation of that good understanding which it has ever been our desire to cultivate.

Of pending questions the most important is that which exists with the Government of Great Britain in respect to our northeastern boundary. It is with unfeigned regret that the people of the United States must look back upon the abortive efforts made by the Executive, for a period of more than half a century, to determine what no nation should suffer long to remain in dispute—the true line which divides its possessions from those of other powers. The nature of the settlements on the borders of the United States and of the neighboring territory was for a season such that this, perhaps, was not indispensable to a faithful performance of the duties of the Federal Government. Time has, however, changed this state of things, and has brought about a condition of affairs in which the true interests of both countries imperatively require that this question should be put at rest. It is not to be disguised that, with full confidence, often expressed, in the desire of the British Government to terminate it, we are apparently as far from its adjustment as we were at the time of signing the treaty of peace in 1783. The sole result of long-pending negotiations and a perplexing arbitration appears to be a conviction on its part that a conventional line must be adopted, from the impossibility of ascertaining the true one according to the description contained in that treaty. Without coinciding in this opinion, which is not thought to be well founded, my predecessor gave the strongest proof of the earnest desire of the United States to terminate satisfactorily this dispute by proposing the substitution of a conventional line if the consent of the States interested in the question could be obtained. To this proposition no answer has as yet been received. The attention of the British Government has, however, been urgently invited to the subject, and its reply can not, I am confident, be much longer delayed. The general relations between Great Britain and the United States are of the most friendly character, and I am well satisfied of the sincere disposition of that Government to maintain them upon their present footing. This disposition has also, I am persuaded, become more general with the people of England than at any previous period. It is scarcely necessary to say to you how cordially it is reciprocated by the Government and people of the United States. The conviction, which must be common to all, of the injurious consequences that result from keeping open this irritating question, and the certainty that its final settlement can not be much longer deferred, will, I trust, lead to an early and satisfactory adjustment. At your last session I laid before you the recent communications between the two Governments and between this Government and that of the State of Maine, in whose solicitude concerning a subject in which she has so deep an interest every portion of the Union participates.

The feelings produced by a temporary interruption of those harmonious relations between France and the United States which are due as well to the recollections of former times as to a correct appreciation of existing interests have been happily succeeded by a cordial disposition on both sides to cultivate an active friendship in their future intercourse. The opinion, undoubtedly correct, and steadily entertained by us, that the commercial relations at present existing between the two countries are susceptible of great and reciprocally beneficial improvements is obviously gaining ground in France, and I am assured of the disposition of that Government to favor the accomplishment of such an object. This disposition shall be met in a proper spirit on our part. The few and comparatively unimportant questions that remain to be adjusted between us can, I have no doubt, be settled with entire satisfaction and without difficulty.

Between Russia and the United States sentiments of good will continue to be mutually cherished. Our minister recently accredited to that Court has been received with a frankness and cordiality and with evidences of respect for his country which leave us no room to doubt the preservation in future of those amicable and liberal relations which have so long and so uninterruptedly existed between the two countries. On the few subjects under discussion between us an early and just decision is confidently anticipated.

A correspondence has been opened with the Government of Austria for the establishment of diplomatic relations, in conformity with the wishes of Congress as indicated by an appropriation act of the session of 1837, and arrangements made for the purpose, which will be duly carried into effect.

With Austria and Prussia and with the States of the German Empire (now composing with the latter the Commercial League) our political relations are of the most friendly character, whilst our commercial intercourse is gradually extending, with benefit to all who are engaged in it.

Civil war yet rages in Spain, producing intense suffering to its own people, and to other nations inconvenience and regret. Our citizens who have claims upon that country will be prejudiced for a time by the condition of its treasury, the inevitable consequence of long-continued and exhausting internal wars. The last installment of the interest of the debt due under the convention with the Queen of Spain has not been paid and similar failures may be expected to happen until a portion of the resources of her Kingdom can be devoted to the extinguishment of its foreign debt.

Having received satisfactory evidence that discriminating tonnage duties were charged upon the vessels of the United States in the ports of Portugal, a proclamation was issued on the 11th day of October last, in compliance with the act of May 25, 1832, declaring that fact, and the duties on foreign tonnage which were levied upon Portuguese vessels in the United States previously to the passage of that act are accordingly revived.

The act of July 4, 1836, suspending the discriminating duties upon the produce of Portugal imported into this country in Portuguese vessels, was passed, upon the application of that Government through its representative here, under the belief that no similar discrimination existed in Portugal to the prejudice of the United States. I regret to state that such duties are now exacted in that country upon the cargoes of American vessels, and as the act referred to vests no discretion in the Executive, it is for Congress to determine upon the expediency of further legislation on the subject. Against these discriminations affecting the vessels of this country and their cargoes seasonable remonstrance was made, and notice was given to the Portuguese Government that unless they should be discontinued the adoption of countervailing measures on the part of the United States would become necessary; but the reply of that Government, received at the Department of State through our chargé d'affaires at Lisbon in the month of September last, afforded no ground to hope for the abandonment of a system so little in harmony with the treatment shown to the vessels of Portugal and their cargoes in the ports of this country and so contrary to the expectations we had a right to entertain.

With Holland, Sweden, Denmark, Naples, and Belgium a friendly intercourse has been uninterruptedly maintained.

With the Government of the Ottoman Porte and its dependencies on the coast of the Mediterranean peace and good will are carefully cultivated, and have been fostered by such good offices as the relative distance and the condition of those countries would permit.

Our commerce with Greece is carried on under the laws of the two Governments, reciprocally beneficial to the navigating interests of both; and I have reason to look forward to the adoption of other measures which will be more extensively and permanently advantageous.

Copies of the treaties concluded with the Governments of Siam and Muscat are transmitted for the information of Congress, the ratifications having been received and the treaties made public since the close of the last annual session. Already have we reason to congratulate ourselves on the prospect of considerable commercial benefit; and we have, besides, received from the Sultan of Muscat prompt evidence of his desire to cultivate the most friendly feelings, by liberal acts toward one of our vessels, bestowed in a manner so striking as to require on our part a grateful acknowledgment.

Our commerce with the islands of Cuba and Porto Rico still labors under heavy restrictions, the continuance of which is a subject of regret. The only effect of an adherence to them will be to benefit the navigation of other countries at the expense of both the United States and Spain.

The independent nations of this continent have ever since they emerged from the colonial state experienced severe trials in their progress to the permanent establishment of liberal political institutions. Their unsettled condition not only interrupts their own advances to prosperity, but has often seriously injured the other powers of the world. The claims of our citizens upon Peru, Chili, Brazil, the Argentine Republic, the Governments formed out of the Republics of Colombia and Mexico, are still pending, although many of them have been presented for examination more than twenty years. New Granada, Venezuela, and Ecuador have recently formed a convention for the purpose of ascertaining and adjusting claims upon the Republic of Colombia, from which it is earnestly hoped our citizens will ere long receive full compensation for the injuries inflicted upon them and for the delay in affording it.

An advantageous treaty of commerce has been concluded by the United States with the Peru-Bolivian Confederation, which wants only the ratification of that Government. The progress of a subsequent negotiation for the settlement of claims upon Peru has been unfavorably affected by the war between that power and Chili and the Argentine Republic, and the same event is also likely to produce delays in the settlement of our demands on those powers.

The aggravating circumstances connected with our claims upon Mexico and a variety of events touching the honor and integrity of our Government led my predecessor to make at the second session of the last Congress a special recommendation of the course to be pursued to obtain a speedy and final satisfaction of the injuries complained of by this Government and by our citizens. He recommended a final demand of redress, with a contingent authority to the Executive to make reprisals if that demand should be made in vain. From the proceedings of Congress on that recommendation it appeared that the opinion of both branches of the Legislature coincided with that of the Executive, that any mode of redress known to the law of nations might justifiably be used. It was obvious, too, that Congress believed with the President that another demand should be made, in order to give undeniable and satisfactory proof of our desire to avoid extremities with a neighboring power, but that there was an indisposition to vest a discretionary authority in the Executive to take redress should it unfortunately be either denied or unreasonably delayed by the Mexican Government.

So soon as the necessary documents were prepared, after entering upon the duties of my office, a special messenger was sent to Mexico to make a final demand of redress, with the documents required by the provisions of our treaty. The demand was made on the 20th of July last. The reply, which bears date the 29th of the same month, contains assurances of a desire on the part of that Government to give a prompt and explicit answer respecting each of the complaints, but that the examination of them would necessarily be deliberate; that in this examination it would be guided by the principles of public law and the obligation of treaties; that nothing should be left undone that might lead to the most speedy and equitable adjustment of our demands, and that its determination in respect to each case should be communicated through the Mexican minister here.

Since that time an envoy extraordinary and minister plenipotentiary has been accredited to this Government by that of the Mexican Republic. He brought with him assurances of a sincere desire that the pending differences between the two Governments should be terminated in a manner satisfactory to both. He was received with reciprocal assurances, and a hope was entertained that his mission would lead to a speedy, satisfactory, and final adjustment of all existing subjects of complaint. A sincere believer in the wisdom of the pacific policy by which the United States have always been governed in their intercourse with foreign nations, it was my particular desire, from the proximity of the Mexican Republic and well-known occurrences on our frontier, to be instrumental in obviating all existing difficulties with that Government and in restoring to the intercourse between the two Republics that liberal and friendly character by which they should always be distinguished. I regret, therefore, the more deeply to have found in the recent communications of that Government so little reason to hope that any future efforts of mine for the accomplishment of those desirable objects would be successful.

Although the larger number—and many of them aggravated cases of personal wrongs—have been now for years before the Mexican Government, and some of the causes of national complaint, and those of the most offensive character, admitted of immediate, simple, and satisfactory replies, it is only within a few days past that any specific communication in answer to our last demand, made five months ago, has been received from the Mexican minister. By the report of the Secretary of State herewith presented and the accompanying documents it will be seen that for not one of our public complaints has satisfaction been given or offered, that but one of the cases of personal wrong has been favorably considered, and that but four cases of both descriptions out of all those formally presented and earnestly pressed have as yet been decided upon by the Mexican Government.

Not perceiving in what manner any of the powers given to the Executive alone could be further usefully employed in bringing this unfortunate controversy to a satisfactory termination, the subject was by my predecessor referred to Congress as one calling for its interposition. In accordance with the clearly understood wishes of the Legislature, another and formal demand for satisfaction has been made upon the Mexican Government, with what success the documents now communicated will show. On a careful and deliberate examination of their contents, and considering the spirit manifested by the Mexican Government, it has become my painful duty to return the subject as it now stands to Congress, to whom it belongs to decide upon the time, the mode, and the measure of redress. Whatever may be your decision, it shall be faithfully executed, confident that it will be characterized by that moderation and justice which will, I trust, under all circumstances govern the councils of our country.

The balance in the Treasury on the 1st January, 1837, was $45,968,523. The receipts during the present year from all sources, including the amount of Treasury notes issued, are estimated at $23,499,981, constituting an aggregate of $69,468,504. Of this amount about $35,281,361 will have been expended at the end of the year on appropriations made by Congress, and the residue, amounting to $34,187,143, will be the nominal balance in the Treasury on the 1st of January next; but of that sum only $1,085,498 is considered as immediately available for and applicable to public purposes. Those portions of it which will be for some time unavailable consist chiefly of sums deposited with the States and due from the former deposit banks. The details upon this subject will be found in the annual report of the Secretary of the Treasury. The amount of Treasury notes which it will be necessary to issue during the year on account of those funds being unavailable will, it is supposed, not exceed four and a half millions. It seemed proper, in the condition of the country, to have the estimates on all subjects made as low as practicable without prejudice to any great public measures. The Departments were therefore desired to prepare their estimates accordingly, and I am happy to find that they have been able to graduate them on so economical a scale. In the great and often unexpected fluctuations to which the revenue is subjected it is not possible to compute the receipts beforehand with great certainty, but should they not differ essentially from present anticipations, and should the appropriations not much exceed the estimates, no difficulty seems likely to happen in defraying the current expenses with promptitude and fidelity.

Notwithstanding the great embarrassments which have recently occurred in commercial affairs, and the liberal indulgence which in consequence of these embarrassments has been extended to both the merchants and the banks, it is gratifying to be able to anticipate that the Treasury notes which have been issued during the present year will be redeemed and that the resources of the Treasury, without any resort to loans or increased taxes, will prove ample for defraying all charges imposed on it during 1838.

The report of the Secretary of the Treasury will afford you a more minute exposition of all matters connected with the administration of the finances during the current year—a period which for the amount of public moneys disbursed and deposited with the States, as well as the financial difficulties encountered and overcome, has few parallels in our history.

Your attention was at the last session invited to the necessity of additional legislative provisions in respect to the collection, safe-keeping, and transfer of the public money. No law having been then matured, and not understanding the proceedings of Congress as intended to be final, it becomes my duty again to bring the subject to your notice.

On that occasion three modes of performing this branch of the public service were presented for consideration. These were, the creation of a national bank; the revival, with modifications, of the deposit system established by the act of the 23d of June, 1836, permitting the use of the public moneys by the banks; and the discontinuance of the use of such institutions for the purposes referred to, with suitable provisions for their accomplishment through the agency of public officers. Considering the opinions of both Houses of Congress on the first two propositions as expressed in the negative, in which I entirely concur, it is unnecessary for me again to recur to them. In respect to the last, you have had an opportunity since your adjournment not only to test still further the expediency of the measure by the continued practical operation of such parts of it as are now in force, but also to discover what should ever be sought for and regarded with the utmost deference—the opinions and wishes of the people.

The national will is the supreme law of the Republic, and on all subjects within the limits of his constitutional powers should be faithfully obeyed by the public servant. Since the measure in question was submitted to your consideration most of you have enjoyed the advantage of personal communication with your constituents. For one State only has an election been held for the Federal Government; but the early day at which it took place deprived the measure under consideration of much of the support it might otherwise have derived from the result. Local elections for State officers have, however, been held in several of the States, at which the expediency of the plan proposed by the Executive has been more or less discussed. You will, I am confident, yield to their results the respect due to every expression of the public voice. Desiring, however, to arrive at truth and a just view of the subject in all its bearings, you will at the same time remember that questions of far deeper and more immediate local interest than the fiscal plans of the National Treasury were involved in those elections. Above all, we can not overlook the striking fact that there were at the time in those States more than one hundred and sixty millions of bank capital, of which large portions were subject to actual forfeiture, other large portions upheld only by special and limited legislative indulgences, and most of it, if not all, to a greater or less extent dependent for a continuance of its corporate existence upon the will of the State legislatures to be then chosen. Apprised of this circumstance, you will judge whether it is not most probable that the peculiar condition of that vast interest in these respects, the extent to which it has been spread through all the ramifications of society, its direct connection with the then pending elections, and the feelings it was calculated to infuse into the canvass have exercised a far greater influence over the result than any which could possibly have been produced by a conflict of opinion in respect to a question in the administration of the General Government more remote and far less important in its bearings upon that interest.

I have found no reason to change my own opinion as to the expediency of adopting the system proposed, being perfectly satisfied that there will be neither stability nor safety either in the fiscal affairs of the Government or in the pecuniary transactions of individuals and corporations so long as a connection exists between them which, like the past, offers such strong inducements to make them the subjects of political agitation. Indeed, I am more than ever convinced of the dangers to which the free and unbiased exercise of political opinion—the only sure foundation and safeguard of republican government—would be exposed by any further increase of the already overgrown influence of corporate authorities. I can not, therefore, consistently with my views of duty, advise a renewal of a connection which circumstances have dissolved.

The discontinuance of the use of State banks for fiscal purposes ought not to be regarded as a measure of hostility toward those institutions. Banks properly established and conducted are highly useful to the business of the country, and will doubtless continue to exist in the States so long as they conform to their laws and are found to be safe and beneficial. How they should be created, what privileges they should enjoy, under what responsibilities they should act, and to what restrictions they should be subject are questions which, as I observed on a previous occasion, belong to the States to decide. Upon their rights or the exercise of them the General Government can have no motive to encroach. Its duty toward them is well performed when it refrains from legislating for their special benefit, because such legislation would violate the spirit of the Constitution and be unjust to other interests; when it takes no steps to impair their usefulness, but so manages its own affairs as to make it the interest of those institutions to strengthen and improve their condition for the security and welfare of the community at large. They have no right to insist on a connection with the Federal Government, nor on the use of the public money for their own benefit. The object of the measure under consideration is to avoid for the future a compulsory connection of this kind. It proposes to place the General Government, in regard to the essential points of the collection, safe-keeping, and transfer of the public money, in a situation which shall relieve it from all dependence on the will of irresponsible individuals or corporations; to withdraw those moneys from the uses of private trade and confide them to agents constitutionally selected and controlled by law; to abstain from improper interference with the industry of the people and withhold inducements to improvident dealings on the part of individuals; to give stability to the concerns of the Treasury; to preserve the measures of the Government from the unavoidable reproaches that flow from such a connection, and the banks themselves from the injurious effects of a supposed participation in the political conflicts of the day, from which they will otherwise find it difficult to escape.

These are my views upon this important subject, formed after careful reflection and with no desire but to arrive at what is most likely to promote the public interest. They are now, as they were before, submitted with unfeigned deference for the opinions of others. It was hardly to be hoped that changes so important on a subject so interesting could be made without producing a serious diversity of opinion; but so long as those conflicting views are kept above the influence of individual or local interests, so long as they pursue only the general good and are discussed with moderation and candor, such diversity is a benefit, not an injury. If a majority of Congress see the public welfare in a different light, and more especially if they should be satisfied that the measure proposed would not be acceptable to the people, I shall look to their wisdom to substitute such as may be more conducive to the one and more satisfactory to the other. In any event, they may confidently rely on my hearty cooperation to the fullest extent to which my views of the Constitution and my sense of duty will permit.

It is obviously important to this branch of the public service and to the business and quiet of the country that the whole subject should in some way be settled and regulated by law, and, if possible, at your present session. Besides the plans above referred to, I am not aware that any one has been suggested except that of keeping the public money in the State banks in special deposit. This plan is to some extent in accordance with the practice of the Government and with the present arrangements of the Treasury Department, which, except, perhaps, during the operation of the late deposit act, has always been allowed, even during the existence of a national bank, to make a temporary use of the State banks in particular places for the safe-keeping of portions of the revenue. This discretionary power might be continued if Congress deem it desirable, whatever general system be adopted. So long as the connection is voluntary we need, perhaps, anticipate few of those difficulties and little of that dependence on the banks which must attend every such connection when compulsory in its nature and when so arranged as to make the banks a fixed part of the machinery of government. It is undoubtedly in the power of Congress so to regulate and guard it as to prevent the public money from being applied to the use or intermingled with the affairs of individuals. Thus arranged, although it would not give to the Government that entire control over its own funds which I desire to secure to it by the plan I have proposed, it would, it must be admitted, in a great degree accomplish one of the objects which has recommended that plan to my judgment—the separation of the fiscal concerns of the Government from those of individuals or corporations.

With these observations I recommend the whole matter to your dispassionate reflection, confidently hoping that some conclusion may be reached by your deliberations which on the one hand shall give safety and stability to the fiscal operations of the Government, and be consistent, on the other, with the genius of our institutions and with the interests and wishes of the great mass of our constituents.

It was my hope that nothing would occur to make necessary on this occasion any allusion to the late national bank. There are circumstances, however, connected with the present state of its affairs that bear so directly on the character of the Government and the welfare of the citizen that I should not feel myself excused in neglecting to notice them. The charter which terminated its banking privileges on the 4th of March, 1836, continued its corporate power two years more for the sole purpose of closing its affairs, with authority "to use the corporate name, style. and capacity for the purpose of suits for a final settlement and liquidation of the affairs and acts of the corporation, and for the sale and disposition of their estate—real, personal, and mixed—but for no other purpose or in any other manner whatsoever." Just before the banking privileges ceased, its effects were transferred by the bank to a new State institution, then recently incorporated, in trust, for the discharge of its debts and the settlement of its affairs. With this trustee, by authority of Congress, an adjustment was subsequently made of the large interest which the Government had in the stock of the institution. The manner in which a trust unexpectedly created upon the act granting the charter, and involving such great public interests, has been executed would under any circumstances be a fit subject of inquiry; but much more does it deserve your attention when it embraces the redemption of obligations to which the authority and credit of the United States have given value. The two years allowed are now nearly at an end. It is well understood that the trustee has not redeemed and canceled the outstanding notes of the bank, but has reissued and is actually reissuing, since the 3d of March, 1836, the notes which have been received by it to a vast amount. According to its own official statement, so late as the 1st of October last, nineteen months after the banking privileges given by the charter had expired, it had under its control uncanceled notes of the late Bank of the United States to the amount of $27,561,866, of which $6,175,861 were in actual circulation, $1,468,627 at State bank agencies, and $3,002,390 *in transitu*, thus showing that upward of ten millions and a half of the notes of the old bank were then still kept outstanding.

The impropriety of this procedure is obvious, it being the duty of the trustee to cancel and not to put forth the notes of an institution whose concerns it had undertaken to wind up. If the trustee has a right to reissue these notes now, I can see no reason why it may not continue to do so after the expiration of the two years. As no one could have anticipated a course so extraordinary, the prohibitory clause of the charter above quoted was not accompanied by any penalty or other special provision for enforcing it, nor have we any general law for the prevention of similar acts in future.

But it is not in this view of the subject alone that your interposition is required. The United States in settling with the trustee for their stock have withdrawn their funds from their former direct liability to the creditors of the old bank, yet notes of the institution continue to be sent forth in its name, and apparently upon the authority of the United States. The transactions connected with the employment of the bills of the old bank are of vast extent, and should they result unfortunately the interests of individuals may be deeply compromised. Without undertaking to decide how far or in what form, if any, the trustee could be made liable for notes which contain no obligation on its part, or the old bank for such as are put in circulation after the expiration of its charter and without its authority, or the Government for indemnity in case of loss, the question still presses itself upon your consideration whether it is consistent with duty and good faith on the part of the Government to witness this proceeding without a single effort to arrest it.

The report of the Commissioner of the General Land Office, which will be laid before you by the Secretary of the Treasury, will show how the affairs of that office have been conducted for the past year. The disposition of the public lands is one of the most important trusts confided to Congress. The practicability of retaining the title and control of such extensive domains in the General Government, and at the same time admitting the Territories embracing them into the Federal Union as coequals with the original States, was seriously doubted by many of our wisest statesmen. All feared that they would become a source of discord, and many carried their apprehensions so far as to see in them the seeds of a future dissolution of the Confederacy. But happily our experience has already been sufficient to quiet in a great degree all such apprehensions. The position at one time assumed, that the admission of new States into the Union on the same footing with the original States was incompatible with a right of soil in the United States and operated as a surrender thereof, notwithstanding the terms of the compacts by which their admission was designed to be regulated, has been wisely abandoned. Whether in the new or the old States, all now agree that the right of soil to the public lands remains in the Federal Government, and that these lands constitute a common property, to be disposed of for the common benefit of all the States, old and new. Acquiescence in this just principle by the people of the new States has naturally promoted a disposition to adopt the most liberal policy in the sale of the public lands. A policy which should be limited to the mere object of selling the lands for the greatest possible sum of money, without regard to higher considerations, finds but few advocates. On the contrary, it is generally conceded that whilst the mode of disposition adopted by the Government should always be a prudent one, yet its leading object ought to be the early settlement

and cultivation of the lands sold, and that it should discountenance, if
it can not prevent, the accumulation of large tracts in the same hands,
which must necessarily retard the growth of the new States or entail
upon them a dependent tenantry and its attendant evils.

A question embracing such important interests and so well calculated
to enlist the feelings of the people in every quarter of the Union has
very naturally given rise to numerous plans for the improvement of the
existing system.   The distinctive features of the policy that has hitherto
prevailed are to dispose of the public lands at moderate prices, thus
enabling a greater number to enter into competition for their purchase
and accomplishing a double object—of promoting their rapid settlement
by the purchasers and at the same time increasing the receipts of the
Treasury; to sell for cash, thereby preventing the disturbing influence
of a large mass of private citizens indebted to the Government which
they have a voice in controlling; to bring them into market no faster
than good lands are supposed to be wanted for improvement, thereby
preventing the accumulation of large tracts in few hands; and to apply
the proceeds of the sales to the general purposes of the Government,
thus diminishing the amount to be raised from the people of the States
by taxation and giving each State its portion of the benefits to be derived
from this common fund in a manner the most quiet, and at the same
time, perhaps, the most equitable, that can be devised.   These provisions,
with occasional enactments in behalf of special interests deemed entitled
to the favor of the Government, have in their execution produced results
as beneficial upon the whole as could reasonably be expected in a matter
so vast, so complicated, and so exciting.   Upward of 70,000,000 acres
have been sold, the greater part of which is believed to have been purchased for actual settlement.   The population of the new States and
Territories created out of the public domain increased between 1800 and
1830 from less than 60,000 to upward of 2,300,000 souls, constituting at
the latter period about one-fifth of the whole people of the United States.
The increase since can not be accurately known, but the whole may now
be safely estimated at over three and a half millions of souls, composing
nine States, the representatives of which constitute above one-third of
the Senate and over one-sixth of the House of Representatives of the
United States.

Thus has been formed a body of free and independent landholders
with a rapidity unequaled in the history of mankind; and this great
result has been produced without leaving anything for future adjustment
between the Government and its citizens.   The system under which
so much has been accomplished can not be intrinsically bad, and with
occasional modifications to correct abuses and adapt it to changes of
circumstances may, I think, be safely trusted for the future.   There is
in the management of such extensive interests much virtue in stability;
and although great and obvious improvements should not be declined,

changes should never be made without the fullest examination and the clearest demonstration of their practical utility. In the history of the past we have an assurance that this safe rule of action will not be departed from in relation to the public lands; nor is it believed that any necessity exists for interfering with the fundamental principles of the system, or that the public mind, even in the new States, is desirous of any radical alterations. On the contrary, the general disposition appears to be to make such modifications and additions only as will the more effectually carry out the original policy of filling our new States and Territories with an industrious and independent population.

The modification most perseveringly pressed upon Congress, which has occupied so much of its time for years past, and will probably do so for a long time to come, if not sooner satisfactorily adjusted, is a reduction in the cost of such portions of the public lands as are ascertained to be unsalable at the rate now established by law, and a graduation according to their relative value of the prices at which they may hereafter be sold. It is worthy of consideration whether justice may not be done to every interest in this matter, and a vexed question set at rest, perhaps forever, by a reasonable compromise of conflicting opinions. Hitherto, after being offered at public sale, lands have been disposed of at one uniform price, whatever difference there might be in their intrinsic value. The leading considerations urged in favor of the measure referred to are that in almost all the land districts, and particularly in those in which the lands have been long surveyed and exposed to sale, there are still remaining numerous and large tracts of every gradation of value, from the Government price downward; that these lands will not be purchased at the Government price so long as better can be conveniently obtained for the same amount; that there are large tracts which even the improvements of the adjacent lands will never raise to that price, and that the present uniform price, combined with their irregular value, operates to prevent a desirable compactness of settlements in the new States and to retard the full development of that wise policy on which our land system is founded, to the injury not only of the several States where the lands lie, but of the United States as a whole.

The remedy proposed has been a reduction of the prices according to the length of time the lands have been in market, without reference to any other circumstances. The certainty that the efflux of time would not always in such cases, and perhaps not even generally, furnish a true criterion of value, and the probability that persons residing in the vicinity, as the period for the reduction of prices approached, would postpone purchases they would otherwise make, for the purpose of availing themselves of the lower price, with other considerations of a similar character, have hitherto been successfully urged to defeat the graduation upon time.

May not all reasonable desires upon this subject be satisfied without encountering any of these objections? All will concede the abstract principle that the price of the public lands should be proportioned to their relative value, so far as can be accomplished without departing from the rule heretofore observed requiring fixed prices in cases of private entries.   The difficulty of the subject seems to lie in the mode of ascertaining what that value is.   Would not the safest plan be that which has been adopted by many of the States as the basis of taxation—an actual valuation of lands and classification of them into different rates? Would it not be practicable and expedient to cause the relative value of the public lands in the old districts which have been for a certain length of time in market to be appraised and classed into two or more rates below the present minimum price by the officers now employed in this branch of the public service or in any other mode deemed preferable, and to make those prices permanent if upon the coming in of the report they shall prove satisfactory to Congress?   Could not all the objects of graduation be accomplished in this way, and the objections which have hitherto been urged against it avoided?   It would seem to me that such a step, with a restriction of the sales to limited quantities and for actual improvement, would be free from all just exception.

By the full exposition of the value of the lands thus furnished and extensively promulgated persons living at a distance would be informed of their true condition and enabled to enter into competition with those residing in the vicinity; the means of acquiring an independent home would be brought within the reach of many who are unable to purchase at present prices; the population of the new States would be made more compact, and large tracts would be sold which would otherwise remain on hand.   Not only would the land be brought within the means of a larger number of purchasers, but many persons possessed of greater means would be content to settle on a larger quantity of the poorer lands rather than emigrate farther west in pursuit of a smaller quantity of better lands. Such a measure would also seem to be more consistent with the policy of the existing laws—that of converting the public domain into cultivated farms owned by their occupants.   That policy is not best promoted by sending emigration up the almost interminable streams of the West to occupy in groups the best spots of land, leaving immense wastes behind them and enlarging the frontier beyond the means of the Government to afford it adequate protection, but in encouraging it to occupy with reasonable denseness the territory over which it advances, and find its best defense in the compact front which it presents to the Indian tribes. Many of you will bring to the consideration of the subject the advantages of local knowledge and greater experience, and all will be desirous of making an early and final disposition of every disturbing question in regard to this important interest.   If these suggestions shall in any degree contribute to the accomplishment of so important a result, it will afford me sincere satisfaction.

In some sections of the country most of the public lands have been sold, and the registers and receivers have very little to do. It is a subject worthy of inquiry whether in many cases two or more districts may not be consolidated and the number of persons employed in this business considerably reduced. Indeed, the time will come when it will be the true policy of the General Government, as to some of the States, to transfer to them for a reasonable equivalent all the refuse and unsold lands and to withdraw the machinery of the Federal land offices altogether. All who take a comprehensive view of our federal system and believe that one of its greatest excellences consists in interfering as little as possible with the internal concerns of the States look forward with great interest to this result.

A modification of the existing laws in respect to the prices of the public lands might also have a favorable influence on the legislation of Congress in relation to another branch of the subject. Many who have not the ability to buy at present prices settle on those lands with the hope of acquiring from their cultivation the means of purchasing under preemption laws from time to time passed by Congress. For this encroachment on the rights of the United States they excuse themselves under the plea of their own necessities; the fact that they dispossess nobody and only enter upon the waste domain; that they give additional value to the public lands in their vicinity, and their intention ultimately to pay the Government price. So much weight has from time to time been attached to these considerations that Congress have passed laws giving actual settlers on the public lands a right of preemption to the tracts occupied by them at the minimum price. These laws have in all instances been retrospective in their operation, but in a few years after their passage crowds of new settlers have been found on the public lands for similar reasons and under like expectations, who have been indulged with the same privilege. This course of legislation tends to impair public respect for the laws of the country. Either the laws to prevent intrusion upon the public lands should be executed, or, if that should be impracticable or inexpedient, they should be modified or repealed. If the public lands are to be considered as open to be occupied by any, they should by law be thrown open to all. That which is intended in all instances to be legalized should at once be made legal, that those who are disposed to conform to the laws may enjoy at least equal privileges with those who are not. But it is not believed to be the disposition of Congress to open the public lands to occupancy without regular entry and payment of the Government price, as such a course must tend to worse evils than the credit system, which it was found necessary to abolish.

It would seem, therefore, to be the part of wisdom and sound policy to remove as far as practicable the causes which produce intrusions upon the public lands, and then take efficient steps to prevent them in future. Would any single measure be so effective in removing all plausible grounds for these intrusions as the graduation of price already suggested? A short period of industry and economy in any part of our country would enable the poorest citizen to accumulate the means to buy him a home at the lower prices, and leave him without apology for settling on lands not his own. If he did not under such circumstances, he would enlist no sympathy in his favor, and the laws would be readily executed without doing violence to public opinion.

A large portion of our citizens have seated themselves on the public lands without authority since the passage of the last preemption law, and now ask the enactment of another to enable them to retain the lands occupied upon payment of the minimum Government price. They ask that which has been repeatedly granted before. If the future may be judged of by the past, little harm can be done to the interests of the Treasury by yielding to their request. Upon a critical examination it is found that the lands sold at the public sales since the introduction of cash payments, in 1820, have produced on an average the net revenue of only 6 cents an acre more than the minimum Government price. There is no reason to suppose that future sales will be more productive. The Government, therefore, has no adequate pecuniary interest to induce it to drive these people from the lands they occupy for the purpose of selling them to others.

Entertaining these views, I recommend the passage of a preemption law for their benefit in connection with the preparatory steps toward the graduation of the price of the public lands, and further and more effectual provisions to prevent intrusions hereafter. Indulgence to those who have settled on these lands with expectations that past legislation would be made a rule for the future, and at the same time removing the most plausible ground on which intrusions are excused and adopting more efficient means to prevent them hereafter, appears to me the most judicious disposition which can be made of this difficult subject. The limitations and restrictions to guard against abuses in the execution of a preemption law will necessarily attract the careful attention of Congress, but under no circumstances is it considered expedient to authorize floating claims in any shape. They have been heretofore, and doubtless would be hereafter, most prolific sources of fraud and oppression, and instead of operating to confer the favor of the Government on industrious settlers are often used only to minister to a spirit of cupidity at the expense of the most meritorious of that class.

The accompanying report of the Secretary of War will bring to your view the state of the Army and all the various subjects confided to the superintendence of that officer.

The principal part of the Army has been concentrated in Florida, with a view and in the expectation of bringing the war in that Territory to a speedy close. The necessity of stripping the posts on the maritime and inland frontiers of their entire garrisons for the purpose of assembling in the field an army of less than 4,000 men would seem to indicate the necessity of increasing our regular forces; and the superior efficiency, as well as greatly diminished expense of that description of troops, recommend this measure as one of economy as well as of expediency. I refer to the report for the reasons which have induced the Secretary of War to urge the reorganization and enlargement of the staff of the Army, and of the Ordnance Corps, in which I fully concur.

It is not, however, compatible with the interests of the people to maintain in time of peace a regular force adequate to the defense of our extensive frontiers. In periods of danger and alarm we must rely principally upon a well-organized militia, and some general arrangement that will render this description of force more efficient has long been a subject of anxious solicitude. It was recommended to the First Congress by General Washington, and has been since frequently brought to your notice, and recently its importance strongly urged by my immediate predecessor. The provision in the Constitution that renders it necessary to adopt a uniform system of organization for the militia throughout the United States presents an insurmountable obstacle to an efficient arrangement by the classification heretofore proposed, and I invite your attention to the plan which will be submitted by the Secretary of War, for the organization of volunteer corps and the instruction of militia officers, as more simple and practicable, if not equally advantageous, as a general arrangement of the whole militia of the United States.

A moderate increase of the corps both of military and topographical engineers has been more than once recommended by my predecessor, and my conviction of the propriety, not to say necessity, of the measure, in order to enable them to perform the various and important duties imposed upon them, induces me to repeat the recommendation.

The Military Academy continues to answer all the purposes of its establishment, and not only furnishes well-educated officers to the Army, but serves to diffuse throughout the mass of our citizens individuals possessed of military knowledge and the scientific attainments of civil and military engineering. At present the cadet is bound, with consent of his parents or guardians, to remain in service five years from the period of his enlistment, unless sooner discharged, thus exacting only one year's service in the Army after his education is completed. This does not appear to me sufficient. Government ought to command for a longer period the services of those who are educated at the public expense, and I recommend that the time of enlistment be extended to seven years, and the terms of the engagement strictly enforced.

The creation of a national foundry for cannon, to be common to the service of the Army and Navy of the United States, has been heretofore recommended, and appears to be required in order to place our ordnance on an equal footing with that of other countries and to enable that branch of the service to control the prices of those articles and graduate the supplies to the wants of the Government, as well as to regulate their quality and insure their uniformity. The same reasons induce me to recommend the erection of a manufactory of gunpowder, to be under the direction of the Ordnance Office. The establishment of a manufactory of small arms west of the Alleghany Mountains, upon the plan proposed by the Secretary of War, will contribute to extend throughout that country the improvements which exist in establishments of a similar description in the Atlantic States, and tend to a much more economical distribution of the armament required in the western portion of our Union.

The system of removing the Indians west of the Mississippi, commenced by Mr. Jefferson in 1804, has been steadily persevered in by every succeeding President, and may be considered the settled policy of the country. Unconnected at first with any well-defined system for their improvement, the inducements held out to the Indians were confined to the greater ab n-dance of game to be found in the West; but when the beneficial effect: of their removal were made apparent a more philanthropic and enlightened policy was adopted in purchasing their lands east of the Mississippi. Liberal prices were given and provisions inserted in all the treaties with them for the application of the funds they received in exchange to such purposes as were best calculated to promote their present welfare and advance their future civilization. These measures have been attended thus far with the happiest results.

It will be seen by referring to the report of the Commissioner of Indian Affairs that the most sanguine expectations of the friends and promoters of this system have been realized. The Choctaws, Cherokees, and othe: tribes that first emigrated beyond the Mississippi have for the most part abandoned the hunter state and become cultivators of the soil. The improvement in their condition has been rapid, and it is believed that they are now fitted to enjoy the advantages of a simple form of government, which has been submitted to them and received their sanction; and I can not too strongly urge this subject upon the attention of Congress.

Stipulations have been made with all the Indian tribes to remove them beyond the Mississippi, except with the bands of the Wyandots, the Six Nations in New York, the Menomonees, Munsees, and Stockbridges in Wisconsin, and Miamies in Indiana. With all but the Menomonees it is expected that arrangements for their emigration will be completed the present year. The resistance which has been opposed to their removal by some of the tribes even after treaties had been made with them to that effect has arisen from various causes, operating differently on each of them. In most instances they have been instigated to resistance by persons to whom the trade with them and the acquisition of their annuities were important, and in some by the personal influence of interested chiefs. These obstacles must be overcome, for the Government can not relinquish the execution of this policy without sacrificing important interests and abandoning the tribes remaining east of the Mississippi to certain destruction.

The decrease in numbers of the tribes within the limits of the States and Territories has been most rapid. If they be removed, they can be protected from those associations and evil practices which exert so pernicious and destructive an influence over their destinies. They can be induced to labor and to acquire property, and its acquisition will inspire them with a feeling of independence. Their minds can be cultivated, and they can be taught the value of salutary and uniform laws and be made sensible of the blessings of free government and capable of enjoying its advantages. In the possession of property, knowledge, and a good government, free to give what direction they please to their labor, and sharers in the legislation by which their persons and the profits of their industry are to be protected and secured, they will have an ever-present conviction of the importance of union and peace among themselves and of the preservation of amicable relations with us. The interests of the United States would also be greatly promoted by freeing the relations between the General and State Governments from what has proved a most embarrassing incumbrance by a satisfactory adjustment of conflicting titles to lands caused by the occupation of the Indians, and by causing the resources of the whole country to be developed by the power of the State and General Governments and improved by the enterprise of a white population.

Intimately connected with this subject is the obligation of the Government to fulfill its treaty stipulations and to protect the Indians thus assembled "at their new residences from all interruptions and disturbances from any other tribes or nations of Indians or from any other person or persons whatsoever," and the equally solemn obligation to guard from Indian hostility its own border settlements, stretching along a line of more than 1,000 miles. To enable the Government to redeem this pledge to the Indians and to afford adequate protection to its own citizens will require the continual presence of a considerable regular force on the frontiers and the establishment of a chain of permanent posts. Examinations of the country are now making, with a view to decide on the most suitable points for the erection of fortresses and other works of defense, the results of which will be presented to you by the Secretary of War at an early day, together with a plan for the effectual protection of the friendly Indians and the permanent defense of the frontier States.

By the report of the Secretary of the Navy herewith communicated it appears that unremitted exertions have been made at the different navy-yards to carry into effect all authorized measures for the extension and employment of our naval force. The launching and preparation of the ship of the line *Pennsylvania* and the complete repairs of the ships of the line *Ohio*, *Delaware*, and *Columbus* may be noticed as forming a respectable addition to this important arm of our national defense. Our commerce and navigation have received increased aid and protection during the present year. Our squadrons in the Pacific and on the Brazilian station have been much increased, and that in the Mediterranean, although small, is adequate to the present wants of our commerce in that sea. Additions have been made to our squadron on the West India station, where the large force under Commodore Dallas has been most actively and efficiently employed in protecting our commerce, in preventing the importation of slaves, and in cooperating with the officers of the Army in carrying on the war in Florida.

The satisfactory condition of our naval force abroad leaves at our disposal the means of conveniently providing for a home squadron for the protection of commerce upon our extensive coast. The amount of appropriations required for such a squadron will be found in the general estimates for the naval service for the year 1838.

The naval officers engaged upon our coast survey have rendered important service to our navigation. The discovery of a new channel into the harbor of New York, through which our largest ships may pass without danger, must afford important commercial advantages to that harbor and add greatly to its value as a naval station. The accurate survey of Georges Shoals, off the coast of Massachusetts, lately completed, will render comparatively safe a navigation hitherto considered dangerous.

Considerable additions have been made to the number of captains, commanders, lieutenants, surgeons, and assistant surgeons in the Navy. These additions were rendered necessary by the increased number of vessels put in commission to answer the exigencies of our growing commerce.

Your attention is respectfully invited to the various suggestions of the Secretary for the improvement of the naval service.

The report of the Postmaster-General exhibits the progress and condition of the mail service. The operations of the Post-Office Department constitute one of the most active elements of our national prosperity, and it is gratifying to observe with what vigor they are conducted. The mail routes of the United States cover an extent of about 142,877 miles, having been increased about 37,103 miles within the last two years. The annual mail transportation on these routes is about 36,228,962 miles, having been increased about 10,359,476 miles within the same period. The number of post-offices has also been increased from 10,770 to 12,099, very few of which receive the mails less than once a week, and a large portion of them daily. Contractors and postmasters in general are represented as attending to their duties with most commendable zeal and fidelity. The revenue of the Department within the year ending on the 30th of June last was $4,137,056.59, and its liabilities accruing within the same time were $3,380,847.75. The increase of revenue over that of the preceding year was $708,166.41.

For many interesting details I refer you to the report of the Postmaster-General, with the accompanying papers. Your particular attention is invited to the necessity of providing a more safe and convenient building for the accommodation of that Department.

I lay before Congress copies of reports submitted in pursuance of a call made by me upon the heads of Departments for such suggestions as their experience might enable them to make as to what further legislative provisions may be advantageously adopted to secure the faithful application of public moneys to the objects for which they are appropriated, to prevent their misapplication or embezzlement by those intrusted with the expenditure of them, and generally to increase the security of the Government against losses in their disbursement. It is needless to dilate on the importance of providing such new safeguards as are within the power of legislation to promote these ends, and I have little to add to the recommendations submitted in the accompanying papers.

By law the terms of service of our most important collecting and disbursing officers in the civil departments are limited to four years, and when reappointed their bonds are required to be renewed. The safety of the public is much increased by this feature of the law, and there can be no doubt that its application to all officers intrusted with the collection or disbursement of the public money, whatever may be the tenure of their offices, would be equally beneficial. I therefore recommend, in addition to such of the suggestions presented by the heads of Departments as you may think useful, a general provision that all officers of the Army or Navy, or in the civil departments, intrusted with the receipt or payment of public money, and whose term of service is either unlimited or for a longer time than four years, be required to give new bonds, with good and sufficient sureties, at the expiration of every such period.

A change in the period of terminating the fiscal year, from the 1st of October to the 1st of April, has been frequently recommended, and appears to be desirable.

The distressing casualties in steamboats which have so frequently happened during the year seem to evince the necessity of attempting to prevent them by means of severe provisions connected with their customhouse papers. This subject was submitted to the attention of Congress by the Secretary of the Treasury in his last annual report, and will be again noticed at the present session, with additional details. It will doubtless receive that early and careful consideration which its pressing importance appears to require.

Your attention has heretofore been frequently called to the affairs of the District of Columbia, and I should not again ask it did not their entire dependence on Congress give them a constant claim upon its notice. Separated by the Constitution from the rest of the Union, limited in extent, and aided by no legislature of its own, it would seem to be a spot where a wise and uniform system of local government might have been easily adopted. This district has, however, unfortunately been left to linger behind the rest of the Union. Its codes, civil and criminal, are not only very defective, but full of obsolete or inconvenient provisions. Being formed of portions of two States, discrepancies in the laws prevail in different parts of the territory, small as it is; and although it was selected as the seat of the General Government, the site of its public edifices, the depository of its archives, and the residence of officers intrusted with large amounts of public property and the management of public business, yet it has never been subjected to or received that special and comprehensive legislation which these circumstances peculiarly demand. I am well aware of the various subjects of greater magnitude and immediate interest that press themselves on the consideration of Congress, but I believe there is not one that appeals more directly to its justice than a liberal and even generous attention to the interests of the District of Columbia and a thorough and careful revision of its local government.

SECOND ANNUAL MESSAGE.

WASHINGTON, *December 3, 1838.*

Fellow-Citizens of the Senate and House of Representatives:

I congratulate you on the favorable circumstances in the condition of our country under which you reassemble for the performance of your official duties. Though the anticipations of an abundant harvest have not everywhere been realized, yet on the whole the labors of the husbandman are rewarded with a bountiful return; industry prospers in its various channels of business and enterprise; general health again prevails through our vast diversity of climate; nothing threatens from abroad the continuance of external peace; nor has anything at home impaired the strength of those fraternal and domestic ties which constitute the only guaranty to the success and permanency of our happy Union, and which, formed in the hour of peril, have hitherto been honorably sustained through every vicissitude in our national affairs. These blessings, which evince the care and beneficence of Providence, call for our devout and fervent gratitude.

We have not less reason to be grateful for other bounties bestowed by the same munificent hand, and more exclusively our own.

The present year closes the first half century of our Federal institutions, and our system, differing from all others in the acknowledged practical and unlimited operation which it has for so long a period given to the sovereignty of the people, has now been fully tested by experience.

The Constitution devised by our forefathers as the framework and bond of that system, then untried, has become a settled form of government; not only preserving and protecting the great principles upon which it was founded, but wonderfully promoting individual happiness and private interests. Though subject to change and entire revocation whenever deemed inadequate to all these purposes, yet such is the wisdom of its construction and so stable has been the public sentiment that it remains unaltered except in matters of detail comparatively unimportant. It has proved amply sufficient for the various emergencies incident to our condition as a nation. A formidable foreign war; agitating collisions between domestic, and in some respects rival, sovereignties; temptations to interfere in the intestine commotions of neighboring countries; the dangerous influences that arise in periods of excessive prosperity, and the antirepublican tendencies of associated wealth—these, with other trials not less formidable, have all been encountered, and thus far successfully resisted.

It was reserved for the American Union to test the advantages of a government entirely dependent on the continual exercise of the popular will, and our experience has shown that it is as beneficent in practice as it is just in theory. Each successive change made in our local institutions has contributed to extend the right of suffrage, has increased the direct influence of the mass of the community, given greater freedom to individual exertion, and restricted more and more the powers of Government; yet the intelligence, prudence, and patriotism of the people have kept pace with this augmented responsibility. In no country has education been so widely diffused. Domestic peace has nowhere so largely reigned. The close bonds of social intercourse have in no instance prevailed with such harmony over a space so vast. All forms of religion have united for the first time to diffuse charity and piety, because for the first time in the history of nations all have been totally untrammeled and absolutely free. The deepest recesses of the wilderness have been penetrated; yet instead of the rudeness in the social condition consequent upon such adventures elsewhere, numerous communities have sprung up, already unrivaled in prosperity, general intelligence, internal tranquillity, and the wisdom of their political institutions. Internal improvement, the fruit of individual enterprise, fostered by the protection of the States, has added new links to the Confederation and fresh rewards to provident industry. Doubtful questions of domestic policy have been quietly settled by mutual forbearance, and agriculture, commerce, and manufactures minister to each other. Taxation and public debt, the burdens which bear so heavily upon all other countries, have pressed with comparative lightness upon us. Without one entangling alliance, our friendship is prized by every nation, and the rights of our citizens are everywhere respected, because they are known to be guarded by a united, sensitive, and watchful people.

To this practical operation of our institutions, so evident and successful, we owe that increased attachment to them which is among the most cheering exhibitions of popular sentiment and will prove their best security in time to come against foreign or domestic assault.

This review of the results of our institutions for half a century, without exciting a spirit of vain exultation, should serve to impress upon us the great principles from which they have sprung—constant and direct supervision by the people over every public measure. strict forbearance on the part of the Government from exercising any doubtful or disputed **powers, and a cautious** abstinence from all interference with concerns which properly belong and are best left to State regulations and individual enterprise.

Full information of the state of our foreign affairs having been recently on different occasions submitted to Congress, I deem it necessary now to bring to your notice only such events as have subsequently occurred or are of such importance as to require particular attention.

The most amicable dispositions continue to be exhibited by all the nations with whom the Government and citizens of the United States have an habitual intercourse. At the date of my last annual message Mexico was the only nation which could not be included in so gratifying a reference to our foreign relations.

I am happy to be now able to inform you that an advance has been made toward the adjustment of our differences with that Republic and the restoration of the customary good feeling between the two nations. This important change has been effected by conciliatory negotiations that have resulted in the conclusion of a treaty between the two Governments, which, when ratified, will refer to the arbitrament of a friendly power all the subjects of controversy between us growing out of injuries to individuals. There is at present also reason to believe that an equitable settlement of all disputed points will be attained without further difficulty or unnecessary delay, and thus authorize the free resumption of diplomatic intercourse with our sister Republic.

With respect to the northeastern boundary of the United States, no official correspondence between this Government and that of Great Britain has passed since that communicated to Congress toward the close of their last session. The offer to negotiate a convention for the appointment of a joint commission of survey and exploration I am, however, assured will be met by Her Majesty's Government in a conciliatory and friendly spirit, and instructions to enable the British minister here to conclude such an arrangement will be transmitted to him without needless delay. It is hoped and expected that these instructions will be of a liberal character, and that this negotiation, if successful, will prove to be an important step toward the satisfactory and final adjustment of the controversy.

I had hoped that the respect for the laws and regard for the peace and honor of their own country which have ever characterized the citizens of the United States would have prevented any portion of them from using any means to promote insurrection in the territory of a power with which we are at peace, and with which the United States are desirous of maintaining the most friendly relations. I regret deeply, however, to be obliged to inform you that this has not been the case. Information has been given to me, derived from official and other sources, that many citizens of the United States have associated together to make hostile incursions from our territory into Canada and to aid and abet insurrection there, in violation of the obligations and laws of the United States and in open disregard of their own duties as citizens. This information has been in part confirmed by a hostile invasion actually made by citizens of the United States, in conjunction with Canadians and others, and accompanied by a forcible seizure of the property of our citizens and an application thereof to the prosecution of military operations against the authorities and people of Canada.

The results of these criminal assaults upon the peace and order of a neighboring country have been, as was to be expected, fatally destructive to the misguided or deluded persons engaged in them and highly injurious to those in whose behalf they are professed to have been undertaken. The authorities in Canada, from intelligence received of such intended movements among our citizens, have felt themselves obliged to take precautionary measures against them; have actually embodied the militia and assumed an attitude to repel the invasion to which they believed the colonies were exposed from the United States. A state of feeling on both sides of the frontier has thus been produced which called for prompt and vigorous interference. If an insurrection existed in Canada, the amicable dispositions of the United States toward Great Britain, as well as their duty to themselves, would lead them to maintain a strict neutrality and to restrain their citizens from all violations of the laws which have been passed for its enforcement. But this Government recognizes a still higher obligation to repress all attempts on the part of its citizens to disturb the peace of a country where order prevails or has been reestablished. Depredations by our citizens upon nations at peace with the United States, or combinations for committing them, have at all times been regarded by the American Government and people with the greatest abhorrence. Military incursions by our citizens into countries so situated, and the commission of acts of violence on the members thereof, in order to effect a change in their government, or under any pretext whatever, have from the commencement of our Government been held equally criminal on the part of those engaged in them, and as much deserving of punishment as would be the disturbance of the public peace by the perpetration of similar acts within our own territory.

By no country or persons have these invaluable principles of international law—principles the strict observance of which is so indispensable to the preservation of social order in the world—been more earnestly

cherished or sacredly respected than by those great and good men who
first declared and finally established the independence of our own country.
They promulgated and maintained them at an early and critical period
in our history; they were subsequently embodied in legislative enactments of a highly penal character, the faithful enforcement of which has
hitherto been, and will, I trust, always continue to be, regarded as a duty
inseparably associated with the maintenance of our national honor.   That
the people of the United States should feel an interest in the spread of
political institutions as free as they regard their own to be is natural,
nor can a sincere solicitude for the success of all those who are at any
time in good faith struggling for their acquisition be imputed to our citizens as a crime.   With the entire freedom of opinion and an undisguised
expression thereof on their part the Government has neither the right
nor, I trust, the disposition to interfere.   But whether the interest or the
honor of the United States requires that they should be made a party to
any such struggle, and by inevitable consequence to the war which is
waged in its support, is a question which by our Constitution is wisely
left to Congress alone to decide.   It is by the laws already made criminal
in our citizens to embarrass or anticipate that decision by unauthorized
military operations on their part.   Offenses of this character, in addition
to their criminality as violations of the laws of our country, have a direct
tendency to draw down upon our own citizens at large the multiplied evils
of a foreign war and expose to injurious imputations the good faith and
honor of the country.   As such they deserve to be put down with promptitude and decision.   I can not be mistaken, I am confident, in counting
on the cordial and general concurrence of our fellow-citizens in this sentiment.   A copy of the proclamation which I have felt it my duty to
issue is herewith communicated.   I can not but hope that the good sense
and patriotism, the regard for the honor and reputation of their country,
the respect for the laws which they have themselves enacted for their
own government, and the love of order for which the mass of our people
have been so long and so justly distinguished will deter the comparatively few who are engaged in them from a further prosecution of such
desperate enterprises.   In the meantime the existing laws have been
and will continue to be faithfully executed, and every effort will be
made to carry them out in their full extent.   Whether they are sufficient
or not to meet the actual state of things on the Canadian frontier it is for
Congress to decide.

It will appear from the correspondence herewith submitted that the
Government of Russia declines a renewal of the fourth article of the convention of April, 1824, between the United States and His Imperial
Majesty, by the third article of which it is agreed that "hereafter there
shall not be formed by the citizens of the United States or under the
authority of the said States any establishment upon the northwest coast
of America, nor in any of the islands adjacent, to the north of 54° 40' of

north latitude, and that in the same manner there shall be none formed by Russian subjects or under the authority of Russia south of the same parallel;'' and by the fourth article, ''that during a term of ten years, counting from the signature of the present convention, the ships of both powers, or which belong to their citizens or subjects, respectively, may reciprocally frequent, without any hindrance whatever, the interior seas, gulfs, harbors, and creeks upon the coast mentioned in the preceding article, for the purpose of fishing and trading with the natives of the country.'' The reasons assigned for declining to renew the provisions of this article are, briefly, that the only use made by our citizens of the privileges it secures to them has been to supply the Indians with spirituous liquors, ammunition, and firearms; that this traffic has been excluded from the Russian trade; and as the supplies furnished from the United States are injurious to the Russian establishments on the northwest coast and calculated to produce complaints between the two Governments, His Imperial Majesty thinks it for the interest of both countries not to accede to the proposition made by the American Government for the renewal of the article last referred to.

The correspondence herewith communicated will show the grounds upon which we contend that the citizens of the United States have, independent of the provisions of the convention of 1824, a right to trade with the natives upon the coast in question at unoccupied places, liable, however, it is admitted, to be at any time extinguished by the creation of Russian establishments at such points. This right is denied by the Russian Government, which asserts that by the operation of the treaty of 1824 each party agreed to waive the general right to land on the vacant coasts on the respective sides of the degree of latitude referred to, and accepted in lieu thereof the mutual privileges mentioned in the fourth article. The capital and tonnage employed by our citizens in their trade with the northwest coast of America will, perhaps, on adverting to the official statements of the commerce and navigation of the United States for the last few years, be deemed too inconsiderable in amount to attract much attention; yet the subject may in other respects deserve the careful consideration of Congress.

I regret to state that the blockade of the principal ports on the eastern coast of Mexico, which, in consequence of differences between that Republic and France, was instituted in May last, unfortunately still continues, enforced by a competent French naval armament, and is necessarily embarrassing to our own trade in the Gulf, in common with that of other nations. Every disposition, however, is believed to exist on the part of the French Government to render this measure as little onerous as practicable to the interests of the citizens of the United States and to those of neutral commerce, and it is to be hoped that an early settlement of the difficulties between France and Mexico will soon reestablish the harmonious relations formerly subsisting between them and again open the ports of that Republic to the vessels of all friendly nations.

A convention for marking that part of the boundary between the United States and the Republic of Texas which extends from the mouth of the Sabine to the Red River was concluded and signed at this city on the 25th of April last. It has since been ratified by both Governments, and seasonable measures will be taken to carry it into effect on the part of the United States.

The application of that Republic for admission into this Union, made in August, 1837, and which was declined for reasons already made known to you, has been formally withdrawn, as will appear from the accompanying copy of the note of the minister plenipotentiary of Texas, which was presented to the Secretary of State on the occasion of the exchange of the ratifications of the convention above mentioned.

Copies of the convention with Texas, of a commercial treaty concluded with the King of Greece, and of a similar treaty with the Peru-Bolivian Confederation, the ratifications of which have been recently exchanged, accompany this message, for the information of Congress and for such legislative enactments as may be found necessary or expedient in relation to either of them.

To watch over and foster the interests of a gradually increasing and widely extended commerce, to guard the rights of American citizens whom business or pleasure or other motives may tempt into distant climes, and at the same time to cultivate those sentiments of mutual respect and good will which experience has proved so beneficial in international intercourse, the Government of the United States has deemed it expedient from time to time to establish diplomatic connections with different foreign states, by the appointment of representatives to reside within their respective territories. I am gratified to be enabled to announce to you that since the close of your last session these relations have been opened under the happiest auspices with Austria and the Two Sicilies, that new nominations have been made in the respective missions of Russia, Brazil, Belgium, and Sweden and Norway in this country, and that a minister extraordinary has been received, accredited to this Government, from the Argentine Confederation.

An exposition of the fiscal affairs of the Government and of their condition for the past year will be made to you by the Secretary of the Treasury.

The available balance in the Treasury on the 1st of January next is estimated at $2,765,342. The receipts of the year from customs and lands will probably amount to $20,615,598. These usual sources of revenue have been increased by an issue of Treasury notes, of which less than $8,000,000, including interest and principal, will be outstanding at the end of the year, and by the sale of one of the bonds of the Bank of the United States for $2,254,871. The aggregate of means from these and other sources, with the balance on hand on the 1st of January last, has been applied to the payment of appropriations by Congress. The whole expenditure for the year on their account, including the redemption of more than eight millions of Treasury notes, constitutes an aggregate of about $40,000,000, and will still leave in the Treasury the balance before stated.

Nearly $8,000,000 of Treasury notes are to be paid during the coming year in addition to the ordinary appropriations for the support of Government. For both these purposes the resources of the Treasury will undoubtedly be sufficient if the charges upon it are not increased beyond the annual estimates. No excess, however, is likely to exist. Nor can the postponed installment of the surplus revenue be deposited with the States nor any considerable appropriations beyond the estimates be made without causing a deficiency in the Treasury. The great caution, advisable at all times, of limiting appropriations to the wants of the public service is rendered necessary at present by the prospective and rapid reduction of the tariff, while the vigilant jealousy evidently excited among the people by the occurrences of the last few years assures us that they expect from their representatives, and will sustain them in the exercise of, the most rigid economy. Much can be effected by postponing appropriations not immediately required for the ordinary public service or for any pressing emergency, and much by reducing the expenditures where the entire and immediate accomplishment of the objects in view is not indispensable.

When we call to mind the recent and extreme embarrassments produced by excessive issues of bank paper, aggravated by the unforeseen withdrawal of much foreign capital and the inevitable derangement arising from the distribution of the surplus revenue among the States as required by Congress, and consider the heavy expenses incurred by the removal of Indian tribes, by the military operations in Florida, and on account of the unusually large appropriations made at the last two annual sessions of Congress for other objects, we have striking evidence in the present efficient state of our finances of the abundant resources of the country to fulfill all its obligations. Nor is it less gratifying to find that the general business of the community, deeply affected as it has been, is reviving with additional vigor, chastened by the lessons of the past and animated by the hopes of the future. By the curtailment of paper issues, by curbing the sanguine and adventurous spirit of speculation, and by the honorable application of all available means to the fulfillment of obligations, confidence has been restored both at home and abroad, and ease and facility secured to all the operations of trade.

The agency of the Government in producing these results has been as efficient as its powers and means permitted. By withholding from the States the deposit of the fourth installment, and leaving several millions at long credits with the banks, principally in one section of the country, and more immediately beneficial to it, and at the same time aiding the banks and commercial communities in other sections by postponing the payment of bonds for duties to the amount of between four and five millions of dollars; by an issue of Treasury notes as a means to enable the Government to meet the consequences of their indulgences, but affording at the same time facilities for remittance and exchange; and by steadily declining to employ as general depositories of the public revenues, or receive the notes of, all banks which refused to redeem them with specie— by these measures, aided by the favorable action of some of the banks and by the support and cooperation of a large portion of the community, we have witnessed an early resumption of specie payments in our great commercial capital, promptly followed in almost every part of the United States.   This result has been alike salutary to the true interests of agriculture, commerce, and manufactures; to public morals, respect for the laws, and that confidence between man and man which is so essential in all our social relations.

The contrast between the suspension of 1814 and that of 1837 is most striking.   The short duration of the latter, the prompt restoration of business, the evident benefits resulting from an adherence by the Government to the constitutional standard of value instead of sanctioning the suspension by the receipt of irredeemable paper, and the advantages derived from the large amount of specie introduced into the country previous to 1837 afford a valuable illustration of the true policy of the Government in such a crisis.   Nor can the comparison fail to remove the impression that a national bank is necessary in such emergencies. Not only were specie payments resumed without its aid, but exchanges have also been more rapidly restored than when it existed, thereby showing that private capital, enterprise, and prudence are fully adequate to these ends.   On all these points experience seems to have confirmed the views heretofore submitted to Congress.   We have been saved the mortification of seeing the distresses of the community for the third time seized on to fasten upon the country so dangerous an institution, and we may also hope that the business of individuals will hereafter be relieved from the injurious effects of a continued agitation of that disturbing subject. The limited influence of a national bank in averting derangement in the exchanges of the country or in compelling the resumption of specie payments is now not less apparent than its tendency to increase inordinate speculation by sudden expansions and contractions; its disposition to create panic and embarrassment for the promotion of its own designs; its interference with politics, and its far greater power for evil than for good, either in regard to the local institutions or the operations of Government itself.   What was in these respects but apprehension or opinion when a national bank was first established now stands confirmed by humiliating experience.   The scenes through which we have passed conclusively prove how little our commerce, agriculture, manufactures, or finances require such an institution, and what dangers are attendant on its power—a power, I trust, never to be conferred by the American people upon their Government, and still less upon individuals not responsible to them for its unavoidable abuses.

My conviction of the necessity of further legislative provisions for the safe-keeping and disbursement of the public moneys and my opinion in regard to the measures best adapted to the accomplishment of those objects have been already submitted to you. These have been strengthened by recent events, and in the full conviction that time and experience must still further demonstrate their propriety I feel it my duty, with respectful deference to the conflicting views of others, again to invite your attention to them.

With the exception of limited sums deposited in the few banks still employed under the act of 1836, the amounts received for duties, and, with very inconsiderable exceptions, those accruing from lands also, have since the general suspension of specie payments by the deposit banks been kept and disbursed by the Treasurer under his general legal powers, subject to the superintendence of the Secretary of the Treasury. The propriety of defining more specifically and of regulating by law the exercise of this wide scope of Executive discretion has been already submitted to Congress.

A change in the office of collector at one of our principal ports has brought to light a defalcation of the gravest character, the particulars of which will be laid before you in a special report from the Secretary of the Treasury. By his report and the accompanying documents it will be seen that the weekly returns of the defaulting officer apparently exhibited throughout a faithful administration of the affairs intrusted to his management. It, however, now appears that he commenced abstracting the public moneys shortly after his appointment and continued to do so, progressively increasing the amount, for the term of more than seven years, embracing a portion of the period during which the public moneys were deposited in the Bank of the United States, the whole of that of the State bank deposit system, and concluding only on his retirement from office, after that system had substantially failed in consequence of the suspension of specie payments.

The way in which this defalcation was so long concealed and the steps taken to indemnify the United States, as far as practicable, against loss will also be presented to you. The case is one which imperatively claims the attention of Congress and furnishes the strongest motive for the establishment of a more severe and secure system for the safe-keeping and disbursement of the public moneys than any that has heretofore existed.

It seems proper, at all events, that by an early enactment similar to that of other countries the application of public money by an officer of Government to private uses should be made a felony and visited with severe and ignominious punishment. This is already in effect the law in respect to the Mint, and has been productive of the most salutary results. Whatever system is adopted, such an enactment would be wise as an independent measure, since much of the public moneys must in their collection and ultimate disbursement pass twice through the hands of public officers, in whatever manner they are intermediately kept. The Government, it must be admitted, has been from its commencement comparatively fortunate in this respect. But the appointing power can not always be well advised in its selections, and the experience of every country has shown that public officers are not at all times proof against temptation. It is a duty, therefore, which the Government owes, as well to the interests committed to its care as to the officers themselves, to provide every guard against transgressions of this character that is consistent with reason and humanity. Congress can not be too jealous of the conduct of those who are intrusted with the public money, and I shall at all times be disposed to encourage a watchful discharge of this duty.

If a more direct cooperation on the part of Congress in the supervision of the conduct of the officers intrusted with the custody and application of the public money is deemed desirable, it will give me pleasure to assist in the establishment of any judicious and constitutional plan by which that object may be accomplished. You will in your wisdom determine upon the propriety of adopting such a plan and upon the measures necessary to its effectual execution. When the late Bank of the United States was incorporated and made the depository of the public moneys, a right was reserved to Congress to inspect at its pleasure, by a committee of that body, the books and the proceedings of the bank. In one of the States, whose banking institutions are supposed to rank amongst the first in point of stability, they are subjected to constant examination by commissioners appointed for that purpose, and much of the success of its banking system is attributed to this watchful supervision.

The same course has also, in view of its beneficial operation, been adopted by an adjoining State, favorably known for the care it has always bestowed upon whatever relates to its financial concerns. I submit to your consideration whether a committee of Congress might not be profitably employed in inspecting, at such intervals as might be deemed proper, the affairs and accounts of officers intrusted with the custody of the public moneys. The frequent performance of this duty might be made obligatory on the committee in respect to those officers who have large sums in their possession, and left discretionary in respect to others. They might report to the Executive such defalcations as were found to exist, with a view to a prompt removal from office unless the default was satisfactorily accounted for, and report also to Congress, at the commencement of each session, the result of their examinations and proceedings. It does appear to me that with a subjection of this class of public officers to the general supervision of the Executive, to examinations by a committee of Congress at periods of which they should have no previous notice, and to prosecution and punishment as for felony for every breach of trust, the safe-keeping of the public moneys might under the system proposed be placed on a surer foundation than it has ever occupied since the establishment of the Government.

The Secretary of the Treasury will lay before you additional information containing new details on this interesting subject. To these I ask your early attention. That it should have given rise to great diversity of opinion can not be a subject of surprise. After the collection and custody of the public moneys had been for so many years connected with and made subsidiary to the advancement of private interests, a return to the simple self-denying ordinances of the Constitution could not but be difficult. But time and free discussion, eliciting the sentiments of the people, and aided by that conciliatory spirit which has ever characterized their course on great emergencies, were relied upon for a satisfactory settlement of the question. Already has this anticipation, on one important point at least—the impropriety of diverting public money to private purposes—been fully realized. There is no reason to suppose that legislation upon that branch of the subject would now be embarrassed by a difference of opinion, or fail to receive the cordial support of a large majority of our constituents.

The connection which formerly existed between the Government and banks was in reality injurious to both, as well as to the general interests of the community at large. It aggravated the disasters of trade and the derangements of commercial intercourse, and administered new excitements and additional means to wild and reckless speculations, the disappointment of which threw the country into convulsions of panic, and all but produced violence and bloodshed. The imprudent expansion of bank credits, which was the natural result of the command of the revenues of the State, furnished the resources for unbounded license in every species of adventure, seduced industry from its regular and salutary occupations by the hope of abundance without labor, and deranged the social state by tempting all trades and professions into the vortex of speculation on remote contingencies.

The same wide-spreading influence impeded also the resources of the Government, curtailed its useful operations, embarrassed the fulfillment of its obligations, and seriously interfered with the execution of the laws. Large appropriations and oppressive taxes are the natural consequences of such a connection, since they increase the profits of those who are allowed to use the public funds, and make it their interest that money should be accumulated and expenditures multiplied. It is thus that a concentrated money power is tempted to become an active agent in political affairs; and all past experience has shown on which side that influence will be arrayed. We deceive ourselves if we suppose that it will ever be found asserting and supporting the rights of the community at large in opposition to the claims of the few.

In a government whose distinguishing characteristic should be a diffusion and equalization of its benefits and burdens the advantage of individuals will be augmented at the expense of the community at large. Nor is it the nature of combinations for the acquisition of legislative influence to confine their interference to the single object for which they were originally formed. The temptation to extend it to other matters is on the contrary, not unfrequently too strong to be resisted. The rightful influence in the direction of public affairs of the mass of the people is therefore in no slight danger of being sensibly and injuriously affected by giving to a comparatively small but very efficient class a direct and exclusive personal interest in so important a portion of the legislation of Congress as that which relates to the custody of the public moneys. If laws acting upon private interests can not always be avoided, they should be confined within the narrowest limits, and left wherever possible to the legislatures of the States. When not thus restricted they lead to combinations of powerful associations, foster an influence necessarily selfish, and turn the fair course of legislation to sinister ends rather than to objects that advance public liberty and promote the general good.

The whole subject now rests with you, and I can not but express a hope that some definite measure will be adopted at the present session.

It will not, I am sure, be deemed out of place for me here to remark that the declaration of my views in opposition to the policy of employing banks as depositories of the Government funds can not justly be construed as indicative of hostility, official or personal, to those institutions; or to repeat in this form and in connection with this subject opinions which I have uniformly entertained and on all proper occasions expressed. Though always opposed to their creation in the form of exclusive privileges, and, as a State magistrate, aiming by appropriate legislation to secure the community against the consequences of their occasional mismanagement, I have yet ever wished to see them protected in the exercise of rights conferred by law, and have never doubted their utility when properly managed in promoting the interests of trade, and through that channel the other interests of the community. To the General Government they present themselves merely as State institutions, having no necessary connection with its legislation or its administration. Like other State establishments, they may be used or not in conducting the affairs of the Government, as public policy and the general interests of the Union may seem to require. The only safe or proper principle upon which their intercourse with the Government can be regulated is that which regulates their intercourse with the private citizen—the conferring of mutual benefits. When the Government can accomplish a financial operation better with the aid of the banks than without it, it should be at liberty to seek that aid as it would the services of a private banker or other capitalist or agent, giving the preference to those who will serve it on the best terms. Nor can there ever exist an interest in the officers of the General Government, as such, inducing them to embarrass or annoy the State banks any more than to incur the hostility of any other class of State institutions or of private citizens. It is not in the nature of things that hostility to these institutions can spring from this source, or any opposition to their course of business, except when they themselves depart from the objects of their creation and attempt to usurp powers not conferred upon them or to subvert the standard of value established by the Constitution. While opposition to their regular operations can not exist in this quarter, resistance to any attempt to make the Government dependent upon them for the success-ful administration of public affairs is a matter of duty, as I trust it ever will be of inclination, no matter from what motive or consideration the attempt may originate.

It is no more than just to the banks to say that in the late emergency most of them firmly resisted the strongest temptations to extend their paper issues when apparently sustained in a suspension of specie pay-ments by public opinion, even though in some cases invited by legisla-tive enactments. To this honorable course, aided by the resistance of the General Government, acting in obedience to the Constitution and laws of the United States, to the introduction of an irredeemable paper medium, may be attributed in a great degree the speedy restoration of our currency to a sound state and the business of the country to its wonted prosperity.

The banks have but to continue in the same safe course and be content in their appropriate sphere to avoid all interference from the General Government and to derive from it all the protection and benefits which it bestows on other State establishments, on the people of the States, and on the States themselves. In this, their true position, they can not but secure the confidence and good will of the people and the Government, which they can only lose when, leaping from their legitimate sphere, they attempt to control the legislation of the country and pervert the opera-tions of the Government to their own purposes.

Our experience under the act, passed at the last session, to grant preemption rights to settlers on the public lands has as yet been too limited to enable us to pronounce with safety upon the efficacy of its pro-visions to carry out the wise and liberal policy of the Government in that respect. There is, however, the best reason to anticipate favorable results from its operation. The recommendations formerly submitted to you in respect to a graduation of the price of the public lands remain to be finally acted upon. Having found no reason to change the views then expressed, your attention to them is again respectfully requested.

Every proper exertion has been made and will be continued to carry out the wishes of Congress in relation to the tobacco trade, as indicated in the several resolutions of the House of Representatives and the legislation of the two branches.   A favorable impression has, I trust, been made in the different foreign countries to which particular attention has been directed; and although we can not hope for an early change in their policy, as in many of them a convenient and large revenue is derived from monopolies in the fabrication and sale of this article, yet, as these monopolies are really injurious to the people where they are established, and the revenue derived from them may be less injuriously and with equal facility obtained from another and a liberal system of administration, we can not doubt that our efforts will be eventually crowned with success if persisted in with temperate firmness and sustained by prudent legislation.

In recommending to Congress the adoption of the necessary provisions at this session for taking the next census or enumeration of the inhabitants of the United States, the suggestion presents itself whether the scope of the measure might not be usefully extended by causing it to embrace authentic statistical returns of the great interests specially intrusted to or necessarily affected by the legislation of Congress.

The accompanying report of the Secretary of War presents a satisfactory account of the state of the Army and of the several branches of the public service confided to the superintendence of that officer.

The law increasing and organizing the military establishment of the United States has been nearly carried into effect, and the Army has been extensively and usefully employed during the past season.

I would again call to your notice the subjects connected with and essential to the military defenses of the country which were submitted to you at the last session, but which were not acted upon, as is supposed, for want of time.   The most important of them is the organization of the militia on the maritime and inland frontiers.   This measure is deemed important, as it is believed that it will furnish an effective volunteer force in aid of the Regular Army, and may form the basis of a general system of organization for the entire militia of the United States.   The erection of a national foundry and gunpowder manufactory, and one for making small arms, the latter to be situated at some point west of the Allegany Mountains, all appear to be of sufficient importance to be again urged upon your attention.

The plan proposed by the Secretary of War for the distribution of the forces of the United States in time of peace is well calculated to promote regularity and economy in the fiscal administration of the service, to preserve the discipline of the troops, and to render them available for the maintenance of the peace and tranquillity of the country.   With this view, likewise, I recommend the adoption of the plan presented by that officer for the defense of the western frontier.   The preservation of the lives and property of our fellow-citizens who are settled upon that border country, as well as the existence of the Indian population, which might be tempted by our want of preparation to rush on their own destruction and attack the white settlements, all seem to require that this subject should be acted upon without delay, and the War Department authorized to place that country in a state of complete defense against any assault from the numerous and warlike tribes which are congregated on that border.

It affords me sincere pleasure to be able to apprise you of the entire removal of the Cherokee Nation of Indians to their new homes west of the Mississippi. The measures authorized by Congress at its last session, with a view to the long-standing controversy with them, have had the happiest effects. By an agreement concluded with them by the commanding general in that country, who has performed the duties assigned to him on the occasion with commendable energy and humanity, their removal has been principally under the conduct of their own chiefs, and they have emigrated without any apparent reluctance.

The successful accomplishment of this important object, the removal also of the entire Creek Nation with the exception of a small number of fugitives amongst the Seminoles in Florida, the progress already made toward a speedy completion of the removal of the Chickasaws, the Choctaws, the Pottawatamies, the Ottawas, and the Chippewas, with the extensive purchases of Indian lands during the present year, have rendered the speedy and successful result of the long-established policy of the Government upon the subject of Indian affairs entirely certain. The occasion is therefore deemed a proper one to place this policy in such a point of view as will exonerate the Government of the United States from the undeserved reproach which has been cast upon it through several successive Administrations. That a mixed occupancy of the same territory by the white and red man is incompatible with the safety or happiness of either is a position in respect to which there has long since ceased to be room for a difference of opinion. Reason and experience have alike demonstrated its impracticability. The bitter fruits of every attempt heretofore to overcome the barriers interposed by nature have only been destruction, both physical and moral, to the Indian, dangerous conflicts of authority between the Federal and State Governments, and detriment to the individual prosperity of the citizen as well as to the general improvement of the country. The remedial policy, the principles of which were settled more than thirty years ago under the Administration of Mr. Jefferson, consists in an extinction, for a fair consideration, of the title to all the lands still occupied by the Indians within the States and Territories of the United States; their removal to a country west of the Mississippi much more extensive and better adapted to their condition than that on which they then resided; the guarantee to them by the United States of their exclusive possession of that country forever, exempt from all intrusions by white men, with ample provisions for their security against external violence and internal dissensions, and the extension to them of suitable facilities for their advancement in civilization. This has not been the policy of particular Administrations only, but of each in succession since the first attempt to carry it out under that of Mr. Monroe. All have labored for its accomplishment, only with different degrees of success. The manner of its execution has, it is true, from time to time given rise to conflicts of opinion and unjust imputations; but in respect to the wisdom and necessity of the policy itself there has not from the beginning existed a doubt in the mind of any calm, judicious, disinterested friend of the Indian race accustomed to reflection and enlightened by experience.

Occupying the double character of contractor on its own account and guardian for the parties contracted with, it was hardly to be expected that the dealings of the Federal Government with the Indian tribes would escape misrepresentation. That there occurred in the early settlement of this country, as in all others where the civilized race has succeeded to the possessions of the savage, instances of oppression and fraud on the part of the former there is too much reason to believe. No such offenses can, however, be justly charged upon this Government since it became free to pursue its own course. Its dealings with the Indian tribes have been just and friendly throughout; its efforts for their civilization constant, and directed by the best feelings of humanity; its watchfulness in protecting them from individual frauds unremitting; its forbearance under the keenest provocations, the deepest injuries, and the most flagrant outrages may challenge at least a comparison with any nation, ancient or modern, in similar circumstances; and if in future times a powerful, civilized, and happy nation of Indians shall be found to exist within the limits of this northern continent it will be owing to the consummation of that policy which has been so unjustly assailed. Only a very brief reference to facts in confirmation of this assertion can in this form be given, and you are therefore necessarily referred to the report of the Secretary of War for further details. To the Cherokees, whose case has perhaps excited the greatest share of attention and sympathy, the United States have granted in fee, with a perpetual guaranty of exclusive and peaceable possession, 13,554,135 acres of land on the west side of the Mississippi, eligibly situated, in a healthy climate, and in all respects better suited to their condition than the country they have left, in exchange for only 9,492,160 acres on the east side of the same river. The United States have in addition stipulated to pay them $5,600,000 for their interest in and improvements on the lands thus relinquished, and $1,160,000 for subsistence and other beneficial purposes, thereby putting it in their power to become one of the most wealthy and independent separate communities of the same extent in the world.

By the treaties made and ratified with the Miamies, the Chippewas, the Sioux, the Sacs and Foxes, and the Winnebagoes during the last year the Indian title to 18,458,000 acres has been extinguished. These purchases have been much more extensive than those of any previous year, and have, with other Indian expenses, borne very heavily upon the Treasury. They leave, however, but a small quantity of unbought Indian lands within the States and Territories, and the Legislature and Executive were equally sensible of the propriety of a final and more speedy extinction of Indian titles within those limits. The treaties, which were with a single exception made in pursuance of previous appropriations for defraying the expenses, have subsequently been ratified by the Senate, and received the sanction of Congress by the appropriations necessary to carry them into effect. Of the terms upon which these important negotiations were concluded I can speak from direct knowledge, and I feel no difficulty in affirming that the interest of the Indians in the extensive territory embraced by them is to be paid for at its fair value, and that no more favorable terms have been granted to the United States than would have been reasonably expected in a negotiation with civilized men fully capable of appreciating and protecting their own rights. For the Indian title to 116,349,897 acres acquired since the 4th of March, 1829, the United States have paid $72,560,056 in permanent annuities, lands, reservations for Indians, expenses of removal and subsistence, merchandise, mechanical and agricultural establishments and implements. When the heavy expenses incurred by the United States and the circumstance that so large a portion of the entire territory will be forever unsalable are considered, and this price is compared with that for which the United States sell their own lands, no one can doubt that justice has been done to the Indians in these purchases also. Certain it is that the transactions of the Federal Government with the Indians have been uniformly characterized by a sincere and paramount desire to promote their welfare; and it must be a source of the highest gratification to every friend to justice and humanity to learn that notwithstanding the obstructions from time to time thrown in its way and the difficulties which have arisen from the peculiar and impracticable nature of the Indian character, the wise, humane, and undeviating policy of the Government in this the most difficult of all our relations, foreign or domestic, has at length been justified to the world in its near approach to a happy and certain consummation.

The condition of the tribes which occupy the country set apart for them in the West is highly prosperous, and encourages the hope of their early civilization. They have for the most part abandoned the hunter state and turned their attention to agricultural pursuits. All those who have been established for any length of time in that fertile region maintain themselves by their own industry. There are among them traders of no inconsiderable capital, and planters exporting cotton to some extent, but the greater number are small agriculturists, living in comfort upon the produce of their farms. The recent emigrants, although they have

in some instances removed reluctantly, have readily acquiesced in their
unavoidable destiny.   They have found at once a recompense for past
sufferings and an incentive to industrious habits in the abundance and
comforts around them.   There is reason to believe that all these tribes
are friendly in their feelings toward the United States; and it is to be
hoped that the acquisition of individual wealth, the pursuits of agriculture, and habits of industry will gradually subdue their warlike propensities and incline them to maintain peace among themselves.   To effect
this desirable object the attention of Congress is solicited to the measures
recommended by the Secretary of War for their future government and
protection, as well from each other as from the hostility of the warlike
tribes around them and the intrusions of the whites.   The policy of the
Government has given them a permanent home and guaranteed to them
its peaceful and undisturbed possession.   It only remains to give them a
government and laws which will encourage industry and secure to them
the rewards of their exertions.   The importance of some form of government can not be too much insisted upon.   The earliest effects will be
to diminish the causes and occasions for hostilities among the tribes, to
inspire an interest in the observance of laws to which they will have
themselves assented, and to multiply the securities of property and the
motives for self-improvement.   Intimately connected with this subject
is the establishment of the military defenses recommended by the Secretary of War, which have been already referred to.   Without them the
Government will be powerless to redeem its pledge of protection to the
emigrating Indians against the numerous warlike tribes that surround
them and to provide for the safety of the frontier settlers of the bordering
States.

The case of the Seminoles constitutes at present the only exception
to the successful efforts of the Government to remove the Indians to the
homes assigned them west of the Mississippi.   Four hundred of this
tribe emigrated in 1836 and 1,500 in 1837 and 1838, leaving in the country, it is supposed, about 2,000 Indians.   The continued treacherous
conduct of these people; the savage and unprovoked murders they have
lately committed, butchering whole families of the settlers of the Territory without distinction of age or sex, and making their way into the
very center and heart of the country, so that no part of it is free from
their ravages; their frequent attacks on the light-houses along that dangerous coast, and the barbarity with which they have murdered the passengers and crews of such vessels as have been wrecked upon the reefs
and keys which border the Gulf, leave the Government no alternative
but to continue the military operations against them until they are totally
expelled from Florida.   There are other motives which would urge the
Government to pursue this course toward the Seminoles.   The United
States have fulfilled in good faith all their treaty stipulations with the
Indian tribes, and have in every other instance insisted upon a like per-

formance of their obligations. To relax from this salutary rule because the Seminoles have maintained themselves so long in the territory they had relinquished, and in defiance of their frequent and solemn engagements still continue to wage a ruthless war against the United States, would not only evince a want of constancy on our part, but be of evil example in our intercourse with other tribes. Experience has shown that but little is to be gained by the march of armies through a country so intersected with inaccessible swamps and marshes, and which, from the fatal character of the climate, must be abandoned at the end of the winter. I recommend, therefore, to your attention the plan submitted by the Secretary of War in the accompanying report, for the permanent occupation of the portion of the Territory freed from the Indians and the more efficient protection of the people of Florida from their inhuman warfare.

From the report of the Secretary of the Navy herewith transmitted it will appear that a large portion of the disposable naval force is either actively employed or in a state of preparation for the purposes of experience and discipline and the protection of our commerce. So effectual has been this protection that so far as the information of Government extends not a single outrage has been attempted on a vessel carrying the flag of the United States within the present year, in any quarter, however distant or exposed.

The exploring expedition sailed from Norfolk on the 19th of August last, and information has been received of its safe arrival at the island of Madeira. The best spirit animates the officers and crews, and there is every reason to anticipate from its efforts results beneficial to commerce and honorable to the nation.

It will also be seen that no reduction of the force now in commission is contemplated. The unsettled state of a portion of South America renders it indispensable that our commerce should receive protection in that quarter; the vast and increasing interests embarked in the trade of the Indian and China seas, in the whale fisheries of the Pacific Ocean, and in the Gulf of Mexico require equal attention to their safety, and a small squadron may be employed to great advantage on our Atlantic coast in meeting sudden demands for the reenforcement of other stations, in aiding merchant vessels in distress, in affording active service to an additional number of officers, and in visiting the different ports of the United States, an accurate knowledge of which is obviously of the highest importance.

The attention of Congress is respectfully called to that portion of the report recommending an increase in the number of smaller vessels, and to other suggestions contained in that document. The rapid increase and wide expansion of our commerce, which is every day seeking new avenues of profitable adventure; the absolute necessity of a naval force for its protection precisely in the degree of its extension; a due regard to the national rights and honor; the recollection of its former exploits, and the anticipation of its future triumphs whenever opportunity presents itself, which we may rightfully indulge from the experience of the past—all seem to point to the Navy as a most efficient arm of our national defense and a proper object of legislative encouragement.

The progress and condition of the Post-Office Department will be seen by reference to the report of the Postmaster-General. The extent of post-roads covered by mail contracts is stated to be 134,818 miles, and the annual transportation upon them 34,580,202 miles. The number of post-offices in the United States is 12,553, and rapidly increasing. The gross revenue for the year ending on the 30th day of June last was $4,262,145; the accruing expenditures, $4,680,068; excess of expenditures, $417,923. This has been made up out of the surplus previously on hand. The cash on hand on the 1st instant was $314,068. The revenue for the year ending June 30, 1838, was $161,540 more than that for the year ending June 30, 1837. The expenditures of the Department had been graduated upon the anticipation of a largely increased revenue. A moderate curtailment of mail service consequently became necessary, and has been effected, to shield the Department against the danger of embarrassment. Its revenue is now improving, and it will soon resume its onward course in the march of improvement.

Your particular attention is requested to so much of the Postmaster-General's report as relates to the transportation of the mails upon railroads. The laws on that subject do not seem adequate to secure that service, now become almost essential to the public interests, and at the same time protect the Department from combinations and unreasonable demands.

Nor can I too earnestly request your attention to the necessity of providing a more secure building for this Department. The danger of destruction to which its important books and papers are continually exposed, as well from the highly combustible character of the building occupied as from that of others in the vicinity, calls loudly for prompt action.

Your attention is again earnestly invited to the suggestions and recommendations submitted at the last session in respect to the District of Columbia.

I feel it my duty also to bring to your notice certain proceedings at law which have recently been prosecuted in this District in the name of the United States, on the relation of Messrs. Stockton & Stokes, of the State of Maryland, against the Postmaster-General, and which have resulted in the payment of money out of the National Treasury, for the first time since the establishment of the Government, by judicial compulsion exercised by the common-law writ of mandamus issued by the circuit court of this District.

The facts of the case and the grounds of the proceedings will be found fully stated in the report of the decision, and any additional information which you may desire will be supplied by the proper Department. No interference in the particular case is contemplated. The money has been paid, the claims of the prosecutors have been satisfied, and the whole subject, so far as they are concerned, is finally disposed of; but it is on the supposition that the case may be regarded as an authoritative exposition of the law as it now stands that I have thought it necessary to present it to your consideration.

The object of the application to the circuit court was to compel the Postmaster-General to carry into effect an award made by the Solicitor of the Treasury, under a special act of Congress for the settlement of certain claims of the relators on the Post-Office Department, which award the Postmaster-General declined to execute in full until he should receive further legislative direction on the subject. If the duty imposed on the Postmaster-General by that law was to be regarded as one of an official nature, belonging to his office as a branch of the executive, then it is obvious that the constitutional competency of the judiciary to direct and control him in its discharge was necessarily drawn in question; and if the duty so imposed on the Postmaster-General was to be considered as merely ministerial, and not executive, it yet remained to be shown that the circuit court of this District had authority to interfere by mandamus, such a power having never before been asserted or claimed by that court. With a view to the settlement of these important questions, the judgment of the circuit court was carried by a writ of error to the Supreme Court of the United States. In the opinion of that tribunal the duty imposed on the Postmaster-General was not an official executive duty, but one of a merely ministerial nature. The grave constitutional questions which had been discussed were therefore excluded from the decision of the case, the court, indeed, expressly admitting that with powers and duties properly belonging to the executive no other department can interfere by the writ of mandamus; and the question therefore resolved itself into this: Has Congress conferred upon the circuit court of this District the power to issue such a writ to an officer of the General Government commanding him to perform a ministerial act? A majority of the court have decided that it has, but have founded their decision upon a process of reasoning which in my judgment renders further legislative provision indispensable to the public interests and the equal administration of justice.

It has long since been decided by the Supreme Court that neither that tribunal nor the circuit courts of the United States, held within the respective States, possess the power in question; but it is now held that this power, denied to both of these high tribunals (to the former by the Constitution and to the latter by Congress), has been by its legislation vested in the circuit court of this District. No such direct grant of power to the circuit court of this District is claimed, but it has been held to result by necessary implication from several sections of the law establishing the court. One of these sections declares that the laws of Maryland, as they existed at the time of the cession, should be in force in that part of the District ceded by that State, and by this provision the common law in civil and criminal cases, as it prevailed in Maryland in 1801, was established in that part of the District.

In England the court of king's bench—because the Sovereign, who, according to the theory of the constitution, is the fountain of justice, originally sat there in person, and is still deemed to be present in construction of law—alone possesses the high power of issuing the writ of mandamus, not only to inferior jurisdictions and corporations, but also to magistrates and others, commanding them in the King's name to do what their duty requires in cases where there is a vested right and no other specific remedy. It has been held in the case referred to that as the Supreme Court of the United States is by the Constitution rendered incompetent to exercise this power, and as the circuit court of this District is a court of general jurisdiction in cases at common law, and the highest court of original jurisdiction in the District, the right to issue the writ of mandamus is incident to its common-law powers. Another ground relied upon to maintain the power in question is that it was included by fair construction in the powers granted to the circuit courts of the United States by the act "to provide for the more convenient organization of the courts of the United States," passed 13th February, 1801; that the act establishing the circuit court of this District, passed the 27th day of February, 1801, conferred upon that court and the judges thereof the same powers as were by law vested in the circuit courts of the United States and in the judges of the said courts; that the repeal of the first-mentioned act, which took place in the next year, did not divest the circuit court of this District of the authority in dispute, but left it still clothed with the powers over the subject which, it is conceded, were taken away from the circuit courts of the United States by the repeal of the act of 13th February, 1801.

Admitting that the adoption of the laws of Maryland for a portion of this District confers on the circuit court thereof, in that portion, the transcendent extrajudicial prerogative powers of the court of king's bench in England, or that either of the acts of Congress by necessary implication authorizes the former court to issue a writ of mandamus to an officer of the United States to compel him to perform a ministerial duty, the consequences are in one respect the same. The result in either case is that the officers of the United States stationed in different parts of the United States are, in respect to the performance of their official duties, subject to different laws and a different supervision—those in the States to one rule, and those in the District of Columbia to another and a very different one. In the District their official conduct is subject to a judicial control from which in the States they are exempt.

Whatever difference of opinion may exist as to the expediency of vesting such a power in the judiciary in a system of government constituted like that of the United States, all must agree that these disparaging discrepancies in the law and in the administration of justice ought not to be permitted to continue; and as Congress alone can provide the remedy, the subject is unavoidably presented to your consideration.

THIRD ANNUAL MESSAGE.

WASHINGTON, *December 2, 1839.*

Fellow-Citizens of the Senate and House of Representatives:

I regret that I can not on this occasion congratulate you that the past year has been one of unalloyed prosperity. The ravages of fire and disease have painfully afflicted otherwise flourishing portions of our country, and serious embarrassments yet derange the trade of many of our cities. But notwithstanding these adverse circumstances, that general prosperity which has been heretofore so bountifully bestowed upon us by the Author of All Good still continues to call for our warmest gratitude. Especially have we reason to rejoice in the exuberant harvests which have lavishly recompensed well-directed industry and given to it that sure reward which is vainly sought in visionary speculations. I can not, indeed, view without peculiar satisfaction the evidences afforded by the past season of the benefits that spring from the steady devotion of the husbandman to his honorable pursuit. No means of individual comfort is more certain and no source of national prosperity is so sure. Nothing can compensate a people for a dependence upon others for the bread they eat, and that cheerful abundance on which the happiness of everyone so much depends is to be looked for nowhere with such sure reliance as in the industry of the agriculturist and the bounties of the earth.

With foreign countries our relations exhibit the same favorable aspect which was presented in my last annual message, and afford continued proof of the wisdom of the pacific, just, and forbearing policy adopted by the first Administration of the Federal Government and pursued by its successors. The extraordinary powers vested in me by an act of Congress for the defense of the country in an emergency, considered so far probable as to require that the Executive should possess ample means to meet it, have not been exerted. They have therefore been attended with no other result than to increase, by the confidence thus reposed in me, my obligations to maintain with religious exactness the cardinal principles that govern our intercourse with other nations.   Happily, in our pending questions with Great Britain, out of which this unusual grant of authority arose, nothing has occurred to require its exertion, and as it is about to return to the Legislature I trust that no future necessity may call for its exercise by them or its delegation to another Department of the Government.

For the settlement of our northeastern boundary the proposition promised by Great Britain for a commission of exploration and survey has been received, and a counter project, including also a provision for the certain and final adjustment of the limits in dispute, is now before the British Government for its consideration.   A just regard to the delicate state of this question and a proper respect for the natural impatience of the State of Maine, not less than a conviction that the negotiation has been already protracted longer than is prudent on the part of either Government, have led me to believe that the present favorable moment should on no account be suffered to pass without putting the question forever at rest.   I feel confident that the Government of Her Britannic Majesty will take the same view of this subject, as I am persuaded it is governed by desires equally strong and sincere for the amicable termination of the controversy.

To the intrinsic difficulties of questions of boundary lines, especially those described in regions unoccupied and but partially known, is to be added in our country the embarrassment necessarily arising out of our Constitution by which the General Government is made the organ of negotiating and deciding upon the particular interests of the States on whose frontiers these lines are to be traced.   To avoid another controversy in which a State government might rightfully claim to have her wishes consulted previously to the conclusion of conventional arrangements concerning her rights of jurisdiction or territory, I have thought it necessary to call the attention of the Government of Great Britain to another portion of our conterminous dominion of which the division still remains to be adjusted   I refer to the line from the entrance of Lake Superior to the most northwestern point of the Lake of the Woods, stipulations for the settlement of which are to be found in the seventh article of the treaty of Ghent.   The commissioners appointed under that article by the two Governments having differed in their opinions, made separate reports, according to its stipulations, upon the points of disagreement, and these differences are now to be submitted to the arbitration of some friendly sovereign or state.   The disputed points should be settled and the line designated before the Territorial government of which it is one of the boundaries takes its place in the Union as a State, and I rely upon the cordial cooperation of the British Government to effect that object.

There is every reason to believe that disturbances like those which lately agitated the neighboring British Provinces will not again prove the sources of border contentions or interpose obstacles to the continuance of that good understanding which it is the mutual interest of Great Britain and the United States to preserve and maintain.

Within the Provinces themselves tranquillity is restored, and on our frontier that misguided sympathy in favor of what was presumed to be a general effort in behalf of popular rights, and which in some instances misled a few of our more inexperienced citizens, has subsided into a rational conviction strongly opposed to all intermeddling with the internal affairs of our neighbors. The people of the United States feel, as it is hoped they always will, a warm solicitude for the success of all who are sincerely endeavoring to improve the political condition of mankind. This generous feeling they cherish toward the most distant nations, and it was natural, therefore, that it should be awakened with more than common warmth in behalf of their immediate neighbors; but it does not belong to their character as a community to seek the gratification of those feelings in acts which violate their duty as citizens, endanger the peace of their country, and tend to bring upon it the stain of a violated faith toward foreign nations. If, zealous to confer benefits on others, they appear for a moment to lose sight of the permanent obligations imposed upon them as citizens, they are seldom long misled. From all the information I receive, confirmed to some extent by personal observation, I am satisfied that no one can now hope to engage in such enterprises without encountering public indignation, in addition to the severest penalties of the law.

Recent information also leads me to hope that the emigrants from Her Majesty's Provinces who have sought refuge within our boundaries are disposed to become peaceable residents and to abstain from all attempts to endanger the peace of that country which has afforded them an asylum. On a review of the occurrences on both sides of the line it is satisfactory to reflect that in almost every complaint against our country the offense may be traced to emigrants from the Provinces who have sought refuge here. In the few instances in which they were aided by citizens of the United States the acts of these misguided men were not only in direct contravention of the laws and well-known wishes of their own Government, but met with the decided disapprobation of the people of the United States.

I regret to state the appearance of a different spirit among Her Majesty's subjects in the Canadas. The sentiments of hostility to our people and institutions which have been so frequently expressed there, and the disregard of our rights which has been manifested on some occasions, have, I am sorry to say, been applauded and encouraged by the people, and even by some of the subordinate local authorities, of the Provinces. The chief officers in Canada, fortunately, have not entertained the same feeling, and have probably prevented excesses that must have been fatal to the peace of the two countries.

I look forward anxiously to a period when all the transactions which have grown out of this condition of our affairs, and which have been made the subjects of complaint and remonstrance by the two Governments, respectively, shall be fully examined, and the proper satisfaction given where it is due from either side.

Nothing has occurred to disturb the harmony of our intercourse with Austria, Belgium, Denmark, France, Naples, Portugal, Prussia, Russia, or Sweden.   The internal state of Spain has sensibly improved, and a well-grounded hope exists that the return of peace will restore to the people of that country their former prosperity and enable the Government to fulfill all its obligations at home and abroad.   The Government of Portugal, I have the satisfaction to state, has paid in full the eleventh and last installment due to our citizens for the claims embraced in the settlement made with it on the 3d of March, 1837.

I lay before you treaties of commerce negotiated with the Kings of Sardinia and of the Netherlands, the ratifications of which have been exchanged since the adjournment of Congress.   The liberal principles of these treaties will recommend them to your approbation.   That with Sardinia is the first treaty of commerce formed by that Kingdom, and it will, I trust, answer the expectations of the present Sovereign by aiding the development of the resources of his country and stimulating the enterprise of his people.   That with the Netherlands happily terminates a long-existing subject of dispute and removes from our future commercial intercourse all apprehension of embarrassment.   The King of the Netherlands has also, in further illustration of his character for justice and of his desire to remove every cause of dissatisfaction, made compensation for an American vessel captured in 1800 by a French privateer, and carried into Curaçoa, where the proceeds were appropriated to the use of the colony, then, and for a short time after, under the dominion of Holland.

The death of the late Sultan has produced no alteration in our relations with Turkey.   Our newly appointed minister resident has reached Constantinople, and I have received assurances from the present ruler that the obligations of our treaty and those of friendship will be fulfilled by himself in the same spirit that actuated his illustrious father.

I regret to be obliged to inform you that no convention for the settlement of the claims of our citizens upon Mexico has yet been ratified by the Government of that country.   The first convention formed for that purpose was not presented by the President of Mexico for the approbation of its Congress, from a belief that the King of Prussia, the arbitrator in case of disagreement in the joint commission to be appointed by the United States and Mexico, would not consent to take upon himself that friendly office.   Although not entirely satisfied with the course pursued by Mexico, I felt no hesitation in receiving in the most conciliatory spirit the explanation offered, and also cheerfully consented to a new convention, in order to arrange the payments proposed to be made to our citizens in a manner which, while equally just to them, was deemed less onerous and inconvenient to the Mexican Government. Relying confidently upon the intentions of that Government, Mr. Ellis was directed to repair to Mexico, and diplomatic intercourse has been resumed between the two countries. The new convention has, he informs us, been recently submitted by the President of that Republic to its Congress under circumstances which promise a speedy ratification, a result which I can not allow myself to doubt.

Instructions have been given to the commissioner of the United States under our convention with Texas for the demarcation of the line which separates us from that Republic. The commissioners of both Governments met in New Orleans in August last. The joint commission was organized, and adjourned to convene at the same place on the 12th of October. It is presumed to be now in the performance of its duties.

The new Government of Texas has shown its desire to cultivate friendly relations with us by a prompt reparation for injuries complained of in the cases of two vessels of the United States.

With Central America a convention has been concluded for the renewal of its former treaty with the United States. This was not ratified before the departure of our late chargé d'affaires from that country, and the copy of it brought by him was not received before the adjournment of the Senate at the last session. In the meanwhile, the period limited for the exchange of ratifications having expired, I deemed it expedient, in consequence of the death of the chargé d'affaires, to send a special agent to Central America to close the affairs of our mission there and to arrange with the Government an extension of the time for the exchange of ratifications.

The commission created by the States which formerly composed the Republic of Colombia for adjusting the claims against that Government has by a very unexpected construction of the treaty under which it acts decided that no provision was made for those claims of citizens of the United States which arose from captures by Colombian privateers and were adjudged against the claimants in the judicial tribunals. This decision will compel the United States to apply to the several Governments formerly united for redress. With all these—New Granada, Venezuela, and Ecuador—a perfectly good understanding exists. Our treaty with Venezuela is faithfully carried into execution, and that country, in the enjoyment of tranquillity, is gradually advancing in prosperity under the guidance of its present distinguished President, General Paez. With Ecuador a liberal commercial convention has lately been concluded, which will be transmitted to the Senate at an early day.

With the great American Empire of Brazil our relations continue unchanged, as does our friendly intercourse with the other Governments of South America—the Argentine Republic and the Republics of Uruguay, Chili, Peru, and Bolivia. The dissolution of the Peru-Bolivian

Confederation may occasion some temporary inconvenience to our citizens in that quarter, but the obligations on the new Governments which have arisen out of that Confederation to observe its treaty stipulations will no doubt be soon understood, and it is presumed that no indisposition will exist to fulfill those which it contracted with the United States.

The financial operations of the Government during the present year have, I am happy to say, been very successful. The difficulties under which the Treasury Department has labored, from known defects in the existing laws relative to the safe-keeping of the public moneys, aggravated by the suspension of specie payments by several of the banks holding public deposits or indebted to public officers for notes received in payment of public dues, have been surmounted to a very gratifying extent. The large current expenditures have been punctually met, and the faith of the Government in all its pecuniary concerns has been scrupulously maintained.

The nineteen millions of Treasury notes authorized by the act of Congress of 1837, and the modifications thereof with a view to the indulgence of merchants on their duty bonds and of the deposit banks in the payment of public moneys held by them, have been so punctually redeemed as to leave less than the original ten millions outstanding at any one time, and the whole amount unredeemed now falls short of three millions. Of these the chief portion is not due till next year, and the whole would have been already extinguished could the Treasury have realized the payments due to it from the banks. If those due from them during the next year shall be punctually made, and if Congress shall keep the appropriations within the estimates, there is every reason to believe that all the outstanding Treasury notes can be redeemed and the ordinary expenses defrayed without imposing on the people any additional burden, either of loans or increased taxes.

To avoid this and to keep the expenditures within reasonable bounds is a duty second only in importance to the preservation of our national character and the protection of our citizens in their civil and political rights. The creation in time of peace of a debt likely to become permanent is an evil for which there is no equivalent. The rapidity with which many of the States are apparently approaching to this condition admonishes us of our own duties in a manner too impressive to be disregarded. One, not the least important, is to keep the Federal Government always in a condition to discharge with ease and vigor its highest functions should their exercise be required by any sudden conjuncture of public affairs—a condition to which we are always exposed and which may occur when it is least expected. To this end it is indispensable that its finances should be untrammeled and its resources as far as practicable unencumbered. No circumstance could present greater obstacles to the accomplishment of these vitally important objects than the creation of an onerous national debt. Our own experience and also that of other nations have demonstrated the unavoidable and fearful rapidity with which a public debt is increased when the Government has once surrendered itself to the ruinous practice of supplying its supposed necessities by new loans. The struggle, therefore, on our part to be successful must be made at the threshold. To make our efforts effective, severe economy is necessary. This is the surest provision for the national welfare, and it is at the same time the best preservative of the principles on which our institutions rest. Simplicity and economy in the affairs of state have never failed to chasten and invigorate republican principles, while these have been as surely subverted by national prodigality, under whatever specious pretexts it may have been introduced or fostered.

These considerations can not be lost upon a people who have never been inattentive to the effect of their policy upon the institutions they have created for themselves, but at the present moment their force is augmented by the necessity which a decreasing revenue must impose. The check lately given to importations of articles subject to duties, the derangements in the operations of internal trade, and especially the reduction gradually taking place in our tariff of duties, all tend materially to lessen our receipts; indeed, it is probable that the diminution resulting from the last cause alone will not fall short of $5,000,000 in the year 1842, as the final reduction of all duties to 20 per cent then takes effect. The whole revenue then accruing from the customs and from the sales of public lands, if not more, will undoubtedly be wanted to defray the necessary expenses of the Government under the most prudent administration of its affairs. These are circumstances that impose the necessity of rigid economy and require its prompt and constant exercise. With the Legislature rest the power and duty of so adjusting the public expenditure as to promote this end. By the provisions of the Constitution it is only in consequence of appropriations made by law that money can be drawn from the Treasury. No instance has occurred since the establishment of the Government in which the Executive, though a component part of the legislative power, has interposed an objection to an appropriation bill on the sole ground of its extravagance. His duty in this respect has been considered fulfilled by requesting such appropriations only as the public service may be reasonably expected to require. In the present earnest direction of the public mind toward this subject both the Executive and the Legislature have evidence of the strict responsibility to which they will be held; and while I am conscious of my own anxious efforts to perform with fidelity this portion of my public functions, it is a satisfaction to me to be able to count on a cordial cooperation from you.

At the time I entered upon my present duties our ordinary disbursements, without including those on account of the public debt, the Post-Office, and the trust funds in charge of the Government, had been largely increased by appropriations for the removal of the Indians, for repelling Indian hostilities, and for other less urgent expenses which

grew out of an overflowing Treasury.   Independent of the redemption
of the public debt and trusts, the gross expenditures of seventeen and
eighteen millions in 1834 and 1835 had by these causes swelled to
twenty-nine millions in 1836, and the appropriations for 1837, made
previously to the 4th of March, caused the expenditure to rise to the
very large amount of thirty-three millions.   We were enabled during
the year 1838, notwithstanding the continuance of our Indian embarrassments, somewhat to reduce this amount, and that for the present
year (1839) will not in all probability exceed twenty-six millions, or
six millions less than it was last year.   With a determination, so far as
depends on me, to continue this reduction, I have directed the estimates
for 1840 to be subjected to the severest scrutiny and to be limited to the
absolute requirements of the public service.   They will be found less
than the expenditures of 1839 by over $5,000,000.

The precautionary measures which will be recommended by the Secretary of the Treasury to protect faithfully the public credit under the
fluctuations and contingencies to which our receipts and expenditures
are exposed, and especially in a commercial crisis like the present, are
commended to your early attention.

On a former occasion your attention was invited to various considerations in support of a preemption law in behalf of the settlers on the public lands, and also of a law graduating the prices for such lands as had
long been in the market unsold in consequence of their inferior quality.
The execution of the act which was passed on the first subject has been
attended with the happiest consequences in quieting titles and securing
improvements to the industrious, and it has also to a very gratifying
extent been exempt from the frauds which were practiced under previous
preemption laws.   It has at the same time, as was anticipated, contributed liberally during the present year to the receipts of the Treasury.

The passage of a graduation law, with the guards before recommended, would also, I am persuaded, add considerably to the revenue
for several years, and prove in other respects just and beneficial.

Your early consideration of the subject is therefore once more earnestly requested.

The present condition of the defenses of our principal seaports and
navy-yards, as represented by the accompanying report of the Secretary
of War, calls for the early and serious attention of Congress; and, as
connecting itself intimately with this subject, I can not recommend too
strongly to your consideration the plan submitted by that officer for the
organization of the militia of the United States.

In conformity with the expressed wishes of Congress, an attempt was
made in the spring to terminate the Florida war by negotiation.   It is to
be regretted that these humane intentions should have been frustrated
and that the effort to bring these unhappy difficulties to a satisfactory
conclusion should have failed; but after entering into solemn engage-

ments with the commanding general, the Indians, without any provocation, recommenced their acts of treachery and murder. The renewal of hostilities in that Territory renders it necessary that I should recommend to your favorable consideration the plan which will be submitted to you by the Secretary of War, in order to enable that Department to conduct them to a successful issue.

Having had an opportunity of personally inspecting a portion of the troops during the last summer, it gives me pleasure to bear testimony to the success of the effort to improve their discipline by keeping them together in as large bodies as the nature of our service will permit. I recommend, therefore, that commodious and permanent barracks be constructed at the several posts designated by the Secretary of War. Notwithstanding the high state of their discipline and excellent police, the evils resulting to the service from the deficiency of company officers were very apparent, and I recommend that the staff officers be permanently separated from the line.

The Navy has been usefully and honorably employed in protecting the rights and property of our citizens wherever the condition of affairs seemed to require its presence. With the exception of one instance, where an outrage, accompanied by murder, was committed on a vessel of the United States while engaged in a lawful commerce, nothing is known to have occurred to impede or molest the enterprise of our citizens on that element, where it is so signally displayed. On learning this daring act of piracy, Commodore Reed proceeded immediately to the spot, and receiving no satisfaction, either in the surrender of the murderers or the restoration of the plundered property, inflicted severe and merited chastisement on the barbarians.

It will be seen by the report of the Secretary of the Navy respecting the disposition of our ships of war that it has been deemed necessary to station a competent force on the coast of Africa to prevent a fraudulent use of our flag by foreigners.

Recent experience has shown that the provisions in our existing laws which relate to the sale and transfer of American vessels while abroad are extremely defective. Advantage has been taken of these defects to give to vessels wholly belonging to foreigners and navigating the ocean an apparent American ownership. This character has been so well simulated as to afford them comparative security in prosecuting the slave trade—a traffic emphatically denounced in our statutes, regarded with abhorrence by our citizens, and of which the effectual suppression is nowhere more sincerely desired than in the United States. These circumstances make it proper to recommend to your early attention a careful revision of these laws, so that without impeding the freedom and facilities of our navigation or impairing an important branch of our industry connected with it the integrity and honor of our flag may be carefully preserved. Information derived from our consul at Havana showing the necessity of this was communicated to a committee of the Senate near the close of the last session, but too late, as it appeared, to be acted upon.   It will be brought to your notice by the proper Department, with additional communications from other sources.

The latest accounts from the exploring expedition represent it as proceeding successfully in its objects and promising results no less useful to trade and navigation than to science.

The extent of post-roads covered by mail service on the 1st of July last was about 133,999 miles and the rate of annual transportation upon them 34,496,878 miles.   The number of post-offices on that day was 12,780 and on the 30th ultimo 13,028.

The revenue of the Post-Office Department for the year ending with the 30th of June last was $4,476,638, exhibiting an increase over the preceding year of $241,560.   The engagements and liabilities of the Department for the same period are $4,624,117.

The excess of liabilities over the revenue for the last two years has been met out of the surplus which had previously accumulated.   The cash on hand on the 30th ultimo was about $206,701.95, and the current income of the Department varies very little from the rate of current expenditures.   Most of the service suspended last year has been restored, and most of the new routes established by the act of 7th July, 1838, have been set in operation, at an annual cost of $136,963.   Notwithstanding the pecuniary difficulties of the country, the revenue of the Department appears to be increasing, and unless it shall be seriously checked by the recent suspension of payment by so many of the banks it will be able not only to maintain the present mail service, but in a short time to extend it.   It is gratifying to witness the promptitude and fidelity with which the agents of this Department in general perform their public duties.

Some difficulties have arisen in relation to contracts for the transportation of the mails by railroad and steamboat companies.   It appears that the maximum of compensation provided by Congress for the transportation of the mails upon railroads is not sufficient to induce some of the companies to convey them at such hours as are required for the accommodation of the public.   It is one of the most important duties of the General Government to provide and maintain for the use of the people of the States the best practicable mail establishment.   To arrive at that end it is indispensable that the Post-Office Department shall be enabled to control the hours at which the mails shall be carried over railroads, as it now does over all other roads.   Should serious inconveniences arise from the inadequacy of the compensation now provided by law, or from unreasonable demands by any of the railroad companies, the subject is of such general importance as to require the prompt attention of Congress.

In relation to steamboat lines, the most efficient remedy is obvious and has been suggested by the Postmaster-General.   The War and Navy

Departments already employ steamboats in their service; and although it is by no means desirable that the Government should undertake the transportation of passengers or freight as a business, there can be no reasonable objection to running boats, temporarily, whenever it may be necessary to put down attempts at extortion, to be discontinued as soon as reasonable contracts can be obtained.

The suggestions of the Postmaster-General relative to the inadequacy of the legal allowance to witnesses in cases of prosecutions for mail depredations merit your serious consideration. The safety of the mails requires that such prosecutions shall be efficient, and justice to the citizen whose time is required to be given to the public demands not only that his expenses shall be paid, but that he shall receive a reasonable compensation.

The reports from the War, Navy, and Post-Office Departments will accompany this communication, and one from the Treasury Department will be presented to Congress in a few days.

For various details in respect to the matters in charge of these Departments I would refer you to those important documents, satisfied that you will find in them many valuable suggestions which will be found well deserving the attention of the Legislature.

From a report made in December of last year by the Secretary of State to the Senate, showing the trial docket of each of the circuit courts and the number of miles each judge has to travel in the performance of his duties, a great inequality appears in the amount of labor assigned to each judge. The number of terms to be held in each of the courts composing the ninth circuit, the distances between the places at which they sit and from thence to the seat of Government, are represented to be such as to render it impossible for the judge of that circuit to perform in a manner corresponding with the public exigencies his term and circuit duties. A revision, therefore, of the present arrangement of the circuit seems to be called for and is recommended to your notice.

I think it proper to call your attention to the power assumed by Territorial legislatures to authorize the issue of bonds by corporate companies on the guaranty of the Territory. Congress passed a law in 1836 providing that no act of a Territorial legislature incorporating banks should have the force of law until approved by Congress, but acts of a very exceptionable character previously passed by the legislature of Florida were suffered to remain in force, by virtue of which bonds may be issued to a very large amount by those institutions upon the faith of the Territory. A resolution, intending to be a joint one, passed the Senate at the same session, expressing the sense of Congress that the laws in question ought not to be permitted to remain in force unless amended in many material respects; but it failed in the House of Representatives for want of time, and the desired amendments have not been made. The interests involved are of great importance, and the subject deserves your early and careful attention.

The continued agitation of the question relative to the best mode of keeping and disbursing the public money still injuriously affects the business of the country. The suspension of specie payments in 1837 rendered the use of deposit banks as prescribed by the act of 1836 a source rather of embarrassment than aid, and of necessity placed the custody of most of the public money afterwards collected in charge of the public officers. The new securities for its safety which this required were a principal cause of my convening an extra session of Congress, but in consequence of a disagreement between the two Houses neither then nor at any subsequent period has there been any legislation on the subject. The effort made at the last session to obtain the authority of Congress to punish the use of public money for private purposes as a crime—a measure attended under other governments with signal advantage—was also unsuccessful, from diversities of opinion in that body, notwithstanding the anxiety doubtless felt by it to afford every practicable security. The result of this is still to leave the custody of the public money without those safeguards which have been for several years earnestly desired by the Executive, and as the remedy is only to be found in the action of the Legislature it imposes on me the duty of again submitting to you the propriety of passing a law providing for the safe-keeping of the public moneys, and especially to ask that its use for private purposes by any officers intrusted with it may be declared to be a felony, punishable with penalties proportioned to the magnitude of the offense.

These circumstances, added to known defects in the existing laws and unusual derangement in the general operations of trade, have during the last three years much increased the difficulties attendant on the collection, keeping, and disbursement of the revenue, and called forth corresponding exertions from those having them in charge. Happily these have been successful beyond expectation. Vast sums have been collected and disbursed by the several Departments with unexpected cheapness and ease, transfers have been readily made to every part of the Union, however distant, and defalcations have been far less than might have been anticipated from the absence of adequate legal restraints. Since the officers of the Treasury and Post-Office Departments were charged with the custody of most of the public moneys received by them there have been collected $66,000,000, and, excluding the case of the late collector at New York, the aggregate amount of losses sustained in the collection can not, it is believed, exceed $60,000. The defalcation of the late collector at that city, of the extent and circumstances of which Congress have been fully informed, ran through all the modes of keeping the public money that have been hitherto in use, and was distinguished by an aggravated disregard of duty that broke through the restraints of every system, and can not, therefore, be usefully referred to as a test of the comparative safety of either. Additional information will also be furnished by the report of the Secretary of the Treasury, in reply to a call made upon that officer by the House of Representatives at the last session requiring detailed information on the subject of defaults by public officers or agents under each Administration from 1789 to 1837. This document will be submitted to you in a few days. The general results (independent of the Post-Office, which is kept separately and will be stated by itself), so far as they bear upon this subject, are that the losses which have been and are likely to be sustained by any class of agents have been the greatest by banks, including, as required in the resolution, their depreciated paper received for public dues; that the next largest have been by disbursing officers, and the least by collectors and receivers. If the losses on duty bonds are included, they alone will be threefold those by both collectors and receivers. Our whole experience, therefore, furnishes the strongest evidence that the desired legislation of Congress is alone wanting to insure in those operations the highest degree of security and facility. Such also appears to have been the experience of other nations. From the results of inquiries made by the Secretary of the Treasury in regard to the practice among them I am enabled to state that in twenty-two out of twenty-seven foreign governments from which undoubted information has been obtained the public moneys are kept in charge of public officers. This concurrence of opinion in favor of that system is perhaps as great as exists on any question of internal administration.

In the modes of business and official restraints on disbursing officers no legal change was produced by the suspension of specie payments. The report last referred to will be found to contain also much useful information in relation to this subject.

I have heretofore assigned to Congress my reasons for believing that the establishment of an independent National Treasury, as contemplated by the Constitution, is necessary to the safe action of the Federal Government. The suspension of specie payments in 1837 by the banks having the custody of the public money showed in so alarming a degree our dependence on those institutions for the performance of duties required by law that I then recommended the entire dissolution of that connection. This recommendation has been subjected, as I desired it should be, to severe scrutiny and animated discussion, and I allow myself to believe that notwithstanding the natural diversities of opinion which may be anticipated on all subjects involving such important considerations, it has secured in its favor as general a concurrence of public sentiment as could be expected on one of such magnitude.

Recent events have also continued to develop new objections to such a connection. Seldom is any bank, under the existing system and practice, able to meet on demand all its liabilities for deposits and notes in circulation. It maintains specie payments and transacts a profitable business only by the confidence of the public in its solvency, and whenever this is destroyed the demands of its depositors and note holders, pressed more rapidly than it can make collections from its debtors,

force it to stop payment.   This loss of confidence, with its consequences,
occurred in 1837, and afforded the apology of the banks for their suspension.   The public then acquiesced in the validity of the excuse, and while
the State legislatures did not exact from them their forfeited charters,
Congress, in accordance with the recommendation of the Executive,
allowed them time to pay over the public money they held, although
compelled to issue Treasury notes to supply the deficiency thus created.

It now appears that there are other motives than a want of public
confidence under which the banks seek to justify themselves in a refusal
to meet their obligations.   Scarcely were the country and Government
relieved in a degree from the difficulties occasioned by the general suspension of 1837 when a partial one, occurring within thirty months of
the former, produced new and serious embarrassments, though it had no
palliation in such circumstances as were alleged in justification of that
which had previously taken place.   There was nothing in the condition
of the country to endanger a well-managed banking institution; commerce was deranged by no foreign war; every branch of manufacturing
industry was crowned with rich rewards, and the more than usual abundance of our harvests, after supplying our domestic wants, had left our
granaries and storehouses filled with a surplus for exportation.   It is in
the midst of this that an irredeemable and depreciated paper currency
is entailed upon the people by a large portion of the banks.   They are
not driven to it by the exhibition of a loss of public confidence or of a
sudden pressure from their depositors or note holders, but they excuse
themselves by alleging that the current of business and exchange with
foreign countries, which draws the precious metals from their vaults,
would require in order to meet it a larger curtailment of their loans to a
comparatively small portion of the community than it will be convenient
for them to bear or perhaps safe for the banks to exact.   The plea has
ceased to be one of necessity.   Convenience and policy are now deemed
sufficient to warrant these institutions in disregarding their solemn obligations.   Such conduct is not merely an injury to individual creditors,
but it is a wrong to the whole community, from whose liberality they hold
most valuable privileges, whose rights they violate, whose business they
derange, and the value of whose property they render unstable and insecure.   It must be evident that this new ground for bank suspensions, in
reference to which their action is not only disconnected with, but wholly
independent of, that of the public, gives a character to their suspensions more alarming than any which they exhibited before, and greatly
increases the impropriety of relying on the banks in the transactions of
the Government.

A large and highly respectable portion of our banking institutions
are, it affords me unfeigned pleasure to state, exempted from all blame
on account of this second delinquency.   They have, to their great credit,
not only continued to meet their engagements, but have even repudiated

the grounds of suspension now resorted to. It is only by such a course that the confidence and good will of the community can be preserved, and in the sequel the best interests of the institutions themselves promoted

New dangers to the banks are also daily disclosed from the extension of that system of extravagant credit of which they are the pillars. Formerly our foreign commerce was principally founded on an exchange of commodities, including the precious metals, and leaving in its transactions but little foreign debt. Such is not now the case. Aided by the facilities afforded by the banks, mere credit has become too commonly the basis of trade. Many of the banks themselves, not content with largely stimulating this system among others, have usurped the business, while they impair the stability, of the mercantile community; they have become borrowers instead of lenders; they establish their agencies abroad; they deal largely in stocks and merchandise; they encourage the issue of State securities until the foreign market is glutted with them; and, unsatisfied with the legitimate use of their own capital and the exercise of their lawful privileges, they raise by large loans additional means for every variety of speculation. The disasters attendant on this deviation from the former course of business in this country are now shared alike by banks and individuals to an extent of which there is perhaps no previous example in the annals of our country. So long as a willingness of the foreign lender and a sufficient export of our productions to meet any necessary partial payments leave the flow of credit undisturbed all appears to be prosperous, but as soon as it is checked by any hesitation abroad or by an inability to make payment there in our productions the evils of the system are disclosed. The paper currency, which might serve for domestic purposes, is useless to pay the debt due in Europe. Gold and silver are therefore drawn in exchange for their notes from the banks. To keep up their supply of coin these institutions are obliged to call upon their own debtors, who pay them principally in their own notes, which are as unavailable to them as they are to the merchants to meet the foreign demand. The calls of the banks, therefore, in such emergencies of necessity exceed that demand, and produce a corresponding curtailment of their accommodations and of the currency at the very moment when the state of trade renders it most inconvenient to be borne. The intensity of this pressure on the community is in proportion to the previous liberality of credit and consequent expansion of the currency. Forced sales of property are made at the time when the means of purchasing are most reduced, and the worst calamities to individuals are only at last arrested by an open violation of their obligations by the banks—a refusal to pay specie for their notes and an imposition upon the community of a fluctuating and depreciated currency.

These consequences are inherent in the present system. They are not influenced by the banks being large or small, created by National or State Governments. They are the results of the irresistible laws of

trade or credit. In the recent events, which have so strikingly illustrated the certain effects of these laws, we have seen the bank of the
largest capital in the Union, established under a national charter, and
lately strengthened, as we were authoritatively informed, by exchanging
that for a State charter with new and unusual privileges—in a condition,
too, as it was said, of entire soundness and great prosperity—not merely
unable to resist these effects, but the first to yield to them.

Nor is it to be overlooked that there exists a chain of necessary dependence among these institutions which obliges them to a great extent
to follow the course of others, notwithstanding its injustice to their own
immediate creditors or injury to the particular community in which they
are placed. This dependence of a bank, which is in proportion to the
extent of its debts for circulation and deposits, is not merely on others
in its own vicinity, but on all those which connect it with the center of
trade. Distant banks may fail without seriously affecting those in our
principal commercial cities, but the failure of the latter is felt at the
extremities of the Union. The suspension at New York in 1837 was
everywhere, with very few exceptions, followed as soon as it was known.
That recently at Philadelphia immediately affected the banks of the
South and West in a similar manner. This dependence of our whole
banking system on the institutions in a few large cities is not found in
the laws of their organization, but in those of trade and exchange. The
banks at that center, to which currency flows and where it is required in
payments for merchandise, hold the power of controlling those in regions
whence it comes, while the latter possess no means of restraining them;
so that the value of individual property and the prosperity of trade
through the whole interior of the country are made to depend on the
good or bad management of the banking institutions in the great seats
of trade on the seaboard.

But this chain of dependence does not stop here. It does not terminate at Philadelphia or New York. It reaches across the ocean and ends
in London, the center of the credit system. The same laws of trade
which give to the banks in our principal cities power over the whole
banking system of the United States subject the former, in their turn, to
the money power in Great Britain. It is not denied that the suspension
of the New York banks in 1837, which was followed in quick succession
throughout the Union, was produced by an application of that power,
and it is now alleged, in extenuation of the present condition of so large
a portion of our banks, that their embarrassments have arisen from the
same cause.

From this influence they can not now entirely escape, for it has its
origin in the credit currencies of the two countries; it is strengthened by
the current of trade and exchange which centers in London, and is rendered almost irresistible by the large debts contracted there by our merchants, our banks, and our States. It is thus that an introduction of a

new bank into the most distant of our villages places the business of that village within the influence of the money power in England; it is thus that every new debt which we contract in that country seriously affects our own currency and extends over the pursuits of our citizens its powerful influence. We can not escape from this by making new banks, great or small, State or national. The same chains which bind those now existing to the center of this system of paper credit must equally fetter every similar institution we create. It is only by the extent to which this system has been pushed of late that we have been made fully aware of its irresistible tendency to subject our own banks and currency to a vast controlling power in a foreign land, and it adds a new argument to those which illustrate their precarious situation. Endangered in the first place by their own mismanagement and again by the conduct of every institution which connects them with the center of trade in our own country, they are yet subjected beyond all this to the effect of whatever measures policy, necessity, or caprice may induce those who control the credits of England to resort to. I mean not to comment upon these measures, present or past, and much less to discourage the prosecution of fair commercial dealing between the two countries, based on reciprocal benefits; but it having now been made manifest that the power of inflicting these and similar injuries is by the resistless law of a credit currency and credit trade equally capable of extending their consequences through all the ramifications of our banking system, and by that means indirectly obtaining, particularly when our banks are used as depositories of the public moneys, a dangerous political influence in the United States, I have deemed it my duty to bring the subject to your notice and ask for it your serious consideration.

Is an argument required beyond the exposition of these facts to show the impropriety of using our banking institutions as depositories of the public money? Can we venture not only to encounter the risk of their individual and mutual mismanagement, but at the same time to place our foreign and domestic policy entirely under the control of a foreign moneyed interest? To do so is to impair the independence of our Government, as the present credit system has already impaired the independence of our banks; it is to submit all its important operations, whether of peace or war, to be controlled or thwarted, at first by our own banks and then by a power abroad greater than themselves. I can not bring myself to depict the humiliation to which this Government and people might be sooner or later reduced if the means for defending their rights are to be made dependent upon those who may have the most powerful of motives to impair them.

Nor is it only in reference to the effect of this state of things on the independence of our Government or of our banks that the subject presents itself for consideration; it is to be viewed also in its relations to the general trade of our country. The time is not long passed when a

deficiency of foreign crops was thought to afford a profitable market for
the surplus of our industry, but now we await with feverish anxiety the
news of the English harvest, not so much from motives of commendable
sympathy, but fearful lest its anticipated failure should narrow the field
of credit there.   Does not this speak volumes to the patriot?   Can a
system be beneficent, wise, or just which creates greater anxiety for
interests dependent on foreign credit than for the general prosperity of
our own country and the profitable exportation of the surplus produce
of our labor?

The circumstances to which I have thus adverted appear to me to
afford weighty reasons, developed by late events, to be added to those
which I have on former occasions offered when submitting to your better
knowledge and discernment the propriety of separating the custody of
the public money from banking institutions.   Nor has anything occurred
to lessen, in my opinion, the force of what has been heretofore urged.
The only ground on which that custody can be desired by the banks is
the profitable use which they may make of the money.   Such use would
be regarded in individuals as a breach of trust or a crime of great magnitude, and yet it may be reasonably doubted whether, first and last,
it is not attended with more mischievous consequences when permitted
to the former than to the latter.   The practice of permitting the public
money to be used by its keepers, as here, is believed to be peculiar to
this country and to exist scarcely anywhere else.   To procure it here
improper influences are appealed to, unwise connections are established
between the Government and vast numbers of powerful State institutions,
other motives than the public good are brought to bear both on the executive and legislative departments, and selfish combinations leading to
special legislation are formed.   It is made the interest of banking institutions and their stockholders throughout the Union to use their exertions
for the increase of taxation and the accumulation of a surplus revenue,
and while an excuse is afforded the means are furnished for those excessive issues which lead to extravagant trading and speculation and are
the forerunners of a vast debt abroad and a suspension of the banks at
home.

Impressed, therefore, as I am with the propriety of the funds of the
Government being withdrawn from the private use of either banks or
individuals, and the public money kept by duly appointed public agents,
and believing as I do that such also is the judgment which discussion,
reflection, and experience have produced on the public mind, I leave the
subject with you.   It is, at all events, essential to the interests of the
community and the business of the Government that a decision should
be made.

Most of the arguments that dissuade us from employing banks in the
custody and disbursement of the public money apply with equal force to
the receipt of their notes for public dues.   The difference is only in form.

In one instance the Government is a creditor for its deposits, and in the other for the notes it holds. They afford the same opportunity for using the public moneys, and equally lead to all the evils attendant upon it, since a bank can as safely extend its discounts on a deposit of its notes in the hands of a public officer as on one made in its own vaults. On the other hand, it would give to the Government no greater security, for in case of failure the claim of the note holder would be no better than that of a depositor.

I am aware that the danger of inconvenience to the public and unreasonable pressure upon sound banks have been urged as objections to requiring the payment of the revenue in gold and silver. These objections have been greatly exaggerated. From the best estimates we may safely fix the amount of specie in the country at $85,000,000, and the portion of that which would be employed at any one time in the receipts and disbursements of the Government, even if the proposed change were made at once, would not, it is now, after fuller investigation, believed exceed four or five millions. If the change were gradual, several years would elapse before that sum would be required, with annual opportunities in the meantime to alter the law should experience prove it to be oppressive or inconvenient. The portions of the community on whose business the change would immediately operate are comparatively small, nor is it believe. that its effect would be in the least unjust or injurious to them.

In the payment of duties, which constitute by far the greater portion of the revenue, a very large proportion is derived from foreign commission houses and agents of foreign manufacturers, who sell the goods consigned to them generally at auction, and after paying the duties out of the avails remit the rest abroad in specie or its equivalent. That the amount of duties should in such cases be also retained in specie can hardly be made a matter of complaint. Our own importing merchants, by whom the residue of the duties is paid, are not only peculiarly interested in maintaining a sound currency, which the measure in question will especially promote, but are from the nature of their dealings best able to know when specie will be needed and to procure it with the least difficulty or sacrifice. Residing, too, almost universally in places where the revenue is received and where the drafts used by the Government for its disbursements must concentrate, they have every opportunity to obtain and use them in place of specie should it be for their interest or convenience. Of the number of these drafts and the facilities they may afford, as well as of the rapidity with which the public funds are drawn and disbursed, an idea may be formed from the fact that of nearly $20,000,000 paid to collectors and receivers during the present year the average amount in their hands at any one time has not exceeded a million and a half, and of the fifteen millions received by the collector of New York alone during the present year the average amount held by him subject to draft during each week has been less than half a million.

The ease and safety of the operations of the Treasury in keeping the public money are promoted by the application of its own drafts to the public dues. The objection arising from having them too long outstanding might be obviated and they yet made to afford to merchants and banks holding them an equivalent for specie, and in that way greatly lessen the amount actually required. Still less inconvenience will attend the requirement of specie in purchases of public lands. Such purchases, except when made on speculation, are in general but single transactions, rarely repeated by the same person; and it is a fact that for the last year and a half, during which the notes of sound banks have been received, more than a moiety of these payments has been voluntarily made in specie, being a larger proportion than would have been required in three years under the graduation proposed.

It is, moreover, a principle than which none is better settled by experience that the supply of the precious metals will always be found adequate to the uses for which they are required. They abound in countries where no other currency is allowed. In our own States, where small notes are excluded, gold and silver supply their place. When driven to their hiding places by bank suspensions, a little firmness in the community soon restores them in a sufficient quantity for ordinary purposes. Postage and other public dues have been collected in coin without serious inconvenience even in States where a depreciated paper currency has existed for years, and this, with the aid of Treasury notes for a part of the time, was done without interruption during the suspension of 1837. At the present moment the receipts and disbursements of the Government are made in legal currency in the largest portion of the Union. No one suggests a departure from this rule, and if it can now be successfully carried out it will be surely attended with even less difficulty when bank notes are again redeemed in specie.

Indeed, I can not think that a serious objection would anywhere be raised to the receipt and payment of gold and silver in all public transactions were it not from an apprehension that a surplus in the Treasury might withdraw a large portion of it from circulation and lock it up unprofitably in the public vaults. It would not, in my opinion, be difficult to prevent such an inconvenience from occurring; but the authentic statements which I have already submitted to you in regard to the actual amount in the public Treasury at any one time during the period embraced in them and the little probability of a different state of the Treasury for at least some years to come seem to render it unnecessary to dwell upon it. Congress, moreover, as I have before observed, will in every year have an opportunity to guard against it should the occurrence of any circumstances lead us to apprehend injury from this source. Viewing the subject in all its aspects, I can not believe that any period will be more auspicious than the present for the adoption of all measures necessary to maintain the sanctity of our own engagements and to aid in securing to the community that abundant supply of the precious metals which adds so much to their prosperity and gives such increased stability to all their dealings.

In a country so commercial as ours banks in some form will probably always exist, but this serves only to render it the more incumbent on us, notwithstanding the discouragements of the past, to strive in our respective stations to mitigate the evils they produce; to take from them as rapidly as the obligations of public faith and a careful consideration of the immediate interests of the community will permit the unjust character of monopolies; to check, so far as may be practicable, by prudent legislation those temptations of interest and those opportunities for their dangerous indulgence which beset them on every side, and to confine them strictly to the performance of their paramount duty—that of aiding the operations of commerce rather than consulting their own exclusive advantage. These and other salutary reforms may, it is believed, be accomplished without the violation of any of the great principles of the social compact, the observance of which is indispensable to its existence, or interfering in any way with the useful and profitable employment of real capital.

Institutions so framed have existed and still exist elsewhere, giving to commercial intercourse all necessary facilities without inflating or depreciating the currency or stimulating speculation. Thus accomplishing their legitimate ends, they have gained the surest guaranty for their protection and encouragement in the good will of the community. Among a people so just as ours the same results could not fail to attend a similar course. The direct supervision of the banks belongs, from the nature of our Government, to the States who authorize them. It is to their legislatures that the people must mainly look for action on that subject. But as the conduct of the Federal Government in the management of its revenue has also a powerful, though less immediate, influence upon them, it becomes our duty to see that a proper direction is given to it. While the keeping of the public revenue in a separate and independent treasury and of collecting it in gold and silver will have a salutary influence on the system of paper credit with which all banks are connected, and thus aid those that are sound and well managed, it will at the same time sensibly check such as are otherwise by at once withholding the means of extravagance afforded by the public funds and restraining them from excessive issues of notes which they would be constantly called upon to redeem.

I am aware it has been urged that this control may be best attained and exerted by means of a national bank. The constitutional objections which I am well known to entertain would prevent me in any event from proposing or assenting to that remedy; but in addition to this, I can not after past experience bring myself to think that it can any

longer be extensively regarded as effective for such a purpose.   The
history of the late national bank, through all its mutations, shows that it
was not so.   On the contrary, it may, after a careful consideration of the
subject, be, I think, safely stated that at every period of banking excess
it took the lead; that in 1817 and 1818, in 1823, in 1831, and in 1834 its
vast expansions, followed by distressing contractions, led to those of the
State institutions.   It swelled and maddened the tides of the banking
system, but seldom allayed or safely directed them.   At a few periods
only was a salutary control exercised, but an eager desire, on the contrary, exhibited for profit in the first place; and if afterwards its measures
were severe toward other institutions, it was because its own safety compelled it to adopt them.   It did not differ from them in principle or in
form; its measures emanated from the same spirit of gain; it felt the
same temptation to overissues; it suffered from and was totally unable
to avert those inevitable laws of trade by which it was itself affected
equally with them; and at least on one occasion, at an early day, it was
saved only by extraordinary exertions from the same fate that attended
the weakest institution it professed to supervise.   In 1837 it failed
equally with others in redeeming its notes (though the two years allowed
by its charter for that purpose had not expired), a large amount of which
remains to the present time outstanding.   It is true that, having so
vast a capital and strengthened by the use of all the revenues of the
Government, it possessed more power; but while it was itself by that
circumstance freed from the control which all banks require, its paramount object and inducement were left the same—to make the most for
its stockholders, not to regulate the currency of the country.   Nor has it,
as far as we are advised, been found to be greatly otherwise elsewhere.
The national character given to the Bank of England has not prevented
excessive fluctuations in their currency, and it proved unable to keep off
a suspension of specie payments, which lasted for nearly a quarter of a
century.   And why should we expect it to be otherwise?   A national institution, though deriving its charter from a different source than the State
banks, is yet constituted upon the same principles, is conducted by men
equally exposed to temptation, and is liable to the same disasters, with
the additional disadvantage that its magnitude occasions an extent of
confusion and distress which the mismanagement of smaller institutions
could not produce.   It can scarcely be doubted that the recent suspension of the United States Bank of Pennsylvania, of which the effects are
felt not in that State alone, but over half the Union, had its origin in a
course of business commenced while it was a national institution, and
there is no good reason for supposing that the same consequences would
not have followed had it still derived its powers from the General Government.   It is in vain, when the influences and impulses are the same,
to look for a difference in conduct or results.   By such creations we do,
therefore, but increase the mass of paper credit and paper currency,

without checking their attendant evils and fluctuations. The extent of power and the efficiency of organization which we give, so far from being beneficial, are in practice positively injurious. They strengthen the chain of dependence throughout the Union, subject all parts more certainly to common disaster, and bind every bank more effectually in the first instance to those of our commercial cities, and in the end to a foreign power. In a word, I can not but believe that, with the full understanding of the operations of our banking system which experience has produced, public sentiment is not less opposed to the creation of a national bank for purposes connected with currency and commerce than for those connected with the fiscal operations of the Government.

Yet the commerce and currency of the country are suffering evils from the operations of the State banks which can not and ought not to be overlooked. By their means we have been flooded with a depreciated paper, which it was evidently the design of the framers of the Constitution to prevent when they required Congress to ''coin money and regulate the value of foreign coins,'' and when they forbade the States ''to coin money, emit bills of credit, make anything but gold and silver a tender in payment of debts,'' or ''pass any law impairing the obligation of contracts.'' If they did not guard more explicitly against the present state of things, it was because they could not have anticipated that the few banks then existing were to swell to an extent which would expel to so great a degree the gold and silver for which they had provided from the channels of circulation, and fill them with a currency that defeats the objects they had in view. The remedy for this must chiefly rest with the States from whose legislation it has sprung. No good that might accrue in a particular case from the exercise of powers not obviously conferred on the General Government would authorize its interference or justify a course that might in the slightest degree increase at the expense of the States the power of the Federal authorities; nor do I doubt that the States will apply the remedy. Within the last few years events have appealed to them too strongly to be disregarded. They have seen that the Constitution, though theoretically adhered to, is subverted in practice; that while on the statute books there is no legal tender but gold and silver, no law impairing the obligations of contracts, yet that in point of fact the privileges conferred on banking corporations have made their notes the currency of the country; that the obligations imposed by these notes are violated under the impulses of interest or convenience, and that the number and power of the persons connected with these corporations or placed under their influence give them a fearful weight when their interest is in opposition to the spirit of the Constitution and laws. To the people it is immaterial whether these results are produced by open violations of the latter or by the workings of a system of which the result is the same. An inflexible execution even of the existing statutes of most of the States would redress many evils now endured, would effectually show the banks the dangers of mismanagement which impunity encourages them to repeat, and would teach all corporations the useful lesson that they are the subjects of the law and the servants of the people. What is still wanting to effect these objects must be sought in additional legislation, or, if that be inadequate, in such further constitutional grants or restrictions as may bring us back into the path from which we have so widely wandered.

In the meantime it is the duty of the General Government to cooperate with the States by a wise exercise of its constitutional powers and the enforcement of its existing laws. The extent to which it may do so by further enactments I have already adverted to, and the wisdom of Congress may yet enlarge them. But above all, it is incumbent upon us to hold erect the principles of morality and law, constantly executing our own contracts in accordance with the provisions of the Constitution, and thus serving as a rallying point by which our whole country may be brought back to that safe and honored standard.

Our people will not long be insensible to the extent of the burdens entailed upon them by the false system that has been operating on their sanguine, energetic, and industrious character, nor to the means necessary to extricate themselves from these embarrassments. The weight which presses upon a large portion of the people and the States is an enormous debt, foreign and domestic. The foreign debt of our States, corporations, and men of business can scarcely be less than $200,000,000, requiring more than $10,000,000 a year to pay the interest. This sum has to be paid out of the exports of the country, and must of necessity cut off imports to that extent or plunge the country more deeply in debt from year to year. It is easy to see that the increase of this foreign debt must augment the annual demand on the exports to pay the interest, and to the same extent diminish the imports, and in proportion to the enlargement of the foreign debt and the consequent increase of interest must be the decrease of the import trade. In lieu of the comforts which it now brings us we might have our gigantic banking institutions and splendid, but in many instances profitless, railroads and canals absorbing to a great extent in interest upon the capital borrowed to construct them the surplus fruits of national industry for years to come, and securing to posterity no adequate return for the comforts which the labors of their hands might otherwise have secured. It is not by the increase of this debt that relief is to be sought, but in its diminution. Upon this point there is, I am happy to say, hope before us; not so much in the return of confidence abroad, which will enable the States to borrow more money, as in a change of public feeling at home, which prompts our people to pause in their career and think of the means by which debts are to be paid before they are contracted. If we would escape embarrassment, public and private, we must cease to run in debt except for objects of necessity or such as will yield a certain return. Let the faith of the States, corporations, and individuals already pledged be kept with the most punctilious regard. It is due to our national character as well as to justice that this should on the part of each be a fixed principle of conduct. But it behooves us all to be more chary in pledging it hereafter. By ceasing to run in debt and applying the surplus of our crops and incomes to the discharge of existing obligations, buying less and selling more, and managing all affairs, public and private, with strict economy and frugality, we shall see our country soon recover from a temporary depression, arising not from natural and permanent causes, but from those I have enumerated, and advance with renewed vigor in her career of prosperity.

Fortunately for us at this moment, when the balance of trade is greatly against us and the difficulty of meeting it enhanced by the disturbed state of our money affairs, the bounties of Providence have come to relieve us from the consequences of past errors. A faithful application of the immense results of the labors of the last season will afford partial relief for the present, and perseverance in the same course will in due season accomplish the rest. We have had full experience in times past of the extraordinary results which can in this respect be brought about in a short period by the united and well-directed efforts of a community like ours. Our surplus profits, the energy and industry of our population, and the wonderful advantages which Providence has bestowed upon our country in its climate, its various productions, indispensable to other nations, will in due time afford abundant means to perfect the most useful of those objects for which the States have been plunging themselves of late in embarrassment and debt, without imposing on ourselves or our children such fearful burdens.

But let it be indelibly engraved on our minds that relief is not to be found in expedients. Indebtedness can not be lessened by borrowing more money or by changing the form of the debt. The balance of trade is not to be turned in our favor by creating new demands upon us abroad. Our currency can not be improved by the creation of new banks or more issues from those which now exist. Although these devices sometimes appear to give temporary relief, they almost invariably aggravate the evil in the end. It is only by retrenchment and reform—by curtailing public and private expenditures, by paying our debts, and by reforming our banking system—that we are to expect effectual relief, security for the future, and an enduring prosperity. In shaping the institutions and policy of the General Government so as to promote as far as it can with its limited powers these important ends, you may rely on my most cordial cooperation.

That there should have been in the progress of recent events doubts in many quarters and in some a heated opposition to every change can not surprise us. Doubts are properly attendant on all reform, and it is peculiarly in the nature of such abuses as we are now encountering to seek to perpetuate their power by means of the influence they have been

permitted to acquire. It is their result, if not their object, to gain for
the few an ascendency over the many by securing to them a monopoly
of the currency, the medium through which most of the wants of mankind are supplied; to produce throughout society a chain of dependence
which leads all classes to look to privileged associations for the means of
speculation and extravagance; to nourish, in preference to the manly
virtues that give dignity to human nature, a craving desire for luxuri-
ous enjoyment and sudden wealth, which renders those who seek them
dependent on those who supply them; to substitute for republican simplicity and economical habits a sickly appetite for effeminate indulgence
and an imitation of that reckless extravagance which impoverished and
enslaved the industrious people of foreign lands, and at last to fix upon
us, instead of those equal political rights the acquisition of which was
alike the object and supposed reward of our Revolutionary struggle, a
system of exclusive privileges conferred by partial legislation.   To remove
the influences which had thus gradually grown up among us, to deprive
them of their deceptive advantages, to test them by the light of wisdom and truth, to oppose the force which they concentrate in their support—all this was necessarily the work of time, even among a people so
enlightened and pure as that of the United States.   In most other countries, perhaps, it could only be accomplished through that series of revolutionary movements which are too often found necessary to effect any
great and radical reform; but it is the crowning merit of our institutions
that they create and nourish in the vast majority of our people a disposition and a power peaceably to remedy abuses which have elsewhere
caused the effusion of rivers of blood and the sacrifice of thousands of the
human race.   The result thus far is most honorable to the self-denial,
the intelligence, and the patriotism of our citizens; it justifies the confident hope that they will carry through the reform which has been so
well begun, and that they will go still further than they have yet gone
in illustrating the important truth that a people as free and enlightened
as ours will, whenever it becomes necessary, show themselves to be indeed
capable of self-government by voluntarily adopting appropriate remedies
for every abuse, and submitting to temporary sacrifices, however great,
to insure their permanent welfare.

My own exertions for the furtherance of these desirable objects have
been bestowed throughout my official career with a zeal that is nourished
by ardent wishes for the welfare of my country, and by an unlimited
reliance on the wisdom that marks its ultimate decision on all great
and controverted questions.   Impressed with the solemn obligations
imposed upon me by the Constitution, desirous also of laying before my
fellow-citizens, with whose confidence and support I have been so highly
honored, such measures as appear to me conducive to their prosperity,
and anxious to submit to their fullest consideration the grounds upon
which my opinions are formed, I have on this as on preceding occasions

freely offered my views on those points of domestic policy that seem at the present time most prominently to require the action of the Government. I know that they will receive from Congress that full and able consideration which the importance of the subjects merits, and I can repeat the assurance heretofore made that I shall cheerfully and readily cooperate with you in every measure that will tend to promote the welfare of the Union.

FOURTH ANNUAL MESSAGE.

Washington, *December 5, 1840.*

Fellow-Citizens of the Senate and House of Representatives:

Our devout gratitude is due to the Supreme Being for having graciously continued to our beloved country through the vicissitudes of another year the invaluable blessings of health, plenty, and peace. Seldom has this favored land been so generally exempted from the ravages of disease or the labor of the husbandman more amply rewarded, and never before have our relations with other countries been placed on a more favorable basis than that which they so happily occupy at this critical conjuncture in the affairs of the world. A rigid and persevering abstinence from all interference with the domestic and political relations of other States, alike due to the genius and distinctive character of our Government and to the principles by which it is directed; a faithful observance in the management of our foreign relations of the practice of speaking plainly, dealing justly, and requiring truth and justice in return as the best conservatives of the peace of nations; a strict impartiality in our manifestations of friendship in the commercial privileges we concede and those we require from others—these, accompanied by a disposition as prompt to maintain in every emergency our own rights as we are from principle averse to the invasion of those of others, have given to our country and Government a standing in the great family of nations of which we have just cause to be proud and the advantages of which are experienced by our citizens throughout every portion of the earth to which their enterprising and adventurous spirit may carry them. Few, if any, remain insensible to the value of our friendship or ignorant of the terms on which it can be acquired and by which it can alone be preserved.

A series of questions of long standing, difficult in their adjustment and important in their consequences, in which the rights of our citizens and the honor of the country were deeply involved, have in the course of a few years (the most of them during the successful Administration of my immediate predecessor) been brought to a satisfactory conclusion; and the most important of those remaining are, I am happy to believe, in a fair way of being speedily and satisfactorily adjusted.

With all the powers of the world our relations are those of honorable peace. Since your adjournment nothing serious has occurred to interrupt or threaten this desirable harmony. If clouds have lowered above the other hemisphere, they have not cast their portentous shadows upon our happy shores. Bound by no entangling alliances, yet linked by a common nature and interest with the other nations of mankind, our aspirations are for the preservation of peace, in whose solid and civilizing triumphs all may participate with a generous emulation. Yet it behooves us to be prepared for any event and to be always ready to maintain those just and enlightened principles of national intercourse for which this Government has ever contended. In the shock of contending empires it is only by assuming a resolute bearing and clothing themselves with defensive armor that neutral nations can maintain their independent rights.

The excitement which grew out of the territorial controversy between the United States and Great Britain having in a great measure subsided, it is hoped that a favorable period is approaching for its final settlement. Both Governments must now be convinced of the dangers with which the question is fraught, and it must be their desire, as it is their interest, that this perpetual cause of irritation should be removed as speedily as practicable. In my last annual message you were informed that the proposition for a commission of exploration and survey promised by Great Britain had been received, and that a counter project, including also a provision for the certain and final adjustment of the limits in dispute, was then before the British Government for its consideration. The answer of that Government, accompanied by additional propositions of its own, was received through its minister here since your separation. These were promptly considered, such as were deemed correct in principle and consistent with a due regard to the just rights of the United States and of the State of Maine concurred in, and the reasons for dissenting from the residue, with an additional suggestion on our part, communicated by the Secretary of State to Mr. Fox. That minister, not feeling himself sufficiently instructed upon some of the points raised in the discussion, felt it to be his duty to refer the matter to his own Government for its further decision. Having now been for some time under its advisement, a speedy answer may be confidently expected. From the character of the points still in difference and the undoubted disposition of both parties to bring the matter to an early conclusion, I look with entire confidence to a prompt and satisfactory termination of the negotiation. Three commissioners were appointed shortly after the adjournment of Congress under the act of the last session providing for the exploration and survey of the line which separates the States of Maine and New Hampshire from the British Provinces. They have been actively employed until their progress was interrupted by the inclemency of the season, and will resume their labors as soon as practicable in the ensuing year.

It is understood that their respective examinations will throw new light upon the subject in controversy and serve to remove any erroneous impressions which may have been made elsewhere prejudicial to the rights of the United States. It was, among other reasons, with a view of preventing the embarrassments which in our peculiar system of government impede and complicate negotiations involving the territorial rights of a State that I thought it my duty, as you have been informed on a previous occasion, to propose to the British Government, through its minister at Washington, that early steps should be taken to adjust the points of difference on the line of boundary from the entrance of Lake Superior to the most northwestern point of the Lake of the Woods by the arbitration of a friendly power in conformity with the seventh article of the treaty of Ghent. No answer has yet been returned by the British Government to this proposition.

With Austria, France, Prussia, Russia, and the remaining powers of Europe I am happy to inform you our relations continue to be of the most friendly character. With Belgium a treaty of commerce and navigation, based upon liberal principles of reciprocity and equality, was concluded in March last, and, having been ratified by the Belgian Government, will be duly laid before the Senate. It is a subject of congratulation that it provides for the satisfactory adjustment of a long-standing question of controversy, thus removing the only obstacle which could obstruct the friendly and mutually advantageous intercourse between the two nations. A messenger has been dispatched with the Hanoverian treaty to Berlin, where, according to stipulation, the ratifications are to be exchanged. I am happy to announce to you that after many delays and difficulties a treaty of commerce and navigation between the United States and Portugal was concluded and signed at Lisbon on the 26th of August last by the plenipotentiaries of the two Governments. Its stipulations are founded upon those principles of mutal liberality and advantage which the United States have always sought to make the basis of their intercourse with foreign powers, and it is hoped they will tend to foster and strengthen the commercial intercourse of the two countries.

Under the appropriation of the last session of Congress an agent has been sent to Germany for the purpose of promoting the interests of our tobacco trade.

The commissioners appointed under the convention for the adjustment of claims of citizens of the United States upon Mexico having met and organized at Washington in August last, the papers in the possession of the Government relating to those claims were communicated to the board. The claims not embraced by that convention are now the subject of negotiation between the two Governments through the medium of our minister at Mexico.

Nothing has occurred to disturb the harmony of our relations with the different Governments of South America. I regret, however, to be obliged to inform you that the claims of our citizens upon the late Republic of Colombia have not yet been satisfied by the separate Governments into which it has been resolved.

The chargé d'affaires of Brazil having expressed the intention of his Government not to prolong the treaty of 1828, it will cease to be obligatory upon either party on the 12th day of December, 1841, when the extensive commercial intercourse between the United States and that vast Empire will no longer be regulated by express stipulations.

It affords me pleasure to communicate to you that the Government of Chili has entered into an agreement to indemnify the claimants in the case of the *Macedonian* for American property seized in 1819, and to add that information has also been received which justifies the hope of an early adjustment of the remaining claims upon that Government.

The commissioners appointed in pursuance of the convention between the United States and Texas for marking the boundary between them have, according to the last report received from our commissioner, surveyed and established the whole extent of the boundary north along the western bank of the Sabine River from its entrance into the Gulf of Mexico to the thirty-second degree of north latitude. The commission adjourned on the 16th of June last, to reassemble on the 1st of November for the purpose of establishing accurately the intersection of the thirty-second degree of latitude with the western bank of the Sabine and the meridian line thence to Red River. It is presumed that the work will be concluded in the present season.

The present sound condition of their finances and the success with which embarrassments in regard to them, at times apparently insurmountable, have been overcome are matters upon which the people and Government of the United States may well congratulate themselves. An overflowing Treasury, however it may be regarded as an evidence of public prosperity, is seldom conducive to the permanent welfare of any people, and experience has demonstrated its incompatibility with the salutary action of political institutions like those of the United States. Our safest reliance for financial efficiency and independence has, on the contrary, been found to consist in ample resources unencumbered with debt, and in this respect the Federal Government occupies a singularly fortunate and truly enviable position.

When I entered upon the discharge of my official duties in March, 1837, the act for the distribution of the surplus revenue was in a course of rapid execution. Nearly $28,000,000 of the public moneys were, in pursuance of its provisions, deposited with the States in the months of January, April, and July of that year. In May there occurred a general suspension of specie payments by the banks, including, with very few exceptions, those in which the public moneys were deposited and upon whose fidelity the Government had unfortunately made itself dependent for the revenues which had been collected from the people and were indispensable to the public service.

This suspension and the excesses in banking and commerce out of which it arose, and which were greatly aggravated by its occurrence, made to a great extent unavailable the principal part of the public money then on hand, suspended the collection of many millions accruing on merchants' bonds, and greatly reduced the revenue arising from customs and the public lands. These effects have continued to operate in various degrees to the present period, and in addition to the decrease in the revenue thus produced two and a half millions of duties have been relinquished by two biennial reductions under the act of 1833, and probably as much more upon the importation of iron for railroads by special legislation.

Whilst such has been our condition for the last four years in relation to revenue, we have during the same period been subjected to an unavoidable continuance of large extraordinary expenses necessarily growing out of past transactions, and which could not be immediately arrested without great prejudice to the public interest. Of these, the charge upon the Treasury in consequence of the Cherokee treaty alone, without adverting to others arising out of Indian treaties, has already exceeded $5,000,000; that for the prosecution of measures for the removal of the Seminole Indians, which were found in progress, has been nearly fourteen millions, and the public buildings have required the unusual sum of nearly three millions.

It affords me, however, great pleasure to be able to say that from the commencement of this period to the present day every demand upon the Government, at home or abroad, has been promptly met. This has been done not only without creating a permanent debt or a resort to additional taxation in any form, but in the midst of a steadily progressive reduction of existing burdens upon the people, leaving still a considerable balance of available funds which will remain in the Treasury at the end of the year. The small amount of Treasury notes, not exceeding $4,500,000, still outstanding, and less by twenty-three millions than the United States have in deposit with the States, is composed of such only as are not yet due or have not been presented for payment. They may be redeemed out of the accruing revenue if the expenditures do not exceed the amount within which they may, it is thought, be kept without prejudice to the public interest, and the revenue shall prove to be as large as may justly be anticipated.

Among the reflections arising from the contemplation of these circumstances, one, not the least gratifying, is the consciousness that the Government had the resolution and the ability to adhere in every emergency to the sacred obligations of law, to execute all its contracts according to the requirements of the Constitution, and thus to present when most needed a rallying point by which the business of the whole country might be brought back to a safe and unvarying standard—a result vitally important as well to the interests as to the morals of the people. There can surely now be no difference of opinion in regard to the incalculable evils that would have arisen if the Government at that critical moment had suffered itself to be deterred from upholding the only true standard of value, either by the pressure of adverse circumstances or the violence of unmerited denunciation. The manner in which the people sustained the performance of this duty was highly honorable to their fortitude and patriotism. It can not fail to stimulate their agents to adhere under all circumstances to the line of duty and to satisfy them of the safety with which a course really right and demanded by a financial crisis may in a community like ours be pursued, however apparently severe its immediate operation.

The policy of the Federal Government in extinguishing as rapidly as possible the national debt, and subsequently in resisting every temptation to create a new one, deserves to be regarded in the same favorable light. Among the many objections to a national debt, the certain tendency of public securities to concentrate ultimately in the coffers of foreign stockholders is one which is every day gathering strength. Already have the resources of many of the States and the future industry of their citizens been indefinitely mortgaged to the subjects of European Governments to the amount of twelve millions annually to pay the constantly accruing interest on borrowed money—a sum exceeding half the ordinary revenues of the whole United States. The pretext which this relation affords to foreigners to scrutinize the management of our domestic affairs, if not actually to intermeddle with them, presents a subject for earnest attention, not to say of serious alarm. Fortunately, the Federal Government, with the exception of an obligation entered into in behalf of the District of Columbia, which must soon be discharged, is wholly exempt from any such embarrassment. It is also, as is believed, the only Government which, having fully and faithfully paid all its creditors, has also relieved itself entirely from debt. To maintain a distinction so desirable and so honorable to our national character should be an object of earnest solicitude. Never should a free people, if it be possible to avoid it, expose themselves to the necessity of having to treat of the peace, the honor, or the safety of the Republic with the governments of foreign creditors, who, however well disposed they may be to cultivate with us in general friendly relations, are nevertheless by the law of their own condition made hostile to the success and permanency of political institutions like ours. Most humiliating may be the embarrassments consequent upon such a condition. Another objection, scarcely less formidable, to the commencement of a new debt is its inevitable tendency to increase in magnitude and to foster national extravagance. He has been an unprofitable observer of events who needs at this day to be admonished of the difficulties which a government habitually dependent on loans to sustain its ordinary expenditures has to encounter in resisting the influences constantly exerted in favor of additional loans; by capitalists, who enrich themselves by government securities for amounts much exceeding the money they actually advance—a prolific source of individual aggrandizement in all borrowing countries; by stockholders, who seek their gains in the rise and fall of public stocks; and by the selfish importunities of applicants for appropriations for works avowedly for the accommodation of the public, but the real objects of which are too frequently the advancement of private interests. The known necessity which so many of the States will be under to impose taxes for the payment of the interest on their debts furnishes an additional and very cogent reason why the Federal Government should refrain from creating a national debt, by which the people would be exposed to double taxation for a similar object. We possess within ourselves ample resources for every emergency, and we may be quite sure that our citizens in no future exigency will be unwilling to supply the Government with all the means asked for the defense of the country. In time of peace there can, at all events, be no justification for the creation of a permanent debt by the Federal Government. Its limited range of constitutional duties may certainly under such circumstances be performed without such a resort. It has, it is seen, been avoided during four years of greater fiscal difficulties than have existed in a similar period since the adoption of the Constitution, and one also remarkable for the occurrence of extraordinary causes of expenditures.

But to accomplish so desirable an object two things are indispensable: First, that the action of the Federal Government be kept within the boundaries prescribed by its founders, and, secondly, that all appropriations for objects admitted to be constitutional, and the expenditure of them also, be subjected to a standard of rigid but well-considered and practical economy. The first depends chiefly on the people themselves—the opinions they form of the true construction of the Constitution and the confidence they repose in the political sentiments of those they select as their representatives in the Federal Legislature; the second rests upon the fidelity with which their more immediate representatives and other public functionaries discharge the trusts committed to them. The duty of economizing the expenses of the public service is admitted on all hands; yet there are few subjects upon which there exists a wider difference of opinion than is constantly manifested in regard to the fidelity with which that duty is discharged. Neither diversity of sentiment nor even mutual recriminations upon a point in respect to which the public mind is so justly sensitive can well be entirely avoided, and least so at periods of great political excitement.   An intelligent people, however, seldom fail to arrive in the end at correct conclusions in such a matter.   Practical economy in the management of public affairs can have no adverse influ- ence to contend with more powerful than a large surplus revenue, and the unusually large appropriations for 1837 may without doubt, independ- ently of the extraordinary requisitions for the public service growing out of the state of our Indian relations, be in no inconsiderable degree traced to this source.   The sudden and rapid distribution of the large surplus then in the Treasury and the equally sudden and unprecedentedly severe revulsion in the commerce and business of the country, pointing with unerring certainty to a great and protracted reduction of the revenue, strengthened the propriety of the earliest practicable reduction of the public expenditures.

But to change a system operating upon so large a surface and applicable to such numerous and diversified interests and objects was more than the work of a day.   The attention of every department of the Govern- ment was immediately and in good faith directed to that end, and has been so continued to the present moment.   The estimates and appropria- tions for the year 1838 (the first.over which I had any control) were some- what diminished.   The expenditures of 1839 were reduced $6,000,000. Those of 1840, exclusive of disbursements for public debt and trust claims, will probably·not exceed twenty-two and a half millions, being between two and three millions less than those of the preceding year and nine or ten millions less than those of 1837.   Nor has it been found necessary in order to produce this result to resort to the power conferred by Congress of postponing certain classes of the public works, except by deferring expenditures for a short period upon a limited portion of them, and which postponement terminated some time since—at the moment the Treasury Department by further receipts from the indebted banks became fully assured of its ability to meet them without prejudice to the public service in other respects.   Causes are in operation which will, it is believed, justify a still further reduction without injury to any important national interest.   The expenses of sustaining the troops employed in Florida have been gradually and greatly reduced through the persevering efforts of the War Department, and a reasonable hope may be entertained that the necessity for military operations in that quarter will soon cease.   The removal of the Indians from within our settled borders is nearly completed.   The pension list, one of the heav- iest charges upon the Treasury, is rapidly diminishing by death.   The most costly of our public buildings are either finished or nearly so, and we may, I think, safely promise ourselves a continued exemption from border difficulties.

The available balance in the Treasury on the 1st of January next is estimated at $1,500,000.   This sum, with the expected receipts from all sources during the next year, will, it is believed, be sufficient to enable the Government to meet every engagement and have a suitable balance in the Treasury at the end of the year, if the remedial measures connected with the customs and the public lands heretofore recommended are adopted and the new appropriations by Congress shall not carry the expenditures beyond the official estimates.

The new system established by Congress for the safe-keeping of the public money, prescribing the kind of currency to be received for the public revenue and providing additional guards and securities against losses, has now been several months in operation. Although it might be premature upon an experience of such limited duration to form a definite opinion in regard to the extent of its influences in correcting many evils under which the Federal Government and the country have hitherto suffered, especially those that have grown out of banking expansions, a depreciated currency, and official defalcations, yet it is but right to say that nothing has occurred in the practical operation of the system to weaken in the slightest degree, but much to strengthen, the confident anticipations of its friends. The grounds of these have been heretofore so fully explained as to require no recapitulation. In respect to the facility and convenience it affords in conducting the public service, and the ability of the Government to discharge through its agency every duty attendant on the collection, transfer, and disbursement of the public money with promptitude and success, I can say with confidence that the apprehensions of those who felt it to be their duty to oppose its adoption have proved to be unfounded. On the contrary, this branch of the fiscal affairs of the Government has been, and it is believed may always be, thus carried on with every desirable facility and security. A few changes and improvements in the details of the system, without affecting any principles involved in it, will be submitted to you by the Secretary of the Treasury, and will, I am sure, receive at your hands that attention to which they may on examination be found to be entitled.

I have deemed this brief summary of our fiscal affairs necessary to the due performance of a duty specially enjoined upon me by the Constitution. It will serve also to illustrate more fully the principles by which I have been guided in reference to two contested points in our public policy which were earliest in their development and have been more important in their consequences than any that have arisen under our complicated and difficult, yet admirable, system of government. I allude to a national debt and a national bank. It was in these that the political contests by which the country has been agitated ever since the adoption of the Constitution in a great measure originated, and there is too much reason to apprehend that the conflicting interests and opposing principles thus marshaled will continue as heretofore to produce similar if not aggravated consequences.

Coming into office the declared enemy of both, I have earnestly endeavored to prevent a resort to either.

The consideration that a large public debt affords an apology, and produces in some degree a necessity also, for resorting to a system and extent of taxation which is not only oppressive throughout, but is likewise so apt to lead in the end to the commission of that most odious of all offenses against the principles of republican government, the prostitution of political power, conferred for the general benefit, to the aggrandizement of particular classes and the gratification of individual cupidity, is alone sufficient, independently of the weighty objections which have already been urged, to render its creation and existence the sources of bitter and unappeasable discord. If we add to this its inevitable tendency to produce and foster extravagant expenditures of the public moneys, by which a necessity is created for new loans and new burdens on the people, and, finally, refer to the examples of every government which has existed for proof, how seldom it is that the system, when once adopted and implanted in the policy of a country, has failed to expand itself until public credit was exhausted and the people were no longer able to endure its increasing weight, it seems impossible to resist the conclusion that no benefits resulting from its career, no extent of conquest, no accession of wealth to particular classes, nor any nor all its combined advantages, can counterbalance its ultimate but certain results—a splendid government and an impoverished people.

If a national bank was, as is undeniable, repudiated by the framers of the Constitution as incompatible with the rights of the States and the liberties of the people; if from the beginning it has been regarded by large portions of our citizens as coming in direct collision with that great and vital amendment of the Constitution which declares that all powers not conferred by that instrument on the General Government are reserved to the States and to the people; if it has been viewed by them as the first great step in the march of latitudinous construction, which unchecked would render that sacred instrument of as little value as an unwritten constitution, dependent, as it would alone be, for its meaning on the interested interpretation of a dominant party, and affording no security to the rights of the minority—if such is undeniably the case, what rational grounds could have been conceived for anticipating aught but determined opposition to such an institution at the present day.

Could a different result have been expected when the consequences which have flowed from its creation, and particularly from its struggles to perpetuate its existence, had confirmed in so striking a manner the apprehensions of its earliest opponents; when it had been so clearly demonstrated that a concentrated money power, wielding so vast a capital and combining such incalculable means of influence, may in those peculiar conjunctures to which this Government is unavoidably exposed prove an overmatch for the political power of the people themselves; when the true character of its capacity to regulate according to its will and its interests and the interests of its favorites the value and production of the labor and property of every man in this extended country had been so fully and fearfully developed; when it was notorious that all classes of this great community had, by means of the power and influence it thus possesses, been infected to madness with a spirit of heedless speculation; when it had been seen that, secure in the support of the combination of influences by which it was surrounded, it could violate its charter and set the laws at defiance with impunity; and when, too, it had become most apparent that to believe that such an accumulation of powers can ever be granted without the certainty of being abused was to indulge in a fatal delusion?

To avoid the necessity of a permanent debt and its inevitable consequences I have advocated and endeavored to carry into effect the policy of confining the appropriations for the public service to such objects only as are clearly within the constitutional authority of the Federal Government; of excluding from its expenses those improvident and unauthorized grants of public money for works of internal improvement which were so wisely arrested by the constitutional interposition of my predecessor, and which, if they had not been so checked, would long before this time have involved the finances of the General Government in embarrassments far greater than those which are now experienced by any of the States; of limiting all our expenditures to that simple, unostentatious, and economical administration of public affairs which is alone consistent with the character of our institutions; of collecting annually from the customs, and the sales of public lands a revenue fully adequate to defray all the expenses thus incurred; but under no pretense whatsoever to impose taxes upon the people to a greater amount than was actually necessary to the public service conducted upon the principles I have stated.

In lieu of a national bank or a dependence upon banks of any description for the management of our fiscal affairs, I recommended the adoption of the system which is now in successful operation. That system affords every requisite facility for the transaction of the pecuniary concerns of the Government; will, it is confidently anticipated, produce in other respects many of the benefits which have been from time to time expected from the creation of a national bank, but which have never been realized; avoid the manifold evils inseparable from such an institution; diminish to a greater extent than could be accomplished by any other measure of reform the patronage of the Federal Government—a wise policy in all governments, but more especially so in one like ours, which works well only in proportion as it is made to rely for its support upon the unbiased and unadulterated opinions of its constituents; do away forever all dependence on corporate bodies either in the raising, collecting, safekeeping, or disbursing the public revenues, and place the Government equally above the temptation of fostering a dangerous and unconstitutional institution at home or the necessity of adapting its policy to the views and interests of a still more formidable money power abroad.

It is by adopting and carrying out these principles under circumstances the most arduous and discouraging that the attempt has been made, thus far successfully, to demonstrate to the people of the United States that a national bank at all times, and a national debt except it be incurred at a period when the honor and safety of the nation demand the temporary sacrifice of a policy which should only be abandoned in such exigencies, are not merely unnecessary, but in direct and deadly hostility to the principles of their Government and to their own permanent welfare.

The progress made in the development of these positions appears in the preceding sketch of the past history and present state of the finin-cial concerns of the Federal Government. The facts there stated fully authorize the assertion that all the purposes for which this Government was instituted have been accomplished during four years of greater pecuniary embarrassment than were ever before experienced in time of peace, and in the face of opposition as formidable as any that was ever before arrayed against the policy of an Administration; that this has been done when the ordinary revenues of the Government were generally decreasing as well from the operation of the laws as the condition of the country, without the creation of a permanent public debt or incurring any liability other than such as the ordinary resources of the Government will speedily discharge, and without the agency of a national bank.

If this view of the proceedings of the Government for the period it embraces be warranted by the facts as they are known to exist; if the Army and Navy have been sustained to the full extent authorized by law, and which Congress deemed sufficient for the defense of the country and the protection of its rights and its honor; if its civil and diplomatic service has been equally sustained; if ample provision has been made for the administration of justice and the execution of the laws; if the claims upon public gratitude in behalf of the soldiers of the Revolution have been promptly met and faithfully discharged; if there have been no failures in defraying the very large expenditures growing out of that long-continued and salutary policy of peacefully removing the Indians to regions of comparative safety and prosperity; if the public faith has at all times and everywhere been most scrupulously maintained by a prompt discharge of the numerous, extended, and diversified claims on the Treas-ury—if all these great and permanent objects, with many others that might be stated, have for a series of years, marked by peculiar obstacles and difficulties, been successfully accomplished without a resort to a permanent debt or the aid of a national bank, have we not a right to expect that a policy the object of which has been to sustain the public service independently of either of these fruitful sources of discord will receive the final sanction of a people whose unbiased and fairly elicited judgment upon public affairs is never ultimately wrong?

That embarrassments in the pecuniary concerns of individuals of unexampled extent and duration have recently existed in this as in other commercial nations is undoubtedly true. To suppose it necessary now to trace these reverses to their sources would be a reflection on the intelligence of my fellow-citizens. Whatever may have been the obscurity in which the subject was involved during the earlier stages of the revulsion, there can not now be many by whom the whole question is not fully understood.

Not deeming it within the constitutional powers of the General Government to repair private losses sustained by reverses in business having no connection with the public service, either by direct appropriations from the Treasury or by special legislation designed to secure exclusive privileges and immunities to individuals or classes in preference to or at the expense of the great majority necessarily debarred from any participation in them, no attempt to do so has been either made, recommended, or encouraged by the present Executive.

It is believed, however, that the great purposes for the attainment of which the Federal Government was instituted have not been lost sight of. Intrusted only with certain limited powers, cautiously enumerated, distinctly specified, and defined with a precision and clearness which would seem to defy misconstruction, it has been my constant aim to confine myself within the limits so clearly marked out and so carefully guarded. Having always been of opinion that the best preservative of the union of the States is to be found in a total abstinence from the exercise of all doubtful powers on the part of the Federal Government rather than in attempts to assume them by a loose construction of the Constitution or an ingenious perversion of its words, I have endeavored to avoid recommending any measure which I had reason to apprehend would, in the opinion even of a considerable minority of my fellow-citizens, be regarded as trenching on the rights of the States or the provisions of the hallowed instrument of our Union. Viewing the aggregate powers of the Federal Government as a voluntary concession of the States, it seemed to me that such only should be exercised as were at the time intended to be given.

I have been strengthened, too, in the propriety of this course by the conviction that all efforts to go beyond this tend only to produce dissatisfaction and distrust, to excite jealousies, and to provoke resistance. Instead of adding strength to the Federal Government, even when successful they must ever prove a source of incurable weakness by alienating a portion of those whose adhesion is indispensable to the great aggregate of united strength and whose voluntary attachment is in my estimation far more essential to the efficiency of a government strong in the best of all possible strength—the confidence and attachment of all those who make up its constituent elements.

Thus believing, it has been my purpose to secure to the whole people and to every member of the Confederacy, by general, salutary, and equal laws alone, the benefit of those republican institutions which it was the end and aim of the Constitution to establish, and the impartial influence of which is in my judgment indispensable to their preservation. I can not bring myself to believe that the lasting happiness of the people, the prosperity of the States, or the permanency of their Union can be maintained by giving preference or priority to any class of citizens in the distribution of benefits or privileges, or by the adoption of measures which enrich one portion of the Union at the expense of another; nor can I see in the interference of the Federal Government with the local legislation and reserved rights of the States a remedy for present or a security against future dangers.

The first, and assuredly not the least, important step toward relieving the country from the condition into which it had been plunged by excesses in trade, banking, and credits of all kinds was to place the business transactions of the Government itself on a solid basis, giving and receiving in all cases value for value, and neither countenancing nor encouraging in others that delusive system of credits from which it has been found so difficult to escape, and which has left nothing behind it but the wrecks that mark its fatal career.

That the financial affairs of the Government are now and have been during the whole period of these wide-spreading difficulties conducted with a strict and invariable regard to this great fundamental principle, and that by the assumption and maintenance of the stand thus taken on the very threshold of the approaching crisis more than by any other cause or causes whatever the community at large has been shielded from the incalculable evils of a general and indefinite suspension of specie payments, and a consequent annihilation for the whole period it might have lasted of a just and invariable standard of value, will, it is believed, at this period scarcely be questioned.

A steady adherence on the part of the Government to the policy which has produced such salutary results, aided by judicious State legislation and, what is not less important, by the industry, enterprise, perseverance, and economy of the American people, can not fail to raise the whole country at an early period to a state of solid and enduring prosperity, not subject to be again overthrown by the suspension of banks or the explosion of a bloated credit system. It is for the people and their representatives to decide whether or not the permanent welfare of the country (which all good citizens equally desire, however widely they may differ as to the means of its accomplishment) shall be in this way secured, or whether the management of the pecuniary concerns of the Government, and by consequence to a great extent those of individuals also, shall be carried back to a condition of things which fostered those contractions and expansions of the currency and those reckless abuses of credit from the baleful effects of which the country has so deeply suffered—a return that can promise in the end no better results than to reproduce the embarrassments the Government has experienced, and to remove from the shoulders of the present to those of fresh victims the bitter fruits of that spirit of speculative enterprise to which our country-men are so liable and upon which the lessons of experience are so una-vailing. The choice is an important one, and I sincerely hope that it may be wisely made.

A report from the Secretary of War, presenting a detailed view of the affairs of that Department, accompanies this communication.

The desultory duties connected with the removal of the Indians, in which the Army has been constantly engaged on the northern and west-ern frontiers and in Florida, have rendered it impracticable to carry into full effect the plan recommended by the Secretary for improving its dis-cipline. In every instance where the regiments have been concentrated they have made great progress, and the best results may be anticipated from a continuance of this system. During the last season a part of the troops have been employed in removing Indians from the interior to the territory assigned them in the West—a duty which they have performed efficiently and with praiseworthy humanity—and that portion of them which has been stationed in Florida continued active operations there throughout the heats of summer.

The policy of the United States in regard to the Indians, of which a succinct account is given in my message of 1838, and of the wisdom and expediency of which I am fully satisfied, has been continued in active operation throughout the whole period of my Administration. Since the spring of 1837 more than 40,000 Indians have been removed to their new homes west of the Mississippi, and I am happy to add that all accounts concur in representing the result of this measure as eminently beneficial to that people.

The emigration of the Seminoles alone has been attended with serious difficulty and occasioned bloodshed, hostilities having been commenced by the Indians in Florida under the apprehension that they would be com-pelled by force to comply with their treaty stipulations. The execution of the treaty of Paynes Landing, signed in 1832, but not ratified until 1834, was postponed at the solicitation of the Indians until 1836, when they again renewed their agreement to remove peaceably to their new homes in the West. In the face of this solemn and renewed compact they broke their faith and commenced hostilities by the massacre of Major Dade's command, the murder of their agent, General Thompson, and other acts of cruel treachery. When this alarming and unexpected intelligence reached the seat of Government, every effort appears to have been made to reenforce General Clinch, who commanded the troops then in Florida. General Eustis was dispatched with reenforcements from Charleston, troops were called out from Alabama, Tennessee, and Geor-gia, and General Scott was sent to take the command, with ample powers and ample means. At the first alarm General Gaines organized a force at New Orleans, and without waiting for orders landed in Florida, where he delivered over the troops he had brought with him to General Scott.

Governor Call was subsequently appointed to conduct a summer campaign, and at the close of it was replaced by General Jesup. These events and changes took place under the Administration of my predecessor. Notwithstanding the exertions of the experienced officers who had command there for eighteen months, on entering upon the administration of the Government I found the Territory of Florida a prey to Indian atrocities. A strenuous effort was immediately made to bring those hostilities to a close, and the army under General Jesup was reenforced until it amounted to 10,000 men, and furnished with abundant supplies of every description. In this campaign a great number of the enemy were captured and destroyed, but the character of the contest only was changed. The Indians, having been defeated in every engagement, dispersed in small bands throughout the country and became an enterprising, formidable, and ruthless banditti. General Taylor, who succeeded General Jesup, used his best exertions to subdue them, and was seconded in his efforts by the officers under his command; but he too failed to protect the Territory from their depredations. By an act of signal and cruel treachery they broke the truce made with them by General Macomb, who was sent from Washington for the purpose of carrying into effect the expressed wishes of Congress, and have continued their devastations ever since. General Armistead, who was in Florida when General Taylor left the army by permission, assumed the command, and after active summer operations was met by propositions for peace, and from the fortunate coincidence of the arrival in Florida at the same period of a delegation from the Seminoles who are happily settled west of the Mississippi and are now anxious to persuade their countrymen to join them there hopes were for some time entertained that the Indians might be induced to leave the Territory without further difficulty. These hopes have proved fallacious and hostilities have been renewed throughout the whole of the Territory. That this contest has endured so long is to be attributed to causes beyond the control of the Government. Experienced generals have had the command of the troops, officers and soldiers have alike distinguished themselves for their activity, patience, and enduring courage, the army has been constantly furnished with supplies of every description, and we must look for the causes which have so long procrastinated the issue of the contest in the vast extent of the theater of hostilities, the almost insurmountable obstacles presented by the nature of the country, the climate, and the wily character of the savages.

The sites for marine hospitals on the rivers and lakes which I was authorized to select and cause to be purchased have all been designated, but the appropriation not proving sufficient, conditional arrangements only have been made for their acquisition. It is for Congress to decide whether these conditional purchases shall be sanctioned and the humane intentions of the law carried into full effect.

The Navy, as will appear from the accompanying report of the Secretary, has been usefully and honorably employed in the protection of our commerce and citizens in the Mediterranean, the Pacific, on the coast of Brazil, and in the Gulf of Mexico. A small squadron, consisting of the frigate *Constellation* and the sloop of war *Boston*, under Commodore Kearney, is now on its way to the China and Indian seas for the purpose of attending to our interests in that quarter, and Commander Aulick, in the sloop of war *Yorktown*, has been instructed to visit the Sandwich and Society islands, the coasts of New Zealand and Japan, together with other ports and islands frequented by our whale ships, for the purpose of giving them countenance and protection should they be required. Other smaller vessels have been and still are employed in prosecuting the surveys of the coast of the United States directed by various acts of Congress, and those which have been completed will shortly be laid before you.

The exploring expedition at the latest date was preparing to leave the Bay of Islands, New Zealand, in further prosecution of objects which have thus far been successfully accomplished. The discovery of a new continent, which was first seen in latitude 66° 2' south, longitude 154° 27' east, and afterwards in latitude 66° 31' south, longitude 153° 40' east, by Lieutenants Wilkes and Hudson, for an extent of 1,800 miles, but on which they were prevented from landing by vast bodies of ice which encompassed it, is one of the honorable results of the enterprise. Lieutenant Wilkes bears testimony to the zeal and good conduct of his officers and men, and it is but justice to that officer to state that he appears to have performed the duties assigned him with an ardor, ability, and perseverance which give every assurance of an honorable issue to the undertaking.

The report of the Postmaster-General herewith transmitted will exhibit the service of that Department the past year and its present condition. The transportation has been maintained during the year to the full extent authorized by the existing laws; some improvements have been effected which the public interest seemed urgently to demand, but not involving any material additional expenditure; the contractors have generally performed their engagements with fidelity; the postmasters, with few exceptions, have rendered their accounts and paid their quarterly balances with promptitude, and the whole service of the Department has maintained the efficiency for which it has for several years been distinguished.

The acts of Congress establishing new mail routes and requiring more expensive services on others and the increasing wants of the country have for three years past carried the expenditures something beyond the accruing revenues, the excess having been met until the past year by the surplus which had previously accumulated. That surplus having been exhausted and the anticipated increase in the revenue not having been realized owing to the depression in the commercial business of the country, the finances of the Department exhibit a small deficiency

at the close of the last fiscal year.   Its resources, however, are ample, and
the reduced rates of compensation for the transportation service which
may be expected on the future lettings from the general reduction of
prices, with the increase of revenue that may reasonably be anticipated
from the revival of commercial activity, must soon place the finances of
the Department in a prosperous condition.

Considering the unfavorable circumstances which have existed during
the past year, it is a gratifying result that the revenue has not declined
as compared with the preceding year, but, on the contrary, exhibits a
small increase, the circumstances referred to having had no other effect
than to check the expected income.

It will be seen that the Postmaster-General suggests certain improvements in the establishment designed to reduce the weight of the mails,
cheapen the transportation, insure greater regularity in the service, and
secure a considerable reduction in the rates of letter postage—an object
highly desirable.   The subject is one of general interest to the community, and is respectfully recommended to your consideration.

The suppression of the African slave trade has received the continued
attention of the Government.   The brig *Dolphin* and schooner *Grampus*
have been employed during the last season on the coast of Africa for
the purpose of preventing such portions of that trade as were said to be
prosecuted under the American flag.   After cruising off those parts of
the coast most usually resorted to by slavers until the commencement
of the rainy season, these vessels returned to the United States for supplies, and have since been dispatched on a similar service.

From the reports of the commanding officers it appears that the trade
is now principally carried on under Portuguese colors, and they express
the opinion that the apprehension of their presence on the slave coast
has in a great degree arrested the prostitution of the American flag to
this inhuman purpose.   It is hoped that by continuing to maintain this
force in that quarter and by the exertions of the officers in command
much will be done to put a stop to whatever portion of this traffic may
have been carried on under the American flag and to prevent its use
in a trade which, while it violates the laws, is equally an outrage on the
rights of others and the feelings of humanity.   The efforts of the several
Governments who are anxiously seeking to suppress this traffic must,
however, be directed against the facilities afforded by what are now recognized as legitimate commercial pursuits before that object can be fully
accomplished.

Supplies of provisions, water casks, merchandise, and articles connected with the prosecution of the slave trade are, it is understood,
freely carried by vessels of different nations to the slave factories, and
the effects of the factors are transported openly from one slave station to
another without interruption or punishment by either of the nations
to which they belong engaged in the commerce of that region.   I sub-

mit to your judgments whether this Government, having been the first to prohibit by adequate penalties the slave trade, the first to declare it piracy, should not be the first also to forbid to its citizens all trade with the slave factories on the coast of Africa, giving an example to all nations in this respect which if fairly followed can not fail to produce the most effective results in breaking up those dens of iniquity.

William Henry Harrison

March 4 to April 4, 1841

(Died prior to delivering any Annual Messages)

John Tyler

April 4, 1841 to March 4, 1845

FIRST ANNUAL MESSAGE.

WASHINGTON, *December 7, 1841.*

To the Senate and House of Representatives of the United States:

In coming together, fellow-citizens, to enter again upon the discharge of the duties with which the people have charged us severally, we find great occasion to rejoice in the general prosperity of the country. We are in the enjoyment of all the blessings of civil and religious liberty, with unexampled means of education, knowledge, and improvement. Through the year which is now drawing to a close peace has been in our borders and plenty in our habitations, and although disease has visited some few portions of the land with distress and mortality, yet in general the health of the people has been preserved, and we are all called upon by the highest obligations of duty to renew our thanks and our devotion to our Heavenly Parent, who has continued to vouchsafe to us the eminent blessings which surround us and who has so signally crowned the year with His goodness. If we find ourselves increasing beyond example in numbers, in strength, in wealth, in knowledge, in everything which promotes human and social happiness, let us ever remember our dependence for all these on the protection and merciful dispensations of Divine Providence.

Since your last adjournment Alexander McLeod, a British subject who was indicted for the murder of an American citizen, and whose case has been the subject of a correspondence heretofore communicated to you, has been acquitted by the verdict of an impartial and intelligent jury, and has under the judgment of the court been regularly discharged.

Great Britain having made known to this Government that the expedition which was fitted out from Canada for the destruction of the steamboat *Caroline* in the winter of 1837, and which resulted in the destruction of said boat and in the death of an American citizen, was undertaken by orders emanating from the authorities of the British Government in Canada, and demanding the discharge of McLeod upon the ground that if engaged in that expedition he did but fulfill the orders of his Government, has thus been answered in the only way in which she could be answered by a government the powers of which are distributed among its several departments by the fundamental law. Happily for the people of Great Britain, as well as those of the United States, the only mode by which an individual arraigned for a criminal offense before the courts of either can obtain his discharge is by the independent action of the judiciary and by proceedings equally familiar to the courts of both countries.

If in Great Britain a power exists in the Crown to cause to be entered a *nolle prosequi*, which is not the case with the Executive power of the United States upon a prosecution pending in a State court, yet *there* no more than *here* can the chief executive power rescue a prisoner from custody without an order of the proper tribunal directing his discharge. The precise stage of the proceedings at which such order may be made is a matter of municipal regulation exclusively, and not to be complained of by any other government. In cases of this kind a government becomes politically responsible only when its tribunals of last resort are shown to have rendered unjust and injurious judgments in matters not doubtful. To the establishment and elucidation of this principle no nation has lent its authority more efficiently than Great Britain. Alexander McLeod, having his option either to prosecute a writ of error from the decision of the supreme court of New York, which had been rendered upon his application for a discharge, to the Supreme Court of the United States, or to submit his case to the decision of a jury, preferred the latter, deeming it the readiest mode of obtaining his liberation; and the result has fully sustained the wisdom of his choice. The manner in which the issue submitted was tried will satisfy the English Government that the principles of justice will never fail to govern the enlightened decision of an American tribunal. I can not fail, however, to suggest to Congress the propriety, and in some degree the necessity, of making such provisions by law, so far as they may constitutionally do so, for the removal at their commencement and at the option of the party of all such cases as may hereafter arise, and which may involve the faithful observance and execution of our international obligations, from the State to the Federal judiciary. This Government, by our institutions, is charged with the maintenance of peace and the preservation of amicable relations with the nations of the earth, and ought to possess without question all the reasonable and proper means of maintaining the one and preserving the other. While just confidence is felt in the judiciary of the States, yet this Government ought to be competent in itself for the fulfillment of the high duties which have been devolved upon it under the organic law by the States themselves.

In the month of September a party of armed men from Upper Canada invaded the territory of the United States and forcibly seized upon the person of one Grogan, and under circumstances of great harshness hurriedly carried him beyond the limits of the United States and delivered him up to the authorities of Upper Canada. His immediate discharge was ordered by those authorities upon the facts of the case being brought to their knowledge—a course of procedure which was to have been expected from a nation with whom we are at peace, and which was not more due to the rights of the United States than to its own regard for justice. The correspondence which passed between the Department of State and the British envoy, Mr. Fox, and with the governor of Vermont, as soon as the facts had been made known to this department, are herewith communicated.

I regret that it is not in my power to make known to you an equally satisfactory conclusion in the case of the *Caroline* steamer, with the circumstances connected with the destruction of which, in December, 1837, by an armed force fitted out in the Province of Upper Canada, you are already made acquainted. No such atonement as was due for the public wrong done to the United States by this invasion of her territory, so wholly irreconcilable with her rights as an independent power, has yet been made. In the view taken by this Government the inquiry whether the vessel was in the employment of those who were prosecuting an unauthorized war against that Province or was engaged by the owner in the business of transporting passengers to and from Navy Island in hopes of private gain, which was most probably the case, in no degree alters the real question at issue between the two Governments. This Government can never concede to any foreign government the power, except in a case of the most urgent and extreme necessity, of invading its territory, either to arrest the persons or destroy the property of those who may have violated the municipal laws of such foreign government or have disregarded their obligations arising under the law of nations. The territory of the United States must be regarded as sacredly secure against all such invasions until they shall voluntarily acknowledge their inability to acquit themselves of their duties to others. And in announcing this sentiment I do but affirm a principle which no nation on earth would be more ready to vindicate at all hazards than the people and Government of Great Britain. If upon a full investigation of all the facts it shall appear that the owner of the *Caroline* was governed by a hostile intent or had made common cause with those who were in the occupancy of Navy Island, then so far as he is concerned there can be no claim to indemnity for the destruction of his boat which this Government would feel itself bound to prosecute, since he would have acted not only in derogation of the rights of Great Britain, but in clear violation of the laws of the United States; but that is a question which, however settled, in no manner involves the higher consideration of the violation of territorial sovereignty and jurisdiction. To recognize it as an admissible practice that each Government in its turn, upon any sudden and unauthorized outbreak which, on a frontier the extent of which renders it impossible for either to have an efficient force on every mile of it, and which outbreak, therefore, neither may be able to suppress in a day, may take vengeance into its own hands, and without even a remonstrance, and in the absence of any pressing or overruling necessity may invade the territory of the other, would inevitably lead to results equally to be deplored by both. When border collisions come to receive the sanction or to be made on the authority of either Government general war must be the inevitable result. While it is the ardent desire of the United States to cultivate the relations of peace with all nations and to fulfill all the duties of good neighborhood toward those who possess territories adjoining their own, that very desire would lead them to deny the right of any foreign power to invade their boundary with an armed force. The correspondence between the two Governments on this subject will at a future day of your session be submitted to your consideration; and in the meantime I can not but indulge the hope that the British Government will see the propriety of renouncing as a rule of future action the precedent which has been set in the affair at Schlosser.

I herewith submit the correspondence which has recently taken place between the American minister at the Court of St. James, Mr. Stevenson, and the minister of foreign affairs of that Government on the right claimed by that Government to visit and detain vessels sailing under the American flag and engaged in prosecuting lawful commerce in the African seas. Our commercial interests in that region have experienced considerable increase and have become an object of much importance, and it is the duty of this Government to protect them against all improper and vexatious interruption. However desirous the United States may be for the suppression of the slave trade, they can not consent to interpolations into the maritime code at the mere will and pleasure of other governments. We deny the right of any such interpolation to any one or all the nations of the earth without our consent. We claim to have a voice in all amendments or alterations of that code, and when we are given to understand, as in this instance, by a foreign government that its treaties with other nations can not be executed without the establishment and enforcement of new principles of maritime police, to be applied without our consent, we must employ a language neither of equivocal import or susceptible of misconstruction. American citizens prosecuting a lawful commerce in the African seas under the flag of their country are not responsible for the abuse or unlawful use of that flag by others; nor can they rightfully on account of any such alleged abuses be interrupted, molested, or detained while on the ocean, and if thus molested and detained while pursuing honest voyages in the usual way and violating no law themselves they are unquestionably entitled to indemnity. This Government has manifested its repugnance to the slave trade in a manner which can not be misunderstood. By its fundamental law it prescribed limits in point of time to its continuance, and against its own citizens who might so far forget the rights of humanity as to engage in that wicked traffic it has long since by its municipal laws denounced the most condign punishment. Many of the States composing this Union had made appeals to the civilized world for its suppression long before the moral sense of other nations had become shocked by the iniquities of the traffic. Whether this Government should now enter into treaties containing mutual stipulations upon this subject is a question for its mature deliberation. Certain it is that if the right to detain American ships on the high seas can be justified on the plea of a necessity for such detention arising out of the existence of treaties between other nations, the same plea may be extended and enlarged by the new stipulations of new treaties to which the United States may not be a party. This Government will not cease to urge upon that of Great Britain full and ample remuneration for all losses, whether arising from detention or otherwise, to which American citizens have heretofore been or may hereafter be subjected by the exercise of rights which this Government can not recognize as legitimate and proper. Nor will I indulge a doubt but that the sense of justice of Great Britain will constrain her to make retribution for any wrong or loss which any American citizen engaged in the prosecution of lawful commerce may have experienced at the hands of her cruisers or other public authorities. This Government, at the same time, will relax no effort to prevent its citizens, if there be any so disposed, from prosecuting a traffic so revolting to the feelings of humanity. It seeks to do no more than to protect the fair and honest trader from molestation and injury; but while the enterprising mariner engaged in the pursuit of an honorable trade is entitled to its protection, it will visit with condign punishment others of an opposite character.

I invite your attention to existing laws for the suppression of the African slave trade, and recommend all such alterations as may give to them greater force and efficacy. That the American flag is grossly abused by the abandoned and profligate of other nations is but too probable. Congress has not long since had this subject under its consideration, and its importance well justifies renewed and anxious attention.

I also communicate herewith the copy of a correspondence between Mr. Stevenson and Lord Palmerston upon the subject, so interesting to several of the Southern States, of the rice duties, which resulted honorably to the justice of Great Britain and advantageously to the United States.

At the opening of the last annual session the President informed Congress of the progress which had then been made in negotiating a convention between this Government and that of England with a view to the final settlement of the question of the boundary between the territorial limits of the two countries. I regret to say that little further advancement of the object has been accomplished since last year, but this is owing to circumstances no way indicative of any abatement of the desire of both parties to hasten the negotiation to its conclusion and to settle the question in dispute as early as possible. In the course of the session it is my hope to be able to announce some further degree of progress toward the accomplishment of this highly desirable end.

The commission appointed by this Government for the exploration and survey of the line of boundary separating the States of Maine and New Hampshire from the conterminous British Provinces is, it is believed, about to close its field labors and is expected soon to report the results of its examinations to the Department of State. The report, when received, will be laid before Congress.

The failure on the part of Spain to pay with punctuality the interest due under the convention of 1834 for the settlement of claims between the two countries has made it the duty of the Executive to call the particular attention of that Government to the subject. A disposition has been manifested by it, which is believed to be entirely sincere, to fulfill its obligations in this respect so soon as its internal condition and the state of its finances will permit. An arrangement is in progress from the result of which it is trusted that those of our citizens who have claims under the convention will at no distant day receive the stipulated payments.

A treaty of commerce and navigation with Belgium was concluded and signed at Washington on the 29th of March, 1840, and was duly sanctioned by the Senate of the United States. The treaty was ratified by His Belgian Majesty, but did not receive the approbation of the Belgian Chambers within the time limited by its terms, and has therefore become void.

This occurrence assumes the graver aspect from the consideration that in 1833 a treaty negotiated between the two Governments and ratified on the part of the United States failed to be ratified on the part of Belgium. The representative of that Government at Washington informs the Department of State that he has been instructed to give explanations of the causes which occasioned delay in the approval of the late treaty by the legislature, and to express the regret of the King at the occurrence.

The joint commission under the convention with Texas to ascertain the true boundary between the two countries has concluded its labors, but the final report of the commissioner of the United States has not been received. It is understood, however, that the meridian line as traced by the commission lies somewhat farther east than the position hitherto generally assigned to it, and consequently includes in Texas some part of the territory which had been considered as belonging to the States of Louisiana and Arkansas.

The United States can not but take a deep interest in whatever relates to this young but growing Republic. Settled principally by emigrants from the United States, we have the happiness to know that the great principles of civil liberty are there destined to flourish under wise institutions and wholesome laws, and that through its example another evidence is to be afforded of the capacity of popular institutions to advance the prosperity, happiness, and permanent glory of the human race. The great truth that government was made for the people and not the people for government has already been established in the practice and by the example of these United States, and we can do no other than contemplate its further exemplification by a sister republic with the deepest interest.

Our relations with the independent States of this hemisphere, formerly under the dominion of Spain, have not undergone any material change within the past year. The incessant sanguinary conflicts in or between those countries are to be greatly deplored as necessarily tending to disable them from performing their duty as members of the community of nations and rising to the destiny which the position and natural resources of many of them might lead them justly to anticipate, as constantly giving occasion also, directly or indirectly, for complaints on the part of our citizens who resort thither for purposes of commercial intercourse, and as retarding reparation for wrongs already committed, some of which are by no means of recent date.

The failure of the Congress of Ecuador to hold a session at the time appointed for that purpose, in January last, will probably render abortive a treaty of commerce with that Republic, which was signed at Quito on the 13th of June, 1839, and had been duly ratified on our part, but which required the approbation of that body prior to its ratification by the Ecuadorian Executive.

A convention which has been concluded with the Republic of Peru, providing for the settlement of certain claims of citizens of the United States upon the Government of that Republic, will be duly submitted to the Senate.

The claims of our citizens against the Brazilian Government originating from captures and other causes are still unsatisfied. The United States have, however, so uniformly shown a disposition to cultivate relations of amity with that Empire that it is hoped the unequivocal tokens of the same spirit toward us which an adjustment of the affairs referred to would afford will be given without further avoidable delay.

The war with the Indian tribes on the peninsula of Florida has during the last summer and fall been prosecuted with untiring activity and zeal. A summer campaign was resolved upon as the best mode of bringing it to a close. Our brave officers and men who have been engaged in that service have suffered toils and privations and exhibited an energy which in any other war would have won for them unfading laurels. In despite of the sickness incident to the climate, they have penetrated the fastnesses of the Indians, broken up their encampments, and harassed them unceasingly. Numbers have been captured, and still greater numbers have surrendered and have been transported to join their brethren on the lands elsewhere allotted to them by the Government, and a strong hope is entertained that under the conduct of the gallant officer at the head of the troops in Florida that troublesome and expensive war is destined to a speedy termination. With all the other Indian tribes we are enjoying the blessings of peace. Our duty as well as our best interests prompts us to observe in all our intercourse with them fidelity in fulfilling our engagements, the practice of strict justice, as well as the constant exercise of acts of benevolence and kindness. These are the great instruments of civilization, and through the use of them alone can the untutored child of the forest be induced to listen to its teachings.

The Secretary of State, on whom the acts of Congress have devolved the duty of directing the proceedings for the taking of the sixth census or enumeration of the inhabitants of the United States, will report to the two Houses the progress of that work. The enumeration of persons has been completed, and exhibits a grand total of 17,069,453, making an increase over the census of 1830 of 4,202,646 inhabitants, and showing a gain in a ratio exceeding 32½ per cent for the last ten years.

From the report of the Secretary of the Treasury you will be informed of the condition of the finances. The balance in the Treasury on the 1st of January last, as stated in the report of the Secretary of the Treasury submitted to Congress at the extra session, was $987,345.03. The receipts into the Treasury during the first three quarters of this year from all sources amount to $23,467,072.52; the estimated receipts for the fourth quarter amount to $6,943,095.25, amounting to $30,410,167.77, and making with the balance in the Treasury on the 1st of January last $31,397,512.80. The expenditures for the first three quarters of this year amount to $24,734,346.97. The expenditures for the fourth quarter as estimated will amount to $7,290,723.73, thus making a total of $32,025,070.70, and leaving a deficit to be provided for on the 1st of January next of about $627,557.90.

Of the loan of $12,000,000 which was authorized by Congress at its late session only $5,432,726.88 have been negotiated. The shortness of time which it had to run has presented no inconsiderable impediment in the way of its being taken by capitalists at home, while the same cause would have operated with much greater force in the foreign market. For that reason the foreign market has not been resorted to; and it is now submitted whether it would not be advisable to amend the law by making what remains undisposed of payable at a more distant day.

Should it be necessary, in any view that Congress may take of the subject, to revise the existing tariff of duties, I beg leave to say that in the performance of that most delicate operation moderate counsels would seem to be the wisest. The Government under which it is our happiness to live owes its existence to the spirit of compromise which prevailed among its framers; jarring and discordant opinions could only have been reconciled by that noble spirit of patriotism which prompted conciliation and resulted in harmony. In the same spirit the compromise bill, as it is commonly called, was adopted at the session of 1833. While the people of no portion of the Union will ever hesitate to pay all necessary taxes for the support of Government, yet an innate repugnance exists to the imposition of burthens not really necessary for that object. In imposing duties, however, for the purposes of revenue a right to discriminate as to the articles on which the duty shall be laid, as well as the amount, necessarily and most properly exists; otherwise the Government would be placed in the condition of having to levy the same duties upon all articles, the productive as well as the unproductive. The slightest duty upon some might have the effect of causing their importation to cease, whereas others, entering extensively into the consumption of the country, might bear the heaviest without any sensible diminution in the amount imported. So also the Government may be justified in so discriminating by reference to other considerations of domestic policy connected with our manufactures. So long as the duties shall be laid with distinct reference to the wants of the Treasury no well-founded objection can exist against them. It might be esteemed desirable that no such augmentation of the taxes should take place as would have the effect of annulling the land-proceeds distribution act of the last session, which act is declared to be inoperative the moment the duties are increased beyond 20 per cent, the maximum rate established by the compromise act. Some of the provisions of the compromise act, which will go into effect on the 30th day of June next, may, however, be found exceedingly inconvenient in practice under any regulations that Congress may adopt. I refer more particularly to that relating to the home valuation. A difference in value of the same articles to some extent will necessarily exist at different ports, but that is altogether insignificant when compared with the conflicts in valuation which are likely to arise from the differences of opinion among the numerous appraisers of merchandise. In many instances the estimates of value must be conjectural, and thus as many different rates of value may be established as there are appraisers. These differences in valuation may also be increased by the inclination which, without the slightest imputation on their honesty, may arise on the part of the appraisers in favor of their respective ports of entry. I recommend this whole subject to the consideration of Congress with a single additional remark. Certainty and permanency in any system of governmental policy are in all respects eminently desirable, but more particularly is this true in all that affects trade and commerce, the operations of which depend much more on the certainty of their returns and calculations which embrace distant periods of time than on high bounties or duties, which are liable to constant fluctuations.

At your late session I invited your attention to the condition of the currency and exchanges and urged the necessity of adopting such measures as were consistent with the constitutional competency of the Government in order to correct the unsoundness of the one and, as far as practicable, the inequalities of the other. No country can be in the enjoyment of its full measure of prosperity without the presence of a medium of exchange approximating to uniformity of value. What is necessary as between the different nations of the earth is also important as between the inhabitants of different parts of the same country. With the first the precious metals constitute the chief medium of circulation, and such also would be the case as to the last but for inventions comparatively modern, which have furnished in place of gold and silver a paper circulation. I do not propose to enter into a comparative analysis of the merits of the two systems. Such belonged more properly to the period of the introduction of the paper system. The speculative philosopher might find inducements to prosecute the inquiry, but his researches could only lead him to conclude that the paper system had probably better never have been introduced and that society might have been much happier without it. The practical statesman has a very different task to perform. He has to look at things as they are, to take them as he finds them, to supply deficiencies and to prune excesses as far as in him lies. The task of furnishing a corrective for derangements of the paper medium with us is almost inexpressibly great. The power exerted by the States to charter banking corporations, and which, having been carried to a great excess, has filled the country with, in most of the States, an irredeemable paper medium, is an evil which in some way or other requires a corrective. The rates at which bills of exchange are negotiated between different parts of the country furnish an index of the value of the local substitute for gold and silver, which is in many parts so far depreciated as not to be received except at a large discount in payment of debts or in the purchase of produce. It could earnestly be desired that every bank not possessing the means of resumption should follow the example of the late United States Bank of Pennsylvania and go into liquidation rather than by refusing to do so to continue embarrassments in the way of solvent institutions, thereby augmenting the difficulties incident to the present condition of things. Whether this Government, with due regard to the rights of the States, has any power to constrain the banks either to resume specie payments or to force them into liquidation, is an inquiry which will not fail to claim your consideration. In view of the great advantages which are allowed the corporators, not among the least of which is the authority contained in most of their charters to make loans to three times the amount of their capital, thereby often deriving three times as much interest on the same amount of money as any individual is permitted by law to receive, no sufficient apology can be urged for a long-continued suspension of specie payments. Such suspension is productive of the greatest detriment to the public by expelling from circulation the precious metals and seriously hazarding the success of any effort that this Government can make to increase commercial facilities and to advance the public interests.

This is the more to be regretted and the indispensable necessity for a sound currency becomes the more manifest when we reflect on the vast amount of the internal commerce of the country. Of this we have no statistics nor just data for forming adequate opinions. But there can be no doubt but that the amount of transportation coastwise by sea, and the transportation inland by railroads and canals, and by steamboats and other modes of conveyance over the surface of our vast rivers and immense lakes, and the value of property carried and interchanged by these means form a general aggregate to which the foreign commerce of the country, large as it is, makes but a distant approach.

In the absence of any controlling power over this subject, which, by forcing a general resumption of specie payments, would at once have the effect of restoring a sound medium of exchange and would leave to the country but little to desire, what measure of relief falling within the limits of our constitutional competency does it become this Government to adopt? It was my painful duty at your last session, under the weight of most solemn obligations, to differ with Congress on the measures which it proposed for my approval, and which it doubtless regarded as corrective of existing evils. Subsequent reflection and events since occurring have only served to confirm me in the opinions then entertained and frankly expressed. I must be permitted to add that no scheme of governmental policy unaided by individual exertions can be available for ameliorating the present condition of things. Commercial modes of exchange and a good currency are but the necessary means of commerce and intercourse, not the direct productive sources of wealth. Wealth can only be accumulated by the earnings of industry and the savings of frugality, and nothing can be more ill judged than to look to facilities in borrowing or to a redundant circulation for the power of discharging pecuniary obligations. The country is full of resources and the people full of energy, and the great and permanent remedy for present embarrassments must be sought in industry, economy, the observance of good faith, and the favorable influence of time. In pursuance of a pledge given to you in my last message to Congress, which pledge I urge as an apology for adventuring to present you the details of any plan, the Secretary of the Treasury will be ready to submit to you, should you require it, a plan of finance which, while it throws around the public treasure reasonable guards for its protection and rests on powers acknowledged in practice to exist from the origin of the Government, will at the same time furnish to the country a sound paper medium and afford all reasonable facilities for regulating the exchanges. When submitted, you will perceive in it a plan amendatory of the existing laws in relation to the Treasury Department, subordinate in all respects to the will of Congress directly and the will of the people indirectly, self-sustaining should it be found in practice to realize its promises in theory, and repealable at the pleasure of Congress. It proposes by effectual restraints and by invoking the true spirit of our institutions to separate the purse from the sword, or, more properly to speak, denies any other control to the President over the agents who may be selected to carry it into execution but what may be indispensably necessary to secure the fidelity of such agents, and by wise regulations keeps plainly apart from each other private and public funds. It contemplates the establishment of a board of control at the seat of government, with agencies at prominent commercial points or wherever else Congress shall direct, for the safe-keeping and disbursement of the public moneys and a substitution at the option of the public creditor of Treasury notes in lieu of gold and silver. It proposes to limit the issues to an amount not to exceed $15,000,000 without the express sanction of the legislative power. It also authorizes the receipt of individual deposits of gold and silver to a limited amount, and the granting certificates of deposit divided into such sums as may be called for by the depositors. It proceeds a step further and authorizes the purchase and sale of domestic bills and drafts resting on a real and substantial basis, payable at sight or having but a short time to run, and drawn on places not less than 100 miles apart, which authority, except in so far as may be necessary for Government purposes exclusively, is only to be exerted upon the express condition that its exercise shall not be prohibited by the State in which the agency is situated. In order to cover the expenses incident to the plan, it will be authorized to receive moderate premiums for certificates issued on deposits and on bills bought and sold, and thus, as far as its dealings extend, to furnish facilities to commercial intercourse at the lowest possible rates and to subduct from the earnings of industry the least possible sum. It uses the State banks at a distance from the agencies as auxiliaries without imparting any power to trade in its name. It is subjected to such guards and restraints as have appeared to be necessary. It is the creature of law and exists only at the pleasure of the Legislature. It is made to rest on an actual specie basis in order to redeem the notes at the places of issue, produces no dangerous redundancy of circulation, affords no temptation to speculation, is attended by no inflation of prices, is equable in its operation, makes the Treasury notes (which it may use along with the certificates of deposit and the notes of specie-paying banks) convertible at the place where collected, receivable in payment of Government dues, and without violating any principle of the Constitution affords the Government and the people such facilities as are called for by the wants of both. Such, it has appeared to me, are its recommendations, and in view of them it will be submitted, whenever you may require it, to your consideration.

I am not able to perceive that any fair and candid objection can be urged against the plan, the principal outlines of which I have thus presented. I can not doubt but that the notes which it proposes to furnish at the voluntary option of the public creditor, issued in lieu of the revenue and its certificates of deposit, will be maintained at an equality with gold and silver everywhere. They are redeemable in gold and silver on demand at the places of issue. They are receivable everywhere in payment of Government dues. The Treasury notes are limited to an amount of one-fourth less than the estimated annual receipts of the Treasury, and in addition they rest upon the faith of the Government for their redemption. If all these assurances are not sufficient to make them available, then the idea, as it seems to me, of furnishing a sound paper medium of exchange may be entirely abandoned.

If a fear be indulged that the Government may be tempted to run into excess in its issues at any future day, it seems to me that no such apprehension can reasonably be entertained until all confidence in the representatives of the States and of the people, as well as of the people themselves, shall be lost. The weightiest considerations of policy require that the restraints now proposed to be thrown around the measure should not for light causes be removed. To argue against any proposed plan its liability to possible abuse is to reject every expedient, since everything dependent on human action is liable to abuse. Fifteen millions of Treasury notes may be issued as the *maximum*, but a discretionary power is to be given to the board of control under that sum, and every consideration will unite in leading them to feel their way with caution. For the first eight years of the existence of the late Bank of the United States its circulation barely exceeded $4,000,000, and for five of its most prosperous years it was about equal to $16,000,000; furthermore, the authority given to receive private deposits to a limited amount and to issue certificates in such sums as may be called for by the depositors may so far fill up the channels of circulation as greatly to diminish the necessity of any considerable issue of Treasury notes. A restraint upon the amount of private deposits has seemed to be indispensably necessary from an apprehension, thought to be well founded, that in any emergency of trade confidence might be so far shaken in the banks as to induce a withdrawal from them of private deposits with a view to insure their unquestionable safety when deposited with the Government, which might prove eminently disastrous to the State banks. Is it objected that it is proposed to authorize the agencies to deal in bills of exchange? It is answered that such dealings are to be carried on at the lowest possible premium, are made to rest on an unquestionably sound basis, are designed to reimburse merely the expenses which would otherwise devolve upon the Treasury, and are in strict subordination to the decision of the Supreme Court in the case of the Bank of Augusta against Earle, and other reported cases, and thereby avoids all conflict with State jurisdiction, which I hold to be indispensably requisite. It leaves the banking privileges of the States without interference, looks to the Treasury and the Union, and while furnishing every facility to the first is careful of the interests of the last. But above all, it is created by law, is amendable by law, and is repealable by law, and, wedded as I am to no theory, but looking solely to the advancement of the public good, I shall be among the very first to urge its repeal if it be found not to subserve the purposes and objects for which it may be created. Nor will the plan be submitted in any overweening confidence in the sufficiency of my own judgment, but with much greater reliance on the wisdom and patriotism of Congress. I can not abandon this subject without urging upon you in the most emphatic manner, whatever may be your action on the suggestions which I have felt it to be my duty to submit, to relieve the Chief Executive

Magistrate, by any and all constitutional means, from a controlling power over the public Treasury. If in the plan proposed, should you deem it worthy of your consideration, that separation is not as complete as you may desire, you will doubtless amend it in that particular. For myself, I disclaim all desire to have any control over the public moneys other than what is indispensably necessary to execute the laws which you may pass.

Nor can I fail to advert in this connection to the debts which many of the States of the Union have contracted abroad and under which they continue to labor. That indebtedness amounts to a sum not less than $200,000,000, and which has been retributed to them for the most part in works of internal improvement which are destined to prove of vast importance in ultimately advancing their prosperity and wealth. For the debts thus contracted the States are alone responsible. I can do no more than express the belief that each State will feel itself bound by every consideration of honor as well as of interest to meet its engagements with punctuality. The failure, however, of any one State to do so should in no degree affect the credit of the rest, and the foreign capitalist will have no just cause to experience alarm as to all other State stocks because any one or more of the States may neglect to provide with punctuality the means of redeeming their engagements. Even such States, should there be any, considering the great rapidity with which their resources are developing themselves, will not fail to have the means at no very distant day to redeem their obligations to the uttermost farthing; nor will I doubt but that, in view of that honorable conduct which has evermore governed the States and the people of the Union, they will each and all resort to every legitimate expedient before they will forego a faithful compliance with their obligations.

From the report of the Secretary of War and other reports accompanying it you will be informed of the progress which has been made in the fortifications designed for the protection of our principal cities, roadsteads, and inland frontier during the present year, together with their true state and condition. They will be prosecuted to completion with all the expedition which the means placed by Congress at the disposal of the Executive will allow.

I recommend particularly to your consideration that portion of the Secretary's report which proposes the establishment of a chain of military posts from Council Bluffs to some point on the Pacific Ocean within our limits. The benefit thereby destined to accrue to our citizens engaged in the fur trade over that wilderness region, added to the importance of cultivating friendly relations with savage tribes inhabiting it, and at the same time of giving protection to our frontier settlements and of establishing the means of safe intercourse between the American settlements at the mouth of the Columbia River and those on this side of the Rocky Mountains, would seem to suggest the importance of carrying into effect the recommendations upon this head with as little delay as may be practicable.

The report of the Secretary of the Navy will place you in possession of the present condition of that important arm of the national defense. Every effort will be made to add to its efficiency, and I can not too strongly urge upon you liberal appropriations to that branch of the public service.   Inducements of the weightiest character exist for the adoption of this course of policy.   Our extended and otherwise exposed maritime frontier calls for protection, to the furnishing of which an efficient naval force is indispensable.   We look to no foreign conquests, nor do we propose to enter into competition with any other nation for supremacy on the ocean; but it is due not only to the honor but to the security of the people of the United States that no nation should be permitted to invade our waters at pleasure and subject our towns and villages to conflagration or pillage.   Economy in all branches of the public service is due from all the public agents to the people, but parsimony alone would suggest the withholding of the necessary means for the protection of our domestic firesides from invasion and our national honor from disgrace. I would most earnestly recommend to Congress to abstain from all appropriations for objects not absolutely necessary; but I take upon myself, without a moment of hesitancy, all the responsibility of recommending the increase and prompt equipment of that gallant Navy which has lighted up every sea with its victories and spread an imperishable glory over the country.

The report of the Postmaster-General will claim your particular attention, not only because of the valuable suggestions which it contains, but because of the great importance which at all times attaches to that interesting branch of the public service.   The increased expense of transporting the mail along the principal routes necessarily claims the public attention, and has awakened a corresponding solicitude on the part of the Government.   The transmission of the mail must keep pace with those facilities of intercommunication which are every day becoming greater through the building of railroads and the application of steam power, but it can not be disguised that in order to do so the Post-Office Department is subjected to heavy exactions.   The lines of communication between distant parts of the Union are to a great extent occupied by railroads, which, in the nature of things, possess a complete monopoly, and the Department is therefore liable to heavy and unreasonable charges. This evil is destined to great increase in future, and some timely measure may become necessary to guard against it.

I feel it my duty to bring under your consideration a practice which has grown up in the administration of the Government, and which, I am deeply convinced, ought to be corrected.   I allude to the exercise of the power which usage rather than reason has vested in the Presidents of removing incumbents from office in order to substitute others more in favor with the dominant party.   My own conduct in this respect has been governed by a conscientious purpose to exercise the removing power only in cases of unfaithfulness or inability, or in those in which its exercise appeared necessary in order to discountenance and suppress that spirit of active partisanship on the part of holders of office which not only withdraws them from the steady and impartial discharge of their official duties, but exerts an undue and injurious influence over elections and degrades the character of the Government itself, inasmuch as it exhibits the Chief Magistrate as being a party through his agents in the secret plots or open workings of political parties.

In respect to the exercise of this power nothing should be left to discretion which may safely be regulated by law, and it is of high importance to restrain as far as possible the stimulus of personal interests in public elections. Considering the great increase which has been made in public offices in the last quarter of a century and the probability of further increase, we incur the hazard of witnessing violent political contests, directed too often to the single object of retaining office by those who are in or obtaining it by those who are out. Under the influence of these convictions I shall cordially concur in any constitutional measure for regulating and, by regulating, restraining the power of removal.

I suggest for your consideration the propriety of making without further delay some specific application of the funds derived under the will of Mr. Smithson, of England, for the diffusion of knowledge, and which have heretofore been vested in public stocks until such time as Congress should think proper to give them a specific direction. Nor will you, I feel confident, permit any abatement of the principal of the legacy to be made should it turn out that the stocks in which the investments have been made have undergone a depreciation.

In conclusion I commend to your care the interests of this District, for which you are the exclusive legislators. Considering that this city is the residence of the Government and for a large part of the year of Congress, and considering also the great cost of the public buildings and the propriety of affording them at all times careful protection, it seems not unreasonable that Congress should contribute toward the expense of an efficient police.

SECOND ANNUAL MESSAGE.

WASHINGTON, *December 6, 1842.*

To the Senate and House of Representatives of the United States:

We have continued reason to express our profound gratitude to the Great Creator of All Things for numberless benefits conferred upon us as

a people.   Blessed with genial seasons, the husbandman has his garners
filled with abundance, and the necessaries of life, not to speak of its luxuries, abound in every direction.   While in some other nations steady
and industrious labor can hardly find the means of subsistence, the greatest evil which we have to encounter is a surplus of production beyond
the home demand, which seeks, and with difficulty finds, a partial market in other regions.   The health of the country, with partial exceptions,
has for the past year been well preserved, and under their free and wise
institutions the United States are rapidly advancing toward the consummation of the high destiny which an overruling Providence seems to have
marked out for them.   Exempt from domestic convulsion and at peace
with all the world, we are left free to consult as to the best means of
securing and advancing the happiness of the people.   Such are the circumstances under which you now assemble in your respective chambers
and which should lead us to unite in praise and thanksgiving to that
great Being who made us and who preserves us as a nation.

I congratulate you, fellow-citizens, on the happy change in the aspect
of our foreign affairs since my last annual message.   Causes of complaint
at that time existed between the United States and Great Britain which,
attended by irritating circumstances, threatened most seriously the public peace.   The difficulty of adjusting amicably the questions at issue
between the two countries was in no small degree augmented by the
lapse of time since they had their origin.   The opinions entertained by
the Executive on several of the leading topics in dispute were frankly
set forth in the message at the opening of your late session.   The
appointment of a special minister by Great Britain to the United States
with power to negotiate upon most of the points of difference indicated
a desire on her part amicably to adjust them, and that minister was met
by the Executive in the same spirit which had dictated his mission.
The treaty consequent thereon having been duly ratified by the two
Governments, a copy, together with the correspondence which accompanied it, is herewith communicated.   I trust that whilst you may see in
it nothing objectionable, it may be the means of preserving for an indefinite period the amicable relations happily existing between the two Governments.   The question of peace or war between the United States and
Great Britain is a question of the deepest interest, not only to themselves, but to the civilized world, since it is scarcely possible that a war
could exist between them without endangering the peace of Christendom.   The immediate effect of the treaty upon ourselves will be felt in
the security afforded to mercantile enterprise, which, no longer apprehensive of interruption, adventures its speculations in the most distant
seas, and, freighted with the diversified productions of every land, returns
to bless our own.   There is nothing in the treaty which in the slightest
degree compromits the honor or dignity of either nation.   Next to the
settlement of the boundary line, which must always be a matter of diffi-

culty between states as between individuals, the question which seemed to threaten the greatest embarrassment was that connected with the African slave trade.

By the tenth article of the treaty of Ghent it was expressly declared that—

Whereas the traffic in slaves is irreconcilable with the principles of humanity and justice, and whereas both His Majesty and the United States are desirous of continuing their efforts to promote its entire abolition, it is hereby agreed that both the contracting parties shall use their best endeavors to accomplish so desirable an object.

In the enforcement of the laws and treaty stipulations of Great Britain a practice had threatened to grow up on the part of its cruisers of subjecting to visitation ships sailing under the American flag, which, while it seriously involved our maritime rights, would subject to vexation a branch of our trade which was daily increasing, and which required the fostering care of Government. And although Lord Aberdeen in his correspondence with the American envoys at London expressly disclaimed all right to detain an American ship on the high seas, even if found with a cargo of slaves on board, and restricted the British pretension to a mere claim to visit and inquire, yet it could not well be discerned by the Executive of the United States how such visit and inquiry could be made without detention on the voyage and consequent interruption to the trade. It was regarded as the right of search presented only in a new form and expressed in different words, and I therefore felt it to be my duty distinctly to declare in my annual message to Congress that no such concession could be made, and that the United States had both the will and the ability to enforce their own laws and to protect their flag from being used for purposes wholly forbidden by those laws and obnoxious to the moral censure of the world. Taking the message as his letter of instructions, our then minister at Paris felt himself required to assume the same ground in a remonstrance which he felt it to be his duty to present to Mr. Guizôt, and through him to the King of the French, against what has been called the "quintuple treaty;" and his conduct in this respect met with the approval of this Government. In close conformity with these views the eighth article of the treaty was framed, which provides "that each nation shall keep afloat in the African seas a force not less than 80 guns, to act separately and apart, under instructions from their respective Governments, and for the enforcement of their respective laws and obligations." From this it will be seen that the ground assumed in the message has been fully maintained at the same time that the stipulations of the treaty of Ghent are to be carried out in good faith by the two countries, and that all pretense is removed for interference with our commerce for any purpose whatever by a foreign government. While, therefore, the United States have been standing up for the freedom of the seas, they have not thought proper to make that a pretext for avoiding a fulfillment of their treaty stipulations or a ground for giving countenance to a trade reprobated by our laws. A similar arrangement by the other great powers could not fail to sweep from the ocean the slave trade without the interpolation of any new principle into the maritime code. We may be permitted to hope that the example thus set will be followed by some if not all of them. We thereby also afford suitable protection to the fair trader in those seas, thus fulfilling at the same time the dictates of a sound policy and complying with the claims of justice and humanity.

It would have furnished additional cause for congratulation if the treaty could have embraced all subjects calculated in future to lead to a misunderstanding between the two Governments. The Territory of the United States commonly called the Oregon Territory, lying on the Pacific Ocean north of the forty-second degree of latitude, to a portion of which Great Britain lays claim, begins to attract the attention of our fellow-citizens, and the tide of population which has reclaimed what was so lately an unbroken wilderness in more contiguous regions is preparing to flow over those vast districts which stretch from the Rocky Mountains to the Pacific Ocean. In advance of the acquirement of individual rights to these lands, sound policy dictates that every effort should be resorted to by the two Governments to settle their respective claims. It became manifest at an early hour of the late negotiations that any attempt for the time being satisfactorily to determine those rights would lead to a protracted discussion, which might embrace in its failure other more pressing matters, and the Executive did not regard it as proper to waive all the advantages of an honorable adjustment of other difficulties of great magnitude and importance because this, not so immediately pressing, stood in the way. Although the difficulty referred to may not for several years to come involve the peace of the two countries, yet I shall not delay to urge on Great Britain the importance of its early settlement. Nor will other matters of commercial importance to the two countries be overlooked, and I have good reason to believe that it will comport with the policy of England, as it does with that of the United States, to seize upon this moment, when most of the causes of irritation have passed away, to cement the peace and amity of the two countries by wisely removing all grounds of probable future collision.

With the other powers of Europe our relations continue on the most amicable footing. Treaties now existing with them should be rigidly observed, and every opportunity compatible with the interests of the United States should be seized upon to enlarge the basis of commercial intercourse. Peace with all the world is the true foundation of our policy, which can only be rendered permanent by the practice of equal and impartial justice to all. Our great desire should be to enter only into that rivalry which looks to the general good in the cultivation of the sciences, the enlargement of the field for the exercise of the mechanical arts, and the spread of commerce—that great civilizer—to every land and sea. Carefully abstaining from interference in all questions exclusively referring themselves to the political interests of Europe, we may be permitted to hope an equal exemption from the interference of European Governments in what relates to the States of the American continent.

On the 23d of April last the commissioners on the part of the United States under the convention with the Mexican Republic of the 11th of April, 1839, made to the proper Department a final report in relation to the proceedings of the commission. From this it appears that the total amount awarded to the claimants by the commissioners and the umpire appointed under that convention was $2,026,079.68. The arbiter having considered that his functions were required by the convention to terminate at the same time with those of the commissioners, returned to the board, undecided for want of time, claims which had been allowed by the American commissioners to the amount of $928,620.88. Other claims, in which the amount sought to be recovered was $3,336,837.05, were submitted to the board too late for its consideration. The minister of the United States at Mexico has been duly authorized to make demand for payment of the awards according to the terms of the convention and the provisions of the act of Congress of the 12th of June, 1840. He has also been instructed to communicate to that Government the expectations of the Government of the United States in relation to those claims which were not disposed of according to the provisions of the convention, and all others of citizens of the United States against the Mexican Government. He has also been furnished with other instructions, to be followed by him in case the Government of Mexico should not find itself in a condition to make present payment of the amount of the awards in specie or its equivalent.

I am happy to be able to say that information which is esteemed favorable both to a just satisfaction of the awards and a reasonable provision for other claims has been recently received from Mr. Thompson, the minister of the United States, who has promptly and efficiently executed the instructions of his Government in regard to this important subject.

The citizens of the United States who accompanied the late Texan expedition to Santa Fe, and who were wrongfully taken and held as prisoners of war in Mexico, have all been liberated.

A correspondence has taken place between the Department of State and the Mexican minister of foreign affairs upon the complaint of Mexico that citizens of the United States were permitted to give aid to the inhabitants of Texas in the war existing between her and that Republic. Copies of this correspondence are herewith communicated to Congress, together with copies of letters on the same subject addressed to the diplomatic corps at Mexico by the American minister and the Mexican secretary of state.

Mexico has thought proper to reciprocate the mission of the United

States to that Government by accrediting to this a minister of the same rank as that of the representative of the United States in Mexico. From the circumstances connected with his mission favorable results are anticipated from it. It is so obviously for the interest of both countries as neighbors and friends that all just causes of mutual dissatisfaction should be removed that it is to be hoped neither will omit or delay the employment of any practicable and honorable means to accomplish that end.

The affairs pending between this Government and several others of the States of this hemisphere formerly under the dominion of Spain have again within the past year been materially obstructed by the military revolutions and conflicts in those countries.

The ratifications of the treaty between the United States and the Republic of Ecuador of the 13th of June, 1839, have been exchanged, and that instrument has been duly promulgated on the part of this Government. Copies are now communicated to Congress with a view to enable that body to make such changes in the laws applicable to our intercourse with that Republic as may be deemed requisite.

Provision has been made by the Government of Chile for the payment of the claim on account of the illegal detention of the brig *Warrior* at Coquimbo in 1820. This Government has reason to expect that other claims of our citizens against Chile will be hastened to a final and satisfactory close.

The Empire of Brazil has not been altogether exempt from those convulsions which so constantly afflict the neighboring republics. Disturbances which recently broke out are, however, now understood to be quieted. But these occurrences, by threatening the stability of the governments, or by causing incessant and violent changes in them or in the persons who administer them, tend greatly to retard provisions for a just indemnity for losses and injuries suffered by individual subjects or citizens of other states. The Government of the United States will feel it to be its duty, however, to consent to no delay not unavoidable in making satisfaction for wrongs and injuries sustained by its own citizens. Many years having in some cases elapsed, a decisive and effectual course of proceeding will be demanded of the respective governments against whom claims have been preferred.

The vexatious, harassing, and expensive war which so long prevailed with the Indian tribes inhabiting the peninsula of Florida has happily been terminated, whereby our Army has been relieved from a service of the most disagreeable character and the Treasury from a large expenditure. Some casual outbreaks may occur, such as are incident to the close proximity of border settlers and the Indians, but these, as in all other cases, may be left to the care of the local authorities, aided when occasion may require by the forces of the United States. A sufficient number of troops will be maintained in Florida so long as the remotest apprehensions of danger shall exist, yet their duties will be limited rather to the garrisoning of the necessary posts than to the maintenance of active hostilities. It is to be hoped that a territory so long retarded in its growth will now speedily recover from the evils incident to a protracted war, exhibiting in the increased amount of its rich productions true evidences of returning wealth and prosperity. By the practice of rigid justice toward the numerous Indian tribes residing within our territorial limits and the exercise of a parental vigilance over their interests, protecting them against fraud and intrusion, and at the same time using every proper expedient to introduce among them the arts of civilized life, we may fondly hope not only to wean them from their love of war, but to inspire them with a love for peace and all its avocations. With several of the tribes great progress in civilizing them has already been made. The schoolmaster and the missionary are found side by side, and the remnants of what were once numerous and powerful nations may yet be preserved as the builders up of a new name for themselves and their posterity.

The balance in the Treasury on the 1st of January, 1842, exclusive of the amount deposited with the States, trust funds, and indemnities, was $230,483.68. The receipts into the Treasury during the three first quarters of the present year from all sources amount to $26,616,593.78, of which more than fourteen millions were received from customs and about one million from the public lands. The receipts for the fourth quarter are estimated at nearly eight millions, of which four millions are expected from customs and three millions and a half from loans and Treasury notes. The expenditures of the first three quarters of the present year exceed twenty-six millions, and those estimated for the fourth quarter amount to about eight millions; and it is anticipated there will be a deficiency of half a million on the 1st of January next, but that the amount of outstanding warrants (estimated at $800,000) will leave an actual balance of about $224,000 in the Treasury. Among the expenditures of this year are more than eight millions for the public debt and about $600,000 on account of the distribution to the States of the proceeds of sales of the public lands.

The present tariff of duties was somewhat hastily and hurriedly passed near the close of the late session of Congress. That it should have defects can therefore be surprising to no one. To remedy such defects as may be found to exist in any of its numerous provisions will not fail to claim your serious attention. It may well merit inquiry whether the exaction of all duties in cash does not call for the introduction of a system which has proved highly beneficial in countries where it has been adopted. I refer to the warehousing system. The first and most prominent effect which it would produce would be to protect the market alike against redundant or deficient supplies of foreign fabrics, both of which in the long run are injurious as well to the manufacturer as the importer. The quantity of goods in store being at all times readily known, it would

enable the importer with an approach to accuracy to ascertain the actual
wants of the market and to regulate himself accordingly. If, however,
he should fall into error by importing an excess above the public wants,
he could readily correct its evils by availing himself of the benefits and
advantages of the system thus established. In the storehouse the goods
imported would await the demand of the market and their issues would
be governed by the fixed principles of demand and supply. Thus an
approximation would be made to a steadiness and uniformity of price,
which if attainable would conduce to the decided advantage of mercantile and mechanical operations.

The apprehension may be well entertained that without something to
ameliorate the rigor of cash payments the entire import trade may fall
into the hands of a few wealthy capitalists in this country and in Europe.
The small importer, who requires all the money he can raise for investments abroad, and who can but ill afford to pay the lowest duty, would
have to subduct in advance a portion of his funds in order to pay the
duties, and would lose the interest upon the amount thus paid for all
the time the goods might remain unsold, which might absorb his profits.
The rich capitalist, abroad as well as at home, would thus possess after
a short time an almost exclusive monopoly of the import trade, and laws
designed for the benefit of all would thus operate for the benefit of a
few—a result wholly uncongenial with the spirit of our institutions and
antirepublican in all its tendencies. The warehousing system would
enable the importer to watch the market and to select his own time for
offering his goods for sale. A profitable portion of the carrying trade in
articles entered for the benefit of drawback must also be most seriously
affected without the adoption of some expedient to relieve the cash system. The warehousing system would afford that relief, since the carrier
would have a safe recourse to the public storehouses and might without
advancing the duty reship within some reasonable period to foreign ports.
A further effect of the measure would be to supersede the system of
drawbacks, thereby effectually protecting the Government against fraud,
as the right of debenture would not attach to goods after their withdrawal
from the public stores.

In revising the existing tariff of duties, should you deem it proper to
do so at your present session, I can only repeat the suggestions and recommendations which upon several occasions I have heretofore felt it to
be my duty to offer to Congress. The great primary and controlling
interest of the American people is union—union not only in the mere
forms of government, forms which may be broken, but union founded
in an attachment of States and individuals for each other. This union
in sentiment and feeling can only be preserved by the adoption of that
course of policy which, neither giving exclusive benefits to some nor
imposing unnecessary burthens upon others, shall consult the interests
of all by pursuing a course of moderation and thereby seeking to harmo-

nize public opinion, and causing the people everywhere to feel and to know that the Government is careful of the interests of all alike. Nor is there any subject in regard to which moderation, connected with a wise discrimination, is more necessary than in the imposition of duties on imports. Whether reference be had to revenue, the primary object in the imposition of taxes, or to the incidents which necessarily flow from their imposition, this is entirely true. Extravagant duties defeat their end and object, not only by exciting in the public mind an hostility to the manufacturing interests, but by inducing a system of smuggling on an extensive scale and the practice of every manner of fraud upon the revenue, which the utmost vigilance of Government can not effectually suppress. An opposite course of policy would be attended by results essentially different, of which every interest of society, and none more than those of the manufacturer, would reap important advantages. Among the most striking of its benefits would be that derived from the general acquiescence of the country in its support and the consequent permanency and stability which would be given to all the operations of industry. It can not be too often repeated that no system of legislation can be wise which is fluctuating and uncertain. No interest can thrive under it. The prudent capitalist will never adventure his capital in manufacturing establishments, or in any other leading pursuit of life, if there exists a state of uncertainty as to whether the Government will repeal to-morrow what it has enacted to-day. Fitful profits, however high, if threatened with a ruinous reduction by a vacillating policy on the part of Government, will scarcely tempt him to trust the money which he has acquired by a life of labor upon the uncertain adventure. I therefore, in the spirit of conciliation, and influenced by no other desire than to rescue the great interests of the country from the vortex of political contention, and in the discharge of the high and solemn duties of the place which I now occupy, recommend moderate duties, imposed with a wise discrimination as to their several objects, as being not only most likely to be durable, but most advantageous to every interest of society.

The report of the Secretary of the War Department exhibits a very full and satisfactory account of the various and important interests committed to the charge of that officer. It is particularly gratifying to find that the expenditures for the military service are greatly reduced in amount—that a strict system of economy has been introduced into the service and the abuses of past years greatly reformed. The fortifications on our maritime frontier have been prosecuted with much vigor, and at many points our defenses are in a very considerable state of forwardness. The suggestions in reference to the establishment of means of communication with our territories on the Pacific and to the surveys so essential to a knowledge of the resources of the intermediate country are entitled to the most favorable consideration. While I would propose nothing inconsistent with friendly negotiations to settle the extent of our claims in that region, yet a prudent forecast points out the necessity of such measures as may enable us to maintain our rights.   The arrangements made for preserving our neutral relations on the boundary between us and Texas and keeping in check the Indians in that quarter will be maintained so long as circumstances may require.   For several years angry contentions have grown out of the disposition directed by law to be made of the mineral lands held by the Government in several of the States.   The Government is constituted the landlord, and the citizens of the States wherein lie the lands are its tenants.   The relation is an unwise one, and it would be much more conducive of the public interest that a sale of the lands should be made than that they should remain in their present condition.   The supply of the ore would be more abundantly and certainly furnished when to be drawn from the enterprise and the industry of the proprietor than under the present system.

The recommendations of the Secretary in regard to the improvements of the Western waters and certain prominent harbors on the Lakes merit, and I doubt not will receive, your serious attention.   The great importance of these subjects to the prosperity of the extensive region referred to and the security of the whole country in time of war can not escape observation.   The losses of life and property which annually occur in the navigation of the Mississippi alone because of the dangerous obstructions in the river make a loud demand upon Congress for the adoption of efficient measures for their removal.

The report of the Secretary of the Navy will bring you acquainted with that important branch of the public defenses.   Considering the already vast and daily increasing commerce of the country, apart from the exposure to hostile inroad of an extended seaboard, all that relates to the Navy is calculated to excite particular attention.   Whatever tends to add to its efficiency without entailing unnecessary charges upon the Treasury is well worthy of your serious consideration.   It will be seen that while an appropriation exceeding by more than a million the appropriations of the current year is asked by the Secretary, yet that in this sum is proposed to be included $400,000 for the purchase of clothing, which when once expended will be annually reimbursed by the sale of the clothes, and will thus constitute a perpetual fund without any new appropriation to the same object.   To this may also be added $50,000 asked to cover the arrearages of past years and $250,000 in order to maintain a competent squadron on the coast of Africa; all of which when deducted will reduce the expenditures nearly within the limits of those of the current year.   While, however, the expenditures will thus remain very nearly the same as of the antecedent year, it is proposed to add greatly to the operations of the marine, and in lieu of only 25 ships in commission and but little in the way of building, to keep with the same expenditure 41 vessels afloat and to build 12 ships of a small class.

A strict system of accountability is established and great pains are taken to insure industry, fidelity, and economy in every department of duty. Experiments have been instituted to test the quality of various materials, particularly copper, iron, and coal, so as to prevent fraud and imposition.

It will appear by the report of the Postmaster-General that the great point which for several years has been so much desired has during the current year been fully accomplished. The expenditures of the Department for current service have been brought within its income without lessening its general usefulness. There has been an increase of revenue equal to $166,000 for the year 1842 over that of 1841, without, as it is believed, any addition having been made to the number of letters and newspapers transmitted through the mails. The post-office laws have been honestly administered, and fidelity has been observed in accounting for and paying over by the subordinates of the Department the moneys which have been received. For the details of the service I refer you to the report.

I flatter myself that the exhibition thus made of the condition of the public administration will serve to convince you that every proper attention has been paid to the interests of the country by those who have been called to the heads of the different Departments. The reduction in the annual expenditures of the Government already accomplished furnishes a sure evidence that economy in the application of the public moneys is regarded as a paramount duty.

At peace with all the world, the personal liberty of the citizen sacredly maintained and his rights secured under political institutions deriving all their authority from the direct sanction of the people, with a soil fertile almost beyond example and a country blessed with every diversity of climate and production, what remains to be done in order to advance the happiness and prosperity of such a people? Under ordinary circumstances this inquiry could readily be answered. The best that probably could be done for a people inhabiting such a country would be to fortify their peace and security in the prosecution of their various pursuits by guarding them against invasion from without and violence from within. The rest for the greater part might be left to their own energy and enterprise. The chief embarrassments which at the moment exhibit themselves have arisen from overaction, and the most difficult task which remains to be accomplished is that of correcting and overcoming its effects. Between the years 1833 and 1838 additions were made to bank capital and bank issues, in the form of notes designed for circulation, to an extent enormously great. The question seemed to be not how the best currency could be provided, but in what manner the greatest amount of bank paper could be put in circulation. Thus a vast amount of what was called money—since for the time being it answered the purposes of money—was thrown upon the country, an overissue which was attended, as a necessary consequence, by an extravagant increase of the prices of all articles of property, the spread of a speculative mania all over the country, and has finally ended in a general indebtedness on the part of States and individuals, the prostration of public and private credit, a depreciation in the market value of real and personal estate, and has left large districts of country almost entirely without any circulating medium. In view of the fact that in 1830 the whole bank-note circulation within the United States amounted to but $61,323,898, according to the Treasury statements, and that an addition had been made thereto of the enormous sum of $88,000,000 in seven years (the circulation on the 1st of January, 1837, being stated at $149,185,890), aided by the great facilities afforded in obtaining loans from European capitalists, who were seized with the same speculative *mania* which prevailed in the United States, and the large importations of funds from abroad—the result of stock sales and loans—no one can be surprised at the apparent but unsubstantial state of prosperity which everywhere prevailed over the land; and as little cause of surprise should be felt at the present prostration of everything and the ruin which has befallen so many of our fellow-citizens in the sudden withdrawal from circulation of so large an amount of bank issues since 1837—exceeding, as is believed, the amount added to the paper currency for a similar period antecedent to 1837—it ceases to be a matter of astonishment that such extensive shipwreck should have been made of private fortunes or that difficulties should exist in meeting their engagements on the part of the debtor States; apart from which, if there be taken into account the immense losses sustained in the dishonor of numerous banks, it is less a matter of surprise that insolvency should have visited many of our fellow-citizens than that so many should have escaped the blighting influences of the times.

In the solemn conviction of these truths and with an ardent desire to meet the pressing necessities of the country, I felt it to be my duty to cause to be submitted to you at the commencement of your last session the plan of an exchequer, the whole power and duty of maintaining which in purity and vigor was to be exercised by the representatives of the people and the States, and therefore virtually by the people themselves. It was proposed to place it under the control and direction of a Treasury board to consist of three commissioners, whose duty it should be to see that the law of its creation was faithfully executed and that the great end of supplying a paper medium of exchange at all times convertible into gold and silver should be attained. The board thus constituted was given as much permanency as could be imparted to it without endangering the proper share of responsibility which should attach to all public agents. In order to insure all the advantages of a well-matured experience, the commissioners were to hold their offices for the respective periods of two, four, and six years, thereby securing at all times in the management of the exchequer the services of two men of experience; and

to place them in a condition to exercise perfect independence of mind
and action it was provided that their removal should only take place for
actual incapacity or infidelity to the trust, and to be followed by the President with an exposition of the causes of such removal, should it occur.
It was proposed to establish subordinate boards in each of the States,
under the same restrictions and limitations of the power of removal, which,
with the central board, should receive, safely keep, and disburse the public moneys.   And in order to furnish a sound paper medium of exchange
the exchequer should retain of the revenues of the Government a sum not
to exceed $5,000,000 in specie, to be set apart as required by its opera-
tions, and to pay the public creditor at his own option either in specie or
Treasury notes of denominations not less than $5 nor exceeding $100,
which notes should be redeemed at the several places of issue, and to be
receivable at all times and everywhere in payment of Government dues,
with a restraint upon such issue of bills that the same should not exceed
the *maximum* of $15,000,000.   In order to guard against all the haz-
ards incident to fluctuations in trade, the Secretary of the Treasury was
invested with authority to issue $5,000,000 of Government stock, should
the same at any time be regarded as necessary in order to place beyond
hazard the prompt redemption of the bills which might be thrown into
circulation; thus in fact making the issue of $15,000,000 of exchequer
bills rest substantially on $10,000,000, and keeping in circulation never
more than one and one-half dollars for every dollar in specie. When to this
it is added that the bills are not only everywhere receivable in Government dues, but that the Government itself would be bound for their ultimate redemption, no rational doubt can exist that the paper which the
exchequer would furnish would readily enter into general circulation
and be maintained at all times at or above par with gold and silver,
thereby realizing the great want of the age and fulfilling the wishes of
the people.   In order to reimburse the Government the expenses of the
plan, it was proposed to invest the exchequer with the limited authority
to deal in bills of exchange (unless prohibited by the State in which an
agency might be situated) having only thirty days to run and resting on a
fair and *bona fide* basis.   The legislative will on this point might be so
plainly announced as to avoid all pretext for partiality or favoritism.
It was furthermore proposed to invest this Treasury agent with authority
to receive on deposit to a limited amount the specie funds of individuals
and to grant certificates therefor to be redeemed on presentation, under
the idea, which is believed to be well founded, that such certificates would
come in aid of the exchequer bills in supplying a safe and ample paper
circulation.   Or if in place of the contemplated dealings in exchange the
exchequer should be authorized not only to exchange its bills for actual
deposits of specie, but, for specie or its equivalent, to sell drafts, charging
therefor a small but reasonable premium, I can not doubt but that the
benefits of the law would be speedily manifested in the revival of the credit,

trade, and business of the whole country. Entertaining this opinion, it becomes my duty to urge its adoption upon Congress by reference to the strongest considerations of the public interests, with such alterations in its details as Congress may in its wisdom see fit to make.

I am well aware that this proposed alteration and amendment of the laws establishing the Treasury Department has encountered various objections, and that among others it has been proclaimed a Government bank of fearful and dangerous import. It is proposed to confer upon it no extraordinary power. It purports to do no more than pay the debts of the Government with the redeemable paper of the Government, in which respect it accomplishes precisely what the Treasury does daily at this time in issuing to the public creditors the Treasury notes which under law it is authorized to issue. It has no resemblance to an ordinary bank, as it furnishes no profits to private stockholders and lends no capital to individuals. If it be objected to as a Government bank and the objection be available, then should all the laws in relation to the Treasury be repealed and the capacity of the Government to collect what is due to it or pay what it owes be abrogated.

This is the chief purpose of the proposed exchequer, and surely if in the accomplishment of a purpose so essential it affords a sound circulating medium to the country and facilities to trade it should be regarded as no slight recommendation of it to public consideration. Properly guarded by the provisions of law, it can run into no dangerous evil, nor can any abuse arise under it but such as the Legislature itself will be answerable for if it be tolerated, since it is but the creature of the law and is susceptible at all times of modification, amendment, or repeal at the pleasure of Congress. I know that it has been objected that the system would be liable to be abused by the Legislature, by whom alone it could be abused, in the party conflicts of the day; that such abuse would manifest itself in a change of the law which would authorize an excessive issue of paper for the purpose of inflating prices and winning popular favor. To that it may be answered that the ascription of such a motive to Congress is altogether gratuitous and inadmissible. The theory of our institutions would lead us to a different conclusion. But a perfect security against a proceeding so reckless would be found to exist in the very nature of things. The political party which should be so blind to the true interests of the country as to resort to such an expedient would inevitably meet with final overthrow in the fact that the moment the paper ceased to be convertible into specie or otherwise promptly redeemed it would become worthless, and would in the end dishonor the Government, involve the people in ruin and such political party in hopeless disgrace. At the same time, such a view involves the utter impossibility of furnishing any currency other than that of the precious metals; for if the Government itself can not forego the temptation of excessive paper issues what reliance can be placed in corporations upon whom the temptations of individual aggrandizement would most strongly operate? The people would have to blame none but themselves for any injury that might arise from a course so reckless, since their agents would be the wrongdoers and they the passive spectators.

There can be but three kinds of public currency—first, gold and silver; second, the paper of State institutions; or, third, a representative of the precious metals provided by the General Government or under its authority. The subtreasury system rejected the last in any form, and as it was believed that no reliance could be placed on the issues of local institutions for the purposes of general circulation it necessarily and unavoidably adopted specie as the exclusive currency for its own use; and this must ever be the case unless one of the other kinds be used. The choice in the present state of public sentiment lies between an exclusive specie currency on the one hand and Government issues of some kind on the other. That these issues can not be made by a chartered institution is supposed to be conclusively settled. They must be made, then, directly by Government agents. For several years past they have been thus made in the form of Treasury notes, and have answered a valuable purpose. Their usefulness has been limited by their being transient and temporary; their ceasing to bear interest at given periods necessarily causes their speedy return and thus restricts their range of circulation, and being used only in the disbursements of Government they can not reach those points where they are most required. By rendering their use permanent, to the moderate extent already mentioned, by offering no inducement for their return and by exchanging them for coin and other values, they will constitute to a certain extent the general currency so much needed to maintain the internal trade of the country. And this is the exchequer plan so far as it may operate in furnishing a currency.

I can not forego the occasion to urge its importance to the credit of the Government in a financial point of view. The great necessity of resorting to every proper and becoming expedient in order to place the Treasury on a footing of the highest respectability is entirely obvious. The credit of the Government may be regarded as the very soul of the Government itself—a principle of vitality without which all its movements are languid and all its operations embarrassed. In this spirit the Executive felt itself bound by the most imperative sense of duty to submit to Congress at its last session the propriety of making a specific pledge of the land fund as the basis for the negotiation of the loans authorized to be contracted. I then thought that such an application of the public domain would without doubt have placed at the command of the Government ample funds to relieve the Treasury from the temporary embarrassments under which it labored. American credit has suffered a considerable shock in Europe from the large indebtedness of the States and the temporary inability of some of them to meet the interest on their debts. The utter and disastrous prostration of the United States Bank of Pennsylvania had contributed largely to increase the sentiment of distrust by reason of the loss and ruin sustained by the holders of its stock, a large portion of whom were foreigners and many of whom were alike ignorant of our political organization and of our actual responsibilities.

It was the anxious desire of the Executive that in the effort to negotiate the loan abroad the American negotiator might be able to point the money lender to the fund mortgaged for the redemption of the principal and interest of any loan he might contract, and thereby vindicate the Government from all suspicion of bad faith or inability to meet its engagements. Congress differed from the Executive in this view of the subject. It became, nevertheless, the duty of the Executive to resort to every expedient in its power to do so.

After a failure in the American market a citizen of high character and talent was sent to Europe, with no better success; and thus the mortifying spectacle has been presented of the inability of this Government to obtain a loan so small as not in the whole to amount to more than one-fourth of its ordinary annual income, at a time when the Governments of Europe, although involved in debt and with their subjects heavily burthened with taxation, readily obtained loans of any amount at a greatly reduced rate of interest. It would be unprofitable to look further into this anomalous state of things, but I can not conclude without adding that for a Government which has paid off its debts of two wars with the largest maritime power of Europe, and now owing a debt which is almost next to nothing when compared with its boundless resources—a Government the strongest in the world, because emanating from the popular will and firmly rooted in the affections of a great and free people, and whose fidelity to its engagements has never been questioned—for such a Government to have tendered to the capitalists of other countries an opportunity for a small investment in its stock, and yet to have failed, implies either the most unfounded distrust in its good faith or a purpose to obtain which the course pursued is the most fatal which could have been adopted. It has now become obvious to all men that the Government must look to its own means for supplying its wants, and it is consoling to know that these means are altogether adequate for the object. The exchequer, if adopted, will greatly aid in bringing about this result. Upon what I regard as a well-founded supposition that its bills would be readily sought for by the public creditors and that the issue would in a short time reach the maximum of $15,000,000, it is obvious that $10,000,000 would thereby be added to the available means of the Treasury without cost or charge. Nor can I fail to urge the great and beneficial effects which would be produced in aid of all the active pursuits of life. Its effects upon the solvent State banks, while it would force into liquidation those of an opposite character through its weekly settlements, would be highly beneficial; and with the advantages of a sound currency the restoration of confidence and credit would follow with a numerous train of blessings. My convictions are most strong that these benefits would flow from the adoption of this measure; but if the result should be adverse there is this security in connection with it—that the law creating it may be repealed at the pleasure of the Legislature without the slightest implication of its good faith.

I recommend to Congress to take into consideration the propriety o. reimbursing a fine imposed on General Jackson at New Orleans at the time of the attack and defense of that city, and paid by him. Without designing any reflection on the judicial tribunal which imposed the fine, the remission at this day may be regarded as not unjust or inexpedient The voice of the civil authority was heard amidst the glitter of arms and obeyed by those who held the sword, thereby giving additional luster to a memorable military achievement. If the laws were offended, thei majesty was fully vindicated; and although the penalty incurred and paid is worthy of little regard in a pecuniary point of view, it can hardly be doubted that it would be gratifying tc the war-worn veteran, now in retire. ment and in the winter of his days, to be relieved from the circumstances in which that judgment placed him. There are cases in which public functionaries may be called on to weigh the public interest against their own personal hazards, and if the civil law be violated from praiseworthy motives or an overruling sense of public danger and public necessity punishment may well be restrained within that limit which asserts and maintains the authority of the law and the subjection of the military to the civil power. The defense of New Orleans, while it saved a city from the hands of the enemy, placed the name of General Jackson among those of the greatest captains of the age and illustrated one of the brightest pages of our history. Now that the causes of excitement existing at the time have ceased to operate, it is believed that the remission of this fine and whatever of gratification that remission might cause the eminent man who incurred and paid it would be in accordance with the general feeling and wishes of the American people.

I have thus, fellow-citizens, acquitted myself of my duty under the Constitution by laying before you as succinctly as I have been able the state of the Union and by inviting your attention to measures of much importance to the country. The executive will most zealously unite its efforts with those of the legislative department in the accomplishment of all that is required to relieve the wants of a common constituency or elevate the destinies of a beloved country.

THIRD ANNUAL MESSAGE.

WASHINGTON, *December, 1843.*

To the Senate and House of Representatives of the United States:

If any people ever had cause to render up thanks to the Supreme Being for parental care and protection extended to them in all the trials and difficulties to which they have been from time to time exposed, we certainly are that people.   From the first settlement of our forefathers on this continent, through the dangers attendant upon the occupation of a savage wilderness, through a long period of colonial dependence, through the War of the Revolution, in the wisdom which led to the adoption of the existing forms of republican government, in the hazards incident to a war subsequently waged with one of the most powerful nations of the earth, in the increase of our population, in the spread of the arts and sciences, and in the strength and durability conferred on political institutions emanating from the people and sustained by their will, the superintendence of an overruling Providence has been plainly visible.   As preparatory, therefore, to entering once more upon the high duties of legislation, it becomes us humbly to acknowledge our dependence upon Him as our guide and protector and to implore a continuance of His parental watchfulness over our beloved country.   We have new cause for the expression of our gratitude in the preservation of the health of our fellow-citizens, with some partial and local exceptions, during the past season, for the abundance with which the earth has yielded up its fruits to the labors of the husbandman, for the renewed activity which has been imparted to commerce, for the revival of trade in all its departments, for the increased rewards attendant on the exercise of the mechanic arts, for the continued growth of our population and the rapidly reviving prosperity of the whole country.   I shall be permitted to exchange congratulations with you, gentlemen of the two Houses of Congress, on these auspicious circumstances, and to assure you in advance of my ready disposition to concur with you in the adoption of all such measures as shall be calculated to increase the happiness of our constituents and to advance the glory of our common country.

Since the last adjournment of Congress the Executive has relaxed no effort to render indestructible the relations of amity which so happily exist between the United States and other countries.   The treaty lately concluded with Great Britain has tended greatly to increase the good understanding which a reciprocity of interests is calculated to encourage, and it is most ardently to be hoped that nothing may transpire to interrupt the relations of amity which it is so obviously the policy of both nations to cultivate.   A question of much importance still remains to be adjusted between them.   The territorial limits of the two countries in relation to what is commonly known as the Oregon Territory still remain in dispute. The United States would be at all times indisposed to aggrandize itself at the expense of any other nation; but while they would be restrained by principles of honor, which should govern the conduct of nations as well as that of individuals, from setting up a demand for territory which does not belong to them, they would as unwillingly consent to a surrender of their rights. After the most rigid and, as far as practicable, unbiased examination of the subject, the United States have always contended that their rights appertain to the entire region of country lying on the Pacific and embraced within 42° and 54° 40′ of north latitude. This claim being controverted by Great Britain, those who have preceded the present Executive — actuated, no doubt, by an earnest desire to adjust the matter upon terms mutually satisfactory to both countries — have caused to be submitted to the British Government propositions for settlement and final adjustment, which, however, have not proved heretofore acceptable to it. Our minister at London has, under instructions, again brought the subject to the consideration of that Government, and while nothing will be done to compromit the rights or honor of the United States, every proper expedient will be resorted to in order to bring the negotiation now in the progress of resumption to a speedy and happy termination. In the meantime it is proper to remark that many of our citizens are either already established in the Territory or are on their way thither for the purpose of forming permanent settlements, while others are preparing to follow; and in view of these facts I must repeat the recommendation contained in previous messages for the establishment of military posts at such places on the line of travel as will furnish security and protection to our hardy adventurers against hostile tribes of Indians inhabiting those extensive regions. Our laws should also follow them, so modified as the circumstances of the case may seem to require. Under the influence of our free system of government new republics are destined to spring up at no distant day on the shores of the Pacific similar in policy and in feeling to those existing on this side of the Rocky Mountains, and giving a wider and more extensive spread to the principles of civil and religious liberty.

I am happy to inform you that the cases which have from time to time arisen of the detention of American vessels by British cruisers on the coast of Africa under pretense of being engaged in the slave trade have been placed in a fair train of adjustment. In the case of the *William and Francis* full satisfaction will be allowed. In the cases of the *Tygris* and *Seamew* the British Government admits that satisfaction is due. In the case of the *Jones* the sum accruing from the sale of that vessel and cargo will be paid to the owners, while I can not but flatter myself that full indemnification will be allowed for all damages sustained by the detention of the vessel; and in the case of the *Douglas* Her Majesty's Government has expressed its determination to make indemnification.

Strong hopes are therefore entertained that most, if not all, of these cases will be speedily adjusted. No new cases have arisen since the ratification of the treaty of Washington, and it is confidently anticipated that the slave trade, under the operation of the eighth article of that treaty, will be altogether suppressed.

The occasional interruption experienced by our fellow-citizens engaged in the fisheries on the neighboring coast of Nova Scotia has not failed to claim the attention of the Executive. Representations upon this subject have been made, but as yet no definitive answer to those representations has been received from the British Government.

Two other subjects of comparatively minor importance, but nevertheless of too much consequence to be neglected, remain still to be adjusted between the two countries. By the treaty between the United States and Great Britain of July, 1815, it is provided that no higher duties shall be levied in either country on articles imported from the other than on the same articles imported from any other place. In 1836 rough rice by act of Parliament was admitted from the coast of Africa into Great Britain on the payment of a duty of 1 penny a quarter, while the same article from all other countries, including the United States, was subjected to the payment of a duty of 20 shillings a quarter. Our minister at London has from time to time brought this subject to the attention of the British Government, but so far without success. He is instructed to renew his representations upon it.

Some years since a claim was preferred against the British Government on the part of certain American merchants for the return of export duties paid by them on shipments of woolen goods to the United States after the duty on similar articles exported to other countries had been repealed, and consequently in contravention of the commercial convention between the two nations securing to us equality in such cases. The principle on which the claim rests has long since been virtually admitted by Great Britain, but obstacles to a settlement have from time to time been interposed, so that a large portion of the amount claimed has not yet been refunded. Our minister is now engaged in the prosecution of the claim, and I can not but persuade myself that the British Government will no longer delay its adjustment.

I am happy to be able to say that nothing has occurred to disturb in any degree the relations of amity which exist between the United States and France, Austria, and Russia, as well as with the other powers of Europe, since the adjournment of Congress. Spain has been agitated with internal convulsions for many years, from the effects of which, it is hoped, she is destined speedily to recover, when, under a more liberal system of commercial policy on her part, our trade with her may again fill its old and, so far as her continental possessions are concerned, its almost forsaken channels, thereby adding to the mutual prosperity of the two countries.

The Germanic Association of Customs and Commerce, which since its establishment in 1833 has been steadily growing in power and importance, and consists at this time of more than twenty German States, and embraces a population of 27,000,000 people united for all the purposes of commercial intercourse with each other and with foreign states, offers to the latter the most valuable exchanges on principles more liberal than are offered in the fiscal system of any other European power. From its origin the importance of the German union has never been lost sight of by the United States. The industry, morality, and other valuable qualities of the German nation have always been well known and appreciated. On this subject I invite the attention of Congress to the report of the Secretary of State, from which it will be seen that while our cotton is admitted free of duty and the duty on rice has been much reduced (which has already led to a greatly increased consumption), a strong disposition has been recently evinced by that great body to reduce, upon certain conditions, their present duty upon tobacco. This being the first intimation of a concession on this interesting subject ever made by any European power, I can not but regard it as well calculated to remove the only impediment which has so far existed to the most liberal commercial intercourse between us and them. In this view our minister at Berlin, who has heretofore industriously pursued the subject, has been instructed to enter upon the negotiation of a commercial treaty, which, while it will open new advantages to the agricultural interests of the United States and a more free and expanded field for commercial operations, will affect injuriously no existing interest of the Union. Should the negotiation be crowned with success, its results will be communicated to both Houses of Congress.

I communicate herewith certain dispatches received from our minister at Mexico, and also a correspondence which has recently occurred between the envoy from that Republic and the Secretary of State. It must but be regarded as not a little extraordinary that the Government of Mexico, in anticipation of a public discussion (which it has been pleased to infer from newspaper publications as likely to take place in Congress, relating to the annexation of Texas to the United States), should have so far anticipated the result of such discussion as to have announced its determination to visit any such anticipated decision by a formal declaration of war against the United States. If designed to prevent Congress from introducing that question as a fit subject for its calm deliberation and final judgment, the Executive has no reason to doubt that it will entirely fail of its object. The representatives of a brave and patriotic people will suffer no apprehension of future consequences to embarrass them in the course of their proposed deliberations, nor will the executive department of the Government fail for any such cause to discharge its whole duty to the country.

The war which has existed for so long a time between Mexico and

Texas has since the battle of San Jacinto consisted for the most part of predatory incursions, which, while they have been attended with much of suffering to individuals and have kept the borders of the two countries in a state of constant alarm, have failed to approach to any definitive result. Mexico has fitted out no formidable armament by land or by sea for the subjugation of Texas. Eight years have now elapsed since Texas declared her independence of Mexico, and during that time she has been recognized as a sovereign power by several of the principal civilized states. Mexico, nevertheless, perseveres in her plans of reconquest, and refuses to recognize her independence. The predatory incursions to which I have alluded have been attended in one instance with the breaking up of the courts of justice, by the seizing upon the persons of the judges, jury, and officers of the court and dragging them along with unarmed, and therefore noncombatant, citizens into a cruel and oppressive bondage, thus leaving crime to go unpunished and immorality to pass unreproved. A border warfare is evermore to be deprecated, and over such a war as has existed for so many years between these two States humanity has had great cause to lament. Nor is such a condition of things to be deplored only because of the individual suffering attendant upon it. The effects are far more extensive. The Creator of the Universe has given man the earth for his resting place and its fruits for his subsistence. Whatever, therefore, shall make the first or any part of it a scene of desolation affects injuriously his heritage and may be regarded as a general calamity. Wars may sometimes be necessary, but all nations have a common interest in bringing them speedily to a close. The United States have an immediate interest in seeing an end put to the state of hostilities existing between Mexico and Texas. They are our neighbors, of the same continent, with whom we are not only desirous of cultivating the relations of amity, but of the most extended commercial intercourse, and to practice all the rites of a neighborhood hospitality. Our own interests are involved in the matter, since, however neutral may be our course of policy, we can not hope to escape the effects of a spirit of jealousy on the part of both of the powers. Nor can this Government be indifferent to the fact that a warfare such as is waged between those two nations is calculated to weaken both powers and finally to render them—and especially the weaker of the two— the subjects of interference on the part of stronger and more powerful nations, who, intent only on advancing their own peculiar views, may sooner or later attempt to bring about a compliance with terms as the condition of their interposition alike derogatory to the nation granting them and detrimental to the interests of the United States. We could not be expected quietly to permit any such interference to our disadvantage. Considering that Texas is separated from the United States by a mere geographical line; that her territory, in the opinion of many, down to a late period formed a portion of the territory of the United

States; that it is homogeneous in its population and pursuits with the adjoining States, makes contributions to the commerce of the world in the same articles with them, and that most of her inhabitants have been citizens of the United States, speak the same language, and live under similar political institutions with ourselves, this Government is bound by every consideration of interest as well as of sympathy to see that she shall be left free to act, especially in regard to her domestic affairs, unawed by force and unrestrained by the policy or views of other countries. In full view of all these considerations, the Executive has not hesitated to express to the Government of Mexico how deeply it deprecated a continuance of the war and how anxiously it desired to witness its termination. I can not but think that it becomes the United States, as the oldest of the American Republics, to hold a language to Mexico upon this subject of an unambiguous character. It is time that this war had ceased. There must be a limit to all wars, and if the parent state after an eight years' struggle has failed to reduce to submission a portion of its subjects standing out in revolt against it, and who have not only proclaimed themselves to be independent, but have been recognized as such by other powers, she ought not to expect that other nations will quietly look on, to their obvious injury, upon a protraction of hostilities. These United States threw off their colonial dependence and established independent governments, and Great Britain, after having wasted her energies in the attempt to subdue them for a less period than Mexico has attempted to subjugate Texas, had the wisdom and justice to acknowledge their independence, thereby recognizing the obligation which rested on her as one of the family of nations. An example thus set by one of the proudest as well as most powerful nations of the earth it could in no way disparage Mexico to imitate. While, therefore, the Executive would deplore any collision with Mexico or any disturbance of the friendly relations which exist between the two countries, it can not permit that Government to control its policy, whatever it may be, toward Texas, but will treat her—as by the recognition of her independence the United States have long since declared they would do—as entirely independent of Mexico. The high obligations of public duty may enforce from the constituted authorities of the United States a policy which the course persevered in by Mexico will have mainly contributed to produce, and the Executive in such a contingency will with confidence throw itself upon the patriotism of the people to sustain the Government in its course of action.

Measures of an unusual character have recently been adopted by the Mexican Government, calculated in no small degree to affect the trade of other nations with Mexico and to operate injuriously to the United States. All foreigners, by a decree of the 23d day of September, and after six months from the day of its promulgation, are forbidden to carry on the business of selling by retail any goods within the confines of Mexico. Against this decree our minister has not failed to remonstrate.

The trade heretofore carried on by our citizens with Santa Fe, in which much capital was already invested and which was becoming of daily increasing importance, has suddenly been arrested by a decree of virtual prohibition on the part of the Mexican Government. Whatever may be the right of Mexico to prohibit any particular course of trade to the citizens or subjects of foreign powers, this late procedure, to say the least of it, wears a harsh and unfriendly aspect.

The installments on the claims recently settled by the convention with Mexico have been punctually paid as they have fallen due, and our minister is engaged in urging the establishment of a new commission in pursuance of the convention for the settlement of unadjusted claims.

With the other American States our relations of amity and good will have remained uninterrupted. Our minister near the Republic of New Granada has succeeded in effecting an adjustment of the claim upon that Govenrment for the schooner *By Chance*, which had been pending for many years. The claim for the brig *Morris*, which had its origin during the existence of the Republic of Colombia, and indemnification for which since the dissolution of that Republic has devolved upon its several members, will be urged with renewed zeal.

I have much pleasure in saying that the Government of Brazil has adjusted the claim upon that Government in the case of the schooner *John S. Bryan*, and that sanguine hopes are entertained that the same spirit of justice will influence its councils in arriving at an early decision upon the remaining claims, thereby removing all cause of dissension between two powers whose interests are to some extent interwoven with each other.

Our minister at Chili has succeeded in inducing a recognition by that Government of the adjustment effected by his predecessor of the first claim in the case of the *Macedonian*. The first installment has been received by the claimants in the United States.

Notice of the exchange of ratifications of the treaty with Peru, which will take place at Lima, has not yet reached this country, but is shortly expected to be received, when the claims upon that Republic will doubtless be liquidated and paid.

In consequence of a misunderstanding between this Government and that of Buenos Ayres, occurring several years ago, this Government has remained unrepresented at that Court, while a minister from it has been constantly resident here. The causes of irritation have in a great measure passed away, and it is in contemplation, in view of important interests which have grown up in that country, at some early period during the present session of Congress, with the concurrence of the Senate, to restore diplomatic relations between the two countries.

Under the provisions of an act of Congress of the last session a minister was dispatched from the United States to China in August of the present year, who, from the latest accounts we have from him, was at Suez, in Egypt, on the 25th of September last, on his route to China.

In regard to the Indian tribes residing within our jurisdictional limits, the greatest vigilance of the Government has been exerted to preserve them at peace among themselves and to inspire them with feelings of confidence in the justice of this Government and to cultivate friendship with the border inhabitants. This has happily succeeded to a great extent, but it is a subject of regret that they suffer themselves in some instances to be imposed upon by artful and designing men, and this notwithstanding all efforts of the Government to prevent it.

The receipts into the Treasury for the calendar year 1843, exclusive of loans, were little more than $18,000,000, and the expenditures, exclusive of the payments on the public debt, will have been about $23,000,000. By the act of 1842 a new arrangement of the fiscal year was made, so that it should commence on the 1st day of July in each year. The accounts and estimates for the current fiscal year will show that the loans and Treasury notes made and issued before the close of the last Congress to meet the anticipated deficiency have not been entirely adequate. Although on the 1st of October last there was a balance in the Treasury, in consequence of the provisions thus made, of $3,914,082.77, yet the appropriations already made by Congress will absorb that balance and leave a probable deficiency of $2,000,000 at the close of the present fiscal year. There are outstanding Treasury notes to about the amount of $4,600,000, and should they be returned upon the Treasury during the fiscal year they will require provision for their redemption. I do not, however, regard this as probable, since they have obviously entered into the currency of the country and will continue to form a portion of it if the system now adopted be continued. The loan of 1841, amounting to $5,672,976.88, falls due on the 1st day of January, 1845, and must be provided for or postponed by a new loan; and unless the resources of revenue should be materially increased by you there will be a probable deficiency for the service of the fiscal year ending June 30, 1845, of upward of $4,000,000.

The delusion incident to an enormously excessive paper circulation, which gave a fictitious value to everything and stimulated adventure and speculation to an extravagant extent, has been happily succeeded by the substitution of the precious metals and paper promptly redeemable in specie; and thus false values have disappeared and a sounder condition of things has been introduced. This transition, although intimately connected with the prosperity of the country, has nevertheless been attended with much embarrassment to the Government in its financial concerns. So long as the foreign importers could receive payment for their cargoes in a currency of greatly less value than that in Europe, but fully available here in the purchase of our agricultural productions (their profits being immeasurably augmented by the operation), the shipments were large and the revenues of the Government became superabundant. But the change in the character of the circulation from a nominal and apparently real value in the first stage of its existence to an obviously depreciated value in its second, so that it no longer answered the purposes of exchange or barter, and its ultimate substitution by a sound metallic and paper circulation combined, has been attended by diminished importations and a consequent falling off in the revenue. This has induced Congress, from 1837, to resort to the expedient of issuing Treasury notes, and finally of funding them, in order to supply deficiencies. I can not, however, withhold the remark that it is in no way compatible with the dignity of the Government that a public debt should be created in time of peace to meet the current expenses of the Government, or that temporary expedients should be resorted to an hour longer than it is possible to avoid them. The Executive can do no more than apply the means which Congress places in its hands for the support of Government, and, happily for the good of the country and for the preservation of its liberties, it possesses no power to levy exactions on the people or to force from them contributions to the public revenue in any form. It can only recommend such measures as may in its opinion be called for by the wants of the public service to Congress, with whom alone rests the power to "lay and collect taxes, duties, imposts, and excises." This duty has upon several occasions heretofore been performed. The present condition of things gives flattering promise that trade and commerce are rapidly reviving, and, fortunately for the country, the sources of revenue have only to be opened in order to prove abundant.

While we can anticipate no considerable increase in the proceeds of the sales of the public lands, for reasons perfectly obvious to all, for several years to come, yet the public lands can not otherwise than be regarded as the foundation of the public credit. With so large a body of the most fertile lands in the world under the control and at the disposal of this Government, no one can reasonably doubt the entire ability to meet its engagements under every emergency. In seasons of trial and difficulty similar to those through which we are passing the capitalist makes his investments in the Government stocks with the most assured confidence of ultimate reimbursement; and whatever may be said of a period of great financial prosperity, such as existed for some years after 1833, I should regard it as suicidal in a season of financial embarrassment either to alienate the lands themselves or the proceeds arising from their sales. The first and paramount duty of those to whom may be intrusted the administration of public affairs is to guard the public credit. In reestablishing the credit of this central Government the readiest and most obvious mode is taken to restore the credit of the States. The extremities can only be made sound by producing a healthy action in the central Government, and the history of the present day fully establishes the fact that an increase in the value of the stocks of this Government will in a great majority of instances be attended by an increase in the value of the stocks of the States. It should therefore be a matter of general congratulation that amidst all the embarrassments arising from surrounding circumstances the credit of the Government should have been so fully restored that it has been enabled to effect a loan of $7,000,000 to redeem that amount of Treasury notes on terms more favorable than any that have been offered for many years. And the 6 per cent stock which was created in 1842 has advanced in the hands of the holders nearly 20 per cent above its par value. The confidence of the people in the integrity of their Government has thus been signally manifested. These opinions relative to the public lands do not in any manner conflict with the observance of the most liberal policy toward those of our fellow-citizens who press forward into the wilderness and are the pioneers in the work of its reclamation. In securing to all such their rights of preemption the Government performs but an act of retributive justice for sufferings encountered and hardships endured, and finds ample remuneration in the comforts which its policy insures and the happiness which it imparts.

Should a revision of the tariff with a view to revenue become necessary in the estimation of Congress, I doubt not you will approach the subject with a just and enlightened regard to the interests of the whole Union. The principles and views which I have heretofore had occasion to submit remain unchanged. It can, however, never be too often repeated that the prominent interest of every important pursuit of life requires for success permanency and stability in legislation. These can only be attained by adopting as the basis of action moderation in all things, which is as indispensably necessary to secure the harmonious action of the political as of the animal system. In our political organization no one section of the country should desire to have its supposed interests advanced at the sacrifice of all others, but union, being the great interest, equally precious to all, should be fostered and sustained by mutual concessions and the cultivation of that spirit of compromise from which the Constitution itself proceeded.

You will be informed by the report from the Treasury Department of the measures taken under the act of the last session authorizing the reissue of Treasury notes in lieu of those then outstanding. The system adopted in pursuance of existing laws seems well calculated to save the country a large amount of interest, while it affords conveniences and obviates dangers and expense in the transmission of funds to disbursing agents. I refer you also to that report for the means proposed by the Secretary to increase the revenue, and particularly to that portion of it which relates to the subject of the warehousing system, which I earnestly urged upon Congress at its last session and as to the importance of which my opinion has undergone no change.

In view of the disordered condition of the currency at the time and the high rates of exchange between different parts of the country, I felt it to be incumbent on me to present to the consideration of your predecessors a proposition conflicting in no degree with the Constitution or with the rights of the States and having the sanction (not in detail, but in principle) of some of the eminent men who have preceded me in the Executive office. That proposition contemplated the issuing of Treasury notes of denominations of not less than $5 nor more than $100, to be employed in the payment of the obligations of the Government in lieu of gold and silver at the option of the public creditor, and to an amount not exceeding $15,000,000. It was proposed to make them receivable everywhere and to establish at various points depositories of gold and silver to be held in trust for the redemption of such notes, so as to insure their convertibility into specie. No doubt was entertained that such notes would have maintained a par value with gold and silver, thus furnishing a paper currency of equal value over the Union, thereby meeting the just expectations of the people and fulfilling the duties of a parental government. Whether the depositories should be permitted to sell or purchase bills under very limited restrictions, together with all its other details, was submitted to the wisdom of Congress and was regarded as of secondary importance. I thought then and think now that such an arrangement would have been attended with the happiest results. The whole matter of the currency would have been placed where by the Constitution it was designed to be placed—under the immediate supervision and control of Congress. The action of the Government would have been independent of all corporations, and the same eye which rests unceasingly on the specie currency and guards it against adulteration would also have rested on the paper currency, to control and regulate its issues and protect it against depreciation. The same reasons which would forbid Congress from parting with the power over the coinage would seem to operate with nearly equal force in regard to any substitution for the precious metals in the form of a circulating medium. Paper when substituted for specie constitutes a standard of value by which the operations of society are regulated, and whatsoever causes its depreciation affects society to an extent nearly, if not quite, equal to the adulteration of the coin. Nor can I withhold the remark that its advantages contrasted with a bank of the United States, apart from the fact that a bank was esteemed as obnoxious to the public sentiment as well on the score of expediency as of constitutionalty, appeared to me to be striking and obvious. The relief which a bank would afford by an issue of $15,000,000 of its notes, judging from the experience of the late United States Bank, would not have occurred in less than fifteen years, whereas under the proposed arrangement the relief arising from the issue of $15,000,000 of Treasury notes would have been consummated in one year, thus furnishing in one-fifteenth part of the time in which a bank could have accomplished it a paper medium of exchange equal in amount to the real wants of the country at par value with gold and silver. The saving to the Government would have been equal to all the interest which it has had to pay on Treasury notes of previous as well as subsequent issues, thereby relieving the Government and at the same time affording relief to the people. Under all the responsibilities attached to the station which I occupy, and in redemption of a pledge given to the last Congress at the close of its first session, I submitted the suggestion to its consideration at two consecutive sessions. The recommendation, however, met with no favor at its hands. While I am free to admit that the necessities of the times have since become greatly ameliorated and that there is good reason to hope that the country is safely and rapidly emerging from the difficulties and embarrassments which everywhere surrounded it in 1841, yet I can not but think that its restoration to a sound and healthy condition would be greatly expedited by a resort to the expedient in a modified form.

The operations of the Treasury now rest upon the act of 1789 and the resolution of 1816, and those laws have been so administered as to produce as great a quantum of good to the country as their provisions are capable of yielding. If there had been any distinct expression of opinion going to show that public sentiment is averse to the plan, either as heretofore recommended to Congress or in a modified form, while my own opinion in regard to it would remain unchanged I should be very far from again presenting it to your consideration. The Government has originated with the States and the people, for their own benefit and advantage, and it would be subversive of the foundation principles of the political edifice which they have reared to persevere in a measure which in their mature judgments they had either repudiated or condemned. The will of our constituents clearly expressed should be regarded as the light to guide our footsteps, the true difference between a monarchical or aristocratical government and a republic being that in the first the will of the few prevails over the will of the many, while in the last the will of the many should be alone consulted.

The report of the Secretary of War will bring you acquainted with the condition of that important branch of the public service. The Army may be regarded, in consequence of the small number of the rank and file in each company and regiment, as little more than a nucleus around which to rally the military force of the country in case of war, and yet its services in preserving the peace of the frontiers are of a most important nature. In all cases of emergency the reliance of the country is properly placed in the militia of the several States, and it may well deserve the consideration of Congress whether a new and more perfect organization might not be introduced, looking mainly to the volunteer companies of the Union for the present and of easy application to the great body of the militia in time of war.

The expenditures of the War Department have been considerably reduced in the last two years. Contingencies, however, may arise which would call for the filling up of the regiments with a full complement of men and make it very desirable to remount the corps of dragoons, which by an act of the last Congress was directed to be dissolved.

I refer you to the accompanying report of the Secretary for information in relation to the Navy of the United States. While every effort has been and will continue to be made to retrench all superfluities and lop off all excrescences which from time to time may have grown up, yet it has not been regarded as wise or prudent to recommend any material change in the annual appropriations. The interests which are involved are of too important a character to lead to the recommendation of any other than a liberal policy. Adequate appropriations ought to be made to enable the Executive to fit out all the ships that are now in a course of building or that require repairs for active service in the shortest possible time should any emergency arise which may require it. An efficient navy, while it is the cheapest means of public defense, enlists in its support the feelings of pride and confidence which brilliant deeds and heroic valor have heretofore served to strengthen and confirm.

I refer you particularly to that part of the Secretary's report which has reference to recent experiments in the application of steam and in the construction of our war steamers, made under the superintendence of distinguished officers of the Navy. In addition to other manifest improvements in the construction of the steam engine and application of the motive power which has rendered them more appropriate to the uses of ships of war, one of those officers has brought into use a power which makes the steamship most formidable either for attack or defense. I can not too strongly recommend this subject to your consideration and do not hesitate to express my entire conviction of its great importance.

I call your particular attention also to that portion of the Secretary's report which has reference to the act of the late session of Congress which prohibited the transfer of any balance of appropriation from other heads of appropriation to that for building, equipment, and repair. The repeal of that prohibition will enable the Department to give renewed employment to a large class of workmen who have been necessarily discharged in consequence of the want of means to pay them—a circumstance attended, especially at this season of the year, with much privation and suffering.

It gives me great pain to announce to you the loss of the steamship the *Missouri* by fire in the Bay of Gibraltar, where she had stopped to renew her supplies of coal on her voyage to Alexandria, with Mr. Cushing, the American minister to China, on board. There is ground for high commendation of the officers and men for the coolness and intrepidity and perfect submission to discipline evinced under the most trying circumstances. Surrounded by a raging fire, which the utmost exertions could not subdue, and which threatened momentarily the explosion of her well-supplied magazines, the officers exhibited no signs of fear and the men obeyed every order with alacrity. Nor was she abandoned until the last gleam of hope of saving her had expired. It is well worthy of your consideration whether the losses sustained by the officers and crew in this unfortunate affair should not be reimbursed to them.

I can not take leave of this painful subject without adverting to the aid rendered upon the occasion by the British authorities at Gibraltar and the commander, officers, and crew of the British ship of the line the *Malabar*, which was lying at the time in the bay. Everything that generosity or humanity could dictate was promptly performed. It is by such acts of good will by one to another of the family of nations that fraternal feelings are nourished and the blessings of permanent peace secured.

The report of the Postmaster-General will bring you acquainted with the operations of that Department during the past year, and will suggest to you such modifications of the existing laws as in your opinion the exigencies of the public service may require. The change which the country has undergone of late years in the mode of travel and transportation has afforded so many facilities for the transmission of mail matter out of the regular mail as to require the greatest vigilance and circumspection in order to enable the officer at the head of the Department to restrain the expenditures within the income. There is also too much reason to fear that the franking privilege has run into great abuse. The Department, nevertheless, has been conducted with the greatest vigor, and has attained at the least possible expense all the useful objects for which it was established.

In regard to all the Departments, I am quite happy in the belief that nothing has been left undone which was called for by a true spirit of economy or by a system of accountability rigidly enforced. This is in some degree apparent from the fact that the Government has sustained no loss by the default of any of its agents. In the complex, but at the same time beautiful, machinery of our system of government, it is not a matter of surprise that some remote agency may have failed for an instant to fulfill its desired office; but I feel confident in the assertion that nothing has occurred to interrupt the harmonious action of the Government itself, and that, while the laws have been executed with efficiency and vigor, the rights neither of States nor individuals have been trampled on or disregarded.

In the meantime the country has been steadily advancing in all that contributes to national greatness. The tide of population continues unbrokenly to flow into the new States and Territories, where a refuge is found not only for our native-born fellow-citizens, but for emigrants from all parts of the civilized world, who come among us to partake of the blessings of our free institutions and to aid by their labor to swell the current of our wealth and power.

It is due to every consideration of public policy that the lakes and rivers of the West should receive all such attention at the hands of Congress as the Constitution will enable it to bestow. Works in favorable and proper situations on the Lakes would be found to be as indispensably necessary, in case of war, to carry on safe and successful naval operations as fortifications on the Atlantic seaboard.   The appropriation made by the last Congress for the improvement of the navigation of the Mississippi River has been diligently and efficiently applied.

I can not close this communication, gentlemen, without recommending to your most favorable consideration the interests of this District. Appointed by the Constitution its exclusive legislators, and forming in this particular the only anomaly in our system of government—of the legislative body being elected by others than those for whose advantage they are to legislate—you will feel a superadded obligation to look well into their condition and to leave no cause for complaint or regret.   The seat of Government of our associated republics can not but be regarded as worthy of your parental care.

In connection with its other interests, as well as those of the whole country, I recommend that at your present session you adopt such measures in order to carry into effect the Smithsonian bequest as in your judgment will be best calculated to consummate the liberal intent of the testator.

When, under a dispensation of Divine Providence, I succeeded to the Presidential office, the state of public affairs was embarrassing and critical. To add to the irritation consequent upon a long-standing controversy with one of the most powerful nations of modern times, involving not only questions of boundary (which under the most favorable circumstances are always embarrassing), but at the same time important and high principles of maritime law, border controversies between the citizens and subjects of the two countries had engendered a state of feeling and of conduct which threatened the most calamitous consequences.   The hazards incident to this state of things were greatly heightened by the arrest and imprisonment of a subject of Great Britain, who, acting (as it was alleged) as a part of a military force, had aided in the commission of an act violative of the territorial jurisdiction of the United States and involving the murder of a citizen of the State of New York.   A large amount of claims against the Government of Mexico remained unadjusted and a war of several years' continuance with the savage tribes of Florida still prevailed, attended with the desolation of a large portion of that beautiful Territory and with the sacrifice of many valuable lives. To increase the embarrassments of the Government, individual and State credit had been nearly stricken down and confidence in the General Government was so much impaired that loans of a small amount could only be negotiated at a considerable sacrifice.   As a necessary consequence of the blight which had fallen on commerce and mechanical industry, the ships of the one were thrown out of employment and the operations of the other had been greatly diminished.   Owing to the condition of the currency, exchanges between different parts of the country had become ruinously high and trade had to depend on a depreciated paper currency in conducting its transactions.   I shall be permitted to congratulate the country that under an overruling Providence peace was preserved without a sacrifice of the national honor; the war in Florida was brought to a speedy termination; a large portion of the claims on Mexico have been fully adjudicated and are in a course of payment, while justice has been rendered to us in other matters by other nations; confidence between man and man is in a great measure restored and the credit of this Government fully and perfectly reestablished; commerce is becoming more and more extended in its operations and manufacturing and mechanical industry once more reap the rewards of skill and labor honestly applied; the operations of trade rest on a sound currency and the rates of exchange are reduced to their lowest amount.

In this condition of things I have felt it to be my duty to bring to your favorable consideration matters of great interest in their present and ultimate results; and the only desire which I feel in connection with the future is and will continue to be to leave the country prosperous and its institutions unimpaired.

FOURTH ANNUAL MESSAGE.

WASHINGTON, *December 3, 1844.*

To the Senate and House of Representatives of the United States:

We have continued cause for expressing our gratitude to the Supreme Ruler of the Universe for the benefits and blessings which our country, under His kind providence, has enjoyed during the past year. Notwithstanding the exciting scenes through which we have passed, nothing has occurred to disturb the general peace or to derange the harmony of our political system. The great moral spectacle has been exhibited of a nation approximating in number to 20,000,000 people having performed the high and important function of electing their Chief Magistrate for the term of four years without the commission of any acts of violence or the manifestation of a spirit of insubordination to the laws. The great and inestimable right of suffrage has been exercised by all who were invested with it under the laws of the different States in a spirit dictated alone by a desire, in the selection of the agent, to advance the interests of the country and to place beyond jeopardy the institutions under which it is our happiness to live. That the deepest interest has been manifested by all our countrymen in the result of the election is not less true than highly creditable to them. Vast multitudes have assembled from time to time at various places for the purpose of canvassing the merits and pretensions of those who were presented for their suffrages, but no armed soldiery has been necessary to restrain within proper limits the popular zeal or to prevent violent outbreaks.   A principle much more controlling was found in the love of order and obedience to the laws, which, with mere individual exceptions, everywhere possesses the American mind, and controls with an influence far more powerful than hosts of armed men.   We can not dwell upon this picture without recognizing in it that deep and devoted attachment on the part of the people to the institutions under which we live which proclaims their perpetuity.   The great objection which has always prevailed against the election by the people of their chief executive officer has been the apprehension of tumults and disorders which might involve in ruin the entire Government.   A security against this is found not only in the fact before alluded to, but in the additional fact that we live under a Confederacy embracing already twenty-six States, no one of which has power to control the election.   The popular vote in each State is taken at the time appointed by the laws, and such vote is announced by the electoral college without reference to the decision of other States.   The right of suffrage and the mode of conducting the election are regulated by the laws of each State, and the election is distinctly federative in all its prominent features. Thus it is that, unlike what might be the results under a consolidated system, riotous proceedings, should they prevail, could only affect the elections in single States without disturbing to any dangerous extent the tranquillity of others.   The great experiment of a political confederation each member of which is supreme as to all matters appertaining to its local interests and its internal peace and happiness, while by a voluntary compact with others it confides to the united power of all the protection of its citizens in matters not domestic has been so far crowned with complete success.   The world has witnessed its rapid growth in wealth and population, and under the guide and direction of a superintending Providence the developments of the past may be regarded but as the shadowing forth of the mighty future.   In the bright prospects of that future we shall find, as patriots and philanthropists, the highest inducements to cultivate and cherish a love of union and to frown down every measure or effort which may be made to alienate the States or the people of the States in sentiment and feeling from each other.   A rigid and close adherence to the terms of our political compact and, above all, a sacred observance of the guaranties of the Constitution will preserve union on a foundation which can not be shaken, while personal liberty is placed beyond hazard or jeopardy.   The guaranty of religious freedom, of the freedom of the press, of the liberty of speech, of the trial by jury, of the habeas corpus, and of the domestic institutions of each of the States, leaving the private citizen in the full exercise of the high and ennobling attributes of his nature and to each State the privilege (which can only be judiciously exerted by itself) of consulting the means best calculated to advance its own happiness—these are the great and important guaranties of the Constitution which the lovers of liberty must cherish and the advocates of union must ever cultivate. Preserving these and avoiding all interpolations by forced construction under the guise of an imagined expediency upon the Constitution, the influence of our political system is destined to be as actively and as beneficially felt on the distant shores of the Pacific as it is now on those of the Atlantic Ocean. The only formidable impediments in the way of its successful expansion (time and space) are so far in the progress of modification by the improvements of the age as to render no longer speculative the ability of representatives from that remote region to come up to the Capitol, so that their constituents shall participate in all the benefits of Federal legislation. Thus it is that in the progress of time the inestimable principles of civil liberty will be enjoyed by millions yet unborn and the great benefits of our system of government be extended to now distant and uninhabited regions. In view of the vast wilderness yet to be reclaimed, we may well invite the lover of freedom of every land to take up his abode among us and assist us in the great work of advancing the standard of civilization and giving a wider spread to the arts and refinements of cultivated life. Our prayers should evermore be offered up to the Father of the Universe for His wisdom to direct us in the path of our duty so as to enable us to consummate these high purposes.

One of the strongest objections which has been urged against confederacies by writers on government is the liability of the members to be tampered with by foreign governments or the people of foreign states, either in their local affairs or in such as affected the peace of others or endangered the safety of the whole confederacy. We can not hope to be entirely exempt from such attempts on our peace and safety. The United States are becoming too important in population and resources not to attract the observation of other nations. It therefore may in the progress of time occur that opinions entirely abstract in the States in which they may prevail and in no degree affecting their domestic institutions may be artfully but secretly encouraged with a view to undermine the Union. Such opinions may become the foundation of political parties, until at last the conflict of opinion, producing an alienation of friendly feeling among the people of the different States, may involve in general destruction the happy institutions under which we live. It should ever be borne in mind that what is true in regard to individuals is equally so in regard to states. An interference of one in the affairs of another is the fruitful cause of family dissensions and neighborhood disputes, and the same cause affects the peace, happiness, and prosperity of states. It may be most devoutly hoped that the good sense of the American people will ever be ready to repel all such attempts should they ever be made.

There has been no material change in our foreign relations since my last annual message to Congress. With all the powers of Europe we continue on the most friendly terms. Indeed, it affords me much satisfaction to state that at no former period has the peace of that enlightened and important quarter of the globe ever been, apparently, more firmly established. The conviction that peace is the true policy of nations would seem to be growing and becoming deeper amongst the enlightened everywhere, and there is no people who have a stronger interest in cherishing the sentiments and adopting the means of preserving and giving it permanence than those of the United States. Amongst these, the first and most effective are, no doubt, the strict observance of justice and the honest and punctual fulfillment of all engagements. But it is not to be forgotten that in the present state of the world it is no less necessary to be ready to enforce their observance and fulfillment in reference to ourselves than to observe and fulfill them on our part in regard to others.

Since the close of your last session a negotiation has been formally entered upon between the Secretary of State and Her Britannic Majesty's minister plenipotentiary and envoy extraordinary residing at Washington relative to the rights of their respective nations in and over the Oregon Territory. That negotiation is still pending. Should it during your session be brought to a definitive conclusion, the result will be promptly communicated to Congress. I would, however, again call your attention to the recommendations contained in previous messages designed to protect and facilitate emigration to that Territory. The establishment of military posts at suitable points upon the extended line of land travel would enable our citizens to emigrate in comparative safety to the fertile regions below the Falls of the Columbia, and make the provision of the existing convention for the joint occupation of the territory by subjects of Great Britain and the citizens of the United States more available than heretofore to the latter. These posts would constitute places of rest for the weary emigrant, where he would be sheltered securely against the danger of attack from the Indians and be enabled to recover from the exhaustion of a long line of travel. Legislative enactments should also be made which should spread over him the ægis of our laws, so as to afford protection to his person and property when he shall have reached his distant home. In this latter respect the British Government has been much more careful of the interests of such of her people as are to be found in that country than the United States. She has made necessary provision for their security and protection against the acts of the viciously disposed and lawless, and her emigrant reposes in safety under the panoply of her laws. Whatever may be the result of the pending negotiation, such measures are necessary. It will afford me the greatest pleasure to witness a happy and favorable termination to the existing negotiation upon terms compatible with the public honor, and the best efforts of the Government will continue to be directed to this end.

It would have given me the highest gratification in this my last annual communication to Congress to have been able to announce to you the complete and entire settlement and adjustment of other matters in difference between the United States and the Government of Her Britannic Majesty, which were adverted to in a previous message. It is so obviously the interest of both countries, in respect to the large and valuable commerce which exists between them, that all causes of complaint, however inconsiderable, should be with the greatest promptitude removed that it must be regarded as cause of regret that any unnecessary delays should be permitted to intervene. It is true that in a pecuniary point of view the matters alluded to are altogether insignificant in amount when compared with the ample resources of that great nation, but they nevertheless, more particularly that limited class which arise under seizures and detentions of American ships on the coast of Africa upon the mistaken supposition indulged in at the time the wrong was committed of their being engaged in the slave trade, deeply affect the sensibilities of this Government and people. Great Britain, having recognized her responsibility to repair all such wrongs by her action in other cases, leaves nothing to be regretted upon the subject as to all cases arising prior to the treaty of Washington than the delay in making suitable reparation in such of them as fall plainly within the principle of others which she has long since adjusted. The injury inflicted by delays in the settlement of these claims falls with severity upon the individual claimants and makes a strong appeal to her magnanimity and sense of justice for a speedy settlement. Other matters arising out of the construction of existing treaties also remain unadjusted, and will continue to be urged upon her attention.

The labors of the joint commission appointed by the two Governments to run the dividing line established by the treaty of Washington were, unfortunately, much delayed in the commencement of the season by the failure of Congress at its last session to make a timely appropriation of funds to meet the expenses of the American party, and by other causes. The United States commissioner, however, expresses his expectation that by increased diligence and energy the party will be able to make up for lost time.

We continue to receive assurances of the most friendly feelings on the part of all the other European powers, with each and all of whom it is so obviously our interest to cultivate the most amicable relations; nor can I anticipate the occurrence of any event which would be likely in any degree to disturb those relations. Russia, the great northern power, under the judicious sway of her Emperor, is constantly advancing in the road of science and improvement, while France, guided by the counsels of her wise Sovereign, pursues a course calculated to consolidate the general peace. Spain has obtained a breathing spell of some duration from the internal convulsions which have through so many years marred her prosperity, while Austria, the Netherlands, Prussia, Belgium, and the other powers of Europe reap a rich harvest of blessings from the prevailing peace.

I informed the two Houses of Congress in my message of December last that instructions had been given to Mr. Wheaton, our minister at Berlin, to negotiate a treaty with the Germanic States composing the Zollverein if it could be done, stipulating, as far as it was practicable to accomplish it, for a reduction of the heavy and onerous duties levied on our tobacco and other leading articles of agricultural production, and yielding in return on our part a reduction of duties on such articles the product of their industry as should not come into competition, or but a limited one, with articles the product of our manufacturing industry. The Executive in giving such instructions considered itself as acting in strict conformity with the wishes of Congress as made known through several measures which it had adopted, all directed to the accomplishment of this important result. The treaty was therefore negotiated, by which essential reductions were secured in the duties levied by the Zollverein on tobacco, rice, and lard, accompanied by a stipulation for the admission of raw cotton free of duty; in exchange for which highly important concessions a reduction of duties imposed by the laws of the United States on a variety of articles, most of which were admitted free of all duty under the act of Congress commonly known as the compromise law, and but few of which were produced in the United States, was stipulated for on our part. This treaty was communicated to the Senate at an early day of its last session, but not acted upon until near its close, when, for the want (as I am bound to presume) of full time to consider it, it was laid upon the table. This procedure had the effect of virtually rejecting it, in consequence of a stipulation contained in the treaty that its ratifications should be exchanged on or before a day which has already passed. The Executive, acting upon the fair inference that the Senate did not intend its absolute rejection, gave instructions to our minister at Berlin to reopen the negotiations so far as to obtain an extension of time for the exchange of ratifications. I regret, however, to say that his efforts in this respect have been unsuccessful. I am nevertheless not without hope that the great advantages which were intended to be secured by the treaty may yet be realized.

I am happy to inform you that Belgium has, by an *"arrêté royale"* issued in July last, assimilated the flag of the United States to her own, so far as the direct trade between the two countries is concerned. This measure will prove of great service to our shipping interest, the trade having heretofore been carried on chiefly in foreign bottoms. I flatter myself that she will speedily resort to a modification of her system relating to the tobacco trade, which would decidedly benefit the agriculture of the United States and operate to the mutual advantage of both countries.

No definitive intelligence has yet been received from our minister of the conclusion of a treaty with the Chinese Empire, but enough is known to induce the strongest hopes that the mission will be crowned with success.

With Brazil our relations continue on the most friendly footing. The commercial intercourse between that growing Empire and the United States is becoming daily of greater importance to both, and it is to the interest of both that the firmest relations of amity and good will should continue to be cultivated between them.

The Republic of New Granada still withholds, notwithstanding the most persevering efforts have been employed by our chargé d'affaires, Mr. Blackford, to produce a different result, indemnity in the case of the brig *Morris;* and the Congress of Venezuela, although an arrangement has been effected between our minister and the minister of foreign affairs of that Government for the payment of $18,000 in discharge of its liabilities in the same case, has altogether neglected to make provision for its payment. It is to be hoped that a sense of justice will soon induce a settlement of these claims.

Our late minister to Chili, Mr. Pendleton, has returned to the United States without having effected an adjustment in the second claim of the *Macedonian,* which is delayed on grounds altogether frivolous and untenable. Mr. Pendleton's successor has been directed to urge the claim in the strongest terms, and, in the event of a failure to obtain a prompt adjustment, to report the fact to the Executive at as early a day as possible, so that the whole matter may be communicated to Congress.

At your last session I submitted to the attention of Congress the convention with the Republic of Peru of the 17th March, 1841, providing for the adjustment of the claims of citizens of the United States against that Republic, but no definitive action was taken upon the subject. I again invite to it your attention and prompt action.

In my last annual message I felt it to be my duty to make known to Congress, in terms both plain and emphatic, my opinion in regard to the war which has so long existed between Mexico and Texas, which since the battle of San Jacinto has consisted altogether of predatory incursions, attended by circumstances revolting to humanity. I repeat now what I then said, that after eight years of feeble and ineffectual efforts to reconquer Texas it was time that the war should have ceased. The United States have a direct interest in the question. The contiguity of the two nations to our territory was but too well calculated to involve our peace. Unjust suspicions were engendered in the mind of one or the other of the belligerents against us, and as a necessary consequence American interests were made to suffer and our peace became daily endangered; in addition to which it must have been obvious to all that the exhaustion produced by the war subjected both Mexico and Texas to the interference of other powers, which, without the interposition of this Government, might eventuate in the most serious injury to the United States. This Government from time to time exerted its friendly offices to bring about a termination of hostilities upon terms honorable alike to both the belligerents. Its efforts in this behalf proved unavailing. Mexico

seemed almost without an object to persevere in the war, and no other
alternative was left the Executive but to take advantage of the well-
known dispositions of Texas and to invite her to enter into a treaty for
annexing her territory to that of the United States.

Since your last session Mexico has threatened to renew the war, and
has either made or proposes to make formidable preparations for invading Texas. She has issued decrees and proclamations, preparatory to
the commencement of hostilities, full of threats revolting to humanity,
and which if carried into effect would arouse the attention of all Christendom. This new demonstration of feeling, there is too much reason to
believe, has been produced in consequence of the negotiation of the late
treaty of annexation with Texas. The Executive, therefore, could not
be indifferent to such proceedings, and it felt it to be due as well to
itself as to the honor of the country that a strong representation should
be made to the Mexican Government upon the subject. This was
accordingly done, as will be seen by the copy of the accompanying dispatch from the Secretary of State to the United States envoy at Mexico.
Mexico has no right to jeopard the peace of the world by urging any
longer a useless and fruitless contest. Such a condition of things would
not be tolerated on the European continent. Why should it be on this?
A war of desolation, such as is now threatened by Mexico, can not be
waged without involving our peace and tranquillity. It is idle to believe
that such a war could be looked upon with indifference by our own citizens inhabiting adjoining States; and our neutrality would be violated
in despite of all efforts on the part of the Government to prevent it. The
country is settled by emigrants from the United States under invitations
held out to them by Spain and Mexico. Those emigrants have left
behind them friends and relatives, who would not fail to sympathize with
them in their difficulties, and who would be led by those sympathies to
participate in their struggles, however energetic the action of the Government to prevent it. Nor would the numerous and formidable bands
of Indians — the most warlike to be found in any land — which occupy the
extensive regions contiguous to the States of Arkansas and Missouri, and
who are in possession of large tracts of country within the limits of Texas,
be likely to remain passive. The inclinations of those numerous tribes
lead them invariably to war whenever pretexts exist.

Mexico had no just ground of displeasure against this Government or
people for negotiating the treaty. What interest of hers was affected
by the treaty? She was despoiled of nothing, since Texas was forever
lost to her. The independence of Texas was recognized by several of
the leading powers of the earth. She was free to treat, free to adopt
her own line of policy, free to take the course which she believed was
best calculated to secure her happiness.

Her Government and people decided on annexation to the United
States, and the Executive saw in the acquisition of such a territory the

means of advancing their permanent happiness and glory. What principle of good faith, then, was violated? What rule of political morals trampled under foot? So far as Mexico herself was concerned, the measure should have been regarded by her as highly beneficial. Her inability to reconquer Texas had been exhibited, I repeat, by eight (now nine) years of fruitless and ruinous contest. In the meantime Texas has been growing in population and resources. Emigration has flowed into her territory from all parts of the world in a current which continues to increase in strength. Mexico requires a permanent boundary between that young Republic and herself. Texas at no distant day, if she continues separate and detached from the United States, will inevitably seek to consolidate her strength by adding to her domain the contiguous Provinces of Mexico. The spirit of revolt from the control of the central Government has heretofore manifested itself in some of those Provinces, and it is fair to infer that they would be inclined to take the first favorable opportunity to proclaim their independence and to form close alliances with Texas. The war would thus be endless, or if cessations of hostilities should occur they would only endure for a season. The interests of Mexico, therefore, could in nothing be better consulted than in a peace with her neighbors which would result in the establishment of a permanent boundary. Upon the ratification of the treaty the Executive was prepared to treat with her on the most liberal basis. Hence the boundaries of Texas were left undefined by the treaty. The Executive proposed to settle these upon terms that all the world should have pronounced just and reasonable. No negotiation upon that point could have been undertaken between the United States and Mexico in advance of the ratification of the treaty. We should have had no right, no power, no authority, to have conducted such a negotiation, and to have undertaken it would have been an assumption equally revolting to the pride of Mexico and Texas and subjecting us to the charge of arrogance, while to have proposed in advance of annexation to satisfy Mexico for any contingent interest she might have in Texas would have been to have treated Texas not as an independent power, but as a mere dependency of Mexico. This assumption could not have been acted on by the Executive without setting at defiance your own solemn declaration that that Republic was an independent State. Mexico had, it is true, threatened war against the United States in the event the treaty of annexation was ratified. The Executive could not permit itself to be influenced by this threat. It represented in this the spirit of our people, who are ready to sacrifice much for peace, but nothing to intimidation. A war under any circumstances is greatly to be deplored, and the United States is the last nation to desire it; but if, as the condition of peace, it be required of us to forego the unquestionable right of treating with an independent power of our own continent upon matters highly interesting to both, and that upon a naked and unsustained pretension of claim by a third power to control the free will of the power with whom we treat, devoted as we may be to peace and anxious to cultivate friendly relations with the whole world, the Executive does not hesitate to say that the people of the United States would be ready to brave all consequences sooner than submit to such condition. But no apprehension of war was entertained by the Executive, and I must express frankly the opinion that had the treaty been ratified by the Senate it would have been followed by a prompt settlement, to the entire satisfaction of Mexico, of every matter in difference between the two countries. Seeing, then, that new preparations for hostile invasion of Texas were about to be adopted by Mexico, and that these were brought about because Texas had adopted the suggestions of the Executive upon the subject of annexation, it could not passively have folded its arms and permitted a war, threatened to be accompanied by every act that could mark a barbarous age, to be waged against her because she had done so.

Other considerations of a controlling character influenced the course of the Executive. The treaty which had thus been negotiated had failed to receive the ratification of the Senate. One of the chief objections which was urged against it was found to consist in the fact that the question of annexation had not been submitted to the ordeal of public opinion in the United States. However untenable such an objection was esteemed to be, in view of the unquestionable power of the Executive to negotiate the treaty and the great and lasting interests involved in the question, I felt it to be my duty to submit the whole subject to Congress as the best expounders of popular sentiment. No definitive action having been taken on the subject by Congress, the question referred itself directly to the decision of the States and people. The great popular election which has just terminated afforded the best opportunity of ascertaining the will of the States and the people upon it. Pending that issue it became the imperative duty of the Executive to inform Mexico that the question of annexation was still before the American people, and that until their decision was pronounced any serious invasion of Texas would be regarded as an attempt to forestall their judgment and could not be looked upon with indifference. I am most happy to inform you that no such invasion has taken place; and I trust that whatever your action may be upon it Mexico will see the importance of deciding the matter by a resort to peaceful expedients in preference to those of arms. The decision of the people and the States on this great and interesting subject has been decisively manifested. The question of annexation has been presented nakedly to their consideration. By the treaty itself all collateral and incidental issues which were calculated to divide and distract the public councils were carefully avoided. These were left to the wisdom of the future to determine. It presented, I repeat, the isolated question of annexation, and in that form it has been submitted to the ordeal of public sentiment. A controlling majority of the people and a large majority of the States have declared in favor of immediate annexation. Instructions have thus come up to both branches of Congress from their respective constituents in terms the most emphatic. It is the will of both the people and the States that Texas shall be annexed to the Union promptly and immediately. It may be hoped that in carrying into execution the public will thus declared all collateral issues may be avoided. Future Legislatures can best decide as to the number of States which should be formed out of the territory when the time has arrived for deciding that question. So with all others. By the treaty the United States assumed the payment of the debts of Texas to an amount not exceeding $10,000,000, to be paid, with the exception of a sum falling short of $400,000, exclusively out of the proceeds of the sales of her public lands. We could not with honor take the lands without assuming the full payment of all incumbrances upon them.

Nothing has occurred since your last session to induce a doubt that the dispositions of Texas remain unaltered. No intimation of an altered determination on the part of her Government and people has been furnished to the Executive. She still desires to throw herself under the protection of our laws and to partake of the blessings of our federative system, while every American interest would seem to require it. The extension of our coastwise and foreign trade to an amount almost incalculable, the enlargement of the market for our manufactures, a constantly growing market for our agricultural productions, safety to our frontiers, and additional strength and stability to the Union—these are the results which would rapidly develop themselves upon the consummation of the measure of annexation. In such event I will not doubt but that Mexico would find her true interest to consist in meeting the advances of this Government in a spirit of amity. Nor do I apprehend any serious complaint from any other quarter; no sufficient ground exists for such complaint. We should interfere in no respect with the rights of any other nation. There can not be gathered from the act any design on our part to do so with their possessions on this continent. We have interposed no impediments in the way of such acquisitions of territory, large and extensive as many of them are, as the leading powers of Europe have made from time to time in every part of the world. We seek no conquest made by war. No intrigue will have been resorted to or acts of diplomacy essayed to accomplish the annexation of Texas. Free and independent herself, she asks to be received into our Union. It is a question for our own decision whether she shall be received or not.

The two Governments having already agreed through their respective organs on the terms of annexation, I would recommend their adoption by Congress in the form of a joint resolution or act to be perfected and made binding on the two countries when adopted in like manner by the Government of Texas.

In order that the subject may be fully presented in all its bearings, the correspondence which has taken place in reference to it since the adjournment of Congress between the United States, Texas, and Mexico is herewith transmitted.

The amendments proposed by the Senate to the convention concluded between the United States and Mexico on the 20th of November, 1843, have been transmitted through our minister for the concurrence of the Mexican Government, but, although urged thereto, no action has yet been had on the subject, nor has any answer been given which would authorize a favorable conclusion in the future.

The decree of September, 1843, in relation to the retail trade, the order for the expulsion of foreigners, and that of a more recent date in regard to passports—all which are considered as in violation of the treaty of amity and commerce between the two countries—have led to a correspondence of considerable length between the minister for foreign relations and our representatives at Mexico, but without any satisfactory result. They remain still unadjusted, and many and serious inconveniences have already resulted to our citizens in consequence of them.

Questions growing out of the act of disarming a body of Texan troops under the command of Major Snively by an officer in the service of the United States, acting under the orders of our Government, and the forcible entry into the custom-house at Bryarlys Landing, on Red River, by certain citizens of the United States, and taking away therefrom the goods seized by the collector of the customs as forfeited under the laws of Texas, have been adjusted so far as the powers of the Executive extend. The correspondence between the two Governments in reference to both subjects will be found amongst the accompanying documents. It contains a full statement of all the facts and circumstances, with the views taken on both sides and the principles on which the questions have been adjusted. It remains for Congress to make the necessary appropriation to carry the arrangement into effect, which I respectfully recommend.

The greatly improved condition of the Treasury affords a subject for general congratulation. The paralysis which had fallen on trade and commerce, and which subjected the Government to the necessity of resorting to loans and the issue of Treasury notes to a large amount, has passed away, and after the payment of upward of $7,000,000 on account of the interest, and in redemption of more than $5,000,000 of the public debt which falls due on the 1st of January next, and setting apart upward of $2,000,000 for the payment of outstanding Treasury notes and meeting an installment of the debts of the corporate cities of the District of Columbia, an estimated surplus of upward of $7,000,000 over and above the existing appropriations will remain in the Treasury at the close of the fiscal year. Should the Treasury notes continue outstanding as heretofore, that surplus will be considerably augmented. Although all interest has ceased upon them and the Government has invited their return to the Treasury, yet they remain outstanding, affording great facilities to commerce, and establishing the fact that under a well-regulated system of finance the Government has resources within itself which render it independent in time of need, not only of private loans, but also of bank facilities.

The only remaining subject of regret is that the remaining stocks of the Government do not fall due at an earlier day, since their redemption would be entirely within its control. As it is, it may be well worthy the consideration of Congress whether the law establishing the sinking fund (under the operation of which the debts of the Revolution and last war with Great Britain were to a great extent extinguished) should not, with proper modifications, so as to prevent an accumulation of surpluses, and limited in amount to a specific sum, be reenacted. Such provision, which would authorize the Government to go into the market for a purchase of its own stock on fair terms, would serve to maintain its credit at the highest point and prevent to a great extent those fluctuations in the price of its securities which might under other circumstances affect its credit. No apprehension of this sort is at this moment entertained, since the stocks of the Government, which but two years ago were offered for sale to capitalists at home and abroad at a depreciation, and could find no purchasers, are now greatly above par in the hands of the holders; but a wise and prudent forecast admonishes us to place beyond the reach of contingency the public credit.

It must also be a matter of unmingled gratification that under the existing financial system (resting upon the act of 1789 and the resolution of 1816) the currency of the country has attained a state of perfect soundness; and the rates of exchange between different parts of the Union, which in 1841 denoted by their enormous amount the great depreciation and, in fact, worthlessness of the currency in most of the States, are now reduced to little more than the mere expense of transporting specie from place to place and the risk incident to the operation. In a new country like that of the United States, where so many inducements are held out for speculation, the depositories of the surplus revenue, consisting of banks of any description, when it reaches any considerable amount, require the closest vigilance on the part of the Government. All banking institutions, under whatever denomination they may pass, are governed by an almost exclusive regard to the interest of the stockholders. That interest consists in the augmentation of profits in the form of dividends, and a large surplus revenue intrusted to their custody is but too apt to lead to excessive loans and to extravagantly large issues of paper. As a necessary consequence prices are nominally increased and the speculative mania very soon seizes upon the public mind. A fictitious state of prosperity for a season exists, and, in the language of the day, money becomes plenty. Contracts are entered into by individuals resting on this unsubstantial state of things, but the delusion speedily passes away and the country is overrun with an indebtedness so weighty as to overwhelm many and to visit every department of industry with great and ruinous embarrassment. The greatest vigilance becomes necessary on the part of Government to guard against this state of things. The depositories must be given distinctly to understand that the favors of the Government will be altogether withdrawn, or substantially diminished, if its revenues shall be regarded as additions to their banking capital or as the foundation of an enlarged circulation.

The Government, through its revenue, has at all times an important part to perform in connection with the currency, and it greatly depends upon its vigilance and care whether the country be involved in embarrassments similar to those which it has had recently to encounter, or, aided by the action of the Treasury, shall be preserved in a sound and healthy condition.

The dangers to be guarded against are greatly augmented by too large a surplus of revenue. When that surplus greatly exceeds in amount what shall be required by a wise and prudent forecast to meet unforeseen contingencies, the Legislature itself may come to be seized with a disposition to indulge in extravagant appropriations to objects many of which may, and most probably would, be found to conflict with the Constitution. A fancied expediency is elevated above constitutional authority, and a reckless and wasteful extravagance but too certainly follows.

The important power of taxation, which when exercised in its most restricted form is a burthen on labor and production, is resorted to under various pretexts for purposes having no affinity to the motives which dictated its grant, and the extravagance of Government stimulates individual extravagance until the spirit of a wild and ill-regulated speculation involves one and all in its unfortunate results. In view of such fatal consequences, it may be laid down as an axiom founded in moral and political truth that no greater taxes should be imposed than are necessary for an economical administration of the Government, and that whatever exists beyond should be reduced or modified. This doctrine does in no way conflict with the exercise of a sound discrimination in the selection of the articles to be taxed, which a due regard to the public weal would at all times suggest to the legislative mind. It leaves the range of selection undefined; and such selection should always be made with an eye to the great interests of the country. Composed as is the Union of separate and independent States, a patriotic Legislature will not fail in consulting the interests of the parts to adopt such course as will be best calculated to advance the harmony of the whole, and thus insure that permanency in the policy of the Government without which all efforts to advance the public prosperity are vain and fruitless.

This great and vitally important task rests with Congress, and the Executive can do no more than recommend the general principles which should govern in its execution.

I refer you to the report of the Secretary of War for an exhibition of the condition of the Army, and recommend to you as well worthy your best consideration many of the suggestions it contains. The Secretary in no degree exaggerates the great importance of pressing forward without delay in the work of erecting and finishing the fortifications to which he particularly alludes. Much has been done toward placing our cities and roadsteads in a state of security against the hazards of hostile attack within the last four years; but considering the new elements which have been of late years employed in the propelling of ships and the formidable implements of destruction which have been brought into service, we can not be too active or vigilant in preparing and perfecting the means of defense. I refer you also to his report for a full statement of the condition of the Indian tribes within our jurisdiction. The Executive has abated no effort in carrying into effect the well-established policy of the Government which contemplates a removal of all the tribes residing within the limits of the several States beyond those limits, and it is now enabled to congratulate the country at the prospect of an early consummation of this object. Many of the tribes have already made great progress in the arts of civilized life, and through the operation of the schools established among them, aided by the efforts of the pious men of various religious denominations who devote themselves to the task of their improvement, we may fondly hope that the remains of the formidable tribes which were once masters of this country will in their transition from the savage state to a condition of refinement and cultivation add another bright trophy to adorn the labors of a well-directed philanthropy.

The accompanying report of the Secretary of the Navy will explain to you the situation of that branch of the service. The present organization of the Department imparts to its operations great efficiency, but I concur fully in the propriety of a division of the Bureau of Construction, Equipment, Increase, and Repairs into two bureaus. The subjects as now arranged are incongruous, and require to a certain extent information and qualifications altogether dissimilar.

The operations of the squadron on the coast of Africa have been conducted with all due attention to the object which led to its origination, and I am happy to say that the officers and crews have enjoyed the best possible health under the system adopted by the officer in command. It is believed that the United States is the only nation which has by its laws subjected to the punishment of death as pirates those who may be engaged in the slave trade. A similar enactment on the part of other nations would not fail to be attended by beneficial results.

In consequence of the difficulties which have existed in the way of securing titles for the necessary grounds, operations have not yet been commenced toward the establishment of the navy-yard at Memphis. So soon as the title is perfected no further delay will be permitted to intervene. It is well worthy of your consideration whether Congress should not direct the establishment of a ropewalk in connection with the contemplated navy-yard, as a measure not only of economy, but as highly useful and necessary. The only establishment of the sort now connected with the service is located at Boston, and the advantages of a similar establishment convenient to the hemp-growing region must be apparent to all.

The report of the Secretary presents other matters to your consideration of an important character in connection with the service.

In referring you to the accompanying report of the Postmaster-General it affords me continued cause of gratification to be able to advert to the fact that the affairs of the Department for the last four years have been so conducted as from its unaided resources to meet its large expenditures. On my coming into office a debt of nearly $500,000 existed against the Department, which Congress discharged by an appropriation from the Treasury. The Department on the 4th of March next will be found, under the management of its present efficient head, free of debt or embarrassment, which could only have been done by the observance and practice of the greatest vigilance and economy. The laws have contemplated throughout that the Department should be self-sustained, but it may become necessary, with the wisest regard to the public interests, to introduce amendments and alterations in the system.

There is a strong desire manifested in many quarters so to alter the tariff of letter postage as to reduce the amount of tax at present imposed. Should such a measure be carried into effect to the full extent desired, it can not well be doubted but that for the first years of its operation a diminished revenue would be collected, the supply of which would necessarily constitute a charge upon the Treasury. Whether such a result would be desirable it will be for Congress in its wisdom to determine. It may in general be asserted as true that radical alterations in any system should rather be brought about gradually than by sudden changes, and by pursuing this prudent policy in the reduction of letter postage the Department might still sustain itself through the revenue which would accrue by the increase of letters. The state and condition of the public Treasury has heretofore been such as to have precluded the recommendation of any material change. The difficulties upon this head have, however, ceased, and a larger discretion is now left to the Government.

I can not too strongly urge the policy of authorizing the establishment of a line of steamships regularly to ply between this country and foreign ports and upon our own waters for the transportation of the mail. The example of the British Government is well worthy of imitation in this respect. The belief is strongly entertained that the emoluments arising from the transportation of mail matter to foreign countries would operate of itself as an inducement to cause individual enterprise to undertake that branch of the task, and the remuneration of the Government would consist in the addition readily made to our steam navy in case of emergency by the ships so employed. Should this suggestion meet your approval, the propriety of placing such ships under the command of experienced officers of the Navy will not escape your observation. The application of steam to the purposes of naval warfare cogently recommends an extensive steam marine as important in estimating the defenses of the country. Fortunately this may be obtained by us to a great extent without incurring any large amount of expenditure. Steam vessels to be engaged in the transportation of the mails on our principal water courses, lakes, and ports of our coast could also be so constructed as to be efficient as war vessels when needed, and would of themselves constitute a formidable force in order to repel attacks from abroad. We can not be blind to the fact that other nations have already added large numbers of steamships to their naval armaments and that this new and powerful agent is destined to revolutionize the condition of the world. It becomes the United States, therefore, looking to their security, to adopt a similar policy, and the plan suggested will enable them to do so at a small comparative cost.

I take the greatest pleasure in bearing testimony to the zeal and untiring industry which has characterized the conduct of the members of the Executive Cabinet. Each in his appropriate sphere has rendered me the most efficient aid in carrying on the Government, and it will not, I trust, appear out of place for me to bear this public testimony. The cardinal objects which should ever be held in view by those intrusted with the administration of public affairs are rigidly, and without favor or affection, so to interpret the national will expressed in the laws as that injustice should be done to none, justice to all. This has been the rule upon which they have acted, and thus it is believed that few cases, if any, exist wherein our fellow-citizens, who from time to time have been drawn to the seat of Government for the settlement of their transactions with the Government, have gone away dissatisfied. Where the testimony has been perfected and was esteemed satisfactory their claims have been promptly audited, and this in the absence of all favoritism or partiality. The Government which is not just to its own people can neither claim their affection nor the respect of the world. At the same time, the closest attention has been paid to those matters which relate more immediately to the great concerns of the country. Order and efficiency in each branch of the public service have prevailed, accompanied by a system of the most rigid responsibility on the part of the receiving and disbursing agents. The fact, in illustration of the truth of this remark, deserves to be noticed that the revenues of the Government, amounting in the last four years to upward of \$120,000,000, have been collected and disbursed through the numerous governmental agents without the loss by default of any amount worthy of serious commentary.

The appropriations made by Congress for the improvement of the rivers of the West and of the harbors on the Lakes are in a course of judicious expenditure under suitable agents, and are destined, it is to be hoped, to realize all the benefits designed to be accomplished by Congress. I can not, however, sufficiently impress upon Congress the great importance of withholding appropriations from improvements which are not ascertained by previous examination and survey to be necessary for the shelter and protection of trade from the dangers of storms and tempests. Without this precaution the expenditures are but too apt to inure to the benefit of individuals, without reference to the only consideration which can render them constitutional—the public interests and the general good.

I can not too earnestly urge upon you the interests of this District, over which by the Constitution Congress has exclusive jurisdiction. It would be deeply to be regretted should there be at any time ground to complain of neglect on the part of a community which, detached as it is from the parental care of the States of Virginia and Maryland, can only expect aid from Congress as its local legislature. Amongst the subjects which claim your attention is the prompt organization of an asylum for the insane who may be found from time to time sojourning within the District. Such course is also demanded by considerations which apply to branches of the public service. For the necessities in this behalf I invite your particular attention to the report of the Secretary of the Navy.

I have thus, gentlemen of the two Houses of Congress, presented you a true and faithful picture of the condition of public affairs, both foreign and domestic. The wants of the public service are made known to you, and matters of no ordinary importance are urged upon your consideration. Shall I not be permitted to congratulate you on the happy auspices under which you have assembled and at the important change in the condition of things which has occurred in the last three years? During that period questions with foreign powers of vital importance to the peace of our country have been settled and adjusted. A desolating and wasting war with savage tribes has been brought to a close. The internal tranquillity of the country, threatened by agitating questions, has been preserved. The credit of the Government, which had experienced a temporary embarrassment, has been thoroughly restored. Its coffers, which for a season were empty, have been replenished. A currency nearly uniform in its value has taken the place of one depreciated and almost worthless. Commerce and manufactures, which had suffered in common with every other interest, have once more revived, and the whole country exhibits an aspect of prosperity and happiness. Trade and barter, no longer governed by a wild and speculative mania, rest upon a solid and substantial footing, and the rapid growth of our cities in every direction bespeaks most strongly the favorable circumstances by which we are surrounded. My happiness in the retirement which shortly awaits me is the ardent hope which I experience that this state of prosperity is neither deceptive nor destined to be short lived, and that measures which have not yet received its sanction, but which I can not but regard as closely connected with the honor, the glory, and still more enlarged prosperity of the country, are destined at an early day to receive the approval of Congress. Under these circumstances and with these anticipations I shall most gladly leave to others more able than myself the noble and pleasing task of sustaining the public prosperity. I shall carry with me into retirement the gratifying reflection that as my sole object throughout has been to advance the public good I may not entirely have failed in accomplishing it; and this gratification is heightened in no small degree by the fact that when under a deep and abiding sense of duty I have found myself constrained to resort to the qualified veto it has neither been followed by disapproval on the part of the people nor weakened in any degree their attachment to that great conservative feature of our Government.

James K. Polk

March 4, 1845 to March 4, 1849

FIRST ANNUAL MESSAGE.

WASHINGTON, *December 2, 1845.*

Fellow-Citizens of the Senate and House of Representatives:

It is to me a source of unaffected satisfaction to meet the representatives of the States and the people in Congress assembled, as it will be to receive the aid of their combined wisdom in the administration of public affairs. In performing for the first time the duty imposed on me by the Constitution of giving to you information of the state of the Union and recommending to your consideration such measures as in my judgment are necessary and expedient, I am happy that I can congratulate you on the continued prosperity of our country. Under the blessings of Divine Providence and the benign influence of our free institutions, it stands before the world a spectacle of national happiness.

With our unexampled advancement in all the elements of national greatness, the affection of the people is confirmed for the Union of the States and for the doctrines of popular liberty which lie at the foundation of our Government.

It becomes us in humility to make our devout acknowledgments to the Supreme Ruler of the Universe for the inestimable civil and religious blessings with which we are favored.

In calling the attention of Congress to our relations with foreign powers, I am gratified to be able to state that though with some of them there have existed since your last session serious causes of irritation and misunderstanding, yet no actual hostilities have taken place. Adopting the maxim in the conduct of our foreign affairs "to ask nothing that is not right and submit to nothing that is wrong," it has been my anxious desire to preserve peace with all nations, but at the same time to be prepared to resist aggression and maintain all our just rights.

In pursuance of the joint resolution of Congress "for annexing Texas to the United States," my predecessor, on the 3d day of March, 1845, elected to submit the first and second sections of that resolution to the Republic of Texas as an overture on the part of the United States for her admission as a State into our Union. This election I approved, and accordingly the chargé d'affaires of the United States in Texas, under instructions of the 10th of March, 1845, presented these sections of the resolution for the acceptance of that Republic. The executive government, the Congress, and the people of Texas in convention have successively complied with all the terms and conditions of the joint resolution. A constitution for the government of the State of Texas, formed by a convention of deputies, is herewith laid before Congress. It is well known, also, that the people of Texas at the polls have accepted the terms of annexation and ratified the constitution. I communicate to Congress the correspondence between the Secretary of State and our chargé d'affaires in Texas, and also the correspondence of the latter with the authorities of Texas, together with the official documents transmitted by him to his own Government. The terms of annexation which were offered by the United States having been accepted by Texas, the public faith of both parties is solemnly pledged to the compact of their union. Nothing remains to consummate the event but the passage of an act by Congress to admit the State of Texas into the Union upon an equal footing with the original States. Strong reasons exist why this should be done at an early period of the session. It will be observed that by the constitution of Texas the existing government is only continued temporarily till Congress can act, and that the third Monday of the present month is the day appointed for holding the first general election. On that day a governor, a lieutenant-governor, and both branches of the legislature will be chosen by the people. The President of Texas is required, immediately after the receipt of official information that the new State has been admitted into our Union by Congress, to convene the legislature, and upon its meeting the existing government will be superseded and the State government organized. Questions deeply interesting to Texas, in common with the other States, the extension of our revenue laws and judicial system over her people and territory, as well as measures of a local character, will claim the early attention of Congress, and therefore upon every principle of republican government she ought to be represented in that body without unnecessary delay. I can not too earnestly recommend prompt action on this important subject. As soon as the act to admit Texas as a State shall be passed the union of the two Republics will be consummated by their own voluntary consent.

This accession to our territory has been a bloodless achievement. No arm of force has been raised to produce the result. The sword has had no part in the victory. We have not sought to extend our territorial possessions by conquest, or our republican institutions over a reluctant people. It was the deliberate homage of each people to the great principle of our federative union. If we consider the extent of territory involved in the annexation, its prospective influence on America, the means by which it has been accomplished, springing purely from the choice of the people themselves to share the blessings of our union, the history of the world may be challenged to furnish a parallel. The jurisdiction of the United States, which at the formation of the Federal Constitution was bounded by the St. Marys on the Atlantic, has passed the capes of Florida and been peacefully extended to the Del Norte. In contemplating the grandeur of this event it is not to be forgotten that the result was achieved in despite of the diplomatic interference of European monarchies. Even France, the country which had been our ancient ally, the country which has a common interest with us in maintaining the freedom of the seas, the country which, by the cession of Louisiana, first opened to us access to the Gulf of Mexico, the country with which we have been every year drawing more and more closely the bonds of successful commerce, most unexpectedly, and to our unfeigned regret, took part in an effort to prevent annexation and to impose on Texas, as a condition of the recognition of her independence by Mexico, that she would never join herself to the United States. We may rejoice that the tranquil and pervading influence of the American principle of self-government was sufficient to defeat the purposes of British and French interference, and that the almost unanimous voice of the people of Texas has given to that interference a peaceful and effective rebuke. From this example European Governments may learn how vain diplomatic arts and intrigues must ever prove upon this continent against that system of self-government which seems natural to our soil, and which will ever resist foreign interference.

Toward Texas I do not doubt that a liberal and generous spirit will actuate Congress in all that concerns her interests and prosperity, and that she will never have cause to regret that she has united her "lone star" to our glorious constellation.

I regret to inform you that our relations with Mexico since your last session have not been of the amicable character which it is our desire to cultivate with all foreign nations. On the 6th day of March last the Mexican envoy extraordinary and minister plenipotentiary to the United States made a formal protest in the name of his Government against the joint resolution passed by Congress "for the annexation of Texas to the United States," which he chose to regard as a violation of the rights of Mexico, and in consequence of it he demanded his passports. He was informed that the Government of the United States did not consider this joint resolution as a violation of any of the rights of Mexico, or that it afforded any just cause of offense to his Government; that the Republic of Texas was an independent power, owing no allegiance to Mexico and constituting no part of her territory or rightful sovereignty and jurisdiction. He was also assured that it was the sincere desire of this Government to maintain with that of Mexico relations of peace and good understanding. That functionary, however, notwithstanding these representations and assurances, abruptly terminated his mission and shortly afterwards left the country. Our envoy extraordinary and minister plenipotentiary to Mexico was refused all official intercourse with that Government, and, after remaining several months, by the permission of his own Government he returned to the United States. Thus, by the acts of Mexico, all diplomatic intercourse between the two countries was suspended.

Since that time Mexico has until recently occupied an attitude of hostility toward the United States—has been marshaling and organizing armies, issuing proclamations, and avowing the intention to make war on the United States, either by an open declaration or by invading Texas. Both the Congress and convention of the people of Texas invited this

Government to send an army into that territory to protect and defend them against the menaced attack. The moment the terms of annexation offered by the United States were accepted by Texas the latter became so far a part of our own country as to make it our duty to afford such protection and defense. I therefore deemed it proper, as a precautionary measure, to order a strong squadron to the coasts of Mexico and to concentrate an efficient military force on the western frontier of Texas. Our Army was ordered to take position in the country between the Nueces and the Del Norte, and to repel any invasion of the Texan territory which might be attempted by the Mexican forces. Our squadron in the Gulf was ordered to cooperate with the Army. But though our Army and Navy were placed in a position to defend our own and the rights of Texas, they were ordered to commit no act of hostility against Mexico unless she declared war or was herself the aggressor by striking the first blow. The result has been that Mexico has made no aggressive movement, and our military and naval commanders have executed their orders with such discretion that the peace of the two Republics has not been disturbed. Texas had declared her independence and maintained it by her arms for more than nine years. She has had an organized government in successful operation during that period. Her separate existence as an independent state had been recognized by the United States and the principal powers of Europe. Treaties of commerce and navigation had been concluded with her by different nations, and it had become manifest to the whole world that any further attempt on the part of Mexico to conquer her or overthrow her Government would be vain. Even Mexico herself had become satisfied of this fact, and whilst the question of annexation was pending before the people of Texas during the past summer the Government of Mexico, by a formal act, agreed to recognize the independence of Texas on condition that she would not annex herself to any other power. The agreement to acknowledge the independence of Texas, whether with or without this condition, is conclusive against Mexico. The independence of Texas is a fact conceded by Mexico herself, and she had no right or authority to prescribe restrictions as to the form of government which Texas might afterwards choose to assume. But though Mexico can not complain of the United States on account of the annexation of Texas, it is to be regretted that serious causes of misunderstanding between the two countries continue to exist, growing out of unredressed injuries inflicted by the Mexican authorities and people on the persons and property of citizens of the United States through a long series of years. Mexico has admitted these injuries, but has neglected and refused to repair them. Such was the character of the wrongs and such the insults repeatedly offered to American citizens and the American flag by Mexico, in palpable violation of the laws of nations and the treaty between the two countries of the 5th of April, 1831, that they have been repeatedly brought to the notice of Congress by my predecessors. As early as the 6th of February, 1837, the President of the United States declared in a message to Congress that—

The length of time since some of the injuries have been committed, the repeated and unavailing applications for redress, the wanton character of some of the outrages upon the property and persons of our citizens, upon the officers and flag of the United States, independent of recent insults to this Government and people by the late extraordinary Mexican minister, would justify in the eyes of all nations immediate war.

He did not, however, recommend an immediate resort to this extreme measure, which, he declared, "should not be used by just and generous nations, confiding in their strength for injuries committed, if it can be honorably avoided," but, in a spirit of forbearance, proposed that another demand be made on Mexico for that redress which had been so long and unjustly withheld.   In these views committees of the two Houses of Congress, in reports made to their respective bodies, concurred.   Since these proceedings more than eight years have elapsed, during which, in addition to the wrongs then complained of, others of an aggravated character have been committed on the persons and property of our citizens. A special agent was sent to Mexico in the summer of 1838 with full authority to make another and final demand for redress.   The demand was made; the Mexican Government promised to repair the wrongs of which we complained, and after much delay a treaty of indemnity with that view was concluded between the two powers on the 11th of April, 1839, and was duly ratified by both Governments.   By this treaty a joint commission was created to adjudicate and decide on the claims of American citizens on the Government of Mexico.   The commission was organized at Washington on the 25th day of August, 1840.   Their time was limited to eighteen months, at the expiration of which they had adjudicated and decided claims amounting to $2,026,139.68 in favor of citizens of the United States against the Mexican Government, leaving a large amount of claims undecided.   Of the latter the American commissioners had decided in favor of our citizens claims amounting to $928,627.88, which were left unacted on by the umpire authorized by the treaty.   Still further claims, amounting to between three and four millions of dollars, were submitted to the board too late to be considered, and were left undisposed of.   The sum of $2,026,139.68, decided by the board, was a liquidated and ascertained debt due by Mexico to the claimants, and there was no justifiable reason for delaying its payment according to the terms of the treaty.   It was not, however, paid. Mexico applied for further indulgence, and, in that spirit of liberality and forbearance which has ever marked the policy of the United States toward that Republic, the request was granted, and on the 30th of January, 1843, a new treaty was concluded.   By this treaty it was provided that the interest due on the awards in favor of claimants under the convention of the 11th of April, 1839, should be paid on the 30th of April, 1843, and that—

The principal of the said awards and the interest accruing thereon shall be paid in five years, in equal installments every three months, the said term of five years to commence on the 30th day of April, 1843, aforesaid.

The interest due on the 30th day of April, 1843, and the three first of the twenty installments have been paid. Seventeen of these installments remain unpaid, seven of which are now due.

The claims which were left undecided by the joint commission, amounting to more than $3,000,000, together with other claims for spoliations on the property of our citizens, were subsequently presented to the Mexican Government for payment, and were so far recognized that a treaty providing for their examination and settlement by a joint commission was concluded and signed at Mexico on the 20th day of November, 1843. This treaty was ratified by the United States with certain amendments to which no just exception could have been taken, but it has not yet received the ratification of the Mexican Government. In the meantime our citizens, who suffered great losses—and some of whom have been reduced from affluence to bankruptcy—are without remedy unless their rights be enforced by their Government. Such a continued and unprovoked series of wrongs could never have been tolerated by the United States had they been committed by one of the principal nations of Europe. Mexico was, however, a neighboring sister republic, which, following our example, had achieved her independence, and for whose success and prosperity all our sympathies were early enlisted. The United States were the first to recognize her independence and to receive her into the family of nations, and have ever been desirous of cultivating with her a good understanding. We have therefore borne the repeated wrongs she has committed with great patience, in the hope that a returning sense of justice would ultimately guide her councils and that we might, if possible, honorably avoid any hostile collision with her. Without the previous authority of Congress the Executive possessed no power to adopt or enforce adequate remedies for the injuries we had suffered, or to do more than to be prepared to repel the threatened aggression on the part of Mexico. After our Army and Navy had remained on the frontier and coasts of Mexico for many weeks without any hostile movement on her part, though her menaces were continued, I deemed it important to put an end, if possible, to this state of things. With this view I caused steps to be taken in the month of September last to ascertain distinctly and in an authentic form what the designs of the Mexican Government were—whether it was their intention to declare war, or invade Texas, or whether they were disposed to adjust and settle in an amicable manner the pending differences between the two countries. On the 9th of November an official answer was received that the Mexican Government consented to renew the diplomatic relations which had been suspended in March last, and for that purpose were willing to accredit a minister from the United States. With a sincere desire to preserve peace and restore relations of good understanding between the two Republics, I waived all ceremony as to the manner of renewing diplomatic intercourse between them, and, assuming the initiative, on the 10th of November a distinguished citizen of Louisiana was appointed envoy extraordinary and minister plenipotentiary to Mexico, clothed with full powers to adjust and definitively settle all pending differences between the two countries, including those of boundary between Mexico and the State of Texas. The minister appointed has set out on his mission and is probably by this time near the Mexican capital. He has been instructed to bring the negotiation with which he is charged to a conclusion at the earliest practicable period, which it is expected will be in time to enable me to communicate the result to Congress during the present session. Until that result is known I forbear to recommend to Congress such ulterior measures of redress for the wrongs and injuries we have so long borne as it would have been proper to make had no such negotiation been instituted.

Congress appropriated at the last session the sum of $275,000 for the payment of the April and July installments of the Mexican indemnities for the year 1844:

Provided it shall be ascertained to the satisfaction of the American Government that said installments have been paid by the Mexican Government to the agent appointed by the United States to receive the same in such manner as to discharge all claim on the Mexican Government, and said agent to be delinquent in remitting the money to the United States.

The unsettled state of our relations with Mexico has involved this subject in much mystery. The first information in an authentic form from the agent of the United States, appointed under the Administration of my predecessor, was received at the State Department on the 9th of November last. This is contained in a letter, dated the 17th of October, addressed by him to one of our citizens then in Mexico with a view of having it communicated to that Department. From this it appears that the agent on the 20th of September, 1844, gave a receipt to the treasury of Mexico for the amount of the April and July installments of the indemnity. In the same communication, however, he asserts that he had not received a single dollar in cash, but that he holds such securities as warranted him at the time in giving the receipt, and entertains no doubt but that he will eventually obtain the money. As these installments appear never to have been actually paid by the Government of Mexico to the agent, and as that Government has not, therefore, been released so as to discharge the claim, I do not feel myself warranted in directing payment to be made to the claimants out of the Treasury without further legislation. Their case is undoubtedly one of much hardship, and it remains for Congress to decide whether any, and what, relief ought to be granted to them. Our minister to Mexico has been instructed to ascertain the facts of the case from the Mexican Government in an authentic and official form and report the result with as little delay as possible.

My attention was early directed to the negotiation which on the 4th of March last I found pending at Washington between the United States and Great Britain on the subject of the Oregon Territory. Three several attempts had been previously made to settle the questions in dispute between the two countries by negotiation upon the principle of compromise, but each had proved unsuccessful. These negotiations took place at London in the years 1818, 1824, and 1826—the two first under the Administration of Mr. Monroe and the last under that of Mr. Adams. The negotiation of 1818, having failed to accomplish its object, resulted in the convention of the 20th of October of that year.

By the third article of that convention it was —

Agreed that any country that may be claimed by either party on the northwest coast of America westward of the Stony Mountains shall, together with its harbors, bays, and creeks, and the navigation of all rivers within the same, be free and open for the term of ten years from the date of the signature of the present convention to the vessels, citizens, and subjects of the two powers ; it being well understood that this agreement is not to be construed to the prejudice of any claim which either of the two high contracting parties may have to any part of the said country, nor shall it be taken to affect the claims of any other power or state to any part of the said country, the only object of the high contracting parties in that respect being to prevent disputes and differences amongst themselves.

The negotiation of 1824 was productive of no result, and the convention of 1818 was left unchanged.

The negotiation of 1826, having also failed to effect an adjustment by compromise, resulted in the convention of August 6, 1827, by which it was agreed to continue in force for an indefinite period the provisions of the third article of the convention of the 20th of October, 1818; and it was further provided that—

It shall be competent, however, to either of the contracting parties, in case either should think fit, at any time after the 20th of October, 1828, on giving due notice of twelve months to the other contracting party, to annul and abrogate this convention; and it shall in such case be accordingly entirely annulled and abrogated after the expiration of the said term of notice.

In these attempts to adjust the controversy the parallel of the forty-ninth degree of north latitude had been offered by the United States to Great Britain, and in those of 1818 and 1826, with a further concession of the free navigation of the Columbia River south of that latitude. The parallel of the forty-ninth degree from the Rocky Mountains to its intersection with the northeasternmost branch of the Columbia, and thence down the channel of that river to the sea, had been offered by Great Britain, with an addition of a small detached territory north of the Columbia. Each of these propositions had been rejected by the parties respectively. In October, 1843, the envoy extraordinary and minister plenipotentiary of the United States in London was authorized to make a similar offer to those made in 1818 and 1826. Thus stood the question when the negotiation was shortly afterwards transferred to Washington, and on the 23d of August, 1844, was formally opened under the direction of my immediate predecessor. Like all the previous negotiations, it was based upon principles of "compromise," and the avowed purpose of the parties was "to treat of the respective claims of the two countries to the Oregon Territory with the view to establish a permanent boundary between them westward of the Rocky Mountains to the Pacific Ocean."

Accordingly, on the 26th of August, 1844, the British plenipotentiary offered to divide the Oregon Territory by the forty-ninth parallel of north latitude from the Rocky Mountains to the point of its intersection with the northeasternmost branch of the Columbia River, and thence down that river to the sea, leaving the free navigation of the river to be enjoyed in common by both parties, the country south of this line to belong to the United States and that north of it to Great Britain. At the same time he proposed in addition to yield to the United States a detached territory north of the Columbia extending along the Pacific and the Straits of Fuca from Bulfinchs Harbor, inclusive, to Hoods Canal, and to make free to the United States any port or ports south of latitude 49° which they might desire, either on the mainland or on Quadra and Vancouvers Island. With the exception of the free ports, this was the same offer which had been made by the British and rejected by the American Government in the negotiation of 1826. This proposition was properly rejected by the American plenipotentiary on the day it was submitted. This was the only proposition of compromise offered by the British plenipotentiary. The proposition on the part of Great Britain having been rejected, the British plenipotentiary requested that a proposal should be made by the United States for "an equitable adjustment of the question." When I came into office I found this to be the state of the negotiation. Though entertaining the settled conviction that the British pretensions of title could not be maintained to any portion of the Oregon Territory upon any principle of public law recognized by nations, yet in deference to what had been done by my predecessors, and especially in consideration that propositions of compromise had been thrice made by two preceding Administrations to adjust the question on the parallel of 49°, and in two of them yielding to Great Britain the free navigation of the Columbia, and that the pending negotiation had been commenced on the basis of compromise, I deemed it to be my duty not abruptly to break it off. In consideration, too, that under the conventions of 1818 and 1827 the citizens and subjects of the two powers held a joint occupancy of the country, I was induced to make another effort to settle this long-pending controversy in the spirit of moderation which had given birth to the renewed discussion. A proposition was accordingly made, which was rejected by the British plenipotentiary, who, without submitting any other proposition, suffered the negotiation on his part to drop, expressing his trust that the United States would offer what he saw fit to call "some further proposal for the settlement of the Oregon question more consistent with fairness and equity and with the reasonable expectations of the British Government." The proposition thus offered and rejected repeated the offer of the parallel of 49° of north latitude, which had been made by two preceding Administrations, but without proposing to surrender to Great Britain, as they had done, the free navigation of the Columbia River. The right of any foreign power to the free navigation of any of our rivers through the heart of our country was one which I was unwilling to concede. It also embraced a provision to make free to Great Britain any port or ports on the cap of Quadra and Vancouvers Island south of this parallel. Had this been a new question, coming under discussion for the first time, this proposition would nct have been made. The extraordinary and wholly inadmissible demands of the British Government and the rejection of the proposition made in deference alone to what had been done by my predecessors and the implied obligation which their acts seemed to impose afford satisfactory evidence that no compromise which the United States ought to accept can be effected. With this conviction the proposition of compromise which had been made and rejected was by my direction subsequently withdrawn and our title to the whole Oregon Territory asserted, and, as is believed, maintained by irrefragable facts and arguments.

The civilized world will see in these proceedings a spirit of liberal concession on the part of the United States, and this Government will be relieved from all responsibility which may follow the failure to settle the controversy.

All attempts at compromise having failed, it becomes the duty of Congress to consider what measures it may be proper to adopt for the security and protection of our citizens now inhabiting or who may hereafter inhabit Oregon, and for the maintenance of our just title to that Territory. In adopting measures for this purpose care should be taken that nothing be done to violate the stipulations of the convention of 1827, which is still in force. The faith of treaties, in their letter and spirit, has ever been, and, I trust, will ever be, scrupulously observed by the United States. Under that convention a year's notice is required to be given by either party to the other before the joint occupancy shall terminate and before either can rightfully assert or exercise exclusive jurisdiction over any portion of the territory. This notice it would, in my judgment, be propei to give, and I recommend that provision be made by law for giving it accordingly, and terminating in this manner the convention of the 6th of August, 1827.

It will become proper for Congress to determine what legislation they can in the meantime adopt without violating this convention. Beyond all question the protection of our laws and our jurisdiction, civil and criminal, ought to be immediately extended over our citizens in Oregon. They have had just cause to complain of our long neglect in this particular, and have in consequence been compelled for their own security and protection to establish a provisional government for themselves. Strong in their allegiance and ardent in their attachment to the United States, they have been thus cast upon their own resources. They are anxious that our laws should be extended over them, and I recommend that this be done by Congress with as little delay as possible in the full extent to which the British Parliament have proceeded in regard to British subjects in that Territory by their act of July 2, 1821, "for regulating the fur trade and establishing a criminal and civil jurisdiction within certain parts of North America." By this act Great Britain extended her laws and jurisdiction, civil and criminal, over her subjects engaged in the fur trade in that Territory. By it the courts of the Province of Upper Canada were empowered to take cognizance of causes civil and criminal. Justices of the peace and other judicial officers were authorized to be appointed in Oregon with power to execute all process issuing from the courts of that Province, and to "sit and hold courts of record for the trial of criminal offenses and misdemeanors" not made the subject of capital punishment, and also of civil cases where the cause of action shall not "exceed in value the amount or sum of £200."

Subsequent to the date of this act of Parliament a grant was made from the "British Crown" to the Hudsons Bay Company of the exclusive trade with the Indian tribes in the Oregon Territory, subject to a reservation that it shall not operate to the exclusion " of the subjects of any foreign states who, under or by force of any convention for the time being between us and such foreign states, respectively, may be entitled to and shall be engaged in the said trade." It is much to be regretted that while under this act British subjects have enjoyed the protection of British laws and British judicial tribunals throughout the whole of Oregon, American citizens in the same Territory have enjoyed no such protection from their Government. At the same time, the result illustrates the character of our people and their institutions. In spite of this neglect they have multiplied, and their number is rapidly increasing in that Territory. They have made no appeal to arms, but have peacefully fortified themselves in their new homes by the adoption of republican institutions for themselves, furnishing another example of the truth that self-government is inherent in the American breast and must prevail. It is due to them that they should be embraced and protected by our laws. It is deemed important that our laws regulating trade and intercourse with the Indian tribes east of the Rocky Mountains should be extended to such tribes as dwell beyond them. The increasing emigration to Oregon and the care and protection which is due from the Government to its citizens in that distant region make it our duty, as it is our interest, to cultivate amicable relations with the Indian tribes of that Territory. For this purpose I recommend that provision be made for establishing an Indian agency and such subagencies as may be deemed necessary beyond the Rocky Mountains.

For the protection of emigrants whilst on their way to Oregon against the attacks of the Indian tribes occupying the country through which they pass, I recommend that a suitable number of stockades and block-house forts be erected along the usual route between our frontier settlements on the Missouri and the Rocky Mountains, and that an adequate force of mounted riflemen be raised to guard and protect them on their journey. The immediate adoption of these recommendations by Congress will not violate the provisions of the existing treaty. It will be doing nothing more for American citizens than British laws have long since done for British subjects in the same territory.

It requires several months to perform the voyage by sea from the Atlantic States to Oregon, and although we have a large number of whale ships in the Pacific, but few of them afford an opportunity of interchanging intelligence without great delay between our settlements in that distant region and the United States. An overland mail is believed to be entirely practicable, and the importance of establishing such a mail at least once a month is submitted to the favorable consideration of Congress.

It is submitted to the wisdom of Congress to determine whether at their present session, and until after the expiration of the year's notice, any other measures may be adopted consistently with the convention of 1827 for the security of our rights and the government and protection of our citizens in Oregon. That it will ultimately be wise and proper to make liberal grants of land to the patriotic pioneers who amidst privations and dangers lead the way through savage tribes inhabiting the vast wilderness intervening between our frontier settlements and Oregon, and who cultivate and are ever ready to defend the soil, I am fully satisfied. To doubt whether they will obtain such grants as soon as the convention between the United States and Great Britain shall have ceased to exist would be to doubt the justice of Congress; but, pending the year's notice, it is worthy of consideration whether a stipulation to this effect may be made consistently with the spirit of that convention.

The recommendations which I have made as to the best manner of securing our rights in Oregon are submitted to Congress with great deference. Should they in their wisdom devise any other mode better calculated to accomplish the same object, it shall meet with my hearty concurrence.

At the end of the year's notice, should Congress think it proper to make provision for giving that notice, we shall have reached a period when the national rights in Oregon must either be abandoned or firmly maintained. That they can not be abandoned without a sacrifice of both national honor and interest is too clear to admit of doubt.

Oregon is a part of the North American continent, to which, it is confidently affirmed, the title of the United States is the best now in existence.

For the grounds on which that title rests I refer you to the correspondence of the late and present Secretary of State with the British plenipotentiary during the negotiation.   The British proposition of compromise,
which would make the Columbia the line south of 49°, with a trifling
addition of detached territory to the United States north of that river,
and would leave on the British side two-thirds of the whole Oregon Territory, including the free navigation of the Columbia and all the valuable
harbors on the Pacific, can never for a moment be entertained by the
United States without an abandonment of their just and clear territorial
rights, their own self-respect, and the national honor.   For the information of Congress, I communicate herewith the correspondence which took
place between the two Governments during the late negotiation.

    The rapid extension of our settlements over our territories heretofore
unoccupied, the addition of new States to our Confederacy, the expansion
of free principles, and our rising greatness as a nation are attracting
the attention of the powers of Europe, and lately the doctrine has been
broached in some of them of a ''balance of power'' on this continent to
check our advancement.   The United States, sincerely desirous of preserving relations of good understanding with all nations, can not in
silence permit any European interference on the North American continent, and should any such interference be attempted will be ready to
resist it at any and all hazards.

    It is well known to the American people and to all nations that this
Government has never interfered with the relations subsisting between
other governments.   We have never made ourselves parties to their
wars or their alliances; we have not sought their territories by conquest;
we have not mingled with parties in their domestic struggles; and believing our own form of government to be the best, we have never attempted
to propagate it by intrigues, by diplomacy, or by force.   We may claim
on this continent a like exemption from European interference.   The
nations of America are equally sovereign and independent with those of
Europe.   They possess the same rights, independent of all foreign interposition, to make war, to conclude peace, and to regulate their internal
affairs.   The people of the United States can not, therefore, view with
indifference attempts of European powers to interfere with the independent action of the nations on this continent.   The American system of
government is entirely different from that of Europe.   Jealousy among
the different sovereigns of Europe, lest any one of them might become
too powerful for the rest, has caused them anxiously to desire the establishment of what they term the ''balance of power.''   It can not be
permitted to have any application on the North American continent, and
especially to the United States.   We must ever maintain the principle
that the people of this continent alone have the right to decide their
own destiny.   Should any portion of them, constituting an independent
state, propose to unite themselves with our Confederacy, this will be a

question for them and us to determine without any foreign interposition. We can never consent that European powers shall interfere to prevent such a union because it might disturb the "balance of power" which they may desire to maintain upon this continent. Near a quarter of a century ago the principle was distinctly announced to the world, in the annual message of one of my predecessors, that—

The American continents, by the free and independent condition which they have assumed and maintain, are henceforth not to be considered as subjects for future colonization by any European powers.

This principle will apply with greatly increased force should any European power attempt to establish any new colony in North America. In the existing circumstances of the world the present is deemed a proper occasion to reiterate and reaffirm the principle avowed by Mr. Monroe and to state my cordial concurrence in its wisdom and sound policy. The reassertion of this principle, especially in reference to North America, is at this day but the promulgation of a policy which no European power should cherish the disposition to resist. Existing rights of every European nation should be respected, but it is due alike to our safety and our interests that the efficient protection of our laws should be extended over our whole territorial limits, and that it should be distinctly announced to the world as our settled policy that no future European colony or dominion shall with our consent be planted or established on any part of the North American continent.

A question has recently arisen under the tenth article of the subsisting treaty between the United States and Prussia. By this article the consuls of the two countries have the right to sit as judges and arbitrators "in such differences as may arise between the captains and crews of the vessels belonging to the nation whose interests are committed to their charge without the interference of the local authorities, unless the conduct of the crews or of the captain should disturb the order or tranquillity of the country, or the said consuls should require their assistance to cause their decisions to be carried into effect or supported."

The Prussian consul at New Bedford in June, 1844, applied to Mr. Justice Story to carry into effect a decision made by him between the captain and crew of the Prussian ship *Borussia*, but the request was refused on the ground that without previous legislation by Congress the judiciary did not possess the power to give effect to this article of the treaty. The Prussian Government, through their minister here, have complained of this violation of the treaty, and have asked the Government of the United States to adopt the necessary measures to prevent similar violations hereafter. Good faith to Prussia, as well as to other nations with whom we have similar treaty stipulations, requires that these should be faithfully observed. I have deemed it proper, therefore, to lay the subject before Congress and to recommend such legislation as may be necessary to give effect to these treaty obligations.

By virtue of an arrangement made between the Spanish Government and that of the United States in December, 1831, American vessels, since the 29th of April, 1832, have been admitted to entry in the ports of Spain, including those of the Balearic and Canary islands, on payment of the same tonnage duty of 5 cents per ton, as though they had been Spanish vessels; and this whether our vessels arrive in Spain directly from the United States or indirectly from any other country. When Congress, by the act of 13th July, 1832, gave effect to this arrangement between the two Governments, they confined the reduction of tonnage duty merely to Spanish vessels ''coming from a port in Spain,'' leaving the former discriminating duty to remain against such vessels coming from a port in any other country. It is manifestly unjust that whilst American vessels arriving in the ports of Spain from other countries pay no more duty than Spanish vessels, Spanish vessels arriving in the ports of the United States from other countries should be subjected to heavy discriminating tonnage duties. This is neither equality nor reciprocity, and is in violation of the arrangement concluded in December, 1831, between the two countries. The Spanish Government have made repeated and earnest remonstrances against this inequality, and the favorable attention of Congress has been several times invoked to the subject by my predecessors. I recommend, as an act of justice to Spain, that this inequality be removed by Congress and that the discriminating duties which have been levied under the act of the 13th of July, 1832, on Spanish vessels coming to the United States from any other foreign country be refunded. This recommendation does not embrace Spanish vessels arriving in the United States from Cuba and Porto Rico, which will still remain subject to the provisions of the act of June 30, 1834, concerning tonnage duty on such vessels. By the act of the 14th of July, 1832, coffee was exempted from duty altogether. This exemption was universal, without reference to the country where it was produced or the national character of the vessel in which it was imported. By the tariff act of the 30th of August, 1842, this exemption from duty was restricted to coffee imported in American vessels from the place of its production, whilst coffee imported under all other circumstances was subjected to a duty of 20 per cent *ad valorem*. Under this act and our existing treaty with the King of the Netherlands Java coffee imported from the European ports of that Kingdom into the United States, whether in Dutch or American vessels, now pays this rate of duty. The Government of the Netherlands complains that such a discriminating duty should have been imposed on coffee the production of one of its colonies, and which is chiefly brought from Java to the ports of that Kingdom and exported from thence to foreign countries. Our trade with the Netherlands is highly beneficial to both countries and our relations with them have ever been of the most friendly character. Under all the circumstances of the case, I recommend that this discrimination should be abolished and that the coffee of Java imported from the Netherlands be placed upon the same footing with that imported directly from Brazil and other countries where it is produced.

Under the eighth section of the tariff act of the 30th of August, 1842, a duty of 15 cents per gallon was imposed on port wine in casks, while on the red wines of several other countries, when imported in casks, a duty of only 6 cents per gallon was imposed. This discrimination, so far as regarded the port wine of Portugal, was deemed a violation of our treaty with that power, which provides that—

No higher or other duties shall be imposed on the importation into the United States of America of any article the growth, produce, or manufacture of the Kingdom and possessions of Portugal than such as are or shall be payable on the like article being the growth, produce, or manufacture of any other foreign country.

Accordingly, to give effect to the treaty as well as to the intention of Congress, expressed in a proviso to the tariff act itself, that nothing therein contained should be so construed as to interfere with subsisting treaties with foreign nations, a Treasury circular was issued on the 16th of July, 1844, which, among other things, declared the duty on the port wine of Portugal, in casks, under the existing laws and treaty to be 6 cents per gallon, and directed that the excess of duties which had been collected on such wine should be refunded. By virtue of another clause in the same section of the act it is provided that all imitations of port or any other wines "shall be subject to the duty provided for the genuine article." Imitations of port wine, the production of France, are imported to some extent into the United States, and the Government of that country now claims that under a correct construction of the act these imitations ought not to pay a higher duty than that imposed upon the original port wine of Portugal. It appears to me to be unequal and unjust that French imitations of port wine should be subjected to a duty of 15 cents, while the more valuable article from Portugal should pay a duty of 6 cents only per gallon. I therefore recommend to Congress such legislation as may be necessary to correct the inequality.

The late President, in his annual message of December last, recommended an appropriation to satisfy the claims of the Texan Government against the United States, which had been previously adjusted so far as the powers of the Executive extend. These claims arose out of the act of disarming a body of Texan troops under the command of Major Snively by an officer in the service of the United States, acting under the orders of our Government, and the forcible entry into the custom-house at Bryarlys Landing, on Red River, by certain citizens of the United States and taking away therefrom the goods seized by the collector of the customs as forfeited under the laws of Texas. This was a liquidated debt ascertained to be due to Texas when an independent state. Her acceptance of the terms of annexation proposed by the United States does not discharge or invalidate the claim. I recommend that provision be made for its payment.

The commissioner appointed to China during the special session of the Senate in March last shortly afterwards set out on his mission in the United States ship *Columbus*. On arriving at Rio de Janeiro on his passage the state of his health had become so critical that by the advice of his medical attendants he returned to the United States early in the month of October last. Commodore Biddle, commanding the East India Squadron, proceeded on his voyage in the *Columbus*, and was charged by the commissioner with the duty of exchanging with the proper authorities the ratifications of the treaty lately concluded with the Emporer of China. Since the return of the commissioner to the United States his health has been much improved, and he entertains the confident belief that he will soon be able to proceed on his mission.

Unfortunately, differences continue to exist among some of the nations of South America which, following our example, have established their independence, while in others internal dissensions prevail. It is natural that our sympathies should be warmly enlisted for their welfare; that we should desire that all controversies between them should be amicably adjusted and their Governments administered in a manner to protect the rights and promote the prosperity of their people. It is contrary, however, to our settled policy to interfere in their controversies, whether external or internal.

I have thus adverted to all the subjects connected with our foreign relations to which I deem it necessary to call your attention. Our policy is not only peace with all, but good will toward all the powers of the earth. While we are just to all, we require that all shall be just to us. Excepting the differences with Mexico and Great Britain, our relations with all civilized nations are of the most satisfactory character. It is hoped that in this enlightened age these differences may be amicably adjusted.

The Secretary of the Treasury in his annual report to Congress will communicate a full statement of the condition of our finances. The imports for the fiscal year ending on the 30th of June last were of the value of $117,254,564, of which the amount exported was $15,346,830, leaving a balance of $101,907,734 for domestic consumption. The exports for the same year were of the value of $114,646,606, of which the amount of domestic articles was $99,299,776. The receipts into the Treasury during the same year were $29,769,133.56, of which there were derived from customs $27,528,112.70, from sales of public lands $2,077,022.30, and from incidental and miscellaneous sources $163,998.56. The expenditures for the same period were $29,968,206.98, of which $8,588,157.62 were applied to the payment of the public debt. The balance in the Treasury on the 1st of July last was $7,658,306.22. The amount of the public debt remaining unpaid on the 1st of October last was $17,075,445.52. Further payments of the public debt would have been made, in anticipation of the period of its reimbursement under the authority conferred upon the Secretary of the Treasury by the acts of July 21, 1841, and of April 15, 1842, and March 3, 1843, had not the unsettled state of our relations with Mexico menaced hostile collision with that power. In view of such a contingency it was deemed prudent to retain in the Treasury an amount unusually large for ordinary purposes.

A few years ago our whole national debt growing out of the Revolution and the War of 1812 with Great Britain was extinguished, and we presented to the world the rare and noble spectacle of a great and growing people who had fully discharged every obligation. Since that time the existing debt has been contracted, and, small as it is in comparison with the similar burdens of most other nations, it should be extinguished at the earliest practicable period. Should the state of the country permit, and especially if our foreign relations interpose no obstacle, it is contemplated to apply all the moneys in the Treasury as they accrue, beyond what is required for the appropriations by Congress, to its liquidation. I cherish the hope of soon being able to congratulate the country on its recovering once more the lofty position which it so recently occupied. Our country, which exhibits to the world the benefits of self-government, in developing all the sources of national prosperity owes to mankind the permanent example of a nation free from the blighting influence of a public debt.

The attention of Congress is invited to the importance of making suitable modifications and reductions of the rates of duty imposed by our present tariff laws. The object of imposing duties on imports should be to raise revenue to pay the necessary expenses of Government. Congress may undoubtedly, in the exercise of a sound discretion, discriminate in arranging the rates of duty on different articles, but the discriminations should be within the revenue standard and be made with the view to raise money for the support of Government.

It becomes important to understand distinctly what is meant by a revenue standard the maximum of which should not be exceeded in the rates of duty imposed. It is conceded, and experience proves, that duties may be laid so high as to diminish or prohibit altogether the importation of any given article, and thereby lessen or destroy the revenue which at lower rates would be derived from its importation. Such duties exceed the revenue rates and are not imposed to raise money for the support of Government. If Congress levy a duty for revenue of 1 per cent on a given article, it will produce a given amount of money to the Treasury and will incidentally and necessarily afford protection or advantage to the amount of 1 per cent to the home manufacturer of a similar or like article over the importer. If the duty be raised to 10 per cent, it will produce a greater amount of money and afford greater protection. If it be still raised to 20, 25, or 30 per cent, and if as it is raised the revenue derived from it is found to be increased, the protection or advantage will also be increased; but if it be raised to 31 per cent, and it is found that the revenue produced at that rate is less than at 30 per cent, it ceases to be a revenue duty.   The precise point in the ascending scale of duties at which it is ascertained from experience that the revenue is greatest is the maximum rate of duty which can be laid for the *bona fide* purpose of collecting money for the support of Government.   To raise the duties higher than that point, and thereby diminish the amount collected, is to levy them for protection merely, and not for revenue.   As long, then, as Congress may gradually increase the rate of duty on a given article, and the revenue is increased by such increase of duty, they are within the revenue standard.   When they go beyond that point, and as they increase the duties, the revenue is diminished or destroyed; the act ceases to have for its object the raising of money to support Government, but is for protection merely.   It does not follow that Congress should levy the highest duty on all articles of import which they will bear within the revenue standard, for such rates would probably produce a much larger amount than the economical administration of the Government would require. Nor does it follow that the duties on all articles should be at the same or a horizontal rate.   Some articles will bear a much higher revenue duty than others.   Below the maximum of the revenue standard Congress may and ought to discriminate in the rates imposed, taking care so to adjust them on different articles as to produce in the aggregate the amount which, when added to the proceeds of the sales of public lands, may be needed to pay the economical expenses of the Government.

In levying a tariff of duties Congress exercise the taxing power, and for purposes of revenue may select the objects of taxation.   They may exempt certain articles altogether and permit their importation free of duty.   On others they may impose low duties.   In these classes should be embraced such articles of necessity as are in general use, and especially such as are consumed by the laborer and poor as well as by the wealthy citizen.   Care should be taken that all the great interests of the country, including manufactures, agriculture, commerce, navigation, and the mechanic arts, should, as far as may be practicable, derive equal advantages from the incidental protection which a just system of revenue duties may afford.   Taxation, direct or indirect, is a burden, and it should be so imposed as to operate as equally as may be on all classes in the proportion of their ability to bear it.   To make the taxing power an actual benefit to one class necessarily increases the burden of the others beyond their proportion, and would be manifestly unjust.   The terms "protection to domestic industry" are of popular import, but they should apply under a just system to all the various branches of industry in our country.   The farmer or planter who toils yearly in his fields is engaged in "domestic industry," and is as much entitled to have his labor "protected" as the manufacturer, the man of commerce, the navigator, or the mechanic, who are engaged also in "domestic industry" in their different pursuits.   The joint labors of all these classes constitute the aggregate of the "domestic industry" of the nation, and they are equally entitled to the nation's "protection." No one of them can justly claim to be the exclusive recipient of "protection," which can only be afforded by increasing burdens on the "domestic industry" of the others.

If these views be correct, it remains to inquire how far the tariff act of 1842 is consistent with them. That many of the provisions of that act are in violation of the cardinal principles here laid down all must concede. The rates of duty imposed by it on some articles are prohibitory and on others so high as greatly to diminish importations and to produce a less amount of revenue than would be derived from lower rates. They operate as "protection merely" to one branch of "domestic industry" by taxing other branches.

By the introduction of minimums, or assumed and false values, and by the imposition of specific duties the injustice and inequality of the act of 1842 in its practical operations on different classes and pursuits are seen and felt. Many of the oppressive duties imposed by it under the operation of these principles range from 1 per cent to more than 200 per cent. They are prohibitory on some articles and partially so on others, and bear most heavily on articles of common necessity and but lightly on articles of luxury. It is so framed that much the greatest burden which it imposes is thrown on labor and the poorer classes, who are least able to bear it, while it protects capital and exempts the rich from paying their just proportion of the taxation required for the support of Government. While it protects the capital of the wealthy manufacturer and increases his profits, it does not benefit the operatives or laborers in his employment, whose wages have not been increased by it. Articles of prime necessity or of coarse quality and low price, used by the masses of the people, are in many instances subjected by it to heavy taxes, while articles of finer quality and higher price, or of luxury, which can be used only by the opulent, are lightly taxed. It imposes heavy and unjust burdens on the farmer, the planter, the commercial man, and those of all other pursuits except the capitalist who has made his investments in manufactures. All the great interests of the country are not as nearly as may be practicable equally protected by it.

The Government in theory knows no distinction of persons or classes, and should not bestow upon some favors and privileges which all others may not enjoy. It was the purpose of its illustrious founders to base the institutions which they reared upon the great and unchanging principles of justice and equity, conscious that if administered in the spirit in which they were conceived they would be felt only by the benefits which they diffused, and would secure for themselves a defense in the hearts of the people more powerful than standing armies and all the means and appliances invented to sustain governments founded in injustice and oppression.

The well-known fact that the tariff act of 1842 was passed by a majority of one vote in the Senate and two in the House of Representatives, and

that some of those who felt themselves constrained, under the peculiar
circumstances existing at the time, to vote in its favor, proclaimed its
defects and expressed their determination to aid in its modification on
the first opportunity, affords strong and conclusive evidence that it was
not intended to be permanent, and of the expediency and necessity of its
thorough revision.

In recommending to Congress a reduction of the present rates of duty
and a revision and modification of the act of 1842, I am far from entertaining opinions unfriendly to the manufacturers. On the contrary, I
desire to see them prosperous as far as they can be so without imposing
unequal burdens on other interests. The advantage under any system of
indirect taxation, even within the revenue standard, must be in favor
of the manufacturing interest, and of this no other interest will complain.

I recommend to Congress the abolition of the minimum principle, or
assumed, arbitrary, and false values, and of specific duties, and the substitution in their place of *ad valorem* duties as the fairest and most equitable indirect tax which can be imposed. By the *ad valorem* principle all
articles are taxed according to their cost or value, and those which are of
inferior quality or of small cost bear only the just proportion of the tax
with those which are of superior quality or greater cost. The articles
consumed by all are taxed at the same rate. A system of *ad valorem*
revenue duties, with proper discriminations and proper guards against
frauds in collecting them, it is not doubted will afford ample incidental
advantages to the manufacturers and enable them to derive as great
profits as can be derived from any other regular business. It is believed
that such a system strictly within the revenue standard will place the
manufacturing interests on a stable footing and inure to their permanent advantage, while it will as nearly as may be practicable extend
to all the great interests of the country the incidental protection which
can be afforded by our revenue laws. Such a system, when once firmly
established, would be permanent, and not be subject to the constant complaints, agitations, and changes which must ever occur when duties are
not laid for revenue, but for the ''protection merely'' of a favored interest.

In the deliberations of Congress on this subject it is hoped that a
spirit of mutual concession and compromise between conflicting interests
may prevail, and that the result of their labors may be crowned with the
happiest consequences.

By the Constitution of the United States it is provided that ''no money
shall be drawn from the Treasury but in consequence of appropriations
made by law.'' A public treasury was undoubtedly contemplated and
intended to be created, in which the public money should be kept from
the period of collection until needed for public uses. In the collection and
disbursement of the public money no agencies have ever been employed
by law except such as were appointed by the Government, directly responsible to it and under its control. The safe-keeping of the public money

should be confided to a public treasury created by law and under like responsibility and control. It is not to be imagined that the framers of the Constitution could have intended that a treasury should be created as a place of deposit and safe-keeping of the public money which was irresponsible to the Government. The first Congress under the Constitution, by the act of the 2d of September, 1789, "to establish the Treasury Department," provided for the appointment of a Treasurer, and made it his duty "to receive and keep the moneys of the United States" and "at all times to submit to the Secretary of the Treasury and the Comptroller, or either of them, the inspection of the moneys in his hands."

That banks, national or State, could not have been intended to be used as a substitute for the Treasury spoken of in the Constitution as keepers of the public money is manifest from the fact that at that time there was no national bank, and but three or four State banks, of limited capital, existed in the country. Their employment as depositories was at first resorted to to a limited extent, but with no avowed intention of continuing them permanently in place of the Treasury of the Constitution. When they were afterwards from time to time employed, it was from motives of supposed convenience. Our experience has shown that when banking corporations have been the keepers of the public money, and been thereby made in effect the Treasury, the Government can have no guaranty that it can command the use of its own money for public purposes. The late Bank of the United States proved to be faithless. The State banks which were afterwards employed were faithless. But a few years ago, with millions of public money in their keeping, the Government was brought almost to bankruptcy and the public credit seriously impaired because of their inability or indisposition to pay on demand to the public creditors in the only currency recognized by the Constitution. Their failure occurred in a period of peace, and great inconvenience and loss were suffered by the public from it. Had the country been involved in a foreign war, that inconvenience and loss would have been much greater, and might have resulted in extreme public calamity. The public money should not be mingled with the private funds of banks or individuals or be used for private purposes. When it is placed in banks for safe-keeping, it is in effect loaned to them without interest, and is loaned by them upon interest to the borrowers from them. The public money is converted into banking capital, and is used and loaned out for the private profit of bank stockholders, and when called for, as was the case in 1837, it may be in the pockets of the borrowers from the banks instead of being in the public Treasury contemplated by the Constitution. The framers of the Constitution could never have intended that the money paid into the Treasury should be thus converted to private use and placed beyond the control of the Government.

Banks which hold the public money are often tempted by a desire of gain to extend their loans, increase their circulation, and thus stimulate, if not produce, a spirit of speculation and extravagance which sooner or later must result in ruin to thousands. If the public money be not permitted to be thus used, but be kept in the Treasury and paid out to the public creditors in gold and silver, the temptation afforded by its deposit with banks to an undue expansion of their business would be checked, while the amount of the constitutional currency left in circulation would be enlarged by its employment in the public collections and disbursements, and the banks themselves would in consequence be found in a safer and sounder condition. At present State banks are employed as depositories, but without adequate regulation of law whereby the public money can be secured against the casualties and excesses, revulsions, suspensions, and defalcations to which from overissues, overtrading, an inordinate desire for gain, or other causes they are constantly exposed. The Secretary of the Treasury has in all cases when it was practicable taken collateral security for the amount which they hold, by the pledge of stocks of the United States or such of the States as were in good credit. Some of the deposit banks have given this description of security and others have declined to do so.

Entertaining the opinion that "the separation of the moneys of the Government from banking institutions is indispensable for the safety of the funds of the Government and the rights of the people," I recommend to Congress that provision be made by law for such separation, and that a constitutional treasury be created for the safe-keeping of the public money. The constitutional treasury recommended is designed as a secure depository for the public money, without any power to make loans or discounts or to issue any paper whatever as a currency or circulation. I can not doubt that such a treasury as was contemplated by the Constitution should be independent of all banking corporations. The money of the people should be kept in the Treasury of the people created by law, and be in the custody of agents of the people chosen by themselves according to the forms of the Constitution—agents who are directly responsible to the Government, who are under adequate bonds and oaths, and who are subject to severe punishments for any embezzlement, private use, or misapplication of the public funds, and for any failure in other respects to perform their duties. To say that the people or their Government are incompetent or not to be trusted with the custody of their own money in their own Treasury, provided by themselves, but must rely on the presidents, cashiers, and stockholders of banking corporations, not appointed by them nor responsible to them, would be to concede that they are incompetent for self-government

In recommending the establishment of a constitutional treasury in which the public money shall be kept, I desire that adequate provision be made by law for its safety and that all Executive discretion or control over it shall be removed, except such as may be necessary in directing its disbursement in pursuance of appropriations made by law.

Under our present land system, limiting the minimum price at which the public lands can be entered to $1.25 per acre, large quantities of lands of inferior quality remain unsold because they will not command that price. From the records of the General Land Office it appears that of the public lands remaining unsold in the several States and Territories in which they are situated, 39,105,577 acres have been in the market subject to entry more than twenty years, 49,638,644 acres for more than fifteen years, 73,074,600 acres for more than ten years, and 106,176,961 acres for more than five years. Much the largest portion of these lands will continue to be unsalable at the minimum price at which they are permitted to be sold so long as large territories of lands from which the more valuable portions have not been selected are annually brought into market by the Government. With the view to the sale and settlement of these inferior lands, I recommend that the price be graduated and reduced below the present minimum rate, confining the sales at the reduced prices to settlers and cultivators, in limited quantities. If graduated and reduced in price for a limited term to $1 per acre, and after the expiration of that period for a second and third term to lower rates, a large portion of these lands would be purchased, and many worthy citizens who are unable to pay higher rates could purchase homes for themselves and their families. By adopting the policy of graduation and reduction of price these inferior lands will be sold for their real value, while the States in which they lie will be freed from the inconvenience, if not injustice, to which they are subjected in consequence of the United States continuing to own large quantities of the public lands within their borders not liable to taxation for the support of their local governments.

I recommend the continuance of the policy of granting preemptions in its most liberal extent to all those who have settled or may hereafter settle on the public lands, whether surveyed or unsurveyed, to which the Indian title may have been extinguished at the time of settlement. It has been found by experience that in consequence of combinations of purchasers and other causes a very small quantity of the public lands, when sold at public auction, commands a higher price than the minimum rates established by law. The settlers on the public lands are, however, but rarely able to secure their homes and improvements at the public sales at that rate, because these combinations, by means of the capital they command and their superior ability to purchase, render it impossible for the settler to compete with them in the market. By putting down all competition these combinations of capitalists and speculators are usually enabled to purchase the lands, including the improvements of the settlers, at the minimum price of the Government, and either turn them out of their homes or extort from them, according to their ability to pay, double or quadruple the amount paid for them to the Government. It is to the enterprise and perseverance of the hardy pioneers of the West, who penetrate the wilderness with their families, suffer the dangers, the privations, and hardships attending the settlement of a new country, and prepare the way for the body of emigrants who in the course of a few years usually follow them, that we are in a great degree indebted for the rapid extension and aggrandizement of our country.

Experience has proved that no portion of our population are more patriotic than the hardy and brave men of the frontier, or more ready to obey the call of their country and to defend her rights and her honor whenever and by whatever enemy assailed. They should be protected from the grasping speculator and secured, at the minimum price of the public lands, in the humble homes which they have improved by their labor. With this end in view, all vexatious or unnecessary restrictions imposed upon them by the existing preemption laws should be repealed or modified. It is the true policy of the Government to afford facilities to its citizens to become the owners of small portions of our vast public domain at low and moderate rates.

The present system of managing the mineral lands of the United States is believed to be radically defective. More than 1,000,000 acres of the public lands, supposed to contain lead and other minerals, have been reserved from sale, and numerous leases upon them have been granted to individuals upon a stipulated rent. The system of granting leases has proved to be not only unprofitable to the Government, but unsatisfactory to the citizens who have gone upon the lands, and must, if continued, lay the foundation of much future difficulty between the Government and the lessees. According to the official records, the amount of rents received by the Government for the years 1841, 1842, 1843, and 1844 was $6,354.74, while the expenses of the system during the same period, including salaries of superintendents, agents, clerks, and incidental expenses, were $26,111.11, the income being less than one-fourth of the expenses. To this pecuniary loss may be added the injury sustained by the public in consequence of the destruction of timber and the careless and wasteful manner of working the mines. The system has given rise to much litigation between the United States and individual citizens, producing irritation and excitement in the mineral region, and involving the Government in heavy additional expenditures. It is believed that similar losses and embarrassments will continue to occur while the present system of leasing these lands remains unchanged. These lands are now under the superintendence and care of the War Department, with the ordinary duties of which they have no proper or natural connection. I recommend the repeal of the present system, and that these lands be placed under the superintendence and management of the General Land Office, as other public lands, and be brought into market and sold upon such terms as Congress in their wisdom may prescribe, reserving to the Government an equitable percentage of the gross amount of mineral product, and that the preemption principle be extended to resident miners and settlers upon them at the minimum price which may be established by Congress.

I refer you to the accompanying report of the Secretary of War for information respecting the present situation of the Army and its operations during the past year, the state of our defenses, the condition of the public works, and our relations with the various Indian tribes within our limits or upon our borders. I invite your attention to the suggestions contained in that report in relation to these prominent objects of national interest. When orders were given during the past summer for concentrating a military force on the western frontier of Texas, our troops were widely dispersed and in small detachments, occupying posts remote from each other. The prompt and expeditious manner in which an army embracing more than half our peace establishment was drawn together on an emergency so sudden reflects great credit on the officers who were intrusted with the execution of these orders, as well as upon the discipline of the Army itself. To be in strength to protect and defend the people and territory of Texas in the event Mexico should commence hostilities or invade her territories with a large army, which she threatened, I authorized the general assigned to the command of the army of occupation to make requisitions for additional forces from several of the States nearest the Texan territory, and which could most expeditiously furnish them, if in his opinion a larger force than that under his command and the auxiliary aid which under like circumstances he was authorized to receive from Texas should be required. The contingency upon which the exercise of this authority depended has not occurred. The circumstances under which two companies of State artillery from the city of New Orleans were sent into Texas and mustered into the service of the United States are fully stated in the report of the Secretary of War. I recommend to Congress that provision be made for the payment of these troops, as well as a small number of Texan volunteers whom the commanding general thought it necessary to receive or muster into our service.

During the last summer the First Regiment of Dragoons made extensive excursions through the Indian country on our borders, a part of them advancing nearly to the possessions of the Hudsons Bay Company in the north, and a part as far as the South Pass of the Rocky Mountains and the head waters of the tributary streams of the Colorado of the West. The exhibition of this military force among the Indian tribes in those distant regions and the councils held with them by the commanders of the expeditions, it is believed, will have a salutary influence in restraining them from hostilities among themselves and maintaining friendly relations between them and the United States. An interesting account of one of these excursions accompanies the report of the Secretary of War. Under the directions of the War Department Brevet Captain Frémont, of the Corps of Topographical Engineers, has been employed since 1842 in exploring the country west of the Mississippi and beyond the Rocky Mountains. Two expeditions have already been brought to a close, and the reports of that scientific and enterprising officer have furnished much interesting and valuable information. He is now engaged in a third expedition, but it is not expected that this arduous service will be completed in season to enable me to communicate the result to Congress at the present session.

Our relations with the Indian tribes are of a favorable character. The policy of removing them to a country designed for their permanent residence west of the Mississippi, and without the limits of the organized States and Territories, is better appreciated by them than it was a few years ago, while education is now attended to and the habits of civilized life are gaining ground among them.

Serious difficulties of long standing continue to distract the several parties into which the Cherokees are unhappily divided. The efforts of the Government to adjust the difficulties between them have heretofore proved unsuccessful, and ·there remains no probability that this desirable object can be accomplished without the aid of further legislation by Congress. I will at an early period of your session present the subject for your consideration, accompanied with an exposition of the complaints and claims of the several parties into which the nation is divided, with a view to the adoption of such measures by Congress as may enable the Executive to do justice to them, respectively, and to put an end, if possible, to the dissensions which have long prevailed and still prevail among them.

I refer you to the report of the Secretary of the Navy for the present condition of that branch of the national defense and for grave suggestions having for their object the increase of its efficiency and a greater economy in its management. During the past year the officers and men have performed their duty in a satisfactory manner. The orders which have been given have been executed with promptness and fidelity. A larger force than has often formed one squadron under our flag was readily concentrated in the Gulf of Mexico, and apparently without unusual effort. It is especially to be observed that notwithstanding the union of so considerable a force, no act was committed that even the jealousy of an irritated power could construe as an act of aggression, and that the commander of the squadron and his officers, in strict conformity with their instructions, holding themselves ever ready for the most active duty, have achieved the still purer glory of contributing to the preservation of peace. It is believed that at all our foreign stations the honor of our flag has been maintained and that generally our ships of war have been distinguished for their good discipline and order. I am happy to add that the display of maritime force which was required by the events of the summer has been made wholly within the usual appropriations for the service of the year, so that no additional appropriations are required.

The commerce of the United States, and with it the navigating interests, have steadily and rapidly increased since the organization of our Government, until, it is believed, we are now second to but one power in the world, and at no distant day we shall probably be inferior to none. Exposed as they must be, it has been a wise policy to afford to these important interests protection with our ships of war distributed in the great highways of trade throughout the world. For more than thirty years appropriations have been made and annually expended for the gradual increase of our naval forces. In peace our Navy performs the important duty of protecting our commerce, and in the event of war will be, as it has been, a most efficient means of defense.

The successful use of steam navigation on the ocean has been followed by the introduction of war steamers in great and increasing numbers into the navies of the principal maritime powers of the world. A due regard to our own safety and to an efficient protection to our large and increasing commerce demands a corresponding increase on our part. No country has greater facilities for the construction of vessels of this description than ours, or can promise itself greater advantages from their employment. They are admirably adapted to the protection of our commerce, to the rapid transmission of intelligence, and to the coast defense. In pursuance of the wise policy of a gradual increase of our Navy, large supplies of live-oak timber and other materials for shipbuilding have been collected and are now under shelter and in a state of good preservation, while iron steamers can be built with great facility in various parts of the Union. The use of iron as a material, especially in the construction of steamers which can enter with safety many of the harbors along our coast now inaccessible to vessels of greater draft, and the practicability of constructing them in the interior, strongly recommend that liberal appropriations should be made for this important object. Whatever may have been our policy in the earlier stages of the Government, when the nation was in its infancy, our shipping interests and commerce comparatively small, our resources limited, our population sparse and scarcely extending beyond the limits of the original thirteen States, that policy must be essentially different now that we have grown from three to more than twenty millions of people, that our commerce, carried in our own ships, is found in every sea, and that our territorial boundaries and settlements have been so greatly expanded. Neither our commerce nor our long line of coast on the ocean and on the Lakes can be successfully defended against foreign aggression by means of fortifications alone. These are essential at important commercial and military points, but our chief reliance for this object must be on a well-organized, efficient navy. The benefits resulting from such a navy are not confined to the Atlantic States. The productions of the interior which seek a market abroad are directly dependent on the safety and freedom of our commerce. The occupation of the Balize below New Orleans by a hostile force would embarrass, if not stagnate, the whole export trade of the Mississippi and affect the value of the agricultural products of the entire valley of that mighty river and its tributaries.

It has never been our policy to maintain large standing armies in time of peace. They are contrary to the genius of our free institutions, would impose heavy burdens on the people and be dangerous to public liberty. Our reliance for protection and defense on the land must be mainly on our citizen soldiers, who will be ever ready, as they ever have been ready in times past, to rush with alacrity, at the call of their country, to her defense. This description of force, however, can not defend our coast, harbors, and inland seas, nor protect our commerce on the ocean or the Lakes. These must be protected by our Navy.

Considering an increased naval force, and especially of steam vessels, corresponding with our growth and importance as a nation, and proportioned to the increased and increasing naval power of other nations, of vast importance as regards our safety, and the great and growing interests to be protected by it, I recommend the subject to the favorable consideration of Congress.

The report of the Postmaster-General herewith communicated contains a detailed statement of the operations of his Department during the past year. It will be seen that the income from postages will fall short of the expenditures for the year between $1,000,000 and $2,000,000. This deficiency has been caused by the reduction of the rates of postage, which was made by the act of the 3d of March last. No principle has been more generally acquiesced in by the people than that this Department should sustain itself by limiting its expenditures to its income. Congress has never sought to make it a source of revenue for general purposes except for a short period during the last war with Great Britain, nor should it ever become a charge on the general Treasury. If Congress shall adhere to this principle, as I think they ought, it will be necessary either to curtail the present mail service so as to reduce the expenditures, or so to modify the act of the 3d of March last as to improve its revenues. The extension of the mail service and the additional facilities which will be demanded by the rapid extension and increase of population on our western frontier will not admit of such curtailment as will materially reduce the present expenditures. In the adjustment of the tariff of postages the interests of the people demand that the lowest rates be adopted which will produce the necessary revenue to meet the expenditures of the Department. I invite the attention of Congress to the suggestions of the Postmaster-General on this subject, under the belief that such a modification of the late law may be made as will yield sufficient revenue without further calls on the Treasury, and with very little change in the present rates of postage. Proper measures have been taken in pursuance of the act of the 3d of March last for the establishment of lines of mail steamers between this and foreign countries. The importance of this service commends itself strongly to favorable consideration.

With the growth of our country the public business which devolves on the heads of the several Executive Departments has greatly increased. In some respects the distribution of duties among them seems to be incongruous, and many of these might be transferred from one to another with advantage to the public interests. A more auspicious time for the consideration of this subject by Congress, with a view to system in the organization of the several Departments and a more appropriate division of the public business, will not probably occur.

The most important duties of the State Department relate to our foreign affairs. By the great enlargement of the family of nations, the increase of our commerce, and the corresponding extension of our consular system the business of this Department has been greatly increased. In its present organization many duties of a domestic nature and consisting of details are devolved on the Secretary of State, which do not appropriately belong to the foreign department of the Government and may properly be transferred to some other Department. One of these grows out of the present state of the law concerning the Patent Office, which a few years since was a subordinate clerkship, but has become a distinct bureau of great importance. With an excellent internal organization, it is still connected with the State Department. In the transaction of its business questions of much importance to inventors and to the community frequently arise, which by existing laws are referred for decision to a board of which the Secretary of State is a member. These questions are legal, and the connection which now exists between the State Department and the Patent Office may with great propriety and advantage be transferred to the Attorney-General.

In his last annual message to Congress Mr. Madison invited attention to a proper provision for the Attorney-General as ''an important improvement in the executive establishment.'' This recommendation was repeated by some of his successors. The official duties of the Attorney-General have been much increased within a few years, and his office has become one of great importance. His duties may be still further increased with advantage to the public interests. As an executive officer his residence and constant attention at the seat of Government are required. Legal questions involving important principles and large amounts of public money are constantly referred to him by the President and Executive Departments for his examination and decision. The public business under his official management before the judiciary has been so augmented by the extension of our territory and the acts of Congress authorizing suits against the United States for large bodies of valuable public lands as greatly to increase his labors and responsibilities. I therefore recommend that the Attorney-General be placed on the same footing with the heads of the other Executive Departments, with such subordinate officers provided by law for his Department as may be required to discharge the additional duties which have been or may be devolved upon him.

Congress possess the power of exclusive legislation over the District of

Columbia, and I commend the interests of its inhabitants to your favorable consideration. The people of this District have no legislative body of their own, and must confide their local as well as their general interests to representatives in whose election they have no voice and over whose official conduct they have no control. Each member of the National Legislature should consider himself as their immediate representative, and should be the more ready to give attention to their interests and wants because he is not responsible to them. I recommend that a liberal and generous spirit may characterize your measures in relation to them. I shall be ever disposed to show a proper regard for their wishes and, within constitutional limits, shall at all times cheerfully cooperate with you for the advancement of their welfare.

I trust it may not be deemed inappropriate to the occasion for me to dwell for a moment on the memory of the most eminent citizen of our country who during the summer that is gone by has descended to the tomb. The enjoyment of contemplating, at the advanced age of near fourscore years, the happy condition of his country cheered the last hours of Andrew Jackson, who departed this life in the tranquil hope of a blessed immortality. His death was happy, as his life had been eminently useful. He had an unfaltering confidence in the virtue and capacity of the people and in the permanence of that free Government which he had largely contributed to establish and defend. His great deeds had secured to him the affections of his fellow-citizens, and it was his happiness to witness the growth and glory of his country, which he loved so well. He departed amidst the benedictions of millions of freemen. The nation paid its tribute to his memory at his tomb. Coming generations will learn from his example the love of country and the rights of man. In his language on a similar occasion to the present, "I now commend you, fellow-citizens, to the guidance of Almighty God, with a full reliance on His merciful providence for the maintenance of our free institutions, and with an earnest supplication that whatever errors it may be my lot to commit in discharging the arduous duties which have devolved on me will find a remedy in the harmony and wisdom of your counsels."

SECOND ANNUAL MESSAGE.

WASHINGTON, *December 8, 1846.*
Fellow-Citizens of the Senate and of the House of Representatives:

In resuming your labors in the service of the people it is a subject of congratulation that there has been no period in our past history when all the elements of national prosperity have been so fully developed. Since your last session no afflicting dispensation has visited our country. General good health has prevailed, abundance has crowned the toil of the husbandman, and labor in all its branches is receiving an ample reward, while education, science, and the arts are rapidly enlarging the means of social happiness. The progress of our country in her career of greatness, not only in the vast extension of our territorial limits and the rapid increase of our population, but in resources and wealth and in the happy condition of our people, is without an example in the history of nations.

As the wisdom, strength, and beneficence of our free institutions are unfolded, every day adds fresh motives to contentment and fresh incentives to patriotism.

Our devout and sincere acknowledgments are due to the gracious Giver of All Good for the numberless blessings which our beloved country enjoys.

It is a source of high satisfaction to know that the relations of the United States with all other nations, with a single exception, are of the most amicable character. Sincerely attached to the policy of peace early adopted and steadily pursued by this Government, I have anxiously desired to cultivate and cherish friendship and commerce with every foreign power. The spirit and habits of the American people are favorable to the maintenance of such international harmony. In adhering to this wise policy, a preliminary and paramount duty obviously consists in the protection of our national interests from encroachment or sacrifice and our national honor from reproach. These must be maintained at any hazard. They admit of no compromise or neglect, and must be scrupulously and constantly guarded. In their vigilant vindication collision and conflict with foreign powers may sometimes become unavoidable. Such has been our scrupulous adherence to the dictates of justice in all our foreign intercourse that, though steadily and rapidly advancing in prosperity and power, we have given no just cause of complaint to any nation and have enjoyed the blessings of peace for more than thirty years. From a policy so sacred to humanity and so salutary in its effects upon our political system we should never be induced voluntarily to depart.

The existing war with Mexico was neither desired nor provoked by the United States. On the contrary, all honorable means were resorted to to avert it. After years of endurance of aggravated and unredressed wrongs on our part, Mexico, in violation of solemn treaty stipulations and of every principle of justice recognized by civilized nations, commenced hostilities, and thus by her own act forced the war upon us. Long before the advance of our Army to the left bank of the Rio Grande we had ample cause of war against Mexico, and had the United States resorted to this extremity we might have appealed to the whole civilized world for the justice of our cause. I deem it to be my duty to present to you on the present occasion a condensed review of the injuries we had sustained, of the causes which led to the war, and of its progress since its commencement. This is rendered the more necessary because of the misapprehensions which have to some extent prevailed as to its origin and true character. The war has been represented as unjust and unnecessary and as one of aggression on our part upon a weak and injured enemy. Such erroneous views, though entertained by but few, have been widely and extensively circulated, not only at home, but have been spread throughout Mexico and the whole world. A more effectual means could not have been devised to encourage the enemy and protract the war than to advocate and adhere to their cause, and thus give them "aid and comfort." It is a source of national pride and exultation that the great body of our people have thrown no such obstacles in the way of the Government in prosecuting the war successfully, but have shown themselves to be eminently patriotic and ready to vindicate their country's honor and interests at any sacrifice. The alacrity and promptness with which our volunteer forces rushed to the field on their country's call prove not only their patriotism, but their deep conviction that our cause is just.

The wrongs which we have suffered from Mexico almost ever since she became an independent power and the patient endurance with which we have borne them are without a parallel in the history of modern civilized nations. There is reason to believe that if these wrongs had been resented and resisted in the first instance the present war might have been avoided. One outrage, however, permitted to pass with impunity almost necessarily encouraged the perpetration of another, until at last Mexico seemed to attribute to weakness and indecision on our part a forbearance which was the offspring of magnanimity and of a sincere desire to preserve friendly relations with a sister republic.

Scarcely had Mexico achieved her independence, which the United States were the first among the nations to acknowledge, when she commenced the system of insult and spoliation which she has ever since pursued. Our citizens engaged in lawful commerce were imprisoned, their vessels seized, and our flag insulted in her ports. If money was wanted, the lawless seizure and confiscation of our merchant vessels and their cargoes was a ready resource, and if to accomplish their purposes it became necessary to imprison the owners, captains, and crews, it was done. Rulers superseded rulers in Mexico in rapid succession, but still there was no change in this system of depredation. The Government of the United States made repeated reclamations on behalf of its citizens, but these were answered by the perpetration of new outrages. Promises of redress made by Mexico in the most solemn forms were postponed or evaded. The files and records of the Department of State contain conclusive proofs of numerous lawless acts perpetrated upon the property and persons of our citizens by Mexico, and of wanton insults to our national flag. The interposition of our Government to obtain redress was again and again invoked under circumstances which no nation ought to disregard. It was hoped that these outrages would cease and that Mexico would be restrained by the laws which regulate the conduct of civilized nations in their intercourse with each other after the treaty of amity, commerce, and navigation of the 5th of April, 1831, was concluded between the two Republics; but this hope soon proved to be vain. The course of seizure and confiscation of the property of our citizens, the violation of their persons, and the insults to our flag pursued by Mexico previous to that time were scarcely suspended for even a brief period, although the treaty so clearly defines the rights and duties of the respective parties that it is impossible to misunderstand or mistake them. In less than seven years after the conclusion of that treaty our grievances had become so intolerable that in the opinion of President Jackson they should no longer be endured. In his message to Congress in February, 1837, he presented them to the consideration of that body, and declared that—

The length of time since some of the injuries have been committed, the repeated and unavailing applications for redress, the wanton character of some of the outrages upon the property and persons of our citizens, upon the officers and flag of the United States, independent of recent insults to this Government and people by the late extraordinary Mexican minister, would justify in the eyes of all nations immediate war.

In a spirit of kindness and forbearance, however, he recommended reprisals as a milder mode of redress. He declared that war should not be used as a remedy "by just and generous nations, confiding in their strength for injuries committed, if it can be honorably avoided," and added:

It has occurred to me that, considering the present embarrassed condition of that country, we should act with both wisdom and moderation by giving to Mexico one more opportunity to atone for the past before we take redress into our own hands. To avoid all misconception on the part of Mexico, as well as to protect our own national character from reproach, this opportunity should be given with the avowed design and full preparation to take immediate satisfaction if it should not be obtained on a repetition of the demand for it. To this end I recommend that an act be passed authorizing reprisals, and the use of the naval force of the United States by the Executive against Mexico to enforce them, in the event of a refusal by the Mexican Government to come to an amicable adjustment of the matters in controversy between us upon another demand thereof made from on board one of our vessels of war on the coast of Mexico.

Committees of both Houses of Congress, to which this message of the President was referred, fully sustained his views of the character of the wrongs which we had suffered from Mexico, and recommended that another demand for redress should be made before authorizing war or reprisals. The Committee on Foreign Relations of the Senate, in their report, say:

After such a demand, should prompt justice be refused by the Mexican Government, we may appeal to all nations, not only for the equity and moderation with which we shall have acted toward a sister republic, but for the necessity which will then compel us to seek redress for our wrongs, either by actual war or by reprisals. The subject will then be presented before Congress, at the commencement of the next session, in a clear and distinct form, and the committee can not doubt but that such measures will be immediately adopted as may be necessary to vindicate the honor of the country and insure ample reparation to our injured fellow-citizens.

The Committee on Foreign Affairs of the House of Representatives made a similar recommendation. In their report they say that—

They fully concur with the President that ample cause exists for taking redress into our own hands, and believe that we should be justified in the opinion of other nations for taking such a step. But they are willing to try the experiment of another demand, made in the most solemn form, upon the justice of the Mexican Government before any further proceedings are adopted.

No difference of opinion upon the subject is believed to have existed in Congress at that time; the executive and legislative departments concurred; and yet such has been our forbearance and desire to preserve peace with Mexico that the wrongs of which we then complained, and which gave rise to these solemn proceedings, not only remain unredressed to this day, but additional causes of complaint of an aggravated character have ever since been accumulating. Shortly after these proceedings a special messenger was dispatched to Mexico to make a final demand for redress, and on the 20th of July, 1837, the demand was made. The reply of the Mexican Government bears date on the 29th of the same month, and contains assurances of the "anxious wish" of the Mexican Government "not to delay the moment of that final and equitable adjustment which is to terminate the existing difficulties between the two Governments;" that "nothing should be left undone which may contribute to the most speedy and equitable determination of the subjects which have so seriously engaged the attention of the American Government;" that the "Mexican Government would adopt as the only guides for its conduct the plainest principles of public right, the sacred obligations imposed by international law, and the religious faith of treaties," and that "whatever reason and justice may dictate respecting each case will be done." The assurance was further given that the decision of the Mexican Government upon each cause of complaint for which redress had been demanded should be communicated to the Government of the United States by the Mexican minister at Washington.

These solemn assurances in answer to our demand for redress were disregarded. By making them, however, Mexico obtained further delay. President Van Buren, in his annual message to Congress of the 5th of December, 1837, states that "although the larger number" of our demands for redress, "and many of them aggravated cases of personal wrongs, have been now for years before the Mexican Government, and some of the causes of national complaint, and those of the most offensive character, admitted of immediate, simple, and satisfactory replies, it is only within a few days past that any specific communication in answer to our last demand, made five months ago, has been received from the Mexican minister;'' and that "for not one of our public complaints has satisfaction been given or offered, that but one of the cases of personal wrong has been favorably considered, and that but four cases of both descriptions out of all those formally presented and earnestly pressed have as yet been decided upon by the Mexican Government.'' President Van Buren, believing that it would be vain to make any further attempt to obtain redress by the ordinary means within the power of the Executive, communicated this opinion to Congress in the message referred to, in which he said:

> On a careful and deliberate examination of their contents [of the correspondence with the Mexican Government], and considering the spirit manifested by the Mexican Government, it has become my painful duty to return the subject as it now stands to Congress, to whom it belongs to decide upon the time, the mode, and the measure of redress.

Had the United States at that time adopted compulsory measures and taken redress into their own hands, all our difficulties with Mexico would probably have been long since adjusted and the existing war have been averted. Magnanimity and moderation on our part only had the effect to complicate these difficulties and render an amicable settlement of them the more embarrassing. That such measures of redress under similar provocations committed by any of the powerful nations of Europe would have been promptly resorted to by the United States can not be doubted. The national honor and the preservation of the national character throughout the world, as well as our own self-respect and the protection due to our own citizens, would have rendered such a resort indispensable. The history of no civilized nation in modern times has presented within so brief a period so many wanton attacks upon the honor of its flag and upon the property and persons of its citizens as had at that time been borne by the United States from the Mexican authorities and people. But Mexico was a sister republic on the North American continent, occupying a territory contiguous to our own, and was in a feeble and distracted condition, and these considerations, it is presumed, induced Congress to forbear still longer.

Instead of taking redress into our own hands, a new negotiation was entered upon with fair promises on the part of Mexico, but with the real purpose, as the event has proved, of indefinitely postponing the reparation which we demanded, and which was so justly due. This negotiation, after more than a year's delay, resulted in the convention of the 11th of April, 1839, "for the adjustment of claims of citizens of the United States of America upon the Government of the Mexican Republic.'' The joint board of commissioners created by this convention to examine and decide upon these claims was not organized until the month of

August, 1840, and under the terms of the convention they were to terminate their duties within eighteen months from that time. Four of the eighteen months were consumed in preliminary discussions on frivolous and dilatory points raised by the Mexican commissioners, and it was not until the month of December, 1840, that they commenced the examination of the claims of our citizens upon Mexico. Fourteen months only remained to examine and decide upon these numerous and complicated cases. In the month of February, 1842, the term of the commission expired, leaving many claims undisposed of for want of time. The claims which were allowed by the board and by the umpire authorized by the convention to decide in case of disagreement between the Mexican and American commissioners amounted to $2,026,139.68. There were pending before the umpire when the commission expired additional claims, which had been examined and awarded by the American commissioners and had not been allowed by the Mexican commissioners, amounting to $928,627.88, upon which he did not decide, alleging that his authority had ceased with the termination of the joint commission. Besides these claims, there were others of American citizens amounting to $3,336,837.05, which had been submitted to the board, and upon which they had not time to decide before their final adjournment.

The sum of $2,026,139.68, which had been awarded to the claimants, was a liquidated and ascertained debt due by Mexico, about which there could be no dispute, and which she was bound to pay according to the terms of the convention. Soon after the final awards for this amount had been made the Mexican Government asked for a postponement of the time of making payment, alleging that it would be inconvenient to make the payment at the time stipulated. In the spirit of forbearing kindness toward a sister republic, which Mexico has so long abused, the United States promptly complied with her request. A second convention was accordingly concluded between the two Governments on the 30th of January, 1843, which upon its face declares that "this new arrangement is entered into for the accommodation of Mexico." By the terms of this convention all the interest due on the awards which had been made in favor of the claimants under the convention of the 11th of April, 1839, was to be paid to them on the 30th of April, 1843, and "the principal of the said awards and the interest accruing thereon" was stipulated to "be paid in five years, in equal installments every three months." Notwithstanding this new convention was entered into at the request of Mexico and for the purpose of relieving her from embarrassment, the claimants have only received the interest due on the 30th of April, 1843, and three of the twenty installments. Although the payment of the sum thus liquidated and confessedly due by Mexico to our citizens as indemnity for acknowledged acts of outrage and wrong was secured by treaty, the obligations of which are ever held sacred by all just nations, yet Mexico has violated this solemn engagement by failing and refusing to make the payment. The two installments due in April and July, 1844, under the peculiar circumstances connected with them, have been assumed by the United States and discharged to the claimants, but they are still due by Mexico. But this is not all of which we have just cause of complaint. To provide a remedy for the claimants whose cases were not decided by the joint commission under the convention of April 11, 1839, it was expressly stipulated by the sixth article of the convention of the 30th of January, 1843, that—

A new convention shall be entered into for the settlement of all claims of the Government and citizens of the United States against the Republic of Mexico which were not finally decided by the late commission which met in the city of Washington, and of all claims of the Government and citizens of Mexico against the United States.

In conformity with this stipulation, a third convention was concluded and signed at the city of Mexico on the 20th of November, 1843, by the plenipotentiaries of the two Governments, by which provision was made for ascertaining and paying these claims. In January, 1844, this convention was ratified by the Senate of the United States with two amendments, which were manifestly reasonable in their character. Upon a reference of the amendments proposed to the Government of Mexico, the same evasions, difficulties, and delays were interposed which have so long marked the policy of that Government toward the United States. It has not even yet decided whether it would or would not accede to them, although the subject has been repeatedly pressed upon its consideration. Mexico has thus violated a second time the faith of treaties by failing or refusing to carry into effect the sixth article of the convention of January, 1843.

Such is the history of the wrongs which we have suffered and patiently endured from Mexico through a long series of years. So far from affording reasonable satisfaction for the injuries and insults we had borne, a great aggravation of them consists in the fact that while the United States, anxious to preserve a good understanding with Mexico, have been constantly but vainly employed in seeking redress for past wrongs, new outrages were constantly occurring, which have continued to increase our causes of complaint and to swell the amount of our demands. While the citizens of the United States were conducting a lawful commerce with Mexico under the guaranty of a treaty of "amity, commerce, and navigation," many of them have suffered all the injuries which would have resulted from open war. This treaty, instead of affording protection to our citizens, has been the means of inviting them into the ports of Mexico that they might be, as they have been in numerous instances, plundered of their property and deprived of their personal liberty if they dared insist on their rights. Had the unlawful seizures of American property and the violation of the personal liberty of our citizens, to say nothing of the insults to our flag, which have occurred in the ports of

Mexico taken place on the high seas, they would themselves long since have constituted a state of actual war between the two countries. In so long suffering Mexico to violate her most solemn treaty obligations, plunder our citizens of their property, and imprison their persons without affording them any redress we have failed to perform one of the first and highest duties which every government owes to its citizens, and the consequence has been that many of them have been reduced from a state of affluence to bankruptcy. The proud name of American citizen, which ought to protect all who bear it from insult and injury throughout the world, has afforded no such protection to our citizens in Mexico. We had ample cause of war against Mexico long before the breaking out of hostilities; but even then we forbore to take redress into our own hands until Mexico herself became the aggressor by invading our soil in hostile array and shedding the blood of our citizens.

Such are the grave causes of complaint on the part of the United States against Mexico—causes which existed long before the annexation of Texas to the American Union; and yet, animated by the love of peace and a magnanimous moderation, we did not adopt those measures of redress which under such circumstances are the justified resort of injured nations.

The annexation of Texas to the United States constituted no just cause of offense to Mexico. The pretext that it did so is wholly inconsistent and irreconcilable with well-authenticated facts connected with the revolution by which Texas became independent of Mexico. That this may be the more manifest, it may be proper to advert to the causes and to the history of the principal events of that revolution.

Texas constituted a portion of the ancient Province of Louisiana, ceded to the United States by France in the year 1803. In the year 1819 the United States, by the Florida treaty, ceded to Spain all that part of Louisiana within the present limits of Texas, and Mexico, by the revolution which separated her from Spain and rendered her an independent nation, succeeded to the rights of the mother country over this territory. In the year 1824 Mexico established a federal constitution, under which the Mexican Republic was composed of a number of sovereign States confederated together in a federal union similar to our own. Each of these States had its own executive, legislature, and judiciary, and for all except federal purposes was as independent of the General Government and that of the other States as is Pennsylvania or Virginia under our Constitution. Texas and Coahuila united and formed one of these Mexican States. The State constitution which they adopted, and which was approved by the Mexican Confederacy, asserted that they were "free and independent of the other Mexican United States and of every other power and dominion whatsoever," and proclaimed the great principle of human liberty that "the sovereignty of the state resides originally and essentially in the general mass of the individuals who compose it." To the Government under this constitution, as well as to that under the federal constitution, the people of Texas owed allegiance.

Emigrants from foreign countries, including the United States, were invited by the colonization laws of the State and of the Federal Government to settle in Texas. Advantageous terms were offered to induce them to leave their own country and become Mexican citizens. This invitation was accepted by many of our citizens in the full faith that in their new home they would be governed by laws enacted by representatives elected by themselves, and that their lives, liberty, and property would be protected by constitutional guaranties similar to those which existed in the Republic they had left. Under a Government thus organized they continued until the year 1835, when a military revolution broke out in the City of Mexico which entirely subverted the federal and State constitutions and placed a military dictator at the head of the Government. By a sweeping decree of a Congress subservient to the will of the Dictator the several State constitutions were abolished and the States themselves converted into mere departments of the central Government. The people of Texas were unwilling to submit to this usurpation. Resistance to such tyranny became a high duty. Texas was fully absolved from all allegiance to the central Government of Mexico from the moment that Government had abolished her State constitution and in its place substituted an arbitrary and despotic central government. Such were the principal causes of the Texan revolution. The people of Texas at once determined upon resistance and flew to arms. In the midst of these important and exciting events, however, they did not omit to place their liberties upon a secure and permanent foundation. They elected members to a convention, who in the month of March, 1836, issued a formal declaration that their "political connection with the Mexican nation has forever ended, and that the people of Texas do now constitute a *free, sovereign, and independent Republic*, and are fully invested with all the rights and attributes which properly belong to independent nations." They also adopted for their government a liberal republican constitution. About the same time Santa Anna, then the Dictator of Mexico, invaded Texas with a numerous army for the purpose of subduing her people and enforcing obedience to his arbitrary and despotic Government. On the 21st of April, 1836, he was met by the Texan citizen soldiers, and on that day was achieved by them the memorable victory of San Jacinto, by which they conquered their independence. Considering the numbers engaged on the respective sides, history does not record a more brilliant achievement. Santa Anna himself was among the captives.

In the month of May, 1836, Santa Anna acknowledged by a treaty with the Texan authorities in the most solemn form "the full, entire, and perfect independence of the Republic of Texas." It is true he was then a prisoner of war, but it is equally true that he had failed to reconquer Texas, and had met with signal defeat; that his authority had not been revoked, and that by virtue of this treaty he obtained his personal release. By it hostilities were suspended, and the army which had invaded Texas under his command returned in pursuance of this arrangement unmolested to Mexico.

From the day that the battle of San Jacinto was fought until the present hour Mexico has never possessed the power to reconquer Texas. In the language of the Secretary of State of the United States in a dispatch to our minister in Mexico under date of the 8th of July, 1842—

Mexico may have chosen to consider, and may still choose to consider, Texas as having been at all times since 1835, and as still continuing, a rebellious province; but the world has been obliged to take a very different view of the matter. From the time of the battle of San Jacinto, in April, 1836, to the present moment, Texas has exhibited the same external signs of national independence as Mexico herself, and with quite as much stability of government. Practically free and independent, acknowledged as a political sovereignty by the principal powers of the world, no hostile foot finding rest within her territory for six or seven years, and Mexico herself refraining for all that period from any further attempt to reestablish her own authority over that territory, it can not but be surprising to find Mr. De Bocanegra [the secretary of foreign affairs of Mexico] complaining that for that whole period citizens of the United States or its Government have been favoring the rebels of Texas and supplying them with vessels, ammunition, and money, as if the war for the reduction of the Province of Texas had been constantly prosecuted by Mexico, and her success prevented by these influences from abroad.

In the same dispatch the Secretary of State affirms that—

Since 1837 the United States have regarded Texas as an independent sovereignty as much as Mexico, and that trade and commerce with citizens of a government at war with Mexico can not on that account be regarded as an intercourse by which assistance and succor are given to Mexican rebels. The whole current of Mr. De Bocanegra's remarks runs in the same direction, as if the independence of Texas had not been acknowledged. It has been acknowledged; it was acknowledged in 1837 against the remonstrance and protest of Mexico, and most of the acts of any importance of which Mr. De Bocanegra complains flow necessarily from that recognition. He speaks of Texas as still being "an integral part of the territory of the Mexican Republic," but he can not but understand that the United States do not so regard it. The real complaint of Mexico, therefore, is in substance neither more nor less than a complaint against the recognition of Texan independence. It may be thought rather late to repeat that complaint, and not quite just to confine it to the United States to the exemption of England, France, and Belgium, unless the United States, having been the first to acknowledge the independence of Mexico herself, are to be blamed for setting an example for the recognition of that of Texas.

And he added that—

The Constitution, public treaties, and the laws oblige the President to regard Texas as an independent state, and its territory as no part of the territory of Mexico.

Texas had been an independent state, with an organized government, defying the power of Mexico to overthrow or reconquer her, for more than ten years before Mexico commenced the present war against the United States. Texas had given such evidence to the world of her ability to maintain her separate existence as an independent nation that she had been formally recognized as such not only by the United States, but by several of the principal powers of Europe. These powers had entered into treaties of amity, commerce, and navigation with her. They had received and accredited her ministers and other diplomatic agents at their respective courts, and they had commissioned ministers and diplomatic agents on their part to the Government of Texas. If Mexico, notwithstanding all this and her utter inability to subdue or reconquer Texas, still stubbornly refused to recognize her as an independent nation, she was none the less so on that account. Mexico herself had been recognized as an independent nation by the United States and by other powers many years before Spain, of which before her revolution she had been a colony, would agree to recognize her as such; and yet Mexico was at that time in the estimation of the civilized world, and in fact, none the less an independent power because Spain still claimed her as a colony. If Spain had continued until the present period to assert that Mexico was one of her colonies in rebellion against her, this would not have made her so or changed the fact of her independent existence. Texas at the period of her annexation to the United States bore the same relation to Mexico that Mexico had borne to Spain for many years before Spain acknowledged her independence, with this important difference, that before the annexation of Texas to the United States was consummated Mexico herself, by a formal act of her Government, had acknowledged the independence of Texas as a nation. It is true that in the act of recognition she prescribed a condition which she had no power or authority to impose—that Texas should not annex herself to any other power—but this could not detract in any degree from the recognition which Mexico then made of her actual independence. Upon this plain statement of facts, it is absurd for Mexico to allege as a pretext for commencing hostilities against the United States that Texas is still a part of her territory.

But there are those who, conceding all this to be true, assume the ground that the true western boundary of Texas is the Nueces instead of the Rio Grande, and that therefore in marching our Army to the east bank of the latter river we passed the Texan line and invaded the territory of Mexico. A simple statement of facts known to exist will conclusively refute such an assumption. Texas, as ceded to the United States by France in 1803, has been always claimed as extending west to the Rio Grande or Rio Bravo. This fact is established by the authority of our most eminent statesmen at a period when the question was as well, if not better, understood than it is at present. During Mr. Jefferson's Administration Messrs. Monroe and Pinckney, who had been sent on a special mission to Madrid, charged among other things with the adjustment of boundary between the two countries, in a note addressed to the Spanish minister of foreign affairs under date of the 28th of January, 1805, assert that the boundaries of Louisiana, as ceded to the United States by France, "are the river Perdido on the east and the river Bravo on the west," and they add that "the facts and principles which justify this conclusion are so satisfactory to our Government as to convince it that the United States have not a better right to the island of New Orleans under the cession referred to than they have to the whole district of territory which is above described.'' Down to the conclusion of the Florida treaty, in February, 1819, by which this territory was ceded to Spain, the United States asserted and maintained their territorial rights to this extent. In the month of June, 1818, during Mr. Monroe's Administration, information having been received that a number of foreign adventurers had landed at Galveston with the avowed purpose of forming a settlement in that vicinity, a special messenger was dispatched by the Government of the United States with instructions from the Secretary of State to warn them to desist, should they be found there, ''or any other place north of the Rio Bravo, and within the territory claimed by the United States.'' He was instructed, should they be found in the country north of that river, to make known to them ''the surprise with which the President has seen possession thus taken, without authority from the United States, of a place within their territorial limits, and upon which no lawful settlement can be made without their sanction.'' He was instructed to call upon them to ''avow under what national authority they profess to act,'' and to give them due warning ''that the place is within the United States, who will suffer no permanent settlement to be made there under any authority other than their own.'' As late as the 8th of July, 1842, the Secretary of State of the United States, in a note addressed to our minister in Mexico, maintains that by the Florida treaty of 1819 the territory as far west as the Rio Grande was confirmed to Spain. In that note he states that—

By the treaty of the 22d of February, 1819, between the United States and Spain, the Sabine was adopted as the line of boundary between the two powers. Up to that period no considerable colonization had been effected in Texas; but the territory between the Sabine and the Rio Grande being confirmed to Spain by the treaty, applications were made to that power for grants of land, and such grants or permissions of settlement were in fact made by the Spanish authorities in favor of citizens of the United States proposing to emigrate to *Texas* in numerous families before the declaration of independence by Mexico.

The Texas which was ceded to Spain by the Florida treaty of 1819 embraced all the country now claimed by the State of Texas between the Nueces and the Rio Grande. The Republic of Texas always claimed this river as her western boundary, and in her treaty made with Santa Anna in May, 1836, he recognized it as such. By the constitution which Texas adopted in March, 1836, senatorial and representative districts were organized extending west of the Nueces. The Congress of Texas on the 19th of December, 1836, passed ''An act to define the boundaries of the Republic of Texas,'' in which they declared the Rio Grande from its mouth to its source to be their boundary, and by the said act they extended their ''civil and political jurisdiction'' over the country up to that boundary. During a period of more than nine years which intervened between the adoption of her constitution and her annexation as one of the States of our Union Texas asserted and exercised many acts of sovereignty and jurisdiction over the territory and inhabitants west of the Nueces. She organized and defined the limits of counties extending to the Rio Grande; she established courts of justice and extended her judicial system over the territory; she established a custom-house and collected duties, and also post-offices and post-roads, in it; she established a land office and issued numerous grants for land within its limits; a senator and a representative residing in it were elected to the Congress of the Republic and served as such before the act of annexation took place. In both the Congress and convention of Texas which gave their assent to the terms of annexation to the United States proposed by our Congress were representatives residing west of the Nueces, who took part in the act of annexation itself. This was the Texas which by the act of our Congress of the 29th of December, 1845, was admitted as one of the States of our Union. That the Congress of the United States understood the State of Texas which they admitted into the Union to extend beyond the Nueces is apparent from the fact that on the 31st of December, 1845, only two days after the act of admission, they passed a law "to establish a collection district in the State of Texas," by which they created a port of delivery at Corpus Christi, situated west of the Nueces, and being the same point at which the Texas custom-house under the laws of that Republic had been located, and directed that a surveyor to collect the revenue should be appointed for that port by the President, by and with the advice and consent of the Senate. A surveyor was accordingly nominated, and confirmed by the Senate, and has been ever since in the performance of his duties. All these acts of the Republic of Texas and of our Congress preceded the orders for the advance of our Army to the east bank of the Rio Grande. Subsequently Congress passed an act "establishing certain post routes" extending west of the Nueces. The country west of that river now constitutes a part of one of the Congressional districts of Texas and is represented in the House of Representatives. The Senators from that State were chosen by a legislature in which the country west of that river was represented. In view of all these facts it is difficult to conceive upon what ground it can be maintained that in occupying the country west of the Nueces with our Army, with a view solely to its security and defense, we invaded the territory of Mexico. But it would have been still more difficult to justify the Executive, whose duty it is to see that the laws be faithfully executed, if in the face of all these proceedings, both of the Congress of Texas and of the United States, he had assumed the responsibility of yielding up the territory west of the Nueces to Mexico or of refusing to protect and defend this territory and its inhabitants, including Corpus Christi as well as the remainder of Texas, against the threatened Mexican invasion.

But Mexico herself has never placed the war which she has waged

upon the ground that our Army occupied the intermediate territory between the Nueces and the Rio Grande. Her refuted pretension that
Texas was not in fact an independent state, but a rebellious province,
was obstinately persevered in, and her avowed purpose in commencing
a war with the United States was to reconquer Texas and to restore
Mexican authority over the whole territory—not to the Nueces only,
but to the Sabine. In view of the proclaimed menaces of Mexico to this
effect, I deemed it my duty, as a measure of precaution and defense, to
order our Army to occupy a position on our frontier as a military post,
from which our troops could best resist and repel any attempted invasion which Mexico might make. Our Army had occupied a position at
Corpus Christi, west of the Nueces, as early as August, 1845, without
complaint from any quarter. Had the Nueces been regarded as the
true western boundary of Texas, that boundary had been passed by our
Army many months before it advanced to the eastern bank of the Rio
Grande. In my annual message of December last I informed Congress
that upon the invitation of both the Congress and convention of Texas I
had deemed it proper to order a strong squadron to the coasts of Mexico
and to concentrate an efficient military force on the western frontier of
Texas to protect and defend the inhabitants against the menaced invasion of Mexico. In that message I informed Congress that the moment
the terms of annexation offered by the United States were accepted by
Texas the latter became so far a part of our own country as to make
it our duty to afford such protection and defense, and that for that purpose our squadron had been ordered to the Gulf and our Army to take a
"position between the Nueces and the Del Norte" or Rio Grande and
to "repel any invasion of the Texan territory which might be attempted
by the Mexican forces."

It was deemed proper to issue this order, because soon after the President of Texas, in April, 1845, had issued his proclamation convening the
Congress of that Republic for the purpose of submitting to that body
the terms of annexation proposed by the United States the Government
of Mexico made serious threats of invading the Texan territory. These
threats became more imposing as it became more apparent in the progress of the question that the people of Texas would decide in favor of
accepting the terms of annexation, and finally they had assumed such
a formidable character as induced both the Congress and convention of
Texas to request that a military force should be sent by the United States
into her territory for the purpose of protecting and defending her against
the threatened invasion. It would have been a violation of good faith
toward the people of Texas to have refused to afford the aid which they
desired against a threatened invasion to which they had been exposed
by their free determination to annex themselves to our Union in compliance with the overture made to them by the joint resolution of our Congress. Accordingly, a portion of the Army was ordered to advance into

Texas. Corpus Christi was the position selected by General Taylor. He encamped at that place in August, 1845, and the Army remained in that position until the 11th of March, 1846, when it moved westward, and on the 28th of that month reached the east bank of the Rio Grande opposite to Matamoras. This movement was made in pursuance of orders from the War Department, issued on the 13th of January, 1846. Before these orders were issued the dispatch of our minister in Mexico transmitting the decision of the council of government of Mexico advising that he should not be received, and also the dispatch of our consul residing in the City of Mexico, the former bearing date on the 17th and the latter on the 18th of December, 1845, copies of both of which accompanied my message to Congress of the 11th of May last, were received at the Department of State. These communications rendered it highly probable, if not absolutely certain, that our minister would not be received by the Government of General Herrera. It was also well known that but little hope could be entertained of a different result from General Paredes in case the revolutionary movement which he was prosecuting should prove successful, as was highly probable. The partisans of Paredes, as our minister in the dispatch referred to states, breathed the fiercest hostility against the United States, denounced the proposed negotiation as treason, and openly called upon the troops and the people to put down the Government of Herrera by force. The reconquest of Texas and war with the United States were openly threatened. These were the circumstances existing when it was deemed proper to order the Army under the command of General Taylor to advance to the western frontier of Texas and occupy a position on or near the Rio Grande.

The apprehensions of a contemplated Mexican invasion have been since fully justified by the event. The determination of Mexico to rush into hostilities with the United States was afterwards manifested from the whole tenor of the note of the Mexican minister of foreign affairs to our minister bearing date on the 12th of March, 1846. Paredes had then revolutionized the Government, and his minister, after referring to the resolution for the annexation of Texas which had been adopted by our Congress in March, 1845, proceeds to declare that—

A fact such as this, or, to speak with greater exactness, so notable an act of usurpation, created an imperious necessity that Mexico, for her own honor, should repel it with proper firmness and dignity. The supreme Government had beforehand declared that it would look upon such an act as a *casus belli*, and as a consequence of this declaration negotiation was by its very nature at an end, and war was the only recourse of the Mexican Government.

It appears also that on the 4th of April following General Paredes, through his minister of war, issued orders to the Mexican general in command on the Texan frontier to "attack" our Army "by every means which war permits." To this General Paredes had been pledged to the army and people of Mexico during the military revolution which had brought him into power.   On the 18th of April, 1846, General Paredes addressed a letter to the commander on that frontier in which he stated to him: "At the present date I suppose you, at the head of that valiant army, either fighting already or preparing for the operations of a campaign;" and, "Supposing you already on the theater of operations and with all the forces assembled, it is indispensable that hostilities be commenced, yourself taking the initiative against the enemy."

The movement of our Army to the Rio Grande was made by the commanding general under positive orders to abstain from all aggressive acts toward Mexico or Mexican citizens, and to regard the relations between the two countries as peaceful unless Mexico should declare war or commit acts of hostility indicative of a state of war, and these orders he faithfully executed.   Whilst occupying his position on the east bank of the Rio Grande, within the limits of Texas, then recently admitted as one of the States of our Union, the commanding general of the Mexican forces, who, in pursuance of the orders of his Government, had collected a large army on the opposite shore of the Rio Grande, crossed the river, invaded our territory, and commenced hostilities by attacking our forces. Thus, after all the injuries which we had received and borne from Mexico, and after she had insultingly rejected a minister sent to her on a mission of peace, and whom she had solemnly agreed to receive, she consummated her long course of outrage against our country by commencing an offensive war and shedding the blood of our citizens on our own soil.

The United States never attempted to acquire Texas by conquest.   On the contrary, at an early period after the people of Texas had achieved their independence they sought to be annexed to the United States.   At a general election in September, 1836, they decided with great unanimity in favor of "annexation," and in November following the Congress of the Republic authorized the appointment of a minister to bear their request to this Government.   This Government, however, having remained neutral between Texas and Mexico during the war between them, and considering it due to the honor of our country and our fair fame among the nations of the earth that we should not at this early period consent to annexation, nor until it should be manifest to the whole world that the reconquest of Texas by Mexico was impossible, refused to accede to the overtures made by Texas.   On the 12th of April, 1844, after more than seven years had elapsed since Texas had established her independence, a treaty was concluded for the annexation of that Republic to the United States, which was rejected by the Senate.   Finally, on the 1st of March, 1845, Congress passed a joint resolution for annexing her to the United States upon certain preliminary conditions to which her assent was required.   The solemnities which characterized the deliberations and conduct of the Government and people of Texas on the deeply interesting questions presented by these resolutions are known to the world. The Congress, the Executive, and the people of Texas, in a convention elected for that purpose, accepted with great unanimity the proposed terms of annexation, and thus consummated on her part the great act of restoring to our Federal Union a vast territory which had been ceded to Spain by the Florida treaty more than a quarter of a century before.

After the joint resolution for the annexation of Texas to the United States had been passed by our Congress the Mexican minister at Washington addressed a note to the Secretary of State, bearing date on the 6th of March, 1845, protesting against it as "an act of aggression the most unjust which can be found recorded in the annals of modern history, namely, that of despoiling a friendly nation like Mexico of a considerable portion of her territory," and protesting against the resolution of annexation as being an act "whereby the Province of Texas, an integral portion of the Mexican territory, is agreed and admitted into the American Union;" and he announced that as a consequence his mission to the United States had terminated, and demanded his passports, which were granted. It was upon the absurd pretext, made by Mexico (herself indebted for her independence to a successful revolution), that the Republic of Texas still continued to be, notwithstanding all that had passed, a Province of Mexico that this step was taken by the Mexican minister.

Every honorable effort has been used by me to avoid the war which followed, but all have proved vain. All our attempts to preserve peace have been met by insult and resistance on the part of Mexico. My efforts to this end commenced in the note of the Secretary of State of the 10th of March, 1845, in answer to that of the Mexican minister. Whilst declining to reopen a discussion which had already been exhausted, and proving again what was known to the whole world, that Texas had long since achieved her independence, the Secretary of State expressed the regret of this Government that Mexico should have taken offense at the resolution of annexation passed by Congress, and gave assurance that our "most strenuous efforts shall be devoted to the amicable adjustment of every cause of complaint between the two Governments and to the cultivation of the kindest and most friendly relations between the sister Republics." That I have acted in the spirit of this assurance will appear from the events which have since occurred. Notwithstanding Mexico had abruptly terminated all diplomatic intercourse with the United States, and ought, therefore, to have been the first to ask for its resumption, yet, waiving all ceremony, I embraced the earliest favorable opportunity "to ascertain from the Mexican Government whether they would receive an envoy from the United States intrusted with full power to adjust all the questions in dispute between the two Governments." In September, 1845, I believed the propitious moment for such an overture had arrived. Texas, by the enthusiastic and almost unanimous will of her people, had pronounced in favor of annexation Mexico herself had agreed to acknowledge the independence of Texas, subject to a condition, it is true, which she had no right to impose and no power to enforce. The last lingering hope of Mexico, if she still could have retained any, that Texas would ever again become one of her Provinces, must have been abandoned.

The consul of the United States at the City of Mexico was therefore instructed by the Secretary of State on the 15th of September, 1845, to make the inquiry of the Mexican Government. The inquiry was made, and on the 15th of October, 1845, the minister of foreign affairs of the Mexican Government, in a note addressed to our consul, gave a favorable response, requesting at the same time that our naval force might be withdrawn from Vera Cruz while negotiations should be pending. Upon the receipt of this note our naval force was promptly withdrawn from Vera Cruz. A minister was immediately appointed, and departed to Mexico. Everything bore a promising aspect for a speedy and peaceful adjustment of all our difficulties. At the date of my annual message to Congress in December last no doubt was entertained but that he would be received by the Mexican Government, and the hope was cherished that all cause of misunderstanding between the two countries would be speedily removed. In the confident hope that such would be the result of his mission, I informed Congress that I forbore at that time to "recommend such ulterior measures of redress for the wrongs and injuries we had so long borne as it would have been proper to make had no such negotiation been instituted." To my surprise and regret the Mexican Government, though solemnly pledged to do so, upon the arrival of our minister in Mexico refused to receive and accredit him. When he reached Vera Cruz, on the 30th of November, 1845, he found that the aspect of affairs had undergone an unhappy change. The Government of General Herrera, who was at that time President of the Republic, was tottering to its fall. General Paredes, a military leader, had manifested his determination to overthrow the Government of Herrera by a military revolution, and one of the principal means which he employed to effect his purpose and render the Government of Herrera odious to the army and people of Mexico was by loudly condemning its determination to receive a minister of peace from the United States, alleging that it was the intention of Herrera, by a treaty with the United States, to dismember the territory of Mexico by ceding away the department of Texas. The Government of Herrera is believed to have been well disposed to a pacific adjustment of existing difficulties, but probably alarmed for its own security, and in order to ward off the danger of the revolution led by Paredes, violated its solemn agreement and refused to receive or accredit our minister; and this although informed that he had been invested with full power to adjust all questions in dispute between the two Governments. Among the frivolous pretexts for this refusal, the principal one was that our minister had not gone upon a special mission confined to the question of Texas alone, leaving all the outrages upon our flag and our citizens unredressed. The Mexican Government well knew that both our national honor and the protection due to our citizens imperatively required that the two questions of boundary and indemnity should be treated of together, as naturally and inseparably blended, and they ought to have seen that this course was best calculated to enable the United States to extend to them the most liberal justice. On the 30th of December, 1845, General Herrera resigned the Presidency and yielded up the Government to General Paredes without a struggle. Thus a revolution was accomplished solely by the army commanded by Paredes, and the supreme power in Mexico passed into the hands of a military usurper who was known to be bitterly hostile to the United States.

Although the prospect of a pacific adjustment with the new Government was unpromising from the known hostility of its head to the United States, yet, determined that nothing should be left undone on our part to restore friendly relations between the two countries, our minister was instructed to present his credentials to the new Government and ask to be accredited by it in the diplomatic character in which he had been commissioned. These instructions he executed by his note of the 1st of March, 1846, addressed to the Mexican minister of foreign affairs, but his request was insultingly refused by that minister in his answer of the 12th of the same month. No alternative remained for our minister but to demand his passports and return to the United States.

Thus was the extraordinary spectacle presented to the civilized world of a Government, in violation of its own express agreement, having twice rejected a minister of peace invested with full powers to adjust all the existing differences between the two countries in a manner just and honorable to both. I am not aware that modern history presents a parallel case in which in time of peace one nation has refused even to hear propositions from another for terminating existing difficulties between them. Scarcely a hope of adjusting our difficulties, even at a remote day, or of preserving peace with Mexico, could be cherished while Paredes remained at the head of the Government. He had acquired the supreme power by a military revolution and upon the most solemn pledges to wage war against the United States and to reconquer Texas, which he claimed as a revolted province of Mexico. He had denounced as guilty of treason all those Mexicans who considered Texas as no longer constituting a part of the territory of Mexico and who were friendly to the cause of peace. The duration of the war which he waged against the United States was indefinite, because the end which he proposed of the reconquest of Texas was hopeless. Besides, there was good reason to believe from all his conduct that it was his intention to convert the Republic of Mexico into a monarchy and to call a foreign European prince to the throne. Preparatory to this end, he had during his short rule destroyed the liberty of the press, tolerating that portion of it only which openly advocated the establishment of a monarchy. The better to secure the success of his ultimate designs, he had by an arbitrary decree convoked a Congress, not to be elected by the free voice of the people, but to be chosen in a manner to make them subservient to his will and to give him absolute control over their deliberations.

Under all these circumstances it was believed that any revolution in Mexico founded upon opposition to the ambitious projects of Paredes would tend to promote the cause of peace as well as prevent any attempted European interference in the affairs of the North American continent, both objects of deep interest to the United States. Any such foreign interference, if attempted, must have been resisted by the United States. My views upon that subject were fully communicated to Congress in my last annual message. In any event, it was certain that no change whatever in the Government of Mexico which would deprive Paredes of power could be for the worse so far as the United States were concerned, while it was highly probable that any change must be for the better. This was the state of affairs existing when Congress, on the 13th of May last, recognized the existence of the war which had been commenced by the Government of Paredes; and it became an object of much importance, with a view to a speedy settlement of our difficulties and the restoration of an honorable peace, that Paredes should not retain power in Mexico.

Before that time there were symptoms of a revolution in Mexico, favored, as it was understood to be, by the more liberal party, and especially by those who were opposed to foreign interference and to the monarchical form of government. Santa Anna was then in exile in Havana, having been expelled from power and banished from his country by a revolution which occurred in December, 1844; but it was known that he had still a considerable party in his favor in Mexico. It was also equally well known that no vigilance which could be exerted by our squadron would in all probability have prevented him from effecting a landing somewhere on the extensive Gulf coast of Mexico if he desired to return to his country. He had openly professed an entire change of policy, had expressed his regret that he had subverted the federal constitution of 1824, and avowed that he was now in favor of its restoration. He had publicly declared his hostility, in strongest terms, to the establishment of a monarchy and to European interference in the affairs of his country. Information to this effect had been received, from sources believed to be reliable, at the date of the recognition of the existence of the war by Congress, and was afterwards fully confirmed by the receipt of the dispatch of our consul in the City of Mexico, with the accompanying documents, which are herewith transmitted. Besides, it was reasonable to suppose that he must see the ruinous consequences to Mexico of a war with the United States, and that it would be his interest to favor peace.

It was under these circumstances and upon these considerations that it was deemed expedient not to obstruct his return to Mexico should he attempt to do so. Our object was the restoration of peace, and, with that view, no reason was perceived why we should take part with Paredes and aid him by means of our blockade in preventing the return of his rival to Mexico. On the contrary, it was believed that the intestine divisions which ordinary sagacity could not but anticipate as the fruit of Santa Anna's return to Mexico, and his contest with Paredes, might strongly tend to produce a disposition with both parties to restore and preserve peace with the United States. Paredes was a soldier by profession and a monarchist in principle. He had but recently before been successful in a military revolution, by which he had obtained power. He was the sworn enemy of the United States, with which he had involved his country in the existing war. Santa Anna had been expelled from power by the army, was known to be in open hostility to Paredes, and publicly pledged against foreign intervention and the restoration of monarchy in Mexico. In view of these facts and circumstances it was that when orders were issued to the commander of our naval forces in the Gulf, on the 13th day of May last, the same day on which the existence of the war was recognized by Congress, to place the coasts of Mexico under blockade, he was directed not to obstruct the passage of Santa Anna to Mexico should he attempt to return.

A revolution took place in Mexico in the early part of August following, by which the power of Paredes was overthrown, and he has since been banished from the country, and is now in exile. Shortly afterwards Santa Anna returned. It remains to be seen whether his return may not yet prove to be favorable to a pacific adjustment of the existing difficulties, it being manifestly his interest not to persevere in the prosecution of a war commenced by Paredes to accomplish a purpose so absurd as the reconquest of Texas to the Sabine. Had Paredes remained in power, it is morally certain that any pacific adjustment would have been hopeless.

Upon the commencement of hostilities by Mexico against the United States the indignant spirit of the nation was at once aroused. Congress promptly responded to the expectations of the country, and by the act of the 13th of May last recognized the fact that war existed, by the act of Mexico, between the United States and that Republic, and granted the means necessary for its vigorous prosecution. Being involved in a war thus commenced by Mexico, and for the justice of which on our part we may confidently appeal to the whole world, I resolved to prosecute it with the utmost vigor. Accordingly the ports of Mexico on the Gulf and on the Pacific have been placed under blockade and her territory invaded at several important points. The reports from the Departments of War and of the Navy will inform you more in detail of the measures adopted in the emergency in which our country was placed and of the gratifying results which have been accomplished.

The various columns of the Army have performed their duty under great disadvantages with the most distinguished skill and courage. The victories of Palo Alto and Resaca de la Palma and of Monterey, won against greatly superior numbers and against most decided advantages in other respects on the part of the enemy, were brilliant in their execution, and entitle our brave officers and soldiers to the grateful thanks of their country. The nation deplores the loss of the brave officers and men who have gallantly fallen while vindicating and defending their country's rights and honor.

It is a subject of pride and satisfaction that our volunteer citizen soldiers, who so promptly responded to their country's call, with an experience of the discipline of a camp of only a few weeks, have borne their part in the hard-fought battle of Monterey with a constancy and courage equal to that of veteran troops and worthy of the highest admiration. The privations of long marches through the enemy's country and through a wilderness have been borne without a murmur. By rapid movements the Province of New Mexico, with Santa Fe, its capital, has been captured without bloodshed. The Navy has cooperated with the Army and rendered important services; if not so brilliant, it is because the enemy had no force to meet them on their own element and because of the defenses which nature has interposed in the difficulties of the navigation on the Mexican coast. Our squadron in the Pacific, with the cooperation of a gallant officer of the Army and a small force hastily collected in that distant country, has acquired bloodless possession of the Californias, and the American flag has been raised at every important point in that Province.

I congratulate you on the success which has thus attended our military and naval operations. In less than seven months after Mexico commenced hostilities, at a time selected by herself, we have taken possession of many of her principal ports, driven back and pursued her invading army, and acquired military possession of the Mexican Provinces of New Mexico, New Leon, Coahuila, Tamaulipas, and the Californias, a territory larger in extent than that embraced in the original thirteen States of the Union, inhabited by a considerable population, and much of it more than 1,000 miles from the points at which we had to collect our forces and commence our movements. By the blockade the import and export trade of the enemy has been cut off. Well may the American people be proud of the energy and gallantry of our regular and volunteer officers and soldiers. The events of these few months afford a gratifying proof that our country can under any emergency confidently rely for the maintenance of her honor and the defense of her rights on an effective force, ready at all times voluntarily to relinquish the comforts of home for the perils and privations of the camp. And though such a force may be for the time expensive, it is in the end economical, as the ability to command it removes the necessity of employing a large standing army in time of peace, and proves that our people love their institutions and are ever ready to defend and protect them.

While the war was in a course of vigorous and successful prosecution, being still anxious to arrest its evils, and considering that after the brilliant victories of our arms on the 8th and 9th of May last the national honor could not be compromitted by it, another overture was made to Mexico, by my direction, on the 27th of July last to terminate hostilities by a peace just and honorable to both countries. On the 31st of August following the Mexican Government declined to accept this friendly overture, but referred it to the decision of a Mexican Congress to be assembled in the early part of the present month. I communicate to you herewith a copy of the letter of the Secretary of State proposing to reopen negotiations, of the answer of the Mexican Government, and of the reply thereto of the Secretary of State.

The war will continue to be prosecuted with vigor as the best means of securing peace. It is hoped that the decision of the Mexican Congress, to which our last overture has been referred, may result in a speedy and honorable peace. With our experience, however, of the unreasonable course of the Mexican authorities, it is the part of wisdom not to relax in the energy of our military operations until the result is made known. In this view it is deemed important to hold military possession of all the Provinces which have been taken until a definitive treaty of peace shall have been concluded and ratified by the two countries.

The war has not been waged with a view to conquest, but, having been commenced by Mexico, it has been carried into the enemy's country and will be vigorously prosecuted there with a view to obtain an honorable peace, and thereby secure ample indemnity for the expenses of the war, as well as to our much-injured citizens, who hold large pecuniary demands against Mexico.

By the laws of nations a conquered country is subject to be governed by the conqueror during his military possession and until there is either a treaty of peace or he shall voluntarily withdraw from it. The old civil government being necessarily superseded, it is the right and duty of the conqueror to secure his conquest and to provide for the maintenance of civil order and the rights of the inhabitants. This right has been exercised and this duty performed by our military and naval commanders by the establishment of temporary governments in some of the conquered Provinces of Mexico, assimilating them as far as practicable to the free institutions of our own country. In the Provinces of New Mexico and of the Californias little, if any, further resistance is apprehended from the inhabitants to the temporary governments which have thus, from the necessity of the case and according to the laws of war, been established. It may be proper to provide for the security of these important conquests by making an adequate appropriation for the purpose of erecting fortifications and defraying the expenses necessarily incident to the maintenance of our possession and authority over them.

Near the close of your last session, for reasons communicated to Congress, I deemed it important as a measure for securing a speedy peace with Mexico, that a sum of money should be appropriated and placed in the power of the Executive, similar to that which had been made upon two former occasions during the Administration of President Jefferson.

On the 26th of February, 1803, an appropriation of $2,000,000 was made and placed at the disposal of the President. Its object is well known. It was at that time in contemplation to acquire Louisiana from France, and it was intended to be applied as a part of the consideration which might be paid for that territory. On the 13th of February, 1806, the same sum was in like manner appropriated, with a view to the purchase of the Floridas from Spain. These appropriations were made to facilitate negotiations and as a means to enable the President to accomplish the important objects in view. Though it did not become necessary for the President to use these appropriations, yet a state of things might have arisen in which it would have been highly important for him to do so, and the wisdom of making them can not be doubted. It is believed that the measure recommended at your last session met with the. approbation of decided majorities in both Houses of Congress. Indeed, in different forms, a bill making an appropriation of $2,000,000 passed each House, and it is much to be regretted that it did not become a law. The reasons which induced me to recommend the measure at that time still exist, and I again submit the subject for your consideration and suggest the importance of early action upon it. Should the appropriation be made and be not needed, it will remain in the Treasury; should it be deemed proper to apply it in whole or in part, it will be accounted for as other public expenditures.

Immediately after Congress had recognized the existence of the war with Mexico my attention was directed to the danger that privateers might be fitted out in the ports of Cuba and Porto Rico to prey upon the commerce of the United States, and I invited the special attention of the Spanish Government to the fourteenth article of our treaty with that power of the 27th of October, 1795, under which the citizens and subjects of either nation who shall take commissions or letters of marque to act as privateers against the other "shall be punished as pirates."

It affords me pleasure to inform you that I have received assurances from the Spanish Government that this article of the treaty shall be faithfully observed on its part. Orders for this purpose were immediately transmitted from that Government to the authorities of Cuba and Porto Rico to exert their utmost vigilance in preventing any attempts to fit out privateers in those islands against the United States. From the good faith of Spain I am fully satisfied that this treaty will be executed in its spirit as well as its letter, whilst the United States will on their part faithfully perform all the obligations which it imposes on them.

Information has been recently received at the Department of State that the Mexican Government has sent to Havana blank commissions to privateers and blank certificates of naturalization signed by General

Salas, the present head of the Mexican Government. There is also reason to apprehend that similar documents have been transmitted to other parts of the world. Copies of these papers, in translation, are herewith transmitted.

As the preliminaries required by the practice of civilized nations for commissioning privateers and regulating their conduct appear not to have been observed, and as these commissions are in blank, to be filled up with the names of citizens and subjects of all nations who may be willing to purchase them, the whole proceeding can only be construed as an invitation to all the freebooters upon earth who are willing to pay for the privilege to cruise against American commerce. It will be for our courts of justice to decide whether under such circumstances these Mexican letters of marque and reprisal shall protect those who accept them, and commit robberies upon the high seas under their authority, from the pains and penalties of piracy.

If the certificates of naturalization thus granted be intended by Mexico to shield Spanish subjects from the guilt and punishment of pirates under our treaty with Spain, they will certainly prove unavailing. Such a subterfuge would be but a weak device to defeat the provisions of a solemn treaty.

I recommend that Congress should immediately provide by law for the trial and punishment as pirates of Spanish subjects who, escaping the vigilance of their Government, shall be found guilty of privateering against the United States. I do not apprehend serious danger from these privateers. Our Navy will be constantly on the alert to protect our commerce. Besides, in case prizes should be made of American vessels, the utmost vigilance will be exerted by our blockading squadron to prevent the captors from taking them into Mexican ports, and it is not apprehended that any nation will violate its neutrality by suffering such prizes to be condemned and sold within its jurisdiction.

I recommend that Congress should immediately provide by law for granting letters of marque and reprisal against vessels under the Mexican flag. It is true that there are but few, if any, commercial vessels of Mexico upon the high seas, and it is therefore not probable that many American privateers would be fitted out in case a law should pass authorizing this mode of warfare. It is, notwithstanding, certain that such privateers may render good service to the commercial interests of the country by recapturing our merchant ships should any be taken by armed vessels under the Mexican flag, as well as by capturing these vessels themselves. Every means within our power should be rendered available for the protection of our commerce.

The annual report of the Secretary of the Treasury will exhibit a detailed statement of the condition of the finances. The imports for the fiscal year ending on the 30th of June last were of the value of $121,691,797, of which the amount exported was $11,346,623, leaving

the amount retained in the country for domestic consumption $110,345,-
174.   The value of the exports for the same period was $113,488,516, of
which $102,141,893 consisted of domestic productions and $11,346,623
of foreign articles.

The receipts into the Treasury for the same year were $29,499,247.06,
of which there was derived from customs $26,712,667.87, from the sales
of public lands $2,694,452.48, and from incidental and miscellaneous
sources $92,126.71.   The expenditures for the same period were $28,-
031,114.20, and the balance in the Treasury on the 1st day of July last
was $9,126,439.08.

The amount of the public debt, including Treasury notes, on the 1st of
the present month was $24,256,494.60, of which the sum of $17,788,-
799.62 was outstanding on the 4th of March, 1845, leaving the amount
incurred since that time $6,467,694.98.

In order to prosecute the war with Mexico with vigor and energy, as
the best means of bringing it to a speedy and honorable termination, a
further loan will be necessary to meet the expenditures for the present
and the next fiscal year.   If the war should be continued until the 30th
of June, 1848, being the end of the next fiscal year, it is estimated that
an additional loan of $23,000,000 will be required.   This estimate is
made upon the assumption that it will be necessary to retain constantly
in the Treasury $4,000,000 to guard against contingencies.   If such
surplus were not required to be retained, then a loan of $19,000,000
would be sufficient.   If, however, Congress should at the present session
impose a revenue duty on the principal articles now embraced in the free
list, it is estimated that an additional annual revenue of about two millions and a half, amounting, it is estimated, on the 30th of June, 1848, to
$4,000,000, would be derived from that source, and the loan required
would be reduced by that amount.   It is estimated also that should Congress graduate and reduce the price of such of the public lands as have
been long in the market the additional revenue derived from that source
would be annually, for several years to come, between half a million and
a million dollars; and the loan required may be reduced by that amount
also.   Should these measures be adopted, the loan required would not
probably exceed $18,000,000 or $19,000,000, leaving in the Treasury a
constant surplus of $4,000,000.   The loan proposed, it is estimated, will
be sufficient to cover the necessary expenditures both for the war and
for all other purposes up to the 30th of June, 1848, and an amount of
this loan not exceeding one-half may be required during the present fiscal
year, and the greater part of the remainder during the first half of the
fiscal year succeeding.

In order that timely notice may be given and proper measures taken to
effect the loan, or such portion of it as may be required, it is important
that the authority of Congress to make it be given at an early period of
your present session.   It is suggested that the loan should be contracted
for a period of twenty years, with authority to purchase the stock and
pay it off at an earlier period at its market value out of any surplus

which may at any time be in the Treasury applicable to that purpose. After the establishment of peace with Mexico, it is supposed that a considerable surplus will exist, and that the debt may be extinguished in a much shorter period than that for which it may be contracted. The period of twenty years, as that for which the proposed loan may be contracted, in preference to a shorter period, is suggested, because all experience, both at home and abroad, has shown that loans are effected upon much better terms upon long time than when they are reimbursable at short dates.

Necessary as this measure is to sustain the honor and the interests of the country engaged in a foreign war, it is not doubted but that Congress will promptly authorize it.

The balance in the Treasury on the 1st July last exceeded $9,000,000, notwithstanding considerable expenditures had been made for the war during the months of May and June preceding. But for the war the whole public debt could and would have been extinguished within a short period; and it was a part of my settled policy to do so, and thus relieve the people from its burden and place the Government in a position which would enable it to reduce the public expenditures to that economical standard which is most consistent with the general welfare and the pure and wholesome progress of our institutions.

Among our just causes of complaint against Mexico arising out of her refusal to treat for peace, as well before as since the war so unjustly commenced on her part, are the extraordinary expenditures in which we have been involved. Justice to our own people will make it proper that Mexico should be held responsible for these expenditures.

Economy in the public expenditures is at all times a high duty which all public functionaries of the Government owe to the people. This duty becomes the more imperative in a period of war, when large and extraordinary expenditures become unavoidable. During the existence of the war with Mexico all our resources should be husbanded, and no appropriations made except such as are absolutely necessary for its vigorous prosecution and the due administration of the Government. Objects of appropriation which in peace may be deemed useful or proper, but which are not indispensable for the public service, may when the country is engaged in a foreign war be well postponed to a future period. By the observance of this policy at your present session large amounts may be saved to the Treasury and be applied to objects of pressing and urgent necessity, and thus the creation of a corresponding amount of public debt may be avoided.

It is not meant to recommend that the ordinary and necessary appropriations for the support of Government should be withheld; but it is well known that at every session of Congress appropriations are proposed for numerous objects which may or may not be made without materially affecting the public interests, and these it is recommended should not be granted.

The act passed at your last session "reducing the duties on imports" not having gone into operation until the 1st of the present month, there has not been time for its practical effect upon the revenue and the business of the country to be developed. It is not doubted, however, that the just policy which it adopts will add largely to our foreign trade and promote the general prosperity. Although it can not be certainly foreseen what amount of revenue it will yield, it is estimated that it will exceed that produced by the act of 1842, which it superseded. The leading principles established by it are to levy the taxes with a view to raise revenue and to impose them upon the articles imported according to their actual value.

The act of 1842, by the excessive rates of duty which it imposed on many articles, either totally excluded them from importation or greatly reduced the amount imported, and thus diminished instead of producing revenue. By it the taxes were imposed not for the legitimate purpose of raising revenue, but to afford advantages to favored classes at the expense of a large majority of their fellow-citizens. Those employed in agriculture, mechanical pursuits, commerce, and navigation were compelled to contribute from their substance to swell the profits and overgrown wealth of the comparatively few who had invested their capital in manufactures. The taxes were not levied in proportion to the value of the articles upon which they were imposed, but, widely departing from this just rule, the lighter taxes were in many cases levied upon articles of luxury and high price and the heavier taxes on those of necessity and low price, consumed by the great mass of the people. It was a system the inevitable effect of which was to relieve favored classes and the wealthy few from contributing their just proportion for the support of Government, and to lay the burden on the labor of the many engaged in other pursuits than manufactures.

A system so unequal and unjust has been superseded by the existing law, which imposes duties not for the benefit or injury of classes or pursuits, but distributes and, as far as practicable, equalizes the public burdens among all classes and occupations. The favored classes who under the unequal and unjust system which has been repealed have heretofore realized large profits, and many of them amassed large fortunes at the expense of the many who have been made tributary to them, will have no reason to complain if they shall be required to bear their just proportion of the taxes necessary for the support of Government. So far from it, it will be perceived by an examination of the existing law that discriminations in the rates of duty imposed within the revenue principle have been retained in their favor. The incidental aid against foreign competition which they still enjoy gives them an advantage which no other pursuits possess, but of this none others will complain, because the duties levied are necessary for revenue. These revenue duties, including freights and charges, which the importer must pay before he can come in competition with the home manufacturer in our markets, amount on nearly all our leading branches of manufacture to more than one-third of the value of the imported article, and in some cases to almost one-half its value.   With such advantages it is not doubted that our domestic manufacturers will continue to prosper, realizing in well-conducted establishments even greater profits than can be derived from any other regular business.   Indeed, so far from requiring the protection of even incidental revenue duties, our manufacturers in several leading branches are extending their business, giving evidence of great ingenuity and skill and of their ability to compete, with increased prospect of success, for the open market of the world.   Domestic manufactures to the value of several millions of dollars, which can not find a market at home, are annually exported to foreign countries.   With such rates of duty as those established by the existing law the system will probably be permanent, and capitalists who are made or shall hereafter make their investments in manufactures will know upon what to rely.   The country will be satisfied with these rates, because the advantages which the manufacturers still enjoy result necessarily from the collection of revenue for the support of Government.   High protective duties, from their unjust operation upon the masses of the people, can not fail to give rise to extensive dissatisfaction and complaint and to constant efforts to change or repeal them, rendering all investments in manufactures uncertain and precarious.   Lower and more permanent rates of duty, at the same time that they will yield to the manufacturer fair and remunerating profits, will secure him against the danger of frequent changes in the system, which can not fail to ruinously affect his interests.

Simultaneously with the relaxation of the restrictive policy by the United States, Great Britain, from whose example we derived the system, has relaxed hers.   She has modified her corn laws and reduced many other duties to moderate revenue rates.   After ages of experience the statesmen of that country have been constrained by a stern necessity and by a public opinion having its deep foundation in the sufferings and wants of impoverished millions to abandon a system the effect of which was to build up immense fortunes in the hands of the few and to reduce the laboring millions to pauperism and misery.   Nearly in the same ratio that labor was depressed capital was increased and concentrated by the British protective policy.

The evils of the system in Great Britain were at length rendered intolerable, and it has been abandoned, but not without a severe struggle on the part of the protected and favored classes to retain the unjust advantages which they have so long enjoyed.   It was to be expected that a similar struggle would be made by the same classes in the United States whenever an attempt was made to modify or abolish the same unjust system here.   The protective policy had been in operation in the United States for a much shorter period, and its pernicious effects were not, therefore, so clearly perceived and felt. Enough, however, was known of these effects to induce its repeal.

It would be strange if in the face of the example of *Great Britain*, our principal foreign customer, and of the evils of a system rendered manifest in that country by long and painful experience, and in the face of the immense advantages which under a more liberal commercial policy we are already deriving, and must continue to derive, by supplying her starving population with food, the United States should restore a policy which she has been compelled to abandon, and thus diminish her ability to purchase from us the food and other articles which she so much needs and we so much desire to sell. By the simultaneous abandonment of the protective policy by Great Britain and the United States new and important markets have already been opened for our agricultural and other products, commerce and navigation have received a new impulse, labor and trade have been released from the artificial trammels which have so long fettered them, and to a great extent reciprocity in the exchange of commodities has been introduced at the same time by both countries, and greatly for the benefit of both. Great Britain has been forced by the pressure of circumstances at home to abandon a policy which has been upheld for ages, and to open her markets for our immense surplus of breadstuffs, and it is confidently believed that other powers of Europe will ultimately see the wisdom, if they be not compelled by the pauperism and sufferings of their crowded population, to pursue a similar policy.

Our farmers are more deeply interested in maintaining the just and liberal policy of the existing law than any other class of our citizens. They constitute a large majority of our population, and it is well known that when they prosper all other pursuits prosper also. They have heretofore not only received none of the bounties or favors of Government, but by the unequal operations of the protective policy have been made by the burdens of taxation which it imposed to contribute to the bounties which have enriched others.

When a foreign as well as a home market is opened to them, they must receive, as they are now receiving, increased prices for their products. They will find a readier sale, and at better prices, for their wheat, flour, rice, Indian corn, beef, pork, lard, butter, cheese, and other articles which they produce. The home market alone is inadequate to enable them to dispose of the immense surplus of food and other articles which they are capable of producing, even at the most reduced prices, for the manifest reason that they can not be consumed in the country. The United States can from their immense surplus supply not only the home demand, but the deficiencies of food required by the whole world.

That the reduced production of some of the chief articles of food in Great Britain and other parts of Europe may have contributed to increase the demand for our breadstuffs and provisions is not doubted, but that the great and efficient cause of this increased demand and of increased prices consists in the removal of artificial restrictions heretofore imposed is deemed to be equally certain. That our exports of food, already increased and increasing beyond former example under the more liberal policy which has been adopted, will be still vastly enlarged unless they be checked or prevented by a restoration of the protective policy can not be doubted. That our commercial and navigating interests will be enlarged in a corresponding ratio with the increase of our trade is equally certain, while our manufacturing interests will still be the favored interests of the country and receive the incidental protection afforded them by revenue duties; and more than this they can not justly demand.

In my annual message of December last a tariff of revenue duties based upon the principles of the existing law was recommended, and I have seen no reason to change the opinions then expressed. In view of the probable beneficial effects of that law, I recommend that the policy established by it be maintained. It has but just commenced to operate, and to abandon or modify it without giving it a fair trial would be inexpedient and unwise. Should defects in any of its details be ascertained by actual experience to exist, these may be hereafter corrected; but until such defects shall become manifest the act should be fairly tested.

It is submitted for your consideration whether it may not be proper, as a war measure, to impose revenue duties on some of the articles now embraced in the free list. Should it be deemed proper to impose such duties with a view to raise revenue to meet the expenses of the war with Mexico or to avoid to that extent the creation of a public debt, they may be repealed when the emergency which gave rise to them shall cease to exist, and constitute no part of the permanent policy of the country.

The act of the 6th of August last, "to provide for the better organization of the Treasury and for the collection, safe-keeping, transfer, and disbursement of the public revenue," has been carried into execution as rapidly as the delay necessarily arising out of the appointment of new officers, taking and approving their bonds, and preparing and securing proper places for the safe-keeping of the public money would permit. It is not proposed to depart in any respect from the principles or policy on which this great measure is founded. There are, however, defects in the details of the measure, developed by its practical operation, which are fully set forth in the report of the Secretary of the Treasury, to which the attention of Congress is invited. These defects would impair to some extent the successful operation of the law at all times, but are especially embarrassing when the country is engaged in a war, when the expenditures are greatly increased, when loans are to be effected and the disbursements are to be made at points many hundred miles distant, in some cases, from any depository, and a large portion of them in a foreign country. The modifications suggested in the report of the Secretary of the Treasury are recommended to your favorable consideration.

In connection with this subject I invite your attention to the importance of establishing a branch of the Mint of the United States at New York. Two-thirds of the revenue derived from customs being collected at that point, the demand for specie to pay the duties will be large, and a branch mint where foreign coin and bullion could be immediately converted into American coin would greatly facilitate the transaction of the public business, enlarge the circulation of gold and silver, and be at the same time a safe depository of the public money.

The importance of graduating and reducing the price of such of the public lands as have been long offered in the market at the minimum rate authorized by existing laws, and remain unsold, induces me again to recommend the subject to your favorable consideration. Many millions of acres of these lands have been offered in the market for more than thirty years and larger quantities for more than ten or twenty years, and, being of an inferior quality, they must remain unsalable for an indefinite period unless the price at which they may be purchased shall be reduced. To place a price upon them above their real value is not only to prevent their sale, and thereby deprive the Treasury of any income from that source, but is unjust to the States in which they lie, because it retards their growth and increase of population, and because they have no power to levy a tax upon them as upon other lands within their limits, held by other proprietors than the United States, for the support of their local governments.

The beneficial effects of the graduation principle have been realized by some of the States owning the lands within their limits in which it has been adopted. They have been demonstrated also by the United States acting as the trustee of the Chickasaw tribe of Indians in the sale of their lands lying within the States of Mississippi and Alabama. The Chickasaw lands, which would not command in the market the minimum price established by the laws of the United States for the sale of their lands, were, in pursuance of the treaty of 1834 with that tribe, subsequently offered for sale at graduated and reduced rates for limited periods. The result was that large quantities of these lands were purchased which would otherwise have remained unsold. The lands were disposed of at their real value, and many persons of limited means were enabled to purchase small tracts, upon which they have settled with their families. That similar results would be produced by the adoption of the graduation policy by the United States in all the States in which they are the owners of large bodies of lands which have been long in the market can not be doubted. It can not be a sound policy to withhold large quantities of the public lands from the use and occupation of our citizens by fixing upon them prices which experience has shown they will not command. On the contrary, it is a wise policy to afford facilities to our citizens to become the owners at low and moderate rates of freeholds of their own instead of being the tenants and dependents of others. If it be apprehended that these lands if reduced in price would be secured in large quantities by speculators or capitalists, the sales may be restricted in limited quantities to actual settlers or persons purchasing for purposes of cultivation.

In my last annual message I submitted for the consideration of Congress the present system of managing the mineral lands of the United States, and recommended that they should be brought into market and sold upon such terms and under such restrictions as Congress might prescribe. By the act of the 11th of July last "the reserved lead mines and contiguous lands in the States of Illinois and Arkansas and Territories of Wisconsin and Iowa" were authorized to be sold. The act is confined in its operation to "lead mines and contiguous lands." A large portion of the public lands, containing copper and other ores, is represented to be very valuable, and I recommend that provision be made authorizing the sale of these lands upon such terms and conditions as from their supposed value may in the judgment of Congress be deemed advisable, having due regard to the interests of such of our citizens as may be located upon them.

It will be important during your present session to establish a Territorial government and to extend the jurisdiction and laws of the United States over the Territory of Oregon. Our laws regulating trade and intercourse with the Indian tribes east of the Rocky Mountains should be extended to the Pacific Ocean; and for the purpose of executing them and preserving friendly relations with the Indian tribes within our limits, an additional number of Indian agencies will be required, and should be authorized by law. The establishment of custom-houses and of post-offices and post-roads and provision for the transportation of the mail via such routes as the public convenience will suggest require legislative authority. It will be proper also to establish a surveyor-general's office in that Territory and to make the necessary provision for surveying the public lands and bringing them into market. As our citizens who now reside in that distant region have been subjected to many hardships, privations, and sacrifices in their emigration, and by their improvements have enhanced the value of the public lands in the neighborhood of their settlements, it is recommended that liberal grants be made to them of such portions of these lands as they may occupy, and that similar grants or rights of preemption be made to all who may emigrate thither within a limited period, prescribed by law.

The report of the Secretary of War contains detailed information relative to the several branches of the public service connected with that Department. The operations of the Army have been of a satisfactory and highly gratifying character. I recommend to your early and favorable consideration the measures proposed by the Secretary of War for speedily filling up the rank and file of the Regular Army, for its greater efficiency in the field, and for raising an additional force to serve during the war with Mexico.

Embarrassment is likely to arise for want of legal provision authorizing compensation to be made to the agents employed in the several States and Territories to pay the Revolutionary and other pensioners the amounts allowed them by law. Your attention is invited to the recommendations of the Secretary of War on this subject. These agents incur heavy responsibilities and perform important duties, and no reason exists why they should not be placed on the same footing as to compensation with other disbursing officers.

Our relations with the various Indian tribes continue to be of a pacific character. The unhappy dissensions which have existed among the Cherokees for many years past have been healed. Since my last annual message important treaties have been negotiated with some of the tribes, by which the Indian title to large tracts of valuable land within the limits of the States and Territories has been extinguished and arrangements made for removing them to the country west of the Mississippi. Between 3,000 and 4,000 of different tribes have been removed to the country provided for them by treaty stipulations, and arrangements have been made for others to follow.

In our intercourse with the several tribes particular attention has been given to the important subject of education. The number of schools established among them has been increased, and additional means provided not only for teaching them the rudiments of education, but of instructing them in agriculture and the mechanic arts.

I refer you to the report of the Secretary of the Navy for a satisfactory view of the operations of the Department under his charge during the past year. It is gratifying to perceive that while the war with Mexico has rendered it necessary to employ an unusual number of our armed vessels on her coasts, the protection due to our commerce in other quarters of the world has not proved insufficient. No means will be spared to give efficiency to the naval service in the prosecution of the war; and I am happy to know that the officers and men anxiously desire to devote themselves to the service of their country in any enterprise, however difficult of execution.

I recommend to your favorable consideration the proposition to add to each of our foreign squadrons an efficient sea steamer, and, as especially demanding attention, the establishment at Pensacola of the necessary means of repairing and refitting the vessels of the Navy employed in the Gulf of Mexico.

There are other suggestions in the report which deserve and I doubt not will receive your consideration.

The progress and condition of the mail service for the past year are fully presented in the report of the Postmaster-General. The revenue for the year ending on the 30th of June last amounted to $3,487,199, which is $802,642.45 less than that of the preceding year. The payments for that Department during the same time amounted to $4,084,297.22. Of this sum $597,097.80 have been drawn from the Treasury. The disbursements for the year were $236,434.77 less than those of the preceding year. While the disbursements have been thus diminished, the ᴍail facilities have been enlarged by new mail routes of 5,739 miles, an increase of transportation of 1,764,145 miles, and the establishment of 418 new post-offices. Contractors, postmasters, and others engaged in this branch of the service have performed their duties with energy and faithfulness deserving commendation. For many interesting details connected with the operations of this establishment you are referred to the report of the Postmaster-General, and his suggestions for improving its revenues are recommended to your favorable consideration. I repeat the opinion expressed in my last annual message that the business of this Department should be so regulated that the revenues derived from it should be made to equal the expenditures, and it is believed that this may be done by proper modifications of the present laws, as suggested in the report of the Postmaster-General, without changing the present rates of postage.

With full reliance upon the wisdom and patriotism of your deliberations, it will be my duty, as it will be my anxious desire, to cooperate with you in every constitutional effort to promote the welfare and maintain the honor of our common country.

THIRD ANNUAL MESSAGE.

WASHINGTON, *December 7, 1847.*

Fellow-Citizens of the Senate and of the House of Representatives:

The annual meeting of Congress is always an interesting event. The representatives of the States and of the people come fresh from their constituents to take counsel together for the common good.

After an existence of near three-fourths of a century as a free and independent Republic, the problem no longer remains to be solved whether man is capable of self-government. The success of our admirable system is a conclusive refutation of the theories of those in other countries who maintain that a "favored few" are born to rule and that the mass of mankind must be governed by force. Subject to no arbitrary or hereditary authority, the people are the only sovereigns recognized by our Constitution.

Numerous emigrants, of every lineage and language, attracted by the civil and religious freedom we enjoy and by our happy condition, annually crowd to our shores, and transfer their heart, not less than their allegiance, to the country whose dominion belongs alone to the people.

No country has been so much favored, or should acknowledge with deeper reverence the manifestations of the divine protection. An all-wise Creator directed and guarded us in our infant struggle for freedom and has constantly watched over our surprising progress until we have become one of the great nations of the earth.

It is in a country thus favored, and under a Government in which the executive and legislative branches hold their authority for limited periods alike from the people, and where all are responsible to their respective constituencies, that it is again my duty to communicate with Congress upon the state of the Union and the present condition of public affairs.

During the past year the most gratifying proofs are presented that our country has been blessed with a widespread and universal prosperity. There has been no period since the Government was founded when all the industrial pursuits of our people have been more successful or when labor in all branches of business has received a fairer or better reward. From our abundance we have been enabled to perform the pleasing duty of furnishing food for the starving millions of less favored countries.

In the enjoyment of the bounties of Providence at home such as have rarely fallen to the lot of any people, it is cause of congratulation that our intercourse with all the powers of the earth except Mexico continues to be of an amicable character.

It has ever been our cherished policy to cultivate peace and good will with all nations, and this policy has been steadily pursued by me.

No change has taken place in our relations with Mexico since the adjournment of the last Congress. The war in which the United States were forced to engage with the Government of that country still continues.

I deem it unnecessary, after the full exposition of them contained in my message of the 11th of May, 1846, and in my annual message at the commencement of the session of Congress in December last, to reiterate the serious causes of complaint which we had against Mexico before she commenced hostilities.

It is sufficient on the present occasion to say that the wanton violation of the rights of person and property of our citizens committed by Mexico, her repeated acts of bad faith through a long series of years, and her disregard of solemn treaties stipulating for indemnity to our injured citizens not only constituted ample cause of war on our part, but were of such an aggravated character as would have justified us before the whole world in resorting to this extreme remedy. With an anxious desire to avoid a rupture between the two countries, we forbore for years to assert our clear rights by force, and continued to seek redress for the wrongs we had suffered by amicable negotiation in the hope that Mexico might yield to pacific counsels and the demands of justice. In this hope we were disappointed. Our minister of peace sent to Mexico was insultingly rejected. The Mexican Government refused even to hear the terms of adjustment which he was authorized to propose, and finally, under wholly unjustifiable pretexts, involved the two countries in war by invading the territory of the State of Texas, striking the first blow, and shedding the blood of our citizens on our own soil.

Though the United States were the aggrieved nation, Mexico commenced the war, and we were compelled in self-defense to repel the invader and to vindicate the national honor and interests by prosecuting it with vigor until we could obtain a just and honorable peace.

On learning that hostilities had been commenced by Mexico I promptly communicated that fact, accompanied with a succinct statement of our other causes of complaint against Mexico, to Congress, and that body, by the act of the 13th of May, 1846, declared that "by the act of the Republic of Mexico a state of war exists between that Government and the United States." This act declaring "the war to exist by the act of the Republic of Mexico," and making provision for its prosecution "to a speedy and successful termination," was passed with great unanimity by Congress, there being but two negative votes in the Senate and but fourteen in the House of Representatives.

The existence of the war having thus been declared by Congress, it became my duty under the Constitution and the laws to conduct and prosecute it. This duty has been performed, and though at every stage of its progress I have manifested a willingness to terminate it by a just peace, Mexico has refused to accede to any terms which could be accepted by the United States consistently with the national honor and interest.

The rapid and brilliant successes of our arms and the vast extent of the enemy's territory which had been overrun and conquered before the close of the last session of Congress were fully known to that body. Since that time the war has been prosecuted with increased energy, and, I am gratified to state, with a success which commands universal admiration. History presents no parallel of so many glorious victories achieved by any nation within so short a period. Our Army, regulars and volunteers, have covered themselves with imperishable honors. Whenever and wherever our forces have encountered the enemy, though he was in vastly superior numbers and often intrenched in fortified positions of his own selection and of great strength, he has been defeated. Too much praise can not be bestowed upon our officers and men, regulars and volunteers, for their gallantry, discipline, indomitable courage, and perseverance, all seeking the post of danger and vying with each other in deeds of noble daring.

While every patriot's heart must exult and a just national pride animate every bosom in beholding the high proofs of courage, consummate military skill, steady discipline, and humanity to the vanquished enemy exhibited by our gallant Army, the nation is called to mourn over the loss of many brave officers and soldiers, who have fallen in defense of their country's honor and interests. The brave dead met their melancholy fate in a foreign land, nobly discharging their duty, and with their country's flag waving triumphantly in the face of the foe. Their patriotic deeds are justly appreciated, and will long be remembered by their grateful countrymen. The parental care of the Government they loved and served should be extended to their surviving families.

Shortly after the adjournment of the last session of Congress the gratifying intelligence was received of the signal victory of Buena Vista, and of the fall of the city of Vera Cruz, and with it the strong castle of San Juan de Ulloa, by which it was defended. Believing that after these and other successes so honorable to our arms and so disastrous to Mexico the period was propitious to afford her another opportunity, if she thought proper to embrace it, to enter into negotiations for peace, a commissioner was appointed to proceed to the headquarters of our Army with full powers to enter upon negotiations and to conclude a just and honorable treaty of peace. He was not directed to make any new overtures of peace, but was the bearer of a dispatch from the Secretary of State of the United States to the minister of foreign affairs of Mexico, in reply to one received from the latter of the 22d of February, 1847, in which the Mexican Government was informed of his appointment and of his presence at the headquarters of our Army, and that he was invested with full powers to conclude a definitive treaty of peace whenever the Mexican Government might signify a desire to do so. While I was unwilling to subject the United States to another indignant refusal, I was yet resolved that the evils of the war should not be protracted a day longer than might be rendered absolutely necessary by the Mexican Government.

Care was taken to give no instructions to the commissioner which could in any way interfere with our military operations or relax our energies in the prosecution of the war. He possessed no authority in any manner to control these operations. He was authorized to exhibit his instructions to the general in command of the Army, and in the event of a treaty being concluded and ratified on the part of Mexico he was directed to give him notice of that fact. On the happening of such contingency, and on receiving notice thereof, the general in command was instructed by the Secretary of War to suspend further active military operations until further orders. These instructions were given with a view to intermit hostilities until the treaty thus ratified by Mexico could be transmitted to Washington and receive the action of the Government of the United States. The commissioner was also directed on reaching the Army to deliver to the general in command the dispatch which he bore from the Secretary of State to the minister of foreign affairs of Mexico, and on receiving it the general was instructed by the Secretary of War to cause it to be transmitted to the commander of the Mexican forces, with a request that it might be communicated to his Government.

The commissioner did not reach the headquarters of the Army until after another brilliant victory had crowned our arms at Cerro Gordo.

The dispatch which he bore from the Secretary of War to the general in command of the Army was received by that officer, then at Jalapa, on the 7th of May, 1847, together with the dispatch from the Secretary of State to the minister of foreign affairs of Mexico, having been transmitted to him from Vera Cruz. The commissioner arrived at the headquarters of the Army a few days afterwards. His presence with the Army and his diplomatic character were made known to the Mexican Government from Puebla on the 12th of June, 1847, by the transmission of the dispatch from the Secretary of State to the minister of foreign affairs of Mexico.

Many weeks elapsed after its receipt, and no overtures were made nor was any desire expressed by the Mexican Government to enter into negotiations for peace.

Our Army pursued its march upon the capital, and as it approached it was met by formidable resistance. Our forces first encountered the enemy, and achieved signal victories in the severely contested battles of Contreras and Churubusco. It was not until after these actions had resulted in decisive victories and the capital of the enemy was within our power that the Mexican Government manifested any disposition to enter into negotiations for peace, and even then, as events have proved, there is too much reason to believe they were insincere, and that in agreeing to go through the forms of negotiation the object was to gain time to strengthen the defenses of their capital and to prepare for fresh resistance.

The general in command of the Army deemed it expedient to suspend hostilities temporarily by entering into an armistice with a view to the opening of negotiations. Commissioners were appointed on the part of Mexico to meet the commissioner on the part of the United States. The result of the conferences which took place between these functionaries of the two Governments was a failure to conclude a treaty of peace.

The commissioner of the United States took with him the project of a treaty already prepared, by the terms of which the indemnity required by the United States was a cession of territory.

It is well known that the only indemnity which it is in the power of Mexico to make in satisfaction of the just and long-deferred claims of our citizens against her and the only means by which she can reimburse the United States for the expenses of the war is a cession to the United States of a portion of her territory. Mexico has no money to pay, and no other means of making the required indemnity. If we refuse this, we can obtain nothing else. To reject indemnity by refusing to accept a cession of territory would be to abandon all our just demands, and to wage the war, bearing all its expenses, without a purpose or definite object.

A state of war abrogates treaties previously existing between the belligerents and a treaty of peace puts an end to all claims for indemnity for tortious acts committed under the authority of one government against the citizens or subjects of another unless they are provided for in its stipulations. A treaty of peace which would terminate the existing war without providing for indemnity would enable Mexico, the acknowledged debtor and herself the aggressor in the war, to relieve herself from her just liabilities. By such a treaty our citizens who hold just demands against her would have no remedy either against Mexico or their own Government. Our duty to these citizens must forever prevent such a peace, and no treaty which does not provide ample means of discharging these demands can receive my sanction.

A treaty of peace should settle all existing differences between the two countries. If an adequate cession of territory should be made by such a treaty, the United States should release Mexico from all her liabilities and assume their payment to our own citizens. If instead of this the United States were to consent to a treaty by which Mexico should again engage to pay the heavy amount of indebtedness which a just indemnity to our Government and our citizens would impose on her, it is notorious that she does not possess the means to meet such an undertaking. From such a treaty no result could be anticipated but the same irritating disappointments which have heretofore attended the violations of similar treaty stipulations on the part of Mexico. Such a treaty would be but a temporary cessation of hostilities, without the restoration of the friendship and good understanding which should characterize the future intercourse between the two countries.

That Congress contemplated the acquisition of territorial indemnity when that body made provision for the prosecution of the war is obvious. Congress could not have meant when, in May, 1846, they appropriated $10,000,000 and authorized the President to employ the militia and naval and military forces of the United States and to accept the services of 50,000 volunteers to enable him to prosecute the war, and when, at their last session, and after our Army had invaded Mexico, they made additional appropriations and authorized the raising of additional troops for the same purpose, that no indemnity was to be obtained from Mexico at the conclusion of the war; and yet it was certain that if no Mexican territory was acquired no indemnity could be obtained. It is further manifest that Congress contemplated territorial indemnity from the fact that at their last session an act was passed, upon the Executive recommendation, appropriating $3,000,000 with that express object. This appropriation was made "to enable the President to conclude a treaty of peace, limits, and boundaries with the Republic of Mexico, to be used by him in the event that said treaty, when signed by the authorized agents of the two Governments and duly ratified by Mexico, shall call for the expenditure of the same or any part thereof." The object of asking this appropriation was distinctly stated in the several messages on the subject which I communicated to Congress. Similar appropriations made in 1803 and 1806, which were referred to, were intended to be applied in part consideration for the cession of Louisiana and the Floridas. In like manner it was anticipated that in settling the terms of a treaty of "limits and boundaries" with Mexico a cession of territory estimated to be of greater value than the amount of our demands against her might be obtained, and that the prompt payment of this sum in part consideration for the territory ceded, on the conclusion of a treaty and its ratification on her part, might be an inducement with her to make such a cession of territory as would be satisfactory to the United States; and although the failure to conclude such a treaty has rendered it unnecessary to use any part of the $3,000,000 appropriated by that act, and the entire sum remains in the Treasury, it is still applicable to that object should the contingency occur making such application proper.

The doctrine of no territory is the doctrine of no indemnity, and if sanctioned would be a public acknowledgment that our country was wrong and that the war declared by Congress with extraordinary unanimity was unjust and should be abandoned—an admission unfounded in fact and degrading to the national character.

The terms of the treaty proposed by the United States were not only just to Mexico, but, considering the character and amount of our claims, the unjustifiable and unprovoked commencement of hostilities by her, the expenses of the war to which we have been subjected, and the success which had attended our arms, were deemed to be of a most liberal character.

The commissioner of the United States was authorized to agree to the establishment of the Rio Grande as the boundary from its entrance into the Gulf to its intersection with the southern boundary of New Mexico, in north latitude about 32°, and to obtain a cession to the United States of the Provinces of New Mexico and the Californias and the privilege of the right of way across the Isthmus of Tehuantepec. The boundary of the Rio Grande and the cession to the United States of New Mexico and Upper California constituted an ultimatum which our commissioner was under no circumstances to yield.

That it might be manifest, not only to Mexico, but to all other nations, that the United States were not disposed to take advantage of a feeble power by insisting upon wresting from her all the other Provinces, including many of her principal towns and cities, which we had conquered and held in our military occupation, but were willing to conclude a treaty in a spirit of liberality, our commissioner was authorized to stipulate for the restoration to Mexico of all our other conquests.

As the territory to be acquired by the boundary proposed might be estimated to be of greater value than a fair equivalent for our just demands, our commissioner was authorized to stipulate for the payment of such additional pecuniary consideration as was deemed reasonable.

The terms of a treaty proposed by the Mexican commissioners were wholly inadmissible. They negotiated as if Mexico were the victorious, and not the vanquished, party. They must have known that their ultimatum could never be accepted. It required the United States to dismember Texas by surrendering to Mexico that part of the territory of that State lying between the Nueces and the Rio Grande, included within her limits by her laws when she was an independent republic, and when she was annexed to the United States and admitted by Congress as one of the States of our Union. It contained no provision for the payment by Mexico of the just claims of our citizens. It required indemnity to Mexican citizens for injuries they may have sustained by our troops in the prosecution of the war. It demanded the right for Mexico to levy and collect the Mexican tariff of duties on goods imported into her ports while in our military occupation during the war, and the owners of which had paid to officers of the United States the military contributions which had been levied upon them; and it offered to cede to the United States, for a pecuniary consideration, that part of Upper California lying north of latitude 37°. Such were the unreasonable terms proposed by the Mexican commissioners.

The cession to the United States by Mexico of the Provinces of New Mexico and the Californias, as proposed by the commissioner of the United States, it was believed would be more in accordance with the convenience and interests of both nations than any other cession of territory which it was probable Mexico could be induced to make.

It is manifest to all who have observed the actual condition of the Mexican Government for some years past and at present that if these Provinces should be retained by her she could not long continue to hold and govern them. Mexico is too feeble a power to govern these Provinces, lying as they do at a distance of more than 1,000 miles from her capital, and if attempted to be retained by her they would constitute but for a short time even nominally a part of her dominions. This would be especially the case with Upper California.

The sagacity of powerful European nations has long since directed their attention to the commercial importance of that Province, and there can be little doubt that the moment the United States shall relinquish their present occupation of it and their claim to it as indemnity an effort would be made by some foreign power to possess it, either by conquest or by purchase. If no foreign government should acquire it in either of these modes, an independent revolutionary government would probably be established by the inhabitants and such foreigners as may remain in or remove to the country as soon as it shall be known that the United States have abandoned it. Such a government would be too feeble long to maintain its separate independent existence, and would finally become annexed to or be a dependent colony of some more powerful state.

Should any foreign government attempt to possess it as a colony, or otherwise to incorporate it with itself, the principle avowed by President Monroe in 1824, and reaffirmed in my first annual message, that no foreign power shall with our consent be permitted to plant or establish any new colony or dominion on any part of the North American continent must be maintained. In maintaining this principle and in resisting its invasion by any foreign power we might be involved in other wars more expensive and more difficult than that in which we are now engaged.

The Provinces of New Mexico and the Californias are contiguous to the territories of the United States, and if brought under the government of our laws their resources—mineral, agricultural, manufacturing, and commercial—would soon be developed.

Upper California is bounded on the north by our Oregon possessions, and if held by the United States would soon be settled by a hardy, enterprising, and intelligent portion of our population. The Bay of San Francisco and other harbors along the Californian coast would afford shelter for our Navy, for our numerous whale ships, and other merchant vessels employed in the Pacific Ocean, and would in a short period become the marts of an extensive and profitable commerce with China and other countries of the East.

These advantages, in which the whole commercial world would participate, would at once be secured to the United States by the cession of this territory; while it is certain that as long as it remains a part of the Mexican dominions they can be enjoyed neither by Mexico herself nor by any other nation.

New Mexico is a frontier Province, and has never been of any considerable value to Mexico. From its locality it is naturally connected with our Western settlements. The territorial limits of the State of Texas, too, as defined by her laws before her admission into our Union, embrace all that portion of New Mexico lying east of the Rio Grande, while Mexico still claims to hold this territory as a part of her dominions. The adjustment of this question of boundary is important.

There is another consideration which induced the belief that the Mexican Government might even desire to place this Province under the protection of the Government of the United States. Numerous bands of fierce and warlike savages wander over it and upon its borders. Mexico has been and must continue to be too feeble to restrain them from committing depredations, robberies, and murders, not only upon the inhabitants of New Mexico itself, but upon those of the other northern States of Mexico. It would be a blessing to all these northern States to have their citizens protected against them by the power of the United States. At this moment many Mexicans, principally females and children, are in captivity among them. If New Mexico were held and governed by the United States, we could effectually prevent these tribes from committing such outrages, and compel them to release these captives and restore them to their families and friends.

In proposing to acquire New Mexico and the Californias, it was known that but an inconsiderable portion of the Mexican people would be transferred with them, the country embraced within these Provinces being chiefly an uninhabited region.

These were the leading considerations which induced me to authorize the terms of peace which were proposed to Mexico. They were rejected, and, negotiations being at an end, hostilities were renewed. An assault was made by our gallant Army upon the strongly fortified places near the gates of the City of Mexico and upon the city itself, and after several days of severe conflict the Mexican forces, vastly superior in number to our own, were driven from the city, and it was occupied by our troops.

Immediately after information was received of the unfavorable result of the negotiations, believing that his continued presence with the Army could be productive of no good, I determined to recall our commissioner. A dispatch to this effect was transmitted to him on the 6th of October last. The Mexican Government will be informed of his recall, and that in the existing state of things I shall not deem it proper to make any further overtures of peace, but shall be at all times ready to receive and consider any proposals which may be made by Mexico.

Since the liberal proposition of the United States was authorized to be made, in April last, large expenditures have been incurred and the precious blood of many of our patriotic fellow-citizens has been shed in the prosecution of the war. This consideration and the obstinate perseverance of Mexico in protracting the war must influence the terms of peace which it may be deemed proper hereafter to accept.

Our arms having been everywhere victorious, having subjected to our military occupation a large portion of the enemy's country, including his capital, and negotiations for peace having failed, the important questions arise, in what manner the war ought to be prosecuted and what should be our future policy. I can not doubt that we should secure and render available the conquests which we have already made, and that with this view we should hold and occupy by our naval and military forces all the ports, towns, cities, and Provinces now in our occupation or which may hereafter fall into our possession; that we should press forward our military operations and levy such military contributions on the enemy as may, as far as practicable, defray the future expenses of the war.

Had the Government of Mexico acceded to the equitable and liberal terms proposed, that mode of adjustment would have been preferred. Mexico having declined to do this and failed to offer any other terms which could be accepted by the United States, the national honor, no less than the public interests, requires that the war should be prosecuted with increased energy and power until a just and satisfactory peace can be obtained. In the meantime, as Mexico refuses all indemnity, we should adopt measures to indemnify ourselves by appropriating permanently a portion of her territory. Early after the commencement of the war New Mexico and the Californias were taken possession of by our forces. Our military and naval commanders were ordered to conquer and hold them, subject to be disposed of by a treaty of peace.

These Provinces are now in our undisputed occupation, and have been so for many months, all resistance on the part of Mexico having ceased within their limits. I am satisfied that they should never be surrendered to Mexico. Should Congress concur with me in this opinion, and that they should be retained by the United States as indemnity, I can perceive no good reason why the civil jurisdiction and laws of the United States should not at once be extended over them. To wait for a treaty of peace such as we are willing to make, by which our relations toward them would not be changed, can not be good policy; whilst our own interest and that of the people inhabiting them require that a stable, responsible, and free government under our authority should as soon as possible be established over them. Should Congress, therefore, determine to hold these Provinces permanently, and that they shall hereafter be considered as constituent parts of our country, the early establishment of Territorial governments over them will be important for the more perfect protection of persons and property; and I recommend that such Territorial governments be established. It will promote peace and tranquillity among the inhabitants, by allaying all apprehension that they may still entertain of being again subjected to the jurisdiction of Mexico. I invite the early and favorable consideration of Congress to this important subject.

Besides New Mexico and the Californias, there are other Mexican Provinces which have been reduced to our possession by conquest. These other Mexican Provinces are now governed by our military and naval commanders under the general authority which is conferred upon a conqueror by the laws of war. They should continue to be held, as a means of coercing Mexico to accede to just terms of peace. Civil as well as military officers are required to conduct such a government. Adequate compensation, to be drawn from contributions levied on the enemy, should be fixed by law for such officers as may be thus employed. What further provision may become necessary and what final disposition it may be proper to make of them must depend on the future progress of the war and the course which Mexico may think proper hereafter to pursue.

With the views I entertain I can not favor the policy which has been suggested, either to withdraw our Army altogether or to retire to a designated line and simply hold and defend it. To withdraw our Army altogether from the conquests they have made by deeds of unparalleled bravery, and at the expense of so much blood and treasure, in a just war on our part, and one which, by the act of the enemy, we could not honorably have avoided, would be to degrade the nation in its own estimation and in that of the world. To retire to a line and simply hold and defend it would not terminate the war. On the contrary, it would encourage Mexico to persevere and tend to protract it indefinitely. It is not to be expected that Mexico, after refusing to establish such a line as a permanent boundary when our victorious Army are in possession of her capital and in the heart of her country, would permit us to hold it without resistance.   That she would continue the war, and in the most harassing and annoying forms, there can be no doubt.   A border warfare of the most savage character, extending over a long line, would be unceasingly waged. It would require a large army to be kept constantly in the field, stationed at posts and garrisons along such a line, to protect and defend it.   The enemy, relieved from the pressure of our arms on his coasts and in the populous parts of the interior, would direct his attention to this line, and, selecting an isolated post for attack, would concentrate his forces upon it. This would be a condition of affairs which the Mexicans, pursuing their favorite system of guerrilla warfare, would probably prefer to any other. Were we to assume a defensive attitude on such a line, all the advantages of such a state of war would be on the side of the enemy.   We could levy no contributions upon him, or in any other way make him feel the pressure of the war, but must remain inactive and await his approach, being in constant uncertainty at what point on the line or at what time he might make an assault.   He may assemble and organize an overwhelming force in the interior on his own side of the line, and, concealing his purpose, make a sudden assault upon some one of our posts so distant from any other as to prevent the possibility of timely succor or reenforcements, and in this way our gallant Army would be exposed to the danger of being cut off in detail; or if by their unequaled bravery and prowess everywhere exhibited during this war they should repulse the enemy, their numbers stationed at any one post may be too small to pursue him. If the enemy be repulsed in one attack, he would have nothing to do but to retreat to his own side of the line, and, being in no fear of a pursuing army, may reenforce himself at leisure for another attack on the same or some other post.   He may, too, cross the line between our posts, make rapid incursions into the country which we hold, murder the inhabitants, commit depredations on them, and then retreat to the interior before a sufficient force can be concentrated to pursue him.   Such would probably be the harassing character of a mere defensive war on our part.   If our forces when attacked, or threatened with attack, be permitted to cross the line, drive back the enemy, and conquer him, this would be again to invade the enemy's country after having lost all the advantages of the conquests we have already made by having voluntarily abandoned them. To hold such a line successfully and in security it is far from being certain that it would not require as large an army as would be necessary to hold all the conquests we have already made and to continue the prosecution of the war in the heart of the enemy's country.   It is also far from being certain that the expenses of the war would be diminished by such a policy.

I am persuaded that the best means of vindicating the national honor and interest and of bringing the war to an honorable close will be to prosecute it with increased energy and power in the vital parts of the enemy's country.

In my annual message to Congress of December last I declared that—

The war has not been waged with a view to conquest, but, having been commenced by Mexico, it has been carried into the enemy's country and will be vigorously prosecuted there with a view to obtain an honorable peace, and thereby secure ample indemnity for the expenses of the war, as well as to our much-injured citizens, who hold large pecuniary demands against Mexico.

Such, in my judgment, continues to be our true policy; indeed, the only policy which will probably secure a permanent peace.

It has never been contemplated by me, as an object of the war, to make a permanent conquest of the Republic of Mexico or to annihilate her separate existence as an independent nation. On the contrary, it has ever been my desire that she should maintain her nationality, and under a good government adapted to her condition be a free, independent, and prosperous Republic. The United States were the first among the nations to recognize her independence, and have always desired to be on terms of amity and good neighborhood with her. This she would not suffer. By her own conduct we have been compelled to engage in the present war. In its prosecution we seek not her overthrow as a nation, but in vindicating our national honor we seek to obtain redress for the wrongs she has done us and indemnity for our just demands against her. We demand an honorable peace, and that peace must bring with it indemnity for the past and security for the future. Hitherto Mexico has refused all accommodation by which such a peace could be obtained.

Whilst our armies have advanced from victory to victory from the commencement of the war, it has always been with the olive branch of peace in their hands, and it has been in the power of Mexico at every step to arrest hostilities by accepting it.

One great obstacle to the attainment of peace has undoubtedly arisen from the fact that Mexico has been so long held in subjection by one faction or military usurper after another, and such has been the condition of insecurity in which their successive governments have been placed that each has been deterred from making peace lest for this very cause a rival faction might expel it from power. Such was the fate of President Herrera's administration in 1845 for being disposed even to listen to the overtures of the United States to prevent the war, as is fully confirmed by an official correspondence which took place in the month of August last between him and his Government, a copy of which is herewith communicated. "For this cause alone the revolution which displaced him from power was set on foot" by General Paredes. Such may be the condition of insecurity of the present Government.

There can be no doubt that the peaceable and well-disposed inhabitants of Mexico are convinced that it is the true interest of their country to conclude an honorable peace with the United States, but the apprehension of becoming the victims of some military faction or usurper may

have prevented them from manifesting their feelings by any public act.
The removal of any such apprehension would probably cause them to
speak their sentiments freely and to adopt the measures necessary for the
restoration of peace.   With a people distracted and divided by contending factions and a Government subject to constant changes by successive
revolutions, the continued successes of our arms may fail to secure a satisfactory peace.   In such event it may become proper for our commanding
generals in the field to give encouragement and assurances of protection
to the friends of peace in Mexico in the establishment and maintenance
of a free republican government of their own choice, able and willing
to conclude a peace which would be just to them and secure to us the
indemnity we demand.   This may become the only mode of obtaining
such a peace.   Should such be the result, the war which Mexico has
forced upon us would thus be converted into an enduring blessing to
herself.   After finding her torn and distracted by factions, and ruled by
military usurpers, we should then leave her with a republican government in the enjoyment of real independence and domestic peace and
prosperity, performing all her relative duties in the great family of
nations and promoting her own happiness by wise laws and their faithful
execution.

If, after affording this encouragement and protection, and after all the
persevering and sincere efforts we have made from the moment Mexico
commenced the war, and prior to that time, to adjust our differences with
her, we shall ultimately fail, then we shall have exhausted all honorable
means in pursuit of peace, and must continue to occupy her country with
our troops, taking the full measure of indemnity into our own hands,
and must enforce the terms which our honor demands.

To act otherwise in the existing state of things in Mexico, and to withdraw our Army without a peace, would not only leave all the wrongs of
which we complain unredressed, but would be the signal for new and
fierce civil dissensions and new revolutions—all alike hostile to peaceful
relations with the United States.   Besides, there is danger, if our troops
were withdrawn before a peace was concluded, that the Mexican people,
wearied with successive revolutions and deprived of protection for their
persons and property, might at length be inclined to yield to foreign
influences and to cast themselves into the arms of some European monarch for protection from the anarchy and suffering which would ensue.
This, for our own safety and in pursuance of our established policy, we
should be compelled to resist.   We could never consent that Mexico
should be thus converted into a monarchy governed by a foreign prince.

Mexico is our near neighbor, and her boundaries are coterminous with
our own through the whole extent across the North American continent,
from ocean to ocean.   Both politically and commercially we have the
deepest interest in her regeneration and prosperity.   Indeed, it is impossible that, with any just regard to our own safety, we can ever become

indifferent to her fate.

It may be that the Mexican Government and people have misconstrued or misunderstood our forbearance and our objects in desiring to conclude an amicable adjustment of the existing differences between the two countries. They may have supposed that we would submit to terms degrading to the nation, or they may have drawn false inferences from the supposed division of opinion in the United States on the subject of the war, and may have calculated to gain much by protracting it, and, indeed, that we might ultimately abandon it altogether without insisting on any indemnity, territorial or otherwise. Whatever may be the false impressions under which they have acted, the adoption and prosecution of the energetic policy proposed must soon undeceive them.

In the future prosecution of the war the enemy must be made to feel its pressure more than they have heretofore done. At its commencement it was deemed proper to conduct it in a spirit of forbearance and liberality. With this end in view, early measures were adopted to conciliate, as far as a state of war would permit, the mass of the Mexican population; to convince them that the war was waged, not against the peaceful inhabitants of Mexico, but against their faithless Government, which had commenced hostilities; to remove from their minds the false impressions which their designing and interested rulers had artfully attempted to make, that the war on our part was one of conquest, that it was a war against their religion and their churches, which were to be desecrated and overthrown, and that their rights of person and private property would be violated. To remove these false impressions, our commanders in the field were directed scrupulously to respect their religion, their churches, and their church property, which were in no manner to be violated; they were directed also to respect the rights of persons and property of all who should not take up arms against us.

Assurances to this effect were given to the Mexican people by Major-General Taylor in a proclamation issued in pursuance of instructions from the Secretary of War in the month of June, 1846, and again by Major-General Scott, who acted upon his own convictions of the propriety of issuing it, in a proclamation of the 11th of May, 1847. In this spirit of liberality and conciliation, and with a view to prevent the body of the Mexican population from taking up arms against us, was the war conducted on our part. Provisions and other supplies furnished to our Army by Mexican citizens were paid for at fair and liberal prices, agreed upon by the parties. After the lapse of a few months it became apparent that these assurances and this mild treatment had failed to produce the desired effect upon the Mexican population. While the war had been conducted on our part according to the most humane and liberal principles observed by civilized nations, it was waged in a far different spirit on the part of Mexico. Not appreciating our forbearance, the Mexican people generally became hostile to the United States, and availed themselves of every opportunity to commit the most savage excesses upon our troops. Large numbers of the population took up arms, and, engaging in guerrilla warfare, robbed and murdered in the most cruel manner individual soldiers or small parties whom accident or other causes had separated from the main body of our Army; bands of guerrilleros and robbers infested the roads, harassed our trains, and whenever it was in their power cut off our supplies.

The Mexicans having thus shown themselves to be wholly incapable of appreciating our forbearance and liberality, it was deemed proper to change the manner of conducting the war, by making them feel its pressure according to the usages observed under similar circumstances by all other civilized nations.

Accordingly, as early as the 22d of September, 1846, instructions were given by the Secretary of War to Major-General Taylor to "draw supplies" for our Army "from the enemy without paying for them, and to require contributions for its support, if in that way he was satisfied he could get abundant supplies for his forces." In directing the execution of these instructions much was necessarily left to the discretion of the commanding officer, who was best acquainted with the circumstances by which he was surrounded, the wants of the Army, and the practicability of enforcing the measure. General Taylor, on the 26th of October, 1846, replied from Monterey that "it would have been impossible hitherto, and is so now, to sustain the Army to any extent by forced contributions of money or supplies." For the reasons assigned by him, he did not adopt the policy of his instructions, but declared his readiness to do so "should the Army in its future operations reach a portion of the country which may be made to supply the troops with advantage." He continued to pay for the articles of supply which were drawn from the enemy's country.

Similar instructions were issued to Major-General Scott on the 3d of April, 1847, who replied from Jalapa on the 20th of May, 1847, that if it be expected "that the Army is to support itself by forced contributions levied upon the country we may ruin and exasperate the inhabitants and starve ourselves." The same discretion was given to him that had been to General Taylor in this respect. General Scott, for the reasons assigned by him, also continued to pay for the articles of supply for the Army which were drawn from the enemy.

After the Army had reached the heart of the most wealthy portion of Mexico it was supposed that the obstacles which had before that time prevented it would not be such as to render impracticable the levy of forced contributions for its support, and on the 1st of September and again on the 6th of October, 1847, the order was repeated in dispatches addressed by the Secretary of War to General Scott, and his attention was again called to the importance of making the enemy bear the burdens of the war by requiring them to furnish the means of supporting our Army, and he was directed to adopt this policy unless by doing so there was danger of depriving the Army of the necessary supplies. Copies of these dispatches were forwarded to General Taylor for his government.

On the 31st of March last I caused an order to be issued to our military and naval commanders to levy and collect a military contribution upon all vessels and merchandise which might enter any of the ports of Mexico in our military occupation, and to apply such contributions toward defraying the expenses of the war. By virtue of the right of conquest and the laws of war, the conqueror, consulting his own safety or convenience, may either exclude foreign commerce altogether from all such ports or permit it upon such terms and conditions as he may prescribe. Before the principal ports of Mexico were blockaded by our Navy the revenue derived from import duties under the laws of Mexico was paid into the Mexican treasury. After these ports had fallen into our military possession the blockade was raised and commerce with them permitted upon prescribed terms and conditions. They were opened to the trade of all nations upon the payment of duties more moderate in their amount than those which had been previously levied by Mexico, and the revenue, which was formerly paid into the Mexican treasury, was directed to be collected by our military and naval officers and applied to the use of our Army and Navy. Care was taken that the officers, soldiers, and sailors of our Army and Navy should be exempted from the operations of the order, and, as the merchandise imported upon which the order operated must be consumed by Mexican citizens, the contributions exacted were in effect the seizure of the public revenues of Mexico and the application of them to our own use. In directing this measure the object was to compel the enemy to contribute as far as practicable toward the expenses of the war.

For the amount of contributions which have been levied in this form I refer you to the accompanying reports of the Secretary of War and of the Secretary of the Navy, by which it appears that a sum exceeding half a million of dollars has been collected. This amount would undoubtedly have been much larger but for the difficulty of keeping open communications between the coast and the interior, so as to enable the owners of the merchandise imported to transport and vend it to the inhabitants of the country. It is confidently expected that this difficulty will to a great extent be soon removed by our increased forces which have been sent to the field.

Measures have recently been adopted by which the internal as well as the external revenues of Mexico in all places in our military occupation will be seized and appropriated to the use of our Army and Navy.

The policy of levying upon the enemy contributions in every form consistently with the laws of nations, which it may be practicable for our military commanders to adopt, should, in my judgment, be rigidly enforced, and orders to this effect have accordingly been given. By such a policy, at the same time that our own Treasury will be relieved from a heavy drain, the Mexican people will be made to feel the burdens of the war, and, consulting their own interests, may be induced the more readily to require their rulers to accede to a just peace.

After the adjournment of the last session of Congress events transpired in the prosecution of the war which in my judgment required a greater number of troops in the field than had been anticipated. The strength of the Army was accordingly increased by "accepting" the services of all the volunteer forces authorized by the act of the 13th of May, 1846, without putting a construction on that act the correctness of which was seriously questioned. The volunteer forces now in the field, with those which had been "accepted" to "serve for twelve months" and were discharged at the end of their term of service, exhaust the 50,000 men authorized by that act. Had it been clear that a proper construction of the act warranted it, the services of an additional number would have been called for and accepted; but doubts existing upon this point, the power was not exercised. It is deemed important that Congress should at an early period of their session confer the authority to raise an additional regular force to serve during the war with Mexico and to be discharged upon the conclusion and ratification of a treaty of peace. I invite the attention of Congress to the views presented by the Secretary of War in his report upon this subject.

I recommend also that authority be given by law to call for and accept the services of an additional number of volunteers, to be exercised at such time and to such extent as the emergencies of the service may require.

In prosecuting the war with Mexico, whilst the utmost care has been taken to avoid every just cause of complaint on the part of neutral nations, and none has been given, liberal privileges have been granted to their commerce in the ports of the enemy in our military occupation.

The difficulty with the Brazilian Government, which at one time threatened to interrupt the friendly relations between the two countries, will, I trust, be speedily adjusted. I have received information that an envoy extraordinary and minister plenipotentiary to the United States will shortly be appointed by His Imperial Majesty, and it is hoped that he will come instructed and prepared to adjust all remaining differences between the two Governments in a manner acceptable and honorable to both. In the meantime, I have every reason to believe that nothing will occur to interrupt our amicable relations with Brazil.

It has been my constant effort to maintain and cultivate the most intimate relations of friendship with all the independent powers of South America, and this policy has been attended with the happiest results. It is true that the settlement and payment of many just claims of American citizens against these nations have been long delayed. The peculiar position in which they have been placed and the desire on the part of my predecessors as well as myself to grant them the utmost indulgence have hitherto prevented these claims from being urged in a manner demanded by strict justice. The time has arrived when they ought to be finally adjusted and liquidated, and efforts are now making for that purpose.

It is proper to inform you that the Government of Peru has in good faith paid the first two installments of the indemnity of $30,000 each, and the greater portion of the interest due thereon, in execution of the convention between that Government and the United States the ratifications of which were exchanged at Lima on the 31st of October, 1846. The Attorney-General of the United States early in August last completed the adjudication of the claims under this convention, and made his report thereon in pursuance of the act of the 8th of August, 1846. The sums to which the claimants are respectively entitled will be paid on demand at the Treasury.

I invite the early attention of Congress to the present condition of our citizens in China. Under our treaty with that power American citizens are withdrawn from the jurisdiction, whether civil or criminal, of the Chinese Government and placed under that of our public functionaries in that country. By these alone can our citizens be tried and punished for the commission of any crime; by these alone can questions be decided between them involving the rights of persons and property, and by these alone can contracts be enforced into which they may have entered with the citizens or subjects of foreign powers. The merchant vessels of the United States lying in the waters of the five ports of China open to foreign commerce are under the exclusive jurisdiction of officers of their own Government. Until Congress shall establish competent tribunals to try and punish crimes and to exercise jurisdiction in civil cases in China, American citizens there are subject to no law whatever. Crimes may be committed with impunity and debts may be contracted without any means to enforce their payment. Inconveniences have already resulted from the omission of Congress to legislate upon the subject, and still greater are apprehended. The British authorities in China have already complained that this Government has not provided for the punishment of crimes or the enforcement of contracts against American citizens in that country, whilst their Government has established tribunals by which an American citizen can recover debts due from British subjects.

Accustomed, as the Chinese are, to summary justice, they could not be made to comprehend why criminals who are citizens of the United States should escape with impunity, in violation of treaty obligations, whilst the punishment of a Chinese who had committed any crime against an American citizen would be rigorously exacted. Indeed, the consequences might be fatal to American citizens in China should a flagrant crime be committed by any one of them upon a Chinese, and should trial and punishment not follow according to the requisitions of the treaty. This might disturb, if not destroy, our friendly relations with that Empire, and cause an interruption of our valuable commerce.

Our treaties with the Sublime Porte, Tripoli, Tunis, Morocco, and

Muscat also require the legislation of Congress to carry them into execution, though the necessity for immediate action may not be so urgent as in regard to China.

The Secretary of State has submitted an estimate to defray the expense of opening diplomatic relations with the Papal States. The interesting political events now in progress in these States, as well as a just regard to our commercial interests, have, in my opinion, rendered such a measure highly expedient.

Estimates have also been submitted for the outfits and salaries of chargés d'affaires to the Republics of Bolivia, Guatemala, and Ecuador. The manifest importance of cultivating the most friendly relations with all the independent States upon this continent has induced me to recommend appropriations necessary for the maintenance of these missions.

I recommend to Congress that an appropriation be made to be paid to the Spanish Government for the purpose of distribution among the claimants in the *Amistad* case. I entertain the conviction that this is due to Spain under the treaty of the 20th of October, 1795, and, moreover, that from the earnest manner in which the claim continues to be urged so long as it shall remain unsettled it will be a source of irritation and discord between the two countries, which may prove highly prejudicial to the interests of the United States. Good policy, no less than a faithful compliance with our treaty obligations, requires that the inconsiderable appropriation demanded should be made.

A detailed statement of the condition of the finances will be presented in the annual report of the Secretary of the Treasury. The imports for the last fiscal year, ending on the 30th of June, 1847, were of the value of $146,545,638, of which the amount exported was $8,011,158, leaving $138,534,480 in the country for domestic use. The value of the exports for the same period was $158,648,622, of which $150,637,464 consisted of domestic productions and $8,011,158 of foreign articles.

The receipts into the Treasury for the same period amounted to $26,-346,790.37, of which there was derived from customs $23,747,864.66, from sales of public lands $2,498,335.20, and from incidental and miscellaneous sources $100,570.51. The last fiscal year, during which this amount was received, embraced five months under the operation of the tariff act of 1842 and seven months during which the tariff act of 1846 was in force. During the five months under the act of 1842 the amount received from customs was $7,842,306.90, and during the seven months under the act of 1846 the amount received was $15,905,557.76.

The net revenue from customs during the year ending on the 1st of December, 1846, being the last year under the operation of the tariff act of 1842, was $22,971,403.10, and the net revenue from customs during the year ending on the 1st of December, 1847, being the first year under the operations of the tariff act of 1846, was about $31,500,000, being an increase of revenue for the first year under the tariff of 1846 of more than

$8,500,000 over that of the last year under the tariff of 1842.

The expenditures during the fiscal year ending on the 30th of June last were $59,451,177.65, of which $3,522,082.37 was on account of payment of principal and interest of the public debt, including Treasury notes redeemed and not funded. The expenditures exclusive of payment of public debt were $55,929,095.28.

It is estimated that the receipts into the Treasury for the fiscal year ending on the 30th of June, 1848, including the balance in the Treasury on the 1st of July last, will amount to $42,886,545.80, of which $31,000,000, it is estimated, will be derived from customs, $3,500,000 from the sale of the public lands, $400,000 from incidental .sources, including sales made by the Solicitor of the Treasury, and $6,285,294.55 from loans already authorized by law, which, together with the balance in the Treasury on the 1st of July last, make the sum estimated.

The expenditures for the same period, if peace with Mexico shall not be concluded and the Army shall be increased as is proposed, will amount, including the necessary payments on account of principal and interest of the public debt and Treasury notes, to $58,615,660.07.

On the 1st of the present month the amount of the public debt actually incurred, including Treasury notes, was $45,659,659.40. The public debt due on the 4th of March, 1845, including Treasury notes, was $17,788,799.62, and consequently the addition made to the public debt since that time is $27,870,859.78.

Of the loan of twenty-three millions authorized by the act of the 28th of January, 1847, the sum of five millions was paid out to the public creditors or exchanged at par for specie; the remaining eighteen millions was offered for specie to the highest bidder not below par, by an advertisement issued by the Secretary of the Treasury and published from the 9th of February until the 10th of April, 1847, when it was awarded to the several highest bidders at premiums varying from one-eighth of 1 per cent to 2 per cent above par. The premium has been paid into the Treasury and the sums awarded deposited in specie in the Treasury as fast as it was required by the wants of the Government.

To meet the expenditures for the remainder of the present and for the next fiscal year, ending on the 30th of June, 1849, a further loan in aid of the ordinary revenues of the Government will be necessary. Retaining a sufficient surplus in the Treasury, the loan required for the remainder of the present fiscal year will be about $18,500,000. If the duty on tea and coffee be imposed and the graduation of the price of the public lands shall be made at an early period of your session, as recommended, the loan for the present fiscal year may be reduced to $17,000,000. The loan may be further reduced by whatever amount of expenditures can be saved by military contributions collected in Mexico. The most vigorous measures for the augmentation of these contributions have been directed and a very considerable sum is expected from that source. Its amount can not, however, be calculated with any certainty. It is recommended that the loan to be made be authorized upon the same terms and for the same time as that which was authorized under the provisions of the act of the 28th of January, 1847.

Should the war with Mexico be continued until the 30th of June, 1849, it is estimated that a further loan of $20,500,000 will be required for the fiscal year ending on that day, in case no duty be imposed on tea and coffee, and the public lands be not reduced and graduated in price, and no military contributions shall be collected in Mexico. If the duty on tea and coffee be imposed and the lands be reduced and graduated in price as proposed, the loan may be reduced to $17,000,000, and will be subject to be still further reduced by the amount of the military contributions which may be collected in Mexico. It is not proposed, however, at present to ask Congress for authority to negotiate this loan for the next fiscal year, as it is hoped that the loan asked for the remainder of the present fiscal year, aided by military contributions which may be collected in Mexico, may be sufficient. If, contrary to my expectation, there should be a necessity for it, the fact will be communicated to Congress in time for their action during the present session. In no event will a sum exceeding $6,000,000 of this amount be needed before the meeting of the session of Congress in December, 1848.

The act of the 30th of July, 1846, "reducing the duties on imports," has been in force since the 1st of December last, and I am gratified to state that all the beneficial effects which were anticipated from its operation have been fully realized. The public revenue derived from customs during the year ending on the 1st of December, 1847, exceeds by more than $8,000,000 the amount received in the preceding year under the operation of the act of 1842, which was superseded and repealed by it. Its effects are visible in the great and almost unexampled prosperity which prevails in every branch of business.

While the repeal of the prohibitory and restrictive duties of the act of 1842 and the substitution in their place of reasonable revenue rates levied on articles imported according to their actual value has increased the revenue and augmented our foreign trade, all the great interests of the country have been advanced and promoted.

The great and important interests of agriculture, which had been not only too much neglected, but actually taxed under the protective policy for the benefit of other interests, have been relieved of the burdens which that policy imposed on them; and our farmers and planters, under a more just and liberal commercial policy, are finding new and profitable markets abroad for their augmented products. Our commerce is rapidly increasing, and is extending more widely the circle of international exchanges. Great as has been the increase of our imports during the past year, our exports of domestic products sold in foreign markets have been still greater.

Our navigating interest is eminently prosperous. The number of vessels built in the United States has been greater than during any preceding period of equal length. Large profits have been derived by those who have constructed as well as by those who have navigated them. Should the ratio of increase in the number of our merchant vessels be progressive, and be as great for the future as during the past year, the time is not distant when our tonnage and commercial marine will be larger than that of any other nation in the world.

Whilst the interests of agriculture, of commerce, and of navigation have been enlarged and invigorated, it is highly gratifying to observe that our manufactures are also in a prosperous condition. None of the ruinous effects upon this interest which were apprehended by some as the result of the operation of the revenue system established by the act of 1846 have been experienced. On the contrary, the number of manufactories and the amount of capital invested in them is steadily and rapidly increasing, affording gratifying proofs that American enterprise and skill employed in this branch of domestic industry, with no other advantages than those fairly and incidentally accruing from a just system of revenue duties, are abundantly able to meet successfully all competition from abroad and still derive fair and remunerating profits. While capital invested in manufactures is yielding adequate and fair profits under the new system, the wages of labor, whether employed in manufactures, agriculture, commerce, or navigation, have been augmented. The toiling millions whose daily labor furnishes the supply of food and raiment and all the necessaries and comforts of life are receiving higher wages and more steady and permanent employment than in any other country or at any previous period of our own history.

So successful have been all branches of our industry that a foreign war, which generally diminishes the resources of a nation, has in no essential degree retarded our onward progress or checked our general prosperity.

With such gratifying evidences of prosperity and of the successful operation of the revenue act of 1846, every consideration of public policy recommends that it shall remain unchanged. It is hoped that the system of impost duties which it established may be regarded as the permanent policy of the country, and that the great interests affected by it may not again be subject to be injuriously disturbed, as they have heretofore been, by frequent and sometimes sudden changes.

For the purpose of increasing the revenue, and without changing or modifying the rates imposed by the act of 1846 on the dutiable articles embraced by its provisions, I again recommend to your favorable consideration the expediency of levying a revenue duty on tea and coffee. The policy which exempted these articles from duty during peace, and when the revenue to be derived from them was not needed, ceases to exist when the country is engaged in war and requires the use of all of its available resources. It is a tax which would be so generally diffused among the people that it would be felt oppressively by none and be complained of by none. It is believed that there are not in the list of imported articles any which are more properly the subject of war duties than tea and coffee.

It is estimated that $3,000,000 would be derived annually by a moderate duty imposed on these articles.

Should Congress avail itself of this additional source of revenue, not only would the amount of the public loan rendered necessary by the war with Mexico be diminished to that extent, but the public credit and the public confidence in the ability and determination of the Government to meet all its engagements promptly would be more firmly established, and the reduced amount of the loan which it may be necessary to negotiate could probably be obtained at cheaper rates.

Congress is therefore called upon to determine whether it is wiser to impose the war duties recommended or by omitting to do so increase the public debt annually $3,000,000 so long as loans shall be required to prosecute the war, and afterwards provide in some other form to pay the semiannual interest upon it, and ultimately to extinguish the principal. If in addition to these duties Congress should graduate and reduce the price of such of the public lands as experience has proved will not command the price placed upon them by the Government, an additional annual income to the Treasury of between half a million and a million of dollars, it is estimated, would be derived from this source. Should both measures receive the sanction of Congress, the annual amount of public debt necessary to be contracted during the continuance of the war would be reduced near $4,000,000. The duties recommended to be levied on tea and coffee it is proposed shall be limited in their duration to the end of the war, and until the public debt rendered necessary to be contracted by it shall be discharged. The amount of the public debt to be contracted should be limited to the lowest practicable sum, and should be extinguished as early after the conclusion of the war as the means of the Treasury will permit.

With this view, it is recommended that as soon as the war shall be over all the surplus in the Treasury not needed for other indispensable objects shall constitute a sinking fund and be applied to the purchase of the funded debt, and that authority be conferred by laws for that purpose.

The act of the 6th of August, 1846, "to establish a warehousing system," has been in operation more than a year, and has proved to be an important auxiliary to the tariff act of 1846 in augmenting the revenue and extending the commerce of the country. Whilst it has tended to enlarge commerce, it has been beneficial to our manufactures by diminishing forced sales at auction of foreign goods at low prices to raise the duties to be advanced on them, and by checking fluctuations in the market. The system, although sanctioned by the experience of other countries, was entirely new in the United States, and is susceptible of improvement in some of its provisions. The Secretary of the Treasury, upon whom was devolved large discretionary powers in carrying this measure into effect, has collected and is now collating the practical results of the system in other countries where it has long been established, and will report at an early period of your session such further regulations suggested by the investigation as may render it still more effective and beneficial.

By the act to "provide for the better organization of the Treasury and for the collection, safe-keeping, and disbursement of the public revenue" all banks were discontinued as fiscal agents of the Government, and the paper currency issued by them was no longer permitted to be received in payment of public dues. The constitutional treasury created by this act went into operation on the 1st of January last. Under the system established by it the public moneys have been collected, safely kept, and disbursed by the direct agency of officers of the Government in gold and silver, and transfers of large amounts have been made from points of collection to points of disbursement without loss to the Treasury or injury or inconvenience to the trade of the country.

While the fiscal operations of the Government have been conducted with regularity and ease under this system, it has had a salutary effect in checking and preventing an undue inflation of the paper currency issued by the banks which exist under State charters. Requiring, as it does, all dues to the Government to be paid in gold and silver, its effect is to restrain excessive issues of bank paper by the banks disproportioned to the specie in their vaults, for the reason that they are at all times liable to be called on by the holders of their notes for their redemption in order to obtain specie for the payment of duties and other public dues. The banks, therefore, must keep their business within prudent limits, and be always in a condition to meet such calls, or run the hazard of being compelled to suspend specie payments and be thereby discredited. The amount of specie imported into the United States during the last fiscal year was $24,121,289, of which there was retained in the country $22,276,170. Had the former financial system prevailed and the public moneys been placed on deposit in the banks, nearly the whole of this amount would have gone into their vaults, not to be thrown into circulation by them, but to be withheld from the hands of the people as a currency and made the basis of new and enormous issues of bank paper. A large proportion of the specie imported has been paid into the Treasury for public dues, and after having been to a great extent recoined at the Mint has been paid out to the public creditors and gone into circulation as a currency among the people. The amount of gold and silver coin now in circulation in the country is larger than at any former period.

The financial system established by the constitutional treasury has been thus far eminently successful in its operations, and I recommend an adherence to all its essential provisions, and especially to that vital provision which wholly separates the Government from all connection with banks and excludes bank paper from all revenue receipts.

In some of its details, not involving its general principles, the system is defective and will require modification. These defects and such amendments as are deemed important were set forth in the last annual report of the Secretary of the Treasury. These amendments are again recommended to the early and favorable consideration of Congress.

During the past year the coinage at the Mint and its branches has exceeded $20,000,000. This has consisted chiefly in converting the coins of foreign countries into American coin.

The largest amount of foreign coin imported has been received at New York, and if a branch mint were established at that city all the foreign coin received at that port could at once be converted into our own coin without the expense, risk, and delay of transporting it to the Mint for that purpose, and the amount recoined would be much larger.

Experience has proved that foreign coin, and especially foreign gold coin, will not circulate extensively as a currency among the people. The important measure of extending our specie circulation, both of gold and silver, and of diffusing it among the people can only be effected by converting such foreign coin into American coin. I repeat the recommendation contained in my last annual message for the establishment of a branch of the Mint of the United States at the city of New York.

All the public lands which had been surveyed and were ready for market have been proclaimed for sale during the past year. The quantity offered and to be offered for sale under proclamations issued since the 1st of January last amounts to 9,138,531 acres. The prosperity of the Western States and Territories in which these lands lie will be advanced by their speedy sale. By withholding them from market their growth and increase of population would be retarded, while thousands of our enterprising and meritorious frontier population would be deprived of the opportunity of securing freeholds for themselves and their families. But in addition to the general considerations which rendered the early sale of these lands proper, it was a leading object at this time to derive as large a sum as possible from this source, and thus diminish by that amount the public loan rendered necessary by the existence of a foreign war.

It is estimated that not less than 10,000,000 acres of the public lands will be surveyed and be in a condition to be proclaimed for sale during the year 1848.

In my last annual message I presented the reasons which in my judgment rendered it proper to graduate and reduce the price of such of the public lands as have remained unsold for long periods after they had been offered for sale at public auction.

Many millions of acres of public lands lying within the limits of several of the Western States have been offered in the market and been subject to sale at private entry for more than twenty years and large quantities for more than thirty years at the lowest price prescribed by the existing laws, and it has been found that they will not command that price. They must remain unsold and uncultivated for an indefinite period unless the price demanded for them by the Government shall be reduced. No satisfactory reason is perceived why they should be longer held at rates above their real value. At the present period an additional reason exists for adopting the measure recommended. When the country is engaged in a foreign war, and we must necessarily resort to loans, it would seem to be the dictate of wisdom that we should avail ourselves of all our resources and thus limit the amount of the public indebtedness to the lowest possible sum.

I recommend that the existing laws on the subject of preemption rights be amended and modified so as to operate prospectively and to embrace all who may settle upon the public lands and make improvements upon them, before they are surveyed as well as afterwards, in all cases where such settlements may be made after the Indian title shall have been extinguished.

If the right of preemption be thus extended, it will embrace a large and meritorious class of our citizens. It will increase the number of small freeholders upon our borders, who will be enabled thereby to educate their children and otherwise improve their condition, while they will be found at all times, as they have ever proved themselves to be in the hour of danger to their country, among our hardiest and best volunteer soldiers, ever ready to attend to their services in cases of emergencies and among the last to leave the field as long as an enemy remains to be encountered. Such a policy will also impress these patriotic pioneer emigrants with deeper feelings of gratitude for the parental care of their Government, when they find their dearest interests secured to them by the permanent laws of the land and that they are no longer in danger of losing their homes and hard-earned improvements by being brought into competition with a more wealthy class of purchasers at the land sales.

The attention of Congress was invited at their last and the preceding session to the importance of establishing a Territorial government over our possessions in Oregon, and it is to be regretted that there was no legislation on the subject. Our citizens who inhabit that distant region of country are still left without the protection of our laws, or any regularly organized government. Before the question of limits and boundaries of the Territory of Oregon was definitely settled, from the necessity of their condition the inhabitants had established a temporary government of their own. Besides the want of legal authority for continuing such a government, it is wholly inadequate to protect them in their rights of person and property, or to secure to them the enjoyment of the privileges of other citizens, to which they are entitled under the Constitution of the United States. They should have the right of suffrage, be represented in a Territorial legislature and by a Delegate in Congress, and possess all the rights and privileges which citizens of other portions of the territories of the United States have heretofore enjoyed or may now enjoy.

Our judicial system, revenue laws, laws regulating trade and intercourse with the Indian tribes, and the protection of our laws generally should be extended over them.

In addition to the inhabitants in that Territory who had previously emigrated to it, large numbers of our citizens have followed them during the present year, and it is not doubted that during the next and subsequent years their numbers will be greatly increased.

Congress at its last session established post routes leading to Oregon, and between different points within that Territory, and authorized the establishment of post-offices at "Astoria and such other places on the coasts of the Pacific within the territory of the United States as the public interests may require." Post-offices have accordingly been established, deputy postmasters appointed, and provision made for the transportation of the mails.

The preservation of peace with the Indian tribes residing west of the Rocky Mountains will render it proper that authority should be given by law for the appointment of an adequate number of Indian agents to reside among them.

I recommend that a surveyor-general's office be established in that Territory, and that the public lands be surveyed and brought into market at an early period.

I recommend also that grants, upon liberal terms, of limited quantities of the public lands be made to all citizens of the United States who have emigrated, or may hereafter within a prescribed period emigrate, to Oregon and settle upon them. These hardy and adventurous citizens, who have encountered the dangers and privations of a long and toilsome journey, and have at length found an abiding place for themselves and their families upon the utmost verge of our western limits, should be secured in the homes which they have improved by their labor.

I refer you to the accompanying report of the Secretary of War for a detailed account of the operations of the various branches of the public service connected with the Department under his charge. The duties devolving on this Department have been unusually onerous and responsible during the past year, and have been discharged with ability and success.

Pacific relations continue to exist with the various Indian tribes, and most of them manifest a strong friendship for the United States. Some depredations were committed during the past year upon our trains transporting supplies for the Army, on the road between the western border of Missouri and Santa Fe. These depredations, which are supposed to have been committed by bands from the region of New Mexico, have been arrested by the presence of a military force ordered out for that purpose. Some outrages have been perpetrated by a portion of the northwestern bands upon the weaker and comparatively defenseless neighboring tribes. Prompt measures were taken to prevent such occurrences in future.

Between 1,000 and 2,000 Indians, belonging to several tribes, have been removed during the year from the east of the Mississippi to the country allotted to them west of that river as their permanent home, and arrangements have been made for others to follow.

Since the treaty of 1846 with the Cherokees the feuds among them appear to have subsided, and they have become more united and contented than they have been for many years past. The commissioners appointed in pursuance of the act of June 27, 1846, to settle claims arising under the treaty of 1835–36 with that tribe have executed their duties, and after a patient investigation and a full and fair examination of all the cases brought before them closed their labors in the month of July last. This is the fourth board of commissioners which has been organized under this treaty. Ample opportunity has been afforded to all those interested to bring forward their claims. No doubt is entertained that impartial justice has been done by the late board, and that all valid claims embraced by the treaty have been considered and allowed. This result and the final settlement to be made with this tribe under the treaty of 1846, which will be completed and laid before you during your session, will adjust all questions of controversy between them and the United States and produce a state of relations with them simple, well defined, and satisfactory.

Under the discretionary authority conferred by the act of the 3d of March last the annuities due to the various tribes have been paid during the present year to the heads of families instead of to their chiefs or such persons as they might designate, as required by the law previously existing. This mode of payment has given general satisfaction to the great body of the Indians. Justice has been done to them, and they are grateful to the Government for it. A few chiefs and interested persons may object to this mode of payment, but it is believed to be the only mode of preventing fraud and imposition from being practiced upon the great body of common Indians, constituting a majority of all the tribes.

It is gratifying to perceive that a number of the tribes have recently manifested an increased interest in the establishment of schools among them, and are making rapid advances in agriculture, some of them producing a sufficient quantity of food for their support and in some cases a surplus to dispose of to their neighbors. The comforts by which those who have received even a very limited education and have engaged in agriculture are surrounded tend gradually to draw off their less civilized brethren from the precarious means of subsistence by the chase to habits of labor and civilization.

The accompanying report of the Secretary of the Navy presents a satisfactory and gratifying account of the condition and operations of the naval service during the past year. Our commerce has been pursued with increased activity and with safety and success in every quarter of

the globe under the protection of our flag, which the Navy has caused
to be respected in the most distant seas.

In the Gulf of Mexico and in the Pacific the officers and men of
our squadrons have displayed distinguished gallantry and performed
valuable services.   In the early stages of the war with Mexico her ports
on both coasts were blockaded, and more recently many of them have
been captured and held by the Navy.   When acting in cooperation with
the land forces, the naval officers and men have performed gallant and
distinguished services on land as well as on water, and deserve the high
commendation of the country.

While other maritime powers are adding to their navies large numbers of war steamers, it was a wise policy on our part to make similar
additions to our Navy.   The four war steamers authorized by the act
of the 3d of March, 1847, are in course of construction.

In addition to the four war steamers authorized by this act, the Secretary of the Navy has, in pursuance of its provisions, entered into contracts
for the construction of five steamers to be employed in the transportation
of the United States mail ''from New York to New Orleans, touching at
Charleston, Savannah, and Havana, and from Havana to Chagres;'' for
three steamers to be employed in like manner from Panama to Oregon,
''so as to connect with the mail from Havana to Chagres across the
Isthmus;'' and for five steamers to be employed in like manner from
New York to Liverpool.   These steamers will be the property of the
contractors, but are to be built ''under the superintendence and direction
of a naval constructor in the employ of the Navy Department, and to be
so constructed as to render them convertible at the least possible expense
into war steamers of the first class.''   A prescribed number of naval officers, as well as a post-office agent, are to be on board of them, and
authority is reserved to the Navy Department at all times to ''exercise
control over said steamships'' and ''to have the right to take them for
the exclusive use and service of the United States upon making proper
compensation to the contractors therefor.''

Whilst these steamships will be employed in transporting the mails of
the United States coastwise and to foreign countries upon an annual compensation to be paid to the owners, they will be always ready, upon an
emergency requiring it, to be converted into war steamers; and the right
reserved to take them for public use will add greatly to the efficiency
and strength of this description of our naval force.   To the steamers thus
authorized under contracts made by the Secretary of the Navy should be
added five other steamers authorized under contracts made in pursuance
of laws by the Postmaster-General, making an addition, in the whole, of
eighteen war steamers subject to be taken for public use.   As further
contracts for the transportation of the mail to foreign countries may be
authorized by Congress, this number may be enlarged indefinitely.

The enlightened policy by which a rapid communication with the various distant parts of the globe is established, by means of American-built sea steamers, would find an ample reward in the increase of our commerce and in making our country and its resources more favorably known abroad; but the national advantage is still greater—of having our naval officers made familiar with steam navigation and of having the privilege of taking the ships already equipped for immediate service at a moment's notice, and will be cheaply purchased by the compensation to be paid for the transportation of the mail in them over and above the postages received.

A just national pride, no less than our commercial interests, would seem to favor the policy of augmenting the number of this description of vessels. They can be built in our country cheaper and in greater numbers than in any other in the world.

I refer you to the accompanying report of the Postmaster-General for a detailed and satisfactory account of the condition and operations of that Department during the past year. It is gratifying to find that within so short a period after the reduction in the rates of postage, and notwithstanding the great increase of mail service, the revenue received for the year will be sufficient to defray all the expenses, and that no further aid will be required from the Treasury for that purpose.

The first of the American mail steamers authorized by the act of the 3d of March, 1845, was completed and entered upon the service on the 1st of June last, and is now on her third voyage to Bremen and other intermediate ports. The other vessels authorized under the provisions of that act are in course of construction, and will be put upon the line as soon as completed. Contracts have also been made for the transportation of the mail in a steamer from Charleston to Havana.

A reciprocal and satisfactory postal arrangement has been made by the Postmaster-General with the authorities of Bremen, and no difficulty is apprehended in making similar arrangements with all other powers with which we may have communications by mail steamers, except with Great Britain.

On the arrival of the first of the American steamers bound to Bremen at Southampton, in the month of June last, the British post-office directed the collection of discriminating postages on all letters and other mailable matter which she took out to Great Britain or which went into the British post-office on their way to France and other parts of Europe. The effect of the order of the British post-office is to subject all letters and other matter transported by American steamers to double postage, one postage having been previously paid on them to the United States, while letters transported in British steamers are subject to pay but a single postage. This measure was adopted with the avowed object of protecting the British line of mail steamers now running between Boston and Liverpool, and if permitted to continue must speedily put an end to the transportation of all letters and other matter by American steamers and give to British steamers a monopoly of the business. A just

and fair reciprocity is all that we desire, and on this we must insist.
By our laws no such discrimination is made against British steamers
bringing letters into our ports, but all letters arriving in the United
States are subject to the same rate of postage, whether brought in
British or American vessels.   I refer you to the report of the Postmaster-
General for a full statement of the facts of the case and of the steps
taken by him to correct this inequality.   He has exerted all the power
conferred upon him by the existing laws.

The minister of the United States at London has brought the subject
to the attention of the British Government, and is now engaged in negotiations for the purpose of adjusting reciprocal postal arrangements
which shall be equally just to both countries.   Should he fail in concluding such arrangements, and should Great Britain insist on enforcing the
unequal and unjust measure she has adopted, it will become necessary to
confer additional powers on the Postmaster-General in order to enable
him to meet the emergency and to put our own steamers on an equal
footing with British steamers engaged in transporting the mails between
the two countries, and I recommend that such powers be conferred.

In view of the existing state of our country, I trust it may not be inappropriate, in closing this communication, to call to mind the words of wisdom and admonition of the first and most illustrious of my predecessors
in his Farewell Address to his countrymen.

That greatest and best of men, who served his country so long and
loved it so much, foresaw with "serious concern" the danger to our
Union of "characterizing parties by *geographical* discriminations—*Northern* and *Southern*, *Atlantic* and *Western*—whence designing men may
endeavor to excite a belief that there is a real difference of local interests
and views," and warned his countrymen against it.

So deep and solemn was his conviction of the importance of the Union
and of preserving harmony between its different parts, that he declared
to his countrymen in that address:

It is of infinite moment that you should properly estimate the immense value of
your national union to your collective and individual happiness; that you should
cherish a cordial, habitual, and immovable attachment to it; accustoming yourselves
to think and speak of it as of the palladium of your political safety and prosperity;
watching for its preservation with jealous anxiety; discountenancing whatever may
suggest even a suspicion that it can in any event be abandoned, and indignantly
frowning upon the first dawning of every attempt to alienate any portion of our
country from the rest or to enfeeble the sacred ties which now link together the
various parts.

After the lapse of half a century these admonitions of Washington
fall upon us with all the force of truth.   It *is* difficult to estimate the
"immense value" of our glorious Union of confederated States, to which
we are so much indebted for our growth in population and wealth and
for all that constitutes us a great and a happy nation.   How unimportant are all our differences of opinion upon minor questions of public
policy compared with its preservation, and how scrupulously should we

avoid all agitating topics which may tend to distract and divide us into contending parties, separated by geographical lines, whereby it may be weakened or endangered.

Invoking the blessing of the Almighty Ruler of the Universe upon your deliberations, it will be my highest duty, no less than my sincere pleasure, to cooperate with you in all measures which may tend to promote the honor and enduring welfare of our common country.

FOURTH ANNUAL MESSAGE.

WASHINGTON, *December 5, 1848.*

Fellow-Citizens of the Senate and of the House of Representatives:

Under the benignant providence of Almighty God the representatives of the States and of the people are again brought together to deliberate for the public good. The gratitude of the nation to the Sovereign Arbiter of All Human Events should be commensurate with the boundless blessings which we enjoy.

Peace, plenty, and contentment reign throughout our borders, and our beloved country presents a sublime moral spectacle to the world.

The troubled and unsettled condition of some of the principal European powers has had a necessary tendency to check and embarrass trade and to depress prices throughout all commercial nations, but notwithstanding these causes, the United States, with their abundant products, have felt their effects less severely than any other country, and all our great interests are still prosperous and successful.

In reviewing the great events of the past year and contrasting the agitated and disturbed state of other countries with our own tranquil and happy condition, we may congratulate ourselves that we are the most favored people on the face of the earth. While the people of other countries are struggling to establish free institutions, under which man may govern himself, we are in the actual enjoyment of them—a rich inheritance from our fathers. While enlightened nations of Europe are convulsed and distracted by civil war or intestine strife, we settle all our political controversies by the peaceful exercise of the rights of freemen at the ballot box.

The great republican maxim, so deeply engraven on the hearts of our people, that the will of the majority, constitutionally expressed, shall prevail, is our sure safeguard against force and violence. It is a subject of just pride that our fame and character as a nation continue rapidly to advance in the estimation of the civilized world.

To our wise and free institutions it is to be attributed that while other nations have achieved glory at the price of the suffering, distress, and impoverishment of their people, we have won our honorable position in the midst of an uninterrupted prosperity and of an increasing individual comfort and happiness.

I am happy to inform you that our relations with all nations are friendly and pacific. Advantageous treaties of commerce have been concluded within the last four years with New Granada, Peru, the Two Sicilies, Belgium, Hanover, Oldenburg, and Mecklenburg-Schwerin. Pursuing our example, the restrictive system of Great Britain, our principal foreign customer, has been relaxed, a more liberal commercial policy has been adopted by other enlightened nations, and our trade has been greatly enlarged and extended. Our country stands higher in the respect of the world than at any former period. To continue to occupy this proud position, it is only necessary to preserve peace and faithfully adhere to the great and fundamental principle of our foreign policy of noninterference in the domestic concerns of other nations. We recognize in all nations the right which we enjoy ourselves, to change and reform their political institutions according to their own will and pleasure. Hence we do not look behind existing governments capable of maintaining their own authority. We recognize all such actual governments, not only from the dictates of true policy, but from a sacred regard for the independence of nations. While this is our settled policy, it does not follow that we can ever be indifferent spectators of the progress of liberal principles. The Government and people of the United States hailed with enthusiasm and delight the establishment of the French Republic, as we now hail the efforts in progress to unite the States of Germany in a confederation similar in many respects to our own Federal Union. If the great and enlightened German States, occupying, as they do, a central and commanding position in Europe, shall succeed in establishing such a confederated government, securing at the same time to the citizens of each State local governments adapted to the peculiar condition of each, with unrestricted trade and intercourse with each other, it will be an important era in the history of human events. Whilst it will consolidate and strengthen the power of Germany, it must essentially promote the cause of peace, commerce, civilization, and constitutional liberty throughout the world.

With all the Governments on this continent our relations, it is believed, are now on a more friendly and satisfactory footing than they have ever been at any former period.

Since the exchange of ratifications of the treaty of peace with Mexico our intercourse with the Government of that Republic has been of the most friendly character. The envoy extraordinary and minister plenipotentiary of the United States to Mexico has been received and accredited, and a diplomatic representative from Mexico of similar rank has been received and accredited by this Government   The amicable relations between the two countries, which had been suspended, have been happily restored, and are destined, I trust, to be long preserved.   The two Republics, both situated on this continent, and with coterminous territories, have every motive of sympathy and of interest to bind them together in perpetual amity.

This gratifying condition of our foreign relations renders it unnecessary for me to call your attention more specifically to them.

It has been my constant aim and desire to cultivate peace and commerce with all nations.   Tranquillity at home and peaceful relations abroad constitute the true permanent policy of our country.   War, the scourge of nations, sometimes becomes inevitable, but is always to be avoided when it can be done consistently with the rights and honor of a nation.

One of the most important results of the war into which we were recently forced with a neighboring nation is the demonstration it has afforded of the military strength of our country.   Before the late war with Mexico European and other foreign powers entertained imperfect and erroneous views of our physical strength as a nation and of our ability to prosecute war, and especially a war waged out of our own country.   They saw that our standing Army on the peace establishment did not exceed 10,000 men.   Accustomed themselves to maintain in peace large standing armies for the protection of thrones against their own subjects, as well as against foreign enemies, they had not conceived that it was possible for a nation without such an army, well disciplined and of long service, to wage war successfully.   They held in low repute our militia, and were far from regarding them as an effective force, unless it might be for temporary defensive operations when invaded on our own soil.   The events of the late war with Mexico have not only undeceived them, but have removed erroneous impressions which prevailed to some extent even among a portion of our own countrymen.   That war has demonstrated that upon the breaking out of hostilities not anticipated, and for which no previous preparation had been made, a volunteer army of citizen soldiers equal to veteran troops, and in numbers equal to any emergency, can in a short period be brought into the field.   Unlike what would have occurred in any other country, we were under no necessity of resorting to drafts or conscriptions.   On the contrary, such was the number of volunteers who patriotically tendered their services that the chief difficulty was in making selections and determining who should be disappointed and compelled to remain at home.   Our citizen soldiers are unlike those drawn from the population of any other country. They are composed indiscriminately of all professions and pursuits—of farmers, lawyers, physicians, merchants, manufacturers, mechanics, and laborers—and this not only among the officers, but the private soldiers in the ranks.   Our citizen soldiers are unlike those of any other country in other respects.   They are armed, and have been accustomed from their youth up to handle and use firearms, and a large proportion of them, especially in the Western and more newly settled States, are expert marksmen.   They are men who have a reputation to maintain at home by their good conduct in the field.   They are intelligent, and there is an individuality of character which is found in the ranks of no other army.   In battle each private man, as well as every officer, fights not only for his country, but for glory and distinction among his fellow-citizens when he shall return to civil life.

The war with Mexico has demonstrated not only the ability of the Government to organize a numerous army upon a sudden call, but also to provide it with all the munitions and necessary supplies with dispatch, convenience, and ease, and to direct its operations with efficiency.   The strength of our institutions has not only been displayed in the valor and skill of our troops engaged in active service in the field, but in the organization of those executive branches which were charged with the general direction and conduct of the war.   While too great praise can not be bestowed upon the officers and men who fought our battles, it would be unjust to withhold from those officers necessarily stationed at home, who were charged with the duty of furnishing the Army in proper time and at proper places with all the munitions of war and other supplies so necessary to make it efficient, the commendation to which they are entitled.   The credit due to this class of our officers is the greater when it is considered that no army in ancient or modern times was ever better appointed or provided than our Army in Mexico.   Operating in an enemy's country, removed 2,000 miles from the seat of the Federal Government, its different corps spread over a vast extent of territory, hundreds and even thousands of miles apart from each other, nothing short of the untiring vigilance and extraordinary energy of these officers could have enabled them to provide the Army at all points and in proper season with all that was required for the most efficient service.

It is but an act of justice to declare that the officers in charge of the several executive bureaus, all under the immediate eye and supervision of the Secretary of War, performed their respective duties with ability, energy, and efficiency.   They have reaped less of the glory of the war, not having been personally exposed to its perils in battle, than their companions in arms; but without their forecast, efficient aid, and cooperation those in the field would not have been provided with the ample means they possessed of achieving for themselves and their country the unfading honors which they have won for both.

When all these facts are considered, it may cease to be a matter of so much amazement abroad how it happened that our noble Army in Mexico, regulars and volunteers, were victorious upon every battlefield, however fearful the odds against them.

The war with Mexico has thus fully developed the capacity of republican governments to prosecute successfully a just and necessary foreign war with all the vigor usually attributed to more arbitrary forms of government. It has been usual for writers on public law to impute to republics a want of that unity, concentration of purpose, and vigor of execution which are generally admitted to belong to the monarchical and aristocratic forms; and this feature of popular government has been supposed to display itself more particularly in the conduct of a war carried on in an enemy's territory. The war with Great Britain in 1812 was to a great extent confined within our own limits, and shed but little light on this subject; but the war which we have just closed by an honorable peace evinces beyond all doubt that a popular representative government is equal to any emergency which is likely to arise in the affairs of a nation.

The war with Mexico has developed most strikingly and conspicuously another feature in our institutions. It is that without cost to the Government or danger to our liberties we have in the bosom of our society of freemen, available in a just and necessary war, virtually a standing army of 2,000,000 armed citizen soldiers, such as fought the battles of Mexico. But our military strength does not consist alone in our capacity for extended and successful operations on land. The Navy is an important arm of the national defense. If the services of the Navy were not so brilliant as those of the Army in the late war with Mexico, it was because they had no enemy to meet on their own element. While the Army had opportunity of performing more conspicuous service, the Navy largely participated in the conduct of the war. Both branches of the service performed their whole duty to the country. For the able and gallant services of the officers and men of the Navy, acting independently as well as in cooperation with our troops, in the conquest of the Californias, the capture of Vera Cruz, and the seizure and occupation of other important positions on the Gulf and Pacific coasts, the highest praise is due. Their vigilance, energy, and skill rendered the most effective service in excluding munitions of war and other supplies from the enemy, while they secured a safe entrance for abundant supplies for our own Army. Our extended commerce was nowhere interrupted, and for this immunity from the evils of war the country is indebted to the Navy.

High praise is due to the officers of the several executive bureaus, navy-yards, and stations connected with the service, all under the immediate direction of the Secretary of the Navy, for the industry, foresight, and energy with which everything was directed and furnished to give efficiency to that branch of the service. The same vigilance existed in directing the operations of the Navy as of the Army. There was concert of action and of purpose between the heads of the two arms of the service. By the orders which were from time to time issued, our vessels of war on the Pacific and the Gulf of Mexico were stationed in proper time and in proper positions to cooperate efficiently with the Army. By this means their combined power was brought to bear successfully on the enemy.

The great results which have been developed and brought to light by this war will be of immeasurable importance in the future progress of our country. They will tend powerfully to preserve us from foreign collisions, and to enable us to pursue uninterruptedly our cherished policy of "peace with all nations, entangling alliances with none."

Occupying, as we do, a more commanding position among nations than at any former period, our duties and our responsibilities to ourselves and to posterity are correspondingly increased. This will be the more obvious when we consider the vast additions which have been recently made to our territorial possessions and their great importance and value.

Within less than four years the annexation of Texas to the Union has been consummated; all conflicting title to the Oregon Territory south of the forty-ninth degree of north latitude, being all that was insisted on by any of my predecessors, has been adjusted, and New Mexico and Upper California have been acquired by treaty. The area of these several Territories, according to a report carefully prepared by the Commissioner of the General Land Office from the most authentic information in his possession, and which is herewith transmitted, contains 1,193,061 square miles, or 763,559,040 acres; while the area of the remaining twenty-nine States and the territory not yet organized into States east of the Rocky Mountains contains 2,059,513 square miles, or 1,318,126,058 acres. These estimates show that the territories recently acquired, and over which our exclusive jurisdiction and dominion have been extended, constitute a country more than half as large as all that which was held by the United States before their acquisition. If Oregon be excluded from the estimate, there will still remain within the limits of Texas, New Mexico, and California 851,598 square miles, or 545,012,720 acres, being an addition equal to more than one-third of all the territory owned by the United States before their acquisition, and, including Oregon, nearly as great an extent of territory as the whole of Europe, Russia only excepted. The Mississippi, so lately the frontier of our country, is now only its center. With the addition of the late acquisitions, the United States are now estimated to be nearly as large as the whole of Europe. It is estimated by the Superintendent of the Coast Survey in the accompanying report that the extent of the seacoast of Texas on the Gulf of Mexico is upward of 400 miles; of the coast of Upper California on the Pacific, of 970 miles, and of Oregon, including the Straits of Fuca, of 650 miles, making the whole extent of seacoast on the Pacific 1,620 miles and the whole extent on both the Pacific and the Gulf of Mexico 2,020 miles. The length of the coast on the Atlantic from the northern limits of the United States around the capes of Florida to the Sabine, on the eastern boundary of Texas, is estimated to be 3,100 miles; so that the addition of seacoast, including Oregon, is very nearly two-thirds as great as all we possessed before, and, excluding Oregon, is an addition of 1,370 miles, being nearly equal to one-half of the extent of coast which we possessed before these acquisitions. We have now three great maritime fronts— on the Atlantic, the Gulf of Mexico, and the Pacific—making in the whole an extent of seacoast exceeding 5,000 miles. This is the extent of the seacoast of the United States, not including bays, sounds, and small irregularities of the main shore and of the sea islands. If these be included, the length of the shore line of coast, as estimated by the Super- intendent of the Coast Survey in his report, would be 33,063 miles.

It would be difficult to calculate the value of these immense additions to our territorial possessions. Texas, lying contiguous to the western boundary of Louisiana, embracing within its limits a part of the naviga- ble tributary waters of the Mississippi and an extensive seacoast, could not long have remained in the hands of a foreign power without endan- gering the peace of our southwestern frontier. Her products in the vicinity of the tributaries of the Mississippi must have sought a market through these streams, running into and through our territory, and the danger of irritation and collision of interests between Texas as a foreign state and ourselves would have been imminent, while the embarrass- ments in the commercial intercourse between them must have been con- stant and unavoidable. Had Texas fallen into the hands or under the influence and control of a strong maritime or military foreign power, as she might have done, these dangers would have been still greater. They have been avoided by her voluntary and peaceful annexation to the United States. Texas, from her position, was a natural and almost indispensable part of our territories. Fortunately, she has been restored to our country, and now constitutes one of the States of our Confed- eracy, ''upon an equal footing with the original States.'' The salubrity of climate, the fertility of soil, peculiarly adapted to the production of some of our most valuable staple commodities, and her commercial advan- tages must soon make her one of our most populous States.

New Mexico, though situated in the interior and without a seacoast, is known to contain much fertile land, to abound in rich mines of the precious metals, and to be capable of sustaining a large population. From its position it is the intermediate and connecting territory between our settlements and our possessions in Texas and those on the Pacific Coast.

Upper California, irrespective of the vast mineral wealth recently devel- oped there, holds at this day, in point of value and importance, to the rest of the Union the same relation that Louisiana did when that fine terri- tory was acquired from France forty-five years ago. Extending nearly ten degrees of latitude along the Pacific, and embracing the only safe and commodious harbors on that coast for many hundred miles, with a temperate climate and an extensive interior of fertile lands, it is scarcely possible to estimate its wealth until it shall be brought under the govern- ment of our laws and its resources fully developed. From its position it must command the rich commerce of China, of Asia, of the islands of the Pacific, of western Mexico, of Central America, the South American States, and of the Russian possessions bordering on that ocean. A great emporium will doubtless speedily arise on the Californian coast which may be destined to rival in importance New Orleans itself. The depot of the vast commerce which must exist on the Pacific will probably be at some point on the Bay of San Francisco, and will occupy the same relation to the whole western coast of that ocean as New Orleans does to the valley of the Mississippi and the Gulf of Mexico. To this depot our numerous whale ships will resort with their cargoes to trade, refit, and obtain supplies. This of itself will largely contribute to build up a city, which would soon become the center of a great and rapidly increasing commerce. Situated on a safe harbor, sufficiently capacious for all the navies as well as the marine of the world, and convenient to excellent timber for shipbuilding, owned by the United States, it must become our great Western naval depot.

It was known that mines of the precious metals existed to a considerable extent in California at the time of its acquisition. Recent discoveries render it probable that these mines are more extensive and valuable than was anticipated. The accounts of the abundance of gold in that territory are of such an extraordinary character as would scarcely command belief were they not corroborated by the authentic reports of officers in the public service who have visited the mineral district and derived the facts which they detail from personal observation. Reluctant to credit the reports in general circulation as to the quantity of gold, the officer commanding our forces in California visited the mineral district in July last for the purpose of obtaining accurate information on the subject. His report to the War Department of the result of his examination and the facts obtained on the spot is herewith laid before Congress. When he visited the country there were about 4,000 persons engaged in collecting gold. There is every reason to believe that the number of persons so employed has since been augmented. The explorations already made warrant the belief that the supply is very large and that gold is found at various places in an extensive district of country.

Information received from officers of the Navy and other sources, though not so full and minute, confirms the accounts of the commander of our military force in California. It appears also from these reports that mines of quicksilver are found in the vicinity of the gold region. One of them is now being worked, and is believed to be among the most productive in the world.

The effects produced by the discovery of these rich mineral deposits and the success which has attended the labors of those who have resorted to them have produced a surprising change in the state of affairs in California. Labor commands a most exorbitant price, and all other pursuits but that of searching for the precious metals are abandoned. Nearly the whole of the male population of the country have gone to the gold districts. Ships arriving on the coast are deserted by their crews and their voyages suspended for want of sailors. Our commanding officer there entertains apprehensions that soldiers can not be kept in the public service without a large increase of pay. Desertions in his command have become frequent, and he recommends that those who shall withstand the strong temptation and remain faithful should be rewarded.

This abundance of gold and the all-engrossing pursuit of it have already caused in California an unprecedented rise in the price of all the necessaries of life.

That we may the more speedily and fully avail ourselves of the undeveloped wealth of these mines, it is deemed of vast importance that a branch of the Mint of the United States be authorized to be established at your present session in California. Among other signal advantages which would result from such an establishment would be that of raising the gold to its par value in that territory. A branch mint of the United States at the great commercial depot on the west coast would convert into our own coin not only the gold derived from our own rich mines, but also the bullion and specie which our commerce may bring from the whole west coast of Central and South America. The west coast of America and the adjacent interior embrace the richest and best mines of Mexico, New Granada, Central America, Chili, and Peru. The bullion and specie drawn from these countries, and especially from those of western Mexico and Peru, to an amount in value of many millions of dollars, are now annually diverted and carried by the ships of Great Britain to her own ports, to be recoined or used to sustain her national bank, and thus contribute to increase her ability to command so much of the commerce of the world. If a branch mint be established at the great commercial point upon that coast, a vast amount of bullion and specie would flow thither to be recoined, and pass thence to New Orleans, New York, and other Atlantic cities. The amount of our constitutional currency at home would be greatly increased, while its circulation abroad would be promoted. It is well known to our merchants trading to China and the west coast of America that great inconvenience and loss are experienced from the fact that our coins are not current at their par value in those countries.

The powers of Europe, far removed from the west coast of America by the Atlantic Ocean, which intervenes, and by a tedious and dangerous navigation around the southern cape of the continent of America, can never successfully compete with the United States in the rich and extensive commerce which is opened to us at so much less cost by the acquisition of California.

The vast importance and commercial advantages of California have heretofore remained undeveloped by the Government of the country of which it constituted a part. Now that this fine province is a part of our country, all the States of the Union, some more immediately and directly than others, are deeply interested in the speedy development of its wealth and resources. No section of our country is more interested or will be more benefited than the commercial, navigating, and manufacturing interests of the Eastern States. Our planting and farming interests in every part of the Union will be greatly benefited by it. As our commerce and navigation are enlarged and extended, our exports of agricultural products and of manufactures will be increased, and in the new markets thus opened they can not fail to command remunerating and profitable prices.

The acquisition of California and New Mexico, the settlement of the Oregon boundary, and the annexation of Texas, extending to the Rio Grande, are results which, combined, are of greater consequence and will add more to the strength and wealth of the nation than any which have preceded them since the adoption of the Constitution.

But to effect these great results not only California, but New Mexico, must be brought under the control of regularly organized governments. The existing condition of California and of that part of New Mexico lying west of the Rio Grande and without the limits of Texas imperiously demands that Congress should at its present session organize Territorial governments over them.

Upon the exchange of ratifications of the treaty of peace with Mexico, on the 30th of May last, the temporary governments which had been established over New Mexico and California by our military and naval commanders by virtue of the rights of war ceased to derive any obligatory force from that source of authority, and having been ceded to the United States, all government and control over them under the authority of Mexico had ceased to exist. Impressed with the necessity of establishing Territorial governments over them, I recommended the subject to the favorable consideration of Congress in my message communicating the ratified treaty of peace, on the 6th of July last, and invoked their action at that session. Congress adjourned without making any provision for their government. The inhabitants by the transfer of their country had become entitled to the benefit of our laws and Constitution, and yet were left without any regularly organized government. Since that time the very limited power possessed by the Executive has been exercised to preserve and protect them from the inevitable consequences of a state of anarchy. The only government which remained was that established by the military authority during the war. Regarding this to be a *de facto* government, and that by the presumed consent of the inhabitants it might be continued temporarily, they were advised to conform and submit to it for the short intervening period before Congress would again assemble and could legislate on the subject. The views entertained by the Executive on this point are contained in a communication of the Secretary of State dated the 7th of October last, which was forwarded for publication to California and New Mexico, a copy of which is herewith transmitted. The small military force of the Regular Army which was serving within the limits of the acquired territories at the close of the war was retained in them, and additional forces have been ordered there for the protection of the inhabitants and to preserve and secure the rights and interests of the United States.

No revenue has been or could be collected at the ports in California, because Congress failed to authorize the establishment of custom-houses or the appointment of officers for that purpose.

The Secretary of the Treasury, by a circular letter addressed to collectors of the customs on the 7th day of October last, a copy of which is herewith transmitted, exercised all the power with which he was invested by law.

In pursuance of the act of the 14th of August last, extending the benefit of our post-office laws to the people of California, the Postmaster-General has appointed two agents, who have proceeded, the one to California and the other to Oregon, with authority to make the necessary arrangements for carrying its provisions into effect.

The monthly line of mail steamers from Panama to Astoria has been required to "stop and deliver and take mails at San Diego, Monterey, and San Francisco." These mail steamers, connected by the Isthmus of Panama with the line of mail steamers on the Atlantic between New York and Chagres, will establish a regular mail communication with California.

It is our solemn duty to provide with the least practicable delay for New Mexico and California regularly organized Territorial governments. The causes of the failure to do this at the last session of Congress are well known and deeply to be regretted. With the opening prospects of increased prosperity and national greatness which the acquisition of these rich and extensive territorial possessions affords, how irrational it would be to forego or to reject these advantages by the agitation of a domestic question which is coeval with the existence of our Government itself, and to endanger by internal strifes, geographical divisions, and heated contests for political power, or for any other cause, the harmony of the glorious Union of our confederated States—that Union which binds us together as one people, and which for sixty years has been our shield and protection against every danger. In the eyes of the world and of posterity how trivial and insignificant will be all our internal divisions and struggles compared with the preservation of this Union of the States in all its vigor and with all its countless blessings! No patriot would foment and excite geographical and sectional divisions. No lover of his country would deliberately calculate the value of the Union. Future generations would look in amazement upon the folly of such a course. Other nations at the present day would look upon it with astonishment, and such of them as desire to maintain and perpetuate thrones and monarchical or aristocratical principles will view it with exultation and delight, because in it they will see the elements of faction, which they hope must ultimately overturn our system. Ours is the great example of a prosperous and free self-governed republic, commanding the admiration and the imitation of all the lovers of freedom throughout the world. How solemn, therefore, is the duty, how impressive the call upon us and upon all parts of our country, to cultivate a patriotic spirit of harmony, of good-fellowship, of compromise and mutual concession, in the administration of the incomparable system of government formed by our fathers in the midst of almost insuperable difficulties, and transmitted to us with the injunction that we should enjoy its blessings and hand it down unimpaired to those who may come after us.

In view of the high and responsible duties which we owe to ourselves and to mankind, I trust you may be able at your present session to approach the adjustment of the only domestic question which seriously threatens, or probably ever can threaten, to disturb the harmony and successful operations of our system.

The immensely valuable possessions of New Mexico and California are already inhabited by a considerable population. Attracted by their great fertility, their mineral wealth, their commercial advantages, and the salubrity of the climate, emigrants from the older States in great numbers are already preparing to seek new homes in these inviting regions. Shall the dissimilarity of the domestic institutions in the different States prevent us from providing for them suitable governments? These institutions existed at the adoption of the Constitution, but the obstacles which they interposed were overcome by that spirit of compromise which is now invoked. In a conflict of opinions or of interests, real or imaginary, between different sections of our country, neither can justly demand all which it might desire to obtain. Each, in the true spirit of our institutions, should concede something to the other.

Our gallant forces in the Mexican war, by whose patriotism and unparalleled deeds of arms we obtained these possessions as an indemnity for our just demands against Mexico, were composed of citizens who belonged to no one State or section of our Union. They were men from slaveholding and nonslaveholding States, from the North and the South, from the East and the West. They were all companions in arms and fellow-citizens of the same common country, engaged in the same common cause. When prosecuting that war they were brethren and friends, and shared alike with each other common toils, dangers, and sufferings. Now, when their work is ended, when peace is restored, and they return again to their homes, put off the habiliments of war, take their places in society, and resume their pursuits in civil life, surely a spirit of harmony and concession and of equal regard for the rights of all and of all sections of the Union ought to prevail in providing governments for the acquired territories—the fruits of their common service. The whole people of the United States, and of every State, contributed to defray the expenses of that war, and it would not be just for any one section to exclude another from all participation in the acquired territory. This would not be in consonance with the just system of government which the framers of the Constitution adopted.

The question is believed to be rather abstract than practical, whether slavery ever can or would exist in any portion of the acquired territory even if it were left to the option of the slaveholding States themselves. From the nature of the climate and productions in much the larger portion of it it is certain it could never exist, and in the remainder the probabilities are it would not. But however this may be, the question, involving, as it does, a principle of equality of rights of the separate and several States as equal copartners in the Confederacy, should not be disregarded.

In organizing governments over these territories no duty imposed on Congress by the Constitution requires that they should legislate on the subject of slavery, while their power to do so is not only seriously questioned, but denied by many of the soundest expounders of that instrument. Whether Congress shall legislate or not, the people of the acquired territories, when assembled in convention to form State constitutions, will possess the sole and exclusive power to determine for themselves whether slavery shall or shall not exist within their limits. If Congress shall abstain from interfering with the question, the people of these territories will be left free to adjust it as they may think proper when they apply for admission as States into the Union. No enactment of Congress could restrain the people of any of the sovereign States of the Union, old or new, North or South, slaveholding or nonslaveholding, from determining the character of their own domestic institutions as they may deem wise and proper. Any and all the States possess this right, and Congress can not deprive them of it. The people of Georgia might if they chose so alter their constitution as to abolish slavery within its limits, and the people of Vermont might so alter their constitution as to admit slavery within its limits. Both States would possess the right, though, as all know, it is not probable that either would exert it.

It is fortunate for the peace and harmony of the Union that this question is in its nature temporary and can only continue for the brief period which will intervene before California and New Mexico may be admitted as States into the Union. From the tide of population now flowing into them it is highly probable that this will soon occur.

Considering the several States and the citizens of the several States as equals and entitled to equal rights under the Constitution, if this were an original question it might well be insisted on that the principle of noninterference is the true doctrine and that Congress could not, in the absence of any express grant of power, interfere with their relative rights. Upon a great emergency, however, and under menacing dangers to the Union, the Missouri compromise line in respect to slavery was adopted. The same line was extended farther west in the acquisition of Texas. After an acquiescence of nearly thirty years in the principle of compromise recognized and established by these acts, and to avoid the danger to the Union which might follow if it were now disregarded, I have heretofore expressed the opinion that that line of compromise should be extended on the parallel of 36° 30′ from the western boundary of Texas, where it now terminates, to the Pacific Ocean. This is the middle ground of compromise, upon which the different sections of the Union may meet, as they have heretofore met. If this be done, it is confidently believed a large majority of the people of every section of the country, however widely their abstract opinions on the subject of slavery may differ, would cheerfully and patriotically acquiesce in it, and peace and harmony would again fill our borders.

The restriction north of the line was only yielded to in the case of Missouri and Texas upon a principle of compromise, made necessary for the sake of preserving the harmony and possibly the existence of the Union.

It was upon these considerations that at the close of your last session I gave my sanction to the principle of the Missouri compromise line by approving and signing the bill to establish "the Territorial government of Oregon." From a sincere desire to preserve the harmony of the Union, and in deference for the acts of my predecessors, I felt constrained to yield my acquiescence to the extent to which they had gone in compromising this delicate and dangerous question. But if Congress shall now reverse the decision by which the Missouri compromise was effected, and shall propose to extend the restriction over the whole territory, south as well as north of the parallel of 36° 30′, it will cease to be a compromise, and must be regarded as an original question.

If Congress, instead of observing the course of noninterference, leaving the adoption of their own domestic institutions to the people who may inhabit these territories, or if, instead of extending the Missouri compromise line to the Pacific, shall prefer to submit the legal and constitutional questions which may arise to the decision of the judicial tribunals, as was proposed in a bill which passed the Senate at your last session, an adjustment may be effected in this mode. If the whole subject be referred to the judiciary, all parts of the Union should cheerfully acquiesce in the final decision of the tribunal created by the Constitution for the settlement of all questions which may arise under the Constitution, treaties, and laws of the United States.

Congress is earnestly invoked, for the sake of the Union, its harmony, and our continued prosperity as a nation, to adjust at its present session this, the only dangerous question which lies in our path, if not in some one of the modes suggested, in some other which may be satisfactory.

In anticipation of the establishment of regular governments over the acquired territories, a joint commission of officers of the Army and Navy has been ordered to proceed to the coast of California and Oregon for the purpose of making reconnoissances and a report as to the proper sites for the erection of fortifications or other defensive works on land and of suitable situations for naval stations. The information which may be expected from a scientific and skillful examination of the whole face of the coast will be eminently useful to Congress when they come to con· sider the propriety of making appropriations for these great national objects. Proper defenses on land will be necessary for the security and protection of our possessions, and the establishment of navy-yards and a dock for the repair and construction of vessels will be important alike to our Navy and commercial marine. Without such establishments every vessel, whether of the Navy or of the merchant service, requiring repair must at great expense come round Cape Horn to one of our Atlantic yards for that purpose. With such establishments vessels, it is believed, may be built or repaired as cheaply in California as upon the Atlantic coast. They would give employment to many of our enterprising ship-builders and mechanics and greatly facilitate and enlarge our commerce in the Pacific.

As it is ascertained that mines of gold, silver, copper, and quicksilver exist in New Mexico and California, and that nearly all the lands where they are found belong to the United States, it is deemed important to the public interest that provision be made for a geological and mineral-ogical examination of these regions. Measures should be adopted to pre-serve the mineral lands, especially such as contain the precious metals, for the use of the United States, or, if brought into market, to sepa-rate them from the farming lands and dispose of them in such manner as to secure a large return of money to the Treasury and at the same time to lead to the development of their wealth by individual proprie-tors and purchasers. To do this it will be necessary to provide for an immediate survey and location of the lots. If Congress should deem it proper to dispose of the mineral lands, they should be sold in small quantities and at a fixed minimum price.

I recommend that surveyors-general's offices be authorized to be estab-lished in New Mexico and California and provision made for surveying and bringing the public lands into market at the earliest practicable period. In disposing of these lands, I recommend that the right of pre-emption be secured and liberal grants made to the early emigrants who have settled or may settle upon them.

It will be important to extend our revenue laws over these territories, and especially over California, at an early period. There is already a considerable commerce with California, and until ports of entry shall be established and collectors appointed no revenue can be received.

If these and other necessary and proper measures be adopted for the development of the wealth and resources of New Mexico and California and regular Territorial governments be established over them, such will probably be the rapid enlargement of our commerce and navigation and such the addition to the national wealth that the present generation may live to witness the controlling commercial and monetary power of the world transferred from London and other European emporiums to the city of New York.

The apprehensions which were entertained by some of our statesmen in the earlier periods of the Government that our system was incapable of operating with sufficient energy and success over largely extended territorial limits, and that if this were attempted it would fall to pieces by its own weakness, have been dissipated by our experience.   By the division of power between the States and Federal Government the latter is found to operate with as much energy in the extremes as in the center. It is as efficient in the remotest of the thirty States which now compose the Union as it was in the thirteen States which formed our Constitution.   Indeed, it may well be doubted whether if our present population had been confined within the limits of the original thirteen States the tendencies to centralization and consolidation would not have been such as to have encroached upon the essential reserved rights of the States, and thus to have made the Federal Government a widely different one, practically, from what it is in theory and was intended to be by its framers.   So far from entertaining apprehensions of the safety of our system by the extension of our territory, the belief is confidently entertained that each new State gives strength and an additional guaranty for the preservation of the Union itself.

In pursuance of the provisions of the thirteenth article of the treaty of peace, friendship, limits, and settlement with the Republic of Mexico, and of the act of July 29, 1848, claims of our citizens, which had been "already liquidated and decided, against the Mexican Republic" amounting, with the interest thereon, to $2,023,832.51 have been liquidated and paid.   There remain to be paid of these claims $74,192.26.

Congress at its last session having made no provision for executing the fifteenth article of the treaty, by which the United States assume to make satisfaction for the "unliquidated claims" of our citizens against Mexico to "an amount not exceeding three and a quarter millions of dollars," the subject is again recommended to your favorable consideration.

The exchange of ratifications of the treaty with Mexico took place on the 30th of May, 1848.   Within one year after that time the commissioner and surveyor which each Government stipulates to appoint are required to meet "at the port of San Diego and proceed to run and mark the said boundary in its whole course to the mouth of the Rio Bravo del Norte."   It will be seen from this provision that the period within which a commissioner and surveyor of the respective Governments are to meet at San Diego will expire on the 30th of May, 1849.   Congress at the close of its last session made an appropriation for "the expenses of running and marking the boundary line" between the two countries, but did not fix the amount of salary which should be paid to the commissioner and surveyor to be appointed on the part of the United States.   It is desirable that the amount of compensation which they shall receive should be prescribed by law, and not left, as at present, to Executive discretion.

Measures were adopted at the earliest practicable period to organize the "Territorial government of Oregon," as authorized by the act of the 14th of August last. The governor and marshal of the Territory, accompanied by a small military escort, left the frontier of Missouri in September last, and took the southern route, by the way of Santa Fe and the river Gila, to California, with the intention of proceeding thence in one of our vessels of war to their destination. The governor was fully advised of the great importance of his early arrival in the country, and it is confidently believed he may reach Oregon in the latter part of the present month or early in the next. The other officers for the Territory have proceeded by sea.

In the month of May last I communicated information to Congress that an Indian war had broken out in Oregon, and recommended that authority be given to raise an adequate number of volunteers to proceed without delay to the assistance of our fellow-citizens in that Territory. The authority to raise such a force not having been granted by Congress, as soon as their services could be dispensed with in Mexico orders were issued to the regiment of mounted riflemen to proceed to Jefferson Barracks, in Missouri, and to prepare to march to Oregon as soon as the necessary provision could be made. Shortly before it was ready to march it was arrested by the provision of the act passed by Congress on the last day of the last session, which directed that all the noncommissioned officers, musicians, and privates of that regiment who had been in service in Mexico should, upon their application, be entitled to be discharged. The effect of this provision was to disband the rank and file of the regiment, and before their places could be filled by recruits the season had so far advanced that it was impracticable for it to proceed until the opening of the next spring.

In the month of October last the accompanying communication was received from the governor of the temporary government of Oregon, giving information of the continuance of the Indian disturbances and of the destitution and defenseless condition of the inhabitants. Orders were immediately transmitted to the commander of our squadron in the Pacific to dispatch to their assistance a part of the naval forces on that station, to furnish them with arms and ammunition, and to continue to give them such aid and protection as the Navy could afford until the Army could reach the country.

It is the policy of humanity, and one which has always been pursued by the United States, to cultivate the good will of the aboriginal tribes of this continent and to restrain them from making war and indulging in excesses by mild means rather than by force. That this could have been done with the tribes in Oregon had that Territory been brought under the government of our laws at an earlier period, and had other suitable measures been adopted by Congress, such as now exist in our intercourse with the other Indian tribes within our limits, can not be doubted. Indeed, the immediate and only cause of the existing hostility of the Indians of Oregon is represented to have been the long delay of the United States in making to them some trifling compensation, in such articles as they wanted, for the country now occupied by our emigrants, which the Indians claimed and over which they formerly roamed. This compensation had been promised to them by the temporary government established in Oregon, but its fulfillment had been postponed from time to time for nearly two years, whilst those who made it had been anxiously waiting for Congress to establish a Territorial government over the country. The Indians became at length distrustful of their good faith and sought redress by plunder and massacre, which finally led to the present difficulties. A few thousand dollars in suitable presents, as a compensation for the country which had been taken possession of by our citizens, would have satisfied the Indians and have prevented the war. A small amount properly distributed, it is confidently believed, would soon restore quiet. In this Indian war our fellow-citizens of Oregon have been compelled to take the field in their own defense, have performed valuable military services, and been subjected to expenses which have fallen heavily upon them. Justice demands that provision should be made by Congress to compensate them for their services and to refund to them the necessary expenses which they have incurred.

I repeat the recommendation heretofore made to Congress, that provision be made for the appointment of a suitable number of Indian agents to reside among the tribes of Oregon, and that a small sum be appropriated to enable these agents to cultivate friendly relations with them. If this be done, the presence of a small military force will be all that is necessary to keep them in check and preserve peace. I recommend that similar provisions be made as regards the tribes inhabiting northern Texas, New Mexico, California, and the extensive region lying between our settlements in Missouri and these possessions, as the most effective means of preserving peace upon our borders and within the recently acquired territories.

The Secretary of the Treasury will present in his annual report a highly satisfactory statement of the condition of the finances.

The imports for the fiscal year ending on the 30th of June last were of the value of $154,977,876, of which the amount exported was $21,128,010, leaving $133,849,866 in the country for domestic use. The value of the exports for the same period was $154,032,131, consisting of domestic productions amounting to $132,904,121 and $21,128,010 of foreign articles. The receipts into the Treasury for the same period, exclusive of loans, amounted to $35,436,750.59, of which there was derived from customs $31,757,070.96, from sales of public lands $3,328,642.56, and from miscellaneous and incidental sources $351,037.07.

It will be perceived that the revenue from customs for the last fiscal year exceeded by $757,070.96 the estimate of the Secretary of the Treasury in his last annual report, and that the aggregate receipts during the same period from customs, lands, and miscellaneous sources also exceeded the estimate by the sum of $536,750.59, indicating, however, a very near approach in the estimate to the actual result.

The expenditures during the fiscal year ending on the 30th of June last, including those for the war and exclusive of payments of principal and interest for the public debt, were $42,811,970.03.

It is estimated that the receipts into the Treasury for the fiscal year ending on the 30th of June, 1849, including the balance in the Treasury on the 1st of July last, will amount to the sum of $57,048,969.90, of which $32,000,000, it is estimated, will be derived from customs, $3,000,000 from the sales of the public lands, and $1,200,000 from miscellaneous and incidental sources, including the premium upon the loan, and the amount paid and to be paid into the Treasury on account of military contributions in Mexico, and the sales of arms and vessels and other public property rendered unnecessary for the use of the Government by the termination of the war, and $20,695,435.30 from loans already negotiated, including Treasury notes funded, which, together with the balance in the Treasury on the 1st of July last, make the sum estimated.

The expenditures for the same period, including the necessary payment on account of the principal and interest of the public debt, and the principal and interest of the first installment due to Mexico on the 30th of May next, and other expenditures growing out of the war to be paid during the present year, will amount, including the reimbursement of Treasury notes, to the sum of $54,195,275.06, leaving an estimated balance in the Treasury on the 1st of July, 1849, of $2,853,694.84.

The Secretary of the Treasury will present, as required by law, the estimate of the receipts and expenditures for the next fiscal year. The expenditures as estimated for that year are $33,213,152.73, including $3,799,102.18 for the interest on the public debt and $3,540,000 for the principal and interest due to Mexico on the 30th of May, 1850, leaving the sum of $25,874,050.35, which, it is believed, will be ample for the ordinary peace expenditures.

The operations of the tariff act of 1846 have been such during the past year as fully to meet the public expectation and to confirm the opinion heretofore expressed of the wisdom of the change in our revenue system which was effected by it. The receipts under it into the Treasury for the first fiscal year after its enactment exceeded by the sum of $5,044,403.09 the amount collected during the last fiscal year under the tariff act of 1842, ending the 30th of June, 1846. The total revenue realized from the commencement of its operation, on the 1st of December, 1846, until the close of the last quarter, on the 30th of September last, being twenty-two months, was $56,654,563.79, being a much larger sum than was ever before received from duties during any equal period under the tariff acts of 1824, 1828, 1832, and 1842. Whilst by the repeal of highly protective and prohibitory duties the revenue has been increased, the taxes on the people have been diminished. They have been relieved from the heavy amounts with which they were burthened under former laws in the form of increased prices or bounties paid to favored classes and pursuits.

The predictions which were made that the tariff act of 1846 would reduce the amount of revenue below that collected under the act of 1842, and would prostrate the business and destroy the prosperity of the country, have not been verified. With an increased and increasing revenue, the finances are in a highly flourishing condition. Agriculture, commerce, and navigation are prosperous; the prices of manufactured fabrics and of other products are much less injuriously affected than was to have been anticipated from the unprecedented revulsions which during the last and the present year have overwhelmed the industry and paralyzed the credit and commerce of so many great and enlightened nations of Europe.

Severe commercial revulsions abroad have always heretofore operated to depress and often to affect disastrously almost every branch of American industry. The temporary depression of a portion of our manufacturing interests is the effect of foreign causes, and is far less severe than has prevailed on all former similar occasions.

It is believed that, looking to the great aggregate of all our interests, the whole country was never more prosperous than at the present period, and never more rapidly advancing in wealth and population. Neither the foreign war in which we have been involved, nor the loans which have absorbed so large a portion of our capital, nor the commercial revulsion in Great Britain in 1847, nor the paralysis of credit and commerce throughout Europe in 1848, have affected injuriously to any considerable extent any of the great interests of the country or arrested our onward march to greatness, wealth, and power.

Had the disturbances in Europe not occurred, our commerce would undoubtedly have been still more extended, and would have added still more to the national wealth and public prosperity. But notwithstanding these disturbances, the operations of the revenue system established by the tariff act of 1846 have been so generally beneficial to the Government and the business of the country that no change in its provisions is demanded by a wise public policy, and none is recommended.

The operations of the constitutional treasury established by the act of the 6th of August, 1846, in the receipt, custody, and disbursement of the public money have continued to be successful. Under this system the public finances have been carried through a foreign war, involving the necessity of loans and extraordinary expenditures and requiring distant transfers and disbursements, without embarrassment, and no loss has occurred of any of the public money deposited under its provisions.

Whilst it has proved to be safe and useful to the Government, its effects have been most beneficial upon the business of the country. It has tended powerfully to secure an exemption from that inflation and fluctuation of the paper currency so injurious to domestic industry and rendering so uncertain the rewards of labor, and, it is believed, has largely contributed to preserve the whole country from a serious commercial revulsion, such as often occurred under the bank deposit system. In the year 1847 there was a revulsion in the business of Great Britain of great extent and intensity, which was followed by failures in that Kingdom unprecedented in number and amount of losses. This is believed to be the first instance when such disastrous bankruptcies, occurring in a country with which we have such extensive commerce, produced little or no injurious effect upon our trade or currency. We remained but little affected in our money market, and our business and industry were still prosperous and progressive.

During the present year nearly the whole continent of Europe has been convulsed by civil war and revolutions, attended by numerous bankruptcies, by an unprecedented fall in their public securities, and an almost universal paralysis of commerce and industry; and yet, although our trade and the prices of our products must have been somewhat unfavorably affected by these causes, we have escaped a revulsion, our money market is comparatively easy, and public and private credit have advanced and improved.

It is confidently believed that we have been saved from their effect by the salutary operation of the constitutional treasury. It is certain that if the twenty-four millions of specie imported into the country during the fiscal year ending on the 30th of June, 1847, had gone into the banks, as to a great extent it must have done, it would in the absence of this system have been made the basis of augmented bank paper issues, probably to an amount not less than $60,000,000 or $70,000,000, producing, as an inevitable consequence of an inflated currency, extravagant prices for a time and wild speculation, which must have been followed, on the reflux to Europe the succeeding year of so much of that specie, by the prostration of the business of the country, the suspension of the banks, and most extensive bankruptcies. Occurring, as this would have done, at a period when the country was engaged in a foreign war, when considerable loans of specie were required for distant disbursements, and when the banks, the fiscal agents of the Government and the depositories of its money, were suspended, the public credit must have sunk, and many millions of dollars, as was the case during the War of 1812, must have been sacrificed in discounts upon loans and upon the depreciated paper currency which the Government would have been compelled to use.

Under the operations of the constitutional treasury not a dollar has been lost by the depreciation of the currency. The loans required to prosecute the war with Mexico were negotiated by the Secretary of the Treasury above par, realizing a large premium to the Government. The restraining effect of the system upon the tendencies to excessive paper issues by banks has saved the Government from heavy losses and thousands of our business men from bankruptcy and ruin. The wisdom of the system has been tested by the experience of the last two years, and it is the dictate of sound policy that it should remain undisturbed. The modifications in some of the details of this measure, involving none of its essential principles, heretofore recommended, are again presented for your favorable consideration.

In my message of the 6th of July last, transmitting to Congress the ratified treaty of peace with Mexico, I recommended the adoption of measures for the speedy payment of the public debt. In reiterating that recommendation I refer you to the considerations presented in that message in its support. The public debt, including that authorized to be negotiated in pursuance of existing laws, and including Treasury notes, amounted at that time to $65,778,450.41.

Funded stock of the United States amounting to about half a million of dollars has been purchased, as authorized by law, since that period, and the public debt has thus been reduced, the details of which will be presented in the annual report of the Secretary of the Treasury.

The estimates of expenditures for the next fiscal year, submitted by the Secretary of the Treasury, it is believed will be ample for all necessary purposes. If the appropriations made by Congress shall not exceed the amount estimated, the means in the Treasury will be sufficient to defray all the expenses of the Government, to pay off the next installment of $3,000,000 to Mexico, which will fall due on the 30th of May next, and still a considerable surplus will remain, which should be applied to the further purchase of the public stock and reduction of the debt. Should enlarged appropriations be made, the necessary consequence will be to postpone the payment of the debt. Though our debt, as compared with that of most other nations, is small, it is our true policy, and in harmony with the genius of our institutions, that we should present to the world the rare spectacle of a great Republic, possessing vast resources and wealth, wholly exempt from public indebtedness. This would add still more to our strength, and give to us a still more commanding position among the nations of the earth.

The public expenditures should be economical, and be confined to such necessary objects as are clearly within the powers of Congress. All such as are not absolutely demanded should be postponed, and the payment of the public debt at the earliest practicable period should be a cardinal principle of our public policy.

For the reason assigned in my last annual message, I repeat the recommendation that a branch of the Mint of the United States be established at the city of New York. The importance of this measure is greatly increased by the acquisition of the rich mines of the precious metals in New Mexico and California, and especially in the latter.

I repeat the recommendation heretofore made in favor of the graduation and reduction of the price of such of the public lands as have been long offered in the market and have remained unsold, and in favor of extending the rights of preemption to actual settlers on the unsurveyed as well as the surveyed lands.

The condition and operations of the Army and the state of other branches of the public service under the supervision of the War Department are satisfactorily presented in the accompanying report of the Secretary of War.

On the return of peace our forces were withdrawn from Mexico, and the volunteers and that portion of the Regular Army engaged for the war were disbanded. Orders have been issued for stationing the forces of our permanent establishment at various positions in our extended country where troops may be required. Owing to the remoteness of some of these positions, the detachments have not yet reached their destination. Notwithstanding the extension of the limits of our country and the forces required in the new territories, it is confidently believed that our present military establishment is sufficient for all exigencies so long as our peaceful relations remain undisturbed.

Of the amount of military contributions collected in Mexico, the sum of $769,650 was applied toward the payment of the first installment due under the treaty with Mexico. The further sum of $346,369.30 has been paid into the Treasury, and unexpended balances still remain in the hands of disbursing officers and those who were engaged in the collection of these moneys. After the proclamation of peace no further disbursements were made of any unexpended moneys arising from this source. The balances on hand were directed to be paid into the Treasury, and individual claims on the fund will remain unadjusted until Congress shall authorize their settlement and payment. These claims are not considerable in number or amount.

I recommend to your favorable consideration the suggestions of the Secretary of War and the Secretary of the Navy in regard to legislation on this subject.

Our Indian relations are presented in a most favorable view in the report from the War Department. The wisdom of our policy in regard to the tribes within our limits is clearly manifested by their improved and rapidly improving condition.

A most important treaty with the Menomonies has been recently negotiated by the Commissioner of Indian Affairs in person, by which all their land in the State of Wisconsin—being about 4,000,000 acres—has been ceded to the United States. This treaty will be submitted to the Senate for ratification at an early period of your present session.

Within the last four years eight important treaties have been negotiated with different Indian tribes, and at a cost of $1,842,000; Indian lands to the amount of more than 18,500,000 acres have been ceded to the United States, and provision has been made for settling in the country west of the Mississippi the tribes which occupied this large extent of the public domain. The title to all the Indian lands within the several States of our Union, with the exception of a few small reservations, is now extinguished, and a vast region opened for settlement and cultivation.

The accompanying report of the Secretary of the Navy gives a satisfactory exhibit of the operations and condition of that branch of the public service.

A number of small vessels, suitable for entering the mouths of rivers, were judiciously purchased during the war, and gave great efficiency to the squadron in the Gulf of Mexico. On the return of peace, when no longer valuable for naval purposes, and liable to constant deterioration, they were sold and the money placed in the Treasury.

The number of men in the naval service authorized by law during the war has been reduced by discharges below the maximum fixed for the peace establishment. Adequate squadrons are maintained in the several quarters of the globe where experience has shown their services may be most usefully employed, and the naval service was never in a condition of higher discipline or greater efficiency.

I invite attention to the recommendation of the Secretary of the Navy on the subject of the Marine Corps. The reduction of the Corps at the end of the war required that four officers of each of the three lower grades should be dropped from the rolls. A board of officers made the selection, and those designated were necessarily dismissed, but without any alleged fault. I concur in opinion with the Secretary that the service would be improved by reducing the number of landsmen and increasing the marines. Such a measure would justify an increase of the number of officers to the extent of the reduction by dismissal, and still the Corps would have fewer officers than a corresponding number of men in the Army.

The contracts for the transportation of the mail in steamships, convertible into war steamers, promise to realize all the benefits to our commerce and to the Navy which were anticipated. The first steamer thus secured to the Government was launched in January, 1847. There are now seven, and in another year there will probably be not less than seventeen afloat. While this great national advantage is secured, our social and commercial intercourse is increased and promoted with Germany, Great Britain, and other parts of Europe, with all the countries on the west coast of our continent, especially with Oregon and California, and between the northern and southern sections of the United States. Considerable revenue may be expected from postages, but the connected line from New York to Chagres, and thence across the Isthmus to Oregon, can not fail to exert a beneficial influence, not now to be estimated, on the interests of the manufactures, commerce, navigation, and currency of the United States. As an important part of the system, I recommend to your favorable consideration the establishment of the proposed line of steamers between New Orleans and Vera Cruz. It promises the most happy results in cementing friendship between the two Republics and extending reciprocal benefits to the trade and manufactures of both.

The report of the Postmaster-General will make known to you the operations of that Department for the past year.

It is gratifying to find the revenues of the Department, under the rates of postage now established by law, so rapidly increasing. The gross amount of postages during the last fiscal year amounted to $4,371,077, exceeding the annual average received for the nine years immediately preceding the passage of the act of the 3d of March, 1845, by the sum of $6,453, and exceeding the amount received for the year ending the 30th of June, 1847, by the sum of $425,184.

The expenditures for the year, excluding the sum of $94,672, allowed by Congress at its last session to individual claimants, and including the sum of $100,500, paid for the services of the line of steamers between Bremen and New York, amounted to $4,198,845, which is less than the annual average for the nine years previous to the act of 1845 by $300,748.

The mail routes on the 30th day of June last were 163,208 miles in extent, being an increase during the last year of 9,390 miles. The mails were transported over them during the same time 41,012,579 miles, making an increase of transportation for the year of 2,124,680 miles, whilst the expense was less than that of the previous year by $4,235.

The increase in the mail transportation within the last three years has been 5,378,310 miles, whilst the expenses were reduced $456,738, making an increase of service at the rate of 15 per cent and a reduction in the expenses of more than 15 per cent.

During the past year there have been employed, under contracts with the Post-Office Department, two ocean steamers in conveying the mails monthly between New York and Bremen, and one, since October last, performing semimonthly service between Charleston and Havana; and a contract has been made for the transportation of the Pacific mails across the Isthmus from Chagres to Panama.

Under the authority given to the Secretary of the Navy, three ocean steamers have been constructed and sent to the Pacific, and are expected to enter upon the mail service between Panama and Oregon and the intermediate ports on the 1st of January next; and a fourth has been engaged by him for the service between Havana and Chagres, so that a regular monthly mail line will be kept up after that time between the United States and our territories on the Pacific.

Notwithstanding this great increase in the mail service, should the revenue continue to increase the present year as it did in the last, there will be received near $450,000 more than the expenditures.

These considerations have satisfied the Postmaster-General that, with certain modifications of the act of 1845, the revenue may be still further increased and a reduction of postages made to a uniform rate of 5 cents, without an interference with the principle, which has been constantly and properly enforced, of making that Department sustain itself.

A well-digested cheap-postage system is the best means of diffusing intelligence among the people, and is of so much importance in a country so extensive as that of the United States that I recommend to your favorable consideration the suggestions of the Postmaster-General for its improvement.

Nothing can retard the onward progress of our country and prevent us from assuming and maintaining the first rank among nations but a disregard of the experience of the past and a recurrence to an unwise public policy. We have just closed a foreign war by an honorable peace— a war rendered necessary and unavoidable in vindication of the national rights and honor. The present condition of the country is similar in some respects to that which existed immediately after the close of the war with Great Britain in 1815, and the occasion is deemed to be a proper one to take a retrospect of the measures of public policy which followed that war. There was at that period of our history a departure from our earlier policy. The enlargement of the powers of the Federal Government by *construction*, which obtained, was not warranted by any just interpretation of the Constitution. A few years after the close of that war a series of measures was adopted which, united and combined, constituted what was termed by their authors and advocates the "American system."

The introduction of the new policy was for a time favored by the condition of the country, by the heavy debt which had been contracted during the war, by the depression of the public credit, by the deranged state of the finances and the currency, and by the commercial and pecuniary embarrassment which extensively prevailed. These were not the only causes which led to its establishment. The events of the war with Great Britain and the embarrassments which had attended its prosecution had left on the minds of many of our statesmen the impression that our Government was not strong enough, and that to wield its resources successfully in great emergencies, and especially in war, more power should be concentrated in its hands. This increased power they did not seek to obtain by the legitimate and prescribed mode—an amendment of the Constitution—but by *construction*. They saw Governments in the Old World based upon different orders of society, and so constituted as to throw the whole power of nations into the hands of a few, who taxed and controlled the many without responsibility or restraint. In that arrangement they conceived the strength of nations in war consisted. There was also something fascinating in the ease, luxury, and display of the higher orders, who drew their wealth from the toil of the laboring millions. The authors of the system drew their ideas of political economy from what they had witnessed in Europe, and particularly in Great Britain. They had viewed the enormous wealth concentrated in few hands and had seen the splendor of the overgrown establishments of an aristocracy which was upheld by the restrictive policy. They forgot to look down upon the poorer classes of the English population, upon whose daily and yearly labor the great establishments they so much admired were sustained and supported. They failed to perceive that the scantily fed and half-clad operatives were not only in abject poverty, but were bound in chains of oppressive servitude for the benefit of favored classes, who were the exclusive objects of the care of the Government.

It was not possible to reconstruct society in the United States upon the European plan. Here there was a written Constitution, by which orders and titles were not recognized or tolerated. A system of measures was therefore divised, calculated, if not intended, to withdraw power gradually and silently from the States and the mass of the people, and by *construction* to approximate our Government to the European models, substituting an aristocracy of wealth for that of orders and titles.

Without reflecting upon the dissimilarity of our institutions and of the condition of our people and those of Europe, they conceived the vain idea of building up in the United States a system similar to that which they admired abroad. Great Britain had a national bank of large capital, in whose hands was concentrated the controlling monetary and financial power of the nation—an institution wielding almost kingly power, and exerting vast influence upon all the operations of trade and upon the policy of the Government itself. Great Britain had an enormous public debt, and it had become a part of her public policy to regard this as a "public blessing." Great Britain had also a restrictive policy, which placed fetters and burdens on trade and trammeled the productive industry of the mass of the nation. By her combined system of policy the landlords and other property holders were protected and enriched by the enormous taxes which were levied upon the labor of the country for their advantage. Imitating this foreign policy, the first step in establishing the new system in the United States was the creation of a national bank. Not foreseeing the dangerous power and countless evils which such an institution might entail on the country, nor perceiving the connection which it was designed to form between the bank and the other branches of the miscalled "American system," but feeling the embarrassments of the Treasury and of the business of the country consequent upon the war, some of our statesmen who had held different and sounder views were induced to yield their scruples and, indeed, settled convictions of its unconstitutionality, and to give it their sanction as an expedient which they vainly hoped might produce relief. It was a most unfortunate error, as the subsequent history and final catastrophe of that

dangerous and corrupt institution have abundantly proved. The bank,
with its numerous branches ramified into the States, soon brought many
of the active political and commercial men in different sections of the
country into the relation of debtors to it and dependents upon it for
pecuniary favors, thus diffusing throughout the mass of society a great
number of individuals of power and influence to give tone to public
opinion and to act in concert in cases of emergency. The corrupt power
of such a political engine is no longer a matter of speculation, having
been displayed in numerous instances, but most signally in the political
struggles of 1832, 1833, and 1834 in opposition to the public will represented by a fearless and patriotic President.

But the bank was but one branch of the new system. A public debt
of more than $120,000,000 existed, and it is not to be disguised that
many of the authors of the new system did not regard its speedy payment
as essential to the public prosperity, but looked upon its continuance as
no national evil. Whilst the debt existed it furnished aliment to the
national bank and rendered increased taxation necessary to the amount
of the interest, exceeding $7,000,000 annually.

This operated in harmony with the next branch of the new system,
which was a high protective tariff. This was to afford bounties to
favored classes and particular pursuits at the expense of all others. A
proposition to tax the whole people for the purpose of enriching a few
was too monstrous to be openly made. The scheme was therefore veiled
under the plausible but delusive pretext of a measure to protect "home
industry," and many of our people were for a time led to believe that a
tax which in the main fell upon labor was for the benefit of the laborer
who paid it. This branch of the system involved a partnership between
the Government and the favored classes, the former receiving the proceeds of the tax imposed on articles imported and the latter the increased price of similar articles produced at home, caused by such tax.
It is obvious that the portion to be received by the favored classes would,
as a general rule, be increased in proportion to the increase of the rates of
tax imposed and diminished as those rates were reduced to the revenue
standard required by the wants of the Government. The rates required
to produce a sufficient revenue for the ordinary expenditures of Government for necessary purposes were not likely to give to the private
partners in this scheme profits sufficient to satisfy their cupidity, and
hence a variety of expedients and pretexts were resorted to for the purpose of enlarging the expenditures and thereby creating a necessity for
keeping up a high protective tariff. The effect of this policy was to interpose artificial restrictions upon the natural course of the business
and trade of the country, and to advance the interests of large capitalists and monopolists at the expense of the great mass of the people, who
were taxed to increase their wealth.

Another branch of this system was a comprehensive scheme of internal improvements, capable of indefinite enlargement and sufficient to swallow up as many millions annually as could be exacted from the foreign commerce of the country. This was a convenient and necessary adjunct of the protective tariff. It was to be the great absorbent of any surplus which might at any time accumulate in the Treasury and of the taxes levied on the people, not for necessary revenue purposes, but for the avowed object of affording protection to the favored classes.

Auxiliary to the same end, if it was not an essential part of the system itself, was the scheme, which at a later period obtained, for distributing the proceeds of the sales of the public lands among the States. Other expedients were devised to take money out of the Treasury and prevent its coming in from any other source than the protective tariff. The authors and supporters of the system were the advocates of the largest expenditures, whether for necessary or useful purposes or not, because the larger the expenditures the greater was the pretext for high taxes in the form of protective duties.

These several measures were sustained by popular names and plausible arguments, by which thousands were deluded. The bank was represented to be an indispensable fiscal agent for the Government; was to equalize exchanges and to regulate and furnish a sound currency, always and everywhere of uniform value. The protective tariff was to give employment to "American labor" at advanced prices; was to protect "home industry" and furnish a steady market for the farmer. Internal improvements were to bring trade into every neighborhood and enhance the value of every man's property. The distribution of the land money was to enrich the States, finish their public works, plant schools throughout their borders, and relieve them from taxation. But the fact that for every dollar taken out of the Treasury for these objects a much larger sum was transferred from the pockets of the people to the favored classes was carefully concealed, as was also the tendency, if not the ultimate design, of the system to build up an aristocracy of wealth, to control the masses of society, and monopolize the political power of the country.

The several branches of this system were so intimately blended together that in their operation each sustained and strengthened the others. Their joint operation was to add new burthens of taxation and to encourage a largely increased and wasteful expenditure of public money. It was the interest of the bank that the revenue collected and the disbursements made by the Government should be large, because, being the depository of the public money, the larger the amount the greater would be the bank profits by its use. It was the interest of the favored classes, who were enriched by the protective tariff, to have the rates of that protection as high as possible, for the higher those rates the greater would be their advantage. It was the interest of the people of all those sections and localities who expected to be benefited by expenditures for internal improvements that the amount collected should be as large as possible, to the end that the sum disbursed might also be the larger. The States, being the beneficiaries in the distribution of the land money, had an interest in having the rates of tax imposed by the protective tariff large enough to yield a sufficient revenue from that source to meet the wants of the Government without disturbing or taking from them the land fund; so that each of the branches constituting the system had a common interest in swelling the public expenditures. They had a direct interest in maintaining the public debt unpaid and increasing its amount, because this would produce an annual increased drain upon the Treasury to the amount of the interest and render augmented taxes necessary. The operation and necessary effect of the whole system were to encourage large and extravagant expenditures, and thereby to increase the public patronage, and maintain a rich and splendid government at the expense of a taxed and impoverished people.

It is manifest that this scheme of enlarged taxation and expenditures, had it continued to prevail, must soon have converted the Government of the Union, intended by its framers to be a plain, cheap, and simple confederation of States, united together for common protection and charged with a few specific duties, relating chiefly to our foreign affairs, into a consolidated empire, depriving the States of their reserved rights and the people of their just power and control in the administration of their Government. In this manner the whole form and character of the Government would be changed, not by an amendment of the Constitution, but by resorting to an unwarrantable and unauthorized construction of that instrument.

The indirect mode of levying the taxes by a duty on imports prevents the mass of the people from readily perceiving the amount they pay, and has enabled the few who are thus enriched, and who seek to wield the political power of the country, to deceive and delude them. Were the taxes collected by a direct levy upon the people, as is the case in the States, this could not occur.

The whole system was resisted from its inception by many of our ablest statesmen, some of whom doubted its constitutionality and its expediency, while others believed it was in all its branches a flagrant and dangerous infraction of the Constitution.

That a national bank, a protective tariff—levied not to raise the revenue needed, but for protection merely—internal improvements, and the distribution of the proceeds of the sale of the public lands are measures without the warrant of the Constitution would, upon the maturest consideration, seem to be clear. It is remarkable that no one of these measures, involving such momentous consequences, is authorized by any express grant of power in the Constitution. No one of them is ''incident to, as being necessary and proper for the execution of, the specific powers'' granted by the Constitution. The authority under which it has been attempted to justify each of them is derived from inferences and constructions of the Constitution which its letter and its whole object and design do not warrant. Is it to be conceived that such immense powers would have been left by the framers of the Constitution to mere inferences and doubtful constructions? Had it been intended to confer them on the Federal Government, it is but reasonable to conclude that it would have been done by plain and unequivocal grants. This was not done; but the whole structure of which the "American system" consisted was reared on no other or better foundation than forced implications and inferences of power, which its authors assumed might be deduced by construction from the Constitution.

But it has been urged that the national bank, which constituted so essential a branch of this combined system of measures, was not a new measure, and that its constitutionality had been previously sanctioned, because a bank had been chartered in 1791 and had received the official signature of President Washington. A few facts will show the just weight to which this precedent should be entitled as bearing upon the question of constitutionality.

Great division of opinion upon the subject existed in Congress. It is well known that President Washington entertained serious doubts both as to the constitutionality and expediency of the measure, and while the bill was before him for his official approval or disapproval so great were these doubts that he required "the opinion in writing" of the members of his Cabinet to aid him in arriving at a decision. His Cabinet gave their opinions and were divided upon the subject, *General Hamilton* being in favor of and *Mr. Jefferson* and *Mr. Randolph* being opposed to the constitutionality and expediency of the bank. It is well known also that President Washington retained the bill from Monday, the 14th, when it was presented to him, until Friday, the 25th of February, being the last moment permitted him by the Constitution to deliberate, when he finally yielded to it his reluctant assent and gave it his signature. It is certain that as late as the 23d of February, being the ninth day after the bill was presented to him, he had arrived at no satisfactory conclusion, for on that day he addressed a note to General Hamilton in which he informs him that "this bill was presented to me by the joint committee of Congress at 12 o'clock on Monday, the 14th instant," and he requested his opinion "to what precise period, by legal interpretation of the Constitution, can the President retain it in his possession before it becomes a law by the lapse of ten days." If the proper construction was that the day on which the bill was presented to the President and the day on which his action was had upon it were both to be counted inclusive, then the time allowed him within which it would be competent for him to return it to the House in which it originated with his objections would expire on Thursday, the 24th of February. General Hamilton on the same day returned an answer, in which he states:

I give it as my opinion that you have ten days exclusive of that on which the bill was delivered to you and Sundays; hence, in the present case if it is returned on Friday it will be in time.

By this construction, which the President adopted, he gained another day for deliberation, and it was not until the 25th of February that he signed the bill, thus affording conclusive proof that he had at last obtained his own consent to sign it not without great and almost insuperable difficulty. Additional light has been recently shed upon the serious doubts which he had on the subject, amounting at one time to a conviction that it was his duty to withhold his approval from the bill. This is found among the manuscript papers of *Mr. Madison*, authorized to be purchased for the use of the Government by an act of the last session of Congress, and now for the first time accessible to the public. From these papers it appears that President Washington, while he yet held the bank bill in his hands, actually requested *Mr. Madison*, at that time a member of the House of Representatives, to prepare the draft of a veto message for him. *Mr. Madison*, at his request, did prepare the draft of such a message, and sent it to him on the 21st of February, 1791. A copy of this original draft, in Mr. Madison's own handwriting, was carefully preserved by him, and is among the papers lately purchased by Congress. It is preceded by a note, written on the same sheet, which is also in Mr. Madison's handwriting, and is as follows:

February 21, 1791.—Copy of a paper made out and sent to the President, *at his request*, to be ready in case his judgment should finally decide against the bill for incorporating a national bank, the bill being then before him.

Among the objections assigned in this paper to the bill, and which were submitted for the consideration of the President, are the following:

I object to the bill, because it is an essential principle of the Government that powers not delegated by the Constitution can not be rightfully exercised; because the power proposed by the bill to be exercised is not expressly delegated, and because I can not satisfy myself that it results from any express power by fair and safe rules of interpretation.

The weight of the precedent of the bank of 1791 and the sanction of the great name of Washington, which has been so often invoked in its support, are greatly weakened by the development of these facts.

The experiment of that bank satisfied the country that it ought not to be continued, and at the end of twenty years Congress refused to recharter it. It would have been fortunate for the country, and saved thousands from bankruptcy and ruin, had our public men of 1816 resisted the temporary pressure of the times upon our financial and pecuniary interests and refused to charter the second bank. Of this the country became abundantly satisfied, and at the close of its twenty years' duration, as in the case of the first bank, it also ceased to exist. Under the repeated blows of *President Jackson* it reeled and fell, and a subsequent attempt to charter a similar institution was arrested by the *veto* of President

Tyler.

Mr. Madison, in yielding his signature to the charter of 1816, did so upon the ground of the respect due to precedents; and, as he subsequently declared—

The Bank of the United States, though on the original question held to be unconstitutional, received the Executive signature.

It is probable that neither the bank of 1791 nor that of 1816 would have been chartered but for the embarrassments of the Government in its finances, the derangement of the currency, and the pecuniary pressure which existed, the first the consequence of the War of the Revolution and the second the consequence of the War of 1812. Both were resorted to in the delusive hope that they would restore public credit and afford relief to the Government and to the business of the country.

Those of our public men who opposed the whole "American system" at its commencement and throughout its progress foresaw and predicted that it was fraught with incalculable mischiefs and must result in serious injury to the best interests of the country. For a series of years their wise counsels were unheeded, and the system was established. It was soon apparent that its practical operation was unequal and unjust upon different portions of the country and upon the people engaged in different pursuits. All were equally entitled to the favor and protection of the Government. It fostered and elevated the money power and enriched the favored few by taxing labor, and at the expense of the many. Its effect was to "make the rich richer and the poor poorer." Its tendency was to create distinctions in society based on wealth and to give to the favored classes undue control and sway in our Government. It was an organized money power, which resisted the popular will and sought to shape and control the public policy.

Under the pernicious workings of this combined system of measures the country witnessed alternate seasons of temporary apparent prosperity, of sudden and disastrous commercial revulsions, of unprecedented fluctuation of prices and depression of the great interests of agriculture, navigation, and commerce, of general pecuniary suffering, and of final bankruptcy of thousands. After a severe struggle of more than a quarter of a century, the system was overthrown.

The bank has been succeeded by a practical system of finance, conducted and controlled solely by the Government. The constitutional currency has been restored, the public credit maintained unimpaired even in a period of a foreign war, and the whole country has become satisfied that banks, national or State, are not necessary as fiscal agents of the Government. Revenue duties have taken the place of the protective tariff. The distribution of the money derived from the sale of the public lands has been abandoned and the corrupting system of internal improvements, it is hoped, has been effectually checked.

It is not doubted that if this whole train of measures, designed to take wealth from the many and bestow it upon the few, were to prevail the effect would be to change the entire character of the Government.   One only danger remains.   It is the seductions of that branch of the system which consists in internal improvements, holding out, as it does, inducements to the people of particular sections and localities to embark the Government in them without stopping to calculate the inevitable consequences.   This branch of the system is so intimately combined and linked with the others that as surely as an effect is produced by an adequate cause, if it be resuscitated and revived and firmly established it requires no sagacity to foresee that it will necessarily and speedily draw after it the reestablishment of a national bank, the revival of a protective tariff, the distribution of the land money, and not only the postponement to the distant future of the payment of the present national debt, but its annual increase.

I entertain the solemn conviction that it the internal-improvement branch of the "American system" be not firmly resisted at this time the whole series of measures composing it will be speedily reestablished and the country be thrown back from its present high state of prosperity, which the existing policy has produced, and be destined again to witness all the evils, commercial revulsions, depression of prices, and pecuniary embarrassments through which we have passed during the last twenty-five years.

To guard against consequences so ruinous is an object of high national importance, involving, in my judgment, the continued prosperity of the country.

I have felt it to be an imperative obligation to withhold my constitutional sanction from two bills which had passed the two Houses of Congress, involving the principle of the internal-improvement branch of the "American system" and conflicting in their provisions with the views here expressed.

This power, conferred upon the President by the Constitution, I have on three occasions during my administration of the executive department of the Government deemed it my duty to exercise, and on this last occasion of making to Congress an annual communication "of the state of the Union" it is not deemed inappropriate to review the principles and considerations which have governed my action.   I deem this the more necessary because, after the lapse of nearly sixty years since the adoption of the Constitution, the propriety of the exercise of this undoubted constitutional power by the President has for the first time been drawn seri· ously in question by a portion of my fellow-citizens.

The Constitution provides that—

Every bill which shall have passed the House of Representatives and the Senate shall, before it become a law, be presented to the President of the United States.   If he approve he *shall* sign it, but if not he *shall* return it with his objections to that House in which it shall have originated, who shall enter the objections at large on their Journal and proceed to reconsider it.

The preservation of the Constitution from infraction is the President's highest duty. He is bound to discharge that duty at whatever hazard of incurring the displeasure of those who may differ with him in opinion. He is bound to discharge it as well by his obligations to the people who have clothed him with his exalted trust as by his oath of office, which he may not disregard. Nor are the obligations of the President in any degree lessened by the prevalence of views different from his own in one or both Houses of Congress. It is not alone hasty and inconsiderate legislation that he is required to check; but if at any time Congress shall, after apparently full deliberation, resolve on measures which he deems subversive of the Constitution or of the vital interests of the country, it is his solemn duty to stand in the breach and resist them. The President is bound to approve or disapprove every bill which passes Congress and is presented to him for his signature. The Constitution makes this his duty, and he can not escape it if he would. He has no election. In deciding upon any bill presented to him he must exercise his own best judgment. If he can not approve, the Constitution commands him to return the bill to the House in which it originated with his objections, and if he fail to do this within ten days (Sundays excepted) it shall become a law without his signature. Right or wrong, he may be overruled by a vote of two-thirds of each House, and in that event the bill becomes a law without his sanction. If his objections be not thus overruled, the subject is only postponed, and is referred to the States and the people for their consideration and decision. The President's power is negative merely, and not affirmative. He can enact no law. The only effect, therefore, of his withholding his approval of a bill passed by Congress is to suffer the existing laws to remain unchanged, and the delay occasioned is only that required to enable the States and the people to consider and act upon the subject in the election of public agents who will carry out their wishes and instructions. Any attempt to coerce the President to yield his sanction to measures which he can not approve would be a violation of the spirit of the Constitution, palpable and flagrant, and if successful would break down the independence of the executive department and make the President, elected by the people and clothed by the Constitution with power to defend their rights, the mere instrument of a majority of Congress. A surrender on his part of the powers with which the Constitution has invested his office would effect a practical alteration of that instrument without resorting to the prescribed process of amendment.

With the motives or considerations which may induce Congress to pass any bill the President can have nothing to do. He must presume them to be as pure as his own, and look only to the practical effect of their measures when compared with the Constitution or the public good.

But it has been urged by those who object to the exercise of this undoubted constitutional power that it assails the representative principle and the capacity of the people to govern themselves; that there is greater safety in a numerous representative body than in the single Executive created by the Constitution, and that the Executive veto is a "one-man power," despotic in its character. To expose the fallacy of this objection it is only necessary to consider the frame and true character of our system. Ours is not a consolidated empire, but a confederated union. The States before the adoption of the Constitution were coordinate, coequal, and separate independent sovereignties, and by its adoption they did not lose that character. They clothed the Federal Government with certain powers and reserved all others, including their own sovereignty, to themselves. They guarded their own rights as States and the rights of the people by the very limitations which they incorporated into the Federal Constitution, whereby the different departments of the General Government were checks upon each other. That the majority should govern is a general principle controverted by none, but they must govern according to the Constitution, and not according to an undefined and unrestrained discretion, whereby they may oppress the minority.

The people of the United States are not blind to the fact that they may be temporarily misled, and that their representatives, legislative and executive, may be mistaken or influenced in their action by improper motives. They have therefore interposed between themselves and the laws which may be passed by their public agents various representations, such as assemblies, senates, and governors in their several States, a House of Representatives, a Senate, and a President of the United States. The people can by their own direct agency make no law, nor can the House of Representatives, immediately elected by them, nor can the Senate, nor can both together without the concurrence of the President or a vote of two-thirds of both Houses.

Happily for themselves, the people in framing our admirable system of government were conscious of the infirmities of their representatives, and in delegating to them the power of legislation they have fenced them around with checks to guard against the effects of hasty action, of error, of combination, and of possible corruption. Error, selfishness, and faction have often sought to rend asunder this web of checks and subject the Government to the control of fanatic and sinister influences, but these efforts have only satisfied the people of the wisdom of the checks which they have imposed and of the necessity of preserving them unimpaired.

The true theory of our system is not to govern by the acts or decrees of any one set of representatives. The Constitution interposes checks upon all branches of the Government, in order to give time for error to be corrected and delusion to pass away; but if the people settle down into a firm conviction different from that of their representatives they give effect to their opinions by changing their public servants. The checks which the people imposed on their public servants in the adoption of the Constitution are the best evidence of their capacity for self-government. They know that the men whom they elect to public stations are of like infirmities and passions with themselves, and not to be trusted without being restricted by coordinate authorities and constitutional limitations. Who that has witnessed the legislation of Congress for the last thirty years will say that he knows of no instance in which measures not demanded by the public good have been carried? Who will deny that in the State governments, by combinations of individuals and sections, in derogation of the general interest, banks have been chartered, systems of internal improvements adopted, and debts entailed upon the people repressing their growth and impairing their energies for years to come?

After so much experience it can not be said that absolute unchecked power is safe in the hands of any one set of representatives, or that the capacity of the people for self-government, which is admitted in its broadest extent, is a conclusive argument to prove the prudence, wisdom, and integrity of their representatives.

The people, by the Constitution, have commanded the President, as much as they have commanded the legislative branch of the Government, to execute their will. They have said to him in the Constitution, which they require he shall take a solemn oath to support, that if Congress pass any bill which he can not approve "he shall return it to the House in which it originated with his objections." In withholding from it his approval and signature he is executing the will of the people, constitutionally expressed, as much as the Congress that passed it. No bill is presumed to be in accordance with the popular will until it shall have passed through all the branches of the Government required by the Constitution to make it a law. A bill which passes the House of Representatives may be rejected by the Senate, and so a bill passed by the Senate may be rejected by the House. In each case the respective Houses exercise the veto power on the other.

Congress, and each House of Congress, hold under the Constitution a check upon the President, and he, by the power of the qualified veto, a check upon Congress. When the President recommends measures to Congress, he avows in the most solemn form his opinions, gives his voice in their favor, and pledges himself in advance to approve them if passed by Congress. If he acts without due consideration, or has been influenced by improper or corrupt motives, or if from any other cause Congress, or either House of Congress, shall differ with him in opinion, they exercise their *veto* upon his recommendations and reject them; and there is no appeal from their decision but to the people at the ballot box. These are proper checks upon the Executive, wisely interposed by the Constitution. None will be found to object to them or to wish them removed. It is equally important that the constitutional checks of the Executive upon the legislative branch should be preserved.

If it be said that the Representatives in the popular branch of Congress are chosen directly by the people, it is answered, the people elect the President. If both Houses represent the States and the people, so does the President. The President represents in the executive department the whole people of the United States, as each member of the legislative department represents portions of them.

The doctrine of restriction upon legislative and executive power, while a well-settled public opinion is enabled within a reasonable time to accomplish its ends, has made our country what it is, and has opened to us a career of glory and happiness to which all other nations have been strangers.

In the exercise of the power of the veto the President is responsible not only to an enlightened public opinion, but to the people of the whole Union, who elected him, as the representatives in the legislative branches who differ with him in opinion are responsible to the people of particular States or districts, who compose their respective constituencies. To deny to the President the exercise of this power would be to repeal that provision of the Constitution which confers it upon him. To charge that its exercise unduly controls the legislative will is to complain of the Constitution itself.

If the Presidential veto be objected to upon the ground that it checks and thwarts the popular will, upon the same principle the equality of representation of the States in the Senate should be stricken out of the Constitution. The vote of a Senator from Delaware has equal weight in deciding upon the most important measures with the vote of a Senator from New York, and yet the one represents a State containing, according to the existing apportionment of Representatives in the House of Representatives, but one thirty-fourth part of the population of the other. By the constitutional composition of the Senate a majority of that body from the smaller States represent less than one-fourth of the people of the Union. There are thirty States, and under the existing apportionment of Representatives there are 230 Members in the House of Representatives. Sixteen of the smaller States are represented in that House by but 50 Members, and yet the Senators from these States constitute a majority of the Senate. So that the President may recommend a measure to Congress, and it may receive the sanction and approval of more than three-fourths of the House of Representatives and of all the Senators from the large States, containing more than three-fourths of the whole population of the United States, and yet the measure may be defeated by the votes of the Senators from the smaller States. None, it is presumed, can be found ready to change the organization of the Senate on this account, or to strike that body practically out of existence by requiring that its action shall be conformed to the will of the more numerous branch.

Upon the same principle that the *veto* of the President should be practically abolished the power of the Vice-President to give the casting vote upon an equal division of the Senate should be abolished also. The Vice-President exercises the *veto* power as effectually by rejecting a bill by his casting vote as the President does by refusing to approve and sign it. This power has been exercised by the Vice-President in a few instances, the most important of which was the rejection of the bill to recharter the Bank of the United States in 1811. It may happen that a bill may be passed by a large majority of the House of Representatives, and may be supported by the Senators from the larger States, and the Vice-President may reject it by giving his vote with the Senators from the smaller States; and yet none, it is presumed, are prepared to deny to him the exercise of this power under the Constitution.

But it is, in point of fact, untrue that an act passed by Congress is conclusive evidence that it is an emanation of the popular will. A majority of the whole number elected to each House of Congress constitutes a quorum, and a majority of that quorum is competent to pass laws. It might happen that a quorum of the House of Representatives, consisting of a single member more than half of the whole number elected to that House, might pass a bill by a majority of a single vote, and in that case a fraction more than one-fourth of the people of the United States would be represented by those who voted for it. It might happen that the same bill might be passed by a majority of one of a quorum of the Senate, composed of Senators from the fifteen smaller States and a single Senator from a sixteenth State; and if the Senators voting for it happened to be from the eight of the smallest of these States, it would be passed by the votes of Senators from States having but fourteen Representatives in the House of Representatives, and containing less than one-sixteenth of the whole population of the United States. This extreme case is stated to illustrate the fact that the mere passage of a bill by Congress is no conclusive evidence that those who passed it represent the majority of the people of the United States or truly reflect their will. If such an extreme case is not likely to happen, cases that approximate it are of constant occurrence. It is believed that not a single law has been passed since the adoption of the Constitution upon which all the members elected to both Houses have been present and voted. Many of the most important acts which have passed Congress have been carried by a close vote in thin Houses. Many instances of this might be given. Indeed, our experience proves that many of the most important acts of Congress are postponed to the last days, and often the last hours, of a session, when they are disposed of in haste, and by Houses but little exceeding the number necessary to form a quorum.

Besides, in most of the States the members of the House of Representatives are chosen by pluralities, and not by majorities of all the voters in their respective districts, and it may happen that a majority of that House may be returned by a less aggregate vote of the people than that received by the minority.

If the principle insisted on be sound, then the Constitution should be so changed that no bill shall become a law unless it is voted for by members representing in each House a majority of the whole people of the United States. We must remodel our whole system, strike down and abolish not only the salutary checks lodged in the executive branch, but must strike out and abolish those lodged in the Senate also, and thus practically invest the whole power of the Government in a majority of a single assembly—a majority uncontrolled and absolute, and which may become despotic. To conform to this doctrine of the right of majorities to rule, independent of the checks and limitations of the Constitution, we must revolutionize our whole system; we must destroy the constitutional compact by which the several States agreed to form a Federal Union and rush into consolidation, which must end in monarchy or despotism. No one advocates such a proposition, and yet the doctrine maintained, if carried out, must lead to this result.

One great object of the Constitution in conferring upon the President a qualified negative upon the legislation of Congress was to protect minorities from injustice and oppression by majorities. The equality of their representation in the Senate and the veto power of the President are the constitutional guaranties which the smaller States have that their rights will be respected. Without these guaranties all their interests would be at the mercy of majorities in Congress representing the larger States. To the smaller and weaker States, therefore, the preservation of this power and its exercise upon proper occasions demanding it is of vital importance. They ratified the Constitution and entered into the Union, securing to themselves an equal representation with the larger States in the Senate; and they agreed to be bound by all laws passed by Congress upon the express condition, and none other, that they should be approved by the President or passed, his objections to the contrary notwithstanding, by a vote of two-thirds of both Houses. Upon this condition they have a right to insist as a part of the compact to which they gave their assent.

A bill might be passed by Congress against the will of the whole people of a particular State and against the votes of its Senators and all its Representatives. However prejudicial it might be to the interests of such State, it would be bound by it if the President shall approve it or it shall be passed by a vote of two-thirds of both Houses; but it has a right to demand that the President shall exercise his constitutional power and arrest it if his judgment is against it. If he surrender this power, or fail to exercise it in a case where he can not approve, it would make his formal approval a mere mockery, and would be itself a violation of the Constitution, and the dissenting State would become bound by a law which had not been passed according to the sanctions of the Constitution.

The objection to the exercise of the *veto* power is founded upon an idea respecting the popular will, which, if carried out, would annihilate State sovereignty and substitute for the present Federal Government a consolidation directed by a supposed numerical majority. A revolution of the Government would be silently effected and the States would be subjected to laws to which they had never given their constitutional consent.

The Supreme Court of the United States is invested with the power to declare, and has declared, acts of Congress passed with the concurrence of the Senate, the House of Representatives, and the approval of the President to be unconstitutional and void, and yet none, it is presumed, can be found who will be disposed to strip this highest judicial tribunal under the Constitution of this acknowledged power—a power necessary alike to its independence and the rights of individuals.

For the same reason that the Executive veto should, according to the doctrine maintained, be rendered nugatory, and be practically expunged from the Constitution, this power of the court should also be rendered nugatory and be expunged, because it restrains the legislative and Executive will, and because the exercise of such a power by the court may be regarded as being in conflict with the capacity of the people to govern themselves. Indeed, there is more reason for striking this power of the court from the Constitution than there is that of the qualified veto of the President, because the decision of the court is final, and can never be reversed even though both Houses of Congress and the President should be unanimous in opposition to it, whereas the veto of the President may be overruled by a vote of two-thirds of both Houses of Congress or by the people at the polls.

It is obvious that to preserve the system established by the Constitution each of the coordinate branches of the Government—the executive, legislative, and judicial—must be left in the exercise of its appropriate powers. If the executive or the judicial branch be deprived of powers conferred upon either as checks on the legislative, the preponderance of the latter will become disproportionate and absorbing and the others impotent for the accomplishment of the great objects for which they were established. Organized, as they are, by the Constitution, they work together harmoniously for the public good. If the Executive and the judiciary shall be deprived of the constitutional powers invested in them, and of their due proportions, the equilibrium of the system must be destroyed, and consolidation, with the most pernicious results, must ensue— a consolidation of unchecked, despotic power, exercised by majorities of the legislative branch.

The executive, legislative, and judicial each constitutes a separate coordinate department of the Government, and each is independent of the others. In the performance of their respective duties under the Constitution neither can in its legitimate action control the others. They each act upon their several responsibilities in their respective spheres. But if the doctrines now maintained be correct, the executive must become practically subordinate to the legislative, and the judiciary must become subordinate to both the legislative and the executive; and thus the whole power of the Government would be merged in a single department. Whenever, if ever, this shall occur, our glorious system of well-regulated self-government will crumble into ruins, to be succeeded, first

by anarchy, and finally by monarchy or despotism. I am far from believing that this doctrine is the sentiment of the American people; and
during the short period which remains in which it will be my duty to
administer the executive department it will be my aim to maintain its
independence and discharge its duties without infringing upon the powers or duties of either of the other departments of the Government.

The power of the Executive veto was exercised by the first and most
illustrious of my predecessors and by four of his successors who preceded me in the administration of the Government, and it is believed in
no instance prejudicially to the public interests. It has never been and
there is but little danger that it ever can be abused. No President will
ever desire unnecessarily to place his opinion in opposition to that of
Congress. He must always exercise the power reluctantly, and only in
cases where his convictions make it a matter of stern duty, which he can
not escape. Indeed, there is more danger that the President, from the
repugnance he must always feel to come in collision with Congress, may
fail to exercise it in cases where the preservation of the Constitution
from infraction, or the public good, may demand it than that he will
ever exercise it unnecessarily or wantonly.

During the period I have administered the executive department of
the Government great and important questions of public policy, foreign
and domestic, have arisen, upon which it was my duty to act. It may,
indeed, be truly said that my Administration has fallen upon eventful
times. I have felt most sensibly the weight of the high responsibilities
devolved upon me. With no other object than the public good, the
enduring fame, and permanent prosperity of my country, I have pursued
the convictions of my own best judgment. The impartial arbitrament of
enlightened public opinion, present and future, will determine how far
the public policy I have maintained and the measures I have from time
to time recommended may have tended to advance or retard the public
prosperity at home and to elevate or depress the estimate of our national
character abroad.

Invoking the blessings of the Almighty upon your deliberations at
your present important session, my ardent hope is that in a spirit of
harmony and concord you may be guided to wise results, and such as
may redound to the happiness, the honor, and the glory of our beloved
country.

Zachary Taylor

March 5, 1849 to July 9, 1850

FIRST ANNUAL MESSAGE.

WASHINGTON, *December 4, 1849.*

Fellow-Citizens of the Senate and House of Representatives:

Sixty years have elapsed since the establishment of this Government, and the Congress of the United States again assembles to legislate for an empire of freemen.   The predictions of evil prophets, who formerly pretended to foretell the downfall of our institutions, are now remembered only to be derided, and the United States of America at this moment present to the world the most stable and permanent Government on earth.

Such is the result of the labors of those who have gone before us. Upon Congress will eminently depend the future maintenance of our system of free government and the transmission of it unimpaired to posterity.

We are at peace with all the other nations of the world, and seek to maintain our cherished relations of amity with them.   During the past year we have been blessed by a kind Providence with an abundance of the fruits of the earth, and although the destroying angel for a time visited extensive portions of our territory with the ravages of a dreadful pestilence, yet the Almighty has at length deigned to stay his hand and to restore the inestimable blessing of general health to a people who have acknowledged His power, deprecated His wrath, and implored His merciful protection.

While enjoying the benefits of amicable intercourse with foreign nations, we have not been insensible to the distractions and wars which have prevailed in other quarters of the world.   It is a proper theme of thanksgiving to Him who rules the destinies of nations that we have been able to maintain amidst all these contests an independent and neutral position toward all belligerent powers.

Our relations with Great Britain are of the most friendly character.   In consequence of the recent alteration of the British navigation acts, British vessels, from British and other foreign ports, will under our existing laws, after the 1st day of January next, be admitted to entry in our ports with cargoes of the growth, manufacture, or production of any part of the world on the same terms as to duties, imposts, and charges as vessels of the United States with their cargoes, and our vessels will be admitted to the same advantages in British ports, entering therein on the same terms as British vessels.   Should no order in council disturb this legislative arrangement, the late act of the British Parliament, by which Great Britain is brought within the terms proposed by the act of Congress of the 1st of March, 1817, it is hoped will be productive of benefit to both countries.

A slight interruption of diplomatic intercourse which occurred between this Government and France, I am happy to say, has been terminated, and our minister there has been received. It is therefore unnecessary to refer now to the circumstances which led to that interruption. I need not express to you the sincere satisfaction with which we shall welcome the arrival of another envoy extraordinary and minister plenipotentiary from a sister Republic to which we have so long been, and still remain, bound by the strongest ties of amity.

Shortly after I had entered upon the discharge of the Executive duties I was apprised that a war steamer belonging to the German Empire was being fitted out in the harbor of New York with the aid of some of our naval officers, rendered under the permission of the late Secretary of the Navy. This permission was granted during an armistice between that Empire and the Kingdom of Denmark, which had been engaged in the Schleswig-Holstein war. Apprehensive that this act of intervention on our part might be viewed as a violation of our neutral obligations incurred by the treaty with Denmark and of the provisions of the act of Congress of the 20th of April, 1818, I directed that no further aid should be rendered by any agent or officer of the Navy; and I instructed the Secretary of State to apprise the minister of the German Empire accredited to this Government of my determination to execute the law of the United States and to maintain the faith of treaties with all nations. The correspondence which ensued between the Department of State and the minister of the German Empire is herewith laid before you. The execution of the law and the observance of the treaty were deemed by me to be due to the honor of the country, as well as to the sacred obligations of the Constitution. I shall not fail to pursue the same course should a similar case arise with any other nation. Having avowed the opinion on taking the oath of office that in disputes between conflicting foreign governments it is our interest not less than our duty to remain strictly neutral, I shall not abandon it. You will perceive from the correspondence submitted to you in connection with this subject that the course adopted in this case has been properly regarded by the belligerent powers interested in the matter.

Although a minister of the United States to the German Empire was appointed by my predecessor in August, 1848, and has for a long time been in attendance at Frankfort-on-the-Main, and although a minister appointed to represent that Empire was received and accredited here, yet no such government as that of the German Empire has been definitively constituted. Mr. Donelson, our representative at Frankfort, remained there several months in the expectation that a union of the German States under one constitution or form of government might at length be organized. It is believed by those well acquainted with the existing relations between Prussia and the States of Germany that no such union can be permanently established without her cooperation. In the event of the formation of such a union and the organization of a central power in Germany of which she should form a part, it would become necessary to withdraw our minister at Berlin; but while Prussia exists as an independent kingdom and diplomatic relations are maintained with her there can be no necessity for the continuance of the mission to Frankfort. I have therefore recalled Mr. Donelson and directed the archives of the legation at Frankfort to be transferred to the American legation at Berlin.

Having been apprised that a considerable number of adventurers were engaged in fitting out a military expedition within the United States against a foreign country, and believing from the best information I could obtain that it was destined to invade the island of Cuba, I deemed it due to the friendly relations existing between the United States and Spain, to the treaty between the two nations, to the laws of the United States, and, above all, to the American honor to exert the lawful authority of this Government in suppressing the expedition and preventing the invasion. To this end I issued a proclamation enjoining it upon the officers of the United States, civil and military, to use all lawful means within their power. A copy of that proclamation is herewith submitted. The expedition has been suppressed. So long as the act of Congress of the 20th of April, 1818, which owes its existence to the law of nations and to the policy of Washington himself, shall remain on our statute books, I hold it to be the duty of the Executive faithfully to obey its injunctions.

While this expedition was in progress I was informed that a foreigner who claimed our protection had been clandestinely and, as was supposed, forcibly carried off in a vessel from New Orleans to the island of Cuba. I immediately caused such steps to be taken as I thought necessary, in case the information I had received should prove correct, to vindicate the honor of the country and the right of every person seeking an asylum on our soil to the protection of our laws. The person alleged to have been abducted was promptly restored, and the circumstances of the case are now about to undergo investigation before a judicial tribunal. I would respectfully suggest that although the crime charged to have been committed in this case is held odious, as being in conflict with our opinions on the subject of national sovereignty and personal freedom, there is no prohibition of it or punishment for it provided in any act of Congress. The expediency of supplying this defect in our criminal code is therefore recommended to your consideration.

I have scrupulously avoided any interference in the wars and contentions which have recently distracted Europe. During the late conflict between Austria and Hungary there seemed to be a prospect that the latter might become an independent nation. However faint that prospect at the time appeared, I thought it my duty, in accordance with the general sentiment of the American people, who deeply sympathized with the Magyar patriots, to stand prepared, upon the contingency of the establishment by her of a permanent government, to be the first to welcome independent Hungary into the family of nations. For this purpose I invested an agent then in Europe with power to declare our willingness promptly to recognize her independence in the event of her ability to sustain it. The powerful intervention of Russia in the contest extinguished the hopes of the struggling Magyars. The United States did not at any time interfere in the contest, but the feelings of the nation were strongly enlisted in the cause, and by the sufferings of a brave people, who had made a gallant, though unsuccessful, effort to be free.

Our claims upon Portugal have been during the past year prosecuted with renewed vigor, and it has been my object to employ every effort of honorable diplomacy to procure their adjustment. Our late chargé d'affaires at Lisbon, the Hon. George W. Hopkins, made able and energetic, but unsuccessful, efforts to settle these unpleasant matters of controversy and to obtain indemnity for the wrongs which were the subjects of complaint. Our present chargé d'affaires at that Court will also bring to the prosecution of these claims ability and zeal. The revolutionary and distracted condition of Portugal in past times has been represented as one of the leading causes of her delay in indemnifying our suffering citizens. But I must now say it is matter of profound regret that these claims have not yet been settled. The omission of Portugal to do justice to the American claimants has now assumed a character so grave and serious that I shall shortly make it the subject of a special message to Congress, with a view to such ultimate action as its wisdom and patriotism may suggest.

With Russia, Austria, Prussia, Sweden, Denmark, Belgium, the Netherlands, and the Italian States we still maintain our accustomed amicable relations.

During the recent revolutions in the Papal States our chargé d'affaires at Rome has been unable to present his letter of credence, which, indeed, he was directed by my predecessor to withhold until he should receive further orders. Such was the unsettled condition of things in those States that it was not deemed expedient to give him any instructions on the subject of presenting his credential letter different from those with which he had been furnished by the late Administration until the 25th of June last, when, in consequence of the want of accurate information of the exact state of things at that distance from us, he was instructed to exercise his own discretion in presenting himself to the then existing Government if in his judgment sufficiently stable, or, if not, to await further events. Since that period Rome has undergone another revolution, and he abides the establishment of a government sufficiently permanent to justify him in opening diplomatic intercourse with it.

With the Republic of Mexico it is our true policy to cultivate the most friendly relations. Since the ratification of the treaty of Guadalupe

Hidalgo nothing has occurred of a serious character to disturb them. A faithful observance of the treaty and a sincere respect for her rights can not fail to secure the lasting confidence and friendship of that Republic. The message of my predecessor to the House of Representatives of the 8th of February last, communicating, in compliance with a resolution of that body, a copy of a paper called a protocol, signed at Queretaro on the 30th of May, 1848, by the commissioners of the United States and the minister of foreign affairs of the Mexican Government, having been a subject of correspondence between the Department of State and the envoy extraordinary and minister plenipotentiary of that Republic accredited to this Government, a transcript of that correspondence is herewith submitted.

The commissioner on the part of the United States for marking the boundary between the two Republics, though delayed in reaching San Diego by unforeseen obstacles, arrived at that place within a short period after the time required by the treaty, and was there joined by the commissioner on the part of Mexico. They entered upon their duties, and at the date of the latest intelligence from that quarter some progress had been made in the survey. The expenses incident to the organization of the commission and to its conveyance to the point where its operations were to begin have so much reduced the fund appropriated by Congress that a further sum, to cover the charges which must be incurred during the present fiscal year, will be necessary. The great length of frontier along which the boundary extends, the nature of the adjacent territory, and the difficulty of obtaining supplies except at or near the extremes of the line render it also indispensable that a liberal provision should be made to meet the necessary charges during the fiscal year ending on the 30th of June, 1851. I accordingly recommend this subject to your attention.

In the adjustment of the claims of American citizens on Mexico, provided for by the late treaty, the employment of counsel on the part of the Government may become important for the purpose of assisting the commissioners in protecting the interests of the United States. I recommend this subject to the early and favorable consideration of Congress.

Complaints have been made in regard to the inefficiency of the means provided by the Government of New Granada for transporting the United States mail across the Isthmus of Panama, pursuant to our postal convention with that Republic of the 6th of March, 1844. Our chargé d'affaires at Bogota has been directed to make such representations to the Government of New Granada as will, it is hoped, lead to a prompt removal of this cause of complaint.

The sanguinary civil war with which the Republic of Venezuela has for some time past been ravaged has been brought to a close. In its progress the rights of some of our citizens resident or trading there have been violated. The restoration of order will afford the Venezuelan Government an opportunity to examine and redress these grievances and others of longer standing which our representatives at Caracas have hitherto ineffectually urged upon the attention of that Government.

The extension of the coast of the United States on the Pacific and the unexampled rapidity with which the inhabitants of California especially are increasing in numbers have imparted new consequence to our relations with the other countries whose territories border upon that ocean. It is probable that the intercourse between those countries and our possessions in that quarter, particularly with the Republic of Chili, will become extensive and mutually advantageous in proportion as California and Oregon shall increase in population and wealth. It is desirable, therefore, that this Government should do everything in its power to foster and strengthen its relations with those States, and that the spirit of amity between us should be mutual and cordial.

I recommend the observance of the same course toward all other American States. The United States stand as the great American power, to which, as their natural ally and friend, they will always be disposed first to look for mediation and assistance in the event of any collision between them and any European nation. As such we may often kindly mediate in their behalf without entangling ourselves in foreign wars or unnecessary controversies. Whenever the faith of our treaties with any of them shall require our interference, we must necessarily interpose.

A convention has been negotiated with Brazil providing for the satisfaction of American claims on that Government, and it will be submitted to the Senate. Since the last session of Congress we have received an envoy extraordinary and minister plenipotentiary from that Empire, and our relations with it are founded upon the most amicable understanding.

Your attention is earnestly invited to an amendment of our existing laws relating to the African slave trade with a view to the effectual suppression of that barbarous traffic. It is not to be denied that this trade is still in part carried on by means of vessels built in the United States and owned or navigated by some of our citizens. The correspondence between the Department of State and the minister and consul of the United States at Rio de Janeiro, which has from time to time been laid before Congress, represents that it is a customary device to evade the penalties of our laws by means of sea letters. Vessels sold in Brazil, when provided with such papers by the consul, instead of returning to the United States for a new register proceed at once to the coast of Africa for the purpose of obtaining cargoes of slaves. Much additional information of the same character has recently been transmitted to the Department of State. It has not been considered the policy of our laws to subject an American citizen who in a foreign country purchases a vessel built in the United States to the inconvenience of sending her home for a new register before permitting her to proceed on a voyage. Any alteration of the laws which might have a tendency to impede the free transfer of property in vessels between our citizens, or the free navi-

gation of those vessels between different parts of the world when employed in lawful commerce, should be well and cautiously considered;
but I trust that your wisdom will devise a method by which our general
policy in this respect may be preserved, and at the same time the abuse
of our flag by means of sea letters, in the manner indicated, may be
prevented.

Having ascertained that there is no prospect of the reunion of the five
States of Central America which formerly composed the Republic of
that name, we have separately negotiated with some of them treaties
of amity and commerce, which will be laid before the Senate.

A contract having been concluded with the State of Nicaragua by a
company composed of American citizens for the purpose of constructing
a ship canal through the territory of that State to connect the Atlantic
and Pacific oceans, I have directed the negotiation of a treaty with Nicaragua pledging both Governments to protect those who shall engage in
and perfect the work.   All other nations are invited by the State of
Nicaragua to enter into the same treaty stipulations with her; and the
benefit to be derived by each from such an arrangement will be the protection of this great interoceanic communication against any power which
might seek to obstruct it or to monopolize its advantages.   All States
entering into such a treaty will enjoy the right of passage through the
canal on payment of the same tolls.   The work, if constructed under
these guaranties, will become a bond of peace instead of a subject of
contention and strife between the nations of the earth.   Should the
great maritime States of Europe consent to this arrangement (and we
have no reason to suppose that a proposition so fair and honorable will
be opposed by any), the energies of their people and ours will cooperate
in promoting the success of the enterprise.   I do not recommend any
appropriation from the National Treasury for this purpose, nor do I
believe that such an appropriation is necessary.   Private enterprise, if
properly protected, will complete the work should it prove to be feasible.   The parties who have procured the charter from Nicaragua for its
construction desire no assistance from this Government beyond its protection; and they profess that, having examined the proposed line of
communication, they will be ready to commence the undertaking whenever that protection shall be extended to them.   Should there appear to
be reason, on examining the whole evidence, to entertain a serious doubt
of the practicability of constructing such a canal, that doubt could be
speedily solved by an actual exploration of the route.

Should such a work be constructed under the common protection of
all nations, for equal benefits to all, it would be neither just nor expedient that any great maritime state should command the communication.
The territory through which the canal may be opened ought to be freed
from the claims of any foreign power.   No such power should occupy a
position that would enable it hereafter to exercise so controlling an influ-

ence over the commerce of the world or to obstruct a highway which ought to be dedicated to the common uses of mankind.

The routes across the Isthmus at Tehuantepec and Panama are also worthy of our serious consideration. They did not fail to engage the attention of my predecessor. The negotiator of the treaty of Guadalupe Hidalgo was instructed to offer a very large sum of money for the right of transit across the Isthmus of Tehuantepec. The Mexican Government did not accede to the proposition for the purchase of the right of way, probably because it had already contracted with private individuals for the construction of a passage from the Guasacualco River to Tehuantepec. I shall not renew any proposition to purchase for money a right which ought to be equally secured to all nations on payment of a reasonable toll to the owners of the improvement, who would doubtless be well contented with that compensation and the guaranties of the maritime states of the world in separate treaties negotiated with Mexico, binding her and them to protect those who should construct the work. Such guaranties would do more to secure the completion of the communication through the territory of Mexico than any other reasonable consideration that could be offered ; and as Mexico herself would be the greatest gainer by the opening of this communication between the Gulf and the Pacific Ocean, it is presumed that she would not hesitate to yield her aid in the manner proposed to accomplish an improvement so important to her own best interests.

We have reason to hope that the proposed railroad across the Isthmus at Panama will be successfully constructed under the protection of the late treaty with New Granada, ratified and exchanged by my predecessor on the 10th day of June, 1848, which guarantees the perfect neutrality of the Isthmus and the rights of sovereignty and property of New Granada over that territory, "with a view that the free transit from ocean to ocean may not be interrupted or embarrassed" during the existence of the treaty. It is our policy to encourage every practicable route across the isthmus which connects North and South America, either by railroad or canal, which the energy and enterprise of our citizens may induce them to complete, and I consider it obligatory upon me to adopt that policy, especially in consequence of the absolute necessity of facilitating intercourse with our possessions on the Pacific.

The position of the Sandwich Islands with reference to the territory of the United States on the Pacific, the success of our persevering and benevolent citizens who have repaired to that remote quarter in Christianizing the natives and inducing them to adopt a system of government and laws suited to their capacity and wants, and the use made by our numerous whale ships of the harbors of the islands as places of resort for obtaining refreshments and repairs all combine to render their destiny peculiarly interesting to us. It is our duty to encourage the authorities of those islands in their efforts to improve and elevate the moral and political condition of the inhabitants, and we should make reasonable allowances for the difficulties inseparable from this task. We desire that the islands may maintain their independence and that other nations should concur with us in this sentiment. We could in no event be indifferent to their passing under the dominion of any other power. The principal commercial states have in this a common interest, and it is to be hoped that no one of them will attempt to interpose obstacles to the entire independence of the islands.

The receipts into the Treasury for the fiscal year ending on the 30th of June last were, in cash, $48,830,097.50, and in Treasury notes funded $10,833,000, making an aggregate of $59,663,097.50; and the expenditures for the same time were, in cash, $46,798,667.82, and in Treasury notes funded $10,833,000, making an aggregate of $57,631,667.82.

The accounts and estimates which will be submitted to Congress in the report of the Secretary of the Treasury show that there will probably be a deficit occasioned by the expenses of the Mexican War and treaty on the 1st day of July next of $5,828,121.66, and on the 1st day of July, 1851, of $10,547,092.73, making in the whole a probable deficit to be provided for of $16,375,214.39. The extraordinary expenses of the war with Mexico and the purchase of California and New Mexico exceed in amount this deficit, together with the loans heretofore made for those objects. I therefore recommend that authority be given to borrow what ever sum may be necessary to cover that deficit. I recommend the observ ance of strict economy in the appropriation and expenditure of public money.

I recommend a revision of the existing tariff and its adjustment on a basis which may augment the revenue. I do not doubt the right or duty of Congress to encourage domestic industry, which is the great source of national as well as individual wealth and prosperity. I look to the wis- dom and patriotism of Congress for the adoption of a system which may place home labor at last on a sure and permanent footing and by due encouragement of manufactures give a new and increased stimulus to agriculture and promote the development of our vast resources and the extension of our commerce. Believing that to the attainment of these ends, as well as the necessary augmentation of the revenue and the pre- vention of frauds, a system of specific duties is best adapted, I strongly recommend to Congress the adoption of that system, fixing the duties at rates high enough to afford substantial and sufficient encouragement to our own industry and at the same time so adjusted as to insure stability.

The question of the continuance of the subtreasury system is respect- fully submitted to the wisdom of Congress. If continued, important modifications of it appear to be indispensable.

For further details and views on the above and other matters connected with commerce, the finances, and revenue I refer to the report of the Secretary of the Treasury.

No direct aid has been given by the General Government to the improvement of agriculture except by the expenditure of small sums for the collection and publication of agricultural statistics and for some chemical analyses, which have been thus far paid for out of the patent fund. This aid is, in my opinion, wholly inadequate. To give to this leading branch of American industry the encouragement which it merits, I respectfully recommend the establishment of an agricultural bureau, to be connected with the Department of the Interior. To elevate the social condition of the agriculturist, to increase his prosperity, and to extend his means of usefulness to his country, by multiplying his sources of information, should be the study of every statesman and a primary object with every legislator.

No civil government having been provided by Congress for California, the people of that Territory, impelled by the necessities of their political condition, recently met in convention for the purpose of forming a constitution and State government, which the latest advices give me reason to suppose has been accomplished; and it is believed they will shortly apply for the admission of California into the Union as a sovereign State. Should such be the case, and should their constitution be conformable to the requisitions of the Constitution of the United States, I recommend their application to the favorable consideration of Congress. The people of New Mexico will also, it is believed, at no very distant period present themselves for admission into the Union. Preparatory to the admission of California and New Mexico the people of each will have instituted for themselves a republican form of government, "laying its foundation in such principles and organizing its powers in such form as to them shall seem most likely to effect their safety and happiness." By awaiting their action all causes of uneasiness may be avoided and confidence and kind feeling preserved. With a view of maintaining the harmony and tranquillity so dear to all, we should abstain from the introduction of those exciting topics of a sectional character which have hitherto produced painful apprehensions in the public mind; and I repeat the solemn warning of the first and most illustrious of my predecessors against furnishing "any ground for characterizing parties by geographical discriminations."

A collector has been appointed at San Francisco under the act of Congress extending the revenue laws over California, and measures have been taken to organize the custom-houses at that and the other ports mentioned in that act at the earliest period practicable. The collector proceeded overland, and advices have not yet been received of his arrival at San Francisco. Meanwhile, it is understood that the customs have continued to be collected there by officers acting under the military authority, as they were during the Administration of my predecessor. It will, I think, be expedient to confirm the collections thus made, and direct the avails (after such allowances as Congress may think fit to authorize) to be expended within the Territory or to be paid into the Treasury for the purpose of meeting appropriations for the improvement of its rivers and harbors.

A party engaged on the coast survey was dispatched to Oregon in January last. According to the latest advices, they had not left California; and directions have been given to them, as soon as they shall have fixed on the sites of the two light-houses and the buoys authorized to be constructed and placed in Oregon, to proceed without delay to make reconnoissances of the most important points on the coast of California, and especially to examine and determine on sites for light-houses on that coast, the speedy erection of which is urgently demanded by our rapidly increasing commerce.

I have transferred the Indian agencies from upper Missouri and Council Bluffs to Santa Fe and Salt Lake, and have caused to be appointed subagents in the valleys of the Gila, the Sacramento, and the San Joaquin rivers. Still further legal provisions will be necessary for the effective and successful extension of our system of Indian intercourse over the new territories.

I recommend the establishment of a branch mint in California, as it will, in my opinion, afford important facilities to those engaged in mining, as well as to the Government in the disposition of the mineral lands.

I also recommend that commissions be organized by Congress to examine and decide upon the validity of the present subsisting land titles in California and New Mexico, and that provision be made for the establishment of offices of surveyor-general in New Mexico, California, and Oregon and for the surveying and bringing into market the public lands in those Territories. Those lands, remote in position and difficult of access, ought to be disposed of on terms liberal to all, but especially favorable to the early emigrants.

In order that the situation and character of the principal mineral deposits in California may be ascertained, I recommend that a geological and mineralogical exploration be connected with the linear surveys, and that the mineral lands be divided into small lots suitable for mining and be disposed of by sale or lease, so as to give our citizens an opportunity of procuring a permanent right of property in the soil. This would seem to be as important to the success of mining as of agricultural pursuits.

The great mineral wealth of California and the advantages which its ports and harbors and those of Oregon afford to commerce, especially with the islands of the Pacific and Indian oceans and the populous regions of eastern Asia, make it certain that there will arise in a few years large and prosperous communities on our western coast. It therefore becomes important that a line of communication, the best and most expeditious which the nature of the country will admit, should be opened within the territory of the United States from the navigable waters of the Atlantic or the Gulf of Mexico to the Pacific. Opinion, as elicited and expressed by two large and respectable conventions lately assembled at St. Louis and Memphis, points to a railroad as that which, if practicable, will best meet the wishes and wants of the country. But while this, if in successful operation, would be a work of great national importance and of a value to the country which it would be difficult to estimate, it ought also to be regarded as an undertaking of vast magnitude and expense, and one which must, if it be indeed practicable, encounter many difficulties in its construction and use. Therefore, to avoid failure and disappointment; to enable Congress to judge whether in the condition of the country through which it must pass the work be feasible, and, if it be found so, whether it should be undertaken as a national improvement or left to individual enterprise, and in the latter alternative what aid, if any, ought to be extended to it by the Government, I recommend as a preliminary measure a careful reconnoissance of the several proposed routes by a scientific corps and a report as to the practicability of making such a road, with an estimate of the cost of its construction and support.

For further views on these and other matters connected with the duties of the home department I refer you to the report of the Secretary of the Interior.

I recommend early appropriations for continuing the river and harbor improvements which have been already begun, and also for the construction of those for which estimates have been made, as well as for examinations and estimates preparatory to the commencement of such others as the wants of the country, and especially the advance of our population over new districts and the extension of commerce, may render necessary. An estimate of the amount which can be advantageously expended within the next fiscal year under the direction of the Bureau of Topographical Engineers accompanies the report of the Secretary of War, to which I respectfully invite the attention of Congress.

The cession of territory made by the late treaty with Mexico has greatly extended our exposed frontier and rendered its defense more difficult. That treaty has also brought us under obligations to Mexico, to comply with which a military force is requisite. But our military establishment is not materially changed as to its efficiency from the condition in which it stood before the commencement of the Mexican War. Some addition to it will therefore be necessary, and I recommend to the favorable consideration of Congress an increase of the several corps of the Army at our distant Western posts, as proposed in the accompanying report of the Secretary of War.

Great embarrassment has resulted from the effect upon rank in the Army heretofore given to brevet and staff commissions. The views of the Secretary of War on this subject are deemed important, and if carried into effect will, it is believed, promote the harmony of the service. The plan proposed for retiring disabled officers and providing an asylum for such of the rank and file as from age, wounds, and other infirmities occasioned by service have become unfit to perform their respective duties is recommended as a means of increasing the efficiency of the Army and as an act of justice due from a grateful country to the faithful soldier.

The accompanying report of the Secretary of the Navy presents a full and satisfactory account of the condition and operations of the naval service during the past year. Our citizens engaged in the legitimate pursuits of commerce have enjoyed its benefits. Wherever our national vessels have gone they have been received with respect, our officers have been treated with kindness and courtesy, and they have on all occasions pursued a course of strict neutrality, in accordance with the policy of our Government.

The naval force at present in commission is as large as is admissible with the number of men authorized by Congress to be employed.

I invite your attention to the recommendation of the Secretary of the Navy on the subject of a reorganization of the Navy in its various grades of officers, and the establishing of a retired list for such of the officers as are disqualified for active and effective service. Should Congress adopt some such measure as is recommended, it will greatly increase the efficiency of the Navy and reduce its expenditures.

I also ask your attention to the views expressed by him in reference to the employment of war steamers and in regard to the contracts for the transportation of the United States mails and the operation of the system upon the prosperity of the Navy.

By an act of Congress passed August 14, 1848, provision was made for extending post-office and mail accommodations to California and Oregon. Exertions have been made to execute that law, but the limited provisions of the act, the inadequacy of the means it authorizes, the ill adaptation of our post-office laws to the situation of that country, and the measure of compensation for services allowed by those laws, compared with the prices of labor and rents in California, render those exertions in a great degree ineffectual. More particular and efficient provision by law is required on this subject.

The act of 1845 reducing postage has now, by its operation during four years, produced results fully showing that the income from such reduced postage is sufficient to sustain the whole expense of the service of the Post-Office Department, not including the cost of transportation in mail steamers on the lines from New York to Chagres and from Panama to Astoria, which have not been considered by Congress as properly belonging to the mail service.

It is submitted to the wisdom of Congress whether a further reduction of postage should not now be made, more particularly on the letter correspondence. This should be relieved from the unjust burden of transporting and delivering the franked matter of Congress, for which public service provision should be made from the Treasury. I confidently believe that a change may safely be made reducing all single-letter postage to the uniform rate of 5 cents, regardless of distance, without thereby imposing any greater tax on the Treasury than would constitute a very moderate compensation for this public service; and I therefore respectfully recommend such a reduction. Should Congress prefer to abolish the franking privilege entirely, it seems probable that no demand on the Treasury would result from the proposed reduction of postage. Whether any further diminution should now be made, or the result of the reduction to 5 cents, which I have recommended, should be first tested, is submitted to your decision.

Since the commencement of the last session of Congress a postal treaty with Great Britain has been received and ratified, and such relations have been formed by the post-office departments of the two countries in pursuance of that treaty as to carry its provisions into full operation. The attempt to extend this same arrangement through England to France has not been equally successful, but the purpose has not been abandoned.

For a particular statement of the condition of the Post-Office Department and other matters connected with that branch of the public service I refer you to the report of the Postmaster-General.

By the act of the 3d of March, 1849, a board was constituted to make arrangements for taking the Seventh Census, composed of the Secretary of State, the Attorney-General, and the Postmaster-General; and it was made the duty of this board " to prepare and cause to be printed such forms and schedules as might be necessary for the full enumeration of the inhabitants of the United States, and also proper forms and schedules for collecting in statistical tables, under proper heads, such information as to mines, agriculture, commerce, manufactures, education, and other topics as would exhibit a full view of the pursuits, industry, education, and resources of the country." The duties enjoined upon the census board thus established having been performed, it now rests with Congress to enact a law for carrying into effect the provision of the Constitution which requires an actual enumeration of the people of the United States within the ensuing year.

Among the duties assigned by the Constitution to the General Government is one of local and limited application, but not on that account the less obligatory. I allude to the trust committed to Congress as the exclusive legislator and sole guardian of the interests of the District of Columbia. I beg to commend these interests to your kind attention. As the national metropolis the city of Washington must be an object of general interest; and founded, as it was, under the auspices of him whose immortal name it bears, its claims to the fostering care of Congress present themselves with additional strength. Whatever can contribute to its prosperity must enlist the feelings of its constitutional guardians and command their favorable consideration.

Our Government is one of limited powers, and its successful administration eminently depends on the confinement of each of its coordinate branches within its own appropriate sphere. The first section of the

Constitution ordains that—

All legislative powers herein granted shall be vested in a Congress of the United States, which shall consist of a Senate and House of Representatives.

The Executive has authority to recommend (not to dictate) measures to Congress. Having performed that duty, the executive department of the Government can not rightfully control the decision of Congress on any subject of legislation until that decision shall have been officially submitted to the President for approval. The check provided by the Constitution in the clause conferring the qualified veto will never be exercised by me except in the cases contemplated by the fathers of the Republic. I view it as an extreme measure, to be resorted to only in extraordinary cases, as where it may become necessary to defend the executive against the encroachments of the legislative power or to prevent hasty and inconsiderate or unconstitutional legislation. By cautiously confining this remedy within the sphere prescribed to it in the cotemporaneous expositions of the framers of the Constitution, the will of the people, legitimately expressed on all subjects of legislation through their constitutional organs, the Senators and Representatives of the United States, will have its full effect. As indispensable to the preservation of our system of self-government, the independence of the representatives of the States and the people is guaranteed by the Constitution, and they owe no responsibility to any human power but their constituents. By holding the representative responsible only to the people, and exempting him from all other influences, we elevate the character of the constituent and quicken his sense of responsibility to his country. It is under these circumstances only that the elector can feel that in the choice of the lawmaker he is himself truly a component part of the sovereign power of the nation. With equal care we should study to defend the rights of the executive and judicial departments. Our Government can only be preserved in its purity by the suppression and entire elimination of every claim or tendency of one coordinate branch to encroachment upon another. With the strict observance of this rule and the other injunctions of the Constitution, with a sedulous inculcation of that respect and love for the Union of the States which our fathers cherished and enjoined upon their children, and with the aid of that overruling Providence which has so long and so kindly guarded our liberties and institutions, we may reasonably expect to transmit them, with their innumerable blessings, to the remotest posterity.

But attachment to the Union of the States should be habitually fostered in every American heart. For more than half a century, during which kingdoms and empires have fallen, this Union has stood unshaken. The patriots who formed it have long since descended to the grave; yet still it remains, the proudest monument to their memory and the object of affection and admiration with everyone worthy to bear the American name.   In my judgment its dissolution would be the greatest of calamities, and to avert that should be the study of every American.   Upon its preservation must depend our own happiness and that of countless generations to come.   Whatever dangers may threaten it, I shall stand by it and maintain it in its integrity to the full extent of the obligations imposed and the powers conferred upon me by the Constitution.

Millard Fillmore

July 10, 1850 to March 4, 1853

FIRST ANNUAL MESSAGE.

WASHINGTON, *December 2, 1850.*

Fellow-Citizens of the Senate and of the House of Representatives:

Being suddenly called in the midst of the last session of Congress by a painful dispensation of Divine Providence to the responsible station which I now hold, I contented myself with such communications to the Legislature as the exigency of the moment seemed to require. The country was shrouded in mourning for the loss of its venerable Chief Magistrate and all hearts were penetrated with grief. Neither the time nor the occasion appeared to require or to justify on my part any general expression of political opinions or any announcement of the principles which would govern me in the discharge of the duties to the performance of which I had been so unexpectedly called. I trust, therefore, that it may not be deemed inappropriate if I avail myself of this opportunity of the reassembling of Congress to make known my sentiments in a general manner in regard to the policy which ought to be pursued by the Government both in its intercourse with foreign nations and its management and administration of internal affairs.

Nations, like individuals in a state of nature, are equal and independent, possessing certain rights and owing certain duties to each other, arising from their necessary and unavoidable relations; which rights and duties there is no common human authority to protect and enforce. Still, they are rights and duties, binding in morals, in conscience, and in honor, although there is no tribunal to which an injured party can appeal but the disinterested judgment of mankind, and ultimately the arbitrament of the sword.

Among the acknowledged rights of nations is that which each possesses of establishing that form of government which it may deem most conducive to the happiness and prosperity of its own citizens, of changing that form as circumstances may require, and of managing its internal affairs according to its own will. The people of the United States claim this right for themselves, and they readily concede it to others. Hence it becomes an imperative duty not to interfere in the government or internal policy of other nations; and although we may sympathize with the unfortunate or the oppressed everywhere in their struggles for freedom, our principles forbid us from taking any part in such foreign contests. We make no wars to promote or to prevent successions to thrones, to maintain any theory of a balance of power, or to suppress the actual government which any country chooses to establish for itself. We instigate no revolutions, nor suffer any hostile military expeditions to be fitted out in the United States to invade the territory or provinces of a friendly nation. The great law of morality ought to have a national as well as a personal and individual application. We should act toward other nations as we wish them to act toward us, and justice and conscience should form the rule of conduct between governments, instead of mere power, self-interest, or the desire of aggrandizement. To maintain a strict neutrality in foreign wars, to cultivate friendly relations, to reciprocate every noble and generous act, and to perform punctually and scrupulously every treaty obligation—these are the duties which we owe to other states, and by the performance of which we best entitle ourselves to like treatment from them; or, if that, in any case, be refused, we can enforce our own rights with justice and a clear conscience.

In our domestic policy the Constitution will be my guide, and in questions of doubt I shall look for its interpretation to the judicial decisions of that tribunal which was established to expound it and to the usage of the Government, sanctioned by the acquiescence of the country. I regard all its provisions as equally binding. In all its parts it is the will of the people expressed in the most solemn form, and the constituted authorities are but agents to carry that will into effect. Every power which it has granted is to be exercised for the public good; but no pretense of utility, no honest conviction, even, of what might be expedient, can justify the assumption of any power not granted. The powers conferred upon the Government and their distribution to the several departments are as clearly expressed in that sacred instrument as the imperfection of human language will allow, and I deem it my first duty not to question its wisdom, add to its provisions, evade its requirements, or nullify its commands.

Upon you, fellow-citizens, as the representatives of the States and the people, is wisely devolved the legislative power. I shall comply with my duty in laying before you from time to time any information calculated to enable you to discharge your high and responsible trust for the benefit of our common constituents.

My opinions will be frankly expressed upon the leading subjects of legislation; and if—which I do not anticipate—any act should pass the two Houses of Congress which should appear to me unconstitutional, or an encroachment on the just powers of other departments, or with provisions hastily adopted and likely to produce consequences injurious and unforeseen, I should not shrink from the duty of returning it to you, with my reasons, for your further consideration. Beyond the due performance of these constitutional obligations, both my respect for the Legislature and my sense of propriety will restrain me from any attempt to control or influence your proceedings. With you is the power, the honor, and the responsibility of the legislation of the country.

The Government of the United States is a limited Government. It is confined to the exercise of powers expressly granted and such others as may be necessary for carrying those powers into effect; and it is at all times an especial duty to guard against any infringement on the just rights of the States. Over the objects and subjects intrusted to Congress its legislative authority is supreme. But here that authority ceases, and every citizen who truly loves the Constitution and desires the continuance of its existence and its blessings will resolutely and firmly resist any interference in those domestic affairs which the Constitution has clearly and unequivocally left to the exclusive authority of the States. And every such citizen will also deprecate useless irritation among the several members of the Union and all reproach and crimination tending to alienate one portion of the country from another. The beauty of our system of government consists, and its safety and durability must consist, in avoiding mutual collisions and encroachments and in the regular separate action of all, while each is revolving in its own distinct orbit.

The Constitution has made it the duty of the President to take care that the laws be faithfully executed. In a government like ours, in which all laws are passed by a majority of the representatives of the people, and these representatives are chosen for such short periods that any injurious or obnoxious law can very soon be repealed, it would appear unlikely that any great numbers should be found ready to resist the execution of the laws. But it must be borne in mind that the country is extensive; that there may be local interests or prejudices rendering a law odious in one part which is not so in another, and that the thoughtless and inconsiderate, misled by their passions or their imaginations, may be induced madly to resist such laws as they disapprove. Such persons should recollect that without law there can be no real practical liberty; that when law is trampled under foot tyranny rules, whether it appears in the form of a military despotism or of popular violence. The law is the only sure protection of the weak and the only efficient restraint upon the strong. When impartially and faithfully administered, none is beneath its protection and none above its control. You, gentlemen, and the country may be assured that to the utmost of my ability and to the extent of the power vested in me I shall at all times and in all places take care that the laws be faithfully executed. In the discharge of this duty, solemnly imposed upon me by the Constitution and by my oath of office, I shall shrink from no responsibility, and shall endeavor to meet events as they may arise with firmness, as well as with prudence and discretion.

The appointing power is one of the most delicate with which the Executive is invested. I regard it as a sacred trust, to be exercised with the sole view of advancing the prosperity and happiness of the people. It shall be my effort to elevate the standard of official employment by selecting for places of importance individuals fitted for the posts to which they are assigned by their known integrity, talents, and virtues. In so extensive a country, with so great a population, and where few persons appointed to office can be known to the appointing power, mistakes will sometimes unavoidably happen and unfortunate appointments be made notwithstanding the greatest care. In such cases the power of removal may be properly exercised; and neglect of duty or malfeasance in office will be no more tolerated in individuals appointed by myself than in those appointed by others.

I am happy in being able to say that no unfavorable change in our foreign relations has taken place since the message at the opening of the last session of Congress. We are at peace with all nations and we enjoy in an eminent degree the blessings of that peace in a prosperous and growing commerce and in all the forms of amicable national intercourse. The unexampled growth of the country, the present amount of its population, and its ample means of self-protection assure for it the respect of all nations, while it is trusted that its character for justice and a regard to the rights of other States will cause that respect to be readily and cheerfully paid.

A convention was negotiated between the United States and Great Britain in April last for facilitating and protecting the construction of a ship canal between the Atlantic and Pacific oceans and for other purposes. The instrument has since been ratified by the contracting parties, the exchange of ratifications has been effected, and proclamation thereof has been duly made.

In addition to the stipulations contained in this convention, two other objects remain to be accomplished between the contracting powers:

First. The designation and establishment of a free port at each end of the canal.

Second. An agreement fixing the distance from the shore within which belligerent maritime operations shall not be carried on.

On these points there is little doubt that the two Governments will come to an understanding.

The company of citizens of the United States who have acquired from the State of Nicaragua the privilege of constructing a ship canal between the two oceans through the territory of that State have made progress in their preliminary arrangements. The treaty between the United States and Great Britain of the 19th of April last, above referred to, being now in operation, it is to be hoped that the guaranties which it offers will be sufficient to secure the completion of the work with all practicable expedition. It is obvious that this result would be indefinitely postponed if any other than peaceful measures for the purpose of harmonizing conflicting claims to territory in that quarter should be adopted. It will consequently be my endeavor to cause any further negotiations on the part of this Government which may be requisite for this purpose to be so conducted as to bring them to a speedy and successful close.

Some unavoidable delay has occurred, arising from distance and the difficulty of intercourse between this Government and that of Nicaragua, but as intelligence has just been received of the appointment of an envoy extraordinary and minister plenipotentiary of that Government to reside at Washington, whose arrival may soon be expected, it is hoped that no further impediments will be experienced in the prompt transaction of business between the two Governments.

Citizens of the United States have undertaken the connection of the two oceans by means of a railroad across the Isthmus of Tehuantepec, under grants of the Mexican Government to a citizen of that Republic. It is understood that a thorough survey of the course of the communication is in preparation, and there is every reason to expect that it will be prosecuted with characteristic energy, especially when that Government shall have consented to such stipulations with the Government of the United States as may be necessary to impart a feeling of security to those who may embark their property in the enterprise. Negotiations are pending for the accomplishment of that object, and a hope is confidently entertained that when the Government of Mexico shall become duly sensible of the advantages which that country can not fail to derive from the work, and learn that the Government of the United States desires that the right of sovereignty of Mexico in the Isthmus shall remain unimpaired, the stipulations referred to will be agreed to with alacrity.

By the last advices from Mexico it would appear, however, that that Government entertains strong objections to some of the stipulations which the parties concerned in the project of the railroad deem necessary for their protection and security. Further consideration, it is to be hoped, or some modification of terms, may yet reconcile the differences existing between the two Governments in this respect.

Fresh instructions have recently been given to the minister of the United States in Mexico, who is prosecuting the subject with promptitude and ability.

Although the negotiations with Portugal for the payment of claims of citizens of the United States against that Government have not yet resulted in a formal treaty, yet a proposition, made by the Government of Portugal for the final adjustment and payment of those claims, has recently been accepted on the part of the United States. It gives me pleasure to say that Mr. Clay, to whom the negotiation on the part of the United States had been intrusted, discharged the duties of his appointment with ability and discretion, acting always within the instructions of his Government.

It is expected that a regular convention will be immediately negotiated for carrying the agreement between the two Governments into effect.

The commissioner appointed under the act of Congress for carrying into effect the convention with Brazil of the 27th of January, 1849, has entered upon the performance of the duties imposed upon him by that act. It is hoped that those duties may be completed within the time which it prescribes. The documents, however, which the Imperial Government, by the third article of the convention, stipulates to furnish to the Government of the United States have not yet been received. As it is presumed that those documents will be essential for the correct disposition of the claims, it may become necessary for Congress to extend the period limited for the duration of the commission. The sum stipulated by the fourth article of the convention to be paid to this Government has been received.

The collection in the ports of the United States of discriminating duties upon the vessels of Chili and their cargoes has been suspended, pursuant to the provisions of the act of Congress of the 24th of May, 1828. It is to be hoped that this measure will impart a fresh impulse to the commerce between the two countries, which of late, and especially since our acqui-sition of California, has, to the mutual advantage of the parties, been much augmented.

Peruvian guano has become so desirable an article to the agricultural interest of the United States that it is the duty of the Government to employ all the means properly in its power for the purpose of causing that article to be imported into the country at a reasonable price. Nothing will be omitted on my part toward accomplishing this desirable end. I am persuaded that in removing any restraints on this traffic the Peruvian Government will promote its own best interests, while it will afford a proof of a friendly disposition toward this country, which will be duly appreciated.

The treaty between the United States and His Majesty the King of the Hawaiian Islands, which has recently been made public, will, it is believed, have a beneficial effect upon the relations between the two countries.

The relations between those parts of the island of St. Domingo which were formerly colonies of Spain and France, respectively, are still in an unsettled condition. The proximity of that island to the United States and the delicate questions involved in the existing controversy there render it desirable that it should be permanently and speedily adjusted. The interests of humanity and of general commerce also demand this; and as intimations of the same sentiment have been received from other governments, it is hoped that some plan may soon be devised to effect the object in a manner likely to give general satisfaction. The Government of the United States will not fail, by the exercise of all proper friendly offices, to do all in its power to put an end to the destructive war which has raged between the different parts of the island and to secure to them both the benefits of peace and commerce.

I refer you to the report of the Secretary of the Treasury for a detailed statement of the finances.

The total receipts into the Treasury for the year ending 30th of June last were $47,421,748.90.

The total expenditures during the same period were $43,002,168.90.

The public debt has been reduced since the last annual report from the Treasury Department $495,276.79.

By the nineteenth section of the act of 28th January, 1847, the proceeds of the sales of the public lands were pledged for the interest and principal of the public debt. The great amount of those lands subsequently granted by Congress for military bounties will, it is believed, very nearly supply the public demand for several years to come, and but little reliance can, therefore, be placed on that hitherto fruitful source of revenue.   Aside from the permanent annual expenditures, which have necessarily largely increased, a portion of the public debt, amounting to $8,075,986.59, must be provided for within the next two fiscal years.   It is most desirable that these accruing demands should be met without resorting to new loans.

All experience has demonstrated the wisdom and policy of raising a large portion of revenue for the support of Government from duties on goods imported.   The power to lay these duties is unquestionable, and its chief object, of course, is to replenish the Treasury.   But if in doing this an incidental advantage may be gained by encouraging the industry of our own citizens, it is our duty to avail ourselves of that advantage.

A duty laid upon an article which can not be produced in this country, such as tea or coffee, adds to the cost of the article, and is chiefly or wholly paid by the consumer.   But a duty laid upon an article which may be produced here stimulates the skill and industry of our own country to produce the same article, which is brought into the market in competition with the foreign article, and the importer is thus compelled to reduce his price to that at which the domestic article can be sold, thereby throwing a part of the duty upon the producer of the foreign article.   The continuance of this process creates the skill and invites the capital which finally enable us to produce the article much cheaper than it could have been procured from abroad, thereby benefiting both the producer and the consumer at home.   The consequence of this is that the artisan and the agriculturist are brought together, each affords a ready market for the produce of the other, the whole country becomes prosperous, and the ability to produce every necessary of life renders us independent in war as well as in peace.

A high tariff can never be permanent.   It will cause dissatisfaction, and will be changed.   It excludes competition, and thereby invites the investment of capital in manufactures to such excess that when changed it brings distress, bankruptcy, and ruin upon all who have been misled by its faithless protection.   What the manufacturer wants is uniformity and permanency, that he may feel a confidence that he is not to be ruined by sudden changes.   But to make a tariff uniform and permanent it is not only necessary that the laws should not be altered, but that the duty should not fluctuate.   To effect this all duties should be specific wherever the nature of the article is such as to admit of it.   *Ad valorem* duties fluctuate with the price and offer strong temptations to fraud and perjury.   Specific duties, on the contrary, are equal and uniform in all ports and at all times, and offer a strong inducement to the importer to bring the best article, as he pays no more duty upon that than upon one of inferior quality. I therefore strongly recommend a modification of the present tariff, which has prostrated some of our most important and necessary manufactures, and that specific duties be imposed sufficient to raise the requisite revenue, making such discriminations in favor of the industrial pursuits of our own country as to encourage home production without excluding foreign competition. It is also important that an unfortunate provision in the present tariff, which imposes a much higher duty upon the raw material that enters into our manufactures than upon the manufactured article, should be remedied.

The papers accompanying the report of the Secretary of the Treasury will disclose frauds attempted upon the revenue, in variety and amount so great as to justify the conclusion that it is impossible under any system of *ad valorem* duties levied upon the foreign cost or value of the article to secure an honest observance and an effectual administration of the laws. The fraudulent devices to evade the law which have been detected by the vigilance of the appraisers leave no room to doubt that similar impositions not discovered, to a large amount, have been successfully practiced since the enactment of the law now in force. This state of things has already had a prejudicial influence upon those engaged in foreign commerce. It has a tendency to drive the honest trader from the business of importing and to throw that important branch of employment into the hands of unscrupulous and dishonest men, who are alike regardless of law and the obligations of an oath. By these means the plain intentions of Congress, as expressed in the law, are daily defeated. Every motive of policy and duty, therefore, impels me to ask the earnest attention of Congress to this subject. If Congress should deem it unwise to attempt any important changes in the system of levying duties at this session, it will become indispensable to the protection of the revenue that such remedies as in the judgment of Congress may mitigate the evils complained of should be at once applied.

As before stated, specific duties would, in my opinion, afford the most perfect remedy for this evil; but if you should not concur in this view, then, as a partial remedy, I beg leave respectfully to recommend that instead of taking the invoice of the article abroad as a means of determining its value here, the correctness of which invoice it is in many cases impossible to verify, the law be so changed as to require a home valuation or appraisal, to be regulated in such manner as to give, as far as practicable, uniformity in the several ports.

There being no mint in California, I am informed that the laborers in the mines are compelled to dispose of their gold dust at a large discount. This appears to me to be a heavy and unjust tax upon the labor of those employed in extracting this precious metal, and I doubt not you will be disposed at the earliest period possible to relieve them from it by the establishment of a mint. In the meantime, as an assayer's office is established there, I would respectfully submit for your consideration the propriety of authorizing gold bullion which has been assayed and stamped to be received in payment of Government dues. I can not conceive that the Treasury would suffer any loss by such a provision, which will at once raise bullion to its par value, and thereby save (if I am rightly informed) many millions of dollars to the laborers which are now paid in brokerage to convert this precious metal into available funds. This discount upon their hard earnings is a heavy tax, and every effort should be made by the Government to relieve them from so great a burden.

More than three-fourths of our population are engaged in the cultivation of the soil. The commercial, manufacturing, and navigating interests are all to a great extent dependent on the agricultural. It is therefore the most important interest of the nation, and has a just claim to the fostering care and protection of the Government so far as they can be extended consistently with the provisions of the Constitution. As this can not be done by the ordinary modes of legislation, I respectfully recommend the establishment of an agricultural bureau, to be charged with the duty of giving to this leading branch of American industry the encouragement which it so well deserves. In view of the immense mineral resources of our country, provision should also be made for the employment of a competent mineralogist and chemist, who should be required, under the direction of the head of the bureau, to collect specimens of the various minerals of our country and to ascertain by careful analysis their respective elements and properties and their adaptation to useful purposes. He should also be required to examine and report upon the qualities of different soils and the manures best calculated to improve their productiveness. By publishing the results of such experiments, with suitable explanations, and by the collection and distribution of rare seeds and plants, with instructions as to the best system of cultivation, much may be done to promote this great national interest.

In compliance with the act of Congress passed on the 23d of May, 1850, providing, among other things, for taking the Seventh Census, a superintendent was appointed and all other measures adopted which were deemed necessary to insure the prompt and faithful performance of that duty. The appropriation already made will, it is believed, be sufficient to defray the whole expense of the work, but further legislation may be necessary in regard to the compensation of some of the marshals of the Territories. It will also be proper to make provision by law at an early day for the publication of such abstracts of the returns as the public interests may require.

The unprecedented growth of our territories on the Pacific in wealth and population and the consequent increase of their social and commercial relations with the Atlantic States seem to render it the duty of the Government to use all its constitutional power to improve the means of intercourse with them. The importance of opening "a line of communication, the best and most expeditious of which the nature of the country will admit," between the Valley of the Mississippi and the Pacific was brought to your notice by my predecessor in his annual message; and as the reasons which he presented in favor of the measure still exist in full force, I beg leave to call your attention to them and to repeat the recommendations then made by him.

The uncertainty which exists in regard to the validity of land titles in California is a subject which demands your early consideration. Large bodies of land in that State are claimed under grants said to have been made by authority of the Spanish and Mexican Governments. Many of these have not been perfected, others have been revoked, and some are believed to be fraudulent. But until they shall have been judicially investigated they will continue to retard the settlement and improvement of the country. I therefore respectfully recommend that provision be made by law for the appointment of commissioners to examine all such claims with a view to their final adjustment.

I also beg leave to call your attention to the propriety of extending at an early day our system of land laws, with such modifications as may be necessary, over the State of California and the Territories of Utah and New Mexico. The mineral lands of California will, of course, form an exception to any general system which may be adopted. Various methods of disposing of them have been suggested. I was at first inclined to favor the system of leasing, as it seemed to promise the largest revenue to the Government and to afford the best security against monopolies; but further reflection and our experience in leasing the lead mines and selling lands upon credit have brought my mind to the conclusion that there would be great difficulty in collecting the rents, and that the relation of debtor and creditor between the citizens and the Government would be attended with many mischievous consequences. I therefore recommend that instead of retaining the mineral lands under the permanent control of the Government they be divided into small parcels and sold, under such restrictions as to quantity and time as will insure the best price and guard most effectually against combinations of capitalists to obtain monopolies.

The annexation of Texas and the acquisition of California and New Mexico have given increased importance to our Indian relations. The various tribes brought under our jurisdiction by these enlargements of our boundaries are estimated to embrace a population of 124,000.

Texas and New Mexico are surrounded by powerful tribes of Indians, who are a source of constant terror and annoyance to the inhabitants. Separating into small predatory bands, and always mounted, they overrun the country, devastating farms, destroying crops, driving off whole herds of cattle, and occasionally murdering the inhabitants or carrying them into captivity. The great roads leading into the country are infested with them, whereby traveling is rendered extremely dangerous and immigration is almost entirely arrested. The Mexican frontier, which by the eleventh article of the treaty of Guadalupe Hidalgo we are bound to protect against the Indians within our border, is exposed to these incursions equally with our own. The military force stationed in that country, although forming a large proportion of the Army, is represented as entirely inadequate to our own protection and the fulfillment of our treaty stipulations with Mexico. The principal deficiency is in cavalry, and I recommend that Congress should, at as early a period as practicable, provide for the raising of one or more regiments of mounted men.

For further suggestions on this subject and others connected with our domestic interests and the defense of our frontier, I refer you to the reports of the Secretary of the Interior and of the Secretary of War.

I commend also to your favorable consideration the suggestion contained in the last-mentioned report and in the letter of the General in Chief relative to the establishment of an asylum for the relief of disabled and destitute soldiers. This subject appeals so strongly to your sympathies that it would be superfluous in me to say anything more than barely to express my cordial approbation of the proposed object.

The Navy continues to give protection to our commerce and other national interests in the different quarters of the globe, and, with the exception of a single steamer on the Northern lakes, the vessels in commission are distributed in six different squadrons.

The report of the head of that Department will exhibit the services of these squadrons and of the several vessels employed in each during the past year. It is a source of gratification that, while they have been constantly prepared for any hostile emergency, they have everywhere met with the respect and courtesy due as well to the dignity as to the peaceful dispositions and just purposes of the nation.

The two brigantines accepted by the Government from a generous citizen of New York and placed under the command of an officer of the Navy to proceed to the Arctic Seas in quest of the British commander Sir John Franklin and his companions, in compliance with the act of Congress approved in May last, had when last heard from penetrated into a high northern latitude; but the success of this noble and humane enterprise is yet uncertain.

I invite your attention to the view of our present naval establishment and resources presented in the report of the Secretary of the Navy, and the suggestions therein made for its improvement, together with the naval policy recommended for the security of our Pacific Coast and the protection and extension of our commerce with eastern Asia. Our facilities for a larger participation in the trade of the East, by means of our recent settlements on the shores of the Pacific, are too obvious to be overlooked or disregarded.

The questions in relation to rank in the Army and Navy and relative rank between officers of the two branches of the service, presented to the

Executive by certain resolutions of the House of Representatives at the last session of Congress, have been submitted to a board of officers in each branch of the service, and their report may be expected at an early day.

I also earnestly recommend the enactment of a law authorizing officers of the Army and Navy to be retired from the service when incompetent for its vigorous and active duties, taking care to make suitable provision for those who have faithfully served their country and awarding distinctions by retaining in appropriate commands those who have been particularly conspicuous for gallantry and good conduct. While the obligation of the country to maintain and honor those who, to the exclusion of other pursuits, have devoted themselves to its arduous service is acknowledged, this obligation should not be permitted to interfere with the efficiency of the service itself.

I am gratified in being able to state that the estimates of expenditure for the Navy in the ensuing year are less by more than $1,000,000 than those of the present, excepting the appropriation which may become necessary for the construction of a dock on the coast of the Pacific, propositions for which are now being considered and on which a special report may be expected early in your present session.

There is an evident justness in the suggestion of the same report that appropriations for the naval service proper should be separated from those for fixed and permanent objects, such as building docks and navy-yards and the fixtures attached, and from the extraordinary objects under the care of the Department which, however important, are not essentially naval.

A revision of the code for the government of the Navy seems to require the immediate consideration of Congress. Its system of crimes and punishments had undergone no change for half a century until the last session, though its defects have been often and ably pointed out; and the abolition of a particular species of corporal punishment, which then took place, without providing any substitute, has left the service in a state of defectiveness which calls for prompt correction. I therefore recommend that the whole subject be revised without delay and such a system established for the enforcement of discipline as shall be at once humane and effectual.

The accompanying report of the Postmaster-General presents a satisfactory view of the operations and condition of that Department.

At the close of the last fiscal year the length of the inland mail routes in the United States (not embracing the service in Oregon and California) was 178,672 miles, the annual transportation thereon 46,541,423 miles, and the annual cost of such transportation $2,724,426.

The increase of the annual transportation over that of the preceding year was 3,997,354 miles and the increase in cost was $342,440.

The number of post-offices in the United States on the 1st day of July last was 18,417, being an increase of 1,670 during the preceding year.

The gross revenues of the Department for the fiscal year ending June 30, 1850, amounted to $5,552,971.48, including the annual appropriation of $200,000 for the franked matter of the Departments and excluding the foreign postages collected for and payable to the British Government.

The expenditures for the same period were $5,212,953.43, leaving a balance of revenue over expenditures of $340,018.05.

I am happy to find that the fiscal condition of the Department is such as to justify the Postmaster-General in recommending the reduction of our inland letter postage to 3 cents the single letter when prepaid and 5 cents when not prepaid. He also recommends that the prepaid rate shall be reduced to 2 cents whenever the revenues of the Department, after the reduction, shall exceed its expenditures by more than 5 per cent for two consecutive years; that the postage upon California and other letters sent by our ocean steamers shall be much reduced, and that the rates of postage on newspapers, pamphlets, periodicals, and other printed matter shall be modified and some reduction thereon made.

It can not be doubted that the proposed reductions will for the present diminish the revenues of the Department. It is believed that the deficiency, after the surplus already accumulated shall be exhausted, may be almost wholly met either by abolishing the existing privileges of sending free matter through the mails or by paying out of the Treasury to the Post-Office Department a sum equivalent to the postage of which it is deprived by such privileges. The last is supposed to be the preferable mode, and will, if not entirely, so nearly supply that deficiency as to make any further appropriation that may be found necessary so inconsiderable as to form no obstacle to the proposed reductions.

I entertain no doubt of the authority of Congress to make appropriations for leading objects in that class of public works comprising what are usually called works of internal improvement. This authority I suppose to be derived chiefly from the power of regulating commerce with foreign nations and among the States and the power of laying and collecting imposts. Where commerce is to be carried on and imposts collected there must be ports and harbors as well as wharves and custom-houses. If ships laden with valuable cargoes approach the shore or sail along the coast, light-houses are necessary at suitable points for the protection of life and property. Other facilities and securities for commerce and navigation are hardly less important; and those clauses of the Constitution, therefore, to which I have referred have received from the origin of the Government a liberal and beneficial construction. Not only have light-houses, buoys, and beacons been established and floating lights maintained, but harbors have been cleared and improved, piers constructed, and even breakwaters for the safety of shipping and sea walls to protect harbors from being filled up and rendered useless by the action of the ocean, have been erected at very great expense. And this construction of the Constitution appears the more reasonable from the consideration that if these works, of such evident importance and utility, are not to be accomplished by Congress they can not be accomplished at all. By the adoption of the Constitution the several States voluntarily parted with the power of collecting duties of imposts in their own ports, and it is not to be expected that they should raise money by internal taxation, direct or indirect, for the benefit of that commerce the revenues derived from which do not, either in whole or in part, go into their own treasuries. Nor do I perceive any difference between the power of Congress to make appropriations for objects of this kind on the ocean and the power to make appropriations for similar objects on lakes and rivers, wherever they are large enough to bear on their waters an extensive traffic. The magnificent Mississippi and its tributaries and the vast lakes of the North and Northwest appear to me to fall within the exercise of the power as justly and as clearly as the ocean and the Gulf of Mexico. It is a mistake to regard expenditures judiciously made for these objects as expenditures for local purposes. The position or sight of the work is necessarily local, but its utility is general. A ship canal around the Falls of St. Mary of less than a mile in length, though local in its construction, would yet be national in its purpose and its benefits, as it would remove the only obstruction to a navigation of more than 1,000 miles, affecting several States, as well as our commercial relations with Canada. So, too, the breakwater at the mouth of the Delaware is erected, not for the exclusive benefit of the States bordering on the bay and river of that name, but for that of the whole coastwise navigation of the United States and, to a considerable extent, also of foreign commerce. If a ship be lost on the bar at the entrance of a Southern port for want of sufficient depth of water, it is very likely to be a Northern ship; and if a steamboat be sunk in any part of the Mississippi on account of its channel not having been properly cleared of obstructions, it may be a boat belonging to either of eight or ten States. I may add, as somewhat remarkable, that among all the thirty-one States there is none that is not to a greater or less extent bounded on the ocean, or the Gulf of Mexico, or one of the Great Lakes, or some navigable river.

In fulfilling our constitutional duties, fellow-citizens, on this subject, as in carrying into effect all other powers conferred by the Constitution, we should consider ourselves as deliberating and acting for one and the same country, and bear constantly in mind that our regard and our duty are due not to a particular part only, but to the whole.

I therefore recommend that appropriations be made for completing such works as have been already begun and for commencing such others as may seem to the wisdom of Congress to be of public and general importance.

The difficulties and delays incident to the settlement of private claims by Congress amount in many cases to a denial of justice. There is reason to apprehend that many unfortunate creditors of the Government have thereby been unavoidably ruined. Congress has so much business of a public character that it is impossible it should give much attention to mere private claims, and their accumulation is now so great that many claimants must despair of ever being able to obtain a hearing. It may well be doubted whether Congress, from the nature of its organization, is properly constituted to decide upon such cases. It is impossible that each member should examine the merits of every claim on which he is compelled to vote, and it is preposterous to ask a judge to decide a case which he has never heard. Such decisions may, and frequently must, do injustice either to the claimant or the Government, and I perceive no better remedy for this growing evil than the establishment of some tribunal to adjudicate upon such claims. I beg leave, therefore, most respectfully to recommend that provision be made by law for the appointment of a commission to settle all private claims against the United States; and as an *ex parte* hearing must in all contested cases be very unsatisfactory, I also recommend the appointment of a solicitor, whose duty it shall be to represent the Government before such commission and protect it against all illegal, fraudulent, or unjust claims which may be presented for their adjudication.

This District, which has neither voice nor vote in your deliberations, looks to you for protection and aid, and I commend all its wants to your favorable consideration, with a full confidence that you will meet them not only with justice, but with liberality. It should be borne in mind that in this city, laid out by Washington and consecrated by his name, is located the Capitol of our nation, the emblem of our Union and the symbol of our greatness. Here also are situated all the public buildings necessary for the use of the Government, and all these are exempt from taxation. It should be the pride of Americans to render this place attractive to the people of the whole Republic and convenient and safe for the transaction of the public business and the preservation of the public records. The Government should therefore bear a liberal proportion of the burdens of all necessary and useful improvements. And as nothing could contribute more to the health, comfort, and safety of the city and the security of the public buildings and records than an abundant supply of pure water, I respectfully recommend that you make such provisions for obtaining the same as in your wisdom you may deem proper.

The act, passed at your last session, making certain propositions to Texas for settling the disputed boundary between that State and the Territory of New Mexico was, immediately on its passage, transmitted by express to the governor of Texas, to be laid by him before the general assembly for its agreement thereto. Its receipt was duly acknowledged, but no official information has yet been received of the action of the general assembly thereon. It may, however, be very soon expected, as, by the terms of the propositions submitted they were to have been acted upon on or before the first day of the present month.

It was hardly to have been expected that the series of measures passed at your last session with the view of healing the sectional differences which had sprung from the slavery and territorial questions should at once have realized their beneficent purpose. All mutual concession in the nature of a compromise must necessarily be unwelcome to men of extreme opinions. And though without such concessions our Constitution could not have been formed, and can not be permanently sustained, yet we have seen them made the subject of bitter controversy in both sections of the Republic. It required many months of discussion and deliberation to secure the concurrence of a majority of Congress in their favor. It would be strange if they had been received with immediate approbation by people and States prejudiced and heated by the exciting controversies of their representatives. I believe those measures to have been required by the circumstances and condition of the country. I believe they were necessary to allay asperities and animosities that were rapidly alienating one section of the country from another and destroying those fraternal sentiments which are the strongest supports of the Constitution. They were adopted in the spirit of conciliation and for the purpose of conciliation. I believe that a great majority of our fellow-citizens sympathize in that spirit and that purpose, and in the main approve and are prepared in all respects to sustain these enactments. I can not doubt that the American people, bound together by kindred blood and common traditions, still cherish a paramount regard for the Union of their fathers, and that they are ready to rebuke any attempt to violate its integrity, to disturb the compromises on which it is based, or to resist the laws which have been enacted under its authority.

The series of measures to which I have alluded are regarded by me as a settlement in principle and substance—a final settlement of the dangerous and exciting subjects which they embraced. Most of these subjects, indeed, are beyond your reach, as the legislation which disposed of them was in its character final and irrevocable. It may be presumed from the opposition which they all encountered that none of those measures was free from imperfections, but in their mutual dependence and connection they formed a system of compromise the most conciliatory and best for the entire country that could be obtained from conflicting sectional interests and opinions.

For this reason I recommend your adherence to the adjustment established by those measures until time and experience shall demonstrate the necessity of further legislation to guard against evasion or abuse.

By that adjustment we have been rescued from the wide and boundless agitation that surrounded us, and have a firm, distinct, and legal ground to rest upon. And the occasion, I trust, will justify me in exhorting my countrymen to rally upon and maintain that ground as the best, if not the only, means of restoring peace and quiet to the country and maintaining inviolate the integrity of the Union.

And now, fellow-citizens, I can not bring this communication to a close without invoking you to join me in humble and devout thanks to the Great Ruler of Nations for the multiplied blessings which He has graciously bestowed upon us. His hand, so often visible in our preservation, has stayed the pestilence, saved us from foreign wars and domestic disturbances, and scattered plenty throughout the land.

Our liberties, religious and civil, have been maintained, the fountains of knowledge have all been kept open, and means of happiness widely spread and generally enjoyed greater than have fallen to the lot of any other nation. And while deeply penetrated with gratitude for the past, let us hope that His all-wise providence will so guide our counsels as that they shall result in giving satisfaction to our constituents, securing the peace of the country, and adding new strength to the united Government under which we live.

SECOND ANNUAL MESSAGE.

WASHINGTON, *December 2, 1851.*

Fellow-Citizens of the Senate and of the House of Representatives:

I congratulate you and our common constituency upon the favorable auspices under which you meet for your first session. Our country is at peace with all the world. The agitation which for a time threatened to disturb the fraternal relations which make us one people is fast subsiding, and a year of general prosperity and health has crowned the nation with unusual blessings. None can look back to the dangers which are passed or forward to the bright prospect before us without feeling a thrill of gratification, at the same time that he must be impressed with a grateful sense of our profound obligations to a beneficent Providence, whose paternal care is so manifest in the happiness of this highly favored land.

Since the close of the last Congress certain Cubans and other foreigners resident in the United States, who were more or less concerned in the previous invasion of Cuba, instead of being discouraged by its failure have again abused the hospitality of this country by making it the scene of the equipment of another military expedition against that possession of Her Catholic Majesty, in which they were countenanced, aided, and joined by citizens of the United States. On receiving intelligence that such designs were entertained, I lost no time in issuing such instructions to the proper officers of the United States as seemed to be called for by the occasion. By the proclamation a copy of which is herewith submitted I also warned those who might be in danger of being inveigled into this scheme of its unlawful character and of the penalties which they would incur. For some time there was reason to hope that these measures had sufficed to prevent any such attempt. This hope, however, proved to be delusive. Very early in the morning of the 3d of August a steamer called the *Pampero* departed from New Orleans for Cuba, having on board upward of 400 armed men with evident intentions to make war upon the authorities of the island. This expedition was set on foot in palpable violation of the laws of the United States. Its leader was a Spaniard, and several of the chief officers and some others engaged in it were foreigners. The persons composing it, however, were mostly citizens of the United States.

Before the expedition set out, and probably before it was organized, a slight insurrectionary movement, which appears to have been soon suppressed, had taken place in the eastern quarter of Cuba. The importance of this movement was, unfortunately, so much exaggerated in the accounts of it published in this country that these adventurers seem to have been led to believe that the Creole population of the island not only desired to throw off the authority of the mother country, but had resolved upon that step and had begun a well-concerted enterprise for effecting it. The persons engaged in the expedition were generally young and ill informed. The steamer in which they embarked left New Orleans stealthily and without a clearance. After touching at Key West, she proceeded to the coast of Cuba, and on the night between the 11th and 12th of August landed the persons on board at Playtas, within about 20 leagues of Havana.

The main body of them proceeded to and took possession of an inland village 6 leagues distant, leaving others to follow in charge of the baggage as soon as the means of transportation could be obtained. The latter, having taken up their line of march to connect themselves with the main body, and having proceeded about 4 leagues into the country, were attacked on the morning of the 13th by a body of Spanish troops, and a bloody conflict ensued, after which they retreated to the place of disembarkation, where about 50 of them obtained boats and reembarked therein. They were, however, intercepted among the keys near the shore by a Spanish steamer cruising on the coast, captured and carried to Havana, and after being examined before a military court were sentenced to be publicly executed, and the sentence was carried into effect on the 16th of August.

On receiving information of what had occurred Commodore Foxhall A. Parker was instructed to proceed in the steam frigate *Saranac* to Havana and inquire into the charges against the persons executed, the circumstances under which they were taken, and whatsoever referred to their trial and sentence. Copies of the instructions from the Department of

State to him and of his letters to that Department are herewith submitted.

According to the record of the examination, the prisoners all admitted the offenses charged against them, of being hostile invaders of the island. At the time of their trial and execution the main body of the invaders was still in the field making war upon the Spanish authorities and Spanish subjects. After the lapse of some days, being overcome by the Spanish troops, they dispersed on the 24th of August. Lopez, their leader, was captured some days after, and executed on the 1st of September. Many of his remaining followers were killed or died of hunger and fatigue, and the rest were made prisoners. Of these none appear to have been tried or executed. Several of them were pardoned upon application of their friends and others, and the rest, about 160 in number, were sent to Spain. Of the final disposition made of these we have no official information.

Such is the melancholy result of this illegal and ill-fated expedition. Thus thoughtless young men have been induced by false and fraudulent representations to violate the law of their country through rash and unfounded expectations of assisting to accomplish political revolutions in other states, and have lost their lives in the undertaking. Too severe a judgment can hardly be passed by the indignant sense of the community upon those who, being better informed themselves, have yet led away the ardor of youth and an ill-directed love of political liberty. The correspondence between this Government and that of Spain relating to this transaction is herewith communicated.

Although these offenders against the laws have forfeited the protection of their country, yet the Government may, so far as consistent with its obligations to other countries and its fixed purpose to maintain and enforce the laws, entertain sympathy for their unoffending families and friends, as well as a feeling of compassion for themselves. Accordingly, no proper effort has been spared and none will be spared to procure the release of such citizens of the United States engaged in this unlawful enterprise as are now in confinement in Spain; but it is to be hoped that such interposition with the Government of that country may not be considered as affording any ground of expectation that the Government of the United States will hereafter feel itself under any obligation of duty to intercede for the liberation or pardon of such persons as are flagrant offenders against the law of nations and the laws of the United States. These laws must be executed. If we desire to maintain our respectability among the nations of the earth, it behooves us to enforce steadily and sternly the neutrality acts passed by Congress and to follow as far as may be the violation of those acts with condign punishment.

But what gives a peculiar criminality to this invasion of Cuba is that, under the lead of Spanish subjects and with the aid of citizens of the

United States, it had its origin with many in motives of cupidity. Money was advanced by individuals, probably in considerable amounts, to purchase Cuban bonds, as they have been called, issued by Lopez, sold, doubtless, at a very large discount, and for the payment of which the public lands and public property of Cuba, of whatever kind, and the fiscal resources of the people and government of that island, from whatever source to be derived, were pledged, as well as the good faith of the government expected to be established. All these means of payment, it is evident, were only to be obtained by a process of bloodshed, war, and revolution. None will deny that those who set on foot military expeditions against foreign states by means like these are far more culpable than the ignorant and the necessitous whom they induce to go forth as the ostensible parties in the proceeding. These originators of the invasion of Cuba seem to have determined with coolness and system upon an undertaking which should disgrace their country, violate its laws, and put to hazard the lives of ill-informed and deluded men. You will consider whether further legislation be necessary to prevent the perpetration of such offenses in future.

No individuals have a right to hazard the peace of the country or to violate its laws upon vague notions of altering or reforming governments in other states. This principle is not only reasonable in itself and in accordance with public law, but is ingrafted into the codes of other nations as well as our own. But while such are the sentiments of this Government, it may be added that every independent nation must be presumed to be able to defend its possessions against unauthorized individuals banded together to attack them. The Government of the United States at all times since its establishment has abstained and has sought to restrain the citizens of the country from entering into controversies between other powers, and to observe all the duties of neutrality. At an early period of the Government, in the Administration of Washington, several laws were passed for this purpose. The main provisions of these laws were reenacted by the act of April, 1818, by which, amongst other things, it was declared that—

If any person shall, within the territory or jurisdiction of the United States, begin, or set on foot, or provide or prepare the means for, any military expedition or enterprise to be carried on from thence against the territory or dominions of any foreign prince or state, or of any colony, district, or people, with whom the United States are at peace, every person so offending shall be deemed guilty of a high misdemeanor, and shall be fined not exceeding $3,000 and imprisoned not more than three years.

And this law has been executed and enforced to the full extent of the power of the Government from that day to this.

In proclaiming and adhering to the doctrine of neutrality and nonintervention, the United States have not followed the lead of other civilized nations; they have taken the lead themselves and have been followed by others. This was admitted by one of the most eminent of modern British statesmen, who said in Parliament, while a minister of the Crown, "that if he wished for a guide in a system of neutrality he should take that laid down by America in the days of Washington and the secretaryship of Jefferson;" and we see, in fact, that the act of Congress of 1818 was followed the succeeding year by an act of the Parliament of England substantially the same in its general provisions.   Up to that time there had been no similar law in England, except certain highly penal statutes passed in the reign of George II, prohibiting English subjects from enlisting in foreign service, the avowed object of which statutes was that foreign armies, raised for the purpose of restoring the house of Stuart to the throne, should not be strengthened by recruits from England herself.

All must see that difficulties may arise in carrying the laws referred to into execution in a country now having 3,000 or 4,000 miles of seacoast, with an infinite number of ports and harbors and small inlets, from some of which unlawful expeditions may suddenly set forth, without the knowledge of Government, against the possessions of foreign states.

"Friendly relations with all, but entangling alliances with none," has long been a maxim with us.   Our true mission is not to propagate our opinions or impose upon other countries our form of government by artifice or force, but to teach by example and show by our success, moderation, and justice the blessings of self-government and the advantages of free institutions.   Let every people choose for itself and make and alter its political institutions to suit its own condition and convenience.   But while we avow and maintain this neutral policy ourselves, we are anxious to see the same forbearance on the part of other nations whose forms of government are different from our own.   The deep interest which we feel in the spread of liberal principles and the establishment of free governments and the sympathy with which we witness every struggle against oppression forbid that we should be indifferent to a case in which the strong arm of a foreign power is invoked to stifle public sentiment and repress the spirit of freedom in any country.

The Governments of Great Britain and France have issued orders to their naval commanders on the West India station to prevent, by force if necessary, the landing of adventurers from any nation on the island of Cuba with hostile intent.   The copy of a memorandum of a conversation on this subject between the chargé d'affaires of Her Britannic Majesty and the Acting Secretary of State and of a subsequent note of the former to the Department of State are herewith submitted, together with a copy of a note of the Acting Secretary of State to the minister of the French Republic and of the reply of the latter on the same subject.   These papers will acquaint you with the grounds of this interposition of two leading commercial powers of Europe, and with the apprehensions, which this Government could not fail to entertain, that such interposition, if carried into effect, might lead to abuses in derogation of the maritime rights of the United States.   The maritime rights of the United States are founded on a firm, secure, and well-defined basis; they stand upon the ground of national independence and public law, and will be maintained in all their full and just extent. The principle which this Government has heretofore solemnly announced it still adheres to, and will maintain under all circumstances and at all hazards. That principle is that in every regularly documented merchant vessel the crew who navigate it and those on board of it will find their protection in the flag which is over them. No American ship can be allowed to be visited or searched for the purpose of ascertaining the character of individuals on board, nor can there be allowed any watch by the vessels of any foreign nation over American vessels on the coast of the United States or the seas adjacent thereto. It will be seen by the last communication from the British chargé d'affaires to the Department of State that he is authorized to assure the Secretary of State that every care will be taken that in executing the preventive measures against the expeditions which the United States Government itself has denounced as not being entitled to the protection of any government no interference shall take place with the lawful commerce of any nation.

In addition to the correspondence on this subject herewith submitted, official information has been received at the Department of State of assurances by the French Government that in the orders given to the French naval forces they were expressly instructed, in any operations they might engage in, to respect the flag of the United States wherever it might appear, and to commit no act of hostility upon any vessel or armament under its protection.

Ministers and consuls of foreign nations are the means and agents of communication between us and those nations, and it is of the utmost importance that while residing in the country they should feel a perfect security so long as they faithfully discharge their respective duties and are guilty of no violation of our laws. This is the admitted law of nations and no country has a deeper interest in maintaining it than the United States. Our commerce spreads over every sea and visits every clime, and our ministers and consuls are appointed to protect the interests of that commerce as well as to guard the peace of the country and maintain the honor of its flag. But how can they discharge these duties unless they be themselves protected? And if protected it must be by the laws of the country in which they reside. And what is due to our own public functionaries residing in foreign nations is exactly the measure of what is due to the functionaries of other governments residing here. As in war the bearers of flags of truce are sacred, or else wars would be interminable, so in peace ambassadors, public ministers, and consuls, charged with friendly national intercourse, are objects of especial respect and protection, each according to the rights belonging to his rank and station. In view of these important principles, it is with deep mortification and regret I announce to you that during the excitement growing out of the executions at Havana the office of Her Catholic Majesty's consul at New Orleans was assailed by a mob, his property destroyed, the Spanish flag found in the office carried off and torn in pieces, and he himself induced to flee for his personal safety, which he supposed to be in danger. On receiving intelligence of these events I forthwith directed the attorney of the United States residing at New Orleans to inquire into the facts and the extent of the pecuniary loss sustained by the consul, with the intention of laying them before you, that you might make provision for such indemnity to him as a just regard for the honor of the nation and the respect which is due to a friendly power might, in your judgment, seem to require. The correspondence upon this subject between the Secretary of State and Her Catholic Majesty's minister plenipotentiary is herewith transmitted.

The occurrence at New Orleans has led me to give my attention to the state of our laws in regard to foreign ambassadors, ministers, and consuls. I think the legislation of the country is deficient in not providing sufficiently either for the protection or the punishment of consuls. I therefore recommend the subject to the consideration of Congress.

Your attention is again invited to the question of reciprocal trade between the United States and Canada and other British possessions near our frontier. Overtures for a convention upon this subject have been received from Her Britannic Majesty's minister plenipotentiary, but it seems to be in many respects preferable that the matter should be regulated by reciprocal legislation. Documents are laid before you showing the terms which the British Government is willing to offer and the measures which it may adopt if some arrangement upon this subject shall not be made.

From the accompanying copy of a note from the British legation at Washington and the reply of the Department of State thereto it will appear that Her Britannic Majesty's Government is desirous that a part of the boundary line between Oregon and the British possessions should be authoritatively marked out, and that an intention was expressed to apply to Congress for an appropriation to defray the expense thereof on the part of the United States. Your attention to this subject is accordingly invited and a proper appropriation recommended.

A convention for the adjustment of claims of citizens of the United States against Portugal has been concluded and the ratifications have been exchanged. The first installment of the amount to be paid by Portugal fell due on the 30th of September last and has been paid.

The President of the French Republic, according to the provisions of the convention, has been selected as arbiter in the case of the *General Armstrong*, and has signified that he accepts the trust and the high satisfaction he feels in acting as the common friend of two nations with which France is united by sentiments of sincere and lasting amity.

The Turkish Government has expressed its thanks for the kind reception given to the Sultan's agent, Amin Bey, on the occasion of his recent visit to the United States. On the 28th of February last a dispatch was addressed by the Secretary of State to Mr. Marsh, the American minister at Constantinople, instructing him to ask of the Turkish Government permission for the Hungarians then imprisoned within the dominions of the Sublime Porte to remove to this country. On the 3d of March last both Houses of Congress passed a resolution requesting the President to authorize the employment of a public vessel to convey to this country Louis Kossuth and his associates in captivity.

The instruction above referred to was complied with, and the Turkish Government having released Governor Kossuth and his companions from prison, on the 10th of September last they embarked on board of the United States steam frigate *Mississippi*, which was selected to carry into effect the resolution of Congress. Governor Kossuth left the *Mississippi* at Gibraltar for the purpose of making a visit to England, and may shortly be expected in New York. By communications to the Department of State he has expressed his grateful acknowledgments for the interposition of this Government in behalf of himself and his associates. This country has been justly regarded as a safe asylum for those whom political events have exiled from their own homes in Europe, and it is recommended to Congress to consider in what manner Governor Kossuth and his companions, brought hither by its authority, shall be received and treated.

It is earnestly to be hoped that the differences which have for some time past been pending between the Government of the French Republic and that of the Sandwich Islands may be peaceably and durably adjusted so as to secure the independence of those islands. Long before the events which have of late imparted so much importance to the possessions of the United States on the Pacific we acknowledged the independence of the Hawaiian Government. This Government was first in taking that step, and several of the leading powers of Europe immediately followed. We were influenced in this measure by the existing and prospective importance of the islands as a place of refuge and refreshment for our vessels engaged in the whale fishery, and by the consideration that they lie in the course of the great trade which must at no distant day be carried on between the western coast of North America and eastern Asia.

We were also influenced by a desire that those islands should not pass under the control of any other great maritime state, but should remain in an independent condition, and so be accessible and useful to the commerce of all nations. I need not say that the importance of these considerations has been greatly enhanced by the sudden and vast development which the interests of the United States have attained in California and Oregon, and the policy heretofore adopted in regard to those islands will be steadily pursued.

It is gratifying, not only to those who consider the commercial interests of nations, but also to all who favor the progress of knowledge and the diffusion of religion, to see a community emerge from a savage state and attain such a degree of civilization in those distant seas.

It is much to be deplored that the internal tranquillity of the Mexican Republic should again be seriously disturbed, for since the peace between that Republic and the United States it had enjoyed such comparative repose that the most favorable anticipations for the future might with a degree of confidence have been indulged. These, however, have been thwarted by the recent outbreak in the State of Tamaulipas, on the right bank of the Rio Bravo. Having received information that persons from the United States had taken part in the insurrection, and apprehending that their example might be followed by others, I caused orders to be issued for the purpose of preventing any hostile expeditions against Mexico from being set on foot in violation of the laws of the United States. I likewise issued a proclamation upon the subject, a copy of which is herewith laid before you. This appeared to be rendered imperative by the obligations of treaties and the general duties of good neighborhood.

In my last annual message I informed Congress that citizens of the United States had undertaken the connection of the two oceans by means of a railroad across the Isthmus of Tehuantepec, under a grant of the Mexican Government to a citizen of that Republic, and that this enterprise would probably be prosecuted with energy whenever Mexico should consent to such stipulations with the Government of the United States as should impart a feeling of security to those who should invest their property in the enterprise.

A convention between the two Governments for the accomplishment of that end has been ratified by this Government, and only awaits the decision of the Congress and the Executive of that Republic.

Some unexpected difficulties and delays have arisen in the ratification of that convention by Mexico, but it is to be presumed that her decision will be governed by just and enlightened views, as well of the general importance of the object as of her own interests and obligations.

In negotiating upon this important subject this Government has had in view one, and only one, object. That object has been, and is, the construction or attainment of a passage from ocean to ocean, the shortest and the best for travelers and merchandise, and equally open to all the world. It has sought to obtain no territorial acquisition, nor any advantages peculiar to itself; and it would see with the greatest regret that Mexico should oppose any obstacle to the accomplishment of an enterprise which promises so much convenience to the whole commercial world and such eminent advantages to Mexico herself. Impressed with these sentiments and these convictions, the Government will continue to exert all proper efforts to bring about the necessary arrangement with the Republic of Mexico for the speedy completion of the work.

For some months past the Republic of Nicaragua has been the theater of one of those civil convulsions from which the cause of free institutions and the general prosperity and social progress of the States of Central America have so often and so severely suffered. Until quiet shall have been restored and a government apparently stable shall have been organized, no advance can prudently be made in disposing of the questions pending between the two countries.

I am happy to announce that an interoceanic communication from the mouth of the St. John to the Pacific has been so far accomplished as that passengers have actually traversed it and merchandise has been transported over it, and when the canal shall have been completed according to the original plan the means of communication will be further improved. It is understood that a considerable part of the railroad across the Isthmus of Panama has been completed, and that the mail and passengers will in future be conveyed thereon.

Whichever of the several routes between the two oceans may ultimately prove most eligible for travelers to and from the different States on the Atlantic and Gulf of Mexico and our coast on the Pacific, there is little reason to doubt that all of them will be useful to the public, and will liberally reward that individual enterprise by which alone they have been or are expected to be carried into effect.

Peace has been concluded between the contending parties in the island of St. Domingo, and, it is hoped, upon a durable basis. Such is the extent of our commercial relations with that island that the United States can not fail to feel a strong interest in its tranquillity.

The office of commissioner to China remains unfilled. Several persons have been appointed, and the place has been offered to others, all of whom have declined its acceptance on the ground of the inadequacy of the compensation. The annual allowance by law is $6,000, and there is no provision for any outfit. I earnestly recommend the consideration of this subject to Congress. Our commerce with China is highly important, and is becoming more and more so in consequence of the increasing intercourse between our ports on the Pacific Coast and eastern Asia. China is understood to be a country in which living is very expensive, and I know of no reason why the American commissioner sent thither should not be placed, in regard to compensation, on an equal footing with ministers who represent this country at the Courts of Europe.

By reference to the report of the Secretary of the Treasury it will be seen that the aggregate receipts for the last fiscal year amounted to $52,312,979.87, which, with the balance in the Treasury on the 1st July, 1850, gave as the available means for the year the sum of $58,917,-524.36.

The total expenditures for the same period were $48,005,878.68. The total imports for the year ending June 30, 1851, were $215,725,995, of which there were in specie $4,967,901. The exports for the same period were $217,517,130, of which there were of domestic products $178,546,555; foreign goods reexported, $9,738,695; specie, $29,231,880.

Since the 1st of December last the payments in cash on account of the public debt, exclusive of interest, have amounted to $7,501,456.56, which, however, includes the sum of $3,242,400, paid under the twelfth article of the treaty with Mexico, and the further sum of $2,591,213.45, being the amount of awards to American citizens under the late treaty with Mexico, for which the issue of stock was authorized, but which was paid in cash from the Treasury.

The public debt on the 20th ultimo, exclusive of the stock authorized to be issued to Texas by the act of 9th September, 1850, was $62,560,-395.26.

The receipts for the next fiscal year are estimated at $51,800,000, which, with the probable unappropriated balance in the Treasury on the 30th June next, will give as the probable available means for that year the sum of $63,258,743.09.

It has been deemed proper, in view of the large expenditures consequent upon the acquisition of territory from Mexico, that the estimates for the next fiscal year should be laid before Congress in such manner as to distinguish the expenditures so required from the otherwise ordinary demands upon the Treasury.

The total expenditures for the next fiscal year are estimated at $42,-892,299.19, of which there is required for the ordinary purposes of the Government, other than those consequent upon the acquisition of our new territories, and deducting the payments on account of the public debt, the sum of $33,343,198.08, and for the purposes connected, directly or indirectly, with those territories and in the fulfillment of the obligations of the Government contracted in consequence of their acquisition the sum of $9,549,101.11.

If the views of the Secretary of the Treasury in reference to the expenditures required for these territories shall be met by corresponding action on the part of Congress, and appropriations made in accordance therewith, there will be an estimated unappropriated balance in the Treasury on the 30th June, 1853, of $20,366,443.90 wherewith to meet that portion of the public debt due on the 1st of July following, amounting to $6,237,931.35, as well as any appropriations which may be made beyond the estimates.

In thus referring to the estimated expenditures on account of our newly acquired territories, I may express the hope that Congress will concur with me in the desire that a liberal course of policy may be pursued toward them, and that every obligation, express or implied, entered into in consequence of their acquisition shall be fulfilled by the most liberal appropriations for that purpose.

The values of our domestic exports for the last fiscal year, as compared with those of the previous year, exhibit an increase of $43,646,322. At first view this condition of our trade with foreign nations would seem to present the most flattering hopes of its future prosperity. An examination of the details of our exports, however, will show that the increased value of our exports for the last fiscal year is to be found in the high price of cotton which prevailed during the first half of that year, which price has since declined about one-half.

The value of our exports of breadstuffs and provisions, which it was supposed the incentive of a low tariff and large importations from abroad would have greatly augmented, has fallen from $68,701,921 in 1847 to $26,051,373 in 1850 and to $21,948,653 in 1851, with a strong probability, amounting almost to a certainty, of a still further reduction in the current year.

The aggregate values of rice exported during the last fiscal year, as compared with the previous year, also exhibit a decrease, amounting to $460,917, which, with a decline in the values of the exports of tobacco for the same period, make an aggregate decrease in these two articles of $1,156,751.

The policy which dictated a low rate of duties on foreign merchandise, it was thought by those who promoted and established it, would tend to benefit the farming population of this country by increasing the demand and raising the price of agricultural products in foreign markets.

The foregoing facts, however, seem to show incontestably that no such result has followed the adoption of this policy. On the contrary, notwithstanding the repeal of the restrictive corn laws in England, the foreign demand for the products of the American farmer has steadily declined, since the short crops and consequent famine in a portion of Europe have been happily replaced by full crops and comparative abundance of food.

It will be seen by recurring to the commercial statistics for the past year that the value of our domestic exports has been increased in the single item of raw cotton by $40,000,000 over the value of that export for the year preceding. This is not due to any increased general demand for that article, but to the short crop of the preceding year, which created an increased demand and an augmented price for the crop of last year. Should the cotton crop now going forward to market be only equal in quantity to that of the year preceding and be sold at the present prices, then there would be a falling off in the value of our exports for the present fiscal year of at least $40,000,000 compared with the amount exported for the year ending 30th June, 1851.

The production of gold in California for the past year seems to promise a large supply of that metal from that quarter for some time to come. This large annual increase of the currency of the world must be attended with its usual results. These have been already partially disclosed in the enhancement of prices and a rising spirit of speculation and adventure, tending to overtrading, as well at home as abroad. Unless some salutary check shall be given to these tendencies it is to be feared that importations of foreign goods beyond a healthy demand in this country will lead to a sudden drain of the precious metals from us, bringing with it, as it has done in former times, the most disastrous consequences to the business and capital of the American people.

The exports of specie to liquidate our foreign debt during the past fiscal year have been $24,263,979 over the amount of specie imported. The exports of specie during the first quarter of the present fiscal year have been $14,651,827. Should specie continue to be exported at this rate for the remaining three quarters of this year, it will drain from our metallic currency during the year ending 30th June, 1852, the enormous amount of $58,607,308.

In the present prosperous condition of the national finances it will become the duty of Congress to consider the best mode of paying off the public debt. If the present and anticipated surplus in the Treasury should not be absorbed by appropriations of an extraordinary character, this surplus should be employed in such way and under such restrictions as Congress may enact in extinguishing the outstanding debt of the nation.

By reference to the act of Congress approved 9th September, 1850, it will be seen that, in consideration of certain concessions by the State of Texas, it is provided that—

The United States shall pay to the State of Texas the sum of $10,000,000 in a stock bearing 5 per cent interest and redeemable at the end of fourteen years, the interest payable half-yearly at the Treasury of the United States.

In the same section of the law it is further provided—

That no more than five millions of said stock shall be issued until the creditors of the State holding bonds and other certificates of stock of Texas, *for which duties on imports were specially* pledged, shall first file at the Treasury of the United States releases of all claims against the United States for or on account of said bonds or certificates, in such form as shall be prescribed by the Secretary of the Treasury and approved by the President of the United States.

The form of release thus provided for has been prescribed by the Secretary of the Treasury and approved. It has been published in all the leading newspapers in the commercial cities of the United States, and all persons holding claims of the kind specified in the foregoing proviso were required to file their releases (in the form thus prescribed) in the Treasury of the United States on or before the 1st day of October, 1851. Although this publication has been continued from the 25th day of March, 1851, yet up to the 1st of October last comparatively few releases had been filed by the creditors of Texas.

The authorities of the State of Texas, at the request of the Secretary of the Treasury, have furnished a schedule of the public debt of that State created prior to her admission into the Union, with a copy of the laws under which each class was contracted.

I have, from the documents furnished by the State of Texas, determined the classes of claims which in my judgment fall within the provisions of the act of Congress of the 9th of September, 1850.

On being officially informed of the acceptance by Texas of the propositions contained in the act referred to I caused the stock to be prepared, and the five millions which are to be issued unconditionally, bearing an interest of 5 per cent from the 1st day of January, 1851, have been for some time ready to be delivered to the State of Texas. The authorities of Texas up to the present time have not authorized anyone to receive this stock, and it remains in the Treasury Department subject to the order of Texas.

The releases required by law to be deposited in the Treasury not having been filed there, the remaining five millions have not been issued. This last amount of the stock will be withheld from Texas until the conditions upon which it is to be delivered shall be complied with by the creditors of that State, unless Congress shall otherwise direct by a modification of the law.

In my last annual message, to which I respectfully refer, I stated briefly the reasons which induced me to recommend a modification of the present tariff by converting the *ad valorem* into a specific duty wherever the article imported was of such a character as to permit it, and that such a discrimination should be made in favor of the industrial pursuits of our own country as to encourage home production without excluding foreign competition.

The numerous frauds which continue to be practiced upon the revenue by false invoices and undervaluations constitute an unanswerable reason for adopting specific instead of *ad valorem* duties in all cases where the nature of the commodity does not forbid it. A striking illustration of these frauds will be exhibited in the report of the Secretary of the Treasury, showing the custom-house valuation of articles imported under a former law, subject to specific duties, when there was no inducement to undervaluation, and the custom-house valuations of the same articles under the present system of *ad valorem* duties, so greatly reduced as to leave no doubt of the existence of the most flagrant abuses under the existing laws. This practical evasion of the present law, combined with the languishing condition of some of the great interests of the country, caused by overimportations and consequent depressed prices, and with the failure in obtaining a foreign market for our increasing surplus of breadstuffs and provisions, has induced me again to recommend a modification of the existing tariff.

The report of the Secretary of the Interior, which accompanies this communication, will present a condensed statement of the operations of that important Department of the Government.

It will be seen that the cash sales of the public lands exceed those of the preceding year, and that there is reason to anticipate a still further increase, notwithstanding the large donations which have been made to many of the States and the liberal grants to individuals as a reward for military services.   This fact furnishes very gratifying evidence of the growing wealth and prosperity of our country.

Suitable measures have been adopted for commencing the survey of the public lands in California and Oregon. Surveying parties have been organized and some progress has been made in establishing the principal base and meridian lines.   But further legislation and additional appropriations will be necessary before the proper subdivisions can be made and the general land system extended over those remote parts of our territory.

On the 3d of March last an act was passed providing for the appointment of three commissioners to settle private land claims in California. Three persons were immediately appointed, all of whom, however, declined accepting the office in consequence of the inadequacy of the compensation.   Others were promptly selected, who for the same reason also declined, and it was not until late in the season that the services of suitable persons could be secured.   A majority of the commissioners convened in this city on the 10th of September last, when detailed instructions were given to them in regard to their duties.   Their first meeting for the transaction of business will be held in San Francisco on the 8th day of the present month.

I have thought it proper to refer to these facts, not only to explain the causes of the delay in filling the commission, but to call your attention to the propriety of increasing the compensation of the commissioners. The office is one of great labor and responsibility, and the compensation should be such as to command men of a high order of talents and the most unquestionable integrity.

The proper disposal of the mineral lands of California is a subject surrounded by great difficulties.   In my last annual message I recommended the survey and sale of them in small parcels under such restrictions as would effectually guard against monopoly and speculation; but upon further information, and in deference to the opinions of persons familiar with the subject, I am inclined to change that recommendation and to advise that they be permitted to remain as at present, a common field, open to the enterprise and industry of all our citizens, until further experience shall have developed the best policy to be ultimately adopted in regard to them.   It is safer to suffer the inconveniences that now exist for a short period than by premature legislation to fasten on the country a system founded in error, which may place the whole subject beyond the future control of Congress.

The agricultural lands should, however, be surveyed and brought into market with as little delay as possible, that the titles may become settled and the inhabitants stimulated to make permanent improvements and enter on the ordinary pursuits of life.   To effect these objects it is desirable that the necessary provision be made by law for the establishment of land offices in California and Oregon and for the efficient prosecution of the surveys at an early day.

Some difficulties have occurred in organizing the Territorial governments of New Mexico and Utah, and when more accurate information shall be obtained of the causes a further communication will be made on that subject.

In my last annual communication to Congress I recommended the establishment of an agricultural bureau, and I take this occasion again to invoke your favorable consideration of the subject.

Agriculture may justly be regarded as the great interest of our people. Four-fifths of our active population are employed in the cultivation of the soil, and the rapid expansion of our settlements over new territory is daily adding to the number of those engaged in that vocation. Justice and sound policy, therefore, alike require that the Government should use all the means authorized by the Constitution to promote the interests and welfare of that important class of our fellow-citizens. And yet it is a singular fact that whilst the manufacturing and commercial interests have engaged the attention of Congress during a large portion of every session and our statutes abound in provisions for their protection and encouragement, little has yet been done directly for the advancement of agriculture. It is time that this reproach to our legislation should be removed, and I sincerely hope that the present Congress will not close their labors without adopting efficient means to supply the omissions of those who have preceded them.

An agricultural bureau, charged with the duty of collecting and disseminating correct information as to the best modes of cultivation and of the most effectual means of preserving and restoring the fertility of the soil and of procuring and distributing seeds and plants and other vegetable productions, with instructions in regard to the soil, climate, and treatment best adapted to their growth, could not fail to be, in the language of Washington in his last annual message to Congress, a "very cheap instrument of immense national benefit."

Regarding the act of Congress approved 28th September, 1850, granting bounty lands to persons who had been engaged in the military service of the country, as a great measure of national justice and munificence, an anxious desire has been felt by the officers intrusted with its immediate execution to give prompt effect to its provisions. All the means within their control were therefore brought into requisition to expedite the adjudication of claims, and I am gratified to be able to state that near 100,000 applications have been considered and about 70,000 warrants issued within the short space of nine months. If adequate provision be made by law to carry into effect the recommendations of the Department, it is confidently expected that before the close of the next fiscal year all who are entitled to the benefits of the act will have received their warrants.

The Secretary of the Interior has suggested in his report various amendments of the laws relating to pensions and bounty lands for the purpose of more effectually guarding against abuses and frauds on the Government, to all of which I invite your particular attention.

The large accessions to our Indian population consequent upon the acquisition of New Mexico and California and the extension of our settlements into Utah and Oregon have given increased interest and importance to our relations with the aboriginal race.

No material change has taken place within the last year in the condition and prospects of the Indian tribes who reside in the Northwestern Territory and west of the Mississippi River. We are at peace with all of them, and it will be a source of pleasure to you to learn that they are gradually advancing in civilization and the pursuits of social life.

Along the Mexican frontier and in California and Oregon there have been occasional manifestations of unfriendly feeling and some depredations committed. I am satisfied, however, that they resulted more from the destitute and starving condition of the Indians than from any settled hostility toward the whites. As the settlements of our citizens progress toward them, the game, upon which they mainly rely for subsistence, is driven off or destroyed, and the only alternative left to them is starvation or plunder. It becomes us to consider, in view of this condition of things, whether justice and humanity, as well as an enlightened economy, do not require that instead of seeking to punish them for offenses which are the result of our own policy toward them we should not provide for their immediate wants and encourage them to engage in agriculture and to rely on their labor instead of the chase for the means of support.

Various important treaties have been negotiated with different tribes during the year, by which their title to large and valuable tracts of country has been extinguished, all of which will at the proper time be submitted to the Senate for ratification.

The joint commission under the treaty of Guadalupe Hidalgo has been actively engaged in running and marking the boundary line between the United States and Mexico. It was stated in the last annual report of the Secretary of the Interior that the initial point on the Pacific and the point of junction of the Gila with the Colorado River had been determined and the intervening line, about 150 miles in length, run and marked by temporary monuments. Since that time a monument of marble has been erected at the initial point, and permanent landmarks of iron have been placed at suitable distances along the line.

The initial point on the Rio Grande has also been fixed by the commissioners, at latitude 32° 22', and at the date of the last communication the survey of the line had been made thence westward about 150 miles to the neighborhood of the copper mines.

The commission on our part was at first organized on a scale which experience proved to be unwieldy and attended with unnecessary expense. Orders have therefore been issued for the reduction of the number of persons employed within the smallest limits consistent with the safety of those engaged in the service and the prompt and efficient execution of their important duties.

Returns have been received from all the officers engaged in taking the census in the States and Territories except California. The superintendent employed to make the enumeration in that State has not yet made his full report, from causes, as he alleges, beyond his control. This failure is much to be regretted, as it has prevented the Secretary of the Interior from making the decennial apportionment of Representatives among the States, as required by the act approved May 23, 1850. It is hoped, however, that the returns will soon be received, and no time will then be lost in making the necessary apportionment and in transmitting the certificates required by law.

The Superintendent of the Seventh Census is diligently employed, under the direction of the Secretary of the Interior, in classifying and arranging in tabular form all the statistical information derived from the returns of the marshals, and it is believed that when the work shall be completed it will exhibit a more perfect view of the population, wealth, occupations, and social condition of a great country than has ever been presented to the world. The value of such a work as the basis of enlightened legislation can hardly be overestimated, and I earnestly hope that Congress will lose no time in making the appropriations necessary to complete the classifications and to publish the results in a style worthy of the subject and of our national character.

The want of a uniform fee bill, prescribing the compensation to be allowed district attorneys, clerks, marshals, and commissioners in civil and criminal cases, is the cause of much vexation, injustice, and complaint. I would recommend a thorough revision of the laws on the whole subject and the adoption of a tariff of fees which, as far as practicable, should be uniform, and prescribe a specific compensation for every service which the officer may be required to perform. This subject will be fully presented in the report of the Secretary of the Interior.

In my last annual message I gave briefly my reasons for believing that you possessed the constitutional power to improve the harbors of our Great Lakes and seacoast and the navigation of our principal rivers, and recommended that appropriations should be made for completing such works as had already been commenced and for commencing such others as might seem to the wisdom of Congress to be of public and general importance. Without repeating the reasons then urged, I deem it my duty again to call your attention to this important subject. The works on many of the harbors were left in an unfinished state, and consequently exposed to the action of the elements, which is fast destroying them. Great numbers of lives and vast amounts of property are annually lost for want of safe and convenient harbors on the Lakes. None but those who have been exposed to that dangerous navigation can fully appreciate the importance of this subject. The whole Northwest appeals to you for relief, and I trust their appeal will receive due consideration at your hands.

The same is in a measure true in regard to some of the harbors and inlets on the seacoast.

The unobstructed navigation of our large rivers is of equal importance. Our settlements are now extending to the sources of the great rivers which empty into and form a part of the Mississippi, and the value of the public lands in those regions would be greatly enhanced by freeing the navigation of those waters from obstructions. In view, therefore, of this great interest, I deem it my duty again to urge upon Congress to make such appropriations for these improvements as they may deem necessary.

The surveys of the Delta of the Mississippi, with a view to the prevention of the overflows that have proved so disastrous to that region of country, have been nearly completed, and the reports thereof are now in course of preparation and will shortly be laid before you.

The protection of our southwestern frontier and of the adjacent Mexican States against the Indian tribes within our border has claimed my earnest and constant attention. Congress having failed at the last session to adopt my recommendation that an additional regiment of mounted men specially adapted to that service should be raised, all that remained to be done was to make the best use of the means at my disposal. Accordingly, all the troops adapted to that service that could properly be spared from other quarters have been concentrated on that frontier and officers of high reputation selected to command them. A new arrangement of the military posts has also been made, whereby the troops are brought nearer to the Mexican frontier and to the tribes they are intended to overawe.

Sufficient time has not yet elapsed to realize all the benefits that are expected to result from these arrangements, but I have every reason to hope that they will effectually check their marauding expeditions. The nature of the country, which furnishes little for the support of an army and abounds in places of refuge and concealment, is remarkably well adapted to this predatory warfare, and we can scarcely hope that any military force, combined with the greatest vigilance, can entirely suppress it.

By the treaty of Guadalupe Hidalgo we are bound to protect the territory of Mexico against the incursions of the savage tribes within our border "with equal diligence and energy" as if the same were made within our territory or against our citizens. I have endeavored to comply as far as possible with this provision of the treaty. Orders have been given to the officers commanding on that frontier to consider the Mexican territory and its inhabitants as equally with our own entitled to their protection, and to make all their plans and arrangements with a view to the attainment of this object. Instructions have also been given to the Indian commissioners and agents among these tribes in all treaties to make the clauses designed for the protection of our own citizens apply also to those of Mexico. I have no reason to doubt that these instructions have been fully carried into effect; nevertheless, it is probable that in spite of all our efforts some of the neighboring States of Mexico may have suffered, as our own have, from depredations by the Indians.

To the difficulties of defending our own territory, as above mentioned, are superadded, in defending that of Mexico, those that arise from its remoteness, from the fact that we have no right to station our troops within her limits and that there is no efficient military force on the Mexican side to cooperate with our own. So long as this shall continue to be the case the number and activity of our troops will rather increase than diminish the evil, as the Indians will naturally turn toward that country where they encounter the least resistance. Yet these troops are necessary to subdue them and to compel them to make and observe treaties. Until this shall have been done neither country will enjoy any security from their attacks.

The Indians in California, who had previously appeared of a peaceable character and disposed to cultivate the friendship of the whites, have recently committed several acts of hostility. As a large portion of the reenforcements sent to the Mexican frontier were drawn from the Pacific, the military force now stationed there is considered entirely inadequate to its defense. It can not be increased, however, without an increase of the Army, and I again recommend that measure as indispensable to the protection of the frontier.

I invite your attention to the suggestions on this subject and on others connected with his Department in the report of the Secretary of War.

The appropriations for the support of the Army during the current fiscal year ending 30th June next were reduced far below the estimate submitted by the Department. The consequence of this reduction is a considerable deficiency, to which I invite your early attention.

The expenditures of that Department for the year ending 30th June last were $9,060,268.58. The estimates for the year commencing 1st July next and ending June 30, 1853, are $7,898,775.83, showing a reduction of $1,161,492.75.

The board of commissioners to whom the management of the affairs of the military asylum created by the act of 3d March last was intrusted have selected a site for the establishment of an asylum in the vicinity of this city, which has been approved by me subject to the production of a satisfactory title.

The report of the Secretary of the Navy will exhibit the condition of the public service under the supervision of that Department. Our naval force afloat during the present year has been actively and usefully employed in giving protection to our widely extended and increasing commerce and interests in the various quarters of the globe, and our flag has everywhere afforded the security and received the respect inspired by the justice and liberality of our intercourse and the dignity and power of the nation.

The expedition commanded by Lieutenant De Haven, dispatched in search of the British commander Sir John Franklin and his companions in the Arctic Seas, returned to New York in the month of October, after having undergone great peril and suffering from an unknown and dangerous navigation and the rigors of a northern climate, without any satisfactory information of the objects of their search, but with new contributions to science and navigation from the unfrequented polar regions. The officers and men of the expedition having been all volunteers for this service and having so conducted it as to meet the entire approbation of the Government, it is suggested, as an act of grace and generosity, that the same allowance of extra pay and emoluments be extended to them that were made to the officers and men of like rating in the late exploring expedition to the South Seas.

I earnestly recommend to your attention the necessity of reorganizing the naval establishment, apportioning and fixing the number of officers in each grade, providing some mode of promotion to the higher grades of the Navy having reference to merit and capacity rather than seniority or date of entry into the service, and for retiring from the effective list upon reduced pay those who may be incompetent to the performance of active duty. As a measure of economy, as well as of efficiency, in this arm of the service, the provision last mentioned is eminently worthy of your consideration.

The determination of the questions of relative rank between the sea officers and civil officers of the Navy, and between officers of the Army and Navy, in the various grades of each, will also merit your attention. The failure to provide any substitute when corporal punishment was abolished for offenses in the Navy has occasioned the convening of numerous courts-martial upon the arrival of vessels in port, and is believed to have had an injurious effect upon the discipline and efficiency of the service. To moderate punishment from one grade to another is among the humane reforms of the age, but to abolish one of severity, which applied so generally to offenses on shipboard, and provide nothing in its stead is to suppose a progress of improvement in every individual among seamen which is not assumed by the Legislature in respect to any other class of men. It is hoped that Congress, in the ample opportunity afforded by the present session, will thoroughly investigate this important subject, and establish such modes of determining guilt and such gradations of punishment as are consistent with humanity and the personal rights of individuals, and at the same time shall insure the most energetic and efficient performance of duty and the suppression of crime in our ships of war.

The stone dock in the navy-yard at New York, which was ten years in process of construction, has been so far finished as to be surrendered up to the authorities of the yard. The dry dock at Philadelphia is reported as completed, and is expected soon to be tested and delivered over to the agents of the Government. That at Portsmouth, N. H., is also nearly ready for delivery; and a contract has been concluded, agreeably to the act of Congress at its last session, for a floating sectional dock on the Bay of San Francisco. I invite your attention to the recommendation of the Department touching the establishment of a navy-yard in conjunction with this dock on the Pacific. Such a station is highly necessary to the convenience and effectiveness of our fleet in that ocean, which must be expected to increase with the growth of commerce and the rapid extension of our whale fisheries over its waters.

The Naval Academy at Annapolis, under a revised and improved system of regulations, now affords opportunities of education and instruction to the pupils quite equal, it is believed, for professional improvement, to those enjoyed by the cadets in the Military Academy. A large class of acting midshipmen was received at the commencement of the last academic term, and a practice ship has been attached to the institution to afford the amplest means for regular instruction in seamanship, as well as for cruises during the vacations of three or four months in each year.

The advantages of science in nautical affairs have rarely been more strikingly illustrated than in the fact, stated in the report of the Navy Department, that by means of the wind and current charts projected and prepared by Lieutenant Maury, the Superintendent of the Naval Observatory, the passage from the Atlantic to the Pacific ports of our country has been shortened by about forty days.

The estimates for the support of the Navy and Marine Corps the ensuing fiscal year will be found to be $5,856,472.19, the estimates for the current year being $5,900,621.

The estimates for special objects under the control of this Department amount to $2,684,220.89, against $2,210,980 for the present year, the increase being occasioned by the additional mail service on the Pacific Coast and the construction of the dock in California, authorized at the last session of Congress, and some slight additions under the head of improvements and repairs in navy-yards, buildings, and machinery.

I deem it of much importance to a just economy and a correct understanding of naval expenditures that there should be an entire separation of the appropriations for the support of the naval service proper from those for permanent improvements at navy-yards and stations and from ocean steam mail service and other special objects assigned to the supervision of this Department.

The report of the Postmaster-General, herewith communicated, presents an interesting view of the progress, operations, and condition of his Department.

At the close of the last fiscal year the length of mail routes within the United States was 196,290 miles, the annual transportation thereon 53,-272,252 miles, and the annual cost of such transportation $3,421,754.

The length of the foreign mail routes is estimated at 18,349 miles and the annual transportation thereon at 615,206 miles. The annual cost of this service is $1,472,187, of which $448,937 are paid by the Post-Office Department and $1,023,250 are paid through the Navy Department.

The annual transportation within the United States, excluding the service in California and Oregon, which is now for the first time reported and embraced in the tabular statements of the Department, exceeds that of the preceding year 6,162,855 miles, at an increased cost of $547,110.

The whole number of post-offices in the United States on the 30th day of June last was 19,796. There were 1,698 post-offices established and 256 discontinued during the year.

The gross revenues of the Department for the fiscal year, including the appropriations for the franked matter of Congress, of the Departments, and officers of Government, and excluding the foreign postages collected for and payable to the British post-office, amounted to $6,727,-866.78.

The expenditures for the same period, excluding $20,599.49, paid under an award of the Auditor, in pursuance of a resolution of the last Congress, for mail service on the Ohio and Mississippi rivers in 1832 and 1833, and the amount paid to the British post-office for foreign postages collected for and payable to that office, amounted to $6,024,566.79, leaving a balance of revenue over the proper expenditures of the year of $703,299.99.

The receipts for postages during the year, excluding the foreign postages collected for and payable to the British post-office, amounted to $6,345,747.21, being an increase of $997,610.79, or 18.65 per cent, over the like receipts for the preceding year.

The reduction of postage under the act of March last did not take effect until the commencement of the present fiscal year. The accounts for the first quarter under the operation of the reduced rates will not be settled before January next, and no reliable estimate of the receipts for the present year can yet be made. It is believed, however, that they will fall far short of those of the last year. The surplus of the revenues now on hand is, however, so large that no further appropriation from the Treasury in aid of the revenues of the Department is required for the current fiscal year, but an additional appropriation for the year ending June 30, 1853, will probably be found necessary when the receipts of the first two quarters of the fiscal year are fully ascertained.

In his last annual report the Postmaster-General recommended a reduction of postage to rates which he deemed as low as could be prudently adopted unless Congress was prepared to appropriate from the Treasury for the support of the Department a sum more than equivalent to the mail services performed by it for the Government. The recommendations of the Postmaster-General in respect to letter postage, except on letters from and to California and Oregon, were substantially adopted by the last Congress. He now recommends adherence to the present letter rates and advises against a further reduction until justified by the revenue of the Department.

He also recommends that the rates of postage on printed matter be so revised as to render them more simple and more uniform in their operation upon all classes of printed matter. I submit the recommendations of the report to your favorable consideration.

The public statutes of the United States have now been accumulating for more than sixty years, and, interspersed with private acts, are scattered through numerous volumes, and, from the cost of the whole, have become almost inaccessible to the great mass of the community. They also exhibit much of the incongruity and imperfection of hasty legislation. As it seems to be generally conceded that there is no "common law" of the United States to supply the defects of their legislation, it is most important that that legislation should be as perfect as possible, defining every power intended to be conferred, every crime intended to be made punishable, and prescribing the punishment to be inflicted. In addition to some particular cases spoken of more at length, the whole criminal code is now lamentably defective. Some offenses are imperfectly described and others are entirely omitted, so that flagrant crimes may be committed with impunity. The scale of punishment is not in all cases graduated according to the degree and nature of the offense, and is often rendered more unequal by the different modes of imprisonment or penitentiary confinement in the different States.

Many laws of a permanent character have been introduced into appropriation bills, and it is often difficult to determine whether the particular clause expires with the temporary act of which it is a part or continues in force. It has also frequently happened that enactments and provisions of law have been introduced into bills with the title or general subject of which they have little or no connection or relation. In this mode of legislation so many enactments have been heaped upon each other, and often with but little consideration, that in many instances it is difficult to search out and determine what is the law.

The Government of the United States is emphatically a government of written laws. The statutes should therefore, as far as practicable, not only be made accessible to all, but be expressed in language so plain and simple as to be understood by all and arranged in such method as to give perspicuity to every subject. Many of the States have revised their public acts with great and manifest benefit, and I recommend that provision be made by law for the appointment of a commission to revise the public statutes of the United States, arranging them in order, supplying deficiencies, correcting incongruities, simplifying their language, and reporting them to Congress for its action.

An act of Congress approved 30th September, 1850, contained a provision for the extension of the Capitol according to such plan as might be approved by the President, and appropriated $100,000 to be expended under his direction by such architect as he should appoint to execute the same. On examining the various plans which had been submitted by different architects in pursuance of an advertisement by a committee of the Senate no one was found to be entirely satisfactory, and it was therefore deemed advisable to combine and adopt the advantages of several.

The great object to be accomplished was to make such an addition as would afford ample and convenient halls for the deliberations of the two Houses of Congress, with sufficient accommodations for spectators and suitable apartments for the committees and officers of the two branches of the Legislature. It was also desirable not to mar the harmony and beauty of the present structure, which, as a specimen of architecture, is so universally admired. Keeping these objects in view, I concluded to make the addition by wings, detached from the present building, yet connected with it by corridors. This mode of enlargement will leave the present Capitol uninjured and afford great advantages for ventilation and the admission of light, and will enable the work to progress without interrupting the deliberations of Congress. To carry this plan into effect I have appointed an experienced and competent architect. The corner stone was laid on the 4th day of July last with suitable ceremonies, since which time the work has advanced with commendable rapidity, and the foundations of both wings are now nearly complete.

I again commend to your favorable regard the interests of the District of Columbia, and deem it only necessary to remind you that although its inhabitants have no voice in the choice of Representatives in Congress, they are not the less entitled to a just and liberal consideration in your legislation. My opinions on this subject were more fully expressed in my last annual communication.

Other subjects were brought to the attention of Congress in my last annual message, to which I would respectfully refer. But there was one of more than ordinary interest, to which I again invite your special attention. I allude to the recommendation for the appointment of a commission to settle private claims against the United States. Justice to individuals, as well as to the Government, imperatively demands that some more convenient and expeditious mode than an appeal to Congress should be adopted.

It is deeply to be regretted that in several instances officers of the Government, in attempting to execute the law for the return of fugitives from labor, have been openly resisted and their efforts frustrated and defeated by lawless and violent mobs; that in one case such resistance resulted in the death of an estimable citizen, and in others serious injury ensued to those officers and to individuals who were using their endeavors to sustain the laws. Prosecutions have been instituted against the alleged offenders so far as they could be identified, and are still pending. I have regarded it as my duty in these cases to give all aid legally in my power to the enforcement of the laws, and I shall continue to do so wherever and whenever their execution may be resisted.

The act of Congress for the return of fugitives from labor is one required and demanded by the express words of the Constitution.

The Constitution declares that—

No person held to service or labor in one State, under the laws thereof, escaping into another, shall, in consequence of any law or regulation therein, be discharged from such service or labor, but shall be delivered up on claim of the party to whom such service or labor may be due.

This constitutional provision is equally obligatory upon the legislative, the executive, and judicial departments of the Government, and upon every citizen of the United States.

Congress, however, must from necessity first act upon the subject by prescribing the proceedings necessary to ascertain that the person is a fugitive and the means to be used for his restoration to the claimant. This was done by an act passed during the first term of President Washington, which was amended by that enacted by the last Congress, and it now remains for the executive and judicial departments to take care that these laws be faithfully executed. This injunction of the Constitution is as peremptory and as binding as any other; it stands exactly on the same foundation as that clause which provides for the return of fugitives from justice, or that which declares that no bill of attainder or *ex post facto* law shall be passed, or that which provides for an equality of taxation according to the census, or the clause declaring that all duties shall be uniform throughout the United States, or the important provision that the trial of all crimes shall be by jury. These several articles and clauses of the Constitution, all resting on the same authority, must stand or fall together. Some objections have been urged against the details of the act for the return of fugitives from labor, but it is worthy of remark that the main opposition is aimed against the Constitution itself, and proceeds from persons and classes of persons many of whom declare their wish to see that Constitution overturned. They avow their hostility to any law which shall give full and practical effect to this requirement of the Constitution. Fortunately, the number of these persons is comparatively small, and is believed to be daily diminishing; but the issue which they present is one which involves the supremacy and even the existence of the Constitution.

Cases have heretofore arisen in which individuals have denied the binding authority of acts of Congress, and even States have proposed to nullify such acts upon the ground that the Constitution was the supreme law of the land, and that those acts of Congress were repugnant to that instrument; but nullification is now aimed not so much against particular laws as being inconsistent with the Constitution as against the Constitution itself, and it is not to be disguised that a spirit exists, and has been actively at work, to rend asunder this Union, which is our cherished inheritance from our Revolutionary fathers.

In my last annual message I stated that I considered the series of measures which had been adopted at the previous session in reference to the agitation growing out of the Territorial and slavery questions as a final settlement in principle and substance of the dangerous and exciting subjects which they embraced, and I recommended adherence to the adjustment established by those measures until time and experience should demonstrate the necessity of further legislation to guard against evasion or abuse. I was not induced to make this recommendation because I thought those measures perfect, for no human legislation can be perfect. Wide differences and jarring opinions can only be reconciled by yielding something on all sides, and this result had been reached after an angry conflict of many months, in which one part of the country was arrayed against another, and violent convulsion seemed to be imminent. Looking at the interests of the whole country, I felt it to be my duty to seize upon this compromise as the best that could be obtained amid conflicting interests and to insist upon it as a final settlement, to be adhered to by all who value the peace and welfare of the country. A year has now elapsed since that recommendation was made. To that recommendation I still adhere, and I congratulate you and the country upon the general acquiescence in these measures of peace which has been exhibited in all parts of the Republic, And not only is there this general acquiescence in these measures, but the spirit of conciliation which has been manifested in regard to them in all parts of the country has removed doubts and uncertainties in the minds of thousands of good men concerning the durability of our popular institutions and given renewed assurance that our liberty and our Union may subsist together for the benefit of this and all succeeding generations.

THIRD ANNUAL MESSAGE.

WASHINGTON, *December 6, 1852.*

Fellow-Citizens of the Senate and of the House of Representatives:

The brief space which has elapsed since the close of your last session has been marked by no extraordinary political event. The quadrennial election of Chief Magistrate has passed off with less than the usual excitement. However individuals and parties may have been disappointed in the result, it is, nevertheless, a subject of national congratulation that the choice has been effected by the independent suffrages of a free people, undisturbed by those influences which in other countries have too often affected the purity of popular elections.

Our grateful thanks are due to an all-merciful Providence, not only for staying the pestilence which in different forms has desolated some of our cities, but for crowning the labors of the husbandman with an abundant harvest and the nation generally with the blessings of peace and prosperity.

Within a few weeks the public mind has been deeply affected by the death of Daniel Webster, filling at his decease the office of Secretary of State. His associates in the executive government have sincerely sympathized with his family and the public generally on this mournful occasion. His commanding talents, his great political and professional eminence, his well-tried patriotism, and his long and faithful services in the most important public trusts have caused his death to be lamented throughout the country and have earned for him a lasting place in our history.

In the course of the last summer considerable anxiety was caused for a short time by an official intimation from the Government of Great Britain that orders had been given for the protection of the fisheries upon the coasts of the British Provinces in North America against the alleged encroachments of the fishing vessels of the United States and France. The shortness of this notice and the season of the year seemed to make it a matter of urgent importance. It was at first apprehended that an increased naval force had been ordered to the fishing grounds to carry into effect the British interpretation of those provisions in the convention of 1818 in reference to the true intent of which the two Governments differ. It was soon discovered that such was not the design of Great Britain, and satisfactory explanations of the real objects of the measure have been given both here and in London.

The unadjusted difference, however, between the two Governments as to the interpretation of the first article of the convention of 1818 is still a matter of importance. American fishing vessels, within nine or ten years, have been excluded from waters to which they had free access for twenty-five years after the negotiation of the treaty. In 1845 this exclusion was relaxed so far as concerns the Bay of Fundy, but the just and liberal intention of the home Government, in compliance with what we think the true construction of the convention, to open all the other outer bays to our fishermen was abandoned in consequence of the opposition of the colonies. Notwithstanding this, the United States have, since the Bay of Fundy was reopened to our fishermen in 1845, pursued the most liberal course toward the colonial fishing interests. By the revenue law of 1846 the duties on colonial fish entering our ports were very greatly reduced, and by the warehousing act it is allowed to be entered in bond without payment of duty. In this way colonial fish has acquired the monopoly of the export trade in our market and is entering to some extent into the home consumption. These facts were among those which increased the sensibility of our fishing interest at the movement in question.

These circumstances and the incidents above alluded to have led me to think the moment favorable for a reconsideration of the entire subject of the fisheries on the coasts of the British Provinces, with a view to place them upon a more liberal footing of reciprocal privilege. A willingness to meet us in some arrangement of this kind is understood to exist on the part of Great Britain, with a desire on her part to include in one comprehensive settlement as well this subject as the commercial intercourse between the United States and the British Provinces. I have thought that, whatever arrangements may be made on these two subjects, it is expedient that they should be embraced in separate conventions. The illness and death of the late Secretary of State prevented the commencement of the contemplated negotiation. Pains have been taken to collect the information required for the details of such an arrangement. The subject is attended with considerable difficulty. If it is found practicable to come to an agreement mutually acceptable to the two parties, conventions may be concluded in the course of the present winter. The control of Congress over all the provisions of such an arrangement affecting the revenue will of course be reserved.

The affairs of Cuba formed a prominent topic in my last annual message. They remain in an uneasy condition, and a feeling of alarm and irritation on the part of the Cuban authorities appears to exist. This feeling has interfered with the regular commercial intercourse between the United States and the island and led to some acts of which we have a right to complain. But the Captain-General of Cuba is clothed with no power to treat with foreign governments, nor is he in any degree under the control of the Spanish minister at Washington. Any communication which he may hold with an agent of a foreign power is informal and matter of courtesy. Anxious to put an end to the existing inconveniences (which seemed to rest on a misconception), I directed the newly appointed minister to Mexico to visit Havana on his way to Vera Cruz. He was respectfully received by the Captain-General, who conferred with him freely on the recent occurrences, but no permanent arrangement was effected.

In the meantime the refusal of the Captain-General to allow passengers and the mail to be landed in certain cases, for a reason which does not furnish, in the opinion of this Government, even a good presumptive ground for such prohibition, has been made the subject of a serious remonstrance at Madrid, and I have no reason to doubt that due respect will be paid by the Government of Her Catholic Majesty to the representations which our minister has been instructed to make on the subject.

It is but justice to the Captain-General to add that his conduct toward the steamers employed to carry the mails of the United States to Havana has, with the exceptions above alluded to, been marked with kindness and liberality, and indicates no general purpose of interfering with the commercial correspondence and intercourse between the island and this country.

Early in the present year official notes were received from the ministers of France and England inviting the Government of the United States to become a party with Great Britain and France to a tripartite convention, in virtue of which the three powers should severally and collectively disclaim now and for the future all intention to obtain possession of the island of Cuba, and should bind themselves to discountenance all attempts to that effect on the part of any power or individual whatever. This invitation has been respectfully declined, for reasons which it would occupy too much space in this communication to state in detail, but which led me to think that the proposed measure would be of doubtful constitutionality, impolitic, and unavailing. I have, however, in common with several of my predecessors, directed the ministers of France and England to be assured that the United States entertain no designs against Cuba, but that, on the contrary, I should regard its incorporation into the Union at the present time as fraught with serious peril.

Were this island comparatively destitute of inhabitants or occupied by a kindred race, I should regard it, if voluntarily ceded by Spain, as a most desirable acquisition. But under existing circumstances I should look upon its incorporation into our Union as a very hazardous measure. It would bring into the Confederacy a population of a different national stock, speaking a different language, and not likely to harmonize with the other members. It would probably affect in a prejudicial manner the industrial interests of the South, and it might revive those conflicts of opinion between the different sections of the country which lately shook the Union to its center, and which have been so happily compromised.

The rejection by the Mexican Congress of the convention which had been concluded between that Republic and the United States for the protection of a transit way across the Isthmus of Tehuantepec and of the interests of those citizens of the United States who had become proprietors of the rights which Mexico had conferred on one of her own citizens in regard to that transit has thrown a serious obstacle in the way of the attainment of a very desirable national object. I am still willing to hope that the differences on the subject which exist, or may hereafter arise, between the Governments will be amicably adjusted. This subject, however, has already engaged the attention of the Senate of the United States, and requires no further comment in this communication.

The settlement of the question respecting the port of San Juan de

Nicaragua and of the controversy between the Republics of Costa Rica and Nicaragua in regard to their boundaries was considered indispensable to the commencement of the ship canal between the two oceans, which was the subject of the convention between the United States and Great Britain of the 19th of April, 1850. Accordingly, a proposition for the same purposes, addressed to the two Governments in that quarter and to the Mosquito Indians, was agreed to in April last by the Secretary of State and the minister of Her Britannic Majesty. Besides the wish to aid in reconciling the differences of the two Republics, I engaged in the negotiation from a desire to place the great work of a ship canal between the two oceans under one jurisdiction and to establish the important port of San Juan de Nicaragua under the government of a civilized power. The proposition in question was assented to by Costa Rica and the Mosquito Indians. It has not proved equally acceptable to Nicaragua, but it is to be hoped that the further negotiations on the subject which are in train will be carried on in that spirit of conciliation and compromise which ought always to prevail on such occasions, and that they will lead to a satisfactory result.

I have the satisfaction to inform you that the executive government of Venezuela has acknowledged some claims of citizens of the United States which have for many years past been urged by our chargé d'affaires at Caracas. It is hoped that the same sense of justice will actuate the Congress of that Republic in providing the means for their payment.

The recent revolution in Buenos Ayres and the Confederated States having opened the prospect of an improved state of things in that quarter, the Governments of Great Britain and France determined to negotiate with the chief of the new confederacy for the free access of their commerce to the extensive countries watered by the tributaries of the La Plata; and they gave a friendly notice of this purpose to the United States, that we might, if we thought proper, pursue the same course. In compliance with this invitation, our minister at Rio Janeiro and our chargé d'affaires at Buenos Ayres have been fully authorized to conclude treaties with the newly organized confederation or the States composing it. The delays which have taken place in the formation of the new government have as yet prevented the execution of those instructions, but there is every reason to hope that these vast countries will be eventually opened to our commerce.

A treaty of commerce has been concluded between the United States and the Oriental Republic of Uruguay, which will be laid before the Senate. Should this convention go into operation, it will open to the commercial enterprise of our citizens a country of great extent and unsurpassed in natural resources, but from which foreign nations have hitherto been almost wholly excluded.

The correspondence of the late Secretary of State with the Peruvian chargé d'affaires relative to the Lobos Islands was communicated to Congress toward the close of the last session. Since that time, on further investigation of the subject, the doubts which had been entertained of the title of Peru to those islands have been removed, and I have deemed it just that the temporary wrong which had been unintentionally done her from want of information should be repaired by an unreserved acknowledgment of her sovereignty.

I have the satisfaction to inform you that the course pursued by Peru has been creditable to the liberality of her Government. Before it was known by her that her title would be acknowledged at Washington, her minister of foreign affairs had authorized our chargé d'affaires at Lima to announce to the American vessels which had gone to the Lobos for guano that the Peruvian Government was willing to freight them on its own account. This intention has been carried into effect by the Peruvian minister here by an arrangement which is believed to be advantageous to the parties in interest.

Our settlements on the shores of the Pacific have already given a great extension, and in some respects a new direction, to our commerce in that ocean. A direct and rapidly increasing intercourse has sprung up with eastern Asia. The waters of the Northern Pacific, even into the Arctic Sea, have of late years been frequented by our whalemen. The application of steam to the general purposes of navigation is becoming daily more common, and makes it desirable to obtain fuel and other necessary supplies at convenient points on the route between Asia and our Pacific shores. Our unfortunate countrymen who from time to time suffer shipwreck on the coasts of the eastern seas are entitled to protection. Besides these specific objects, the general prosperity of our States on the Pacific requires that an attempt should be made to open the opposite regions of Asia to a mutually beneficial intercourse. It is obvious that this attempt could be made by no power to so great advantage as by the United States, whose constitutional system excludes every idea of distant colonial dependencies. I have accordingly been led to order an appropriate naval force to Japan, under the command of a discreet and intelligent officer of the highest rank known to our service. He is instructed to endeavor to obtain from the Government of that country some relaxation of the inhospitable and antisocial system which it has pursued for about two centuries. He has been directed particularly to remonstrate in the strongest language against the cruel treatment to which our shipwrecked mariners have often been subjected and to insist that they shall be treated with humanity. He is instructed, however, at the same time, to give that Government the amplest assurances that the objects of the United States are such, and such only, as I have indicated, and that the expedition is friendly and peaceful. Notwithstanding the jealousy with which the Governments of eastern Asia regard all overtures from foreigners, I am not without hopes of a beneficial result of the expedition. Should it be crowned with success, the advantages will not be confined to the United States, but, as in the case of China, will be equally enjoyed by all the other maritime powers. I have much satisfaction in stating that in all the steps preparatory to this expedition the Government of the United States has been materially aided by the good offices of the King of the Netherlands, the only European power having any commercial relations with Japan.

In passing from this survey of our foreign relations, I invite the attention of Congress to the condition of that Department of the Government to which this branch of the public business is intrusted. Our intercourse with foreign powers has of late years greatly increased, both in consequence of our own growth and the introduction of many new states into the family of nations. In this way the Department of State has become overburdened. It has by the recent establishment of the Department of the Interior been' relieved of some portion of the domestic business. If the residue of the business of that kind—such as the distribution of Congressional documents, the keeping, publishing, and distribution of the laws of the United States, the execution of the copyright law, the subject of reprieves and pardons, and some other subjects relating to interior administration—should be transferred from the Department of State, it would unquestionably be for the benefit of the public service. I would also suggest that the building appropriated to the State Department is not fireproof; that there is reason to think there are defects in its construction, and that the archives of the Government in charge of the Department, with the precious collections of the manuscript papers of Washington, Jefferson, Hamilton, Madison, and Monroe, are exposed to destruction by fire. A similar remark may be made of the buildings appropriated to the War and Navy Departments.

The condition of the Treasury is exhibited in the annual report from that Department.

The cash receipts into the Treasury for the fiscal year ending the 30th June last, exclusive of trust funds, were $49,728,386.89, and the expenditures for the same period, likewise exclusive of trust funds, were $46,-007,896.20, of which $9,455,815.83 was on account of the principal and interest of the public debt, including the last installment of the indemnity to Mexico under the treaty of Guadalupe Hidalgo, leaving a balance of $14,632,136.37 in the Treasury on the 1st day of July last. Since this latter period further purchases of the principal of the public debt have been made to the extent of $2,456,547.49, and the surplus in the Treasury will continue to be applied to that object whenever the stock can be procured within the limits as to price authorized by law.

The value of foreign merchandise imported during the last fiscal year was $207,240,101, and the value of domestic productions exported was $149,861,911, besides $17,204,026 of foreign merchandise exported, making the aggregate of the entire exports $167,065,937. Exclusive of the above, there was exported $42,507,285 in specie, and imported from foreign ports $5,262,643.

In my first annual message to Congress I called your attention to what seemed to me some defects in the present tariff, and recommended such modifications as in my judgment were best adapted to remedy its evils and promote the prosperity of the country. Nothing has since occurred to change my views on this important question.

Without repeating the arguments contained in my former message in favor of discriminating protective duties, I deem it my duty to call your attention to one or two other considerations affecting this subject. The first is the effect of large importations of foreign goods upon our currency. Most of the gold of California, as fast as it is coined, finds its way directly to Europe in payment for goods purchased. In the second place, as our manufacturing establishments are broken down by competition with foreigners, the capital invested in them is lost, thousands of honest and industrious citizens are thrown out of employment, and the farmer, to that extent, is deprived of a home market for the sale of his surplus produce. In the third place, the destruction of our manufactures leaves the foreigner without competition in our market, and he consequently raises the price of the article sent here for sale, as is now seen in the increased cost of iron imported from England. The prosperity and wealth of every nation must depend upon its productive industry. The farmer is stimulated to exertion by finding a ready market for his surplus products, and benefited by being able to exchange them without loss of time or expense of transportation for the manufactures which his comfort or convenience requires. This is always done to the best advantage where a portion of the community in which he lives is engaged in other pursuits. But most manufactures require an amount of capital and a practical skill which can not be commanded unless they be protected for a time from ruinous competition from abroad. Hence the necessity of laying those duties upon imported goods which the Constitution authorizes for revenue in such a manner as to protect and encourage the labor of our own citizens. Duties, however, should not be fixed at a rate so high as to exclude the foreign article, but should be so graduated as to enable the domestic manufacturer fairly to compete with the foreigner in our own markets, and by this competition to reduce the price of the manufactured article to the consumer to the lowest rate at which it can be produced. This policy would place the mechanic by the side of the farmer, create a mutual interchange of their respective commodities, and thus stimulate the industry of the whole country and render us independent of foreign nations for the supplies required by the habits or necessities of the people.

Another question, wholly independent of protection, presents itself, and that is, whether the duties levied should be upon the value of the article at the place of shipment, or, where it is practicable, a specific duty, graduated according to quantity, as ascertained by weight or measure. All

our duties are at present *ad valorem*.   A certain percentage is levied on
the price of the goods at the port of shipment in a foreign country.   Most
commercial nations have found it indispensable, for the purpose of preventing fraud and perjury, to make the duties specific whenever the
article is of such a uniform value in weight or measure as to justify such
a duty.   Legislation should never encourage dishonesty or crime.   It
is impossible that the revenue officers at the port where the goods are
entered and the duties paid should know with certainty what they cost
in the foreign country.   Yet the law requires that they should levy the
duty according to such cost.   They are therefore compelled to resort to
very unsatisfactory evidence to ascertain what that cost was.   They take
the invoice of the importer, attested by his oath, as the best evidence of
which the nature of the case admits.   But everyone must see that the
invoice may be fabricated and the oath by which it is supported false,
by reason of which the dishonest importer pays a part only of the duties
which are paid by the honest one, and thus indirectly receives from the
Treasury of the United States a reward for his fraud and perjury.   The
reports of the Secretary of the Treasury heretofore made on this subject
show conclusively that these frauds have been practiced to a great extent.
The tendency is to destroy that high moral character for which our merchants have long been distinguished, to defraud the Government of its
revenue, to break down the honest importer by a dishonest competition,
and, finally, to transfer the business of importation to foreign and irresponsible agents, to the great detriment of our own citizens.   I therefore
again most earnestly recommend the adoption of specific duties wherever it is practicable, or a home valuation, to prevent these frauds.

I would also again call your attention to the fact that the present
tariff in some cases imposes a higher duty upon the raw material imported than upon the article manufactured from it, the consequence of
which is that the duty operates to the encouragement of the foreigner
and the discouragement of our own citizens.

For full and detailed information in regard to the general condition of
our Indian affairs, I respectfully refer you to the report of the Secretary
of the Interior and the accompanying documents.

The Senate not having thought proper to ratify the treaties which have
been negotiated with the tribes of Indians in California and Oregon, our
relations with them have been left in a very unsatisfactory condition.

In other parts of our territory particular districts of country have been
set apart for the exclusive occupation of the Indians, and their right to
the lands within those limits has been acknowledged and respected.   But
in California and Oregon there has been no recognition by the Government of the exclusive right of the Indians to any part of the country.
They are therefore mere tenants at sufferance, and liable to be driven
from place to place at the pleasure of the whites.

The treaties which have been rejected proposed to remedy this evil by allotting to the different tribes districts of country suitable to their habits of life and sufficient for their support. This provision, more than any other, it is believed, led to their rejection; and as no substitute for it has been adopted by Congress, it has not been deemed advisable to attempt to enter into new treaties of a permanent character, although no effort has been spared by temporary arrangements to preserve friendly relations with them.

If it be the desire of Congress to remove them from the country altogether, or to assign to them particular districts more remote from the settlements of the whites, it will be proper to set apart by law the territory which they are to occupy and to provide the means necessary for removing them to it. Justice alike to our own citizens and to the Indians requires the prompt action of Congress on this subject.

The amendments proposed by the Senate to the treaties which were negotiated with the Sioux Indians of Minnesota have been submitted to the tribes who were parties to them, and have received their assent. A large tract of valuable territory has thus been opened for settlement and cultivation, and all danger of collision with these powerful and warlike bands has been happily removed.

The removal of the remnant of the tribe of Seminole Indians from Florida has long been a cherished object of the Government, and it is one to which my attention has been steadily directed. Admonished by past experience of the difficulty and cost of the attempt to remove them by military force, resort has been had to conciliatory measures. By the invitation of the Commissioner of Indian Affairs, several of the principal chiefs recently visited Washington, and whilst here acknowledged in writing the obligation of their tribe to remove with the least possible delay. Late advices from the special agent of the Government represent that they adhere to their promise, and that a council of their people has been called to make their preliminary arrangements. A general emigration may therefore be confidently expected at an early day.

The report from the General Land Office shows increased activity in its operations. The survey of the northern boundary of Iowa has been completed with unexampled dispatch. Within the last year 9,522,953 acres of public land have been surveyed and 8,032,463 acres brought into market.

	Acres.
In the last fiscal year there were sold	1,553,071
Located with bounty-land warrants	3,201,314
Located with other certificates	115,682
Making a total of	4,870,067
In addition there were—	
Reported under swamp-land grants	5,219,188
For internal improvements, railroads, etc	3,025,920
Making an aggregate of	13,115,175

Being an increase of the amount sold and located under land warrants of 569,220 acres over the previous year.

The whole amount thus sold, located under land warrants, reported under swamp-land grants, and selected for internal improvements exceeds that of the previous year by 3,342,372 acres; and the sales would without doubt have been much larger but for the extensive reservations for railroads in Missouri, Mississippi, and Alabama.

	Acres.
For the quarter ending 30th September, 1852, there were sold	243,255
Located with bounty-land warrants	1,387,116
Located with other certificates	15,649
Reported under swamp-land grants	2,485,233
Making an aggregate for the quarter of	4,131,253

Much the larger portion of the labor of arranging and classifying the returns of the last census has been finished, and it will now devolve upon Congress to make the necessary provision for the publication of the results in such form as shall be deemed best. The apportionment of representation on the basis of the new census has been made by the Secretary of the Interior in conformity with the provisions of law relating to that subject, and the recent elections have been made in accordance with it.

I commend to your favorable regard the suggestion contained in the report of the Secretary of the Interior that provision be made by law for the publication and distribution, periodically, of an analytical digest of all the patents which have been or may hereafter be granted for useful inventions and discoveries, with such descriptions and illustrations as may be necessary to present an intelligible view of their nature and operation. The cost of such publication could easily be defrayed out of the patent fund, and I am persuaded that it could be applied to no object more acceptable to inventors and beneficial to the public at large.

An appropriation of $100,000 having been made at the last session for the purchase of a suitable site and for the erection, furnishing, and fitting up of an asylum for the insane of the District of Columbia and of the Army and Navy of the United States, the proper measures have been adopted to carry this beneficent purpose into effect.

By the latest advices from the Mexican boundary commission it appears that the survey of the river Gila from its confluence with the Colorado to its supposed intersection with the western line of New Mexico has been completed. The survey of the Rio Grande has also been finished from the point agreed on by the commissioners as "the point where it strikes the southern boundary of New Mexico" to a point 135 miles below Eagle Pass, which is about two-thirds of the distance along the course of the river to its mouth.

The appropriation which was made at the last session of Congress for the continuation of the survey is subject to the following proviso:

Provided, That no part of this appropriation shall be used or expended until it shall be made satisfactorily to appear to the President of the United States that the southern boundary of New Mexico is not established by the commissioner and surveyor of the United States farther north of the town called "Paso" than the same is laid down in Disturnell's map, which is added to the treaty.

My attention was drawn to this subject by a report from the Department of the Interior, which reviewed all the facts of the case and submitted for my decision the question whether under existing circumstances any part of the appropriation could be lawfully used or expended for the further prosecution of the work. After a careful consideration of the subject I came to the conclusion that it could not, and so informed the head of that Department. Orders were immediately issued by him to the commissioner and surveyor to make no further requisitions on the Department, as they could not be paid, and to discontinue all operations on the southern line of New Mexico. But as the Department had no exact information as to the amount of provisions and money which remained unexpended in the hands of the commissioner and surveyor, it was left discretionary with them to continue the survey down the Rio Grande as far as the means at their disposal would enable them or at once to disband the commission. A special messenger has since arrived from the officer in charge of the survey on the river with information that the funds subject to his control were exhausted and that the officers and others employed in the service were destitute alike of the means of prosecuting the work and of returning to their homes.

The object of the proviso was doubtless to arrest the survey of the southern and western lines of New Mexico, in regard to which different opinions have been expressed; for it is hardly to be supposed that there could be any objection to that part of the line which extends along the channel of the Rio Grande. But the terms of the law are so broad as to forbid the use of any part of the money for the prosecution of the work, or even for the payment to the officers and agents of the arrearages of pay which are justly due to them.

I earnestly invite your prompt attention to this subject, and recommend a modification of the terms of the proviso, so as to enable the Department to use as much of the appropriation as will be necessary to discharge the existing obligations of the Government and to complete the survey of the Rio Grande to its mouth.

It will also be proper to make further provision by law for the fulfillment of our treaty with Mexico for running and marking the residue of the boundary line between the two countries.

Permit me to invite your particular attention to the interests of the District of Columbia, which are confided by the Constitution to your peculiar care.

Among the measures which seem to me of the greatest importance to its prosperity are the introduction of a copious supply of water into the city of Washington and the construction of suitable bridges across the Potomac to replace those which were destroyed by high water in the early part of the present year.

At the last session of Congress an appropriation was made to defray the cost of the surveys necessary for determining the best means of affording an unfailing supply of good and wholesome water. Some progress has been made in the survey, and as soon as it is completed the result will be laid before you.

Further appropriations will also be necessary for grading and paving the streets and avenues and inclosing and embellishing the public grounds within the city of Washington.

I commend all these objects, together with the charitable institutions of the District, to your favorable regard.

Every effort has been made to protect our frontier and that of the adjoining Mexican States from the incursions of the Indian tribes. Of about 11,000 men of which the Army is composed, nearly 8,000 are employed in the defense of the newly acquired territory (including Texas) and of emigrants proceeding thereto. I am gratified to say that these efforts have been unusually successful. With the exception of some partial outbreaks in California and Oregon and occasional depredations on a portion of the Rio Grande, owing, it is believed, to the disturbed state of that border region, the inroads of the Indians have been effectually restrained.

Experience has shown, however, that whenever the two races are brought into contact collisions will inevitably occur. To prevent these collisions the United States have generally set apart portions of their territory for the exclusive occupation of the Indian tribes. A difficulty occurs, however, in the application of this policy to Texas. By the terms of the compact by which that State was admitted into the Union she retained the ownership of all the vacant lands within her limits. The government of that State, it is understood, has assigned no portion of her territory to the Indians, but as fast as her settlements advance lays it off into counties and proceeds to survey and sell it. This policy manifestly tends not only to alarm and irritate the Indians, but to compel them to resort to plunder for subsistence. It also deprives this Government of that influence and control over them without which no durable peace can ever exist between them and the whites. I trust, therefore, that a due regard for her own interests, apart from considerations of humanity and justice, will induce that State to assign a small portion of her vast domain for the provisional occupancy of the small remnants of tribes within her borders, subject, of course, to her ownership and eventual jurisdiction. If she should fail to do this, the fulfillment of our treaty stipulations with Mexico and our duty to the Indians themselves will, it is feared, become a subject of serious embarrassment to the Government. It is hoped, however, that a timely and just provision by Texas may avert this evil.

No appropriations for fortifications were made at the two last sessions of Congress. The cause of this omission is probably to be found in a growing belief that the system of fortifications adopted in 1816, and heretofore acted on, requires revision.

The subject certainly deserves full and careful investigation, but it should not be delayed longer than can be avoided. In the meantime there are certain works which have been commenced, some of them nearly completed, designed to protect our principal seaports from Boston to New Orleans and a few other important points. In regard to the necessity for these works, it is believed that little difference of opinion exists among military men. I therefore recommend that the appropriations necessary to prosecute them be made.

I invite your attention to the remarks on this subject and on others connected with his Department contained in the accompanying report of the Secretary of War.

Measures have been taken to carry into effect the law of the last session making provision for the improvement of certain rivers and harbors, and it is believed that the arrangements made for that purpose will combine efficiency with economy. Owing chiefly to the advanced season when the act was passed, little has yet been done in regard to many of the works beyond making the necessary preparations. With respect to a few of the improvements, the sums already appropriated will suffice to complete them; but most of them will require additional appropriations. I trust that these appropriations will be made, and that this wise and beneficent policy, so auspiciously resumed, will be continued. Great care should be taken, however, to commence no work which is not of sufficient importance to the commerce of the country to be viewed as national in its character. But works which have been commenced should not be discontinued until completed, as otherwise the sums expended will in most cases be lost.

The report from the Navy Department will inform you of the prosperous condition of the branch of the public service committed to its charge. It presents to your consideration many topics and suggestions of which I ask your approval. It exhibits an unusual degree of activity in the operations of the Department during the past year. The preparations for the Japan expedition, to which I have already alluded; the arrangements made for the exploration and survey of the China Seas, the Northern Pacific, and Behrings Straits; the incipient measures taken toward a reconnoissance of the continent of Africa eastward of Liberia; the preparation for an early examination of the tributaries of the river La Plata, which a recent decree of the provisional chief of the Argentine Confederation has opened to navigation—all these enterprises and the means by which they are proposed to be accomplished have commanded my full approbation, and I have no doubt will be productive of most useful results.

Two officers of the Navy were heretofore instructed to explore the whole extent of the Amazon River from the confines of Peru to its mouth. The return of one of them has placed in the possession of the Government an interesting and valuable account of the character and resources of a country abounding in the materials of commerce, and which if opened to the industry of the world will prove an inexhaustible fund of wealth. The report of this exploration will be communicated to you as soon as it is completed.

Among other subjects offered to your notice by the Secretary of the Navy, I select for special commendation, in view of its connection with the interests of the Navy, the plan submitted by him for the establishment of a permanent corps of seamen and the suggestions he has presented for the reorganization of the Naval Academy.

In reference to the first of these, I take occasion to say that I think it will greatly improve the efficiency of the service, and that I regard it as still more entitled to favor for the salutary influence it must exert upon the naval discipline, now greatly disturbed by the increasing spirit of insubordination resulting from our present system. The plan proposed for the organization of the seamen furnishes a judicious substitute for the law of September, 1850, abolishing corporal punishment, and satisfactorily sustains the policy of that act under conditions well adapted to maintain the authority of command and the order and security of our ships. It is believed that any change which proposes permanently to dispense with this mode of punishment should be preceded by a system of enlistment which shall supply the Navy with seamen of the most meritorious class, whose good deportment and pride of character may preclude all occasion for a resort to penalties of a harsh or degrading nature. The safety of a ship and her crew is often dependent upon immediate obedience to a command, and the authority to enforce it must be equally ready. The arrest of a refractory seaman in such moments not only deprives the ship of indispensable aid, but imposes a necessity for double service on others, whose fidelity to their duties may be relied upon in such an emergency. The exposure to this increased and arduous labor since the passage of the act of 1850 has already had, to a most observable and injurious extent, the effect of preventing the enlistment of the best seamen in the Navy. The plan now suggested is designed to promote a condition of service in which this objection will no longer exist. The details of this plan may be established in great part, if not altogether, by the Executive under the authority of existing laws, but I have thought it proper, in accordance with the suggestion of the Secretary of the Navy, to submit it to your approval.

The establishment of a corps of apprentices for the Navy, or boys to be enlisted until they become of age, and to be employed under such regulations as the Navy Department may devise, as proposed in the report, I cordially approve and commend to your consideration; and I also concur in the suggestion that this system for the early training of seamen may be most usefully ingrafted upon the service of our merchant marine.

The other proposition of the report to which I have referred—the reorganization of the Naval Academy—I recommend to your attention as a project worthy of your encouragement and support. The valuable services already rendered by this institution entitle it to the continuance of your fostering care.

Your attention is respectfully called to the report of the Postmaster-General for the detailed operation of his Department during the last fiscal year, from which it will be seen that the receipts from postages for that time were less by $1,431,696 than for the preceding fiscal year, being a decrease of about 23 per cent.

This diminution is attributable to the reduction in the rates of postage made by the act of March 3, 1851, which reduction took effect at the commencement of the last fiscal year.

Although in its operation during the last year the act referred to has not fulfilled the predictions of its friends by increasing the correspondence of the country in proportion to the reduction of postage, I should, nevertheless, question the policy of returning to higher rates. Experience warrants the expectation that as the community becomes accustomed to cheap postage correspondence will increase. It is believed that from this cause and from the rapid growth of the country in population and business the receipts of the Department must ultimately exceed its expenses, and that the country may safely rely upon the continuance of the present cheap rate of postage.

In former messages I have, among other things, respectfully recommended to the consideration of Congress the propriety and necessity of further legislation for the protection and punishment of foreign consuls residing in the United States; to revive, with certain modifications, the act of 10th March, 1838, to restrain unlawful military expeditions against the inhabitants of conterminous states or territories; for the preservation and protection from mutilation or theft of the papers, records, and archives of the nation; for authorizing the surplus revenue to be applied to the payment of the public debt in advance of the time when it will become due; for the establishment of land offices for the sale of the public lands in California and the Territory of Oregon; for the construction of a road from the Mississippi Valley to the Pacific Ocean; for the establishment of a bureau of agriculture for the promotion of that interest, perhaps the most important in the country; for the prevention of frauds upon the Government in applications for pensions and bounty lands; for the establishment of a uniform fee bill, prescribing a specific compensation for every service required of clerks, district attorneys, and marshals; for authorizing an additional regiment of mounted men for the defense of our frontiers against the Indians and for fulfilling our treaty stipulations with Mexico to defend her citizens against the Indians "with equal diligence and energy as our own;" for determining the relative rank between the naval and civil officers in our public ships and between the officers of the Army and Navy in the various grades of each; for reorganizing the naval establishment by fixing the number of officers in each grade, and providing for a retired list upon reduced pay of those unfit for active duty; for prescribing and regulating punishments in the Navy; for the appointment of a commission to revise the public statutes of the United States by arranging them in order, supplying deficiencies, correcting incongruities, simplifying their language, and reporting them to Congress for its final action; and for the establishment of a commission to adjudicate and settle private claims against the United States. I am not aware, however, that any of these subjects have been finally acted upon by Congress. Without repeating the reasons for legislation on these subjects which have been assigned in former messages, I respectfully recommend them again to your favorable consideration.

I think it due to the several Executive Departments of this Government to bear testimony to the efficiency and integrity with which they are conducted. With all the careful superintendence which it is possible for the heads of those Departments to exercise, still the due administration and guardianship of the public money must very much depend on the vigilance, intelligence, and fidelity of the subordinate officers and clerks, and especially on those intrusted with the settlement and adjustment of claims and accounts. I am gratified to believe that they have generally performed their duties faithfully and well. They are appointed to guard the approaches to the public Treasury, and they occupy positions that expose them to all the temptations and seductions which the cupidity of peculators and fraudulent claimants can prompt them to employ. It will be but a wise precaution to protect the Government against that source of mischief and corruption, as far as it can be done, by the enactment of all proper legal penalties. The laws in this respect are supposed to be defective, and I therefore deem it my duty to call your attention to the subject and to recommend that provision be made by law for the punishment not only of those who shall accept bribes, but also of those who shall either promise, give, or offer to give to any of those officers or clerks a bribe or reward touching or relating to any matter of their official action or duty.

It has been the uniform policy of this Government, from its foundation to the present day, to abstain from all interference in the domestic affairs of other nations. The consequence has been that while the nations of Europe have been engaged in desolating wars our country has pursued its peaceful course to unexampled prosperity and happiness. The wars in which we have been compelled to engage in defense of the rights and honor of the country have been, fortunately, of short duration. During the terrific contest of nation against nation which succeeded the French Revolution we were enabled by the wisdom and firmness of President Washington to maintain our neutrality. While other nations were drawn into this wide-sweeping whirlpool, we sat quiet and unmoved upon our own shores. While the flower of their numerous armies was wasted by disease or perished by hundreds of thousands upon the battle-field, the youth of this favored land were permitted to enjoy the bless-ings of peace beneath the paternal roof. While the States of Europe incurred enormous debts, under the burden of which their subjects still groan, and which must absorb no small part of the product of the honest industry of those countries for generations to come, the United States have once been enabled to exhibit the proud spectacle of a nation free from public debt, and if permitted to pursue our prosperous way for a few years longer in peace we may do the same again.

But it is now said by some that this policy must be changed. Europe is no longer separated from us by a voyage of months, but steam navi-gation has brought her within a few days' sail of our shores. We see more of her movements and take a deeper interest in her controversies. Although no one proposes that we should join the fraternity of potentates who have for ages lavished the blood and treasure of their subjects in maintaining ''the balance of power,'' yet it is said that we ought to inter-fere between contending sovereigns and their subjects for the purpose of overthrowing the monarchies of Europe and establishing in their place republican institutions. It is alleged that we have heretofore pursued a different course from a sense of our weakness, but that now our conscious strength dictates a change of policy, and that it is consequently our duty to mingle in these contests and aid those who are struggling for liberty.

This is a most seductive but dangerous appeal to the generous sym-pathies of freemen. Enjoying, as we do, the blessings of a free Govern-ment, there is no man who has an American heart that would not rejoice to see these blessings extended to all other nations. We can not witness the struggle between the oppressed and his oppressor anywhere without the deepest sympathy for the former and the most anxious desire for his triumph. Nevertheless, is it prudent or is it wise to involve ourselves in these foreign wars? Is it indeed true that we have heretofore refrained from doing so merely from the degrading motive of a conscious weakness? For the honor of the patriots who have gone before us, I can not admit it. Men of the Revolution, who drew the sword against the oppressions of the mother country and pledged to Heaven ''their lives, their fortunes, and their sacred honor'' to maintain their freedom, could never have been actuated by so unworthy a motive. They knew no weakness or fear where right or duty pointed the way, and it is a libel upon their fair fame for us, while we enjoy the blessings for which they so nobly fought and bled, to insinuate it. The truth is that the course which they pursued was dictated by a stern sense of international justice, by a statesmanlike prudence and a far-seeing wisdom, looking not merely to the present necessities but to the permanent safety and interest of the country. They knew that the world is governed less by sympathy than by reason and force; that it was not possible for this nation to become a ''propagan-dist'' of free principles without arraying against it the combined powers of Europe, and that the result was more likely to be the overthrow of republican liberty here than its establishment there.   History has been written in vain for those who can doubt this.   France had no sooner estab-- lished a republican form of government than she manifested a desire to force its blessings on all the world.   Her own historian informs us that, hearing of some petty acts of tyranny in a neighboring principality, "the National Convention declared that she would afford succor and fraternity to all nations who wished to recover their liberty, and she gave it in charge to the executive power to give orders to the generals of the French armies to aid all citizens who might have been or should be oppressed in the cause of liberty."   Here was the false step which led to her subsequent misfortunes.   She soon found herself involved in war with all the rest of Europe.   In less than ten years her Government was changed from a republic to an empire, and finally, after shedding rivers of blood, foreign powers restored her exiled dynasty and exhausted Europe sought peace and repose in the unquestioned ascendency of monarchical principles.   Let us learn wisdom from her example.   Let us remember that revolutions do not always establish freedom.   Our own free institu- tions were not the offspring of our Revolution.   They existed before. They were planted in the free charters of self-government under which the English colonies grew up, and our Revolution only freed us from the dominion of a foreign power whose government was at variance with those institutions.   But European nations have had no such training for self-government, and every effort to establish it by bloody revolutions has been, and must without that preparation continue to be, a failure. Liberty unregulated by law degenerates into anarchy, which soon becomes the most horrid of all despotisms.   Our policy is wisely to govern our- selves, and thereby to set such an example of national justice, prosperity, and true glory as shall teach to all nations the blessings of self-govern- ment and the unparalleled enterprise and success of a free people.

We live in an age of progress, and ours is emphatically a country of progress.   Within the last half century the number of States in this Union has nearly doubled, the population has almost quadrupled, and our boundaries have been extended from the Mississippi to the Pacific. Our territory is checkered over with railroads and furrowed with canals. The inventive talent of our country is excited to the highest pitch, and the numerous applications for patents for valuable improvements distinguish this age and this people from all others.   The genius of one American has enabled our commerce to move against wind and tide and that of another has annihilated distance in the transmission of intelli- gence.   The whole country is full of enterprise.   Our common schools are diffusing intelligence among the people and our industry is fast accu- mulating the comforts and luxuries of life.   This is in part owing to our peculiar position, to our fertile soil and comparatively sparse population; but much of it is also owing to the popular institutions under which we live, to the freedom which every man feels to engage in any useful pursuit according to his taste or inclination, and to the entire confidence that his person and property will be protected by the laws. But whatever may be the cause of this unparalleled growth in population, intelligence, and wealth, one thing is clear—that the Government must keep pace with the progress of the people. It must participate in their spirit of enterprise, and while it exacts obedience to the laws and restrains all unauthorized invasions of the rights of neighboring states, it should foster and protect home industry and lend its powerful strength to the improvement of such means of intercommunication as are necessary to promote our internal commerce and strengthen the ties which bind us together as a people.

It is not strange, however much it may be regretted, that such an exuberance of enterprise should cause some individuals to mistake change for progress and the invasion of the rights of others for national prowess and glory. The former are constantly agitating for some change in the organic law, or urging new and untried theories of human rights. The latter are ever ready to engage in any wild crusade against a neighboring people, regardless of the justice of the enterprise and without looking at the fatal consequences to ourselves and to the cause of popular government. Such expeditions, however, are often stimulated by mercenary individuals, who expect to share the plunder or profit of the enterprise without exposing themselves to danger, and are led on by some irresponsible foreigner, who abuses the hospitality of our own Government by seducing the young and ignorant to join in his scheme of personal ambition or revenge under the false and delusive pretense of extending the area of freedom. These reprehensible aggressions but retard the true progress of our nation and tarnish its fair fame. They should therefore receive the indignant frowns of every good citizen who sincerely loves his country and takes a pride in its prosperity and honor.

Our Constitution, though not perfect, is doubtless the best that ever was formed. Therefore let every proposition to change it be well weighed and, if found beneficial, cautiously adopted. Every patriot will rejoice to see its authority so exerted as to advance the prosperity and honor of the nation, whilst he will watch with jealousy any attempt to mutilate this charter of our liberties or pervert its powers to acts of aggression or injustice. Thus shall conservatism and progress blend their harmonious action in preserving the form and spirit of the Constitution and at the same time carry forward the great improvements of the country with a rapidity and energy which freemen only can display.

In closing this my last annual communication, permit me, fellow-citizens, to congratulate you on the prosperous condition of our beloved country. Abroad its relations with all foreign powers are friendly, its rights are respected, and its high place in the family of nations cheerfully recognized. At home we enjoy an amount of happiness, public and private, which has probably never fallen to the lot of any other people. Besides affording to our own citizens a degree of prosperity of which on so large a scale I know of no other instance, our country is annually affording a refuge and a home to multitudes, altogether without example, from the Old World.

We owe these blessings, under Heaven, to the happy Constitution and Government which were bequeathed to us by our fathers, and which it is our sacred duty to transmit in all their integrity to our children. We must all consider it a great distinction and privilege to have been chosen by the people to bear a part in the administration of such a Government. Called by an unexpected dispensation to its highest trust at a season of embarrassment and alarm, I entered upon its arduous duties with extreme diffidence. I claim only to have discharged them to the best of an humble ability, with a single eye to the public good, and it is with devout gratitude in retiring from office that I leave the country in a state of peace and prosperity.

Franklin Pierce

March 4, 1853 to March 4, 1857

FIRST ANNUAL MESSAGE.

WASHINGTON, D. C., *December 5, 1853.*

Fellow-Citizens of the Senate and of the House of Representatives:

The interest with which the people of the Republic anticipate the assembling of Congress and the fulfillment on that occasion of the duty imposed upon a new President is one of the best evidences of their capacity to realize the hopes of the founders of a political system at once complex and symmetrical. While the different branches of the Government are to a certain extent independent of each other, the duties of all alike have direct reference to the source of power. Fortunately, under this system no man is so high and none so humble in the scale of public station as to escape from the scrutiny or to be exempt from the responsibility which all official functions imply.

Upon the justice and intelligence of the masses, in a government thus organized, is the sole reliance of the confederacy and the only security for honest and earnest devotion to its interests against the usurpations and encroachments of power on the one hand and the assaults of personal ambition on the other.

The interest of which I have spoken is inseparable from an inquiring, self-governing community, but stimulated, doubtless, at the present time by the unsettled condition of our relations with several foreign powers, by the new obligations resulting from a sudden extension of the field of enterprise, by the spirit with which that field has been entered and the amazing energy with which its resources for meeting the demands of humanity have been developed.

Although disease, assuming at one time the characteristics of a widespread and devastating pestilence, has left its sad traces upon some portions of our country, we have still the most abundant cause for reverent thankfulness to God for an accumulation of signal mercies showered upon us as a nation. It is well that a consciousness of rapid advancement and increasing strength be habitually associated with an abiding sense of dependence upon Him who holds in His hands the destiny of men and of nations.

Recognizing the wisdom of the broad principle of absolute religious toleration proclaimed in our fundamental law, and rejoicing in the benign influence which it has exerted upon our social and political condition, I should shrink from a clear duty did I fail to express my deepest conviction that we can place no secure reliance upon any apparent progress if it be not sustained by national integrity, resting upon the great truths affirmed and illustrated by divine revelation. In the midst of our sorrow for the afflicted and suffering, it has been consoling to see how promptly disaster made true neighbors of districts and cities separated widely from each other, and cheering to watch the strength of that common bond of brotherhood which unites all hearts, in all parts of this Union, when danger threatens from abroad or calamity impends over us at home.

Our diplomatic relations with foreign powers have undergone no essential change since the adjournment of the last Congress. With some of them questions of a disturbing character are still pending, but there are good reasons to believe that these may all be amicably adjusted.

For some years past Great Britain has so construed the first article of the convention of the 20th of April, 1818, in regard to the fisheries on the northeastern coast, as to exclude our citizens from some of the fishing grounds to which they freely resorted for nearly a quarter of a century subsequent to the date of that treaty. The United States have never acquiesced in this construction, but have always claimed for their fishermen all the rights which they had so long enjoyed without molestation. With a view to remove all difficulties on the subject, to extend the rights of our fishermen beyond the limits fixed by the convention of 1818, and to regulate trade between the United States and the British North American Provinces, a negotiation has been opened with a fair prospect of a favorable result. To protect our fishermen in the enjoyment of their rights and prevent collision between them and British fishermen, I deemed it expedient to station a naval force in that quarter during the fishing season.

Embarrassing questions have also arisen between the two Governments in regard to Central America. Great Britain has proposed to settle them by an amicable arrangement, and our minister at London is instructed to enter into negotiations on that subject.

A commission for adjusting the claims of our citizens against Great Britain and those of British subjects against the United States, organized under the convention of the 8th of February last, is now sitting in London for the transaction of business.

It is in many respects desirable that the boundary line between the United States and the British Provinces in the northwest, as designated in the convention of the 15th of June, 1846, and especially that part which separates the Territory of Washington from the British possessions on the north, should be traced and marked. I therefore present the subject to your notice.

With France our relations continue on the most friendly footing. The extensive commerce between the United States and that country might, it is conceived, be released from some unnecessary restrictions to the mutual advantage of both parties. With a view to this object, some progress has been made in negotiating a treaty of commerce and navigation.

Independently of our valuable trade with Spain, we have important political relations with her growing out of our neighborhood to the islands of Cuba and Porto Rico. I am happy to announce that since the last Congress no attempts have been made by unauthorized expeditions within the United States against either of those colonies. Should any movement be manifested within our limits, all the means at my command will be vigorously exerted to repress it. Several annoying occurrences have taken place at Havana, or in the vicinity of the island of Cuba, between our citizens and the Spanish authorities. Considering the proximity of that island to our shores, lying, as it does, in the track of trade between some of our principal cities, and the suspicious vigilance with which foreign intercourse, particularly that with the United States, is there guarded, a repetition of such occurrences may well be apprehended.

As no diplomatic intercourse is allowed between our consul at Havana and the Captain-General of Cuba, ready explanations can not be made or prompt redress afforded where injury has resulted. All complaint on the part of our citizens under the present arrangement must be, in the first place, presented to this Government and then referred to Spain. Spain again refers it to her local authorities in Cuba for investigation, and postpones an answer till she has heard from those authorities. To avoid these irritating and vexatious delays, a proposition has been made to provide for a direct appeal for redress to the Captain-General by our consul in behalf of our injured fellow-citizens. Hitherto the Government of Spain has declined to enter into any such arrangement. This course on her part is deeply regretted, for without some arrangement of this kind the good understanding between the two countries may be exposed to occasional interruption. Our minister at Madrid is instructed to renew the proposition and to press it again upon the consideration of Her Catholic Majesty's Government.

For several years Spain has been calling the attention of this Government to a claim for losses by some of her subjects in the case of the schooner *Amistad*. This claim is believed to rest on the obligations imposed by our existing treaty with that country. Its justice was admitted in our diplomatic correspondence with the Spanish Government as early as March, 1847, and one of my predecessors, in his annual message of that year, recommended that provision should be made for its payment. In January last it was again submitted to Congress by the Executive. It has received a favorable consideration by committees of both branches, but as yet there has been no final action upon it. I conceive that good faith requires its prompt adjustment, and I present it to your early and favorable consideration.

Martin Koszta, a Hungarian by birth, came to this country in 1850, and declared his intention in due form of law to become a citizen of the United States. After remaining here nearly two years he visited Turkey. While at Smyrna he was forcibly seized, taken on board an Austrian brig of war then lying in the harbor of that place, and there confined in irons, with the avowed design to take him into the dominions of Austria. Our consul at Smyrna and legation at Constantinople interposed for his release, but their efforts were ineffectual. While thus in prison Commander Ingraham, with the United States ship of war *St. Louis*, arrived at Smyrna, and after inquiring into the circumstances of the case came to the conclusion that Koszta was entitled to the protection of this Government, and took energetic and prompt measures for his release. Under an arrangement between the agents of the United States and of Austria, he was transferred to the custody of the French consul-general at Smyrna, there to remain until he should be disposed of by the mutual agreement of the consuls of the respective Governments at that place. Pursuant to that agreement, he has been released, and is now in the United States. The Emperor of Austria has made the conduct of our officers who took part in this transaction a subject of grave complaint. Regarding Koszta as still his subject, and claiming a right to seize him within the limits of the Turkish Empire, he has demanded of this Government its consent to the surrender of the prisoner, a disavowal of the acts of its agents, and satisfaction for the alleged outrage. After a careful consideration of the case I came to the conclusion that Koszta was seized without legal authority at Smyrna; that he was wrongfully detained on board of the Austrian brig of war; that at the time of his seizure he was clothed with the nationality of the United States, and that the acts of our officers, under the circumstances of the case, were justifiable, and their conduct has been fully approved by me, and a compliance with the several demands of the Emperor of Austria has been declined.

For a more full account of this transaction and my views in regard to it I refer to the correspondence between the chargé d'affaires of Austria and the Secretary of State, which is herewith transmitted. The principles and policy therein maintained on the part of the United States will, whenever a proper occasion occurs, be applied and enforced.

The condition of China at this time renders it probable that some important changes will occur in that vast Empire which will lead to a more unrestricted intercourse with it. The commissioner to that country who has been recently appointed is instructed to avail himself of all occasions to open and extend our commercial relations, not only with the Empire of China, but with other Asiatic nations.

In 1852 an expedition was sent to Japan, under the command of Commodore Perry, for the purpose of opening commercial intercourse with that Empire. Intelligence has been received of his arrival there and of his having made known to the Emperor of Japan the object of his visit. But it is not yet ascertained how far the Emperor will be disposed to abandon his restrictive policy and open that populous country to a commercial intercourse with the United States.

It has been my earnest desire to maintain friendly intercourse with the Governments upon this continent and to aid them in preserving good understanding among themselves. With Mexico a dispute has arisen as to the true boundary line between our Territory of New Mexico and the

Mexican State of Chihuahua. A former commissioner of the United States, employed in running that line pursuant to the treaty of Guadalupe Hidalgo, made a serious mistake in determining the initial point on the Rio Grande; but inasmuch as his decision was clearly a departure from the directions for tracing the boundary contained in that treaty, and was not concurred in by the surveyor appointed on the part of the United States, whose concurrence was necessary to give validity to that decision, this Government is not concluded thereby; but that of Mexico takes a different view of the subject.

There are also other questions of considerable magnitude pending between the two Republics. Our minister in Mexico has ample instructions to adjust them. Negotiations have been opened, but sufficient progress has not been made therein to enable me to speak of the probable result. Impressed with the importance of maintaining amicable relations with that Republic and of yielding with liberality to all her just claims, it is reasonable to expect that an arrangement mutually satisfactory to both countries may be concluded and a lasting friendship between them confirmed and perpetuated.

Congress having provided for a full mission to the States of Central America, a minister was sent thither in July last. As yet he has had time to visit only one of these States (Nicaragua), where he was received in the most friendly manner. It is hoped that his presence and good offices will have a benign effect in composing the dissensions which prevail among them, and in establishing still more intimate and friendly relations between them respectively and between each of them and the United States.

Considering the vast regions of this continent and the number of states which would be made accessible by the free navigation of the river Amazon, particular attention has been given to this subject. Brazil, through whose territories it passes into the ocean, has hitherto persisted in a policy so restricted in regard to the use of this river as to obstruct and nearly exclude foreign commercial intercourse with the States which lie upon its tributaries and upper branches. Our minister to that country is instructed to obtain a relaxation of that policy and to use his efforts to induce the Brazilian Government to open to common use, under proper safeguards, this great natural highway for international trade. Several of the South American States are deeply interested in this attempt to secure the free navigation of the Amazon, and it is reasonable to expect their cooperation in the measure. As the advantages of free commercial intercourse among nations are better understood, more liberal views are generally entertained as to the common rights of all to the free use of those means which nature has provided for international communication. To these more liberal and enlightened views it is hoped that Brazil will conform her policy and remove all unnecessary restrictions upon the free use of a river which traverses so many states and so large a part of the continent. I am happy to inform you that the Republic of

Paraguay and the Argentine Confederation have yielded to the liberal policy still resisted by Brazil in regard to the navigable rivers within their respective territories. Treaties embracing this subject, among others, have been negotiated with these Governments, which will be submitted to the Senate at the present session.

A new branch of commerce, important to the agricultural interests of the United States, has within a few years past been opened with Peru. Notwithstanding the inexhaustible deposits of guano upon the islands of that country, considerable difficulties are experienced in obtaining the requisite supply. Measures have been taken to remove these difficulties and to secure a more abundant importation of the article. Unfortunately, there has been a serious collision between our citizens who have resorted to the Chincha Islands for it and the Peruvian authorities stationed there. Redress for the outrages committed by the latter was promptly demanded by our minister at Lima. This subject is now under consideration, and there is reason to believe that Peru is disposed to offer adequate indemnity to the aggrieved parties.

We are thus not only at peace with all foreign countries, but, in regard to political affairs, are exempt from any cause of serious disquietude in our domestic relations.

The controversies which have agitated the country heretofore are passing away with the causes which produced them and the passions which they had awakened; or, if any trace of them remains, it may be reasonably hoped that it will only be perceived in the zealous rivalry of all good citizens to testify their respect for the rights of the States, their devotion to the Union, and their common determination that each one of the States, its institutions, its welfare, and its domestic peace, shall be held alike secure under the sacred ægis of the Constitution.

This new league of amity and of mutual confidence and support into which the people of the Republic have entered happily affords inducement and opportunity for the adoption of a more comprehensive and unembarrassed line of policy and action as to the great material interests of the country, whether regarded in themselves or in connection with the powers of the civilized world.

The United States have continued gradually and steadily to expand through acquisitions of territory, which, how much soever some of them may have been questioned, are now universally seen and admitted to have been wise in policy, just in character, and a great element in the advancement of our country, and with it of the human race, in freedom, in prosperity, and in happiness. The thirteen States have grown to be thirty-one, with relations reaching to Europe on the one side and on the other to the distant realms of Asia.

I am deeply sensible of the immense responsibility which the present magnitude of the Republic and the diversity and multiplicity of its interests devolves upon me, the alleviation of which so far as relates to the immediate conduct of the public business, is, first, in my reliance on the wisdom and patriotism of the two Houses of Congress, and, secondly, in the directions afforded me by the principles of public polity affirmed by our fathers of the epoch of 1798, sanctioned by long experience, and consecrated anew by the overwhelming voice of the people of the United States.

Recurring to these principles, which constitute the organic basis of union, we perceive that vast as are the functions and the duties of the Federal Government, vested in or intrusted to its three great departments—the legislative, executive, and judicial—yet the substantive power, the popular force, and the large capacities for social and material development exist in the respective States, which, all being of themselves well-constituted republics, as they preceded so they alone are capable of maintaining and perpetuating the American Union. The Federal Government has its appropriate line of action in the specific and limited powers conferred on it by the Constitution, chiefly as to those things in which the States have a common interest in their relations to one another and to foreign governments, while the great mass of interests which belong to cultivated men—the ordinary business of life, the springs of industry, all the diversified personal and domestic affairs of society—rest securely upon the general reserved powers of the people of the several States. There is the effective democracy of the nation, and there the vital essence of its being and its greatness.

Of the practical consequences which flow from the nature of the Federal Government, the primary one is the duty of administering with integrity and fidelity the high trust reposed in it by the Constitution, especially in the application of the public funds as drawn by taxation from the people and appropriated to specific objects by Congress.

Happily, I have no occasion to suggest any radical changes in the financial policy of the Government. Ours is almost, if not absolutely, the solitary power of Christendom having a surplus revenue drawn immediately from imposts on commerce, and therefore measured by the spontaneous enterprise and national prosperity of the country, with such indirect relation to agriculture, manufactures, and the products of the earth and sea as to violate no constitutional doctrine and yet vigorously promote the general welfare. Neither as to the sources of the public treasure nor as to the manner of keeping and managing it does any grave controversy now prevail, there being a general acquiescence in the wisdom of the present system.

The report of the Secretary of the Treasury will exhibit in detail the state of the public finances and the condition of the various branches of the public service administered by that Department of the Government.

The revenue of the country, levied almost insensibly to the taxpayer, goes on from year to year, increasing beyond either the interests or the prospective wants of the Government.

At the close of the fiscal year ending June 30, 1852, there remained in the Treasury a balance of $14,632,136. The public revenue for the fiscal year ending June 30, 1853, amounted to $58,931,865 from customs and to $2,405,708 from public lands and other miscellaneous sources, amounting together to $61,337,574, while the public expenditures for the same period, exclusive of payments on account of the public debt, amounted to $43,554,262, leaving a balance of $32,425,447 of receipts above expenditures.

This fact of increasing surplus in the Treasury became the subject of anxious consideration at a very early period of my Administration, and the path of duty in regard to it seemed to me obvious and clear, namely: First, to apply the surplus revenue to the discharge of the public debt so far as it could judiciously be done, and, secondly, to devise means for the gradual reduction of the revenue to the standard of the public exigencies.

Of these objects the first has been in the course of accomplishment in a manner and to a degree highly satisfactory. The amount of the public debt of all classes was on the 4th of March, 1853, $69,190,037, payments on account of which have been made since that period to the amount of $12,703,329, leaving unpaid and in continuous course of liquidation the sum of $56,486,708. These payments, although made at the market price of the respective classes of stocks, have been effected readily and to the general advantage of the Treasury, and have at the same time proved of signal utility in the relief they have incidentally afforded to the money market and to the industrial and commercial pursuits of the country.

The second of the above-mentioned objects, that of the reduction of the tariff, is of great importance, and the plan suggested by the Secretary of the Treasury, which is to reduce the duties on certain articles and to add to the free list many articles now taxed, and especially such as enter into manufactures and are not largely, or at all, produced in the country, is commended to your candid and careful consideration.

You will find in the report of the Secretary of the Treasury, also, abundant proof of the entire adequacy of the present fiscal system to meet all the requirements of the public service, and that, while properly administered, it operates to the advantage of the community in ordinary business relations.

I respectfully ask your attention to sundry suggestions of improvements in the settlement of accounts, especially as regards the large sums of outstanding arrears due to the Government, and of other reforms in the administrative action of his Department which are indicated by the Secretary; as also to the progress made in the construction of marine hospitals, custom-houses, and of a new mint in California and assay office in the city of New York, heretofore provided for by Congress, and also to the eminently successful progress of the Coast Survey and of the Light-House Board.

Among the objects meriting your attention will be important recommendations from the Secretaries of War and Navy. I am fully satisfied that the Navy of the United States is not in a condition of strength and efficiency commensurate with the magnitude of our commercial and other interests, and commend to your especial attention the suggestions on this subject made by the Secretary of the Navy. I respectfully submit that the Army, which under our system must always be regarded with the highest interest as a nucleus around which the volunteer forces of the nation gather in the hour of danger, requires augmentation, or modification, to adapt it to the present extended limits and frontier relations of the country and the condition of the Indian tribes in the interior of the continent, the necessity of which will appear in the communications of the Secretaries of War and the Interior.

In the administration of the Post-Office Department for the fiscal year ending June 30, 1853, the gross expenditure was $7,982,756, and the gross receipts during the same period $5,942,734, showing that the current revenue failed to meet the current expenses of the Department by the sum of $2,042,032. The causes which, under the present postal system and laws, led inevitably to this result are fully explained by the report of the Postmaster-General, one great cause being the enormous rates the Department has been compelled to pay for mail service rendered by railroad companies.

The exhibit in the report of the Postmaster-General of the income and expenditures by mail steamers will be found peculiarly interesting and of a character to demand the immediate action of Congress.

Numerous and flagrant frauds upon the Pension Bureau have been brought to light within the last year, and in some instances merited punishments inflicted; but, unfortunately, in others guilty parties have escaped, not through the want of sufficient evidence to warrant a conviction, but in consequence of the provisions of limitation in the existing laws.

From the nature of these claims, the remoteness of the tribunals to pass upon them, and the mode in which the proof is of necessity furnished, temptations to crime have been greatly stimulated by the obvious difficulties of detection. The defects in the law upon this subject are so apparent and so fatal to the ends of justice that your early action relating to it is most desirable.

During the last fiscal year 9,819,411 acres of the public lands have been surveyed and 10,363,891 acres brought into market. Within the same period the sales by public purchase and private entry amounted to 1,083,-495 acres; located under military bounty-land warrants, 6,142,360 acres; located under other certificates, 9,427 acres; ceded to the States as swamp lands, 16,684,253 acres; selected for railroad and other objects under acts of Congress, 1,427,457 acres; total amount of lands disposed of within the fiscal year, 25,346,902 acres, which is an increase in quantity sold and located under land warrants and grants of 12,231,818 acres over the fiscal year immediately preceding. The quantity of land sold during the second and third quarters of 1852 was 334,451 acres; the amount received therefor was $623,687. The quantity sold the second and third quarters of the year 1853 was 1,609,919 acres, and the amount received therefor $2,226,876.

The whole number of land warrants issued under existing laws prior to the 30th of September last was 266,042, of which there were outstanding at that date 66,947. The quantity of land required to satisfy these outstanding warrants is 4,778,120 acres.

Warrants have been issued to 30th of September last under the act of 11th February, 1847, calling for 12,879,280 acres, under acts of September 28, 1850, and March 22, 1852, calling for 12,505,360 acres, making a total of 25,384,640 acres.

It is believed that experience has verified the wisdom and justice of the present system with regard to the public domain in most essential particulars.

You will perceive from the report of the Secretary of the Interior that opinions which have often been expressed in relation to the operation of the land system as not being a source of revenue to the Federal Treasury were erroneous. The net profits from the sale of the public lands to June 30, 1853, amounted to the sum of $53,289,465.

I recommend the extension of the land system over the Territories of Utah and New Mexico, with such modifications as their peculiarities may require.

Regarding our public domain as chiefly valuable to provide homes for the industrious and enterprising, I am not prepared to recommend any essential change in the land system, except by modifications in favor of the actual settler and an extension of the preemption principle in certain cases, for reasons and on grounds which will be fully developed in the reports to be laid before you.

Congress, representing the proprietors of the territorial domain and charged especially with power to dispose of territory belonging to the United States, has for a long course of years, beginning with the Administration of Mr. Jefferson, exercised the power to construct roads within the Territories, and there are so many and obvious distinctions between this exercise of power and that of making roads within the States that the former has never been considered subject to such objections as apply to the latter; and such may now be considered the settled construction of the power of the Federal Government upon the subject.

Numerous applications have been and no doubt will continue to be made for grants of land in aid of the construction of railways. It is not believed to be within the intent and meaning of the Constitution that the power to dispose of the public domain should be used otherwise than might be expected from a prudent proprietor, and therefore that grants of land to aid in the construction of roads should be restricted to cases where it would be for the interest of a proprietor under like circumstances thus to contribute to the construction of these works. For the practical operation of such grants thus far in advancing the interests of the States in which the works are located, and at the same time the substantial interests of all the other States, by enhancing the value and promoting the rapid sale of the public domain, I refer you to the report of the Secretary of the Interior. A careful examination, however, will show that this experience is the result of a just discrimination and will be far from affording encouragement to a reckless or indiscriminate extension of the·principle.

I commend to your favorable consideration the men of genius of our country who by their inventions and discoveries in science and arts have contributed largely to the improvements of the age without, in many instances, securing for themselves anything like an adequate reward. For many interesting details upon this subject I refer you to the appropriate reports, and especially urge upon your early attention the apparently slight, but really important, modifications of existing laws therein suggested.

The liberal spirit which has so long marked the action of Congress in relation to the District of Columbia will, I have no doubt, continue to be manifested.

The erection of an asylum for the insane of the District of Columbia and of the Army and Navy of the United States has been somewhat retarded by the great demand for materials and labor during the past summer, but full preparation for the reception of patients before the return of another winter is anticipated; and there is the best reason to believe, from the plan and contemplated arrangements which have been devised, with the large experience furnished within the last few years in relation to the nature and treatment of the disease, that it will prove an asylum indeed to this most helpless and afflicted class of sufferers and stand as a noble monument of wisdom and mercy.

Under the acts of Congress of August 31, 1852, and of March 3, 1853, designed to secure for the cities of Washington and Georgetown an abundant supply of good and wholesome water, it became my duty to examine the report and plans of the engineer who had charge of the surveys under the act first named. The best, if not the only, plan calculated to secure permanently the object sought was that which contemplates taking the water from the Great Falls of the Potomac, and consequently I gave to it my approval.

For the progress and present condition of this important work and for its demands so far as appropriations are concerned I refer you to the report of the Secretary of War.

The present judicial system of the United States has now been in operation for so long a period of time and has in its general theory and much of its details become so familiar to the country and acquired so entirely the public confidence that if modified in any respect it should only be in those particulars which may adapt it to the increased extent, population, and legal business of the United States. In this relation the organization of the courts is now confessedly inadequate to the duties to be performed by them, in consequence of which the States of Florida, Wisconsin, Iowa, Texas, and California, and districts of other States, are in effect excluded from the full benefits of the general system by the functions of the circuit court being devolved on the district judges in all those States or parts of States.

The spirit of the Constitution and a due regard to justice require that all the States of the Union should be placed on the same footing in regard to the judicial tribunals. I therefore commend to your consideration this important subject, which in my judgment demands the speedy action of Congress. I will present to you, if deemed desirable a plan which I am prepared to recommend for the enlargement and modification of the present judicial system.

The act of Congress establishing the Smithsonian Institution provided that the President of the United States and other persons therein designated should constitute an "establishment" by that name, and that the members should hold stated and special meetings for the supervision of the affairs of the Institution. The organization not having taken place, it seemed to me proper that it should be effected without delay. This has been done; and an occasion was thereby presented for inspecting the condition of the Institution and appreciating its successful progress thus far and its high promise of great and general usefulness.

I have omitted to ask your favorable consideration for the estimates of works of a local character in twenty-seven of the thirty-one States, amounting to $1,754,500, because, independently of the grounds which have so often been urged against the application of the Federal revenue for works of this character, inequality, with consequent injustice, is inherent in the nature of the proposition, and because the plan has proved entirely inadequate to the accomplishment of the objects sought.

The subject of internal improvements, claiming alike the interest and good will of all, has, nevertheless, been the basis of much political discussion and has stood as a deep-graven line of division between statesmen of eminent ability and patriotism. The rule of strict construction of all powers delegated by the States to the General Government has arrayed itself from time to time against the rapid progress of expenditures from the National Treasury on works of a local character within the States. Memorable as an epoch in the history of this subject is the message of President Jackson of the 27th of May, 1830, which met the system of internal improvements in its comparative infancy; but so rapid had been its growth that the projected appropriations in that year for works of this character had risen to the alarming amount of more than $100,000,000.

In that message the President admitted the difficulty of bringing back the operations of the Government to the construction of the Constitution set up in 1798, and marked it as an admonitory proof of the necessity of guarding that instrument with sleepless vigilance against the authority of precedents which had not the sanction of its most plainly defined powers.

Our Government exists under a written compact between sovereign States, uniting for specific objects and with specific grants to their general agent.   If, then, in the progress of its administration there have been departures from the terms and intent of the compact, it is and will ever be proper to refer back to the fixed standard which our fathers left us and to make a stern effort to conform our action to it.   It would seem that the fact of a principle having been resisted from the first by many of the wisest and most patriotic men of the Republic, and a policy having provoked constant strife without arriving at a conclusion which can be regarded as satisfactory to its most earnest advocates, should suggest the inquiry whether there may not be a plan likely to be crowned by happier results.   Without perceiving any sound distinction or intending to assert any principle as opposed to improvements needed for the protection of internal commerce which does not equally apply to improvements upon the seaboard for the protection of foreign commerce, I submit to you whether it may not be safely anticipated that if the policy were once settled against appropriations by the General Government for local improvements for the benefit of commerce, localities requiring expenditures would not, by modes and means clearly legitimate and proper, raise the fund necessary for such constructions as the safety or other interests of their commerce might require.

If that can be regarded as a system which in the experience of more than thirty years has at no time so commanded the public judgment as to give it the character of a settled policy; which, though it has produced some works of conceded importance, has been attended with an expenditure quite disproportionate to their value and has resulted in squandering large sums upon objects which have answered no valuable purpose, the interests of all the States require it to be abandoned unless hopes may be indulged for the future which find no warrant in the past.

With an anxious desire for the completion of the works which are regarded by all good citizens with sincere interest, I have deemed it my duty to ask at your hands a deliberate reconsideration of the question, with a hope that, animated by a desire to promote the permanent and substantial interests of the country, your wisdom may prove equal to the task of devising and maturing a plan which, applied to this subject, may promise something better than constant strife, the suspension of the powers of local enterprise, the exciting of vain hopes, and the disappointment of cherished expectations.

In expending the appropriations made by the last Congress several cases have arisen in relation to works for the improvement of harbors which involve questions as to the right of soil and jurisdiction, and have threatened conflict between the authority of the State and General Governments. The right to construct a breakwater, jetty, or dam would seem necessarily to carry with it the power to protect and preserve such constructions. This can only be effectually done by having jurisdiction over the soil. But no clause of the Constitution is found on which to rest the claim of the United States to exercise jurisdiction over the soil of a State except that conferred by the eighth section of the first article of the Constitution. It is, then, submitted whether, in all cases where constructions are to be erected by the General Government, the right of soil should not first be obtained and legislative provision be made to cover all such cases.

For the progress made in the construction of roads within the Territories, as provided for in the appropriations of the last Congress, I refer you to the report of the Secretary of War.

There is one subject of a domestic nature which, from its intrinsic importance and the many interesting questions of future policy which it involves, can not fail to receive your early attention. I allude to the means of communication by which different parts of the wide expanse of our country are to be placed in closer connection for purposes both of defense and commercial intercourse, and more especially such as appertain to the communication of those great divisions of the Union which lie on the opposite sides of the Rocky Mountains.

That the Government has not been unmindful of this heretofore is apparent from the aid it has afforded through appropriations for mail facilities and other purposes. But the general subject will now present itself under aspects more imposing and more purely national by reason of the surveys ordered by Congress, and now in the process of completion, for communication by railway across the continent, and wholly within the limits of the United States.

The power to declare war, to raise and support armies, to provide and maintain a navy, and to call forth the militia to execute the laws, suppress insurrections, and repel invasions was conferred upon Congress as means to provide for the common defense and to protect a territory and a population now widespread and vastly multiplied. As incidental to and indispensable for the exercise of this power, it must sometimes be necessary to construct military roads and protect harbors of refuge. To appropriations by Congress for such objects no sound objection can be raised. Happily for our country, its peaceful policy and rapidly increasing population impose upon us no urgent necessity for preparation, and leave but few trackless deserts between assailable points and a patriotic people ever ready and generally able to protect them. These necessary links the enterprise and energy of our people are steadily and boldly struggling to supply. All experience affirms that wherever private enterprise will avail it is most wise for the General Government to leave to that and individual watchfulness the location and execution of all means of communication.

The surveys before alluded to were designed to ascertain the most practicable and economical route for a railroad from the river Mississippi to the Pacific Ocean. Parties are now in the field making explorations, where previous examinations had not supplied sufficient data and where there was the best reason to hope the object sought might be found. The means and time being both limited, it is not to be expected that all the accurate knowledge desired will be obtained, but it is hoped that much and important information will be added to the stock previously possessed, and that partial, if not full, reports of the surveys ordered will be received in time for transmission to the two Houses of Congress on or before the first Monday in February next, as required by the act of appropriation. The magnitude of the enterprise contemplated has aroused and will doubtless continue to excite a very general interest throughout the country. In its political, its commercial, and its military bearings it has varied, great, and increasing claims to consideration. The heavy expense, the great delay, and, at times, fatality attending travel by either of the Isthmus routes have demonstrated the advantage which would result from interterritorial communication by such safe and rapid means as a railroad would supply.

These difficulties, which have been encountered in a period of peace, would be magnified and still further increased in time of war. But whilst the embarrassments already encountered and others under new contingencies to be anticipated may serve strikingly to exhibit the importance of such a work, neither these nor all considerations combined can have an appreciable value when weighed against the obligation strictly to adhere to the Constitution and faithfully to execute the powers it confers.

Within this limit and to the extent of the interest of the Government involved it would seem both expedient and proper if an economical and practicable route shall be found to aid by all constitutional means in the construction of a road which will unite by speedy transit the populations of the Pacific and Atlantic States. To guard against misconception, it should be remarked that although the power to construct or aid in the construction of a road within the limits of a Territory is not embarrassed by that question of jurisdiction which would arise within the limits of a State, it is, nevertheless, held to be of doubtful power and more than doubtful propriety, even within the limits of a Territory, for the General Government to undertake to administer the affairs of a railroad, a canal, or other similar construction, and therefore that its connection with a work of this character should be incidental rather than primary. I will only add at present that, fully appreciating the magnitude of the subject and solicitous that the Atlantic and Pacific shores of the Republic may be bound together by inseparable ties of common interest, as well as of common fealty and attachment to the Union, I shall be disposed, so far as my own action is concerned, to follow the lights of the Constitution as expounded and illustrated by those whose opinions and expositions constitute the standard of my political faith in regard to the powers of the Federal Government. It is, I trust, not necessary to say that no grandeur of enterprise and no present urgent inducement promising popular favor will lead me to disregard those lights or to depart from that path which experience has proved to be safe, and which is now radiant with the glow of prosperity and legitimate constitutional progress. We can afford to wait, but we can not afford to overlook the ark of our security.

It is no part of my purpose to give prominence to any subject which may properly be regarded as set at rest by the deliberate judgment of the people. But while the present is bright with promise and the future full of demand and inducement for the exercise of active intelligence, the past can never be without useful lessons of admonition and instruction. If its dangers serve not as beacons, they will evidently fail to fulfill the object of a wise design. When the grave shall have closed over all who are now endeavoring to meet the obligations of duty, the year 1850 will be recurred to as a period filled with anxious apprehension. A successful war had just terminated. Peace brought with it a vast augmentation of territory. Disturbing questions arose bearing upon the domestic institutions of one portion of the Confederacy and involving the constitutional rights of the States. But notwithstanding differences of opinion and sentiment which then existed in relation to details and specific provisions, the acquiescence of distinguished citizens, whose devotion to the Union can never be doubted, has given renewed vigor to our institutions and restored a sense of repose and security to the public mind throughout the Confederacy. That this repose is to suffer no shock during my official term, if I have power to avert it, those who placed me here may be assured. The wisdom of men who knew what independence cost, who had put all at stake upon the issue of the Revolutionary struggle, disposed of the subject to which I refer in the only way consistent with the Union of these States and with the march of power and prosperity which has made us what we are. It is a significant fact that from the adoption of the Constitution until the officers and soldiers of the Revolution had passed to their graves, or, through the infirmities of age and wounds, had ceased to participate actively in public affairs, there was not merely a quiet acquiescence in, but a prompt vindication of, the constitutional rights of the States. The reserved powers were scrupulously respected. No statesman put forth the narrow views of casuists to justify interference and agitation, but the spirit of the compact was regarded as sacred in the eye of honor and indispensable for the great experiment of civil liberty, which, environed by inherent difficulties, was yet borne forward in apparent weakness by a power superior to all obstacles. There is no condemnation which the voice of freedom will not pronounce upon us should we prove faithless to this great trust. While men inhabiting different parts of this vast continent can no more be expected to hold the same opinions or entertain the same sentiments than every variety of climate or soil can be expected to furnish the same agricultural products, they can unite in a common object and sustain common principles essential to the maintenance of that object. The gallant men of the South and the North could stand together during the struggle of the Revolution; they could stand together in the more trying period which succeeded the clangor of arms. As their united valor was adequate to all the trials of the camp and dangers of the field, so their united wisdom proved equal to the greater task of founding upon a deep and broad basis institutions which it has been our privilege to enjoy and will ever be our most sacred duty to sustain. It is but the feeble expression of a faith strong and universal to say that their sons, whose blood mingled so often upon the same field during the War of 1812 and who have more recently borne in triumph the flag of the country upon a foreign soil, will never permit alienation of feeling to weaken the power of their united efforts nor internal dissensions to paralyze the great arm of freedom, uplifted for the vindication of self-government.

I have thus briefly presented such suggestions as seem to me especially worthy of your consideration. In providing for the present you can hardly fail to avail yourselves of the light which the experience of the past casts upon the future.

The growth of our population has now brought us, in the destined career of our national history, to a point at which it well behooves us to expand our vision over the vast prospective.

The successive decennial returns of the census since the adoption of the Constitution have revealed a law of steady, progressive development, which may be stated in general terms as a duplication every quarter century. Carried forward from the point already reached for only a short period of time, as applicable to the existence of a nation, this law of progress, if unchecked, will bring us to almost incredible results. A large allowance for a diminished proportional effect of emigration would not very materially reduce the estimate, while the increased average duration of human life known to have already resulted from the scientific and hygienic improvements of the past fifty years will tend to keep up through the next fifty, or perhaps hundred, the same ratio of growth which has been thus revealed in our past progress; and to the influence of these causes may be added the influx of laboring masses from eastern Asia to the Pacific side of our possessions, together with the probable accession of the populations already existing in other parts of our hemisphere, which within the period in question will feel with yearly increasing force the natural attraction of so vast, powerful, and prosperous a confederation of self-governing republics and will seek the privilege of being admitted within its safe and happy bosom, transferring with themselves, by a peaceful and healthy process of incorporation, spacious regions of virgin and exuberant soil, which are destined to swarm with the fast-growing and fast-spreading millions of our race.

These considerations seem fully to justify the presumption that the law of population above stated will continue to act with undiminished effect through at least the next half century, and that thousands of persons who have already arrived at maturity and are now exercising the rights of freemen will close their eyes on the spectacle of more than 100,000,000 of population embraced within the majestic proportions of the American Union. It is not merely as an interesting topic of speculation that I present these views for your consideration. They have important practical bearings upon all the political duties we are called upon to perform. Heretofore our system of government has worked on what may be termed a miniature scale in comparison with the development which it must thus assume within a future so near at hand as scarcely to be beyond the present of the existing generation.

It is evident that a confederation so vast and so varied, both in numbers and in territorial extent, in habits and in interests, could only be kept in national cohesion by the strictest fidelity to the principles of the Constitution as understood by those who have adhered to the most restricted construction of the powers granted by the people and the States. Interpreted and applied according to those principles, the great compact adapts itself with healthy ease and freedom to an unlimited extension of that benign system of federative self-government of which it is our glorious and, I trust, immortal charter. Let us, then, with redoubled vigilance, be on our guard against yielding to the temptation of the exercise of doubtful powers, even under the pressure of the motives of conceded temporary advantage and apparent temporary expediency.

The minimum of Federal government compatible with the maintenance of national unity and efficient action in our relations with the rest of the world should afford the rule and measure of construction of our powers under the general clauses of the Constitution. A spirit of strict deference to the sovereign rights and dignity of every State, rather than a disposition to subordinate the States into a provincial relation to the central authority, should characterize all our exercise of the respective powers temporarily vested in us as a sacred trust from the generous confidence of our constituents.

In like manner, as a manifestly indispensable condition of the perpetuation of the Union and of the realization of that magnificent national future adverted to, does the duty become yearly stronger and clearer upon us, as citizens of the several States, to cultivate a fraternal and affectionate spirit, language, and conduct in regard to other States and in relation to the varied interests, institutions, and habits of sentiment and opinion which may respectively characterize them. Mutual forbearance, respect, and noninterference in our personal action as citizens and an enlarged exercise of the most liberal principles of comity in the public dealings of State with State, whether in legislation or in the execution of laws, are the means to perpetuate that confidence and fraternity the decay of which a mere political union, on so vast a scale, could not long survive.

In still another point of view is an important practical duty suggested by this consideration of the magnitude of dimensions to which our political system, with its corresponding machinery of government, is so rapidly expanding. With increased vigilance does it require us to cultivate the cardinal virtues of public frugality and official integrity and purity. Public affairs ought to be so conducted that a settled conviction shall pervade the entire Union that nothing short of the highest tone and standard of public morality marks every part of the administration and legislation of the General Government. Thus will the federal system, whatever expansion time and progress may give it, continue more and more deeply rooted in the love and confidence of the people.

That wise economy which is as far removed from parsimony as from corrupt and corrupting extravagance; that single regard for the public good which will frown upon all attempts to approach the Treasury with insidious projects of private interest cloaked under public pretexts; that sound fiscal administration which, in the legislative department, guards against the dangerous temptations incident to overflowing revenue, and, in the executive, maintains an unsleeping watchfulness against the tendency of all national expenditure to extravagance, while they are admitted elementary political duties, may, I trust, be deemed as properly adverted to and urged in view of the more impressive sense of that necessity which is directly suggested by the considerations now presented.

Since the adjournment of Congress the Vice-President of the United States has passed from the scenes of earth, without having entered upon the duties of the station to which he had been called by the voice of his countrymen. Having occupied almost continuously for more than thirty years a seat in one or the other of the two Houses of Congress, and having by his singular purity and wisdom secured unbounded confidence and universal respect, his failing health was watched by the nation with painful solicitude. His loss to the country, under all the circumstances, has been justly regarded as irreparable.

In compliance with the act of Congress of March 2, 1853, the oath of office was administered to him on the 24th of that month at Ariadne estate, near Matanzas, in the island of Cuba; but his strength gradually declined, and was hardly sufficient to enable him to return to his home in Alabama, where, on the 18th day of April, in the most calm and peaceful way, his long and eminently useful career was terminated.

Entertaining unlimited confidence in your intelligent and patriotic devotion to the public interest, and being conscious of no motives on my part which are not inseparable from the honor and advancement of my country, I hope it may be my privilege to deserve and secure not only your cordial cooperation in great public measures, but also those relations of mutual confidence and regard which it is always so desirable to cultivate between members of coordinate branches of the Government.

SECOND ANNUAL MESSAGE.

WASHINGTON, *December 4, 1854.*

Fellow-Citizens of the Senate and of the House of Representatives:

The past has been an eventful year, and will be hereafter referred to as a marked epoch in the history of the world. While we have been happily preserved from the calamities of war, our domestic prosperity has not been entirely uninterrupted. The crops in portions of the country have been nearly cut off. Disease has prevailed to a greater extent than usual, and the sacrifice of human life through casualties by sea and land is without parallel. But the pestilence has swept by, and restored salubrity invites the absent to their homes and the return of business to its ordinary channels. If the earth has rewarded the labor of the husbandman less bountifully than in preceding seasons, it has left him with abundance for domestic wants and a large surplus for exportation. In the present, therefore, as in the past, we find ample grounds for reverent thankfulness to the God of grace and providence for His protecting care and merciful dealings with us as a people.

Although our attention has been arrested by painful interest in passing events, yet our country feels no more than the slight vibrations of the convulsions which have shaken Europe. As individuals we can not repress sympathy with human suffering nor regret for the causes which produce it; as a nation we are reminded that whatever interrupts the peace or checks the prosperity of any part of Christendom tends more or less to involve our own. The condition of States is not unlike that of individuals; they are mutually dependent upon each other. Amicable relations between them and reciprocal good will are essential for the promotion of whatever is desirable in their moral, social, and political condition. Hence it has been my earnest endeavor to maintain peace and friendly intercourse with all nations.

The wise theory of this Government, so early adopted and steadily pursued, of avoiding all entangling alliances has hitherto exempted it from many complications in which it would otherwise have become involved. Notwithstanding this our clearly defined and well-sustained course of action and our geographical position, so remote from Europe, increasing disposition has been manifested by some of its Governments to supervise and in certain respects to direct our foreign policy. In plans for adjusting the balance of power among themselves they have assumed to take us into account, and would constrain us to conform our conduct to their views. One or another of the powers of Europe has from time to time undertaken to enforce arbitrary regulations contrary in many respects to established principles of international law. That law the United States have in their foreign intercourse uniformly respected and observed, and they can not recognize any such interpolations therein as the temporary interests of others may suggest. They do not admit that the sovereigns of one continent or of a particular community of states can legislate for all others.

Leaving the transatlantic nations to adjust their political system in the way they may think best for their common welfare, the independent powers of this continent may well assert the right to be exempt from all annoying interference on their part. Systematic abstinence from intimate political connection with distant foreign nations does not conflict with giving the widest range to our foreign commerce. This distinction, so clearly marked in history, seems to have been overlooked or disregarded by some leading foreign states. Our refusal to be brought within and subjected to their peculiar system has, I fear, created a jealous distrust of our conduct and induced on their part occasional acts of disturbing effect upon our foreign relations. Our present attitude and past course give assurances, which should not be questioned, that our purposes are not aggressive nor threatening to the safety and welfare of other nations. Our military establishment in time of peace is adapted to maintain exterior defenses and to preserve order among the aboriginal tribes within the limits of the Union. Our naval force is intended only for the protection of our citizens abroad and of our commerce, diffused, as it is, over all the seas of the globe. The Government of the United States, being essentially pacific in policy, stands prepared to repel invasion by the voluntary service of a patriotic people, and provides no permanent means of foreign aggression. These considerations should allay all apprehension that we are disposed to encroach on the rights or endanger the security of other states.

Some European powers have regarded with disquieting concern the territorial expansion of the United States. This rapid growth has resulted from the legitimate exercise of sovereign rights belonging alike to all nations, and by many liberally exercised. Under such circumstances it could hardly have been expected that those among them which have within a comparatively recent period subdued and absorbed ancient kingdoms, planted their standards on every continent, and now possess or claim the control of the islands of every ocean as their appropriate domain would look with unfriendly sentiments upon the acquisitions of this country, in every instance honorably obtained, or would feel themselves justified in imputing our advancement to a spirit of aggression or to a passion for political predominance.

Our foreign commerce has reached a magnitude and extent nearly equal to that of the first maritime power of the earth, and exceeding that of any other. Over this great interest, in which not only our merchants, but all classes of citizens, at least indirectly, are concerned, it is the duty of the executive and legislative branches of the Government to exercise a careful supervision and adopt proper measures for its protection. The policy which I had in view in regard to this interest embraces its future as well as its present security. Long experience has shown that, in general, when the principal powers of Europe are engaged in war the rights of neutral nations are endangered. This consideration led, in the progress of the War of our Independence, to the formation of the celebrated confederacy of armed neutrality, a primary object of which was to assert the doctrine that free ships make free goods, except in the case of articles contraband of war—a doctrine which from the very commencement of our national being has been a cherished idea of the statesmen of this country. At one period or another every maritime power has by some solemn treaty stipulation recognized that principle, and it might have been hoped that it would come to be universally received and respected as a rule of international law. But the refusal of one power prevented this, and in the next great war which ensued—that of the French Revolution—it failed to be respected among the belligerent States of Europe. Notwithstanding this, the principle is generally admitted to be a sound and salutary one, so much so that at the commencement of the existing war in Europe Great Britain and France announced their purpose to observe it for the present; not, however, as a recognized international right, but as a mere concession for the time being. The cooperation, however, of these two powerful maritime nations in the interest of neutral rights appeared to me to afford an occasion inviting and justifying on the part of the United States a renewed effort to make the doctrine in question a principle of international law, by means of special conventions between the several powers of Europe and America. Accordingly, a proposition embracing not only the rule that free ships make free goods, except contraband articles, but also the less contested one that neutral property other than contraband, though on board enemy's ships, shall be exempt from confiscation, has been submitted by this Government to those of Europe and America.

Russia acted promptly in this matter, and a convention was concluded between that country and the United States providing for the observance of the principles announced, not only as between themselves, but also as between them and all other nations which shall enter into like stipulations. None of the other powers have as yet taken final action on the subject. I am not aware, however, that any objection to the proposed stipulations has been made, but, on the contrary, they are acknowledged to be essential to the security of neutral commerce, and the only apparent obstacle to their general adoption is in the possibility that it may be encumbered by inadmissible conditions.

The King of the Two Sicilies has expressed to our minister at Naples his readiness to concur in our proposition relative to neutral rights and to enter into a convention on that subject.

The King of Prussia entirely approves of the project of a treaty to the same effect submitted to him, but proposes an additional article providing for the renunciation of privateering. Such an article, for most obvious reasons, is much desired by nations having naval establishments large in proportion to their foreign commerce. If it were adopted as an international rule, the commerce of a nation having comparatively a small naval force would be very much at the mercy of its enemy in case of war with a power of decided naval superiority. The bare statement of the condition in which the United States would be placed, after having surrendered the right to resort to privateers, in the event of war with a belligerent of naval supremacy will show that this Government could never listen to such a proposition. The navy of the first maritime power in Europe is at least ten times as large as that of the United States. The foreign commerce of the two countries is nearly equal, and about equally exposed to hostile depredations. In war between that power and the United States, without resort on our part to our mercantile marine the means of our enemy to inflict injury upon our commerce would be tenfold greater than ours to retaliate. We could not extricate our country from this unequal condition, with such an enemy, unless we at once departed from our present peaceful policy and became a great naval power. Nor would this country be better situated in war with one of the secondary naval powers. Though the naval disparity would be less, the greater extent and more exposed condition of our widespread commerce would give any of them a like advantage over us.

The proposition to enter into engagements to forego a resort to privateers in case this country should be forced into war with a great naval power is not entitled to more favorable consideration than would be a proposition to agree not to accept the services of volunteers for operations on land. When the honor or the rights of our country require it to assume a hostile attitude, it confidently relies upon the patriotism of its citizens, not ordinarily devoted to the military profession, to augment the Army and the Navy so as to make them fully adequate to the emergency which calls them into action. The proposal to surrender the right to employ privateers is professedly founded upon the principle that private property of unoffending noncombatants, though enemies, should be exempt from the ravages of war; but the proposed surrender goes but little way in carrying out that principle, which equally requires that such private property should not be seized or molested by national ships of war.

Should the leading powers of Europe concur in proposing as a rule of international law to exempt private property upon the ocean from seizure by public armed cruisers as well as by privateers, the United States will readily meet them upon that broad ground.

Since the adjournment of Congress the ratifications of the treaty between the United States and Great Britain relative to coast fisheries and to reciprocal trade with the British North American Provinces have been exchanged, and some of its anticipated advantages are already enjoyed by us, although its full execution was to abide certain acts of legislation not yet fully performed. So soon as it was ratified Great Britain opened to our commerce the free navigation of the river St. Lawrence and to our fishermen unmolested access to the shores and bays, from which they had been previously excluded, on the coasts of her North American Provinces; in return for which she asked for the introduction free of duty into the ports of the United States of the fish caught on the same coast by British fishermen. This being the compensation stipulated in the treaty for privileges of the highest importance and value to the United States, which were thus voluntarily yielded before it became effective, the request seemed to me to be a reasonable one; but it could not be acceded to from want of authority to suspend our laws imposing duties upon all foreign fish. In the meantime the Treasury Department issued a regulation for ascertaining the duties paid or secured by bonds on fish caught on the coasts of the British Provinces and brought to our markets by British subjects after the fishing grounds had been made fully accessible to the citizens of the United States. I recommend to your favorable consideration a proposition, which will be submitted to you, for authority to refund the duties and cancel the bonds thus received. The Provinces of Canada and New Brunswick have also anticipated the full operation of the treaty by legislative arrangements, respectively, to admit free of duty the products of the United States mentioned in the free list of the treaty; and an arrangement similar to that regarding British fish has been made for duties now chargeable on the products of those Provinces enumerated in the same free list and introduced therefrom into the United States, a proposition for refunding which will, in my judgment, be in like manner entitled to your favorable consideration.

There is difference of opinion between the United States and Great Britain as to the boundary line of the Territory of Washington adjoining the British possessions on the Pacific, which has already led to difficulties on the part of the citizens and local authorities of the two Governments I recommend that provision be made for a commission, to be joined by one on the part of Her Britannic Majesty, for the purpose of running and establishing the line in controversy. Certain stipulations of the third and fourth articles of the treaty concluded by the United States and Great Britain in 1846, regarding possessory rights of the Hudsons Bay Company and property of the Pugets Sound Agricultural Company, have given rise to serious disputes, and it is important to all concerned that summary means of settling them amicably should be devised. I have reason to believe that an arrangement can be made on just terms for the extinguishment of the rights in question, embracing also the right of the Hudsons Bay Company to the navigation of the river Columbia; and I therefore suggest to your consideration the expediency of making a contingent appropriation for that purpose.

France was the early and efficient ally of the United States in their struggle for independence. From that time to the present, with occasional slight interruptions, cordial relations of friendship have existed between the Governments and people of the two countries. The kindly sentiments cherished alike by both nations have led to extensive social and commercial intercourse, which I trust will not be interrupted or checked by any casual event of an apparently unsatisfactory character. The French consul at San Francisco was not long since brought into the United States district court at that place by compulsory process as a witness in favor of another foreign consul, in violation, as the French Government conceives, of his privileges under our consular convention with France. There being nothing in the transaction which could imply any disrespect to France or its consul, such explanation has been made as, I hope, will be satisfactory. Subsequently misunderstanding arose on the subject of the French Government having, as it appeared, abruptly excluded the American minister to Spain from passing through France on his way from London to Madrid. But that Government has unequivocally disavowed any design to deny the right of transit to the minister of the United States, and after explanations to this effect he has resumed his journey and actually returned through France to Spain. I herewith lay before Congress the correspondence on this subject between our envoy at Paris and the minister of foreign relations of the French Government.

The position of our affairs with Spain remains as at the close of the last session. Internal agitation, assuming very nearly the character of political revolution, has recently convulsed that country. The late ministers were violently expelled from power, and men of very different views in relation to its internal affairs have succeeded. Since this change there has been no propitious opportunity to resume and press on negotiations for the adjustment of serious questions of difficulty between the Spanish Government and the United States. There is reason to believe that our minister will find the present Government more favorably inclined than the preceding to comply with our just demands and to make suitable arrangements for restoring harmony and preserving peace between the two countries.

Negotiations are pending with Denmark to discontinue the practice of levying tolls on our vessels and their cargoes passing through the Sound. I do not doubt that we can claim exemption therefrom as a matter of right. It is admitted on all hands that this exaction is sanctioned, not by the general principles of the law of nations, but only by special conventions which most of the commercial nations have entered into with Denmark. The fifth article of our treaty of 1826 with Denmark provides that there shall not be paid on the vessels of the United States and their cargoes when passing through the Sound higher duties than those of the most favored nations. This may be regarded as an implied agreement to submit to the tolls during the continuance of the treaty, and consequently may embarrass the assertion of our right to be released therefrom. There are also other provisions in the treaty which ought to be modified. It was to remain in force for ten years and until one year after either party should give notice to the other of intention to terminate it. I deem it expedient that the contemplated notice should be given to the Government of Denmark.

The naval expedition dispatched about two years since for the purpose of establishing relations with the Empire of Japan has been ably and skillfully conducted to a successful termination by the officer to whom it was intrusted. A treaty opening certain of the ports of that populous country has been negotiated, and in order to give full effect thereto it only remains to exchange ratifications and adopt requisite commercial regulations.

The treaty lately concluded between the United States and Mexico settled some of our most embarrassing difficulties with that country, but numerous claims upon it for wrongs and injuries to our citizens remained unadjusted, and many new cases have been recently added to the former list of grievances. Our legation has been earnest in its endeavors to obtain from the Mexican Government a favorable consideration of these claims, but hitherto without success. This failure is probably in some measure to be ascribed to the disturbed condition of that country. It has been my anxious desire to maintain friendly relations with the Mexican Republic and to cause its rights and territories to be respected, not only by our citizens, but by foreigners who have resorted to the United States for the purpose of organizing hostile expeditions against some of the States of that Republic. The defenseless condition in which its frontiers have been left has stimulated lawless adventurers to embark in these enterprises and greatly increased the difficulty of enforcing our obligations of neutrality. Regarding it as my solemn duty to fulfill efficiently these obligations, not only toward Mexico, but other foreign nations, I have exerted all the powers with which I am invested to defeat such proceedings and bring to punishment those who by taking a part therein violated our laws. The energy and activity of our civil and military authorities have frustrated the designs of those who meditated expeditions of this character except in two instances. One of these, composed of foreigners, was at first countenanced and aided by the Mexican Government itself, it having been deceived as to their real object. The other, small in number, eluded the vigilance of the magistrates at San

Francisco and succeeded in reaching the Mexican territories; but the effective measures taken by this Government compelled the abandonment of the undertaking.

The commission to establish the new line between the United States and Mexico, according to the provisions of the treaty of the 30th of December last, has been organized, and the work is already commenced.

Our treaties with the Argentine Confederation and with the Republics of Uruguay and Paraguay secure to us the free navigation of the river La Plata and some of its larger tributaries, but the same success has not attended our endeavors to open the Amazon. The reasons in favor of the free use of that river I had occasion to present fully in a former message, and, considering the cordial relations which have long existed between this Government and Brazil, it may be expected that pending negotiations will eventually reach a favorable result.

Convenient means of transit between the several parts of a country are not only desirable for the objects of commercial and personal communication, but essential to its existence under one government. Separated, as are the Atlantic and Pacific coasts of the United States, by the whole breadth of the continent, still the inhabitants of each are closely bound together by community of origin and institutions and by strong attachment to the Union. Hence the constant and increasing intercourse and vast interchange of commercial productions between these remote divisions of the Republic. At the present time the most practicable and only commodious routes for communication between them are by the way of the isthmus of Central America. It is the duty of the Government to secure these avenues against all danger of interruption.

In relation to Central America, perplexing questions existed between the United States and Great Britain at the time of the cession of California. These, as well as questions which subsequently arose concerning interoceanic communication across the Isthmus, were, as it was supposed, adjusted by the treaty of April 19, 1850, but, unfortunately, they have been reopened by serious misunderstanding as to the import of some of its provisions, a readjustment of which is now under consideration. Our minister at London has made strenuous efforts to accomplish this desirable object, but has not yet found it possible to bring the negotiations to a termination.

As incidental to these questions, I deem it proper to notice an occurrence which happened in Central America near the close of the last session of Congress. So soon as the necessity was perceived of establishing interoceanic communications across the Isthmus a company was organized, under the authority of the State of Nicaragua, but composed for the most part of citizens of the United States, for the purpose of opening such a transit way by the river San Juan and Lake Nicaragua, which soon became an eligible and much used route in the transportation of our citizens and their property between the Atlantic and Pacific. Meanwhile, and in anticipation of the completion and importance of this transit way, a number of adventurers had taken possession of the old Spanish port at the mouth of the river San Juan in open defiance of the State or States of Central America, which upon their becoming independent had rightfully succeeded to the local sovereignty and jurisdiction of Spain. These adventurers undertook to change the name of the place from San Juan del Norte to Greytown, and though at first pretending to act as the subjects of the fictitious sovereign of the Mosquito Indians, they subsequently repudiated the control of any power whatever, assumed to adopt a distinct political organization, and declared themselves an independent sovereign state. If at some time a faint hope was entertained that they might become a stable and respectable community, that hope soon vanished. They proceeded to assert unfounded claims to civil jurisdiction over Punta Arenas, a position on the opposite side of the river San Juan, which was in possession, under a title wholly independent of them, of citizens of the United States interested in the Nicaragua Transit Company, and which was indispensably necessary to the prosperous operation of that route across the Isthmus. The company resisted their groundless claims, whereupon they proceeded to destroy some of its buildings and attempted violently to dispossess it.

At a later period they organized a strong force for the purpose of demolishing the establishment at Punta Arenas, but this mischievous design was defeated by the interposition of one of our ships of war at that time in the harbor of San Juan. Subsequently to this, in May last, a body of men from Greytown crossed over to Punta Arenas, arrogating authority to arrest on the charge of murder a captain of one of the steamboats of the Transit Company. Being well aware that the claim to exercise jurisdiction there would be resisted then, as it had been on previous occasions, they went prepared to assert it by force of arms. Our minister to Central America happened to be present on that occasion. Believing that the captain of the steamboat was innocent (for he witnessed the transaction on which the charge was founded), and believing also that the intruding party, having no jurisdiction over the place where they proposed to make the arrest, would encounter desperate resistance if they persisted in their purpose, he interposed, effectually, to prevent violence and bloodshed. The American minister afterwards visited Greytown, and whilst he was there a mob, including certain of the so-called public functionaries of the place, surrounded the house in which he was, avowing that they had come to arrest him by order of some person exercising the chief authority. While parleying with them he was wounded by a missile from the crowd. A boat dispatched from the American steamer *Northern Light* to release him from the perilous situation in which he was understood to be was fired into by the town guard and compelled to return. These incidents, together with the known character of the population of Greytown and their excited state, induced just apprehensions that the lives and property of our citizens at Punta Arenas would be in imminent danger after the departure of the steamer, with her passengers, for New York, unless a guard was left for their protection.   For this purpose, and in order to insure the safety of passengers and property passing over the route, a temporary force was organized, at considerable expense to the United States, for which provision was made at the last session of Congress.

This pretended community, a heterogeneous assemblage gathered from various countries, and composed for the most part of blacks and persons of mixed blood, had previously given other indications of mischievous and dangerous propensities.   Early in the same month property was clandestinely abstracted from the depot of the Transit Company and taken to Greytown.   The plunderers obtained shelter there and their pursuers were driven back by its people, who not only protected the wrongdoers and shared the plunder, but treated with rudeness and violence those who sought to recover their property.

Such, in substance, are the facts submitted to my consideration, and proved by trustworthy evidence.   I could not doubt that the case demanded the interposition of this Government.   Justice required that reparation should be made for so many and such gross wrongs, and that a course of insolence and plunder, tending directly to the insecurity of the lives of numerous travelers and of the rich treasure belonging to our citizens passing over this transit way, should be peremptorily arrested. Whatever it might be in other respects, the community in question, in power to do mischief, was not despicable.   It was well provided with ordnance, small arms, and ammunition, and might easily seize on the unarmed boats, freighted with millions of property, which passed almost daily within its reach.   It did not profess to belong to any regular government, and had, in fact, no recognized dependence on or connection with anyone to which the United States or their injured citizens might apply for redress or which could be held responsible in any way for the outrages committed.   Not standing before the world in the attitude of an organized political society, being neither competent to exercise the rights nor to discharge the obligations of a government, it was, in fact, a marauding establishment too dangerous to be disregarded and too guilty to pass unpunished, and yet incapable of being treated in any other way than as a piratical resort of outlaws or a camp of savages depredating on emigrant trains or caravans and the frontier. settlements of civilized states.

Seasonable notice was given to the people of Greytown that this Government required them to repair the injuries they had done to our citizens and to make suitable apology for their insult of our minister, and that a ship of war would be dispatched thither to enforce compliance with these demands.   But the notice passed unheeded.   Thereupon a commander of the Navy, in charge of the sloop of war *Cyane*, was ordered to repeat the demands and to insist upon a compliance therewith. Finding that neither the populace nor those assuming to have authority over them manifested any disposition to make the required reparation, or even to offer excuse for their conduct, he warned them by a public proclamation that if they did not give satisfaction within a time specified he would bombard the town. By this procedure he afforded them opportunity to provide for their personal safety. To those also who desired to avoid loss of property in the punishment about to be inflicted on the offending town he furnished the means of removing their effects by the boats of his own ship and of a steamer which he procured and tendered to them for that purpose. At length, perceiving no disposition on the part of the town to comply with his requisitions, he appealed to the commander of Her Britannic Majesty's schooner *Bermuda*, who was seen to have intercourse and apparently much influence with the leaders among them, to interpose and persuade them to take some course calculated to save the necessity of resorting to the extreme measure indicated in his proclamation; but that officer, instead of acceding to the request, did nothing more than to protest against the contemplated bombardment. No steps of any sort were taken by the people to give the satisfaction required. No individuals, if any there were, who regarded themselves as not responsible for the misconduct of the community adopted any means to separate themselves from the fate of the guilty. The several charges on which the demands for redress were founded had been publicly known to all for some time, and were again announced to them. They did not deny any of these charges; they offered no explanation, nothing in extenuation of their conduct, but contumaciously refused to hold any intercourse with the commander of the *Cyane*. By their obstinate silence they seemed rather desirous to provoke chastisement than to escape it. There is ample reason to believe that this conduct of wanton defiance on their part is imputable chiefly to the delusive idea that the American Government would be deterred from punishing them through fear of displeasing a formidable foreign power, which they presumed to think looked with complacency upon their aggressive and insulting deportment toward the United States. The *Cyane* at length fired upon the town. Before much injury had been done the fire was twice suspended in order to afford opportunity for an arrangement, but this was declined. Most of the buildings of the place, of little value generally, were in the sequel destroyed, but, owing to the considerate precautions taken by our naval commander, there was no destruction of life.

When the *Cyane* was ordered to Central America, it was confidently hoped and expected that no occasion would arise for "a resort to violence and destruction of property and loss of life." Instructions to that effect were given to her commander; and no extreme act would have been requisite had not the people themselves, by their extraordinary conduct in the affair, frustrated all the possible mild measures for obtaining satisfaction. A withdrawal from the place, the object of his visit entirely defeated, would under the circumstances in which the commander of the *Cyane* found himself have been absolute abandonment of all claim of our citizens for indemnification and submissive acquiescence in national indignity. It would have encouraged in these lawless men a spirit of insolence and rapine most dangerous to the lives and property of our citizens at Punta Arenas, and probably emboldened them to grasp at the treasures and valuable merchandise continually passing over the Nicaragua route. It certainly would have been most satisfactory to me if the objects of the *Cyane's* mission could have been consummated without any act of public force, but the arrogant contumacy of the offenders rendered it impossible to avoid the alternative either to break up their establishment or to leave them impressed with the idea that they might persevere with impunity in a career of insolence and plunder.

This transaction has been the subject of complaint on the part of some foreign powers, and has been characterized with more of harshness than of justice. If comparisons were to be instituted, it would not be difficult to present repeated instances in the history of states standing in the very front of modern civilization where communities far less offending and more defenseless than Greytown have been chastised with much greater severity, and where not cities only have been laid in ruins, but human life has been recklessly sacrificed and the blood of the innocent made profusely to mingle with that of the guilty.

Passing from foreign to domestic affairs, your attention is naturally directed to the financial condition of the country, always a subject of general interest. For complete and exact information regarding the finances and the various branches of the public service connected therewith I refer you to the report of the Secretary of the Treasury, from which it will appear that the amount of revenue during the last fiscal year from all sources was $73,549,705, and that the public expenditures for the same period, exclusive of payments on account of the public debt, amounted to $51,018,249. During the same period the payments made in redemption of the public debt, including interest and premium, amounted to $24,336,-380. To the sum total of the receipts of that year is to be added a balance remaining in the Treasury at the commencement thereof, amounting to $21,942,892; and at the close of the same year a corresponding balance, amounting to $20,137,967, of receipts above expenditures also remained in the Treasury. Although, in the opinion of the Secretary of the Treasury, the receipts of the current fiscal year are not likely to equal in amount those of the last, yet they will undoubtedly exceed the amount of expenditures by at least $15,000,000. I shall therefore continue to direct that the surplus revenue be applied, so far as it can be judiciously and economically done, to the reduction of the public debt, the amount of which at the commencement of the last fiscal year was $67,340,628; of which there had been paid on the 20th day of November, 1854, the sum of $22,365,172, leaving a balance of outstanding public debt of only $44,975,456, redeemable at different periods within fourteen years. There are also remnants of other Government stocks, most of which are already due, and on which the interest has ceased, but which have not yet been presented for payment, amounting to $233,179. This statement exhibits the fact that the annual income of the Government greatly exceeds the amount of its public debt, which latter remains unpaid only because the time of payment has not yet matured, and it can not be discharged at once except at the option of public creditors, who prefer to retain the securities of the United States; and the other fact, not less striking, that the annual revenue from all sources exceeds by many millions of dollars the amount needed for a prudent and economical administration of the Government.

The estimates presented to Congress from the different Executive Departments at the last session amounted to $38,406,581 and the appropriations made to the sum of $58,116,958. Of this excess of appropriations over estimates, however, more than twenty millions was applicable to extraordinary objects, having no reference to the usual annual expenditures. Among these objects was embraced ten millions to meet the third article of the treaty between the United States and Mexico; so that, in fact, for objects of ordinary expenditure the appropriations were limited to considerably less than $40,000,000. I therefore renew my recommendation for a reduction of the duties on imports. The report of the Secretary of the Treasury presents a series of tables showing the operation of the revenue system for several successive years; and as the general principle of reduction of duties with a view to revenue, and not protection, may now be regarded as the settled policy of the country, I trust that little difficulty will be encountered in settling the details of a measure to that effect.

In connection with this subject I recommend a change in the laws, which recent experience has shown to be essential to the protection of the Government. There is no express provision of law requiring the records and papers of a public character of the several officers of the Government to be left in their offices for the use of their successors, nor any provision declaring it felony on their part to make false entries in the books or return false accounts. In the absence of such express provision by law, the outgoing officers in many instances have claimed and exercised the right to take into their own possession important books and papers, on the ground that these were their private property, and have placed them beyond the reach of the Government. Conduct of this character, brought in several instances to the notice of the present Secretary of the Treasury, naturally awakened his suspicion, and resulted in the disclosure that at four ports—namely, Oswego, Toledo, Sandusky, and Milwaukee—the Treasury had, by false entries, been defrauded within the four years next preceding March, 1853, of the sum of $198,000. The great difficulty with which the detection of these frauds has been attended, in consequence of the abstraction of books and papers by the retiring officers, and the facility with which similar frauds in the public service may be perpetrated render the necessity of new legal enactments in the respects above referred to quite obvious. For other material modifications of the revenue laws which seem to me desirable, I refer you to the report of the Secretary of the Treasury. That report and the tables which accompany it furnish ample proofs of the solid foundation on which the financial security of the country rests and of the salutary influence of the independent-treasury system upon commerce and all monetary operations.

The experience of the last year furnishes additional reasons, I regret to say, of a painful character, for the recommendation heretofore made to provide for increasing the military force employed in the Territory inhabited by the Indians. The settlers on the frontier have suffered much from the incursions of predatory bands, and large parties of emigrants to our Pacific possessions have been massacred with impunity. The recurrence of such scenes can only be prevented by teaching these wild tribes the power of and their responsibility to the United States. From the garrisons of our frontier posts it is only possible to detach troops in small bodies; and though these have on all occasions displayed a gallantry and a stern devotion to duty which on a larger field would have commanded universal admiration, they have usually suffered severely in these conflicts with superior numbers, and have sometimes been entirely sacrificed. All the disposable force of the Army is already employed on this service, and is known to be wholly inadequate to the protection which should be afforded. The public mind of the country has been recently shocked by savage atrocities committed upon defenseless emigrants and border settlements, and hardly less by the unnecessary destruction of valuable lives where inadequate detachments of troops have undertaken to furnish the needed aid. Without increase of the military force these scenes will be repeated, it is to be feared, on a larger scale and with more disastrous consequences. Congress, I am sure, will perceive that the plainest duties and responsibilities of Government are involved in this question, and I doubt not that prompt action may be confidently anticipated when delay must be attended by such fearful hazards.

The bill of the last session providing for an increase of the pay of the rank and file of the Army has had beneficial results, not only in facilitating enlistments, but in obvious improvement in the class of men who enter the service. I regret that corresponding consideration was not bestowed on the officers, who, in view of their character and services and the expenses to which they are necessarily subject, receive at present what is, in my judgment, inadequate compensation.

The valuable services constantly rendered by the Army and its inestimable importance as the nucleus around which the volunteer forces of the nation can promptly gather in the hour of danger, sufficiently attest the wisdom of maintaining a military peace establishment; but the theory of our system and the wise practice under it require that any proposed augmentation in time of peace be only commensurate with our extended limits and frontier relations. While scrupulously adhering to this principle, I find in existing circumstances a necessity for increase of our military force, and it is believed that four new regiments, two of infantry and two of mounted men, will be sufficient to meet the present exigency. If it were necessary carefully to weigh the cost in a case of such urgency, it would be shown that the additional expense would be comparatively light.

With the increase of the numerical force of the Army should, I think, be combined certain measures of reform in its organic arrangement and administration. The present organization is the result of partial legislation often directed to special objects and interests; and the laws regulating rank and command, having been adopted many years ago from the British code, are not always applicable to our service. It is not surprising, therefore, that the system should be deficient in the symmetry and simplicity essential to the harmonious working of its several parts, and require a careful revision.

The present organization, by maintaining large staff corps or departments, separates many officers from that close connection with troops and those active duties in the field which are deemed requisite to qualify them for the varied responsibilities of high command. Were the duties of the Army staff mainly discharged by officers detached from their regiments, it is believed that the special service would be equally well performed and the discipline and instruction of the Army be improved. While due regard to the security of the rights of officers and to the nice sense of honor which should be cultivated among them would seem to exact compliance with the established rule of promotion in ordinary cases, still it can hardly be doubted that the range of promotion by selection, which is now practically confined to the grade of general officers, might be somewhat extended with benefit to the public service. Observance of the rule of seniority sometimes leads, especially in time of peace, to the promotion of officers who, after meritorious and even distinguished service, may have been rendered by age or infirmity incapable of performing active duty, and whose advancement, therefore, would tend to impair the efficiency of the Army. Suitable provision for this class of officers, by the creation of a retired list, would remedy the evil without wounding the just pride of men who by past services have established a claim to high consideration. In again commending this measure to the favorable consideration of Congress I would suggest that the power of placing officers on the retired list be limited to one year. The practical operation of the measure would thus be tested, and if after the lapse of years there should be occasion to renew the provision it can be reproduced with any improvements which experience may indicate. The present organization of the artillery into regiments is liable to obvious objections. The service of artillery is that of batteries, and an organization of batteries into a corps of artillery would be more consistent with the nature of their duties. A large part of the troops now called artillery are, and have been, on duty as infantry, the distinction between the two arms being merely nominal. This nominal artillery in our service is disproportionate to the whole force and greater than the wants of the country demand. I therefore commend the discontinuance of a distinction which has no foundation in either the arms used or the character of the service expected to be performed.

In connection with the proposition for the increase of the Army, I have presented these suggestions with regard to certain measures of reform as the complement of a system which would produce the happiest results from a given expenditure, and which, I hope, may attract the early attention and be deemed worthy of the approval of Congress.

The recommendation of the Secretary of the Navy having reference to more ample provisions for the discipline and general improvement in the character of seamen and for the reorganization and gradual increase of the Navy I deem eminently worthy of your favorable consideration. The principles which have controlled our policy in relation to the permanent military force by sea and land are sound, consistent with the theory of our system, and should by no means be disregarded. But, limiting the force to the objects particularly set forth in the preceding part of this message, we should not overlook the present magnitude and prospective extension of our commercial marine, nor fail to give due weight to the fact that besides the 2,000 miles of Atlantic seaboard we have now a Pacific coast stretching from Mexico to the British possessions in the north, teeming with wealth and enterprise and demanding the constant presence of ships of war. The augmentation of the Navy has not kept pace with the duties properly and profitably assigned to it in time of peace, and it is inadequate for the large field of its operations, not merely in the present, but still more in the progressively increasing exigencies of the commerce of the United States. I cordially approve of the proposed apprentice system for our national vessels recommended by the Secretary of the Navy.

The occurrence during the last few months of marine disasters of the most tragic nature, involving great loss of human life, has produced intense emotions of sympathy and sorrow throughout the country. It may well be doubted whether all these calamitous events are wholly attributable to the necessary and inevitable dangers of the sea. The merchants, mariners, and shipbuilders of the United States are, it is true, unsurpassed in far-reaching enterprise, skill, intelligence, and courage by any others in the world. But with the increasing amount of our commercial tonnage in the aggregate and the larger size and improved equipment of the ships now constructed a deficiency in the supply of reliable seamen begins to be very seriously felt. The inconvenience may perhaps be met in part by due regulation for the introduction into our merchant ships of indented apprentices, which, while it would afford useful and eligible occupation to numerous young men, would have a tendency to raise the character of seamen as a class. And it is deserving of serious reflection whether it may not be desirable to revise the existing laws for the maintenance of discipline at sea, upon which the security of life and property on the ocean must to so great an extent depend. Although much attention has already been given by Congress to the proper construction and arrangement of steam vessels and all passenger ships, still it is believed that the resources of science and mechanical skill in this direction have not been exhausted. No good reason exists for the marked distinction which appears upon our statutes between the laws for protecting life and property at sea and those for protecting them on land. In most of the States severe penalties are provided to punish conductors of trains, engineers, and others employed in the transportation of persons by railway or by steamboats on rivers. Why should not the same principle be applied to acts of insubordination, cowardice, or other misconduct on the part of masters and mariners producing injury or death to passengers on the high seas, beyond the jurisdiction of any of the States, and where such delinquencies can be reached only by the power of Congress? The whole subject is earnestly commended to your consideration.

The report of the Postmaster-General, to which you are referred for many interesting details in relation to this important and rapidly extending branch of the public service, shows that the expenditure of the year ending June 30, 1854, including $133,483 of balance due to foreign offices, amounted to $8,710,907. The gross receipts during the same period amounted to $6,955,586, exhibiting an expenditure over income of $1,755,321 and a diminution of deficiency as compared with the last year of $361,756. The increase of the revenue of the Department for the year ending June 30, 1854, over the preceding year was $970,399. No proportionate increase, however, can be anticipated for the current year, in consequence of the act of Congress of June 23, 1854, providing for increased compensation to all postmasters. From these statements it is apparent that the Post-Office Department, instead of defraying its expenses according to the design at the time of its creation, is now, and under existing laws must continue to be, to no small extent a charge upon the general Treasury. The cost of mail transportation during the year ending June 30, 1854, exceeds the cost of the preceding year by $495,074. I again call your attention to the subject of mail transportation by ocean steamers, and commend the suggestions of the Postmaster-General to your early attention.

During the last fiscal year 11,070,935 acres of the public lands have been surveyed and 8,190,017 acres brought into market. The number of acres sold is 7,035,735 and the amount received therefor $9,285,533. The aggregate amount of lands sold, located under military scrip and land warrants, selected as swamp lands by States, and by locating under grants for roads is upward of 23,000,000 acres. The increase of lands sold over the previous year is about 6,000,000 acres, and the sales during the first two quarters of the current year present the extraordinary result of five and a half millions sold, exceeding by nearly 4,000,000 acres the sales of the corresponding quarters of the last year.

The commendable policy of the Government in relation to setting apart public domain for those who have served their country in time of war is illustrated by the fact that since 1790 no less than 30,000,000 acres have been applied to this object.

The suggestions which I submitted in my annual message of last year in reference to grants of land in aid of the construction of railways were less full and explicit than the magnitude of the subject and subsequent developments would seem to render proper and desirable. Of the soundness of the principle then asserted with regard to the limitation of the power of Congress I entertain no doubt, but in its application it is not enough that the value of lands in a particular locality may be enhanced; that, in fact, a larger amount of money may probably be received in a given time for alternate sections than could have been realized for all the sections without the impulse and influence of the proposed improvements. A prudent proprietor looks beyond limited sections of his domain, beyond present results to the ultimate effect which a particular line of policy is likely to produce upon all his possessions and interests. The Government, which is trustee in this matter for the people of the States, is bound to take the same wise and comprehensive view. Prior to and during the last session of Congress upward of 30,000,000 acres of land were withdrawn from public sale with a view to applications for grants of this character pending before Congress. A careful review of the whole subject led me to direct that all such orders be abrogated and the lands restored to market, and instructions were immediately given to that effect. The applications at the last session contemplated the construction of more than 5,000 miles of road and grants to the amount of nearly 20,000,000 acres of the public domain. Even admitting the right on the part of Congress to be unquestionable, is it quite clear that the proposed grants would be productive of good, and not evil? The different projects are confined for the present to eleven States of this Union and one Territory. The reasons assigned for the grants show that it is proposed to put the works speedily in process of construction. When we reflect that since the commencement of the construction of railways in the United States, stimulated, as they have been, by the large dividends realized from the earlier works over the great thoroughfares and between the most important points of commerce and population, encouraged by State legislation, and pressed forward by the amazing energy of private enterprise, only 17,000 miles have been completed in all the States in a quarter of a century; when we see the crippled condition of many works commenced and prosecuted upon what were deemed to be sound principles and safe calculations; when we contemplate the enormous absorption of capital withdrawn from the ordinary channels of business, the extravagant rates of interest at this moment paid to continue operations, the bankruptcies, not merely in money but in character, and the inevitable effect upon finances generally, can it be doubted that the tendency is to run to excess in this matter? Is it wise to augment this excess by encouraging hopes of sudden wealth expected to flow from magnificent schemes dependent upon the action of Congress? Does the spirit which has produced such results need to be stimulated or checked? Is it not the better rule to leave all these works to private enterprise, regulated and, when expedient, aided by the cooperation of States? If constructed by private capital the stimulant and the check go together and furnish a salutary restraint against speculative schemes and extravagance. But it is manifest that with the most effective guards there is danger of going too fast and too far.

We may well pause before a proposition contemplating a simultaneous movement for the construction of railroads which in extent will equal, exclusive of the great Pacific road and all its branches, nearly one-third of the entire length of such works now completed in the United States, and which can not cost with equipments less than $150,000,000. The dangers likely to result from combinations of interests of this character can hardly be overestimated. But independently of these considerations, where is the accurate knowledge, the comprehensive intelligence, which shall discriminate between the relative claims of these twenty-eight proposed roads in eleven States and one Territory? Where will you begin and where end? If to enable these companies to execute their proposed works it is necessary that the aid of the General Government be primarily given, the policy will present a problem so comprehensive in its bearings and so important to our political and social well-being as to claim in anticipation the severest analysis. Entertaining these views, I recur with satisfaction to the experience and action of the last session of Congress as furnishing assurance that the subject will not fail to elicit a careful reexamination and rigid scrutiny.

It was my intention to present on this occasion some suggestions regarding internal improvements by the General Government, which want of time at the close of the last session prevented my submitting on the return to the House of Representatives with objections of the bill entitled "An act making appropriations for the repair, preservation, and completion of certain public works heretofore commenced under the authority of law;" but the space in this communication already occupied with other matter of immediate public exigency constrains me to reserve that subject for a special message, which will be transmitted to the two Houses of Congress at an early day.

The judicial establishment of the United States requires modification, and certain reforms in the manner of conducting the legal business of the Government are also much needed; but as I have addressed you upon both of these subjects at length before, I have only to call your attention to the suggestions then made.

My former recommendations in relation to suitable provision for various objects of deep interest to the inhabitants of the District of Columbia are renewed. Many of these objects partake largely of a national character, and are important independently of their relation to the prosperity of the only considerable organized community in the Union entirely unrepresented in Congress.

I have thus presented suggestions on such subjects as appear to me to be of particular interest or importance, and therefore most worthy of consideration during the short remaining period allotted to the labors of the present Congress.

Our forefathers of the thirteen united colonies, in acquiring their independence and in founding this Republic of the United States of America, have devolved upon us, their descendants, the greatest and the most noble trust ever committed to the hands of man, imposing upon all, and especially such as the public will may have invested for the time being with political functions, the most sacred obligations. We have to maintain inviolate the great doctrine of the inherent right of popular self-government; to reconcile the largest liberty of the individual citizen with complete security of the public order; to render cheerful obedience to the laws of the land, to unite in enforcing their execution, and to frown indignantly on all combinations to resist them; to harmonize a sincere and ardent devotion to the institutions of religious faith with the most universal religious toleration; to preserve the rights of all by causing each to respect those of the other; to carry forward every social improvement to the uttermost limit of human perfectibility, by the free action of mind upon mind, not by the obtrusive intervention of misapplied force; to uphold the integrity and guard the limitations of our organic law; to preserve sacred from all touch of usurpation, as the very palladium of our political salvation, the reserved rights and powers of the several States and of the people; to cherish with loyal fealty and devoted affection this Union, as the only sure foundation on which the hopes of civil liberty rest; to administer government with vigilant integrity and rigid economy; to cultivate peace and friendship with foreign nations, and to demand and exact equal justice from all, but to do wrong to none; to eschew intermeddling with the national policy and the domestic repose of other governments, and to repel it from our own; never to shrink from war when the rights and the honor of the country call us to arms, but to cultivate in preference the arts of peace, seek enlargement of the rights of neutrality, and elevate and liberalize the intercourse of nations; and by such just and honorable means, and such only, whilst exalting the condition of the Republic, to assure to it the legitimate influence and the benign authority of a great example amongst all the powers of Christendom.

Under the solemnity of these convictions the blessing of Almighty God is earnestly invoked to attend upon your deliberations and upon all the counsels and acts of the Government, to the end that, with common zeal and common efforts, we may, in humble submission to the divine will, cooperate for the promotion of the supreme good of these United States.

THIRD ANNUAL MESSAGE.

WASHINGTON, *December 31, 1855.*

Fellow-Citizens of the Senate and of the House of Representatives:

The Constitution of the United States provides that Congress shall assemble annually on the first Monday of December, and it has been usual for the President to make no communication of a public character to the Senate and House of Representatives until advised of their readiness to receive it. I have deferred to this usage until the close of the first month of the session, but my convictions of duty will not permit me longer to postpone the discharge of the obligation enjoined by the Constitution upon the President "to give to the Congress information of the state of the Union and recommend to their consideration such measures as he shall judge necessary and expedient."

It is matter of congratulation that the Republic is tranquilly advancing in a career of prosperity and peace.

Whilst relations of amity continue to exist between the United States and all foreign powers, with some of them grave questions are depending which may require the consideration of Congress.

Of such questions, the most important is that which has arisen out of the negotiations with Great Britain in reference to Central America.

By the convention concluded between the two Governments on the 19th of April, 1850, both parties covenanted that "neither will ever" "occupy, or fortify, or colonize, or assume or exercise any dominion over Nicaragua. Costa Rica, the Mosquito Coast, or any part of Central America."

It was the undoubted understanding of the United States in making this treaty that all the present States of the former Republic of Central America and the entire territory of each would thenceforth enjoy complete independence, and that both contracting parties engaged equally and to the same extent, for the present and for the future, that if either then had any claim of right in Central America such claim and all occupation or authority under it were unreservedly relinquished by the stipulations of the convention, and that no dominion was thereafter to be exercised or assumed in any part of Central America by Great Britain or the United States.

This Government consented to restrictions in regard to a region of country wherein we had specific and peculiar interests only upon the conviction that the like restrictions were in the same sense obligatory on Great Britain. But for this understanding of the force and effect of the convention it would never have been concluded by us.

So clear was this understanding on the part of the United States that in correspondence contemporaneous with the ratification of the convention it was distinctly expressed that the mutual covenants of nonoccupation were not intended to apply to the British establishment at the Balize. This qualification is to be ascribed to the fact that, in virtue of successive treaties with previous sovereigns of the country, Great Britain had obtained a concession of the right to cut mahogany or dyewoods at the Balize, but with positive exclusion of all domain or sovereignty; and thus it confirms the natural construction and understood import of the treaty as to all the rest of the region to which the stipulations applied.

It, however, became apparent at an early day after entering upon the discharge of my present functions that Great Britain still continued in the exercise or assertion of large authority in all that part of Central America commonly called the Mosquito Coast, and covering the entire length of the State of Nicaragua and a part of Costa Rica; that she regarded the Balize as her absolute domain and was gradually extending its limits at the expense of the State of Honduras, and that she had formally colonized a considerable insular group known as the Bay Islands, and belonging of right to that State.

All these acts or pretensions of Great Britain, being contrary to the rights of the States of Central America and to the manifest tenor of her stipulations with the United States as understood by this Government, have been made the subject of negotiation through the American minister in London. I transmit herewith the instructions to him on the subject and the correspondence between him and the British secretary for foreign affairs, by which you will perceive that the two Governments differ widely and irreconcilably as to the construction of the convention and its effect on their respective relations to Central America.

Great Britain so construes the convention as to maintain unchanged all her previous pretensions over the Mosquito Coast and in different parts of Central America. These pretensions as to the Mosquito Coast are founded on the assumption of political relation between Great Britain and the remnant of a tribe of Indians on that coast, entered into at a time when the whole country was a colonial possession of Spain. It can not be successfully controverted that by the public law of Europe and America no possible act of such Indians or their predecessors could confer on Great Britain any political rights.

Great Britain does not allege the assent of Spain as the origin of her claims on the Mosquito Coast. She has, on the contrary, by repeated and successive treaties renounced and relinquished all pretensions of her own and recognized the full and sovereign rights of Spain in the most unequivocal terms. Yet these pretensions, so without solid foundation in the beginning and thus repeatedly abjured, were at a recent period revived by Great Britain against the Central American States, the legitimate successors to all the ancient jurisdiction of Spain in that region. They were first applied only to a defined part of the coast of Nicaragua, afterwards to the whole of its Atlantic coast, and lastly to a part of the coast of Costa Rica, and they are now reasserted to this extent notwithstanding engagements to the United States.

On the eastern coast of Nicaragua and Costa Rica the interference of Great Britain, though exerted at one time in the form of military occupation of the port of San Juan del Norte, then in the peaceful possession of the appropriate authorities of the Central American States, is now presented by her as the rightful exercise of a protectorship over the Mosquito tribe of Indians.

But the establishment at the Balize, now reaching far beyond its treaty limits into the State of Honduras, and that of the Bay Islands, appertaining of right to the same State, are as distinctly colonial governments as those of Jamaica or Canada, and therefore contrary to the very letter, as well as the spirit, of the convention with the United States as it was at the time of ratification and now is understood by this Government.

The interpretation which the British Government thus, in assertion and act, persists in ascribing to the convention entirely changes its character. While it holds us to all our obligations, it in a great measure releases Great Britain from those which constituted the consideration of this Government for entering into the convention. It is impossible, in my judgment, for the United States to acquiesce in such a construction of the respective relations of the two Governments to Central America.

To a renewed call by this Government upon Great Britain to abide by and carry into effect the stipulations of the convention according to its obvious import by withdrawing from the possession or colonization of portions of the Central American States of Honduras, Nicaragua, and Costa Rica, the British Government has at length replied, affirming that the operation of the treaty is prospective only and did not require Great Britain to abandon or contract any possessions held by her in Central America at the date of its conclusion.

This reply substitutes a partial issue in the place of the general one presented by the United States. The British Government passes over the question of the rights of Great Britain, real or supposed, in Central America, and assumes that she had such rights at the date of the treaty and that those rights comprehended the protectorship of the Mosquito Indians, the extended jurisdiction and limits of the Balize, and the colony of the Bay Islands, and thereupon proceeds by implication to infer that if the stipulations of the treaty be merely future in effect Great Britain may still continue to hold the contested portions of Central America. The United States can not admit either the inference or the premises. We steadily deny that at the date of the treaty Great Britain had any possessions there other than the limited and peculiar establishment at the Balize, and maintain that if she had any they were surrendered by the convention.

This Government, recognizing the obligations of the treaty, has, of course, desired to see it executed in good faith by both parties, and in the discussion, therefore, has not looked to rights which we might assert independently of the treaty in consideration of our geographical position and of other circumstances which create for us relations to the Central American States different from those of any government of Europe.

The British Government, in its last communication, although well knowing the views of the United States, still declares that it sees no reason why a conciliatory spirit may not enable the two Governments to overcome all obstacles to a satisfactory adjustment of the subject.

Assured of the correctness of the construction of the treaty constantly adhered to by this Government and resolved to insist on the rights of the United States, yet actuated also by the same desire which is avowed by the British Government, to remove all causes of serious misunderstanding between two nations associated by so many ties of interest and kindred, it has appeared to me proper not to consider an amicable solution of the controversy hopeless.

There is, however, reason to apprehend that with Great Britain in the actual occupation of the disputed territories, and the treaty therefore practically null so far as regards our rights, this international difficulty can not long remain undetermined without involving in serious danger the friendly relations which it is the interest as well as the duty of both countries to cherish and preserve. It will afford me sincere gratification if future efforts shall result in the success anticipated heretofore with more confidence than the aspect of the case permits me now to entertain.

One other subject of discussion between the United States and Great Britain has grown out of the attempt, which the exigencies of the war in which she is engaged with Russia induced her to make, to draw recruits from the United States.

It is the traditional and settled policy of the United States to maintain impartial neutrality during the wars which from time to time occur among the great powers of the world. Performing all the duties of neutrality toward the respective belligerent states, we may reasonably expect them not to interfere with our lawful enjoyment of its benefits. Notwithstanding the existence of such hostilities, our citizens retained the individual right to continue all their accustomed pursuits, by land or by sea, at home or abroad, subject only to such restrictions in this relation as the laws of war, the usage of nations, or special treaties may impose; and it is our sovereign right that our territory and jurisdiction shall not be invaded by either of the belligerent parties for the transit of their armies, the operations of their fleets, the levy of troops for their service, the fitting out of cruisers by or against either, or any other act or incident of war. And these undeniable rights of neutrality, individual and national, the United States will under no circumstances surrender.

In pursuance of this policy, the laws of the United States do not forbid their citizens to sell to either of the belligerent powers articles contraband of war or take munitions of war or soldiers on board their private ships for transportation; and although in so doing the individual citizen exposes his property or person to some of the hazards of war, his acts do not involve any breach of national neutrality nor of themselves implicate the Government. Thus, during the progress of the present war in Europe, our citizens have, without national responsibility therefor, sold gunpowder and arms to all buyers, regardless of the destination of those articles. Our merchantmen have been, and still continue to be, largely employed by Great Britain and by France in transporting troops, provisions, and munitions of war to the principal seat of military operations and in bringing home their sick and wounded soldiers; but such use of our mercantile marine is not interdicted either by the international or by our municipal law, and therefore does not compromit our neutral relations with Russia.

But our municipal law, in accordance with the law of nations, peremptorily forbids not only foreigners, but our own citizens, to fit out within the United States a vessel to commit hostilities against any state with which the United States are at peace, or to increase the force of any foreign armed vessel intended for such hostilities against a friendly state.

Whatever concern may have been felt by either of the belligerent powers lest private armed cruisers or other vessels in the service of one might be fitted out in the ports of this country to depredate on the property of the other, all such fears have proved to be utterly groundless. Our citizens have been withheld from any such act or purpose by good faith and by respect for the law.

While the laws of the Union are thus peremptory in their prohibition of the equipment or armament of belligerent cruisers in our ports, they provide not less absolutely that no person shall, within the territory or jurisdiction of the United States, enlist or enter himself, or hire or retain another person to enlist or enter himself, or to go beyond the limits or jurisdiction of the United States with intent to be enlisted or entered, in the service of any foreign state, either as a soldier or as a marine or seaman on board of any vessel of war, letter of marque, or privateer. And these enactments are also in strict conformity with the law of nations, which declares that no state has the right to raise troops for land or sea service in another state without its consent, and that, whether forbidden by the municipal law or not, the very attempt to do it without such consent is an attack on the national sovereignty.

Such being the public rights and the municipal law of the United States, no solicitude on the subject was entertained by this Government when, a year since, the British Parliament passed an act to provide for the enlistment of foreigners in the military service of Great Britain. Nothing on the face of the act or in its public history indicated that the British Government proposed to attempt recruitment in the United States, nor did it ever give intimation of such intention to this Government. It was matter of surprise, therefore, to find subsequently that the engagement of persons within the United States to proceed to Halifax, in the British Province of Nova Scotia, and there enlist in the service of Great Britain, was going on extensively, with little or no disguise. Ordinary legal steps were immediately taken to arrest and punish parties concerned, and so put an end to acts infringing the municipal law and derogatory to our sovereignty. Meanwhile suitable representations on the subject were addressed to the British Government.

Thereupon it became known, by the admission of the British Government itself, that the attempt to draw recruits from this country originated with it, or at least had its approval and sanction; but it also appeared that the public agents engaged in it had "stringent instructions" not to violate the muncipal law of the United States.

It is difficult to understand how it should have been supposed that troops could be raised here by Great Britain without violation of the municipal law. The unmistakable object of the law was to prevent every such act which if performed must be either in violation of the law or in studied evasion of it, and in either alternative the act done would be alike injurious to the sovereignty of the United States.

In the meantime the matter acquired additional importance by the recruitments in the United States not being discontinued, and the disclosure of the fact that they were prosecuted upon a systematic plan devised by official authority; that recruiting rendezvous had been opened in our principal cities and depots for the reception of recruits established on our frontier, and the whole business conducted under the supervision and by the regular cooperation of British officers, civil and military, some in the North American Provinces and some in the United States. The complicity of those officers in an undertaking which could only be accomplished by defying our laws, throwing suspicion over our attitude of neutrality, and disregarding our territorial rights is conclusively proved by the evidence elicited on the trial of such of their agents as have been apprehended and convicted. Some of the officers thus implicated are of high official position, and many of them beyond our jurisdiction, so that legal proceedings could not reach the source of the mischief.

These considerations, and the fact that the cause of complaint was not a mere casual occurrence, but a deliberate design, entered upon with full knowledge of our laws and national policy and conducted by responsible public functionaries, impelled me to present the case to the British Government, in order to secure not only a cessation of the·wrong, but its reparation. The subject is still under discussion, the result of which will be communicated to you in due time.

I repeat the recommendation submitted to the last Congress, that provision be made for the appointment of a commissioner, in connection with Great Britain, to survey and establish the boundary line which divides the Territory of Washington from the contiguous British possessions. By reason of the extent and importance of the country in dispute, there has been imminent danger of collision between the subjects of Great Britain and the citizens of the United States, including their respective authorities, in that quarter. The prospect of a speedy arrangement has contributed hitherto to induce on both sides forbearance to assert by force what each claims as a right. Continuance of delay on the part of the two Governments to act in the matter·will increase the dangers and difficulties of the controversy.

Misunderstanding exists as to the extent, character, and value of the possessory rights of the Hudsons Bay Company and the property of the Pugets Sound Agricultural Company reserved in our treaty with Great Britain relative to the Territory of Oregon. I have reason to believe that a cession of the rights of both companies to the United States, which would be the readiest means of terminating all questions, can be obtained on reasonable terms, and with a view to this end I present the subject to the attention of Congress.

The colony of Newfoundland, having enacted the laws required by the treaty of the 5th of June, 1854, is now placed on the same footing in respect to commercial intercourse with the United States as the other British North American Provinces.

The commission which that treaty contemplated, for determining the rights of fishery in rivers and mouths of rivers on the coasts of the United States and the British North American Provinces, has been organized, and has commenced its labors, to complete which there are needed further appropriations for the service of another season.

In pursuance of the authority conferred by a resolution of the Senate of the United States passed on the 3d of March last, notice was given to Denmark on the 14th day of April of the intention of this Government to avail itself of the stipulation of the subsisting convention of friendship, commerce, and navigation between that Kingdom and the United States whereby either party might after ten years terminate the same at the expiration of one year from the date of notice for that purpose.

The considerations which led me to call the attention of Congress to that convention and induced the Senate to adopt the resolution referred to still continue in full force. The convention contains an article which, although it does not directly engage the United States to submit to the imposition of tolls on the vessels and cargoes of Americans passing into or from the Baltic Sea during the continuance of the treaty, yet may by possibility be construed as implying such submission. The exaction of those tolls not being justified by any principle of international law, it became the right and duty of the United States to relieve themselves from the implication of engagement on the subject, so as to be perfectly free to act in the premises in such way as their public interests and honor shall demand.

I remain of the opinion that the United States ought not to submit to the payment of the Sound dues, not so much because of their amount, which is a secondary matter, but because it is in effect the recognition of the right of Denmark to treat one of the great maritime highways of nations as a close sea, and prevent the navigation of it as a privilege, for which tribute may be imposed upon those who have occasion to use it.

This Government on a former occasion, not unlike the present, signalized its determination to maintain the freedom of the seas and of the great natural channels of navigation. The Barbary States had for a long time coerced the payment of tribute from all nations whose ships frequented the Mediterranean. To the last demand of such payment made by them the United States, although suffering less by their depredations than many other nations, returned the explicit answer that we preferred war to tribute, and thus opened the way to the relief of the commerce of the world from an ignominious tax, so long submitted to by the more powerful nations of Europe.

If the manner of payment of the Sound dues differ from that of the tribute formerly conceded to the Barbary States, still their exaction by Denmark has no better foundation in right. Each was in its origin nothing but a tax on a common natural right, extorted by those who were at that time able to obstruct the free and secure enjoyment of it, but who no longer possess that power.

Denmark, while resisting our assertion of the freedom of the Baltic Sound and Belts, has indicated a readiness to make some new arrangement on the subject, and has invited the governments interested, including the United States, to be represented in a convention to assemble for the purpose of receiving and considering a proposition which she intends to submit for the capitalization of the Sound dues and the distribution of the sum to be paid as commutation among the governments according to the respective proportions of their maritime commerce to and from the Baltic. I have declined, in behalf of the United States, to accept this invitation, for the most cogent reasons. One is that Denmark does not offer to submit to the convention the question of her right to levy the

Sound dues. The second is that if the convention were allowed to take cognizance of that particular question, still it would not be competent to deal with the great international principle involved, which affects the right in other cases of navigation and commercial freedom, as well as that of access to the Baltic. Above all, by the express terms of the proposition it is contemplated that the consideration of the Sound dues shall be commingled with and made subordinate to a matter wholly extraneous—the balance of power among the Governments of Europe.

While, however, rejecting this proposition and insisting on the right of free transit into and from the Baltic, I have expressed to Denmark a willingness on the part of the United States to share liberally with other powers in compensating her for any advantages which commerce shall hereafter derive from expenditures made by her for the improvement and safety of the navigation of the Sound or Belts.

I lay before you herewith sundry documents on the subject, in which my views are more fully disclosed. Should no satisfactory arrangement be soon concluded, I shall again call your attention to the subject, with recommendation of such measures as may appear to be required in order to assert and secure the rights of the United States, so far as they are affected by the pretensions of Denmark.

I announce with much gratification that since the adjournment of the last Congress the question then existing between this Government and that of France respecting the French consul at San Francisco has been satisfactorily determined, and that the relations of the two Governments continue to be of the most friendly nature.

A question, also, which has been pending for several years between the United States and the Kingdom of Greece, growing out of the sequestration by public authorities of that country of property belonging to the present American consul at Athens, and which had been the subject of very earnest discussion heretofore, has recently been settled to the satisfaction of the party interested and of both Governments.

With Spain peaceful relations are still maintained, and some progress has been made in securing the redress of wrongs complained of by this Government. Spain has not only disavowed and disapproved the conduct of the officers who illegally seized and detained the steamer *Black Warrior* at Havana, but has also paid the sum claimed as indemnity for the loss thereby inflicted on citizens of the United States.

In consequence of a destructive hurricane which visited Cuba in 1844, the supreme authority of that island issued a decree permitting the importation for the period of six months of certain building materials and provisions free of duty, but revoked it when about half the period only had elapsed, to the injury of citizens of the United States who had proceeded to act on the faith of that decree. The Spanish Government refused indemnification to the parties aggrieved until recently, when it was assented to, payment being promised to be made so soon as the amount due can be ascertained.

Satisfaction claimed for the arrest and search of the steamer *El Dorado* has not yet been accorded, but there is reason to believe that it will be; and that case, with others, continues to be urged on the attention of the Spanish Government. I do not abandon the hope of concluding with Spain some general arrangement which, if it do not wholly prevent the recurrence of difficulties in Cuba, will render them less frequent, and, whenever they shall occur, facilitate their more speedy settlement.

The interposition of this Government has been invoked by many of its citizens on account of injuries done to their persons and property for which the Mexican Republic is responsible. The unhappy situation of that country for some time past has not allowed its Government to give due consideration to claims of private reparation, and has appeared to call for and justify some forbearance in such matters on the part of this Government. But if the revolutionary movements which have lately occurred in that Republic end in the organization of a stable government, urgent appeals to its justice will then be made, and, it may be hoped, with success, for the redress of all complaints of our citizens.

In regard to the American Republics, which from their proximity and other considerations have peculiar relations to this Government, while it has been my constant aim strictly to observe all the obligations of political friendship and of good neighborhood, obstacles to this have arisen in some of them from their own insufficient power to check lawless irruptions, which in effect throws most of the task on the United States. Thus it is that the distracted internal condition of the State of Nicaragua has made it incumbent on me to appeal to the good faith of our citizens to abstain from unlawful intervention in its affairs and to adopt preventive measures to the same end, which on a similar occasion had the best results in reassuring the peace of the Mexican States of Sonora and Lower California.

Since the last session of Congress a treaty of amity, commerce, and navigation and for the surrender of fugitive criminals with the Kingdom of the Two Sicilies; a treaty of friendship, commerce, and navigation with Nicaragua, and a convention of commercial reciprocity with the Hawaiian Kingdom have been negotiated. The latter Kingdom and the State of Nicaragua have also acceded to a declaration recognizing as international rights the principles contained in the convention between the United States and Russia of July 22, 1854. These treaties and conventions will be laid before the Senate for ratification.

The statements made in my last annual message respecting the anticipated receipts and expenditures of the Treasury have been substantially verified.

It appears from the report of the Secretary of the Treasury that the receipts during the last fiscal year, ending June 30, 1855, from all sources were $65,003,930, and that the public expenditures for the same period, exclusive of payments on account of the public debt, amounted to $56,-365,393. During the same period the payments made in redemption of the public debt, including interest and premium, amounted to $9,844,528.

The balance in the Treasury at the beginning of the present fiscal year, July 1, 1855, was $18,931,976; the receipts for the first quarter and the estimated receipts for the remaining three quarters amount together to $67,918,734; thus affording in all, as the available resources of the current fiscal year, the sum of $86,856,710.

If to the actual expenditures of the first quarter of the current fiscal year be added the probable expenditures for the remaining three quarters, as estimated by the Secretary of the Treasury, the sum total will be $71,226,846, thereby leaving an estimated balance in the Treasury on July 1, 1856, of $15,623,863.41.

In the above-estimated expenditures of the present fiscal year are included $3,000,000 to meet the last installment of the ten millions provided for in the late treaty with Mexico and $7,750,000 appropriated on account of the debt due to Texas, which two sums make an aggregate amount of $10,750,000 and reduce the expenditures, actual or estimated, for ordinary objects of the year to the sum of $60,476,000.

The amount of the public debt at the commencement of the present fiscal year was $40,583,631, and, deduction being made of subsequent payments, the whole public debt of the Federal Government remaining at this time is less than $40,000,000. The remnant of certain other Government stocks, amounting to $243,000, referred to in my last message as outstanding, has since been paid.

I am fully persuaded that it would be difficult to devise a system superior to that by which the fiscal business of the Government is now conducted. Notwithstanding the great number of public agents of collection and disbursement, it is believed that the checks and guards provided, including the requirement of monthly returns, render it scarcely possible for any considerable fraud on the part of those agents or neglect involving hazard of serious public loss to escape detection. I renew, however, the recommendation heretofore made by me of the enactment of a law declaring it felony on the part of public officers to insert false entries in their books of record or account or to make false returns, and also requiring them on the termination of their service to deliver to their successors all books, records, and other objects of a public nature in their custody.

Derived, as our public revenue is, in chief part from duties on imports, its magnitude affords gratifying evidence of the prosperity, not only of our commerce, but of the other great interests upon which that depends.

The principle that all moneys not required for the current expenses of the Government should remain for active employment in the hands of the people and the conspicuous fact that the annual revenue from all sources exceeds by many millions of dollars the amount needed for a prudent and economical administration of public affairs can not fail to suggest the propriety of an early revision and reduction of the tariff of duties on imports. It is now so generally conceded that the purpose of revenue alone can justify the imposition of duties on imports that in readjusting the impost tables and schedules, which unquestionably require essential modifications, a departure from the principles of the present tariff is not anticipated.

The Army during the past year has been actively engaged in defending the Indian frontier, the state of the service permitting but few and small garrisons in our permanent fortifications. The additional regiments authorized at the last session of Congress have been recruited and organized, and a large portion of the troops have already been sent to the field. All the duties which devolve on the military establishment have been satisfactorily performed, and the dangers and privations incident to the character of the service required of our troops have furnished additional evidence of their courage, zeal, and capacity to meet any requisition which their country may make upon them. For the details of the military operations, the distribution of the troops, and additional provisions required for the military service, I refer to the report of the Secretary of War and the accompanying documents.

Experience gathered from events which have transpired since my last annual message has but served to confirm the opinion then expressed of the propriety of making provision by a retired list for disabled officers and for increased compensation to the officers retained on the list for active duty. All the reasons which existed when these measures were recommended on former occasions continue without modification, except so far as circumstances have given to some of them additional force.

The recommendations heretofore made for a partial reorganization of the Army are also renewed. The thorough elementary education given to those officers who commence their service with the grade of cadet qualifies them to a considerable extent to perform the duties of every arm of the service; but to give the highest efficiency to artillery requires the practice and special study of many years, and it is not, therefore, believed to be advisable to maintain in time of peace a larger force of that arm than can be usually employed in the duties appertaining to the service of field and siege artillery. The duties of the staff in all its various branches belong to the movements of troops, and the efficiency of an army in the field would materially depend upon the ability with which those duties are discharged. It is not, as in the case of the artillery, a specialty, but requires also an intimate knowledge of the duties of an officer of the line, and it is not doubted that to complete the education of an officer for either the line or the general staff it is desirable that he shall have served in both. With this view, it was recommended on a former occasion that the duties of the staff should be mainly performed by details from the line, and, with conviction of the advantages which would result from such a change, it is again presented for the consideration of Congress.

The report of the Secretary of the Navy, herewith submitted, exhibits in full the naval operations of the past year, together with the present condition of the service, and it makes suggestions of further legislation, to which your attention is invited.

The construction of the six steam frigates for which appropriations were made by the last Congress has proceeded in the most satisfactory manner and with such expedition as to warrant the belief that they will be ready for service early in the coming spring. Important as this addition to our naval force is, it still remains inadequate to the contingent exigencies of the protection of the extensive seacoast and vast commercial interests of the United States. In view of this fact and of the acknowledged wisdom of the policy of a gradual and systematic increase of the Navy an appropriation is recommended for the construction of six steam sloops of war.

In regard to the steps taken in execution of the act of Congress to promote the efficiency of the Navy, it is unnecessary for me to say more than to express entire concurrence in the observations on that subject presented by the Secretary in his report.

It will be perceived by the report of the Postmaster-General that the gross expenditure of the Department for the last fiscal year was $9,968,-342 and the gross receipts $7,342,136, making an excess of expenditure over receipts of $2,626,206; and that the cost of mail transportation during that year was $674,952 greater than the previous year. Much of the heavy expenditures to which the Treasury is thus subjected is to be ascribed to the large quantity of printed matter conveyed by the mails, either franked or liable to no postage by law or to very low rates of postage compared with that charged on letters, and to the great cost of mail service on railroads and by ocean steamers. The suggestions of the Postmaster-General on the subject deserve the consideration of Congress.

The report of the Secretary of the Interior will engage your attention as well for useful suggestions it contains as for the interest and importance of the subjects to which they refer.

The aggregate amount of public land sold during the last fiscal year, located with military scrip or land warrants, taken up under grants for roads, and selected as swamp lands by States is 24,557,409 acres, of which the portion sold was 15,729,524 acres, yielding in receipts the sum of $11,485,380. In the same period of time 8,723,854 acres have been surveyed, but, in consideration of the quantity already subject to entry, no additional tracts have been brought into market.

The peculiar relation of the General Government to the District of Columbia renders it proper to commend to your care not only its material but also its moral interests, including education, more especially in those parts of the District outside of the cities of Washington and Georgetown.

The commissioners appointed to revise and codify the laws of the District have made such progress in the performance of their task as to insure its completion in the time prescribed by the act of Congress.

Information has recently been received that the peace of the settlements in the Territories of Oregon and Washington is disturbed by hostilities on the part of the Indians, with indications of extensive combinations of a hostile character among the tribes in that quarter, the more serious in their possible effect by reason of the undetermined foreign interests existing in those Territories, to which your attention has already been especially invited. Efficient measures have been taken, which, it is believed, will restore quiet and afford protection to our citizens.

In the Territory of Kansas there have been acts prejudicial to good order, but as yet none have occurred under circumstances to justify the interposition of the Federal Executive. That could only be in case of obstruction to Federal law or of organized resistance to Territorial law, assuming the character of insurrection, which, if it should occur, it would be my duty promptly to overcome and suppress. I cherish the hope, however, that the occurrence of any such untoward event will be prevented by the sound sense of the people of the Territory, who by its organic law, possessing the right to determine their own domestic institutions, are entitled while deporting themselves peacefully to the free exercise of that right, and must be protected in the enjoyment of it without interference on the part of the citizens of any of the States.

The southern boundary line of this Territory has never been surveyed and established. The rapidly extending settlements in that region and the fact that the main route between Independence, in the State of Missouri, and New Mexico is contiguous in this line suggest the probability that embarrassing questions of jurisdiction may consequently arise. For these and other considerations I commend the subject to your early attention.

I have thus passed in review the general state of the Union, including such particular concerns of the Federal Government, whether of domestic or foreign relation, as it appeared to me desirable and useful to bring to the special notice of Congress. Unlike the great States of Europe and Asia and many of those of America, these United States are wasting their strength neither in foreign war nor domestic strife. Whatever of discontent or public dissatisfaction exists is attributable to the imperfections of human nature or is incident to all governments, however perfect, which human wisdom can devise. Such subjects of political agitation as occupy the public mind consist to a great extent of exaggeration of inevitable evils, or overzeal in social improvement, or mere imagination of grievance, having but remote connection with any of the constitutional functions or duties of the Federal Government. To whatever extent these questions exhibit a tendency menacing to the stability of the Constitution or the integrity of the Union, and no further, they demand the consideration of the Executive and require to be presented by him to Congress.

Before the thirteen colonies became a confederation of independent

States they were associated only by community of transatlantic origin, by geographical position, and by the mutual tie of common dependence on Great Britain. When that tie was sundered they severally assumed the powers and rights of absolute self-government. The municipal and social institutions of each, its laws of property and of personal relation, even its political organization, were such only as each one chose to establish, wholly without interference from any other. In the language of the Declaration of Independence, each State had "full power to levy war, conclude peace, contract alliances, establish commerce, and to do all other acts and things which independent states may of right do." The several colonies differed in climate, in soil, in natural productions, in religion, in systems of education, in legislation, and in the forms of political administration, and they continued to differ in these respects when they voluntarily allied themselves as States to carry on the War of the Revolution.

The object of that war was to disenthrall the united colonies from foreign rule, which had proved to be oppressive, and to separate them permanently from the mother country. The political result was the foundation of a Federal Republic of the free white men of the colonies, constituted, as they were, in distinct and reciprocally independent State governments. As for the subject races, whether Indian or African, the wise and brave statesmen of that day, being engaged in no extravagant scheme of social change, left them as they were, and thus preserved themselves and their posterity from the anarchy and the ever-recurring civil wars which have prevailed in other revolutionized European colonies of America.

When the confederated States found it convenient to modify the conditions of their association by giving to the General Government direct access in some respects to the people of the States, instead of confining it to action on the States as such, they proceeded to frame the existing ˜onstitution, adhering steadily to one guiding thought, which was to delegate only such power as was necessary and proper to the execution of specific purposes, or, in other words, to retain as much as possible consistently with those purposes of the independent powers of the individual States. For objects of common defense and security, they intrusted to the General Government certain carefully defined functions, leaving all others as the undelegated rights of the separate independent sovereignties.

Such is the constitutional theory of our Government, the practical observance of which has carried us, and us alone among modern republics, through nearly three generations of time without the cost of one drop of blood shed in civil war. With freedom and concert of action, it has enabled us to contend successfully on the battlefield against foreign foes, has elevated the feeble colonies into powerful States, and has raised our industrial productions and our commerce which transports them to the level of the richest and the greatest nations of Europe. And the admirable adaptation of our political institutions to their objects, combining local self-government with aggregate strength, has established the practicability of a government like ours to cover a continent with confederate states.

The Congress of the United States is in effect that congress of sovereignties which good men in the Old World have sought for, but could never attain, and which imparts to America an exemption from the mutable leagues for common action, from the wars, the mutual invasions, and vague aspirations after the balance of power which convulse from time to time the Governments of Europe. Our cooperative action rests in the conditions of permanent confederation prescribed by the Constitution. Our balance of power is in the separate reserved rights of the States and their equal representation in the Senate. That independent sovereignty in every one of the States, with its reserved rights of local self-government assured to each by their coequal power in the Senate, was the fundamental condition of the Constitution. Without it the Union would never have existed. However desirous the larger States might be to reorganize the Government so as to give to their population its proportionate weight in the common counsels, they knew it was impossible unless they conceded to the smaller ones authority to exercise at least a negative influence on all the measures of the Government, whether legislative or executive, through their equal representation in the Senate. Indeed, the larger States themselves could not have failed to perceive that the same power was equally necessary to them for the security of their own domestic interests against the aggregate force of the General Government. In a word, the original States went into this permanent league on the agreed premises of exerting their common **strength for the defense of the whole and of all its parts, but of utterly** excluding all capability of reciprocal aggression. Each solemnly bound itself to all the others neither to undertake nor permit any encroachment upon or intermeddling with another's reserved rights.

Where it was deemed expedient particular rights of the States were expressly guaranteed by the Constitution, but in all things besides these rights were guarded by the limitation of the powers granted and by express reservation of all powers not granted in the compact of union. Thus the great power of taxation was limited to purposes of common defense and general welfare, excluding objects appertaining to the local legislation of the several States; and those purposes of general welfare and common defense were afterwards defined by specific enumeration as being matters only of co-relation between the States themselves or between them and foreign governments, which, because of their common and general nature, could not be left to the separate control of each State.

Of the circumstances of local condition, interest, and rights in which a portion of the States, constituting one great section of the Union, differed from the rest and from another section, the most important was the peculiarity of a larger relative colored population in the Southern than in the Northern States.

A population of this class, held in subjection, existed in nearly all the States, but was more numerous and of more serious concernment in the South than in the North on account of natural differences of climate and production; and it was foreseen that, for the same reasons, while this population would diminish and sooner or later cease to exist in some States, it might increase in others. The peculiar character and magnitude of this question of local rights, not in material relations only, but still more in social ones, caused it to enter into the special stipulations of the Constitution.

Hence, while the General Government, as well by the enumerated powers granted to it as by those not enumerated, and therefore refused to it, was forbidden to touch this matter in the sense of attack or offense, it was placed under the general safeguard of the Union in the sense of defense against either invasion or domestic violence, like all other local interests of the several States. Each State expressly stipulated, as well for itself as for each and all of its citizens, and every citizen of each State became solemnly bound by his allegiance to the Constitution that any person held to service or labor in one State, escaping into another, should not, in consequence of any law or regulation thereof, be discharged from such service or labor, but should be delivered up on claim of the party to whom such service or labor might be due by the laws of his State.

Thus and thus only, by the reciprocal guaranty of all the rights of every State against interference on the part of another, was the present form of government established by our fathers and transmitted to us, and by no other means is it possible for it to exist. If one State ceases to respect the rights of another and obtrusively intermeddles with its local interests; if a portion of the States assume to impose their institutions on the others or refuse to fulfill their obligations to them, we are no longer united, friendly States, but distracted, hostile ones, with little capacity left of common advantage, but abundant means of reciprocal injury and mischief. Practically it is immaterial whether aggressive interference between the States or deliberate refusal on the part of any one of them to comply with constitutional obligations arise from erroneous conviction or blind prejudice, whether it be perpetrated by direction or indirection. In either case it is full of threat and of danger to the durability of the Union.

Placed in the office of Chief Magistrate as the executive agent of the whole country, bound to take care that the laws be faithfully executed, and specially enjoined by the Constitution to give information to Congress on the state of the Union, it would be palpable neglect of duty on my part to pass over a subject like this, which beyond all things at the present time vitally concerns individual and public security.

It has been matter of painful regret to see States conspicuous for their services in founding this Republic and equally sharing its advantages disregard their constitutional obligations to it. Although conscious of their inability to heal admitted and palpable social evils of their own, and which are completely within their jurisdiction, they engage in the offensive and hopeless undertaking of reforming the domestic institutions of other States, wholly beyond their control and authority. In the vain pursuit of ends by them entirely unattainable, and which they may not legally attempt to compass, they peril the very existence of the Constitution and all the countless benefits which it has conferred. While the people of the Southern States confine their attention to their own affairs, not presuming officiously to intermeddle with the social institutions of the Northern States, too many of the inhabitants of the latter are permanently organized in associations to inflict injury on the former by wrongful acts, which would be cause of war as between foreign powers and only fail to be such in our system because perpetrated under cover of the Union.

Is it possible to present this subject as truth and the occasion require without noticing the reiterated but groundless allegation that the South has persistently asserted claims and obtained advantages in the practical administration of the General Government to the prejudice of the North, and in which the latter has acquiesced? That is, the States which either promote or tolerate attacks on the rights of persons and of property in other States, to disguise their own injustice, pretend or imagine, and constantly aver, that they, whose constitutional rights are thus systematically assailed, are themselves the aggressors. At the present time this imputed aggression, resting, as it does, only in the vague declamatory charges of political agitators, resolves itself into misapprehension or misinterpretation, of the principles and facts of the political organization of the new Territories of the United States.

What is the voice of history? When the ordinance which provided for the government of the territory northwest of the river Ohio and for its eventual subdivision into new States was adopted in the Congress of the Confederation, it is not to be supposed that the question of future relative power as between the States which retained and those which did not retain a numerous colored population escaped notice or failed to be considered. And yet the concession of that vast territory to the interests and opinions of the Northern States, a territory now the seat of five among the largest members of the Union, was in great measure the act of the State of Virginia and of the South.

When Louisiana was acquired by the United States, it was an acquisition not less to the North than to the South; for while it was important to the country at the mouth of the river Mississippi to become the emporium of the country above it, so also it was even more important to the whole Union to have that emporium; and although the new province, by reason of its imperfect settlement, was mainly regarded as on the Gulf of Mexico, yet in fact it extended to the opposite boundaries of the United States, with far greater breadth above than below, and was in territory, as in everything else, equally at least an accession to the Northern States. It is mere delusion and prejudice, therefore, to speak of Louisiana as acquisition in the special interest of the South.

The patriotic and just men who participated in that act were influenced by motives far above all sectional jealousies. It was in truth the great event which, by completing for us the possession of the Valley of the Mississippi, with commercial access to the Gulf of Mexico, imparted unity and strength to the whole Confederation and attached together by indissoluble ties the East and the West, as well as the North and the South.

As to Florida, that was but the transfer by Spain to the United States of territory on the east side of the river Mississippi in exchange for large territory which the United States transferred to Spain on the west side of that river, as the entire diplomatic history of the transaction serves to demonstrate. Moreover, it was an acquisition demanded by the commercial interests and the security of the whole Union.

In the meantime the people of the United States had grown up to a proper consciousness of their strength, and in a brief contest with France and in a second serious war with Great Britain they had shaken off all which remained of undue reverence for Europe, and emerged from the atmosphere of those transatlantic influences which surrounded the infant Republic, and had begun to turn their attention to the full and systematic development of the internal resources of the Union.

Among the evanescent controversies of that period the most conspicuous was the question of regulation by Congress of the social condition of the future States to be founded in the territory of Louisiana.

The ordinance for the government of the territory northwest of the river Ohio had contained a provision which prohibited the use of servile labor therein, subject to the condition of the extraditions of fugitives from service due in any other part of the United States. Subsequently to the adoption of the Constitution this provision ceased to remain as a law, for its operation as such was absolutely superseded by the Constitution. But the recollection of the fact excited the zeal of social propagandism in some sections of the Confederation, and when a second State, that of Missouri, came to be formed in the territory of Louisiana proposition was made to extend to the latter territory the restriction originally applied to the country situated between the rivers Ohio and Mississippi.

Most questionable as was this proposition in all its constitutional relations, nevertheless it received the sanction of Congress, with some slight modifications of line, to save the existing rights of the intended new State. It was reluctantly acquiesced in by Southern States as a sacrifice to the cause of peace and of the Union, not only of the rights stipulated by the treaty of Louisiana, but of the principle of equality among the States guaranteed by the Constitution. It was received by the Northern States with angry and resentful condemnation and complaint, because it did not concede all which they had exactingly demanded. Having passed through the forms of legislation, it took its place in the statute book, standing open to repeal, like any other act of doubtful constitutionality, subject to be pronounced null and void by the courts of law, and possessing no possible efficacy to control the rights of the States which might thereafter be organized out of any part of the original territory of Louisiana.

In all this, if any aggression there were, any innovation upon preexisting rights, to which portion of the Union are they justly chargeable?

This controversy passed away with the occasion, nothing surviving it save the dormant letter of the statute.

But long afterwards, when by the proposed accession of the Republic of Texas the United States were to take their next step in territorial greatness, a similar contingency occurred and became the occasion for systematized attempts to intervene in the domestic affairs of one section of the Union, in defiance of their rights as States and of the stipulations of the Constitution. These attempts assumed a practical direction in the shape of persevering endeavors by some of the Representatives in both Houses of Congress to deprive the Southern States of the supposed benefit of the provisions of the act authorizing the organization of the State of Missouri.

But the good sense of the people and the vital force of the Constitution triumphed over sectional prejudice and the political errors of the day, and the State of Texas returned to the Union as she was, with social institutions which her people had chosen for themselves and with express agreement by the reannexing act that she should be susceptible of subdivision into a plurality of States.

Whatever advantage the interests of the Southern States, as such, gained by this were far inferior in results, as they unfolded in the progress of time, to those which sprang from previous concessions made by the South.

To every thoughtful friend of the Union, to the true lovers of their country, to all who longed and labored for the full success of this great experiment of republican institutions, it was cause of gratulation that such an opportunity had occurred to illustrate our advancing power on this continent and to furnish to the world additional assurance of the strength and stability of the Constitution. Who would wish to see Florida still a European colony? Who would rejoice to hail Texas as a lone star instead of one in the galaxy of States? Who does not appreciate the incalculable benefits of the acquisition of Louisiana? And yet narrow views and sectional purposes would inevitably have excluded them all from the Union.

But another struggle on the same point ensued when our victorious armies returned from Mexico and it devolved on Congress to provide for the territories acquired by the treaty of Guadalupe Hidalgo. The great relations of the subject had now become distinct and clear to the perception of the public mind, which appreciated the evils of sectional controversy upon the question of the admission of new States. In that crisis intense solicitude pervaded the nation. But the patriotic impulses of the popular heart, guided by the admonitory advice of the Father of his Country, rose superior to all the difficulties of the incorporation of a new empire into the Union. In the counsels of Congress there was manifested extreme antagonism of opinion and action between some Representatives, who sought by the abusive and unconstitutional employment of the legislative powers of the Government to interfere in the condition of the inchoate States and to impose their own social theories upon the latter, and other Representatives, who repelled the interposition of the General Government in this respect and maintained the self-constituting rights of the States. In truth, the thing attempted was in form alone action of the General Government, while in reality it was the endeavor, by abuse of legislative power, to force the ideas of internal policy entertained in particular States upon allied independent States. Once more the Constitution and the Union triumphed signally. The new territories were organized without restrictions on the disputed point, and were thus left to judge in that particular for themselves; and the sense of constitutional faith proved vigorous enough in Congress not only to accomplish this primary object, but also the incidental and hardly less important one of so amending the provisions of the statute for the extradition of fugitives from service as to place that public duty under the safeguard of the General Government, and thus relieve it from obstacles raised up by the legislation of some of the States.

Vain declamation regarding the provisions of law for the extradition of fugitives from service, with occasional episodes of frantic effort to obstruct their execution by riot and murder, continued for a brief time to agitate certain localities. But the true principle of leaving each State and Territory to regulate its own laws of labor according to its own sense of right and expediency had acquired fast hold of the public judgment, to such a degree that by common consent it was observed in the organization of the Territory of Washington.

When, more recently, it became requisite to organize the Territories of Nebraska and Kansas, it was the natural and legitimate, if not the inevitable, consequence of previous events and legislation that the same great and sound principle which had already been applied to Utah and New Mexico should be applied to them—that they should stand exempt from the restrictions proposed in the act relative to the State of Missouri.

These restrictions were, in the estimation of many thoughtful men, null from the beginning, unauthorized by the Constitution, contrary to the treaty stipulations for the cession of Louisiana, and inconsistent with the equality of these States.

They had been stripped of all moral authority by persistent efforts to procure their indirect repeal through contradictory enactments. They had been practically abrogated by the legislation attending the organization of Utah, New Mexico, and Washington. If any vitality remained in them it would have been taken away, in effect, by the new Territorial acts in the form originally proposed to the Senate at the first session of the last Congress. It was manly and ingenuous, as well as patriotic and just, to do this directly and plainly, and thus relieve the statute book of an act which might be of possible future injury, but of no possible future benefit; and the measure of its repeal was the final consummation and complete recognition of the principle that no portion of the United States shall undertake through assumption of the powers of the General Government to dictate the social institutions of any other portion.

The scope and effect of the language of repeal were not left in doubt. It was declared in terms to be "the true intent and meaning of this act not to legislate slavery into any Territory or State, nor to exclude it therefrom, but to leave the people thereof perfectly free to form and regulate their domestic institutions in their own way, subject only to the Constitution of the United States."

The measure could not be withstood upon its merits alone. It was attacked with violence on the false or delusive pretext that it constituted a breach of faith.   Never was objection more utterly destitute of substantial justification.   When before was it imagined by sensible men that a regulative or declarative statute, whether enacted ten or forty years ago, is irrepealable ; that an act of Congress is above the Constitution?   If indeed, there were in the facts any cause to impute bad faith, it would attach to those only who have never ceased, from the time of the enactment of the restrictive provision to the present day, to denounce and condemn it; who have constantly refused to complete it by needful supplementary legislation; who have spared no exertion to deprive it of moral force; who have themselves again and again attempted its repeal by the enactment of incompatible provisions, and who, by the inevitable reactionary effect of their own violence on the subject, awakened the country to perception of the true constitutional principle of leaving the matter involved to the discretion of the people of the respective existing or incipient States.

It is not pretended that this principle or any other precludes the possibility of evils in practice, disturbed, as political action is liable to be, by human passions.   No form of government is exempt from inconveniences; but in this case they are the result of the abuse, and not of the legitimate exercise, of the powers reserved or conferred in the organization of a Territory.   They are not to be charged to the great principle of popular sovereignty.   On the contrary, they disappear before the intelligence and patriotism of the people, exerting through the ballot box their peaceful and silent but irresistible power.

If the friends of the Constitution are to have another struggle, its enemies could not present a more acceptable issue than that of a State whose constitution clearly embraces "a republican form of government" being excluded from the Union because its domestic institutions may not in all respects comport with the ideas of what is wise and expedient entertained in some other State. Fresh from groundless imputations of breach of faith against others, men will commence the agitation of this new question with indubitable violation of an express compact between the independent sovereign powers of the United States and of the Republic of Texas, as well as of the older and equally solemn compacts which assure the equality of all the States.

But deplorable as would be such a violation of compact in itself and in all its direct consequences, that is the very least of the evils involved. When sectional agitators shall have succeeded in forcing on this issue, can their pretensions fail to be met by counter pretensions? Will not different States be compelled, respectively, to meet extremes with extremes? And if either extreme carry its point, what is that so far forth but dissolution of the Union? If a new State, formed from the territory of the United States, be absolutely excluded from admission therein, that fact of itself constitutes the disruption of union between it and the other States. But the process of dissolution could not stop there. Would not a sectional decision producing such result by a majority of votes, either Northern or Southern, of necessity drive out the oppressed and aggrieved minority and place in presence of each other two irreconcilably hostile confederations?

It is necessary to speak thus plainly of projects the offspring of that sectional agitation now prevailing in some of the States, which are as impracticable as they are unconstitutional, and which if persevered in must and will end calamitously. It is either disunion and civil war or it is mere angry, idle, aimless disturbance of public peace and tranquillity. Disunion for what? If the passionate rage of fanaticism and partisan spirit did not force the fact upon our attention, it would be difficult to believe that any considerable portion of the people of this enlightened country could have so surrendered themselves to a fanatical devotion to the supposed interests of the relatively few Africans in the United States as totally to abandon and disregard the interests of the 25,000,000 Americans; to trample under foot the injunctions of moral and constitutional obligation, and to engage in plans of vindictive hostility against those who are associated with them in the enjoyment of the common heritage of our national institutions.

Nor is it hostility against their fellow-citizens of one section of the Union alone. The interests, the honor, the duty, the peace, and the prosperity of the people of all sections are equally involved and imperiled in this question. And are patriotic men in any part of the Union prepared on such issue thus madly to invite all the consequences of the forfeiture of their constitutional engagements? It is impossible. The storm of frenzy and faction must inevitably dash itself in vain against the unshaken rock of the Constitution. I shall never doubt it. I know that the Union is stronger a thousand times than all the wild and chimerical schemes of social change which are generated one after another in the unstable minds of visionary sophists and interested agitators. I rely confidently on the patriotism of the people, on the dignity and self-respect of the States, on the wisdom of Congress, and, above all, on the continued gracious favor of Almighty God to maintain against all enemies, whether at home or abroad, the sanctity of the Constitution and the integrity of the Union.

FOURTH ANNUAL MESSAGE.

WASHINGTON, *December 2, 1856.*

Fellow-Citizens of the Senate and of the House of Representatives:

The Constitution requires that the President shall from time to time not only recommend to the consideration of Congress such measures as he may judge necessary and expedient, but also that he shall give information to them of the state of the Union. To do this fully involves exposition of all matters in the actual condition of the country, domestic or foreign, which essentially concern the general welfare. While performing his constitutional duty in this respect, the President does not speak merely to express personal convictions, but as the executive minister of the Government, enabled by his position and called upon by his official obligations to scan with an impartial eye the interests of the whole and of every part of the United States.

Of the condition of the domestic interests of the Union—its agriculture, mines, manufactures, navigation, and commerce—it is necessary only to say that the internal prosperity of the country, its continuous and steady advancement in wealth and population and in private as well as public well-being, attest the wisdom of our institutions and the predominant spirit of intelligence and patriotism which, notwithstanding occasional irregularities of opinion or action resulting from popular freedom, has distinguished and characterized the people of America.

In the brief interval between the termination of the last and the commencement of the present session of Congress the public mind has been occupied with the care of selecting for another constitutional term the President and Vice-President of the United States.

The determination of the persons who are of right, or contingently, to preside over the administration of the Government is under our system committed to the States and the people. We appeal to them, by their voice pronounced in the forms of law, to call whomsoever they will to the high post of Chief Magistrate.

And thus it is that as the Senators represent the respective States of the Union and the members of the House of Representatives the several constituencies of each State, so the President represents the aggregate population of the United States. Their election of him is the explicit and solemn act of the sole sovereign authority of the Union.

It is impossible to misapprehend the great principles which by their recent political action the people of the United States have sanctioned and announced.

They have asserted the constitutional equality of each and all of the States of the Union as States: they have affirmed the constitutional equality of each and all of the citizens of the United States as citizens, whatever their religion, wherever their birth or their residence; they have maintained the inviolability of the constitutional rights of the different sections of the Union, and they have proclaimed their devoted and unalterable attachment to the Union and to the Constitution, as objects of interest superior to all subjects of local or sectional controversy, as the safeguard of the rights of all, as the spirit and the essence of the liberty, peace, and greatness of the Republic.

In doing this they have at the same time emphatically condemned the idea of organizing in these United States mere geographical parties, of marshaling in hostile array toward each other the different parts of the country, North or South, East or West.

Schemes of this nature, fraught with incalculable mischief, and which the considerate sense of the people has rejected, could have had countenance in no part of the country had they not been disguised by suggestions plausible in appearance, acting upon an excited state of the public mind, induced by causes temporary in their character and, it is to be hoped, transient in their influence.

Perfect liberty of association for political objects and the widest scope of discussion are the received and ordinary conditions of government in our country. Our institutions, framed in the spirit of confidence in the intelligence and integrity of the people, do not forbid citizens, either individually or associated together, to attack by writing, speech, or any other methods short of physical force the Constitution and the very existence of the Union. Under the shelter of this great liberty, and protected by the laws and usages of the Government they assail, associations have been formed in some of the States of individuals who, pretending to seek only to prevent the spread of the institution of slavery into the present or future inchoate States of the Union, are really inflamed with desire to change the domestic institutions of existing States. To accomplish their objects they dedicate themselves to the odious task of depreciating the government organization which stands in their way and of calumniating with indiscriminate invective not only the citizens of particular States with whose laws they find fault, but all others of their fellow-citizens throughout the country who do not participate with them in their assaults upon the Constitution, framed and adopted by our fathers, and claiming for the privileges it has secured and the blessings it has conferred the steady support and grateful reverence of their children. They seek an object which they well know to be a revolutionary one. They are perfectly aware that the change in the relative condition of the white and black races in the slaveholding States which they would promote is beyond their lawful authority; that to them it is a foreign object; that it can not be effected by any peaceful instrumentality of theirs; that for them and the States of which they are citizens the only path to its accomplishment is through burning cities, and ravaged fields, and slaughtered populations, and all there is most terrible in foreign complicated with civil and servile war; and that the first step in the attempt is the forcible disruption of a country embracing in its broad bosom a degree of liberty and an amount of individual and public prosperity to which there is no parallel in history, and substituting in its place hostile governments, driven at once and inevitably into mutual devastation and fratricidal carnage, transforming the now peaceful and felicitous brotherhood into a vast permanent camp of armed men like the rival monarchies of Europe and Asia. Well knowing that such, and such only, are the means and the consequences of their plans and purposes, they endeavor to prepare the people of the United States for civil war by doing everything in their power to deprive the Constitution and the laws of moral authority and to undermine the fabric of the Union by appeals to passion and sectional prejudice, by indoctrinating its people with reciprocal hatred, and by educating them to stand face to face as enemies, rather than shoulder to shoulder as friends.

It is by the agency of such unwarrantable interference, foreign and domestic, that the minds of many otherwise good citizens have been so inflamed into the passionate condemnation of the domestic institutions of the Southern States as at length to pass insensibly to almost equally passionate hostility toward their fellow-citizens of those States, and thus finally to fall into temporary fellowship with the avowed and active enemies of the Constitution. Ardently attached to liberty in the abstract, they do not stop to consider practically how the objects they would attain can be accomplished, nor to reflect that, even if the evil were as great as they deem it, they have no remedy to apply, and that it can be only aggravated by their violence and unconstitutional action. A question which is one of the most difficult of all the problems of social institution, political economy, and statesmanship they treat with unreasoning intemperance of thought and language. Extremes beget extremes. Violent attack from the North finds its inevitable consequence in the growth of a spirit of angry defiance at the South. Thus in the progress of events we had reached that consummation, which the voice of the people has now so pointedly rebuked, of the attempt of a portion of the States, by a sectional organization and movement, to usurp the control of the Government of the United States.

I confidently believe that the great body of those who inconsiderately took this fatal step are sincerely attached to the Constitution and the Union. They would upon deliberation shrink with unaffected horror from any conscious act of disunion or civil war. But they have entered into a path which leads nowhere unless it be to civil war and disunion, and which has no other possible outlet. They have proceeded thus far in that direction in consequence of the successive stages of their progress having consisted of a series of secondary issues, each of which professed to be confined within constitutional and peaceful limits, but which attempted indirectly what few men were willing to do directly; that is, to act aggressively against the constitutional rights of nearly one-half of the thirty-one States.

In the long series of acts of indirect aggression, the first was the strenuous agitation by citizens of the Northern States, in Congress and out of it, of the question of negro emancipation in the Southern States.

The second step in this path of evil consisted of acts of the people of the Northern States, and in several instances of their governments, aimed to facilitate the escape of persons held to service in the Southern States and to prevent their extradition when reclaimed according to law and in virtue of express provisions of the Constitution. To promote this object, legislative enactments and other means were adopted to take away or defeat rights which the Constitution solemnly guaranteed. In order to nullify the then existing act of Congress concerning the extradition of fugitives from service, laws were enacted in many States forbidding their officers, under the severest penalties, to participate in the execution of any act of Congress whatever. In this way that system of harmonious cooperation between the authorities of the United States and of the several States, for the maintenance of their common institutions, which existed in the early years of the Republic was destroyed; conflicts of jurisdiction came to be frequent, and Congress found itself compelled, for the support of the Constitution and the vindication of its power, to authorize the appointment of new officers charged with the execution of its acts, as if they and the officers of the States were the ministers, respectively, of foreign governments in a state of mutual hostility rather than fellow-magistrates of a common country peacefully subsisting under the protection of one well-constituted Union. Thus here also aggression was followed by reaction, and the attacks upon the Constitution at this point did but serve to raise up new barriers for its defense and security.

The third stage of this unhappy sectional controversy was in connection with the organization of Territorial governments and the admission of new States into the Union. When it was proposed to admit the State of Maine, by separation of territory from that of Massachusetts, and the State of Missouri, formed of a portion of the territory ceded by France to the United States, representatives in Congress objected to the admission of the latter unless with conditions suited to particular views of public policy. The imposition of such a condition was successfully resisted; but at the same period the question was presented of imposing restrictions upon the residue of the territory ceded by France. That question was for the time disposed of by the adoption of a geographical line of limitation.

In this connection it should not be forgotten that when France, of her own accord, resolved, for considerations of the most far-sighted sagacity, to cede Louisiana to the United States, and that accession was accepted by the United States, the latter expressly engaged that "the inhabitants of the ceded territory shall be incorporated in the Union of the United States and admitted as soon as possible, according to the principles of the Federal Constitution, to the enjoyment of all the rights, advantages, and immunities of citizens of the United States; and in the meantime they shall be maintained and protected in the free enjoyment of their *liberty*, *property*, and the religion which they profess;" that is to say, while it remains in a Territorial condition its inhabitants are maintained and protected in the free enjoyment of their liberty and property, with a right then to pass into the condition of States on a footing of perfect equality with the original States.

The enactment which established the restrictive geographical line was acquiesced in rather than approved by the States of the Union. It stood on the statute book, however, for a number of years; and the people of the respective States acquiesced in the reenactment of the principle as applied to the State of Texas, and it was proposed to acquiesce in its further application to the territory acquired by the United States from Mexico. But this proposition was successfully resisted by the representatives from the Northern States, who, regardless of the statute line, insisted upon applying restriction to the new territory generally, whether lying north or south of it, thereby repealing it as a legislative compromise, and, on the part of the North, persistently violating the compact, if compact there was.

Thereupon this enactment ceased to have binding virtue in any sense, whether as respects the North or the South, and so in effect it was treated on the occasion of the admission of the State of California and the organization of the Territories of New Mexico, Utah, and Washington.

Such was the state of this question when the time arrived for the organization of the Territories of Kansas and Nebraska. In the progress of constitutional inquiry and reflection it had now at length come to be seen clearly that Congress does not possess constitutional power to impose restrictions of this character upon any present or future State of the Union. In a long series of decisions, on the fullest argument and after the most deliberate consideration, the Supreme Court of the United States had finally determined this point in every form under which the question could arise, whether as affecting public or private rights—in questions of the public domain, of religion, of navigation, and of servitude.

The several States of the Union are by force of the Constitution coequal in domestic legislative power. Congress can not change a law of domestic relation in the State of Maine; no more can it in the State of Missouri. Any statute which proposes to do this is a mere nullity; it takes away no right, it confers none. If it remains on the statute book unrepealed, it remains there only as a monument of error and a beacon of warning to the legislator and the statesman. To repeal it will be only to remove imperfection from the statutes, without affecting, either in the sense of permission. or of prohibition, the action of the States or of their citizens.

Still when the nominal restriction of this nature, already a dead letter in law, was in terms repealed by the last Congress, in a clause of the act organizing the Territories of Kansas and Nebraska, that repeal was made the occasion of a widespread and dangerous agitation.

It was alleged that the original enactment being a compact of perpetual moral obligation, its repeal constituted an odious breach of faith.

An act of Congress, while it remains unrepealed, more especially if it be constitutionally valid in the judgment of those public functionaries whose duty it is to pronounce on that point, is undoubtedly binding on the conscience of each good citizen of the Republic. But in what sense can it be asserted that the enactment in question was invested with perpetuity and entitled to the respect of a solemn compact? Between whom was the compact? No distinct contending powers of the Government, no separate sections of the Union treating as such, entered into treaty stipulations on the subject. It was a mere clause of an act of Congress, and, like any other controverted matter of legislation, received its final shape and was passed by compromise of the conflicting opinions or sentiments of the members of Congress. But if it had moral authority over men's consciences, to whom did this authority attach? Not to those of the North, who had repeatedly refused to confirm it by extension and who had zealously striven to establish other and incompatible regulations upon the subject. And if, as it thus appears, the supposed compact had no obligatory force as to the North, of course it could not have had any as to the South, for all such compacts must be mutual and of reciprocal obligation.

It has not unfrequently happened that lawgivers, with undue estimation of the value of the law they give or in the view of imparting to it peculiar strength, make it perpetual in terms; but they can not thus bind the conscience, the judgment, and the will of those who may succeed them, invested with similar responsibilities and clothed with equal authority. More careful investigation may prove the law to be unsound in principle. Experience may show it to be imperfect in detail and impracticable in execution. And then both reason and right combine not merely to justify but to require its repeal.

The Constitution, supreme, as it is, over all the departments of the Government—legislative, executive, and judicial—is open to amendment by its very terms; and Congress or the States may, in their discretion, propose amendment to it, solemn compact though it in truth is between the sovereign States of the Union. In the present instance a political enactment which had ceased to have legal power or authority of any kind was repealed. The position assumed that Congress had no moral right to enact such repeal was strange enough, and singularly so in view of the fact that the argument came from those who openly refused obedience to existing laws of the land, having the same popular designation and quality as compromise acts; nay, more, who unequivocally disregarded and condemned the most positive and obligatory injunctions of the Constitution itself, and sought by every means within their reach to deprive a portion of their fellow-citizens of the equal enjoyment of those rights and privileges guaranteed alike to all by the fundamental compact of our Union.

This argument against the repeal of the statute line in question was accompanied by another of congenial character and equally with the former destitute of foundation in reason and truth. It was imputed that the measure originated in the conception of extending the limits of slave labor beyond those previously assigned to it, and that such was its natural as well as intended effect; and these baseless assumptions were made, in the Northern States, the ground of unceasing assault upon constitutional right.

The repeal in terms of a statute, which was already obsolete and also null for unconstitutionality, could have no influence to obstruct or to promote the propagation of conflicting views of political or social institution. When the act organizing the Territories of Kansas and Nebraska was passed, the inherent effect upon that portion of the public domain thus opened to legal settlement was to admit settlers from all the States of the Union alike, each with his convictions of public policy and private interest, there to found, in their discretion, subject to such limitations as the Constitution and acts of Congress might prescribe, new States, hereafter to be admitted into the Union. It was a free field, open alike to all, whether the statute line of assumed restriction were repealed or not. That repeal did not open to free competition of the diverse opinions and domestic institutions a field which without such repeal would have been closed against them; it found that field of competition already opened, in fact and in law. All the repeal did was to relieve the statute book of an objectionable enactment, unconstitutional in effect and injurious in terms to a large portion of the States.

Is it the fact that in all the unsettled regions of the United States, if emigration be left free to act in this respect for itself, without legal prohibitions on either side, slave labor will spontaneously go everywhere in preference to free labor? Is it the fact that the peculiar domestic institutions of the Southern States possess relatively so much of vigor that wheresoever an avenue is freely opened to all the world they will penetrate to the exclusion of those of the Northern States? Is it the fact that the former enjoy, compared with the latter, such irresistibly superior vitality, independent of climate, soil, and all other accidental circumstances, as to be able to produce the supposed result in spite of the assumed moral and natural obstacles to its accomplishment and of the more numerous population of the Northern States?

The argument of those who advocate the enactment of new laws of restriction and condemn the repeal of old ones in effect avers that their particular views of government have no self-extending or self-sustaining power of their own, and will go nowhere unless forced by act of Congress. And if Congress do but pause for a moment in the policy of stern coercion; if it venture to try the experiment of leaving men to judge for themselves what institutions will best suit them; if it be not strained up to perpetual legislative exertion on this point—if Congress proceed thus to act in the very spirit of liberty, it is at once charged with aiming to extend slave labor into all the new Territories of the United States.

Of course these imputations on the intentions of Congress in this respect, conceived, as they were, in prejudice and disseminated in passion, are utterly destitute of any justification in the nature of things and contrary to all the fundamental doctrines and principles of civil liberty and self-government.

While, therefore, in general, the people of the Northern States have never at any time arrogated for the Federal Government the power to interfere directly with the domestic condition of persons in the Southern States, but, on the contrary, have disavowed all such intentions and have shrunk from conspicuous affiliation with those few who pursue their fanatical objects avowedly through the contemplated means of revolutionary change of the Government and with acceptance of the necessary consequences—a civil and servile war—yet many citizens have suffered themselves to be drawn into one evanescent political issue of agitation after another, appertaining to the same set of opinions, and which subsided as rapidly as they arose when it came to be seen, as it uniformly did, that they were incompatible with the compacts of the Constitution and the existence of the Union. Thus when the acts of some of the States to nullify the existing extradition law imposed upon Congress the duty of passing a new one, the country was invited by agitators to enter into party organization for its repeal; but that agitation speedily ceased by reason of the impracticability of its object. So when the statute restriction upon the institutions of new States by a geographical line had been repealed, the country was urged to demand its restoration, and that project also died almost with its birth. Then followed the cry of alarm from the North against imputed Southern encroachments, which cry sprang in reality from the spirit of revolutionary attack on the domestic institutions of the South, and, after a troubled existence of a few months, has been rebuked by the voice of a patriotic people.

Of this last agitation, one lamentable feature was that it was carried on at the immediate expense of the peace and happiness of the people of the Territory of Kansas. That was made the battlefield, not so much of opposing factions or interests within itself as of the conflicting passions of the whole people of the United States. Revolutionary disorder in Kansas had its origin in projects of intervention deliberately arranged by certain members of that Congress which enacted the law for the organization of the Territory; and when propagandist colonization of Kansas had thus been undertaken in one section of the Union for the systematic promotion of its peculiar views of policy there ensued as a matter of course a counteraction with opposite views in other sections of the Union.

In consequence of these and other incidents, many acts of disorder, it is undeniable, have been perpetrated in Kansas, to the occasional interruption rather than the permanent suspension of regular government. Aggressive and most reprehensible incursions into the Territory were undertaken both in the North and the South, and entered it on its northern border by the way of Iowa, as well as on the eastern by way of Missouri; and there has existed within it a state of insurrection against the constituted authorities, not without countenance from inconsiderate persons in each of the great sections of the Union. But the difficulties in that Territory have been extravagantly exaggerated for purposes of political agitation elsewhere. The number and gravity of the acts of violence have been magnified partly by statements entirely untrue and partly by reiterated accounts of the same rumors or facts. Thus the Territory has been seemingly filled with extreme violence, when the whole amount of such acts has not been greater than what occasionally passes before us in single cities to the regret of all good citizens, but without being regarded as of general or permanent political consequence.

Imputed irregularities in the elections had in Kansas, like occasional irregularities of the same description in the States, were beyond the sphere of action of the Executive. But incidents of actual violence or of organized obstruction of law, pertinaciously renewed from time to time, have been met as they occurred by such means as were available and as the circumstances required, and nothing of this character now remains to affect the general peace of the Union. The attempt of a part of the inhabitants of the Territory to erect a revolutionary government, though sedulously encouraged and supplied with pecuniary aid from active agents of disorder in some of the States, has completely failed. Bodies of armed men, foreign to the Territory, have been prevented from entering or compelled to leave it; predatory bands, engaged in acts of rapine under cover of the existing political disturbances, have been arrested or dispersed, and every well-disposed person is now enabled once more to devote himself in peace to the pursuits of prosperous industry, for the prosecution of which he undertook to participate in the settlement of the Territory.

It affords me unmingled satisfaction thus to announce the peaceful condition of things in Kansas, especially considering the means to which it was necessary to have recourse for the attainment of the end, namely, the employment of a part of the military force of the United States. The withdrawal of that force from its proper duty of defending the country against foreign foes or the savages of the frontier to employ it for the suppression of domestic insurrection is, when the exigency occurs, a matter of the most earnest solicitude. On this occasion of imperative necessity it has been done with the best results, and my satisfaction in the attainment of such results by such means is greatly enhanced by the consideration that, through the wisdom and energy of the present executive of Kansas and the prudence, firmness, and vigilance of the military officers on duty there tranquillity has been restored without one drop of blood having been shed in its accomplishment by the forces of the United States.

The restoration of comparative tranquillity in that Territory furnishes the means of observing calmly and appreciating at their just value the events which have occurred there and the discussions of which the government of the Territory has been the subject.

We perceive that controversy concerning its future domestic institutions was inevitable; that no human prudence, no form of legislation, no wisdom on the part of Congress, could have prevented it.

It is idle to suppose that the particular provisions of their organic law were the cause of agitation. Those provisions were but the occasion, or the pretext, of an agitation which was inherent in the nature of things. Congress legislated upon the subject in such terms as were most consonant with the principle of popular sovereignty which underlies our Government. It could not have legislated otherwise without doing violence to another great principle of our institutions—the imprescriptible right of equality of the several States.

We perceive also that sectional interests and party passions have been the great impediment to the salutary operation of the organic principles adopted and the chief cause of the successive disturbances in Kansas. The assumption that because in the organization of the Territories of Nebraska and Kansas Congress abstained from imposing restraints upon them to which certain other Territories had been subject, therefore disorders occurred in the latter Territory, is emphatically contradicted by the fact that none have occurred in the former. Those disorders were not the consequence, in Kansas, of the freedom of self-government conceded to that Territory by Congress, but of unjust interference on the part of persons not inhabitants of the Territory. Such interference, wherever it has exhibited itself by acts of insurrectionary character or of obstruction to process of law, has been repelled or suppressed by all the means which the Constitution and the laws place in the hands of the

Executive.

In those parts of the United States where, by reason of the inflamed state of the public mind, false rumors and misrepresentations have the greatest currency it has been assumed that it was the duty of the Executive not only to suppress insurrectionary movements in Kansas, but also to see to the regularity of local elections. It needs little argument to show that the President has no such power. All government in the United States rests substantially upon popular election. The freedom of elections is liable to be impaired by the intrusion of unlawful votes or the exclusion of lawful ones, by improper influences, by violence, or by fraud. But the people of the United States are themselves the all-sufficient guardians of their own rights, and to suppose that they will not remedy in due season any such incidents of civil freedom is to suppose them to have ceased to be capable of self-government. The President of the United States has not power to interpose in elections, to see to their freedom, to canvass their votes, or to pass upon their legality in the Territories any more than in the States. If he had such power the Government might be republican in form, but it would be a monarchy in fact; and if he had undertaken to exercise it in the case of Kansas he would have been justly subject to the charge of usurpation and of violation of the dearest rights of the people of the United States.

Unwise laws, equally with irregularities at elections, are in periods of great excitement the occasional incidents of even the freest and best political institutions; but all experience demonstrates that in a country like ours, where the right of self-constitution exists in the completest form, the attempt to remedy unwise legislation by resort to revolution is totally out of place, inasmuch as existing legal institutions afford more prompt and efficacious means for the redress of wrong.

I confidently trust that now, when the peaceful condition of Kansas affords opportunity for calm reflection and wise legislation, either the legislative assembly of the Territory or Congress will see that no act shall remain on its statute book violative of the provisions of the Constitution or subversive of the great objects for which that was ordained and established, and will take all other necessary steps to assure to its inhabitants the enjoyment, without obstruction or abridgment, of all the constitutional rights, privileges, and immunities of citizens of the United States, as contemplated by the organic law of the Territory.

Full information in relation to recent events in this Territory will be found in the documents communicated herewith from the Departments of State and War.

I refer you to the report of the Secretary of the Treasury for particular information concerning the financial condition of the Government and the various branches of the public service connected with the Treasury Department.

During the last fiscal year the receipts from customs were for the first time more than $64,000,000, and from all sources $73,918,141, which, with the balance on hand up to the 1st of July, 1855, made the total resources of the year amount to $92,850,117. The expenditures, including $3,000,000 in execution of the treaty with Mexico and excluding sums paid on account of the public debt, amounted to $60,172,401, and including the latter to $72,948,792, the payment on this account having amounted to $12,776,390.

On the 4th of March, 1853, the amount of the public debt was $69,-129,937. There was a subsequent increase of $2,750,000 for the debt of Texas, making a total of $71,879,937. Of this the sum of $45,525,319, including premium, has been discharged, reducing the debt to $30,963,-909, all which might be paid within a year without embarrassing the public service, but being not yet due and only redeemable at the option of the holder, can not be pressed to payment by the Government.

On examining the expenditures of the last five years it will be seen that the average, deducting payments on account of the public debt and $10,000,000 paid by treaty to Mexico, has been but about $48,000,000. It is believed that under an economical administration of the Government the average expenditure for the ensuing five years will not exceed that sum, unless extraordinary occasion for its increase should occur. The acts granting bounty lands will soon have been executed, while the extension of our frontier settlements will cause a continued demand for lands and augmented receipts, probably, from that source. These considerations will justify a reduction of the revenue from customs so as not to exceed forty-eight or fifty million dollars. I think the exigency for such reduction is imperative, and again urge it upon the consideration of Congress.

The amount of reduction, as well as the manner of effecting it, are questions of great and general interest, it being essential to industrial enterprise and the public prosperity, as well as the dictate of obvious justice, that the burden of taxation be made to rest as equally as possible upon all classes and all sections and interests of the country.

I have heretofore recommended to your consideration the revision of the revenue laws, prepared under the direction of the Secretary of the Treasury, and also legislation upon some special questions affecting the business of that Department, more especially the enactment of a law to punish the abstraction of official books or papers from the files of the Government and requiring all such books and papers and all other public property to be turned over by the outgoing officer to his successor; of a law requiring disbursing officers to deposit all public money in the vaults of the Treasury or in other legal depositories, where the same are conveniently accessible, and a law to extend existing penal provisions to all persons who may become possessed of public money by deposit or otherwise and who shall refuse or neglect on due demand to pay the same into the Treasury. I invite your attention anew to each of these objects.

The Army during the past year has been so constantly employed against hostile Indians in various quarters that it can scarcely be said, with propriety of language, to have been a peace establishment. Its duties have been satisfactorily performed, and we have reason to expect as a result of the year's operations greater security to the frontier inhabitants than has been hitherto enjoyed. Extensive combinations among the hostile Indians of the Territories of Washington and Oregon at one time threatened the devastation of the newly formed settlements of that remote portion of the country. From recent information we are permitted to hope that the energetic and successful operations conducted there will prevent such combinations in future and secure to those Territories an opportunity to make steady progress in the development of their agricultural and mineral resources.

Legislation has been recommended by me on previous occasions to cure defects in the existing organization and to increase the efficiency of the Army, and further observation has but served to confirm me in the views then expressed and to enforce on my mind the conviction that such measures are not only proper, but necessary.

I have, in addition, to invite the attention of Congress to a change of policy in the distribution of troops and to the necessity of providing a more rapid increase of the military armament. For details of these and other subjects relating to the Army I refer to the report of the Secretary of War.

The condition of the Navy is not merely satisfactory, but exhibits the most gratifying evidences of increased vigor. As it is comparatively small, it is more important that it should be as complete as possible in all the elements of strength; that it should be efficient in the character of its officers, in the zeal and discipline of its men, in the reliability of its ordnance, and in the capacity of its ships. In all these various qualities the Navy has made great progress within the last few years. The execution of the law of Congress of February 28, 1855, "to promote the efficiency of the Navy," has been attended by the most advantageous results. The law for promoting discipline among the men is found convenient and salutary. The system of granting an honorable discharge to faithful seamen on the expiration of the period of their enlistment and permitting them to reenlist after a leave of absence of a few months without cessation of pay is highly beneficial in its influence. The apprentice system recently adopted is evidently destined to incorporate into the service a large number of our countrymen, hitherto so difficult to procure. Several hundred American boys are now on a three years' cruise in our national vessels and will return well-trained seamen. In the Ordnance Department there is a decided and gratifying indication of progress, creditable to it and to the country. The suggestions of the Secretary of the Navy in regard to further improvement in that branch of the service I commend to your favorable action.

The new frigates ordered by Congress are now afloat and two of them in active service. They are superior models of naval architecture, and with their formidable battery add largely to public strength and security. I concur in the views expressed by the Secretary of the Department in favor of a still further increase of our naval force.

The report of the Secretary of the Interior presents facts and views in relation to internal affairs over which the supervision of his Department extends of much interest and importance.

The aggregate sales of the public lands during the last fiscal year amount to 9,227,878 acres, for which has been received the sum of $8,821,414. During the same period there have been located with military scrip and land warrants and for other purposes 30,100,230 acres, thus making a total aggregate of 39,328,108 acres. On the 30th of September last surveys had been made of 16,873,699 acres, a large proportion of which is ready for market.

The suggestions in this report in regard to the complication and progressive expansion of the business of the different bureaus of the Department, to the pension system, to the colonization of Indian tribes, and the recommendations in relation to various improvements in the District of Columbia are especially commended to your consideration.

The report of the Postmaster-General presents fully the condition of that Department of the Government. Its expenditures for the last fiscal year were $10,407,868 and its gross receipts $7,620,801, making an excess of expenditure over receipts of $2,787,046. The deficiency of this Department is thus $744,000 greater than for the year ending June 30, 1853. Of this deficiency $330,000 is to be attributed to the additional compensation allowed to postmasters by the act of Congress of June 22, 1854. The mail facilities in every part of the country have been very much increased in that period, and the large addition of railroad service, amounting to 7,908 miles, has added largely to the cost of transportation.

The inconsiderable augmentation of the income of the Post-Office Department under the reduced rates of postage and its increasing expenditures must for the present make it dependent to some extent upon the Treasury for support. The recommendations of the Postmaster-General in relation to the abolition of the franking privilege and his views on the establishment of mail steamship lines deserve the consideration of Congress. I also call the special attention of Congress to the statement of the Postmaster-General respecting the sums now paid for the transportation of mails to the Panama Railroad Company, and commend to their early and favorable consideration the suggestions of that officer in relation to new contracts for mail transportation upon that route, and also upon the Tehuantepec and Nicaragua routes.

The United States continue in the enjoyment of amicable relations with all foreign powers.

When my last annual message was transmitted to Congress two subjects of controversy, one relating to the enlistment of soldiers in this country for foreign service and the other to Central America, threatened to disturb the good understanding between the United States and Great Britain. Of the progress and termination of the former question you were informed at the time, and the other is now in the way of satisfactory adjustment.

The object of the convention between the United States and Great Britain of the 19th of April, 1850, was to secure for the benefit of all nations the neutrality and the common use of any transit way or interoceanic communication across the Isthmus of Panama which might be opened within the limits of Central America. The pretensions subsequently asserted by Great Britain to dominion or control over territories in or near two of the routes, those of Nicaragua and Honduras, were deemed by the United States not merely incompatible with the main object of the treaty, but opposed even to its express stipulations. Occasion of controversy on this point has been removed by an additional treaty, which our minister at London has concluded, and which will be immediately submitted to the Senate for its consideration. Should the proposed supplemental arrangement be concurred in by all the parties to be affected by it, the objects contemplated by the original convention will have been fully attained.

The treaty between the United States and Great Britain of the 5th of June, 1854, which went into effective operation in 1855, put an end to causes of irritation between the two countries, by securing to the United States the right of fishery on the coast of the British North American Provinces, with advantages equal to those enjoyed by British subjects. Besides the signal benefits of this treaty to a large class of our citizens engaged in a pursuit connected to no inconsiderable degree with our national prosperity and strength, it has had a favorable effect upon other interests in the provision it made for reciprocal freedom of trade between the United States and the British Provinces in America.

The exports of domestic articles to those Provinces during the last year amounted to more than $22,000,000, exceeding those of the preceding year by nearly $7,000,000; and the imports therefrom during the same period amounted to more than twenty-one million, an increase of six million upon those of the previous year.

The improved condition of this branch of our commerce is mainly attributable to the above-mentioned treaty.

Provision was made in the first article of that treaty for a commission to designate the mouths of rivers to which the common right of fishery on the coast of the United States and the British Provinces was not to extend. This commission has been employed a part of two seasons, but without much progress in accomplishing the object for which it was instituted, in consequence of a serious difference of opinion between the commissioners, not only as to the precise point where the rivers terminate, but in many instances as to what constitutes a river. These difficulties, however, may be overcome by resort to the umpirage provided for by the treaty.

The efforts perseveringly prosecuted since the commencement of my Administration to relieve our trade to the Baltic from the exaction of Sound dues by Denmark have not yet been attended with success. Other governments have also sought to obtain a like relief to their commerce, and Denmark was thus induced to propose an arrangement to all the European powers interested in the subject, and the manner in which her proposition was received warranting her to believe that a satisfactory arrangement with them could soon be concluded, she made a strong appeal to this Government for temporary suspension of definite action on its part, in consideration of the embarrassment which might result to her European negotiations by an immediate adjustment of the question with the United States. This request has been acceded to upon the condition that the sums collected after the 16th of June last and until the 16th of June next from vessels and cargoes belonging to our merchants are to be considered as paid under protest and subject to future adjustment. There is reason to believe that an arrangement between Denmark and the maritime powers of Europe on the subject will be soon concluded, and that the pending negotiation with the United States may then be resumed and terminated in a satisfactory manner.

With Spain no new difficulties have arisen, nor has much progress been made in the adjustment of pending ones.

Negotiations entered into for the purpose of relieving our commercial intercourse with the island of Cuba of some of its burdens and providing for the more speedy settlement of local disputes growing out of that intercourse have not yet been attended with any results.

Soon after the commencement of the late war in Europe this Government submitted to the consideration of all maritime nations two principles for the security of neutral commerce—one that the neutral flag should cover enemies' goods, except articles contraband of war, and the other that neutral property on board merchant vessels of belligerents should be exempt from condemnation, with the exception of contraband articles. These were not presented as new rules of international law, having been generally claimed by neutrals, though not always admitted by belligerents. One of the parties to the war (Russia), as well as several neutral powers, promptly acceded to these propositions, and the two other principal belligerents (Great Britain and France) having consented to observe them for the present occasion, a favorable opportunity seemed to be presented for obtaining a general recognition of them, both in Europe and America.

But Great Britain and France, in common with most of the States of Europe, while forbearing to reject, did not affirmatively act upon the overtures of the United States.

While the question was in this position the representatives of Russia, France, Great Britain, Austria, Prussia, Sardinia, and Turkey, assembled at Paris, took into consideration the subject of maritime rights, and put forth a declaration containing the two principles which this Government had submitted nearly two years before to the consideration of maritime powers, and adding thereto the following propositions: "Privateering is and remains abolished," and "Blockades in order to be binding must be effective; that is to say, maintained by a force sufficient really to prevent access to the coast of the enemy;" and to the declaration thus composed of four points, two of which had already been proposed by the United States, this Government has been invited to accede by all the powers represented at Paris except Great Britain and Turkey. To the last of the two additional propositions—that in relation to blockades—there can certainly be no objection. It is merely the definition of what shall constitute the effectual investment of a blockaded place, a definition for which this Government has always contended, claiming indemnity for losses where a practical violation of the rule thus defined has been injurious to our commerce. As to the remaining article of the declaration of the conference of Paris, that "privateering is and remains abolished," I certainly can not ascribe to the powers represented in the conference of Paris any but liberal and philanthropic views in the attempt to change the unquestionable rule of maritime law in regard to privateering. Their proposition was doubtless intended to imply approval of the principle that private property upon the ocean, although it might belong to the citizens of a belligerent state, should be exempted from capture; and had that proposition been so framed as to give full effect to the principle, it would have received my ready assent on behalf of the United States. But the measure proposed is inadequate to that purpose. It is true that if adopted private property upon the ocean would be withdrawn from one mode of plunder, but left exposed meanwhile to another mode, which could be used with increased effectiveness. The aggressive capacity of great naval powers would be thereby augmented, while the defensive ability of others would be reduced. Though the surrender of the means of prosecuting hostilities by employing privateers, as proposed by the conference of Paris, is mutual in terms, yet in practical effect it would be the relinquishment of a right of little value to one class of states, but of essential importance to another and a far larger class. It ought not to have been anticipated that a measure so inadequate to the accomplishment of the proposed object and so unequal in its operation would receive the assent of all maritime powers. Private property would be still left to the depredations of the public armed cruisers.

I have expressed a readiness on the part of this Government to accede to all the principles contained in the declaration of the conference of

Paris provided that the one relating to the abandonment of privateering can be so amended as to effect the object for which, as is presumed, it was intended—the immunity of private property on the ocean from hostile capture. To effect this object, it is proposed to add to the declaration that "privateering is and remains abolished" the following amendment:

And that the private property of subjects and citizens of a belligerent on the high seas shall be exempt from seizure by the public armed vessels of the other belligerent, except it be contraband.

This amendment has been presented not only to the powers which have asked our assent to the declaration to abolish privateering, but to all other maritime states. Thus far it has not been rejected by any, and is favorably entertained by all which have made any communication in reply.

Several of the governments regarding with favor the proposition of the United States have delayed definitive action upon it only for the purpose of consulting with others, parties to the conference of Paris. I have the satisfaction of stating, however, that the Emperor of Russia has entirely and explicitly approved of that modification and will cooperate in endeavoring to obtain the assent of other powers, and that assurances of a similar purport have been received in relation to the disposition of the Emperor of the French.

The present aspect of this important subject allows us to cherish the hope that a principle so humane in its character, so just and equal in its operation, so essential to the prosperity of commercial nations, and so consonant to the sentiments of this enlightened period of the world will command the approbation of all maritime powers, and thus be incorporated into the code of international law.

My views on the subject are more fully set forth in the reply of the Secretary of State, a copy of which is herewith transmitted, to the communications on the subject made to this Government, especially to the communication of France.

The Government of the United States has at all times regarded with friendly interest the other States of America, formerly, like this country, European colonies, and now independent members of the great family of nations. But the unsettled condition of some of them, distracted by frequent revolutions, and thus incapable of regular and firm internal administration, has tended to embarrass occasionally our public intercourse by reason of wrongs which our citizens suffer at their hands, and which they are slow to redress.

Unfortunately, it is against the Republic of Mexico, with which it is our special desire to maintain a good understanding, that such complaints are most numerous; and although earnestly urged upon its attention, they have not as yet received the consideration which this Government had a right to expect. While reparation for past injuries has been withheld, others have been added. The political condition of that country, however, has been such as to demand forbearance on the part of the United States. I shall continue my efforts to procure for the wrongs of our citizens that redress which is indispensable to the continued friendly association of the two Republics.

The peculiar condition of affairs in Nicaragua in the early part of the present year rendered it important that this Government should have diplomatic relations with that State. Through its territory had been opened one of the principal thoroughfares across the isthmus connecting North and South America, on which a vast amount of property was transported and to which our citizens resorted in great numbers in passing between the Atlantic and Pacific coasts of the United States. The protection of both required that the existing power in that State should be regarded as a responsible Government, and its minister was accordingly received. But he remained here only a short time. Soon thereafter the political affairs of Nicaragua underwent unfavorable change and became involved in much uncertainty and confusion. Diplomatic representatives from two contending parties have been recently sent to this Government, but with the imperfect information possessed it was not possible to decide which was the Government *de facto*, and, awaiting further developments, I have refused to receive either.

Questions of the most serious nature are pending between the United States and the Republic of New Granada. The Government of that Republic undertook a year since to impose tonnage duties on foreign vessels in her ports, but the purpose was resisted by this Government as being contrary to existing treaty stipulations with the United States and to rights conferred by charter upon the Panama Railroad Company, and was accordingly relinquished at that time, it being admitted that our vessels were entitled to be exempt from tonnage duty in the free ports of Panama and Aspinwall. But the purpose has been recently revived on the part of New Granada by the enactment of a law to subject vessels visiting her ports to the tonnage duty of 40 cents per ton, and although the law has not been put in force, yet the right to enforce it is still asserted and may at any time be acted on by the Government of that Republic.

The Congress of New Granada has also enacted a law during the last year which levies a tax of more than $3 on every pound of mail matter transported across the Isthmus. The sum thus required to be paid on the mails of the United States would be nearly $2,000,000 annually in addition to the large sum payable by contract to the Panama Railroad Company. If the only objection to this exaction were the exorbitancy of its amount, it could not be submitted to by the United States.

The imposition of it, however, would obviously contravene our treaty with New Granada and infringe the contract of that Republic with the Panama Railroad Company. The law providing for this tax was by its terms to take effect on the 1st of September last, but the local authorities on the Isthmus have been induced to suspend its execution and to await further instructions on the subject from the Government of the Republic. I am not yet advised of the determination of that Government. If a measure so extraordinary in its character and so clearly contrary to treaty stipulations and the contract rights of the Panama Railroad Company, composed mostly of American citizens, should be persisted in, it will be the duty of the United States to resist its execution.

I regret exceedingly that occasion exists to invite your attention to a subject of still graver import in our relations with the Republic of New Granada. On the 15th day of April last a riotous assemblage of the inhabitants of Panama committed a violent and outrageous attack on the premises of the railroad company and the passengers and other persons in or near the same, involving the death of several citizens of the United States, the pillage of many others, and the destruction of a large amount of property belonging to the railroad company. I caused full investigation of that event to be made, and the result shows satisfactorily that complete responsibility for what occurred attaches to the Government of New Granada. I have therefore demanded of that Government that the perpetrators of the wrongs in question should be punished; that provision should be made for the families of citizens of the United States who were killed, with full indemnity for the property pillaged or destroyed.

The present condition of the Isthmus of Panama, in so far as regards the security of persons and property passing over it, requires serious consideration. Recent incidents tend to show that the local authorities can not be relied on to maintain the public peace of Panama, and there is just ground for apprehension that a portion of the inhabitants are meditating further outrages, without adequate measures for the security and protection of persons or property having been taken, either by the State of Panama or by the General Government of New Granada.

Under the guaranties of treaty, citizens of the United States have, by the outlay of several million dollars, constructed a railroad across the Isthmus, and it has become the main route between our Atlantic and Pacific possessions, over which multitudes of our citizens and a vast amount of property are constantly passing; to the security and protection of all which and the continuance of the public advantages involved it is impossible for the Government of the United States to be indifferent.

I have deemed the danger of the recurrence of scenes of lawless violence in this quarter so imminent as to make it my duty to station a part of our naval force in the harbors of Panama and Aspinwall, in order to protect the persons and property of the citizens of the United States in those ports and to insure to them safe passage across the Isthmus. And it would, in my judgment, be unwise to withdraw the naval force now in those ports until, by the spontaneous action of the Republic of New Granada or otherwise, some adequate arrangement shall have been made for the protection and security of a line of interoceanic communication, so important at this time not to the United States only, but to all other maritime states, both of Europe and America.

Meanwhile negotiations have been instituted, by means of a special commission, to obtain from New Granada full indemnity for injuries sustained by our citizens on the Isthmus and satisfactory security for the general interests of the United States.

In addressing to you my last annual message the occasion seems to me an appropriate one to express my congratulations, in view of the peace, greatness, and felicity which the United States now possess and enjoy. To point you to the state of the various Departments of the Government and of all the great branches of the public service, civil and military, in order to speak of the intelligence and the integrity which pervades the whole, would be to indicate but imperfectly the administrative condition of the country and the beneficial effects of that on the general welfare. Nor would it suffice to say that the nation is actually at peace at home and abroad; that its industrial interests are prosperous; that the canvas of its mariners whitens every sea, and the plow of its husbandmen is marching steadily onward to the bloodless conquest of the continent; that cities and populous States are springing up, as if by enchantment, from the bosom of our Western wilds, and that the courageous energy of our people is making of these United States the great Republic of the world. These results have not been attained without passing through trials and perils, by experience of which, and thus only, nations can harden into manhood. Our forefathers were trained to the wisdom which conceived and the courage which achieved independence by the circumstances which surrounded them, and they were thus made capable of the creation of the Republic. It devolved on the next generation to consolidate the work of the Revolution, to deliver the country entirely from the influences of conflicting transatlantic partialities or antipathies which attached to our colonial and Revolutionary history, and to organize the practical operation of the constitutional and legal institutions of the Union. To us of this generation remains the not less noble task of maintaining and extending the national power. We have at length reached that stage of our country's career in which the dangers to be encountered and the exertions to be made are the incidents, not of weakness, but of strength. In foreign relations we have to attemper our power to the less happy condition of other Republics in America and to place ourselves in the calmness and conscious dignity of right by the side of the greatest and wealthiest of the Empires of Europe. In domestic relations we have to guard against the shock of the discontents, the ambitions, the interests, and the exuberant, and therefore sometimes irregular, impulses of opinion or of action which are the natural product of the present political elevation, the self-reliance, and the restless spirit of enterprise of the people of the United States.

I shall prepare to surrender the Executive trust to my successor and retire to private life with sentiments of profound gratitude to the good Providence which during the period of my Administration has vouchsafed to carry the country through many difficulties, domestic and foreign, and which enables me to contemplate the spectacle of amicable and respectful relations between ours and all other governments and the establishment of constitutional order and tranquillity throughout the Union.

James Buchanan

March 4, 1857 to March 4, 1861

FIRST ANNUAL MESSAGE.

WASHINGTON, *December 8, 1857.*

Fellow-Citizens of the Senate and House of Representatives:

In obedience to the command of the Constitution, it has now become my duty "to give to Congress information of the state of the Union and recommend to their consideration such measures" as I judge to be "necessary and expedient."

But first and above all, our thanks are due to Almighty God for the numerous benefits which He has bestowed upon this people, and ·our united prayers ought to ascend to Him that He would continue to bless our great Republic in time to come as He has blessed it in time past. Since the adjournment of the last Congress our constituents have enjoyed an unusual degree of health. The earth has yielded her fruits abundantly and has bountifully rewarded the toil of the husbandman. Our great staples have commanded high prices, and up till within a brief period our manufacturing, mineral, and mechanical occupations have largely partaken of the general prosperity. We have possessed all the elements of material wealth in rich abundance, and yet, notwithstanding all these advantages, our country in its monetary interests is at the present moment in a deplorable condition. In the midst of unsurpassed plenty in all the productions of agriculture and in all the elements of national wealth, we find our manufactures suspended, our public works retarded, our private enterprises of different kinds abandoned, and thousands of useful laborers thrown out of employment and reduced to want. The revenue of the Government, which is chiefly derived from duties on imports from abroad, has been greatly reduced, whilst the appropriations made by Congress at its last session for the current fiscal year are very large in amount.

Under these circumstances a loan may be required before the close of your present session; but this, although deeply to be regretted, would prove to be only a slight misfortune when compared with the suffering and distress prevailing among the people. With this the Government can not fail deeply to sympathize, though it may be without the power to extend relief.

It is our duty to inquire what has produced such unfortunate results and whether their recurrence can be prevented. In all former revulsions the blame might have been fairly attributed to a variety of cooperating causes, but not so upon the present occasion. It is apparent that our existing misfortunes have proceeded solely from our extravagant and vicious system of paper currency and bank credits, exciting the people to wild speculations and gambling in stocks. These revulsions must continue to recur at successive intervals so long as the amount of the paper currency and bank loans and discounts of the country shall be left to the discretion of 1,400 irresponsible banking institutions, which from the very law of their nature will consult the interest of their stockholders rather than the public welfare.

The framers of the Constitution, when they gave to Congress the power "to coin money and to regulate the value thereof" and prohibited the States from coining money, emitting bills of credit, or making anything but gold and silver coin a tender in payment of debts, supposed they had protected the people against the evils of an excessive and irredeemable paper currency. They are not responsible for the existing anomaly that a Government endowed with the sovereign attribute of coining money and regulating the value thereof should have no power to prevent others from driving this coin out of the country and filling up the channels of circulation with paper which does not represent gold and silver.

It is one of the highest and most responsible duties of Government to insure to the people a sound circulating medium, the amount of which ought to be adapted with the utmost possible wisdom and skill to the wants of internal trade and foreign exchanges. If this be either greatly above or greatly below the proper standard, the marketable value of every man's property is increased or diminished in the same proportion, and injustice to individuals as well as incalculable evils to the community are the consequence.

Unfortunately, under the construction of the Federal Constitution which has now prevailed too long to be changed this important and delicate duty has been dissevered from the coining power and virtually transferred to more than 1,400 State banks acting independently of each other and regulating their paper issues almost exclusively by a regard to the present interest of their stockholders. Exercising the sovereign power of providing a paper currency instead of coin for the country, the first duty which these banks owe to the public is to keep in their vaults a sufficient amount of gold and silver to insure the convertibility of their notes into coin at all times and under all circumstances. No bank ought ever to be chartered without such restrictions on its business as to secure this result. All other restrictions are comparatively vain. This is the only true touchstone, the only efficient regulator of a paper currency—the only one which can guard the public against overissues and bank suspensions. As a collateral and eventual security, it is doubtless wise, and in all cases ought to be required, that banks shall hold an amount of United States or State securities equal to their notes in circulation and pledged for their redemption. This, however, furnishes no adequate security against overissues. On the contrary, it may be perverted to inflate the currency. Indeed, it is possible by this means to convert all the debts of the United States and State Governments into bank notes, without reference to the specie required to redeem them. However valuable these securities may

be in themselves, they can not be converted into gold and silver at the
moment of pressure, as our experience teaches, in sufficient time to prevent bank suspensions and the depreciation of bank notes.   In England,
which is to a considerable extent a paper-money country, though vastly
behind our own in this respect, it was deemed advisable, anterior to the
act of Parliament of 1844, which wisely separated the issue of notes from
the banking department, for the Bank of England always to keep on
hand gold and silver equal to one-third of its combined circulation and
deposits.   If this proportion was no more than sufficient to secure the
convertibility of its notes with the whole of Great Britain and to some
extent the continent of Europe as a field for its circulation, rendering
it almost impossible that a sudden and immediate run to a dangerous
amount should be made upon it, the same proportion would certainly be
insufficient under our banking system.   Each of our 1,400 banks has but
a limited circumference for its circulation, and in the course of a very few
days the depositors and note holders might demand from such a bank
a sufficient amount in specie to compel it to suspend, even although it
had coin in its vaults equal to one-third of its immediate liabilities.   And
yet I am not aware, with the exception of the banks of Louisiana, that
any State bank throughout the Union has been required by its charter
to keep this or any other proportion of gold and silver compared with
the amount of its combined circulation and deposits.   What has been the
consequence?   In a recent report made by the Treasury Department on
the condition of the banks throughout the different States, according
to returns dated nearest to January, 1857, the aggregate amount of actual
specie in their vaults is $58,349,838, of their circulation $214,778,822,
and of their deposits $230,351,352.   Thus it appears that these banks in
the aggregate have considerably less than one dollar in seven of gold and
silver compared with their circulation and deposits.   It was palpable,
therefore, that the very first pressure must drive them to suspension and
deprive the people of a convertible currency, with all its disastrous consequences.   It is truly wonderful that they should have so long continued
to preserve their credit when a demand for the payment of one-seventh
of their immediate liabilities would have driven them into insolvency.
And this is the condition of the banks, notwithstanding that four hundred millions of gold from California have flowed in upon us within the
last eight years, and the tide still continues to flow.   Indeed, such has
been the extravagance of bank credits that the banks now hold a considerably less amount of specie, either in proportion to their capital or to
their circulation and deposits combined, than they did before the discovery
of gold in California.   Whilst in the year 1848 their specie in proportion
to their capital was more than equal to one dollar for four and a half, in
1857 it does not amount to one dollar for every six dollars and thirty-
three cents of their capital.   In the year 1848 the specie was equal
within a very small fraction to one dollar in five of their circulation and

deposits; in 1857 it is not equal to one dollar in seven and a half of their circulation and deposits.

From this statement it is easy to account for our financial history for the last forty years. It has been a history of extravagant expansions in the business of the country, followed by ruinous contractions. At successive intervals the best and most enterprising men have been tempted to their ruin by excessive bank loans of mere paper credit, exciting them to extravagant importations of foreign goods, wild speculations, and ruinous and demoralizing stock gambling. When the crisis arrives, as arrive it must, the banks can extend no relief to the people. In a vain struggle to redeem their liabilities in specie they are compelled to contract their loans and their issues, and at last, in the hour of distress, when their assistance is most needed, they and their debtors together sink into insolvency.

It is this paper system of extravagant expansion, raising the nominal price of every article far beyond its real value when compared with the cost of similar articles in countries whose circulation is wisely regulated, which has prevented us from competing in our own markets with foreign manufacturers, has produced extravagant importations, and has counteracted the effect of the large incidental protection afforded to our domestic manufactures by the present revenue tariff. But for this the branches of our manufactures composed of raw materials, the production of our own country —such as cotton, iron, and woolen fabrics—would not only have acquired almost exclusive possession of the home market, but would have created for themselves a foreign market throughout the world.

Deplorable, however, as may be our present financial condition, we may yet indulge in bright hopes for the future. No other nation has ever existed which could have endured such violent expansions and contractions of paper credits without lasting injury; yet the buoyancy of youth, the energies of our population, and the spirit which never quails before difficulties will enable us soon to recover from our present financial embarrassments, and may even occasion us speedily to forget the lesson which they have taught.

In the meantime it is the duty of the Government, by all proper means within its power, to aid in alleviating the sufferings of the people occasioned by the suspension of the banks and to provide against a recurrence of the same calamity. Unfortunately, in either aspect of the case it can do but little. Thanks to the independent treasury, the Government has not suspended payment, as it was compelled to do by the failure of the banks in 1837. It will continue to discharge its liabilities to the people in gold and silver. Its disbursements in coin will pass into circulation and materially assist in restoring a sound currency. From its high credit, should we be compelled to make a temporary loan, it can be effected on advantageous terms. This, however, shall if possible be avoided, but if not, then the amount shall be limited to the lowest practicable sum.

I have therefore determined that whilst no useful Government works already in progress shall be suspended, new works not already commenced will be postponed if this can be done without injury to the country. Those necessary for its defense shall proceed as though there had been no crisis in our monetary affairs.

But the Federal Government can not do much to provide against a recurrence of existing evils. Even if insurmountable constitutional objections did not exist against the creation of a national bank, this would furnish no adequate preventive security. The history of the last Bank of the United States abundantly proves the truth of this assertion. Such a bank could not, if it would, regulate the issues and credits of 1,400 State banks in such a manner as to prevent the ruinous expansions and contractions in our currency which afflicted the country throughout the existence of the late bank, or secure us against future suspensions. In 1825 an effort was made by the Bank of England to curtail the issues of the country banks under the most favorable circumstances. The paper currency had been expanded to a ruinous extent, and the bank put forth all its power to contract it in order to reduce prices and restore the equilibrium of the foreign exchanges. It accordingly commenced a system of curtailment of its loans and issues, in the vain hope that the joint stock and private banks of the Kingdom would be compelled to follow its example. It found, however, that as it contracted they expanded, and at the end of the process, to employ the language of a very high official authority, "whatever reduction of the paper circulation was effected by the Bank of England (in 1825) was more than made up by the issues of the country banks."

But a bank of the United States would not, if it could, restrain the issues and loans of the State banks, because its duty as a regulator of the currency must often be in direct conflict with the immediate interest of its stockholders. If we expect one agent to restrain or control another, their interests must, at least in some degree, be antagonistic. But the directors of a bank of the United States would feel the same interest and the same inclination with the directors of the State banks to expand the currency, to accommodate their favorites and friends with loans, and to declare large dividends. Such has been our experience in regard to the last bank.

After all, we must mainly rely upon the patriotism and wisdom of the States for the prevention and redress of the evil. If they will afford us a real specie basis for our paper circulation by increasing the denomination of bank notes, first to twenty and afterwards to fifty dollars; if they will require that the banks shall at all times keep on hand at least one dollar of gold and silver for every three dollars of their circulation and deposits, and if they will provide by a self-executing enactment, which nothing can arrest, that the moment they suspend they shall go into liquidation, I believe that such provisions, with a weekly publication by each bank of a statement of its condition, would go far to secure us against future suspensions of specie payments.

Congress, in my opinion, possess the power to pass a uniform bank rupt law applicable to all banking institutions throughout the United States, and I strongly recommend its exercise. This would make it the irreversible organic law of each bank's existence that a suspension of specie payments shall produce its civil death. The instinct of self-preservation would then compel it to perform its duties in such a manner as to escape the penalty and preserve its life.

The existence of banks and the circulation of bank paper are so identified with the habits of our people that they can not at this day be suddenly abolished without much immediate injury to the country. If we could confine them to their appropriate sphere and prevent them from administering to the spirit of wild and reckless speculation by extravagant loans and issues, they might be continued with advantage to the public.

But this I say, after long and much reflection: If experience shall prove it to be impossible to enjoy the facilities which well-regulated banks might afford without at the same time suffering the calamities which the excesses of the banks have hitherto inflicted upon the country, it would then be far the lesser evil to deprive them altogether of the power to issue a paper currency and confine them to the functions of banks of deposit and discount.

Our relations with foreign governments are upon the whole in a satisfactory condition.

The diplomatic difficulties which existed between the Government of the United States and that of Great Britain at the adjournment of the last Congress have been happily terminated by the appointment of a British minister to this country, who has been cordially received.

Whilst it is greatly to the interest, as I am convinced it is the sincere desire, of the Governments and people of the two countries to be on terms of intimate friendship with each other, it has been our misfortune almost always to have had some irritating, if not dangerous, outstanding question with Great Britain.

Since the origin of the Government we have been employed in negotiating treaties with that power, and afterwards in discussing their true intent and meaning. In this respect the convention of April 19, 1850, commonly called the Clayton and Bulwer treaty, has been the most unfortunate of all, because the two Governments place directly opposite and contradictory constructions upon its first and most important article. Whilst in the United States we believed that this treaty would place both powers upon an exact equality by the stipulation that neither will ever "occupy, or fortify, or colonize, or assume, or exercise any dominion" over any part of Central America, it is contended by the British Government that the true construction of this language has left them in the rightful possession of all that portion of Central America which was in their occupancy at the date of the treaty; in fact, that the treaty is a virtual recognition on the part of the United States of the right of Great Britain, either as owner or protector, to the whole extensive coast of Central America, sweeping round from the Rio Hondo to the port and harbor of San Juan de Nicaragua, together with the adjacent Bay Islands, except the comparatively small portion of this between the Sarstoon and Cape Honduras. According to their construction, the treaty does no more than simply prohibit them from extending their possessions in Central America beyond the present limits. It is not too much to assert that if in the United States the treaty had been considered susceptible of such a construction it never would have been negotiated under the authority of the President, nor would it have received the approbation of the Senate. The universal conviction in the United States was that when our Government consented to violate its traditional and time-honored policy and to stipulate with a foreign government never to occupy or acquire territory in the Central American portion of our own continent, the consideration for this sacrifice was that Great Britain should, in this respect at least, be placed in the same position with ourselves. Whilst we have no right to doubt the sincerity of the British Government in their construction of the treaty, it is at the same time my deliberate conviction that this construction is in opposition both to its letter and its spirit.

Under the late Administration negotiations were instituted between the two Governments for the purpose, if possible, of removing these difficulties, and a treaty having this laudable object in view was signed at London on the 17th October, 1856, and was submitted by the President to the Senate on the following 10th of December. Whether this treaty, either in its original or amended form, would have accomplished the object intended without giving birth to new and embarrassing complications between the two Governments, may perhaps be well questioned. Certain it is, however, it was rendered much less objectionable by the different amendments made to it by the Senate. The treaty as amended was ratified by me on the 12th March, 1857, and was transmitted to London for ratification by the British Government. That Government expressed its willingness to concur in all the amendments made by the Senate with the single exception of the clause relating to Ruatan and the other islands in the Bay of Honduras. The article in the original treaty as submitted to the Senate, after reciting that these islands and their inhabitants "having been, by a convention bearing date the 27th day of August, 1856, between Her Britannic Majesty and the Republic of Honduras, constituted and declared a free territory under the sovereignty of the said Republic of Honduras," stipulated that "the two contracting parties do hereby mutually engage to recognize and respect in all future time the independence and rights of the said free territory as a part of the Republic of Honduras."

Upon an examination of this convention between Great Britain and Honduras of the 27th August, 1856, it was found that whilst declaring the Bay Islands to be "a free territory under the sovereignty of the Republic of Honduras" it deprived that Republic of rights without which its sovereignty over them could scarcely be said to exist. It divided them from the remainder of Honduras and gave to their inhabitants a separate government of their own, with legislative, executive, and judicial officers elected by themselves. It deprived the Government of Honduras of the taxing power in every form and exempted the people of the islands from the performance of military duty except for their own exclusive defense. It also prohibited that Republic from erecting fortifications upon them for their protection, thus leaving them open to invasion from any quarter; and, finally, it provided "that slavery shall not at any time hereafter be permitted to exist therein."

Had Honduras ratified this convention, she would have ratified the establishment of a state substantially independent within her own limits, and a state at all times subject to British influence and control. Moreover, had the United States ratified the treaty with Great Britain in its original form, we should have been bound "to recognize and respect in all future time" these stipulations to the prejudice of Honduras. Being in direct opposition to the spirit and meaning of the Clayton and Bulwer treaty as understood in the United States, the Senate rejected the entire clause, and substituted in its stead a simple recognition of the sovereign right of Honduras to these islands in the following language:

The two contracting parties do hereby mutually engage to recognize and respect the islands of Ruatan, Bonaco, Utila, Barbaretta, Helena, and Morat, situate in the Bay of Honduras and off the coast of the Republic of Honduras, as under the sovereignty and as part of the said Republic of Honduras.

Great Britain rejected this amendment, assigning as the only reason that the ratifications of the convention of the 27th August, 1856, between her and Honduras had not been "exchanged, owing to the hesitation of that Government." Had this been done, it is stated that "Her Majesty's Government would have had little difficulty in agreeing to the modification proposed by the Senate, which then would have had in effect the same signification as the original wording." Whether this would have been the effect, whether the mere circumstance of the exchange of the ratifications of the British convention with Honduras prior in point of time to the ratification of our treaty with Great Britain would "in effect" have had "the same signification as the original wording," and thus have nullified the amendment of the Senate, may well be doubted. It is, perhaps, fortunate that the question has never arisen.

The British Government, immediately after rejecting the treaty as amended, proposed to enter into a new treaty with the United States, similar in all respects to the treaty which they had just refused to ratify, if the United States would consent to add to the Senate's clear and unqualified recognition of the sovereignty of Honduras over the Bay Islands the following conditional stipulation:

> Whenever and so soon as the Republic of Honduras shall have concluded and ratified a treaty with Great Britain by which Great Britain shall have ceded and the Republic of Honduras shall have accepted the said islands, subject to the provisions and conditions contained in such treaty.

This proposition was, of course, rejected. After the Senate had refused to recognize the British convention with Honduras of the 27th August, 1856, with full knowledge of its contents, it was impossible for me, necessarily ignorant of "the provisions and conditions" which might be contained in a future convention between the same parties, to sanction them in advance.

The fact is that when two nations like Great Britain and the United States, mutually desirous, as they are, and I trust ever may be, of maintaining the most friendly relations with each other, have unfortunately concluded a treaty which they understand in senses directly opposite, the wisest course is to abrogate such a treaty by mutual consent and to commence anew. Had this been done promptly, all difficulties in Central America would most probably ere this have been adjusted to the satisfaction of both parties. The time spent in discussing the meaning of the Clayton and Bulwer treaty would have been devoted to this praiseworthy purpose, and the task would have been the more easily accomplished because the interest of the two countries in Central America is identical, being confined to securing safe transits over all the routes across the Isthmus.

Whilst entertaining these sentiments, I shall, nevertheless, not refuse to contribute to any reasonable adjustment of the Central American questions which is not practically inconsistent with the American interpretation of the treaty. Overtures for this purpose have been recently made by the British Government in a friendly spirit, which I cordially reciprocate, but whether this renewed effort will result in success I am not yet prepared to express an opinion. A brief period will determine.

With France our ancient relations of friendship still continue to exist. The French Government have in several recent instances, which need not be enumerated, evinced a spirit of good will and kindness toward our country, which I heartily reciprocate. It is, notwithstanding, much to be regretted that two nations whose productions are of such a character as to invite the most extensive exchanges and freest commercial intercourse should continue to enforce ancient and obsolete restrictions of trade against each other. Our commercial treaty with France is in this respect an exception from our treaties with all other commercial nations. It jealously levies discriminating duties both on tonnage and on articles the growth, produce, or manufacture of the one country when arriving in vessels belonging to the other.

More than forty years ago, on the 3d March, 1815, Congress passed an act offering to all nations to admit their vessels laden with their national productions into the ports of the United States upon the same terms with our own vessels provided they would reciprocate to us similar advantages. This act confined the reciprocity to the productions of the respective foreign nations who might enter into the proposed arrangement with the United States. The act of May 24, 1828, removed this restriction and offered a similar reciprocity to all such vessels without reference to the origin of their cargoes. Upon these principles our commercial treaties and arrangements have been founded, except with France, and let us hope that this exception may not long exist.

Our relations with Russia remain, as they have ever been, on the most friendly footing. The present Emperor, as well as his predecessors, have never failed when the occasion offered to manifest their good will to our country, and their friendship has always been highly appreciated by the Government and people of the United States.

With all other European Governments, except that of Spain, our relations are as peaceful as we could desire. I regret to say that no progress whatever has been made since the adjournment of Congress toward the settlement of any of the numerous claims of our citizens against the Spanish Government. Besides, the outrage committed on our flag by the Spanish war frigate *Ferrolana* on the high seas off the coast of Cuba in March, 1855, by firing into the American mail steamer *El Dorado* and detaining and searching her, remains unacknowledged and unredressed. The general tone and temper of the Spanish Government toward that of the United States are much to be regretted. Our present envoy extraordinary and minister plenipotentiary to Madrid has asked to be recalled, and it is my purpose to send out a new minister to Spain with special instructions on all questions pending between the two Governments, and with a determination to have them speedily and amicably adjusted if this be possible. In the meantime, whenever our minister urges the just claims of our citizens on the notice of the Spanish Government he is met with the objection that Congress has never made the appropriation recommended by President Polk in his annual message of December, 1847, "to be paid to the Spanish Government for the purpose of distribution among the claimants in the *Amistad* case." A similar recommendation was made by my immediate predecessor in his message of December, 1853, and entirely concurring with both in the opinion that this indemnity is justly due under the treaty with Spain of the 27th of October, 1795, I earnestly recommend such an appropriation to the favorable consideration of Congress.

A treaty of friendship and commerce was concluded at Constantinople on the 13th December, 1856, between the United States and Persia, the ratifications of which were exchanged at Constantinople on the 13th June, 1857, and the treaty was proclaimed by the President on the 18th August, 1857. This treaty, it is believed, will prove beneficial to American commerce. The Shah has manifested an earnest disposition to cultivate friendly relations with our country, and has expressed a strong wish that we should be represented at Teheran by a minister plenipotentiary; and I recommend that an appropriation be made for this purpose.

Recent occurrences in China have been unfavorable to a revision of the treaty with that Empire of the 3d July, 1844, with a view to the security and extension of our commerce. The twenty-fourth article of this treaty stipulated for a revision of it in case experience should prove this to be requisite, "in which case the two Governments will, at the expiration of twelve years from the date of said convention, treat amicably concerning the same by means of suitable persons appointed to conduct such negotiations." These twelve years expired on the 3d July, 1856, but long before that period it was ascertained that important changes in the treaty were necessary, and several fruitless attempts were made by the commissioner of the United States to effect these changes. Another effort was about to be made for the same purpose by our commissioner in conjunction with the ministers of England and France, but this was suspended by the occurrence of hostilities in the Canton River between Great Britain and the Chinese Empire. These hostilities have necessarily interrupted the trade of all nations with Canton, which is now in a state of blockade, and have occasioned a serious loss of life and property. Meanwhile the insurrection within the Empire against the existing imperial dynasty still continues, and it is difficult to anticipate what will be the result.

Under these circumstances I have deemed it advisable to appoint a distinguished citizen of Pennsylvania envoy extraordinary and minister plenipotentiary to proceed to China and to avail himself of any opportunities which may offer to effect changes in the existing treaty favorable to American commerce. He left the United States for the place of his destination in July last in the war steamer *Minnesota*. Special ministers to China have also been appointed by the Governments of Great Britain and France.

Whilst our minister has been instructed to occupy a neutral position in reference to the existing hostilities at Canton, he will cordially cooperate with the British and French ministers in all peaceful measures to secure by treaty stipulations those just concessions to commerce which the nations of the world have a right to expect and which China can not long be permitted to withhold. From assurances received I entertain no doubt that the three ministers will act in harmonious concert to obtain similar commercial treaties for each of the powers they represent.

We can not fail to feel a deep interest in all that concerns the welfare of the independent Republics on our own continent, as well as of the Empire of Brazil.

Our difficulties with New Granada, which a short time since bore so threatening an aspect, are, it is to be hoped, in a fair train of settlement in a manner just and honorable to both parties.

The isthmus of Central America, including that of Panama, is the great highway between the Atlantic and Pacific over which a large portion of the commerce of the world is destined to pass. The United States are more deeply interested than any other nation in preserving the freedom and security of all the communications across this isthmus. It is our duty, therefore, to take care that they shall not be interrupted either by invasions from our own country or by wars between the independent States of Central America. Under our treaty with New Granada of the 12th December, 1846, we are bound to guarantee the neutrality of the Isthmus of Panama, through which the Panama Railroad passes, "as well as the rights of sovereignty and property which New Granada has and possesses over the said territory." This obligation is founded upon equivalents granted by the treaty to the Government and people of the United States.

Under these circumstances I recommend to Congress the passage of an act authorizing the President, in case of necessity, to employ the land and naval forces of the United States to carry into effect this guaranty of neutrality and protection. I also recommend similar legislation for the security of any other route across the Isthmus in which we may acquire an interest by treaty.

With the independent Republics on this continent it is both our duty and our interest to cultivate the most friendly relations. We can never feel indifferent to their fate, and must always rejoice in their prosperity. Unfortunately both for them and for us, our example and advice have lost much of their influence in consequence of the lawless expeditions which have been fitted out against some of them within the limits of our country. Nothing is better calculated to retard our steady material progress or impair our character as a nation than the toleration of such enterprises in violation of the law of nations.

It is one of the first and highest duties of any independent state in its relations with the members of the great family of nations to restrain its people from acts of hostile aggression against their citizens or subjects. The most eminent writers on public law do not hesitate to denounce such hostile acts as robbery and murder.

Weak and feeble states like those of Central America may not feel themselves able to assert and vindicate their rights. The case would be far different if expeditions were set on foot within our own territories to make private war against a powerful nation. If such expeditions were fitted out from abroad against any portion of our own country, to burn down our cities, murder and plunder our people, and usurp our Government, we should call any power on earth to the strictest account for not preventing such enormities.

Ever since the Administration of General Washington acts of Congress have been enforced to punish severely the crime of setting on foot a military expedition within the limits of the United States to proceed from thence against a nation or state with whom we are at peace. The present neutrality act of April 20, 1818, is but little more than a collection of preexisting laws. Under this act the President is empowered to employ the land and naval forces and the militia "for the purpose of preventing the carrying on of any such expedition or enterprise from the territories and jurisdiction of the United States," and the collectors of customs are authorized and required to detain any vessel in port when there is reason to believe she is about to take part in such lawless enterprises.

When it was first rendered probable that an attempt would be made to get up another unlawful expedition against Nicaragua, the Secretary of State issued instructions to the marshals and district attorneys, which were directed by the Secretaries of War and the Navy to the appropriate army and navy officers, requiring them to be vigilant and to use their best exertions in carrying into effect the provisions of the act of 1818. Notwithstanding these precautions, the expedition has escaped from our shores. Such enterprises can do no possible good to the country, but have already inflicted much injury both on its interests and its character. They have prevented peaceful emigration from the United States to the States of Central America, which could not fail to prove highly beneficial to all the parties concerned. In a pecuniary point of view alone our citizens have sustained heavy losses from the seizure and closing of the transit route by the San Juan between the two oceans.

The leader of the recent expedition was arrested at New Orleans, but was discharged on giving bail for his appearance in the insufficient sum of $2,000.

I commend the whole subject to the serious attention of Congress, believing that our duty and our interest, as well as our national character, require that we should adopt such measures as will be effectual in restraining our citizens from committing such outrages.

I regret to inform you that the President of Paraguay has refused to ratify the treaty between the United States and that State as amended by the Senate, the signature of which was mentioned in the message of my predecessor to Congress at the opening of its session in December, 1853. The reasons assigned for this refusal will appear in the correspondence herewith submitted.

It being desirable to ascertain the fitness of the river La Plata and its tributaries for navigation by steam, the United States steamer *Water Witch* was sent thither for that purpose in 1853. This enterprise was successfully carried on until February, 1855, when, whilst in the peaceful prosecution of her voyage up the Parana River, the steamer was fired upon by a Paraguayan fort. The fire was returned, but as the *Water Witch* was of small force and not designed for offensive operations, she retired from the conflict. The pretext upon which the attack was made was a decree of the President of Paraguay of October, 1854, prohibiting foreign vessels of war from navigating the rivers of that State. As Paraguay, however, was the owner of but one bank of the river of that name, the other belonging to Corientes, a State of the Argentine Confederation, the right of its Government to expect that such a decree would be obeyed can not be acknowledged. But the *Water Witch* was not, properly speaking, a vessel of war. She was a small steamer engaged in a scientific enterprise intended for the advantage of commercial states generally. Under these circumstances I am constrained to consider the attack upon her as unjustifiable and as calling for satisfaction from the Paraguayan Government.

Citizens of the United States also who were established in business in Paraguay have had their property seized and taken from them, and have otherwise been treated by the authorities in an insulting and arbitrary manner, which requires redress.

A demand for these purposes will be made in a firm but conciliatory spirit. This will the more probably be granted if the Executive shall have authority to use other means in the event of a refusal. This is accordingly recommended.

It is unnecessary to state in detail the alarming condition of the Territory of Kansas at the time of my inauguration. The opposing parties then stood in hostile array against each other, and any accident might have relighted the flames of civil war. Besides, at this critical moment Kansas was left without a governor by the resignation of Governor Geary.

On the 19th of February previous the Territorial legislature had passed a law providing for the election of delegates on the third Monday of June to a convention to meet on the first Monday of September for the purpose of framing a constitution preparatory to admission into the Union. This law was in the main fair and just, and it is to be regretted that all the qualified electors had not registered themselves and voted under its provisions.

At the time of the election for delegates an extensive organization existed in the Territory whose avowed object it was, if need be, to put down the lawful government by force and to establish a government of their own under the so-called Topeka constitution. The persons attached to this revolutionary organization abstained from taking any part in the election.

The act of the Territorial legislature had omitted to provide for submitting to the people the constitution which might be framed by the convention, and in the excited state of public feeling throughout Kansas an apprehension extensively prevailed that a design existed to force upon them a constitution in relation to slavery against their will. In this emergency it became my duty, as it was my unquestionable right, having in view the union of all good citizens in support of the Territorial laws, to express an opinion on the true construction of the provisions concerning slavery contained in the organic act of Congress of the 30th May, 1854. Congress declared it to be "the true intent and meaning of this act not to legislate slavery into any Territory or State, nor to exclude it therefrom, but to leave the people thereof perfectly free to form and regulate their domestic institutions in their own way." Under it Kansas, "when admitted as a State," was to "be received into the Union with or without slavery, as their constitution may prescribe at the time of their admission."

Did Congress mean by this language that the delegates elected to frame a constitution should have authority finally to decide the question of slavery, or did they intend by leaving it to the people that the people of Kansas themselves should decide this question by a direct vote? On this subject I confess I had never entertained a serious doubt, and therefore in my instructions to Governor Walker of the 28th March last I merely said that when "a constitution shall be submitted to the people of the Territory they must be protected in the exercise of their right of voting for or against that instrument, and the fair expression of the popular will must not be interrupted by fraud or violence."

In expressing this opinion it was far from my intention to interfere with the decision of the people of Kansas, either for or against slavery. From this I have always carefully abstained. Intrusted with the duty of taking "care that the laws be faithfully executed," my only desire was that the people of Kansas should furnish to Congress the evidence required by the organic act, whether for or against slavery, and in this manner smooth their passage into the Union. In emerging from the condition of Territorial dependence into that of a sovereign State it was their duty, in my opinion, to make known their will by the votes of the majority on the direct question whether this important domestic institution should or should not continue to exist. Indeed, this was the only possible mode in which their will could be authentically ascertained.

The election of delegates to a convention must necessarily take place in separate districts. From this cause it may readily happen, as has often been the case, that a majority of the people of a State or Territory are on one side of a question, whilst a majority of the representatives from the several districts into which it is divided may be upon the other side. This arises from the fact that in some districts delegates may be elected by small majorities, whilst in others those of different sentiments may receive majorities sufficiently great not only to overcome the votes given for the former, but to leave a large majority of the whole people in direct opposition to a majority of the delegates. Besides, our history proves that influences may be brought to bear on the representative sufficiently powerful to induce him to disregard the will of his constituents. The truth is that no other authentic and satisfactory mode exists of ascertaining the will of a majority of the people of any State or Territory on an important and exciting question like that of slavery in Kansas except by leaving it to a direct vote. How wise, then, was it for Congress to pass over all subordinate and intermediate agencies and proceed directly to the source of all legitimate power under our institutions!

How vain would any other principle prove in practice! This may be illustrated by the case of Kansas. Should she be admitted into the Union with a constitution either maintaining or abolishing slavery against the sentiment of the people, this could have no other effect than to continue and to exasperate the existing agitation during the brief period required to make the constitution conform to the irresistible will of the majority.

The friends and supporters of the Nebraska and Kansas act, when struggling on a recent occasion to sustain its wise provisions before the great tribunal of the American people, never differed about its true meaning on this subject. Everywhere throughout the Union they publicly pledged their faith and their honor that they would cheerfully submit the question of slavery to the decision of the *bona fide* people of Kansas, without any restriction or qualification whatever. All were cordially united upon the great doctrine of popular sovereignty, which is the vital principle of our free institutions. Had it then been insinuated from any quarter that it would be a sufficient compliance with the requisitions of the organic law for the members of a convention thereafter to be elected to withhold the question of slavery from the people and to substitute their own will for that of a legally ascertained majority of all their constituents, this would have been instantly rejected. Everywhere they remained true to the resolution adopted on a celebrated occasion recognizing ''the right of the people of all the Territories, including Kansas and Nebraska, acting through the legally and fairly expressed will of a majority of actual residents, and whenever the number of their inhabitants justifies it, to form a constitution with or without slavery and be admitted into the Union upon terms of perfect equality with the other States.''

The convention to frame a constitution for Kansas met on the first Monday of September last. They were called together by virtue of an act of the Territorial legislature, whose lawful existence had been recognized by Congress in different forms and by different enactments. A large proportion of the citizens of Kansas did not think proper to register their names and to vote at the election for delegates; but an opportunity to do this having been fairly afforded, their refusal to avail themselves of their right could in no manner affect the legality of the convention.

This convention proceeded to frame a constitution for Kansas, and finally adjourned on the 7th day of November. But little difficulty occurred in the convention except on the subject of slavery. The truth is that the general provisions of our recent State constitutions are so similar and, I may add, so excellent that the difference between them is not essential. Under the earlier practice of the Government no constitution framed by the convention of a Territory preparatory to its admission into the Union as a State had been submitted to the people.

I trust, however, the example set by the last Congress, requiring that
the constitution of Minnesota "should be subject to the approval and
ratification of the people of the proposed State," may be followed on
future occasions.   I took it for granted that the convention of Kansas
would act in accordance with this example, founded, as it is, on correct
principles, and hence my instructions to Governor Walker in favor of
submitting the constitution to the people were expressed in general and
unqualified terms.

In the Kansas-Nebraska act, however, this requirement, as applicable
to the whole constitution, had not been inserted, and the convention
were not bound by its terms to submit any other portion of the instrument to an election except that which relates to the "domestic institution" of slavery.   This will be rendered clear by a simple reference to
its language.   It was "not to legislate slavery into any Territory or
State, nor to exclude it therefrom, but to leave the people thereof perfectly free to form and regulate their domestic institutions in their own
way."   According to the plain construction of the sentence, the words
"domestic institutions" have a direct, as they have an appropriate, reference to slavery.   "Domestic institutions" are limited to the family
The relation between master and slave and a few others are "domestic
institutions," and are entirely distinct from institutions of a political
character.   Besides, there was no question then before Congress, nor,
indeed, has there since been any serious question before the people of
Kansas or the country, except that which relates to the "domestic institution" of slavery.

The convention, after an angry and excited debate, finally determined,
by a majority of only two, to submit the question of slavery to the people,
though at the last forty-three of the fifty delegates present affixed their
signatures to the constitution.

A large majority of the convention were in favor of establishing slavery
in Kansas.   They accordingly inserted an article in the constitution for
this purpose similar in form to those which had been adopted by other
Territorial conventions.   In the schedule, however, providing for the
transition from a Territorial to a State government the question has
been fairly and explicitly referred to the people whether they will have
a constitution "with or without slavery."   It declares that before the
constitution adopted by the convention "shall be sent to Congress for
admission into the Union as a State" an election shall be held to decide
this question, at which all the white male inhabitants of the Territory
above the age of 21 are entitled to vote.   They are to vote by ballot, and
"the ballots cast at said election shall be indorsed 'constitution with
slavery' and 'constitution with no slavery.'"   If there be a majority in
favor of the "constitution with slavery," then it is to be transmitted to
Congress by the president of the convention in its original form; if, on
the contrary, there shall be a majority in favor of the "constitution with

no slavery," "then the article providing for slavery shall be stricken from the constitution by the president of this convention;" and it is expressly declared that "no slavery shall exist in the State of Kansas, except that the right of property in slaves now in the Territory shall in no manner be interfered with;" and in that event it is made his duty to have the constitution thus ratified transmitted to the Congress of the United States for the admission of the State into the Union.

At this election every citizen will have an opportunity of expressing his opinion by his vote "whether Kansas shall be received into the Union with or without slavery," and thus this exciting question may be peacefully settled in the very mode required by the organic law. The election will be held under legitimate authority, and if any portion of the inhabitants shall refuse to vote, a fair opportunity to do so having been presented, this will be their own voluntary act and they alone will be responsible for the consequences.

Whether Kansas shall be a free or a slave State must eventually, under some authority, be decided by an election; and the question can never be more clearly or distinctly presented to the people than it is at the present moment. Should this opportunity be rejected she may be involved for years in domestic discord, and possibly in civil war, before she can again make up the issue now so fortunately tendered and again reach the point she has already attained.

Kansas has for some years occupied too much of the public attention. It is high time this should be directed to far more important objects. When once admitted into the Union, whether with or without slavery, the excitement beyond her own limits will speedily pass away, and she will then for the first time be left, as she ought to have been long since, to manage her own affairs in her own way. If her constitution on the subject of slavery or on any other subject be displeasing to a majority of the people, no human power can prevent them from changing it within a brief period. Under these circumstances it may well be questioned whether the peace and quiet of the whole country are not of greater importance than the mere temporary triumph of either of the political parties in Kansas.

Should the constitution without slavery be adopted by the votes of the majority, the rights of property in slaves now in the Territory are reserved. The number of these is very small, but if it were greater the provision would be equally just and reasonable. The slaves were brought into the Territory under the Constitution of the United States and are now the property of their masters. This point has at length been finally decided by the highest judicial tribunal of the country, and this upon the plain principle that when a confederacy of sovereign States acquire a new territory at their joint expense both equality and justice demand that the citizens of one and all of them shall have the right to take into it whatsoever is recognized as property by the common Constitution.

To have summarily confiscated the property in slaves already in the Territory would have been an act of gross injustice and contrary to the practice of the older States of the Union which have abolished slavery.

A Territorial government was established for Utah by act of Congress approved the 9th September, 1850, and the Constitution and laws of the United States were thereby extended over it "so far as the same or any provisions thereof may be applicable." This act provided for the appointment by the President, by and with the advice and consent of the Senate, of a governor (who was to be *ex officio* superintendent of Indian affairs), a secretary, three judges of the supreme court, a marshal, and a district attorney. Subsequent acts provided for the appointment of the officers necessary to extend our land and our Indian system over the Territory. Brigham Young was appointed the first governor on the 20th September, 1850, and has held the office ever since. Whilst Governor Young has been both governor and superintendent of Indian affairs throughout this period, he has been at the same time the head of the church called the Latter-day Saints, and professes to govern its members and dispose of their property by direct inspiration and authority from the Almighty. His power has been, therefore, absolute over both church and state.

The people of Utah almost exclusively belong to this church, and believing with a fanatical spirit that he is governor of the Territory by divine appointment, they obey his commands as if these were direct revelations from Heaven. If, therefore, he chooses that his government shall come into collision with the Government of the United States, the members of the Mormon Church will yield implicit obedience to his will. Unfortunately, existing facts leave but little doubt that such is his determination. Without entering upon a minute history of occurrences, it is sufficient to say that all the officers of the United States, judicial and executive, with the single exception of two Indian agents, have found it necessary for their own personal safety to withdraw from the Territory, and there no longer remains any government in Utah but the despotism of Brigham Young. This being the condition of affairs in the Territory, I could not mistake the path of duty. As Chief Executive Magistrate I was bound to restore the supremacy of the Constitution and laws within its limits. In order to effect this purpose, I appointed a new governor and other Federal officers for Utah and sent with them a military force for their protection and to aid as a *posse comitatus* in case of need in the execution of the laws.

With the religious opinions of the Mormons, as long as they remained mere opinions, however deplorable in themselves and revolting to the moral and religious sentiments of all Christendom, I had no right to interfere. Actions alone, when in violation of the Constitution and laws of the United States, become the legitimate subjects for the jurisdiction of the civil magistrate. My instructions to Governor Cumming have therefore been framed in strict accordance with these principles. At their date a hope was indulged that no necessity might exist for employing the military in restoring and maintaining the authority of the law, but this hope has now vanished. Governor Young has by proclamation declared his determination to maintain his power by force, and has already committed acts of hostility against the United States. Unless he should retrace his steps the Territory of Utah will be in a state of open rebellion. He has committed these acts of hostility notwithstanding Major Van Vliet, an officer of the Army, sent to Utah by the Commanding General to purchase provisions for the troops, had given him the strongest assurances of the peaceful intentions of the Government, and that the troops would only be employed as a *posse comitatus* when called on by the civil authority to aid in the execution of the laws.

There is reason to believe that Governor Young has long contemplated this result. He knows that the continuance of his despotic power depends upon the exclusion of all settlers from the Territory except those who will acknowledge his divine mission and implicitly obey his will, and that an enlightened public opinion there would soon prostrate institutions at war with the laws both of God and man. He has therefore for several years, in order to maintain his independence, been industriously employed in collecting and fabricating arms and munitions of war and in disciplining the Mormons for military service. As superintendent of Indian affairs he has had an opportunity of tampering with the Indian tribes and exciting their hostile feelings against the United States. This, according to our information, he has accomplished in regard to some of these tribes, while others have remained true to their allegiance and have communicated his intrigues to our Indian agents. He has laid in a store of provisions for three years, which in case of necessity, as he informed Major Van Vliet, he will conceal, "and then take to the mountains and bid defiance to all the powers of the Government."

A great part of all this may be idle boasting, but yet no wise government will lightly estimate the efforts which may be inspired by such frenzied fanaticism as exists among the Mormons in Utah. This is the first rebellion which has existed in our Territories, and humanity itself requires that we should put it down in such a manner that it shall be the last. To trifle with it would be to encourage it and to render it formidable. We ought to go there with such an imposing force as to convince these deluded people that resistance would be vain, and thus spare the effusion of blood. We can in this manner best convince them that we are their friends, not their enemies. In order to accomplish this object it will be necessary, according to the estimate of the War Department, to raise four additional regiments; and this I earnestly recommend to Congress. At the present moment of depression in the revenues of the country I am sorry to be obliged to recommend such a measure; but I feel confident of the support of Congress, cost what it may, in suppressing the insurrection and in restoring and maintaining the sovereignty of the Constitution and laws over the Territory of Utah.

I recommend to Congress the establishment of a Territorial government over Arizona, incorporating with it such portions of New Mexico as they may deem expedient. I need scarcely adduce arguments in support of this recommendation. We are bound to protect the lives and the property of our citizens inhabiting Arizona, and these are now without any efficient protection. Their present number is already considerable, and is rapidly increasing, notwithstanding the disadvantages under which they labor. Besides, the proposed Territory is believed to be rich in mineral and agricultural resources, especially in silver and copper. The mails of the United States to California are now carried over it throughout its whole extent, and this route is known to be the nearest and believed to be the best to the Pacific.

Long experience has deeply convinced me that a strict construction of the powers granted to Congress is the only true, as well as the only safe, theory of the Constitution. Whilst this principle shall guide my public conduct, I consider it clear that under the war-making power Congress may appropriate money for the construction of a military road through the Territories of the United States when this is absolutely necessary for the defense of any of the States against foreign invasion. The Constitution has conferred upon Congress power ''to declare war,'' ''to raise and support armies,'' ''to provide and maintain a navy,'' and to call forth the militia to ''repel invasions.'' These high sovereign powers necessarily involve important and responsible public duties, and among them there is none so sacred and so imperative as that of preserving our soil from the invasion of a foreign enemy. The Constitution has therefore left nothing on this point to construction, but expressly requires that ''the United States shall protect each of them [the States] against invasion.'' Now if a military road over our own Territories be indispensably necessary to enable us to meet and repel the invader, it follows as a necessary consequence not only that we possess the power, but it is our imperative duty to construct such a road. It would be an absurdity to invest a government with the unlimited power to make and conduct war and at the same time deny to it the only means of reaching and defeating the enemy at the frontier. Without such a road it is quite evident we can not ''protect'' California and our Pacific possessions ''against invasion.'' We can not by any other means transport men and munitions of war from the Atlantic States in sufficient time successfully to defend these remote and distant portions of the Republic.

Experience has proved that the routes across the isthmus of Central America are at best but a very uncertain and unreliable mode of communication. But even if this were not the case, they would at once be closed against us in the event of war with a naval power so much stronger than our own as to enable it to blockade the ports at either end of these routes. After all, therefore, we can only rely upon a military road through our own Territories; and ever since the origin of the Government Congress has been in the practice of appropriating money from the public Treasury for the construction of such roads.

The difficulties and the expense of constructing a military railroad to connect our Atlantic and Pacific States have been greatly exaggerated. The distance on the Arizona route, near the thirty-second parallel of north latitude, between the western boundary of Texas, on the Rio Grande, and the eastern boundary of California, on the Colorado, from the best explorations now within our knowledge, does not exceed 470 miles, and the face of the country is in the main favorable. For obvious reasons the Government ought not to undertake the work itself by means of its own agents. This ought to be committed to other agencies, which Congress might assist, either by grants of land or money, or by both, upon such terms and conditions as they may deem most beneficial for the country. Provision might thus be made not only for the safe, rapid, and economical transportation of troops and munitions of war, but also of the public mails. The commercial interests of the whole country, both East and West, would be greatly promoted by such a road, and, above all, it would be a powerful additional bond of union. And although advantages of this kind, whether postal, commercial, or political, can not confer constitutional power, yet they may furnish auxiliary arguments in favor of expediting a work which, in my judgment, is clearly embraced within the war-making power.

For these reasons I commend to the friendly consideration of Congress the subject of the Pacific Railroad, without finally committing myself to any particular route.

The report of the Secretary of the Treasury will furnish a detailed statement of the condition of the public finances and of the respective branches of the public service devolved upon that Department of the Government. By this report it appears that the amount of revenue received from all sources into the Treasury during the fiscal year ending the 30th June, 1857, was $68,631,513.67, which amount, with the balance of $19,901,325.45 remaining in the Treasury at the commencement of the year, made an aggregate for the service of the year of $88,532,839.12.

The public expenditures for the fiscal year ending 30th June, 1857, amounted to $70,822,724.85, of which $5,943,896.91 were applied to the redemption of the public debt, including interest and premium, leaving in the Treasury at the commencement of the present fiscal year, on the 1st July, 1857, $17,710,114.27.

The receipts into the Treasury for the first quarter of the present fiscal year, commencing 1st July, 1857, were $20,929,819.81, and the estimated receipts of the remaining three quarters to the 30th June, 1858, are $36,750,000, making, with the balance before stated, an aggregate of $75,389,934.08 for the service of the present fiscal year.

The actual expenditures during the first quarter of the present fiscal year were $23,714,528.37, of which $3,895,232.39 were applied to the redemption of the public debt, including interest and premium. The probable expenditures of the remaining three quarters to 30th June, 1858, are $51,248,530.04, including interest on the public debt, making an aggregate of $74,963,058.41, leaving an estimated balance in the Treasury at the close of the present fiscal year of $426,875.67.

The amount of the public debt at the commencement of the present fiscal year was $29,060,386.90.

The amount redeemed since the 1st of July was $3,895,232.39, leaving a balance unredeemed at this time of $25,165,154.51.

The amount of estimated expenditures for the remaining three quarters of the present fiscal year will in all probability be increased from the causes set forth in the report of the Secretary. His suggestion, therefore, that authority should be given to supply any temporary deficiency by the issue of a limited amount of Treasury notes is approved, and I accordingly recommend the passage of such a law.

As stated in the report of the Secretary, the tariff of March 3, 1857, has been in operation for so short a period of time and under circumstances so unfavorable to a just development of its results as a revenue measure that I should regard it as inexpedient, at least for the present, to undertake its revision.

I transmit herewith the reports made to me by the Secretaries of War and of the Navy, of the Interior, and of the Postmaster-General. They all contain valuable and important information and suggestions, which I commend to the favorable consideration of Congress.

I have already recommended the raising of four additional regiments, and the report of the Secretary of War presents strong reasons proving this increase of the Army under existing circumstances to be indispensable.

I would call the special attention of Congress to the recommendation of the Secretary of the Navy in favor of the construction of ten small war steamers of light draft. For some years the Government has been obliged on many occasions to hire such steamers from individuals to supply its pressing wants. At the present moment we have no armed vessel in the Navy which can penetrate the rivers of China. We have but few which can enter any of the harbors south of Norfolk, although many millions of foreign and domestic commerce annually pass in and out of these harbors. Some of our most valuable interests and most vulnerable points are thus left exposed. This class of vessels of light draft, great speed, and heavy guns would be formidable in coast defense. The cost of their construction will not be great and they will require but a comparatively small expenditure to keep them in commission. In time of peace they will prove as effective as much larger vessels and more useful. One of them should be at every station where we maintain a squadron, and three or four should be constantly employed on our Atlantic and

Pacific coasts. Economy, utility, and efficiency combine to recommend them as almost indispensable. Ten of these small vessels would be of incalculable advantage to the naval service, and the whole cost of their construction would not exceed $2,300,000, or $230,000 each.

The report of the Secretary of the Interior is worthy of grave consideration. It treats of the numerous important and diversified branches of domestic administration intrusted to him by law. Among these the most prominent are the public lands and our relations with the Indians.

Our system for the disposal of the public lands, originating with the fathers of the Republic, has been improved as experience pointed the way, and gradually adapted to the growth and settlement of our Western States and Territories. It has worked well in practice. Already thirteen States and seven Territories have been carved out of these lands, and still more than a thousand millions of acres remain unsold. What a boundless prospect this presents to our country of future prosperity and power!

We have heretofore disposed of 363,862,464 acres of the public land.

Whilst the public lands, as a source of revenue, are of great importance, their importance is far greater as furnishing homes for a hardy and independent race of honest and industrious citizens who desire to subdue and cultivate the soil. They ought to be administered mainly with a view of promoting this wise and benevolent policy. In appropriating them for any other purpose we ought to use even greater economy than if they had been converted into money and the proceeds were already in the public Treasury. To squander away this richest and noblest inheritance which any people have ever enjoyed upon objects of doubtful constitutionality or expediency would be to violate one of the most important trusts ever committed to any people. Whilst I do not deny to Congress the power, when acting *bona fide* as a proprietor, to give away portions of them for the purpose of increasing the value of the remainder, yet, considering the great temptation to abuse this power, we can not be too cautious in its exercise.

Actual settlers under existing laws are protected against other purchasers at the public sales in their right of preemption to the extent of a quarter section, or 160 acres, of land. The remainder may then be disposed of at public or entered at private sale in unlimited quantities.

Speculation has of late years prevailed to a great extent in the public lands. The consequence has been that large portions of them have become the property of individuals and companies, and thus the price is greatly enhanced to those who desire to purchase for actual settlement. In order to limit the area of speculation as much as possible, the extinction of the Indian title and the extension of the public surveys ought only to keep pace with the tide of emigration.

If Congress should hereafter grant alternate sections to States or companies, as they have done heretofore, I recommend that the intermediate sections retained by the Government should be subject to preemption by actual settlers.

It ought ever to be our cardinal policy to reserve the public lands as much as may be for actual settlers, and this at moderate prices. We shall thus not only best promote the prosperity of the new States and Territories and the power of the Union, but shall secure homes for our posterity for many generations.

The extension of our limits has brought within our jurisdiction many additional and populous tribes of Indians, a large proportion of which are wild, untractable, and difficult to control. Predatory and warlike in their disposition and habits, it is impossible altogether to restrain them from committing aggressions on each other, as well as upon our frontier citizens and those emigrating to our distant States and Territories. Hence expensive military expeditions are frequently necessary to overawe and chastise the more lawless and hostile.

The present system of making them valuable presents to influence them to remain at peace has proved ineffectual. It is believed to be the better policy to colonize them in suitable localities where they can receive the rudiments of education and be gradually induced to adopt habits of industry. So far as the experiment has been tried it has worked well in practice, and it will doubtless prove to be less expensive than the present system.

The whole number of Indians within our territorial limits is believed to be, from the best data in the Interior Department, about 325,000.

The tribes of Cherokees, Choctaws, Chickasaws, and Creeks settled in the Territory set apart for them west of Arkansas are rapidly advancing in education and in all the arts of civilization and self-government, and we may indulge the agreeable anticipation that at no very distant day they will be incorporated into the Union as one of the sovereign States.

It will be seen from the report of the Postmaster-General that the Post-Office Department still continues to depend on the Treasury, as it has been compelled to do for several years past, for an important portion of the means of sustaining and extending its operations. Their rapid growth and expansion are shown by a decennial statement of the number of post-offices and the length of post-roads, commencing with the year 1827. In that year there were 7,000 post-offices; in 1837, 11,177; in 1847, 15,146, and in 1857 they number 26,586. In this year 1,725 post-offices have been established and 704 discontinued, leaving a net increase of 1,021. The postmasters of 368 offices are appointed by the President.

The length of post-roads in 1827 was 105,336 miles; in 1837, 141,242 miles; in 1847, 153,818 miles, and in the year 1857 there are 242,601 miles of post-road, including 22,530 miles of railroad on which the mails are transported.

The expenditures of the Department for the fiscal year ending on the 30th June, 1857, as adjusted by the Auditor, amounted to $11,507,670.

To defray these expenditures there was to the credit of the Department on the 1st July, 1856, the sum of $789,599; the gross revenue of the year, including the annual allowances for the transportation of free mail matter, produced $8,053,951, and the remainder was supplied by the appropriation from the Treasury of $2,250,000 granted by the act of Congress approved August 18, 1856, and by the appropriation of $666,883 made by the act of March 3, 1857, leaving $252,763 to be carried to the credit of the Department in the accounts of the current year. I commend to your consideration the report of the Department in relation to the establishment of the overland mail route from the Mississippi River to San Francisco, Cal. The route was selected with my full concurrence, as the one, in my judgment, best calculated to attain the important objects contemplated by Congress.

The late disastrous monetary revulsion may have one good effect should it cause both the Government and the people to return to the practice of a wise and judicious economy both in public and private expenditures.

An overflowing Treasury has led to habits of prodigality and extravagance in our legislation. It has induced Congress to make large appropriations to objects for which they never would have provided had it been necessary to raise the amount of revenue required to meet them by increased taxation or by loans. We are now compelled to pause in our career and to scrutinize our expenditures with the utmost vigilance; and in performing this duty I pledge my cooperation to the extent of my constitutional competency.

It ought to be observed at the same time that true public economy does not consist in withholding the means necessary to accomplish important national objects intrusted to us by the Constitution, and especially such as may be necessary for the common defense. In the present crisis of the country it is our duty to confine our appropriations to objects of this character, unless in cases where justice to individuals may demand a different course. In all cases care ought to be taken that the money granted by Congress shall be faithfully and economically applied.

Under the Federal Constitution "every bill which shall have passed the House of Representatives and the Senate shall, before it become a law," be approved and signed by the President; and if not approved, "he shall return it with his objections to that House in which it shall have originated." In order to perform this high and responsible duty, sufficient time must be allowed the President to read and examine every bill presented to him for approval. Unless this be afforded, the Constitution becomes a dead letter in this particular, and, even worse, it becomes a means of deception. Our constituents, seeing the President's approval and signature attached to each act of Congress, are induced to believe that he has actually performed his duty, when in truth nothing is in many cases more unfounded.

From the practice of Congress such an examination of each bill as the

Constitution requires has been rendered impossible. The most important business of each session is generally crowded into its last hours, and the alternative presented to the President is either to violate the constitutional duty which he owes to the people and approve bills which for want of time it is impossible he should have examined, or by his refusal to do this subject the country and individuals to great loss and inconvenience.

Besides, a practice has grown up of late years to legislate in appropriation bills at the last hours of the session on new and important subjects. This practice constrains the President either to suffer measures to become laws which he does not approve or to incur the risk of stopping the wheels of the Government by vetoing an appropriation bill. Formerly such bills were confined to specific appropriations for carrying into effect existing laws and the well-established policy of the country, and little time was then required by the President for their examination.

For my own part, I have deliberately determined that I shall approve no bills which I have not examined, and it will be a case of extreme and most urgent necessity which shall ever induce me to depart from this rule. I therefore respectfully but earnestly recommend that the two Houses would allow the President at least two days previous to the adjournment of each session within which no new bill shall be presented to him for approval. Under the existing joint rule one day is allowed, but this rule has been hitherto so constantly suspended in practice that important bills continue to be presented to him up till the very last moments of the session. In a large majority of cases no great public inconvenience can arise from the want of time to examine their provisions, because the Constitution has declared that if a bill be presented to the President within the last ten days of the session he is not required to return it, either with an approval or with a veto, "in which case it shall not be a law." It may then lie over and be taken up and passed at the next session. Great inconvenience would only be experienced in regard to appropriation bills, but, fortunately, under the late excellent law allowing a salary instead of a per diem to members of Congress the expense and inconvenience of a called session will be greatly reduced.

I can not conclude without commending to your favorable consideration the interest of the people of this District. Without a representative on the floor of Congress, they have for this very reason peculiar claims upon our just regard. To this I know, from my long acquaintance with them, they are eminently entitled.

SECOND ANNUAL MESSAGE.

WASHINGTON CITY, *December 6, 1858.*

Fellow-Citizens of the Senate and House of Representatives:

When we compare the condition of the country at the present day with what it was one year ago at the meeting of Congress, we have much reason for gratitude to that Almighty Providence which has never failed to interpose for our relief at the most critical periods of our history. One year ago the sectional strife between the North and the South on the dangerous subject of slavery had again become so intense as to threaten the peace and perpetuity of the Confederacy. The application for the admission of Kansas as a State into the Union fostered this unhappy agitation and brought the whole subject once more before Congress. It was the desire of every patriot that such measures of legislation might be adopted as would remove the excitement from the States and confine it to the Territory where it legitimately belonged. Much has been done, I am happy to say, toward the accomplishment of this object during the last session of Congress.

The Supreme Court of the United States had previously decided that all American citizens have an equal right to take into the Territories whatever is held as property under the laws of any of the States, and to hold such property there under the guardianship of the Federal Constitution so long as the Territorial condition shall remain.

This is now a well-established position, and the proceedings of the last session were alone wanting to give it practical effect. The principle has been recognized in some form or other by an almost unanimous vote of both Houses of Congress that a Territory has a right to come into the Union either as a free or a slave State, according to the will of a majority of its people. The just equality of all the States has thus been vindicated and a fruitful source of dangerous dissension among them has been removed.

Whilst such has been the beneficial tendency of your legislative proceedings outside of Kansas, their influence has nowhere been so happy as within that Territory itself. Left to manage and control its own affairs in its own way, without the pressure of external influence, the revolutionary Topeka organization and all resistance to the Territorial government established by Congress have been finally abandoned. As a natural consequence that fine Territory now appears to be tranquil and prosperous and is attracting increasing thousands of immigrants to make it their happy home.

The past unfortunate experience of Kansas has enforced the lesson, so often already taught, that resistance to lawful authority under our form of government can not fail in the end to prove disastrous to its authors. Had the people of the Territory yielded obedience to the laws enacted by their legislature, it would at the present moment have contained a large additional population of industrious and enterprising citizens, who have been deterred from entering its borders by the existence of civil strife and organized rebellion.

It was the resistance to rightful authority and the persevering attempts to establish a revolutionary government under the Topeka constitution which caused the people of Kansas to commit the grave error of refusing to vote for delegates to the convention to frame a constitution under a law not denied to be fair and just in its provisions. This refusal to vote **has been the prolific source of all the evils which have followed.** In their hostility to the Territorial government they disregarded the principle, absolutely essential to the working of our form of government, that a majority of those who vote, not the majority who may remain at home, from whatever cause, must decide the result of an election. For this reason, seeking to take advantage of their own error, they denied the authority of the convention thus elected to frame a constitution.

The convention, notwithstanding, proceeded to adopt a constitution unexceptionable in its general features, and providing for the submission of the slavery question to a vote of the people, which, in my opinion, they were bound to do under the Kansas and Nebraska act. This was the all-important question which had alone convulsed the Territory; and yet the opponents of the lawful government, persisting in their first error, refrained from exercising their right to vote, and preferred that slavery should continue rather than surrender their revolutionary Topeka organ-ization.

A wiser and better spirit seemed to prevail before the first Monday of January last, when an election was held under the constitution. A majority of the people then voted for a governor and other State officers, for a Member of Congress and members of the State legislature. This election was warmly contested by the two political parties in Kansas, and a greater vote was polled than at any previous election. A large majority of the members of the legislature elect belonged to that party which had previously refused to vote. The antislavery party were thus placed in the ascendant, and the political power of the State was in their own hands. Had Congress admitted Kansas into the Union under the Lecompton constitution, the legislature might at its very first session have submitted the question to a vote of the people whether they would or would not have a convention to amend their constitution, either on the slavery or any other question, and have adopted all necessary means for giving speedy effect to the will of the majority. Thus the Kansas question would have been immediately and finally settled.

Under these circumstances I submitted to Congress the constitution thus framed, with all the officers already elected necessary to put the State government into operation, accompanied by a strong recommendation in favor of the admission of Kansas as a State. In the course of my long public life I have never performed any official act which in the retrospect has afforded me more heartfelt satisfaction. Its admission could have inflicted no possible injury on any human being, whilst it would within a brief period have restored peace to Kansas and harmony to the Union. In that event the slavery question would ere this have been finally settled according to the legally expressed will of a majority of the voters, and popular sovereignty would thus have been vindicated in a constitutional manner.

With my deep convictions of duty I could have pursued no other course. It is true that as an individual I had expressed an opinion, both before and during the session of the convention, in favor of submitting the remaining clauses of the constitution, as well as that concerning slavery, to the people. But, acting in an official character, neither myself nor any human authority had the power to rejudge the proceedings of the convention and declare the constitution which it had framed to be a nullity. To have done this would have been a violation of the Kansas and Nebraska act, which left the people of the Territory "perfectly free to form and regulate their domestic institutions in their own way, subject only to the Constitution of the United States." It would equally have violated the great principle of popular sovereignty, at the foundation of our institutions, to deprive the people of the power, if they thought proper to exercise it, of confiding to delegates elected by themselves the trust of framing a constitution without requiring them to subject their constituents to the trouble, expense, and delay of a second election. It would have been in opposition to many precedents in our history, commencing in the very best age of the Republic, of the admission of Territories as States into the Union without a previous vote of the people approving their constitution.

It is to be lamented that a question so insignificant when viewed in its practical effects on the people of Kansas, whether decided one way or the other, should have kindled such a flame of excitement throughout the country. This reflection may prove to be a lesson of wisdom and of warning for our future guidance. Practically considered, the question is simply whether the people of that Territory should first come into the Union and then change any provision in their constitution not agreeable to themselves, or accomplish the very same object by remaining out of the Union and framing another constitution in accordance with their will. In either case the result would be precisely the same. The only difference, in point of fact, is that the object would have been much sooner attained and the pacification of Kansas more speedily effected had it been admitted as a State during the last session of Congress.

My recommendation, however, for the immediate admission of Kansas failed to meet the approbation of Congress. They deemed it wiser to adopt a different measure for the settlement of the question. For my own part, I should have been willing to yield my assent to almost any constitutional measure to accomplish this object. I therefore cordially acquiesced in what has been called the English compromise and approved the "act for the admission of the State of Kansas into the Union" upon the terms therein prescribed.

Under the ordinance which accompanied the Lecompton constitution the people of Kansas had claimed double the quantity of public lands for the support of common schools which had ever been previously granted to any State upon entering the Union, and also the alternate sections of land for 12 miles on each side of two railroads proposed to be constructed from the northern to the southern boundary and from the eastern to the western boundary of the State. Congress, deeming these claims unreasonable, provided by the act of May 4, 1858, to which I have just referred, for the admission of the State on an equal footing with the original States, but "upon the fundamental condition precedent" that a majority of the people thereof, at an election to be held for that purpose, should, in place of the very large grants of public lands which they had demanded under the ordinance, accept such grants as had been made to Minnesota and other new States. Under this act, should a majority reject the proposition offered them, "it shall be deemed and held that the people of Kansas do not desire admission into the Union with said constitution under the conditions set forth in said proposition." In that event the act authorizes the people of the Territory to elect delegates to form a constitution and State government for themselves "whenever, and not before, it is ascertained by a census, duly and legally taken, that the population of said Territory equals or exceeds the ratio of representation required for a member of the House of Representatives of the Congress of the United States." The delegates thus assembled "shall first determine by a vote whether it is the wish of the people of the proposed State to be admitted into the Union at that time, and, if so, shall proceed to form a constitution and take all necessary steps for the establishment of a State government in conformity with the Federal Constitution." After this constitution shall have been formed, Congress, carrying out the principles of popular sovereignty and nonintervention, have left "the mode and manner of its approval or ratification by the people of the proposed State" to be "prescribed by law," and they "shall then be admitted into the Union as a State under such constitution, thus fairly and legally made, with or without slavery, as said constitution may prescribe."

An election was held throughout Kansas, in pursuance of the provisions of this act, on the 2d day of August last, and it resulted in the rejection by a large majority of the proposition submitted to the people by Congress. This being the case, they are now authorized to form another constitution, preparatory to admission into the Union, but not until their number, as ascertained by a census, shall equal or exceed the ratio required to elect a member to the House of Representatives.

It is not probable, in the present state of the case, that a third constitution can be lawfully framed and presented to Congress by Kansas before its population shall have reached the designated number. Nor is it to be presumed that after their sad experience in resisting the Territorial laws they will attempt to adopt a constitution in express violation of the provisions of an act of Congress. During the session of 1856 much of the time of Congress was occupied on the question of admitting Kansas under the Topeka constitution. Again, nearly the whole of the last session was devoted to the question of its admission under the Lecompton constitution. Surely it is not unreasonable to require the people of Kansas to wait before making a third attempt until the number of their inhabitants shall amount to 93,420. During this brief period the harmony of the States as well as the great business interests of the country demand that the people of the Union shall not for a third time be convulsed by another agitation on the Kansas question. By waiting for a short time and acting in obedience to law Kansas will glide into the Union without the slightest impediment.

This excellent provision, which Congress have applied to Kansas, ought to be extended and rendered applicable to all Territories which may hereafter seek admission into the Union.

Whilst Congress possess the undoubted power of admitting a new State into the Union, however small may be the number of its inhabitants, yet this power ought not, in my opinion, to be exercised before the population shall amount to the ratio required by the act for the admission of Kansas. Had this been previously the rule, the country would have escaped all the evils and misfortunes to which it has been exposed by the Kansas question.

Of course it would be unjust to give this rule a retrospective application, and exclude a State which, acting upon the past practice of the Government, has already formed its constitution, elected its legislature and other officers, and is now prepared to enter the Union.

The rule ought to be adopted, whether we consider its bearing on the people of the Territories or upon the people of the existing States. Many of the serious dissensions which have prevailed in Congress and throughout the country would have been avoided had this rule been established at an earlier period of the Government.

Immediately upon the formation of a new Territory people from different States and from foreign countries rush into it for the laudable purpose of improving their condition. Their first duty to themselves is to open and cultivate farms, to construct roads, to establish schools, to erect places of religious worship, and to devote their energies generally to reclaim the wilderness and to lay the foundations of a flourishing and prosperous commonwealth. If in this incipient condition, with a population of a few thousand, they should prematurely enter the Union, they are oppressed by the burden of State taxation, and the means necessary for the improvement of the Territory and the advancement of their own interests are thus diverted to very different purposes.

The Federal Government has ever been a liberal parent to the Territories and a generous contributor to the useful enterprises of the early settlers. It has paid the expenses of their governments and legislative assemblies out of the common Treasury, and thus relieved them from a heavy charge. Under these circumstances nothing can be better calculated to retard their material progress than to divert them from their useful employments by prematurely exciting angry political contests among themselves for the benefit of aspiring leaders. It is surely no hardship for embryo governors, Senators, and Members of Congress to wait until the number of inhabitants shall equal those of a single Congressional district. They surely ought not to be permitted to rush into the Union with a population less than one-half of several of the large counties in the interior of some of the States. This was the condition of Kansas when it made application to be admitted under the Topeka constitution. Besides, it requires some time to render the mass of a population collected in a new Territory at all homogeneous and to unite them on anything like a fixed policy. Establish the rule, and all will look forward to it and govern themselves accordingly.

But justice to the people of the several States requires that this rule should be established by Congress. Each State is entitled to two Senators and at least one Representative in Congress. Should the people of the States fail to elect a Vice-President, the power devolves upon the Senate to select this officer from the two highest candidates on the list. In case of the death of the President, the Vice-President thus elected by the Senate becomes President of the United States. On all questions of legislation the Senators from the smallest States of the Union have an equal vote with those from the largest. The same may be said in regard to the ratification of treaties and of Executive appointments. All this has worked admirably in practice, whilst it conforms in principle with the character of a Government instituted by sovereign States. I presume no American citizen would desire the slightest change in the arrangement. Still, is it not unjust and unequal to the existing States to invest some 40,000 or 50,000 people collected in a Territory with the attributes of sovereignty and place them on an equal footing with Virginia and New York in the Senate of the United States?

For these reasons I earnestly recommend the passage of a general act which shall provide that, upon the application of a Territorial legislature declaring their belief that the Territory contains a number of inhabitants which, if in a State, would entitle them to elect a Member of Congress, it shall be the duty of the President to cause a census of the inhabitants to be taken, and if found sufficient then by the terms of this act to authorize them to proceed ''in their own way'' to frame a State constitution preparatory to admission into the Union. I also recommend that an appropriation may be made to enable the President to take a census of the people of Kansas.

The present condition of the Territory of Utah, when contrasted with what it was one year ago, is a subject for congratulation. It was then in a state of open rebellion, and, cost what it might, the character of the Government required that this rebellion should be suppressed and the Mormons compelled to yield obedience to the Constitution and the laws. In order to accomplish this object, as I informed you in my last annual message, I appointed a new governor instead of Brigham Young, and other Federal officers to take the place of those who, consulting their personal safety, had found it necessary to withdraw from the Territory. To protect these civil officers, and to aid them, as a *posse comitatus*, in the execution of the laws in case of need, I ordered a detachment of the Army to accompany them to Utah. The necessity for adopting these measures is now demonstrated.

On the 15th of September, 1857, Governor Young issued his proclamation, in the style of an independent sovereign, announcing his purpose to resist by force of arms the entry of the United States troops into our own Territory of Utah. By this he required all the forces in the Territory to "hold themselves in readiness to march at a moment's notice to repel any and all such invasion," and established martial law from its date throughout the Territory. These proved to be no idle threats. Forts Bridger and Supply were vacated and burnt down by the Mormons to deprive our troops of a shelter after their long and fatiguing march. Orders were issued by Daniel H. Wells, styling himself "Lieutenant-General, Nauvoo Legion," to stampede the animals of the United States troops on their march, to set fire to their trains, to burn the grass and the whole country before them and on their flanks, to keep them from sleeping by night surprises, and to blockade the road by felling trees and destroying the fords of rivers, etc.

These orders were promptly and effectually obeyed. On the 4th of October, 1857, the Mormons captured and burned, on Green River, three of our supply trains, consisting of seventy-five wagons loaded with provisions and tents for the army, and carried away several hundred animals. This diminished the supply of provisions so materially that General Johnston was obliged to reduce the ration, and even with this precaution there was only sufficient left to subsist the troops until the 1st of June.

Our little army behaved admirably in their encampment at Fort Bridger under these trying privations. In the midst of the mountains, in a dreary, unsettled, and inhospitable region, more than a thousand miles from home, they passed the severe and inclement winter without a murmur. They looked forward with confidence for relief from their country in due season, and in this they were not disappointed.

The Secretary of War employed all his energies to forward them the necessary supplies and to muster and send such a military force to Utah as would render resistance on the part of the Mormons hopeless, and thus terminate the war without the effusion of blood. In his efforts he was efficiently sustained by Congress. They granted appropriations sufficient to cover the deficiency thus necessarily created, and also provided for raising two regiments of volunteers "for the purpose of quelling disturbances in the Territory of Utah, for the protection of supply and emigrant trains, and the suppression of Indian hostilities on the frontiers." Happily, there was no occasion to call these regiments into service. If there had been, I should have felt serious embarrassment in selecting them, so great was the number of our brave and patriotic citizens anxious to serve their country in this distant and apparently dangerous expedition. Thus it has ever been, and thus may it ever be.

The wisdom and economy of sending sufficient reenforcements to Utah are established, not only by the event, but in the opinion of those who from their position and opportunities are the most capable of forming a correct judgment. General Johnston, the commander of the forces, in addressing the Secretary of War from Fort Bridger under date of October 18, 1857, expresses the opinion that "unless a large force is sent here, from the nature of the country a protracted war on their [the Mormons's] part is inevitable." This he considered necessary to terminate the war "speedily and more economically than if attempted by insufficient means."

In the meantime it was my anxious desire that the Mormons should yield obedience to the Constitution and the laws without rendering it necessary to resort to military force. To aid in accomplishing this object, I deemed it advisable in April last to dispatch two distinguished citizens of the United States, Messrs. Powell and McCulloch, to Utah. They bore with them a proclamation addressed by myself to the inhabitants of Utah, dated on the 6th day of that month, warning them of their true condition and how hopeless it was on their part to persist in rebellion against the United States, and offering all those who should submit to the laws a full pardon for their past seditions and treasons. At the same time I assured those who should persist in rebellion against the United States that they must expect no further lenity, but look to be rigorously dealt with according to their deserts. The instructions to these agents, as well as a copy of the proclamation and their reports, are herewith submitted. It will be seen by their report of the 3d of July last that they have fully confirmed the opinion expressed by General Johnston in the previous October as to the necessity of sending reenforcements to Utah. In this they state that they "are firmly impressed with the belief that the presence of the Army here and the large additional force that had been ordered to this Territory were the chief inducements that caused the Mormons to abandon the idea of resisting the authority of the United States. A less decisive policy would probably have resulted in a long, bloody, and expensive war."

These gentlemen conducted themselves to my entire satisfaction and rendered useful services in executing the humane intentions of the Government.

It also affords me great satisfaction to state that Governor Cumming has performed his duty in an able and conciliatory manner and with the happiest effect. I can not in this connection refrain from mentioning the valuable services of Colonel Thomas L. Kane, who, from motives of pure benevolence and without any official character or pecuniary compensation, visited Utah during the last inclement winter for the purpose of contributing to the pacification of the Territory.

I am happy to inform you that the governor and other civil officers of Utah are now performing their appropriate functions without resistance. The authority of the Constitution and the laws has been fully restored and peace prevails throughout the Territory.

A portion of the troops sent to Utah are now encamped in Cedar Valley, 44 miles southwest of Salt Lake City, and the remainder have been ordered to Oregon to suppress Indian hostilities.

The march of the army to Salt Lake City through the Indian Territory has had a powerful effect in restraining the hostile feelings against the United States which existed among the Indians in that region and in securing emigrants to the far West against their depredations. This will also be the means of establishing military posts and promoting settlements along the route.

I recommend that the benefits of our land laws and preemption system be extended to the people of Utah by the establishment of a land office in that Territory.

I have occasion also to congratulate you on the result of our negotiations with China.

You were informed by my last annual message that our minister had been instructed to occupy a neutral position in the hostilities conducted by Great Britain and France against Canton. He was, however, at the same time directed to cooperate cordially with the British and French ministers in all peaceful measures to secure by treaty those just concessions to foreign commerce which the nations of the world had a right to demand. It was impossible for me to proceed further than this on my own authority without usurping the war-making power, which under the Constitution belongs exclusively to Congress.

Besides, after a careful examination of the nature and extent of our grievances, I did not believe they were of such a pressing and aggravated character as would have justified Congress in declaring war against the Chinese Empire without first making another earnest attempt to adjust them by peaceful negotiation. I was the more inclined to this opinion because of the severe chastisement which had then but recently been inflicted upon the Chinese by our squadron in the capture and destruction of the Barrier forts to avenge an alleged insult to our flag.

The event has proved the wisdom of our neutrality. Our minister has executed his instructions with eminent skill and ability. In conjunction with the Russian plenipotentiary, he has peacefully, but effectually, co-operated with the English and French plenipotentiaries, and each of the four powers has concluded a separate treaty with China of a highly satisfactory character. The treaty concluded by our own plenipotentiary will immediately be submitted to the Senate.

I am happy to announce that through the energetic yet conciliatory efforts of our consul-general in Japan a new treaty has been concluded with that Empire, which may be expected materially to augment our trade and intercourse in that quarter and remove from our countrymen the disabilities which have heretofore been imposed upon the exercise of their religion. The treaty shall be submitted to the Senate for approval without delay.

It is my earnest desire that every misunderstanding with the Government of Great Britain should be amicably and speedily adjusted. It has been the misfortune of both countries, almost ever since the period of the Revolution, to have been annoyed by a succession of irritating and dangerous questions, threatening their friendly relations. This has partially prevented the full development of those feelings of mutual friendship between the people of the two countries so natural in themselves and so conducive to their common interest. Any serious interruption of the commerce between the United States and Great Britain would be equally injurious to both. In fact, no two nations have ever existed on the face of the earth which could do each other so much good or so much harm.

Entertaining these sentiments, I am gratified to inform you that the long-pending controversy between the two Governments in relation to the question of visitation and search has been amicably adjusted. The claim on the part of Great Britain forcibly to visit American vessels on the high seas in time of peace could not be sustained under the law of nations, and it had been overruled by her own most eminent jurists. This question was recently brought to an issue by the repeated acts of British cruisers in boarding and searching our merchant vessels in the Gulf of Mexico and the adjacent seas. These acts were the more injurious and annoying, as these waters are traversed by a large portion of the commerce and navigation of the United States and their free and unrestricted use is essential to the security of the coastwise trade between the different States of the Union. Such vexatious interruptions could not fail to excite the feelings of the country and to require the interposition of the Government. Remonstrances were addressed to the British Government against these violations of our rights of sovereignty, and a naval force was at the same time ordered to the Cuban waters with directions "to protect all vessels of the United States on the high seas from search or detention by the vessels of war of any other nation." These measures received the unqualified and even enthusiastic approbation of the American people. Most fortunately, however, no collision took place, and the British Government promptly avowed its recognition of the principles of international law upon this subject as laid down by the Government of the United States in the note of the Secretary of State to the British minister at Washington of April 10, 1858, which secure the vessels of the United States upon the high seas from visitation or search in time of peace under any circumstances whatever. The claim has been abandoned in a manner reflecting honor on the British Government and evincing a just regard for the law of nations, and can not fail to strengthen the amicable relations between the two countries.

The British Government at the same time proposed to the United States that some mode should be adopted, by mutual arrangement between the two countries, of a character which may be found effective without being offensive, for verifying the nationality of vessels suspected on good grounds of carrying false colors. They have also invited the United States to take the initiative and propose measures for this purpose. Whilst declining to assume so grave a responsibility, the Secretary of State has informed the British Government that we are ready to receive any proposals which they may feel disposed to offer having this object in view, and to consider them in an amicable spirit. A strong opinion is, however, expressed that the occasional abuse of the flag of any nation is an evil far less to be deprecated than would be the establishment of any regulations which might be incompatible with the freedom of the seas. This Government has yet received no communication specifying the manner in which the British Government would propose to carry out their suggestion, and I am inclined to believe that no plan which can be devised will be free from grave embarrassments. Still, I shall form no decided opinion on the subject until I shall have carefully and in the best spirit examined any proposals which they may think proper to make.

I am truly sorry I can not also inform you that the complications between Great Britain and the United States arising out of the Clayton and Bulwer treaty of April, 1850, have been finally adjusted.

At the commencement of your last session I had reason to hope that, emancipating themselves from further unavailing discussions, the two Governments would proceed to settle the Central American questions in a practical manner, alike honorable and satisfactory to both; and this hope I have not yet abandoned. In my last annual message I stated that overtures had been made by the British Government for this purpose in a friendly spirit, which I cordially reciprocated. Their proposal was to withdraw these questions from direct negotiation between the two Governments, but to accomplish the same object by a negotiation between the British Government and each of the Central American Republics whose territorial interests are immediately involved. The settlement was to be made in accordance with the general tenor of the interpretation placed upon the Clayton and Bulwer treaty by the United States, with certain modifications. As negotiations are still pending upon this basis, it would not be proper for me now to communicate their present condition. A final settlement of these questions is greatly to be desired, as this would wipe out the last remaining subject of dispute between the two countries.

Our relations with the great Empires of France and Russia, as well as with all other Governments on the continent of Europe, except that of Spain, continue to be of the most friendly character.

With Spain our relations remain in an unsatisfactory condition. In my message of December last I informed you that our envoy extraordinary and minister plenipotentiary to Madrid had asked for his recall, and it was my purpose to send out a new minister to that Court with special instructions on all questions pending between the two Governments, and with a determination to have them speedily and amicably adjusted if that were possible. This purpose has been hitherto defeated by causes which I need not enumerate.

The mission to Spain has been intrusted to a distinguished citizen of Kentucky, who will proceed to Madrid without delay and make another and a final attempt to obtain justice from that Government.

Spanish officials under the direct control of the Captain-General of Cuba have insulted our national flag and in repeated instances have from time to time inflicted injuries on the persons and property of our citizens. These have given birth to numerous claims against the Spanish Government, the merits of which have been ably discussed for a series of years by our successive diplomatic representatives. Notwithstanding this, we have not arrived at a practical result in any single instance, unless we may except the case of the *Black Warrior*, under the late Administration, and that presented an outrage of such a character as would have justified an immediate resort to war. All our attempts to obtain redress have been baffled and defeated. The frequent and oft-recurring changes in the Spanish ministry have been employed as reasons for delay. We have been compelled to wait again and again until the new minister shall have had time to investigate the justice of our demands.

Even what have been denominated "the Cuban claims," in which more than 100 of our citizens are directly interested, have furnished no exception. These claims were for the refunding of duties unjustly exacted from American vessels at different custom-houses in Cuba so long ago as the year 1844. The principles upon which they rest are so manifestly equitable and just that, after a period of nearly ten years, in 1854 they were recognized by the Spanish Government. Proceedings were afterwards instituted to ascertain their amount, and this was finally fixed, according to their own statement (with which we were satisfied), at the sum of $128,635.54. Just at the moment, after a delay of fourteen years, when we had reason to expect that this sum would be repaid with interest, we have received a proposal offering to refund one-third of that amount ($42,878.41), but without interest, if we would accept this in full satisfaction. The offer is also accompanied by a declaration that this indemnification is not founded on any reason of strict justice, but is made as a special favor.

One alleged cause for procrastination in the examination and adjustment of our claims arises from an obstacle which it is the duty of the Spanish Government to remove. Whilst the Captain-General of Cuba is invested with general despotic authority in the government of that island, the power is withheld from him to examine and redress wrongs committed by officials under his control on citizens of the United States. Instead of making our complaints directly to him at Havana, we are obliged to present them through our minister at Madrid. These are then referred back to the Captain-General for information, and much time is thus consumed in preliminary investigations and correspondence between Madrid and Cuba before the Spanish Government will consent to proceed to negotiation. Many of the difficulties between the two Governments would be obviated and a long train of negotiation avoided if the Captain-General were invested with authority to settle questions of easy solution on the spot, where all the facts are fresh and could be promptly and satisfactorily ascertained. We have hitherto in vain urged upon the Spanish Government to confer this power upon the Captain-General, and our minister to Spain will again be instructed to urge this subject on their notice. In this respect we occupy a different position from the powers of Europe. Cuba is almost within sight of our shores; our commerce with it is far greater than that of any other nation, including Spain itself, and our citizens are in habits of daily and extended personal intercourse with every part of the island. It is therefore a great grievance that when any difficulty occurs, no matter how unimportant, which might be readily settled at the moment, we should be obliged to resort to Madrid, especially when the very first step to be taken there is to refer it back to Cuba.

The truth is that Cuba, in its existing colonial condition, is a constant source of injury and annoyance to the American people. It is the only spot in the civilized world where the African slave trade is tolerated, and we are bound by treaty with Great Britain to maintain a naval force on the coast of Africa, at much expense both of life and treasure, solely for the purpose of arresting slavers bound to that island. The late serious difficulties between the United States and Great Britain respecting the right of search, now so happily terminated, could never have arisen if Cuba had not afforded a market for slaves. As long as this market shall remain open there can be no hope for the civilization of benighted Africa. Whilst the demand for slaves continues in Cuba wars will be waged among the petty and barbarous chiefs in Africa for the purpose of seizing subjects to supply this trade. In such a condition of affairs it is impossible that the light of civilization and religion can ever penetrate these dark abodes.

It has been made known to the world by my predecessors that the United States have on several occasions endeavored to acquire Cuba from Spain by honorable negotiation. If this were accomplished, the last relic of the African slave trade would instantly disappear. We would not, if we could, acquire Cuba in any other manner. This is due to our national character. All the territory which we have acquired since the origin of the Government has been by fair purchase from France, Spain, and Mexico or by the free and voluntary act of the independent State of Texas in blending her destinies with our own. This course we shall ever pursue, unless circumstances should occur which we do not now anticipate, rendering a departure from it clearly justifiable under the imperative and overruling law of self-preservation.

The island of Cuba, from its geographical position, commands the mouth of the Mississippi and the immense and annually increasing trade, foreign and coastwise, from the valley of that noble river, now embracing half the sovereign States of the Union. With that island under the dominion of a distant foreign power this trade, of vital importance to these States, is exposed to the danger of being destroyed in time of war, and it has hitherto been subjected to perpetual injury and annoyance in time of peace. Our relations with Spain, which ought to be of the most friendly character, must always be placed in jeopardy whilst the existing colonial government over the island shall remain in its present condition.

Whilst the possession of the island would be of vast importance to the United States, its value to Spain is comparatively unimportant. Such was the relative situation of the parties when the great Napoleon transferred Louisiana to the United States. Jealous as he ever was of the national honor and interests of France, no person throughout the world has imputed blame to him for accepting a pecuniary equivalent for this cession.

The publicity which has been given to our former negotiations upon this subject and the large appropriation which may be required to effect the purpose render it expedient before making another attempt to renew the negotiation that I should lay the whole subject before Congress. This is especially necessary, as it may become indispensable to success that I should be intrusted with the means of making an advance to the Spanish Government immediately after the signing of the treaty, without awaiting the ratification of it by the Senate. I am encouraged to make this suggestion by the example of Mr. Jefferson previous to the purchase of Louisiana from France and by that of Mr. Polk in view of the acquisition of territory from Mexico. I refer the whole subject to Congress and commend it to their careful consideration.

I repeat the recommendation made in my message of December last in favor of an appropriation "to be paid to the Spanish Government for the purpose of distribution among the claimants in the *Amistad* case." President Polk first made a similar recommendation in December, 1847, and it was repeated by my immediate predecessor in December, 1853. I entertain no doubt that indemnity is fairly due to these claimants under our treaty with Spain of October 27, 1795; and whilst demanding justice we ought to do justice. An appropriation promptly made for this purpose could not fail to exert a favorable influence on our negotiations with Spain.

Our position in relation to the independent States south of us on this continent, and especially those within the limits of North America, is of a peculiar character. The northern boundary of Mexico is coincident with our own southern boundary from ocean to ocean, and we must necessarily feel a deep interest in all that concerns the well-being and the **fate of so near a neighbor. We have always cherished** the kindest wishes for the success of that Republic, and have indulged the hope that it might at last, after all 'its trials, enjoy peace and prosperity under a free and stable government. We have never hitherto interfered, directly or indirectly, with its internal affairs, and it is a duty which we owe to ourselves to protect the integrity of its territory against the hostile interference of any other power. Our geographical position, our direct interest in all that concerns Mexico, and our well-settled policy in regard to the North American continent render this an indispensable duty.

Mexico has been in a state of constant revolution almost ever since it achieved its independence. One military leader after another has usurped the Government in rapid succession, and the various constitutions from time to time adopted have been set at naught almost as soon as they were proclaimed. The successive Governments have afforded no adequate protection, either to Mexican citizens or foreign residents, against lawless violence. Heretofore a seizure of the capital by a military chieftain has been generally followed by at least the nominal submission of the country to his rule for a brief period, but not so at the present crisis of Mexican affairs. A civil war has been raging for some time throughout the Republic between the central Government at the City of Mexico, which has endeavored to subvert the constitution last framed by military power, and those who maintain the authority of that constitution. The antagonist parties each hold possession of different States of the Republic, and the fortunes of the war are constantly changing. Meanwhile the most reprehensible means have been employed by both parties to extort money from foreigners, as well as natives, to carry on this ruinous contest. The truth is that this fine country, blessed with a productive soil and a benign climate, has been reduced by civil dissension to a condition of almost hopeless anarchy and imbecility. It would be vain for this Government to attempt to enforce payment in money of the claims of American citizens, now amounting to more than $10,000,000, against Mexico, because she is destitute of all pecuniary means to satisfy these demands.

Our late minister was furnished with ample powers and instructions for the adjustment of all pending questions with the central Government of Mexico, and he performed his duty with zeal and ability. The claims of our citizens, some of them arising out of the violation of an express provision of the treaty of Guadalupe Hidalgo, and others from gross injuries to persons as well as property, have remained unredressed and even unnoticed. Remonstrances against these grievances have been addressed without effect to that Government. Meantime in various parts of the Republic instances have been numerous of the murder, imprisonment, and plunder of our citizens by different parties claiming and exercising a local jurisdiction; but the central Government, although repeatedly urged thereto, have made no effort either to punish the authors of these outrages or to prevent their recurrence. No American citizen can now visit Mexico on lawful business without imminent danger to his person and property. There is no adequate protection to either, and in this respect our treaty with that Republic is almost a dead letter.

This state of affairs was brought to a crisis in May last by the promulgation of a decree levying a contribution *pro rata* upon all the capital in the Republic between certain specified amounts, whether held by Mexicans or foreigners. Mr. Forsyth, regarding this decree in the light of a "forced loan," formally protested against its application to his countrymen and advised them not to pay the contribution, but to suffer it to be forcibly exacted. Acting upon this advice, an American citizen refused to pay the contribution, and his property was seized by armed men to satisfy the amount. Not content with this, the Government proceeded still further and issued a decree banishing him from the country. Our minister immediately notified them that if this decree should be carried into execution he would feel it to be his duty to adopt "the most decided measures that belong to the powers and obligations of the representative office." Notwithstanding this warning, the banishment was enforced, and Mr. Forsyth promptly announced to the Government the suspension of the political relations of his legation with them until the pleasure of his own Government should be ascertained.

This Government did not regard the contribution imposed by the decree of the 15th May last to be in strictness a "forced loan," and as such prohibited by the tenth article of the treaty of 1826 between Great Britain and Mexico, to the benefits of which American citizens are entitled by treaty; yet the imposition of the contribution upon foreigners was considered an unjust and oppressive measure. Besides, internal factions in other parts of the Republic were at the same time levying similar exactions upon the property of our citizens and interrupting their commerce. There had been an entire failure on the part of our minister to secure redress for the wrongs which our citizens had endured, notwithstanding his persevering efforts. And from the temper manifested by the Mexican Government he had repeatedly assured us that no favorable change could be expected until the United States should "give striking evidence of

their will and power to protect their citizens," and that "severe chasten-
ing is the only earthly remedy for our grievances." From this statement of facts it would have been worse than idle to direct Mr. Forsyth to
retrace his steps and resume diplomatic relations with that Government,
and it was therefore deemed proper to sanction his withdrawal of the
legation from the City of Mexico.

Abundant cause now undoubtedly exists for a resort to hostilities
against the Government still holding possession of the capital. Should
they succeed in subduing the constitutional forces, all reasonable hope
will then have expired of a peaceful settlement of our difficulties.

On the other hand, should the constitutional party prevail and their
authority be established over the Republic, there is reason to hope that
they will be animated by a less unfriendly spirit and may grant that
redress to American citizens which justice requires so far as they may
possess the means. But for this expectation I should at once have recommended to Congress to grant the necessary power to the President to
take possession of a sufficient portion of the remote and unsettled territory of Mexico, to be held in pledge until our injuries shall be redressed
and our just demands be satisfied. We have already exhausted every
milder means of obtaining justice. In such a case this remedy of reprisals
is recognized by the law of nations, not only as just in itself, but as a means
of preventing actual war.

But there is another view of our relations with Mexico, arising from
the unhappy condition of affairs along our southwestern frontier, which
demands immediate action. In that remote region, where there are
but few white inhabitants, large bands of hostile and predatory Indians
roam promiscuously over the Mexican States of Chihuahua and Sonora
and our adjoining Territories. The local governments of these States
are perfectly helpless and are kept in a state of constant alarm by the
Indians. They have not the power, if they possessed the will, even to
restrain lawless Mexicans from passing the border and committing depre
dations on our remote settlers. A state of anarchy and violence prevails
throughout that distant frontier. The laws are a dead letter and life
and property wholly insecure. For this reason the settlement of Arizona
is arrested, whilst it is of great importance that a chain of inhabitants
should extend all along its southern border sufficient for their own protection and that of the United States mail passing to and from California.
Well-founded apprehensions are now entertained that the Indians and
wandering Mexicans, equally lawless, may break up the important stage
and postal communication recently established between our Atlantic and
Pacific possessions. This passes very near to the Mexican boundary
throughout the whole length of Arizona. I can imagine no possible
remedy for these evils and no mode of restoring law and order on that
remote and unsettled frontier but for the Government of the United
States to assume a temporary protectorate over the northern portions of

Chihuahua and Sonora and to establish military posts within the same; and this I earnestly recommend to Congress. This protection may be withdrawn as soon as local governments shall be established in these Mexican States capable of performing their duties to the United States, restraining the lawless, and preserving peace along the border.

I do not doubt that this measure will be viewed in a friendly spirit by the governments and people of Chihuahua and Sonora, as it will prove equally effectual for the protection of their citizens on that remote and lawless frontier as for citizens of the United States.

And in this connection permit me to recall your attention to the condition of Arizona. The population of that Territory, numbering, as is alleged, more than 10,000 souls, are practically without a government, without laws, and without any regular administration of justice. Murder and other crimes are committed with impunity. This state of things calls loudly for redress, and I therefore repeat my recommendation for the establishment of a Territorial government over Arizona.

The political condition of the narrow isthmus of Central America, through which transit routes pass between the Atlantic and Pacific oceans, presents a subject of deep interest to all commercial nations. It is over these transits that a large proportion of the trade and travel between the European and Asiatic continents is destined to pass. To the United States these routes are of incalculable importance as a means of communication between their Atlantic and Pacific possessions. The latter now extend throughout seventeen degrees of latitude on the Pacific coast, embracing the important State of California and the flourishing Territories of Oregon and Washington. All commercial nations therefore have a deep and direct interest that these communications shall be rendered secure from interruption. If an arm of the sea connecting the two oceans penetrated through Nicaragua and Costa Rica, it could not be pretended that these States would have the right to arrest or retard its navigation to the injury of other nations. The transit by land over this narrow isthmus occupies nearly the same position. It is a highway in which they themselves have little interest when compared with the vast interests of the rest of the world. Whilst their rights of sovereignty ought to be respected, it is the duty of other nations to require that this important passage shall not be interrupted by the civil wars and revolutionary outbreaks which have so frequently occurred in that region. The stake is too important to be left at the mercy of rival companies claiming to hold conflicting contracts with Nicaragua. The commerce of other nations is not to stand still and await the adjustment of such petty controversies. The Government of the United States expect no more than this, and they will not be satisfied with less. They would not, if they could, derive any advantage from the Nicaragua transit not common to the rest of the world. Its neutrality and protection for the common use of all nations is their only object. They have no objection that Nicaragua shall demand and receive a fair compensation from the companies and individuals who may traverse the route, but they insist that it shall never hereafter be closed by an arbitrary decree of that Government. If disputes arise between it and those with whom they may have entered into contracts, these must be adjusted by some fair tribunal provided for the purpose, and the route must not be closed pending the controversy. This is our whole policy, and it can not fail to be acceptable to other nations.

All these difficulties might be avoided if, consistently with the good faith of Nicaragua, the use of this transit could be thrown open to general competition, providing at the same time for the payment of a reasonable rate to the Nicaraguan Government on passengers and freight.

In August, 1852, the Accessory Transit Company made its first interoceanic trip over the Nicaraguan route, and continued in successful operation, with great advantage to the public, until the 18th February, 1856, when it was closed and the grant to this company as well as its charter were summarily and arbitrarily revoked by the Government of President Rivas. Previous to this date, however, in 1854, serious disputes concerning the settlement of their accounts had arisen between the company and the Government, threatening the interruption of the route at any moment. These the United States in vain endeavored to compose. It would be useless to narrate the various proceedings which took place between the parties up till the time when the transit was discontinued. Suffice it to say that since February, 1856, it has remained closed, greatly to the prejudice of citizens of the United States. Since that time the competition has ceased between the rival routes of Panama and Nicaragua, and in consequence thereof an unjust and unreasonable amount has been exacted from our citizens for their passage to and from California.

A treaty was signed on the 16th day of November, 1857, by the Secretary of State and minister of Nicaragua, under the stipulations of which the use and protection of the transit route would have been secured, not only to the United States, but equally to all other nations. How and on what pretext this treaty has failed to receive the ratification of the Nicaraguan Government will appear by the papers herewith communicated from the State Department. The principal objection seems to have been to the provision authorizing the United States to employ force to keep the route open in case Nicaragua should fail to perform her duty in this respect. From the feebleness of that Republic, its frequent changes of government, and its constant internal dissensions, this had become a most important stipulation, and one essentially necessary, not only for the security of the route, but for the safety of American citizens passing and repassing to and from our Pacific possessions. Were such a stipulation embraced in a treaty between the United States and Nicaragua, the knowledge of this fact would of itself most probably prevent hostile parties from committing aggressions on the route, and render our actual interference for its protection unnecessary.

The executive government of this country in its intercourse with foreign nations is limited to the employment of diplomacy alone. When this fails it can proceed no further. It can not legitimately resort to force without the direct authority of Congress, except in resisting and repelling hostile attacks. It would have no authority to enter the territories of Nicaragua even to prevent the destruction of the transit and protect the lives and property of our own citizens on their passage. It is true that on a sudden emergency of this character the President would direct any armed force in the vicinity to march to their relief, but in doing this he would act upon his own responsibility.

Under these circumstances I earnestly recommend to Congress the passage of an act authorizing the President, under such restrictions as they may deem proper, to employ the land and naval forces of the United States in preventing the transit from being obstructed or closed by lawless violence, and in protecting the lives and property of American citizens traveling thereupon, requiring at the same time that these forces shall be withdrawn the moment the danger shall have passed away. Without such a provision our citizens will be constantly exposed to interruption in their progress and to lawless violence.

A similar necessity exists for the passage of such an act for the protection of the Panama and Tehuantepec routes.

In reference to the Panama route, the United States, by their existing treaty with New Granada, expressly guarantee the neutrality of the Isthmus, "with the view that the free transit from the one to the other sea may not be interrupted or embarrassed in any future time while this treaty exists."

In regard to the Tehuantepec route, which has been recently opened under the most favorable auspices, our treaty with Mexico of the 30th December, 1853, secures to the citizens of the United States a right of transit over it for their persons and merchandise and stipulates that neither Government shall "interpose any obstacle" thereto. It also concedes to the United States the "right to transport across the Isthmus, in closed bags, the mails of the United States not intended for distribution along the line of the communication; also the effects of the United States Government and its citizens which may be intended for transit and not for distribution on the Isthmus, free of custom-house or other charges by the Mexican Government."

These treaty stipulations with New Granada and Mexico, in addition to the considerations applicable to the Nicaragua route, seem to require legislation for the purpose of carrying them into effect.

The injuries which have been inflicted upon our citizens in Costa Rica and Nicaragua during the last two or three years have received the prompt attention of this Government. Some of these injuries were of the most aggravated character. The transaction at Virgin Bay in April, 1856, when a company of unarmed Americans, who were in no way connected with any belligerent conduct or party, were fired upon by the troops of Costa Rica and numbers of them killed and wounded, was brought to the knowledge of Congress by my predecessor soon after its occurrence, and was also presented to the Government of Costa Rica for that immediate investigation and redress which the nature of the case demanded. A similar course was pursued with reference to other outrages in these countries, some of which were hardly less aggravated in their character than the transaction at Virgin Bay. At the time, however, when our present minister to Nicaragua was appointed, in December, 1857, no redress had been obtained for any of these wrongs and no reply even had been received to the demands which had been made by this Government upon that of Costa Rica more than a year before. Our minister was instructed, therefore, to lose no time in expressing to those Governments the deep regret with which the President had witnessed this inattention to the just claims of the United States and in demanding their prompt and satisfactory adjustment. Unless this demand shall be complied with at an early day it will only remain for this Government to adopt such other measures as may be necessary in order to obtain for itself that justice which it has in vain attempted to secure by peaceful means from the Governments of Nicaragua and Costa Rica. While it has shown, and will continue to show, the most sincere regard for the rights and honor of these Republics, it can not permit this regard to be met by an utter neglect on their part of what is due to the Government and citizens of the United States.

Against New Granada we have long-standing causes of complaint, arising out of the unsatisfied claims of our citizens upon that Republic, and to these have been more recently added the outrages committed upon our citizens at Panama in April, 1856. A treaty for the adjustment of these difficulties was concluded by the Secretary of State and the minister of New Granada in September, 1857, which contained just and acceptable provisions for that purpose. This treaty was transmitted to Bogota and was ratified by the Government of New Granada, but with certain amendments. It was not, however, returned to this city until after the close of the last session of the Senate. It will be immediately transmitted to that body for their advice and consent, and should this be obtained it will remove all our existing causes of complaint against New Granada on the subject of claims.

Questions have arisen between the two Governments as to the right of New Granada to levy a tonnage duty upon the vessels of the United States in its ports of the Isthmus and to levy a passenger tax upon our citizens arriving in that country, whether with a design to remain there or to pass from ocean to ocean by the transit route; and also a tax upon the mail of the United States transported over the Panama Railroad. The Government of New Granada has been informed that the United States would consider the collection of either of these taxes as an act in violation of the treaty between the two countries, and as such would be resisted by the United States.   At the same time, we are prepared to discuss these questions in a spirit of amity and justice and with a sincere desire to adjust them in a satisfactory manner.   A negotiation for that purpose has already been commenced.   No effort has recently been made to collect these taxes nor is any anticipated under present circumstances.

With the Empire of Brazil our relations are of the most friendly character.   The productions of the two countries, and especially those of an agricultural nature, are such as to invite extensive mutual exchanges. A large quantity of American flour is consumed in Brazil, whilst more than treble the amount in value of Brazilian coffee is consumed in the United States.   Whilst this is the case, a heavy duty has been levied until very recently upon the importation of American flour into Brazil. I am gratified, however, to be able to inform you that in September last this has been reduced from \$1.32 to about 49 cents per barrel, and the duties on other articles of our production have been diminished in nearly the same proportion.

I regret to state that the Government of Brazil still continues to levy an export duty of about 11 per cent on coffee, notwithstanding this article is admitted free from duty in the United States.   This is a heavy charge upon the consumers of coffee in our country, as we purchase half of the entire surplus crop of that article raised in Brazil.   Our minister, under instructions, will reiterate his efforts to have this export duty removed, and it is hoped that the enlightened Government of the Emperor will adopt this wise, just, and equal policy.   In that event, there is good reason to believe that the commerce between the two countries will greatly increase, much to the advantage of both.

The claims of our citizens against the Government of Brazil are not in the aggregate of very large amount; but some of these rest upon plain principles of justice and their settlement ought not to be longer delayed. A renewed and earnest, and I trust a successful, effort will be made by our minister to procure their final adjustment.

On the 2d of June last Congress passed a joint resolution authorizing the President "to adopt such measures and use such force as in his judgment may be necessary and advisable" "for the purpose of adjusting the differences between the United States and the Republic of Paraguay in connection with the attack on the United States steamer *Water Witch* and with other measures referred to" in his annual message, and on the 12th of July following they made an appropriation to defray the expenses and compensation of a commissioner to that Republic should the President deem it proper to make such an appointment.

In compliance with these enactments, I have appointed a commissioner, who has proceeded to Paraguay with full powers and instructions to settle these differences in an amicable and peaceful manner if this be practicable. His experience and discretion justify the hope that he may prove successful in convincing the Paraguayan Government that it is due both to honor and justice that they should voluntarily and promptly make atonement for the wrongs which they have committed against the United States and indemnify our injured citizens whom they have forcibly despoiled of their property.

Should our commissioner prove unsuccessful after a sincere and earnest effort to accomplish the object of his mission, then no alternative will remain but the employment of force to obtain "just satisfaction" from Paraguay. In view of this contingency, the Secretary of the Navy, under my direction, has fitted out and dispatched a naval force to rendezvous near Buenos Ayres, which, it is believed, will prove sufficient for the occasion. It is my earnest desire, however, that it may not be found necessary to resort to this last alternative.

When Congress met in December last the business of the country had just been crushed by one of those periodical revulsions which are the inevitable consequence of our unsound and extravagant system of bank credits and inflated currency. With all the elements of national wealth in abundance, our manufactures were suspended, our useful public and private enterprises were arrested, and thousands of laborers were deprived of employment and reduced to want. Universal distress prevailed among the commercial, manufacturing, and mechanical classes. This revulsion was felt the more severely in the United States because similar causes had produced the like deplorable effects throughout the commercial nations of Europe. All were experiencing sad reverses at the same moment. Our manufacturers everywhere suffered severely, not because of the recent reduction in the tariff of duties on imports, but because there was no demand at any price for their productions. The people were obliged to restrict themselves in their purchases to articles of prime necessity. In the general prostration of business the iron manufacturers in different States probably suffered more than any other class, and much destitution was the inevitable consequence among the great number of workmen who had been employed in this useful branch of industry. There could be no supply where there was no demand. To present an example, there could be no demand for railroad iron after our magnificent system of railroads, extending its benefits to every portion of the Union, had been brought to a dead pause. The same consequences have resulted from similar causes to many other branches of useful manufactures. It is self-evident that where there is no ability to purchase manufactured articles these can not be sold, and consequently must cease to be produced.

No government, and especially a government of such limited powers as that of the United States, could have prevented the late revulsion. The whole commercial world seemed for years to have been rushing to this catastrophe. The same ruinous consequences would have followed in the United States whether the duties upon foreign imports had remained as they were under the tariff of 1846 or had been raised to a much higher standard. The tariff of 1857 had no agency in the result. The general causes existing throughout the world could not have been controlled by the legislation of any particular country.

The periodical revulsions which have existed in our past history must continue to return at intervals so long as our present unbounded system of bank credits shall prevail. They will, however, probably be the less severe in future, because it is not to be expected, at least for many years to come, that the commercial nations of Europe, with whose interests our own are so materially involved, will expose themselves to similar calamities. But this subject was treated so much at large in my last annual message that I shall not now pursue it further. Still, I respectfully renew the recommendation in favor of the passage of a uniform bankrupt law applicable to banking institutions. This is all the direct power over the subject which I believe the Federal Government possesses. Such a law would mitigate, though it might not prevent, the evil. The instinct of self-preservation might produce a wholesome restraint upon their banking business if they knew in advance that a suspension of specie payments would inevitably produce their civil death.

But the effects of the revulsion are now slowly but surely passing away. The energy and enterprise of our citizens, with our unbounded resources, will within the period of another year restore a state of wholesome industry and trade. Capital has again accumulated in our large cities. The rate of interest is there very low. Confidence is gradually reviving, and so soon as it is discovered that this capital can be profitably employed in commercial and manufacturing enterprises and in the construction of railroads and other works of public and private improvement prosperity will again smile throughout the land. It is vain, however, to disguise the fact from ourselves that a speculative inflation of our currency without a corresponding inflation in other countries whose manufactures come into competition with our own must ever produce disastrous results to our domestic manufactures. No tariff short of absolute prohibition can prevent these evil consequences.

In connection with this subject it is proper to refer to our financial condition. The same causes which have produced pecuniary distress throughout the country have so reduced the amount of imports from foreign countries that the revenue has proved inadequate to meet the necessary expenses of the Government. To supply the deficiency, Congress, by the act of December 23, 1857, authorized the issue of $20,000,000 of Treasury notes; and this proving inadequate, they authorized, by the act of June 14, 1858, a loan of $20,000,000, "to be applied to the payment of appropriations made by law."

No statesman would advise that we should go on increasing the national debt to meet the ordinary expenses of the Government. This would be a most ruinous policy. In case of war our credit must be our chief resource, at least for the first year, and this would be greatly impaired by having contracted a large debt in time of peace. It is our true policy to increase our revenue so as to equal our expenditures. It would be ruinous to continue to borrow. Besides, it may be proper to observe that the incidental protection thus afforded by a revenue tariff would at the present moment to some extent increase the confidence of the manufacturing interests and give a fresh impulse to our reviving business. To this surely no person will object.

In regard to the mode of assessing and collecting duties under a strictly revenue tariff, I have long entertained and often expressed the opinion that sound policy requires this should be done by specific duties in cases to which these can be properly applied. They are well adapted to commodities which are usually sold by weight or by measure, and which from their nature are of equal or of nearly equal value. Such, for example, are the articles of iron of different classes, raw sugar, and foreign wines and spirits.

In my deliberate judgment specific duties are the best, if not the only, means of securing the revenue against false and fraudulent invoices, and such has been the practice adopted for this purpose by other commercial nations. Besides, specific duties would afford to the American manufacturer the incidental advantages to which he is fairly entitled under a revenue tariff. The present system is a sliding scale to his disadvantage. Under it, when prices are high and business prosperous, the duties rise in amount when he least requires their aid. On the contrary, when prices fall and he is struggling against adversity, the duties are diminished in the same proportion, greatly to his injury.

Neither would there be danger that a higher rate of duty than that intended by Congress could be levied in the form of specific duties. It would be easy to ascertain the average value of any imported article for a series of years, and, instead of subjecting it to an *ad valorem* duty at a certain rate *per centum*, to substitute in its place an equivalent specific duty.

By such an arrangement the consumer would not be injured. It is true he might have to pay a little more duty on a given article in one year, but, if so, he would pay a little less in another, and in a series of years these would counterbalance each other and amount to the same thing so far as his interest is concerned. This inconvenience would be trifling when contrasted with the additional security thus afforded against frauds upon the revenue, in which every consumer is directly interested.

I have thrown out these suggestions as the fruit of my own observation, to which Congress, in their better judgment, will give such weight as they may justly deserve.

The report of the Secretary of the Treasury will explain in detail the operations of that Department of the Government. The receipts into the Treasury from all sources during the fiscal year ending June 30, 1858, including the Treasury notes authorized by the act of December 23, 1857, were $70,273,869.59, which amount, with the balance of $17,710,114.27 remaining in the Treasury at the commencement of the year, made an aggregate for the service of the year of $87,983,983.86.

The public expenditures during the fiscal year ending June 30, 1858, amounted to $81,585,667.76, of which $9,684,537.99 were applied to the payment of the public debt and the redemption of Treasury notes with the interest thereon, leaving in the Treasury on July 1, 1858, being the commencement of the present fiscal year, $6,398,316.10.

The receipts into the Treasury during the first quarter of the present fiscal year, commencing the 1st of July, 1858, including one-half of the loan of $20,000,000, with the premium upon it, authorized by the act of June 14, 1858, were $25,230,879.46, and the estimated receipts for the remaining three quarters to the 30th of June, 1859, from ordinary sources are $38,500,000, making, with the balance before stated, an aggregate of $70,129,195.56.

The expenditures during the first quarter of the present fiscal year were $21,708,198.51, of which $1,010,142.37 were applied to the payment of the public debt and the redemption of Treasury notes and the interest thereon. The estimated expenditures during the remaining three quarters to June 30, 1859, are $52,357,698.48, making an aggregate of $74,065,896.99, being an excess of expenditure beyond the estimated receipts into the Treasury from ordinary sources during the fiscal year to the 30th of June, 1859, of $3,936,701.43. Extraordinary means are placed by law within the command of the Secretary of the Treasury, by the reissue of Treasury notes redeemed and by negotiating the balance of the loan authorized by the act of June 14, 1858, to the extent of $11,000,000, which, if realized during the present fiscal year, will leave a balance in the Treasury on the 1st day of July, 1859, of $7,063,298.57.

The estimated receipts during the next fiscal year, ending June 30, 1860, are $62,000,000, which, with the above-estimated balance of $7,063,298.57 make an aggregate for the service of the next fiscal year of $69,063,298.57. The estimated expenditures during the next fiscal year, ending June 30, 1860, are $73,139,147.46, which leaves a deficit of estimated means, compared with the estimated expenditures, for that year, commencing on July 1, 1859, of $4,075,848.89.

In addition to this sum the Postmaster-General will require from the Treasury for the service of the Post-Office Department $3,838,728, as explained in the report of the Secretary of the Treasury, which will increase the estimated deficit on June 30, 1860, to $7,914,576.89. To provide for the payment of this estimated deficiency, which will be increased by such appropriations as may be made by Congress not estimated for in the report of the Treasury Department, as well as to provide for the gradual redemption from year to year of the outstanding Treasury notes, the Secretary of the Treasury recommends such a revi-

sion of the present tariff as will raise the required amount. After what
I have already said I need scarcely add that I concur in the opinion
expressed in his report—that the public debt should not be increased by
an additional loan—and would therefore strongly urge upon Congress
the duty of making at their present session the necessary provision for
meeting these liabilities.

The public debt on July 1, 1858, the commencement of the present
fiscal year, was $25,155,977.66.

During the first quarter of the present year the sum of $10,000,000
has been negotiated of the loan authorized by the act of June 14, 1858,
making the present outstanding public debt, exclusive of Treasury notes,
$35,155,977.66. There was on the 1st of July, 1858, of Treasury notes
issued by authority of the act of December 23, 1857, unredeemed, the
sum of $19,754,800, making the amount of actual indebtedness at that
date $54,910,777.66. To this will be added $10,000,000 during the present fiscal year, this being the remaining half of the loan of $20,000,000
not yet negotiated.

The rapid increase of the public debt and the necessity which exists
for a modification of the tariff to meet even the ordinary expenses of the
Government ought to admonish us all, in our respective spheres of duty,
to the practice of rigid economy. The objects of expenditure should be
limited in number, as far as this may be practicable, and the appropriations necessary to carry them into effect ought to be disbursed under the
strictest accountability. Enlightened economy does not consist in the refusal to appropriate money for constitutional purposes essential to the
defense, progress, and prosperity of the Republic, but in taking care that
none of this money shall be wasted by mismanagement in its application
to the objects designated by law.

Comparisons between the annual expenditure at the present time and
what it was ten or twenty years ago are altogether fallacious. The
rapid increase of our country in extent and population renders a corresponding increase of expenditure to some extent unavoidable. This
is constantly creating new objects of expenditure and augmenting the
amount required for the old. The true questions, then, are, Have these
objects been unnecessarily multiplied, or has the amount expended upon
any or all of them been larger than comports with due economy? In
accordance with these principles, the heads of the different Executive
Departments of the Government have been instructed to reduce their
estimates for the next fiscal year to the lowest standard consistent with
the efficiency of the service, and this duty they have performed in a spirit
of just economy. The estimates of the Treasury, War, Navy, and Interior Departments have each been in some degree reduced, and unless a
sudden and unforeseen emergency should arise it is not anticipated that
a deficiency will exist in either within the present or the next fiscal year.
The Post-Office Department is placed in a peculiar position, different

from the other Departments, and to this I shall hereafter refer.

I invite Congress to institute a rigid scrutiny to ascertain whether the expenses in all the Departments can not be still further reduced, and I promise them all the aid in my power in pursuing the investigation.

I transmit herewith the reports made to me by the Secretaries of War, of the Navy, of the Interior, and of the Postmaster-General. They each contain valuable information and important recommendations, to which I invite the attention of Congress.

In my last annual message I took occasion to recommend the immediate construction of ten small steamers of light draft, for the purpose of increasing the efficiency of the Navy. Congress responded to the recommendation by authorizing the construction of eight of them. The progress which has been made in executing this authority is stated in the report of the Secretary of the Navy. I concur with him in the opinion that a greater number of this class of vessels is necessary for the purpose of protecting in a more efficient manner the persons and property of American citizens on the high seas and in foreign countries, as well as in guarding more effectually our own coasts. I accordingly recommend the passage of an act for this purpose.

The suggestions contained in the report of the Secretary of the Interior, especially those in regard to the disposition of the public domain, the pension and bounty-land system, the policy toward the Indians, and the amendment of our patent laws, are worthy of the serious consideration of Congress.

The Post-Office Department occupies a position very different from that of the other Departments. For many years it was the policy of the Government to render this a self-sustaining Department; and if this can not now be accomplished, in the present condition of the country, we ought to make as near an approach to it as may be practicable.

The Postmaster-General is placed in a most embarrassing position by the existing laws. He is obliged to carry these into effect. He has no other alternative. He finds, however, that this can not be done without heavy demands upon the Treasury over and above what is received for postage, and these have been progressively increasing from year to year until they amounted for the last fiscal year, ending on the 30th of June, 1858, to more than $4,500,000, whilst it is estimated that for the present fiscal year they will amount to $6,290,000. These sums are exclusive of the annual appropriation of $700,000 for "compensation for the mail service performed for the two Houses of Congress and the other Departments and officers of the Government in the transmission of free matter."

The cause of these large deficits is mainly attributable to the increased expense of transporting the mails. In 1852 the sum paid for this service was but a fraction above four millions and a quarter. Since that year it has annually increased, until in 1858 it has reached more than eight millions and a quarter, and for the service of 1859 it is estimated that it will amount to more than $10,000,000.

The receipts of the Post-Office Department can be made to approach or to equal its expenditure only by means of the legislation of Congress. In applying any remedy care should be taken that the people shall not be deprived of the advantages which they are fairly entitled to enjoy from the Post-Office Department. The principal remedies recommended to the consideration of Congress by the Postmaster-General are to restore the former rate of postage upon single letters to 5 cents; to substitute for the franking privilege the delivery to those now entitled to enjoy it of post-office stamps for their correspondence, and to direct the Department in making contracts for the transportation of the mail to confine itself to the payment of the sum necessary for this single purpose, without requiring it to be transported in post coaches or carriages of any particular description. Under the present system the expense to the Government is greatly increased by requiring that the mail shall be carried in such vehicles as will accommodate passengers. This will be done, without pay from the Department, over all roads where the travel will remunerate the contractors.

These recommendations deserve the grave consideration of Congress.

I would again call your attention to the construction of a Pacific railroad. Time and reflection have but served to confirm me in the truth and justice of the observations which I made on this subject in my last annual message, to which I beg leave respectfully to refer.

It is freely admitted that it would be inexpedient for this Government to exercise the power of constructing the Pacific railroad by its own immediate agents. Such a policy would increase the patronage of the Executive to a dangerous extent, and introduce a system of jobbing and corruption which no vigilance on the part of Federal officials could either prevent or detect. This can only be done by the keen eye and active and careful supervision of individual and private interest. The construction of this road ought therefore to be committed to companies incorporated by the States or other agencies whose pecuniary interests would be directly involved. Congress might then assist them in the work by grants of land or of money, or both, under such conditions and restrictions as would secure the transportation of troops and munitions of war free from any charge and that of the United States mail at a fair and reasonable price.

The progress of events since the commencement of your last session has shown how soon difficulties disappear before a firm and determined resolution. At that time such a road was deemed by wise and patriotic men to be a visionary project. The great distance to be overcome and the intervening mountains and deserts in the way were obstacles which, in the opinion of many, could not be surmounted. Now, after the lapse of but a single year, these obstacles, it has been discovered, are far less formidable than they were supposed to be, and mail stages with passengers now pass and repass regularly twice in each week, by a common wagon road, between San Francisco and St. Louis and Memphis in less than twenty-five days. The service has been as regularly performed as it was in former years between New York and this city.

Whilst disclaiming all authority to appropriate money for the construction of this road, except that derived from the war-making power of the Constitution, there are important collateral considerations urging us to undertake the work as speedily as possible.

The first and most momentous of these is that such a road would be a powerful bond of union between the States east and west of the Rocky Mountains. This is so self-evident as to require no illustration.

But again, in a commercial point of view, I consider this the great question of the day. With the eastern front of our Republic stretching along the Atlantic and its western front along the Pacific, if all the parts should be united by a safe, easy, and rapid intercommunication we must necessarily command a very large proportion of the trade both of Europe and Asia. Our recent treaties with China and Japan will open these rich and populous Empires to our commerce; and the history of the world proves that the nation which has gained possession of the trade with eastern Asia has always become wealthy and powerful. The peculiar geographical position of California and our Pacific possessions invites American capital and enterprise into this fruitful field. To reap the rich harvest, however, it is an indispensable prerequisite that we shall first have a railroad to convey and circulate its products throughout every portion of the Union. Besides, such a railroad through our temperate latitude, which would not be impeded by the frosts and snows of winter nor by the tropical heats of summer, would attract to itself much of the travel and the trade of all nations passing between Europe and Asia.

On the 21st of August last Lieutenant J. N. Maffit, of the United States brig *Dolphin,* captured the slaver *Echo* (formerly the *Putnam,* of New Orleans) near Kay Verde, on the coast of Cuba, with more than 300 African negroes on board. The prize, under the command of Lieutenant Bradford, of the United States Navy, arrived at Charleston on the 27th August, when the negroes, 306 in number, were delivered into the custody of the United States marshal for the district of South Carolina. They were first placed in Castle Pinckney, and afterwards in Fort Sumter, for safe-keeping, and were detained there until the 19th September, when the survivors, 271 in number, were delivered on board the United States steamer *Niagara* to be transported to the coast of Africa under the charge of the agent of the United States, pursuant to the provisions of the act of the 3d March, 1819, "in addition to the acts prohibiting the slave trade." Under the second section of this act the President is "authorized to make such regulations and arrangements as he may deem expedient for the safe-keeping, support, and removal beyond the limits of the United States of all such negroes, mulattoes, or persons of color" captured by vessels of the United States as may be delivered to the marshal of the district into which they are brought, "and to appoint a proper person or persons residing upon the coast of Africa as agent or agents for receiving the negroes, mulattoes, or persons of color delivered from on board vessels seized in the prosecution of the slave trade by commanders of United States armed vessels."

A doubt immediately arose as to the true construction of this act. It is quite clear from its terms that the President was authorized to provide "for the safe-keeping, support, and removal" of these negroes up till the time of their delivery to the agent on the coast of Africa, but no express provision was made for their protection and support after they had reached the place of their destination. Still, an agent was to be appointed to receive them in Africa, and it could not have been supposed that Congress intended he should desert them at the moment they were received and turn them loose on that inhospitable coast to perish for want of food or to become again the victims of the slave trade. Had this been the intention of Congress, the employment of an agent to receive them, who is required to reside on the coast, was unnecessary, and they might have been landed by our vessels anywhere in Africa and left exposed to the sufferings and the fate which would certainly await them.

Mr. Monroe, in his special message of December 17, 1819, at the first session after the act was passed, announced to Congress what in his opinion was its true construction. He believed it to be his duty under it to follow these unfortunates into Africa and make provision for them there until they should be able to provide for themselves. In communicating this interpretation of the act to Congress he stated that some doubt had been entertained as to its true intent and meaning, and he submitted the question to them so that they might, "should it be deemed advisable, amend the same before further proceedings are had under it." Nothing was done by Congress to explain the act, and Mr. Monroe proceeded to carry it into execution according to his own interpretation. This, then, became the practical construction. When the Africans from on board the *Echo* were delivered to the marshal at Charleston, it became my duty to consider what disposition ought to be made of them under the law. For many reasons it was expedient to remove them from that locality as speedily as possible. Although the conduct of the authorities and citizens of Charleston in giving countenance to the execution of the law was just what might have been expected from their high character, yet a prolonged continuance of 300 Africans in the immediate vicinity of that city could not have failed to become a source of inconvenience and anxiety to its inhabitants. Where to send them was the question. There was no portion of the coast of Africa to which they could be removed with any regard to humanity except to Liberia. Under these circumstances an agreement was entered into with the Colonization Society on the 7th of September last, a copy of which is herewith transmitted, under which the society engaged, for the consideration of $45,000, to receive these Africans in Liberia from the agent of the United States and furnish them during the period of one year thereafter with comfortable shelter, clothing, provisions, and medical attendance, causing the children to receive schooling, and all, whether children or adults, to be instructed in the arts of civilized life suitable to their condition. This aggregate of $45,000 was based upon an allowance of $150 for each individual; and as there has been considerable mortality among them and may be more before they reach Africa, the society have agreed, in an equitable spirit, to make such a deduction from the amount as under the circumstances may appear just and reasonable. This can not be fixed until we shall ascertain the actual number which may become a charge to the society.

It was also distinctly agreed that under no circumstances shall this Government be called upon for any additional expenses.

The agents of the society manifested a laudable desire to conform to the wishes of the Government throughout the transaction. They assured me that after a careful calculation they would be required to expend the sum of $150 on each individual in complying with the agreement, and they would have nothing left to remunerate them for their care, trouble, and responsibility. At all events, I could make no better arrangement, and there was no other alternative. During the period when the Government itself, through its own agents, undertook the task of providing for captured negroes in Africa the cost per head was very much greater.

There having been no outstanding appropriation applicable to this purpose, I could not advance any money on the agreement. I therefore recommend that an appropriation may be made of the amount necessary to carry it into effect.

Other captures of a similar character may, and probably will, be made by our naval forces, and I earnestly recommend that Congress may amend the second section of the act of March 3, 1819, so as to free its construction from the ambiguity which has so long existed and render the duty of the President plain in executing its provisions.

I recommend to your favorable regard the local interests of the District of Columbia. As the residence of Congress and the Executive Departments of the Government, we can not fail to feel a deep concern in its welfare. This is heightened by the high character and the peaceful and orderly conduct of its resident inhabitants.

I can not conclude without performing the agreeable duty of expressing my gratification that Congress so kindly responded to the recommendation of my last annual message by affording me sufficient time before the close of their late session for the examination of all the bills presented to me for approval. This change in the practice of Congress has proved to be a wholesome reform. It exerted a beneficial influence on the transaction of legislative business and elicited the general approbation of the country.   It enabled Congress to adjourn with that dignity and deliberation so becoming to the representatives of this great Republic, without having crowded into general appropriation bills provisions foreign to their nature and of doubtful constitutionality and expediency.   Let me warmly and strongly commend this precedent established by themselves as a guide to their proceedings during the present session.

THIRD ANNUAL MESSAGE.

WASHINGTON CITY, *December 19, 1859*

Fellow-Citizens of the Senate and House of Representatives:

Our deep and heartfelt gratitude is due to that Almighty Power which has bestowed upon us such varied and numerous blessings throughout the past year.   The general health of the country has been excellent, our harvests have been unusually plentiful, and prosperity smiles throughout the land.   Indeed, notwithstanding our demerits, we have much reason to believe from the past events in our history that we have enjoyed the special protection of Divine Providence ever since our origin as a nation.   We have been exposed to many threatening and alarming difficulties in our progress, but on each successive occasion the impending cloud has been dissipated at the moment it appeared ready to burst upon our head, and the danger to our institutions has passed away.   May we ever be under the divine guidance and protection.

Whilst it is the duty of the President "from time to time to give to Congress information of the state of the Union," I shall not refer in detail to the recent sad and bloody occurrences at Harpers Ferry.   Still, it is proper to observe that these events, however bad and cruel in themselves, derive their chief importance from the apprehension that they are but symptoms of an incurable disease in the public mind, which may break out in still more dangerous outrages and terminate at last in an open war by the North to abolish slavery in the South.

Whilst for myself I entertain no such apprehension, they ought to afford a solemn warning to us all to beware of the approach of danger. Our Union is a stake of such inestimable value as to demand our constant and watchful vigilance for its preservation.   In this view, let me implore my countrymen, North and South, to cultivate the ancient feelings of mutual forbearance and good will toward each other and strive to allay the demon spirit of sectional hatred and strife now alive in the land.

This advice proceeds from the heart of an old public functionary whose service commenced in the last generation, among the wise and conservative statesmen of that day, now nearly all passed away, and whose first and dearest earthly wish is to leave his country tranquil, prosperous, united, and powerful.

We ought to reflect that in this age, and especially in this country, there is an incessant flux and reflux of public opinion. Questions which in their day assumed a most threatening aspect have now nearly gone from the memory of men. They are "volcanoes burnt out, and on the lava and ashes and squalid scoria of old eruptions grow the peaceful olive, the cheering vine, and the sustaining corn." Such, in my opinion, will prove to be the fate of the present sectional excitement should those who wisely seek to apply the remedy continue always to confine their efforts within the pale of the Constitution. If this course be pursued, the existing agitation on the subject of domestic slavery, like everything human, will have its day and give place to other and less threatening controversies. Public opinion in this country is all-powerful, and when it reaches a dangerous excess upon any question the good sense of the people will furnish the corrective and bring it back within safe limits. Still, to hasten this auspicious result at the present crisis we ought to remember that every rational creature must be presumed to intend the natural consequences of his own teachings. Those who announce abstract doctrines subversive of the Constitution and the Union must not be surprised should their heated partisans advance one step further and attempt by violence to carry these doctrines into practical effect. In this view of the subject, it ought never to be forgotten that however great may have been the political advantages resulting from the Union to every portion of our common country, these would all prove to be as nothing should the time ever arrive when they can not be enjoyed without serious danger to the personal safety of the people of fifteen members of the Confederacy. If the peace of the domestic fireside throughout these States should ever be invaded, if the mothers of families within this extensive region should not be able to retire to rest at night without suffering dreadful apprehensions of what may be their own fate and that of their children before the morning, it would be vain to recount to such a people the political benefits which result to them from the Union. Self-preservation is the first instinct of nature, and therefore any state of society in which the sword is all the time suspended over the heads of the people must at last become intolerable. But I indulge in no such gloomy forebodings. On the contrary, I firmly believe that the events at Harpers Ferry, by causing the people to pause and reflect upon the possible peril to their cherished institutions, will be the means under Providence of allaying the existing excitement and preventing further outbreaks of a similar character. They will resolve that the Constitution and the Union shall not be endangered by rash counsels, knowing that should "the silver

cord be loosed or the golden bowl be broken * * * at the fountain ''
human power could never reunite the scattered and hostile fragments.

I cordially congratulate you upon the final settlement by the Supreme
Court of the United States of the question of slavery in the Territories,
which had presented an aspect so truly formidable at the commencement
of my Administration. The right has been established of every citizen to
take his property of any kind, including slaves, into the common Territories belonging equally to all the States of the Confederacy, and to have
it protected there under the Federal Constitution. Neither Congress
nor a Territorial legislature nor any human power has any authority to
annul or impair this vested right. The supreme judicial tribunal of the
country, which is a coordinate branch of the Government, has 'sanctioned and affirmed these principles of constitutional law, so manifestly
just in themselves and so well calculated to promote peace and harmony
among the States. It is a striking proof of the sense of justice which is
inherent in our people that the property in slaves has never been disturbed, to my knowledge, in any of the Territories. Even throughout
the late troubles in Kansas there has not been any attempt, as I am cred-
ibly informed, to interfere in a single instance with the right of the master. Had any such attempt been made, the judiciary would doubtless
have afforded an adequate remedy. Should they fail to do this hereafter,
it will then be time enough to strengthen their hands by further legislation. Had it been decided that either Congress or the Territorial legislature possess the power to annul or impair the right to property in slaves,
the evil would be intolerable. In the latter event there would be a struggle for a majority of the members of the legislature at each successive
election, and the sacred rights of property held under the Federal Constitution would depend for the time being on the result. The agitation
would thus be rendered incessant whilst the Territorial condition remained, and its baneful influence would keep alive a dangerous excitement among the people of the several States.

Thus has the status of a Territory during the intermediate period
from its first settlement until it shall become a State been irrevocably
fixed by the final decision of the Supreme Court. Fortunate has this
been for the prosperity of the Territories, as well as the tranquillity of
the States. Now emigrants from the North and the South, the East
and the West, will meet in the Territories on a common platform, having
brought with them that species of property best adapted, in their own
opinion, to promote their welfare. From natural causes the slavery
question will in each case soon virtually settle itself, and before the Territory is prepared for admission as a State into the Union this decision,
one way or the other, will have been a foregone conclusion. Meanwhile
the settlement of the new Territory will proceed without serious interruption, and its progress and prosperity will not be endangered or retarded by violent political struggles.

When in the progress of events the inhabitants of any Territory shall have reached the number required to form a State, they will then proceed in a regular manner and in the exercise of the rights of popular sovereignty to form a constitution preparatory to admission into the Union. After this has been done, to employ the language of the Kansas and Nebraska act, they "shall be received into the Union with or without slavery, as their constitution may prescribe at the time of their admission." This sound principle has happily been recognized in some form or other by an almost unanimous vote of both Houses of the last Congress.

All lawful means at my command have been employed, and shall continue to be employed, to execute the laws against the African slave trade. After a most careful and rigorous examination of our coasts and a thorough investigation of the subject, we have not been able to discover that any slaves have been imported into the United States except the cargo by the *Wanderer*, numbering between three and four hundred. Those engaged in this unlawful enterprise have been rigorously prosecuted, but not with as much success as their crimes have deserved. A number of them are still under prosecution.

Our history proves that the fathers of the Republic, in advance of all other nations, condemned the African slave trade. It was, notwithstanding, deemed expedient by the framers of the Constitution to deprive Congress of the power to prohibit "the migration or importation of such persons as any of the States now existing shall think proper to admit" "prior to the year 1808." It will be seen that this restriction on the power of Congress was confined to such States only as might think proper to admit the importation of slaves. It did not extend to other States or to the trade carried on abroad. Accordingly, we find that so early as the 22d March, 1794, Congress passed an act imposing severe penalties and punishments upon citizens and residents of the United States who should engage in this trade between foreign nations. The provisions of this act were extended and enforced by the act of 10th May, 1800.

Again, the States themselves had a clear right to waive the constitutional privilege intended for their benefit, and to prohibit by their own laws this trade at any time they thought proper previous to 1808. Several of them exercised this right before that period, and among them some containing the greatest number of slaves. This gave to Congress the immediate power to act in regard to all such States, because they themselves had removed the constitutional barrier. Congress accordingly passed an act on 28th February, 1803, "to prevent the importation of certain persons into certain States where by the laws thereof their admission is prohibited." In this manner the importation of African slaves into the United States was to a great extent prohibited some years in advance of 1808.

As the year 1808 approached Congress determined not to suffer this trade to exist even for a single day after they had the power to abolish it. On the 2d of March, 1807, they passed an act, to take effect "from and after the 1st day of January, 1808," prohibiting the importation of African slaves into the United States. This was followed by subsequent acts of a similar character, to which I need not specially refer. Such were the principles and such the practice of our ancestors more than fifty years ago in regard to the African slave trade. It did not occur to the revered patriots who had been delegates to the Convention, and afterwards became members of Congress, that in passing these laws they had violated the Constitution which they had framed with so much care and deliberation. They supposed that to prohibit Congress in express terms from exercising a specified power before an appointed day necessarily involved the right to exercise this power after that day had arrived.

If this were not the case, the framers of the Constitution had expended much labor in vain. Had they imagined that Congress would possess no power to prohibit the trade either before or after 1808, they would not have taken so much care to protect the States against the exercise of this power before that period. Nay, more, they would not have attached such vast importance to this provision as to have excluded it from the possibility of future repeal or amendment, to which other portions of the Constitution were exposed. It would, then, have been wholly unnecessary to ingraft on the fifth article of the Constitution, prescribing the mode of its own future amendment, the proviso "that no amendment which may be made prior to the year 1808 shall in any manner affect" the provision in the Constitution securing to the States the right to admit the importation of African slaves previous to that period. According to the adverse construction, the clause itself, on which so much care and discussion had been employed by the members of the Convention, was an absolute nullity from the beginning, and all that has since been done under it a mere usurpation.

It was well and wise to confer this power on Congress, because had it been left to the States its efficient exercise would have been impossible. In that event any one State could have effectually continued the trade, not only for itself, but for all the other slave States, though never so much against their will. And why? Because African slaves, when once brought within the limits of any one State in accordance with its laws, can not practically be excluded from any State where slavery exists. And even if all the States had separately passed laws prohibiting the importation of slaves, these laws would have failed of effect for want of a naval force to capture the slavers and to guard the coast. Such a force no State can employ in time of peace without the consent of Congress.

These acts of Congress, it is believed, have, with very rare and insignificant exceptions, accomplished their purpose. For a period of more than half a century there has been no perceptible addition to the number of our domestic slaves. During this period their advancement in civilization has far surpassed that of any other portion of the African race. The light and the blessings of Christianity have been extended to them, and both their moral and physical condition has been greatly improved.

Reopen the trade and it would be difficult to determine whether the effect would be more deleterious on the interests of the master or on those of the native-born slave. Of the evils to the master, the one most to be dreaded would be the introduction of wild, heathen, and ignorant barbarians among the sober, orderly, and quiet slaves whose ancestors have been on the soil for several generations. This might tend to barbarize, demoralize, and exasperate the whole mass and produce most deplorable consequences.

The effect upon the existing slave would, if possible, be still more deplorable. At present he is treated with kindness and humanity. He is well fed, well clothed, and not overworked. His condition is incomparably better than that of the coolies which modern nations of high civilization have employed as a substitute for African slaves. Both the philanthropy and the self-interest of the master have combined to produce this humane result. But let this trade be reopened and what will be the effect? The same to a considerable extent as on a neighboring island, the only spot now on earth where the African slave trade is openly tolerated, and this in defiance of solemn treaties with a power abundantly able at any moment to enforce their execution. There the master, intent upon present gain, extorts from the slave as much labor as his physical powers are capable of enduring, knowing that when death comes to his relief his place can be supplied at a price reduced to the lowest point by the competition of rival African slave traders. Should this ever be the case in our country, which I do not deem possible, the present useful character of the domestic institution, wherein those too old and too young to work are provided for with care and humanity and those capable of labor are not overtasked, would undergo an unfortunate change. The feeling of reciprocal dependence and attachment which now exists between master and slave would be converted into mutual distrust and hostility.

But we are obliged as a Christian and moral nation to consider what would be the effect upon unhappy Africa itself if we should reopen the slave trade. This would give the trade an impulse and extension which it has never had, even in its palmiest days. The numerous victims required to supply it would convert the whole slave coast into a perfect pandemonium, for which this country would be held responsible in the eyes both of God and man. Its petty tribes would then be constantly engaged in predatory wars against each other for the purpose of seizing slaves to supply the American market. All hopes of African civilization would thus be ended.

On the other hand, when a market for African slaves shall no longer be furnished in Cuba, and thus all the world be closed against this trade, we may then indulge a reasonable hope for the gradual improvement of Africa. The chief motive of war among the tribes will cease whenever there is no longer any demand for slaves. The resources of that fertile but miserable country might then be developed by the hand of industry and afford subjects for legitimate foreign and domestic commerce. In this manner Christianity and civilization may gradually penetrate the existing gloom.

The wisdom of the course pursued by this Government toward China has been vindicated by the event. Whilst we sustained a neutral position in the war waged by Great Britain and France against the Chinese Empire, our late minister, in obedience to his instructions, judiciously cooperated with the ministers of these powers in all peaceful measures to secure by treaty the just concessions demanded by the interests of foreign commerce. The result is that satisfactory treaties have been concluded with China by the respective ministers of the United States, Great Britain, France, and Russia. Our "treaty, or general convention, of peace, amity, and commerce" with that Empire was concluded at Tien-tsin on the 18th June, 1858, and was ratified by the President, by and with the advice and consent of the Senate, on the 21st December following. On the 15th December, 1858, John E. Ward, a distinguished citizen of Georgia, was duly commissioned as envoy extraordinary and minister plenipotentiary to China.

He left the United States for the place of his destination on the 5th of February, 1859, bearing with him the ratified copy of this treaty, and arrived at Shanghai on the 28th May. From thence he proceeded to Peking on the 16th June, but did not arrive in that city until the 27th July. According to the terms of the treaty, the ratifications were to be exchanged on or before the 18th June, 1859. This was rendered impossible by reasons and events beyond his control, not necessary to detail; but still it is due to the Chinese authorities at Shanghai to state that they always assured him no advantage should be taken of the delay, and this pledge has been faithfully redeemed.

On the arrival of Mr. Ward at Peking he requested an audience of the Emperor to present his letter of credence. This he did not obtain, in consequence of his very proper refusal to submit to the humiliating ceremonies required by the etiquette of this strange people in approaching their sovereign. Nevertheless, the interviews on this question were conducted in the most friendly spirit and with all due regard to his personal feelings and the honor of his country. When a presentation to His Majesty was found to be impossible, the letter of credence from the President was received with peculiar honors by Kweiliang, "the Emperor's prime minister and the second man in the Empire to the Emperor himself." The ratifications of the treaty were afterwards, on the 16th of August, exchanged in proper form at Pei-tsang. As the exchange did not take place until after the day prescribed by the treaty, it is deemed proper before its publication again to submit it to the Senate. It is but simple justice to the Chinese authorities to observe that throughout the whole transaction they appear to have acted in good faith and in a friendly spirit toward the United States. It is true this has been done after their own peculiar fashion; but we ought to regard with a lenient eye the ancient customs of an empire dating back for thousands of years, so far as this may be consistent with our own national honor. The conduct of our minister on the occasion has received my entire approbation.

In order to carry out the spirit of this treaty and to give it full effect it became necessary to conclude two supplemental conventions, the one for the adjustment and satisfaction of the claims of our citizens and the other to fix the tariff on imports and exports and to regulate the transit duties and trade of our merchants with China. This duty was satisfactorily performed by our late minister. These conventions bear date at Shanghai on the 8th November, 1858. Having been considered in the light of binding agreements subsidiary to the principal treaty, and to be carried into execution without delay, they do not provide for any formal ratification or exchange of ratifications by the contracting parties. This was not deemed necessary by the Chinese, who are already proceeding in good faith to satisfy the claims of our citizens and, it is hoped, to carry out the other provisions of the conventions. Still, I thought it was proper to submit them to the Senate, by which they were ratified on the 3d of March, 1859. The ratified copies, however, did not reach Shanghai until after the departure of our minister to Peking, and these conventions could not, therefore, be exchanged at the same time with the principal treaty. No doubt is entertained that they will be ratified and exchanged by the Chinese Government should this be thought advisable; but under the circumstances presented I shall consider them binding engagements from their date on both parties, and cause them to be published as such for the information and guidance of our merchants trading with the Chinese Empire.

It affords me much satisfaction to inform you that all our difficulties with the Republic of Paraguay have been satisfactorily adjusted. It happily did not become necessary to employ the force for this purpose which Congress had placed at my command under the joint resolution of 2d June, 1858. On the contrary, the President of that Republic, in a friendly spirit, acceded promptly to the just and reasonable demands of the Government of the United States. Our commissioner arrived at Assumption, the capital of the Republic, on the 25th of January, 1859, and left it on the 17th of February, having in three weeks ably and successfully accomplished all the objects of his mission. The treaties which he has concluded will be immediately submitted to the Senate.

In the view that the employment of other than peaceful means might become necessary to obtain "just satisfaction" from Paraguay, a strong naval force was concentrated in the waters of the La Plata to await contingencies whilst our commissioner ascended the rivers to Assumption. The Navy Department is entitled to great credit for the promptness, efficiency, and economy with which this expedition was fitted out and conducted. It consisted of 19 armed vessels, great and small, carrying 200 guns and 2,500 men, all under the command of the veteran and gallant Shubrick. The entire expenses of the expedition have been defrayed out of the ordinary appropriations for the naval service, except the sum of $289,000, applied to the purchase of seven of the steamers constituting a part of it, under the authority of the naval appropriation act of the 3d March last. It is believed that these steamers are worth more than their cost, and they are all now usefully and actively employed in the naval service.

The appearance of so large a force, fitted out in such a prompt manner, in the far-distant waters of the La Plata, and the admirable conduct of the officers and men employed in it, have had a happy effect in favor of our country throughout a'l that remote portion of the world.

Our relations with the great Empires of France and Russia, as well as with all other governments on the continent of Europe, unless we may except that of Spain, happily continue to be of the most friendly character.

In my last annual message I presented a statement of the unsatisfactory condition of our relations with Spain, and I regret to say that this has not materially improved.

Without special reference to other claims, even the "Cuban claims," the payment of which has been ably urged by our ministers, and in which more than a hundred of our citizens are directly interested, remain unsatisfied, notwithstanding both their justice and their amount ($128,635.54) had been recognized and ascertained by the Spanish Government itself.

I again recommend that an appropriation be made "to be paid to the Spanish Government for the purpose of distribution among the claimants in the *Amistad* case." In common with two of my predecessors, I entertain no doubt that this is required by our treaty with Spain of the 27th October, 1795. The failure to discharge this obligation has been employed by the cabinet of Madrid as a reason against the settlement of our claims.

I need not repeat the arguments which I urged in my last annual message in favor of the acquisition of Cuba by fair purchase. My opinions on that measure remain unchanged. I therefore again invite the serious attention of Congress to this important subject. Without a recognition of this policy on their part it will be almost impossible to institute negotiations with any reasonable prospect of success.

Until a recent period there was good reason to believe that I should be able to announce to you on the present occasion that our difficulties with Great Britain arising out of the Clayton and Bulwer treaty had been finally adjusted in a manner alike honorable and satisfactory to both parties.   From causes, however, which the British Government had not anticipated, they have not yet completed treaty arrangements with the Republics of Honduras and Nicaragua, in pursuance of the understanding between the two Governments.   It is, nevertheless, confidently expected that this good work will ere long be accomplished.

Whilst indulging the hope that no other subject remained which could disturb the good understanding between the two countries, the question arising out of the adverse claims of the parties to the island of San Juan, under the Oregon treaty of the 15th June, 1846, suddenly assumed a threatening prominence.   In order to prevent unfortunate collisions on that remote frontier, the late Secretary of State, on the 17th July, 1855, addressed a note to Mr. Crampton, then British minister at Washington, communicating to him a copy of the instructions which he (Mr. Marcy) had given on the 14th July to Governor Stevens, of Washington Territory, having a special reference to an "apprehended conflict between our citizens and the British subjects on the island of San Juan." To prevent this the governor was instructed "that the officers of the Territory should abstain from all acts on the disputed grounds which are calculated to provoke any conflicts, so far as it can be done without implying the concession to the authorities of Great Britain of an exclusive right over the premises.   The title ought to be settled before either party should attempt to exclude the other by force or exercise complete and exclusive sovereign rights within the fairly disputed limits."

In acknowledging the receipt on the next day of Mr. Marcy's note the British minister expressed his entire concurrence "in the propriety of the course recommended to the governor of Washington Territory by your [Mr. Marcy's] instructions to that officer," and stating that he had "lost no time in transmitting a copy of that document to the Governor-General of British North America" and had "earnestly recommended to His Excellency to take such measures as to him may appear best calculated to secure on the part of the British local authorities and the inhabitants of the neighborhood of the line in question the exercise of the same spirit of forbearance which is inculcated by you [Mr. Marcy] on the authorities and citizens of the United States."

Thus matters remained upon the faith of this arrangement until the 9th July last, when General Harney paid a visit to the island.   He found upon it twenty-five American residents with their families, and also an establishment of the Hudsons Bay Company for the purpose of raising sheep.   A short time before his arrival one of these residents had shot an animal belonging to the company whilst trespassing upon his premises, for which, however, he offered to pay twice its value, but that was refused.   Soon after "the chief factor of the company at Victoria, Mr. Dalles, son-in-law of Governor Douglas, came to the island in the British sloop of war *Satellite* and threatened to take this American [Mr. Cutler] by force to Victoria to answer for the trespass he had committed.   The

American seized his rifle and told Mr. Dalles if any such attempt was made he would kill him upon the spot. The affair then ended."

Under these circumstances the American settlers presented a petition to the General "through the United States inspector of customs, Mr. Hubbs, to place a force upon the island to protect them from the Indians, as well as the oppressive interference of the authorities of the Hudsons Bay Company at Victoria with their rights as American citizens." The General immediately responded to this petition, and ordered Captain George E. Pickett, Ninth Infantry, "to establish his company on Belle-vue, or San Juan Island, on some suitable position near the harbor at the southeastern extremity." This order was promptly obeyed and a military post was established at the place designated. The force was afterwards increased, so that by the last return the whole number of troops then on the island amounted in the aggregate to 691 men.

Whilst I do not deem it proper on the present occasion to go further into the subject and discuss the weight which ought to be attached to the statements of the British colonial authorities contesting the accuracy of the information on which the gallant General acted, it was due to him that I should thus present his own reasons for issuing the order to Captain Pickett. From these it is quite clear his object was to prevent the British authorities on Vancouvers Island from exercising jurisdiction over American residents on the island of San Juan, as well as to protect them against the incursions of the Indians. Much excitement prevailed for some time throughout that region, and serious danger of collision between the parties was apprehended. The British had a large naval force in the vicinity, and it is but an act of simple justice to the admiral on that station to state that he wisely and discreetly forbore to commit any hostile act, but determined to refer the whole affair to his Government and await their instructions.

This aspect of the matter, in my opinion, demanded serious attention. It would have been a great calamity for both nations had they been precipitated into acts of hostility, not on the question of title to the island, but merely concerning what should be its condition during the intervening period whilst the two Governments might be employed in settling the question to which of them it belongs. For this reason Lieutenant-General Scott was dispatched, on the 17th of September last, to Washington Territory to take immediate command of the United States forces on the Pacific Coast, should he deem this necessary. The main object of his mission was to carry out the spirit of the precautionary arrangement between the late Secretary of State and the British minister, and thus to preserve the peace and prevent collision between the British and American authorities pending the negotiations between the two Governments. Entertaining no doubt of the validity of our title, I need scarcely add that in any event American citizens were to be placed on a footing at least as favorable as that of British subjects, it being understood that

Captain Pickett's company should remain on the island. It is proper to observe that, considering the distance from the scene of action and in ignorance of what might have transpired on the spot before the General's arrival, it was necessary to leave much to his discretion; and I am happy to state the event has proven that this discretion could not have been intrusted to more competent hands. General Scott has recently returned from his mission, having successfully accomplished its objects, and there is no longer any good reason to apprehend a collision between the forces of the two countries during the pendency of the existing negotiations.

I regret to inform you that there has been no improvement in the affairs of Mexico since my last annual message, and I am again obliged to ask the earnest attention of Congress to the unhappy condition of that Republic.

The constituent Congress of Mexico, which adjourned on the 17th February, 1857, adopted a constitution and provided for a popular election. This took place in the following July (1857), and General Comonfort was chosen President almost without opposition. At the same election a new Congress was chosen, whose first session commenced on the 16th of September (1857). By the constitution of 1857 the Presidential term was to begin on the 1st of December (1857) and continue for four years. On that day General Comonfort appeared before the assembled Congress in the City of Mexico, took the oath to support the new constitution, and was duly inaugurated as President. Within a month afterwards he had been driven from the capital and a military rebellion had assigned the supreme power of the Republic to General Zuloaga. The constitution provided that in the absence of the President his office should devolve upon the chief justice of the supreme court; and General Comonfort having left the country, this functionary, General Juarez, proceeded to form at Guanajuato a constitutional Government. Before this was officially known, however, at the capital the Government of Zuloaga had been recognized by the entire diplomatic corps, including the minister of the United States, as the *de facto* Government of Mexico. The constitutional President, nevertheless, maintained his position with firmness, and was soon established, with his cabinet, at Vera Cruz. Meanwhile the Government of Zuloaga was earnestly resisted in many parts of the Republic, and even in the capital, a portion of the army having pronounced against it, its functions were declared terminated, and an assembly of citizens was invited for the choice of a new President. This assembly elected General Miramon, but that officer repudiated the plan under which he was chosen, and Zuloaga was thus restored to his previous position. He assumed it, however, only to withdraw from it; and Miramon, having become by his appointment "President substitute," continues with that title at the head of the insurgent party.

In my last annual message I communicated to Congress the circumstances under which the late minister of the United States suspended his official relations with the central Government and withdrew from the country. It was impossible to maintain friendly intercourse with a government like that at the capital, under whose usurped authority wrongs were constantly committed, but never redressed. Had this been an established government, with its power extending by the consent of the people over the whole of Mexico, a resort to hostilities against it would have been quite justifiable, and, indeed, necessary. But the country was a prey to civil war, and it was hoped that the success of the constitutional President might lead to a condition of things less injurious to the United States. This success became so probable that in January last I employed a reliable agent to visit Mexico and report to me the actual condition and prospects of the contending parties. In consequence of his report and from information which reached me from other sources favorable to the prospects of the constitutional cause, I felt justified in appointing a new minister to Mexico, who might embrace the earliest suitable opportunity of restoring our diplomatic relations with that Republic. For this purpose a distinguished citizen of Maryland was selected, who proceeded on his mission on the 8th of March last, with discretionary authority to recognize the Government of President Juarez if on his arrival in Mexico he should find it entitled to such recognition according to the established practice of the United States.

On the 7th of April following Mr. McLane presented his credentials to President Juarez, having no hesitation "in pronouncing the Government of Juarez to be the only existing government of the Republic." He was cordially received by the authorities at Vera Cruz, and they have ever since manifested the most friendly disposition toward the United States.

Unhappily, however, the constitutional Government has not been able to establish its power over the whole Republic.

It is supported by a large majority of the people and the States, but there are important parts of the country where it can enforce no obedience.

General Miramon maintains himself at the capital, and in some of the distant Provinces there are military governors who pay little respect to the decrees of either Government. In the meantime the excesses which always attend upon civil war, especially in Mexico, are constantly recurring. Outrages of the worst description are committed both upon persons and property. There is scarcely any form of injury which has not been suffered by our citizens in Mexico during the last few years. We have been nominally at peace with that Republic, but "so far as the interests of our commerce, or of our citizens who have visited the country as merchants, shipmasters, or in other capacities, are concerned, we might as well have been at war." Life has been insecure, property unprotected, and trade impossible except at a risk of loss which prudent men can not be expected to incur. Important contracts, involving large expenditures, entered into by the central Government, have been set at defiance by the local governments. Peaceful American residents, occupying their rightful possessions, have been suddenly expelled the country, in defiance of treaties and by the mere force of arbitrary power. Even the course of justice has not been safe from control, and a recent decree of Miramon permits the intervention of Government in all suits where either party is a foreigner. Vessels of the United States have been seized without law, and a consular officer who protested against such seizure has been fined and imprisoned for disrespect to the authorities. Military contributions have been levied in violation of every principle of right, and the American who resisted the lawless demand has had his property forcibly taken away and has been himself banished. From a conflict of authority in different parts of the country tariff duties which have been paid in one place have been exacted over again in another place. Large numbers of our citizens have been arrested and imprisoned without any form of examination or any opportunity for a hearing, and even when released have only obtained their liberty after much suffering and injury, and without any hope of redress. The wholesale massacre of Crabbe and his associates without trial in Sonora, as well as the seizure and murder of four sick Americans who had taken shelter in the house of an American upon the soil of the United States, was communicated to Congress at its last session. Murders of a still more atrocious character have been committed in the very heart of Mexico, under the authority of Miramon's Government, during the present year. Some of these were only worthy of a barbarous age, and if they had not been clearly proven would have seemed impossible in a country which claims to be civilized. Of this description was the brutal massacre in April last, by order of General Marquez, of three American physicians who were seized in the hospital at Tacubaya while attending upon the sick and the dying of both parties, and without trial, as without crime, were hurried away to speedy execution. Little less shocking was the recent fate of Ormond Chase, who was shot in Tepic on the 7th of August by order of the same Mexican general, not only without a trial, but without any conjecture by his friends of the cause of his arrest. He is represented as a young man of good character and intelligence, who had made numerous friends in Tepic by the courage and humanity which he had displayed on several trying occasions; and his death was as unexpected as it was shocking to the whole community. Other outrages might be enumerated, but these are sufficient to illustrate the wretched state of the country and the unprotected condition of the persons and property of our citizens in Mexico.

In all these cases our ministers have been constant and faithful in their demands for redress, but both they and this Government, which they have successively represented, have been wholly powerless to make their demands effective. Their testimony in this respect and in reference to the only remedy which in their judgments would meet the exigency has been both uniform and emphatic. "Nothing but a manifestation of the power of the Government of the United States," wrote our late min-

ister in 1856, "and of its purpose to punish these wrongs will avail. I
assure you that the universal belief here is that there is nothing to be
apprehended from the Government of the United States, and that local
Mexican officials can commit these outrages upon American citizens
with absolute impunity." "I hope the President," wrote our present
minister in August last, "will feel authorized to ask from Congress the
power to enter Mexico with the military forces of the United States at
the call of the constitutional authorities, in order to protect the citizens
and the treaty rights of the United States. Unless such a power is conferred upon him, neither the one nor the other will be respected in the
existing state of anarchy and disorder, and the outrages already perpetrated will never be chastised; and, as I assured you in my No. 23, all
these evils must increase until every vestige of order and government
disappears from the country." I have been reluctantly led to the same
opinion, and in justice to my countrymen who have suffered wrongs
from Mexico and who may still suffer them I feel bound to announce
this conclusion to Congress.

The case presented, however, is not merely a case of individual claims,
although our just claims against Mexico have reached a very large
amount; nor is it merely the case of protection to the lives and property of the few Americans who may still remain in Mexico, although the
life and property of every American citizen ought to be sacredly protected in every quarter of the world; but it is a question which relates
to the future as well as to the present and the past, and which involves,
indirectly at least, the whole subject of our duty to Mexico as a neighboring State. The exercise of the power of the United States in that
country to redress the wrongs and protect the rights of our own citizens
is none the less to be desired because efficient and necessary aid may
thus be rendered at the same time to restore peace and order to Mexico
itself. In the accomplishment of this result the people of the United
States must necessarily feel a deep and earnest interest. Mexico ought
to be a rich and prosperous and powerful Republic. She possesses an
extensive territory, a fertile soil, and an incalculable store of mineral
wealth. She occupies an important position between the Gulf and the
ocean for transit routes and for commerce. Is it possible that such a
country as this can be given up to anarchy and ruin without an effort
from any quarter for its rescue and its safety? Will the commercial
nations of the world, which have so many interests connected with it,
remain wholly indifferent to such a result? Can the United States
especially, which ought to share most largely in its commercial intercourse, allow their immediate neighbor thus to destroy itself and injure
them? Yet without support from some quarter it is impossible to perceive how Mexico can resume her position among nations and enter upon
a career which promises any good results. The aid which she requires,
and which the interests of all commercial countries require that she

should have, it belongs to this Government to render, not only by virtue of our neighborhood to Mexico, along whose territory we have a continuous frontier of nearly a thousand miles, but by virtue also of our established policy, which is inconsistent with the intervention of any European power in the domestic concerns of that Republic.

The wrongs which we have suffered from Mexico are before the world and must deeply impress every American citizen. A government which is either unable or unwilling to redress such wrongs is derelict to its highest duties. The difficulty consists in selecting and enforcing the remedy. We may in vain apply to the constitutional Government at Vera Cruz, although it is well disposed to do us justice, for adequate redress. Whilst its authority is acknowledged in all the important ports and throughout the seacoasts of the Republic, its power does not extend to the City of Mexico and the States in its vicinity, where nearly all the recent outrages have been committed on American citizens. We must penetrate into the interior before we can reach the offenders, and this can only be done by passing through the territory in the occupation of the constitutional Government. The most acceptable and least difficult mode of accomplishing the object will be to act in concert with that Government. Their consent and their aid might, I believe, be obtained; but if not, our obligation to protect our own citizens in their just rights secured by treaty would not be the less imperative. For these reasons I recommend to Congress to pass a law authorizing the President, under such conditions as they may deem expedient, to employ a sufficient military force to enter Mexico for the purpose of obtaining indemnity for the past and security for the future. I purposely refrain from any suggestion as to whether this force shall consist of regular troops or volunteers, or both. This question may be most appropriately left to the decision of Congress. I would merely observe that should volunteers be selected such a force could be easily raised in this country among those who sympathize with the sufferings of our unfortunate fellow-citizens in Mexico and with the unhappy condition of that Republic. Such an accession to the forces of the constitutional Government would enable it soon to reach the City of Mexico and extend its power over the whole Republic. In that event there is no reason to doubt that the just claims of our citizens would be satisfied and adequate redress obtained for the injuries inflicted upon them. The constitutional Government have ever evinced a strong desire to do justice, and this might be secured in advance by a preliminary treaty.

It may be said that these measures will, at least indirectly, be inconsistent with our wise and settled policy not to interfere in the domestic concerns of foreign nations. But does not the present case fairly constitute an exception? An adjoining Republic is in a state of anarchy and confusion from which she has proved wholly unable to extricate herself. She is entirely destitute of the power to maintain peace upon her borders or to prevent the incursions of banditti into our territory. In her fate and in her fortune, in her power to establish and maintain a settled government, we have a far deeper interest, socially, commercially, and politically, than any other nation. She is now a wreck upon the ocean, drifting about as she is impelled by different factions. As a good neighbor, shall we not extend to her a helping hand to save her? If we do not, it would not be surprising should some other nation undertake the task, and thus force us to interfere at last, under circumstances of increased difficulty, for the maintenance of our established policy.

I repeat the recommendation contained in my last annual message that authority may be given to the President to establish one or more temporary military posts across the Mexican line in Sonora and Chihuahua, where these may be necessary to protect the lives and property of American and Mexican citizens against the incursions and depredations of the Indians, as well as of lawless rovers, on that remote region. The establishment of one such post at a point called Arispe, in Sonora, in a country now almost depopulated by the hostile inroads of the Indians from our side of the line, would, it is believed, have prevented much injury and many cruelties during the past season. A state of lawlessness and violence prevails on that distant frontier. Life and property are there wholly insecure. The population of Arizona, now numbering more than 10,000 souls, are practically destitute of government, of laws, or of any regular administration of justice. Murder, rapine, and other crimes are committed with impunity. I therefore again call the attention of Congress to the necessity for establishing a Territorial government over Arizona.

The treaty with Nicaragua of the 16th of February, 1857, to which I referred in my last annual message, failed to receive the ratification of the Government of that Republic, for reasons which I need not enumerate. A similar treaty has been since concluded between the parties, bearing date on the 16th March, 1859, which has already been ratified by the Nicaraguan Congress. This will be immediately submitted to the Senate for their ratification. Its provisions can not, I think, fail to be acceptable to the people of both countries.

Our claims against the Governments of Costa Rica and Nicaragua remain unredressed, though they are pressed in an earnest manner and not without hope of success.

I deem it to be my duty once more earnestly to recommend to Congress the passage of a law authorizing the President to employ the naval force at his command for the purpose of protecting the lives and property of American citizens passing in transit across the Panama, Nicaragua, and Tehuantepec routes against sudden and lawless outbreaks and depredations. I shall not repeat the arguments employed in former messages in support of this measure. Suffice it to say that the lives of many of our people and the security of vast amounts of treasure passing and repassing over one or more of these routes between the Atlantic and

Pacific may be deeply involved in the action of Congress on this subject.

I would also again recommend to Congress that authority be given to the President to employ the naval force to protect American merchant vessels, their crews and cargoes, against violent and lawless seizure and confiscation in the ports of Mexico and the Spanish American States when these countries may be in a disturbed and revolutionary condition. The mere knowledge that such an authority had been conferred, as I have already stated, would of itself in a great degree prevent the evil. Neither would this require any additional appropriation for the naval service.

The chief objection urged against the grant of this authority is that Congress by conferring it would violate the Constitution; that it would be a transfer of the war-making, or, strictly speaking, the war-declaring, power to the Executive. If this were well founded, it would, of course, be conclusive. A very brief examination, however, will place this objection at rest.

Congress possess the sole and exclusive power under the Constitution "to declare war." They alone can "raise and support armies" and "provide and maintain a navy." But after Congress shall have declared war and provided the force necessary to carry it on the President, as Commander in Chief of the Army and Navy, can alone employ this force in making war against the enemy. This is the plain language, and history proves that it was the well-known intention of the framers, of the Constitution.

It will not be denied that the general "power to declare war" is without limitation and embraces within itself not only what writers on the law of nations term a public or perfect war, but also an imperfect war, and, in short, every species of hostility, however confined or limited. Without the authority of Congress the President can not fire a hostile gun in any case except to repel the attacks of an enemy. It will not be doubted that under this power Congress could, if they thought proper, authorize the President to employ the force at his command to seize a vessel belonging to an American citizen which had been illegally and unjustly captured in a foreign port and restore it to its owner. But can Congress only act after the fact, after the mischief has been done? Have they no power to confer upon the President the authority in advance to furnish instant redress should such a case afterwards occur? Must they wait until the mischief has been done, and can they apply the remedy only when it is too late? To confer this authority to meet future cases under circumstances strictly specified is as clearly within the war-declaring power as such an authority conferred upon the President by act of Congress after the deed had been done. In the progress of a great nation many exigencies must arise imperatively requiring that Congress should authorize the President to act promptly on certain conditions which may or may not afterwards arise. Our history has already presented a number of such cases. I shall refer only to the latest.

Under the resolution of June 2, 1858, "for the adjustment of difficulties with the Republic of Paraguay," the President is "authorized to adopt such measures and use such force as in his judgment may be necessary and advisable in the event of a refusal of just satisfaction by the Government of Paraguay." "Just satisfaction" for what? For "the attack on the United States steamer *Water Witch*" and "other matters referred to in the annual message of the President." Here the power is expressly granted upon the condition that the Government of Paraguay shall refuse to render this "just satisfaction." In this and other similar cases Congress have conferred upon the President power in advance to employ the Army and Navy upon the happening of contingent future events; and this most certainly is embraced within the power to declare war.

Now, if this conditional and contingent power could be constitutionally conferred upon the President in the case of Paraguay, why may it not be conferred for the purpose of protecting the lives and property of American citizens in the event that they may be violently and unlawfully attacked in passing over the transit routes to and from California or assailed by the seizure of their vessels in a foreign port? To deny this power is to render the Navy in a great degree useless for the protection of the lives and property of American citizens in countries where neither protection nor redress can be otherwise obtained.

The Thirty-fifth Congress terminated on the 3d of March, 1859, without having passed the "act making appropriations for the service of the Post-Office Department during the fiscal year ending the 30th of June, 1860." This act also contained an appropriation "to supply deficiencies in the revenue of the Post-Office Department for the year ending 30th June, 1859." I believe this is the first instance since the origin of the Federal Government, now more than seventy years ago, when any Congress went out of existence without having passed all the general appropriation bills necessary to carry on the Government until the regular period for the meeting of a new Congress. This event imposed on the Executive a grave responsibility. It presented a choice of evils.

Had this omission of duty occurred at the first session of the last Congress, the remedy would have been plain. I might then have instantly recalled them to complete their work, and this without expense to the Government. But on the 4th of March last there were fifteen of the thirty-three States which had not elected any Representatives to the present Congress. Had Congress been called together immediately, these States would have been virtually disfranchised. If an intermediate period had been selected, several of the States would have been compelled to hold extra sessions of their legislatures, at great inconvenience and expense, to provide for elections at an earlier day than that previously fixed by law. In the regular course ten of these States would not elect until after the beginning of August, and five of these ten not until October and November.

On the other hand, when I came to examine carefully the condition of the Post-Office Department, I did not meet as many or as great difficulties as I had apprehended. Had the bill which failed been confined to appropriations for the fiscal year ending on the 30th June next, there would have been no reason of pressing importance for the call of an extra session. Nothing would become due on contracts (those with railroad companies only excepted) for carrying the mail for the first quarter of the present fiscal year, commencing on the 1st of July, until the 1st of December—less than one week before the meeting of the present Congress. The reason is that the mail contractors for this and the current year did not complete their first quarter's service until the 30th September last, and by the terms of their contracts sixty days more are allowed for the settlement of their accounts before the Department could be called upon for payment.

The great difficulty and the great hardship consisted in the failure to provide for the payment of the deficiency in the fiscal year ending the 30th June, 1859. The Department had entered into contracts, in obedience to existing laws, for the service of that fiscal year, and the contractors were fairly entitled to their compensation as it became due. The deficiency as stated in the bill amounted to $3,838,728, but after a careful settlement of all these accounts it has been ascertained that it amounts to $4,296,009. With the scanty means at his command the Postmaster-General has managed to pay that portion of this deficiency which occurred in the first two quarters of the past fiscal year, ending on the 31st December last. In the meantime the contractors themselves, under these trying circumstances, have behaved in a manner worthy of all commendation. They had one resource in the midst of their embarrassments. After the amount due to each of them had been ascertained and finally settled according to law, this became a specific debt of record against the United States, which enabled them to borrow money on this unquestionable security. Still, they were obliged to pay interest in consequence of the default of Congress, and on every principle of justice ought to receive interest from the Government. This interest should commence from the date when a warrant would have issued for the payment of the principal had an appropriation been made for this purpose. Calculated up to the 1st December, it will not exceed $96,660—a sum not to be taken into account when contrasted with the great difficulties and embarrassments of a public and private character, both to the people and the States, which would have resulted from convening and holding a special session of Congress.

For these reasons I recommend the passage of a bill at as early a day as may be practicable to provide for the payment of the amount, with interest, due to these last-mentioned contractors, as well as to make the necessary appropriations for the service of the Post-Office Department for the current fiscal year.

The failure to pass the Post-Office bill necessarily gives birth to serious reflections. Congress, by refusing to pass the general appropriation bills necessary to carry on the Government, may not only arrest its action, but might even destroy its existence. The Army, the Navy, the judiciary, in short, every department of the Government, can no longer perform their functions if Congress refuse the money necessary for their support. If this failure should teach the country the necessity of electing a full Congress in sufficient time to enable the President to convene them in any emergency, even immediately after the old Congress has expired, it will have been productive of great good. In a time of sudden and alarming danger, foreign or domestic, which all nations must expect to encounter in their progress, the very salvation of our institutions may be staked upon the assembling of Congress without delay. If under such circumstances the President should find himself in the condition in which he was placed at the close of the last Congress, with nearly half the States of the Union destitute of representatives, the consequences might be disastrous. I therefore recommend to Congress to carry into effect the provisions of the Constitution on this subject, and to pass a law appointing some day previous to the 4th March in each year of odd number for the election of Representatives throughout all the States. They have already appointed a day for the election of electors for President and Vice-President, and this measure has been approved by the country.

I would again express a most decided opinion in favor of the construction of a Pacific railroad, for the reasons stated in my two last annual messages. When I reflect upon what would be the defenseless condition of our States and Territories west of the Rocky Mountains in case of a war with a naval power sufficiently strong to interrupt all intercourse with them by the routes across the Isthmus, I am still more convinced than ever of the vast importance of this railroad. I have never doubted the constitutional competency of Congress to provide for its construction, but this exclusively under the war-making power. Besides, the Constitution expressly requires as an imperative duty that "the United States shall protect each of them [the States] against invasion." I am at a loss to conceive how this protection can be afforded to California and Oregon against such a naval power by any other means. I repeat the opinion contained in my last annual message that it would be inexpedient for the Government to undertake this great work by agents of its own appointment and under its direct and exclusive control. This would increase the patronage of the Executive to a dangerous extent and would foster a system of jobbing and corruption which no vigilance on the part of Federal officials could prevent. The construction of this road ought, therefore, to be intrusted to incorporated companies or other agencies who would exercise that active and vigilant supervision over it which can be inspired alone by a sense of corporate and individual interest. I venture to assert that the additional cost of transporting troops, munitions of war, and necessary supplies for the Army across the vast intervening plains to our possessions on the Pacific Coast would be greater in such a war than the whole amount required to construct the road. And yet this resort would after all be inadequate for their defense and protection.

We have yet scarcely recovered from the habits of extravagant expenditure produced by our overflowing Treasury during several years prior to the commencement of my Administration. The financial reverses which we have since experienced ought to teach us all to scrutinize our expenditures with the greatest vigilance and to reduce them to the lowest possible point. The Executive Departments of the Government have devoted themselves to the accomplishment of this object with considerable success, as will appear from their different reports and estimates. To these I invite the scrutiny of Congress, for the purpose of reducing them still lower, if this be practicable consistent with the great public interests of the country. In aid of the policy of retrenchment, I pledge myself to examine closely the bills appropriating lands or money, so that if any of these should inadvertently pass both Houses, as must sometimes be the case, I may afford them an opportunity for reconsideration. At the same time, we ought never to forget that true public economy consists not in withholding the means necessary to accomplish important national objects confided to us by the Constitution, but in taking care that the money appropriated for these purposes shall be faithfully and frugally expended.

It will appear from the report of the Secretary of the Treasury that it is extremely doubtful, to say the least, whether we shall be able to pass through the present and the next fiscal year without providing additional revenue. This can only be accomplished by strictly confining the appropriations within the estimates of the different Departments, without making an allowance for any additional expenditures which Congress may think proper, in their discretion, to authorize, and without providing for the redemption of any portion of the $20,000,000 of Treasury notes which have been already issued. In the event of a deficiency, which I consider probable, this ought never to be supplied by a resort to additional loans. It would be a ruinous practice in the days of peace and prosperity to go on increasing the national debt to meet the ordinary expenses of the Government. This policy would cripple our resources and impair our credit in case the existence of war should render it necessary to borrow money. Should such a deficiency occur as I apprehend, I would recommend that the necessary revenue be raised by an increase of our present duties on imports. I need not repeat the opinions expressed in my last annual message as to the best mode and manner of accomplishing this object, and shall now merely observe that these have since undergone no change.

The report of the Secretary of the Treasury will explain in detail the operations of that Department of the Government.

The receipts into the Treasury from all sources during the fiscal year ending June 30, 1859, including the loan authorized by the act of June

14, 1858, and the issues of Treasury notes authorized by existing laws, were $81,692,471.01, which sum, with the balance of $6,398,316.10 remaining in the Treasury at the commencement of that fiscal year, made an aggregate for the service of the year of $88,090,787.11.

The public expenditures during the fiscal year ending June 30, 1859, amounted to $83,751,511.57. Of this sum $17,405,285.44 were applied to the payment of interest on the public debt and the redemption of the issues of Treasury notes. The expenditures for all other branches of the public service during that fiscal year were therefore $66,346,226.13.

The balance remaining in the Treasury on the 1st July, 1859, being the commencement of the present fiscal year, was $4,339,275.54.

The receipts into the Treasury during the first quarter of the present fiscal year, commencing July 1, 1859, were $20,618,865.85. Of this amount $3,821,300 was received on account of the loan and the issue of Treasury notes, the amount of $16,797,565.85 having been received during the quarter from the ordinary sources of public revenue. The estimated receipts for the remaining three quarters of the present fiscal year, to June 30, 1860, are $50,426,400. Of this amount it is estimated that $5,756,400 will be received for Treasury notes which may be reissued under the fifth section of the act of 3d March last, and $1,170,000 on account of the loan authorized by the act of June 14, 1858, making $6,926,400 from these extraordinary sources, and $43,500,000 from the ordinary sources of the public revenue, making an aggregate, with the balance in the Treasury on the 1st July, 1859, of $75,384,541.89 for the estimated means of the present fiscal year, ending June 30, 1860.

The expenditures during the first quarter of the present fiscal year were $20,007,174.76. Four million six hundred and sixty-four thousand three hundred and sixty-six dollars and seventy-six cents of this sum were applied to the payment of interest on the public debt and the redemption of the issues of Treasury notes, and the remainder, being $15,342,808, were applied to ordinary expenditures during the quarter. The estimated expenditures during the remaining three quarters, to June 30, 1860, are $40,995,558.23, of which sum $2,886,621.34 are estimated for the interest on the public debt. The ascertained and estimated expenditures for the fiscal year ending June 30, 1860, on account of the public debt are accordingly $7,550,988.10, and for the ordinary expenditures of the Government $53,451,744.89, making an aggregate of $61,-002,732.99, leaving an estimated balance in the Treasury on June 30, 1860, of $14,381,808.40.

The estimated receipts during the next fiscal year, ending June 30, 1861, are $66,225,000, which, with the balance estimated, as before stated, as remaining in the Treasury on the 30th June, 1860, will make an aggregate for the service of the next fiscal year of $80,606,808.40.

The estimated expenditures during the next fiscal year, ending 30th June, 1861, are $66,714,928.79. Of this amount $3,386,621.34 will be required to pay the interest on the public debt, leaving the sum of $63,328,307.45 for the estimated ordinary expenditures during the fiscal year ending 30th June, 1861. Upon these estimates a balance will be left in the Treasury on the 30th June, 1861, of $13,891,879.61.

But this balance, as well as that estimated to remain in the Treasury on the 1st July, 1860, will be reduced by such appropriations as shall be made by law to carry into effect certain Indian treaties during the present fiscal year, asked for by the Secretary of the Interior, to the amount of $539,350; and upon the estimates of the Postmaster-General for the service of his Department the last fiscal year, ending 30th June, 1859, amounting to $4,296,009, together with the further estimate of that officer for the service of the present fiscal year, ending 30th June, 1860, being $5,526,324, making an aggregate of $10,361,683.

Should these appropriations be made as requested by the proper Departments, the balance in the Treasury on the 30th June, 1861, will not, it is estimated, exceed $3,530,196.61.

I transmit herewith the reports of the Secretaries of War, of the Navy, of the Interior, and of the Postmaster-General. They each contain valuable information and important recommendations well worthy of the serious consideration of Congress.

It will appear from the report of the Secretary of War that the Army expenditures have been materially reduced by a system of rigid economy, which in his opinion offers every guaranty that the reduction will be permanent. The estimates of the Department for the next have been reduced nearly $2,000,000 below the estimates for the present fiscal year and $500,000 below the amount granted for this year at the last session of Congress.

The expenditures of the Post-Office Department during the past fiscal year, ending on the 30th June, 1859, exclusive of payments for mail service specially provided for by Congress out of the general Treasury, amounted to $14,964,493.33 and its receipts to $7,968,484.07, showing a deficiency to be supplied from the Treasury of $6,996,009.26, against $5,235,677.15 for the year ending 30th June, 1858. The increased cost of transportation, growing out of the expansion of the service required by Congress, explains this rapid augmentation of the expenditures. It is gratifying, however, to observe an increase of receipts for the year ending on the 30th of June, 1859, equal to $481,691.21 compared with those in the year ending on the 30th June, 1858.

It is estimated that the deficiency for the current fiscal year will be $5,988,424.04, but that for the year ending 30th June, 1861, it will not exceed $1,342,473.90 should Congress adopt the measures of reform proposed and urged by the Postmaster-General. Since the month of March retrenchments have been made in the expenditures amounting to $1,826,471 annually, which, however, did not take effect until after the commencement of the present fiscal year. The period seems to have arrived for determining the question whether this Department shall become a permanent and ever-increasing charge upon the Treasury, or shall be permitted to resume the self-sustaining policy which had so long controlled its administration. The course of legislation recommended by the Postmaster-General for the relief of the Department from its present embarrassments and for restoring it to its original independence is deserving of your early and earnest consideration.

In conclusion I would again commend to the just liberality of Congress the local interests of the District of Columbia. Surely the city bearing the name of Washington, and destined, I trust, for ages to be the capital of our united, free, and prosperous Confederacy, has strong claims on our favorable regard.

FOURTH ANNUAL MESSAGE.

WASHINGTON CITY, *December 3, 1860.*

Fellow-Citizens of the Senate and House of Representatives:

Throughout the year since our last meeting the country has been eminently prosperous in all its material interests. The general health has been excellent, our harvests have been abundant, and plenty smiles throughout the land. Our commerce and manufactures have been prosecuted with energy and industry, and have yielded fair and ample returns. In short, no nation in the tide of time has ever presented a spectacle of greater material prosperity than we have done until within a very recent period.

Why is it, then, that discontent now so extensively prevails, and the Union of the States, which is the source of all these blessings, is threatened with destruction?

The long-continued and intemperate interference of the Northern people with the question of slavery in the Southern States has at length produced its natural effects. The different sections of the Union are now arrayed against each other, and the time has arrived, so much dreaded by the Father of his Country, when hostile geographical parties have been formed.

I have long foreseen and often forewarned my countrymen of the now impending danger. This does not proceed solely from the claim on the part of Congress or the Territorial legislatures to exclude slavery from the Territories, nor from the efforts of different States to defeat the execution of the fugitive-slave law. All or any of these evils might have been endured by the South without danger to the Union (as others have been) in the hope that time and reflection might apply the remedy. The immediate peril arises not so much from these causes as from the fact that the incessant and violent agitation of the slavery question throughout the North for the last quarter of a century has at length produced its malign influence on the slaves and inspired them with vague notions of freedom.   Hence a sense of security no longer exists around the family altar.   This feeling of peace at home has given place to apprehensions of servile insurrections.   Many a matron throughout the South retires at night in dread of what may befall herself and children before the morning.   Should this apprehension of domestic danger, whether real or imaginary, extend and intensify itself until it shall pervade the masses of the Southern people, then disunion will become inevitable.   Self-preservation is the first law of nature, and has been implanted in the heart of man by his Creator for the wisest purpose; and no political union, however fraught with blessings and benefits in all other respects, can long continue if the necessary consequence be to render the homes and the firesides of nearly half the parties to it habitually and hopelessly insecure.   Sooner or later the bonds of such a union must be severed. It is my conviction that this fatal period has not yet arrived, and my prayer to God is that He would preserve the Constitution and the Union throughout all generations.

But let us take warning in time and remove the cause of danger.   It can not be denied that for five and twenty years the agitation at the North against slavery has been incessant.   In 1835 pictorial handbills and inflammatory appeals were circulated extensively throughout the South of a character to excite the passions of the slaves, and, in the language of General Jackson, "to stimulate them to insurrection and produce all the horrors of a servile war."   This agitation has ever since been continued by the public press, by the proceedings of State and county conventions and by abolition sermons and lectures.   The time of Congress has been occupied in violent speeches on this never-ending subject, and appeals, in pamphlet and other forms, indorsed by distinguished names, have been sent forth from this central point and spread broadcast over the Union.

How easy would it be for the American people to settle the slavery question forever and to restore peace and harmony to this distracted country!   They, and they alone, can do it.   All that is necessary to accomplish the object, and all for which the slave States have ever contended, is to be let alone and permitted to manage their domestic institutions in their own way.   As sovereign States, they, and they alone, are responsible before God and the world for the slavery existing among them.   For this the people of the North are not more responsible and have no more right to interfere than with similar institutions in Russia or in Brazil.

Upon their good sense and patriotic forbearance I confess I still greatly rely. Without their aid it is beyond the power of any President, no matter what may be his own political proclivities, to restore peace and harmony among the States. Wisely limited and restrained as is his power under our Constitution and laws, he alone can accomplish but little for good or for evil on such a momentous question.

And this brings me to observe that the election of any one of our fellow-citizens to the office of President does not of itself afford just cause for dissolving the Union. This is more especially true if his election has been effected by a mere plurality, and not a majority of the people, and has resulted from transient and temporary causes, which may probably never again occur. In order to justify a resort to revolutionary resistance, the Federal Government must be guilty of "a deliberate, palpable, and dangerous exercise" of powers not granted by the Constitution. The late Presidential election, however, has been held in strict conformity with its express provisions. How, then, can the result justify a revolution to destroy this very Constitution? Reason, justice, a regard for the Constitution, all require that we shall wait for some overt and dangerous act on the part of the President elect before resorting to such a remedy. It is said, however, that the antecedents of the President elect have been sufficient to justify the fears of the South that he will attempt to invade their constitutional rights. But are such apprehensions of contingent danger in the future sufficient to justify the immediate destruction of the noblest system of government ever devised by mortals? From the very nature of his office and its high responsibilities he must necessarily be conservative. The stern duty of administering the vast and complicated concerns of this Government affords in itself a guaranty that he will not attempt any violation of a clear constitutional right.

After all, he is no more than the chief executive officer of the Government. His province is not to make but to execute the laws. And it is a remarkable fact in our history that, notwithstanding the repeated efforts of the antislavery party, no single act has ever passed Congress, unless we may possibly except the Missouri compromise, impairing in the slightest degree the rights of the South to their property in slaves; and it may also be observed, judging from present indications, that no probability exists of the passage of such an act by a majority of both Houses, either in the present or the next Congress. Surely under these circumstances we ought to be restrained from present action by the precept of Him who spake as man never spoke, that "sufficient unto the day is the evil thereof." The day of evil may never come unless we shall rashly bring it upon ourselves.

It is alleged as one cause for immediate secession that the Southern States are denied equal rights with the other States in the common Territories. But by what authority are these denied? Not by Congress.

which has never passed, and I believe never will pass, any act to exclude slavery from these Territories; and certainly not by the Supreme Court, which has solemnly decided that slaves are property, and, like all other property, their owners have a right to take them into the common Territories and hold them there under the protection of the Constitution.

So far then, as Congress is concerned, the objection is not to anything they have already done, but to what they may do hereafter. It will surely be admitted that this apprehension of future danger is no good reason for an immediate dissolution of the Union. It is true that the Territorial legislature of Kansas, on the 23d February, 1860, passed in great haste an act over the veto of the governor declaring that slavery "is and shall be forever prohibited in this Territory." Such an act, however, plainly violating the rights of property secured by the Constitution, will surely be declared void by the judiciary whenever it shall be presented in a legal form.

Only three days after my inauguration the Supreme Court of the United States solemnly adjudged that this power did not exist in a Territorial legislature. Yet such has been the factious temper of the times that the correctness of this decision has been extensively impugned before the people, and the question has given rise to angry political conflicts throughout the country. Those who have appealed from this judgment of our highest constitutional tribunal to popular assemblies would, if they could, invest a Territorial legislature with power to annul the sacred rights of property. This power Congress is expressly forbidden by the Federal Constitution to exercise. Every State legislature in the Union is forbidden by its own constitution to exercise it. It can not be exercised in any State except by the people in their highest sovereign capacity, when framing or amending their State constitution. In like manner it can only be exercised by the people of a Territory represented in a convention of delegates for the purpose of framing a constitution preparatory to admission as a State into the Union. Then, and not until then, are they invested with power to decide the question whether slavery shall or shall not exist within their limits. This is an act of sovereign authority, and not of subordinate Territorial legislation. Were it otherwise, then indeed would the equality of the States in the Territories be destroyed, and the rights of property in slaves would depend not upon the guaranties of the Constitution, but upon the shifting majorities of an irresponsible Territorial legislature. Such a doctrine, from its intrinsic unsoundness, can not long influence any considerable portion of our people, much less can it afford a good reason for a dissolution of the Union.

The most palpable violations of constitutional duty which have yet been committed consist in the acts of different State legislatures to defeat the execution of the fugitive-slave law. It ought to be remembered, however, that for these acts neither Congress nor any President can justly be held responsible. Having been passed in violation of the Federal Constitution, they are therefore null and void. All the courts, both State and national, before whom the question has arisen have from the beginning declared the fugitive-slave law to be constitutional. The single exception is that of a State court in Wisconsin, and this has not only been reversed by the proper appellate tribunal, but has met with such universal reprobation that there can be no danger from it as a precedent. The validity of this law has been established over and over again by the Supreme Court of the United States with perfect unanimity. It is founded upon an express provision of the Constitution, requiring that fugitive slaves who escape from service in one State to another shall be "delivered up" to their masters. Without this provision it is a well-known historical fact that the Constitution itself could never have been adopted by the Convention. In one form or other, under the acts of 1793 and 1850, both being substantially the same, the fugitive-slave law has been the law of the land from the days of Washington until the present moment. Here, then, a clear case is presented in which it will be the duty of the next President, as it has been my own, to act with vigor in executing this supreme law against the conflicting enactments of State legislatures. Should he fail in the performance of this high duty, he will then have manifested a disregard of the Constitution and laws, to the great injury of the people of nearly one-half of the States of the Union. But are we to presume in advance that he will thus violate his duty? This would be at war with every principle of justice and of Christian charity. Let us wait for the overt act. The fugitive-slave law has been carried into execution in every contested case since the commencement of the present Administration, though often, it is to be regretted, with great loss and inconvenience to the master and with considerable expense to the Government. Let us trust that the State legislatures will repeal their unconstitutional and obnoxious enactments. Unless this shall be done without unnecessary delay, it is impossible for any human power to save the Union.

The Southern States, standing on the basis of the Constitution, have a right to demand this act of justice from the States of the North. Should it be refused, then the Constitution, to which all the States are parties, will have been willfully violated by one portion of them in a provision essential to the domestic security and happiness of the remainder. In that event the injured States, after having first used all peaceful and constitutional means to obtain redress, would be justified in revolutionary resistance to the Government of the Union.

I have purposely confined my remarks to revolutionary resistance, because it has been claimed within the last few years that any State, whenever this shall be its sovereign will and pleasure, may secede from the Union in accordance with the Constitution and without any violation of the constitutional rights of the other members of the Confederacy; that as each became parties to the Union by the vote of its own people assembled in convention, so any one of them may retire from the Union in a similar manner by the vote of such a convention.

In order to justify secession as a constitutional remedy, it must be on the principle that the Federal Government is a mere voluntary association of States, to be dissolved at pleasure by any one of the contracting parties. If this be so, the Confederacy is a rope of sand, to be penetrated and dissolved by the first adverse wave of public opinion in any of the States. In this manner our thirty-three States may resolve themselves into as many petty, jarring, and hostile republics, each one retiring from the Union without responsibility whenever any sudden excitement might impel them to such a course. By this process a Union might be entirely broken into fragments in a few weeks which cost our forefathers many years of toil, privation, and blood to establish.

Such a principle is wholly inconsistent with the history as well as the character of the Federal Constitution. After it was framed with the greatest deliberation and care it was submitted to conventions of the people of the several States for ratification. Its provisions were discussed at length in these bodies, composed of the first men of the country. Its opponents contended that it conferred powers upon the Federal Government dangerous to the rights of the States, whilst its advocates maintained that under a fair construction of the instrument there was no foundation for such apprehensions. In that mighty struggle between the first intellects of this or any other country it never occurred to any individual, either among its opponents or advocates, to assert or even to intimate that their efforts were all vain labor, because the moment that any State felt herself aggrieved she might secede from the Union. What a crushing argument would this have proved against those who dreaded that the rights of the States would be endangered by the Constitution! The truth is that it was not until many years after the origin of the Federal Government that such a proposition was first advanced. It was then met and refuted by the conclusive arguments of General Jackson, who in his message of the 16th of January, 1833, transmitting the nullifying ordinance of South Carolina to Congress, employs the following language:

The right of the people of a single State to absolve themselves at will and without the consent of the other States from their most solemn obligations, and hazard the liberties and happiness of the millions composing this Union, can not be acknowledged. Such authority is believed to be utterly repugnant both to the principles upon which the General Government is constituted and to the objects which it is expressly formed to attain.

It is not pretended that any clause in the Constitution gives countenance to such a theory. It is altogether founded upon inference; not from any language contained in the instrument itself, but from the sovereign character of the several States by which it was ratified. But is it beyond the power of a State, like an individual, to yield a portion of its sovereign rights to secure the remainder? In the language of Mr. Madison, who has been called the father of the Constitution—

It was formed by the States; that is, by the people in each of the States acting in their highest sovereign capacity, and formed, consequently, by the same authority which formed the State constitutions. * * * Nor is the Government of the United States, created by the Constitution, less a government, in the strict sense of the term, within the sphere of its powers than the governments created by the constitutions of the States are within their several spheres. It is, like them, organized into legislative, executive, and judiciary departments. It operates, like them directly on persons and things, and, like them, it has at command a physical force for executing the powers committed to it.

It was intended to be perpetual, and not to be annulled at the pleasure of any one of the contracting parties. The old Articles of Confederation were entitled "Articles of Confederation and Perpetual Union between the States," and by the thirteenth article it is expressly declared that "the articles of this Confederation shall be inviolably observed by every State, and the Union shall be perpetual." The preamble to the Constitution of the United States, having express reference to the Articles of Confederation, recites that it was established "in order to form a more perfect union." And yet it is contended that this "more perfect union" does not include the essential attribute of perpetuity.

But that the Union was designed to be perpetual appears conclusively from the nature and extent of the powers conferred by the Constitution on the Federal Government. These powers embrace the very highest attributes of national sovereignty. They place both the sword and the purse under its control. Congress has power to make war and to make peace, to raise and support armies and navies, and to conclude treaties with foreign governments. It is invested with the power to coin money and to regulate the value thereof, and to regulate commerce with foreign nations and among the several States. It is not necessary to enumerate the other high powers which have been conferred upon the Federal Government. In order to carry the enumerated powers into effect, Congress possesses the exclusive right to lay and collect duties on imports, and, in common with the States, to lay and collect all other taxes.

But the Constitution has not only conferred these high powers upon Congress, but it has adopted effectual means to restrain the States from interfering with their exercise. For that purpose it has in strong prohibitory language expressly declared that—

No State shall enter into any treaty, alliance, or confederation; grant letters of marque and reprisal; coin money; emit bills of credit; make anything but gold and silver coin a tender in payment of debts; pass any bill of attainder, *ex post facto* law, or law impairing the obligation of contracts.

Moreover—

No State shall without the consent of the Congress lay any imposts or duties on imports or exports, except what may be absolutely necessary for executing its inspection laws.

And if they exceed this amount the excess shall belong to the United States.   And—

No State shall without the consent of Congress lay any duty of tonnage, keep troops or ships of war in time of peace, enter into any agreement or compact with another State or with a foreign power, or engage in war, unless actually invaded or in such imminent danger as will not admit of delay.

In order still further to secure the uninterrupted exercise of these high powers against State interposition, it is provided that—

This Constitution and the laws of the United States which shall be made in pursuance thereof, and all treaties made or which shall be made under the authority of the United States, shall be the supreme law of the land, and the judges in every State shall be bound thereby, anything in the constitution or laws of any State to the contrary notwithstanding.

The solemn sanction of religion has been superadded to the obligations of official duty, and all Senators and Representatives of the United States, all members of State legislatures, and all executive and judicial officers, ''both of the United States and of the several States, shall be bound by oath or affirmation to support this Constitution.''

In order to carry into effect these powers, the Constitution has established a perfect Government in all its forms—legislative, executive, and judicial; and this Government to the extent of its powers acts directly upon the individual citizens of every State, and executes its own decrees by the agency of its own officers.   In this respect it differs entirely from the Government under the old Confederation, which was confined to making requisitions on the States in their sovereign character.   This left it in the discretion of each whether to obey or to refuse, and they often declined to comply with such requisitions.   It thus became necessary for the purpose of removing this barrier and ''in order to form a more perfect union'' to establish a Government which could act directly upon the people and execute its own laws without the intermediate agency of the States.   This has been accomplished by the Constitution of the United States.   In short, the Government created by the Constitution, and deriving its authority from the sovereign people of each of the several States, has precisely the same right to exercise its power over the people of all these States in the enumerated cases that each one of them possesses over subjects not delegated to the United States, but ''reserved to the States respectively or to the people.''

To the extent of the delegated powers the Constitution of the United States is as much a part of the constitution of each State and is as binding upon its people as though it had been textually inserted therein.

This Government, therefore, is a great and powerful Government, invested with all the attributes of sovereignty over the special subjects to which its authority extends.   Its framers never intended to implant in its bosom the seeds of its own destruction, nor were they at its creation guilty of the absurdity of providing for its own dissolution.   It was not intended by its framers to be the baseless fabric of a vision, which at the touch of the enchanter would vanish into thin air, but a substantial and mighty fabric, capable of resisting the slow decay of time and of defying the storms of ages. Indeed, well may the jealous patriots of that day have indulged fears that a Government of such high powers might violate the reserved rights of the States, and wisely did they adopt the rule of a strict construction of these powers to prevent the danger. But they did not fear, nor had they any reason to imagine, that the Constitution would ever be so interpreted as to enable any State by her own act, and without the consent of her sister States, to discharge her people from all or any of their federal obligations.

It may be asked, then, Are the people of the States without redress against the tyranny and oppression of the Federal Government? By no means. The right of resistance on the part of the governed against the oppression of their governments can not be denied. It exists independently of all constitutions, and has been exercised at all periods of the world's history. Under it old governments have been destroyed and new ones have taken their place. It is embodied in strong and express language in our own Declaration of Independence. But the distinction must ever be observed that this is revolution against an established government, and not a voluntary secession from it by virtue of an inherent constitutional right. In short, let us look the danger fairly in the face. Secession is neither more nor less than revolution. It may or it may not be a justifiable revolution, but still it is revolution.

What, in the meantime, is the responsibility and true position of the Executive? He is bound by solemn oath, before God and the country, "to take care that the laws be faithfully executed," and from this obligation he can not be absolved by any human power. But what if the performance of this duty, in whole or in part, has been rendered impracticable by events over which he could have exercised no control? Such at the present moment is the case throughout the State of South Carolina so far as the laws of the United States to secure the administration of justice by means of the Federal judiciary are concerned. All the Federal officers within its limits through whose agency alone these laws can be carried into execution have already resigned. We no longer have a district judge, a district attorney, or a marshal in South Carolina. In fact, the whole machinery of the Federal Government necessary for the distribution of remedial justice among the people has been demolished, and it would be difficult, if not impossible, to replace it.

The only acts of Congress on the statute book bearing upon this subject are those of February 28, 1795, and March 3, 1807. These authorize the President, after he shall have ascertained that the marshal, with his *posse comitatus*, is unable to execute civil or criminal process in any particular case, to call forth the militia and employ the Army and Navy to aid him in performing this service, having first by proclamation commanded the insurgents "to disperse and retire peaceably to their respective abodes within a limited time." This duty can not by possibility be performed in a State where no judicial authority exists to issue process, and where there is no marshal to execute it, and where, even if there were such an officer, the entire population would constitute one solid combination to resist him.

The bare enumeration of these provisions proves how inadequate they are without further legislation to overcome a united opposition in a single State, not to speak of other States who may place themselves in a similar attitude. Congress alone has power to decide whether the present laws can or can not be amended so as to carry out more effectually the objects of the Constitution.

The same insuperable obstacles do not lie in the way of executing the laws for the collection of the customs. The revenue still continues to be collected as heretofore at the custom-house in Charleston, and should the collector unfortunately resign a successor may be appointed to perform this duty.

Then, in regard to the property of the United States in South Carolina. This has been purchased for a fair equivalent, "by the consent of the legislature of the State," "for the erection of forts, magazines, arsenals," etc., and over these the authority "to exercise exclusive legislation" has been expressly granted by the Constitution to Congress. It is not believed that any attempt will be made to expel the United States from this property by force; but if in this I should prove to be mistaken, the officer in command of the forts has received orders to act strictly on the defensive. In such a contingency the responsibility for consequences would rightfully rest upon the heads of the assailants.

Apart from the execution of the laws, so far as this may be practicable, the Executive has no authority to decide what shall be the relations between the Federal Government and South Carolina. He has been invested with no such discretion. He possesses no power to change the relations heretofore existing between them, much less to acknowledge the independence of that State. This would be to invest a mere executive officer with the power of recognizing the dissolution of the confederacy among our thirty-three sovereign States. It bears no resemblance to the recognition of a foreign *de facto* government, involving no such responsibility. Any attempt to do this would, on his part, be a naked act of usurpation. It is therefore my duty to submit to Congress the whole question in all its bearings. The course of events is so rapidly hastening forward that the emergency may soon arise when you may be called upon to decide the momentous question whether you possess the power by force of arms to compel a State to remain in the Union. I should feel myself recreant to my duty were I not to express an opinion on this important subject.

The question fairly stated is, Has the Constitution delegated to Congress the power to coerce a State into submission which is attempting to withdraw or has actually withdrawn from the Confederacy? If answered in the affirmative, it must be on the principle that the power has been conferred upon Congress to declare and to make war against a State. After much serious reflection I have arrived at the conclusion that no such power has been delegated to Congress or to any other department of the Federal Government. It is manifest upon an inspection of the Constitution that this is not among the specific and enumerated powers granted to Congress, and it is equally apparent that its exercise is not " necessary and proper for carrying into execution " any one of these powers. So far from this power having been delegated to Congress, it was expressly refused by the Convention which framed the Constitution.

It appears from the proceedings of that body that on the 31st May, 1787, the clause "*authorizing an exertion of the force of the whole against a delinquent State*" came up for consideration. Mr. Madison opposed it in a brief but powerful speech, from which I shall extract but a single sentence. He observed:

The use of force against a State would look more like a declaration of war than an infliction of punishment, and would probably be considered by the party attacked as a dissolution of all previous compacts by which it might be bound.

Upon his motion the clause was unanimously postponed, and was never, I believe, again presented. Soon afterwards, on the 8th June, 1787, when incidentally adverting to the subject, he said: "Any government for the United States formed on the supposed practicability of using force against the unconstitutional proceedings of the States would prove as visionary and fallacious as the government of Congress," evidently meaning the then existing Congress of the old Confederation.

Without descending to particulars, it may be safely asserted that the power to make war against a State is at variance with the whole spirit and intent of the Constitution. Suppose such a war should result in the conquest of a State; how are we to govern it afterwards? Shall we hold it as a province and govern it by despotic power? In the nature of things, we could not by physical force control the will of the people and compel them to elect Senators and Representatives to Congress and to perform all the other duties depending upon their own volition and required from the free citizens of a free State as a constituent member of the Confederacy.

But if we possessed this power, would it be wise to exercise it under existing circumstances? The object would doubtless be to preserve the Union. War would not only present the most effectual means of destroying it, but would vanish all hope of its peaceable reconstruction. Besides, in the fraternal conflict a vast amount of blood and treasure would be expended, rendering future reconciliation between the States impossible. In the meantime, who can foretell what would be the sufferings and privations of the people during its existence?

The fact is that our Union rests upon public opinion, and can never be cemented by the blood of its citizens shed in civil war. If it can not live in the affections of the people, it must one day perish. Congress possesses many means of preserving it by conciliation, but the sword was not placed in their hand to preserve it by force.

But may I be permitted solemnly to invoke my countrymen to pause and deliberate before they determine to destroy this the grandest temple which has ever been dedicated to human freedom since the world began? It has been consecrated by the blood of our fathers, by the glories of the past, and by the hopes of the future. The Union has already made us the most prosperous, and ere long will, if preserved, render us the most powerful, nation on the face of the earth. In every foreign region of the globe the title of American citizen is held in the highest respect, and when pronounced in a foreign land it causes the hearts of our countrymen to swell with honest pride. Surely when we reach the brink of the yawning abyss we shall recoil with horror from the last fatal plunge.

By such a dread catastrophe the hopes of the friends of freedom throughout the world would be destroyed, and a long night of leaden despotism would enshroud the nations. Our example for more than eighty years would not only be lost, but it would be quoted as a conclusive proof that man is unfit for self-government.

It is not every wrong—nay, it is not every grievous wrong—which can justify a resort to such a fearful alternative. This ought to be the last desperate remedy of a despairing people, after every other constitutional means of conciliation had been exhausted. We should reflect that under this free Government there is an incessant ebb and flow in public opinion. The slavery question, like everything human, will have its day. I firmly believe that it has reached and passed the culminating point. But if in the midst of the existing excitement the Union shall perish, the evil may then become irreparable.

Congress can contribute much to avert it by proposing and recommending to the legislatures of the several States the remedy for existing evils which the Constitution has itself provided for its own preservation. This has been tried at different critical periods of our history, and always with eminent success. It is to be found in the fifth article, providing for its own amendment. Under this article amendments have been proposed by two-thirds of both Houses of Congress, and have been "ratified by the legislatures of three-fourths of the several States," and have consequently become parts of the Constitution. To this process the country is indebted for the clause prohibiting Congress from passing any law respecting an establishment of religion or abridging the freedom of speech or of the press or of the right of petition. To this we are also indebted for the bill of rights which secures the people against any abuse of power by the Federal Government. Such were the apprehensions justly entertained by the friends of State rights at that period as to have rendered it extremely doubtful whether the Constitution could have long survived without those amendments.

Again the Constitution was amended by the same process, after the election of President Jefferson by the House of Representatives, in February, 1803. This amendment was rendered necessary to prevent a recurrence of the dangers which had seriously threatened the existence of the Government during the pendency of that election. The article for its own amendment was intended to secure the amicable adjustment of conflicting constitutional questions like the present which might arise between the governments of the States and that of the United States. This appears from contemporaneous history. In this connection I shall merely call attention to a few sentences in Mr. Madison's justly celebrated report, in 1799, to the legislature of Virginia. In this he ably and conclusively defended the resolutions of the preceding legislature against the strictures of several other State legislatures. These were mainly founded upon the protest of the Virginia legislature against the "alien and sedition acts," as "palpable and alarming infractions of the Constitution." In pointing out the peaceful and constitutional remedies—and he referred to none other—to which the States were authorized to resort on such occasions, he concludes by saying that—

The legislatures of the States might have made a direct representation to Congress with a view to obtain a rescinding of the two offensive acts, or they might have represented to their respective Senators in Congress their wish that two-thirds thereof would propose an explanatory amendment to the Constitution; or two-thirds of themselves, if such had been their option, might by an application to Congress have obtained a convention for the same object.

This is the very course which I earnestly recommend in order to obtain an "explanatory amendment" of the Constitution on the subject of slavery. This might originate with Congress or the State legislatures, as may be deemed most advisable to attain the object. The explanatory amendment might be confined to the final settlement of the true construction of the Constitution on three special points:

1. An express recognition of the right of property in slaves in the States where it now exists or may hereafter exist.

2. The duty of protecting this right in all the common Territories throughout their Territorial existence, and until they shall be admitted as States into the Union, with or without slavery, as their constitutions may prescribe.

3. A like recognition of the right of the master to have his slave who has escaped from one State to another restored and "delivered up" to him, and of the validity of the fugitive-slave law enacted for this purpose, together with a declaration that all State laws impairing or defeating this right are violations of the Constitution, and are consequently null and void. It may be objected that this construction of the Constitution has already been settled by the Supreme Court of the United States, and what more ought to be required? The answer is that a very

large proportion of the people of the United States still contest the correctness of this decision, and never will cease from agitation and admit
its binding force until clearly established by the people of the several
States in their sovereign character.   Such an explanatory amendment
would, it is believed, forever terminate the existing dissensions, and
restore peace and harmony among the States.

It ought not to be doubted that such an appeal to the arbitrament
established by the Constitution itself would be received with favor by
all the States of the Confederacy.   In any event, it ought to be tried in
a spirit of conciliation before any of these States shall separate themselves from the Union.

When I entered upon the duties of the Presidential office, the aspect
neither of our foreign nor domestic affairs was at all satisfactory.   We
were involved in dangerous complications with several nations, and two
of our Territories were in a state of revolution against the Government.
A restoration of the African slave trade had numerous and powerful
advocates.   Unlawful military expeditions were countenanced by many
of our citizens, and were suffered, in defiance of the efforts of the Government, to escape from our shores for the purpose of making war upon the
unoffending people of neighboring republics with whom we were at peace.
In addition to these and other difficulties, we experienced a revulsion in
monetary affairs soon after my advent to power of unexampled severity
and of ruinous consequences to all the great interests of the country.
When we take a retrospect of what was then our condition and contrast
this with its material prosperity at the time of the late Presidential election, we have abundant reason to return our grateful thanks to that
merciful Providence which has never forsaken us as a nation in all our
past trials.

Our relations with Great Britain are of the most friendly character.
Since the commencement of my Administration the two dangerous questions arising from the Clayton and Bulwer treaty and from the right of
search claimed by the British Government have been amicably and honorably adjusted.

The discordant constructions of the Clayton and Bulwer treaty between
the two Governments, which at different periods of the discussion bore a
threatening aspect, have resulted in a final settlement entirely satisfactory
to this Government.   In my last annual message I informed Congress
that the British Government had not then ''completed treaty arrangements with the Republics of Honduras and Nicaragua in pursuance of
the understanding between the two Governments.   It is, nevertheless,
confidently expected that this good work will ere long be accomplished.''
This confident expectation has since been fulfilled.   Her Britannic Majesty concluded a treaty with Honduras on the 28th November, 1859, and
with Nicaragua on the 28th August, 1860, relinquishing the Mosquito
protectorate.   Besides, by the former the Bay Islands are recognized as

a part of the Republic of Honduras. It may be observed that the stipulations of these treaties conform in every important particular to the amendments adopted by the Senate of the United States to the treaty concluded at London on the 17th October, 1856, between the two Governments. It will be recollected that this treaty was rejected by the British Government because of its objection to the just and important amendment of the Senate to the article relating to Ruatan and the other islands in the Bay of Honduras.

It must be a source of sincere satisfaction to all classes of our fellow-citizens, and especially to those engaged in foreign commerce, that the claim on the part of Great Britain forcibly to visit and search American merchant vessels on the high seas in time of peace has been abandoned. This was by far the most dangerous question to the peace of the two countries which has existed since the War of 1812. Whilst it remained open they might at any moment have been precipitated into a war. This was rendered manifest by the exasperated state of public feeling throughout our entire country produced by the forcible search of American merchant vessels by British cruisers on the coast of Cuba in the spring of 1858. The American people hailed with general acclaim the orders of the Secretary of the Navy to our naval force in the Gulf of Mexico "to protect all vessels of the United States on the high seas from search or detention by the vessels of war of any other nation." These orders might have produced an immediate collision between the naval forces of the two countries. This was most fortunately prevented by an appeal to the justice of Great Britain and to the law of nations as expounded by her own most eminent jurists.

The only question of any importance which still remains open is the disputed title between the two Governments to the island of San Juan, in the vicinity of Washington Territory. As this question is still under negotiation, it is not deemed advisable at the present moment to make any other allusion to the subject.

The recent visit of the Prince of Wales, in a private character, to the people of this country has proved to be a most auspicious event. In its consequences it can not fail to increase the kindred and kindly feelings which I trust may ever actuate the Government and people of both countries in their political and social intercourse with each other.

With France, our ancient and powerful ally, our relations continue to be of the most friendly character. A decision has recently been made by a French judicial tribunal, with the approbation of the Imperial Government, which can not fail to foster the sentiments of mutual regard that have so long existed between the two countries. Under the French law no person can serve in the armies of France unless he be a French citizen. The law of France recognizing the natural right of expatriation, it follows as a necessary consequence that a Frenchman by the fact of having become a citizen of the United States has changed his allegiance and has lost his native character. He can not therefore be compelled to serve in the French armies in case he should return to his native country. These principles were announced in 1852 by the French minister of war. and in two late cases have been confirmed by the French judiciary. In these, two natives of France have been discharged from the French army because they had become American citizens. To employ the language of our present minister to France, who has rendered good service on this occasion, "I do not think our French naturalized fellow-citizens will hereafter experience much annoyance on this subject."

I venture to predict that the time is not far distant when the other continental powers will adopt the same wise and just policy which has done so much honor to the enlightened Government of the Emperor. In any event, our Government is bound to protect the rights of our naturalized citizens everywhere to the same extent as though they had drawn their first breath in this country. We can recognize no distinction between our native and naturalized citizens.

Between the great Empire of Russia and the United States the mutual friendship and regard which has so long existed still continues to prevail, and if possible to increase. Indeed, our relations with that Empire are all that we could desire. Our relations with Spain are now of a more complicated, though less dangerous, character than they have been for many years. Our citizens have long held and continue to hold numerous claims against the Spanish Government. These had been ably urged for a series of years by our successive diplomatic representatives at Madrid, but without obtaining redress. The Spanish Government finally agreed to institute a joint commission for the adjustment of these claims, and on the 5th day of March, 1860, concluded a convention for this purpose with our present minister at Madrid.

Under this convention what have been denominated the "Cuban claims," amounting to $128,635.54, in which more than 100 of our fellow-citizens are interested, were recognized, and the Spanish Government agreed to pay $100,000 of this amount "within three months following the exchange of ratifications." The payment of the remaining $28,635.54 was to await the decision of the commissioners for or against the *Amistad* claim; but in any event the balance was to be paid to the claimants either by Spain or the United States. These terms, I have every reason to know, are highly satisfactory to the holders of the Cuban claims. Indeed, they have made a formal offer authorizing the State Department to settle these claims and to deduct the amount of the *Amistad* claim from the sums which they are entitled to receive from Spain. This offer, of course, can not be accepted. All other claims of citizens of the United States against Spain, or the subjects of the Queen of Spain against the United States, including the *Amistad* claim, were by this convention referred to a board of commissioners in the usual form. Neither the validity of the *Amistad* claim nor of any other claim against either party, with the single exception of the Cuban claims, was recognized by the convention. Indeed, the Spanish Government did not insist that the validity of the *Amistad* claim should be thus recognized, notwithstanding its payment had been recommended to Congress by two of my predecessors, as well as by myself, and an appropriation for that purpose had passed the Senate of the United States.

They were content that it should be submitted to the board for examination and decision like the other claims. Both Governments were bound respectively to pay the amounts awarded to the several claimants "at such times and places as may be fixed by and according to the tenor of said awards."

I transmitted this convention to the Senate for their constitutional action on the 3d of May, 1860, and on the 27th of the succeeding June they determined that they would "not advise and consent" to its ratification.

These proceedings place our relations with Spain in an awkward and embarrassing position. It is more than probable that the final adjustment of these claims will devolve upon my successor.

I reiterate the recommendation contained in my annual message of December, 1858, and repeated in that of December, 1859, in favor of the acquisition of Cuba from Spain by fair purchase. I firmly believe that such an acquisition would contribute essentially to the well-being and prosperity of both countries in all future time, as well as prove the certain means of immediately abolishing the African slave trade throughout the world. I would not repeat this recommendation upon the present occasion if I believed that the transfer of Cuba to the United States upon conditions highly favorable to Spain could justly tarnish the national honor of the proud and ancient Spanish monarchy. Surely no person ever attributed to the first Napoleon a disregard of the national honor of France for transferring Louisiana to the United States for a fair equivalent, both in money and commercial advantages.

With the Emperor of Austria and the remaining continental powers of Europe, including that of the Sultan, our relations continue to be of the most friendly character.

The friendly and peaceful policy pursued by the Government of the United States toward the Empire of China has produced the most satisfactory results. The treaty of Tien-tsin of the 18th June, 1858, has been faithfully observed by the Chinese authorities. The convention of the 8th November, 1858, supplementary to this treaty, for the adjustment and satisfaction of the claims of our citizens on China referred to in my last annual message, has been already carried into effect so far as this was practicable. Under this convention the sum of 500,000 taels, equal to about $700,000, was stipulated to be paid in satisfaction of the claims of American citizens out of the one-fifth of the receipts for tonnage, import, and export duties on American vessels at the ports of Canton,

Shanghai, and Fuchau, and it was "agreed that this amount shall be in full liquidation of all claims of American citizens at the various ports to this date." Debentures for this amount, to wit, 300,000 taels for Canton, 100,000 for Shanghai, and 100,000 for Fuchau, were delivered, according to the terms of the convention, by the respective Chinese collectors of the customs of these ports to the agent selected by our minister to receive the same. Since that time the claims of our citizens have been adjusted by the board of commissioners appointed for that purpose under the act of March 3, 1859, and their awards, which proved satisfactory to the claimants, have been approved by our minister. In the aggregate they amount to the sum of $498,694.78. The claimants have already received a large proportion of the sums awarded to them out of the fund provided, and it is confidently expected that the remainder will ere long be entirely paid. After the awards shall have been satisfied there will remain a surplus of more than $200,000 at the disposition of Congress. As this will, in equity, belong to the Chinese Government, would not justice require its appropriation to some benevolent object in which the Chinese may be specially interested?

Our minister to China, in obedience to his instructions, has remained perfectly neutral in the war between Great Britain and France and the Chinese Empire, although, in conjunction with the Russian minister, he was ever ready and willing, had the opportunity offered, to employ his good offices in restoring peace between the parties. It is but an act of simple justice, both to our present minister and his predecessor, to state that they have proved fully equal to the delicate, trying, and responsible positions in which they have on different occasions been placed.

The ratifications of the treaty with Japan concluded at Yeddo on the 29th July, 1858, were exchanged at Washington on the 22d May last, and the treaty itself was proclaimed on the succeeding day. There is good reason to expect that under its protection and influence our trade and intercourse with that distant and interesting people will rapidly increase.

The ratifications of the treaty were exchanged with unusual solemnity. For this purpose the Tycoon had accredited three of his most distinguished subjects as envoys extraordinary and ministers plenipotentiary, who were received and treated with marked distinction and kindness, both by the Government and people of the United States. There is every reason to believe that they have returned to their native land entirely satisfied with their visit and inspired by the most friendly feelings for our country. Let us ardently hope, in the language of the treaty itself, that "there shall henceforward be perpetual peace and friendship between the United States of America and His Majesty the Tycoon of Japan and his successors."

With the wise, conservative, and liberal Government of the Empire of Brazil our relations continue to be of the most amicable character.

The exchange of the ratifications of the convention with the Republic of New Granada signed at Washington on the 10th of September, 1857, has been long delayed from accidental causes for which neither party is censurable. These ratifications were duly exchanged in this city on the 5th of November last. Thus has a controversy been amicably terminated which had become so serious at the period of my inauguration as to require me, on the 17th of April, 1857, to direct our minister to demand his passports and return to the United States.

Under this convention the Government of New Granada has specially acknowledged itself to be responsible to our citizens "for damages which were caused by the riot at Panama on the 15th April, 1856." These claims, together with other claims of our citizens which had been long urged in vain, are referred for adjustment to a board of commissioners. I submit a copy of the convention to Congress, and recommend the legislation necessary to carry it into effect.

Persevering efforts have been made for the adjustment of the claims of American citizens against the Government of Costa Rica, and I am happy to inform you that these have finally prevailed. A convention was signed at the city of San Jose on the 2d July last, between the minister resident of the United States in Costa Rica and the plenipotentiaries of that Republic, referring these claims to a board of commissioners and providing for the payment of their awards. This convention will be submitted immediately to the Senate for their constitutional action.

The claims of our citizens upon the Republic of Nicaragua have not yet been provided for by treaty, although diligent efforts for this purpose have been made by our minister resident to that Republic. These are still continued, with a fair prospect of success.

Our relations with Mexico remain in a most unsatisfactory condition. In my last two annual messages I discussed extensively the subject of these relations, and do not now propose to repeat at length the facts and arguments then presented. They proved conclusively that our citizens residing in Mexico and our merchants trading thereto had suffered a series of wrongs and outrages such as we have never patiently borne from any other nation. For these our successive ministers, invoking the faith of treaties, had in the name of their country persistently demanded redress and indemnification, but without the slightest effect. Indeed, so confident had the Mexican authorities become of our patient endurance that they universally believed they might commit these outrages upon American citizens with absolute impunity. Thus wrote our minister in 1856, and expressed the opinion that "nothing but a manifestation of the power of the Government and of its purpose to punish these wrongs will avail."

Afterwards, in 1857, came the adoption of a new constitution for Mexico, the election of a President and Congress under its provisions, and the inauguration of the President. Within one short month, however, this President was expelled from the capital by a rebellion in the army, and the supreme power of the Republic was assigned to General Zuloaga. This usurper was in his turn soon compelled to retire and give place to General Miramon.

Under the constitution which had thus been adopted Señor Juarez, as chief justice of the supreme court, became the lawful President of the Republic, and it was for the maintenance of the constitution and his authority derived from it that the civil war commenced and still continues to be prosecuted.

Throughout the year 1858 the constitutional party grew stronger and stronger. In the previous history of Mexico a successful military revolution at the capital had almost universally been the signal for submission throughout the Republic. Not so on the present occasion. A majority of the citizens persistently sustained the constitutional Government. When this was recognized, in April, 1859, by the Government of the United States, its authority extended over a large majority of the Mexican States and people, including Vera Cruz and all the other important seaports of the Republic. From that period our commerce with Mexico began to revive, and the constitutional Government has afforded it all the protection in its power.

Meanwhile the Government of Miramon still held sway at the capital and over the surrounding country, and continued its outrages against the few American citizens who still had the courage to remain within its power. To cap the climax, after the battle of Tacubaya, in April, 1859, General Marquez ordered three citizens of the United States, two of them physicians, to be seized in the hospital at that place, taken out and shot, without crime and without trial. This was done, notwithstanding our unfortunate countrymen were at the moment engaged in the holy cause of affording relief to the soldiers of both parties who had been wounded in the battle, without making any distinction between them.

The time had arrived, in my opinion, when this Government was bound to exert its power to avenge and redress the wrongs of our citizens and to afford them protection in Mexico. The interposing obstacle was that the portion of the country under the sway of Miramon could not be reached without passing over territory under the jurisdiction of the constitutional Government. Under these circumstances I deemed it my duty to recommend to Congress in my last annual message the employment of a sufficient military force to penetrate into the interior, where the Government of Miramon was to be found, with or, if need be, without the consent of the Juarez Government, though it was not doubted that this consent could be obtained. Never have I had a clearer conviction on any subject than of the justice as well as wisdom of such a policy. No other alternative was left except the entire abandonment of our fellow-citizens who had gone to Mexico under the faith of treaties to the systematic injustice, cruelty, and oppression of Miramon's Government. Besides, it is almost certain that the simple authority to employ this force would of itself have accomplished all our objects without striking a single blow. The constitutional Government would then ere this have been established at the City of Mexico, and would have been ready and willing to the extent of its ability to do us justice.

In addition—and I deem this a most important consideration—European Governments would have been deprived of all pretext to interfere in the territorial and domestic concerns of Mexico. We should thus have been relieved from the obligation of resisting, even by force should this become necessary, any attempt by these Governments to deprive our neighboring Republic of portions of her territory—a duty from which we could not shrink without abandoning the traditional and established policy of the American people. I am happy to observe that, firmly relying upon the justice and good faith of these Governments, there is no present danger that such a contingency will happen.

Having discovered that my recommendations would not be sustained by Congress, the next alternative was to accomplish in some degree, if possible, the same objects by treaty stipulations with the constitutional Government. Such treaties were accordingly concluded by our late able and excellent minister to Mexico, and on the 4th of January last were submitted to the Senate for ratification. As these have not yet received the final action of that body, it would be improper for me to present a detailed statement of their provisions. Still, I may be permitted to express the opinion in advance that they are calculated to promote the agricultural, manufacturing, and commercial interests of the country and to secure our just influence with an adjoining Republic as to whose fortunes and fate we can never feel indifferent, whilst at the same time they provide for the payment of a considerable amount toward the satisfaction of the claims of our injured fellow-citizens.

At the period of my inauguration I was confronted in Kansas by a revolutionary government existing under what is called the "Topeka constitution." Its avowed object was to subdue the Territorial government by force and to inaugurate what was called the "Topeka government" in its stead. To accomplish this object an extensive military organization was formed, and its command intrusted to the most violent revolutionary leaders. Under these circumstances it became my imperative duty to exert the whole constitutional power of the Executive to prevent the flames of civil war from again raging in Kansas, which in the excited state of the public mind, both North and South, might have extended into the neighboring States. The hostile parties in Kansas had been inflamed against each other by emissaries both from the North and the South to a degree of malignity without parallel in our history. To prevent actual collision and to assist the civil magistrates in enforcing the laws, a strong detachment of the Army was stationed in the Territory, ready to aid the marshal and his deputies when lawfully called upon as a *posse comitatus* in the execution of civil and criminal process. Still, the troubles in Kansas could not have been permanently settled without an election by the people.

The ballot box is the surest arbiter of disputes among freemen. Under this conviction every proper effort was employed to induce the hostile parties to vote at the election of delegates to frame a State constitution, and afterwards at the election to decide whether Kansas should be a slave or free State.

The insurgent party refused to vote at either, lest this might be considered a recognition on their part of the Territorial government established by Congress. A better spirit, however, seemed soon after to prevail, and the two parties met face to face at the third election, held on the first Monday of January, 1858, for members of the legislature and State officers under the Lecompton constitution. The result was the triumph of the antislavery party at the polls. This decision of the ballot box proved clearly that this party were in the majority, and removed the danger of civil war. From that time we have heard little or nothing of the Topeka government, and all serious danger of revolutionary troubles in Kansas was then at an end.

The Lecompton constitution, which had been thus recognized at this State election by the votes of both political parties in Kansas, was transmitted to me with the request that I should present it to Congress. This I could not have refused to do without violating my clearest and strongest convictions of duty. The constitution and all the proceedings which preceded and followed its formation were fair and regular on their face. I then believed, and experience has proved, that the interests of the people of Kansas would have been best consulted by its admission as a State into the Union, especially as the majority within a brief period could have amended the constitution according to their will and pleasure. If fraud existed in all or any of these proceedings, it was not for the President but for Congress to investigate and determine the question of fraud and what ought to be its consequences. If at the first two elections the majority refused to vote, it can not be pretended that this refusal to exercise the elective franchise could invalidate an election fairly held under lawful authority, even if they had not subsequently voted at the third election. It is true that the whole constitution had not been submitted to the people, as I always desired; but the precedents are numerous of the admission of States into the Union without such submission. It would not comport with my present purpose to review the proceedings of Congress upon the Lecompton constitution. It is sufficient to observe that their final action has removed the last vestige of serious revolutionary troubles. The desperate band recently assembled under a notorious outlaw in the southern portion of the Territory to resist the execution of the laws and to plunder peaceful citizens will, I doubt not, be speedily subdued and brought to justice.

Had I treated the Lecompton constitution as a nullity and refused to transmit it to Congress, it is not difficult to imagine, whilst recalling the position of the country at that moment, what would have been the disastrous consequences, both in and out of the Territory, from such a dereliction of duty on the part of the Executive.

Peace has also been restored within the Territory of Utah, which at the commencement of my Administration was in a state of open rebellion. This was the more dangerous, as the people, animated by a fanatical spirit and intrenched within their distant mountain fastnesses, might have made a long and formidable resistance. Cost what it might, it was necessary to bring them into subjection to the Constitution and the laws. Sound policy, therefore, as well as humanity, required that this object should if possible be accomplished without the effusion of blood. This could only be effected by sending a military force into the Territory sufficiently strong to convince the people that resistance would be hopeless, and at the same time to offer them a pardon for past offenses on condition of immediate submission to the Government. This policy was pursued with eminent success, and the only cause for regret is the heavy expenditure required to march a large detachment of the Army to that remote region and to furnish it subsistence.

Utah is now comparatively peaceful and quiet, and the military force has been withdrawn, except that portion of it necessary to keep the Indians in check and to protect the emigrant trains on their way to our Pacific possessions.

In my first annual message I promised to employ my best exertions in cooperation with Congress to reduce the expenditures of the Government within the limits of a wise and judicious economy. An overflowing Treasury had produced habits of prodigality and extravagance which could only be gradually corrected. The work required both time and patience. I applied myself diligently to this task from the beginning and was aided by the able and energetic efforts of the heads of the different Executive Departments. The result of our labors in this good cause did not appear in the sum total of our expenditures for the first two years, mainly in consequence of the extraordinary expenditure necessarily incurred in the Utah expedition and the very large amount of the contingent expenses of Congress during this period. These greatly exceeded the pay and mileage of the members. For the year ending June 30, 1858, whilst the pay and mileage amounted to $1,490,214, the contingent expenses rose to $2,093,309.79; and for the year ending June 30, 1859, whilst the pay and mileage amounted to $859,093.66, the contingent expenses amounted to $1,431,565.78. I am happy, however, to be able to inform you that during the last fiscal year, ending June 30, 1860, the total expenditures of the Government in all its branches—legislative, executive, and judicial—exclusive of the public debt, were reduced to the sum of $55,402,-

465.46. This conclusively appears from the books of the Treasury. In the year ending June 30, 1858, the total expenditure, exclusive of the public debt, amounted to $71,901,129.77, and that for the year ending June 30, 1859, to $66,346,226.13. Whilst the books of the Treasury show an actual expenditure of $59,848,474.72 for the year ending June 30, 1860, including $1,040,667.71 for the contingent expenses of Congress, there must be deducted from this amount the sum of $4,296,009.26, with the interest upon it of $150,000, appropriated by the act of February 15, 1860, "for the purpose of supplying the deficiency in the revenues and defraying the expenses of the Post-Office Department for the year ending June 30, 1859." This sum, therefore, justly chargeable to the year 1859, must be deducted from the sum of $59,848,474.72 in order to ascertain the expenditure for the year ending June 30, 1860, which leaves a balance for the expenditures of that year of $55,402,465.46. The interest on the public debt, including Treasury notes, for the same fiscal year, ending June 30, 1860, amounted to $3,177,314.62, which, added to the above sum of $55,402,465.46, makes the aggregate of $58,579,780.08.

It ought in justice to be observed that several of the estimates from the Departments for the year ending June 30, 1860, were reduced by Congress below what was and still is deemed compatible with the public interest. Allowing a liberal margin of $2,500,000 for this reduction and for other causes, it may be safely asserted that the sum of $61,000,000, or, at the most, $62,000,000, is amply sufficient to administer the Government and to pay the interest on the public debt, unless contingent events should hereafter render extraordinary expenditures necessary.

This result has been attained in a considerable degree by the care exercised by the appropriate Departments in entering into public contracts. I have myself never interfered with the award of any such contract, except in a single case, with the Colonization Society, deeming it advisable to cast the whole responsibility in each case on the proper head of the Department, with the general instruction that these contracts should always be given to the lowest and best bidder. It has ever been my opinion that public contracts are not a legitimate source of patronage to be conferred upon personal or political favorites, but that in all such cases a public officer is bound to act for the Government as a prudent individual would act for himself.

It is with great satisfaction I communicate the fact that since the date of my last annual message not a single slave has been imported into the United States in violation of the laws prohibiting the African slave trade. This statement is founded upon a thorough examination and investigation of the subject. Indeed, the spirit which prevailed some time since among a portion of our fellow-citizens in favor of this trade seems to have entirely subsided.

I also congratulate you upon the public sentiment which now exists against the crime of setting on foot military expeditions within the limits of the United States to proceed from thence and make war upon the people of unoffending States with whom we are at peace. In this respect a happy change has been effected since the commencement of my Administration. It surely ought to be the prayer of every Christian and patriot that such expeditions may never again receive countenance in our country or depart from our shores.

It would be a useless repetition to do more than refer with earnest commendation to my former recommendations in favor of the Pacific railroad; of the grant of power to the President to employ the naval force in the vicinity for the protection of the lives and property of our fellow-citizens passing in transit over the different Central American routes against sudden and lawless outbreaks and depredations, and also to protect American merchant vessels, their crews and cargoes, against violent and unlawful seizure and confiscation in the ports of Mexico and the South American Republics when these may be in a disturbed and revolutionary condition. It is my settled conviction that without such a power we do not afford that protection to those engaged in the commerce of the country which they have a right to demand.

I again recommend to Congress the passage of a law, in pursuance of the provisions of the Constitution, appointing a day certain previous to the 4th March in each year of an odd number for the election of Representatives throughout all the States. A similar power has already been exercised, with general approbation, in the appointment of the same day throughout the Union for holding the election of electors for President and Vice-President of the United States. My attention was earnestly directed to this subject from the fact that the Thirty-fifth Congress terminated on the 3d March, 1859, without making the necessary appropriation for the service of the Post-Office Department. I was then forced to consider the best remedy for this omission, and an immediate call of the present Congress was the natural resort. Upon inquiry, however, I ascertained that fifteen out of the thirty-three States composing the Confederacy were without Representatives, and that consequently these fifteen States would be disfranchised by such a call. These fifteen States will be in the same condition on the 4th March next. Ten of them can not elect Representatives, according to existing State laws, until different periods, extending from the beginning of August next until the months of October and November. In my last message I gave warning that in a time of sudden and alarming danger the salvation of our institutions might depend upon the power of the President immediately to assemble a full Congress to meet the emergency.

It is now quite evident that the financial necessities of the Government will require a modification of the tariff during your present session for the purpose of increasing the revenue. In this aspect, I desire to reiterate the recommendation contained in my last two annual messages in favor of imposing specific instead of *ad valorem* duties on all imported

articles to which these can be properly applied. From long observation
and experience I am convinced that specific duties are necessary, both to
protect the revenue and to secure to our manufacturing interests that
amount of incidental encouragement which unavoidably results from a
revenue tariff.

As an abstract proposition it may be admitted that *ad valorem* duties
would in theory be the most just and equal. But if the experience of
this and of all other commercial nations has demonstrated that such
duties can not be assessed and collected without great frauds upon the
revenue, then it is the part of wisdom to resort to specific duties. Indeed,
from the very nature of an *ad valorem* duty this must be the result.
Under it the inevitable consequence is that foreign goods will be entered
at less than their true value. The Treasury will therefore lose the duty
on the difference between their real and fictitious value, and to this extent
we are defrauded.

The temptations which *ad valorem* duties present to a dishonest importer are irresistible. His object is to pass his goods through the
custom-house at the very lowest valuation necessary to save them from
confiscation. In this he too often succeeds in spite of the vigilance of
the revenue officers. Hence the resort to false invoices, one for the pur-
chaser and another for the custom-house, and to other expedients to
defraud the Government. The honest importer produces his invoice
to the collector, stating the actual price at which he purchased the
articles abroad. Not so the dishonest importer and the agent of the
foreign manufacturer. And here it may be observed that a very large
proportion of the manufactures imported from abroad are consigned for
sale to commission merchants, who are mere agents employed by the
manufacturers. In such cases no actual sale has been made to fix their
value. The foreign manufacturer, if he be dishonest, prepares an invoice
of the goods, not at their actual value, but at the very lowest rate necessary to escape detection. In this manner the dishonest importer and the
foreign manufacturer enjoy a decided advantage over the honest mer·
chant. They are thus enabled to undersell the fair trader and drive
him from the market. In fact the operation of this system has already
driven from the pursuits of honorable commerce many of that class of
regular and conscientious merchants whose character throughout the
world is the pride of our country.

The remedy for these evils is to be found in specific duties, so far as
this may be practicable. They dispense with any inquiry at the custom-house into the actual cost or value of the article, and it pays the
precise amount of duty previously fixed by law. They present no temptations to the appraisers of foreign goods, who receive but small salaries, and might by undervaluation in a few cases render themselves
independent.

Besides, specific duties best conform to the requisition in the Constitution that "no preference shall be given by any regulation of commerce or revenue to the ports of one State over those of another." Under our *ad valorem* system such preferences are to some extent inevitable, and complaints have often been made that the spirit of this provision has been violated by a lower appraisement of the same articles at one port than at another.

An impression strangely enough prevails to some extent that specific duties are necessarily protective duties. Nothing can be more fallacious. Great Britain glories in free trade, and yet her whole revenue from imports is at the present moment collected under a system of specific duties. It is a striking fact in this connection that in the commercial treaty of January 23, 1860, between France and England one of the articles provides that the *ad valorem* duties which it imposes shall be converted into specific duties within six months from its date, and these are to be ascertained by making an average of the prices for six months previous to that time. The reverse of the propositions would be nearer to the truth, because a much larger amount of revenue would be collected by merely converting the *ad valorem* duties of a tariff into equivalent specific duties. To this extent the revenue would be increased, and in the same proportion the specific duty might be diminished.

Specific duties would secure to the American manufacturer the incidental protection to which he is fairly entitled under a revenue tariff, and to this surely no person would object. The framers of the existing tariff have gone further, and in a liberal spirit have discriminated in favor of large and useful branches of our manufactures, not by raising the rate of duty upon the importation of similar articles from abroad, but, what is the same in effect, by admitting articles free of duty which enter into the composition of their fabrics.

Under the present system it has been often truly remarked that this incidental protection decreases when the manufacturer needs it most and increases when he needs it least, and constitutes a sliding scale which always operates against him. The revenues of the country are subject to similar fluctuations. Instead of approaching a steady standard, as would be the case under a system of specific duties, they sink and rise with the sinking and rising prices of articles in foreign countries. It would not be difficult for Congress to arrange a system of specific duties which would afford additional stability both to our revenue and our manufactures and without injury or injustice to any interest of the country. This might be accomplished by ascertaining the average value of any given article for a series of years at the place of exportation and by simply converting the rate of *ad valorem* duty upon it which might be deemed necessary for revenue purposes into the form of a specific duty. Such an arrangement could not injure the consumer. If he should pay a greater amount of duty one year, this would be counterbalanced by a lesser amount the next, and in the end the aggregate would be the same.

I desire to call your immediate attention to the present condition of the Treasury, so ably and clearly presented by the Secretary in his report to Congress, and to recommend that measures be promptly adopted to enable it to discharge its pressing obligations. The other recommendations of the report are well worthy of your favorable consideration.

I herewith transmit to Congress the reports of the Secretaries of War, of the Navy, of the Interior, and of the Postmaster-General. The recommendations and suggestions which they contain are highly valuable and deserve your careful attention.

The report of the Postmaster-General details the circumstances under which Cornelius Vanderbilt, on my request, agreed in the month of July last to carry the ocean mails between our Atlantic and Pacific coasts. Had he not thus acted this important intercommunication must have been suspended, at least for a season. The Postmaster-General had no power to make him any other compensation than the postages on the mail matter which he might carry. It was known at the time that these postages would fall far short of an adequate compensation, as well as of the sum which the same service had previously cost the Government. Mr. Vanderbilt, in a commendable spirit, was willing to rely upon the justice of Congress to make up the deficiency, and I therefore recommend that an appropriation may be granted for this purpose.

I should do great injustice to the Attorney-General were I to omit the mention of his distinguished services in the measures adopted and prosecuted by him for the defense of the Government against numerous and unfounded claims to land in California purporting to have been made by the Mexican Government previous to the treaty of cession. The successful opposition to these claims has saved the United States public property worth many millions of dollars and to individuals holding title under them to at least an equal amount.

It has been represented to me from sources which I deem reliable that the inhabitants in several portions of Kansas have been reduced nearly to a state of starvation on account of the almost total failure of their crops, whilst the harvests in every other portion of the country have been abundant. The prospect before them for the approaching winter is well calculated to enlist the sympathies of every heart. The destitution appears to be so general that it can not be relieved by private contributions, and they are in such indigent circumstances as to be unable to purchase the necessaries of life for themselves. I refer the subject to Congress. If any constitutional measure for their relief can be devised, I would recommend its adoption.

I cordially commend to your favorable regard the interests of the people of this District. They are eminently entitled to your consideration, especially since, unlike the people of the States, they can appeal to no government except that of the Union.